Jimmy Swaggart Bible Commentary

Psalms

JIMMY SWAGGART BIBLE COMMENTARY

- Genesis (639 pages) (11-201)
- Exodus (639 pages) (11-202)
- Leviticus (435 pages) (11-203)
- Numbers
  Deuteronomy (493 pages) (11-204)
- Joshua
  Judges
  Ruth (329 pages) (11-205)
- I Samuel
  II Samuel (528 pages) (11-206)
- I Kings
  II Kings (560 pages) (11-207)
- I Chronicles
  II Chronicles (528 pages) (11-226)
- Ezra
  Nehemiah
  Esther (288 pages) (11-208)
- Job (320 pages) (11-225)
- Psalms (688 pages) (11-216)
- Proverbs (320 pages) (11-227)
- Ecclesiastes
  Song Of Solomon (245 pages) (11-228)
- Isaiah (688 pages) (11-220)
- Jeremiah
  Lamentations (688 pages) (11-070)
- Ezekiel (508 pages) (11-223)
- Daniel (403 pages) (11-224)
- Hosea
  Joel
  Amos (496 pages) (11-229)
- Obadiah
  Jonah
  Micah
  Naham
  Habakkuk
  Zephaniah *(will be ready Spring 2013)* (11-230)
- Matthew (625 pages) (11-073)
- Mark (606 pages) (11-074)
- Luke (626 pages) (11-075)
- John (532 pages) (11-076)
- Acts (697 pages) (11-077)
- Romans (536 pages) (11-078)
- I Corinthians (632 pages) (11-079)
- II Corinthians (589 pages) (11-080)
- Galatians (478 pages) (11-081)
- Ephesians (550 pages) (11-082)
- Philippians (476 pages) (11-083)
- Colossians (374 pages) (11-084)
- I Thessalonians
  II Thessalonians (498 pages) (11-085)
- I Timothy
  II Timothy
  Titus
  Philemon (687 pages) (11-086)
- Hebrews (831 pages) (11-087)
- James
  I Peter
  II Peter (730 pages) (11-088)
- I John
  II John
  III John
  Jude (377 pages) (11-089)
- Revelation (602 pages) (11-090)

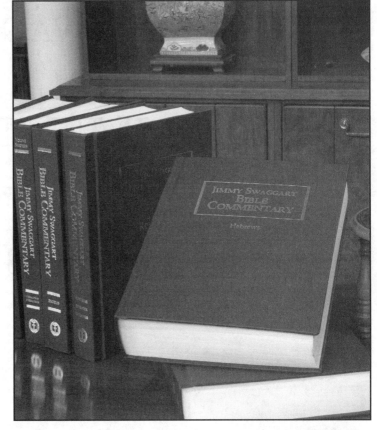

OBADIAH
JONAH
MICAH
NAHAM
HABAKKUK
ZEPHANIAH

For prices and information please call: 1-800-288-8350
Baton Rouge residents please call: (225) 768-7000
Website: www.jsm.org • Email: info@jsm.org

Jimmy Swaggart Bible Commentary

Psalms

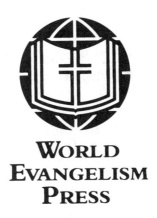

WORLD EVANGELISM PRESS

ISBN 978-0-9769530-8-1
11-216 • COPYRIGHT © 2006 World Evangelism Press®
P.O. Box 262550 • Baton Rouge, Louisiana 70826-2550
Website: www.jsm.org • Email: info@jsm.org • (225) 768-8300
13 14 15 16 17 18 19 20 21 22 23 24 25 26 27 28 / CK / 18 17 16 15 14 13 12 11 10 9 8 7 6 5 4 3
All rights reserved. Printed and bound in U.S.A.
No part of this publication may be reproduced in any form or by any means
without the publisher's prior written permission.

TABLE OF CONTENTS

1. Introduction v
2. Psalms 1
3. Index 661

INTRODUCTION

INTRODUCTION

It is June 6, 2005, as I begin the rewrite of the great Book of Psalms, Earth's First Songbook. Even though much of the material will be the same as in our First Volume on the Book of Psalms, this Volume will contain additional material regarding the Cross of Christ, which the Psalms proclaim in graphic detail.

Since the Lord gave me the Revelation of the Cross in 1997, I now see the Scriptures, which I always have loved, in a much more completed way. That's the reason I feel compelled to rewrite this Volume.

Until one properly understands the Cross of Christ, which is, in effect, the story of the Bible, one cannot really understand the Scriptures as one should. The meaning of the New Covenant is the meaning of the Cross, even as the Cross is the meaning of the New Covenant. And the New Covenant is the revelation of the Old.

On the road to Emmaus, and also in the upper chamber, the Messiah spoke to His Disciples of the things in the Psalms concerning Himself (Lk., Chpt. 24).

The Holy Spirit trained the writers of the Psalms, but He was the Author (Acts 1:16; 2:25, 30; Heb. 3:7). Hence, He says that no Scripture is of human origination (II Pet. 1:20), but that all Scripture is of Divine Inspiration (II Tim. 3:16).

PROPHECY

The Book of the Psalms is a Volume of Prophecy; its principal predictions concern the perfections, the sufferings, and the succeeding glories of the Lord Jesus Christ.

God having been dishonored by human unbelief and disobedience, it was necessary that a Man should be born Who would perfectly love, trust, and serve Him, and Who would be the True Adam, i.e., the True Man, as the True Israel, and the True Church.

God's moral glory demanded that sin should be judged; that sinners should repent, confess, and forsake sin, and worship and obey Him; and being God, His Nature required perfection in these emotions of the heart and will. Such perfection was impossible to fallen man, and it was equally out of his power to provide a Sacrifice that could remove his guilt and restore his relationship with God.

THE LORD JESUS CHRIST

The Psalms reveal Christ as satisfying in these relationships all the Divine requirements. He, though Himself sinless, declares Himself in these Psalms to be the True Advocate, and He expresses to God the abhorrence of sin, accompanied by the Repentance and sorrow which we ought to feel but will not and cannot. Similarly, the faith, love, obedience, and worship which man fails to give, He perfectly renders, all on our behalf!

Thus, as the High Priest of His people, He, the True Advocate, charges Himself with the guilt of our sins; declares them to be His Own; confesses them, repents of them, declaring at the same time His Own sinlessness; and atones for them. Thus, those Psalms in which the Speaker declares His sinfulness and His sinlessness become quite clear of comprehension when it is recognized Who the Speaker actually is.

SON OF GOD AND SON OF MAN

Messiah's other Offices and Ministries as Son of God and Son of Man, as King and Priest, as Servant of Jehovah, as Angel of Jehovah, as the Word of God, and as the Burnt Offering, the Meal Offering, the Peace Offering, the Sin Offering, and the Guilt Offering, and as the Resurrection and the Life, are all sung of, together with the sufferings or the glories appropriate to each Office.

The Gospels record the fact that He prayed; the Psalms furnish the Words of His prayers.

AN INEXHAUSTIBLE DIARY

The Psalter is an inexhaustible source of strength, guidance, consolation and moral teaching to the people of God, and many valuable Commentaries point out these treasures. It may, therefore, in this aspect be justly regarded as a diary kept by the Lord when on Earth, in which are recorded His Own experiences proper to those in whom He dwells. But this Commentary studies the Psalter in relationship to the Messiah; and in its compilation the best Commentaries, together with the Hebrew Text and its Greek, Latin, German, French, Italian, Spanish, and English translations, have been used.

Some of the Messianic experiences were entirely personal, others were representative, others sympathetic, and others proper to Him as the True Israel.

The interpretation of the Book, therefore, belongs to Him as Messiah, to Israel as His people, and to the nations as His possession. Its application is to all who feel their need of a Saviour from sin and from its consequences. As stated in Romans 16:25 and in the Fifth Chapter of Ephesians, the Church, as such, does not appear in the Book.

THE TRUE AND FALSE MESSIAH

The great opposing figures in the Book are the True Messiah and the false messiah. The one is termed the Man of the Earth; the other, the Blessed Man, the Lord of the whole Earth.

The Psalms, ignorantly called vindictive, predict the just doom of the false one and of his followers; other Psalms foretell the glories of the Heavenly Man and of His servants. Vengeance belongs unto God; and He has appointed a Man — the Messiah — Who will righteously execute that vengeance. And He will associate with Himself His people and His Angels as the executors of His Wrath.

The Psalms mainly belong to this coming period of judgment. They predict the Advent of the Day of Christ, when all evil workers shall be cast out of the Earth (Mat. 13:41). These judgment Psalms, which will be so appropriate at that time, do not belong to the present day of Grace, as should be obvious. Rightly dividing the Word of Truth (II Tim. 2:15) will relieve Christian people who, not being skillful in the Word of Righteousness (Heb. 5:13), feel distress when reading these predictions.

(Much of the above introductory material was derived from the writings of George Williams.)[1]

FIVE BOOKS

The Book of Psalms contains five Books corresponding to the five Books of the Pentateuch and to the five Books of the Apocalypse, i.e., *"The Book of Revelation."*

They are as follows:

Book One: Psalms 1-41 — Genesis; Revelation 1-3;

Book Two: Psalms 42-72 — Exodus; Revelation 4-9;

Book Three: Psalms 73-89 — Leviticus; Revelation 10-11;

Book Four: Psalms 90-106 — Numbers; Revelation 12-18; and,

Book Five: Psalms 107-150 — Deuteronomy; Revelation 19-22.

EARTH'S FIRST SONGBOOK

The Psalms were used for many centuries by Israel as they worshipped God at the time of the Sacrifices at the Temple. The Psalms as we know them today are exactly as they were in Jesus' day. In Matthew 26:30, the hymn that was sung was, no doubt, a Psalm. Actually, several Psalms generally were sung at the Passover.

The usual custom was that a cup was filled with wine for every person. A blessing was pronounced, after which the wine was drunk. Then unleavened bread, bitter herbs, and the lamb were brought in. Thanksgiving was offered for the many blessings of life and the food was handed around to each guest.

A second cup of wine was drunk, after which an explanation of the Feast was given with Exodus 12:26-27. The company then sang Psalms 113 and 114, followed by another blessing. Then the food was eaten, and after this a third cup of wine was drunk, and Psalms 115 and 118 were sung.

It is noteworthy to understand that the largest Book in the Bible is given over to praise and worship of God; consequently, worship and praise of God should characterize the majority of our communion and fellowship with the Lord.

It is also noteworthy to understand that this praise and worship of the Lord is instituted in songs; the Book of Psalms was, in fact, Earth's First Songbook, at least of which we have a record.

THE BOOK OF PSALMS

The Book of Psalms is the longest Book in the Bible, containing 150 Chapters, 2,461 Verses, and 43,743 Words. This Scriptural verbiage contains 202

Verses of History, 160 Verses of fulfilled Prophecy, and 274 Verses of unfulfilled Prophecy.

The theme of this great Book is *"Trust, Worship, and Praise."*

As we've already stated, when one reads the Book of Psalms, one is reading Earth's First Songbook. The Hebrew word is *"sepher tehillim,"* which means *"The Book of Praises."* In the Greek the title is *"Psalmoi,"* which means *"songs."* The word, *"Psalter,"* is from the Greek, *"Psalterion,"* which means *"a harp or other stringed instruments."*

THE AUTHORSHIP OF THE PSALMS

According to the titles and the Psalms themselves, seventy-three Psalms are ascribed to David. Of the others, twelve are attributed to Asaph, twelve to the sons of Korah, two to Solomon, one to Moses, one to Ethan, and the remainder are anonymous. David was undoubtedly the author of some of the Psalms that do not name him or another author.

THE DISPENSATIONAL ASPECT OF THE PSALMS

The Dispensational aspect of this great Book must be kept in mind, for repeatedly the First and Second Advents of Christ, the future Tribulation, the Millennium, and the other periods of God's Plan for man are detailed.

MESSIANIC PSALMS

There are fifteen Psalms which are said to be Messianic, which means that they are prophetic in tone and refer to Christ.

It is my contention, however, that all of the Psalms, in some way, are Messianic. This means they refer to Christ in either His Atoning, Mediatorial, or Intercessory Work.

In effect, the Lord Jesus Christ, as the Representative and the Sin Bearer of His people, declares their sins, sorrows, sufferings, and chastisements to be His Own. He did this as the Perfect, sinless One! In every respect was He our Representative Man, our Glorious Substitute, the Last Adam, and the Second Man (I Cor. 15:45, 47).

As someone has well said, "When one reads the Gospels, one is reading the actions and deeds of Christ, and when one reads the Psalms, one is reading the heart of Christ."

THE BOOK OF PSALMS

BOOK ONE
(The Genesis Book)
(Psalms 1-41)

PSALM 1

The Blessedness Of Christ

(1) "BLESSED IS THE MAN WHO WALKS NOT IN THE COUNSEL OF THE UNGODLY, NOR STANDS IN THE WAY OF SINNERS, NOR SITS IN THE SEAT OF THE SCORNFUL.

(2) "BUT HIS DELIGHT IS IN THE LAW OF THE LORD; AND IN HIS LAW DOES HE MEDITATE DAY AND NIGHT."

Even though this Psalm is not called a *"Messianic Psalm,"* still, it speaks totally of Christ. The Blessed Man of this Psalm is the Son of Man, the Messiah. The word *"Blessed"* means *"happy."*

THE BLESSED MAN

Our Lord was blessed, at least in part, because:
1. He walked not in the counsel of the ungodly;
2. He did not stand in the way of sinners; and,
3. He did not sit in the seat of the scornful.

In the day of our Lord, He did not seek or desire the counsel of the Pharisees or the Sadducees; He looked strictly to His Heavenly Father. Presently, it refers to the fact that True Believers will not walk in the counsel of humanistic psychology, or of man in general, but will look to Preachers who point exclusively to the *"Word"* as alone the infallible guide.

"Standing in the way of sinners" refers to accepting their ways and their paths, which Christ never did. Christ was a friend to sinners, but He never adopted even one single *"way"* of sinners.

He never one time was scornful of the Word of God or the Way of God. Rather He learned obedience by the things He suffered.

This does not mean that He learned to be obedient, for had He learned to be obedient, that would have meant that He had been disobedient, which, of course, He never was (Heb. 5:8).

THE LAW OF THE LORD

Following the presentation of three things which the Righteous Man, i.e., *"The Lord Jesus Christ,"* will <u>not</u> do, Verse 2 tells us two things which He will do, i.e., *"delight in the Law of the LORD,"* and *"meditate in it day and night."* His delight is in the Law of the Lord. In essence, while this could refer to any Word from the Lord, more specifically, it refers to the *"Law of Moses."* He delighted in this Law, making it His road map for life and living. He knew that the answer to every problem is found in the Word of God.

A PERSONAL EXPERIENCE

In 1991, a crisis time in this Ministry, a time when I did not know what to do, when all type of demands were being made, in the very midst of sorrow and heartache, I made one of the greatest decisions of my life. I laid my Bible on the table in front of me, and did so in the presence of others, and said, *"I don't know the answer for the Child of God regarding victory over the world, the flesh, and the Devil; however, I know the answer is in this Book. And by the Grace of God, I am going to find that answer."*

It took me some six years — six years of constant prayer, seeking the Lord day and night, before the answer came. But it did come!

The first thing the Lord showed me was from the Sixth Chapter of Romans. He showed me that the problem was the *"sin nature."* I did not then have any knowledge regarding the sin nature, and, when a person does not have correct Biblical knowledge regarding this particular situation, the sin nature will always rule in some way, causing all type of problems.

However, at that particular early morning hour, even though He told me what the problem was, He did not then give me the solution. And yet, I was overjoyed to know what the problem actually was. It is a very disconcerting thing to struggle with all of one's strength, to do the very best that one can, and still fail, despite all of one's efforts! When one doesn't know the reason why, one is left very confused, very hurt, and one has a thousand unanswered questions, all of which begin with *"Why?"*

WHAT IS THE SIN NATURE?

The sin nature is the result of the Fall in the Garden of Eden. Man fell from a place and position of total God-consciousness, down to the far, far lower level of total self-consciousness. As a result, his human nature became totally and completely controlled by the sin nature, meaning that every action, every thought, and every direction of the unbeliever is toward sin in some way. The sinner is ruled by the sin nature twenty-four hours a day, seven days a week, which is the cause of all of man's inhumanity to man, all the problems in the world today, and all the problems that ever have been.

THE CROSS OF CHRIST

A few days later in one of our morning prayer meetings, the Lord opened up to me the solution to this problem of the sin nature. He spoke directly to my heart, and I had absolutely no doubt that it was the Lord speaking.

The following is what He said to me:

"The answer for which you seek is found in the Cross.

"The solution for which you seek is found in the Cross.

"And it is found only in the Cross."

I cannot even begin to relate how I felt that day. I now had the solution to the problem. It was the Cross of Christ, as found in the Sixth Chapter of Romans, actually in Verses 3 through 5.

From that moment, the Lord began to open up more and more this great Message of the Cross, a Message which, I personally feel, is impossible to exhaust. This Message is so perfect, so complete, and so total that it is a Covenant that will never have to be amended in any form or fashion. Paul said so when he referred to it as *"The Everlasting Covenant"* (Heb. 13:20).

THE HOLY SPIRIT

After the Lord opened up to me the answer and the solution of the Cross, I then wondered how the Holy Spirit functioned in all of this. I knew that He most definitely did, but if the price was paid completely at the Cross, what was His Role?

That question may seem strange, considering that I had probably seen, at least at that particular time, more people baptized with the Holy Spirit than any human being alive.

It was two or three weeks before the Lord answered my question. It was during our morning Radio Program, *"A Study In The Word."* Without premeditation, I began to make the statement, *"The Holy Spirit works exclusively within the parameters of the Finished Work of Christ, and He will not work outside of those parameters."*

My own statement shook me a little bit, because, without premeditation, it just sort of came out of my mouth — in reality, it came out of my heart. But I knew it was right!

One of my associates, Loren Larson, was also on the Program with me that day. There was a pause! Loren then said, *"Can you give me Scripture for that?"*

Once again, there was no premeditation on my part. I paused for just a moment, looked down at my Bible, and my eyes fell on Romans 8:2, *"For the Law of the Spirit of Life in Christ Jesus has made me free from the Law of Sin and Death."*

Let's read that Verse from THE EXPOSITOR'S STUDY BIBLE:

"For the Law (that which we are about to give is a Law of God, devised by the Godhead in eternity past [I Pet. 1:18-20]; this Law, in fact, is *'God's Prescribed Order of Victory'*) *of the Spirit* (Holy Spirit, i.e., *'the way the Spirit works'*) *of life* (all life comes from Christ, but through the Holy Spirit [Jn. 16:13-14]) *in Christ Jesus* (any time Paul uses the term or one of its derivatives, he is, without fail, referring to what Christ did at the Cross, which makes this *'life'* possible) *has made me free* (given me total Victory) *from the Law of Sin and Death* (these are the two most powerful Laws in the universe; the *'Law of the Spirit of Life in Christ Jesus'* alone is stronger than the *'Law of Sin and Death'*; this means that if the Believer attempts to live for God by any manner other than Faith in Christ and the Cross, He is doomed to failure)."

Now I knew that when our Faith is placed exclusively in Christ and the Cross (for that's what the phrase, *"In Christ Jesus,"* actually means), then the Holy Spirit will work mightily on our behalf. The Holy Spirit is God! As such, there is nothing He cannot do.

He doesn't require much of us, but He does require that our faith be exclusively in Christ and the Cross (Rom. 6:11). In fact, if our faith is in any thing else other than Christ and the Cross, irrespective as to what the other thing might be, or even how good it might be in its own right, still, faith placed accordingly is looked at by the Lord as one living in *"spiritual adultery"* (Rom. 7:1-4).

To be sure, the Holy Spirit is not going to help someone who is living in spiritual adultery. While the Holy Spirit most definitely will do all that He can for us, still, we limit Him greatly when our faith is misplaced. This is the reason for all Christian failure, all Christian transgression, and all disobedience to the Lord. It can be traced to an improper object of faith.

MEDITATE IN THE WORD DAY AND NIGHT

This means that Jesus meditated on the Word of God constantly. It was in His thoughts every waking moment; it provided a *"joy unspeakable and full of glory,"* as it always will. He is our example, and we must take advantage of that example.

How much do we meditate on the Word of God? Is it in all of our thoughts? Is the Word of God the criteria for every situation? It most definitely should be!

The Word of God, I fear, is under attack by Satan today as never before, at least since the Reformation. The market is being flooded with spurious translations, which are not translations at all, but rather paraphrases and interpretations. I speak of paraphrases such as *"The Message Bible,"* which, to be truthful, is blasphemy! There are scores of others of similar worthlessness!

There is nothing in the world more important than the Word of God. This means that if your Bible is not a word-for-word translation, such as the King James Version, then you would be better off throwing it in the garbage and securing one that is. There are two or three Bible Versions which are word-for-word translations; but, regrettably, they are not in much demand any more.

I strongly advise the Reader to get THE EXPOSITOR'S STUDY BIBLE, which is a King James Version, but yet different from any other Bible that has ever been on the market, at least to our knowledge.

We give an explanation following each Scripture, sometimes after just a phrase, and sometimes even after just a single word.

THE EXPOSITOR'S STUDY BIBLE will help you to understand the Word of God better. Anything that will do that is of great value.

(3) "AND HE SHALL BE LIKE A TREE PLANTED BY THE RIVERS OF WATER, WHO BRINGS FORTH HIS FRUIT IN HIS SEASON; HIS LEAF ALSO SHALL NOT WITHER; AND WHATSOEVER HE DOES SHALL PROSPER."

This Verse proclaims the character of the Son of God and all who follow Him.

A TREE PLANTED BY THE RIVERS OF WATER

The phrase, *"And He shall be like a tree planted by the rivers of water,"* refers to the river that shall flow out from under the threshold of the Millennial Temple (Ezek. 47:1-11).

The *"trees"* which will grow on both sides of this river will be for *"medicine"* for the natural people of the world of that day (Ezek. 47:12).

Another great thing about this *"river"* and the trees which will grow on either side is that *"everything shall live whither the river cometh"* (Ezek. 47:9).

If one desires life, it can be found only in Christ. As stated, He is *"the tree of life."*

FRUIT

The phrase, *"Who brings forth fruit in his season,"* proclaims, as is obvious, *"fruitfulness"*! The *"fruit of the Spirit"* was evidenced in the life of Christ in a perfect manner, and at all times. Due to the Cross, such *"fruit"* is now available to all (Gal. 5:22-23).

However, the only way that Holy Spirit fruit can be developed in our lives is by us *"walking in the Spirit"* (Gal. 5:25).

HOW DOES ONE WALK IN THE SPIRIT?

The phrases, *"Walking after the Spirit"* (Rom. 8:1) and *"Walking in the Spirit,"* have to do with our walk before God, i.e., how we live this life. One cannot *"walk in the Spirit"* until one first *"walks after the Spirit."* This is done by one exhibiting faith in Christ and the Cross, and doing so at all times. When this is done, the Holy Spirit is then given free latitude to work within our hearts and lives, and He Alone can make us what we ought to be.

This *"River"* in Ezekiel, Chapter 47, is symbolic of the Holy Spirit, even though it will be a literal river in the coming Kingdom Age. With Christ as our example, we are to be planted by the side of this River, drawing its nourishment constantly, which will then make us fruitful.

Paul said, *"They who are Christ's have crucified the flesh with the affections and lusts"* (Gal. 5:24).

The *"flesh"* is crucified in the Crucifixion of Christ. We were *"baptized into His Death, buried with Him by baptism into death, and raised with Him in newness of life"* (Rom. 6:3-5).

This is a *"Crucifixion"* in which we must engage every single day.

Jesus said, *"If any man will come after Me, let him deny himself, and take up his cross daily, and follow Me"* (Lk. 9:23), which tells us, from the very lips of the Master, that this is a *"daily"* experience.

NO LEAF WILL WITHER

The phrase, *"His leaf also shall not wither,"* means that whatever is done with Christ and in Christ will last forever.

"His leaf" corresponds to the leaves of the tree that are for the *"healing of the nations"* (Rev. 22:2). The promise is that *"His leaf shall not wither."* He will forever be the Tree of Life.

If it is anchored in Christ, and thereby carried out in Christ, which refers to the Cross of Christ, one can guarantee that such work will last. It will not *"wither."* But if it is built on anything other than Christ and Him Crucified, no matter how it may look on the surface, it ultimately will *"wither"*!

PROSPERITY

The phrase, *"And whatsoever He does shall prosper,"* presents a Promise of unprecedented proportions.

Oftentimes, the Believer says to the Lord, *"Bless me."* This is not an improper request; still, a little more understanding is necessary that we may know of that for which we ask.

First of all, God cannot bless ungodly, flawed, stained, sinful man. He can only bless Christ within us. In that manner we are blessed, and blessed greatly, but only as Christ is in us.

The Psalm opens, *"Blessed is the Man,"* and that Man is *"Christ Jesus."* Consequently, God cannot bless, per se, a Denomination, a Bible College, a Seminary, or an organization; however, within these respective things, He definitely does bless individuals Who have Christ within them.

WHAT IS TRUE PROSPERITY?

True prosperity is being in the direct center of God's Will. It is not money, as some think, even though the Lord does bless financially.

The Scripture plainly tells us that if we seek first of all the Kingdom of God and His Righteousness, then all these other things will be added unto us (Mat. 6:33).

(4) "THE UNGODLY ARE NOT SO: BUT ARE LIKE THE CHAFF WHICH THE WIND DRIVES AWAY."

This Passage leaps ahead and speaks of the Antichrist, who is the opposite of The Christ. It also speaks of all of man's efforts. Without Christ, man, be he ever so brilliant, intelligent, educated, or rich, is likened to no more than *"chaff."*

"Chaff" is used throughout Scripture as an emblem of what is weak and worthless. In ancient times, it was considered of no value at all. When grain was winnowed, it was thrown up in the air until the wind had blown all the chaff away.

"Chaff" is likened to flesh. John the Baptist said:

"I indeed baptize you with water unto Repentance: but He Who comes after me is mightier than I, Whose Shoes I am not worthy to bear: He shall Baptize you with the Holy Spirit and with fire:

"Whose fan is in His Hand, and He will thoroughly purge His floor, and gather His Wheat into the garner; but He will burn up the chaff with unquenchable fire" (Mat. 3:11-12).

We are here told that the Holy Spirit Alone can separate the chaff from the wheat, i.e., *"the flesh from the Spirit."*

A VISION THE LORD GAVE ME

If I remember correctly, the year was 1982.

In obedience to the Lord, in our Magazine <u>The Evangelist</u>, I had written an article entitled, *"A Letter To My Catholic Friends."* In those days, our Magazine went into approximately 800,000 homes each month, and the article created quite a stir.

It seemed like every newspaper in the country vented their spleen against this Evangelist. Television Stations, especially those owned by Charismatics, threatened to take our Telecast off the air. In fact, we received far more criticism from Pentecostal and Charismatic Preachers than we did even from the Catholics.

At the time the Lord told me to address the Catholic situation, we had the largest audience in the world, regarding Gospel Television. Our Telecast was aired all over the world, translated into any number of languages.

NOTES

In fact, we were receiving millions of dollars a year from Catholic Charismatics, money which we desperately needed. I was their fair-haired boy. But then the Lord told me to tell the Catholics, *"The just shall live by faith,"* meaning that works are *"out."*

The firestorm that developed was so intense that I was not certain we could survive. Right in the middle of this situation, we had to leave for a crusade in Guatemala City, Guatemala. We needed desperately to stay in Baton Rouge, or so I thought, but still we had to go.

We left on a Wednesday, and the crusade would begin on a Friday night.

Upon arriving in Guatemala City about noon, we went to our hotel and got settled. Early the next morning, possibly about 1 a.m., I awakened, slipped out of bed, and went to the next room to pray (we had a two-room suite) and seek the Lord.

I was greatly troubled over the problems back in the States, and very concerned that we would lose quite a number of Television Stations, and I did not know quite how to handle these problems. We actually lost only one Station, which was owned by Pat Robertson in Atlanta, Georgia. But almost immediately, Ted Turner put us on his station, which covered not only Atlanta, but much of the United States. (If I remember correctly, it was the station where the CNN Broadcast originated.)

THE THRESHINGFLOOR

As I went to prayer that night, there was a powerful moving of the Holy Spirit that settled on my soul. But yet, it did not seem to involve itself with the problems at hand, but rather with something else altogether!

I can only describe it as a Vision. While I was in prayer, I saw one of the old-fashioned threshingfloors used in Bible times. I saw a worker who was taking stalks of grain, throwing them up into the air, and the chaff being blown to the side of the threshingfloor.

I did not see the manner in which the grain was crushed in order to separate the chaff from the grain, but only the worker throwing the chaff in the air, and the wind blowing it to the side.

Then I saw the worker set fire to the chaff,

and I watched it as it began to burn. I asked the Lord, *"Why is it necessary that the chaff be burned, when it is no longer mixed with the grain? It's not even on the threshingfloor any longer!"*

The Lord's answer was to the point, as it generally is. He said to me, *"The chaff must be burned, because there must be no trace of it left. This is typical of the separation of the flesh from the Spirit of God. The flesh must be separated from the Spirit, with no trace of the flesh left."*

As I have already stated, the Lord completely ignored my petitions concerning our problems back in the States; He dealt with something that was so very important, actually something which I did not really understand at the time. I knew it was for me, and I knew there was much flesh that had to be separated, and burned with the fire of the Holy Spirit, but I did not at all know or understand the significance of what I had seen.

That separation would most definitely come about. It would be a very painful process, so painful that at times I thought I would not be able to stand it. However, it was necessary, as it always is!

Can I say now that all flesh has been separated from the Spirit?

To be frank, I think this is a process that actually never ends. Perhaps the greater bulk has experienced that separation, but I am concerned that this always will be a situation which must be addressed, even on a daily basis.

Again, that's why Paul said, *"And they who are Christ's have crucified the flesh with the affections and lusts"* (Gal. 5:24).

(5) "THEREFORE THE UNGODLY SHALL NOT STAND IN THE JUDGMENT, NOR SINNERS IN THE CONGREGATION OF THE RIGHTEOUS."

The *"ungodly"* stands for any person who does not know the Lord, but more specifically the Antichrist.

"The Judgment" stands for *"The Great White Throne Judgment."* The Antichrist and all who follow in his wake will have no defense regarding their position as they stand on that day at that Judgment.

"The congregation of the righteous" will not include any sinners. To stand in the *"congregation of the righteous,"* one must accept Christ and all that Christ is, which means all that He did for us at the Cross of Calvary.

All sin is then covered by the Precious Blood of the Lord Jesus Christ, which is the only answer for sin. There is no other (Heb. 10:12).

If man attempts to address sin in any way other than by the Cross of Christ, he will fail, as fail he must!

Furthermore, no person can stand in *"the congregation of the righteous"* by his own merit, good works, or personal effort. One <u>can</u> only stand there in Christ, and one <u>will</u> stand there only in Christ, for Christ Alone has paid the price, and did it all on our behalf. It takes faith in Him and what He did for us at the Cross, and that alone is the requirement (Jn. 3:16). The Lord will not convey the attribute *"righteous"* on any other basis than by Faith in Christ and His Finished Work.

(6) "FOR THE LORD KNOWS THE WAY OF THE RIGHTEOUS: BUT THE WAY OF THE UNGODLY SHALL PERISH."

The Lord acknowledged — had respect to — *"the way"* of Abel, but to *"the way"* of Cain, He had no respect (Gen. 4:4), because man's *"way"* is not God's *"Way."* Conversely, God's *"Way"* is not man's *"way."* Satan's greatest effort in the great conflict between good and evil is to insert his *"way"* in place of God's *"Way."*

The Church all too often accepts the *"way of the ungodly"* instead of the *"way of the Righteous"* (Christ). Anytime we deviate from the Word of God, we then go the *"way of the ungodly."*

Concerning this, Pulpit says, *"God is said to 'know' those of whom He approves, and on whom He 'lifts up the light of His Countenance.' The wicked He does not 'know'; He 'casts them out of the sight of His eyes' — 'casts them behind His back': refuses to acknowledge them. God 'knows the way of the righteous,' and therefore they live and prosper; He does not 'know' the way of the wicked, and therefore 'the way of the ungodly shall perish.'"*[2]

WHAT IS GOD'S WAY?

Pure and simple, God's Way is His Word,

and, more particularly, *"Jesus Christ and Him Crucified"* (I Cor. 1:23). One might say, and be correct, that it is the *"Way of the Cross."*

Unfortunately, the far greater majority of the modern Church either completely ignores the Cross, or doesn't understand the Cross, or opposes the Cross. Either way leads one to great hurt.

There is only one way of victory in this world as it regards righteous living. That is, that we understand that every single thing we receive from the Lord comes to us exclusively from Christ as the Source and the Cross as the Means. When one understands that, then, as we have said and will continue to say, the Holy Spirit will help us greatly, for the simple reason that we are functioning in *"God's Way."*

Satan continuously tries to throw up different *"ways,"* and he does so through the medium of the Church. He uses Preachers to carry out his devious designs, and there are all too many who are willing and ready to cooperate with him.

Please allow me to say it even one more time:

God doesn't have ten ways, five ways, not even two ways. He has only one Way, and it is *"Jesus Christ and Him Crucified"* (Rom. 6:1-14; 8:1-2, 11; I Cor. 1:17-18, 23, 2:2; Gal. 6:14; Eph. 2:13-18; Col. 2:14-15).

PSALM 2

A Psalm of David:
Messiah's Kingship and Kingdom

While there is no record as to who wrote Psalm 1, the Second Psalm was written by David. Simon Peter said so (Acts 4:25-26).

The Blessed Man of Psalm 1 and the Crowned King of Psalm 2 are the One and the Same Divine Person, the Messiah, the Son of Man, the Son of God. In both Psalms, He stands in contrast to the first Adam as Man and King in the Earth and over the Earth.

By referring to Verse 8, many people have interpreted this Psalm as pertaining to the carrying out of the Great Commission. In a limited sense, it can be understood in that capacity; however, that is not the real meaning.

This Psalm speaks of the great victory of Christ at the Battle of Armageddon and the beginning of the Millennial Reign.

(1) "WHY DO THE HEATHEN RAGE, AND THE PEOPLE IMAGINE A VAIN THING?"

The *"heathen"* here refer to the Antichrist and all who follow him in his attempt to destroy Israel at the Battle of Armageddon. So this is the great gathering of mighty armies against Christ, as is recorded in the Book of Revelation (Rev., Chpt. 17).

(2) "THE KINGS OF THE EARTH SET THEMSELVES, AND THE RULERS TAKE COUNSEL TOGETHER, AGAINST THE LORD, AND AGAINST HIS ANOINTED, SAYING."

This pertains to the nations of the world joining hands with the Antichrist, all against Israel, and, more specifically, against the Lord Jesus Christ, typified by the phrase, *"His Anointed."*

In other words, at this time, the Antichrist, empowered by Satan as no other man has been, will set himself against the Lord. So, the question is asked, *"How does the Antichrist think that he can defeat Christ?"*

THE PLANS OF THE EVIL ONE

If the Antichrist can destroy Israel, which will make void the Promises of God, he has won this great battle of the ages. If any of the Word of God falls to the ground, even the slightest bit, meaning that the Word fails in some way, then Satan has won. Either the entirety of the Word of God is true in every respect, or none of it can be trusted.

So, the Evil One, working through the Antichrist, seeking to destroy Israel, and coming close to being successful in that attempt, will think to win this conflict of the ages by destroying Israel, which will make void untold numbers of Prophecies in the Word of God. This is the manner in which he thinks to defeat Christ!

(3) "LET US BREAK THEIR BANDS ASUNDER, AND CAST AWAY THEIR CORDS FROM US."

Man has ever tried to disassociate himself from God. The first organized effort was the building of the Tower of Babel

(Gen., Chpt. 11). This effort was stopped when God confounded their languages. The last great organized effort will be the Antichrist who will seek to overcome Christ once and for all by the method previously discussed. As the first failed, so shall the last!

The efforts of the Antichrist and those with him, who will undoubtedly number into the millions, will precipitate the Second Coming of the Lord, which will portray a deluge of power such as the world has never seen before. The Antichrist is going to wish he had not started this fight.

Concerning this battle, the Prophet Zechariah said, *"Then shall the LORD go forth, and fight against those nations, as when He fought in the day of battle"* (Zech. 14:3). The Lord is going to pull off His gloves!

(4) **"HE WHO SITS IN THE HEAVENS SHALL LAUGH: THE LORD SHALL HAVE THEM IN DERISION."**

Man's feeble efforts against God obviously cause Him no consternation. They only produce a *"laugh"* on the part of the Creator, Who holds them in contempt.

HOW DOES SATAN THINK HE CAN OVERTHROW GOD?

Of course, the sponsor of all of this evil is Satan himself, as he uses the Antichrist as a tool. Satan thinks he can win this conflict simply because he is deceived; his greatest weapon is deception, which he uses to deceive the entirety of the world. He is very successful at what he does, simply because he himself is greatly deceived.

As someone has said, *"A false way is most dangerous, when the one promoting such a way actually believes what he is promoting."* Satan believes his own lie!

THE CROSS, THE ONLY CURE FOR DECEPTION

Much, if not most, of the modern Church world is deceived, as it regards false doctrine. Paul addressed this, and I quote from THE EXPOSITOR'S STUDY BIBLE:

"Now the Spirit (Holy Spirit) *speaks expressly* (pointedly), *that in the latter times* (the times in which we now live, the last of the last days, which begin the fulfillment of Endtime Prophecies) *some shall depart from the Faith* (anytime Paul uses the term *'the Faith,'* in short he is referring to the Cross; so we are told here that some will depart from the Cross as the means of Salvation and Victory), *giving heed to seducing spirits* (evil spirits, i.e., *'religious spirits,'* making something seem like what it isn't), *and doctrines of devils* (should have been translated, *'doctrines of demons'*; the *'seducing spirits'* entice Believers away from the true Faith, causing them to believe *'doctrines inspired by demon spirits')"* (I Tim. 4:1).

That's the reason the Apostle also said, and I continue to quote from THE EXPOSITOR'S STUDY BIBLE:

"Examine yourselves, whether you be in the Faith (the words, *'the Faith,'* refer to *'Christ and Him Crucified,'* with the Cross ever being the Object of our Faith)*; prove your own selves* (make certain your Faith is actually in the Cross, and not other things). *Know you not your own selves, how that Jesus Christ is in you* (which He can only be by our Faith expressed in His Sacrifice), *except you be reprobates?* (Rejected)*"* (II Cor. 13:5).

If one doesn't look exclusively to Christ as the Source and the Cross as the Means, he is a perfect candidate for deception. That's why most of the modern Church world is seduced into believing false doctrines.

One Preacher comes along and says the key to victory is taking the Lord's Supper every day. Another comes along and states that the problem is the *"Family Curse."* Another comes along and states that the answer to all things is to memorize several Scriptures, quoting them over and over again, which will then stir God to action and give us what we want.

Yet another comes along and states that one must *"fall out in the Spirit,"* and then one will know complete victory. Another comes along and states that what we need is the *"Buddy System,"* which will then eliminate all failure. Another comes along and states that the problem of Christians is that they have a demon spirit, and if that particular spirit can be cast out, then their problems will be over.

Actually, in the preceding two paragraphs, I've only touched a few of the many unscriptural directions put forth by modern Preachers as ways for a Christian to have victory. While some of these things may have Scriptural validity in their own right, such as *"The Lord's Supper,"* still, all of those things named, plus many we have not named, will not bring anyone any victory whatsoever. The only manner and way in which victory can be obtained by the Child of God is that our faith be placed exclusively in Christ and the Cross. Then the Holy Spirit, Who Alone can do what is needed, will begin to work mightily in our lives. He only requests that our Faith be in the correct object, which is the Cross of Christ (Rom. 6:1-14; 8:1-2, 11).

WHY IS IT SO HARD FOR PREACHERS TO ACCEPT THE CROSS?

Anything and everything else other than the Cross always makes man look good — at least he thinks it does! It's the idea that we have found some secret avenue which, if followed, will bring about some type of utopian paradise, etc. In truth, most Preachers simply look for a gimmick.

And when one mentions the *"Cross,"* it is automatically brushed aside as something elementary, as in *"Oh! I already know all about that!"* But truthfully, most Preachers know just a little something about the Cross as it refers to Salvation, and absolutely nothing as it refers to Sanctification. Consequently, they try to formulate their own avenues of victory, going from one fad to another — and nothing is successful!

Paul addressed this very same thing as it regards the Galatians. He said, and I continue to quote from THE EXPOSITOR'S STUDY BIBLE:

"O foolish Galatians (failure to use one's powers of perception), *who has bewitched you* (malignant influence), *that you should not obey the truth* (refers to *'Jesus Christ and Him Crucified'*), *before whose eyes Jesus Christ has been evidently set forth, crucified among you?* (Paul preached the Cross with such vividness that his hearers could see Jesus Christ Crucified among them. Regrettably, only a few modern Preachers follow his example)" (Gal. 3:1).

Paul then went on to say, *"Are you so foolish? Having begun in the Spirit* (Do you think you can now be brought to a state of spiritual maturity by means of self-effort?), *are you now made perfect by the flesh?* (These Galatians were practicing Salvation by *'Faith,'* and Sanctification by *'self,'* which also is the state of most modern Christians)" (Gal. 3:3).

Theologians have labeled the problem which beset the Galatians as *"Galatianism,"* which means, as stated, that they trusted Christ for Salvation, but they trusted *"self"* for Sanctification. The problem is no less acute presently!

WHAT DOES IT MEAN TO PREACH THE CROSS?

In simple form, it means that we preach the Cross as the Means by which the Lord gives every single thing to Believers. In other words, it is the Cross of Christ that has made possible Salvation, the Baptism with the Holy Spirit, Divine Healing, the Fruit of the Spirit, Gifts of the Spirit, prosperity, and, in fact, every single thing that we receive from the Lord. We preach that Christ is the Source of all of these things, with the Cross as the Means.

But what are most Preachers preaching?

As we have already stated, they are preaching everything but the Cross.

When I turn on Television and hear a Preacher, I only need to listen to him for just a few moments, and I can tell pretty much where he's going. If he is promoting anything as the answer other than Christ and Him Crucified, then what he is preaching will not help anyone. It actually will cause hurt and harm.

If one is not *"preaching the Cross,"* then one is not really preaching the Gospel.

Paul also said:

"For Christ sent me not to baptize (presents to us a cardinal truth), *but to preach the Gospel* (the manner in which one may be saved from sin): *not with wisdom of words* (intellectualism is not the Gospel), *lest the Cross of Christ should be made of none effect.* (This tells us in no uncertain terms that the Cross of Christ must always be the emphasis of the Message)" (I Cor. 1:17).

In this one Verse, we are told what the Gospel of Christ really is. It is the *"preaching of the Cross."* Anything else may be part

Gospel, or no Gospel at all, but it is not the total and full Gospel.

(5) "THEN SHALL HE SPEAK UNTO THEM IN HIS WRATH, AND VEX THEM IN HIS SORE DISPLEASURE."

This is the Battle of Armageddon, with Jesus Christ coming back in Power and Glory, bringing the Wrath of God upon the Antichrist and a sinful world (Rev., Chpt. 19; Ezek., Chpts. 38-39).

What many people do not realize is that the Book of Psalms is one of the greatest Prophetic Books in the entirety of the Bible.

THE SECOND COMING OF THE LORD

The Second Coming will be the most cataclysmic event the world has ever known. There is nothing that could even remotely compare with that which will take place at that particular time. The very elements of the Heavens themselves will cooperate fully with their Creator; everything will be at the disposal of Christ, Who will use the elements against the Antichrist as never seen before in history (Ezek. 38:22).

The Second Coming, as should be obvious, will be a Coming of Judgment. For some 2,000 years, the Lord has spoken to the world in Grace. To be sure, that Grace has been ridiculed and lampooned.

He will not come back this time in Grace, although He never ceases to be a God of Grace, but rather He will come back in Judgment. To be sure, the Antichrist and all who follow him will feel the brunt of that Judgment in no uncertain terms!

(6) "YET HAVE I SET MY KING UPON MY HOLY HILL OF ZION."

The *"King"* is the Lord Jesus Christ.

"Zion" is Jerusalem.

This means that Muhammad will not reign in Jerusalem, and neither will the Antichrist. The contention of man the world over is with the Lord Jesus Christ. To be blunt, at the Second Coming, all are going to know exactly Who is Boss!

(7) "I WILL DECLARE THE DECREE: THE LORD HAS SAID UNTO ME, YOU ARE MY SON; THIS DAY HAVE I BEGOTTEN YOU."

This pertains to the Incarnation, God becoming Man.

NOTES

THE INCARNATION

Before the foundation of the world, God through foreknowledge knew that He would make man, and through foreknowledge He knew that man would fall; consequently, it was decided in the High Counsels of the Godhead that man would be redeemed by God becoming Man and going to the Cross.

Among the many other reasons that God became Man, one of the reasons, perhaps the greatest, is that God cannot die; therefore, in order to die on the Cross, which was absolutely necessary, He would have to become Man (I Pet. 1:18-20). This means that the Cross of Christ is the foundation of the great Plan of God. In other words, every single rudiment of this great Plan is built on the principle of the Cross of Christ; therefore, any doctrine that is not based squarely on the Cross of Christ will somehow be spurious.

That's the reason that the *"Word of Faith"* doctrine is unscriptural. It is not based on the Cross of Christ. Actually, it openly repudiates the Cross, and its Preachers refer to the Cross as *"past miseries"* and *"the greatest defeat in human history."* This is the reason that the *"Government of Twelve"* is not Scriptural, and neither is the *"Purpose Driven Life."* These particular schemes are not at all based on the Cross of Christ, which means they were hatched up out of the minds of men, which also means that God can never bless them, which also means that the end result of these doctrines will not be pleasant things, but rather the very opposite! Anything other than the Cross, in some way or the other, is false doctrine.

THE MEANING OF THE INCARNATION

When God became man, i.e., the Lord Jesus Christ, He never ceased to be God, not even for one moment. As someone has well said: He did lose the *"expression"* of His Deity, but He did not lose the *"possession"* of His Deity.

For mankind to be redeemed, man would have to accomplish the task; however, there was a great problem with that requirement. Due to the Fall, all are born with original sin, actually in the likeness of Adam (Gen. 5:3).

So, there was no way that man could redeem himself. It was utterly impossible!

Love had created man, so Love must redeem man. In order to redeem man, God would have to become Man, which He did! He would become our Substitute, our Representative Man, The Man Christ Jesus, Who would do for man what man could not for himself. So every single thing He did was not at all for Heaven, for Angels, or for Himself, but was altogether for sinners.

As stated, He was our Substitute. He kept the Law perfectly in word, thought, and deed, never failing even one time. He then went to the Cross in order to satisfy the demands of the broken Law, for mankind had broken the Law and had done so repeatedly, and the wages of that was death (Rom. 6:23).

Everything He did was altogether for us, but the crowning achievement of all, that which was an absolute necessity, was the Cross. There He atoned for all sin, making it possible for a thrice-Holy God to justify an obviously guilty sinner. The only way that a just God could justify a guilty sinner, thereby declaring him innocent, not guilty, etc., was for Someone Else to pay the price, and that Someone Else was God's Son. He was, and is, Very God, just as He was, and is, Very Man.

THE DOCTRINE OF SUBSTITUTION AND IDENTIFICATION

The only currency that God will accept in the Bank of Heaven, so to speak, is Faith, but it must be Faith in Christ and what Christ did for us at the Cross. We identify with the Lord Jesus Christ in His Death, Burial, and Resurrection; when we evidence our Faith in that, then the Lord grants to us a perfect, spotless, and pure Righteousness, i.e., *"The Righteousness of Christ,"* which is the only Righteousness that God will accept (Rom. 4:3-5; 6:1-14; Gal. 2:20-21).

Jesus Christ, our Creator, now is also our Saviour! He will retain the badge of the price that He has paid, which is a Glorified human Body, complete with the nail scars in His Hands and Feet, which He will wear forever and forever (Zech. 13:6).

(8) "ASK OF ME, AND I SHALL GIVE YOU THE HEATHEN FOR YOUR INHERITANCE, AND THE UTTERMOST PARTS OF THE EARTH FOR YOUR POSSESSION."

This pertains to the coming Kingdom Age, when every nation in the world will then look to Christ. The majority of the world will give their hearts and lives to Christ as their Saviour.

POSSESSION OF THIS EARTH

The struggle between good and evil, between God and Satan, has raged from the time of Satan's Fall and resultant revolution against God. While other things definitely were at stake, and are at stake, the greatest struggle was for planet Earth.

There is every evidence that Lucifer, who was created by God, and who served the Lord in Righteousness and Holiness for a period of time, was actually given charge of this Earth. There was a creation over which he ruled, a creation of intelligence, of which we now have no information. In fact, it is believed by some Scholars that this creation, whatever it was, is where demon spirits originated.

We know that God did not create evil spirits in this manner. They became this way after some type of cataclysmic event. That event was the Fall of Lucifer, and that creation gave its allegiance to Lucifer, who became Satan.

In Genesis 1:1, the Scripture says, *"In the beginning God created the heaven and the Earth."* It then says, *"And the Earth was without form, and void; and darkness was upon the face of the deep . . ."* (Gen. 1:2).

We know that God did not create the Earth to be a formless void bathed in darkness. That is not God's Way. So it became that way at a point in time. That point in time was Lucifer's Fall, which brought the Judgment of God on the world that then was.

The First Chapter of Genesis proclaims the Lord bringing the Earth back to a habitable state, but we have no way of knowing how old the Earth actually is. We do know, however, that the Earth is much older than the approximate 6,000 years of recorded time.

When the Earth was brought back by the Lord to a habitable state, the Lord then created man, with every evidence that man was actually His highest creation, even higher than the Angels (Ps. 8:4-5). However, man fell from that lofty position, and at present only bears traces of the original creation.

Dominion was given to man, which made man the prince of this Earth (Gen. 1:26). Lucifer was very upset with that, for that which was once his now belonged to man.

So, Satan enticed Eve into disobeying God. Adam followed suit, which plunged the world into chaos. Upon the Fall of man, Satan once again gained the supremacy over this Earth, and the Holy Spirit now refers to him as *"the god of this present world"* (II Cor. 4:4) and *"the prince of the powers of the air"* (Jn. 12:31; Eph. 2:2).

CALVARY, WHERE SATAN WAS DEFEATED

When we speak of the Lord Jesus Christ defeating Satan, plus all the fallen angels and demon spirits, we must understand exactly what we are saying. Jesus Christ is God, while Satan is a creature. As such, Satan a thousand times over is no match for the Lord Jesus Christ. This means that the contest of which we speak was not physical, not in any sense.

So what do we mean by Jesus defeating Satan?

Satan holds men in bondage by virtue of the fact of sin. In other words, it is sin that gives him the legal right to exert dominion over man and place him in captivity, and he has done this with almost all of the human race. God gave Satan that right.

When Jesus went to the Cross, He went there to atone for sin — all sin, past, present, and future — which He did. In fact, had He failed to atone for even one sin, He could not have risen from the dead, for the *"wages of sin is death"* (Rom. 6:23). The very fact that He rose from the dead tells us that all sin was atoned.

When He atoned for all sin by the giving of His Life, and we are speaking of the Cross of Calvary, this removed the legal right that Satan has to hold mankind in captivity. The Scripture says:

"Blotting out the handwriting of Ordinances that was against us (pertains to the Law of Moses, which was God's Standard of Righteousness that man could not reach), *which was contrary to us* (Law is against us, simply because we are unable to keep its precepts, no matter how hard we try), *and took it out of the way* (refers to the penalty of the Law being removed), *nailing it to His Cross* (the Law with its decrees was abolished in Christ's Death, as if Crucified with Him);

"And having spoiled principalities and powers (Satan and all of his henchmen were defeated at the Cross by Christ atoning for all sin; sin was the legal right Satan had to hold man in captivity; with all sin atoned, He has no more legal right to hold anyone in bondage), *He* (Christ) *made a show of them openly* (what Jesus did at the Cross was in the face of the whole universe), *triumphing over them in it.* (The triumph is complete and it was all done for us, meaning we can walk in power and perpetual victory due to the Cross)" (Col. 2:14-15).

IF JESUS ATONED FOR ALL SIN, HOW CAN SATAN CONTINUE TO HOLD MEN IN BONDAGE?

Looking at the unredeemed, Satan continues to hold them in bondage, simply because they will not accept God's free offer of Salvation. By continuing in sin, such persons allow Satan to maintain his legal right to hold them in captivity, which he definitely does!

But why is it that most Christians also are still held in bondage, despite the fact that they have made the Lord Jesus Christ the Saviour of their soul?

The answer to all sin is the Cross of Christ (Heb. 10:12). As long as Believers keep trusting Christ and the Cross, Satan has no more dominion over them. Once they transfer their faith away from the Cross of Christ to something else, a transfer which Satan constantly promotes, then they give Satan once again the legal right to place them in bondage, which he does!

That's why Paul said to the Galatians, *"Stand fast therefore in the liberty wherewith Christ has made us free* (we were made free, which refers to freedom to live a holy life by evidencing faith in Christ and the Cross), *and be not entangled again with the yoke of bondage.* (To abandon the Cross and go under Law of any kind guarantees bondage once again to the sin nature)" (Gal. 5:1).

Let me say it again:

As long as Believers place their faith exclusively in Christ and what He did for us at the Cross, they will know freedom beyond compare. Satan will have no place in them whatsoever. This means that sin in no form will have dominion over them (Rom. 6:14).

Regrettably, most Christians have their faith in anything and everything except the Cross of Christ. That's the reason that Paul said:

"But God forbid that I should glory (boast), *save in the Cross of our Lord Jesus Christ* (what the opponents of Paul sought to escape at the price of insincerity is the Apostle's only basis of exhortation), *by Whom the world is crucified unto me, and I unto the world.* (The only way we can overcome the world, and I mean the only way, is by placing our Faith exclusively in the Cross of Christ and keeping it there)" (Gal. 6:14).

At Calvary, Jesus defeated Satan, and did so in totality. That's why our faith must ever be in Christ as the Source and the Cross as the Means.

(9) "YOU SHALL BREAK THEM WITH A ROD OF IRON; YOU SHALL DASH THEM IN PIECES LIKE A POTTER'S VESSEL."

Once again, this speaks of the great Battle of Armageddon, which will precipitate the Second Coming of the Lord, Who will wreak havoc on the Antichrist and all his armies. In other words, the Lord will not show Mercy at that time.

(10) "BE WISE NOW THEREFORE, O YOU KINGS: BE INSTRUCTED, YOU JUDGES OF THE EARTH."

This Psalm predicts that even though Israel and the Gentiles, along with their princes and rulers, crucified God's Anointed King, yet will God enthrone Him upon Zion's Hill and give Him not only His ancient people for a Kingdom, but also all the nations of the Earth for a possession; and that those who seek refuge in Him shall be blessed, but that His enemies shall suffer wrath.

The leaders of nations are encouraged to use a little common sense, i.e., *"be wise."* Regrettably, almost none ever do; regrettably, almost none will!

(11) "SERVE THE LORD WITH FEAR, AND REJOICE WITH TREMBLING."

NOTES

The idea is this:

If one will not serve the Lord from the position of love, they should have sense enough to do so from the position of fear. *"The fear of the LORD is the beginning of wisdom"* (Ps. 111:10).

If one begins to serve the Lord, even from the baser motive of fear, to be sure, such fear will finally evolve into love, and then into joy.

The word *"trembling"* carries the idea of the great and terrible Power of God, which can be unleashed at any time. The only reason it is not unleashed is because of His Mercy. To be sure, ample reasons are always present for the unleashing of that Power.

Mankind must understand that the only thing which stands between him and eternal Hell is the Cross of Christ. Unfortunately, the world doesn't believe that, and, tragically, much of the Church does not believe it either. Irrespective, it happens to be true.

(12) "KISS THE SON, LEST HE BE ANGRY, AND YOU PERISH FROM THE WAY, WHEN HIS WRATH IS KINDLED BUT A LITTLE. BLESSED ARE ALL THEY WHO PUT THEIR TRUST IN HIM."

In effect, the Lord is saying that despite the unity of the *"kings of the Earth"* and their opposition against the Lord Jesus, there is no way they can win. They will *"perish from the way."* So, the only way to save themselves is to *"kiss the Son."* They who do so will be *"blessed"* because they have *"put their trust in Him."*

PSALM 3

A Psalm of David:
A Prayer of Confidence in the LORD

(1) "LORD, HOW ARE THEY INCREASED WHO TROUBLE ME! MANY ARE THEY WHO RISE UP AGAINST ME."

The Holy Spirit put these words into David's mouth the morning after his flight from Jerusalem because of Absalom's unnatural rebellion. David is here seen as a type of the Messiah rejected by His Own people. Though surrounded by enemies, he slept in confidence upon the mountainside beneath Jehovah's sheltering wing, and, in the assurance of faith, declared that God would lift up his head and destroy his foes.

(2) "MANY THERE BE WHICH SAY OF MY SOUL, THERE IS NO HELP FOR HIM IN GOD. SELAH."

As Israel said this of David, likewise, they said it of the Lord Jesus Christ. When Jesus hung on the Cross, the Jews shouted at Him, *"He trusted in God; let Him deliver Him now, if He will have Him: for He said, I am the Son of God"* (Mat. 27:43).

THE ABSALOM SPIRIT

As Absalom sought to destroy David, which means that he laid his hands on the Lord's anointed, there are many in the modern Church who follow suit. In fact, the Absalom spirit has been abundant from the time that Cain murdered his brother Abel unto the present time.

It was true that David had sinned, and had sinned greatly. David had committed the terrible sins of murder and adultery. He murdered Bathsheba's husband Uriah in cold-blood. His sins were grievous, actually as grievous as sins could ever be.

In view of that, David's enemies, which regrettably included his own son Absalom, felt that they could strike and take the throne of Israel. They reasoned that because David had sinned so grievously, God would no longer help him, which would leave the field wide open for their insurrection.

They thought wrong! Even though David had sinned, and sinned grievously, and would pay dearly, still, the Hand of God was definitely upon him just as much now as at the beginning.

Whatever punishment needed to be inflicted, the Lord would do it, and not man. So whenever man, especially religious man, takes it upon himself to punish for sin, he has just endeavored to step into the place of God, which the Lord will never tolerate. Sooner or later, those who lay their hands on the Lord's anointed are going to suffer the consequences (Ps. 105:15).

In no way does this mean that God condones sin, for He never does! But David had repented of this sin, and, in the Eyes of God, David was as pure and clean as the Blood of the Lord Jesus Christ could make him. And what stands for David, also stands for every other Believer! We must never forget that.

If one denies David this privilege, he has just denied himself!

SELAH

No one quite knows exactly what the word *"Selah"* means. The following are a few of its suggested meanings:

1. A thought-link, connecting ideas in Hebrew poetry.

2. The Septuagint translates it *"diapsalma,"* a pause in the Psalm by the singers.

3. The Chaldee sometimes translates it *"lealmin,"* which means *"forever."*

4. In could be a word equivalent to *"da capo,"* which in music directs the choir to repeat.

5. It could be a word from the Hebrew *"sal,"* meaning to raise or elevate the voices of singers.

6. It could be a word from *"salah,"* meaning to spread out, indicating that the subject should be meditated on by the Reader.

7. It may be a word denoting an instrumental interlude or louder accompaniment.

(3) "BUT YOU, O LORD, ARE A SHIELD FOR ME; MY GLORY, AND THE LIFTER UP OF MY HEAD."

Pulpit says, *"As God had raised up David to the Throne* (II Sam. 2:4; 5:3), *prospered him in his wars* (II Sam. 8:1-14), *and exalted him above all the other kings of the period, so He was well able now, if He so willed, to restore him to his place and reestablish him in the monarchy, which He did"* (II Sam. 15:25; Ps. 43:3).[3]

(4) "I CRIED UNTO THE LORD WITH MY VOICE, AND HE HEARD ME OUT OF HIS HOLY HILL. SELAH."

The *"Holy Hill"* which David mentions has to do with the Holy Hill of Zion, where the Ark of God is situated in the Temple.

At this time of distress, David, as was his habit, took his problems to the Lord. He *"cried unto the LORD,"* because, despite his past sin, he had a tremendous relationship with Jehovah.

PRAYER

David was a man of prayer, which is obvious from the Psalms he wrote. He constantly sought the Lord. Of him, the Scripture says, *"Evening and morning, and at noon, will I pray, and cry aloud: and He shall hear my voice"* (Ps. 55:17).

This means that David set time aside three times a day for prayer to the Lord.

When I was a child, my Grandmother taught me to pray. She taught me that God answers prayer, and she taught me that He was able to do all things. In fact, one of her great statements to me was, *"Jimmy, God is a big God, so ask big!"*

That short line, which instilled faith in my heart, has helped me to touch the world for Christ. Every Believer should *"ask big!"*

At one of the lowest times of my personal Ministry, a time when I did not see how I could continue, the Lord instructed me to begin two prayer meetings a day. I had always had a very strong prayer life, but now the Lord was telling me to continue.

After a short period of time, He spoke to my heart and said, *"Do not seek Me so much for what I can do, but rather for Who I am!"*

He wanted relationship to be established in a greater way than ever. For approximately ten years, several of us met twice a day, with the exception of Sundays. I still personally maintain this regimen myself.

I don't see how any Believer can develop any relationship with the Lord without having a prayer life. I am certainly not saying that all should have three times set aside each day as did David, or two times each day as the Lord instructed me, but, in some manner, every Believer should have a concentrated prayer life.

This means that you should set aside a little time each day, whether it is morning or evening, whether it is fifteen minutes a day, or thirty minutes, etc., devoted to the Lord, to where you can seek His Face and receive His Leading and Guidance.

One should begin each prayer session by thanking the Lord for His Graciousness and His Kindness. He has blessed us with so many Blessings, for which we should ever thank Him and praise Him. Without fail, this should be done before we begin to petition Him for various and different things. Such shows gratitude and also shows faith!

Second, one must ask believing, knowing that the Lord desires to answer prayer.

NOTES

A PERSONAL EXPERIENCE

If I remember, it was November of 2003. Some weeks before, again while in prayer, the Lord had brought to my mind a particular Radio Station we had tried to purchase in Palm Springs, California. At the beginning, I dismissed it, thinking it had already been sold. We had tried to purchase the Station approximately one year earlier, but because we did not have the funds, we had to let it pass.

I had one of my associates to call one of the owners of the Station to see what its present status was. We found out that the Station was even then in the process of being sold. In fact, the man told me they had just signed the contracts.

In my mind, I thought the situation was over. But I still wondered why the Lord had prompted me to make the call! The owner had stated that if anything fell down on the first contract, they would contact us.

The Lord kept bringing this Station to my mind, urging me to continue to pray about the situation. In seeking the Lord, I had made the statement any number of times, *"Lord, we want this Station, if it be Your Will!"*

After two or three days of praying in that manner, the Lord spoke to my heart and said:

"You are praying wrong.

"I know that you want My Will!

"It is not proper for you to continue to question My Will. If you see something that you feel is right for the Ministry, claim what you see. If it's not My Will, I will step in and stop it.

"Every time you make the statement, 'If it be Your Will,' you are hindering your faith. I don't want you to do that any more. Claim what is needed, that your faith be not hindered."

I knew it was the Lord speaking to me and I knew that what I was hearing was a great truth. I began to do exactly as the Lord said, i.e., *"Claim the Station!"*

From that moment, I knew in my heart that we were going to get that Station. And sure enough, a couple of days later, the owner called to tell us, *"The other man has fallen down on his contract. If you are interested, the Station is yours."*

Now, we most definitely wanted the Station, and I believed that the Lord wanted us to have it, but we didn't have any money, not even a dollar of the money. However, Miracle of miracles, the Lord provided that as well. We were given $350,000 for the down payment. I am not at liberty to divulge the source; however, we all know that the True Source was the Lord.

All of us should constantly want and desire the Perfect Will of God. And we must not always just strike out presuming to know what that Will is. But once we do know His Will, we shouldn't hinder our praying by continually questioning His Will.

The Lord had told me, and has told me, to fill this nation with Radio Stations, which we immediately set out to do. So I know it is His Will for this to be done. So now whenever Stations become available, and I think it is a good thing for the Ministry, I begin to claim that Station, plus everything else that the Ministry needs, plus my own personal needs, etc.

Our God is a prayer-answering God. The problem is that most Christians don't pray. As a result, they miss out on His Leading, His Guidance, and His Blessings! Because truthfully, one can have none of these things if one doesn't have a proper prayer life.

(5) "I LAID ME DOWN AND SLEPT; I AWAKED; FOR THE LORD SUSTAINED ME."

When David wrote this Psalm, Absalom and a number of the mighty men of Israel had gathered an army with the intention of killing David and taking the kingdom. However, David sought the Lord, placed himself in the Hands of the Lord (which means that he trusted the Lord), and then laid down and went to sleep.

At this particular time, there would not have been many people in the world who thought that David would come out of this thing victorious. To use some street vernacular, not many people would have bought stock in David's company at that time. But David knew that he had the leading of the Lord, and, despite his past sin (which now was repented of), he also had the Blessings of the Lord. David knew the Lord would watch over and protect him; consequently, he was able to lay down and sleep soundly, because he had put the entirety of the situation in God's Hands.

Considering his situation, that was real Faith!

(6) "I WILL NOT BE AFRAID OF TEN THOUSANDS OF PEOPLE, WHO HAVE SET THEMSELVES AGAINST ME ROUND ABOUT."

David's statement, as given here, is not idle bluster. It is not merely a *"good confession."*

David had taken this problem to the Lord; he had been given the assurance that the Lord would see him through, even though at the time he did not know exactly how; he trusted the Lord implicitly, and with no fear.

FEAR

The Apostle Paul stated, *"For God has not given us the spirit of fear; but of power, and of love, and of a sound mind"* (II Tim. 1:7).

John the Beloved said, *"There is no fear in love; but perfect love casts out fear: because fear has torment. He who fears is not made perfect in love"* (I Jn. 4:18).

This means that if we love the Lord as we should, which means that we have a personal relationship with Him, we know that there is absolutely nothing that can happen to us but that He causes it or allows it. In this, we know that He is not going to allow anything that would be harmful to us. Even though at times certain things seem to be very negative and very detrimental, we still know that whatever the Lord causes or allows is all for our good. We love Him and we trust Him!

A fear-free life is truly *"more abundant life"* (Jn. 10:10).

FEAR AND THE CROSS OF CHRIST

Personally, I do not think that one can know a life free from fear without having a correct understanding of the Cross of Christ as it refers to our Sanctification. Every answer is found in the Cross, every solution to every problem is found in the Cross, and the Cross alone. There are no solutions found outside of the Cross, and there is no victory outside of the Cross!

Understanding the Cross as it refers to our Sanctification goes hand-in-hand with victory over fear. Beginning in 1997, the Lord began to open up to me the Revelation of the Cross; to be sure, during this time, we have faced some difficult situations at the Ministry. However, as I would take it to the Lord in prayer, whatever it may have been, even though at times I did not see how in the world the situation could be rectified, every single time I would commit it to the Lord, I knew that somehow He would meet the need.

To be sure, He always has. When I commit the situation to Him, there has never been any fear.

Before the Revelation of the Cross, I would lay awake all night countless times, worrying and fretting over particular problems. But since the Cross, there is no worry or anxiety. As David said, *"I will not be afraid."*

It doesn't matter what forces Satan brings against you, or how much they may seem to surround you, still, the forces available to the Lord are so much greater than those of the Evil One.

(7) "ARISE, O LORD; SAVE ME, O MY GOD: FOR YOU HAVE SMITTEN ALL MY ENEMIES UPON THE CHEEK BONE; YOU HAVE BROKEN THE TEETH OF THE UNGODLY."

This Verse presents an example of great Faith!

FAITH

Faith records as accomplished that which it confidently expects. Hence, the use of the past tense in this Verse. The particulars of this victory are recorded in John 8:1-12. Every man, including the Disciples, went to his own home. Jesus, having no where to lay His Head, went to the Mount of Olives; He spent the night there; in the morning, anticipating what would occur during the day, He sang this Psalm.

Upon entering the Temple (Jn. 8:2), the Scribes and Pharisees appeared with their victim, the adulteress, but Jesus covered them with shame, i.e., He smote them on the cheekbone and He broke their teeth, for He delivered the woman from their power.

So David, by faith, claims the victory, even though it has not yet happened.

To be sure, victories are won in the spirit world long before the actual happening. Only those who truly know the Lord and have a strong prayer life would understand this of which I here speak.

(8) "SALVATION BELONGS UNTO THE LORD: YOUR BLESSING IS UPON YOUR PEOPLE. SELAH."

Faith again reaches out!

BLESSINGS

David here claims the Blessings of the Lord, which always come upon God's people. He is God's Child, so he claims the Blessing.

Very few in Israel of that day would have believed that the Lord would have blessed David. They did not believe this because they did not understand Justification by Faith. But David knew that he could claim the Blessings of the Lord, which he did!

Furthermore, whatever the people thought, and whatever the people did, had no bearing whatsoever on what the Lord would do with David, that is, if David only would believe Him, which he did!

When one trusts the Lord, one can claim the Blessings of the Lord, and one should claim the Blessings of the Lord. If one has committed sin, one should confess it before the Lord, forsake it, and continue to believe God. That is God's Way!

The Lord longs for and seeks for means and ways to bless His people. We should believe that, understand that, and know that! We should expect the Blessings of the Lord — and bountiful Blessings at that!

PSALM 4

A Psalm of David:
An Evening Prayer of Trust in God

(1) "HEAR ME WHEN I CALL, O GOD OF MY RIGHTEOUSNESS: YOU HAVE ENLARGED ME WHEN I WAS IN DISTRESS; HAVE MERCY UPON ME, AND HEAR MY PRAYER."

This Psalm was composed by David on the same occasion as Psalm 3, when Absalom rebelled.

THE PRAYER

This is a prayer of distress concerning David in a time of great trial. And yet it is a prayer from the Lord Jesus Christ, as well. So, there is a double meaning to the Psalm. It concerns David and the Greater Son of David.

As David cried unto the Lord in this time of great distress when Absalom tried to kill him, likewise, the Lord Jesus Christ cried to God in the same manner when the Scribes and the Pharisees in the spirit of Absalom killed him.

In fact, the rebellion of Absalom against his father David is a type of what the Pharisees and the Scribes did to Christ, and was meant to serve as a type in that respect.

(2) "O YOU SONS OF MEN, HOW LONG WILL YOU TURN MY GLORY INTO SHAME? HOW LONG WILL YOU LOVE VANITY, AND SEEK AFTER LEASING? SELAH."

In this Verse, David refers to the sin of Absalom, which characterizes the sin of all men.

THREE SINS LISTED

There are three sins listed in this second Verse, which, in fact, are universal sins. They are:

1. Turning God's Glory to shame (Rom. 1:22-32). God's greatest Glory is His Creation of man; however, due to the Fall, man has turned after the ways of unrighteousness, thereby turning the Glory of God into shame.

Other than the few hours Adam lived righteously before the Fall, the only True Man Who has ever truly lived is the Lord Jesus Christ.

2. Unredeemed man loves vanity (Rom. 8:20; Eph. 4:17; II Pet. 2:18). Vanity stems from pride, which, within itself is the foundation sin of the human race (Prov. 6:16-17; I Jn. 2:16).

3. Leasing: This word means *"lying"* or *"falsehood"* (Prov. 17:4; 19:22). Satan is the father of lies; consequently, all of his children are liars. Actually, almost the entirety of the human race, in its pursuit of life outside of Christ, is based on a lie.

The sins listed in Verse 2 are the reason that Absalom rebelled against his father; the Scribes and the Pharisees rebelled against Christ; and all men rebel against God.

(3) "BUT KNOW THAT THE LORD HAS SET APART HIM WHO IS GODLY FOR HIMSELF: THE LORD WILL HEAR WHEN I CALL UNTO HIM."

David was God's man; he was called of God and anointed by God. Israel had been blessed immeasurably under his leadership, which, in effect, was the leadership of God. Now David had sinned with Bathsheba. Instead of the nation forgiving him and remembering that all of their blessing depended on him, on the contrary, they rebelled against him.

Why?

WHY DID ISRAEL REBEL AGAINST DAVID?

The reason was rebellion, pride, and lying. It would be the same reason that Israel used to reject the Lord Jesus Christ. The only difference was that David had sinned, but Christ had never sinned. The hearts of the people were the same in both cases.

The Third Verse means that the Lord has set aside Christ as His Own possession — made Him a special subject of Grace and Providence. As well, the Lord did the same for David and will to all who will take upon themselves the Lordship of Christ.

The Lord hears Christ, and He will hear us only because He hears Christ.

Everything is tied to Christ. Actually, when the Holy Spirit through David used the words in the Second Verse, *"My Glory,"* He was speaking of Christ. Christ is *"His Glory."* His Glory was that He was the Son of God, the Saviour. Men turned it into shame, declaring Him to be a devil (Jn. 8:48-54). Even though He saved others, He could not save Himself (Mat. 27:42-43). Truly, He would not save Himself. Had He saved Himself, we could not have been saved.

His traducers loved vanity, for they willingly gratified the passions of their nature (Jn. 8:44), and they followed after falsehood, for their father Satan, whom they willingly imitated, was a liar.

But He Whom they defamed was the Godly One Whom Jehovah had set apart for Himself. Only once was there seen on Earth a Man Whom the Holy Spirit could declare to be absolutely Godly, even as this Verse proclaims, and absolutely *"Righteous."* That Man was, and is, the Lord Jesus Christ.

(4) "STAND IN AWE, AND SIN NOT:

COMMUNE WITH YOUR OWN HEART UPON YOUR BED, AND BE STILL. SELAH."

This was perhaps addressed to David's faithful followers, who were zealous for him, advising them to check their wrath (II Sam. 16:9; 18:5-15).

As well, when reviled, Jesus did not revile again (I Pet. 2:23).

BE STILL

David would tell his followers to *"be still,"* simply because he had learned that he also must *"be still."*

This simply means that we aren't to take matters into our own hands, but rather *"be still"* and wait on the Lord, allowing Him to carry forth that which should be done.

I go back in time regarding my own personal Ministry. The year was 1988.

Something happened which was about as detrimental as it could ever be, as it regards efforts made against my own Ministry, to destroy what little we had left. These efforts were ugly, to say the least; so ugly, in fact, that I would not repeat them. They were totally untrue!

As well, this vile gossip was being carried out by religious leaders.

When it came to my ears, my immediate reaction was to defend myself. In fact, I called our Television Department, telling them that I was going to make a Special and air it over the entire nation to expose the lie and the liars.

I slept very little that night. Long before daylight, I was walking out in front of the house praying, seeking the Lord, asking for guidance and direction.

There were no waves of glory, and there did not seem to be any answer from the Lord, at least not at that time.

However, I've learned that the Lord always answers, that is, if we will earnestly seek Him, but it will be in His Own Way.

About eight o'clock that morning, Gabriel and Matthew (our grandsons), who then were little fellows, came over to the house. I was sitting outside with them, watching them while they were swimming in our pool.

After a few minutes, Frances walked out to where we were. She had the Bible in her hands. Of course, both Frances and I had been discussing the situation all the day before and a good part of the night.

She handed me her Bible and said, *"I believe the Lord has given us His answer as to what we should do!"*

I took the Bible as she pointed out the Verse to me. It read:

"The LORD shall fight for you, and you shall hold your peace" (Ex. 14:14).

The moment I read it, I sensed the Presence of the Lord. The tears began to roll down my face, simply because I knew the Lord had given me His Answer. Almost immediately, I went and called our Television Director to cancel the proposed Television Special.

I had the answer from the Lord. I was to do nothing. The Lord had promised me that He would fight for me. And that He has, from that day until this! Had I taken the steps that I was thinking of taking, it not only would not have done any good, but I would have forfeited the help which the Lord Alone could give me, the latter being the most important of all!

So, in a very limited way, I know David's feelings, as it regards this great Fourth Verse.

(5) "OFFER THE SACRIFICES OF RIGHTEOUSNESS, AND PUT YOUR TRUST IN THE LORD."

Even though these are the words of David, they were, in essence, the Words of Christ.

Jesus is saying that He counsels the Pharisees to commune with their own heart; to be silent in true conversion; and to offer righteous sacrifices and not mere oblations.

The Jews of Jesus' day offered many sacrifices, but not of Righteousness, because they did not put their *"trust in the LORD."*

Trust in the Lord is the Sacrifice of Righteousness. That Sacrifice goes all the way to what Jesus did on the Cross, for that is actually the meaning of the word *"sacrifices."*

(6) "THERE BE MANY WHO SAY, WHO WILL SHOW US ANY GOOD? LORD, LIFT THOU UP THE LIGHT OF YOUR COUNTENANCE UPON US."

David here asks a question, and then gives the answer.

HOW CAN GOD BRING GOOD OUT OF SUCH TRAGEDY?

There were many at this time who seemed

to throw in their lot with David, but who also, in essence, were asking the question, *"Can any good come out of this?"* They had very little, if any, faith! They were hearing the many enemies of David, who were saying that David was finished. Unfortunately, there are always a plethora of individuals of this stripe. They exercise no faith, but yet they don't quite see fit to join the enemy.

If someone will fully trust the Lord, exactly as David said in the previous Verse, the Lord is able to take whatever is, and have nothing left but that which is good. To be sure, only the Lord can do such a thing. It might take some time, even much time, but it is better to trust God and believe for what He will do than to give up and quit.

That's about the only thing the Lord cannot deal with, and I continue to speak of quitters. Irrespective of the past, as long as the person keeps believing and keeps trusting, it might take some time, but the Lord will bring the situation out, and do so with abundant Glory.

THE PRESENCE OF THE LORD

David answered the questions of the doubters by saying, *"LORD, lift Thou up the light of Your Countenance upon us."* In other words, *"If Your Presence is upon us, if Your Presence is with us, then You will make the impossible, possible!"*

The Lord would do exactly that for David, for the Son of David, and for all who follow the Son of David.

If the Presence of the Lord is with a person, there is nothing that cannot be done.

(7) "YOU HAVE PUT GLADNESS IN MY HEART, MORE THAN IN THE TIME THAT THEIR CORN AND THEIR WINE INCREASED."

A great testimony is here given.

THE LORD WILL MAKE A WAY

Being cut off from everything except the Lord, David, no doubt, wondered as to how he would be able to secure provisions for those who were following him!

The majority of Israel was following Absalom, because they were wanting and desiring the riches of Israel to be in their hands, which would happen if Absalom could gain

NOTES

the throne. They had no desire whatsoever for spiritual things, only material things!

So, David says that despite the difficulties, *"The LORD has put gladness in my heart,"* which expresses joy that no material things could ever provide. David's heart was more joyful than it would have been in the time of a great and bountiful harvest. Only the Lord could do such a thing.

To be sure, He can give such *"gladness,"* even when things look their worst!

(8) "I WILL BOTH LAY ME DOWN IN PEACE, AND SLEEP: FOR YOU, LORD, ONLY MAKE ME DWELL IN SAFETY."

Even though his kingdom was in ruins and he was being chased and marked for execution, still, David reposes in the Lord.

THE SON OF DAVID

Likewise, Jesus replied that the conscious Presence of God satisfies the heart with a gladness which wealth, however great, cannot give; He finally declares that though *"in solitude"* amid the shadows and dangers of the night now enwrapping Him, He will both lay Himself down in peace and sleep at once, because of the sure protection of Jehovah's wings. He did not lay Himself down in nervous fear as a Disciple might, but in peace, and went immediately to sleep, for He was the Prince and Perfecter of Faith (Heb. 12:2; Lk. 21:37).

PSALM 5

*A Psalm of David:
A Prayer for Protection*

(1) "GIVE EAR TO MY WORDS, O LORD, CONSIDER MY MEDITATION."

As the Third and Fifth Psalms relate to the Lord's outward enemies, so do the Fourth and Sixth to His inward sorrows. The Third and Fifth are morning Psalms. Thus, *"Jehovah My Shield"* (Ps. 3:3) corresponds to *"Jehovah My God"* (Ps. 5:2). If threatened by enemies, He had a Shield; if needing strength and vindication, He had God.

I believe I can say without fear of Scriptural contradiction that all of David's Psalms are also those of the Greater Son of David. The entirety of the Book of Psalms, more than likely, falls into this category, but most definitely those of David.

So, when one reads these prayers, petitions, praises, and instructions of another nature, one is reading of Christ in either His Atoning, Mediatorial, or Intercessory Work. As previously stated, when one reads the Gospels, one is reading the actions of our Lord, and when one reads the Psalms, one is reading His Heart.

MEDITATION

The word *"meditation"* connects this Psalm with the *"meditation"* of Psalm 1:2. Our Lord meditated in the Word of God (Ps. 1), and in the Ways of God (Ps. 5). It is said of the Lord Jesus, *"The Lord GOD has given Me the tongue of the learned, that I should know how to speak a word in season to him who is weary: He wakens morning by morning, He wakens My ear to hear as the learned"* (Isa. 50:4).

As every Believer is to have a consecrated prayer life, likewise, every Believer ought to have a time of study each day as it regards the Word of God, and then meditate day and night on the Word he has studied. Such will prove to be the most healthy, the most prosperous, function in which one could ever begin to engage.

In this day and age, everything is competing for man's attention. I speak of Television, Radio, publications, plus all types of other activity, etc.

Therefore, in order to meditate on the Word of God, we have to ask the Lord to help us do so, which He most definitely will.

Even though all of us must go about our daily business and duties, still, our thoughts must not be far from the Word of God. That being the case, the Holy Spirit will make meditation natural to us instead of something out of the ordinary.

There is a healing, strengthening, and saving factor about meditation on the Word that cannot be explained in the natural, but which most definitely is the truth. It is because the Word of God is totally unlike anything else, actually being alive, so to speak, because it is the Word of God. As such, it cannot be exhausted.

(2) "HEARKEN UNTO THE VOICE OF MY CRY, MY KING, AND MY GOD: FOR UNTO YOU WILL I PRAY."

Jesus was King of Jerusalem and God of the Temple, but in subjection as Man, He ascribed these titles to Jehovah (Mat. 21:5, 12).

(3) "MY VOICE SHALL YOU HEAR IN THE MORNING, O LORD; IN THE MORNING WILL I DIRECT MY PRAYER UNTO YOU, AND WILL LOOK UP."

In the morning, Christ set out His petitions in order before God, and during the day, He kept looking up for the answer; and the Gospels record how He received them. His enemies, i.e., those who watched Him (Lk. 20:20), were the Pharisees, for they had no faithfulness in their mouth — they were mere professors of the Law; the Sadducees, for their heart was an abyss of hatred (Lk. 19:47; 20:27-38); and the Herodians, for they flattered Him with their tongue while the purpose of their speech was to destroy His Life (Lk. 20:19-26).

Linking particular Scriptures regarding the prayer life of our Lord, they say, *"At evening, and at morning, and at noonday will I pray, and He shall hear My Voice"* (Ps. 55:17; 59:16; 88:13; 119:147).

In this Verse, the *"morning"* time of prayer is repeated, which adds force to the implied injunction. The words translated *"direct My prayer"* mean *"arrange"* or *"set in order"* as the Priests did the Altar before a Sacrifice (Lev. 1:7-8, 12; 6:5; Num. 28:4). In this sense, prayer is viewed as a sacrificial act, referring to the fact that all prayer must be based entirely on the Finished Work of Christ, i.e., the Cross.

THE MESSIAH

Just as the harp is not the author of its music which the hand awakes upon its strings, but yet must be attuned before the musician can use it, so David and the other inspired writers were not the authors of these Psalms. They were attuned by sorrows and joys to be as instruments from which these songs could be drawn.

Only the Messiah as the High Priest of His people can exhaust the language of these songs, but they have precious lessons for the heart that knows what it is to suffer shame and hatred for His Namesake.

So, as a result of His *"Meditation"* in the

Scriptures day and night, He, as a Man, learned that He was to enter Jerusalem; to cleanse the Temple of the Canaanite, the trafficker; to meet the hatred of the leaders of the nation; and to cause His people to rejoice.

In the morning, He set out His Petitions in order before God, and during the day, He kept looking up for the answers. That He received them is recorded in the Gospels.

(4) "FOR YOU ARE NOT A GOD WHO HAS PLEASURE IN WICKEDNESS: NEITHER SHALL EVIL DWELL WITH YOU."

There was no wickedness or evil in the Messiah. There were terrible wickedness and evil in Israel.

God cannot tolerate evil, irrespective as to how much His Name may be claimed, and irrespective of the religious posture, even as the Pharisees and the Sadducees. If it's not God's Way, which is according to His Word, and strictly according to His Word, then whatever the claims might be, the Lord labels it as *"wickedness"* and *"evil."*

To be frank, I think it can be said, and should be said, that anything that purports to be the Gospel outside of *"Jesus Christ and Him Crucified,"* which these Psalms bear out, must be labeled as *"wickedness"* and *"evil."*

(5) "THE FOOLISH SHALL NOT STAND IN YOUR SIGHT: YOU HATE ALL WORKERS OF INIQUITY."

In this Verse, the Holy Spirit brings out the position of those who veer from the Word of God.

WORKERS OF INIQUITY

Israel would be a fool and reject the Messiah; consequently, they would not stand in God's sight. He would put them away because He hated all workers of iniquity, irrespective of who they were.

God had made great Promises to Abraham, Isaac, and Jacob; however, those Promises to the Israel of Jesus' day could not be kept because of the evil that dwelt in Israel's heart.

Let all know and understand this: God cannot abide wickedness or evil even in those He calls His *"chosen."*

THE CROSS AND SANCTIFICATION

There are millions of Christians who truly love the Lord and are trying desperately to live as clean and straight as they know how; however, they have no knowledge as it regards the Cross and their Sanctification. As a result, they attempt to sanctify themselves and to do so by various means and methods, all unscriptural, and all totally ineffective.

This means that in some way, despite the best efforts of these people, whoever they might be, the sin nature is going to rule them in some form or fashion. They do not understand the Sixth Chapter of Romans, which portrays the manner in which the sin nature is to be made ineffective. Paul takes Believers, for it is to Believers that he speaks, directly to the Cross.

As stated, the first two Verses of this Chapter tell us that the problem is sin. Verses 3 through 5 then tell us that the only answer to sin, and in any form, is the Cross of Christ.

In this Sixth Chapter of Romans, the Apostle Paul tells us that if our faith is placed in the Cross as it ought to be, and maintained in the Cross, then the sin nature will be ineffective and cause us no problems, meaning that *"sin shall not have dominion over us"* (Rom. 6:14). Otherwise, and as stated, it most definitely will, and despite the best efforts of the best Christians.

Someone has well said, and rightly so, that the Sixth Chapter of Romans gives to us the *"mechanics of the Holy Spirit,"* which tells us *"how"* He works, and the Eighth Chapter of Romans gives us the *"dynamics of the Holy Spirit,"* which tells us *"what"* He does, once we understand *"how"* He does it.

The Holy Spirit works entirely within the framework of the Finished Work of Christ. He will not work outside of those parameters (Rom. 8:2). He only demands of us that our faith be exclusively in Christ and the Cross, and that it not be allowed to be placed in other things.

That's why the Apostle Paul told the Galatians:

"Behold, I Paul, say unto you, that if you be circumcised, Christ shall profit you nothing" (Gal. 5:2).

Some false teachers had come into the Churches in Galatia, and they were telling the Galatians that in order to be what they ought to be with the Lord, they had to also embrace the Law. They went on to explain to them that *"circumcision"* was the physical sign of the Covenant, and must be entered into by all the men and the little boys, that is, if they wanted to be what they should be with the Lord.

So Paul answers that charge by stating that if they placed their faith in circumcision (or anything else of such a nature, I might quickly add), then *"Christ shall profit you nothing."* This means that all that He did at Calvary's Cross will be to no avail, at least to those who place their faith elsewhere.

The point of this statement is that even though the Christians of which I speak are Godly people who are trying their hardest to live a Godly life, still, due to not having a correct understanding of the Cross of Christ as it affects our Sanctification, the sin nature is going to rule and reign in some manner, which will result in wickedness and evil, which the Lord cannot abide.

These good people, despite their zeal and love for God, will suffer as a result of their sin. And God cannot abide sin in any capacity. Sin is the very reason for the Cross, and that's what makes it so sinful and wicked for the Church to depart from the Cross. There is no other remedy!

(6) "YOU SHALL DESTROY THEM WHO SPEAK LEASING: THE LORD WILL ABHOR THE BLOODY AND DECEITFUL MAN."

This has a double meaning:

The first speaks of Ahithophel, who betrayed David. He was David's closest advisor. The second and foremost meaning speaks of Judas, one of the Lord's Disciples, who betrayed Him.

Ahithophel was angry because of the sin that David had committed with his granddaughter, Bathsheba. He would not forgive David. Judas was angry because the Lord would not use His Power to throw off Rome and set up Israel as the premier nation. In short, he totally rejected the real reason why Jesus came, which was to go to the Cross. In effect, he would not accept the Cross (Jn. 6:53-71).

They both, Ahithophel and Judas, lied. The Holy Spirit called both of them *"bloody and deceitful men."* They specialized *"in the lie."* Someone has said, *"The lie is the greatest weapon that your enemy can use against you, for there is no defense against a lie."*

(7) "BUT AS FOR ME, I WILL COME INTO YOUR HOUSE IN THE MULTITUDE OF YOUR MERCY: AND IN YOUR FEAR WILL I WORSHIP TOWARD YOUR HOLY TEMPLE."

The *"Temple"* referred to here is speaking of the Heavenly Temple, to which David prayed, and the Earthly Temple, into which Jesus went. Jesus called it *"My Father's House"* (Jn. 2:16).

So, He came into this *"House"* in *"Mercy"* and *"Fear"* and cleansed the Temple of its traffickers.

(8) "LEAD ME, O LORD, IN YOUR RIGHTEOUSNESS BECAUSE OF MY ENEMIES; MAKE YOUR WAY STRAIGHT BEFORE MY FACE."

When our Lord went into the Temple and cleansed it, He was led by the Holy Spirit because of Righteousness. As He was led by the Holy Spirit, He did not have to fear His *"enemies."* The *"straight way"* left no doubt about what He had to do. All God's Ways are *"straight." "Strait is the gate and narrow is the way that leads to life, and few there be who find it"* (Mat. 7:14).

(9) "FOR THERE IS NO FAITHFULNESS IN THEIR MOUTH; THEIR INWARD PART IS VERY WICKEDNESS; THEIR THROAT IS AN OPEN SEPULCHER; THEY FLATTER WITH THEIR TONGUE."

Even though David was speaking of those who, under Absalom, had come against him in order to take the kingdom, still, the greater meaning has to do with the Greater Son of David, and speaks of the Pharisees, the Sadducees, and the Herodians.

The phrase, *"Very wickedness,"* actually says, *"Nothing but wickedness."* What they emitted from their throats was from a putrid heart.

To *"flatter with their tongues"* refers to them asking smooth questions, i.e., trying to appear righteous and holy, when they were the very opposite. This applied to all three parties, Pharisees, Sadducees, and Herodians; quite possibly the Herodians were smoother than the others, but just as evil.

RELIGION

Religion can be described as the efforts of

man to better himself by his own devices, or to reach God in some way. In other words, religion is not of God. This means that Christianity is actually not a religion, but rather a relationship with a Man, The Man Christ Jesus.

When people depart from the Cross, trying to devise other ways of Salvation or Victory, they have just engaged in religion, which God can never accept.

In fact, there is nothing in the world more wicked than religion. It has soaked the Earth with blood. Using Cain as an example, religion, in one way or another, murders all who disagree with its concepts.

Self-righteousness is the product of religion and characterizes so much of the Church. It was the bane of the Pharisees during the time of Christ.

In fact, the Pharisees were the religious leaders of Israel. They concluded themselves to be fundamentalists, i.e., they claimed to believe all the Bible. But, in truth, they believed none of the Bible; they constantly changed it to suit their own fancy. They were bitter enemies of Christ, just as the modern variety continue to be bitter enemies of Christ, irrespective that they constantly use His Name.

(10) "DESTROY THOU THEM, O GOD; LET THEM FALL BY THEIR OWN COUNSELS; CAST THEM OUT IN THE MULTITUDE OF THEIR TRANSGRESSIONS; FOR THEY HAVE REBELLED AGAINST YOU."

Even though David prayed this prayer as it regards his enemies at that particular time, the prayer becomes even more powerful and more startling when we realize that this also is the prayer of Christ as it regards the Pharisees, Sadducees, and Herodians.

JUDGMENT

This prayer was answered in totality. Ahithophel committed suicide, and Absalom was killed just a few days later. In fact, the entirety of those who came against David were either destroyed or their effectiveness totally destroyed.

Likewise, in A.D. 70, Israel was completely destroyed by the Romans. In the sack and destruction of Jerusalem, over one million Jews were killed by the Roman Tenth Legion under Titus. Still another million were taken as slaves and sold all over the world, and thousands were given away at trifling prices.

TOUCH NOT MY ANOINTED AND DO MY PROPHETS NO HARM

First of all, let's see what the heading actually means, as it refers to Psalms 105:15.

Many have tried to use this Passage claiming that those who are truly anointed and who are true Prophets must never be questioned or called to account. Nothing could be further from the Truth.

While it definitely is wrong to attempt to harm those who fall into this category, as should be overly obvious, still, if one who is anointed by the Lord, and who would be in the classification of a Prophet, takes a false direction, such must be pointed out to him.

Paul did exactly that when he confronted Simon Peter, the Prince of the Apostles, even though Peter was older than Paul. Peter had been personally selected by Christ and had walked shoulder to shoulder with our Lord for some three and a half years. He was the man who preached the inaugural message on the Day of Pentecost, the man who was used mightily of God in healings, signs, wonders, and miracles.

But yet, Paul confronted him, and did so publicly, when Peter began to vacillate as it regards Law and Grace. If Paul had not done so, the Church could have been destroyed that very day, or at least been greatly weakened (Gal. 2:11-14).

And yet, it is very wrong, which also should be very obvious, for anyone to lay their hand upon one who is truly anointed by the Lord. Concerning new converts, Jesus said, *"Inasmuch as you did it not to one of the least of these, you did it not to Me"* (Mat. 25:45). If He said this about the *"least,"* and He most definitely did, what do you think the reaction of the Lord is, as it regards those who maliciously lay their hands on those who are truly called of God? The answer to that should be overly obvious.

Those who opposed David at this most critical time of his life and Ministry did so for a variety of reasons. The main reason, however, was that they thought this was the time to strike. David had sinned, and his sin was known over the entirety of Israel. Furthermore, the sin had been grievous, to say the least! They had even stated, *"There is no help for Him in God"* (Ps. 3:2). So they did not fear to lay their hands on him.

Yes, David had sinned, but David had also repented. Even if he had not repented, whatever was to be done to him was not at all their prerogative. That belonged to God.

Saul truly was wicked; however, at the leading of the Holy Spirit, David was not allowed to lift his hand against Saul. David opposed Saul's direction, and did so publicly, still, he did him no bodily harm, even when it was in his power to do so.

Let it be clearly known and understood: While it may be early or late, those who lay their hands maliciously on the Lord's anointed will not come away as they began. The Word of God plainly says that judgment will come on those who follow such a course.

(11) "BUT LET ALL THOSE WHO PUT THEIR TRUST IN YOU REJOICE: LET THEM EVER SHOUT FOR JOY, BECAUSE YOU DEFEND THEM: LET THEM ALSO WHO LOVE YOUR NAME BE JOYFUL IN YOU."

This Passage speaks of the Resurrection of the Lord Jesus Christ, as well as the Resurrection of David. Even though David did not literally die, still, as far as Israel was concerned, he was dead.

However, he placed his trust in Jehovah, and the Lord restored (resurrected) him to the Throne; likewise, Jesus rose from the dead with a shout o'er his foes; the Church shouted on the Day of Pentecost; there has been shouting for joy all the way on the line of march from Pentecost until now. When the Lord comes back, He will come back *"with a shout"* (I Thess. 4:16-17).

If we put our trust in the Lord, which brings about a great joy of heart, then the Lord will defend us.

BLESSINGS

One should notice the words which are used in this Scripture. They are *"rejoice," "shout for joy,"* and *"joyful in You."*

This is what trust in the Lord ultimately brings about. Trust in man brings about the very opposite!

(12) "FOR YOU, LORD, WILL BLESS THE RIGHTEOUS; WITH FAVOR WILL YOU COMPASS HIM AS WITH A SHIELD."

We are here shown the protection of the Lord for those who truly trust Him.

THE SHIELD

The Hebrew word used here for *"shield"* is *"zinnah."* It refers to the largest type of shield made, which covers the entirety of the body. So, the Lord is here telling us that those who trust Him will be totally and completely protected, and from every source and in every capacity.

THE RIGHTEOUS

The *"Righteous"* spoken of here is *"The Lord Jesus Christ."* Jehovah will bless His Son, the Lord Jesus Christ, and will bless all those who are in Christ.

PSALM 6

A Psalm of David:
The Intercessory Prayer of Christ

(1) "O LORD, REBUKE ME NOT IN YOUR ANGER, NEITHER CHASTEN ME IN YOUR HOT DISPLEASURE."

David wrote this Psalm.

THE INTERCESSION OF CHRIST

Even though David wrote this Psalm, it is a prayer, not only of David, but also of the Messiah. Our far greater spiritual instruction will be to study it from the vantage point of the Messiah.

Realizing it is difficult for the Reader to grasp or to understand the terminology as coming from the Lord Jesus Christ, still, if that be the case, it is because we do not really understand Christ as becoming our Substitute, and that He functions in three capacities, that of Atoning Saviour, Mediator, and Intercessor.

To more fully understand the implications of Christ as our Substitute, it is necessary to also understand the Incarnation. When God became Man, He fully became Man, and yet never ceased to be God. He laid aside the expression of His Deity, while never losing possession of His Deity. As David cried to be delivered from his enemies, and seemingly even to be forgiven of his sin, likewise, the Messiah cried to God as the High Priest and Advocate of Israel, pleading for them. He makes Himself one of them and prays as though He Himself merited God's just anger and displeasure.

This is the import of the word *"Me"* in this Verse. Most Christians do not fully understand the complete advocacy of Christ in Intercession. He becomes one with the sinner, even though He Himself never sinned. When He pleads to the Father on our behalf as He pleaded on Israel's behalf, He pleads as though He is the One Who actually failed and sinned. This is Advocacy and Intercession that is hard for us to even comprehend.

(2) "HAVE MERCY UPON ME, O LORD; FOR I AM WEAK; O LORD, HEAL ME; FOR MY BONES ARE VEXED."

As David cried these words to the Lord, he was saying that which the Son of David cried for Israel and for every Saint of God. The Writer of Hebrews says, *"He ever lives to make intercession for them"* (Heb. 7:25). Even though it is for us, still, He prays as though it is for Him. He enters into our hurts, our weaknesses, our sicknesses, and our vexation — and in a sense, even into our sins, even though He never failed in any capacity, not even one time.

OPPRESSION

In this petition, Bodily ailment certainly seems to be implied. But it is that sort of Bodily ailment which often is produced by mental distress — a general languor, weariness, and stress. Most of the time when we think of our Lord and the suffering He endured, we think of physical suffering; however, He experienced a mental distress, an oppression, if you will, as no other human being has ever experienced. Some of us have tasted that of which He bore the full brunt, and even the taste discomfited us.

Oppression is caused by demon spirits which afflict a person from without. Some sicknesses are caused by demon oppression, mental distress, as here recorded, plus fear, etc. To be sure, every Believer has experienced such, even as did our Lord! However, that which He experienced, that which He

NOTES

addressed at the Cross, lessened the load on us considerably, to say the least!

(3) "MY SOUL IS ALSO SORE VEXED: BUT YOU, O LORD, HOW LONG?"

Jesus repeated these words later in His Ministry when He said, *"Now is My soul troubled"* (Jn. 12:27). This Passage tells us that it is not the body alone which suffers; the soul also is vexed, and greatly vexed. Clearly the main emphasis is upon the mental suffering.

The question, *"But You, O LORD, how long?"* in essence says, *"How long shall I cry, and You will not hear?"* (Hab. 1:2). The cry is that of one wearied out with long suffering.

DAVID

The idea presented in this prayer of David is that the pressure was so great that minutes seemed like hours. David's situation seemed to grow worse by the hour; therefore, his request for the Lord to step in and help was urgent indeed!

(4) "RETURN, O LORD, DELIVER MY SOUL: OH SAVE ME FOR YOUR MERCIES' SAKE."

As David cries these words, he realizes that it is only the Mercy of God that will save Him. God can only show Mercy to those who do not deserve Mercy, in fact only to those who know they do not deserve Mercy. Millions think they deserve Mercy because of their Church attendance, religious works, or religious occupation. No man, no matter how pious he may seem to be, deserves the Mercy of God.

Mercy is a product of Grace. Only the one who does not deserve Grace can be the recipient of such. (None deserve it; however, the self-righteous think they do.)

In this instance, the Messiah pleads for Mercy for Israel's sake. Sadly, Israel will not receive Mercy because Israel thought she deserved such.

How can this Verse be correlated with Verse 10 of the previous Chapter, where David prays for the destruction of his enemies, which also is the prayer of the Messiah?

MERCY

God can show Mercy only on the premise of true Repentance. If they will not repent, then they must be destroyed. Regrettably, Absalom and those who followed him did not repent, and neither did the Israel of Jesus' day.

So, there is no contradiction of terms here, but only the course which the Lord has always followed. Repentance brings Mercy, while rebellion ultimately brings destruction!

(5) "FOR IN DEATH THERE IS NO REMEMBRANCE OF YOU: IN THE GRAVE WHO SHALL GIVE YOU THANKS?"

First, second, and third opportunities are on this side of the grave. After death there are no more opportunities to get right with God (Lk., Chpt. 16). Consequently, the Catholic doctrine of Purgatory is error. There is no Purgatory.

The Messiah knows that if Israel doesn't turn to God, Israel will die. Israel would not turn to God, and Israel did die. In A.D. 70, Titus, the leader of the great Roman Tenth Legion, completely destroyed Israel. When the Lord of Glory cried these words, Israel was on the eve of death.

How many times has He said the same thing for those who have continued to rebel and who are on the eve of destruction, even though they little know of their personal danger?

SOUL SLEEP?

The doctrine that the soul sleeps in the grave until the First Resurrection is not Scriptural. The Bible does not teach such. What David is addressing here pertains to opportunities that we have in life which will be no more after death.

Before the Cross, when Believers died, the body went back to dust and the soul and the spirit went to Paradise (Lk. 16:19-31). When the unredeemed died, their bodies also went back to dust, but their soul and spirit instantly went to Hell.

Since the Cross, there is a difference. For the Believer, the body goes to the grave and thereby to dust, and the soul and the spirit instantly go to be with Christ (Phil. 1:23).

At the Resurrection of Life, which is the same as the Rapture, the soul and the spirit of every Believer will come back with the Lord, and each will be given a Glorified Body, which will be very similar to the body he or she had on Earth, minus several things (I Thess. 4:13-18).

First of all, there will be no imperfections. Also, the evidence is that babies and little children will receive adult bodies. The body will be Glorified, which means that it will be like Christ when He was raised from the dead. In this Glorified Body, the indication is that it will be flesh and bone, and there will be no blood (Lk. 24:39).

The life of the flesh presently is in the blood, but then it will be in the Spirit, i.e., *"the Holy Spirit"* (I Cor., Chpt. 15).

As it regards the unredeemed dead, while they will experience a resurrection, it will be a thousand years later than the Resurrection of Life (Rev. 20:5-6). At that time, they will be given indestructible bodies, with which they will stand at the Great White Throne Judgment (Rev. 20:11-15). They will then be cast into the Lake of Fire, where they will remain forever and forever (Rev. 20:10, 14-15).

So, when the Bible speaks of death as sleep, or certain things about the grave, it is only speaking of the physical body, and not the soul and the spirit. There is no such thing as soul sleep, as taught by some.

(6) "I AM WEARY WITH MY GROANING; ALL THE NIGHT MAKE I MY BED TO SWIM; I WATER MY COUCH WITH MY TEARS."

Other nights the Messiah would not have a bed; when He was in Jerusalem, He would lodge in the open (most of the time on the Mount of Olives). Tonight He had a bed, for it says, *"He went out to Bethany and lodged there"* (Mat. 21:17).

But He did not sleep, for in secret He wept bitterly over the guilty city, as that day He had wept aloud over it in public (Lk. 19:41). He burdened Himself both day and night with the sins and sorrows of the city He loved.

DAVID

Despite the fact that the Lord had forgiven David and he was assured of the Lord's help, still, his tremendous sorrow was caused by his heartache over what was happening, knowing that he was to blame. Sin carries with it a terrible aftermath, even though the Lord forgives, cleanses, and washes clean. And the closer one is to God, the more that one loves the Lord, knowing the harm that the Work of God has suffered, and knowing that the blame must lie at the doorstep of the perpetrator, the grief knows no end.

There are few, if any, men in history who were closer to the Lord than David. Considering that the Redeemer would come through his family, considering that the Redeemer would be referred to as *"The Son of David,"* this makes the sorrow all the more acute!

At such a time, enemies seem to come out of the woodwork. In all of the aftermath, untold numbers of innocent people are hurt; therefore, David would *"water my couch with my tears."*

(7) "MY EYE IS CONSUMED BECAUSE OF GRIEF; IT WAXES OLD BECAUSE OF ALL MY ENEMIES."

David's enemies were myriad because David was a Type of Christ. Christ also would be surrounded by many enemies — the Pharisees, the Sadducees, and the Herodians, to name a few.

ENEMIES

These enemies are almost always numbered with the people of God, even though they are not of God. The modern Church is filled with such.

What do we mean by the word *"enemies"*?

At the present time, it would refer to all who object to the Message of the Cross; to be sure, that number also is myriad.

Concerning this, the Apostle Paul said, and I quote from THE EXPOSITOR'S STUDY BIBLE:

"For many walk (speaks of those attempting to live for God outside of the victory and rudiments of the Cross of Christ), *of whom I have told you often, and now tell you even weeping* (this is a most serious matter), *that they are the enemies of the Cross of Christ* (those who do not look exclusively to the Cross of Christ must be labeled 'enemies'):

"Whose end is destruction (if the Cross is ignored, and continues to be ignored, the loss of the soul is the only ultimate conclusion), *whose god is their belly* (refers to those who attempt to pervert the Gospel for their own personal gain), *and whose glory is in their shame* (the material things they seek, God labels as *'shame'*), *who mind earthly things.* (This means they have no interest in Heavenly things, which signifies they are using the Lord for their own personal gain)" (Phil. 3:18-19).

Unfortunately, the enemies of the Cross take the same position as did Cain of old. They are not content with opposing the Message of the Cross; they feel they have to use any means at their disposal to stop the voice that proclaims the Message, even as Cain murdered Abel.

The way the Bible described the word *"murder,"* it includes not only the taking of life, but also the destruction of character, etc. In other words, God looks at the efforts to destroy the character of another by gossip, whispering, etc., the same as *"murder."*

(8) "DEPART FROM ME, ALL YOU WORKERS OF INIQUITY; FOR THE LORD HAS HEARD THE VOICE OF MY WEEPING."

For three and a half years of public Ministry, our Lord importuned the leaders of Israel to return to God; however, they persisted in their iniquity and rebellion. Soon He would depart for Glory, and soon they would depart for eternal darkness; He said, *"And where I am, thither you cannot come"* (Jn. 7:34).

David knows that the Lord has heard his prayer; despite what others say, he knows he will be rescued. So he can demand, and rightly so, that those who would hurt him ultimately be taken out by the Lord. In the natural, it did not look that way at all; however, due to the Lord moving greatly on David's heart, despite what others thought, he knew what the outcome would be!

(9) "THE LORD HAS HEARD MY SUPPLICATION; THE LORD WILL RECEIVE MY PRAYER."

The Lord always hears the prayer of the Messiah. He always heeds His Supplication. Every single Intercession that the Lord of Glory has ever made on behalf of a Child of God has always, without fail, been answered; therefore, the Scripture says, *"If we confess our sins, He is faithful and just to forgive us our sins, and to cleanse us from all unrighteousness"* (I Jn. 1:9).

Counting the previous Verse, there is a threefold repetition, which marks the absoluteness of the Psalmist's conviction. The

Lord will come to his rescue!

(10) "LET ALL MY ENEMIES BE ASHAMED AND SORE VEXED: LET THEM RETURN AND BE ASHAMED SUDDENLY."

Concerning the Messiah, this has not yet been answered. It will be answered in the not-too-distant future.

The Prophet Zechariah said, *"And I will pour upon the House of David, and upon the inhabitants of Jerusalem, the Spirit of Grace and of supplications: and they shall look upon Me Whom they have pierced, and they shall mourn for Him as one mourns for his only son, and shall be in bitterness for Him as one who is in bitterness for his firstborn"* (Zech. 12:10).

This will take place at the beginning of the Kingdom Age after Israel has come to Christ. They will accept Him fully as Saviour and as Lord! Then this prayer will be totally and completely answered!

PSALM 7

*A Psalm of David:
A Petition for Protection*

(1) "O LORD MY GOD, IN YOU DO I PUT MY TRUST: SAVE ME FROM ALL THEM WHO PERSECUTE ME, AND DELIVER ME."

David wrote this Psalm more than likely while Saul was attempting to kill him, which, as is obvious, would have been quite some time before the writing of Psalms 3 and 4.

THE SUFFERING OF THE MESSIAH

Even though this Psalm pertained to David as it regards his tremendous difficulties referring to Saul, still, in a greater way it refers to the suffering of the Messiah in sympathy with the elect remnant of Israel under the persecution of the Antichrist. As Jesus is the True Man and the True Church, He is also the True Israel. As such, He calls to God on their behalf. In that coming day, that Remnant, guided by the Spirit of God in them, and we speak of the few Jews who will know the Lord at that time, will use this language and be strengthened by it.

This Psalm, which David sang unto the Lord, concerned the words of Cush the Benjamite. The Bible does not say who Cush was, except that he belonged to the Tribe of Benjamin, Saul's Tribe. The word means *"black."* The original Cush was a grandson of Noah and a progenitor of the Egyptians (Gen. 10:10). Here, he is introduced as a type of the Antichrist, the future Pharaoh.

It was probably during Saul's pursuit of David that this member of Saul's Tribe spoke in a manner against David that furnished the opportunity for the Holy Spirit to inspire this Song and Prophecy.

I think it would be obvious that David's personal experiences and moral character were much below the language of the Psalm. It is, therefore, prophetic of the Messiah.

(2) "LEST HE TEAR MY SOUL LIKE A LION, RENDING IT IN PIECES, WHILE THERE IS NONE TO DELIVER."

Here David's chief persecutor is compared to a lion, and David has no one to deliver him. As the lion is the king of beasts, so Saul was king of the land. As the lion in his fierceness seizes and tears his prey to pieces, so David was in danger of being seized and destroyed by Saul. All this answers to the some twenty-one attempts of Saul to kill David (I Sam. 18:1-26:2).

(3) "O LORD MY GOD, IF I HAVE DONE THIS; IF THERE BE INIQUITY IN MY HANDS;

(4) "IF I HAVE REWARDED EVIL UNTO HIM THAT WAS AT PEACE WITH ME; (YEA, I HAVE DELIVERED HIM THAT WITHOUT CAUSE IS MY ENEMY:)

(5) "LET THE ENEMY PERSECUTE MY SOUL, AND TAKE IT; YEA, LET HIM TREAD DOWN MY LIFE UPON THE EARTH, AND LAY MY HONOR IN THE DUST, SELAH."

David was accused by Saul of seeking the kingdom and the opportunity to kill the king. David denies these charges here before God, offering to lay down his life if such be true (Vss. 3-5). The following are the seven denials of David:

DAVID'S PROCLAMATION TO THE LORD

1. *"I have not plotted to get the kingdom."*
2. *"I have not plotted the murder of Saul."*
3. *"I have not rewarded evil to Saul but have been at peace with him."*
4. *"I am not guilty, or I would not have*

delivered Saul from death after he became my enemy" (I Sam. 24:1-22; 26:1-25).

5. *"If I am guilty, let Saul capture me,"* which he did not (Vs. 5).

6. *"If I am guilty, let him destroy my life,"* which Saul did not (Vs. 5).

7. *"If I am guilty, let him take away my honor,"* which he did not (Vs. 5).

Likewise, in the Great Tribulation, Christ and the Antichrist will confront each other. The man of sin will accuse the Lord Jesus Christ of being the cause of all the problems that beset the people of Israel and the entirety of the world. As Saul repeatedly lied about David, the Antichrist will lie repeatedly about Christ. As the accusations were untrue about David, they will, of course, also be untrue about Christ.

(6) "ARISE, O LORD, IN YOUR ANGER, LIFT UP YOURSELF BECAUSE OF THE RAGE OF MY ENEMIES: AND AWAKE FOR ME TO THE JUDGMENT THAT YOU HAVE COMMANDED."

Addressing this petition, Pulpit Commentary says, *"To call on God to 'arise' is to ask Him to take action, to lay aside the mutual attitude in which He most commonly shows Himself to man, and to interfere openly in the concerns of Earth.*

"To call on Him to 'arise in His anger' is to entreat Him to vindicate our cause against those opposed to us, and to visit them with some open manifestation of His displeasure."[4]

The short phrase, *"Lift up Yourself,"* is even a stronger expression than *"Arise"* (Isa. 33:10). It is a call on God to appear in His full strength.

The idea here presented is that force must be met by force. David justifies his appeal by alleging the violence and fury of those whose attacks he has to meet.

JUDGMENT

The phrase, *"And await for me to the judgment that You have commanded,"* presents two phrases which, in the original, are not connected. It actually reads, *"Await for me: You have commanded judgment."* The meaning seems to be, *"Arise Yourself on my behalf — judgment is a thing which You have ordained — surely now is the time for it."*

THE DISPENSATION OF GRACE

Inasmuch as David was living under the Dispensation of Law, and we presently are living under the Dispensation of Grace, the question must be asked, *"Would it be proper for modern Believers to pray such a prayer as David prayed?"*

Yes, it would!

David did not instigate any type of force or action against these people. He did defend himself against the army of Absalom when he was attacked, and rightly so. But he did not initiate the insurrection, as is overly obvious.

So, he is asking the Lord to either stop the situation as it is, without any type of force having to be used, or else to help him when the time comes to properly defend himself, and more than all to defend the Work of God. And that's exactly what the Lord did!

David is not taking matters into his own hands, and neither should we. By praying as he did, he is putting matters totally in the Hands of the Lord.

It wasn't merely David's feelings at stake, nor his position as king, as important as that definitely was. It was the Work of God which was at stake. If Absalom had had his way, we might not even be here today. That's how critical the situation was!

(7) "SO SHALL THE CONGREGATION OF THE PEOPLE COMPASS YOU ABOUT: FOR THEIR SAKES THEREFORE RETURN THOU ON HIGH."

This Verse proclaims tremendous spiritual knowledge on the part of David.

THE WORK OF THE LORD, PRESENT AND FUTURE!

The phrase, *"So shall the congregation of the people compass you about,"* says the following:

If the Lord will show Himself in Judgment, thereby bringing to a halt this insurrection which threatens the Work of God, *"the congregation of the people"* — not, apparently, Israel only — will crowd around You in acknowledgment of Your Majesty, and recognize in You the Righteous Judge of all the Earth.

It seems that David knew what was at stake.

So he looks beyond Israel to the entirety of the world. By faith, he sees the Church, even as he does Israel. In other words, if the Lord did not intervene, it would jeopardize His Work even unto the distant future. And that was exactly correct! So his petition was predicated on this knowledge.

I'm afraid that all too often our present actions are centered too much on ourselves. We do not properly take into consideration the Work of God and how it is being affected, presently and into the future. Perhaps if we properly did this, even as David here serves as our example, we would do things differently!

(8) "THE LORD SHALL JUDGE THE PEOPLE: JUDGE ME, O LORD, ACCORDING TO MY RIGHTEOUSNESS, AND ACCORDING TO MY INTEGRITY THAT IS IN ME."

The Holy Spirit now moves upon David in answer to the petition that he has made.

THE JUDGMENT OF THE LORD

Previously, judgment had been prayed for; now it is announced. *"The LORD shall judge"* — shall decide between David and his enemies — shall judge them in His anger, and, at the same time, judge David, i.e., vindicate his cause.

RIGHTEOUSNESS

The phrase, *"Judge me, O LORD, according to my righteousness,"* in effect, says, *"Judge me, and if you find righteousness, acquit me, and vindicate me."*

The question may be asked as to how David could claim righteousness, considering his past terrible sins of adultery and murder? In fact, the uprising of Absalom took place about ten years after the situation with Bathsheba.

Irrespective of the sin, whenever a person honestly repents before God, at that moment every sin is washed and cleansed, with God now looking at the person as if they had never sinned. Unfortunately, most of the modern Church does not understand this. I speak of *"Justification by Faith."*

JUSTIFICATION BY FAITH

The great question is, *"How can a thrice-Holy God justify an obviously guilty sinner, thereby proclaiming him clean, and, at the same time, maintain His justness?"*

Paul addressed this by making the following statement, and I quote from THE EXPOSITOR'S STUDY BIBLE:

"Being justified freely by His Grace (made possible by the Cross) *through the Redemption that is in Christ Jesus* (carried out at the Cross):

"Whom God has set forth to be a propitiation (Atonement or Reconciliation) *through Faith in His Blood* (again, all of this is made possible by the Cross), *to declare His Righteousness for the remission of sins that are past* (refers to all who trusted Christ before He actually came, which covers the entirety of the time from the Garden of Eden to the moment Jesus died on the Cross), *through the forbearance* (tolerance) *of God* (meaning that God tolerated the situation before Calvary, knowing the debt would be fully paid at that time);

"To declare, I say, at this time His Righteousness (refers to God's Righteousness, which must be satisfied at all times, and is in Christ and only Christ): *that He* (God) *might be Just* (not overlooking sin in any manner), *and the Justifier of him which believes in Jesus.* (God can justify a believing [although guilty] sinner and His Holiness not be impacted, providing the sinner's Faith is exclusively in Christ. Only in this manner can God be *'just'* and at the same time *'justify'* the sinner)" (Rom. 3:24-26).

An altogether righteous God can declare an altogether unrighteous individual as justified, but only on the basis of the Finished Work of Christ, which necessitates the person's faith in that Finished Work.

Justification by Faith is a declaration of *"Not Guilty!"* on the basis of justice satisfied by what Christ did at the Cross. That's the reason the Cross is so very, very important!

(9) "OH LET THE WICKEDNESS OF THE WICKED COME TO AN END; BUT ESTABLISH THE JUST: FOR THE RIGHTEOUS GOD TRIES THE HEARTS AND REINS."

It is not so much the removal of the wicked that David desires, but rather the removal of their wickedness. Unfortunately, unless such a person comes to Christ, they have to be removed along with their wickedness, because

THE HEART OF MAN

The phrase, *"For the Righteous God tries the hearts and reins,"* refers to the word *"heart"* being used as a catch-all phrase for the seat of understanding and the will. It is the *"reins"* of natural impulses and affections. It is not speaking of the physical organ which we refer to as the *"heart."*

As it regards the *"heart"* as it mostly is used in the Bible, it refers essentially to the whole man, with all his attributes, physical, intellectual, and spiritual, of which the Hebrew thought and spoke; the heart was conceived of as the governing center of all of these. It is the heart which makes a man or a beast what he is, and which governs all his actions (Prov. 4:23). Character, personality, will, and mind are all modern terms which all reflect something of the meaning of *"heart"* in its Biblical usage. This means that *"heart"* comes the nearest to the Old Testament and New Testament terms for *"person."*

THE RIGHT ATTITUDE OF THE HEART

The right attitude of the heart begins with it being broken or crushed (Ps. 51:17), symbolic of humility and penitence, and synonymous with *"a broken spirit."* This brokenness is necessary because it is the heart, or stony heart, which does not submit to the Will of God (Ezek. 11:19).

The Lord knows the heart of each person and is not deceived by outward appearance (I Sam. 16:7), but a worthy prayer is, nevertheless, that He should search and know the heart (Ps. 139:23), and make it clean (Ps. 51:10).

A *"new heart"* must be the aim of all (Ezek. 18:31), and that means that God's Law has to become no longer merely external but *"written on the heart"* to make it clean (Jer. 31:33).

Thus it is that the heart, the spring of all desires, must be guarded (Prov. 4:23), and the teacher aims to win his people's heart to the right way (Prov. 23:26).

It is the pure in heart who shall see God (Mat. 5:8), and it is through Christ's dwelling in the heart by faith that the Saints can comprehend the love of God (Eph. 3:17).

(Much of the material on the heart was derived from the *"New Bible Dictionary."*)

(10) "MY DEFENSE IS OF GOD, WHICH SAVES THE UPRIGHT IN HEART."

God tries the hearts that are so deceitful and desperately wicked (Jer. 17:9-10).

GOD'S SHIELD

The phrase, *"My defense is of God,"* literally, in the original Hebrew, is *"My shield is on God,"* i.e., *"rests on Him"* or *"is upheld by Him."*

There is a shield around every single Believer in the world, and there always has been.

The Lord told Abraham, *"Fear not, Abram: I am your shield, and your exceeding great reward"* (Gen. 15:1).

All of this means that nothing can happen to a Child of God unless the Lord causes it or allows it. The Lord definitely did not cause David's problems, because David himself caused those problems, but the Lord allowed the opposition against him for particular reasons.

If the Lord allows something, whatever it is, it is always for our good.

The Lord in no way causes us to sin or do wrong, as should be overly obvious, but He does cause many good things to happen to us, things which we could never rightly deserve, but which He freely gives to us. In truth, He is the cause of all good things!

Certain negative situations may allow Satan to have much more latitude in the life of a Believer, which will, or may, cause great problems, still, whatever happens to the Child of God, the Lord has to give the Evil One permission; even then, the Lord draws the lines which control the severity of the attack.

Satan is on a leash; he can only do what the Lord allows him to do, which is predicated on our actions, etc. (Job, Chpts. 1-2). That should be a great consolation to the Child of God, and I speak of being under the protection of the Lord at all times. In effect, the Lord is our *"Shield."*

(11) "GOD JUDGES THE RIGHTEOUS, AND GOD IS ANGRY WITH THE WICKED EVERY DAY."

Two great things are here said:

GOD, THE RIGHTEOUS JUDGE

The phrase, *"God judges the righteous,"* should have been translated *"God is a Righteous Judge."* He can judge righteously simply because He is Righteousness, which means that He doesn't merely *"have"* Righteousness, but He, in fact, *"is"* Righteousness.

He knows all things — past, present, and future. He Alone can read the hearts of men and ascertain their motives, their desires, and their true feelings.

Since man cannot do these things, man is not allowed to judge the character and the motives of another (Mat. 7:1-5).

THE ANGER OF GOD

The three words, *"with the wicked,"* were inserted by the translators. They are unnecessary, since, of course, it is with the wicked that God is angry.

What the Psalmist means to assert especially is that God's anger continues against the wicked as long as their wickedness continues.

God is so unalterably opposed to sin that He cannot abide it in any form. The Cross of Christ is the only thing that stops Him from raining Judgment, in a manner heretofore unknown, upon this world. *"God loves the world so much that He gave His Only Begotten Son . . ."* (Jn. 3:16). However, His love cannot overlook sin, so that love became Man in order to go to a Cross, that mankind might be saved.

(12) "IF HE TURN NOT, HE WILL WHET HIS SWORD; HE HAS BENT HIS BOW, AND MADE IT READY."

Concerning this phrase, Bishop Horne said, *"Every new transgression sets a fresh edge to God's sword."*

The Lord takes such action only as long as His Work is threatened.

People who do not know the Lord, whoever they might be, have no protection whatsoever unless a loved one or someone else is praying for them, or else, through foreknowledge, the Lord knows that person will ultimately come to God and be used of Him.

Let me give a personal example.

NOTES

THE WAYS OF THE LORD

On March 15, 1935, I was born into a home that did not know the Lord. Until my Dad was twenty-five years old, he had never been inside of a Church, had never heard a Gospel Message, had never even heard a Gospel Song.

My Mother and Dad tried to live good and moral lives. But, without the Lord, such efforts fall into the category of impossible.

Concerning the occasion of this illustration, I was two years old. My Mother and Dad had gone to another area from their home, where both of them had a few days work. This was in 1937, the very heart of the depression, and money was very, very scarce.

They were staying in a little cottage, where several of these small cottages were linked side-by-side.

After being there for a couple of days and nights, something happened that could be attributed only to the Lord — even though my parents were unsaved.

My Dad awoke in the night and noticed that I was standing on the floor by the side of the door. He called out to me, loudly and several times, to get back into bed. Without explanation, he suddenly realized that I was in bed. Even though he did not then understand what had happened, he had had a Vision.

What did it all mean?

The next morning the area was in an uproar because two people had been murdered – one person in each of the cottages on either side of our cottage. Someone had broken into these cottages, stolen their money (what little they had), and murdered them.

When my Dad investigated the door of our cabin, he found the latch had nearly been broken. Then he realized that when he shouted for me to get back into bed, this must have scared off the intruders, who, no doubt, would have murdered all of us, exactly as they had murdered the others.

As stated, my Mother and Dad did not, at that time, know the Lord. But yet the Lord knew that they would give their hearts to Him about two years later. My Dad, in fact, would be greatly used of the Lord in planting several Churches, and seeing many, many people saved. Then the Lord would save me when I was eight years old, fill me with His Spirit, and call me to preach the Gospel, which we have been able to do all over the world.

Had the Lord, through foreknowledge, not seen that we ultimately would give our hearts to Him, there is a possibility that we also would have been murdered that night.

We serve a wonderful God!

(13) "HE HAS ALSO PREPARED FOR HIM THE INSTRUMENTS OF DEATH; HE ORDAINS HIS ARROWS AGAINST THE PERSECUTORS."

The Lord is deathly opposed to wickedness, which includes those who allow such in their lives, who even harbor and cherish such.

THE INSTRUMENTS OF DEATH

There is a tremendous meaning behind this statement, *"Instruments of death."* It is far more involved than meets the eye.

Considering the horrendous death toll which resulted when the Tsunami hit the Far East during the Christmas Season of 2004, millions asked the question, *"Why?"* Actually, all such similar disasters, whether large or small, evoke the same type of question, and understandably so!

In the Olivet Discourse, Jesus answered the question. He listed particular disasters, such as wars, famines, pestilences, earthquakes, etc., and then said, *"All these are the beginning of sorrows"* (Mat. 24:7-8).

At His First Advent, the Son of God offered the Kingdom to Israel (Mat. 4:17). Had Israel accepted, Jesus still would have had to go to the Cross. But the Romans surely would have taken care of that. Of course, had this happened, the Resurrection, Ascension, and the Exaltation of Christ also would have taken place at that time (Acts 2:33), the Second Coming would have come about very shortly thereafter, and the Millennium would have begun almost immediately. Naturally, the Lord, through foreknowledge, knew this would not happen.

At any rate, because Israel rejected their Messiah, this consigned the balance of the world to continued wars, bloodshed, and troubled elements.

So, Israel's rejection of her Messiah is the cause of much death. In all of this, the Lord allows wars, turbulence, etc., because of man rejecting God.

There is not a problem in the world that could not be solved if nations would turn to God instead of going on in their rebellious ways. This would solve the problems in Africa, in Central and South America, and in every nation of the world, including the United States.

In every country of the world, sin is so pronounced that judgment is inevitable. At certain times, the Lord *"prepares instruments of death."* Considering sin, He has no choice!

(14) "BEHOLD, HE TRAVAILS WITH INIQUITY, AND HAS CONCEIVED MISCHIEF, AND BROUGHT FORTH FALSEHOOD."

In the superscription of this Psalm, it reads, *"Shiggaion of David, which he sang unto the Lord, concerning the words of Cush the Benjamite."*

David says the man *"travailed with iniquity,"* which means that he *"turned everything he touched into iniquity."* He was a *"liar."* As such, and as stated, he prefigures the coming Antichrist.

(15) "HE MADE A PIT, AND DIGGED IT, AND IS FALLEN INTO THE DITCH WHICH HE MADE."

Cush had concocted a scheme to ensnare and kill David; but whatever it was that he did, instead of it destroying David, it destroyed him.

Likewise, in the Battle of Armageddon, as the Antichrist *"makes a pit"* in order to bury Israel, he instead will be buried in that pit himself. The Second Coming of the Lord will guarantee that!

(16) "HIS MISCHIEF SHALL RETURN UPON HIS OWN HEAD, AND HIS VIOLENT DEALING SHALL COME DOWN UPON HIS OWN PATE."

Even though this prefigures the Antichrist, who will also follow this course, this also characterizes all of humanity that is without God. Cush outsmarted himself, which is the lot of all who seek to come against the Lord's Anointed.

(17) "I WILL PRAISE THE LORD ACCORDING TO HIS RIGHTEOUSNESS: AND WILL SING PRAISE TO THE NAME OF THE LORD MOST HIGH."

Victory belongs to the Lord!

THE MOST HIGH

The phrase, *"Most High,"* in the Hebrew is *"Elyon,"* which means *"possessor of Heaven and Earth; the Dispenser of God's Blessings in the Earth."* The word is first used in the Bible in Genesis 14:18. This is the first time it is used in the Book of Psalms. It is one of the titles of the Messiah as *"Most High"* over the Earth, which will take place in the coming Kingdom Age.

In these Prophetic communications, the great fact appears once more that the Lord Jesus Christ is never far from those who love Him; that He sympathizes with us; that He makes our sorrows His Own; and that He will surely deliver us from our strongest foes, whether spiritual or physical.

This fact has comforted and strengthened the servants of God in the past; it comforts and strengthens us in the present; and it will most signally do so in the future.

PSALM 8

A Psalm of David:
The Sovereignty of the Son of Man

(1) "O LORD, OUR LORD, HOW EXCELLENT IS YOUR NAME IN ALL THE EARTH! WHO HAS SET YOUR GLORY ABOVE THE HEAVENS."

The Holy Spirit, in Matthew 21:16, I Corinthians 15:27, Ephesians 1:22, and Hebrews 2:5-8, affirms the Messiah to be the Man of this Song.

These first eight Psalms set the Messiah forth as the True Adam (Ps. 1); as the True King (Ps. 2); but rejected and persecuted (Ps. 3-7); and finally as Lord over all the Earth (Ps. 8).

SOVEREIGN LORD

When one looks at the beginning and the ending of the Psalm, one finds that it ends exactly as it begins. *"LORD"* in the Hebrew means *"Jehovah Adonai."* It means *"Jehovah, our Sovereign."*

Written by David, it is called a Messianic Psalm. It pictures the happiness to fill the Earth when, after the destruction of the Antichrist and his followers, the Messiah will establish His Kingdom of Righteousness and Peace; His right to ascend the Throne is declared in His Glory as God, as Lord of the whole Earth, as Son of Man, and as King of Israel, King of kings.

His Name is not now excellent in all the Earth, for He is still despised and rejected by men. But on the Millennial morn, His Name, over all the Earth and forever, will indeed be excellent!

(2) "OUT OF THE MOUTH OF BABES AND SUCKLINGS HAVE YOU ORDAINED STRENGTH BECAUSE OF YOUR ENEMIES, THAT YOU MIGHT STILL THE ENEMY AND THE AVENGER."

As Verse 1 extols the Glory of the Messiah as Creator, this second Verse extols His Glory as Redeemer.

The word *"babes"* is figurative and portrays the redeemed. The redeemed will praise Him because He has *"stilled the enemy and the avenger"* — namely, Satan.

THE LORD OUR VICTOR

The latter part of this Verse refers to the Antichrist and how he will be defeated in the Battle of Armageddon by the Second Coming. But, even in a greater sense, it pertains to the great victory won at Calvary's Cross.

The victory at Calvary guarantees all other victories. Without the Cross, there could have been no Redemption and no Second Coming. Without the Cross, man would not have had a chance. As previously stated, the only thing standing between man and eternal Hell is the Cross of Christ.

(3) "WHEN I CONSIDER YOUR HEAVENS, THE WORK OF YOUR FINGERS, THE MOON AND THE STARS, WHICH YOU HAVE ORDAINED."

The argument of Verses 3 through 8 is the amazing love of Christ in coming forth from the Highest Glory to redeem a being so insignificant as man. This insignificance is illustrated by contrasting man with the Heavens.

THE WORK OF THE FINGERS OF GOD

In his life as a shepherd, David no doubt had had abundant opportunity to *"consider the Heavens."* David had evidently scanned them with the eye of faith, and they became all the more wonderful to him because he knew God had created them.

(4) "WHAT IS MAN, THAT YOU ARE MINDFUL OF HIM? AND THE SON OF MAN, THAT YOU VISIT HIM?"

The coming forth of the Messiah from Heaven dims the glories of His Creation by His Personal excellency. Then, as the Son of Man, He has the entire Creation placed beneath His Feet and clothes it with a greater glory than it ever previously possessed.

CHRIST, THE TRUE MAN

Even though this Chapter points to Christ as the True Man, still, in a sense, it pertains to mankind in general. All of mankind is to be brought into the Presence of the True Man, Christ Jesus, to be like Him. Until one is like Christ, no man is truly whole. And one cannot be like Christ except by going to the Cross with Christ, at least by Faith (Rom. 6:3-5).

(5) "FOR YOU HAVE MADE HIM A LITTLE LOWER THAN THE ANGELS, AND HAVE CROWNED HIM WITH GLORY AND HONOR."

Here we learn something of Christ and also of mankind in general.

CROWNED WITH GLORY AND HONOR

The phrase, *"For You have made Him a little lower than the Angels,"* should have been translated, *"For You have made Him a little lower than the Godhead."* The Hebrew word translated *"Angels"* is *"Elohim,"* which should have been translated *"Godhead."*

In particular, this speaks of the Incarnation of Christ, but it also speaks of mankind in general. This one phrase means that man is God's highest Creation, even higher than the Angels.

It is difficult for us to understand how this can be, considering the state of man presently, which can be observed by all; however, observing man at present is observing the results of the Fall, which has all but destroyed the *"Image of God"* in man. Even with the redeemed Saints, traces of the Fall still remain; even the redeemed are not, and will not be, as we ought to be until the coming

NOTES

Resurrection, when we then will be glorified.

From this, we know and realize that man is God's highest creation; through the True Man, the Lord Jesus Christ, man will ultimately be brought to his proper place.

At the present, if one desires to know what true mankind is to be like, one has to view Christ, Who Alone was, and is, the True Man.

THE CREATION OF MAN

1. Man's soul is the seat of the emotions, passions, desires, appetites, and all feelings.

2. Man's spirit is the seat of the intellect, will, and conscience. It is capable of all Divine powers, only in a lesser degree.

3. The body is wonderfully made, consisting of various chemicals — iron, sugar, salt, carbon, iodine, phosphorous, lime, calcium, and others. The body has 263 bones; 600 muscles; 970 miles of blood vessels; 400 cups on the tongue for taste; 20,000 hairs in the ears to tune into all sounds; 40 pounds of jaw pressure; 10 million nerves and branches; and 3,500 sweat tubes to each square inch of skin.

There are six hundred million (600,000,000) air cells in the lungs that inhale 2,400 gallons of air daily, and a telephone system that relates to the brain instantly any known sound, taste, sight, touch, or smell. The heart beats approximately 4,200 times an hour and pumps some 12 tons of blood daily.

As stated, the world does not really know what man was like before the Fall. What it now sees is fallen man separated from God (Isa. 59:2); depraved in nature (Eph. 2:1-3); ignorant and blind (Eph. 4:18); evil in conscience (Heb. 10:22); obstinate and rebellious (Acts 7:51; Rom. 8:7); evil in thoughts (Gen. 6:5); lustful and ungodly (Jn. 8:44; Rom. 7:5-23); dominated by Satan (Jn. 8:34); servants of sin (Jn. 8:34); dead in sin (Eph. 2:1-9).

Jesus Christ was *"crowned with glory and honor,"* and man can have such only as he is in Christ. There is no glory or honor outside of Christ! Not any at all!

(6) "YOU MADE HIM TO HAVE DOMINION OVER THE WORKS OF YOUR HANDS; YOU HAVE PUT ALL THINGS UNDER HIS FEET."

This Passage places man at the head of all of God's works — the heavens, including the sun, moon, and stars, and the Earth, including all living things.

It makes him next to God in position and power over all Creation. Thus, Adam was originally made higher than the Angels because, as stated, the word translated *"Angels"* in Verse 5 should have been translated *"Elohim,"* which means *"Godhead."*

THE EXALTED CHRIST

By sin man lost his lofty position and was brought very low and made subject to death. Now, man in his lessened estate (short of God's Glory [Rom. 3:23]) is below Angels — far below Angels!

Christ Himself was made lower for a time to take man's low place and to raise him again higher than Angels, as he originally was. Christ has been exalted to a place higher than Angels or any other being except the Father. Redeemed man is to be raised up to that exalted position with Him, all made possible by the Cross (Eph. 2:6-7).

The great restoration of man back to his original position of honor and glory has already begun. Paul said, *"And has put all things under His feet, and gave Him to be the Head over all things to the Church, which is His Body, the fullness of Him Who fills all in all"* (Eph. 1:22-23).

Christ is the Head of the Church, which is His Body. Ultimately, that which is given by Promise will, upon the Resurrection of Life, be carried to its ultimate, victorious conclusion.

(7) "ALL SHEEP AND OXEN, YEA, AND THE BEASTS OF THE FIELD;

(8) "THE FOWL OF THE AIR, AND THE FISH OF THE SEA, AND WHATSOEVER PASSES THROUGH THE PATHS OF THE SEAS."

Examples of the animal kingdom are here given, as well as the fowl of the air and the fish of the sea. The Lord, as stated, has given man total dominion over all His Creation. Redeemed man ultimately will realize this lofty place and position, and act accordingly, which will take place in the coming Kingdom Age. All redeemed Saints, who will have Glorified Bodies, will then help the Lord administer the affairs of the Universe, and will do so forever!

(9) "O LORD, OUR LORD, HOW EXCELLENT IS YOUR NAME IN ALL THE EARTH!"

The Lord's Name is excellent in all the Earth at present, but not at all recognized as such. In the coming Kingdom Age, this most definitely will change. Christ, reigning Personally from Jerusalem, will so change everything (and for the better, a thousand times better) that the entirety of the world will look to Him in that hour.

The great contention now around the world is with the Name *"Jesus Christ." "God"* is looked at somehow as abstract; therefore, the animosity is directed toward Christ.

Irrespective of that, as it concerns the future, what the Bible says will happen, most definitely will take place. We are living at the very end of the Church Age. The First Resurrection is about to take place, which will involve every Saint of God who has ever lived, and who is living presently.

When the Resurrection takes place, such will signal that it is time for Israel to be restored; however, her Restoration will not come about quickly or easily.

First of all, she will believe that the Antichrist is the Messiah, accept him as such, and will herald it all over the world. Tragically, she will learn the hard way that she has been duped, deceived, and misled.

The Antichrist will then set about in earnest to destroy Israel, and will actually invade this tiny country. Israel will lose this military conflict, which will represent her first defeat since becoming a nation in 1948.

Jesus said that the last three and a half years of the Great Tribulation would be worse than anything there has ever been (Mat. 24:21). But all of this is necessary in order to bring Israel to her spiritual senses.

It will take Israel coming near to annihilation, with the Antichrist and his armies on the verge of taking the entirety of the City of Jerusalem, for Israel to finally cry as never before for the True Messiah. Actually, the very prayer which will be proclaimed at that time is found in the Sixty-fourth Chapter of Isaiah. To be sure, the Lord will hear and answer that prayer, and will do so by the Advent of the Second Coming.

At that time, Israel will accept Him, not only as Saviour, but also as Lord. The evidence is that every single Jew on the face of the Earth will then recognize Christ Jesus as the Messiah.

Israel will then be restored to her rightful place and position as the leading nation in the world, under Christ!

PSALM 9

*A Psalm of David:
Praise to God, the Great Deliverer*

(1) "I WILL PRAISE YOU, O LORD, WITH MY WHOLE HEART; I WILL SHOW FORTH ALL YOUR MARVELOUS WORKS.

(2) "I WILL BE GLAD AND REJOICE IN YOU: I WILL SING PRAISE TO YOUR NAME, O THOU MOST HIGH."

This Psalm was written by David.

PRAISE AND WORSHIP

This Song begins with Praise in order to thank God for the victory that has been given to David over his enemies. Exactly what victory he is speaking of is not known.

The greater fulfillment, however, is praise to the Lord for the victory of the Lord Jesus Christ over the Antichrist, which will take place in the coming Battle of Armageddon. The Holy Spirit through David, some 3,000 years ago, praised God for that coming victory, because it is certain.

This praise of God is truly worship in Spirit and in Truth (Jn. 4:24). It is sectioned as follows:

1. *"I will praise You, O LORD, with my whole heart."*
2. *"I will show forth all Your marvelous works."*
3. *"I will be glad and rejoice in You."*
4. *"I will sing praise to Your Name, O Thou Most High."*

Most so-called praise of God presently is offered in the midst of ceremony, which, in reality, is no praise at all. Most of that which is called *"Christianity"* is really only ceremony and has no validity with the Lord. God will only accept praise from the heart that is made whole by His Grace. We are to praise Him for all His *"marvelous works."*

Praise will always elicit gladness and rejoicing. Whenever we sing Spirit-inspired songs, we are praising the Lord, which is one of the highest forms of praise, which the Psalms here evidence.

ALL PRAISE AND WORSHIP MUST HAVE AS THEIR FOUNDATION THE CROSS OF CHRIST

The Altar of Incense sat in front of the Veil which separated the Holy of Holies from the Holy Place. Twice a day the Priests were to bring coals of fire from the Brazen Altar (which typified Christ and His Crucifixion) and place those coals on the Altar of Incense. They were then to pour Incense over the coals, which would fill the Holy Place with a sweet and pleasant fragrance. All of this typified the Intercession of Christ, all on our behalf, so that our praises, our prayers, and our worship can be accepted.

We must remember that the sweet and pleasant fragrance was all brought about because the coals of fire came from the Brazen Altar. If coals of fire were brought from any other ignition, it meant death for the Priests, which is exactly what happened to Nadab and Abihu when they offered *"strange fire"* on that Altar (Lev. 10:1-2).

Even though these two men were Priests, actually sons of Aaron, still their disobedience to the Lord by ignoring the Shed Blood of the Lamb, which is exactly what the Brazen Altar typifies, brought instant death. It is still doing the same presently.

It might not be so pronounced at present, because we are living in the Dispensation of Grace, but that doesn't mean that God overlooks the situation. It does mean that He withdraws His Spirit, for His Spirit cannot tolerate anything that is not exactly according to the Cross of Christ. This means that whatever is left, even though very religious, is not at all sanctioned by the Lord; in fact, the kiss of death is upon all such actions.

Due to the fact that the Cross of Christ is all but ignored in the modern Church, even ridiculed in a great part of the Church, this means that most praise and worship, so-called, is not recognized by God at all!

(3) "WHEN MY ENEMIES ARE TURNED BACK, THEY SHALL FALL AND PERISH AT YOUR PRESENCE."

Psalms 9 through 15 actually form one Prophecy.

PROPHECY

These Psalms predict the advent, character, career, and doom of *"the man of the Earth,"* i.e., the Antichrist. This group of Psalms stands, therefore, in contrast with the first eight, which deal with the Advent, Character, Career, and Triumph of the Blessed Man, i.e., the Messiah. The period when these Prophecies shall be fulfilled is the future *"Time of Trouble"* of which the Lord speaks in Matthew 24:21. That will be the *"Time of Jacob's Trouble,"* out of which he is to be delivered, and to which Jeremiah 30:7 and Daniel 12:1 point.

The Spirit of Christ in *"Jacob,"* when delivered out of his trouble, will sing the Song of Praise of which this Psalm opens (Vss. 1-2), and review them out of sorrow which shall precede the Deliverance (Vss. 3-14). It is characteristic of faith to make present and real, and to give thanks for, a Redemption yet to be accomplished. This principle, as stated, appears in the first two Verses of this Psalm.

THE SECOND COMING

The expression, *"At Your Presence,"* refers to the visible Coming of the Messiah in Power and Glory, which, of course, is the Second Coming. The brightness of that Coming will occasion the Deliverance of His people Israel, and the doom of the Antichrist.

As this Song of Praise was sung some 3,000 years ago, and rendered for a victory that is even yet future, this should be a great lesson to us.

VICTORY IN JESUS

In these Passages, a great Truth is presented to us.

The Holy Spirit, through the Word of God and what Jesus has done for us at Calvary, has already predicted our victory, and in every capacity, that is, if we will only believe.

As it regards Christ, and the Holy Spirit proclaiming His coming victory over the Antichrist, there is no doubt about this prospect, simply because it is Christ, Who cannot fail. With Believers, it is somewhat different: While the Holy Spirit sings our victory, a victory which most definitely is intended to be ours, and in every capacity, it is predicated on our continued faith. The free will of the Believer is never violated by the Lord. It was faith in Christ and the Cross which got us in, and it is faith in Christ and the Cross which keeps us in.

If, however, our faith wanes and weakens, and is transferred from Christ and the Cross to something else, this can stop the victory which the Lord has planned for us. The entirety of the Book of Hebrews, in fact, was written by the Apostle Paul for this very cause.

As we have already discussed in past Commentary, some Christian Jews were turning their backs on the Lord and going back into Temple Worship, which means that they were repudiating Christ and the Cross. Paul urgently warned them against this by telling them that if they continued on this course, they would be lost (Heb. 6:4-6; 10:26-29).

Let it be understood:

If the Believer abandons the Cross while claiming, at the same time, to be trusting in Christ, such is impossible.

ANOTHER JESUS

If the Cross is ignored or repudiated, as it is in many modern Christian circles, this also abrogates faith in Christ. Paul stated that if such is done, in other words, if the Cross is ignored or disbelieved (I Cor. 1:17-18, 23; 2:2; Gal. 6:14), then the Believer is left with *"another Jesus"* and *"another gospel,"* which, of course, can never be recognized by the Lord (II Cor. 11:4; Gal. 1:6-7).

And I'm afraid that is exactly the case in the faith of most modern Christians. They are serving *"another Jesus,"* which is brought about by *"another spirit,"* which is *"another gospel."*

Because it is so very, very important, please allow me to say it again:

Jesus Christ and Him Crucified is the heart of the Gospel. If that is removed, there is no more Gospel.

THE CROSS OF CHRIST

When we speak of the Cross, we are not putting Jesus back on the Cross. The Lord presently is by the Right Hand of the Father, and He will remain there always (Heb. 1:3).

We also, at least by faith, are seated with Christ in Heavenly Places (Eph. 2:6).

The Cross is something which took place now nearly 2,000 years ago, and will never have to be repeated. So what we are speaking about is the benefits of the Cross, that which the Cross afforded, which, as we have repeatedly stated, is the *"Means"* by which Christ gives us all things.

That's why Paul said, *"God forbid that I should glory, save in the Cross of our Lord Jesus Christ, by Whom the world is crucified unto me, and I unto the world"* (Gal. 6:14).

Is the modern Church preaching the Cross?

Are modern Christians placing their faith exclusively in Christ and the Cross?

All you have to do is turn on Christian Television, and the answer, I think, will be very obvious. The modern Church knows almost nothing about the Cross of Christ. It is putting forth every type of man-devised remedy that one can thing of, in order to address the needs of modern Christians, all to no avail.

It is only Christ and the Cross! Without Faith explicitly placed in that Finished Work, which gives the Holy Spirit latitude to work within our lives to help us live the life we ought to live in Christ Jesus (Rom. 8:1-2, 11), we cannot have the victory for which Christ paid such a price — a price He paid all on our behalf.

(4) "FOR YOU HAVE MAINTAINED MY RIGHT AND MY CAUSE; YOU SAT IN THE THRONE JUDGING RIGHT."

This Verse, as do all of these Verses, picture both David and the Son of David.

THE RIGHTEOUS JUDGMENT OF GOD

David uniformly ascribes his military successes not to his own ability, nor to the valor of his soldiers, but to God's favor. God's favor, which is secured by the justice of his cause, gives David victory after victory.

To an even greater degree, this phrase, *"For You have maintained My right and My cause,"* proclaims the most excellent favor of God toward His Son, our Saviour, the Lord Jesus Christ.

Within itself, that is not a great revelation, because, simply said, it is obvious; however, that which is a great Truth is that, as we are in Christ, everything with which God favors Christ, is also ours! Every victory won by Christ, and He won them all, was all done for you and me, and which we are meant to have, and which we can have, simply by exhibiting faith in Christ and what Christ has done for us at the Cross. Then the Lord will *"maintain my right and my cause."*

THE THRONE OF GOD

It is the Lord Who does the judging, which He does from His Throne.

Judges what?

The Lord judges all things, and His Judgment is final, irrespective as to what man might say or do.

It is not known whether David wrote this Psalm at the time that Absalom and most of Israel rose up against him, trying to kill him and take the throne of Israel. But if that was the time, it was God Who sat on His Throne and judged the situation, not the men of Israel.

At that particular time, i.e., the time of Absalom's insurrection, most of Israel had turned against David. The Bible tells us that Absalom stole the hearts of Israel (II Sam. 15:1-6). However, none of this swayed the justice of God in any manner. God was the final judge, and not the deceived men of Israel.

All of this tells us that if we look to men, we get the help that men can give, which is precious little, if any. If we look to God, we get the help that God can give, which is Almighty.

Exactly as with David, I have watched this same scenario played out in my own life and Ministry. The news media did all they could to destroy us, and, worse yet, the Church world followed suit. In the natural, such would be impossible to overcome. But it was not men who made the final decision, but God.

As a result, this Ministry has not only survived, but, due to the Revelation of the Cross, it is stronger than ever. We give the Lord all the praise and all the glory for this, because He Alone is the One Who has done this thing. The Lord is the final Judge, and not man!

As with David of old, men have to make up their minds as to what they are going to do! Are you going to go with the crowd, or with God?

It is important to remember the following: In any situation, God and one man are a majority!

(5) "YOU HAVE REBUKED THE HEATHEN, YOU HAVE DESTROYED THE WICKED, YOU HAVE PUT OUT THEIR NAME FOREVER AND EVER."

Not only does this Verse speak of one of David's great victories, but, more than all, it speaks of the coming great victory of Jesus Christ over the Antichrist in the Battle of Armageddon.

VICTORY

The phrase, *"You have put out their name forever and ever,"* leaps beyond David's present situation, and directs attention to the Second Coming, when the Lord will destroy the Antichrist and all who follow him. To be sure, this will be the last uprising, at least by man. The victory, therefore, is *"forever and ever."*

None of the nations with which David contended suffered extinction or extermination, but the Antichrist and his followers will most definitely face such an end. Ezekiel, Chapters 38 and 39, proclaim to us exactly how this will happen. (Please see our Commentary on the Book of Ezekiel.)

(6) "O THOU ENEMY, DESTRUCTIONS ARE COME TO A PERPETUAL END: AND YOU HAVE DESTROYED CITIES; THEIR MEMORIAL IS PERISHED WITH THEM."

The first phrase could be translated, *"The enemy had come to an end; they are desolate forever."*

The second phrase could be translated, *"And as for the cities you have destroyed, their very memory has perished."*

DAVID AND THE SON OF DAVID

The Holy Spirit here speaks through David, employing words which proclaim that the enemies of God will ultimately come to an end, and in totality. This Passage, therefore, jumps ahead to the Second Coming; in particular, it speaks of Babylon, which will be rebuilt and then destroyed by an earthquake immediately before the Second Coming (Rev., Chpt. 18). Babylon and all that it represented will be no more — never to rise again!

Even though such speaks of the city itself, it more particularly speaks of the Babylonian system, which has governed this world ever since the Fall. With the Second Coming of Christ, the Babylonian spirit will be forever finished.

(7) "BUT THE LORD SHALL ENDURE FOREVER: HE HAS PREPARED HIS THRONE FOR JUDGMENT."

This speaks of Christ ascending His Throne in Jerusalem, which will take place very shortly after the Second Coming, from which He will judge the nations (Mat. 25:32-46).

(8) "AND HE SHALL JUDGE THE WORLD IN RIGHTEOUSNESS, HE SHALL MINISTER JUDGMENT TO THE PEOPLE IN UPRIGHTNESS."

In referring to the future judgment of the nations, the Apostle Paul quoted this Eighth Verse of this Ninth Psalm to the Athenians (Acts 17:31). This *"judgment"* will be the judgment of the nations, which will take place at the beginning of the Kingdom Age.

Concerning this time, Isaiah said, *"And He shall judge among the nations, and shall rebuke many people: and they shall beat their swords into plowshares, and their spears into pruninghooks: nation shall not lift up sword against nation, neither shall they learn war any more"* (Isa. 2:4).

Isaiah also said, *"And He shall not judge after the sight of His Eyes, and neither reprove after the hearing of His Ears:*

"But with Righteousness shall He judge the poor, and reprove with equity for the meek of the Earth: and He shall smite the Earth with the rod of His Mouth, and with the breath of His Lips shall He slay the wicked.

"And Righteousness shall be the girdle of His Loins, and Faithfulness the girdle of His reins" (Isa. 11:3-5).

"The Government shall be upon His Shoulder. . . .

"Of the increase of His Government and Peace there shall be no end, upon the throne of David, and upon His Kingdom, to order it, and to establish it with judgment and with justice from henceforth even forever. The zeal of the LORD of Hosts will perform this" (Isa. 9:6-7).

The Kingdom Age will be the *"Dispensation of Righteousness."*

The following are the Dispensations of time, as given to us in the Bible.

DISPENSATIONS

1. INNOCENCE: This Dispensation began with the Creation of Adam and Eve and continued unto their Fall, which could have lasted about forty days, although the exact time is not known.

2. CONSCIENCE: This Dispensation began with the Fall of Adam and Eve and lasted unto Noah, a time frame of about 1,600 years.

3. GOVERNMENT: This Dispensation began with Noah and lasted unto Abraham, a time frame of approximately 400 years.

4. PROMISE: This Dispensation began with Abraham and lasted unto Moses, a time frame of approximately 400 years.

5. LAW: This Dispensation began with Moses and lasted unto Christ, a time frame of about 1,500 years.

6. GRACE: This Dispensation began with Christ and continues unto this hour, which has been about 2,000 years.

7. RIGHTEOUSNESS: This Dispensation will begin with the Second Coming and will last a thousand years.

8. PERFECTION: This Dispensation will begin with the Creation of the New Heavens and the New Earth, outlined in the last two Chapters of the Book of Revelation. It will last forever.

(9) "THE LORD ALSO WILL BE A REFUGE FOR THE OPPRESSED, A REFUGE IN TIMES OF TROUBLE."

A great Promise is here given!

A REFUGE

The phrase, *"In times of trouble,"* literally says, *"In times that are steeped in trouble."*

The Lord does not promise a trouble-free existence. We must remember that we are living as Believers in a hostile environment. Satan is the *"god of this present world"* and the *"prince of the powers of the air."* In effect, he controls the system of this world. The only Light in this world is that of the Lord Jesus Christ; His Saints are meant to be a reflection of His Light.

The Lord didn't say there would not be trouble, but He did say that He would be a *"refuge"* in these times of trouble — and no matter how bad the trouble may be!

As no other faith in the world, the followers of Christ, at times, have had to undergo tremendous troubles, trials, tests, and persecutions.

Israel was beset on every side before Christ, and, since Christ, the persecution has continued. The Early Church was rife with persecution. Due to the outpouring of the Holy Spirit in the Latter Rain, which was predicted by the Prophet Joel, and which took place at approximately the turn of the Twentieth Century, persecution around the world, at least to a great degree, has greatly slackened. An exception to that would be the countries which were under the iron yoke of Communism for approximately fifty years, and such persecution continues in China even unto this hour. Irrespective, Christ is ever the Refuge!

HUMANISTIC PSYCHOLOGY

As it regards persecution of the spirit, of which Satan is the chief architect, and which continues unabated, it is a shame that the modern Church has forsaken the refuge of Christ, instead opting for the refuge of humanistic psychology, which is no refuge at all.

Every need that we have is found entirely in Christ, and Christ Alone! However, when we speak of Christ, we must understand, and without fail, that it is the Cross which is the Means by which all of the things are given unto us for which Christ paid such a price. It is the Holy Spirit Who dispenses all that Christ has done, and He works exclusively within the framework of the Finished Work of Christ (Rom. 8:2). In fact, He will function in no other manner.

So, this means that if Believers resort to humanistic psychology, or any other such alleged panacea, the Holy Spirit will not help, which leaves such a Believer defenseless.

The *"refuge"* is available to all, but only on God's terms. Those terms are *"Jesus Christ and Him Crucified"* (I Cor. 1:23).

(10) "AND THEY WHO KNOW YOUR NAME WILL PUT THEIR TRUST IN YOU: FOR YOU, LORD, HAVE NOT FORSAKEN

THEM WHO SEEK YOU."

Pulpit says, *"To know the Name of God is to know Him according to His historical manifestation; when one hears Him named, to call to remembrance all that He has done. His Name is the focus in which all the ways of His actions meet."*[5]

THE LORD WILL NEVER FORSAKE HIS CHILDREN

Never in the past has God forsaken those who faithfully clung to Him. We might be tried, like Job; we might be *"hunted upon the mountains,"* like David himself; we might even have the sense of being forsaken (Ps. 22:1); but, nevertheless, we are not forsaken. The Lord *"forsakes not His Saints; we are preserved forever"* (Ps. 37:28).

(11) "SING PRAISES TO THE LORD, WHICH DWELLS IN ZION: DECLARE AMONG THE PEOPLE HIS DOINGS."

Here we are told what the posture of the Saints ought to be!

SING PRAISES AND DECLARE THE DOINGS OF THE LORD

In this one Verse, we are given the secret of victory, and also a preview of the Great Commission.

It was to David that most of the Psalms were given, which constitute Earth's first songbook. This tells us how valuable is music and singing, as it regards praises to the Lord.

When a Church begins to lose its way, the first thing it actually loses is its song. If it loses everything, neither song nor music is left. Such is the Catholic Church.

Regrettably, the Denominational world falls close to the same category. For the most part, its song and music are stilted and formal. Sadly, such must also be said of most Charismatic and Pentecostal Churches!

If a Church is on fire for God and is preaching the Truth, the Spirit of God will be moving greatly in the music and singing, which will then be exuberant and elicit praise to the Lord.

Under the inspiration of the Holy Spirit, the sweet singer of Israel told us, *"Sing praises to the LORD,"* and that is what we must do!

As stated, we are given here a preview of the Great Commission, which tells us that we are to *"declare among the people His doings."* This means we must tell what the Lord has done, what the Lord is doing, and what the Lord shall do.

All too often, the modern Church is declaring among the people not at all *"His doings,"* but rather our doings, and the latter are of absolutely no consequence.

(12) "WHEN HE MAKES INQUISITION FOR BLOOD, HE REMEMBERS THEM: HE FORGETS NOT THE CRY OF THE HUMBLE."

All who have shed blood wrongly will one day answer to God. Of that one can be certain!

The short phrase, *"He remembers them,"* records the fact that the Lord takes note of everything. It may seem that some, if not most, go unpunished, the truth is that God remembers all; He will one day call it to account, even if it is at the Great White Throne Judgment (Rev. 20:11-15).

THE AVENGER OF BLOOD

The first murder occurred very near the first stage of human history. Cain murdered his brother Abel. Concerning that terrible sin, the Lord said to Cain, *"What have you done? The voice of your brother's blood cries unto Me from the ground"* (Gen. 4:10).

The blood of untold millions, shed from then until now, and we speak of the innocent who have been murdered, will, as stated, be called to account. The blood of all who fall into this category cries to God from the ground.

Although this Passage definitely pertains to any and all, even as we have stated, more directly it is aimed toward those who have shown no mercy upon Israel, and have wantonly slain the sons of Jacob. To be sure, Adolf Hitler, along with all his henchmen, and along with others all down through history, will stand before God one day and answer for the Holocaust and the other massacres against God's ancient people.

But more directly and to the point, the Passage speaks of the coming Great Tribulation, when the Antichrist will seek to annihilate Israel, in effect attempting to blot them from the face of the Earth.

Verse 12 predicts that God will permit the

false Messiah to slaughter multitudes of His beloved people, but that He will avenge their deaths. He may allow their oppressors to torture and kill them, but He will not forget their cry (Rev. 2:10; 6:9; 13:7).

(13) "HAVE MERCY UPON ME, O LORD; CONSIDER MY TROUBLE WHICH I SUFFER OF THEM WHO HATE ME, THOU WHO LIFTS ME UP FROM THE GATES OF DEATH."

This will be the cry of Israel in the coming Great Tribulation, especially when it looks like all is lost.

To be sure, the Lord will hear, and, because Israel will be crying to Him from a repentant heart, He most definitely will show Mercy.

(14) "THAT I MAY SHOW FORTH ALL YOUR PRAISE IN THE GATES OF THE DAUGHTER OF ZION: I WILL REJOICE IN YOUR SALVATION."

The *"daughter of Zion"* is Jerusalem.

It has been a long, long time since Jerusalem has heard the sincere praises of the Lord, and a long time since Jews have rejoiced in His Salvation; however, that time is coming, and coming soon, when every word of these Verses will be totally fulfilled. It will be at the beginning of the Kingdom Age, which is closer today than ever before.

(15) "THE HEATHEN ARE SUNK DOWN IN THE PIT THAT THEY MADE: IN THE NET WHICH THEY HID IS THEIR OWN FOOT TAKEN."

The victory which David mentions is not here revealed; however, the greater meaning has to do with the coming Battle of Armageddon, when the Antichrist will seek to destroy Israel from the face of the Earth. That which the Antichrist seeks to do, which is to totally annihilate Israel and destroy every Jew down to the last man, woman, and child, will instead be the scene of his own undoing.

The efforts of the Antichrist will precipitate the Second Coming, which will be with such power as to defy all description. The *"man of sin"* will be destroyed, along with all of his mighty armies.

(16) "THE LORD IS KNOWN BY THE JUDGMENT WHICH HE EXECUTES: THE WICKED IS SNARED IN THE WORK OF HIS OWN HANDS. HIGGAION. SELAH."

The judgment of the Lord is here outlined.

THE JUDGMENT OF THE LORD

If one understands, even to a small degree, the Omniscience of God (which means that He knows all things, past, present, and future), the Omnipotence of God (which means that He is All-Powerful), and the Omnipresence of God (which means that He is everywhere), then one must come to the conclusion that He sees all, knows all, and has a direct involvement in everything that happens on this Earth, and in every capacity.

To not understand that is to not properly understand God.

This means that the Lord either causes or allows every single thing that happens in this world. Of course, He does not cause sin and transgression in any form, as should be obvious; however, He does allow it, because of the free moral agency of man.

The Scripture says, *"For the Wrath of God is revealed from Heaven against all ungodliness and unrighteousness of men, who hold the truth in unrighteousness"* (Rom. 1:18).

When the Scripture says *"all,"* it means *"all"*!

One must conclude that every accident, so-called, every calamity, no matter how little or large, is, in some way, the Judgment of God, which is revealed from Heaven against all ungodliness and unrighteousness. The judgment against sin is evidenced in this life, has been since the very beginning, and will continue; but there is coming for all unredeemed a *"Great White Throne Judgment,"* where every single unredeemed person who has ever lived will stand and be judged by God according to who they are and how they lived (Rev. 20:11-15).

HUMANISTIC PSYCHOLOGY AND JUDGMENT

The world has been so psychologized that the idea of judgment, which means that man is responsible for his actions, is anathema to most of the human race. Humanistic psychology teaches that man is a victim. This means that something else is the cause of his problems, such as environment, lack of education, or maltreatment by others, etc. The Bible teaches the very opposite, namely that every single person is responsible for his own sinful actions.

However, irrespective as to what the world thinks, every human being on this Earth is ultimately going to be judged, whether in Jesus Christ or at the Great White Throne Judgment.

The Lord, thankfully, has made a way that all sins are judged in Jesus Christ and what He did for us at the Cross, if men only will take advantage of this great Sacrifice. If that Judgment is ignored, a face-to-face Judgment by God will one day most definitely come about.

MEDITATION

The words *"Higgaion"* means *"to meditate."* The Reader is told to meditate on what the Lord has said through the Psalmist. Then it closes with *"Selah."*

(17) "THE WICKED SHALL BE TURNED INTO HELL, AND ALL THE NATIONS THAT FORGET GOD."

The Holy Spirit here means exactly what He says. If Salvation through Jesus Christ, God's only Son, is ignored, *"Hell"* is the final destination.

Most of the nations of the world, and for all time, have forgotten God, i.e., ignored God or disbelieved Him. Actually, most the nations of the world always have worshipped, and presently do worship, a god of their own manufacture. *"Allah"* is a case in point. For the most part, even those who claim to recognize God, recognize Jesus Christ not at all.

Jesus said, *"I am the Way, the Truth, and the Life: no man comes unto the Father, but by Me"* (Jn. 14:6). This means that all nations which reject Jesus Christ as the Son of God, and what He did for us at Calvary, ultimately *"shall be turned into Hell."* As we have previously stated, the only thing standing between mankind and eternal Hell is the Cross of Christ!

(18) "FOR THE NEEDY SHALL NOT ALWAYS BE FORGOTTEN: THE EXPECTATION OF THE POOR SHALL NOT PERISH FOREVER."

In a general sense, this refers to most of the people of the world who, from the beginning, have suffered untold anguish and heartache. So many go to bed hungry each night; they are *"forgotten."* Now the expectation of the poor is never met; it also is *"forgotten."*

When the Lord of Glory returns, this will be the very first thing that He will do, i.e., *"Remember the needy"* and bring to pass *"the expectation of the poor."*

ISRAEL

More particularly, this Verse speaks of Israel, which has been all but forgotten these last 2,000 years — or at least it seems that way! For these last 2,000 years, Israel has lived in expectation, but her expectation has been placed in the wrong thing.

At the Second Coming, their situation finally will be rectified, as they accept the Lord Jesus Christ, the Very One Whom they crucified, as Messiah, Saviour, and Lord.

(19) "ARISE, O LORD; LET NOT MAN PREVAIL: LET THE HEATHEN BE JUDGED IN YOUR SIGHT.

(20) "PUT THEM IN FEAR, O LORD: THAT THE NATIONS MAY KNOW THEMSELVES TO BE BUT MEN. SELAH."

This speaks of the Battle of Armageddon.

ARMAGEDDON

At the Battle of Armageddon, the nations of the world that side with the Antichrist will surely think they have victory in sight. They will, however, be made to realize that, in spite of their might, weaponry, and great armies, they are *"but men,"* and, in comparison to the Lord Jesus Christ, they have no power.

The words, *"Let not man prevail,"* speak of the Antichrist, as well as God's intervention to save man from the very beginning.

THE PLAN OF GOD

The Lord has repeatedly sent judgments on this Earth in order that man's plans and efforts to circumvent the Great Plan of God will not be realized. I speak of the flood (Gen., Chpts. 6-8), the confusion of tongues (Gen., Chpt. 11), and the destruction of Sodom and Gomorrah (Gen., Chpt. 19). There have, no doubt, been many other judgments, but not of the magnitude of those just mentioned.

The judgments which the Lord will send

during the coming Great Tribulation also will fall into the category of those mentioned in the previous paragraph. Whatever plans man has during that time will be stopped short by the intervention of the Lord, especially by the Second Coming.

So, the talk of man destroying himself is not Biblical. It will never happen. The Lord, not man, is in control of this Earth. And the Lord is very close to rectifying the situation of sin and transgression, which has caused so much heartache in the world.

PSALM 10

An Appeal to Punish the Wicked

(1) "WHY DO YOU STAND AFAR OFF, O LORD? WHY DO YOU HIDE YOURSELF IN TIMES OF TROUBLE?"

The author of this Psalm is unknown; however, it very well could have been David.

THE TIME OF JACOB'S TROUBLE

This Psalm very well can apply to the obvious; however, more particularly, it applies to the efforts of the Antichrist in the last three and a half years of his efforts to take over the world. He will have broken his seven-year nonaggression pact with Israel and actually will have declared war on her. His ambition is threefold:
1. To take over the world;
2. To destroy Israel, the people of God; and,
3. To defeat the Lord Jesus Christ.

He will be so lifted up in his own pride and unholy ambition that he actually will believe that he can succeed.

If the Word of God falls to the ground (actually, any Promise or Prediction made), Satan has won. Of course, if the Antichrist can destroy Israel, that will abrogate countless Promises in the Word of God.

In this *"Time of Jacob's Trouble,"* Israel will begin to cry to God. One of the main reasons for the Great Tribulation is that Israel may be brought back to the Lord. Sadly, it will entail much suffering and sorrow. Psalm 10 gives a vivid picture of the appalling sufferings that Israel will undergo at this future time.

(2) "THE WICKED IN HIS PRIDE DOES PERSECUTE THE POOR: LET THEM BE TAKEN IN THE DEVICES THAT THEY HAVE IMAGINED."

"The poor" which here are referred to could refer to any who fit the description. Still, more particularly, it refers to Israel in the last half of the Great Tribulation. This *"wicked"* or *"lawless"* one will, in his pride, think he can take over the whole world and defeat God. He will fall through his own *"devices"* that he has *"imagined"* against the Lord of Glory.

(3) "FOR THE WICKED BOASTS OF HIS HEART'S DESIRE, AND BLESSES THE COVETOUS, WHOM THE LORD ABHORS."

Three thousand years ago, the Holy Spirit proclaims what the Antichrist will attempt to do. It should be obvious, even from these predictions, that the Lord cannot be defeated.

DECEPTION

Daniel said that the Antichrist will have a *"mouth speaking great things"* (Dan. 7:20). The boasts of the *"man of sin"* will fill the headlines and newspapers, television networks, and all means of communication. He will bless the evil *"whom the LORD abhors."* Right will become wrong, and wrong will become right. Evil will become good, and good will become evil. This spirit, to be sure, is already in the world presently.

(4) "THE WICKED, THROUGH THE PRIDE OF HIS COUNTENANCE, WILL NOT SEEK AFTER GOD: GOD IS NOT IN ALL HIS THOUGHTS."

Concerning the countenance of the Antichrist, Daniel said, *"Whose look was more stout than his fellows"* (Dan. 7:20). This man will be filled with the powers of darkness, but yet his charisma will be so great that hundreds of millions will be deceived by this *"work of the flesh."* In his pride, he will declare that there is no God, or that, if there is, He takes no interest in human affairs.

GOD IN THE THOUGHTS OF MAN

The phrase, *"God is not in all his thoughts,"* pertains to the fact that God is not thought of concerning decisions made, etc. Of course, the Antichrist will have no regard for God whatsoever, actually thinking that he himself is God.

The greater principle of this phrase pertains to the idea that God must be in our thinking in every capacity.

As James said, *"Go to now, you who say, Today or tomorrow we will go into such a city, and continue there a year, and buy and sell, and get gain:*

"For that ye ought to say, If the Lord will, we shall live, and do this, or that" (James 4:13, 15).

Concerning individuals, Believers should let the Lord make the plans for them, and then they are guaranteed of success. Our trouble is that we make the plans and then ask God to bless them, which He will never do. In every capacity, God must be in all of our thoughts; we must desire to know His Will about all things, to desire and to walk in His Will.

(5) "HIS WAYS ARE ALWAYS GRIEVOUS; YOUR JUDGMENTS ARE FAR ABOVE OUT OF HIS SIGHT: AS FOR ALL HIS ENEMIES, HE PUFFS AT THEM."

As it regards his own ways, the Antichrist will find them successful, and he will thereby be enabled to despise his enemies. He will declare that the judgments of God cannot reach him. This lawless one will laugh at his enemies. He will think to conquer the world!

(6) "HE HAS SAID IN HIS HEART, I SHALL NOT BE MOVED: FOR I SHALL NEVER BE IN ADVERSITY."

The Antichrist will promise himself exemption from adversity. He will think he is unbeatable, unstoppable, and immovable. Irrespective of the power brought against him, he will prevail — or so he thinks!

THE FALLEN ANGEL

Going back some 2,300 years from this present time, Alexander the Great set out to conquer the world. Alexander also thought he was unstoppable and unbeatable. He held such a record of conquest that some men even thought he was a god, and he actually claimed to be!

But the truth is that he was being aided and abetted by one of Satan's most powerful fallen angels, who helped him with his military conquests, but without his knowledge. When Alexander the Great died, this fallen angel was consigned to *"the bottomless pit"*

NOTES

(Rev. 17:8). This *"beast,"* as he is called in the Book of Revelation, will be released out of this pit in the very near future in order to help the Antichrist; however, the Holy Spirit through John the Beloved proclaimed the destruction of both the Antichrist and the fallen angel (Rev. 17:8).

So, this same fallen angel, which helped Alexander the Great and made him the greatest military leader in history, will also help the Antichrist. Irrespective, the Antichrist will fail just as did Alexander the Great.

(7) "HIS MOUTH IS FULL OF CURSING AND DECEIT AND FRAUD: UNDER HIS TONGUE IS MISCHIEF AND VANITY."

Daniel also said, *"And through his policy also he shall cause craft* (deceit) *to prosper in his hand"* (Dan. 8:25).

(8) "HE SITS IN THE LURKING PLACES OF THE VILLAGES: IN THE SECRET PLACES DOES HE MURDER THE INNOCENT: HIS EYES ARE PRIVILY SET AGAINST THE POOR."

Verses 8 through 10 refer to the efforts of the Antichrist to destroy the *"holy people"* Israel. They are called *"the innocent"* and *"the poor"* (Vss. 9-10).

All of this proclaims the fact that the Lord sees all. He not only sees all, but he also knows all, and can predict the future as far in advance as one can begin to think.

THE ANTICHRIST AND THE WORD OF GOD

Many may ask the question, *"Doesn't the Antichrist read these very Verses? Won't he realize that the Lord is speaking against him?"*

Oh yes! The Antichrist, no doubt, will read these Verses and will know that the Lord, beyond the shadow of a doubt, is speaking of him; however, the Antichrist is so deceived that he does not believe what these predictions state. He really thinks that he will overcome the Jews, despite that which the Lord has said.

That shouldn't seem so strange, because most of the world, and for all time, follow the lies of Satan, despite the fact that the Bible tells us what has been, what is, and what shall be. The problem is *"unbelief"* (Jn. 16:8-9).

(9) "HE LIES IN WAIT SECRETLY AS A LION IN HIS DEN: HE LIES IN WAIT TO CATCH THE POOR: HE DOES CATCH THE POOR, WHEN HE DRAWS HIM INTO HIS NET."

This Verse plainly tells us that the Antichrist will completely ignore the Word of God here given, even as he sets about to destroy Israel.

So, the Holy Spirit not only proclaims what is going to happen, but the very thoughts of the man of sin.

(10) "HE CROUCHES, AND HUMBLES HIMSELF, THAT THE POOR MAY FALL BY HIS STRONG ONES."

The *"strong ones"* are his followers. Their temporary prosperity and successful oppression of the Elect of the Most High are described in Verses 2 through 11.

These Verses detail the fact that the Antichrist will hotly pursue the oppressed (Vs. 2); that they will be captured by him (Vss. 2, 9); that he will boast of the success of his plans (Vs. 3); that he will renounce and revile Jehovah (Vs. 3); that God's judgments will be willingly quite beyond his ken (Vs. 5); that in his pride he will declare that there is no God, and, if there is, then he is powerful enough to overcome God. His actions prove that he thinks such!

(11) "HE HAS SAID IN HIS HEART, GOD HAS FORGOTTEN: HE HIDES HIS FACE; HE WILL NEVER SEE IT."

The mouth, tongue, and eyes of the Antichrist will all be employed in the oppression and destruction of the poor in spirit, i.e., *"Israel"*; finally, he will assure his own heart of two things: that, as to the past, God will forget it; and, as to the future, there never will be a Judgment.

As we have already stated, as the Antichrist will think, so have thought untold millions, even billions, in the past and the present.

(12) "ARISE, O LORD; O GOD, LIFT UP YOUR HAND: FORGET NOT THE HUMBLE."

The *"humble"* refers here to Israel in the Battle of Armageddon, when it seems as if she will suffer total loss.

(13) "WHEREFORE DOES THE WICKED CONTEMN GOD? HE HAS SAID IN HIS HEART, YOU WILL NOT REQUIRE IT."

God's longsuffering does but make the wicked despise Him.

So, that being the case, why does the Lord tarry long with the wicked? Why doesn't he step in immediately?

THE LONGSUFFERING OF THE LORD

Yes, the Lord can do anything He so desires. He is Omniscient, Omnipotent, and Omnipresent. But in all of this, He also is *"Love."* As such, His Nature, despite the fact of the rebuttals, the rejection, and even blasphemy, is to continue to appeal to the wayward souls, even though He knows beforehand that their answer will be rejection.

If God was any other way, this world would have been destroyed a long, long time ago! Not a single one of us would be saved! We all would be eternally lost! But thank God, His Power is tempered with Mercy.

As the songwriter said:
"Mercy rewrote my life!"

(14) YOU HAVE SEEN IT; FOR YOU BEHOLD MISCHIEF AND SPITE, TO REQUITE IT WITH YOUR HAND: THE POOR COMMITS HIMSELF UNTO YOU; YOU ARE THE HELPER OF THE FATHERLESS."

As is obvious, these are songs which were sung by Israel; they should be sung by us, as well!

THE ALL-SEEING EYE OF GOD

The short phrase, *"You have seen it,"* once again proclaims the fact that whatever it is that Satan does, whatever it is that anyone does, *"The Lord sees it."*

Do we really understand that? Do we really believe that?

No one hides anything from God. He sees not only the good things, but also the bad things. There is only one way that all the bad, sorrowful, hurtful things can be erased from our record. That is by our faith placed entirely in Christ and what Christ has done for us at the Cross.

There the slate was wiped clean! There every sin and iniquity were forgiven! There a new beginning was made! There, Mercy rewrote my life!

THE SCORE WILL BE SETTLED

The phrase, *"For You behold mischief and*

spite, to requite it with Your hand," means that a reckoning day is coming.

This is a general statement which applies to all, but, in a more particular way, it applies to Israel, here referred to as *"the poor."* She will at long last commit herself unto the Lord. This is the primary purpose of the Great Tribulation. This is the reason it is called *"The Time of Jacob's Trouble"* (Jer. 30:7).

(15) "BREAK THOU THE ARM OF THE WICKED AND THE EVIL MAN: SEEK OUT HIS WICKEDNESS TILL YOU FIND NONE."

Once again, all of these Passages apply in the general sense, but, in a more particular way, this speaks of the Lord breaking the arm *"of the wicked and the evil man,"* i.e., *"the Antichrist."* It will happen at the Second Coming.

Like a fire, all wickedness will be destroyed, which means that every vestige of the Antichrist will be lifted from the Earth, as well as all who follow him.

(16) "THE LORD IS KING FOREVER AND EVER: THE HEATHEN ARE PERISHED OUT OF HIS LAND."

The *"LORD"* is *"King"* over Israel, and, in fact, over the entirety of the world. This means that the Antichrist will not be king. The Antichrist will, in fact, *"perish"* out of His (the Lord's) Land.

(17) "LORD, YOU HAVE HEARD THE DESIRE OF THE HUMBLE: YOU WILL PREPARE THEIR HEART, YOU WILL CAUSE YOUR EAR TO HEAR."

At the Second Coming, the Lord will not only defeat the Antichrist and all of his armies, but He also will put it in the hearts of those of Israel to accept Him as Saviour and Lord. This will not, however, be an arbitrary act.

The desire of the hearts of Israel will be toward the Lord, giving the Lord something on which to act. That goes not only for Israel, but for anyone. If one wills evil, more evil is willed to him! If one wills Righteousness, more Righteousness is willed to him (Mat. 5:6).

(18) "TO JUDGE THE FATHERLESS AND THE OPPRESSED, THAT THE MAN OF THE EARTH MAY NO MORE OPPRESS."

The Coming of the Lord will result in the disappearance out of the Earth of the hostile heathen. The apparition of the Messiah will so effectually destroy *"the man of the Earth"* (the Antichrist) that he will be terrible no more. In fact, he will be consigned to Eternal Hell (Rev. 19:20).

PSALM 11

A Psalm of David:
The Lord is Our Faithful Defender

(1) "IN THE LORD PUT I MY TRUST: HOW SAY YE TO MY SOUL, FLEE AS A BIRD TO YOUR MOUNTAIN?"

David wrote this Psalm at a time when he was in great distress. Even though we have no way of knowing exactly when it was written, still, there is some indication that it may have been written when Saul was constantly threatening him with death.

This Psalm had to do with David's situation, and, as well, could certainly be applied to our life experience. But, more pointedly, it refers to the Great Tribulation, when the Antichrist will break his seven-year pact with Israel and threaten her destruction.

Psalm 10 portrayed the Lawless One; Psalm 11 describes the lawlessness which will characterize his kingdom and the consequent oppression and suffering of the righteous.

The picture of this Psalm in these times of trouble is very vivid. Immanuel's land is a scene of tumult, and His servants are cruelly oppressed. The phrase, *"Flee as a bird to your mountain,"* could very well refer to Israel's fleeing to Petra, which the Bible says they will do (Isa. 16:1-5). This will happen at approximately the midpoint of the Great Tribulation.

(2) "FOR, LO, THE WICKED BEND THEIR BOW, THEY MAKE READY THEIR ARROW UPON THE STRING, THAT THEY MAY PRIVILY SHOOT AT THE UPRIGHT IN HEART."

As this possibly represented Saul in his effort to destroy David, even more so it represents the Antichrist, who will make every effort to destroy Israel. At this time, Israel will be defeated. (This will occur when the Antichrist breaks his seven-year Covenant with Israel at the midpoint of the Great Tribulation. This will be their first defeat since the forming of themselves as a nation in 1948 [Dan. 9:27].)

(3) "IF THE FOUNDATIONS BE DESTROYED, WHAT CAN THE RIGHTEOUS DO?"

This Verse contains a warning!

THE FOUNDATIONS

World law is based on the Bible, at least in part, whether the participants realize it or not. However, the Antichrist will do all within his power to abolish these foundations of law and will replace them with lawlessness. Righteous men, therefore, will have no legal remedy and will not be able to accomplish anything.

At times like these, it will seem as though Righteousness has died and wickedness prevails. No doubt, it also seemed that way for David at this particular time!

The *"foundations"* here addressed speak of the great principles of the Word of God, i.e., *"the foundation on which the Word of God is based, which is Christ and the Cross."* That is the one and only foundation. If it is destroyed, even those who desire to live for God, i.e., *"the Righteous,"* cannot be successful in their efforts.

THE MESSAGE OF THE CROSS

Sadly and regrettably, the number of Churches truly preaching the Cross is abysmally small. Actually, in most Churches, the Cross has been abandoned in favor of the new fads, such as *"The Purpose Driven Life,"* *"The Government of Twelve,"* or *"The Word of Faith,"* etc. In almost all of these circles, humanistic psychology had taken the place of the Cross of Christ. In other words, precious few Preachers any more are *"preaching the Cross."* The few who do mostly limit it to Salvation, and then only with sentimental value.

The Cross of Christ, however, is the foundation on which all doctrine must be built, or else it will be specious in some way (I Pet. 1:18-20).

So, let all know and understand:

If the Message of the Cross is abrogated, denied, ignored, or disbelieved, that leaves Christianity without Christ, which means that it is then little more than Buddhism or Islam, etc.

Take a look presently at Judaism. It denied Christ to Whom all of Judaism once pointed. Where is it today?

Paul warned all and sundry that if the Church went the way of Israel, which refers to the fact of trying to establish one's own righteousness instead of accepting the Righteousness of Christ, then the Church would also be cut off! (Rom. 10:3; 11:19-21).

(4) "THE LORD IS IN HIS HOLY TEMPLE, THE LORD'S THRONE IS IN HEAVEN: HIS EYES BEHOLD, HIS EYELIDS TRY, THE CHILDREN OF MEN."

Irrespective of what may be happening on Earth or even around us, the Lord is on His Throne, and His Eyes are beholding every single thing that is happening. Nothing escapes His penetrating gaze. Even though He seemingly does not answer, at least at the moment, and even though it may seem that evil rules the day, still, nothing escapes His attention or His scrutiny.

This is perhaps the hardest time for any Child of God to undergo. Catastrophe seems to reign on every hand; trouble abounds. And yet it seems like God cannot be found. Prayers seemingly go unanswered. His hand does not come to the rescue. David faced this particular time. Possibly it could be said that every single Christian, at one time or another, faces these trying times. The reason is given in the following Verse.

(5) "THE LORD TRIES THE RIGHTEOUS: BUT THE WICKED AND HIM WHO LOVES VIOLENCE, HIS SOUL HATES."

The reason is here given!

THE TESTING OF FAITH

All of this is for a purpose and a reason. These are times designed by the Lord so that our faith is put to the test. As painful as they are, these are necessary times. The very ingredient of faith demands that it be tested.

During these trying times, it may seem as though wickedness prevails, i.e., that God no longer cares. Nevertheless, the Lord gives us this Promise that even though at the present He may not seem to be intervening, still, let it always be understood that *"His soul hates the wicked and him who loves violence."*

The Holy Spirit is telling us that just because God doesn't take action immediately, this does not mean that He in any way approves of the wickedness that is being carried out. He hates it, irrespective of His seeming inaction.

Faith must always be tested, and great faith must be tested greatly!

The next Verse tells us what the Lord ultimately will do.

(6) "UPON THE WICKED HE SHALL RAIN SNARES, FIRE AND BRIMSTONE, AND AN HORRIBLE TEMPEST: THIS SHALL BE THE PORTION OF THEIR CUP."

Even though it may seem at the present as though God is doing nothing and that the wicked are getting by with their great sinfulness, still, their *"cup"* is filling up and will ultimately bring terrible judgment upon them from God. (*"The wicked"* more pointedly refers to the Antichrist.)

(7) "FOR THE RIGHTEOUS LORD LOVES RIGHTEOUSNESS; HIS COUNTENANCE DOES BEHOLD THE UPRIGHT."

The matter is simple: God hates evil and loves Righteousness.

THE SHINING FACE OF THE LORD

Even though it may seem, at least for a time, like the Lord has forgotten His people and allowed the wicked to do what they desire, still, His Promise to us is that *"His Countenance does behold the upright."*

He knows everything that the Child of God is undergoing for the moment, and, if we will trust Him, He will bring it out to our good, our benefit, and our blessing. He is beholding us.

In the longer view, the Holy Spirit is saying that the Lord is beholding Israel, and even though it may seem that the Antichrist will have his way and destroy the holy people, still, God is beholding all, and judgment will come upon the Evil One, and those who proclaim Righteousness will ultimately be greatly blessed.

PSALM 12

A Psalm of David:
The Righteous are Delivered

(1) "HELP, LORD; FOR THE GODLY MAN CEASES; FOR THE FAITHFUL FAIL FROM AMONG THE CHILDREN OF MEN."

David wrote this Psalm and it pertains to three things:

1. David and the difficulties he had with Saul before finally becoming King.
2. Present-day circumstances which apply to you and me.
3. The coming Antichrist and his efforts to take over the world and to make the lie the centerpiece of his doctrine.

VIOLENCE AND FALSEHOOD

The two greatest weapons of Satan against the servants of God are *"violence"* and *"falsehood."* The violence of the False Messiah is the theme in the previous Chapter; falsehood is the theme in this Chapter.

There is a reason that the *"Godly man ceases"* and that the *"faithful fail."* It is found in the next Verse.

(2) "THEY SPEAK VANITY EVERY ONE WITH HIS NEIGHBOR: WITH FLATTERING LIPS AND WITH A DOUBLE HEART DO THEY SPEAK."

Whenever the Bible is displaced by human teaching, a logical result is that righteous men will be persecuted. Satan's greatest effort against the cause of Christ is to water down the Word of God, to dilute it, or to do away with it altogether.

THE LIE OF FALSE DOCTRINE

There have never been so many Bibles in America and Canada as there are today; tragically, there has never been less reading and study of the Bible as today.

The Bible is largely an unread Book. The pulpit is almost silent regarding the Word of God. Humanistic, Freudian psychology has become the guru of the modern pulpit. The number of Churches in the land which faithfully adhere to the Word of God is miniscule. The *"lie of false doctrine"* and compromised, human teaching abound.

In David's day, this was the cause of Israel's problem. Saul did not desire to adhere to the Word of God. Likewise, in the Great Tribulation, the Antichrist will make every effort to do away with the Bible. He will, by and large, succeed. Satan's contest is with the Bible. He will do anything within Hell's power to keep Preachers from preaching it, people from studying it, and men from believing it.

FALSE BIBLES

At the present time (2005), the land is being flooded with paraphrases of the Bible, such as *"The Message Bible,"* which, in reality, is no Bible at all. This is one of the great attacks, if not the greatest attack, by Satan against the Word of God. Satan is no longer attacking it frontally, as he did in the past, but is making an end run, so to speak. He is replacing the Word of God with these spurious paraphrases and duping well-known Preachers into recommending this stupidity.

If the Bible you study is not a word-for-word translation, such as the King James Version and two or three others which fall into this category, whatever it is you have, it may be *"about"* the Bible, but it is not the Bible, which means it is not the Word of God!

Remember this:

Jesus said, *"Man shall not live by bread alone, but by every Word that proceeds out of the Mouth of God"* (Mat. 4:4).

This means that every *"Word"* of the original Text is inspired by the Lord and is meant to stay the way it is.

This doesn't mean that word-for-word translations are inspired, for no translation is inspired. I personally believe that the Lord helped the individuals to make the translation, but, as far as Inspiration is concerned, that applies only to the original Text, of which there are none remaining. However, there are tens of thousands of copies of the original Text, some going back to within 300 years of the original writing.

To be frank, the Bible, such as the King James Text, is guaranteed to be free from Textual error. Regarding particular Epistles, this means that the Bible which you hold in your hands is the same as that which was held in the hands of the Apostle Paul.

(3) "THE LORD SHALL CUT OFF ALL FLATTERING LIPS, AND THE TONGUE THAT SPEAKS PROUD THINGS."

The prediction given here means that ultimately all who do not believe the Word of God will be *"cut off."* God's Word will stand; the *"flattering lips"* and the *"proud things"* ultimately will fail.

(4) "WHO HAVE SAID, WITH OUR TONGUE WILL WE PREVAIL; OUR LIPS ARE OUR OWN: WHO IS LORD OVER US?"

In the Great Tribulation, when the Antichrist prevails, false teachers will abound. They will boast that they are their own masters, controlled by no God of the Heavens. They will say that their lips are their own; that their teaching originates with themselves; that it is independent, free, and untrammeled; and that thanks to their tongue and their doctrine, it will prevail.

Every false teacher presently has the same spirit within him that the teachers under the Antichrist will have. It is a spirit of rebellion: *"Who is Lord over us?"*

(5) "FOR THE OPPRESSION OF THE POOR, FOR THE SIGHING OF THE NEEDY, NOW WILL I ARISE, SAITH THE LORD; I WILL SET HIM IN SAFETY FROM HIM WHO PUFFS AT HIM."

David is here given the Promise by the Holy Spirit that his *"oppression"* and his *"sighing"* will soon end. The same could be said for you and me. It also will be said for Israel in the latter days under the Antichrist.

God has given us a Promise that *"now will I arise."* He says three things:

1. *"The Lord will protect David,"* and He did!

2. *"The Lord will protect us from them who 'puff' at us."*

3. *"The Lord will protect Israel when the Antichrist comes against her and it seems that all is lost."*

(6) "THE WORDS OF THE LORD ARE PURE WORDS: AS SILVER TRIED IN A FURNACE OF EARTH, PURIFIED SEVEN TIMES."

Such is the Bible. Not only is it a pure Revelation of God, but the very words with which it is composed are pure words — seven times purified, meaning perfectly pure. The impure teachings of man give birth to vile actions. A true creed, which can only be based on the Word of God, produces pure conduct. A false creed produces vile conduct.

THE CROSS

The Lord's Way is the Way of the Cross. As we have said over and over, the only thing that stands between man and eternal Hell is the Cross of Christ — the only thing! This means that if the Preacher is not *"preaching the Cross,"* he is not preaching the Gospel.

Paul said:

"Christ sent me not to baptize, but to preach the Gospel, not with enticing words, lest the Cross of Christ should be made of none effect" (I Cor. 1:17).

In this one Verse, we are told exactly what the Gospel really is. It is *"the Cross of Christ."*

Other things, such as Water Baptism, most definitely may be important, even very important. But neither Water Baptism nor any other Church Ordinance is to be given preeminence. *"The Message of the Cross"* must ever be preeminent!

Those are the *"pure words of the LORD,"* even *"purified seven times."*

We ask the Reader to note the following:

In the last two Chapters of the Book of Revelation, when all sin is defeated, and when Satan, all who have followed him, his fallen angels, and demon spirits have been cast into the Lake of Fire, where they will remain forever and forever, seven times in these two Chapters, our Lord is referred to as *"the Lamb"* (Rev. 21:9, 14, 22, 23, 27; 22:1, 3).

This is definitely not by chance! It is done accordingly by the Holy Spirit so that all may know that the glory, the grandeur, and the greatness which all Saints will enjoy forever and forever, all and without exception, were made possible by the Cross of Christ.

(7) "YOU SHALL KEEP THEM, O LORD, YOU SHALL PRESERVE THEM FROM THIS GENERATION FOREVER."

The destiny of those who love and obey the Word of God is presented in Verse 7, in contrast to the fate of those who accept man's teaching, which is given in Verse 3. The latter shall be *"cut off,"* but lovers of the Bible itself shall be preserved forever.

(8) "THE WICKED WALK ON EVERY SIDE, WHEN THE VILEST MEN ARE EXALTED."

When those who do not believe the Bible are exalted in religious circles, *"the wicked"* become the order of the day.

Regrettably, this is happening in most institutionalized religion.

In a more particular way, it refers to the coming Great Tribulation, when the *"vilest men will be exalted,"* i.e., those who hate the Bible. Then *"the wicked"* will have the preeminence. However, this will only last for a short time.

PSALM 13

A Psalm of David:
A Prayer of Distress and Faith

(1) "HOW LONG WILL YOU FORGET ME, O LORD? FOREVER? HOW LONG WILL YOU HIDE YOUR FACE FROM ME?

(2) "HOW LONG SHALL I TAKE COUNSEL IN MY SOUL, HAVING SORROW IN MY HEART DAILY? HOW LONG SHALL MY ENEMY BE EXALTED OVER ME?"

This Psalm was written by David but it is not known when he wrote it. Some think it was during the time when Saul was persecuting David. Other Scholars feel that David wrote it after committing the sin concerning Bathsheba and her husband Uriah.

A BROKEN HEART

The first two Verses speak of great heartache, even despair. It seems that David has cried repeatedly to God, but with no answer. In exasperation, he even asks, *"How long will this continue? Forever?"*

If this Psalm really was written after the episode with Bathsheba and her husband Uriah, then we are seeing the aftermath of sin. Even though David had repented, a Repentance he proclaims in Psalm 51, and even though God had forgiven him, still, the hurt remains. Although forgiveness brings about a Restoration of communion and a reunion of fellowship, the hurt lingers, even great hurt.

To the one who truly loves the Lord, even as David most definitely did, the hurt is exacerbated. It seems to have no limitation, because sin is such a loathsome business!

This time, ever how long it was, ultimately would come to an end, even as we shall see. But that did not lessen the impact of the sorrow during the time it did last.

In a far greater and prophetic measure, the Psalm pictures the sufferings of Israel during the *"times of trouble"* under the reign of the False Messiah.

INTERCESSION

The afflicted one in the Psalm is Israel; the Speaker is Immanuel. As the High Priest of His people, He prays for them as if He Himself was suffering the affliction. He makes His people's sorrows His Own. The *"enemy"* in Verse 2 is the Antichrist.

One can look at these first two Verses and read Christ into this heart's cry. As stated, while the Gospels portray the acts of our Lord, the Psalms portray His heart.

These are the words prayed by Christ, words which will stand forever, as Intercession for His people, which includes you and me.

Some may claim that they do not need such Intercession. They may claim that their sin is not nearly as bad as was David's; however, the only ones who would think such would be those who do not fully understand the Cross, or themselves. Truthfully, none of us, even the best of us, whoever that might be, could last twenty-four hours without the constant Intercession of Christ, all on our behalf.

(3) "CONSIDER AND HEAR ME, O LORD MY GOD: LIGHTEN MY EYES, LEST I SLEEP THE SLEEP OF DEATH;

(4) "LEST MY ENEMY SAY, I HAVE PREVAILED AGAINST HIM; AND THOSE WHO TROUBLE ME REJOICE WHEN I AM MOVED."

The sobbing cry of David to his Lord is that the Lord would once again hear him — and if God does not do so, he (David) will die.

Only one, as stated, who has had a close walk with God, as did David, would understand the horror of broken fellowship.

THE SUFFERING OF
THE WORK OF GOD

David's request also concerns his myriad of enemies, who are joyful because of his problems, thinking they now can prevail against him. For a time it looked like they might, especially if this Psalm was written during the time of Absalom's rebellion, which followed the sin with Bathsheba and against Uriah.

In prophetic tone, the cry comes from the Messiah making Intercession for Israel, saying, in effect, that if God does not hear and protect against the *"enemy"* (False Shepherd), then Israel will die.

The prayer of both David and the Son of David will be answered.

Failure brings great hurt to the Work of God, irrespective as to who commits it, or whatever the failure might be. David is extremely concerned about this — in fact, more concerned about this than over anything else.

David feels that if the Lord does not give him Grace, then he simply will not be able to stand the pressure. He will die! However, the Lord never leaves one in the lurch. Irrespective, He always comes to the rescue, especially for those with an honest heart, such as David.

(5) "BUT I HAVE TRUSTED IN YOUR MERCY; MY HEART SHALL REJOICE IN YOUR SALVATION.

(6) "I WILL SING UNTO THE LORD, BECAUSE HE HAS DEALT BOUNTIFULLY WITH ME."

David shouts because the Mercy of God is once again being shown unto him. Perhaps these words were written immediately after the writing of the Fifty-first Psalm. Now, his heart rejoices in the saving Grace of the Lord, Who has cleansed him, forgiven him, and washed him of all iniquity.

THE SONG RETURNS

Whenever the joy returns, then the song returns. Once again, the Lord begins to deal *"bountifully."*

The words, *"Dealt bountifully,"* can be translated *"compensated,"* and thus reaffirm what so often appears in the Scriptures — that the overcomer will be compensated in the future state for all his sufferings as a Christ-confessor in the present life, and that he will learn that perfect wisdom and infinite love will permit and overrule every trial.

The certitude of the faithfulness, love, and power which the Messiah will show to His people in the day of His coming again strengthens the faith of His people during the time of their waiting and suffering. The Antichrist will be defeated, Israel will be brought back to God, and Jesus Christ will be crowned *"KING OF KINGS AND LORD*

OF LORDS" (Rev. 19:16).

PSALM 14

*A Psalm of David:
The Foolishness of Men*

(1) "THE FOOL HAS SAID IN HIS HEART, THERE IS NO GOD. THEY ARE CORRUPT, THEY HAVE DONE ABOMINABLE WORKS, THERE IS NONE WHO DOES GOOD."

David wrote this Psalm and it also has a triple meaning.

THE FOOL

The triple meaning is as follows:

1. It applies to David. As the Lord gave David this Psalm, it was, no doubt, inspired by the nations of the world of which David had knowledge which had refused to serve the God of Israel.

2. The meaning of this Song is also the manner in which it applies to all of humanity, and for all time.

3. It applies to the Antichrist. The first and last Verses prove the folly of the Antichrist, who will be the *"fool"* of II Thessalonians 2:4; the corruption of his followers (Vs. 1); their mutual doom (Vs. 5); and Israel's final redemption (Vs. 7).

The Holy Spirit has labeled a *"fool"* all those who are *"gone aside"* (Vs. 3) and say in their heart, *"There is no God."* There are three things which the Holy Spirit says about individuals who will not reverence or serve the Lord:

A. They are corrupt;
B. They have done abominable works; and,
C. There is none who does good.

The Word is emphatic on this point. Outside of God, it is not possible for one to do good; consequently, all the good that is done in this world is done by those who serve the Lord.

This also means that despite all the Promises the Antichrist will make concerning the bettering of the lot of humanity, still, there will be no good done, only destruction.

(2) "THE LORD LOOKED DOWN FROM HEAVEN UPON THE CHILDREN OF MEN, TO SEE IF THERE WERE ANY WHO DID UNDERSTAND, AND SEEK GOD."

Another great truth is here given!

THE WAYS OF GOD

The word *"looked"* means literally to bow Himself over to get a better and closer examination of men and their wicked ways. This means to minutely inspect the heart of each individual as only God can do to see if *"any did understand, and seek God."* Several things are said in this Verse:

1. No man will be able to stand in the judgment and say that God did not do all that was possible in order to save men. Minute inspection has been made of each heart.

2. God desired to see just how evil that man's heart really is. It seems that the results were a shock even to God.

3. God would find that there was no redeeming quality in man. Yet He would go to great lengths to save man.

Why?

Because God is Love, and Love must go to any length to redeem.

SIN

Sin takes one further than one desires to go, and costs more than one can afford to pay!

When the depths of depravity are a shock to God, then we come to understand, at least somewhat, of the wickedness of the human heart. That's the reason it is such dire foolishness for man to try to save himself. It simply cannot be done! Filth cannot cleanse filth, as pollution cannot cleanse pollution!

For man to be saved, he must be *"born again,"* for nothing else will suffice (Jn. 3:3). And for the Born-Again experience to be brought about, the great price of Christ on the Cross of Calvary had to be paid.

When one looks at the Cross and all of its attendant horror, then one should say, *"Sin did this!"* Even more so, one should say, *"My sin did this!"*

All of this tells us that there is no love like the Love of God. There also is no destruction as bleak as sin. But there is no sin that the Love of God cannot cleanse and wash, which is done solely by Christ and what He did at the Cross.

The greatest surprise of all is that it only

takes faith in that which the Lord has done for us at Calvary in order for us to be the beneficiary of all for which He paid such a price.

As Charles Wesley, the brother of John Wesley, wrote:

"O Love that will not let me go!"

(3) "THEY ARE ALL GONE ASIDE, THEY ARE ALL TOGETHER BECOME FILTHY: THERE IS NONE WHO DOES GOOD, NO, NOT ONE."

This is a statement of fact — the whole race has left God and the straight way for crooked paths.

THE DENIAL OF GOD

The denial of God, as given in Verse 1, is the first step in total apostasy. Paul mentioned this in Romans 1:21-32. This means that America, Canada, and all other nations in the world, for that matter, are labeled by the Holy Spirit as *"fools,"* whenever *"they did not like to retain God in their knowledge."*

Paul further said, *"God gave them over to a reprobate mind"* (Rom. 1:28). In the public educational system, the system of government, and the judicial system of the United States, this country has said, *"We do not want God in our knowledge."* The results are obvious:

1. *"Gone aside after a crooked way"*;
2. *"Altogether become filthy"*; and,
3. *"No good is done, no, not even by one person."*

THE TOTAL DEPRAVITY OF MAN

This teaches the total depravity of man, which means that man, within himself, cannot do anything that is good, nor can he instigate anything that can contribute toward his Salvation. Within himself, he cannot reach God, nor does he have any desire to reach God. And yet, deep in the heart of every person where only God can reach, there is something there that, upon proper Revelation of God by the Holy Spirit to that individual, either will say *"Yes"* or *"No"* to God. God initiates the Revelation, but He in no way forces or manipulates the free will of man.

FREE WILL

"Free will" is taught throughout Scripture (Rev. 22:17). The teaching that God arbitrarily selects some for Salvation and some for destruction is unscriptural and consequently demonic, for all error of doctrine is instigated by demon spirits.

The Holy Spirit never tampers with man's power of choice. The Lord will deal with man, impress man, even speak to man, but He will never force man to do something against his will. This part of man that sets him apart from the animal creation is actually *"the Image of God"* (Gen. 1:27) and *"the Breath of God"* (Gen. 2:7). This factor giving man the power of choice and the ability to create sets man apart from all of God's other creation.

Angels have the power of choice, but there is no record that they have the ability to create. It seems they can do only what God tells them to do. This is one of the reasons that demon spirits, even fallen angels, desire to work through and with mankind. Man has the ability to create, although he cannot create something out of nothing, as can God. Man can only create something out of that which God has initiated in the first place.

With fallen spirits and fallen angels aiding and abetting man, there really is little limit as to what he can do (Gen. 11:6). This is the manner by which the Antichrist will make his great debut in these last days (Rev. 13:11-17).

(4) "HAVE ALL THE WORKERS OF INIQUITY NO KNOWLEDGE? WHO EAT UP MY PEOPLE AS THEY EAT BREAD, AND CALL NOT UPON THE LORD."

David here speaks of the knowledge of the Lord.

THE KNOWLEDGE OF THE LORD

The knowledge that the Lord is speaking of is true understanding of the Fear of the Lord, which is the beginning of wisdom. Irrespective of how much knowledge that men may have, still, if they do not have this knowledge, they really have no knowledge that can address itself to the true questions of life.

These *"workers of iniquity"* will always oppose the people of God. Also, when the Church leaves the Word of God, opting for the *"knowledge of this world,"* they also seek to hinder and even destroy the true people of God.

Actually, down through the centuries, the greatest hindrance to God's people has not been from the world system, per se, but instead has come from an apostate religious system that has turned its back on the Word of God.

(5) "THERE WERE THEY IN GREAT FEAR: FOR GOD IS IN THE GENERATION OF THE RIGHTEOUS."

God's people cannot be attacked without provoking Him; we are in Him, and He in us; He will assuredly come to our relief.

GREAT FEAR

The *"great fear"* mentioned here has to do with the Second Coming. The Antichrist will be bearing down upon Jerusalem, and thousands of television cameras will, no doubt, record the events, transmitting them to the farthest corners of the globe. The Antichrist wants the entirety of the world to observe him as he defeats the hated Jew.

And then, the Second Coming, the most dramatic event in human history, will take place. All of a sudden, even instantly, great bravado will turn to *"great fear."*

The short phrase, *"Great fear,"* actually means that terror seizes on them. It implies a panic terror, and rightly so! At this time, the Lord will use power such as He has never used before, and all for the destruction of the Antichrist and his vast armies.

(6) "YOU HAVE SHAMED THE COUNSEL OF THE POOR, BECAUSE THE LORD IS HIS REFUGE."

Other than to generalize the application of these Passages (Vss. 3-6), this also applies to the future Antichrist, who will seek to destroy Israel. The *"poor"* referred to in the Sixth Verse is actually referring to Israel. The Antichrist will not know that their *"refuge is the LORD,"* but he will soon find out.

(7) "OH THAT THE SALVATION OF ISRAEL WERE COME OUT OF ZION! WHEN THE LORD BRINGS BACK THE CAPTIVITY OF HIS PEOPLE, JACOB SHALL REJOICE, AND ISRAEL SHALL BE GLAD."

This Verse proclaims the Restoration of Israel!

JACOB AND ISRAEL

It is interesting that the Holy Spirit uses both names, *"Jacob"* and *"Israel,"* in this concluding Verse. Jacob is the natural name; Israel is the spiritual name. This Passage shows that as God ultimately brought *"Jacob"* from being a schemer and a fraud to become *"Israel,"* a Prince with God, likewise, the nation of Israel as a whole will be brought from being a schemer and a fraud to being Israel, the Prince of God. Hallelujah!

Back to the Sixth Verse, it is interesting that the covetous Pharisees mocked the counsel of the *"Poor Man"* (Lk. 16:14) when they heard His teaching about serving God and Mammon.

PSALM 15

A Psalm of David:
Who Shall Dwell in Your Holy Hill?

(1) "LORD, WHO SHALL ABIDE IN YOUR TABERNACLE? WHO SHALL DWELL IN YOUR HOLY HILL?"

As noted, David wrote this Psalm.

THE LORD JESUS CHRIST

The theme is: Who shall be entitled to reign on Mount Zion as a King over the Kingdom? In other words, who is to be the chief citizen of the Kingdom of Heaven when it is established on the Earth?

The answer describes a Man Who once lived on Earth and Who has never had a moral peer. That Man is the Messiah. He Alone satisfies the requirements of Verses 2 through 5. Incidentally, the descriptions, *"Your Tabernacle"* and *"Your Holy Hill,"* are not types, but realities. In other words, the Holy Spirit through David is speaking of both the earthly Jerusalem, which will be established in the coming Kingdom Age, and the Heavenly Mount Zion and City of God, the New Jerusalem (Heb. 12:22-23; Rev. 14:1).

Considering that no one has ever met these qualifications, which will be outlined in this Psalm, except the Lord Jesus Christ, how is it possible for anyone to *"abide"* there? The answer is forthcoming!

(2) "HE WHO WALKS UPRIGHTLY, AND WORKS RIGHTEOUSNESS, AND SPEAKS

THE TRUTH IN HIS HEART."

An upright walk is the first requirement.

In the Hebrew, the Text implies continuance, i.e., the Chief Citizen in the Kingdom of Heaven will be a Perfect Man Who perfectly kept, and perfectly keeps, God's Perfect Law. He lives blamelessly and always did so live; He practices Righteousness, and never practiced anything else. He speaks, and always spoke, Truth in His Heart; He always condemns vile persons and continuously honors them who fear Jehovah. He never did backbite with His Tongue, and does not do so, or injure His neighbor; He never did, nor does He receive a malicious story against another; He always kept, and does keep, His Pledges; He never practiced, nor practices, usury; and He never accepted, nor accepts, bribes.

THE LAST ADAM, THE SECOND MAN

The Messiah was such, and is such. He Alone, therefore, can, and shall, sit upon the Throne of Jehovah on Mount Zion.

But the citizens of such a Kingdom must morally resemble the King. All men fail in this resemblance, both by nature and by practice. Those, therefore, who would *"see"* and *"enter"* that Kingdom must, by a birth from above, receive a new moral nature (Jn. 3:3, 5). In such persons, the Messiah, by His Holy Spirit, lives the blameless life here portrayed.

(3) "HE WHO BACKBITES NOT WITH HIS TONGUE, NOR DOES EVIL TO HIS NEIGHBOR, NOR TAKES UP A REPROACH AGAINST HIS NEIGHBOR."

The requirements continue to be given.

THE MANNER IN WHICH BELIEVERS CAN MEET THESE REQUIREMENTS

Having established the fact that it is Jesus Alone Who can meet, and has met, these criteria, Believers can do such, be such, and be acclaimed by the Heavenly Father as such, only by the means of being *"In Christ,"* which comes about by the New Birth. That being accomplished, and our faith being anchored in Christ and the Cross, the Holy Spirit, Who resides within us, then sets about to bring our *"condition"* up to our *"position,"* or our *"state"* up to our *"standing."*

(4) "IN WHOSE EYES A VILE PERSON IS CONTEMNED; BUT HE HONORS THEM WHO FEAR THE LORD. HE WHO SWEARS TO HIS OWN HURT, AND CHANGES NOT."

The Believer has a position in Christ that is perfect, which is the only type of position that God can accept. It is called *"Justification by Faith,"* meaning that we evidence Faith in Christ and what Christ has done for us at the Cross.

However, even though that is the Believer's position, a position, incidentally, that never changes, still, our condition or state is not exactly up to our position or standing. This is a fact that we must realize as it regards our walk with the Lord. Our Salvation is perfect, because it must be, and because it is in Christ, but our condition or state needs improvement, which is the Work of the Holy Spirit.

(5) "HE WHO PUTS NOT OUT HIS MONEY TO USURY, NOR TAKES REWARD AGAINST THE INNOCENT. HE WHO DOES THESE THINGS SHALL NEVER BE MOVED."

The reason it is such a sin for Believers to transfer their faith from Christ and the Cross to something else (and it doesn't really matter what the *"something else"* is), a sin which the Apostle Paul greatly condemned, is because it stops the Holy Spirit from His Work within our lives.

The Holy Spirit doesn't require much of us, but He does require that our Faith be exclusively in Christ and the Cross. We must not deviate from that, whatever else we might do (Rom. 6:1-14; 8:1-2, 11; I Cor. 1:17-18, 21, 23; 2:2; Gal., Chpt. 5; 6:14).

SPIRITUAL ADULTERY

The reason the Holy Spirit refuses to work in our lives under such circumstances, and we continue to speak of our faith being in something other than Christ and the Cross, is because such a Believer is then placed in the position of living in *"spiritual adultery"* (Rom. 7:1-4).

As Paul addressed in the first four Verses of the Seventh Chapter of Romans, Christ is to meet our every need, and in every capacity, which is what the Cross is all about. Whatever and Whoever Christ is, He hasn't changed. He is the same, yesterday, today, and forever. But it is the Cross which made it possible for Him to lavish us with great gifts, all superintended by the Holy Spirit.

That's what Jesus was speaking of when He said:

"If any man thirst, let him come unto Me, and drink.

"He who believes on Me as the Scripture has said, out of his belly shall flow rivers of Living Water."

"But this spoke He of the Spirit" (Jn. 7:37-39).

Let us say it again:

"Christ is the Source, while the Cross is the Means."

Jesus, as stated, has obeyed these precepts given in this Fifteenth Psalm, and has done so in every respect, and has done so perfectly. We qualify only as long as we are in Christ and our faith is properly placed in Him and the Cross.

PSALM 16

A Psalm of David:
The Coming Davidic King

(1) "PRESERVE ME, O GOD: FOR IN YOU DO I PUT MY TRUST."

This Psalm was written by David and it is referred to as a *"Messianic Psalm."*

The personal pronouns of Verses 5 through 11 refer to the Messiah. Verses 1 through 4 refer not only to Him, but also to David.

TRUST

The phrase, *"In You do I put My trust,"* was one of David's favorite statements. It also portrays the Son of David. The cry of the Holy Spirit is for the Saint of God to trust God for everything. Sadly, the modern Church puts most of its trust in man instead of God. The reason for that is that the Church has, for the most part, left the Word of God for fables (II Tim. 4:4).

At this particular time, I speak of humanistic psychology, *"The Purpose Driven Life"* scheme, and *"The Government of Twelve"* scheme. These are the fads for the present, but they will change shortly, as they have done through the many centuries.

Let the Believer understand the following:

Something is not necessarily Scriptural just because Scriptures are used. The Scriptures must first of all be used in the correct manner. That's why we are told to *"study to show ourselves approved unto God, a workman who needs not to be ashamed, rightly dividing the Word of Truth"* (II Tim. 2:15).

PROPER TRUST

While every true Believer claims to trust the Lord, unless one understands the Message of the Cross (I Cor. 1:18), then one cannot truly trust the Lord, at least as one should. Of course, there is a modicum of trust by any and every Believer, as there must be, if one is saved; however, the type of trust of which the Holy Spirit through David here speaks pertains to knowledge that is complete. I speak of the knowledge of Christ and what He has done for us at the Cross.

Without that particular knowledge, which David, as all Old Testament Saints, had by faith, one cannot evidence proper trust. That's why Paul said:

"God forbid that I should glory, save in the Cross of the our Lord Jesus Christ, by Whom the world is crucified unto me, and I unto the world" (Gal. 6:14).

The great Apostle also said, *"For the preaching* (Word) *of the Cross is to them who perish foolishness; but unto us who are saved it is the Power of God"* (I Cor. 1:18).

The Greek word in this Verse translated *"preaching"* is *"logos,"* which should have been translated *"Word,"* making it read, *"For the Word of the Cross is to them who perish foolishness...."*

It involves much more than preaching, even though it certainly includes such. In actuality, it pertains to the entire body of truth, as it regards the Cross — in effect, the entirety of the New Covenant.

So, as stated, if one doesn't understand the Cross, one really doesn't understand Bible faith or Bible trust.

(2) "O MY SOUL, YOU HAVE SAID UNTO THE LORD, YOU ARE MY LORD: MY GOODNESS EXTENDS NOT TO YOU."

In effect, both David and the Messiah are saying, *"You are My Lord, I have no good beyond and apart from You. You are My highest and only good."*

All *"good"* must emanate from God, or else it has at its root unholy motives, which spring from selfish desire, and thereby from the flesh, i.e., *"Satan."*

(3) "BUT TO THE SAINTS WHO ARE IN THE EARTH, AND TO THE EXCELLENT, IN WHOM IS ALL MY DELIGHT."

In essence, the Messiah is saying, *"As for the Saints who are in the Earth, they are the excellent, in whom is all My delight."*

THE MESSIAH

The Messiah in this Passage appears as a Man in His relation to God, and as a Brother in His relation to Israel and the Church. These He calls *"the excellent of the Earth."*

The False Messiah and his followers will regard them as the refuse of the Earth! What is true of the redeemed of Israel is true of God's Saints in all Dispensations, for His delights are with the sons of men (Prov. 8:31).

Actually, there is little difference in God's mind regarding Israel and the Church. As Israel was God's special people in the Earth, likewise, the Church (the true called-out Church) is His delight and special people in the Earth, and will be until Israel is restored, which will be at the beginning of the Kingdom Age.

(4) "THEIR SORROWS SHALL BE MULTIPLIED WHO HASTEN AFTER ANOTHER GOD: THEIR DRINK OFFERINGS OF BLOOD WILL I NOT OFFER, NOR TAKE UP THEIR NAMES INTO MY LIPS."

This Verse presents the Messiah as a True Worshipper, as it also should present the Child of God. It also contrasts the joys of such worshippers with the sorrow of idolaters.

IDOLATRY

The modern Christian too often thinks of idolatry as an Old Testament sin which does not relate to the modern Christian; however, John the Beloved said, *"Little children, keep yourselves from idols"* (I Jn. 5:21).

Anything that replaces God in one's heart and life becomes an idol; consequently, Hollywood is an idol to many Christians; sports is an idol to many Christians; even hobbies become idols to some Christians. In the majority of the lives of most who call themselves *"Christians,"* religion has become an idol. In other words, their allegiance is to a particular Church, Denomination, Doctrine, or Preacher. Christ and the Word of God are no longer the center of their allegiance.

(5) "THE LORD IS THE PORTION OF MY INHERITANCE AND OF MY CUP: YOU MAINTAIN MY LOT."

David and the Messiah could both have said the words pertaining to Verses 1 through 4; but Verses 5 through 11, even though uttered by the mouth of David, pertain solely to the Son of David.

THE DIVISION OF THE LAND

This Verse is taken from the idea of the general division of the Promised Land. The members of the Tribe of Levi had no inheritance, but were to live off the parts of the Offerings which fell to the share of Divine service. Jehovah Himself is called their share (Deut. 10:9; 18:1-2). All Israelites were to be a Kingdom of Priests to God (Ex. 19:6; Jer. 10:16).

Likewise, Jesus mentioned the *"cup"* in Matthew 20:22. This Verse expresses the mission and characterizes the ministry given to the Messiah and declared by Him to be pleasant and goodly.

(6) "THE LINES ARE FALLEN UNTO ME IN PLEASANT PLACES; YEA, I HAVE A GOODLY HERITAGE."

Again, the Master is referring to the division of the Promised Land.

THE GOODLY HERITAGE

David is here speaking of the parceling out of the entirety of the Land of Israel after the enemies had been defeated by Joshua. The account is found in Joshua, Chapters 13 through 21. A brief synopsis is given in Joshua 19:49-51.

When the land finally was conquered, with all enemies defeated, the Holy Spirit, working through the High Priest by the means of the Urim and Thummim, allotted to each Tribe a portion of land, with the largest portion being given to the Tribe of Judah, because from this Tribe the Messiah would come (Gen. 49:10). The Holy Spirit actually drew the lines for each family in Israel.

The people did not come in and select parcels of land themselves; it was all done by the leading and guidance of the Holy Spirit, even down to the minute detail.

Picking up on this, David says in his statement about the Ministry which the Lord gave to him to accomplish, *"The lines are drawn in pleasant places."*

THE PORTION ASSIGNED BY THE HOLY SPIRIT

In Truth, the Lord still works the same way, as it regards Ministry. In other words, He draws the line for each and every Believer, as it regards place, position, and Ministry. Sadly, many Believers never realize the potential outlined for them by Christ, and others are not satisfied with what the Lord has given them; instead they try to infringe upon the allotment of others.

The Holy Spirit has allotted a particular Ministry for every single Believer on the face of the Earth, and He always has done so. If the Believer will kindly ask the Lord what that Ministry is, the Holy Spirit always will show exactly where the lines are drawn. The reason that many Believers do not know is simply because they really don't care that much. As a result, the Work of God is hindered, and hindered greatly, under such circumstances.

A PERSONAL ILLUSTRATION

Many years ago, a dear lady came to the Lord and was baptized with the Holy Spirit. Even though she was in destitute circumstances, she still wanted to do something for the Lord. In prayer, she importuned Him about what her life and ministry should be. The answer soon came.

The Lord said to her, *"Raise the children!"*
That was it! *"Raise the children!"*

What the Lord meant, of course, was that she should raise them according to the Word of God, instilling in their hearts the Word and the need for great consecration to the Lord.

She obeyed the Lord to the fullest. Her daughter, Ruth, married H. B. Garlock, who opened up West Africa to the Gospel, actually to the Pentecostal Message. Her son was A. N. Trotter, who spent some twelve years in Africa, and most of the Churches in certain countries in Africa were established by his Ministry. One of the missionaries there told me that most of the Pastors in an area encompassing several countries of the African continent were Baptized with the Holy Spirit under the Ministry of Brother A. N. Trotter.

So, whenever the Lord told our dear Sister, *"Raise the children,"* that was her Ministry. That's what the Lord wanted her to do. And she accomplished it in a remarkable manner!

Raising the children may seem to be insignificant; however, the end result proved to be the very opposite. It truly was one of the single most important things in the world of that day.

The lines that the Lord draws for each and every Believer are exactly what the Holy Spirit wants. To be sure, He will let the Believer know exactly what those lines are and where they are. We are to stay within those boundaries. But most do not seek the Will of God; they rather try to chart their own course, which always brings disaster. When the Lord draws the lines, they are *"fallen unto me in pleasant places."*

DOING THE WILL OF GOD

Many Believers are fearful of yielding to the Will of God; they fear in their hearts that God will ask something of them that they desperately do not want to do. All of that is wrong!

Whatever the Lord asks a person to do, irrespective as to what it might be, He gives that person a love for that Ministry, whatever it is and wherever it is. He makes that Ministry seem like the greatest thing on the face of the Earth, which, for that person, it really is!

Many years ago, I was speaking to Mark Buntain, who built a tremendous work in Calcutta, India — a work to which our Ministry for years gave support. Mark was visiting here in the USA, actually in Baton Rouge. He had ministered at Family Worship Center.

The next day, Mark was scheduled to leave the States and return to Calcutta. I have been to Calcutta, and, please believe me, it is not a place that one desires to be.

"Mark," I asked, *"are you somewhat sorry to leave the States to return to Calcutta?"*

I will never forget his answer. For a few moments he looked at me, and then he said, *"Brother Swaggart, I can't wait to leave the States. I can't wait to get home to Calcutta."* He felt that way because that's where God called him. He truly was happy in no other place.

No! No one ever has to be fearful of the Will of God. Whatever the Lord wants you to do, He will make you happy in that thing, actually happier than you have ever been in your life. At the same time, you will be grossly dissatisfied with everything else.

So many Believers are unhappy simply because they are not in the Will of God. If you get in His Will, then you will know true joy, true fulfillment, and true happiness!

(7) "I WILL BLESS THE LORD, WHO HAS GIVEN ME COUNSEL: MY REINS ALSO INSTRUCT ME IN THE NIGHT SEASONS."

Our Lord's perfect dependence as a Man, and that which His sinless Body taught Him, are the two statements of Verse 7. He, by dwelling in a human body, *"learned obedience"* (Heb. 5:8). He did not have to learn to be obedient, for that would imply He was a sinner by nature, but He *"learned obedience,"* which is quite another thing.

The *"reins,"* according to Hebrew ideas, are the seat of feeling and emotion.

The idea is this:

The Master would pray Himself to sleep each night, always keeping His heart open to what the Holy Spirit would instruct Him.

(8) "I HAVE SET THE LORD ALWAYS BEFORE ME: BECAUSE HE IS AT MY RIGHT HAND, I SHALL NOT BE MOVED."

Verses 8 through 11 contemplate Christ as a Man about to descend into the realm of the dead. The Messiah, while looking into the black mouth of death, declares He is not afraid.

(9) "THEREFORE MY HEART IS GLAD, AND MY GLORY REJOICES: MY FLESH ALSO SHALL REST IN HOPE."

This means that His Body would rest confidently in expectation of the Resurrection. In fact, His Resurrection was not at all in doubt.

He told His Disciples, and did so repeatedly, that *"He must go to Jerusalem . . . and be killed, and be raised again the third day"* (Mat. 16:21).

Had the Lord failed to atone for even one single sin, He could not have risen from the dead, *"for the wages of sin is death"* (Rom. 6:23). In view of the fact that He was taking the penalty of sin upon Himself, which He did, He had to atone for all sin, past, present, and future, that is, if Death was to be defeated. That He did!

So there was no doubt about His Resurrection. The idea that He had to fight demon spirits, etc., in order to rise from the dead, is not found in the Bible. When He went down into the nether world, He went down there as a Conqueror, not as a victim. The Work was finished at Calvary, and His Resurrection would prove such!

(10) "FOR YOU WILL NOT LEAVE MY SOUL IN HELL; NEITHER WILL YOU SUFFER YOUR HOLY ONE TO SEE CORRUPTION."

When Jesus went to *"Hell,"* which He did upon His Death, it was only to the Paradise side (Lk. 16:19-31), and to the prison compartment of Hell, where He preached to the spirits in prison, which were fallen angels (I Pet. 3:19-20).

There is no record that He went to the burning side of Hell, as some teach.

THE JESUS DIED SPIRITUALLY DOCTRINE

This totally unscriptural doctrine claims that Jesus became a vile sinner on the Cross. Some even go so far as to claim that the Lord became demon-possessed. They claim that He was totally forsaken by God, and He thereby died as a lost sinner. Since He died as a lost sinner (according to their claims), He went to the burning side of Hell, where He was tortured for some three days and nights by demon spirits, and even by Satan himself.

At the end of this 72 hour period, God said, *"It is enough!"* meaning that Jesus had suffered enough, so He was then *"born again,"* exactly as any sinner is Born-Again, and was raised from the dead.

This teaching puts the Atonement in the burning side of Hell, of all places, claiming that the Cross was actually the greatest defeat in human history. This doctrine is totally specious and is a doctrine of devils, exactly as Paul said in I Timothy 4:1.

THE FIRSTBORN OF MANY BRETHREN

Part of the *"Jesus Died Spiritually Doctrine"* comes from Romans 8:29, which says, *"For whom He did foreknow, He also did predestinate to be conformed to be the Image of His Son, that He might be the Firstborn among many brethren."*

The word *"Firstborn"* here in the Greek is *"protokos."* It does not mean, or even hint at, the idea that Jesus was Born-Again, as some teach. It simply means that He is the Father, or the Author, of Salvation.

In fact, when this word *"Firstborn"* is used throughout the Scripture concerning Christ, it has the same connotation.

For instance:

"And He is the Head of the Body, the Church: Who is the Beginning, the Firstborn from the dead; that in all things He might have the preeminence" (Col. 1:18).

The way the word *"Firstborn"* is here used, it refers to Jesus being the Resurrection. In other words, He was not only resurrected, but He *"is"* the Resurrection and the Life, hence, the Father of the Resurrection (Jn. 11:25).

Again, Paul says of Christ, *"Who is the Image of the invisible God, the Firstborn of every creature"* (Col. 1:15).

Paul is not saying that Jesus, as the Image of the invisible God, is a *"creature,"* but rather that He is the Father of all Creation (Jn. 1:3).

Actually, the Greek Scholars tell us that there is no word in English that properly corresponds with the Greek word translated *"firstborn."* In effect, the word *"firstborn"* is the closest word in English to the Greek word *"protokos."*

WHAT IS MEANT BY THE EXPRESSION, *"JESUS DIED SPIRITUALLY"*?

Those who teach this doctrine claim that Jesus became a sinner on the Cross, even demon-possessed, and thereby died under the Judgment of God, as do all sinners. The Bible does not teach such a thing. The Scripture teaches:

"How much more shall the Blood of Christ, Who through the Eternal Spirit offered Himself without spot to God" (Heb. 9:14). If He became a sinner on the Cross, then He could not have offered Himself *"without spot to God."*

Again, the Scripture states, *"Who His Own Self bore our sins in His Own Body on the tree"* (I Pet. 2:24). This means that Jesus paid the price by the giving of Himself. In effect, He gave His Perfect Body as a Sacrifice, which satisfied the Righteousness of a thrice-Holy God. He did not redeem us by going to Hell, as some claim, but by offering Himself in Sacrifice.

Again, Peter said, *"For Christ also has once suffered for sins, the Just for the unjust* (had He become a sinner, He could not be referred to as *"Just"*), *that He might bring us to God, being put to death in the flesh, but quickened by the Spirit"* (I Pet. 3:18). Plainly and clearly, we are here told that Jesus paid for our sins by dying *"in the flesh,"* which means that He did not die spiritually, i.e., as a sinner without God.

Becoming a sinner would not accomplish the task of paying the price for sin; this would only exacerbate the problem. If Jesus had become a sinner, then God could not have accepted Him as a Sacrifice.

When the lambs were chosen for the Sacrificial Offering in Old Testament times, they were minutely inspected by the Priests to insure that there was no blemish (Ex. 12:5). After the lamb was killed, the Priest was instructed to lay open the backbone to see if there was even any discoloration in the flesh. If there was, the carcass was discarded and another lamb was chosen. This was done because the lamb signified the Coming Redeemer, Who had to be Perfect.

When one puts together the types and shadows of the Old Testament concerning Christ with the Scriptures of the New Testament concerning His Death, there is no evidence whatsoever that Jesus died as a sinner, but there is every evidence that He paid the price fully by the giving of Himself in Sacrifice, which was a Perfect Sacrifice, which alone could be accepted by God.

So, truly, God the Father did not allow the *"Holy One,"* the Lord Jesus Christ, *"to see corruption."*

(11) "YOU WILL SHOW ME THE PATH OF LIFE: IN YOUR PRESENCE IS FULLNESS OF JOY; AT YOUR RIGHT HAND THERE ARE PLEASURES FOR EVERMORE."

This is the *"path"* which leads to the Source and Center of all life, even God Himself; it is also the path to Heaven, in contrast with the corruption of Hell.

FULLNESS OF JOY

The phrase, *"In Your Presence is fullness of joy,"* proclaims the fact and literally states *"a satiety of joy,"* which means enough, and more than enough, to satisfy the most extreme cravings of the human heart. Truly, *"there are pleasures for evermore."*

All of this is made possible, totally and completely, by the Cross of Christ. That is the reason that Paul said, *"We preach Christ Crucified"* (I Cor. 1:23).

PSALM 17

*A Psalm of David:
A Prayer for Protection*

(1) "HEAR THE RIGHT, O LORD, ATTEND UNTO MY CRY, GIVE EAR UNTO MY PRAYER, THAT GOES NOT OUT OF FEIGNED LIPS."

This is a Psalm of David written in the form of a prayer. It is also a prayer and a cry of *"The Son of David."*

VERY GOD AND VERY MAN

Many lack understanding regarding the Incarnation of Christ. In the minds of many Christians, Jesus is somewhat half-God and half-Man. That is basely incorrect. Jesus was Very God (fully God) and Very Man (fully Man). In the Incarnation, He functioned only as a Man, but yet never ceased to be God. As someone has well said, *"He laid aside His expression of Deity, but not His possession of Deity."*

Therefore, if we lack understanding regarding His Incarnation, it will be difficult for us to understand His praying, as this Psalm proclaims.

As He prays, He associates His people with Himself; consequently, we should also pray in this manner. Several things are said here in this First Verse. They are as follows:

1. *"Hear the right,"* which means hear the Righteous, Who is Christ. If we pray to the Father in the Name of Jesus (Jn. 16:23) and we ask according to His Will (I Jn. 5:14), we have the assurance that He will hear us.

2. *"Attend unto My cry."* This means to be desperate in prayer. It is prayer which comes from the heart, and, at times, even from a broken heart.

3. *"Not out of feigned lips."* This means with all sincerity. There is no mixture of self-will or the flesh.

This is the only type of prayer that Christ prayed. It is the only type of prayer that we should pray.

(2) "LET MY SENTENCE COME FORTH FROM YOUR PRESENCE; LET YOUR EYES BEHOLD THE THINGS THAT ARE EQUAL."

This Verse may read, *"Let sentence in My favor be pronounced by You, for Your eyes discern upright actions."*

JUDGE

This petition, as given by David and the Son of David, should come from us, as well. It pleads with the Lord for His correct judgment. When men judge, they virtually always judge incorrectly; consequently, that's the reason Jesus said, *"Judge not"* (Mat. 7:1-2). The reason that man is not qualified to judge is because he does not behold all things that are equal. He can only judge from improper knowledge, bias, prejudice, or from personal motivation — hence, *"Judge not."*

(3) "YOU HAVE PROVED MY HEART; YOU HAVE VISITED ME IN THE NIGHT; YOU HAVE TRIED ME, AND SHALL FIND NOTHING; I AM PURPOSED THAT MY MOUTH SHALL NOT TRANSGRESS."

Even though David prayed this prayer, still, only the Son of God could fit this description.

THE PERFECTION OF THE SON OF GOD

Four things are here said:
1. *"Proved"* — a tested Man;
2. *"Find nothing"* — innocent;
3. *"Purposed"* — consecrated mouth; and,
4. *"Not transgress"* — sinless life.

Satan found no imperfection in Him, and God found nothing but perfection.

The only way that God can try us and *"find nothing"* regarding transgression is that we have accepted the Lord's perfection as our perfection. It is called *"Justification by Faith."* It is found only in Christ!

(4) "CONCERNING THE WORKS OF MEN, BY THE WORD OF YOUR LIPS I HAVE KEPT ME FROM THE PATHS OF THE DESTROYER."

The *"paths of the destroyer"* and the *"paths of Jehovah"* are contrasted in Verses 4 and 5. The statement is made that preservation from the one and perseverance in the other alone are secured by allegiance to the Scriptures. This was demonstrated in the temptation in the desert.

"The Destroyer" (Vs. 4), *"The Wicked,"* and *"The Enemies"* (Vs. 9) are proper titles of the future Antichrist and his followers.

(5) "HOLD UP MY GOINGS IN YOUR PATHS, THAT MY FOOTSTEPS SLIP NOT."

This can only be done by the total adherence to the Word of God.

THE CROSS OF CHRIST

To live the life we ought to live, the life that we must live, it can only be done by one's faith placed exclusively in Christ and the Cross, and one's faith maintained exclusively in Christ and the Cross.

The way this is done is found in the Sixth Chapter of Romans. Some have said that Romans presents to us the *"mechanics"* of the Holy Spirit, which tells us *"how"* the Holy Spirit works. Once we understand how the Holy Spirit works, then we know *"what"* He does, as found in the Eighth Chapter of Romans. This Chapter is referred to as the *"dynamics"* of the Holy Spirit.

This is God's Prescribed Order of Victory, and His only Prescribed Order of Victory.

NOTES

This great Plan of Redemption and Victory were given to the Apostle Paul, and he gave it to us in his Epistles, and, more particularly, in the Sixth and Eighth Chapters of Romans.

(6) "I HAVE CALLED UPON YOU, FOR YOU WILL HEAR ME, O GOD: INCLINE YOUR EAR UNTO ME, AND HEAR MY SPEECH."

This Verse proclaims the guarantee of answered prayer, that is, when it is done according to the Will of God.

INTERCESSORY PRAYER

Concentrated intercessory prayer is almost a thing of the past in the modern Church. Most Christians do not even really believe in prayer. If they did, they would engage in it much more.

The modern Church has, by and large, opted for humanistic psychology as the answer to its spiritual and emotional ills. Most of the Church world pays lip service to believing the cry of this Psalm, but they seldom follow its example.

Let it ever be known that there is no help whatsoever that can be derived from man with respect to the problems we have mentioned. God is the only Source of strength and help. He still answers prayer.

(7) "SHOW YOUR MARVELOUS LOVINGKINDNESS, O THOU WHO SAVES BY YOUR RIGHT HAND THEM WHICH PUT THEIR TRUST IN YOU FROM THOSE WHO RISE UP AGAINST THEM."

Another Promise is here given for those who trust the Lord.

TRUST IN GOD

If we honestly seek the Lord, praying according to His Will, as the Master prayed so long ago, we have the assurance of His marvelous lovingkindness, and that He will save us by the Power of His Right Hand. But He will only do that for those who totally put their *"trust"* in Him. Over and over again in the Word of God, but especially in the Psalms, we are told to trust the Lord, and we are told what He will do for them who put their trust totally in Him.

Considering this, and how important that it actually is, let's look at it a little closer.

WHAT DOES IT MEAN FOR ONE TO PUT ONE'S TRUST TOTALLY IN THE LORD?

Let's look, first of all, at doctors, hospitals, and medicine. If one seeks the service of a doctor, or has to go to a hospital, or has to take medicine, is that an abrogation of trust, as it regards the Lord?

No, it isn't!

Regrettably, some people have taken *"trust in the Lord"* to places and positions never intended by the Lord, which then becomes presumption rather than trust.

It's not wrong to seek the help of a doctor, nor to have to go to a hospital, nor to take medicine. In fact, I thank God for competent doctors, for good hospitals, and for medicine that helps to alleviate physical problems.

While the Lord definitely is the Healer, and while He definitely still heals today, He at times does heal through doctors, hospitals, and medicine. If doctors, hospitals, and medicine were wrong, if they represented a lack of trust in the Lord, then what I am about to give you from the Word of God would never have been given to us.

In the last Eight Chapters of the great Book of Ezekiel, the Prophet tells us of the coming Kingdom Age, when Christ will rule Personally from Jerusalem, and when the world will know peace and prosperity as it has never known before. He goes into detail as it concerns the Temple and its arrangements, which will be in Jerusalem.

In the Forty-seventh Chapter of his Book, he speaks of the river that will flow out from under the threshold of the Millennial Temple, which, at a particular distance, will part into two rivers — one going toward the Mediterranean and the other part going toward the Dead Sea, with the latter body of water then literally becoming alive and teeming with fish (Ezek. 47:9-10).

By the side of that river, the Scripture says, *"... shall grow all trees for meat, whose leaf shall not fade, neither shall the fruit thereof be consumed* (meaning the fruit will be so abundant that one crop will not be gathered before the other comes on*): it shall bring forth new fruit according to his months, because their waters they issued out of the Sanctuary: and the fruit thereof shall be for meat, and the leaf thereof for medicine"* (Ezek. 47:12).

As stated, this will be during the Kingdom Age, when Christ will be ruling Personally from Jerusalem. The Scripture here plainly tells us that the fruit and the leaves of these trees will serve as *"meat and medicine."* In other words, the leaves will have healing properties contained within them, and the human race will be able to avoid all sickness by consuming these leaves.

In fact, most medicines we have today come from plants and leaves, etc. But then, the knowledge will be perfect, because Christ will be reigning Personally, and He will put together mixtures which will be perfect in their application and results.

So, if it is a lack of faith and trust to take medicine now, then it would be a lack of faith and trust to take medicine then; however, we see that is not the case.

WHAT DOES BIBLICAL TRUST ACTUALLY MEAN?

It is simple faith in Christ and what Christ has done for us at the Cross. In other words, Christ and His Cross must ever be the Object of our faith, meaning that we must not allow our faith to be moved to other things.

When one makes Christ and the Cross the Object of one's faith and does so constantly, this automatically states that such a person is looking to Christ exclusively for all things, which must be done.

As Paul said, *"Christ is our husband, and He can meet our every need"* (Rom. 7:4).

If one places one's faith in something other than Christ and the Cross, then true Biblical trust cannot be enjoyed. All faith, all trust, all dependence on the Lord, all answers to prayer, actually everything depend solely upon the understanding of the Believer that everything comes to us from Christ as the Source and the Cross as the means.

(8) "KEEP ME AS THE APPLE OF THE EYE, HIDE ME UNDER THE SHADOW OF YOUR WINGS."

In Verses 7 through 14, the Son of David associates His people with Himself; they have the same enemies. If He confides in

Jehovah, so do they; if He trusts in El-Shaddai's wings and is as the apple of His Eye, they are also equally precious to God and trust the same refuge. He describes His enemies and ours in Verses 9 through 12 and prays for Deliverance for us as for Himself in Verses 13 and 14.

JESUS, THE APPLE OF GOD'S EYE

Only of Christ can it be said that He is the apple of the Father's Eye. Such cannot be said of any human being, unless the person is properly in Christ. Always remember that whatever it is that God sees in us, thinks of us, knows of us, or gives to us, all, without exception, is predicated on us being properly *"in Christ."* Outside of Christ there is nothing. In Christ there is everything!

The phrase, *"The apple of His Eye,"* is derived from Deuteronomy 32:10, where the Lord said, *"He found him (Israel) in a desert land, and in the waste howling wilderness; He led him about, He instructed him, He kept him as the apple of His Eye."*

THE SHADOW OF HIS WINGS

The phrase, *"Hide me under the shadow of Your wings,"* was also probably taken from Deuteronomy 32:11-12. The Scripture says:

"As an eagle stirs up her nest, flutters over her young, spreads abroad her wings, takes them, bears them on her wings:

"So the LORD Alone did lead him, and there was no strange god with him."

The phrase about the wings presents a metaphor, which denotes protection, guidance, and provision.

The only thing that can hinder this is the *"strange god,"* which, in modern vernacular, refers to faith in something other than Christ and the Cross. The Apostle Paul called such *"another Jesus,"* presented by *"another spirit,"* which results in *"another gospel"* (II Cor. 11:4).

Unfortunately, the modern Church seems to be enamored with this *"strange god,"* which abrogates the *"shadow of His wings."*

(9) "FROM THE WICKED WHO OPPRESS ME, FROM MY DEADLY ENEMIES, WHO COMPASS ME ABOUT."

This Passage deals with four particulars. The Word of God, being the Word of God and thereby alive and eternal, paints with a broad brush. These four particulars are as follows:

DAVID

As David prayed this prayer, even as the Holy Spirit inspired Him to say these words, his tongue was used for several voices, even as we shall see.

First of all, David was praying about his own problems. He had many enemies, even as do all who are truly called and anointed by the Holy Spirit. Those enemies are almost always from within. They *"who compass me about"* are ever seeking to destroy. David is praying that the Lord will keep him. In truth, the Lord is the only One Who can keep him.

BELIEVERS

As David's voice spoke these words, they are likewise our words. The Holy Spirit through him proclaimed and made these petitions. They are meant to be our example, and we are meant to echo the same words. As the Lord was the only One Who could help David, likewise, the Lord is the only One Who can help us! Never forget that these enemies are *"deadly,"* which means they seek to destroy us. They come in the form of demon spirits and also in the form of institutionalized religion. But no matter how much power they have, if we look to the Lord, He will see us through.

ISRAEL

These words also apply to Israel in a coming day, with the Antichrist closing in. She will cry these words to the Lord and He most definitely will hear her. So, as David prayed that day so long ago, and as the Holy Spirit put the words in his mouth, it was meant to imply so much more than even he could contemplate.

THE LORD JESUS CHRIST

Even more important, these words are the very words of our Master. These *"deadly enemies"* were the Pharisees, the Sadducees, the Scribes, etc., i.e., the religious hierarchy of Israel. They hated Christ because He was *"the Apple of the Eye of God."*

We must not forget that Jesus was not only Very God, which means totally God, but He also was *"Very Man,"* i.e., totally Man. When God became Man, He purposely laid aside the expression of His Deity, an expression which, in a sense, was lost forever, all for you and me, while never losing possession of His Deity. Even though He functioned as a Man, and will do so forever, He nevertheless is God!

As a Man, The Man Christ Jesus, He sought the Father and cried for help and leading exactly as we do. He was meant to serve as our example (I Pet. 2:21).

(10) "THEY ARE ENCLOSED IN THEIR OWN FAT: WITH THEIR MOUTH THEY SPEAK PROUDLY."

David here speaks of his enemies.

A DESCRIPTION OF THE WICKED

The phrase, *"They are enclosed in their own fat,"* refers to the fact that self-indulgence has hardened their feelings and dulled their souls. An organ enclosed in fat cannot work freely. So their feelings, through the coarseness and hardness in which they are, as it were, embedded, cannot work as nature intended.

When Christians attempt to turn the Word of God into a vehicle for their own enrichment, making that effort the sole purpose of their interest in the Word, they have completely abrogated the meaning of the Word of God. This, sadly, is a portrait of the modern Church.

PRIDE

The phrase, *"With their mouth they speak proudly,"* refers to the very opposite of true Christianity. In the modern religious climate, *"money"* and *"control"* present themselves as the criteria. The Salvation of souls is hardly ever considered anymore. It is all *"money"* and *"control,"* hence the *"doctrine of the Nicolaitanes"* (Rev. 2:15), *"which thing"* Jesus said, *"I hate."*

(The word *"Nicolaitanes"* means *"control of the laity."* *"Nico"* in the Greek means *"control,"* while *"laitanes"* means *"the laity."*)

(11) "THEY HAVE NOW COMPASSED US IN OUR STEPS: THEY HAVE SET THEIR EYES BOWING DOWN TO THE EARTH."

Once again, let us not forget that David is speaking here in a fourfold manner:

THE TRAP OF THE ENEMY

The phrase, *"They have now compassed us in our steps,"* could be translated *"They are following our steps; they now compass me."*

The idea pertains to the simile of the lion in David's mind. The lion, before making his spring, fixes his eyes intently upon the prey — not to fascinate it, but to make sure of his distance — with intent, when he springs, to cast the prey down to the earth; so it is now with David's enemies, who have set their eyes upon him.

Who were these enemies?

They were individuals in Israel who had no regard for God or for His Will, who also hated David, especially because he was anointed by God. To be sure, Joseph's coat of many colors will never bring approval, but rather the opposite.

Never mind that Israel was more blessed under David than it had ever known; still, these *"enemies"* hated David, and their modern counterparts follow along the same path.

The phrase, *"They have set their eyes bowing down to the earth,"* could be translated, *"They have set their eyes to cast me down to the earth."*

As Cain with Abel, the enemies of the Lord, who, incidentally, occupy high positions in the world of religion, are not satisfied to merely oppose that which is of God, but feel they must stop its voice, and they will use any tactic to do so. As Cain killed Abel, their direction is the same.

Let the following be understood:

More than all, it is the Message that they oppose; however, to stop the Message, they must, at the same time, stop the Messenger.

A PERSONAL EXPERIENCE

The last few years I was with a particular Pentecostal Denomination (with which I had been associated all my life), the Lord blessed abundantly during that time. We were covering large parts of the world through Television and seeing hundreds of thousands, and I exaggerate not, brought to a saving knowledge of Jesus Christ.

We were building Churches all over the world, all under the name of that particular Denomination. We also were building Bible Colleges and supporting approximately one hundred missionaries. Considering all things, our financial help to that particular Denomination was approximately $1 million a month, if not more.

We also were building schools for children in Third World countries, all under the auspices of that particular Denomination. If I remember correctly, we built 139 schools.

However, the leadership of that particular Denomination did not at all like the Message that I preached. Even then, they were going full bore into humanistic psychology. I was, at the same time, preaching to the largest gospel Television audience in the world, saying that humanistic psychology held no answers whatsoever. They didn't like that at all!

In other words, the direction they were traveling and the direction I was traveling were totally different.

In my naiveté, I thought if they only would come to our meetings and see the great number of souls being saved and the great number of people being baptized with the Holy Spirit, then surely they would not then oppose us. What I did not realize was that the Moving and Operation of the Holy Spirit was the very thing they did not want or desire. I was slow to learn that and fell into their trap.

Despite my zeal at the time, and even despite the fact that God was using me mightily to see hundreds of thousands brought to a saving knowledge of Jesus Christ, tragically, then I understood the Cross only as it regarded Salvation. I did not at all understand it as it regarded Sanctification. Since I was being used by the Lord, I was, therefore, a perfect target for Satan, and he took full advantage of the situation.

Please do not misunderstand. I blame no one but myself for failure. But, at the same time, if a person doesn't understand the Cross as it regards Sanctification, they are going to relive the Seventh Chapter of the Book of Romans all over again, and it does not matter who they are or how much God is using them. Without fail, it will be,

NOTES

"O wretched man that I am! Who shall deliver me from the body of this death?" (Rom. 7:24).

Since I did not know God's Prescribed Order of Victory, there was no way that I could overcome the powers of darkness arrayed against me. The leaders of that Denomination took full advantage of that.

Most of the modern Church believe that the opposition against me was because of what happened; however, that was only an excuse. It was the Message that I preached, and the Message that I preach now, which was bitterly opposed by these religious leaders, and which they continue to oppose unto this hour, and greatly so!

THE GREATEST CHOICE I EVER MADE

In the midst of that horror, a horror worse than death, I will never forget the day that I laid my Bible on a table in front of me, with Frances and others sitting nearby, and stated, *"I don't know the answer to victory over the world, the flesh, and the Devil. But I know the answer is in this Bible, and, by the Grace of God, I am going to find that answer."*

That was the greatest decision I ever made, other than the hour I came to Christ when I was but a child.

From the moment that I made that statement, it was some six years before the answer came. But thank God it came! And when it came, it was over, above, and beyond anything I could ever have begun to think.

The Lord showed me that the problem was my lack of understanding as it regards the *"sin nature."* Then a few days later, He showed me that the solution to the problem was the Cross, and the only solution to the problem was the Cross.

Some days after that, He showed me how the Holy Spirit works in this great scenario. In showing me the meaning of the sin nature, and that the solution was the Cross, and the Cross alone, He took me to the Sixth Chapter of Romans, and explained that great Chapter to me.

Then, when He explained how the Holy Spirit works, He took me to the Eighth Chapter of Romans, more specifically to Romans 8:2.

"For the Law of the Spirit of Life in Christ

Jesus has made me free from the law of sin and death."

As the song says:

"I never shall forget the day,
"When the burdens of my heart rolled away,
"He made me happy, glad, and free,
"I'll sing and shout it, that He's everything to me."

(12) "LIKE AS A LION THAT IS GREEDY OF HIS PREY, AND AS IT WERE A YOUNG LION LURKING IN SECRET PLACES."

Satan comes as a *"roaring lion, seeking whom he may devour"* (I Pet. 5:8).

THE ROARING LION

The phrase, *"Like as a lion that is greedy of his prey,"* could be translated, *"His likeness is as a lion that is greedy to rend."*

The phrase, *"And as it were a young lion,"* could be translated, *"A lion in the first burst of youthful vigor."*

The phrase, *"Lurking in secret places,"* means *"the attitude of the lion when it is preparing to spring."*

The Child of God should ever realize that which he is up against, and we speak of the powers of darkness. To be sure, these powers are far greater than we could ever hope to be. But, at the same time, they are not at all greater than the Lord. In fact, at Calvary, the Lord totally and completely defeated Satan and all of his minions of darkness.

Jesus did so by atoning for all sin, because sin is the legal right that Satan has to hold man in bondage. When Satan's legal right is removed, which Jesus removed when He nailed it to His Cross, the Evil One has been rendered ineffective (Col. 2:14-15).

That's what Paul was talking about when he said, *"Knowing this* (knowing what Jesus did for us at the Cross), *that our old man is crucified with Him* (all that we were before conversion), *that the body of sin might be destroyed* (the power of sin broken), *that henceforth we should not serve sin* (should not serve the sin nature; the guilt of sin is removed at conversion because the sin nature no longer rules within our hearts and lives)" (Rom. 6:6).

The phrase, *"That the body of sin might be destroyed,"* would have been better translated, *"That the body of the sin nature might be made ineffective,"* for that is what the Greek word there means.

Actually, the sin nature is not removed from us at conversion, but is made ineffective. It will remain ineffective as long as our faith is placed in Christ and the Cross and our faith remains in Christ and the Cross. Satan is then made ineffective by the Cross of Calvary and our faith in that Finished Work.

However, the moment we transfer our faith to something else, which, sadly and regrettably, most Christians do, that's when we deprive ourselves of the help of the Holy Spirit (Rom. 8:2), which then gives Satan latitude to work; the sin nature then revives, which gives us untold problems. Unfortunately, because most of the modern Church knows next to nothing about the sin nature, and that the Cross of Christ is the only solution to that problem, most are controlled by the sin nature in some way, even as Romans, Chapter 6, Verse 13 bears out.

If our faith in anchored exclusively in Christ and the Cross and remains there, this *"roaring lion"* will have no effect on us.

(13) "ARISE, O LORD, DISAPPOINT HIM, CAST HIM DOWN: DELIVER MY SOUL FROM THE WICKED, WHICH IS YOUR SWORD."

This speaks of David's enemies and the Lord's enemies, which are Satan and the Antichrist. It speaks of our enemies, as well. The *"sword"* is the Word of God (Eph. 6:17).

THE RECOURSE OF THE CHILD OF GOD

Some may ask the question, *"Is it proper to pray such a prayer in this time and age of Grace?"*

Yes! It is!

First of all, this speaks of individuals who, although very religious, do not, in reality, want the Lord or His Ways. The Church is full of such! That type of person has charted a course that is totally anathema to the Word of God, a course which is extremely hurtful to the Work of God. They are not going to change.

It also speaks of demon spirits, which work

through such individuals, seeking to hinder the Work of the Lord, to even hinder greatly and destroy totally the man or woman who is being used of the Lord.

It is perfectly right, Scriptural, and permissible for us to pray that the Lord will stop such a person and deliver us from that individual so that we might carry out the Work which the Lord has called us to do.

The word *"disappoint"* means to forestall and confront. Even though it addresses itself to the Lord's enemies on every hand, more specifically it speaks of the Antichrist, who in this Verse is called the Lawless One (*"the wicked man"*).

(14) "FROM MEN WHICH ARE YOUR HAND, O LORD, FROM MEN OF THE WORLD, WHICH HAVE THEIR PORTION IN THIS LIFE, AND WHOSE BELLY YOU FILL WITH YOUR HID TREASURE: THEY ARE FULL OF CHILDREN, AND LEAVE THE REST OF THEIR SUBSTANCE TO THEIR BABES."

This Verse has to do with individuals who profess the Lord but whose affections are on the things of this world in totality! They do not see the things of the Lord and do not desire the things of the Lord, even though they may speak of the Lord constantly.

Regrettably and sadly, much of the modern Church falls into this category. It is attempting to build a kingdom of God in this world. It tries to do so through political means, through economic means, and always through religious means.

"The Purpose Driven Life" is an excellent case in point.

The leaders of this scheme have just selected a country in Africa in which they are going to apply *"The Purpose Driven Life"* to make it a model nation for Africa and the world.

THE TRUTH

The truth of the matter is that Africa's problems (which also goes for any nation of the world, including the United States) are not economic, educational, or political, but rather spiritual.

The Lord's Way is for a person to be *"born again."* Regrettably, there aren't but a few people in the world, at least as we consider

NOTES

the magnitude of the entire population, who fall into that category. Those *"few"* are the *"salt"* and the *"light"* of the world, all under Christ, still, even though we have great influence on the world, there are not enough of us to completely change the tide.

Further truth is this:

Satan presently is the *"god of this present world"* and the *"prince of the powers of the air."* This world's system belongs entirely to him.

There is coming a day that all of this is going to change, but not until the Second Coming.

So, what is the modern Church presently doing?

The modern Church, for the most part, is ignoring God's Way; instead, it is substituting its own way. God's Way is to preach the Gospel, not some scheme devised by men. All of these schemes, such as *"The Purpose Driven Life,"* will effect nothing good whatsoever; rather, they will fall out to great harm.

How?

They will fall out to great harm because they steer people always from the true good they can find in the Word of God and in the preaching of the Gospel.

THE GREAT COMMISSION

Let's look at the instructions that Jesus gave to His Disciples. I quote from THE EXPOSITOR'S STUDY BIBLE:

"And Jesus came and spoke unto them (the same meeting on the mountain, and constitutes the Great Commission), *saying, All power is given unto Me in Heaven and in Earth.* (This is not given to Him as Son of God; for, as God, nothing can be added to Him or taken from Him; it is rather a power which He has merited by His Incarnation and His Death at Calvary on the Cross [Phil. 2:8-10]; this authority extends not only over men so that He governs and protects the Church, disposes human events, controls hearts and opinions; but the forces of Heaven also are at His Command; the Holy Spirit is bestowed by Him, and the Angels are in His employ as ministering to the members of His Body. When He said, *'All power,'* He meant *'All Power!'*)

"Go ye therefore (applies to any and all who follow Christ and in all ages), *and teach all nations* (should have been translated, *'and preach to all nations,'* for the word *'teach'* here refers to a proclamation of Truth), *baptizing them in the Name of the Father, and of the Son, and of the Holy Spirit* (presents the only formula for Water Baptism given in the Word of God):

"Teaching them (means to give instruction) *to observe all things* (the whole Gospel for the whole man) *whatsoever I have commanded you* (not a suggestion): *and, lo, I am with you always* (it is I, Myself, God, and Man, Who am — not *'will be'* — hence, forever present among you, and with you, as Companion, Friend, Guide, Saviour, God), *even unto the end of the world* (should have been translated *'age'*). *Amen.* (It is the guarantee of My Promise)" (Mat. 28:18-20).

(15) "AS FOR ME I WILL BEHOLD YOUR FACE IN RIGHTEOUSNESS: I SHALL BE SATISFIED, WHEN I AWAKE, WITH YOUR LIKENESS."

The final Verse of this Psalm deals with the Resurrection.

THE RESURRECTION

This Psalm, in correspondence with the prior one, closes with the assured hope of Resurrection. The statements express the highest joy of the spiritual nature. Not glory, nor the material joys of Heaven, here enrapture the speaker, but the one absorbing desire to see God's Face and to be like Him.

This is measurably true of everyone who has the Spirit of Christ, but immeasurably true of Him Who prayed, *"Glorify Thou Me with Thine Own Self with the Glory which I had with You before the world was"* (Jn. 17:5).

Opposition to truth and the indulgence of self-will in evil or ritualism both make the heart insensible to the influence of the Holy Spirit.

PSALM 18

A Psalm of David:
A Hymn of Thanksgiving

(1) "I WILL LOVE YOU, O LORD, MY STRENGTH."

NOTES

The inscription which goes with the Psalm is:

To the Chief Musician, a Psalm of David, the servant of the Lord, who spoke unto the Lord the words of this song in the day that the Lord delivered him from the hand of all his enemies, from the hand of Saul.

DAVID

The circumstances under which the Holy Spirit inspired David to write this Prophecy are stated in the title. It was first written in the Twenty-second Chapter of II Samuel and here handed to the Chief Musician for use in the public worship. The variations were made and designed by the Divine Author. David himself must have recognized that the experiences of the Psalm went far beyond his own personal deliverance from Saul (I Pet. 1:10-12).

THE MESSIAH

The Holy Spirit states in Romans 15:9 and Hebrews 2:13 that the Speaker here is the Messiah, and that the Psalm predicts the sufferings of His First Advent (Vss. 20-36), the glories of His Second (Vss. 37-50), and the majesty of the Resurrection, which connects the two (Vss. 1-19). These are the great divisions of this Prophecy.

The Messiah was sinless, and He will in Righteousness destroy out of His future kingdom (the Kingdom Age) all the workers of iniquity (Mat. 13:41; Rev. 12:12; 19:1-5). This explains the seemingly self-righteous language of the Speaker and His exultation over the destruction of His enemies; for they were the enemies of His people and of all goodness.

The first Verse should read: *"Fervently do I love You, O Jehovah My Strength!"*

The opening and close of the Prophecy correspond. In Verses 1 and 49, Jehovah is spoken to. He is loved in the one and praised in the other.

LOVE

The verb translated *"our love"* expresses the very tenderest affection and is elsewhere never used to denote the love of man towards God, but only that of God towards man, which is far greater love than that which man could ever know. These are the words of the Messiah, as tendered toward His Heavenly Father.

(2) "THE LORD IS MY ROCK, AND MY FORTRESS, AND MY DELIVERER; MY GOD, MY STRENGTH, IN WHOM I WILL TRUST; MY BUCKLER, AND THE HORN OF MY SALVATION, AND MY HIGH TOWER."

There are seven metaphors used here by the Holy Spirit in praise to God.

SEVEN METAPHORS USED OF GOD

Those metaphors are:
1. Rock;
2. Fortress;
3. Deliverer;
4. Strength;
5. Buckler;
6. Horn; and,
7. High Tower.

As *"seven"* is God's number of completion and perfection, this means that the Protection, Deliverance, and Victory which the Lord provides for each and every Believer, at least for those who will order their lives according to His Prescribed Way, are total and complete. Everything we need is found in this Verse.

First of all, the Lord is a *"Rock,"* and, more particularly, *"my Rock."* That means that He is unmovable.

Second, He is *"my Fortress,"* which pertains to that which Satan cannot penetrate.

Third, He is *"my Deliverer,"* which He has done through the Cross (Col. 2:14-15).

Fourth, I do not trust my personal strength, but rather *"God is my Strength."*

Fifth, He is *"my Buckler,"* which refers to a shield. It is worn on the left arm, and the top half ends immediately under the right eye. The one holding the shield can see to fight.

Sixth, the Lord is also the *"Horn of my Salvation,"* which refers to dominion.

Seventh, the *"High Tower"* refers to a place of refuge.

These words are used by the Holy Spirit for a reason. Demon powers used Saul to try to destroy David; likewise, demon powers come strongly against every Christian, especially those who have a Divine Touch of God on their lives. There is no way to defeat these enemies other than through the Lord. He then becomes all of these things because we could not become them ourselves, nor could any other man become them for us. Man alone is helpless against Satan; likewise, man's methods, such as humanistic psychology, have no effect upon the powers of darkness. There is only one *"Rock"* and one *"Deliverer,"* and that is the Lord. In Him, and in Him Alone, *"I will trust."* Anyone who goes in any other direction from that which is outlined in this Passage will be destroyed.

THE CROSS OF CHRIST

In a sense, we attain to this sevenfold protection by looking exclusively to Christ and the Cross. Concerning this, Jesus said, and I quote from THE EXPOSITOR'S STUDY BIBLE:

"For whosoever will save his life shall lose it (try to live one's life outside of Christ and the Cross): *but whosoever will lose his life for My sake, the same shall save it* (when we place our faith entirely in Christ and the Cross, looking exclusively to Him, we have just found *'more abundant life'* [Jn. 10:10])" (Mat. 16:25).

Anyone who attempts to defeat the powers of darkness outside of God's Prescribed Order, which is Christ and the Cross, is foolish indeed! In the first place, it simply cannot be done in that capacity, nor is it meant to be done. Whatever needs to be done, Jesus did it for us at the Cross.

(3) "I WILL CALL UPON THE LORD, WHO IS WORTHY TO BE PRAISED: SO SHALL I BE SAVED FROM MY ENEMIES."

Zacharias (Lk. 1:69-71) prophesied of the Messiah as the *"Horn of Salvation,"* thus quoting Verse 2. He also quoted from Verse 3, *"We shall be saved from our enemies."*

CALLING UPON THE LORD

The phrase, *"I will call upon the LORD,"* actually says, *"I will call upon the LORD, and do so continually."* He will save me from my enemies, and is *"worthy to be praised."*

In all of these Psalms, the exhortation constantly is given that we call upon the Lord, and He will save us. There is no hint whatsoever of the modern gospel that looks to man for help, where man is taught to depend on self. Such is doomed to failure!

(4) "THE SORROWS OF DEATH

COMPASSED ME, AND THE FLOODS OF UNGODLY MEN MADE ME AFRAID."

David now speaks with the voice of the Messiah!

DAVID AND THE MESSIAH

First of all, David speaks of himself. When Saul was seeking to kill him, he thought that surely he would die, hence him saying, *"The sorrows of death compassed me."*

Saul had many men with him, all seeking to destroy David, hence *"the floods of ungodly men made me afraid."*

However, in a more particular way, the Verse belongs to the Messiah. When He died on the Cross, His Soul and Spirit went down into the death world. This is where He tasted death for every man, at least those who will believe.

The phrase, *"And the floods of ungodly men made Me afraid,"* pertains to the many Pharisees and Sadducees who banded together against Christ, who actually effected His Crucifixion.

Christ being *"made afraid"* (and this certainly does speak of Christ) concerns the feelings of a human being, which He was, venturing into a situation into which no one had ever gone. As God, which He most definitely was, He had no fear. As a Man, He experienced those feelings, exactly as we do!

(5) "THE SORROWS OF HELL COMPASSED ME ABOUT: THE SNARES OF DEATH PREVENTED ME."

In the previous Verse, our Lord experienced *"the sorrows of death,"* while in this Verse, He experiences *"the sorrows of Hell."*

When Jesus died, He went down into the Paradise part of Hell, where He liberated all who were there (Eph. 4:8-10). He also preached to the *"spirits in prison,"* which actually were fallen angels (I Pet. 3:19). There is no record in the Bible that He went into the burning side of Hell, as some teach; however, the parts into which He actually did go were bad enough!

The phrase, *"The snares of death prevented Me,"* actually says, *"came upon Me."* This refers to the moment of His Death on the Cross.

(6) "IN MY DISTRESS I CALLED UPON THE LORD, AND CRIED UNTO MY GOD: HE HEARD MY VOICE OUT OF HIS TEMPLE, AND MY CRY CAME BEFORE HIM, EVEN INTO HIS EARS."

While David definitely did this of which he speaks, still, the greater meaning has to do with the Messiah at the time of His Death.

THE CRY OF THE MESSIAH IS HEARD!

In the four Gospels, we are only given a capsule view of what actually took place on the Cross. The Psalms, as here illustrated, provide the details of that which actually took place. Here we find the Messiah calling upon the LORD at this particular time, the time of His Death. He exclaims that the LORD heard His Voice.

Had He died on the Cross as a sinner, and gone to the burning side of Hell, as some teach, to be sure, this Scripture would have no meaning. The truth is that Jesus, while dying physically, did not die spiritually. To *"die spiritually"* means to die without God and without hope, exactly as any unsaved soul dies. Christ did not do that, and there is nothing in the Bible that even remotely hints at such a thing.

(7) "THEN THE EARTH SHOOK AND TREMBLED; THE FOUNDATIONS ALSO OF THE HILLS MOVED AND WERE SHAKEN, BECAUSE HE WAS WROTH."

This Verse refers to the time of the Death of Christ.

THE GREAT EARTHQUAKE

The Scripture says that when Jesus died, *"The earth did quake, and the rocks rent"* (Mat. 27:51).

The phrase, *"Because He was wroth,"* refers to God being angry at what the religious hierarchy of Jerusalem had done to their Messiah, God's Only Son. His Anger was manifested in the earthquake!

(8) "THERE WENT UP A SMOKE OUT OF HIS NOSTRILS, AND FIRE OUT OF HIS MOUTH DEVOURED: COALS WERE KINDLED BY IT."

These are metaphors used to describe the anger of God at the treatment of Christ by the human race, and, more particularly, by the Jews.

(9) "HE BOWED THE HEAVENS ALSO,

AND CAME DOWN: AND DARKNESS WAS UNDER HIS FEET."

According to the Scriptures, from about 12 noon until about 3 p.m., *"There was a darkness over all the Earth"* (Lk. 23:44). The Psalmist here tells us that this was God manifesting His Anger at what was being done. Even though what was being done was necessary, it was the hardened hearts of these men who crucified Christ which angered God. And rightly so!

In a sense, the darkness spoke of two things:

1. These people wanted spiritual darkness, so they would get darkness, symbolized by the darkness which covered the land.

2. God did not want inquisitive eyes staring at Christ when He did bear the penalty for the sin of all of mankind. So the Heavenly Father blanketed that part of the Earth with darkness.

As stated, the Psalms open up to us so much more about Christ even than we are given in the Gospels. It becomes even more remarkable when we realize that all of these predictions were given at least a thousand years before the First Advent of Christ.

(10) "AND HE RODE UPON A CHERUB, AND DID FLY: YEA, HE DID FLY UPON THE WINGS OF THE WIND."

Even though the Holy Spirit through David is speaking here metaphorically, still, we must not ignore or overlook the underlying Truth.

First of all, there is indication that the Lord does at times travel from place to place. In other words, He leaves His Throne in Heaven in order to attend to certain things. The Scriptural evidence also is clear that He is always accompanied by Cherubim (Ezek., Chpts. 1, 10). Furthermore, the Cherubim denote the Holiness of the God, and that such Holiness is never interrupted (Rev., Chpt. 4).

"The wings of the wind" simply refer to a manner of transportation totally unknown to mankind.

(11) "HE MADE DARKNESS HIS SECRET PLACE; HIS PAVILION ROUND ABOUT HIM WERE DARK WATERS AND THICK CLOUDS OF THE SKIES."

The statements given in this Verse continue to be metaphorical, but probably more

NOTES

so than ever.

The ways of the Lord are *"dark"* to human beings, meaning that we little understand, if at all, the way the Lord does things.

(12) "AT THE BRIGHTNESS THAT WAS BEFORE HIM HIS THICK CLOUDS PASSED, HAIL STONES AND COALS OF FIRE."

This simply states the fact that the LORD created the elements and that they constantly are at His beck and call!

(13) "THE LORD ALSO THUNDERED IN THE HEAVENS, AND THE HIGHEST GAVE HIS VOICE; HAIL STONES AND COALS OF FIRE."

The LORD can use these elements anytime He so desires. He does, in fact, use them constantly for various reasons.

(14) "YEA, HE SENT OUT HIS ARROWS, AND SCATTERED THEM; AND HE SHOT OUT LIGHTNINGS, AND DISCOMFITED THEM."

The effect of the tempest of God's Wrath is to *"scatter"* and *"discomfit"* the enemy, which He has done many times in the past, and which He will also do in the future (Ezek. 38:22).

(15) "THEN THE CHANNELS OF WATERS WERE SEEN, AND THE FOUNDATIONS OF THE WORLD WERE DISCOVERED AT YOUR REBUKE, O LORD, AT THE BLAST OF THE BREATH OF YOUR NOSTRILS."

The meaning of this Verse is wrapped up in the three words, *"At Your rebuke."* Again, the LORD uses the elements to carry out His Will, such as the opening of the Red Sea for the Children of Israel.

(16) "HE SENT FROM ABOVE, HE TOOK ME, HE DREW ME OUT OF MANY WATERS."

While David here speaks of the LORD's Deliverance, the Messiah is, at the same time, speaking of the power that was given to Him at His Resurrection to come out of the death world (Rom. 8:11).

(17) "HE DELIVERED ME FROM MY STRONG ENEMY, AND FROM THEM WHICH HATED ME: FOR THEY WERE TOO STRONG FOR ME."

Once again, the Messiah speaks!

As God, which Jesus most definitely was,

no power was greater than His, as would be obvious; however, as *"Man,"* which, as it regards Redemption and everything that pertains to Redemption, is the manner and way that He functioned, He had to depend upon His Father, exactly as we do.

(18) "THEY PREVENTED ME IN THE DAY OF MY CALAMITY: BUT THE LORD WAS MY STAY."

The power of the LORD prevented Christ from being hindered by demon spirits in the death world.

(19) "HE BROUGHT ME FORTH ALSO INTO A LARGE PLACE; HE DELIVERED ME, BECAUSE HE DELIGHTED IN ME."

The *"large place"* pertains to Paradise, where Jesus went upon His Death, and to which He went in order to deliver all who were held there, which included all the Old Testament Saints, ever how many there were (Eph. 4:8-10).

To be sure, God the Father delighted in Christ. Because He delighted in Christ, He delights in all who are *"in Christ"* (Mat. 3:17).

(20) "THE LORD REWARDED ME ACCORDING TO MY RIGHTEOUSNESS; ACCORDING TO THE CLEANNESS OF MY HANDS HAS HE RECOMPENSED ME."

Even though David is speaking here of himself, more particularly it is the Messiah speaking. The only One Who honestly could use the term *"My Righteousness"* was, and is, the Lord Jesus Christ. All of us who are Believers have *"Righteousness,"* but it definitely is not personal righteousness, but rather than which Christ has given to us by virtue of what He did at the Cross and our faith in that Finished Work.

Christ Alone has Righteousness; Christ Alone has clean hands!

(21) "FOR I HAVE KEPT THE WAYS OF THE LORD, AND HAVE NOT WICKEDLY DEPARTED FROM MY GOD."

There is a twofold statement in this Verse:

DAVID

How could David say that he had always kept the Ways of the Lord and never had departed wickedly from God?

David was not claiming sinless perfection. He was saying that whatever the situation, whatever the circumstances, even in the matter of sin, He took it to the Lord and never departed wickedly to other means.

When the modern Church places its faith and trust in humanistic psychology or anything other than the Cross of Christ, pure and simple, it is not *"keeping the Ways of the LORD,"* which means that it is *"wickedly departing from God."*

(22) "FOR ALL HIS JUDGMENTS WERE BEFORE ME, AND I DID NOT PUT AWAY HIS STATUTES FROM ME."

The criteria for everything done by both David and the Messiah was the Word of God. It must be our criteria also!

THE WORD OF GOD

The story of the Bible is the Story of Jesus Christ and Him Crucified. It runs like a theme from Genesis 1:1 through Revelation 22:21. If we do not understand the Bible in that fashion, then we simply do not properly understand the Bible. Minus the Cross, some certainly will understand some things, but to have a correct interpretation of the entire Word of God, it is absolutely necessary that one understand that every belief system must be built on the Foundation of the Cross.

The Cross of Christ was formulated in the Mind of the Godhead from even before the foundation of the world (I Pet. 1:18-20). Consequently, Jesus Christ and Him Crucified must be the Foundation of all doctrine.

(23) "I WAS ALSO UPRIGHT BEFORE HIM, AND I KEPT MYSELF FROM MY INIQUITY."

The language of Verses 20 through 26 could only be used by the Messiah, for He was sinless.

THE SINLESS SON OF GOD

The words, *"My iniquity,"* as used in this Verse, do not mean that Christ had a besetting sin, nor may they be here understood as intending the iniquity of the Elect, which He made His Own; but they point to a form of iniquity especially planned by Satan for Him, and to which He Alone could be tempted.

Such, for example, was the third temptation in the wilderness (Lk. 4:9).

(24) "THEREFORE HAS THE LORD RECOMPENSED ME ACCORDING TO

MY RIGHTEOUSNESS, ACCORDING TO THE CLEANNESS OF MY HANDS IN HIS EYESIGHT."

The Messiah continues to speak!

The short phrase, *"In His eyesight,"* refers to the only eyes which actually matter, i.e., those of the Lord.

In God's Eyes, the Lord Jesus Christ was absolutely Perfect in every respect, even though the Pharisees and the Sadducees claimed that He was an impostor.

(25) "WITH THE MERCIFUL YOU WILL SHOW YOURSELF MERCIFUL; WITH AN UPRIGHT MAN YOU WILL SHOW YOURSELF UPRIGHT."

A great Truth is brought out in this Verse.

MERCIFUL

The word *"Merciful"* here means the *"Merciful One."* It is a very interesting word to Hebrew Scholars. It is a Messianic Title. He is, and will be, the full depository and witness of God's Mercy — not mercy merely in relation to sinners, but favor and grace shown and enjoyed so as to become an evidence of moral perfection.

It is particularly celebrated in Psalms 86:2 and 89:19, where the Messiah is entitled *"God's Holy One,"* i.e., *"Merciful One"* — the Hebrew word is the same for Merciful and Holy — because all these Mercies center in Him; hence the expression, *"sure mercies of David"* (Acts 13:34).

The Messiah is also the *"Upright Man,"* actually the *"True Man"* (I Cor. 15:47).

(26) "WITH THE PURE YOU WILL SHOW YOURSELF PURE; AND WITH THE FROWARD YOU WILL SHOW YOURSELF FROWARD."

This Scripture, as all others, is extremely interesting!

PURE AND PERVERSE

Jesus is the *"Pure One"* of this Verse. The *"perverse one"* is the future Antichrist.

The Truth of this Verse points to the fact that if one wills righteousness, God wills more righteousness to him. If one wills unrighteousness, God wills more unrighteousness to him. The initiation is not necessarily in God, but rather the individuals. The same sun which hardens clay also softens wax. The action is not in the sun, but in the material.

(27) "FOR YOU WILL SAVE THE AFFLICTED PEOPLE; BUT WILL BRING DOWN HIGH LOOKS."

"Pride goes before destruction, and a haughty spirit before a fall" (Prov. 16:18).

(28) "FOR YOU WILL LIGHT MY CANDLE: THE LORD MY GOD WILL ENLIGHTEN MY DARKNESS."

Outside of the Lord, there is no *"Light"*! In the Lord, all Light resides. Therefore, no matter how much education a person may have, if they do not know the Lord and His Word, there is no Light in them.

(29) "FOR BY YOU I HAVE RUN THROUGH A TROOP, AND BY MY GOD HAVE I LEAPED OVER A WALL."

Probably David had in mind his taking of the city of Jebus when he first became king, the city which later would be named Jerusalem. The Lord gave him the power to do these things, hence him using this type of metaphor.

(30) "AS FOR GOD, HIS WAY IS PERFECT: THE WORD OF THE LORD IS TRIED: HE IS A BUCKLER TO ALL THOSE WHO TRUST IN HIM."

There was a perfect correspondence between the nature of our Lord and the nature of His Heavenly Father. He could rest in full confidence in the just judgment of such a scrutinizing Judge. No one ever trusted the Word of God and was deceived. That Word, whenever tested, has always been found to be trustworthy and true as pure gold.

(31) "FOR WHO IS GOD SAVE THE LORD? OR WHO IS A ROCK SAVE OUR GOD?"

As the One and Only God, absolute confidence may be placed in Jehovah, Who is able to protect and preserve to the uttermost all who serve Him.

(32) "IT IS GOD WHO GIRDS ME WITH STRENGTH, AND MAKES MY WAY PERFECT."

The Heavenly Father made the Way of His Son, our Saviour, Perfect in every respect.

David and every Believer can say this in a limited way, but only Christ can say such in a total way.

(33) "HE MAKES MY FEET LIKE

HINDS' FEET, AND SETS ME UPON MY HIGH PLACES.

(34) "HE TEACHES MY HANDS TO WAR, SO THAT A BOW OF STEEL IS BROKEN BY MY ARMS."

God's manner of warfare is here proclaimed.

SPIRITUAL WARFARE

The Lord Jesus did not use warlike weapons. The language of Verse 34 is, therefore, figurative. When the Herodians, the Pharisees, the Scribes, and the Sadducees warred against Him with their bows of steel, he bent their bows and broke them, i.e., He showed the folly of their hard questions and confounded them.

There have probably been more books written on Spiritual Warfare in the last three or four decades than during the entire balance of Christianity. Regrettably, almost all of them are wrong.

How do I know that?

The Sixth Chapter of Ephesians proclaims to us that given by the Holy Spirit regarding Spiritual Warfare. All of the admonitions lead directly to Christ and the Cross. In other words, when the Believer places his faith and confidence solely in Christ and what Christ did at the Cross, the Holy Spirit, Who Alone can do what needs to done, will then carry out the task, adequately protecting the Child of God from the powers of darkness.

There is no other way, no other means, no other direction, and no other answer. It strictly is *"Jesus Christ and Him Crucified"* (I Cor. 1:23).

Paul told us, *"For the preaching of the Cross is to them who perish foolishness; but unto us which are saved it is the Power of God"* (I Cor. 1:18).

How is the preaching of the Cross the Power of God?

The *"Power"* resides in the Holy Spirit, and, to be sure, in the Holy Spirit Alone! Considering that He works entirely within the framework of the Finished Work of Christ (and in no other way [Rom. 8:2]), this simply means that we as Believers must ever look to Christ and the Cross. When we do this, the Holy Spirit works on our behalf, doing whatever needs to be done to carry out the necessary victory.

Concerning warfare, Paul plainly said, *"Fight the good fight of Faith, lay hold on Eternal Life"* (I Tim. 6:12).

In this *"warfare,"* the *"good fight of Faith"* is the only fight in which we are called upon to engage.

What does that mean?

It means that Satan knows, beyond the shadow of a doubt, that your victory lies completely within Christ and the Cross; as a result, he will do everything within his power to move your Faith from Christ and the Cross to something else, and he doesn't too much care what the *"something else"* is.

Even on a daily basis, we constantly must fight that our faith remains where it ought to be, which is in Christ and the Cross. And please believe me, it is a fight! It is a *"good fight,"* because it's the only fight in which we are called upon to engage, and we are guaranteed of victory if we continue to fight as instructed.

This is the manner in which we should engage in Spiritual Warfare. The reason I can say that all the other directions given are false is simply because the alternatives are being presented by Preachers who are not preaching the Cross. Pure and simple, they are preaching something else. Consequently, there will be no victory from those quarters. The victory is found in the Cross of Christ alone (Rom. 6:1-14; 8:1-2, 11; Gal. 6:14).

(35) "YOU HAVE ALSO GIVEN ME THE SHIELD OF YOUR SALVATION: AND YOUR RIGHT HAND HAS HELD ME UP, AND YOUR GENTLENESS HAS MADE ME GREAT."

The Holy Spirit is here using an example which was common in warfare during the time of David.

When a warrior was engaged in battle and was using his weapons, especially the bow, to be protected from the arrows of the enemy, there was another individual who walked with him and held a shield before him. This is what the Lord is saying regarding His Divine protection for us. He Personally holds a shield in front of us to ward off the attacks of the enemy. It is called *"the shield of faith"* (Eph. 6:16). The *"faith"* here mentioned by Paul refers to faith in Christ and what Christ did for us at the Cross.

THE GENTLENESS OF OUR LORD

The phrase, *"And Your Right Hand has held me up, and Your gentleness has made me great,"* proclaims this quality in God which most nearly corresponds to humility in man. The word *"gentleness,"* as it is here used, is not elsewhere used of God.

When we think of warfare, we definitely do not think of gentleness; however, it fits here, and beautifully so!

Whatever attacks the Lord allows to be placed against us by Satan (and it is the Lord who sets the schedule, not Satan), He guarantees us that He always will uphold us with His Mighty Right Hand, and He will do so with *"gentleness."*

(36) "YOU HAVE ENLARGED MY STEPS UNDER ME, THAT MY FEET DID NOT SLIP."

In this journey of life, and our *"walk"* before God, if we fully trust the Lord, He will see to it that our feet always are on solid ground, and that they will not slip.

Once again we go back to the warrior. During the type of warfare which was engaged some 3,000 years ago, if the warrior slipped and fell, his death warrant was pretty well signed, sealed, and delivered. Here the Lord tells us that in this conflict in which we constantly are engaged in life, that He will see to it that our *"feet do not slip."*

What a Promise!

(37) "I HAVE PURSUED MY ENEMIES, AND OVERTAKEN THEM: NEITHER DID I TURN AGAIN TILL THEY WERE CONSUMED."

In the closing section of this Psalm (Vss. 37-50), the future tense may be used throughout, as in the Hebrew Text, for the language is prophetic; but the past tense also may be used, for, when sung on the Millennial Morn, the facts will be accomplished facts.

This magnificent Passage sets forth the future glory of the Messiah, His destruction of the enemies of His People, and their Restoration.

VICTORY

In this Passage and following, we are told that not only will the Messiah overcome all enemies, which has two meanings, the first being the Cross and the second being the Battle of Armageddon, but also His Victory is our victory.

That is the very reason for God becoming Man. He would do for us that which we could not do for ourselves. Then all that He has done will accrue to us, and in totality, which presents a *"victory"* of unprecedented proportions.

To every Believer who struggles, the statement has already been made and it is placed in the past tense. The Lord has already pursued the enemies and overtaken them. He not only overtook them, but rather *"consumed them."*

Again, I state:

He did this all for you and me. Considering the great price that He paid, and we speak of the Cross, we must make certain that we avail ourselves of all that He has done for us.

Proper faith will claim that the battle has already been fought and won! Proper faith guarantees the victory!

When a Believer lives in this aura of victory already won, all fear regarding the future subsides.

(38) "I HAVE WOUNDED THEM THAT THEY WERE NOT ABLE TO RISE: THEY ARE FALLEN UNDER MY FEET."

This Passage corresponds with another from the New Testament:

"And has put all things under His feet, and gave Him to be the Head over all things to the Church,

"Which is His Body, the fullness of Him Who fills all in all" (Eph. 1:22-23).

A VICTORIOUS CHURCH

Continuing to proclaim the fact that Jesus Christ has done everything for us, and that all things are placed under *"His feet,"* with Him being the *"Head,"* we then become the Body, which includes the *"feet."* This means that Satan and all the cohorts of darkness are under our feet, because they are under the Feet of Christ. Jesus did it all for us at the Cross.

(39) "FOR YOU HAVE GIRDED ME WITH STRENGTH UNTO THE BATTLE: YOU HAVE SUBDUED UNDER ME THOSE WHO ROSE UP AGAINST ME."

Once again, these are the words of the Messiah extolling the Father, Who has given Him the victory — the victory in all capacities — which includes victory over all sin and all the forces of darkness (Col. 2:14-15).

(40) "YOU HAVE ALSO GIVEN ME THE NECKS OF MY ENEMIES; THAT I MIGHT DESTROY THEM WHO HATE ME."

In warfare of old, when the enemy lay prostrate on the ground, with the victor's foot on his neck, that was a sign of total victory. So what does this tell us.

A COMPLETE VICTORY

When Jesus atoned for all sin on Calvary's Cross, He took away the legal right that Satan had to hold man in captivity. That legal right was sin. But with all sin atoned, that legal right was taken away. The Scripture says:

"And having spoiled principalities and powers, He made a show of them openly, triumphing over them in it" (Col. 2:15).

By Christ doing what He did, He literally *"destroyed"* the powers of darkness. So if any Believer today is being held captive in some manner by Satan (and regrettably, untold millions are!), this is a sure sign that such a Believer has his faith in the wrong place. In order to obtain all that Christ has done for us, the Believer must place his faith entirely in Christ and the Cross, and also maintain his faith in Christ and the Cross. Then the Holy Spirit, Who is God and Who can do anything, will work mightily on our behalf.

(41) "THEY CRIED, BUT THERE WAS NONE TO SAVE THEM: EVEN UNTO THE LORD, BUT HE ANSWERED THEM NOT."

This Passage pertains to Israel and her abject defeat at the hands of the Roman General Titus.

THE JUDGMENT OF GOD

This Passage refers to Israel's Crucifixion of her Saviour and then her suffering the consequent vengeance of God. The Roman General Titus, who commanded the famed Tenth Legion, sacked and burned Jerusalem in A.D. 70. Over one million Jews were killed, and another million were sold as slaves. Titus actually crucified so many Jews that there was no more room to place crosses in the ground.

At that time, they cried unto the Lord, *"But He answered them not."*

They were not crying for Deliverance from sin, but rather for deliverance from the hands of the Romans; consequently, they did not provide a ground on which the Lord could act, so *"He answered them not."*

(42) "THEN DID I BEAT THEM SMALL AS THE DUST BEFORE THE WIND: I DID CAST THEM OUT AS THE DIRT IN THE STREETS."

Strangely and regrettably, this is exactly what happened to Israel at the time of their destruction by Titus.

At the Crucifixion of Christ, they had said, *"We have no king but Caesar"* (Jn. 19:15).

They were to find that Caesar would prove to be a hard taskmaster.

In the state they were in, considering that they had crucified the Lord, their Messiah, there was nothing the Lord could do but *"cast them out as the dirt in the streets."*

The Lord cannot save people against their will. He will not force them to serve Him. Service without love is no service at all!

(43) "YOU HAVE DELIVERED ME FROM THE STRIVINGS OF THE PEOPLE; AND YOU HAVE MADE ME THE HEAD OF THE HEATHEN: A PEOPLE WHOM I HAVE NOT KNOWN SHALL SERVE ME."

Despite being the chosen people, Israel would not serve the Lord, so the Holy Spirit turned to the Gentiles. The Lord chose Paul as His Apostle to the Gentiles. Thus began the Church!

Consequently, Gentiles have made up virtually the entirety of the Church, and the Gospel has gone to much of the world.

These words of the Messiah were prophesied some 3,000 years ago, and they have come to pass exactly as here stated.

(44) "AS SOON AS THEY HEAR OF ME, THEY SHALL OBEY ME: THE STRANGERS SHALL SUBMIT THEMSELVES UNTO ME."

The Messiah continues through David to speak of the Gentiles.

And so we have!

(45) "THE STRANGERS SHALL FADE AWAY, AND BE AFRAID OUT OF THEIR CLOSE PLACES."

The word *"strangers"* here refers to Gentiles. The Passage refers to the fact that many Gentiles will come to the Lord out of fear, and rightly so!

(46) "THE LORD LIVES; AND BLESSED BE MY ROCK; AND LET THE GOD OF MY SALVATION BE EXALTED."

"The God of my Salvation" is a favorite phrase with David (Ps. 25:5; 27:9; 38:22; 51:14; 88:1).

The short phrase, *"The LORD lives,"* actually means *"The LORD continuously lives, and will ever live."* As God, He had no beginning, which means He has always been, and will have no ending, meaning that He always will be. That is terminology that we as human beings cannot fully comprehend, but yet it is the only way to properly describe the Lord.

(47) "IT IS GOD WHO AVENGES ME, AND SUBDUES THE PEOPLE UNDER ME."

Here, David gives the Lord all the glory for all the victories that he was able to win. And I might quickly add that he won them all! Even more so, it pertains to the Messiah, Whom the Lord avenged according to Verses 41 and 42.

As Believers, we must leave all vengeance up to the Lord.

Plainly and clearly, the Holy Spirit through Paul says:

"Vengeance belongs unto Me, I will recompense, saith the Lord" (Heb. 10:30); and,

"It is written, Vengeance is Mine; I will repay, saith the Lord" (Rom. 12:19).

God can exact vengeance simply because He knows all things; consequently, He will do all things perfectly. We as human beings know very little; we, therefore, are not equipped, so to speak, to take vengeance. It must be left to the Lord!

(48) "HE DELIVERS ME FROM MY ENEMIES: YEA, YOU DID LIFT ME UP ABOVE THOSE WHO RISE UP AGAINST ME: YOU HAVE DELIVERED ME FROM THE VIOLENT MAN."

More particularly, the Messiah is here thanking the Lord for His victory over *"the violent man,"* i.e., the Antichrist.

This is remarkable, considering that this great prediction was given some 3,000 years ago, and is actually written in the past tense.

NOTES

This means that there is absolutely no way that Satan can take best.

THE CHURCH

In Verses 43 through 45, the Gentile Church is predicted. It has run its course now for nearly 2,000 years. As it regards the Church Age, we are, in fact, at the very closing hours of time.

At any moment, the Rapture of the Church could take place, which will include every single Believer who has ever lived, all the way from Abel up unto the time of the First Resurrection.

After the Rapture of the Church, the Antichrist will make his debut (II Thess. 2:7-12). His defeat is here predicted. It most certainly will come to pass exactly as here stated.

(49) "THEREFORE WILL I GIVE THANKS UNTO YOU, O LORD, AMONG THE HEATHEN, AND SING PRAISES UNTO YOUR NAME."

This Passage has to do with the coming Kingdom Age, when the entirety of the world will have a new song. That song will be *"Praises unto Your Name."*

(50) "GREAT DELIVERANCE GIVES HE TO HIS KING; AND SHOWS MERCY TO HIS ANOINTED, TO DAVID, AND TO HIS SEED FOR EVERMORE."

As stated, this Psalm proclaims the petitions of David, but more so the Son of David, Who really is *"His Anointed."* In fact, the phrase, *"His Anointed,"* is used only of the Messiah!

In this Eighteenth Psalm, we have Israel's rejection of her Messiah, His Crucifixion, the destruction of Israel as a nation, the advent of the Church under Christ, the rise and defeat of the Antichrist, and the Kingdom Age.

PSALM 19

A Psalm of David:
The Wonderful Creation and
Covenants of God

(1) "THE HEAVENS DECLARE THE GLORY OF GOD; AND THE FIRMAMENT SHOWS HIS HANDIWORK."

There is no excuse for man not to believe

in God, for we are plainly told that *"The Heavens declare the Glory of God."* In other words, Creation demands a Creator. That Creator is God, the Creator of the first cause, and thereby of all things.

As noted, this Psalm was written by David.

The structure of the Psalm demonstrates its unity. It contains 126 words in the Hebrew Text, that is, seven multiplied by eighteen (7 x 18 = 126).

"Seven" is the number of completion.

"Eight" is the number of Resurrection.

"Ten" is the number of Divinity.

"Five" is the number of Grace, and *"five"* upon *"five"* expresses *"Grace"* upon *"Grace"* (Jn. 1:16).

GOD IN CREATION

The first four Verses of this Psalm proclaim Creation. It also proclaims the Creator as God. As stated, creation demands a Creator.

The actual Hebrew states, *"The Heavens are recounting the Glory of God, of El, 'The Mighty One'"* — the God of nature.

The *"firmament"* is the entire atmosphere enveloping the Earth, in which the clouds hang and the fowls of the heavens move. Like the starry heavens above, this, too, *"shows,"* or rather *"proclaims,"* God's Handiwork.

The Bible actually begins by assuming the existence of God and His Creation of all things (Gen. 1:1).

In the Bible, the Doctrine of Creation is based on Divine Revelation, this being particularly the case in the New Testament, where Creation is seen in the light of the Divine Revelation in Jesus Christ and the *"new creation"* which has already become a spiritual reality through His Work at Calvary's Cross.

Biblical teaching regarding Creation should not be identified or confused with any scientific theory of origins, for all of these theories try to explain creation outside of God, which, of course, is impossible!

THE ANCIENT HEBREWS

The thought of the ancient Hebrews consistently related all existing phenomena to God as the one ground or source of existence. Because of this specifically monistic attitude, there could never be any place in their concept of Creation for the kind of dualism entertained by other religions.

To God as the sole Creator belonged a responsibility for the world of nature and men, and though there were facets of His Creation which did not reflect His high moral and ethical Character, even these were ultimately reconcilable to belief in the activity of one Deity.

The relationship between God and His Creation is a contingent one, for it is the Lord Who makes all things (Isa. 44:24), and His Handiwork is absolutely dependent upon Him for its ordering and survival. When the Old Testament writers spoke about the idea of Creation, they were making a spiritual affirmation to the effect that God was Sovereign and Lord of the Cosmos.

HOW DID GOD BRING CREATION INTO EXISTENCE?

As an expression of the way in which God formed the world and the universe, the idea of Creation by the *"Word"* is implicit. The account in the First Chapter of Genesis is marked by the phrase, *"And God said . . .",* at the beginning of each new stage in the creative process. This thought is also carried over with other Old Testament writers, notably the Psalmists (Ps. 33:9; 148:5; Isa. 45:12), who emphasize the transcendent Majesty of the Creator.

The best expressions of this concept are found in the New Testament (Jn. 1:1-13; Heb. 11:3; II Pet. 3:5-6), which also attributed dynamic qualities to the Word. All of this is synonymous with the sovereign power which shaped the course of history and the lives of men alike, being supremely manifest in the creation of the world.

Whatever the meaning of the phrase, *"And God said,"* there can be no doubt that the narrative as a whole ascribes the processes of Creation to the free and spontaneous activity of God. The Word of the Lord is that power which, when placed in the mouths of the Prophets, makes them spokesmen for God and gives them a position of authority in dispensing the Divine Oracles (Jer. 1:9-10).

The Word also has a vitality which makes

it sharper than any two-edged sword (Heb. 4:12; Rev. 19:13-15), and, in the Person of the Incarnate Logos (Jn. 1:1-18), establishes a relationship of a particularly efficacious sort between the Creator and His Creation.

MAN'S PLACE IN CREATION

The concept of creation out of nothing applies, of course, to the formulation of the Cosmos, and does not exhaust the Biblical teaching on the subject of Creation. Thus, man was not created *ex nihilo* (out of nothing), but from previously prepared material, the *"dust from the ground"* (Gen. 2:7), as were also the beasts of the field and the fowls of the air (Gen. 2:19).

This has been described as secondary creation, to denote an activity which makes use of material already in existence, but which is nevertheless integral to the concept of primary Creation.

The harmony which is represented in the world and its inhabitants is, in fact, a Divinely-imposed order in which each creature fulfills the Will of God. In every instance the creative fiat not merely brings entities into existence, but relates them to some specific function within the larger structure.

Because of the personal relationship which exists between God and His Creation, there can be no room in Scripture for the idea of *"nature"* as an autonomous power set in motion by a First Cause. God is depicted in the Scriptures as being at all times in control of the world (Job 38:33; Jer. 5:24), which needs His continual undergirding if it is to continue (Ps. 104:29-30). Where there is the expression of the regularity of natural forces, as in the Promise given to Noah (Gen. 8:22), it is based upon the Covenant Mercies and Faithfulness of God.

While the world was intended to display the Glory of God, it was also fashioned as the dwellingplace for man (Isa. 45:18), the crown of Divine Creation. Man was fashioned from the ground to which he ultimately returns when he dies, with death being brought on by the Fall, which was not originally intended.

While the animals and plants stand in an indirect relationship to the Creator, since they were brought forth by the earth, man is the direct product of creative activity, and is dignified in a special manner by being the recipient of the *"Living Breath"* of God. Stress is laid upon the nature of man as the highest form of created life in both accounts, where, in Genesis 1:26-27, man is described as being in the Divine Image.

THE DIVINE IMAGE OF GOD

This can only mean that man in his complete bodily existence was patterned after the Image of God. The fact that the same concept was applied to Seth as a son of Adam (Gen. 5:3) argues firmly against any attempts to reduce this *"Image"* to man's *"spiritual self,"* *"soul,"* or some such concept. The reference in Genesis 2:7 is also illuminating in this connection, for it speaks of man becoming a *"living soul."* The rendering *"living soul"* is less satisfactory than that of *"personality,"* since it is the totality of man which is again in view.

Hebrew thought consistently viewed man as a personality, and the numerous Old Testament references to the relationship between emotions and bodily changes demonstrated concern for the integration of the personality of a kind which has been reemphasized by modern psychosomatic medicine. Man is not just a *"body"* into which a *"soul"* has been placed. Instead, he is a living personality which has physical extension in time and place. When living by Divine Law, he is neither *"body"* nor *"soul,"* but a unified being in which all aspects of existence are designed to function in an integrated manner to the Glory of God.

Because man is, in effect, the Living Image of God upon Earth, he is given the task of serving as the Divine representative and ordering the ways of those aspects of creation which are put under his control (Gen. 1:28). Though he has been made in the Image of God, man is still inferior to the Deity in stature (Ps. 8:6-8). Nevertheless, he is crowned with glory and honor because he has been made especially to enjoy fellowship with the Creator.

THE WILL OF MAN

Unlike the animal creation, which has to obey instinctive impulses and laws, man has been given a freedom of will as part of his spiritual heritage. While his prime vocation is to serve God in the world of nature, he is unique in being the only creature which can respond to God in disobedience as well as in faith and trust. He can revile God as well as praise Him, and can separate himself from the Divine Presence just as easily as he can have fellowship with God.

Certainly the latter function was the clear intention of the Creator, since no other species can articulate the Divine praises. Thus, man was made to communicate meaningfully and intelligently with God, an ideal which was subsequently attributed to the nation in Covenant relationship with Him, and we speak of Israel (Isa. 43:21).

THE FUTURE OF CREATION

The Creation narratives contain no hint of foreboding for the future, for everything has the seal of perfection stamped on it. Until the declension of man and woman from pristine Grace, the prospect for the future was one of continuous and untrammeled fellowship with God. When sin entered human experience, it cast a blemish upon all created life (Hos. 4:7; Rom. 8:21-22) and threatened the future of man by separating his personality from God; thereafter it became necessary for the Creator to make specific provision for human spiritual needs, first by the Promise of One Who should effectively break the power of the Tempter (Gen. 3:15), then by the provision of a Sacrificial System which would enable the penitent worshipper to renew his fellowship with God, and finally by revealing that at some specific point in history the Creator's purpose would be entirely realized, and a New Heaven and Earth would replace the existing order of things.

The end of the sequence does not seem to have concerned the earlier figures in Hebrew history. It was only as the Covenant relationship became progressively weakened that an other-worldly perspective came into prominence.

Even then the eschatology of both pre- and post-exilic Prophets tended to think of a recreated theocratic society upon this Earth rather than the newly-fashioned Heaven and Earth of New Testament proclamation (Rev. 21:1), although Isaiah emphasized recreation in the New Testament sense (Isa. 66:22).

Consistently throughout the Old Testament, however, the greatest menace to the Divine Creation was the fact of sin, particularly where it represented a violation of the Covenant obligations. The Covenant community was itself a special creation intended as a witness in pagan society to the Nature and Power of the One True God and a means of His expression in the world.

Many of the Prophets diagnosed the national malaise in terms of sin and rebellion against God (Isa. 1:3; Jer. 8:7; Hos. 14:1), and Hosea went so far as to assert that the perverted will (Jer. 17:9) of Israel had even affected the natural Creation (Hos. 4:3).

THE NEW CREATION IN CHRIST

The New Testament Authors agreed with Judaism that God Alone was the Creator of the world through His Word, but, in the light of the fuller Revelation of God in Christ, they viewed the process of Creation Christologically. In Jesus, all things cohered (Col. 1:17), and the unity of Creation in Him was demonstrated further as part of the Divine purpose in history (Eph. 1:9-10). He it is Who upholds the universe by His powerful Word (Heb. 1:3), and brings meaning to the historical process as the Saviour and Redeemer of the world.

In the light of this conviction it was possible for the members of the primitive Church to assert that human Salvation was predestined in Christ before the founding of the world (Mat. 25:34; Eph. 1:4; I Pet. 1:18-20). Everything centers upon the Firstborn of all Creation (Col. 1:15), since it has been created through Him and unto Him, Who is the beginning and the end of Salvation.

The New Testament authors were insistent that the new Kingdom of Grace, long promised by Prophecy, had already appeared with the Incarnate Christ. The new creation was actually a Promise of future glory (Eph. 1:14; Rev. 21:1-4), when all redeemed creatures would laud their Creator (Rev. 4:8-11; 5:13).

Christ was the New Man Whom Adam foreshadowed (Rom. 5:12-14; I Cor. 15:21-22), the Image of the invisible God (Col. 1:15), Whose Death would redeem the world from bondage to sin and make individual Salvation possible.

In the Work of Calvary, Christ has paid the penalty for human iniquity and has opened the way for renewal of the individual personality through confession, surrender, and the acceptance of His saving Grace by Faith. When one has identified himself completely with the Work of Calvary and has received cleansing and pardon, he is *"in Christ."* The Saviour has restored the human pattern which God planned at the first. Those who are His are themselves new creations by Divine Grace.

(Bibliography of works used in preparing the above material on Creation: H. W. Robinson, *"Inspiration and Revelation in the Old Testament"*; E. Jacob, *"Old Testament Theology"*; and, G. A. F. Knight, *"A Christian Theology of the Old Testament."*)

(2) "DAY UNTO DAY UTTERS SPEECH, AND NIGHT UNTO NIGHT SHOWS KNOWLEDGE."

The phrases, *"Day unto day"* and *"Night unto night,"* mean day and night continually.

THE PROCLAMATION OF KNOWLEDGE

This Passage tells us that the Creation pours out speech, i.e., *"proclamation,"* as water is poured from a fountain. Each day bears its testimony to the next, and so the stream goes on in a flow that is never broken.

The phrase, *"And night unto night shows knowledge,"* compares with Paul's statement that *"that which may be known of God"* is manifested to man through the Creation (Rom. 1:19-20).

A certain superiority seems to be assigned to the night, *"as though the contemplation of the starry firmament awakened deeper, more spiritual thoughts than the brightness of day."* In fact, much more of God's Creation, as it regards the heavens, can be seen at night.

Once again, this *"knowledge"* is wrapped up in the statement that Creation demands a Creator.

The following story might serve as an excellent illustration.

CREATION DEMANDS A CREATOR

When Communism ruled the former Soviet Union, in one particular biology class, the teacher, extolling the principles of atheism and evolution, made excellent progress with the students, with one exception. The young man insisted that Creation had to have a Creator, and that the Creator was God. Of course, he was laughed at and ridiculed.

One particular morning, when the teacher came into the class, she saw sitting on her desk a model of the universe. It was expertly done, and presented itself as an excellent learning tool

She quickly asked, *"Who made this model?"* When no one spoke up, she finally said, *"Come on! Who made it? It didn't just happen by itself!"*

Slowly, the student who had made the model stood; it was the one who insisted that Creation had to have a Creator, and that the Creator was God.

"That's what I've been trying to tell you!" he said.

Creation didn't just happen. It had to have a Creator!

(3) "THERE IS NO SPEECH NOR LANGUAGE, WHERE THEIR VOICE IS NOT HEARD."

The translation should be, *"There is no speech, there are no words; their voice is not heard."*

The speech which Creation utters is not common speech — it is without sound, without language; no articulate voice is to be heard. By its very creation, that which it carries out on a daily, even hourly, basis, doing so without fail, is the language it speaks.

(4) "THEIR LINE IS GONE OUT THROUGH ALL THE EARTH, AND THEIR WORDS TO THE END OF THE WORLD. IN THEM HAS HE SET A TABERNACLE FOR THE SUN."

TEACHING

The material Earth is the sphere in which the Heavenly Message operates, and the Message itself is addressed to the inhabited *"world."* There is no limitation. All nations are embraced in this gracious Revelation.

The word *"line"* means *"teaching."* Although

no voice is heard, yet the heavens and its constellations keep continually pouring forth teaching respecting the Glory of God, so that all nations are without excuse (Rom. 1:19-20).

We know that the sun is enclosed in an envelope of fire, but this fact has been shown in this Psalm for about 3,000 years.

(5) "WHICH IS AS A BRIDEGROOM COMING OUT OF HIS CHAMBER, AND REJOICES AS A STRONG MAN TO RUN A RACE."

Verses 4 through 6 present another aspect of the Ways of God.

GOD IN ORDINATION

The phrase, *"Which is as a bridegroom coming out of his chamber,"* literally says, *"And he is as a bridegroom,"* speaking of the sun.

The bridegroom went forth to meet the bride in glorious apparel, and was *"preceded"* by a blaze of torchlight.

The sun's *"chamber"* is where he passes the night — below the Earth; from this he bursts forth at morning in his full glory, scattering the darkness, and lighting up his splendid *"tabernacle."*

It is amazing how the Holy Spirit illustrates the Creation.

(6) "HIS GOING FORTH IS FROM THE END OF THE HEAVEN, AND HIS CIRCUIT UNTO THE ENDS OF IT: AND THERE IS NOTHING HID FROM THE HEAT THEREOF."

While many things might be hidden from the light of the Sun, nothing is hidden from its *"heat,"* which is the vital force from where the whole Earth receives life and energy.

The Holy Spirit sets forth the *"Sun"* as the sparkling gem, if you please, in the midst of all of this creation. And rightly so!

First of all, the Sun is approximately one hundred times bigger in radius than the Earth. One could put approximately one million Earths into the same three-dimensional space as the Sun. We learn from this just how great, how powerful, and how big this orb actually is. It actually is beyond our comprehension to think of something that large.

But yet, the Sun has to be that large to send heat some ninety-three million (93,000,000) miles to Earth. When we realize that this heat has no enclosure and has *"leaked"* all the way from the Sun to planet Earth, it begins to become obvious why the Holy Spirit is here highlighting this part of God's Creation.

(7) "THE LAW OF THE LORD IS PERFECT, CONVERTING THE SOUL: THE TESTIMONY OF THE LORD IS SURE, MAKING WISE THE SIMPLE."

Whereas in the last three Verses, we viewed God in ordination, now we view Him in another aspect altogether.

GOD IN REVELATION

We find in this Psalm that the Heavens declare God's Glory, while the Scriptures declare His Grace. The Heavens reveal His Hand; the Scriptures reveal His Heart.

The phrase, *"The Law of the LORD is perfect,"* pertains to the fact that whatsoever proceeds from God is perfect in its kind; His *"Law"* especially — the rule of life to His rational creatures.

That Salvation is not by the Law is not the fault of the Law, but of man, who cannot keep it. *"The Law"* itself *"is holy, and the Commandment holy, and just, and good"* (Rom. 7:12).

The Law is like a mirror which shows man what he is, but actually provides no power to change man. And change is desperately needed!

CONVERTING THE SOUL

The phrase, *"Converting the soul,"* actually means *"to restore the soul."* The Hebrew word is used of restoring from disorder and decay, from sorrow and affliction, and even from death.

The Law, by instructing men, restores them from moral blindness to the light which is theirs by nature (Rom. 1:19), and, as a further consequence in many cases, restores them from sin to righteousness, which it is designed to do. Unfortunately, precious few in Israel, considering the whole, even tried to keep the Law.

THE LAW AND THE MODERN BELIEVER

Jesus Christ came to this world, and came

as a Man, the *"Last Adam"* and the *"Second Man,"* to do in man's place what man could not do. He was our Substitute. As such, He kept the Law perfectly in every respect, never breaking it even one time, not in word, thought, or deed!

He then satisfied the demands of the broken Law by giving Himself in Sacrifice, which atoned for all sin. His Offering of Himself presented a Perfect Sacrifice, which alone a thrice-Holy God could accept.

Concerning this, Paul said, *"Blotting out the handwriting of Ordinances that was against us, which was contrary to us, and took it out of the way, nailing it to His Cross"* (Col. 2:14).

THE MORAL LAW

The Law actually came originally in three parts: the Ceremonial, the Ritual, and the Moral. The Moral was ensconced in the Ten Commandments, given to us in the Twentieth Chapter of the Book of Exodus.

Jesus fulfilled all the Ceremonial, Ritual, and Moral Law, but, as should be obvious, God still commands the Moral part of the Law. If it was wrong to steal 3,500 years ago, it is still wrong to steal presently, despite what Christ did at the Cross. Moral truths are objective, and cannot change.

So, how does the ancient moral Law affect the modern Christian?

Paul addressed this by saying, and I quote from THE EXPOSITOR'S STUDY BIBLE:

"For I through the Law (Christ has perfectly kept the Law and suffered its just penalty, all on my behalf) *am dead to the Law* (the Law is not dead, but I am dead to the Law by virtue of having died with Christ [Rom. 6:3-5]), *that I might live unto God.* (This presents that which can only be done through Christ, and never by the Law.)

"I am Crucified with Christ (as the foundation of all victory; Paul here takes us back to Romans 6:3-5): *nevertheless I live* (have new life); *yet not I* (not by my own strength and ability), *but Christ lives in me* (by virtue of me dying with Him on the Cross, and being raised with Him in newness of life): *and the life which I now live in the flesh* (my daily walk before God) *I live by the Faith of the Son of God* (the Cross is ever the Object of my Faith), *Who loved me, and gave Himself for me"* (which is the only way that I could be saved).

"I do not frustrate the Grace of God (if we make anything other than the Cross of Christ the object of our Faith, we frustrate the Grace of God, which means we stop its action, and the Holy Spirit will no longer help us): *for if Righteousness come by the Law* (any type of Law), *then Christ is dead in vain.* (If I can successfully live for the Lord by any means other than Faith in Christ and the Cross, then the death of Christ was a waste)" (Gal. 2:19-21).

The modern Christian keeps the moral law and does so constantly by simply placing his faith in Christ, Who has kept it on our behalf. When our faith is exclusively in Christ and the Cross, the Holy Spirit will function in our hearts and lives, literally making Christ live through us, with the Law then being perfectly kept without any thought on our part. It is all in Christ and the Cross and our Faith in that Finished Work.

THE TESTIMONY OF THE LORD

The phrase, *"The testimony of the LORD is sure, making wise the simple,"* actually refers to the Decalogue, i.e., *"The Ten Commandments."* It may be regarded as one of the many synonyms under which the whole Law may be spoken of.

In a greater way, this can refer to the entirety of the Word of God.

First of all, it is *"sure,"* meaning that there is no error. It can be trusted in all circumstances.

It is so *"sure"* that it can make *"wise the simple,"* which refers to the fact that one is not truly educated unless one is truly educated in the Bible.

"Making wise the simple" means to *"enlighten the moral judgment,"* which the Bible alone can do.

If the modern Church knew the Bible as the modern Church ought to know the Bible, the stampede toward the *"Purpose Driven Life"* debacle would have no takers. This false direction has gained such acceptance simply because the modern Church has already subscribed to something that is false.

Because the heart is not satisfied, something new is always appealing.

If Believers will anchor their faith exclusively in Christ and the Cross, all these false directions will hold no allurement — none whatsoever! To be sure, Christ is the purpose of all life. When one truly knows Him (and one can only truly know Him by virtue of the Cross), every need is then met.

But when Believers have their faith anchored otherwise, false doctrine, whatever it might be, becomes very appealing!

(8) "THE STATUTES OF THE LORD ARE RIGHT, REJOICING THE HEART: THE COMMANDMENT OF THE LORD IS PURE, ENLIGHTENING THE EYES."

Again, the Word of God is extolled.

REJOICING THE HEART

The Law of the Lord, when looked at as it should be, is not felt as stern commands, but as gracious intimations of what God desires man to do for his own good. When man under the old Law attempted to carry out its precepts, there was a joy that filled his heart.

Presently, when the Believer places his faith in Christ and the Cross exclusively, which is the fulfillment of the Law, the same joy, even to a greater degree and a greater measure, fills the heart.

Where every effort by man is impure, *"the Commandment of the LORD is pure, enlightening the eyes,"* which means to *"give light to the intellect."*

(9) "THE FEAR OF THE LORD IS CLEAN, ENDURING FOREVER: THE JUDGMENTS OF THE LORD ARE TRUE AND RIGHTEOUS ALTOGETHER."

As with all of these Verses, great statements are herein made.

THE FEAR OF THE LORD

The phrase, *"The fear of the LORD is clean, enduring forever,"* actually pertains to *"the instruction afforded by God for fearing Him."*

The Holy Spirit will open the Word of the Lord to the individual. The *"fear"* here addressed is not a slavish fear, but rather the place and position that one should give the Creator and the Saviour. If we have any sense, we fear the Lord.

TRUE AND RIGHTEOUS

The phrase, *"The judgments of the LORD are true and righteous altogether,"* refers to the Word of God, which is perfect. This is the reason it is imperative that the Bible you have is a word-for-word translation. Many of the interpretations and paraphrases which are being placed on the market presently are little more than an abomination. But Satan is very successful at this effort, which means that people are not learning the Word of God, but something else entirely — actually the ideas of man, which are of no benefit whatsoever.

(10) "MORE TO BE DESIRED ARE THEY THAN GOLD, YEA, THAN MUCH FINE GOLD: SWEETER ALSO THAN HONEY AND THE HONEYCOMB."

God's Law, i.e., *"His Word,"* is of far greater good to man and, therefore, far more to be desired than any amount of riches. And yet, most Christians take such little advantage of that which the Word offers.

Every Believer should ask the Lord to help him understand the Word. When such a prayer is prayed, help is guaranteed. The Lord will see to it that such a person does not get pushed into wrong doctrine, but rather that the response will be as it should.

(11) "MOREOVER BY THEM IS YOUR SERVANT WARNED: AND IN KEEPING OF THEM THERE IS GREAT REWARD."

There was but one Man Who ever lived on Earth Who could exhaustively use the words of Verses 10 and 11, and He dwelt in the Scriptures as the sun dwells in the heavens. These Scriptures *"warned Him,"* i.e., they *"admonished or taught Him."*

(12) "WHO CAN UNDERSTAND HIS ERRORS? CLEANSE THOU ME FROM SECRET FAULTS.

(13) "KEEP BACK YOUR SERVANT ALSO FROM PRESUMPTUOUS SINS; LET THEM NOT HAVE DOMINION OVER ME: THEN SHALL I BE UPRIGHT, AND I SHALL BE INNOCENT FROM THE GREAT TRANSGRESSION."

The sense of these two Verses is phenomenal, to say the least!

THE WORD OF GOD

The sense of these Verses is this:

The only way that one can understand his error is by going to the Word of God. The only thing that will probe deep into the heart of man and locate the *"secret faults"* is the Word of God.

The *"great transgression"* spoken of in Verse 13 is that of declaring the Word of God insufficient for the problems at hand. Thus it was with Jehovah's perfect Servant. He prayed that He might be kept back from association with the presumptuous; that He might be guarded from their influence; and He might be clear from the great transgression of stepping outside the Scriptures, as the sun is clear of the great transgression of stepping outside its tabernacle in the heavens.

Such an act on the part of the sun would wreck the universe, and such an act on the part of the Servant of Jehovah would bring eternal ruin upon Angels and men.

Stepping outside the Scriptures is the cause of all spiritual declension and backsliding, all spiritual apostasy, and all departing from God.

The Hebrew verbs employed in Verse 13 are astronomical terms. This is one of the many proofs that the Creator of the heavens also is the Author of the Scripture.

(14) "LET THE WORDS OF MY MOUTH, AND THE MEDITATION OF MY HEART, BE ACCEPTABLE IN YOUR SIGHT, O LORD, MY STRENGTH, AND MY REDEEMER."

Our words and the meditation of our hearts can only be acceptable unto the Lord so long as they remain constant in the Word of God.

The great titles of Elohim (El) and Jehovah occur at the opening and closing of this Psalm, just as they appear at the opening and closing of the Bible, and in the same relationship.

PSALM 20

A Psalm of David:
A Psalm of Trust: Prayer for Victory

(1) "THE LORD HEAR YOU IN THE DAY OF TROUBLE; THE NAME OF THE GOD OF JACOB DEFEND YOU."

As noted, David wrote this Psalm. There are six things given in which we may trust: The Lord's Name, Sanctuary, Sacrifice, Salvation, Prayer, and Power.

THE DAY OF TROUBLE

Much of modern-day faith-teaching pretty well denies the *"day of trouble."* But Jesus, in speaking of two houses, one built upon sand and the other upon rock, said, *"And the rain descended, and the floods came, and the winds blew, and beat upon that house"* (Mat. 7:25, 27). In other words, there is nothing the Christian can do to stop this *"day of trouble"* from coming. The answer is building the house on the *"Rock."* That *"Rock"* is *"The Name of the God of Jacob."*

It is very interesting that the Holy Spirit uses this title, *"The Name of the God of Jacob."* This means the God Who met Jacob when he had nothing and deserved nothing but wrath, and Who gave him everything. It is the equivalent of the New Testament *"God of all Grace"* (I Pet. 5:10).

Satan is constantly accusing the Brethren (Rev., Chpt. 12). The *"God of Jacob"* will defend us.

THE MESSIAH

Even though this Psalm was written by David and applies to David, it also applies to all Believers, even unto this present hour; however, the greater thrust of this Verse and the entire Psalm pertains to the Messiah.

The specific meaning of the *"day of trouble,"* as here given, pertains to Christ while He was on the Cross. He will cry to the Lord at that time. It is even believed that He quoted the entire Twenty-second Psalm, not just the First Verse. The admonition is that the Lord would hear Him at that time; the Lord did hear Him at that time.

This completely sets aside the teaching which claims that Jesus died spiritually on the Cross, i.e., that Jesus died as a sinner and went to Hell, with God forsaking Him in totality. That is not the case, as we shall see, in the Commentary to the First Verse of the Twenty-second Psalm.

The *"Name"* stands for the Person. The

term occurs three times in the Psalm: the Defending Name (Vs. 1); the Displayed Name (Vs. 5); and the Delivering Name (Vs. 7).

It is beautiful here that the Holy Spirit is not ashamed to refer to God as the *"God of Jacob."* This tells us that the Lord does not really look at us as we are, but as what He can make of us, that is, if we only will allow Him to do so. The story of Jacob is the greatest story in the Bible of the Sanctification process. It is a process that every last Believer, even those of us under the New Covenant, must undergo, at least in one way or another.

(2) "SEND THEE HELP FROM THE SANCTUARY, AND STRENGTHEN THEE OUT OF ZION."

Even though the Lord Jesus was not normally close to the Sanctuary during His earthly Ministry, nevertheless, He received great help from what it represented; hence, His cleansing of it two times.

THE SANCTUARY

Before the Cross of Christ, the Holy Spirit dwelt in the Sanctuary, actually between the Mercy Seat and the Cherubim, which were situated in the Holy of Holies, the room immediately behind the Holy Place. At least that is where He was supposed to dwell. He did, in fact, dwell there in the times of the Tabernacle and the Temple, at least until the Temple was destroyed by Nebuchadnezzar.

In the Temple built by Zerubbabel, there was no Ark of the Covenant, and there also was no Ark in Herod's Temple during the time of Christ. The Prophet Ezekiel saw the Holy Spirit leave the Temple not long before it was destroyed by Nebuchadnezzar (Ezek., Chpt. 10; 11:23). The Holy Spirit left because of Israel's great sin. Once the Holy Spirit had gone, Israel no longer served any purpose, so they were taken captive by Nebuchadnezzar.

However, in the time of the coming Kingdom Age, the Prophet Ezekiel saw the Holy Spirit return, meaning that He will occupy the Temple during the thousand-year reign of Christ (Ezek. 43:1-7).

Since the Cross, the Holy Spirit now resides in the hearts and lives of Believers, making Believers His Temple (I Cor. 3:16).

NOTES

Before the Cross, the sin debt remained, simply because animal blood was woefully insufficient to alleviate this debt; however, Christ *"took away all sin"* (Jn. 1:29). This made it possible for the Holy Spirit to come into the hearts and lives of each Believer and to abide permanently. The Cross is what makes it possible!

So that's the reason that help was asked of the Lord from the Sanctuary, because that's where the Holy Spirit then dwelt. We do not pray in the same manner presently, and for all the obvious reasons. We pray to the Heavenly Father exactly as did all Believers before Christ, but with a great difference. We now pray in the Name of Jesus, because Christ has finished His Work (Jn. 16:23).

(3) "REMEMBER ALL YOUR OFFERINGS, AND ACCEPT YOUR BURNT SACRIFICE; SELAH."

The Messiah is praying that the Sacrifice of His sinless Life and atoning Death will be accepted. All the multiple millions of offerings that went before, i.e., the death of countless blemish-free lambs, looked forward to *"Your Burnt Sacrifice."* The *"Burnt Sacrifices"* were always Sacrifices that contained the shedding of blood. They were the basis of all answered prayer in the Old Testament program. They signified the giving of one's all; likewise, Christ gave His all.

THE CROSS OF CHRIST

Everything, i.e., Salvation, the Baptism with the Holy Spirit, answered prayer, blessings of every description, the Fruit of the Spirit, etc., all, without exception, are granted to us from Christ as the Source, but with the Cross as the means. Does the Reader understand that?

If one separates Christ from the Cross in any manner, then he is left with *"another Jesus"* (II Cor. 11:4).

As we have already said several times in this Volume:

1. The only way to God is through Jesus Christ (Jn. 14:6).

2. The only way to Jesus is through the Cross (Lk. 9:23).

3. The only way to the Cross is by a denial

of self (Lk. 9:23).

Because it is so very, very important, please allow us to repeat the following:

If the Cross is separated from Christ, then we are left with a Jesus that is not actually the Son of the Living God.

Do not misunderstand. Jesus is not still on a Cross. He is seated by the Right Hand of the Father (Heb. 1:3). We speak of the benefits of the Cross, benefits which will never end. That is the reason that the Apostle Paul referred to the Cross as *"The Everlasting Covenant"* (Heb. 13:20).

(4) "GRANT THEE ACCORDING TO THINE OWN HEART, AND FULFILL ALL THY COUNSEL."

Most probably these were the words of the High Priest to the people after offering their sacrifices.

A GLORIOUS PETITION

The petition has been offered by the Messiah, and the answer comes back from God the Father, *"Grant Thee according to Thine Own heart,"* which means, *"Whatever Your heart desires in connection with this expedition, all that You hope from it, all that You would have it accomplish."*

The phrase, *"Fulfill all Thy counsel,"* in essence says, *"Make all Your plans to prosper."*

God the Father granted all that which God the Son requested. If it was granted to God the Son, and it most definitely was, it also is granted to us, because He did it all for you and me.

We modern Christians live so far beneath our true spiritual privileges. Unfortunately, far too much of the modern Church looks to material things instead of the spiritual. We have it backwards. If we attend to the spiritual, the physical and the material will take care of themselves. Jesus said so (Mat. 6:33).

The way we obtain these great victories in the spiritual sense, which is the key to all things, is by simple faith in Christ and the Cross (Rom. 6:1-14; 8:1-2, 11; I Cor. 1:17-18; 23; Gal. 6:14).

(5) "WE WILL REJOICE IN YOUR SALVATION, AND IN THE NAME OF OUR GOD WE WILL SET UP OUR BANNERS: THE LORD FULFILL ALL YOUR PETITIONS."

Three things are said in this Verse.

NOTES

THE LORD ANSWERS PRAYER

The phrase, *"The LORD fulfill all Your petitions,"* presents David praying this prayer, which is actually a prayer of the Messiah. He is here guaranteed the answer to His prayers. And if He is granted these petitions as our Substitute Man, which He most definitely is, then we also are granted these petitions, whatever our petitions might be.

Everything He did, He did for you and me; consequently, we are meant to have every single victory for which He paid such a price.

Considering the price that He paid, it grieves our Lord terribly when we do not avail ourselves of all for which He has paid such a price.

Once again, we come back to the idea that Believers should first of all seek for victory in their lives, which only can be obtained by our faith in Christ and the Cross, which then gives the Holy Spirit the latitude to work in our lives, Who Alone can bring forth such victory.

The Holy Spirit is the Dispenser of all that for which Christ has paid such a price (Rom. 8:2).

Jesus said:

"If any man thirst, let him come unto Me, and drink.

"He who believes on Me as the Scripture has said, out of his innermost being shall flow rivers of Living Water."

The Scriptures then add:

"But this spoke He of the Spirit" (Jn. 7:37-39).

BANNERS

The phrase, *"And in the Name of our God we will set up our banners,"* refers to that which is conspicuous.

The Hebrew word for *"banners"* is *"dagal,"* which means *"to raise a flag, to be conspicuous, to flaunt."*

We must not be timid or bashful regarding the Lord and all He has done for us. Relating it to this present time, we must *"preach the Cross," "sing the Cross," "testify the Cross,"* i.e., raise our flag, even flaunt it! People must know what we stand for, and that upon which we stand. We must not hide this light under a bushel.

SALVATION

Knowing that the Lord will fulfill all our petitions, we now will *"rejoice in Your Salvation."* We will be thrilled to say so! In today's vernacular, *"There is therefore now no condemnation to them which are in Christ Jesus, who walk not after the flesh, but after the Spirit"* (Rom. 8:1).

(6) "NOW KNOW I THAT THE LORD SAVES HIS ANOINTED; HE WILL HEAR HIM FROM HIS HOLY HEAVEN WITH THE SAVING STRENGTH OF HIS RIGHT HAND."

The words, *"His Anointed,"* speak of *"His Messiah."* When our Lord prays, the Father always hears and always grants Him the *"saving strength of His Right Hand."*

HIS ANOINTED

Hannah, the mother of the Prophet Samuel, was the first one to use the word *"Anointed"* to refer to the Messiah.

She said:

"And He (God the Father) *shall give strength unto His King, and exalt the Horn of His Anointed"* (I Sam. 2:10).

And then, shortly after Hannah, an unnamed Prophet said, *"And I will raise Me up a faithful Priest . . . and I will build Him a sure house; and He shall walk before My Anointed forever"* (I Sam. 2:35).

The writer of the Second Psalm said, *"And the rulers take counsel together against the LORD, and against His Anointed"* (Ps. 2:2). This speaks of Christ, the Messiah.

David prayed, *"The LORD is their strength, and He is the saving strength of His Anointed"* (Ps. 28:8). Even though David was speaking of himself as being anointed of the Lord, which he definitely was, still, it is actually speaking of the Messiah.

The Prophet Isaiah said, *"The yoke shall be destroyed because of the anointing"* (Isa. 10:27). It should have been translated, *"The yoke shall be destroyed because of The Anointed One."*

GOD THE FATHER ALWAYS HEARS GOD THE SON

The phrase, *"He will hear Him from His Holy Heaven, with the saving strength of His Right Hand,"* refers to two particulars.

First of all, God the Father always hears, without exception, the prayers and petitions of His Son, the Lord Jesus Christ.

Second, *"His Right Hand"* refers to the Almighty Power of God, which is at the disposal of *"His Anointed."*

In connection with this, we must understand that God cannot bless sinful man as sinful man. God can only bless His Son, our Saviour, the Lord Jesus Christ; consequently, the Lord can bless us only as we are *"in Christ."* We must understand this!

Christ, as the Last Adam and the Second Man, is the Source of all things from God the Father. Everything is wrapped up in Christ, and, more particularly, what He did for us at the Cross. It is only as we are properly in Him that we can be the recipients of all that He has done for us. We must never forget that everything He did was done exclusively for us — not at all for Himself.

(7) "SOME TRUST IN CHARIOTS, AND SOME IN HORSES: BUT WE WILL REMEMBER THE NAME OF THE LORD OUR GOD."

Three particulars are here addressed.

TRUST IN THE LORD

1. The Antichrist, by trusting in chariots and horses (military equipment), will be defeated. But the Lord Jesus Christ, by trusting in the Name of the Lord God, will be victorious.

2. David was proclaiming his trust in the Lord, and that he had won all of his many battles by the means of that trust.

3. It is the same for us presently. Do we trust in the things of the world, or do we trust in the Lord?

As someone has well said, if we trust in man, we get what man can give, which is nothing. If we trust in the Lord, we get what the Lord can give, which is everything.

(8) "THEY ARE BROUGHT DOWN AND FALLEN: BUT WE ARE RISEN, AND STAND UPRIGHT."

This Passage leaps forward to the coming Battle of Armageddon, when the Antichrist will fall; however, the Lord, all who follow Him, and Israel shall stand upright.

All who trust in the Lord will conclude by *"standing upright."* All who do not trust in the Lord will be *"brought down and will fall."*

(9) "SAVE, LORD: LET THE KING HEAR US WHEN WE CALL."

Verses 1 through 6 refer to the Messiah's calling to God. Verse 9 refers to Israel in the Battle of Armageddon calling to the God of Glory and to the King, Who will be the Lord Jesus Christ. God will hear when they call. He will *"save."*

He hears now, and, to be sure, He now *"will save."*

PSALM 21

*A Psalm of David:
Thanks and Praise for Victory*

(1) "THE KING SHALL JOY IN YOUR STRENGTH, O LORD; AND IN YOUR SALVATION HOW GREATLY SHALL HE REJOICE!"

As noted, this Psalm was written by David

REJOICING IN THE LORD

Even though David is here speaking of himself, thanking the Lord for the great blessings afforded, still, the greater thrust of the Psalm has to do with the Son of David. The strength and Salvation of this First Verse signalized the Resurrection. Death and Hell have now been defeated. All sin has been atoned. The great Work of Redemption, promised for so many long centuries, has now been finished!

Now the Messiah rejoices, and rightly so!

As we have said several times, when one reads the Psalms, one is reading the heart of the Saviour. Everything that is said in these Psalms, in one way or another, speaks of Christ in either His Atoning, Mediatorial, or High Priestly Work.

However, even though that thread runs throughout all the Psalms, more than all it runs through those which were written by David — and for all the obvious reasons. It was through David that the Messiah would come. And through David He did come!

(2) "YOU HAVE GIVEN HIM HIS HEART'S DESIRE, AND HAVE NOT WITHHELD THE REQUEST OF HIS LIPS. SELAH."

Jesus was raised from the dead by the Power of God (Rom. 8:11). What His Heart desired and His Lips requested may be learned from Verses 3 through 7.

As we have already stated, the Father always heard the petitions of the Son, and He always *"gave Him His heart's desire."* He did not withhold *"any request of His Lips."*

Let us say it again, because it is so very, very important:

Everything Christ did was done for you and for me. When through the Spirit we learn how to fully glorify Christ, which one has to properly understand the Cross in order to do, then our requests will be treated by the Heavenly Father exactly as the requests of His Son, Whom He always answered.

(3) "FOR YOU PREVENT HIM WITH THE BLESSINGS OF GOODNESS: YOU SET A CROWN OF PURE GOLD ON HIS HEAD."

Two things are here said concerning the Messiah!

THE BLESSINGS OF GOODNESS

The phrase, *"For You prevented Him with the Blessings of Goodness,"* refers to the fact that the Father prevented anything and everything that would hinder the Messiah. While He was tempted in all points like as we are, still, the Lord allowed Satan only so much latitude. To be sure, it was far greater latitude than He allows with any of us, but still there was a limit, and that limit was placed there by the Father. The idea is that nothing marred those *"Blessings of Goodness,"* whether of the Messiah receiving them or bestowing them on others, which He constantly did!

THE CROWN OF PURE GOD

The phrase, *"You set a crown of pure gold on His Head,"* refers to something which will be done in the coming Kingdom Age, and by those who previously rejected Him, His Own people, the Jews.

When He came the first time, He was totally rejected. In fact, the religious leaders of Israel, who were the ruling body of Israel, as it regards the Kingship of Christ, plainly and clearly stated, *"We have no king but Caesar"* (Jn. 19:15). They found that king to be a hard taskmaster!

(4) "HE ASKED LIFE OF YOU, AND YOU

GAVE IT HIM, EVEN LENGTH OF DAYS FOREVER AND EVER."

It is difficult for us to understand Christ praying in this manner, but it is because we do not properly understand His humanity. While He definitely was *"Very God,"* He also was *"Very Man."* While He never ceased to be God, still, He conducted Himself totally and completely at all times as a *"Man,"* The Man Christ Jesus. As such, He wept, prayed, cried, pleaded, appealed, and asked. To be sure, He was not turned down in His petitions, except one time!

While Jesus hung on the Cross, He prayed for the Pharisees and the Sadducees, *"Father, forgive them; for they know not what they do"* (Lk. 23:34).

That was a prayer that the Father could not answer, simply because the guilty ones would not seek forgiveness. Had they done so, the prayer would have been instantly and readily answered.

The phrase, *"Even length of days forever and ever,"* pertains to the fact that God raised Jesus from the dead, and, in His Glorified Form, He will live forever.

(5) "HIS GLORY IS GREAT IN YOUR SALVATION: HONOR AND MAJESTY HAVE YOU LAID UPON HIM."

This Passage pertains to the Exaltation of Christ.

THE EXALTATION OF CHRIST

Jesus Christ has always been the Creator (Jn. 1:1-3).

As well, as God He is Perfect; therefore, how is it possible to improve upon such?

While it is not possible to improve upon perfection, one can add to perfection. And that's exactly what happened to Christ.

He is the Creator, but, due to the Cross, He also now is the Saviour.

The Scripture says of Him:

"Wherefore God also has highly exalted Him, and given Him a Name which is above every name:

"That at the Name of Jesus every knee should bow, of things in Heaven, and things in Earth, and things under the Earth;

"And that every tongue should confess that Jesus Christ is Lord, to the Glory of God the Father" (Phil. 2:9-11).

Let's say it again! It is because of the Cross. Concerning His Exaltation, the Scripture says, *"And being found in fashion as a Man, He humbled Himself, and became obedient unto death, even the death of the Cross"* (Phil. 2:8).

(6) "FOR YOU HAVE MADE HIM MOST BLESSED FOREVER: YOU HAVE MADE HIM EXCEEDING GLAD WITH YOUR COUNTENANCE."

Once again, this speaks of the Incarnation and Exaltation of Christ.

BLESSED FOREVER

Two things are here said.

First of all, the Text, *"For You have made Him most blessed forever,"* refers to His Exaltation, which was because of His Incarnation, all in order that He might go to the Cross, and because He did go to the Cross.

When God became a Man, The Man Christ Jesus, He laid aside the expression of Deity, never to take it up again, while, at the same time, never ceasing to be Deity. In essence, He stooped down to a lower level in order to become Man, hence, the Incarnation, God becoming Man, all in order to go to the Cross. For doing this, He has been made *"Most Blessed forever."*

Due to the fact of the Incarnation and what He did at the Cross as it regards the Redemption of humanity, He is Greater today than ever before.

The phrase, *"You have made Him exceeding glad with Your Countenance,"* presents the manner in which the Exaltation was carried out. In essence, the Father smiled on Him, signifying that all He had done at the Cross had been approved and accepted. It is a perfect Redemption, which the Holy Spirit calls *"The Everlasting Covenant"* (Heb. 13:20).

(7) "FOR THE KING TRUSTS IN THE LORD, AND THROUGH THE MERCY OF THE MOST HIGH HE SHALL NOT BE MOVED."

Even though David is speaking of himself here, still, the greater thrust of what the Holy Spirit says through him pertains to the Messiah. In final form, *"the King"* is Christ Jesus.

THE MOST HIGH AND CHRIST

The phrase, *"And through the mercy of*

the Most High He shall not be moved," should be read by every human being on the face of the Earth.

The contention of the world is not so much with God, because God is somewhat an abstract concept. Of course, God is not an abstract concept according to the Bible, but it is in the minds of many, i.e., many things are referred to as God! The contention is with the Lord Jesus Christ.

The *"Most High"* here says that the exalted place which Jesus now occupies, He shall occupy forever, *"He shall not be moved."*

This is the idea:

Everyone on the face of the Earth, all who have ever lived, all who live now, and all who will ever live, must, on the final day, stand before Christ. They will stand before Him at the *"Judgment Seat of Christ,"* which will contain only those who are Born-Again, and will stand there in order to receive rewards.

Otherwise, they will face Christ at *"The Great White Throne Judgment,"* which will contain only those who have rejected Christ, which speaks of every soul in this capacity through the ages. There they will be judged according to the life they lived; there will be a record of everyone, of everything, and for all time. They will then be placed into the Lake of Fire, where they will remain forever and forever (Rev. 20:11-15).

Either way, all are going to have to stand before Christ!

(8) "YOUR HAND SHALL FIND OUT ALL YOUR ENEMIES: YOUR RIGHT HAND SHALL FIND OUT THOSE WHO HATE YOU."

Once again, this refers to the coming Great White Throne Judgment. That particular judgment is going to be a horrifying time. It speaks of those down through the ages who have been *"enemies"* of Christ. Concerning the New Covenant, Paul said, *"They are the enemies of the Cross of Christ: whose end is destruction"* (Phil 3:18-19).

As we have stated, the Lord keeps books regarding every single individual. The Scripture says, *"And I saw the dead, small and great, stand before God; and the Books were opened, and another Book was opened, which is the Book of Life: and the dead were judged out of those things which were written in the Books, according to their works"* (Rev. 20:12).

Everyone on the face of the Earth should read these words and conduct their lives accordingly!

(9) "YOU SHALL MAKE THEM AS A FIERY OVEN IN THE TIME OF YOUR ANGER: THE LORD SHALL SWALLOW THEM UP IN HIS WRATH, AND THE FIRE SHALL DEVOUR THEM."

All should read these words!

THE GREAT WHITE THRONE JUDGMENT

The world has become so psychologized that it no longer believes that a Judgment Day is coming; however, irrespective as to what man may think, most assuredly a Judgment Day is coming. It is referred to as *"The Great White Throne Judgment"* (Rev. 20:11-15).

The Lord Jesus Christ will be the Judge.

Christ wants to be your Saviour; but if you do not allow Him to be your Saviour, one day He will be your Judge.

Every single soul who stands at the Great White Throne Judgment is lost. No redeemed will stand there. Each one will see from the books exactly what he did, how he did it, and why he did it. There will be no argument!

The Final Judgment will be:

"And whosoever was not found written in the Book of Life was cast into the Lake of Fire" (Rev. 20:15).

(10) "THEIR FRUIT SHALL YOU DESTROY FROM THE EARTH, AND THEIR SEED FROM AMONG THE CHILDREN OF MEN."

The idea is this:

Every single person who ever has lived, if they do not accept Christ, there will come an hour when there will not be a single one left on the Earth.

When will this take place?

As stated, it will occur at *"The Great White Throne Judgment"* (Rev. 20:11).

(11) "FOR THEY INTENDED EVIL AGAINST YOU: THEY IMAGINED A MISCHIEVOUS DEVICE, WHICH THEY ARE NOT ABLE TO PERFORM."

The Pharisees and Sadducees *"intended*

evil against the Lord." Untold millions of others fall into the same category.

A MISCHIEVOUS DEVICE

The phrase, *"They imagined a mischievous device, which they are not able to perform,"* speaks of two particulars.

First of all, it speaks of Christ, Whose Name the Pharisees and Sadducees tried to blot out from the face of the Earth. They thought that crucifying Him would prove Him to be an impostor. But He rose from the dead, meaning they were not able to carry out their devices.

Second, it refers to the Antichrist, who will seek to dethrone God in the coming Great Tribulation. He will attempt to take over the entirety of the world; he will attempt to stamp out any semblance of any other type of religion on the face of the Earth except the worship of himself. The climactic efforts will rush toward Armageddon. There he will think to completely annihilate the Jews and prove the Word of God to be untrue, because if he can cause even one Word of the Word of God to fail, he has won!

But in that he will fail, as well, inasmuch as his push to annihilate the Jews from the face of the Earth and to completely destroy Jerusalem will be met by the Second Coming of Christ, the most cataclysmic event the world ever will have known. His *"mischievous device"* will come to pieces before his eyes.

The Antichrist will lose his life at Armageddon and thereby lose his soul for all eternity. Concerning him, the Scripture says, *"The beast* (the Antichrist) *was taken, and with him the false prophet, who wrought miracles before him, with which he deceived them who had received the mark of the beast, and them who worshipped his image. These both were cast alive into a Lake of Fire burning with brimstone"* (Rev. 19:20).

(12) "THEREFORE SHALL YOU MAKE THEM TURN THEIR BACK, WHEN YOU SHALL MAKE READY YOUR ARROWS UPON YOUR STRINGS AGAINST THE FACE OF THEM."

The Antichrist will *"turn his back"* to the onslaught of Christ at the Second Coming, but to no avail. The Antichrist possesses only the equipment available to mere humanity. The Lord can use the elements, which He most definitely will do, even as prophesied by Ezekiel:

"And I will plead against him (against the Antichrist) *with pestilence and with blood; I will rain upon him, and upon his bands, and upon the many people who are with him, an overflowing rain, and great hailstones, fire, and brimstone"* (Ezek. 38:22).

In other words, this is a war the Antichrist is going to wish he had not started.

(13) "BE THOU EXALTED, LORD, IN YOUR OWN STRENGTH: SO WILL WE SING AND PRAISE YOUR POWER."

On the Millennial Morn, Israel will acclaim Christ as King and worship Him as God. At the beginning of the Kingdom Age, Israel, and to a man, will accept Christ. Israel will then *"sing and praise Your power,"* referring to the power used against the Antichrist and his armies.

At His First Advent, they crucified Him. At His Second Advent, they will exalt Him!

PSALM 22

A Psalm of David:
Christ's Suffering and Coming Glory

(1) "MY GOD, MY GOD, WHY HAVE YOU FORSAKEN ME? WHY ARE YOU SO FAR FROM HELPING ME, AND FROM THE WORDS OF MY ROARING?"

As noted, this Psalm was written by David.

DID GOD FORSAKE CHRIST TOTALLY WHEN JESUS WAS ON THE CROSS?

No! He forsook Him in the sense that He would not deliver Him from the Cross; however, Christ did not ask for deliverance at this time, and rightly so! Had He come down from the Cross as the blasphemers demanded (Mat. 27:40), Redemption would never have been effected, and man could not have been saved.

Inasmuch as Jesus was bearing the sin penalty for all of mankind, and for all time, God could not look upon Him, even though Christ was His Only Son. This is what the Prophet Habakkuk said, when he cried, *"You are of purer eyes than to behold evil, and cannot not look on iniquity"* (Hab. 1:13).

This does not mean that Jesus was evil, or that He had committed any type of iniquity, for He had not. He was utterly, purely, and totally sinless; however, He was bearing the sin penalty of mankind; inasmuch as this was being done, God pulled the blinds, so to speak, that not only He would not look, but also that no man saw Jesus die. This *"darkness"* lasted from 12 noon until 3 p.m. (Mat. 27:45).

The moment before Jesus died, He said, *"It is finished; Father, into Your hands I commend My Spirit"* (Jn. 19:30; Lk. 23:46).

Had God forsaken Him totally, as some claim, then He could not have referred to Him as His *"Father,"* and He also could not have commended His Spirit to the Father.

Many use this First Verse from Psalm 22 and Mark 15:34 as the proof that Jesus died spiritually on the Cross, which means that He died as a sinner and went to Hell — the burning side of Hell. However, the Scripture does not at all teach that, as is overly obvious. Jesus did not die as a sinner on the Cross and did not go to the burning side of Hell. The price was totally and completely paid at Calvary. That's why He cried, *"It is finished!"*

Referring to the very moment that Jesus died, the Scriptures say, *"The Veil of the Temple was rent in twain from the top to the bottom"* (Mat. 27:51).

This *"Veil"* hung between the Holy Place and the Holy of Holies. The Veil being rent signified that the way was now open for sinful man to come into the very Presence of God, but only on the basis of the shed Blood of the Crucified Lamb and one's faith in that Finished Work (Jn. 3:16). If Redemption's Plan awaited Jesus going to the burning side of Hell and suffering there for three days and nights, as some teach, then that *"Veil"* would not have been rent until that particular time. But the Veil was torn from top to bottom at the moment that Jesus died, a fact which unequivocally states that the Redemption's Plan was completed at the Cross.

Of course, the Resurrection was of immense significance; however, due to the fact that all sin was atoned at the Cross, the Resurrection was not in doubt. That's the reason that the Plan was carried out and completed, totally and absolutely, at the Cross.

THE SUFFERINGS OF CHRIST

The Twenty-second Psalm predicts the sufferings of Christ (Vss. 1-21) and the glories that are to follow (Vss. 22-31). It presents a sinless Man, the Lord Jesus Christ, forsaken by God in the manner we have explained. Such a fact is unique in history and never will need to be repeated. That sinless Man — Himself God manifest in the flesh — was made to be sin (II Cor. 5:21), that is, a Sin Offering (Isa. 53:10) and, therefore, forsaken, at least for a short period of time. He was pierced with the Sword of Divine Wrath (Zech. 14:7), inasmuch as He suffered the pangs of death, which are sin's wages (Rom. 6:23).

In that Judgment, God dealt infinitely with sin; by so dealing with it in the Person of His Beloved Son, He showed His Wrath against sin and His Love for the sinner. Thus, He vindicated Himself and redeemed man. God revealed Himself at Calvary.

When one looks on the horror of Calvary, one must say, *"Sin did this!"*

PROPHECY

Those who deny the fact of Prophecy cannot explain away this Psalm. Its translation into Greek proves that it was in existence at least 300 years before Christ, and yet it contains a number of minute predictions, the actual and material fulfillment of which the New Testament records.

The Holy Spirit, in Matthew 27:46, states that Christ spoke this Psalm as He hung on the tree. It glorifies Him as the Sin Offering (Isa. 53:10); Psalm 40 glorifies Him as the Burnt Offering; and, Psalm 69 glorifies Him as the Trespass Offering. The Gospels narrate the facts of the Crucifixion; this Psalm, the feelings of the Crucified. Combining these Scriptures, the Believer recognizes that he can accompany the Lord Jesus a little way in His sufferings, but there soon comes a point beyond which we cannot go.

The depth of horror to which the sinless soul of Jesus sank under the Wrath of God, as the Sin Offering, is unfathomable for men or Angels!

DEGREES OF SUFFERING

Four degrees of suffering appear in this Psalm:

1. Suffering from the Hand of God (Vss. 1-6).
2. Suffering from the rejection of Israel (Vss. 7-8).
3. Suffering from the demons which gathered around His Cross in exulting and hellish triumph (Vss. 12-13).
4. The physical suffering of Crucifixion — the most painful form of death (Vss. 14-18).

Had the Messiah been only Man, He would have put His physical sufferings first and His spiritual sufferings last. But to Him, as the Only Begotten Son of God, there was no anguish so infinite as the hiding of the Father's Face. His physical sufferings were agonizing; His mental and spiritual, from the onslaught of the bulls of Bashan, i.e., the demons, still more terrible; the pain of His wounded heart, because of the hatred of those He loved and came to save, was a still deeper depth of agony; but an agony unspeakable was His being forsaken of God, even for some three hours of time.

During His Ministry on Earth, Christ spoke of God as His Father and resumed the title after He had triumphantly shouted, *"Finished!"* But while suffering Divine Wrath as the Sin Offering, He addressed Him as God (Vss. 1-2, 10).

The word *"roaring"* speaks of loud lamentations, which were probably His quoting of this Twenty-second Psalm.

(2) "O MY GOD, I CRY IN THE DAYTIME, BUT YOU HEAR NOT; AND IN THE NIGHT SEASON, AND AM NOT SILENT."

This Passage deals with the time factor on the Cross!

THE NIGHT SEASON

The *"night season"* was that of the three hours of darkness between 12 noon and 3 p.m. During that time, He was the *"Sin Offering"*; consequently, He was not heard. God purposely did not hear His Petitions at this particular time, because He actually could not hear Him, at least as far the act was concerned. For that three hour period, God separated Himself from the Divine Son, because He had to, that is, if man was to be redeemed.

As stated, no one will ever fully know what Christ actually suffered regarding those three hours on the Cross. Even though He was there for a total of six hours — from 9 a.m. until 3 p.m. — still it was the three hours between 12 noon and 3 p.m. when His Father hid His Face from His Only Son.

During that time, our Lord was *"not silent"*; nevertheless, He was not heard!

(3) "BUT YOU ARE HOLY, O THOU WHO INHABIT THE PRAISES OF ISRAEL."

Many Christians speak of God inhabiting the praises of His people. Basically, that is correct; however, this is the Passage from which the statement is derived.

GOD IS HOLY

Irrespective of the acute situation, and I speak of the Cross and all of its horror, and our Lord bearing the sin penalty of mankind, still, none of this abrogated the Holiness of God to the slightest degree. Still God is Holy; as well, the Sufferer casts no reproach upon Him, but *"commits Himself to Him Who judges righteously"* (I Pet. 2:23).

As previously stated, some time in eternity past, even before the foundation of the world (I Pet. 1:18-20), it was deemed necessary by the Godhead that God would become Man and would die on a Cross in order that mankind might be redeemed. The Righteousness of God must be satisfied. Even though God could speak physical healing into being for those who are sick, He could not simply speak Redemption into existence, that is, if He was to maintain His Nature and Character. While He certainly had the Power to do so, His Nature and Character would not allow such. The price must be paid to the full, and the best way it could be paid was by God becoming Man and dying on a Cross. God's Holiness would then be vindicated!

PRAISING GOD

The phrase, *"O Thou Who inhabit the praises of Israel,"* proclaims a phenomenal statement!

First of all, it speaks to the fact that despite what Israel was doing that day, i.e., crucifying her Messiah, still, she ultimately will be restored.

Second, untold tens of thousands in the past, and we speak of redeemed Israelites, have praised the Lord for the coming Redeemer, which now guarantees His Resurrection.

Every true praise to God proclaims something which ultimately will be brought to pass, even though it may take much time to do so. Faith resides in praises, while unbelief reside in murmuring and complaining.

(4) "OUR FATHERS TRUSTED IN YOU: THEY TRUSTED, AND YOU DID DELIVER THEM."

A great Truth is here presented.

TRUST

The words, *"trust"* or *"trusted,"* can be said to be the theme of the Book of Psalms. These words are used some sixty-nine times in this Book. Basically, the word *"trust"* is the same as *"faith."*

So, in all of these Songs, for the Psalms are Songs, the Holy Spirit proclaims *"trust"* as the theme and overriding principle.

The idea of this Verse is that the Lord Alone is the Only One Who can deliver. Man cannot deliver, nor anything that man devises. Jesus Himself said, *"The Spirit of the Lord is upon Me, because He has anointed Me to . . . preach deliverance to the captives."*

DELIVERANCE

He did not say *"to deliver the captives,"* but rather *"to preach deliverance to the captives."*

How is that done?

We are to tell the people that the Lord will deliver them, and that He is the Only One Who can deliver. He only demands that the person give their heart and life to Him.

We also are to tell them that the manner in which *"deliverance"* is effected, irrespective of the problem, is by and through the Means of the Cross. The Believer is to express faith in Christ and Christ exclusively, which actually refers to what He did for us at the Cross. When this is done, the Holy Spirit, Who is God, will effect Deliverance.

Unfortunately, Preachers in the modern Church are recommending everything except the Cross. And it doesn't really matter what else is recommended, no matter how good it might be in its own right, there is no Deliverance from any other source than Christ and what He did at the Cross. This is the manner in which the Holy Spirit works, and this is the only manner in which the Holy Spirit works (Rom. 1-2, 11).

In this great Twenty-second Psalm, we are studying the agony of Christ on the Cross. There He paid the price, and did so by atoning for all sin. By doing that, He removed, as previously stated, the legal right that Satan had to hold mankind in bondage. With all sin atoned, past, present, and future, at least for all who will believe (Jn. 3:16), Satan has no more legal right. So, if any person in the world is laboring under bondage of any nature, it is an unnecessary bondage. It is because the person hasn't availed himself of the great victory won by Christ at Calvary's Cross.

When a person does avail himself of that great victory, then every bondage is broken; however, the Holy Spirit demands that our faith be exclusively in the Cross.

THE SIXTH CHAPTER OF ROMANS

Whenever the Apostle Paul, under the Inspiration of the Holy Spirit, told Believers how to walk in victory, i.e., how to live a Godly life, and how to do so perpetually, he took Believers straight to the Cross.

First of all, in Verses 1 and 2, he lets us know that sin is the problem. And then in Verses 3 and 5, he tells us that the Cross is the only answer to the problem of sin. The Sixth Chapter of Romans is actually where the Apostle Paul addressed the *"Sin Nature."*

THE SIN NATURE

Whenever the believing sinner comes to Christ, at that moment the *"Sin Nature"* is made ineffective (Rom. 6:6). But not understanding Sanctification, as it regards the Cross, the Believer then puts his faith in something other than the Cross, which brings about failure, which also brings about a resurrection of the Sin Nature. The Christian finds himself being ruled in some way by the Sin Nature, and his willpower is simply not strong enough to overcome it. Sadly, almost all Christians at the present time fall into this category.

Paul addressed this also by saying, *"For to will is present with me; but how to perform that which is good I find not"* (Rom. 7:18). In other words, the great Apostle told us that willpower simply is not enough. The Believer definitely is to use his will (whosoever will!), but it is only to be used for direction. Once the right direction is achieved, which is Christ and the Cross, then the Holy Spirit takes over and brings victory to such a Believer.

WILLPOWER

Unfortunately, when most Christians go to their Pastor or a Counselor asking for help for some particular type of problem, mostly they are told, *"You've got to try harder."*

Such advice is worse than useless! It doesn't matter how hard the person tries, how much they use their willpower, they're not going to be able to overcome sin in this manner. That's why Paul said:

"I do not frustrate the Grace of God, for if Righteousness come by the Law, then Christ is dead in vain" (Gal. 2:21).

Unfortunately, the modern Church is not being taught the rudiments of the Cross, at least as it refers to Sanctification. It is being taught everything but the Cross.

Jesus said, *"You shall know the Truth, and the Truth shall make you free"* (Jn. 8:32). Unfortunately, the far greater majority of the modern Church simply do not know the *"Truth,"* so they remain in bondage!

Let us say it again: Jesus Christ is the Source, and the Cross is the Means!

(5) "THEY CRIED UNTO YOU, AND WERE DELIVERED: THEY TRUSTED IN YOU, AND WERE NOT CONFOUNDED."

If one puts one's trust totally and completely in the Lord, which refers to Christ and what He did at the Cross, we have the Promise here given to us that we will not be *"confounded."* In other words, the Lord will do exactly what He says that He will do. He will deliver the individual, irrespective as to what the problem might be!

(6) "BUT I AM A WORM, AND NO MAN; A REPROACH OF MEN, AND DESPISED OF THE PEOPLE."

How deeply Christ was *"despised of the people"* appeared most evidently when they expressed their desire that, instead of Him, a murderer should be granted to them (Acts 3:14).

The *"worm"* is a symbol of extreme weakness and helplessness — it is naturally despised, derided, and trodden upon.

THE WORM

The word *"worm"* has several meanings:

1. The Hebrew is *"tola,"* which means *"a maggot."*

2. It is used of worms in food and plants (Ex. 16:20).

3. It is used of man in his unclean, sinful state, as contrasted with God (Job 25:6; Isa. 41:14).

4. It is used of the conscious or never-dying souls of men in Hell (Isa. 14:11; 66:24; Mk. 9:44, 48).

5. It speaks of Christ, meaning that He took the lowest place among men, to be rejected, scorned, spit upon, and even humiliated in infamy and shame (I Pet. 2:24; Isa. 49:7; 52:14; 53:1-12).

(7) "ALL THEY WHO SEE ME LAUGH ME TO SCORN: THEY SHOOT OUT THE LIP, THEY SHAKE THE HEAD, SAYING."

As David spoke these words, the Holy Spirit through him was actually portraying what would be done to Christ when He was on the Cross; the words were spoken approximately one thousand years before it actually happened.

This was done by His Own people while He hung on the Cross in bitter suffering. They had no kind word for Him. They only laughed and mocked Him (Mat. 27:39-43).

THE HARDENED HEART

When one hears the Gospel, it does one of two things:

1. It softens the heart, with the person accepting Christ; or,

2. If rejected, the heart is hardened, exactly as were the hearts of the religious leaders of Israel who crucified Christ. There is nothing in the world more damnable than religion.

(Religion is that which is devised by man for the purpose of reaching God or bettering himself in some way.)

Inasmuch as it is impossible for fallen

man to devise anything that God can accept, religion only tends to produce self-righteousness.

If the Believer's faith is not exclusively in Christ and the Cross, ultimately self-righteousness will be the result; that being the case, the heart also will ultimately harden. It cannot be otherwise!

(8) "HE TRUSTED ON THE LORD THAT HE WOULD DELIVER HIM: LET HIM DELIVER HIM, SEEING HE DELIGHTED IN HIM."

Actually, these very words were used by the mockers among the religious leaders of Israel (Mat. 27:43).

JESUS CHRIST AND THE CROSS

Had God delivered Christ at the time He was hanging on the Cross, such a deliverance would have abrogated the very Plan of Redemption. He had to go to the Cross, He had to drink the dregs down to the bitter end, that is, if man was to be saved.

Again, let me repeat:

"When one looks at the horror of the Cross, one must say, 'Sin did this!'"

(9) "BUT YOU ARE HE WHO TOOK ME OUT OF THE WOMB: YOU DID MAKE ME HOPE WHEN I WAS UPON MY MOTHER'S BREASTS."

These two Verses (9-10) show the relationship between the Father and the Son, even from the womb of the Virgin Mary. And yet, this relationship, which had never been broken, would now be broken, at least for a short time, because Jesus was bearing the sin penalty of the world.

(10) "I WAS CAST UPON YOU FROM THE WOMB: YOU ARE MY GOD FROM MY MOTHER'S BELLY."

Jesus praying this way may seem to be strange to some people, considering Who He was, and is; however, it must be remembered that He faced all of this as a *"Man."* While He never ceased to be Deity, He never used those powers; He had, in fact, no expression of Deity, so He suffered it all as a Man. As a Man, He cried to God, His Father.

(11) "BE NOT FAR FROM ME; FOR TROUBLE IS NEAR; FOR THERE IS NONE TO HELP."

NOTES

At this time, the time of the Cross, there was not a single solitary soul to help Christ. All His Disciples forsook Him and fled (Mat. 26:56) — He was truly One Who *"had no helper."*

It was God Alone on Whom He could call. In His calling upon God, He did not ask to be delivered from the pain and suffering of the Cross, even the terrible horror of having to be the Bearer of the penalty of sin — which penalty was death. And yet, during this time, from 12 noon to 3 p.m., darkness covered that part of the world; during that time, the Father could have absolutely nothing to do with Christ, which presented a loneliness unparalleled!

To be sure, after the sin penalty was paid through death, the Father most definitely would deliver Him from the death world. Of that, there was never any doubt. But while He was on the Cross, there was no help, even as there could be no help!

(12) "MANY BULLS HAVE COMPASSED ME: STRONG BULLS OF BASHAN HAVE BESET ME ROUND."

Bashan was a district east of Jordan, where cattle were raised. The strongest bulls of Israel came from Bashan.

Jesus used these *"bulls"* as a symbol of the religious rulers of Israel, who were controlled by demon spirits. They determined to destroy Christ (Mat. 27:1-66; Acts 2:36).

RELIGIOUS LEADERS

The greatest hindrance, the greatest bane, to the Work of God on Earth is *"religious leaders."* I also think it not wrong to say that all religious leaders are more or less controlled by demon spirits.

By that, I do not mean that all who serve in capacities of leadership in Denominations fall into this category. They don't! I am personally acquainted with some who are Godly, who provide a tremendous service for the Work of God. But they are not religious leaders, but rather laborers in the Vineyard of the Lord.

Using religious Denominations as an example, however, if such a Denomination begins to stray from the Word of God, unless Revival eventually comes, such a Denomination ultimately will find itself controlled by demon spirits. These spirits work through the leaders. Religion provides the greatest harbor for demon spirits.

Demon spirits control Islam in totality. They control Buddhism, Hinduism, Shintoism, Mormonism, Catholicism, and much of that which goes under the guise of Christianity.

Paul said:

"The Spirit speaks expressly, that in the latter times some shall depart from the Faith, giving heed to seducing spirits, and doctrines of demons" (I Tim. 4:1).

Every Believer should know his or her Bible well enough, and should walk close to the Lord, in order that they know what they are supporting. To support that which actually is controlled by demon spirits, which regrettably is the state of much of the modern Church, is a travesty indeed!

(13) "THEY GAPED UPON ME WITH THEIR MOUTHS, AS A RAVENING AND A ROARING LION."

The religious leaders of Israel were so cruel, so ungodly, and so venomous that even while Jesus was dying on the Cross, they were making fun of Him and demeaning Him, which could be said to have been the most wicked hour in history (Mat. 27:39-43).

Even after this, the Lord continued to deal with these wicked individuals, giving them still an opportunity to repent. But they would not! (Acts 22:1-23:14).

No wonder the Lord, in A.D. 70, allowed Titus the Roman General to completely annihilate Judaea and Jerusalem. Over one million Jews were slaughtered and approximately another one million were sold into slavery all over the world.

(14) "I AM POURED OUT LIKE WATER, AND ALL MY BONES ARE OUT OF JOINT: MY HEART IS LIKE WAX; IT IS MELTED IN THE MIDST OF MY BOWELS."

Verses 14 through 18 proclaim the physical sufferings of the Saviour.

CRUCIFIXION

Crucifixion was one of the most horrifying forms of death ever devised by evil men. When Jesus was crucified, Rome ruled. No Roman citizen was ever crucified. This horrible death was reserved for slaves and for nations which had been conquered by Rome. Crucifixion causes death by literally pulling the bones out of their sockets, i.e., *"out of joint."*

The following is what the Holy Spirit says that Crucifixion was like:

1. *"Poured out like water"* (Vs. 14).
2. *"Bones out of joint"* (Vs. 14).
3. *"Heart like wax"* (Vs. 14).
4. *"Lose control of bowels"* (Vs. 14).
5. *"Strength is dried up"* (Vs. 15).
6. *"Tongue cleaving to the jaws"* (Vs. 15).
7. *"The piercing of the hands and the feet"* (Vs. 16).

(15) "MY STRENGTH IS DRIED UP LIKE A POTSHERD; AND MY TONGUE CLEAVES TO MY JAWS; AND YOU HAVE BROUGHT ME INTO THE DUST OF DEATH."

This Passage proclaims the extreme and agonizing thirst which sets in. The secretions generally fail and the saliva especially is suppressed, so that the mouth is parched and dry. Hence, the cry of suffering which was at last wrung from our Lord when, just before the end, He exclaimed, *"I thirst"* (Jn. 19:28).

THE DUST OF DEATH

The *"dust of death,"* which carried one to the edge of death, is as far as Jesus could be brought, as it regards the Grim Reaper. He did not die from the torture of His Body. In fact, He could not have died by that calamity alone.

He Himself had said, *"Therefore does My Father love Me, because I lay down My Life, that I might take it again.*

"No man takes it from Me, but I lay it down of Myself. I have power to lay it down, and I have power to take it again. This Commandment have I received of My Father" (Jn. 10:17-18).

So, no man took Jesus' Life from Him. He laid it down freely, and did so as a Sacrifice. He did not die until the Holy Spirit told Him to die (Heb. 9:14).

Jesus was not born in original sin as are all other human beings. Joseph was not His father, and Mary really only provided a *"house"* for Him for the nine month gestation period. He was conceived by the Holy Spirit (Mat. 1:18). This simply means that the Holy Spirit decreed the pregnancy, and it instantly happened. It was the same as the Lord saying, *"Let there be light, and there was light"* (Gen. 1:3).

So, *"the dust of death"* was the nearest that Jesus could be brought to that dark void. Having not been born in sin, and having never sinned, He was not subject to death. So, in order to die, He had to purposely lay down His Life, which He did!

(16) "FOR DOGS HAVE COMPASSED ME: THE ASSEMBLY OF THE WICKED HAVE ENCLOSED ME: THEY PIERCED MY HANDS AND MY FEET."

We have here a description of those who crucified Christ!

DOGS

The phrase, *"For dogs have compassed Me,"* refers to the Gentiles who actually carried out the Crucifixion.

The *"assembly of the wicked"* refers to the Scribes, Priests, and the Pharisees.

Approximately a thousand years before Christ, it was predicted that His *"hands and feet"* would be pierced. And so they were!

(17) "I MAY TELL ALL MY BONES: THEY LOOK AND STARE UPON ME."

The idea of this Verse pertains to the heaving of Christ in gasping for breath, which placed such a strain upon His physical Body that every bone hurt. He was, in a sense, suffocating and His bones were not getting enough oxygen.

(18) "THEY PART MY GARMENTS AMONG THEM, AND CAST LOTS UPON MY VESTURE."

Again, some one thousand years before the time, it is here predicted that some would gamble for His garments. Two Evangelists (Mat. 27:35; Jn. 19:24) note the fulfillment of the Prophecy in the conduct of the soldiers at the Crucifixion of Christ. The circumstances were reserved for the final touch in the picture, since it marked that all was over; the victim was on the point of expiring; He would never need His clothes again.

(19) "BUT BE NOT THOU FAR FROM ME, O LORD: O MY STRENGTH, HASTE THEE TO HELP ME."

The idea of the phrase, *"But be not Thou far from Me, O LORD,"* proclaims the fact that God has had to forsake Him, at least to a certain degree, while He did bear the sin penalty of humanity. In essence, our Lord says that He knows this must be, but He requests that the Father not be too far away. This prayer was, no doubt, answered.

The phrase, *"O My Strength, haste Thee to help Me,"* requests that, at the moment the work is finished, which would be at the moment of death, the Lord would come speedily to Him, which He definitely did!

(20) "DELIVER MY SOUL FROM THE SWORD; MY DARLING FROM THE POWER OF THE DOG."

The phrase, *"Deliver My soul from the sword,"* represents Rome's authority as executioner. This prayer also was answered in that the Cross really did not kill Christ. As we have already stated, He laid down His Life freely!

ONLY BEGOTTEN SON

The phrase, *"My darling from the power of the dog,"* is somewhat as the previous phrase. The Romans were Gentile dogs.

The word *"darling"* is a term of affection, which means *"My Only One."* The Father addressed Jesus as *"His Only Begotten Son."* Jesus is saying to the Father, *"I am the Only One You have!"* The term could not be used of anyone else. The Hebrew word occurs eleven times and generally means an only son (Gen. 22:2, 16; Prov. 4:3; Jer. 6:26; Amos 8:10; Zech. 12:10; Ps. 25:16; 35:17; 48:6; Judg. 11:34; and Ps. 22:20).

(21) "SAVE ME FROM THE LION'S MOUTH: FOR YOU HAVE HEARD ME FROM THE HORNS OF THE UNICORNS."

The lion's mouth and the horns of the wild ox are figures of death and of him who has the power of death, namely, Satan (Heb. 2:14).

Jesus was asking the Father that death would not conquer Him when He went into the death world. To be certain, that prayer most definitely was answered!

(22) "I WILL DECLARE YOUR NAME UNTO MY BRETHREN: IN THE MIDST OF THE CONGREGATION WILL I PRAISE YOU."

After the Holy Spirit through David gave us the horror of the Crucifixion, now Verses 22 through 31 give us the Exaltation and Glory of the Messiah.

This Verse speaks to us of the Church, which, of course, was not in existence during David's day. It also speaks to us of the Restoration of Israel, which will take place at the beginning of the Kingdom Age, immediately after the Second Coming. Then the Name of the Lord will be *"declared"* and constantly will be *"praised."*

(23) "YOU WHO FEAR THE LORD, PRAISE HIM; ALL YOU THE SEED OF JACOB, GLORIFY HIM; AND FEAR HIM, ALL YOU THE SEED OF ISRAEL."

Three things are here said:

FEAR THE LORD

What does it mean to *"fear the LORD"*?

Jesus answered that by saying, *"And fear not them who kill the body, but are not able to kill the soul* (don't fear men): *but rather fear Him* (God) *Who is able to destroy both soul and body in Hell"* (Mat. 10:28).

All too often many register fear of man, but no fear at all of God.

The more a Believer truly knows and understands the Lord, at least as far as a poor human can understand Him, the more one will fear the Lord. It doesn't speak of a slavish fear, but rather an understanding that God can do anything, that He means what He says, and that He says what He means!

PRAISE THE LORD

The Praise of God is to be joined with the fear of God, according to the universal teaching of Scripture. If there is no proper fear, there will not be proper praise. And truly, proper praise of the Lord cannot be properly enjoined until the person is Baptized with the Holy Spirit, for the Holy Spirit is the Instigator and the True Helper of Praise on behalf of the Saint.

In regards to this, Jesus said, and I quote from THE EXPOSITOR'S STUDY BIBLE:

"But the hour comes, and now is, when the true worshippers shall worship the Father in spirit and in truth (God is not looking for Holy Worship; He is looking for Holy Worshippers; as stated, Calvary would make possible an entirely different type of worship, which did not require ceremonies or rituals, etc.): *for the Father seeks such to worship Him* (means that by the word *'seeks'* such are not easily found).

"God is a Spirit (simply means that *'God is a Spirit-Being'*): *and they who worship Him must worship Him in spirit and in truth.* (Man worships the Lord through and by his personal spirit, which is moved upon by the Holy Spirit; otherwise, it is not worship which God will accept)" (Jn. 4:23-24).

Again, concerning the Holy Spirit and praise, Jesus also said, *"He* (the Holy Spirit) *shall glorify Me* (will portray Christ and what Christ did at the Cross for dying humanity) . . ." (Jn. 16:14).

GLORIFY HIM

The phrase, *"Glorify Him; and fear Him, all you the seed of Israel,"* looks forward to the coming day when all in Israel, with no exceptions, will glorify the Lord.

To *"glorify"* the Lord means to extol His greatness as our Creator and our Saviour. When Israel properly praises Him, which they most definitely do, which, as stated, will begin at the coming Kingdom Age, then the entirety of the world will follow suit.

(24) "FOR HE HAS NOT DESPISED NOR ABHORRED THE AFFLICTION OF THE AFFLICTED; NEITHER HAS HE HID HIS FACE FROM HIM; BUT WHEN HE CRIED UNTO HIM, HE HEARD."

Two meanings come from this Verse.

THE MESSIAH

First of all, this Passage declares that the Father, even though it seemed not to be so, did, in fact, hear every cry. There was no real turning away, no real forsaking Him, as it seemed! Every cry was heard, and the cries were answered at the fitting moment.

Every pain was marked and every suffering sympathized with. And the reward given by the Father and received by Christ was proportionate. The Prophet Isaiah said, *"Therefore will I divide Him a portion with the great, and He shall divide the spoil with the strong; because He has poured out His soul unto death: and He was numbered with the transgressors; and He bore the sin of many, and made intercession for the transgressors"* (Isa. 53:12).

Paul wrote, *"He became obedient unto death, even the death of the Cross; wherefore*

God also has highly exalted Him, and given Him a Name which is above every name: that at the Name of Jesus every knee should bow, of things in Heaven, and things in Earth, and things under the Earth; and that every tongue should confess that Jesus Christ is Lord, to the Glory of God the Father" (Phil. 2:8-11).

ISRAEL

The double meaning includes Israel. While Christ was the True Israel, still, national Israel is here addressed, as well.

As the Father did not *"despise"* or *"abhor"* what His Son had to go through in order that man might be redeemed, the Son also will not *"despise"* or *"abhor"* Israel, despite their affliction being caused by their terrible sin.

He will not hide His Face from them when they call, which they will do in the Battle of Armageddon, when it looks like all is lost. He most definitely will hear and will most definitely come to their rescue.

(25) "MY PRAISE SHALL BE OF YOU IN THE GREAT CONGREGATION: I WILL PAY MY VOWS BEFORE THEM WHO FEAR HIM."

The phraseology is that of the Mosaic Dispensation, with which alone David was acquainted; however, that *"great congregation"* now includes every nation in the world in which there are some who are praising the Lord.

Our Ministry goes all over the world by means of the Internet, and I speak of both Radio and Television. Every month we receive e-mails from virtually every nation on the face of the Earth, even those which are tightly controlled by Islam. As stated, the *"congregation"* is *"great."*

The word *"vows"* as used in this Verse could have been better translated, in the strict sense, by the word *"devotions,"* for the Hebrew word used here leans more toward the latter than the former.

(26) "THE MEEK SHALL EAT AND BE SATISFIED: THEY SHALL PRAISE THE LORD WHO SEEK HIM: YOUR HEART SHALL LIVE FOREVER."

Three things are said in this Verse.

THE MEEK

The word *"meek"* speaks of those who are broken in spirit. It refers to those who know that they are bankrupt morally, and that if any righteousness is afforded them, it will have to be strictly by the Grace of God. Truthfully, the entirety of the human race, and for all time, falls into that category, but sadly only a few seem to understand that.

The word *"eat"* carries the idea of partaking of Christ in His Atoning, Mediatorial, and Intercessory Work, all made possible by the Cross. This is what Jesus was talking about when He said, *"Except you eat the flesh of the Son of Man, and drink His Blood, you have no life in you"* (Jn. 6:53).

The Master wasn't speaking of literally eating His flesh and literally drinking His Blood, but rather that when one believes on Him, as it regards the Cross, this statement is fulfilled. His words point strictly to the Cross, where He would give His Life in the pouring out of His Blood. We are to so identify with His Sacrifice that, in the Mind of God, our Faith actually places us in Christ when He died, in Him when He was buried, and in Him when He was raised from the dead. In essence, we were baptized into His Death, buried with Him by Baptism into Death, and raised with Him in newness of life (Rom. 6:3-5).

That constitutes *"eating of Him"*; and, to be sure, when this is done, the soul will be *"satisfied."* Actually, the soul will be *"satisfied"* only when this is done!

PRAISING THE LORD

The phrase, *"They shall praise the Lord Who seek Him,"* says that if we properly seek the Lord, we definitely will praise Him, and do so repeatedly. The Scripture tells us that when we begin to pray, we should first of all *"enter into His gates with thanksgiving, and into His courts with praise: be thankful unto Him, and bless His Name"* (Ps. 100:4).

We have so much for which to praise the Lord, so much for which to thank Him, so much for which to lift Him up, for He, and He Alone, is the Source of all Blessings.

Let us say it again:

Christ is the Source, and the Cross is the Means!

ETERNAL LIFE

The phrase, *"Your heart shall live forever,"* speaks of eternal life.

The word *"heart"* is used in the Bible as a metaphor, so to speak, of the innermost being of the individual. It is not speaking of the physical organ.

One might say, and not be far wrong, that the heart represents the spirit and the soul of man.

(27) "ALL THE ENDS OF THE WORLD SHALL REMEMBER AND TURN UNTO THE LORD: AND ALL THE KINDREDS OF THE NATIONS SHALL WORSHIP BEFORE YOU."

This Verse presents a sweeping panorama.

ALL THE KINDREDS OF THE NATIONS

Those who believe upon this Atoning Saviour shall be regarded as a new race — a generation — of which Messiah will be the Head (I Cor. 15:22; Isa. 53:10-11). They shall continually serve Him, they shall keep coming, and they shall keep declaring unto nations yet to be born that God's Righteous One accomplished this annihilation of sin by the oblation of Himself as the Sin Offering.

The fulfillment of this Passage will commence at the beginning of the Kingdom Age; it will continue forever.

(28) "FOR THE KINGDOM IS THE LORD'S: AND HE IS THE GOVERNOR AMONG THE NATIONS."

Two things are here said.

THE KINGDOM

The phrase, *"For the Kingdom is the LORD's,"* speaks volumes. This means that Satan, over whatever it is that he seeks to rule, is an impostor, a charlatan, an intruder, if you will. The Evil One has contested Christ mightily for this Kingdom, but, despite Satanic rule in this world, the Kingdom belongs to the Lord.

It also has a second meaning.

Whatever the conflict between good and evil, between Christ and Satan, has been, and whatever it is presently, the end result, and without fail, is going to be supremacy for Christ and total defeat for Satan. The Bible tells us so (Rev., Chpt. 20).

THE GOVERNOR

The phrase, *"And He is the Governor among the nations,"* refers to the fact that Christ will be the Governor, not of only one nation, but of the entirety of the world. As stated, this will commence immediately after the Second Coming, which within itself will be the most cataclysmic happening the world has ever known. Immediately after that Coming, the Second Advent, the Lord will declare supremacy over all the Earth.

To start things out right, the Scripture says, *"And he* (the Angel under the authority of Christ) *laid hold on the dragon, that old serpent, which is the Devil, and Satan, and bound him a thousand years, and cast him into the bottomless pit, and shut him up, and set a seal upon him, that he should deceive the nations no more"* (Rev. 20:2-3).

In that coming Glad Day, there will be one President over the entirety of the Earth, and He will be the Lord Jesus Christ. The *"Government will be upon His Shoulder"* (Isa. 9:6), which means that He will Personally formulate a new constitution for the entirety of the world, which will be the Word of God.

In preaching city-wide Crusades back in the 1970's and 1980's, oftentimes I would hold up the Bible and say, *"This is the Constitution of the United States of America."* That comment never failed to incense the Media! While the Bible most definitely is the foundation of all the Blessings that this nation has received, which has been more than any country that ever has been, the Bible is respected in its totality only by a few! That all will change in the coming Kingdom Age.

(29) "ALL THEY WHO BE FAT UPON EARTH SHALL EAT AND WORSHIP: ALL THEY WHO GO DOWN TO THE DUST SHALL BOW BEFORE HIM: AND NONE CAN KEEP ALIVE HIS OWN SOUL."

Three things are said in this Passage.

FAT AND PROSPEROUS

The phrase, *"All they who be fat upon Earth shall eat and worship,"* states that the key to spiritual and financial prosperity is to fully partake of Christ, which is symbolized by the word *"eat,"* and then to fully and completely *"worship"* Him.

To be frank, one does not have to wait until the coming Kingdom Age for this to be realized. It is available here and now.

Once again, the word *"eat"* goes back to the Sixth Chapter of the Gospel according to St. John (Vss. 47-63). Pure and plain, it speaks of the Cross, meaning if the Cross is properly understood, and if our faith is properly placed therein, then one can be *"fat."*

THE CROSS, THE SECRET OF ALL PROSPERITY

When we speak of *"prosperity,"* we are speaking of such in every capacity. John the Beloved said, *"Beloved, I wish above all things that you may prosper and be in health, even as your soul prospers"* (III Jn. 2).

To which we alluded some pages back, when Jesus gave forth this amazing Message, which was probably given in Capernaum, it was the most graphic Message the people had ever heard. He plainly said, *"Verily, verily, I say unto you, Except you eat the flesh of the Son of Man, and drink His Blood, you have no life in you."*

He then continued, *"He who eats My flesh, and drinks My Blood, dwells in Me, and I in him"* (Jn. 6:53, 56).

He didn't really bother to explain Himself except by saying, *"It is the Spirit that quickens; the flesh profits nothing: the words that I speak unto you, they are spirit, and they are Life"* (Jn. 6:63).

In actuality, He was speaking of the Cross and the price He would there pay by the giving of His Perfect Life and Perfect Body as a Sacrifice, which would atone for all sin, and, thereby, satisfy the demands of a thrice-Holy God.

The reason that He phrased His statements as He did was to proclaim the import of the Message.

One must understand that the Cross of Christ is the Means by which the Lord gives us all things. It is the Cross that made it all possible, whatever it is.

That means that we have to understand that fully, believe that fully, and hold to that fully.

Is that what is happening in the modern Church?

NOTES

THE CROSS AND UNBELIEF

We teach that the Cross of Christ is the foundation of all Biblical Doctrine. It was formulated in the Mind of the Godhead, even before the foundation of the world (I Pet. 1:18-20). That being the case, every doctrine must be built upon that foundation, or else it is spurious in some way. That's where all false doctrine originates, and I speak of an improper understanding of the Cross.

Second, one must understand that the answer to all sin is the Cross of Christ, and the Cross of Christ alone! This rules out humanistic psychology, and it rules out anything and everything else proposed by man. It is the Cross, and the Cross alone!

Some people complain about my teaching, claiming that we hold up the Cross of Christ as the answer to everything. When they say that, my retort is quick.

"Now you're beginning to get the Message. You are exactly right. The Cross of Christ is the answer to everything. It is the solution. It is, in fact, the only solution."

Unless one believes that, one is not eating the Flesh of Christ and drinking His Blood!

JESUS CHRIST, KING OF KINGS

The phrase, *"All they who go down to the dust shall bow before Him,"* refers to the fact that *"at the Name of Jesus, every knee shall bow, of things in Heaven, and things in Earth, and things under the Earth"* (Phil. 2:10).

ETERNAL LIFE

The phrase, *"And none can keep alive his own soul,"* refers to the fact that Eternal Life is Christ's Gift, and, we might quickly add, a Gift all made possible by the Cross.

In answer to this, Jesus said, *"This is that Bread which came down from Heaven: not as your fathers did eat Manna, and are dead: he who eats of this Bread shall live forever"* (Jn. 6:58). The *"Bread"* is Christ. The way the metaphor is used, it speaks of what He did at the Cross.

(30) "A SEED SHALL SERVE HIM; IT SHALL BE ACCOUNTED TO THE LORD FOR A GENERATION."

Beginning with the Kingdom Age, *"A*

seed shall serve Him," meaning that all children will then be raised to serve the Lord. As well, generation after generation shall continue in that capacity!

(31) "THEY SHALL COME, AND SHALL DECLARE HIS RIGHTEOUSNESS UNTO A PEOPLE WHO SHALL BE BORN, THAT HE HAS DONE THIS."

This speaks of the natural people which will be born and will live in the coming Kingdom Age. When the little children are old enough to think for themselves, they will be taught the Word and the Ways of the Lord.

The phrase, *"That He has done this,"* refers to what Jesus did at the Cross, which will be held up forever and forever for all the world to see!

PSALM 23

*A Psalm of David:
The Shepherd Psalm*

(1) "THE LORD IS MY SHEPHERD; I SHALL NOT WANT."

As it regards a song, this Psalm may very well represent the greatest height of Inspiration that ever rested upon a frail mortal. It was written by David.

It was written from the perspective of the sheep rather than the Shepherd, but yet it greatly extols the Shepherd!

MY SHEPHERD

The great theme is not so much what Jehovah gives or does, but What and Who He is. The admonishment to the Child of God is that the Lord may be our Shepherd and that we may follow Him; however, in its fuller application, it pertains to Christ when He was walking through the dark valley of His earthly life and was looking to Jehovah as His Shepherd.

PROVISION

The short phrase, *"I shall not want,"* proclaims that the pronoun *"my"* refers to the sheep.

Sheep are not too very bright. About all they can do with any degree of success is to *"follow."* In selecting His Disciples, Jesus simply said to them, *"Follow Me."* He was desiring to be their Shepherd. It is simple to follow, and yet it proves to be so very difficult for mankind. To follow Christ will cost one everything. The world, even the religious world, demands that the sheep follow their voice instead of His voice. But Jesus said, *"And the sheep follow Him: for they know His voice"* (Jn. 10:4).

Actually, the greater temptation will always be the lure of another voice. The other voice will always be very religious in the sounding of its siren call; however, to follow that voice will mean death (spiritual death). To follow the voice of the True Shepherd always means life.

The words, *"I shall not want,"* definitely do apply to material things, but apply much more to spiritual things. The Church too often settles for what God can do rather than for Who God is. Truly, He does provide, but more truly *"He is."*

EIGHT TITLES FOR JEHOVAH IN THIS SONG

1. The Hebrew meaning for the title *"Lord"* in Verse 1 is *"Jehovah-Ro'i."* It means *"The LORD is my Shepherd."*

2. The title *"Lord"* also means *"Jehovah-Jireh,"* which means *"The LORD will provide"* (Gen. 22:14).

3. The pronoun *"He"* in Verse 2 actually says, *"Jehovah-Shalom."* It means *"The LORD our Peace"* (Judg. 6:24).

4. The first *"He"* in Verse 3 is *"Jehovah-Ropha,"* which means *"The LORD our Healer"* (Ex. 15:26).

5. The second *"He"* in Verse 3 is *"Jehovah-Tsidkenu,"* which means *"The LORD our Righteousness"* (Jer. 23:6).

6. The pronouns, *"You"* and *"Your,"* in Verse 4 present the Lord as *"Jehovah-Shammah,"* which means *"The LORD is there"* (Ezek. 48:35).

7. The pronoun *"You"* in the first part of Verse 5 is *"Jehovah-Nissi,"* which means *"The LORD my Banner"* (Ex. 17:15).

8. The last pronoun *"You"* in Verse 5 is *"Jehovah-Mekaddischem,"* which means *"The LORD our Sanctifier"* (Ex. 31:13).

RESURRECTION

The number *"eight"* refers to Resurrection,

and constitutes the number of names given to Jehovah in this Psalm. In effect, they are the eight names of Christ, because He Alone as a Man experienced Death and Resurrection, and did it all on our behalf.

The Apostle Paul said, *"But now is Christ risen from the dead, and become the Firstfruits of them who slept"* (I Cor. 15:20).

This is the idea: Because He lives, we shall live also!

In these titles given to Christ in this Psalm, we find the solution for every problem, the answer to every question, the fulfillment of every need. Christ is all of these things to us, and they all are made possible by the Cross.

(2) "HE MAKES ME TO LIE DOWN IN GREEN PASTURES: HE LEADS ME BESIDE THE STILL WATERS."

Following any other voice will lead only to barren pastures. The Lord Alone can lead to *"green pastures."*

GREEN PASTURES

The phrase, *"He makes me to lie down in green pastures,"* proclaims a bountiful supply.

The Twenty-third Psalm makes it abundantly clear that the Church is not the Saviour, neither is Denominational hierarchy the Saviour, neither are rules and regulations the Saviour. Only the Lord is. The majority of that which calls itself *"the Church"* little follows this Shepherd, but rather follows the siren call of religious Denominations, religious hierarchy, or religious activity; consequently, the *"Lord"* is not their Shepherd. Anything that Jesus does not lead is spurious, specious, destructive, and eventually brings death.

The Great Shepherd gives His sheep a conscious Salvation. Each one can say, *"He is mine"* — not, *"I hope He is mine!"* The leading that He does is always to the Word of God. The Bible, being the only Revealed Body of Truth that has ever been given to mankind, is the only *"green pastures"* and *"still waters"* that one will ever need.

Those *"green pastures"* and *"still pastures"* have never been exhausted. They cannot, in fact, ever be exhausted. The Bible holds the answer to every problem of life that may present itself. Sadly, the modern Church seldom grazes in its *"green pastures"* nor drinks from its *"still waters."*

THE STILL WATERS

The phrase, *"He leads me beside the still waters,"* actually means *"waters of refreshment."* Even though it may be a desert, the *"waters"* which here are addressed are always cool waters. These are waters which are sparkling clear and sparkling clean.

Jesus said, and I quote from THE EXPOSITOR'S STUDY BIBLE:

"Whosoever drinks of this water shall thirst again (presents one of the most simple, common, and yet, at the same time, most profound statements ever uttered; the things of the world can never satisfy the human heart and life, irrespective as to how much is acquired):

"But whosoever drinks of the water that I shall give him shall never thirst ('whosoever' means exactly what it says! Christ accepted is spiritual thirst forever slaked!); *but the water that I shall give him shall be in him a well of water springing up into Everlasting Life.* (Everything that the world or religion gives pertains to the external; but this which Jesus gives deals with the very core of one's being, and is a perennial fountain)" (Jn. 4:13-14).

The *"green pastures"* and the *"still waters"* are used as metaphors.

(3) "HE RESTORES MY SOUL: HE LEADS ME IN THE PATHS OF RIGHTEOUSNESS FOR HIS NAMES' SAKE."

Two things are said in this Passage!

RESTORATION

The phrase, *"He restores my soul,"* refers to the soul being revived and reinvigorated. At times, all of us get weary and even exhausted. This journey of life has its pitfalls, its difficulties, and its problems. To be frank, these will not be totally alleviated until the Second Coming.

True Restoration can only come about in one manner.

It is the Holy Spirit Alone Who can bring about that which we need as Believers. He knows our needs! Not only that, He knows the solution for stress, problems, difficulties, etc. All too often, we attempt to treat the symptoms, which is all that the world can do — and not even very well, at that! The Holy Spirit goes to the seat of the problem, whatever it is.

The Believer generally doesn't even know or understand what he personally needs. That's the reason we treat symptoms, which never really solves the problem.

THE MANNER IN WHICH THE HOLY SPIRIT WORKS

We should settle it in our minds that it is the Holy Spirit Alone Who can revive and reinvigorate. Humanistic psychology cannot do it and neither can religious activity. The Holy Spirit works entirely within the framework of the Cross of Christ. It is the Cross which gives the Holy Spirit the legal means to do all that He does within our hearts and lives. It is so legal, in fact, that it is referred to as a *"Law,"* i.e., *"The Law of the Spirit of Life in Christ Jesus"* (Rom. 8:2).

The Holy Spirit doesn't require much of us, but He does require that we place our faith extensively, exclusively, and absolutely in Christ and the Cross, and in nothing else. The Believer must understand that the Cross of Christ is the answer not only for sin, but also the answer for every other problem of life. At the Cross, Jesus paid it all, addressed it all, and did it so well that He wrote *"Finished!"* on His Great Work (Rom. 6:1-14; 8:1-2, 11; I Cor. 1:17-18, 23; 2:2; Gal. 6:14).

Whenever one's faith is properly placed, and we continue to speak of the Cross of Christ, the Holy Spirit will then revive and reinvigorate, and will do so constantly.

THE PATHS OF RIGHTEOUSNESS

The phrase, *"He leads me in the paths of righteousness for His Name's sake,"* also means *"paths of pleasantness and peace"* (Prov. 3:17).

Irrespective of our occupations, providing they are Scriptural, He provides for us *"the paths of righteousness."* He Alone knows these *"paths."* He does it *"for His Name's sake."* In other words, God blesses us for *"Jesus' sake,"* because He is the One Who has paid the price for the things we need.

NOTES

A JEWISH ILLUSTRATION

There is an interesting observation which would be very familiar to the shepherd of old.

At times, a lamb will meander away from the appointed path. Invariably, he becomes tangled in the briars of the rocky byway. Being unable to extricate himself, he begins to *"bleat."* Very soon the shepherd comes and retrieves the lamb from the midst of the thorns, briars, and rocky defiles.

If the little lamb remains there, he will be devoured by a wolf or other wild animal. Too often, the same lamb again leaves the appointed path and finds himself in an area that will lock him in. Every time when he cries out, the shepherd comes and retrieves the little one with his shepherd's *"staff."*

If the lamb refuses to stay on the appointed *"path,"* the final alternative is the following:

CHASTISEMENT

The lamb again leaves the appointed path, and, as usual, finds himself in difficult straits. As before, he begins to cry out for the shepherd to come; however, at this stage, the shepherd must teach the little lamb a lesson.

So, the good shepherd does not come immediately when the little lamb begins to call. Finally, the little voice grows hoarse from *"bleating,"* and it is forced to stop crying out altogether. At long last, the shepherd does finally come. As before, the shepherd extricates the wayward lamb, but now he does something different.

The shepherd takes the same *"staff"* by which he reached down into the rocky crevice and retrieved the wayward one. He pulls out one of the lamb's forelegs and cracks it sharply with the *"staff,"* which instantly breaks the leg. Then the shepherd carefully *"sets"* the leg, and lays the lamb on his shoulder, close to his heart. He carries it until the wound is healed.

Then when he puts the lamb back down on the *"paths of righteousness,"* it no longer desires to go astray. This is called *"chastising the one He loves"* (Heb. 12:6).

In the Third Verse, the pronoun *"He"* in

the Hebrew means *"Jehovah-Ropha"* (Ex. 15:26), which, as stated, means *"The LORD our Healer."*

(4) "YEA, THOUGH I WALK THROUGH THE VALLEY OF THE SHADOW OF DEATH, I WILL FEAR NO EVIL: FOR YOU ARE WITH ME; YOUR ROD AND YOUR STAFF THEY COMFORT ME."

Two things also are said in this Verse.

THE SHADOW OF DEATH

The phrase, *"Yea, though I walk through the valley of the shadow of death, I will fear no evil,"* refers to the *"powers of darkness."* Powerful attacks by Satan can become very threatening; however, the lamb says, *"I will fear no evil."*

Why?

The Good Shepherd has promised to remain with us, irrespective of what Satan may do. Others may jump ship; He never will. The credit of His Name as a *"Shepherd"* is tarnished if He leads the sheep in any wrong paths, or if He loses even one of them.

In this Verse, the words, *"You"* and *"Your,"* in the Hebrew mean *"Jehovah-Tsidkenu"* (Jer. 23:6), which means *"The LORD our Righteousness."* So, His Name is *"Righteousness."*

THE ROD AND THE STAFF

If He has used His *"staff"* (crook) to retrieve us when we were in serious danger, likewise, He will use both His *"rod"* (club) and *"staff"* to help us at this dangerous time. With his *"club,"* He will beat back the demon powers of darkness. With His *"crook,"* He will snatch us back from danger.

Hallelujah!

The ideal position for the *"lamb"* is to allow the shepherd to fight for him. The only fight that we are told to fight is *"the good fight of Faith"* (I Tim. 6:12).

What a comfort it is to know that the *"rod"* and *"staff"* constantly are beating back the powers of darkness on our behalf!

For this to be ever accomplished, all we have to do is understand that it is made possible by Christ and what He has done for us at the Cross. Consequently, our faith must be placed in Christ and the Cross, and it must ever be allowed to remain there.

(5) "YOU PREPARE A TABLE BEFORE ME IN THE PRESENCE OF MY ENEMIES: YOU ANOINT MY HEAD WITH OIL; MY CUP RUNS OVER."

Three things are said in this Verse.

THE PREPARATION OF THE TABLE

The phrase, *"You prepare a table before me in the presence of my enemies,"* tells us that we will have enemies, but that, in the very midst of the presence of these enemies, He will *"prepare a table for us."*

What anger must grip these *"enemies"* when they see their attacks not only thwarted, but to see the great Blessings of God given to the very lambs they desired to destroy!

If Believers fully trust the Lord, which means they place their faith entirely in Christ and the Cross, which means they stand on the Promises of God, i.e., *"the Word,"* such are guaranteed the prepared table right in the midst of the enemies.

This Passage is very real to me personally.

We have suffered the full brunt of the efforts of both the Media and Organized Religion to destroy us with everything within their power. They left no stone unturned.

At one particular crisis time, I had resolved to *"fight back."* I alerted our Television Director that we would make a Special, air it over our Network of Stations, and tell the world what these people were doing. On this occasion, I speak of Organized Religion.

I slept almost not at all that night. Actually, I arose a good while before daylight and attempted to pray and find the Mind of the Lord. I was greatly troubled in spirit, and, during the time of prayer, I received no answer.

Sometime later that morning, possibly about 8 a.m. or 9 a.m., the grandsons, Gabriel and Matthew, came over to our house to go swimming. I was to watch them. They must have been about five or six years old at the time.

While I was sitting and watching them, Frances came out of the house and very quickly walked up to me, handing me her Bible.

She said, *"Read Exodus 14:14."*

I took the Bible in my hands and looked at the Text to which she had just pointed. The words seemed to leap out at me. They said, *"The LORD shall fight for you, and you* shall hold your peace."

The moment I read those words, I knew this was the Mind of the Lord. I did not have a single doubt.

I instantly went back into the house and called our Television people to tell them we would not be making a Special Program after all.

From then until now, I have allowed the Lord to *"fight for us."*

ANOTHER EXAMPLE

If I remember correctly, the account that I am about to address probably took place in the year 1998.

One Television investigative reporter, so-called, had prepared a program designed to destroy us. It would be aired over CNN. To my face, this man said, *"I am going to take you out!"*

When the program aired a few nights later, it was exactly as he said it would be — as destructive as possible. There was no truth in what he reported, but truth was not the idea, but rather destruction.

The day after the *"Special"* aired, we received a call from Larry King, which we did, and do, repeatedly, asking us to be on his program in order to *"defend ourselves."* To be frank, that's my nature. I actually had told Mr. King that I would accept his invitation.

Driving home that night from the office, I was seeking the Lord as I drove, asking Him for His Leading and Guidance, when the Spirit of the Lord came over me. The Lord began to speak to my heart, saying to me, *"Do not try to defend yourself. Let Me defend you."* Then He added, *"Are you willing to suffer loss?"*

When I answered the Lord in the affirmative, *"Lord, if that is what You want, that is exactly what I want. Loss, or no loss, I want Your Perfect Will."*

Yes, we did suffer some loss. People wrote us and told us that they would never again support us, etc. But I had a peace in my heart, and, since that time, the Lord has begun to bless abundantly, giving us many times more than what we lost.

There may be temporary loss in obeying the Lord and doing His Will, but it will be temporary, at most. In the end, the Lord will always make it up. To be sure, in the totality of the situation, there never is any loss in doing the Will of God.

THE ANOINTING

The phrase, *"You anoint my head with oil; my cup runs over,"* refers, as is obvious, to two things.

Sheep have teeth only on their bottom jaw. They have none on the top jaw, so they cannot eat grass like other animals do. When they forage for grass, they have to move their heads in a scoop-like motion, which causes them, at times, to scrape their foreheads on rocks.

Every night, the shepherd will inspect the foreheads of the sheep. He will pour oil on those who have scraped their skin so they might quickly heal. He then gives the animal some cold water in a cup. But both expressions are metaphors.

The *"cup running over"* is an expressive metaphor indicative of a state of bliss rarely experienced in this life. Likewise, the *"anointing the head with oil"* refers to the whole life being full to overflowing with blessedness.

This and more was Israel's when they served God, and this and more can be the lot of every Believer if such a Believer will only dedicate fully to the Lord.

(6) "SURELY GOODNESS AND MERCY SHALL FOLLOW ME ALL THE DAYS OF MY LIFE: AND I WILL DWELL IN THE HOUSE OF THE LORD FOREVER."

As is generally the custom in most of these Verses, two things are said in each one.

GOODNESS AND MERCY

The first phrase, *"Surely goodness and mercy shall follow me all the days of my life,"* proclaims that which the Lord desires to do for all of His Children. As *"goodness and mercy"* are shown to us by the Lord, we are to show the same to others.

How can we not do so, when the Lord has been so good to us?

This Verse does not say that trouble and heartache will follow, but rather *"goodness and mercy."* Furthermore, this is a perpetual *"goodness and mercy,"* not just something that happens occasionally. It is constant!

The two words, *"goodness"* and *"mercy,"*

are to be taken together rather than over-curiously distinguished. Yet they are not mere synonyms. Goodness is the stream, mercy is the fountain; goodness is the open hand of God's bounty, mercy is His loving heart.

"Goodness" reminds us that our nature is a bundle of want; *"mercy,"* that our deepest and highest need can be satisfied — not by all God's Gifts — but only by Himself.

THE HOUSE OF THE LORD

The phrase, *"And I will dwell in the House of the LORD forever,"* carries with it the idea of Eternal Life.

David was speaking of the Temple, because that is all that he then knew. However, the short phrase, *"House of the LORD,"* has an altogether different meaning at present, and all because of Calvary.

Now, Believers are looked at by the Lord as His House (I Cor. 3:16). So, if we want to dwell in His House forever, then He will dwell in our house forever!

The short phrase, *"All the days,"* means not simply that *"I choose and desire,"* but *"I expect assuredly to dwell in my Father's House forever."*

How can one whose life is a *"vapor"* (James 4:14), standing on a point which crumbles beneath his feet, ignorant of what even the next hour will bring, thus boldly challenge the hidden future of earthly life, the boundless future beyond?

The answer comes from the Divine Shepherd, the Faithful Witness — *"Because I live, you shall live also"* (Jn. 14:1-3, 19; 12:26; II Cor. 5:1; Rom. 8:35-39).

PSALM 24

*A Psalm of David:
The King of Glory*

(1) "THE EARTH IS THE LORD'S, AND THE FULLNESS THEREOF; THE WORLD, AND THEY WHO DWELL THEREIN."

As noted, this is a Psalm of David.

THE CREATION

The words *"The Earth is the LORD's,"* refer back to Genesis 1:1. God created the Earth, so it legally belongs to Him. Sadly, it is now in rebellion against Him, being dominated more or less by Satan and evil spirit forces (II Cor. 4:4; Eph. 2:2; I Jn. 5:19).

This Song celebrates the Messiah as Creator (Vss. 1-2), as Redeemer (Vss. 3-6), and as King of Glory (Vss. 7-10).

GOD'S CHILDREN

The phrase, *"The world, and they who dwell therein,"* proclaims the fact that God is Creator of all. On that basis, mankind, in general and in totality, belongs to the Lord.

However, by the mere fact that God has created mankind does not make a person a Child of God, or *"God's Children."* Actually, it was originally intended to be that way; had it not been for the Fall, it most definitely would have been that way.

Man and woman were so created by God that they were destined to bring sons and daughters of God into the world (Lk. 3:38); however, due to the Fall, all children are brought into the world in the likeness of Adam (Gen. 5:3). That's where original sin comes in.

There is, however, a day coming, which will be in the Perfect Age to come, which is outlined in the last two Chapters of Revelation, when the original Plan of God will finally be realized. When parents then bring forth children, they will bring them forth in the *"likeness"* and *"image"* of the Lord.

(2) "FOR HE HAS FOUNDED IT UPON THE SEAS, AND ESTABLISHED IT UPON THE FLOODS."

God has established the Earth above the seas and floods, causing it to *"appear,"* thus making it a fitting habitation for man, hence, His right of property in the Earth and in all the dwellers on it. All exist through His providential care (Pulpit).[6]

(3) "WHO SHALL ASCEND INTO THE HILL OF THE LORD? OR WHO SHALL STAND IN HIS HOLY PLACE?"

The Holy Spirit here sings of the day when the Chief Shepherd will appear (I Pet. 5:4). He will enter the City of Jerusalem with His sheep and take His seat upon the Throne of Jehovah in Mount Zion. This Song celebrates Messiah as Creator, as Redeemer, and as King of Glory.

THE CHIEF SHEPHERD

Two questions are posed in this Psalm:
1. Who is this Chief Shepherd? The answer is *"Jehovah-Messiah."*
2. Who are His sheep? The answer is: *"Such who are pure in doctrine and holy in life."*

The Shepherd's right to the Throne of the whole Earth, to all that is in it, and to the obedience of its inhabitants is the double right of Creation and Redemption. If we misunderstand the question of Verse 3, we will misunderstand its all-important answer.

Self-righteousness will automatically begin to quote its list of accomplishment that surely constitute its *"clean hands"* and *"pure heart,"* or so it thinks! As usual, self-righteousness will be wrong.

The answer is the Lord Jesus Christ. He is the One Who will *"ascend into the hill of the LORD."* He is the One Who will *"stand in His Holy Place."*

We also can follow this path if we properly identify with Him, and I refer to identifying with His Cross and allowing Him to become our Righteous Substitute. God will accept no other!

(4) "HE WHO HAS CLEAN HANDS, AND A PURE HEART; WHO HAS NOT LIFTED UP HIS SOUL UNTO VANITY, NOR SWORN DECEITFULLY."

There are three thoughts to this Passage.

SELF-RIGHTEOUSNESS

The self-righteous are quick to list supposed accomplishments, and think that surely such will guarantee admittance to *"His Holy Place."*

Wrong!

THE BORN-AGAIN BELIEVER

Many think that their new experience in Christ makes them worthy. Wrong again!

John said, *"No man was found worthy"* (Rev. 5:4). The demand is that not only are the hands to be clean now and the heart pure now, but that the hands have always been clean and the heart always pure. No person can say that except Christ.

THE LORD JESUS CHRIST

He is the Only One Who has always had *"clean hands"* and *"a pure heart,"* the Only One Who never has *"lifted up His soul unto vanity, nor sworn deceitfully."* All have tried; all have failed, with the exception of Christ; however, if we fully accept Him as our Substitute, John said, *"As He is, so are we"* (I Jn. 4:17), but only on that basis.

THE CROSS

To be sure, the only means by which a person can be rightly in Christ, thereby the recipient of all that Christ affords, is by the means of the Cross.

In Old Testament times, there was only one answer for the sins, the failures, the transgressions, and the faults. That one answer was the Sacrificial System, i.e., *"the Brazen Altar."* There was no other, because there needed to be no other.

The Sacrificial System and the Brazen Altar constituted a Type of Christ and what He would do at Calvary's Cross. That was the only answer.

If the Priests or the people deviated from the *"Altar,"* their Sacrifices would be unacceptable to God. It had to be done exactly according to God's Prescribed Order, with everything pointing strictly to Christ and the Cross, of which both the Sacrificial System and the Brazen Altar were types.

Presently, it is the same. The Cross of Christ, to which all of these Old Testament types and shadows pointed, is the answer now and in totality. If men try to do it another way, whatever the other way is, it's a way that God will not accept, exactly as it was in Old Testament times. The Message has always been *"Jesus Christ and Him Crucified"* (I Cor. 1:23). That's the story of the Bible.

FAITH

The way to gain all that Christ has done for us at the Cross is by simply evidencing faith in Him and His Finished Work.

Let us say it again:

The Object of our Faith must ever be Christ and the Cross. It must not be transferred to other things, no matter how wonderful those other things might be in their own right. That's the reason Paul said, *"Christ sent me not to baptize, but to preach the Gospel, not with enticing words, lest the Cross of Christ be made of none effect"* (I Cor. 1:17).

In this one Verse, Paul tells us that the emphasis must never stray from the Cross of Christ, no matter how important the other situations or principles might be.

Of course, Water Baptism, of which Paul spoke, is very important; however, there is no Saving Grace in Water Baptism. All Saving Grace is given to us strictly by the principles of Christ and the Cross, and by no other means.

(5) "HE SHALL RECEIVE THE BLESSING FROM THE LORD, AND RIGHTEOUSNESS FROM THE GOD OF HIS SALVATION."

In a sense, we are told here how blessings come to the Believer!

THE LORD JESUS CHRIST

The Lord Jesus Christ is the One Who really receives the Blessing from the Lord. In effect, God cannot bless poor, fallen man. He can only bless His Son, the Lord Jesus Christ. However, when Jesus comes into our heart, then the Blessing that comes to Him also comes to us.

The believing sinner comes *"into Christ"* only by the means of the Cross. It cannot be any other way!

In fact, when the Apostle Paul was charged by the Holy Spirit to tell Believers how to successfully live for God, Believers were taken straight to the Cross (Rom. 6:3-5).

RIGHTEOUSNESS

The right of entry into the King's Court is *"Righteousness."* Christ is Righteousness, and His Righteousness becomes our Righteousness. This is the only raiment suitable to the sinlessness of that Court. A person in foul raiment (self-righteousness) would be totally out of place in the King's Court, if, by some chance, he happened to be there (Mat. 22:11).

All who arrive there will actually have received the Blessing from Jehovah, which admits them to His Kingdom, and also gives them a Righteousness befitting them for its purity. But this Righteousness is not merited, for it is *"received"* from a Personal Saviour — a God of *"Salvation"* — the God of Jacob, that is, the God Who elected Jacob unto Salvation when he only merited condemnation (Gen. 28:12-15).

NOTES

(6) "THIS IS THE GENERATION OF THEM WHO SEEK HIM, WHO SEEK YOUR FACE, O JACOB. SELAH."

A great truth of Righteousness is here unveiled!

JACOB

The great Patriarch Jacob is used here as an example. To prove His point, the Holy Spirit also uses the name *"Jacob,"* which means *"deceiver, supplanter, etc."*

This is the idea:

All men must be changed; however, they can only be changed as Jacob was changed, and that is by admitting their situation, and thereby looking exclusively to the Lord.

Furthermore, of all the billions of people who have lived, and who presently live upon this Earth, the Holy Spirit pulls, irrespective of the timeframe, all true Believers into one group, and labels them as *"the generation of them who seek Him."* Regrettably and sadly, this means that the far greater majority of the world's population are of no consequence.

Jesus truly died for all (Jn. 3:16); however, it is only those who truly believe Him who receive the benefits of what He has done for us at the Cross. The rest, as stated, are of no consequence.

That may sound like a very callous remark, but how else can it be? The free Plan of Salvation is offered to all, the price has been paid, the hand of the Lord is poised to write down one's name in the Lamb's Book of Life; however, this cannot be done unless faith is evidenced. Sadly and regrettably, it is evidenced only by a few. Truly, *"straight is the gate, and narrow is the way, which leads to life, and few there be who find it"* (Mat. 7:14).

The reason that most never find it is because of *"false prophets, which come to you in sheep's clothing, but inwardly they are ravening wolves"* (Mat. 7:15).

THE TRUE ISRAEL

As well, this particular Verse of Scripture pertains to the fact that God looked at those who, as did Jacob of old, truly trusted Him as the True Israel. In fact, one might say there were two Israels, the one who disregarded

His Word and had no regard for His Way, and then the one, as Jacob, who did their best to serve God. To be sure, the second group was much smaller than the first group.

As it regards the True Church, there are only a few who actually fit the Scriptural position. For example:

In the United States, there are approximately one hundred million (100,000,000) people who claim to be Born-Again. But, if the truth be known, which God Alone knows, only a tiny percentage of that number truly are Born-Again.

Which are you?

(7) "LIFT UP YOUR HEADS, O YE GATES; AND BE YE LIFT UP, YOU EVERLASTING DOORS; AND THE KING OF GLORY SHALL COME IN."

Now we are plainly told that the One Who has *"clean hands"* and *"a pure heart"* is the *"King of Glory,"* the Lord Jesus Christ!

When David made this statement, he may very well have had in view the Ark of the Covenant, where God dwelt between the Mercy Seat and the Cherubim. Still, the Holy Spirit had a far greater picture in mind.

The Holy Spirit is speaking of the day that Jesus will enter into the Temple in Jerusalem, not only as the Messiah of Israel, but as the President, so to speak, of the entirety of the world. This will occur at the beginning of the Kingdom Age.

(8) "WHO IS THIS KING OF GLORY? THE LORD STRONG AND MIGHTY, THE LORD MIGHTY IN BATTLE."

This Verse asks two questions.

WHO IS THIS KING OF GLORY?

He is none other than the Lord Jesus Christ, the King of kings and the Lord of lords, the First and the Last, the Alpha and Omega, the Beginning and the End, the Creator of all the ages, the Redeemer of mankind, the Baptizer with the Holy Spirit, the Healer of men's souls and their physical bodies, our Sanctifier, our Keeper, our Eternal Life, our All-in-All, a Gale of Spices swept from Heaven's Door!

WHAT DID THE KING OF GLORY DO?

The phrase, *"The LORD strong and mighty,*

NOTES

the LORD mighty in battle," refers to what Jesus did at the Cross, when He satisfied the demands of the broken Law, thereby atoning for all sin, which defeated Satan and all of his cohorts of darkness. It was, as stated, all done at the Cross (Col. 2:13-15).

(9) "LIFT UP YOUR HEADS, O YE GATES, EVEN LIFT THEM UP, YE EVERLASTING DOORS; AND THE KING OF GLORY SHALL COME IN."

This Verse, as is obvious, is almost identical to Verse 7.

THE KING OF GLORY

Some teach that this Verse pertains to Jesus Christ going back to Heaven after the great work on Earth was completed, as it regards the Cross, and then entering into the Throne Room of Glory — with His Mission completed! Most assuredly, this could very well be at least part of the meaning of this Verse, but the greater fulfillment, as stated, speaks of the Lord going into the Temple in Jerusalem, a triumphant entry, we might quickly add, after the Battle of Armageddon is won.

The most ancient gate of Jerusalem is the Eastern Gate. At present, it is walled up. The Muslims have a tradition that it will never be opened until Jesus of Nazareth returns to Earth, and that He will be the First to pass through it into the City.

They are right about one thing:

"He" will pass through it into the City, not Muhammad.

(10) "WHO IS THIS KING OF GLORY? THE LORD OF HOSTS, HE IS THE KING OF GLORY. SELAH."

Once again, the question is asked, *"Who is this King of Glory?"* Verse 8 asks the question and describes Him; Verse 10 answers it.

Again, we state: The answer is *"Jesus-Jehovah"*; *"He is the King of Glory."*

PSALM 25

A Psalm of David:
A Prayer of Distress

(1) "UNTO YOU, O LORD, DO I LIFT UP MY SOUL."

As noted, this Psalm was written by David.

THE LORD JESUS CHRIST, OUR GREAT HIGH PRIEST

Many of these Psalms set forth the Messiah as Israel's Great High Priest and also as our Great High Priest. As such, He leads our worship, confesses our sins, prays for pardon, voices our confidence, hope, and faith, burdens Himself with our sorrows and fears, and, in every respect, acts as the True Priest of and for His people.

There is an aspect of Christ's High Priestly Work that most do not understand. Most True Christians have a fairly comprehensive understanding of the Sacrifice made at Calvary, at least as it regards Salvation, but almost none of His High Priestly Work.

Even though Christ is Personally sinless, He confesses Israel's sins (and ours) as His Own. He asks forgiveness for them, and yet, at the same time, declares our moral perfection. To many, this is somewhat confusing, but actually it is quite simple.

He takes to Himself His people's sins, and He accredits to us His Own merit. He is at once Priest, Advocate, Mediator, and Substitute.

The beauty of this Psalm is matchless. The Reader is deeply moved as he understands that the Speaker is the Lord of Glory Himself pleading for His people. He has neither sins nor transgressions Personally, but He confesses those of His people as His Own.

(2) "O MY GOD, I TRUST IN YOU: LET ME NOT BE ASHAMED, LET NOT MY ENEMIES TRIUMPH OVER ME.

(3) "YEA, LET NONE WHO WAIT ON YOU BE ASHAMED: LET THEM BE ASHAMED WHICH TRANSGRESS WITHOUT CAUSE."

The theme of the entirety of the Psalms is *"Trust in God."*

TRUST

Three things are said in these Verses. They are:

1. Trust is placed in the Lord!
2. The petition is that the Lord not allow us to be ashamed, in other words, *"Lord, You've got to help me. I have placed my faith in You, and I have made my stand bold for all to see. Please don't let me fall down and thereby be greatly shamed."*

3. The Believer can go in many directions regarding *"trust"*; however, if trust and confidence are not placed solely in the Lord, to be sure, the enemies of one's soul will triumph.

ENEMIES

These enemies of which David speaks are not only the heathen, but also vices of the soul.

To be sure, this prayer was most definitely answered. Instead of the enemies triumphing, Believers triumph!

Let me show you how I know this!

Paul writes and says, and I quote from THE EXPOSITOR'S STUDY BIBLE:

"And having spoiled principalities and powers (Satan and all of his henchmen were defeated at the Cross by Christ atoning for all sin; sin was the legal right Satan had to hold man in captivity; with all sin atoned, he has no more legal right to hold anyone in bondage), *He* (Christ) *made a show of them openly* (what Jesus did at the Cross was in the face of the whole universe), *triumphing over them in it.* (The triumph is complete, and it was all done for us, meaning we can walk in power and perpetual victory due to the Cross)" (Col. 2:15).

Do you the Reader properly understand what Paul is here saying?

He is saying that Jesus at the Cross (Col. 2:14) won every victory, and did so all on our behalf. It is meant for us to have the benefits of each victory, in other words, that each victory becomes our victory, which accrue to us by our evidencing simple faith in Christ and the Cross.

Because Jesus *"triumphed over the enemy,"* this means that we also have triumphed over the enemy. It's not something that is to be done in the future, it is something that already has been done.

The Christian's lot is not in *"doing,"* but rather in trusting in something that already has been *"done."* I speak of Calvary!

(4) "SHOW ME YOUR WAYS, O LORD; TEACH ME YOUR PATHS."

Few Christians actually seek the *"Ways of the LORD."* Most seek His acts. I am Pentecostal; however, I have to admit that much of the Pentecostal and Charismatic part of the Church falls into the category I've just mentioned. They little seek the Lord's Ways.

While it is certainly true that God wants to do great and wonderful things for us, still, His greater desire is that we know Him Personally, that we draw closer to Him, and that we learn His Ways.

THE WAYS OF THE LORD

It was in October of 1991. The Ministry was at a crisis point, and I actually did not know what to do.

The very first thing the Lord told me to do was to establish two prayer meetings each day, with the exception of Service times. This we set out to do immediately.

After the first few sessions of prayer, the Lord gently spoke to my heart and said to me, *"Do not seek Me so much for what I can do, but rather for Who I am!"*

To be sure, the Ministry was in a wilderness. It was absolutely impossible for us to survive without the direct intervention of the Hand of God. In the midst of all of that, the Lord said to me, *"Seek Me for Who I am!"*

We began to conduct, together with a small group of faithful Believers, the prayer meetings, a regimen to which I still personally hold, and, little by little, the Lord began to open up Himself to me. More and more, I began to learn exactly Who He was, and is, and there is nothing more important than that.

I want to know *"His Ways"* and *"His Paths,"* and I know that He Alone can teach me. That, He will do. And He will do it for anyone who has a hunger and thirst for God!

(5) "LEAD ME IN YOUR TRUTH, AND TEACH ME: FOR YOU ARE THE GOD OF MY SALVATION; ON YOU DO I WAIT ALL THE DAY."

Four things are said in this Verse. They are:

1. *"LEAD ME IN YOUR TRUTH"*: This prayer of Christ, for that's exactly what it is, was most definitely answered. Jesus said, *"Howbeit when He, the Spirit of Truth, is come* (which He did on the Day of Pentecost), *He will guide you into all Truth* (if our Faith is properly placed in Christ and the Cross, the Holy Spirit can then bring forth Truth to us; He doesn't guide into some truth, but rather *'all Truth'*): *for He shall not speak of Himself* (tells us not only what He does, but Whom He represents); *but whatsoever He shall hear, that shall He speak* (doesn't refer to lack of knowledge, for the Holy Spirit is God, but rather He will proclaim the Work of Christ only): *and He will show you things to come* (pertains to the New Covenant, which would shortly be given)" (Jn. 16:13).

2. *"TEACH ME"*: The Lord uses a variety of ways to teach His Children. First of all, He uses the Word of God through the fivefold Calling (Eph. 4:11). However, if the Preacher or Teacher is teaching you something wrong, then you have problems. Sad to say, if the Preacher doesn't know and understand the Cross of Christ, as it refers to Sanctification as well as Salvation, what he will be teaching may be very sincere, but it will be wrong!

If the Believer will honestly and sincerely ask the Lord to show him the right way, and not allow him to be led astray, this is a prayer that the Holy Spirit most definitely will answer. If the person seeks Truth, to be sure, Truth will be given to that person. The Lord will see to that!

3. *"THE GOD OF MY SALVATION"*: In David's day, a great problem for Israel was *"idols,"* i.e., *"other gods."* Presently, things are different! Today, the problem for the modern Church is *"another Jesus"* (II Cor. 11:4).

If the Believer separates the Cross from Christ, then he is left with *"another Jesus,"* which means it's not the Jesus of the Bible. Regrettably, that's the state of the far greater majority of the modern Church. The Cross of Christ is ignored, disbelieved, or outright maligned. As a result, it is left with *"another Jesus,"* which means it's not the Jesus of the Bible and, therefore, not the Jesus of Salvation.

4. *"ON YOU DO I WAIT ALL THE DAY"*: In order for the Lord to teach him, David was willing to wait on the Lord all the day. Few are willing to pay this price, to make this sacrifice, or to seek the Presence of the Lord. To be sure, it doesn't take the Lord long to do anything; however, it takes us a great deal of time to be brought to the place

we ought to be. We have to be willing to wait, and that means to wait in Faith.

(6) "REMEMBER, O LORD, YOUR TENDER MERCIES AND YOUR LOVINGKINDNESSES; FOR THEY HAVE BEEN EVER OF OLD."

Past mercies form a ground for the expectation of future Blessings. God's Character cannot change; His Action at one time will always be consistent and harmonious with His Action at another. If He has been kind and merciful to David (and to us) in the past, David (and we also) may count on His continuing the same in the future.

Such mercies and lovingkindnesses did not begin yesterday. From the very beginning of time the Lord has functioned in this capacity.

REMEMBER

There are some things we want the Lord to remember, such as His *"Mercies and Lovingkindnesses,"* and there are some things we want Him to forget, and I speak of past sins, as the next Verse presents.

First of all, we have the Scriptural right, as here given to us, to ask the Lord to remember all the good things which He does, and to remember them on our behalf. In fact, if the Lord has put such in His Word, and He most definitely has, then we have the right to ask for those great attributes. In fact, the Lord desires that we ask for them. We have not, because we ask not! And then all too often, we ask with the wrong spirit and the wrong motives.

If we ask in brokenness and contrition, this is a prayer that the Lord will always answer.

(7) "REMEMBER NOT THE SINS OF MY YOUTH, NOR MY TRANSGRESSIONS: ACCORDING TO YOUR MERCY REMEMBER THOU ME FOR YOUR GOODNESS' SAKE, O LORD."

We want the Lord to remember His *"Mercies and Lovingkindnesses"* toward us, and do so always; but, at the same time, we do not want Him to remember our sins or any of our transgressions — and rightly so! To be sure, He won't!

Sin is an awful thing; however, if the Believer properly confesses such to the Lord, He has promised *"to forgive us, and to cleanse us from all unrighteousness"* (I Jn. 1:9). When we are *"cleansed,"* which we are by His Precious Blood and our Faith in that Finished Work, to be sure, the infraction also is erased, never to be charged against us again.

MERCY

The phrase, *"According to Your mercy remember Thou me, for Your goodness' sake, O LORD,"* provides the ground on which we are to approach the Lord. We dare not ask for justice, only *"mercy."* If we ask for justice, we cannot hope to survive; therefore, we must come to the Lord on the ground of *"mercy,"* and mercy alone!

When blind Bartimaeus approached Jesus for healing, His cry was, *"Jesus, Thou Son of David, have mercy on me"* (Lk. 18:38).

Had he tried to approach the Lord in any other fashion, he would have been met in a different way. Inasmuch as he approached the Lord on the only basis in which the Lord will hear and answer us, he instantly received a Miracle — he received his sight.

The song says:

> "Mercy there was great, and Grace was free.
> "Pardon there was multiplied to me.
> "There my burdened soul found liberty,
> "At Calvary!"

(8) "GOOD AND UPRIGHT IS THE LORD: THEREFORE WILL HE TEACH SINNERS IN THE WAY."

Two great truths are taught in this Scripture.

SINNERS

Regrettably, all men are sinners (Rom. 3:10). And there is only one remedy for sin, and that is the Cross of Christ! Let the Reader survey those words very closely. There is only one remedy for sin, and that is the Cross of Christ. There is no other, as there can be no other, as there need be no other!

If there is anything that teaches man the Love of God, it is Calvary's Cross. In fact, Calvary shows that man is not just a little bit wrong, but totally wrong. There is no earthly way out of his dilemma.

Then Calvary tells us of the great Love of God. When man could not help himself,

God gave His Only Son, Who would hang on a cruel Cross, thereby paying the price for all of humanity, that whosoever will might be saved (Rev. 22:17).

So, the first thing we learn from this Scripture is how *"good and upright is the LORD."* He is so good that He will save sinners, and that means any and all who will come to Him.

Those are the two truths of this Verse:
1. All men are sinners; and,
2. The Lord saves sinners!

(9) "THE MEEK WILL HE GUIDE IN JUDGMENT: AND THE MEEK WILL HE TEACH HIS WAY."

The word *"meek"* refers to those who are broken and contrite in spirit. In other words, this is the very opposite of the prideful.

THE MEEK

It is very difficult for mankind to be brought to a broken condition. Man is stubborn; he is obstinate; he is perverse; he is hard! To bring him to a place of a broken and contrite spirit sometimes takes tragedy!

Irrespective of the manner that man comes to the place to where he can receive of the Lord, in some way he must be brought to that place. The Lord will not hear the proud, will not answer the prayers of the proud, will not cleanse and save the proud — in fact, will have nothing to do with the proud. Only the *"meek will He guide in judgment."* Only the *"meek will He teach His Way."* We must never forget that!

SELF-RIGHTEOUSNESS

This is the reason that self-righteousness is so wrong! It puts man in the driver's seat, when man is woefully inadequate. Self-righteousness makes claims upon God, which no man is worthy to make.

If the Believer attempts to live for God by any means other than simple faith in Christ and the Cross, always and without exception, the results will be self-righteousness. When man embarks upon a course of *"works,"* whatever those works might be, such will always lead the individual away from God instead of toward God.

Paul said, *"If Righteousness come by the Law, then Christ is dead in vain"* (Gal. 2:21).

NOTES

(10) "ALL THE PATHS OF THE LORD ARE MERCY AND TRUTH UNTO SUCH AS KEEP HIS COVENANT AND HIS TESTIMONIES."

If we want *"Mercy"* and *"Truth"* from the Lord, then we must *"keep His Covenant and His Testimonies."*

THE PATHS OF THE LORD

To be able to walk this *"path,"* we must keep the *"Covenants"* and the *"Testimonies"* of the Lord. So where does that leave us?

To use street vernacular, we are shot down!

There has never been any individual who could boast of keeping all the Covenants and Testimonies of the Lord.

After Paul was Saved and baptized with the Holy Spirit, he thought surely he could then keep the Commandments of the Lord. This was before he understood the Message of the Cross.

The Apostle minutely inspected the Commandments, and congratulated himself on having kept them. But when he reached the last one, *"You shall not covet,"* the Holy Spirit then made him realize that he had not kept the Law at all (Rom 7:7).

Perhaps he had not actually broken some of these Commandments in fact, but in spirit he had done so, simply because he coveted to do so in his heart. He realized this and then he knew that if he tried to function in the realm of Covenants and Testimonies that he had lost before he even began.

So, what is the answer?

There is only One Who has perfectly kept all the *"Covenants and Testimonies,"* and has done so for all time, not failing in even one point. That Person is the Lord Jesus Christ.

When the Believer places his faith exclusively in Christ and what Christ has done at the Cross, then all the great victories which belong to Christ (victories, incidentally, which were carried out for us) are then granted to us simply on the merit of faith. It is only by faith that these great victories can be obtained.

Whenever our faith is exclusively in Christ and what He did for us at the Cross, then we are able to walk these *"paths of the LORD,"* which are *"Mercy and Truth."*

That is the only way it can be done, and it is the only way that it is meant to be done!

(11) "FOR YOUR NAME'S SAKE, O LORD, PARDON MY INIQUITY; FOR IT IS GREAT."

This Passage opens up to us two great truths. They are:

SIN AND THE CHARACTER OF GOD

Our Great High Priest, when confessing His people's iniquity as His Own, asks for pardon on two grounds:

1. The magnitude of the sin; and,
2. The Name and Character of God as a pardoning God.

Man tries to minimize his sin and magnify his penitence; he pleads for pardon because the first is so small and the second is so great. However, the Great High Priest, the Lord Jesus Christ, rightly estimates all sin as being great, and urges its magnitude as grounds for pardon.

Believers also have a tendency to magnify the sins of others and to minimize their own. God will have none of it. He demands that we understand the magnitude of any and all sin, ours included. Only on those grounds will He pardon (I Jn. 1:9).

(12) "WHAT MAN IS HE WHO FEARS THE LORD? HIM SHALL HE TEACH IN THE WAY THAT HE SHALL CHOOSE."

Once again, we have two great truths presented here.

THE FEAR OF THE LORD

The question, *"What man is he who fears the LORD?"* proclaims the ground on which God will make His Way clear. A proper *"fear of the LORD"* is the first requirement of any and all things, as it regards the Lord.

It's not possible to have the proper fear of the Lord unless there is proper relationship with the Lord.

TEACHING AS GIVEN BY THE LORD

The phrase, *"Him shall He teach in the way that He shall choose,"* refers to the Lord teaching the individual, which He most definitely will do, providing the individual properly fears the Lord.

Of course, the Holy Spirit is the greatest Teacher of all. If we follow God's Prescribed Order, then we have the assurance of the Lord that we will be properly taught.

John the Beloved wrote, and I quote from THE EXPOSITOR'S STUDY BIBLE:

"But the Anointing which you have received of Him (the Holy Spirit) *abides in you* (abides permanently to help us ascertain if what we are hearing is Scriptural or not), *and you need not that any man teach you: but as the same Anointing teaches you of all things* (no Believer needs anything that's not already found written in the Word), *and is Truth, and is no lie* (the Holy Spirit will guide us into all Truth [Jn. 16:13]), *and even as it* (the Anointing) *has taught you, you shall abide in Him* (refers to the fact that what we are taught by the Spirit, regarding the Word of God, helps us to abide in Christ)" (I Jn. 2:27).

In this statement, John does not mean that God-called Teachers are not needed, but rather that the final word on any subject is the Bible, and not man.

(13) "HIS SOUL SHALL DWELL AT EASE; AND HIS SEED SHALL INHERIT THE EARTH."

This Verse is linked with the previous Verse.

BLESSINGS

The phrase, *"His soul shall dwell at ease,"* actually says, *"His soul shall dwell in bliss."* In other words, while on Earth, such a person will enjoy blessings of every kind.

The phrase, *"And his seed shall inherit the Earth,"* has to do with his children, his posterity after him. They also shall prosper, that is, if they continue in the paths of their father, who fears the Lord, and is thereby taught by the Lord.

Here we are given God's Prescription for *"Blessings."* Everyone wants to be blessed, so now we are taught the manner in which God blesses.

If we properly fear Him, He will teach us, that is, teach us how to believe Him, how to stand upon His Promises, and thereby to receive and to enjoy the Blessings of the Lord.

(14) "THE SECRET OF THE LORD IS WITH THEM WHO FEAR HIM; AND HE WILL SHOW THEM HIS COVENANT."

The instruction continues!

THE SECRET OF THE LORD

God favors those who fear Him with secret and confidential communion. He *"comes unto them, and makes His abode with them"* (Jn. 14:23), *"teaches them"* (Jn. 14:26), enlightens them, leads them in His Way, and further instructs them, in effect, *"sealing their instruction."*

The phrase, *"He will show them His Covenant,"* means that He will help such Believers to see its full force.

If one properly fears the Lord, one is going to have a proper relationship with the Lord. Such a relationship means that one constantly studies and mediates upon the Word. Such a climate will guarantee great *"Blessings."*

(15) "MY EYES ARE EVER TOWARD THE LORD; FOR HE SHALL PLUCK MY FEET OUT OF THE NET."

There is only One who can pluck one's feet out of the net, and that is the Lord!

MODERN PSYCHOLOGY

This Passage flies in the face of much of the Church world. Only God can do such. And yet, Christian man constantly acts as if he also has the power to do so.

Psychology is the rage of the modern Church. Many Pastors are told by their Denominational heads that modern problems are not addressed in the Bible and must have the help of the professional counselor.

Pure and simple, such direction, at the least, is ridiculous, and, at the worst, is blasphemy!

The Bible addresses itself to every single spiritual problem that may beset man. To think that it doesn't either portrays gross unbelief or base ignorance, or both! The Bible alone holds the answer.

Not only can modern psychology not help, but it will lead one away from the true help that can be obtained in the Word of God and from the Lord Jesus Christ.

This *"net"* only further entangles us if we attempt to extricate ourselves. We simply cannot do it in this fashion. Therefore, every Child of God must, for his own protection and security, say, *"My eyes are ever toward the LORD."*

NOTES

OUR GREAT HIGH PRIEST

The Person of this Great High Priest, the Lord Jesus Christ, and His Sympathy with His people shine with great beauty in Verses 15 through 22. He, as our Head, has His Eyes ever toward Jehovah, and we, as His feet, are temporarily caught in the enemy's net, even as Verse 15 proclaims. He, as God's Only One, afflicts Himself with the distresses, afflictions, pains, and sins of His people. Our troubles enlarge His Heart and make it swell with sorrow. The hatred shown to Israel, He accepts as shown to Himself, and He pleads the perfection of His Faith, His Integrity, and His Uprightness as the argument for their (and our) Redemption out of all their (and our) troubles.

Never was there a love like this! Not merely with His Lips does He officially confess His people's sins and accept their distresses as His Own, but He pleads for forgiveness and Deliverance, and, with and from His Heart, He really burdens Himself and bears and makes our sorrows as His Own, as no earthly Priest ever could or did (Mat. 8:17).

(16) "TURN THEE UNTO ME, AND HAVE MERCY UPON ME; FOR I AM DESOLATE AND AFFLICTED."

We are not promised a trouble-free existence on this life's journey, even as this Verse proclaims. We do, however, have the privilege of turning exclusively to the Lord, and requesting His Mercy, which He will never withhold.

Irrespective as to how much faith we have, how close to God we might be, there will come times on this Christian journey that we will seem to be *"desolate and afflicted."* Of course, the Lord could stop all such actions; however, He allows certain types of tribulation in order that our faith in Him be strengthened. If we never had a problem, we would never know how the Lord could solve all of these problems.

(17) "THE TROUBLES OF MY HEART ARE ENLARGED: O BRING THOU ME OUT OF MY DISTRESSES.

(18) "LOOK UPON MY AFFLICTION AND MY PAIN; AND FORGIVE ALL MY SINS."

David looks upon his present situation as being caused by sin, and, to be sure, sin will most definitely cause problems, and of every nature and type.

Moreover, David regarded the problems as a punishment sent on him for his sins. At any rate, it is very obvious that David at this time is deeply conscious of his sins, and deeply repentant. This Psalm very well could have been written by David in the very midst of his terrible sin committed against Bathsheba and her husband Uriah.

THE RESULT OF SIN

Sin is the problem of the human family. It is also the problem of the Believer. Unfortunately, much of the modern gospel which makes the rounds presently, which, in fact, is no Gospel at all, treats sin in a totally unscriptural manner.

Our Word of Faith friends state that sin should not be mentioned by the Christian or the Preacher, because to do so, they claim, only develops a sin consciousness, and thereby causes the person to sin.

Someone should have told the Apostle Paul this great *"truth,"* because he mentions sin some seventeen times in the Sixth Chapter of his Epistle to the Romans alone. No! I'm sorry, denying something doesn't rid one of its terrible results. You won't find such advice in the Bible.

"The Purpose Driven Life" people address sin a little bit differently than *"The Word of Faith"* people. They too will not mention it, but for a different reason. They claim that to mention sin might offend people, and that's not the way to win them, etc.

Once again, I think it's obvious that such foolishness does not match up with the Word of God.

Pure and simple, the problem is sin, whether with an unbeliever or with a Believer. When Paul was led by the Holy Spirit to give directions as to how Believers can live an overcoming life, he starts out with the problem of sin. I speak of Romans 6:1-2.

The great Apostle then gives us the solution to sin, which is the only solution, which is the Cross of Christ, which is found in Romans 6:3-5.

THE OLD TESTAMENT

When one goes to the Old Testament, we see one answer for sin, one panacea, one solution. It is the Cross of Christ, which was foreshadowed in the Sacrificial System. There was no other remedy for sin, only the Sacrifices, which pointed to the coming One!

When Jesus Christ came to this world, He came for one purpose and reason, and that was to go to the Cross. That was His destination, even from before the foundation of the world (I Pet. 1:18-20). While He did many other things, the Cross was ever in view.

The Lord told His chosen Disciples that He must go to Jerusalem *"and suffer many things of the Elders and Chief Priests and Scribes and be killed, and be raised again the third day,*

"Then Peter took Him, and began to rebuke Him, saying, Be it far from You, Lord: this shall not be unto You."

Jesus' retort to Peter was strong to say the least.

He said, *"Get thee behind Me, Satan: you are an offense unto Me: for you savor not the things that be of God, but those that be of men"* (Mat. 16:21-23).

This tells us that our Lord would not tolerate anything, even from His most choice Disciples, which would steer Him away from the Cross. The Cross, as stated, was ever His destination. It was there that all sin would be atoned; it was there where Satan and all his cohorts of darkness would be defeated. It was there that man's Redemption was settled, the price paid, and the door opened for all to come. The Cross! The Cross! The Cross! (I Cor. 1:17-18; 21, 23; 2:2; Gal. 6:14).

As stated, there is only one answer for sin, and that's the Cross. This means there is only one way for sins to be washed, cleansed, and put away. It is the Cross! This also means there is only one way for victory over sin, and that is the Cross!

That's the reason we are so openly opposed to any direction, such as *"The Purpose Driven Life,"* etc., which will pull Believers away from the Cross. Such a road leads to abject disaster.

(19) "CONSIDER MY ENEMIES; FOR THEY ARE MANY; AND THEY HATE ME WITH CRUEL HATRED."

If David wrote this Psalm in the very midst of his terrible sin committed against

Bathsheba and her husband Uriah, which he probably did, the terminology then becomes more understandable.

ENEMIES

The enemies which came against David, and I speak of those from within (for that was by far his greatest problem), did not suddenly become his enemies. They were always his enemies. The situation concerning Bathsheba only gave them an open door by which to pursue their illicit desires.

Israel had been blessed beyond comprehension primarily because of David. Of course, the Source of the Blessings was always the Lord; however, His instrument was David.

Many in Israel, even some of its leaders, who, incidentally, had been appointed by David, didn't have sense enough to see this. The reason?

They were evil at heart, and always had been.

What David did was very wrong, exceedingly wrong! However, using that as an opportunity to get at David and, if possible, to even take the very throne, set these people against God. They didn't realize that, but that's exactly what happened! The end result would not be pleasant or pretty. Absalom, and untold thousands who followed him, would die. Ahithophel would commit suicide!

If these men had had even a degree of spirituality, they would have helped David during this time of great sorrow and trial. To be sure, the attitude and direction of these *"enemies"* could little add to the suffering that David experienced because of his sin.

However, please allow me to make the following statement:

"When a person is down, and anyone can do any negative thing to that person they so desire, and not only not be reprimanded, but rather applauded, then one finds out just exactly how many good Christians there really are."

There aren't many! David found that out!

(20) "O KEEP MY SOUL, AND DELIVER ME: LET ME NOT BE ASHAMED; FOR I PUT MY TRUST IN YOU."

A person can be put in a place to where

NOTES

they have no recourse but the Lord. The Lord actually allows this to happen at times. As unsavory as the situation might be, such a person finds out just how wonderful the Lord can be in such circumstances. The Lord will not allow such a person to be *"ashamed."*

(21) "LET INTEGRITY AND UPRIGHTNESS PRESERVE ME; FOR I WAIT ON YOU."

In this Verse, David is not claiming *"integrity and uprightness"*; he is merely saying that these things belong to the Lord, and, as a result, the Lord will see him through.

David is also stating that to wait on the Lord is, within itself, and regardless of the past problems, *"integrity and uprightness."*

At the same time, this tells us that Believers who look elsewhere have just left the premises of *"integrity and uprightness."* Such are found only in the Lord.

(22) "REDEEM ISRAEL, O GOD, OUT OF ALL HIS TROUBLES."

This prayer has not yet been answered, not because of the Intercessor, be it David or our Lord, but because of Israel's rebellion. Ultimately, it will be answered in all of its totality. To be sure, Israel will be redeemed.

This also can be said for every Child of God who puts his faith and trust in the Lord. Otherwise, there is no Redemption.

PSALM 26

*A Psalm of David:
A Petition for Exoneration*

(1) "JUDGE ME, O LORD; FOR I HAVE WALKED IN MY INTEGRITY: I HAVE TRUSTED ALSO IN THE LORD; THEREFORE I SHALL NOT SLIDE."

This is also a Psalm of David and it has a double meaning:

1. David pleads his own petitions; and,
2. The Son of David pleads for Israel, and also for you and me.

If one will read these Psalms with not only David's petition in mind, but also the petition of the Greater Petitioner, our Intercessor, the Psalm will become much more understandable.

Failure to recognize Who the real Speaker

is in this and similar Psalms leads to the unjust charge that David had a very high opinion of himself, and was, in effect, a self-righteous Pharisee.

INTEGRITY!

In effect, the Lord Jesus Christ is telling Jehovah to judge Him rather than us. The integrity with which He speaks is His Own and not ours. Much of the time the integrity which the Church espouses is a man-made integrity, which has no validity with God. Conversely, the integrity that only God can give, sadly, has little merit with the Church. God's integrity is bound up in His Word. Man's integrity is bound up in his own rules and regulations, which change constantly.

If our trust is in a man-made integrity, we will ultimately *"slide."*

(2) "EXAMINE ME, O LORD, AND PROVE ME; TRY MY REINS AND MY HEART."

David's cry is that the Lord would examine him closely to see if he is anchored in God's Word. The Messiah cries the same for Israel. As our Intercessor, He does the same for us. He becomes one with us, urging us to become one with Him. Only then can the Intercession bring forth its desired results.

Every Child of God should urge the Holy Spirit to probe deep within the heart to *"prove me"* — to see that we are abiding in the Word of God and not in a man-made gospel.

EXAMINATION

This Psalm is rich with instruction for the people of God in all Dispensations, but two facts full of consolation are especially prominent. The one is that help is sure to be given in response to such a Pleader and to such a plea. The second is that this Divine Priest is willing and able to live His blameless Life in whoever trusts Him.

The Hebrew Text employs the phrase, *"I have,"* five times, and the phrase, *"I shall"* seven times. Only the Messiah could thus fully describe His past and guarantee His future action. The words, *"Judge Me,"* in Verse 1, mean *"Vindicate Me"*; the word *"integrity"* should read *"blamelessness"*; and the word *"therefore"* should be omitted. *"Reins"* and *"heart"* are figures of speech for thoughts and feelings.

NOTES

THE LAMB FOR SACRIFICE

In the Temple twice a day, at 9 a.m. and at 3 p.m., a lamb was offered for Israel. On the Sabbath Day, two lambs were offered at each of these particular times.

When the animal was killed and its skin pulled from its little body, a Priest would take a razor-sharp knife, lay open the lamb's flesh all the way to the backbone, and inspect it carefully. If there was even a slight discoloration, the carcass of this lamb was laid aside and another lamb offered. The lamb had to be perfect, because it represented the One Who was to come.

As the Levitical Priest scrutinized, both inwardly and outwardly, the lamb for the daily sacrifice, so the Lamb of God could confidently offer Himself to the searchings of God's Eye. In Him, all was perfection. Every emotion of His Spirit, Soul, and Body, every thought and affection of His Heart, every look, word, and action were absolutely and always sinless!

Only such a One could serve as our Divine Intercessor, our Divine High Priest (Heb. 7:25-28).

(3) "FOR YOUR LOVINGKINDNESS IS BEFORE MY EYES: AND I HAVE WALKED IN YOUR TRUTH."

Only the Lord Jesus Christ could actually say such. Only He has constantly *"walked in Your Truth."*

LOVINGKINDNESS

The phrase, *"For Your lovingkindness is before my eyes,"* pertains to the Mercy and Grace of God. The Lord is not only the Personification of kindness to us, but He is also *"lovingkindness."* In effect, this states that the Lord never conducts Himself in any other fashion. If the truth be known, even when He has to send Judgment, His Judgment is an act of kindness. It is an effort to try to bring man to his senses, etc.

The greatest *"lovingkindness"* of all is the Cross of Christ (Jn. 3:16). Once we fully understand that, then we are beginning to understand the lovingkindness of our Lord extended to us. Failure to understand the Cross is a failure to understand the lovingkindness of God, and results in our looking at Him in an erroneous way.

If the Believer doesn't function entirely within the Cross, then the Believer is going to function in Law, in which there is no lovingkindness, only condemnation. So, when the Church is observed functioning in such an unkind way, to be sure, it is functioning in Law, and not in Grace.

If we fully understand the lovingkindness that is shown to us, which is made possible to us only by the Cross, then we will be quick to show lovingkindness to others.

In no way does this mean that we are to condone sin; however, committing the sin of unkindness in no way answers the problem.

To the Believers who function in Law, whether they realize such or not, my words here will have no meaning. But to those who understand that everything they have from the Lord has come to them solely from Christ as the Source and the Cross as the Means, these understand perfectly that of which I here speak.

TRUTH

The phrase, *"And I have walked in Your Truth,"* proclaims the Word of God as God's Truth, i.e., *"Your Word is Your Truth"* (Jn. 17:17). The Bible proclaims the following:

1. Jesus is Truth (Jn. 14:6);
2. The Word is Truth (Jn. 17:17); and,
3. The Holy Spirit is Truth (I Jn. 5:6).

This means that Truth is not merely here contained, but, in reality, Jesus, the Word, and the Holy Spirit are Truth. As I read and study the Word of God, I *"have"* Truth; however, that is different than literally *"being"* Truth, which proclaims Christ, etc.

All of this means that Truth is not a philosophy, but rather a Person, the Lord Jesus Christ, in essence, the Godhead.

(4) "I HAVE NOT SAT WITH VAIN PERSONS, NEITHER WILL I GO IN WITH DISSEMBLERS."

The idea of this Verse is, at least as it regards David, that he always had sought the Lord and what the Lord wanted instead of consulting those with personal agendas.

We may quickly read over this Verse and miss what really is being said here.

FALSE DIRECTIONS

The Church as a whole all over the world is constantly coming up with fads, schemes, etc., which are not of God, and which seek to ensnare people. To be sure, these fads and schemes generally are very successful.

"The Purpose Driven Life" scheme falls into such a category. This foolishness has been conceived by man, which means that it was not conceived by God.

The word *"dissemblers"* actually means *"hypocrites."*

This speaks of those who know the way, the Way of the Cross, or at least have the opportunity to know the way, but rather reject it, thereby fomenting other ways, etc. The Holy Spirit labels such individuals *"hypocrites"*!

In effect, the Messiah, the Greater Son of David, is saying that He would not accept the leaven of the Pharisees, even though they were the religious leaders of Israel. The Messiah had nothing to do with these *"vain persons."*

THE DIVIDING LINE IS THE CROSS

The Cross always has been the dividing line between the True Church and the apostate Church. It began with Cain and Abel on the first page of human history (Gen., Chpt. 4). But yet I personally feel that the Cross presently is the dividing line as never before.

Let me explain how:

We are living in the last of the last days, actually the last days of the Church Age. Provisions are already being made for the Restoration of Israel, which will take place at the Second Coming. This means that the Rapture of the Church is imminent.

Please allow me to make the following statements:

1. The only thing that stands between mankind and eternal Hell is the Cross of Christ!
2. The only thing that stands between the Church and apostasy is the Cross of Christ!

I wish to deal with the second statement.

If the Church rejects the Cross, then it will go into apostasy. And, to be truthful, virtually the entirety of the modern Church has already apostatized. In fact, the Lord is no longer dealing with the institutionalized Church.

In the First Chapter of the Book of Revelation, John pictures Jesus as standing *"in the midst of the Seven Candlesticks,"* which represent the Churches.

The last part of the Third Chapter of the Book of Revelation proclaims the last Message of Christ to the Seven Churches of Asia. This last Message is to the Church at Laodicea. In this final Message, Jesus is pictured outside the Church, standing at the door and knocking, pleading with man to *"open the door"* (Rev. 3:20).

This means that Christ today is dealing only with individuals. Christ always has dealt with individuals, but He also has, in the past, dealt with the Church as a whole; however, as here pictured, that is no longer being done.

The reason?

Apostasy!

So what are we saying?

We are saying that the Message of the Cross is being presented all over the world. The individuals who accept the Message will be saved; otherwise, they will go into apostasy!

All religious persons outside of the Cross are constituted as *"vain persons"* and *"dissemblers,"* i.e., *"hypocrites."*

(5) "I HAVE HATED THE CONGREGATION OF EVILDOERS; AND WILL NOT SIT WITH THE WICKED."

Everything that is not strictly *"Jesus Christ and Him Crucified"* must be abandoned.

If the Lord hates something, we also must hate it!

However, it is not speaking of hating the individuals per se, but rather what they represent, the way they are traveling, the road which represents their direction.

That's why Paul said:

"But though we, or an Angel from Heaven, preach any other gospel unto you than that which we have preached unto you, let him be accursed" (Gal. 1:8).

As the next Verse will proclaim, everything that is not of the Cross must be labeled as *"wicked."*

(6) "I WILL WASH MY HANDS IN INNOCENCY: SO WILL I COMPASS YOUR ALTAR, O LORD."

NOTES

There is no innocency as such in the human race; consequently, only the Lord Jesus Christ could say such a thing. David said it by faith and we, therefore, can also do so. But Christ Alone, Who is our Substitute, can claim such!

THE ALTAR

The *"Altar"* here addressed concerned the Brazen Altar of the Tabernacle of old. It represented Christ and what He would do at the Cross in order to redeem fallen humanity.

What the *"Altar"* represented, namely, the Lord Jesus Christ and His Atoning Work on Calvary's Cross, is that which gave David perfection, that which gives us perfection presently. It is all in Christ, as it all must ever be in Christ.

However, we must note the following:

ANOTHER JESUS

If the Believer attempts to make only the Lord Jesus the sole object of his faith, thereby eliminating the Cross, he concludes with *"another Jesus"* (II Cor. 11:4). And that is the bane of the modern Church.

To a certain extent, it lauds Christ and speaks His Name constantly; however, for most of the Church, the Cross is either ignored, or even disbelieved. As a result, the object of faith is a *"Cross-less Christ,"* which the Lord will never accept.

This is the same problem which Paul addressed in his Ministry. Jesus, *"Yes!"* The Cross, *"No!"* It is the same presently!

If we try to lift up Christ without the Cross, or ignore the Cross in any way, but claim, at the same time, to be extolling Christ, this represents, in actuality, a Christ which is not in the Bible, and which the Lord will not accept. That's why Paul said, *"We preach Christ Crucified"* (I Cor. 1:23).

Much of the world is willing to accept God without Jesus, and much of the Church is willing to accept Jesus without the Cross. In either case, such is not to be! Anything that proclaims Jesus without the Cross is done so by *"another spirit"* which presents *"another gospel,"* which Paul said *"is not another"* (Gal. 1:6-7; II Cor. 11:4), i.e., *"not valid."*

We can only refer to Jesus as *"Lord"* by

the Holy Spirit (I Cor. 12:3). We cannot know the Holy Spirit except by and through the Cross of Christ (Rom. 8:2).

(7) "THAT I MAY PUBLISH WITH THE VOICE OF THANKSGIVING, AND TELL OF ALL YOUR WONDROUS WORKS."

The idea of this Verse is that we should constantly give thanksgiving unto the Lord, constantly telling of all *"Your wondrous works."*

The Lord has been so good to us. We should constantly thank Him for such. All of our prayer sessions should, in fact, begin with thanksgiving unto the Lord (Ps. 100:4).

"Telling of His wondrous works" produces faith; complaining produces unbelief!

(8) "LORD, I HAVE LOVED THE HABITATION OF YOUR HOUSE, AND THE PLACE WHERE YOUR HONOR DWELLS."

David was speaking of the Tabernacle where the Ark of the Covenant dwelt. Now the Christian becomes the Temple of the Holy Spirit (I Cor. 3:16). That's the reason Paul said, *"I beseech you therefore, Brethren, by the mercies of God, that you present your bodies a living sacrifice, holy, acceptable unto God, which is your reasonable service"* (Rom. 12:1).

THE CROSS OF CHRIST

The only way that one can successfully present one's body as a living sacrifice unto God is by their faith being placed exclusively in Christ and the Cross. Otherwise, it is impossible, no matter the effort!

Actually, in the Tabernacle and Temple of old, it was the Holy Spirit of the Divine Trinity Who dwelt in the Holy of Holies between the Mercy Seat and the Cherubim. As stated, due to what Christ did at the Cross, now it is possible, and has been since the Cross, for the Holy Spirit to dwell in the lives of Believers, which He most definitely does, beginning at conversion.

The *"honor"* here addressed by David pertains to the Glory of God that then was in the Tabernacle, but now, as stated, is in the hearts and lives of Believers.

(9) "GATHER NOT MY SOUL WITH SINNERS, NOR MY LIFE WITH BLOODY MEN."

A tremendous Truth, even in two ways, is here given by David.

NOTES

SEPARATION

The Bible does not teach isolation, but it most definitely does teach separation, and we speak of separation from the world. In fact, Paul wrote and said, *"Wherefore, come out from among them, and be ye separate, saith the Lord, and touch not the unclean thing; and I will receive you"* (II Cor. 6:17).

We Believers are *"in"* the world, but we definitely are not to be *"of"* the world. We do not march to the world's drumbeat or sing its tune. It is to have no bearing on us.

That of which I speak is somewhat like a ship in the water. Such a vessel can haul goods and be an accommodation to many people, that is, as long as the ship stays on the water. But the moment water gets into the ship, then you've got a problem! And that's exactly what happens with the Church. We are in the world, and, as such, we can do great things for the Lord; however, the moment the world gets in us, we have great problems!

FAILURE

The second Truth brought out here is that it is quite possible for even the Godliest, as David, to find themselves in the very place they don't want to be. David probably had at this time hardly any idea that soon he would become a murderer. David was complicit in the murder of Uriah the Hittite by the sword of the children of Ammon, because he had committed idolatry with the man's wife, Bathsheba (II Sam. 12:9).

"Wherefore let him who thinks he stands take heed lest he fall" (I Cor. 10:12).

There is only one way that one can find security, and I speak of guaranteed security, and that is that one's faith is exclusively in Christ and what He has done for us at the Cross (Rom. 6:1-14). In fact, this situation is so critical that Jesus said that we must address it on a daily basis, in effect, taking up the Cross daily (Lk. 9:23).

The Believer is safe only as long as the Believer keeps his faith in Christ and the Cross. The Lord has provided no other safety and protection, because no other safety and protection are needed. It only requires faith on our part, but, of necessity, faith in the correct object.

(10) "IN WHOSE HANDS IS MISCHIEF, AND THEIR RIGHT HAND IS FULL OF BRIBES."

Those who do not serve the Lord serve self. In doing so, they will go to any length and basically do anything to serve their own purpose. Some obviously go much deeper into sin than others. Still, all who do not know the Lord fall into this category of *"mischief"* and *"dishonesty"* in one way or another.

(11) BUT AS FOR ME, I WILL WALK IN MY INTEGRITY: REDEEM ME, AND BE MERCIFUL UNTO ME."

The repeated *"my"* of Verse 9 and the repeated *"me"* of Verse 11 are to be interpreted of Israel as personated by her Advocate.

One can claim the Mercy of God, which has to do with all the Blessings of God, if one looks solely to the Lord, trusting in His integrity. Trust makes His integrity our integrity.

(12) MY FOOT STANDS IN AN EVEN PLACE: IN THE CONGREGATIONS WILL I BLESS THE LORD."

As the Intercessor, the foot of Christ was planted upon the smooth (i.e., righteous) pavement of the Divine audience chamber, and the foot itself was as *"even"* as the pavement on which it stood; for, as prefigured in the Meal Offering, there was an evenness in His Life among men that all their hatred, treachery, and snares failed to roughen. He could therefore say, *"My foot has always stood, always stands, and will continually stand in an even place."*

PSALM 27

*A Psalm of David:
Trust and Commitment to God*

(1) "THE LORD IS MY LIGHT AND MY SALVATION; WHOM SHALL I FEAR? THE LORD IS THE STRENGTH OF MY LIFE; OF WHOM SHALL I BE AFRAID?"

The Messiah in the Garden of Gethsemane (Jn. 18:1-6) is the theme of the first six Verses of this Psalm; its remaining Verses belong to His subsequent experiences in the hands of captors.

NOTES

OUR ALL-SUFFICIENT HIGH PRIEST

The doctrine, therefore, of this Psalm is that the Messiah is an all-sufficient High Priest for His people; and that He can, by His example, by His Ministry, and by His Spirit in us carry us triumphantly through the sharpest trials and through death itself (Heb. 4:14-15). A Priest who can help must be a Priest who has suffered and won, who, having been tempted in all points, can have compassion on the ignorant and defeated.

THE BELIEVER

We are given tremendous Promises in this Verse, for they apply to us as well as to David and to our Lord.

If the Lord is our *"Light"* and *"Salvation,"* then what do we have to fear?

If He is *"the strength of my life,"* then why should I be afraid of anyone?

Every Believer belongs to the Lord, belonging to Him by virtue of the price that He paid for our Redemption. As such, we are very special property. The Lord has planned out every aspect of our life and living, that is, if we will only earnestly seek His Face in order that we may function as He desires that we function.

All too often, regrettably, far too many Believers little understand their place and position in Christ. They little seek His Divine Leading and Direction, which presents a great loss to such a person.

If we follow the Lord, doing so to the best of our ability, which we only can do by evidencing faith in Christ and the Cross, then we need not fear what anyone can do to us, or anything else. If Satan does something to us, it's only because the Lord allows him to do so.

Satan has to go before the Lord, hat in hand, so to speak, asking permission, before he can come against us in any fashion. Even if the Lord then allows Satan any latitude at all, He sets the parameters within which Satan can work; and the Evil One dare go no further!

Regrettably, at times, we give Satan much latitude in our lives by default. In other words, we fail to understand the Cross as it regards Sanctification, and we, therefore, attempt to live for the Lord in all the wrong ways. As a result, most Christians live in a state of spiritual adultery (Rom. 7:1-4). In effect, if Satan governs us, it is by our consent, whether we understand this or not.

THE WAY OF VICTORY

The Lord has provided a way of victory. That Way is His Cross (Rom. 6:1-14). He has provided no other, because no other is needed. The problem is sin, and the only answer to sin is the Cross of Christ. Regrettably and sadly, the Church constantly puts forth other avenues of proposed victory, when, in reality, there is no victory whatsoever in those directions.

That's why Paul said, *"We preach Christ Crucified"* (I Cor. 1:23).

(2) "WHEN THE WICKED, EVEN MY ENEMIES AND MY FOES, CAME UPON ME TO EAT UP MY FLESH, THEY STUMBLED AND FELL."

Approximately a thousand years before Christ, the Holy Spirit through David proclaims what will take place in the Garden of Gethsemane when the enemies of our Lord came to seize Him. In the darkness of that night, as He saw the lanterns and torches of those coming to seize Him, His heart sang in the quiet confidence of all assured faith. *"Jehovah is My Light and My Stronghold. Whom shall I fear?"* And when, a moment later, He, with great majesty, said, *"I Am the I Am,"* they fell backward to the ground (Jn. 18:1-6).

(3) "THOUGH AN HOST SHOULD ENCAMP AGAINST ME, MY HEART SHALL NOT FEAR: THOUGH WAR SHOULD RISE AGAINST ME, IN THIS WILL I BE CONFIDENT."

We are here given the attitude of the heart of the Master when He was arrested in the Garden of Gethsemane.

FEAR

There is torment in fear, but Jesus had no torment at all, simply because there was no fear. Even though they surrounded Him and had every intention of executing the supreme penalty of death, He was *"confident"* that God would see Him through.

Every Child of God should have this same confidence. For us, He has faced the *"wicked,"* the *"enemies,"* the *"foes,"* and the *"host."* He has overcome them all. If we put our trust in Him and what He did for us at the Cross, we can also be certain that total victory will be ours. The Holy Spirit will see to it (Rom. 8:2).

On the way to the palace of Caiaphas, and later on the way to the Judgment Hall of Pilate, abandoned and defenseless, but knowing all things that should come upon Him — He perfectly trusted and perfectly believed that He certainly would be resurrected.

(4) "ONE THING HAVE I DESIRED OF THE LORD, THAT WILL I SEEK AFTER; THAT I MAY DWELL IN THE HOUSE OF THE LORD ALL THE DAYS OF MY LIFE, TO BEHOLD THE BEAUTY OF THE LORD, AND TO ENQUIRE IN HIS TEMPLE."

By faith, we are seated with Christ in the Heavenlies (Eph. 2:6). Upon the event of the First Resurrection, we will be with Him forever. This is really what every Child of God does *"seek after."*

The Lord utters these words as *"The Man Christ Jesus."*

THE TEMPLE

When Christ was on Earth, the Temple was polluted by the Sadducees and the Pharisees. They had actually turned the Court of the Gentiles into a *"den of thieves"* (Lk. 19:46).

In the coming Kingdom Age, this prayer will be answered in totality, and the Millennial Temple will be constantly occupied by the Lord.

That which David desired did not at that time come to pass. The Temple which he envisioned, of which the Lord had given him a complete set of blueprints, was not built by him, but rather by his son, Solomon. But in the coming Kingdom Age, David, along with every other Glorified Believer, will, together with the Master, have constant access to the Temple.

(5) "FOR IN THE TIME OF TROUBLE HE SHALL HIDE ME IN HIS PAVILION: IN THE SECRET OF HIS TABERNACLE SHALL HE HIDE ME; HE SHALL SET ME UP UPON A ROCK."

As David cried these words, little did he

realize that he was saying what the Messiah would say.

Verses 5 and 6 reveal the unshakable confidence that our Lord had in His Father, and His conviction as to Resurrection. He consequently pledges Himself to sing loud praises in the Heavenly Temple. These were among the joys that He set before Him. Because of these, He endured the Cross, despising its shame.

(6) "AND NOW SHALL MY HEAD BE LIFTED UP ABOVE MY ENEMIES ROUND ABOUT ME: THEREFORE WILL I OFFER IN HIS TABERNACLE SACRIFICES OF JOY; I WILL SING, YEA, I WILL SING PRAISES UNTO THE LORD."

This is True Faith. The Messiah, facing an agonizing death on Mount Calvary, instead looked beyond to the Resurrection, where He would be lifted up above *"My enemies."* He spoke of *"joy."* This was undoubtedly the blackest time of the Master's earthly sojourn. In the very midst of it, He said, *"I will sing praises unto the LORD."* Only an unshakable Faith could say such.

(7) "HEAR, O LORD, WHEN I CRY WITH MY VOICE: HAVE MERCY ALSO UPON ME, AND ANSWER ME."

Verses 7 through 10 belong to the moment of the arrest of our Lord and the abandonment by His Disciples.

All He had on Earth were His beloved Disciples (Mk. 3:35). As He looked upon them as they fled, His heart must have been pierced with anguish, but it rested in the consciousness that Jehovah would compensate Him by gathering Him and them into His bosom.

(8) "WHEN YOU SAID, SEEK YE MY FACE; MY HEART SAID UNTO YOU, YOUR FACE, LORD, WILL I SEEK."

The full meaning seems to be: *"To You said My Heart, Have You said unto Me, Seek ye My Face? I for One will obey You. Your Face, LORD, will I seek."*

(9) "HIDE NOT YOUR FACE FAR FROM ME; PUT NOT YOUR SERVANT AWAY IN ANGER: YOU HAVE BEEN MY HELP; LEAVE ME NOT, NEITHER FORSAKE ME, O GOD OF MY SALVATION."

Even though David cries these words, which did truly fit him, still, they pertain more so to the Greater Son of David.

This was not a cry of unbelief on the part of the Master, but of an affection that made God His all and His refuge. To Israel, Jehovah had said, and was continually saying, *"Seek ye My face"* (Deut. 4:29; I Chron. 28:9; Isa. 45:19; Amos 5:4). One heart, the Messiah's, promptly replied, *"Your Face, O Jehovah, will I seek."*

(10) "WHEN MY FATHER AND MY MOTHER FORSAKE ME, THEN THE LORD WILL TAKE ME UP."

The expression here is proverbial.

This is what David is here saying:

Even if he is forsaken by his nearest and dearest, he would not be forsaken by God.

Jesus was forsaken by all except the Father!

We should understand this, as it also regards our own personal lives. Whatever others may do, the Lord will not forsake those who trust Him.

Men may try to claim this, that, or the other, i.e., claim that if they forsake you, that means God has forsaken you.

Let the following be clearly understood:

FORSAKEN BY THE LORD?

It doesn't matter what other people do, what other Churches do, or what religious leaders do, if a person continues to trust the Lord, in spite of what has happened, the Lord will not forsake such a person.

"For He has said, I will never leave you, nor forsake you.

"So that we may boldly say, The Lord is my helper, and I will not fear what man shall do unto me" (Heb. 13:5-6).

Religious men love to claim, just as did the Pharisees and Sadducees, that if they forsake you, that means that God has forsaken you. In other words, your acceptance by the Lord is based upon their acceptance of you, or so they claim. Nothing could be further from the Truth!

God's acceptance of you is not based on what other men think or on what they do. It is based strictly upon one's faith and confidence in Him.

(11) "TEACH ME YOUR WAY, O LORD, AND LEAD ME IN A PLAIN PATH, BECAUSE OF MY ENEMIES."

Unfortunately, David had many enemies,

and the Greater Son of David had even more enemies.

Why?

ENEMIES OF THE LORD

The enemies of our Lord were the religious leaders of Israel. There are far more enemies inside the Church than outside. It was not the thieves and the harlots who crucified Christ, but rather the religious leaders of Israel. In effect, that element is still in the crucifying business.

(12) "DELIVER ME NOT OVER UNTO THE WILL OF MY ENEMIES: FOR FALSE WITNESSES ARE RISEN UP AGAINST ME, AND SUCH AS BREATHE OUT CRUELTY."

There is no cruelty like religious cruelty.

The prayer of Verse 11 contemplates the moment when Christ entered into the palace of Caiaphas. Verse 12 portrays the hour when the false witnesses accused Him, and the Pharisees cruelly determined to crucify Him.

(13) "I HAD FAINTED, UNLESS I HAD BELIEVED TO SEE THE GOODNESS OF THE LORD IN THE LAND OF THE LIVING."

The sense of Verse 13 is: *"I have always believed, I do now believe, and I will continue to believe, that I shall see the goodness of Jehovah in the land of the living."* In other words, Christ firmly believed that He would be raised from the dead. And so He was!

(14) "WAIT ON THE LORD: BE OF GOOD COURAGE, AND HE SHALL STRENGTHEN YOUR HEART: WAIT, I SAY, ON THE LORD."

It is not easy to *"wait."* Perhaps waiting is the hardest thing that any Child of God ever has to do.

The word *"courage"* means *"be encouraged."*

What a statement for Him to make as He travels the way to Calvary!

Due to the agony of the Garden and Satan's efforts to kill Him, He was strengthened in His heart by *"waiting on the LORD."*

What a lesson for the Church! What a lesson for every Child of God! What a lesson for every Believer who is in the midst of a trial!

WAITING ON THE LORD

The Believer is to take a lesson from our Lord, even when our feelings indicate the contrary. We are to conduct ourselves with encouragement, no matter how the situation looks, feels, or seems to be! To conduct oneself accordingly shows faith, and we are here promised by the Lord that such faith will be rewarded by the Lord. He will strengthen our hearts!

PSALM 28

*A Psalm of David:
A Prayer for God's Help*

(1) "UNTO YOU WILL I CRY, O LORD MY ROCK; BE NOT SILENT TO ME: LEST, IF YOU BE SILENT TO ME, I BECOME LIKE THEM WHO GO DOWN INTO THE PIT."

As noted, David wrote this Psalm.

REQUESTS OF OUR LORD

Praying on behalf of His people, He asks in Verses 1 and 2 for audience. In Verses 3 and 4, our Lord makes definite petitions in favor of His people and against His and our enemies. In Verse 5, He sets out the just ground of the judgment which He demands.

To become like them who go down into the sepulcher, which means to go without God, is to be hopeless.

The Lord is the only One Who can meet the need. To be sure, it hasn't changed from then until now. The problem is, however, that Believers look to other men because this is what they are taught to do. If they do so, they get only the pitiful help that poor human beings can give. If they go to God, they receive the help which He gives, which is all-powerful. So we should cry to the Lord, Who can help us in all of our troubles, irrespective as to what those troubles might be. He is our Rock, which refers to the fact that He is unchangeable!

INTERCESSION

Once again, we are brought into the Intercessory petitions of the Great Intercessor Himself. What comfort it is to feel the heartthrob of His petition as He becomes one with us.

The Intercession of Christ on behalf of His people is little understood by most

Christians. Perhaps none can fully understand it.

As we read these Psalms, we are reading the words that the Lord says on our behalf. These are words we would like to say ourselves; but most of the time do not know how to say them, or even that they need to be said. The Holy Spirit categorically says such in the following:

"Likewise the Spirit also helps our infirmities: for we know not what we should pray for as we ought: but the Spirit Itself makes intercession for us with groanings which cannot be uttered" (Rom. 8:26).

Many Pentecostals erroneously think that this Passage in Romans has the meaning of the petitioner praying in tongues. While it certainly is valid to pray in tongues, still, this is not the meaning of the Passage. It does mean that the Holy Spirit, before the Throne of God, literally petitions the Father with inutterable gushings of the heart on our behalf. Moreover, the Christ of Whom we now particularly speak *"ever lives to make Intercession for us"* (Heb. 7:25).

Without this twin Intercession, the Child of God would little know victory, leading, guidance, or overcoming power.

INTERCESSION FOR SIN

The Holy Spirit makes Intercession for us regarding help. He doesn't intercede on our behalf regarding sin, that being the sole domain of our Lord. Christ is the One Who paid the price at Calvary's Cross; therefore, He is the One Who makes Intercession for us, as it regards sin.

This First Verse is powerful. If the Lord is silent, then we will remain in our sin. The word *"pit"* does not refer to Hell, but is used figuratively for the state of sin (Isa. 51:1). In other words, if the Lord doesn't do it, it cannot be done. All too often, the modern Church is placing its hopes on the deceit of humanistic psychology. If such is trusted, or any other avenue of supposed help, there will be no extrication from *"the pit."*

(2) "HEAR THE VOICE OF MY SUPPLICATIONS, WHEN I CRY UNTO YOU, WHEN I LIFT UP MY HANDS TOWARD YOUR HOLY ORACLE."

In the Old Testament, the *"Holy Oracle"* was the *"Most Holy Place,"* which contained the Ark of the Covenant, where God dwelt between the Mercy Seat and the Cherubim.

Under the New Covenant, we are to pray to the Father in Heaven, and do so in the Name of Jesus, with every Believer having, in a sense, the Power of Attorney regarding the use of that Name (Jn. 16:23).

(3) "DRAW ME NOT AWAY WITH THE WICKED, AND WITH THE WORKERS OF INIQUITY, WHICH SPEAK PEACE TO THEIR NEIGHBORS, BUT MISCHIEF IS IN THEIR HEARTS."

The horror that the follower of the Lord has of not having his sins forgiven, i.e., being placed in the same position as the *"wicked,"* is horror indeed!

Verses 1 and 2 proclaim the great chasm that divides the Child of God from the wicked, which is described in Verses 3 through 5.

The wicked actually love their sins because *"mischief is in their hearts."*

(4) "GIVE THEM ACCORDING TO THEIR DEEDS, AND ACCORDING TO THE WICKEDNESS OF THEIR ENDEAVORS: GIVE THEM AFTER THE WORK OF THEIR HANDS; RENDER TO THEM THEIR DESERT."

When one considers that this is the prayer of the Son of God, Who gave Himself for a wicked world, then one should realize the thoughts of God for those who will not repent. There is no way they can escape eternal damnation.

The next Verse tells us why!

(5) "BECAUSE THEY REGARD NOT THE WORKS OF THE LORD, NOR THE OPERATION OF HIS HANDS, HE SHALL DESTROY THEM, AND NOT BUILD THEM UP."

Most of the world falls into the category of Verses 3 through 5. They truly *"regard not the works of the Lord."* If they continue in that direction and refuse to repent, *"He shall destroy them."*

Those who do not understand the nature of God claim that God does not do such. They place the responsibility on the person or on Satan. While it certainly is true that both Satan and the *"wicked"* are responsible, still, God is the One Who will actually destroy the wicked. And no wonder, considering the wicked have spurned God's great Love and Mercy.

Men go to Hell because they want to go to Hell. They die lost because they desire to die lost. Anyone who desires to come to the Lord simply has to call upon His Name (Rom. 10:13).

It does not matter where the person is, who the person is, or what the person has done. If a person will sincerely call upon the Lord, he will be heard, and Salvation will be instant!

(6) "BLESSED BE THE LORD, BECAUSE HE HAS HEARD THE VOICE OF MY SUPPLICATIONS."

This Scripture, as all Scriptures, should be especially meaningful to the Believer.

GUARANTEED INTERCESSION

Now Christ acts as the Great High Priest in the perfection of the faith of which He is the Author and Finisher by declaring that His supplications have been heard. God always hears the Intercession of the Great Intercessor, the Lord Jesus Christ.

In Verse 2, we have the petition that God will hear the *"supplications."* In Verse 6, we have the assurance that He has heard the *"supplications"* — and for all time.

Referring back to Romans 8:26: Even though the Holy Spirit makes Intercession for us, which is so very important, He does not, and cannot, enter into the oneness, as Christ can, of our *"supplication."* Basically, the Holy Spirit *"helps our infirmities,"* which means *"to render assistance"*; however, that is a far different type of Intercession than that which is made by Christ, Who literally becomes one with our sin, our failure, and our disobedience. Only Christ can enter this realm of darkness (and darkness it is!), because He has atoned in totality for all sin, past, present, and future, at least for all who will believe (Col. 2:14-15).

(7) "THE LORD IS MY STRENGTH AND MY SHIELD; MY HEART TRUSTED IN HIM, AND I AM HELPED: THEREFORE MY HEART GREATLY REJOICES; AND WITH MY SONG WILL I PRAISE HIM."

The exclamation is, *"I am helped!"*

THE HELP GIVEN BY THE LORD

This is *"help"* we cannot do without. Let it ever be said, *"There is no other help like this help."* Now we can praise him! Now we have a song! Now we greatly rejoice!

Why?

The Lord Jesus Christ is our Great Intercessor; He ever lives to make Intercession for us. Because of His Intercession, we are guaranteed forgiveness and cleansing from sin. The exclamation, *"I am helped!"* is actually a gross understatement. Truly every sin has been forgiven. We are washed and cleansed by the Precious Blood of the Lamb. Nothing is held against us.

"There is therefore now no condemnation to them who are in Christ Jesus, who walk not after the flesh, but after the Spirit" (Rom. 8:1).

I can sense the Presence of the Lord even as I dictate these notes. When the Lord intercedes on our behalf, we are not left with guilt and condemnation, but rather with a song. The world cannot give such a thing; in fact, the world has absolutely no knowledge of this of which we speak.

(8) "THE LORD IS THEIR STRENGTH, AND HE IS THE SAVING STRENGTH OF HIS ANOINTED."

A great truth is here opened up!

HIS ANOINTED

The two words, *"His Anointed,"* speak of *"His Messiah."*

What does it mean for our Lord to be anointed?

Jesus said of Himself, *"The Spirit of the Lord is upon Me, because He has anointed Me to preach the Gospel to the poor; He has sent Me to heal the brokenhearted, to preach deliverance to the captives, and recovering of sight to the blind, to set at liberty them who are bruised, to preach the acceptable Year of the Lord"* (Lk. 4:18-19).

As God, our Lord needed no anointing, as should be obvious. However, as *"Man,"* He did need the Anointing of the Holy Spirit in every capacity. He, in truth, has a sevenfold Anointing.

THE SEVENFOLD ANOINTING

This means that there is no problem, no difficulty, and no heartache, irrespective as to what it might be, that He cannot solve. He is the answer to every question, the solution to every problem, the power for every weakness, the riches for all poverty, and Salvation from all sin! He is our everything!

This Eighth Verse declares the Trinity. He Who anoints is God the Father, He Who is anointed is God the Son, and the oil with which He is anointed is symbolic of God the Holy Spirit.

(9) "SAVE YOUR PEOPLE, AND BLESS YOUR INHERITANCE: FEED THEM ALSO, AND LIFT THEM UP FOREVER."

Now that the Lord has heard this petition and the sin has been washed away, we are no longer in the *"pit."* Now we are as sheep in *"green pastures"* *"beside the still waters,"* and He is feeding us. He has promised to do so *"forever."*

PSALM 29

*A Psalm of David:
The Voice of God*

(1) "GIVE UNTO THE LORD, O YE MIGHTY, GIVE UNTO THE LORD GLORY AND STRENGTH."

The Name *"Jehovah"* occurs eighteen times in this Psalm — four times in the first two Verses, four times in the last two, and ten times in the intervening Verses.

ALMIGHTY GOD

The Divine Psalmist calls upon the Angels to worship Jehovah; He recites God's Power over Nature; He declares that in the beautiful Temple of Creation, everything, animate and inanimate, proclaims His Glory; He records that Jehovah sat as King at the flood; and He predicts that the strength of Verse 1 and the peace of Verse 11 will be given to His people.

The doctrine of this Psalm is that Jehovah is mightier than the Angels of His Might; that He is stronger than the forces of nature; that He is Almighty; and that all this limitless strength is at the disposition of His weakest child. The forces against His children may be mighty, but He Who loves and cares for us is mightier than they.

The mighty Angels are summoned to hear a Voice mightier than theirs; and the majestic sanctuary of Creation is commanded to ascribe all its glory and power to Jehovah.

(2) "GIVE UNTO THE LORD THE GLORY DUE UNTO HIS NAME; WORSHIP THE LORD IN THE BEAUTY OF HOLINESS."

Two things are said in this Verse:

1. His Name is worthy of all the glory that we can give Him.

2. We should worship the Lord in the beauty of Holiness.

HOLINESS

We are told that *"Holiness"* is beautiful. This expression is found five times in the Bible (Vs. 2; Ps. 96:9; 110:3; I Chron. 16:29; II Chron. 20:21).

At the beginning, everything in Creation was created Holy. When the Plan of Redemption is complete, all will be eternally Holy again, except those who have rebelled against God.

There is a false holiness created by the flesh, which has no beauty, only death; however, the Holiness given by God, which can only be given by God, which has nothing to do with Church rules, regulations, or personal attention to such, is beautiful indeed. Carnal holiness, which, in reality, is no Holiness at all, is only external. True Biblical Holiness, engendered by God, is internal.

WHAT IS HOLINESS?

First of all, we must understand that all Holiness comes from God (Lev. 19:2; 21:8; Isa. 43:15; 47:4). However, this *"Holiness"* is projected to us basically through the Holy Spirit.

Within himself, man has no Holiness, but yet is commanded to be holy (I Pet. 1:15-16).

So, the great question is, *"How can man be holy?"*

There is nothing that man can do, such as religious ceremonies or religious activity, that can make one holy. Belonging to certain Churches doesn't make one holy and neither does carrying out a particular religious regimen. As stated, there is actually nothing man can do to make himself holy.

So, how can one become holy?

As far as *"position"* is concerned, every single Believer in the world, and all who have ever lived, have a *"standing"* of Holiness, or a *"position,"* one might say, of Holiness.

That is given to every Believer at conversion (I Cor. 6:11).

In effect, *"Holiness"* is basically the same thing, at least to a certain extent, as *"Sanctification."* And we all know that a Believer's *"condition"* in a practical sense is not the same as one's *"position."* It is the business of the Holy Spirit to bring our *"state"* up to our *"standing,"* our *"condition"* up to our *"position."*

HOW DOES THE HOLY SPIRIT BRING OUR STATE OF HOLINESS UP TO OUR STANDING OF HOLINESS?

While the Christian can do nothing within himself to make himself holy, he can do many things to make himself unholy — and fast, one might say! All sin constitutes that which is grossly unholy; therefore, it is the business of the Holy Spirit to get all sin out of our lives (Rom. 8:1-2, 11).

How does the Holy Spirit do that?

The Holy Spirit doesn't demand much of us. If He did, all of us would be in a sad situation. But He does demand one thing, and that one thing is faith, and, more particularly, faith in Christ and what Christ did at the Cross.

The Believer exhibiting faith in Christ and what Christ did at the Cross, and doing so on a continual basis, constitutes *"walking after the Spirit"* (Rom. 8:1, 3). Whenever the Believer's faith is properly placed in Christ and the Cross, and remains in that capacity, even as it must, the Holy Spirit can then perform the work needed to be done in our hearts and lives, which will rid us of sin's dominion. The Bible doesn't teach sinless perfection, but it definitely does teach that *"sin shall not have dominion over you"* (Rom. 6:14).

Every Believer must, therefore, think of himself as holy, because in Christ we are holy. It is impossible to be otherwise. And yet, every Believer knows and understands that there are things in his life which are not pleasing to the Lord, things which must be eliminated, whatever they might be. The unending, unceasing Work of the Holy Spirit in our lives is to effectually eliminate all those things in our lives which do not please the Lord.

NOTES

But the problem with the greater majority of the Church is that most Christians have not been taught the fundamental principles of the Cross of Christ as it regards Sanctification; therefore, they attempt to sanctify themselves in one way or another, which is impossible!

So, because most Christians little understand how the Holy Spirit works, their situation, spiritually speaking, is not one of victory, but rather the very opposite.

MODERN FADS

This is the reason that the Church constantly comes up with one scheme after the other. Whether they realize it or not, they are attempting to be what the Lord wants them to be, just doing it all wrong! Because whatever they currently are doing is not working, they gravitate to any new fad or scheme which comes along.

I speak presently of *"The Purpose Driven Life,"* etc.

This scheme is, first of all, not Scriptural. And how do I know it's not Scriptural?

It's not Scriptural because they are not teaching and preaching *"Jesus Christ and Him Crucified"* (I Cor. 1:23). And anything that purports to be Gospel, but emphasizes something other than the Cross of Christ, pure and simple, is unscriptural (I Cor. 1:17).

The very fact that millions of Christians have embraced this particular scheme tells us that whatever it is they are in is not the right thing. If it was the right thing, they would not gravitate toward this foolishness. Once they complete this fad, they will be looking for something else.

Only the Cross of Christ can satisfy the human heart. Only the Cross of Christ can bring about the working of the Holy Spirit in one's life, Who Alone can make us what we ought to be. Only the Cross of Christ is the proper foundation. Everything else plays out to defeat. The Cross alone culminates in victory (Rom. 6:1-14; 8:1-2, 11; Gal. 6:14).

For the Christian who is holy to be holy, i.e., to be what he is, he must evidence faith in Christ and what Christ did at the Cross, and that exclusively (Lk. 9:23-24). That done, and continuing to be done, the Holy Spirit will begin a lifelong work of developing the

Believer into Christlikeness. That and that alone is Holiness!

(3) "THE VOICE OF THE LORD IS UPON THE WATERS: THE GOD OF GLORY THUNDERS: THE LORD IS UPON MANY WATERS."

Regarding the *"waters,"* what David here says has reference to the word *"flood"* in Verse 10. It carries the idea that the elements, even the waters of the Earth, respond to His Voice, and to His Voice alone.

For instance, the Lord has said, *"Neither shall there anymore be a flood to destroy the Earth"* (Gen. 9:11). That being the Word of the Lord, it is guaranteed that the Earth will not again be destroyed by a flood. In fact, all of the things which make man fearful, such as the *"greenhouse effect,"* or the *"warming"* or *"cooling"* of the poles, have no validity. In other words, some scientific organizations are claiming that if the great ice floes of Greenland melted, the elevation of the ocean would increase some fifteen feet. That is not going to happen!

How do I know that?

I know that because the Lord is in control of all things, and there is nothing in His Word which gives any credence to such an idea.

(4) "THE VOICE OF THE LORD IS POWERFUL; THE VOICE OF THE LORD IS FULL OF MAJESTY."

The Lord controls all things, and does so by His Word.

"The Voice of the LORD is powerful" in that He has the Power to do whatever is necessary. But, at the same time, *"the Voice of the LORD is full of majesty,"* meaning that He will never do something that is detrimental in an overall sense to His Creation.

(5) "THE VOICE OF THE LORD BREAKS THE CEDARS; YEA, THE LORD BREAKS THE CEDARS OF LEBANON."

The *"Cedars of Lebanon"* were the most powerful trees known in the entirety of the world at that particular time. They were similar to the great redwoods of California. With a Word, however, the Lord could cause the elements to topple these giants.

(6) "HE MAKES THEM ALSO TO SKIP LIKE A CALF; LEBANON AND SIRION LIKE A YOUNG UNICORN."

NOTES

"Sirion" is another name for *"Mount Hermon"* (Deut. 3:9).

These two mountains, *"Lebanon"* and *"Hermon,"* are visible throughout the greater part of the Holy Land.

Through earthquakes, the Lord is able to make these mountains shake and tremble, which again proclaims His Almighty Power.

These Verses are not given merely to proclaim the Power of God, for that should be evident. But they are given that we may know and understand that this Power, even as the last Verse proclaims, is at the disposal of every Child of God.

(7) "THE VOICE OF THE LORD DIVIDES THE FLAMES OF FIRE."

All of this pertains to the fact that the Lord is in control, which refers to control of everything, especially the elements.

(8) "THE VOICE OF THE LORD SHAKES THE WILDERNESS; THE LORD SHAKES THE WILDERNESS OF KADESH."

"Kadesh" is mentioned because it lies at the opposite extremity from Lebanon, meaning that the Lord covers the entirety of the nation of Israel.

While the Lord definitely has control over the entirety of the world, this Passage is worded as it is in order to proclaim that the Lord has and takes minute control over every part of Israel. It is the same presently with those who name the Name of Christ.

Even though nothing happens but that the Lord has the doing of it, irrespective as to what it is, still, He exerts a protection, a control, if you will, over His people more than over anyone else in the world, which should be obvious.

Every Believer is presented as the *"salt"* of the Earth and the *"light"* of the world, all under and through Christ (Mat. 5:13-14).

(9) "THE VOICE OF THE LORD MAKES THE HINDS TO CALVE, AND DISCOVERS THE FOREST: AND IN HIS TEMPLE DOES EVERY ONE SPEAK OF HIS GLORY."

The actual translation of the last phrase is, *"Everyone says, 'Glory.'"*

The King James translators, obviously not being accustomed to praising the Lord, at least in a manner to where the praises can be heard, seemingly did not quite understand how to translate this particular phrase. We who are Saved and baptized with the Holy Spirit are quite accustomed to saying, *"Glory,"* and many other similar praises, doing so vocally and often.

PRAISE

Praising the Lord is the privilege of every single Believer. It is something that Believers, for all the obvious reasons, should do constantly.

When a Believer is praising the Lord, such evidences faith. Complaining, murmuring, and finding fault obviously are the very opposite.

The Lord cannot bless complainers, but He most definitely can bless *"praisers."*

I have noticed that when a person truly comes to Christ and is baptized with the Holy Spirit, then exactly as the Scripture here portrays, such a person is accustomed to *"saying, 'Glory.'"* It is commonplace and comes naturally. As stated, this pertains more so to Spirit-filled Believers.

Those who are saved but who have not been baptized with the Holy Spirit seemingly do not have a spirit of praise about them, as do those who are Spirit-filled.

In my years of ministering and preaching the Gospel, I have noticed that when a person is baptized with the Holy Spirit, which is always accompanied by the speaking with other tongues, then irrespective as to what that person has been in the past, whether Catholic, Protestant, or whatever, they automatically will begin to praise the Lord, and the praises are all very similar.

Such is characteristic of Spirit-filled people.

About a thousand years before Christ, the Holy Spirit through David stated that *"everyone"* would *"say 'Glory.'"* If you as a Believer aren't accustomed to doing such, you need to break a bad habit and start to praise the Lord. He is worthy of all praise!

(10) "THE LORD SITS UPON THE FLOOD; YEA, THE LORD SITS KING FOREVER."

The special Hebrew word for *"flood"* occurs twelve times in the Hebrew Bible — eleven times in Genesis and once in this Psalm.

The argument of the Verse is that even the Flood — nature's mightiest convulsion, and we speak of Noah's Flood — was controlled by this mightier Power. This is Power beyond our comprehension, but yet Power which is at our disposal, that is, if we only will learn to believe God.

(11) THE LORD WILL GIVE STRENGTH UNTO HIS PEOPLE; THE LORD WILL BLESS HIS PEOPLE WITH PEACE."

We are promised two things in this Verse. They are:
1. Strength!
2. Peace!

This Psalm tells us of the *"Strength"* of the Lord. As stated, it is at our disposal. Understanding that and claiming that, *"The LORD will bless His people with peace."* This, incidentally, is Sanctifying Peace.

PSALM 30

A Psalm of David:
Praise for Deliverance

(1) "I WILL EXTOL YOU, O LORD; FOR YOU HAVE LIFTED ME UP, AND HAVE NOT MADE MY FOES TO REJOICE OVER ME."

The superscription of this Psalm states that it is *"of David,"* i.e., it concerns the Messiah. It is to be sung at the Dedication of the House, that is, at the Dedication of the future Millennial Temple, with the Dedication of Solomon's Temple serving as a type.

It does not definitely say that David wrote this Psalm, and it was not used until the Dedication of the Temple, which was built by Solomon some years after David's death. However, it definitely is possible that David wrote this Psalm for it to be used at the Dedication, which it was, and, more than likely, this is the way it happened.

Most all of David's Psalms are prophetic and picture Christ in either His Atoning, Mediatorial, or Intercessory Work.

THE LORD JESUS CHRIST, THE TRUE ISRAEL!

This Song will actually be sung by the Lord Jesus as the True Israel, Who will intercede for the nation of Israel, and will do so at the Battle of Armageddon, when it looks like Israel will be totally destroyed by the Antichrist.

He begins the petition by thanking the

Lord for victory, stating, in essence, that the Antichrist will not win and cannot, therefore, rejoice over the destruction of Israel, as he thought he would at the beginning!

The reason?

The Lord will lift Israel up.

(2) "O LORD MY GOD, I CRIED UNTO YOU, AND YOU HAVE HEALED ME."

Israel will experience this healing at the Second Coming!

At the darkest time of its history, when it looks like the Antichrist will succeed where Haman, Herod, and Hitler failed, Israel will then cry unto the Lord as never before. To be sure, the Lord will hear their petition!

Why?

It is actually the True Israel, the Lord Jesus Christ, Who will make the petition. The Father never turns Him down!

(3) "O LORD, YOU HAVE BROUGHT UP MY SOUL FROM THE GRAVE: YOU HAVE KEPT ME ALIVE, THAT I SHOULD NOT GO DOWN TO THE PIT."

The True Israel says exactly what should be said in this petition, i.e., *"in this Song."*

He admits that Israel was at the very point of death, i.e., total annihilation. He also admits that it is the Lord Who, because of His Mercy and Grace, kept them alive! For all practical purposes, Israel should have been destroyed and taken down into Hell, i.e., *"to the pit,"* for that was their just deserts. But the Lord said otherwise — again because the Father never will turn down His Son.

(4) "SING UNTO THE LORD, O YE SAINTS OF HIS, AND GIVE THANKS AT THE REMEMBRANCE OF HIS HOLINESS."

This will be the song of redeemed Israel at the conclusion of the Battle of Armageddon, when they, at long last, return from their spiritual exile. They then will have a song to sing!

THE SONG OF SAINTS

While this is pointedly directed toward Israel and their great deliverance that is even yet to come, it can very well apply to any and all Believers, because the Promises of God are without favor. In other words, whatever the Lord will do for Israel, He will also do for all Believers who name His Name.

Israel is here referred to as *"Saints,"* but the designation applies to all who follow Christ (I Cor. 1:2).

God is Holy. Because He is Holy, He will never forfeit His Word, not even to the slightest degree. Whatever He has said, that He will do! Consequently, we should *"give thanks,"* and do so perpetually!

(5) "FOR HIS ANGER ENDURES BUT A MOMENT; IN HIS FAVOR IS LIFE: WEEPING MAY ENDURE FOR A NIGHT, BUT JOY COMES IN THE MORNING."

This Verse proclaims to us several things.

THE PROMISES OF GOD

1. *"For His anger endures but a moment"*: There are many things which anger God, all headed up by the fact of sin. But we have His Promise here that such anger will endure only for a *"moment."*

The idea is this:

While the Lord definitely does chastise His Children, and rightly so, it is only for a short time, and it is always for our good (Heb. 12:5-14).

2. *"In His favor is life"*: As we have said over and over, Jesus Christ is the Source of all things from God, while the Cross is the means. We win *"His favor"* simply by expressing faith in Christ and what He has done for us at the Cross. That is the secret of all Blessings!

3. *"Weeping may endure for a night, but joy comes in the morning"*: The Believer may have problems, which are referred to as a *"night,"* but we also have His Promise that the *"morning"* will bring *"joy."* The world cannot look to such, only a continued night.

Many Saints have gathered strength from this Passage — and rightly so! But more pointedly, this portrays Israel's rebellion and God's Anger at that rebellion. Even though His Anger regarding Israel has now lasted for some 2,500 years, or even longer, still, in the light of eternity, the Holy Spirit calls it *"but a moment."* He will give Israel *"life."* The *"weeping"* that is here mentioned could be said to be on the part of both Israel and Jehovah.

Even though it has lasted for the same length of time as His *"anger,"* still, the Holy Spirit calls it *"a night."* The *"joy"* that will come in the *"morning"* speaks of that

Millennial Morn, when Israel will, at long last, accept the Lord Jesus Christ as her Messiah. In effect, this *"morning"* will then last forever.

(6) "AND IN MY PROSPERITY I SAID, I SHALL NEVER BE MOVED."

The prosperity continued as long as Israel's obedience continued. When her obedience faltered, the prosperity faltered.

PROSPERITY

In His Own time and His Own Way, the Lord most definitely will prosper all who follow Him. If each Believer will look to the Lord and claim His Promises, such a Believer can expect prosperity in the financial sense, in the physical sense, in the domestic sense, and, above all, in the spiritual sense.

All true prosperity comes by and through the Cross. As we have repeatedly stated, Christ is the Source, while the Cross is the means. Outside of the Cross, there is no true prosperity!

Every Christian should give to the Lord liberally and generously. One simply cannot out-give God!

As the Believer gives, He should believe the Lord for the windows of Heaven to open and for the Lord to bless. The Word says that the Lord will bless, and the Word cannot lie!

FROM THIS DAY WILL I BLESS YOU

In September of 2004, if I remember the month correctly, the Lord gave us (this Ministry) a Promise, as it regards His Blessings. Actually, it came through Loren Larson.

We were in the midst of a SonLife Radio drive to raise money for the Network.

Loren mentioned that the Lord had been dealing with him about the Message given by the Prophet Haggai.

Israel had not conducted themselves as they should. The foundation of the Temple had been laid, but the work had languished for years, and the Lord was angry with the situation. Then He began to stir up the Prophet Haggai in connection with this problem, telling them to finish the Temple, i.e., to put His Work first.

Then He told Israel that if they would obey Him, *"from this day will I bless you"* (Hag. 2:19).

NOTES

As Loren was relating this information on that day, the Spirit of the Lord came over me all of a sudden, and I knew this was a Word from the Lord, as it regards SonLife Radio, the entirety of this Ministry, and all who stand with this Ministry.

As I dictate these notes in the month of July of 2005, and as I look back to that time, the Lord has done exactly that which He said He would do, and even much more. In fact, the Blessings have been so abundant that I do not even know how to begin to enumerate that which the Lord has done, is doing, and I know He shall continue to do.

I could enumerate each Blessing, but I'm afraid that people would have a problem believing what I am saying. But this one thing I want all to understand:

This great Promise, *"From this day will I bless you,"* was given not only for this Ministry, but also for all who support this Ministry. You are to give believing that the Lord is going to bless you. He has promised that on a certain day He will begin the Blessing, and it will not let up. And that's exactly what He wants to do.

He only asks one thing of you, which is the same thing He asks of me — and that is faith in that which He has promised. That means that your life and testimony are to be a constant paean of praise. This means that there is to be no faultfinding, none whatsoever, which means there can be no complaints. You are to praise the Lord, doing so constantly, believing exactly what He has said, namely, *"From this day will I bless you."*

The pronoun *"you"* refers to the person who is reading these words who has stood behind this Ministry.

Don't misunderstand! The Lord will bless anyone who supports His Work, wherever that Work is; however, the Promise He gave to us concerned this Ministry, and this Ministry alone. He has said it, *"From this day will I bless you,"* and I believe He means exactly what He has said. In fact, I know that He means it, because we are experiencing it in a way that we previously never thought possible.

To be frank, I'm speaking of prosperity here such as most of you have never known. Believe God for it! Stand upon His Promise!

If you have put His Work first, He has designated a certain day that the Blessings will begin, and it is for *"you"* (Hag. 2:19).

(7) "LORD, BY YOUR FAVOR YOU HAVE MADE MY MOUNTAIN TO STAND STRONG: YOU DID HIDE YOUR FACE, AND I WAS TROUBLED."

The *"favor"* that is spoken of here refers to God's choice of Israel. He is the One Who made that *"mountain to stand strong."* Nevertheless, during the Great Tribulation, the time of Jacob's Trouble, especially when the Antichrist bears down for the *"final solution,"* it will seem that God does hide His Face. Then Israel will be greatly *"troubled."*

During that time, the Battle of Armageddon, there is evidence that not a single nation in the world will come to the aid of Israel; therefore, for a period of time, it will look as if these ancient people finally will be totally and completely annihilated. At any rate, that will be the driving effort of the Antichrist.

Israel will then call on the Name of the Lord as they have never prayed before. It is a prayer that most definitely will be answered.

(8) "I CRIED TO YOU, O LORD; AND UNTO THE LORD I MADE SUPPLICATION."

Of all the many reasons for the coming Great Tribulation, which Jesus said would be worse than has ever happened in human history and would never happen again (Mat. 24:21), the greatest reason of all by far will be to bring Israel back to God, i.e., to push her to the place to where she will *"cry to You, O LORD."* According to Zechariah, she will do just that (Zech. 12:10).

(9) "WHAT PROFIT IS THERE IN MY BLOOD, WHEN I GO DOWN TO THE PIT? SHALL THE DUST PRAISE YOU? SHALL IT DECLARE YOUR TRUTH?"

Israel's argument is that there is profit to God only in Israel's Salvation, not in her destruction. What praise will it be to Him for her to *"go down to the pit"*? In essence, she is saying to God, *"If You will deliver me, then I will praise You and declare Your Truth."*

(10) "HEAR, O LORD, AND HAVE MERCY UPON ME: LORD, BE THOU MY HELPER."

This plea and petition will go up to the Lord during the midst of the Battle of Armageddon. No other nation in the world will help Israel at this time, so her only help must come from the Lord. She will now cry to Him!

The very prayer that Israel will pray at that time is recorded in the Sixty-fourth Chapter of Isaiah. It is a prayer that the Lord surely will answer.

Why?

At long last, Israel's pride is broken. She no longer stands haughty. She cries for mercy and pleads with the Lord that He once again be her *"Helper."* The Lord will hear and answer that prayer, even as He always will hear and answer such a prayer, no matter who prays it.

(11) "YOU HAVE TURNED FOR ME MY MOURNING INTO DANCING: YOU HAVE PUT OFF MY SACKCLOTH, AND GIRDED ME WITH GLADNESS."

This Verse speaks of the Coming of the Lord Jesus Christ and His deliverance of Israel in the Battle of Armageddon. The Antichrist will be defeated. What looked like certain defeat (mourning) will be turned into *"dancing."* Now she will pull off her *"sackcloth,"* because a fountain is open. In the sight of David, she will be *"girded with gladness."*

(12) "TO THE END THAT MY GLORY MAY SING PRAISE TO YOU, AND NOT BE SILENT. O LORD MY GOD, I WILL GIVE THANKS UNTO YOU FOREVER."

Israel has now come to Christ, which, as stated, will take place at the Second Coming; thereupon she says that never again will she discontinue singing praise to the Lord. She will never again be *"silent."* She proclaims, *"I will give thanks unto You forever."* Her wandering is over. She is home at last!

PSALM 31

A Psalm of David:
Prayer for Victory Over Enemies

(1) "IN YOU, O LORD, DO I PUT MY TRUST; LET ME NEVER BE ASHAMED: DELIVER ME IN YOUR RIGHTEOUSNESS."

David wrote this Psalm; more than all, however, it speaks of the Greater Son of David.

THE REJECTION OF CHRIST

The doctrine of this Psalm is that the Messiah was tested in all points, yet without sin; that as Captain of His people's Salvation, He was perfected through sufferings; that having suffered being tempted, He is able to succour them who are tempted (Heb., Chpts. 2-5); that He was a Man of Sorrows and acquainted with grief; and He was hated, despised, and rejected of men (Isa., Chpt. 53).

The cries and the faith of the Psalm reveal the distress and the confidence of Him Who is the Author and Finisher of Faith.

In the first two Verses, He prays to be rescued from the Scribes, Pharisees, and Herodians who were seeking His Life; He cries for deliverance from the net which they in private prepared in order to entangle Him in His talk. On the Cross, He uttered aloud the first sentence of Verse 5. And inwardly, in the next sentence, He gave thanks for His redemption out of death — in the energy of faith, speaking of it as an accomplished fact already performed by Jehovah, the God of Truth. He was the God of Truth, for He had promised to resurrect His Beloved Son.

(2) "BOW DOWN YOUR EAR TO ME; DELIVER ME SPEEDILY: BE THOU MY STRONG ROCK, FOR AN HOUSE OF DEFENSE TO SAVE ME."

In these first two Verses, He prays to be rescued from the Scribes, Pharisees, and Herodians who were seeking His Life.

JESUS CHRIST, VERY MAN

While our Lord was Very God, He also was Very Man. Even though He never ceased to be God, still, He did not function in the capacity of Deity in His Incarnation, but solely as a Man; therefore, He prayed and cried to God for help, exactly as we do, which is the way it should have been done.

Most Believers, however, do not understand this about the Lord. They do not quite understand that He had feelings as any other human being, that He faced difficulties exactly as we do, and that He called on His Father exactly as we do.

Because He was, and is, God, most think that He never had to cry for help. These Psalms tell us differently!

NOTES

As we have previously stated, the four Gospels proclaim the acts of the Saviour, while the Psalms portray His Heart.

(3) "FOR YOU ARE MY ROCK AND MY FORTRESS; THEREFORE FOR YOUR NAME'S SAKE LEAD ME, AND GUIDE ME."

Considering the number of enemies who surrounded Him, if He were to fully obey the Father and carry out His mission, He would say, *"Lead Me, and guide Me."*

LEADING AND GUIDANCE

Our Lord depended on the Father for leading and guidance exactly as we do. He sought accordingly, and, because He always asked in the Will of the Father, His prayers and petitions always were answered.

As Believers, Christ was, and is, our Example. We are to understand that the Lord is our *"Rock"* and our *"Fortress."* We are to seek His Leading and Guidance, and do so for His Name's sake.

His Name carries His Mission. The Name *"Jesus"* was actually *"Joshua"* in the Hebrew, which means *"Jehovah saves"*!

So His very Name tells us that He will save us, and do so in every capacity, if we will only look to Him as we should. Whereas Christ prayed to the Father, we too are to pray to the Father, but with one difference. We are to pray *"in the Name of Jesus"* (Jn. 16:23).

(4) "PULL ME OUT OF THE NET THAT THEY HAVE LAID PRIVILY FOR ME: FOR YOU ARE MY STRENGTH."

The Pharisees, along with the Scribes and Herodians, constantly attempted to entangle Him in His talk. He cries for deliverance.

RELIGIOUS LEADERS

It is ironic that those who hated Him without cause were not the thieves, harlots, or Publicans. It was instead the *"Church"* of that day, so to speak, and, more particularly, the religious leaders of Israel. There are presently, and always have been, two Churches: the True Church and the apostate Church. The True Church is made up of all Born-Again Believers, wherever they might be, and constitutes only a tiny percentage of the size of the apostate Church.

Regrettably, it seems only a precious few are able to discern which is which! However, it is incumbent upon the Children of God to know which is correct. Otherwise, they could lose their soul. The Bible is the yardstick; there is no other.

(5) "INTO YOUR HAND I COMMIT MY SPIRIT: YOU HAVE REDEEMED ME, O LORD GOD OF TRUTH."

On the Cross, Jesus uttered aloud the first sentence of this Verse. Inwardly, in the next sentence, He gave thanks for His Redemption from death in the energy of Faith, speaking of it as an accomplished fact already performed by the Lord of Glory. This was the God of Truth, for He had promised to resurrect His Beloved Son.

DID JESUS DIE SPIRITUALLY?

No! Jesus did not die spiritually.

This error is taught by the *"Word of Faith"* people. They teach that Jesus became a sinner on the Cross, died as a sinner, and some even say He became demon-possessed on the Cross. Their erroneous doctrine then continues on to teach that, as a sinner, He went to Hell, where He was tormented three days and nights until God finally said, *"It is enough!"* Then, they say, Jesus was Born-Again, as any sinner is Born-Again, and raised from the dead.

None of that is true! There is nothing about that in the Bible, and it is not in the Bible because it never happened.

If Jesus had died as a sinner, as they claim, He could not have said with His dying breath, *"Into Your Hand I commit My Spirit."*

From approximately noon to about 3 p.m. on Crucifixion Day, darkness covered that part of the world as Jesus was dying. During that particular time, He had become the Sin Penalty for the human race — in essence, a Sin Offering (Isa. 53:10).

Inasmuch as He was at that time being *"made a curse for us,"* God could not look upon Him (Gal. 3:13). Jesus wasn't cursed by God; rather He was *"made a curse for us,"* which is altogether different.

Had there been sin in any capacity in His Heart or Life, He would have been cursed by God. Inasmuch as there was no sin, He had to be *"made a curse,"* which refers to the fact that He would shed His Life's Blood, and thereby die as a Sacrifice. When He died, even moments before He died, the price was now paid and complete. So He could say, *"Into Your Hand I commit My Spirit."*

The total Plan of Redemption was carried out in totality at the Cross. When He died, it was done! Even though the Resurrection was, of course, of extreme importance, it did not add anything to the Atonement; it rather ratified what already had been done. In other words, due to the fact that all sin was atoned at the Cross, the Resurrection was never in doubt.

No! Jesus did not die spiritually on the Cross, but rather physically.

Concerning this, Peter said, *"Who His Own Self bore our sins in His Own Body on the tree, that we, being dead to sins, should live unto Righteousness"* (I Pet. 2:24).

He then said, *"Forasmuch then as Christ had suffered for us in the flesh, arm yourselves likewise with the same mind: for he who has suffered in the flesh has ceased from sin"* (I Pet. 4:1).

Paul said, *"And, having made peace through the Blood of His Cross, by Him to reconcile all things unto Himself; by Him, I say, whether they be things in Earth, or things in Heaven . . .*

"In the Body of His flesh through death, to present you holy and unblameable and unreproveable in His sight" (Col. 1:20-22).

All of this tells us that Jesus paid the price for man's Redemption *"in His flesh,"* which refers to His Perfect Body offered in Sacrifice. As stated, this means that Redemption was finished at the Cross.

(6) "I HAVE HATED THEM WHO REGARD LYING VANITIES: BUT I TRUST IN THE LORD."

Some strong things are said by our Lord in this Verse.

LYING VANITIES

The *"lying vanities"* spoken of here refer to idols that Israel had worshipped in centuries past, which had caused her so many troubles; the phrase also refers to ritualistic religion of the present time.

Sadly, this reflects on most all who presently call themselves the *"Church."* The Lord's response to the idol of ritualistic religion is *"hatred."*

Why?

Ritualistic religion makes a god out of ritual, ceremony, Denominations, and men. Our *"trust"* is to be in nothing but the Lord.

Paul tells us what the Gospel actually is in the following Verse. He says, *"Christ sent me not to baptize, but to preach the Gospel, not with words of wisdom, lest the Cross of Christ be made of none effect"* (I Cor. 1:17).

If it's not *"Jesus Christ and Him Crucified,"* then it is *"lying vanities."*

(7) "I WILL BE GLAD AND REJOICE IN YOUR MERCY: FOR YOU HAVE CONSIDERED MY TROUBLE; YOU HAVE KNOWN MY SOUL IN ADVERSITIES."

If it were possible, Immanuel was more precious to God when in adversity, trouble, and danger than at any other time. Man refuses generally to recognize a companion when he is in adversity, but God did not so act toward His Servant. He actually recognized both Him and His adversities.

We ask the Reader to notice carefully that when the Patriarch Jacob was in deep trouble, that is exactly when the Lord referred to him as *"Israel"* (Gen. 35:1-10, 21).

The reason?

When one is in trouble, one is much more apt to seek the Lord than otherwise. In Blessings, we learn about ourselves. In adversity and trouble, we learn about God!

(8) "AND HAVE NOT SHUT ME UP INTO THE HAND OF THE ENEMY: YOU HAVE SET MY FEET IN A LARGE ROOM."

As David prays this prayer, can he know that his troubles, as a microcosm of the sufferings of the Coming Son of David, will point to the great Redemption price paid by the Redeemer? Through the Holy Spirit, David probably had some knowledge. But, before the fact, he could not understand, unless perfectly revealed to him by God, as we now after the fact understand.

A LARGE ROOM

The *"large room"* that the Holy Spirit pointed out to David would come to pass with David being made the great king of Israel, but more perfectly will be brought to pass in the great victory won by the Lord Jesus Christ at Calvary's Cross, involving the entirety of Creation, both animate and inanimate. Because of the Cross, all of us now have *"a large room"* in this great Redemption Plan.

(9) "HAVE MERCY UPON ME, O LORD, FOR I AM IN TROUBLE: MY EYE IS CONSUMED WITH GRIEF, YEA, MY SOUL AND MY BELLY."

Mere mortals can only measure imperfectly the *"grief"* that He experienced as He came unto His Own, and His Own received Him not. The three and a half years of His earthly Ministry were spent in *"sighing."*

When Israel rejected Him, He knew this meant that they were, proverbially speaking, signing their own death warrant. He knew they were facing desolation (Mat. 23:38).

(10) "FOR MY LIFE IS SPENT WITH GRIEF, AND MY YEARS WITH SIGNING; MY STRENGTH FAILS BECAUSE OF MY INIQUITY, AND MY BONES ARE CONSUMED."

This in no way means that He had sinned or failed. It means that He took our iniquity as His Own.

What a statement!

(11) "I WAS A REPROACH AMONG ALL MY ENEMIES, BUT ESPECIALLY AMONG MY NEIGHBORS, AND A FEAR TO MY ACQUAINTANCE: THEY WHO DID SEE ME WITHOUT FLED FROM ME."

In this one Verse, we have the cry of His broken heart.

THE REPROACH OF CHRIST

Jesus was a joke to His enemies and a derision to His neighbors. His relatives abandoned Him through fear of being put out of the Synagogue.

To be put out of the Synagogue meant to be denied all religious instruction and shunned in all activity. For a carpenter (or whatever trade one practiced), this meant he would not be able to find work. If a person did not own his own house, he would be evicted by his landlord. His family would be instructed to conduct themselves toward him as though he were dead.

Modern-day religious Denominations are very similar in their attitude. That's the reason that *"Denominationalism"* is an abomination in the Eyes of God. It abrogates the Headship of Christ and places man (a Denominational leader) at the head instead.

"Denominationalism" contains the idea that belonging to a certain Denomination guarantees some type of spiritual superiority, or even Salvation; consequently, other Denominations, or other Christians, are considered to be inferior. While it is not wrong to belong to a religious Denomination, it is wrong to belong to such when it practices *"Denominationalism,"* as almost all do.

The last few years that I was in a particular Denomination, at times I heard certain individuals say, *"If they* (speaking of others) *really are where they ought to be with the Lord, they would be with us. The very fact that they are not with us shows that they are not what they ought to be."* In a nutshell, that is *"Denominationalism."*

"Denominationalism" is very much akin to racism. Racism claims that one particular race is superior to the others, which says, at the same time, that all the other races are inferior.

Those who have been cashiered out of a religious Denomination because of their fidelity to the Bible can take heart that Jesus before them was treated in the same manner. Moreover, down through the centuries, millions have spilled their life's blood because they would not obey religious man, but instead would obey the God of the Bible.

"Neither did His brethren believe in Him" (Jn. 7:5).

(12) "I AM FORGOTTEN AS A DEAD MAN OUT OF MIND: I AM LIKE A BROKEN VESSEL."

This Verse portrays the action of the religious leaders of Israel toward Christ.

A BROKEN VESSEL

Israel flatly refused to believe that Jesus was the Messiah. He did not carry their credentials, neither did He fit their description. They were, in fact, looking for the Messiah, because Daniel had pinpointed in his Prophecies almost the exact time when the Messiah would be born (Dan. 9:24-26). But they were looking for a type of Messiah who would satisfy their ungodly lusts.

They had no desire for the Kingdom of God; they only desired the kingdom of man. It was utterly unthinkable in their minds that this Peasant could be the Messiah. Because He was a *"Broken Vessel,"* to them He was a Reject, One Who could not be taken seriously.

Despite the fact that *"no man ever spoke like this Man"* or performed the miracles that He constantly did, He was not worth serious consideration by these religious leaders. He was a *"Broken Vessel."*

(13) "FOR I HAVE HEARD THE SLANDER OF MANY: FEAR WAS ON EVERY SIDE: WHILE THEY TOOK COUNSEL TOGETHER AGAINST ME, THEY DEVISED TO TAKE AWAY MY LIFE."

All of this definitely was said of David, but more perfectly of the Son of David.

SLANDER

"Slander" is one of Satan's favorite tactics.

The name *"Satan"* actually means *"slanderer."* Someone has well said, *"The greatest weapon which your enemy can use against you is the 'lie,' for there is no defense against a lie."*

The religious world *"takes counsel together"* almost exclusively to oppose that which is of God. Religion constantly feels threatened — and especially by that which truly is of the Lord.

At this Ministry (Jimmy Swaggart Ministries), we make it a practice to never deal with anyone personally in the sense of their life and living. We definitely approve of some things and disapprove of other things, but we leave the judgment of that person personally to the Lord.

We do oppose what we believe to be false doctrine, and do so stringently, but we do not oppose the individuals themselves who are preaching the false message, whoever they might be. At times, we may feel led to call their names and quote what they have stated, but we do not pass judgment upon them personally.

No person is qualified to judge the motives of someone else (Mat. 7:1-2); however, we definitely are called upon to judge what they preach (I Cor. 14:29).

As it regards mere gossip about others, perhaps the following will be of some help. It was given in a Message preached several hundreds of years ago. I feel it is worth repeating:

1. When you hear something negative about someone, you should realize that you are hearing gossip, and it should be treated accordingly.

2. Even if you truly know something about the matter, nevertheless, your knowledge of the spiritual warfare involved is very limited. If you address the matter at all, you must be very, very careful.

3. If you were placed in the same position as the one who failed, whoever they may be, would you have done any better, or even as well?

(14) "BUT I TRUSTED IN YOU, O LORD: I SAID, YOU ARE MY GOD."

As David did not attempt to defend himself, the Son of David did not attempt to defend Himself either. As severe as was the matter, He placed it in the Hands of the Lord. What an example for us to follow!

(15) "MY TIMES ARE IN YOUR HAND: DELIVER ME FROM THE HAND OF MY ENEMIES, AND FROM THEM WHO PERSECUTE ME."

The Master's Faith was never broken. He kept believing that His times and His mission were not in man's hands, but in God's (Lk. 13:33).

This is one of the greatest lessons the Christian can finally learn. Let the whole world say *"No!"* and God say *"Yes!"* Guess Whose Voice is going to count? Total trust in the Lord, as evidenced in the Fourteenth Verse knows that God's Will shall be done. Man does not have the say, only God does. Man cannot *"deliver,"* but God can, and only God can.

OUR TIMES ARE IN HIS HAND

The Text didn't say that our times are in the hands of men, but rather in the *"Hand of God."* As should be obvious, there is a vast difference!

If we fully understand this phrase, then we will not fear what men can do to us; however, if we look to men, we will get the help that men can give, which is nothing.

The *"times"* of every Believer truly are in the *"Hand of the Lord."* Many do not understand that and do not function in that capacity, but that's the way it is, whether they believe it or not. Most of the time, however, the Lord is unable to do all the things with

NOTES

us that He desires to do, simply because we do not properly trust Him.

(16) "MAKE YOUR FACE TO SHINE UPON YOUR SERVANT: SAVE ME FOR YOUR MERCIES' SAKE."

The petition offered in this Verse is so beautiful as to be beyond description. It should be the petition of every single Believer.

THE FACE OF THE LORD SHINING UPON BELIEVERS

The expression, *"Make Your Face to shine upon Your servant,"* is first used in the Blessing of Moses (Num. 6:25). Its intrinsic beauty and poetry recommended it to David even as it should, and to us, as well. This expression is used several times in the Psalms (Ps. 4:6; 67:1; 80:5, 7, 19; 119:135). It may be regarded as equivalent to the expression, *"Be Thou favorable and gracious unto Your servant."* It speaks of the Mercy of God, as it should speak of the Mercy of God!

Many years ago, as I was reading the Word of God, the Holy Spirit emphasized this beautiful expression to my heart. I want the Face of the Lord to shine upon me, and I know that you do, as well. Such signifies acceptance, approval, and the resultant Blessings. So my prayer ever is:

"O Lord, ever make Your Face to shine upon Your servant. I claim such, not because of any good that I have accomplished, but for 'Your Mercies' sake.'"

(17) "LET ME NOT BE ASHAMED, O LORD; FOR I HAVE CALLED UPON YOU: LET THE WICKED BE ASHAMED, AND LET THEM BE SILENT IN THE GRAVE."

All the *"wicked"* ultimately will *"be silent in the grave."* In other words, there is coming a day that the slander of all the wicked will forever cease.

David is saying that he has ever been the true worshipper. Even when he sinned, his sins were not sins of unfaithfulness, but lapses, sins of infirmity, unpremeditated yieldings to temptation.

This did not make the sins right or correct, but neither did they keep David from calling on the Lord. In truth, they caused the sweet singer of Israel to call even more upon the Lord, and for all the obvious reasons!

(18) "LET THE LYING LIPS BE PUT

TO SILENCE; WHICH SPEAK GRIEVOUS THINGS PROUDLY AND CONTEMPTUOUSLY AGAINST THE RIGHTEOUS."

It was religious pride that opposed Jesus Christ. It was religious pride that nailed Him to the Cross. Religious pride showed Him nothing but contempt. The situation has not changed; it is the same now as it was then. Ultimately, those *"lying lips"* will be *"put to silence,"* even as they were put to silence then.

(19) "OH HOW GREAT IS YOUR GOODNESS, WHICH YOU HAVE LAID UP FOR THEM WHO FEAR YOU; WHICH YOU HAVE WROUGHT FOR THEM WHO TRUST IN YOU BEFORE THE SONS OF MEN!"

Verses 19 through 24 proclaim the Lord speaking words of comfort and succour to His people; the argument is that we surely will be delivered because He Himself was delivered. We will not have to tread an untrodden road of suffering, shame, and hatred, for it is a way already trodden by Him.

(20) "YOU SHALL HIDE THEM IN THE SECRET OF YOUR PRESENCE FROM THE PRIDE OF MAN: YOU SHALL KEEP THEM SECRETLY IN A PAVILION FROM THE STRIFE OF TONGUES."

A tremendous lesson is given in this Verse. It is:

TWO TYPES OF SIN

1. Sins of passion; and,
2. Sins of pride.

Both are extremely destructive and thus viewed by God; however, both are not thus viewed by man. Religious man claims to hate the sins of passion, all the while indulging secretly in them, and lauds the sins of pride by not really recognizing this sin for what it is — the most awful of all sin.

It was pride that caused the fall of Satan (Ezek., Chpt. 28; Isa., Chpt. 14). It is pride that keeps man from admitting his terminal spiritual condition — even religious man — especially religious man. It was pride that nailed the Lord Jesus to the Cross. It was pride that caused the Pharisees, Herodians, Scribes, and Sadducees to oppose Christ so terribly. It is *"the pride of man"* that is causing the majority of the human family to be eternally lost.

(21) "BLESSED BE THE LORD: FOR HE HAS SHOWED ME HIS MARVELOUS KINDNESS IN A STRONG CITY."

God showed David His marvelous lovingkindness by giving him an assurance of absolute security.

He does the same for us presently, and even more!

(22) "FOR I SAID IN MY HASTE, I AM CUT OFF FROM BEFORE YOUR EYES: NEVERTHELESS YOU HEARD THE VOICE OF MY SUPPLICATIONS WHEN I CRIED UNTO YOU."

David could very well have been speaking of the time that he went over to the Philistines (I Sam. 27:1).

The Son of Man also knew that, except for God, it was impossible for Him to be delivered; however, when *"He cried,"* God heard, as He always will!

(23) "O LOVE THE LORD, ALL YE HIS SAINTS: FOR THE LORD PRESERVES THE FAITHFUL AND PLENTIFULLY REWARDS THE PROUD DOER.

(24) "BE OF GOOD COURAGE, AND HE SHALL STRENGTHEN YOUR HEART, ALL YE WHO HOPE IN THE LORD."

The Holy Spirit through David and the Son of David tells the Saints of God that, despite the enemies and the powers of darkness, we are to be encouraged.

Why?

Because the Lord *"shall strengthen your heart."* This will only come to those who do not trust in man, but instead have their *"hope in the LORD."*

PSALM 32

A Psalm of David:
The Blessedness of Forgiveness

(1) "BLESSED IS HE WHOSE TRANSGRESSION IS FORGIVEN, WHOSE SIN IS COVERED."

As noted, David wrote this Psalm.

THE BLESSING OF CONFESSED SIN

This Psalm is one of the most powerful in the entirety of this great collection. Every Christian should read it carefully, and over and over.

It speaks of the terror of unconfessed sin, and then the blessing of confessed sin. Even though there is no proof as to the time it was written, still, the description seems to favor the period of time between the terrible sin with Bathsheba and the time when the Lord sent the Prophet Nathan to David.

The Gracious Spirit here instructs the Reader as to: the misery resulting from unconfessed sin; the relief and conscious pardon enjoyed as the result of confession; the peace and safety accompanying companionship with God; and the conditions affecting that fellowship.

Once again the Reader will be taken into the Heart of God, and to the Intercessory Work of Christ, our Great High Priest.

In this Psalm, the Lord will speak in His Own Name, as the Great High Priest of His people, on our behalf as if He Himself were the guilty transgressor.

What a consolation it is to have a Priest Who thus makes Himself one with the repentant sinner, pleads and prays as the sinner ought to plead and pray, but cannot, and uses the very words which will be acceptable to God. Such an High Priest becomes repentant man.

The word *"transgression"* implies rebellion against law; *"sin"* points to moral failure; and *"iniquity"* to corruption in the future.

The first (transgression) is forgiven, that is, its punishment is unbound from off the transgressor. To forgive is to unbind.

The second (sin) is covered, that is, atoned for, by a Blood Sacrifice, namely the Death of Christ at Calvary.

A PROPHETIC PSALM

This Psalm is also prophetic in that it foretells the confession of guilt which, in the coming day of her repentance, Israel will make of her two great sins: of adultery, in having loved idols; and of murder, in having slain the Messiah (Acts 7:52). Because they refused to make this confession, they have, during many centuries, suffered as a nation the anguish which is portrayed in Verses 3 and 4.

Yet in this Psalm, the High Priest encourages them to this confession, and uses for them the language befitting it, bringing them, at the same time, into an intimacy with God into which conscious forgiveness leads.

BLESSED IS THE MAN

The word *"blessed,"* as used in Verses 1 and 2 is in the plural number in the Hebrew Text. The Verse, therefore, may read, *"O the happinesses of the man. . . ."* The construction of Verses 1 and 2 tell us that there is a complete remission, a complete forgiveness of sin. This is, in fact, the only way that God forgives. He never engages in a partial forgiveness, only a total and complete forgiveness.

The Scripture truly says, *"If we confess our sins, He is faithful and just to forgive us our sins, and to cleanse us from all unrighteousness"* (I Jn. 1:9).

It is this way because *"the Blood of Jesus Christ His Son cleanses us from all sin"* (I Jn. 1:7).

(2) "BLESSED IS THE MAN UNTO WHOM THE LORD IMPUTES NOT INIQUITY, AND IN WHOSE SPIRIT THERE IS NO GUILE."

A tremendous truth is here proclaimed.

NO IMPUTATION OF INIQUITY

When sin is properly confessed and then properly forgiven, which the Lord always does, no iniquity is imputed to such a person, i.e., *"placed to our charge."* On the contrary, the spotless Righteousness of Christ is imputed or accounted to the repentant and believing sinner.

Paul explained this in his great treatment on Justification by Faith in the Epistle to the Romans (Rom. 4:7-8).

And we must remember that there is no such thing as a partial justification. A person either is totally justified, or not at all justified!

A full forgiveness dislodges guile from the heart, for who will not declare all his debts to one who engages to discharge them, or who will not hide any symptom of his malady from a physician who can cure perfectly!

Sadly, the bulk of the modern Church little knows or understands *"Justification by Faith."* Or, if they do understand it, they commit the greater sin of attempting to withhold it from others, but accept it for themselves; however, the sad fact is that if they do not allow the same for others, God will not allow it for them. Consequently, multiple hundreds of thousands of Church pulpits are spiritually dead, with the pew following suit.

(3) "WHEN I KEPT SILENCE, MY BONES WAXED OLD THROUGH MY ROARING ALL THE DAY LONG.

(4) "FOR DAY AND NIGHT YOUR HAND WAS HEAVY UPON ME: MY MOISTURE IS TURNED INTO THE DROUGHT OF SUMMER. SELAH."

Another great truth is here proclaimed!

UNCONFESSED SIN

As stated, this Psalm could very well have been written during the timeframe of David's seduction of Bathsheba and the coming of Nathan the Prophet, which induced Repentance. No load is heavier to bear than unconfessed sin; no night so black as the Hand of God held over His Face to shut out the Light.

These two Verses adequately describe the unrepentant Christian. The joy is gone; the burden is heavy; the bones seem to ache; the *"roaring"* speaks of the guilty conscience; spiritual showers turn into *"drought."*

The *"Selah"* of Verse 4 contrasts the misery of unconfessed sin with the relief of forgiven guilt, as evidenced in Verse 5. The *"Selah"* of this latter Verse connects that forgiveness with the future Salvation from wrath of which it is an earnest, and the last *"Selah"* unites that future safety with present Holiness.

(5) "I ACKNOWLEDGED MY SIN UNTO YOU, AND MY INIQUITY HAVE I NOT HID. I SAID, I WILL CONFESS MY TRANSGRESSIONS UNTO THE LORD; AND YOU FORGAVE THE INIQUITY OF MY SIN. SELAH."

Verse 5 proclaims the joy of sins forgiven versus the misery of the unconfessed sin of Verse 4. Salvation is simple, swift, and sure.

The first part of Verse 5 says, *"I acknowledged."* The latter part says, *"You forgave."* The *"acknowledgment"* is the secret of the *"forgiveness."*

It is the Work of the Holy Spirit to bring the person to the place of confession of guilt (acknowledgment). Only then can the sin be forgiven. The question must be asked, *"To whom should it be acknowledged?"*

First of all, it must be acknowledged to God. If it involves other people, it also must be acknowledged to them. Otherwise, it is only *"unto the Lord."*

(6) "FOR THIS SHALL EVERY ONE WHO IS GODLY PRAY UNTO YOU IN A TIME WHEN YOU MAY BE FOUND: SURELY IN THE FLOODS OF GREAT WATERS THEY SHALL NOT COME NEAR UNTO HIM."

This Verse proclaims the following:

THE GODLY

The term *"Godly"* means one to whom God shows Mercy. It expresses the attitude of God toward the repentant sinner, rather than the moral worthiness of the repentant sinner toward God.

The statement, *"When You may be found,"* could pertain toward *"the time of the finding out of sin."* The *"flood of great waters"* pictures the Wrath of God in the day of inquisition and punishment of sin. In that day, God will be the hiding place of the forgiven sinner, who will be compassed with singing and as safe from floods and fears as Noah was when he made the Ark his hiding place.

(7) "YOU ARE MY HIDING PLACE; YOU SHALL PRESERVE ME FROM TROUBLE; YOU SHALL COMPASS ME ABOUT WITH SONGS OF DELIVERANCE. SELAH."

The truth of this great Verse is available to all Believers.

SONGS OF DELIVERANCE

If one is hidden in the Lord, no harm can happen to him.

"Songs of deliverance" are such songs as men sing when they have been delivered from peril. God will make such songs to sound in the Psalmist's ears and in his heart.

(8) "I WILL INSTRUCT YOU AND TEACH YOU IN THE WAY WHICH YOU SHALL GO: I WILL GUIDE YOU WITH MY EYE."

Jerome and others have regarded Verses 8 and 9 as an utterance of God, Who first admonishes David and then passes on to an admonition of the Israelites generally;

however, Pulpit says the following about that particular claim:

"A sudden intrusion of a Divine utterance, without any notice of a change of speaker, is without parallel in the Psalms, and should certainly not be admitted without some plain necessity. Here is no necessity at all." [7]

I personally think that the Pulpit Commentary is correct.

So then, what does this Passage mean?

INSTRUCTION

Every evidence is that David made these statements. When He said, *"I will instruct you and teach you in the way which you shall go,"* he was speaking of that which he would teach Israel.

Some may ask the question, *"How could David teach Israel anything, especially considering his failure regarding Bathsheba and her husband Uriah?"*

Most would not accept his teaching; nevertheless, the Holy Spirit here plainly says that David had much to teach Israel.

In such a case, teaching can be given (and valuable teaching at that!), if the person handles his own situation as he should, even as David did.

In essence, this is what Jesus said of Simon Peter:

"Simon, Simon, behold, Satan has desired to have you, that He may sift you as wheat: but I have prayed for you, that your faith fail not: and when you are converted, strengthen your brethren" (Lk. 22:31-32).

The word *"converted,"* as here used, did not mean that Peter was to get Saved again, but rather that he had come back to the right way.

Jesus was speaking of the hour when Peter would deny Him, which was a grievous sin. But He told him that he would find his way back, and he was to *"strengthen his brethren."*

Now considering that Peter had failed, how could he strengthen anyone?

Once again, even as with David, the answer is obvious! Peter handled it correctly, and now could readily tell Believers how they should conduct themselves. Experience is the greatest teacher of all, and, to be sure, a bad experience also is a good teacher, even though it is an expensive teacher.

The experiences of both David and Peter could be described as very costly educational experiences, to say the least; however, they both handled the situation correctly, taking it to the Lord, exactly as they should, and now could give tremendous instruction to those who would have sense enough to heed and listen.

(9) "BE YE NOT AS THE HORSE, OR AS THE MULE, WHICH HAVE NO UNDERSTANDING: WHOSE MOUTH MUST BE HELD IN WITH BIT AND BRIDLE, LEST THEY COME NEAR UNTO YOU."

This is true concerning a horse or a mule, because they have no understanding; but it should not be true concerning Believers. Our ears should be in tune to the Word of God, and our hearts should be tendered toward that which the Holy Spirit proposes. Unfortunately, that's not the case with most!

As a bit and bridle are necessary with a horse or mule, a bit and bridle are necessary with many Christians. Consequently, such do not learn quickly and do not learn easily!

Perhaps to a certain extent all Believers fall into this category!

(10) "MANY SORROWS SHALL BE TO THE WICKED: BUT HE WHO TRUSTS IN THE LORD, MERCY SHALL COMPASS HIM ABOUT.

(11) "BE GLAD IN THE LORD, AND REJOICE, YE RIGHTEOUS: AND SHOUT FOR JOY, ALL YE WHO ARE UPRIGHT IN HEART."

In these last two Verses, the Holy Spirit instructs His people respecting the sorrows which surely will come upon the self-willed (the *"wicked"*), and the joys unspeakable and full of glory which will be the present and eternal portion of those who trust in Jehovah-Messiah.

PSALM 33

*Probably Written by David:
Praise to the Lord*

(1) "REJOICE IN THE LORD, O YE RIGHTEOUS: FOR PRAISE IS COMELY FOR THE UPRIGHT."

This Psalm contains the first mention in

the Bible of the New Song. The last mention is in the Fourteenth Chapter of the Book of Revelation. Uniting these two Passages together, it is evident that Israel will sing this song on Mount Zion at the opening of the Millennial Reign of Christ, and that He will stand with them and lead the song.

REJOICING

The word *"rejoice"* actually means *"shout for joy."* Even though the Psalm has no title and does not name an author, still, it was probably written by David. Actually, it is joined to the preceding Psalm. It is the rejoicing of a glad heart (and rightly so!) that has had sins covered and transgressions forgiven. The words, *"Comely for the upright,"* mean *"it is suitable."*

Praise constantly should be in the heart of a Child of God. The Church should be filled with *"praise"* upon the assembling of the Saints. A person who does not praise the Lord does not know the Lord. A Church that does not praise the Lord does not know the Lord.

When *"praise"* is an embarrassment to the Christian, that means the Christian is not really following Christ. Actually, he has only embraced a philosophy of Christianity, which means that he really does not know the Christ of the Bible. If he did, *"praise would be comely for him."*

(2) "PRAISE THE LORD WITH HARP: SING UNTO HIM WITH THE PSALTERY AND AN INSTRUMENT OF TEN STRINGS."

A great truth is here given!

MUSIC

Music is an undeniable part of worship of God. It is at this time and will be forever a part of the worship of God in Heaven (Rev. 5:8).

In all the means of worshipping God, music and singing comprise one of the greatest forms of worship found in the Word of God. We know this because the longest Book in the Bible, Psalms (which actually means *"Songs"*), is given over to worship. That's how much the Holy Spirit thinks of this type of worship.

Consequently, whenever a Church loses its way, the first thing that goes is the *"song."* Whatever music there is becomes stilted, formal, cold, and lifeless.

When a Church is on fire for God, the music and the singing, as it constitutes the worship of the Lord, presents itself as vibrant, powerful, and full of life.

THE COMPOSITION OF MUSIC

The composition of music, as designed by God, consists of the following:
1. Rhythm;
2. Harmony; and,
3. Melody.

These three parts are not wrong unless they are perverted.

If the song consists of rhythm only, it would not feed the spirit, but would only draw attention to the flesh, and then it would be perverted. Likewise, most contemporary Christian (so-called) music perverts the harmony and the melody, which prevents worship. As Satan has grossly perverted most of the music of the world, he has likewise perverted most of the music of the Church. It is either dead, lifeless, and without the Spirit, or perverted, as in the contemporary style.

This means that the Christian should be very particular as to the type of music he sings, listens to, and enjoys. Basically, such is a barometer of one's spiritual condition.

A PERSONAL EXPERIENCE

At eight years of age, I fervently asked the Lord to give me the talent to play the piano. I promised Him that I would not use this talent in the world, but would use it for His Glory. The Lord was true to my petition, and He gave me that for which I had asked. And I have been very careful, trying my best to be true to the promise I made to Him.

He not only gave me the talent to play the piano, but He also gave me an understanding of music as it regards worship of the Lord. To a great extent, I can tell whether a song is correctly or incorrectly arranged. There is a certain way that the Holy Spirit desires music to be. If we follow that way, our worship of the Lord will be greatly accepted, and we will be greatly blessed.

At times I have been greatly criticized for taking a bold stand against much of the music that pervades the modern Church, because I know that it is not of God and will not bring blessing to the participant. Regrettably, the Church has done its best to borrow from the world, not only in music, but in many other things, as well! The Church claims it must do such to reach the youth for Christ, etc.

The end result of all of this is that the Church is not reaching anyone, much less the youth.

Besides that, music, at least as it regards the Lord, is not meant to try to draw people to Christ, although, in certain circumstances, it might do that. It is meant to worship the Lord, and that exclusively!

(3) "SING UNTO HIM A NEW SONG; PLAY SKILLFULLY WITH A LOUD NOISE."

This *"Song"* is spoken of seven times in the Old Testament and once in the New Testament (Ps. 33:3; 40:3; 96:1; 93:1; 144:9; 149:1; Isa. 42:10; Rev. 14:3). This *"New Song"* will be sung on Earth during the Kingdom Age by redeemed men. The *"New Song"* of Revelation 5:9 will be sung in Heaven by sinless Angels, Cherubim, and redeemed men. Its theme also is Redemption.

The music that is to accompany this *"New Song"* must be skillfully rendered in a manner that it will be easily heard.

(4) "FOR THE WORD OF THE LORD IS RIGHT; AND ALL HIS WORKS ARE DONE IN TRUTH."

This Passage pertains to far more than merely God's Creation; however, the Holy Spirit is telling us that what the *"Word of the LORD"* says about God's Creation is correct. Man says that Creation is the result of *"nothing working on nothing, from nothing, begetting everything."* God says, *"His Works are done in Truth."*

Here the Lord labels a *"lie"* any claim regarding Creation which is outside the scope of the Bible. That which the Word of God says is *"Truth,"* and only what the Word of God says!

This means that it's not possible for one to believe in evolution and at the same time be Saved.

(5) "HE LOVES RIGHTEOUSNESS AND JUDGMENT: THE EARTH IS FULL OF THE GOODNESS OF THE LORD."

Here we learn some things about the Lord.

NOTES

RIGHTEOUSNESS

The *"Righteousness"* that God is speaking of is the Righteousness of His Son Jesus Christ, which is freely given to the believing sinner, and is made possible by what Christ did at the Cross, and solely by what Christ did at the Cross! God hates self-righteousness. *"Judgment"* actually is the Word of the Lord.

In looking at God's beautiful Creation minus that which has been marred by man, one has to admit the *"Goodness of God."* In observing God's dealings with man regarding the great price He has paid for man's Redemption in the Sacrifice of His Son at Calvary, man has to admit the *"Goodness of God."*

The very meaning of the word *"Righteousness"* is *"that which is right."* However, the definition of what is right must be that of the Lord, and not man! That definition is found in the Word of God, and in the Word of God exclusively!

(6) "BY THE WORD OF THE LORD WERE THE HEAVENS MADE; AND ALL THE HOST OF THEM BY THE BREATH OF HIS MOUTH."

Here we learn other things about the Lord.

THE TRINITY

1. *"The Word of LORD"* speaks of the Lord Jesus Christ (Jn. 1:1-5).

2. *"Of the LORD,"* as given in Verse 5, speaks of Jehovah.

3. *"The Breath of His mouth"* speaks of the Holy Spirit.

Consequently, we have the Trinity outlined in these Passages.

CREATION

God is to be praised, not only for His Goodness, but also for His Greatness, and especially for His Greatness in Creation. The heavens were made *"by His Word"* in a double sense — by the Word, Who is the Second Person of the Trinity (Jn. 1:3; Heb. 1:2, 10), and by a mere utterance, without the employment of any mechanical means, even as we learn from Genesis 1:6-8.

The *"host of Heaven"* is undoubtedly the host of heavenly bodies, i.e., the sun, moon, and stars — as in Genesis 2:1. These were made *"by the Breath of God's Mouth,"* i.e., by His simple utterance of the command, *"Let there be lights in the firmament of the heaven, to divide the day from the night"* (Gen. 1:14).

(7) "HE GATHERS THE WATERS OF THE SEA TOGETHER AS AN HEAP: HE LAYS UP THE DEPTH IN STOREHOUSES."

Concerning this, Pulpit says, *"As if the original gathering and continued retention of the sea in one convex mass were as great a proof of Omnipotence as the miracles related in these Passages."* [8]

Concerning the last phrase, the waters of the great deep are regarded as stored up by the Almighty in the huge cavities of the ocean bed for His Own use, to be employed at some time or other in carrying out His purposes (Gen. 7:11).

(8) "LET ALL THE EARTH FEAR THE LORD: LET ALL THE INHABITANTS OF THE WORLD STAND IN AWE OF HIM."

The Earth as a whole does not *"fear the LORD."* Precious few *"stand in awe of Him."* Nevertheless, the day is soon to come when this Scripture literally will be fulfilled, and in totality!

(9) "FOR HE SPOKE, AND IT WAS DONE; HE COMMANDED, AND IT STOOD FAST."

The word *"done"* was added by the translators. The actual statement is, *"For He spoke, and it was."* In other words, the thing of which He spoke literally came into existence at once.

The phrase, *"He commanded, and it stood fast,"* literally says, *"And it stood."* God's lightest Word, once uttered, presents itself as a standing Law, to which nature absolutely conforms, and to which man ought to conform.

The type of awesome power that is here represented is beyond the comprehension of man; actually, the Lord spoke the Earth into existence; He commanded, and it stood fast — it remains suspended in space and confined to its orbit. These great facts should teach its inhabitants to worship Him and not to worship idols, which are mere figments of someone's imagination.

(10) "THE LORD BRINGS THE COUNSEL OF THE HEATHEN TO NAUGHT: HE MAKES THE DEVICES OF THE PEOPLE OF NONE EFFECT."

Too much and too often man worships the Creation instead of the Creator (Rom., Chpt. 1). God has brought, or will bring, to naught all the foolishness of man, which consists of false doctrine, evolution, false science, psychology, and all false religions.

All of that in the world which is a lie ultimately will be brought to naught. Then there will be nothing left but the Word of the Lord.

(11) "THE COUNSEL OF THE LORD STANDS FOREVER, THE THOUGHTS OF HIS HEART TO ALL GENERATIONS."

All of these Passages contain great truths and, in fact, are Truth.

THE BIBLE

The Bible is and always has been the only Revealed Body of Truth in the world; consequently, Preachers should study it and know it more than they know any other book. Every Christian should master its contents, or seek to do so. In it, and in it alone, are the great questions of life addressed and answered.

(12) "BLESSED IS THE NATION WHOSE GOD IS THE LORD; AND THE PEOPLE WHOM HE HAS CHOSEN FOR HIS OWN INHERITANCE."

Directly, this Verse speaks of Israel. In general, it speaks of any nation in the world *"whose God is the LORD."*

The word *"blessed"* could easily be translated *"happy."* Two things are said in this Verse.

THE BLESSED NATION

1. Any nation that worships and serves God through His Son Jesus Christ and in accordance with God's Word is *"blessed."* Someone has well said, *"Much Bible, much freedom; some Bible, some freedom; no Bible, no freedom."*

Someone once asked a question concerning Brazil and the United States. Both countries are approximately the same age, the same size, both have an abundance of natural resources — in other words, basically equal. The question was, *"Why has the United States advanced to such a greater degree than Brazil?"*

The answer is this:

When settlers founded the country of Brazil, they were looking for gold. When settlers founded the United States, they were looked for God.

Here is another example:

At about the same time that the colonies of America were grappling over the formation of a Constitution (the late 1700's), the little island country of Haiti was (believe it or not!) far outstripping America in advancement and prosperity. A group of native Haitians sought the help of Satan by promising to him the gift of their country if he would give them freedom from the French. At about the same time, Benjamin Franklin was telling the framers of the Constitution that this nation (the U.S.A.) must be given to God.

Now, over two hundred years later, the end results of both countries are obvious. But sadly, the United States is forsaking the God Who gave her freedom and prosperity. More and more, we are turning to atheistic evolution and Godless humanistic psychology, which presents a denial of the Word of God.

ISRAEL AND THE CHURCH

2. The people that God *"has chosen"* was Israel then and the Church now. In the old economy of God, one had to be a Jew, or at least become a proselyte Jew, in order to be Saved. Even then, this did not mean that all Jews were saved, but only those who believed in the atoning work of what the Sacrifices represented.

Likewise, all today who truly are Born-Again, both Jew and Gentile, are a part of God's Church, the mystical Body of Christ. His *"Church"* has nothing to do with Denominational affiliation, such as Catholic, Baptist, Pentecostal, or Methodist. One enters the Church of the Lord Jesus Christ solely be being Born-Again, and by no other means (Jn. 3:16).

(13) "THE LORD LOOKS FROM HEAVEN; HE BEHOLDS ALL THE SONS OF MEN.

(14) "FROM THE PLACE OF HIS HABITATION HE LOOKS UPON ALL THE INHABITANTS OF THE EARTH."

NOTES

Nothing is hidden from God. He is Omnipotent (all-powerful), Omniscient (all-knowing), and Omnipresent (everywhere).

THE OMNIPOTENT AND OMNISCIENCE OF GOD

Everything that happens on this planet is either caused by God or allowed by God. While it is true that God does not cause any of the evil, starvation, famine, sickness, suffering, or war that plagues the human race, still, God allows Satan to do certain things because of the evil hearts of men, things which also affect the innocent.

What *"He looks upon"* at the present and in the past has not been a presentable picture. He sees a world in rebellion against Him, bringing upon themselves untold sorrow and heartache as a result. This will change in the not-too-distant future when the Lord Jesus Christ returns (Rev., Chpt. 19).

That God would have any care at all for man presents a wondrous condescension, and so worthy of all praise; His having regard to all men — all the frail sons of weak and sinful Adam — is still more wonderful, still more deserving of eulogy; however, this He definitely does!

All of this means several things:

First of all, it refers to the fact of His unlimited ability in His beholding all the sons of men.

Second, the idea is given that all men are important in His sight, irrespective as to who they might be, or where they might be, which, again, is beyond our comprehension.

(15) "HE FASHIONS THEIR HEARTS ALIKE; HE CONSIDERS ALL THEIR WORKS."

A great truth is here given to us concerning Salvation or the lack thereof!

THE FASHIONING OF THE HEARTS OF MEN

The phrase, *"He fashions their hearts alike,"* means that all men begin on a level playing field, so to speak.

In other words, God does not fashion some hearts to be evil and some to be righteous. All are fashioned equal, but all have the power of choice. Upon man's choice, God considers man's works.

In this one Verse of Scripture, we are given much information as it regards Salvation, and why some are saved and some aren't. But yet, there is still a mystery attached to the actions of some in rejecting the Lord. How can man reject His Creator?

WHY DO SOME ACCEPT THE LORD AND SOME REJECT THE LORD?

As it regards the heart, which constitutes the faculties, the inner man, the soul and the spirit of the individual, all are fashioned alike. One doesn't have a greater propensity toward God than another. So why is it that some accept the Lord and some reject the Lord?

That is a mystery!

First of all, it has precious little to do with families. In the Bible, we find Abel accepting the Lord and doing God's Will, but Cain rejecting the Lord, even though they are brothers. We find Esau and Jacob, who were twins, taking opposite directions. So family ties have little to do with this!

The mystery of this is found in the free choice of man. In other words, man has the ability to say *"Yes"* to the Lord or *"No"* to the Lord! As to what causes him to make the choice he does, is, as stated, a mystery!

The Holy Spirit can work on two individuals, and do so with equal passion. Oftentimes one will accept and the other reject! Some few times, both accept. Many times, both reject.

PREDESTINATION

The doctrine of *"predestination"* is viable and Scriptural if it is understood correctly; but, unfortunately, mostly is understood incorrectly!

Many believe and teach that God has predestined some to go to Heaven and some to go to Hell, and there is nothing the person can do about whichever place he is predestined to go. That is basely incorrect!

God does predestine His Plans, but who will be in those Plans (whatever those Plans might be) is left up strictly to the individual. It is *"whosoever will"*!

For instance, Paul said the following:

"For whom He did foreknow, He also did predestinate to be conformed to the Image of His Son, that He might be the Firstborn among many brethren" (Rom. 8:29).

In this Passage, as in all Passages referring to predestination or foreknowledge, it is the Plan that is predestined (in this instance, the *"conformity to the Image of His Son"*), and not who will enter the Plan. Once again, it is always *"whosoever will"* (Rev. 22:17).

(16) "THERE IS NO KING SAVED BY THE MULTITUDE OF AN HOST: A MIGHTY MAN IS NOT DELIVERED BY MUCH STRENGTH.

(17) "AN HORSE IS A VAIN THING FOR SAFETY: NEITHER SHALL HE DELIVER ANY BY HIS GREAT STRENGTH."

A nation's safety and protection is not necessarily in their mighty army or navy, but actually is in God. A mighty army and other such things are not condemned by God; however, the instruction is that God is the One Who guides the destiny of kings and nations, not man.

(18) "BEHOLD, THE EYE OF THE LORD IS UPON THEM WHO FEAR HIM, UPON THEM WHO HOPE IN HIS MERCY.

(19) "TO DELIVER THEIR SOUL FROM DEATH, AND TO KEEP THEM ALIVE IN FAMINE."

Safety and protection are promised in these Verses to those who trust the Lord.

THE PROTECTION OF THE LORD

In a certain sense, the Eye of the Lord is upon all, but it rests especially upon the righteous. He notes how all men act, but carefully watches over the safety and prosperity of His faithful ones.

Protection and deliverance, which man's own strength cannot give and which no host, however numerous, can afford, can be furnished freely by the Lord, Who Alone keeps souls from death, and *"delivers"* those who are in peril, at least if they trust in Him!

The phrase, *"And to keep them alive in famine,"* refers to the fact that the Lord is able to provide when there seems to be no provision available.

But, once again, all of this is dependent upon the individual placing his faith and trust exclusively in the Lord, and never in man.

(20) "OUR SOUL WAITS FOR THE LORD:

HE IS OUR HELP AND OUR SHIELD."

Sometimes the Lord doesn't move quite as quickly as we think He should; however, confident in His Goodwill and His Power to help us, we wait patiently and cheerfully for Him to manifest Himself in His Own good time.

The phrase, *"He is our Help and our Shield,"* refers to the fact that we trust in no one and nothing but Him — and above all, not in our own strength, but in Him Alone! We depend on Him, and on Him Alone!

Over and over again, the Word of God stresses the necessity of our trust being solely in the Lord. Again and again, Israel missed the Lord, because they placed their trust in surrounding Gentile nations, who really didn't care for them at all. When the Lord is solely trusted, He solely performs miracles, and even more miracles!

(21) "FOR OUR HEART SHALL REJOICE IN HIM, BECAUSE WE HAVE TRUSTED IN HIS HOLY NAME."

Trust in God secures His Help, and this brings the deliverance over which the heart rejoices.

HOW DOES ONE FULLY TRUST IN HIS HOLY NAME?

His Name is *"Jesus,"* which means *"Jehovah saves."*

How does He save?

Over and over again, we have made the statement, *"Christ is the Source of all good things, but the Cross is the Means by which those good things are given to us."*

The Cross of Christ must ever be the Object of our Faith (Rom. 6:1-14; 8:1-2, 11; I Cor. 1:17-18, 21, 23; 2:2; Gal. 6:14; Eph. 2:13-18; Col. 2:14-15).

In essence, God honors nothing but His Son, the Lord Jesus Christ (Mat. 3:17). To have the honor of God, we must honor what Christ has done for us, which pertains solely to the Cross (Jn. 3:16). That is what is meant by *"trust in His Holy Name."*

(22) "LET YOUR MERCY, O LORD, BE UPON US, ACCORDING AS WE HOPE IN YOU."

The measure of men's hope and trust in God is the measure of His Mercy and Goodness to them. Those who are assured that they have a full trust in Him may confidently expect a full and complete Deliverance and Victory.

The words, *"According as,"* present themselves as *"emphatic."*

PSALM 34

*A Psalm of David:
Thanks for Deliverance*

(1) "I WILL BLESS THE LORD AT ALL TIMES: HIS PRAISE SHALL CONTINUALLY BE IN MY MOUTH."

As noted, this is a Psalm of David.

CONSTANT PRAISE

This Psalm is a Prophecy. It deals with the Government of God in the Earth; His permitting His people to be oppressed; His ultimate deliverance of them; and His destruction of their foes.

In inviting His people to unite with Him in praising Jehovah, the Messiah encourages us by pointing to His Own experience and to the experience of others in whom He dwells.

It is believed that the Holy Spirit gave this Prophecy to David immediately after his degrading conduct in Gath (I Sam., Chpt. 21). Such is incomprehensible to strangers to the spiritual life. However, Verse 18 removes the difficulty.

When the Believer is mortified, shamed, broken, and contrite in spirit, and amazed that such a wretch should find pardon and deliverance, then is the soul restored and fresh revelation given respecting a Divine David, Who found deliverance, not by deceiving man, but in trusting God.

In this Verse, we are told exactly how important that praising the Lord actually is. Especially when we consider that *"His praise shall continually be in my mouth."* This speaks of constant praise.

It is not speaking of vocal praise all the time, but it is meaning that praise should be in our hearts constantly.

BLESSING THE LORD

The phrase, *"I will bless the LORD at all*

times," doesn't leave any room for fault-finding or complaining, as should be obvious.

To *"bless the LORD"* refers to the fact of understanding that He does all things well, and that every single blessing that we have has come from Him. As a result, we should never complain!

(2) "MY SOUL SHALL MAKE HER BOAST IN THE LORD: THE HUMBLE SHALL HEAR THEREOF, AND BE GLAD."

The word *"humble"* should have been translated *"oppressed."*

DEMON OPPRESSION

Every Christian, at one time or another, has experienced demon oppression. This, as should be obvious, is totally different from demon possession.

In fact, a Child of God, can definitely be oppressed by demons, but cannot be possessed by demons.

Possession is that which comes from within, while oppression is that which comes from without.

Oppression can cause nervous disorders, emotional disturbances, fear, depression, discouragement, etc.

Most of the time, *"demon oppression"* takes place in hearts and lives simply because the Believer doesn't understand his place and position in Christ, which means he doesn't understand the Cross, as it refers to Sanctification. All victory is found in Christ and what Christ did at the Cross. When the Believer evidences faith in Christ and the Cross, ever making that the Object of his Faith, this then gives the Holy Spirit great latitude to work within our lives. This is the answer to oppression. In fact, this is the only answer to oppression.

Whatever needs to be done, Jesus has already done it at the Cross. The Scripture says, and I quote from THE EXPOSITOR'S STUDY BIBLE:

"Blotting out the handwriting of Ordinances that was against us (pertains to the Law of Moses, which was God's Standard of Righteousness that man could not reach), *which was contrary to us* (Law is against us, simply because we are unable to keep its precepts, no matter how hard we try), *and took it out of the way* (refers to the penalty of the Law being removed), *nailing it to His Cross* (the Law with its decrees was abolished in Christ's death, as if crucified with Him);

"And having spoiled principalities and powers (Satan and all of his henchmen were defeated at the Cross by Christ atoning for all sin; sin was the legal right Satan had to hold man in captivity; with all sin atoned, he has no more legal right to hold anyone in bondage), *He* (Christ) *made a show of them openly* (what Jesus did at the Cross was in the face of the whole universe), *triumphing over them in it.* (The triumph is complete, and it was all done for us, meaning we can walk in power and perpetual victory due to the Cross)" (Col. 2:14-15).

Satan has great latitude with Believers for the simple reason that most have no idea the part that the Cross plays in our Sanctification process, which pertains to our everyday living for God. In fact, this is the single most important aspect for the Believer. When we consider that most Believers have no understanding of this of which we speak, then we begin to realize the cause and the reason for the high rate of failure and oppression in the hearts and lives of Believers.

Our Lord paid a terrible price for this great Redemption process. To be sure, the great Redemption Plan covers every aspect of our life and living. Nothing is excluded; all are included. So, there is no need for us to walk in defeat, i.e., *"to live in defeat."* Every provision has been made for victory — and perpetual victory, at that!

Once again:

Christ is the Source, and the Cross is the Means.

BOASTING IN THE LORD

The word *"boasting"* actually refers to glorying.

The Prophet Jeremiah said, *"Let him who glories glory in this, that he understands and knows Me, that I am the LORD which executes lovingkindness, judgment, and righteousness in the Earth"* (Jer. 9:24).

In the New Testament, Paul said, *"But God forbid that I should glory* (boast), *save in the Cross of our Lord Jesus Christ* (what the opponents of Paul sought to escape at the price of insincerity is the Apostle's only basis of exultation), *by Whom the world is crucified unto me, and I unto the world."* (The only way we can overcome the world, and I mean the only way, is by placing our faith exclusively in the Cross of Christ and keeping it there [Gal. 6:14].)

(3) "O MAGNIFY THE LORD WITH ME, AND LET US EXALT HIS NAME TOGETHER."

The purpose of the schooling is to so humble the Saint that he will trust the Lord, praise, and magnify Jehovah.

If we put our total dependence in God, victory will be ours without the terrible humiliation. Sadly, it is difficult for man to learn this lesson. Instead of *"magnifying the LORD,"* we tend to *"magnify ourselves"* by engaging in forays (such as David's) which are the products of man-made ideas and ingenuity. They always lead to trouble.

Not content with praising God in his own person, David calls on Israel generally to praise the Lord with him. He then proceeds to assign reasons why God could be praised, which begin with the next Verse.

MAGNIFYING THE LORD

One does not magnify the Lord by finding fault, by complaining, etc. One magnifies the Lord by exalting His Name and by praising Him for the wonderful things He has done.

Let the Reader understand this:

God is not limited. We may limit Him, and all of us have done this at one time or another, but the limitation was our doing and not His. It doesn't matter who we are, where we live, the circumstances of our birth, or how many strikes seem to be against us. If we will believe the Lord, He can bless us where we are, no matter where that is.

Solomon said, *"If the tree fall toward the south, or toward the north, in the place where the tree falls, there it shall be"* (Eccl. 11:3).

What does this Passage mean?

Believers constantly attempt to put God in a box. Their faith is attached to *"what might have been,"* a place and position in which God does not work.

The Lord does not work from *"what might have been,"* but from *"what is."* It doesn't matter which way the tree falls, which means it doesn't matter where we live, who we are,

NOTES

or what the situation is. If we will believe God, He will bless us where we are, and will do so grandly.

The Reader should get it out of his mind that he is in the wrong place at the wrong time, etc. In spite of circumstances and in spite of situations, the Believer should believe God, should stand on the Promises, should speak faith, should speak blessings, and should run over with confidence, for this is the type of faith that God always rewards. He may test us for a while, but, to be sure, He will do great things for us if we only will believe Him.

(4) "I SOUGHT THE LORD, AND HE HEARD ME, AND DELIVERED ME FROM ALL MY FEARS."

Another great truth is here given to us.

SEEKING THE LORD

To *"seek the LORD"* is not merely to trust in Him, but to fly to Him, and make our requests of Him in our troubles.

Verses 4 through 6 give us the prayers of David, but also the Greater Son of David. He is inviting His people to unite with Him in praising Jehovah.

The *"fears"* here addressed refer to the *"fear of man."* It does not speak of the *"fear of God."*

(5) "THEY LOOKED UNTO HIM, AND WERE LIGHTENED: AND THEIR FACES WERE NOT ASHAMED."

We have the Promise that if we look to God, several things will happen.

THE PROMISE OF GOD

1. *"He will hear us"*;
2. *"He will deliver us"*;
3. *"We will be enlightened"*;
4. *"We will not be ashamed"*; and,
5. *"We will be saved out of all our troubles."*

Because these things are the Promises of God, they cannot fail!

At the same time, the Holy Spirit is telling us that if we look to man, then we will be neither delivered nor enlightened, but will rather be ashamed. We will not be saved out of all our troubles. God is not only the answer, He is the only answer.

(6) "THIS POOR MAN CRIED, AND THE LORD HEARD HIM, AND SAVED HIM OUT

OF ALL HIS TROUBLES."

Here the Messiah portrays Himself as a *"poor Man"* because all mankind falls into the same category. We cannot save ourselves; we cannot deliver ourselves. Self cannot improve self, irrespective of the efforts made. To look at self clothes the face with misery. To look at man clothes it with distraction. To look at God makes the face to shine. So it was with Moses (II Cor., Chpt. 3).

(7) "THE ANGEL OF THE LORD ENCAMPS ROUND ABOUT THEM WHO FEAR HIM, AND DELIVERS THEM."

The Hebrew word *"to encamp"* is related to the name *"Mahanaim,"* which means *"two camps"* (Gen. 32:1-2). One was Jacob's feeble camp; the other, the encompassing camp of God's mighty Angels (II Ki. 6:17; Gen. 32:1-2).

The Divine title, *"The Angel of Jehovah,"* taken from the word *"LORD,"* occurs only here and in Psalms 35:5-6. It is given here for deliverance and there for destruction. An Angel delivered Peter, but destroyed Herod (Acts, Chpt. 12).

(8) "O TASTE AND SEE THAT THE LORD IS GOOD: BLESSED IS THE MAN WHO TRUSTS IN HIM."

As we have repeatedly stated, *"Trust in the LORD,"* is the theme of Psalms.

TASTE AND SEE

Here the eternal invitation is given to all, that if they only will *"taste,"* then they will *"see"* that *"the LORD is good."* Regrettably, most will not *"taste."*

The idea is that of a pot of food, surrounded by hungry people, who have it in their minds that the food is not good. The invitation is given to them that if they only will *"taste,"* they will see that it is *"good."*

(9) "O FEAR THE LORD, YE HIS SAINTS: FOR THERE IS NO WANT TO THEM WHO FEAR HIM."

In Verse 4, we are told that the Lord delivered the poor man from all his fears (fear of man). Now we are told that we should *"fear the LORD."* This means to honor, respect, love, and adore Him, and fear Him regarding His Word. In other words, He means what He says, and says what He means.

NOTES

NO WANT

Fear of God, a reverent and Godly fear, will always accompany trust in God, such as God approves. The Saints of God both love and fear Him.

To such a person, there is *"no want,"* since God supplies all our wants.

As Believers, we can have our every need met, be it financial, domestic, physical, or spiritual. Provision has been made at the Cross of Calvary, where the price was totally and completely paid. So, if we do not have an ample provision, then it's our fault, and not God's!

(10) "THE YOUNG LIONS DO LACK, AND SUFFER HUNGER: BUT THEY WHO SEEK THE LORD SHALL NOT WANT ANY GOOD THING."

Even the mighty lions, with their great power, still lack and suffer hunger at times; however, if we trust in the Lord, the Promise is that *"we shall not want any good thing."*

Once again, this is based on that which is good for the soul.

(11) "COME, YE CHILDREN, HEARKEN UNTO ME: I WILL TEACH YOU THE FEAR OF THE LORD."

We are told here that the *"fear of the LORD"* is the secret of receiving good things. We are also now told that the Holy Spirit will *"teach us how to fear the LORD."* Everyone should be immensely interested in this instruction.

The next two Verses give us the answer.

(12) "WHAT MAN IS HE WHO DESIRES LIFE, AND LOVES MANY DAYS, THAT HE MAY SEE GOOD?

(13) "KEEP YOUR TONGUE FROM EVIL, AND YOUR LIPS FROM SPEAKING GUILE."

Pulpit says, *"If the end be happiness, the means will be right moral conduct; and, first of all, right government of the tongue. The sins of the tongue are numerous, and abundantly noted in the Psalms* (Ps. 5:9; 10:7; 12:3; 15:3; 50:19; 57:4; 73:8-9, etc.). *The sins of the tongue are more difficult to avoid than any others; they cling closer to us; they are scarcely ever wholly laid aside."* [9]

The Apostle James said, *"If any man offend not in word, the same is a perfect man, and able also to bridle the whole body"*

(James 3:2). The meek Moses *"spoke unadvisedly with his lips"* (Ps. 106:33). Job *"darkened counsel by words without knowledge"* (Job 38:2).

Peter's words on one occasion drew upon him the rebuke, *"Get thee behind Me, Satan"* (Mat. 16:23).

(14) "DEPART FROM EVIL, AND DO GOOD; SEEK PEACE, AND PURSUE IT."

From words, the Psalmist proceeds to acts, and, in the bleakest possible way, says all that can be said.

First, he tells us to *"depart from evil,"* which refers to the fact that we do nothing that is wrong; break no laws of God, no command of conscience; have a conscience void of offense, both towards God and toward man.

Second, he requires positive goodness — *"do good,"* i.e., actively perform the Will of God from the heart; discharge every duty; practice every virtue; carry out the precepts of the moral law in every particular (Pulpit).[10]

(15) "THE EYES OF THE LORD ARE UPON THE RIGHTEOUS, AND HIS EARS ARE OPEN UNTO THEIR CRY."

Two great Promises are given to us here.

THE EYES OF THE LORD

What a delightful statement! His *"Eyes"* are watching us, and His *"Ears"* are listening to us. He is waiting for us to call on Him.

To those who do not love the Lord, the idea of such minute inspection on a constant basis is unnerving. To be frank, they don't care to have anything to do with such a situation. The reasons are obvious. Their deeds are evil, and they don't want the Lord involved. But He, of course, is involved!

However, while the Lord is Omniscient, meaning that He knows everything that is happening in the world, and at all times, still, this Passage not only speaks of inspection, but it speaks of the Eyes of the Lord upon the righteous in order to do us good. He is like a parent who is always listening for a little child. The moment it gets in trouble and cries, the parent is quickly there! This is what is meant by this Passage, as it regards the Lord and those who serve Him.

(16) "THE FACE OF THE LORD IS AGAINST THEM WHO DO EVIL, TO CUT OFF THE REMEMBRANCE OF THEM FROM THE EARTH."

This is the reason that those who do not serve the Lord do not desire His involvement in any capacity; however, irrespective as to what they like, the Lord knows exactly what is going on at all times.

As well, His *"Face"* is always against them who do evil, meaning that He is opposed to them and their actions. No good will come to them. Even those who seem to be doing well really aren't!

There is coming a day when there will be no more evil, and even the remembrance of those who have done evil will be *"cut off from the Earth."*

(17) "THE RIGHTEOUS CRY, AND THE LORD HEARS, AND DELIVERS THEM OUT OF ALL THEIR TROUBLES."

We have here the Promise of the Lord that when we *"cry"* to Him, He always will hear and will deliver us.

Are there qualifications?

Yes there are, and they are listed in the next Verse.

(18) "THE LORD IS NEAR UNTO THEM WHO ARE OF A BROKEN HEART; AND SAVES SUCH AS BE OF CONTRITE SPIRIT."

This same (or a similar) Passage is given elsewhere in the Word of God, showing us exactly how important this is.

The Prophet Isaiah said, *"But to this man will I look, even to him who is poor and of a contrite spirit, and trembles at My Word"* (Isa. 66:2).

In a later Psalm, David also said, *"The sacrifices of God are a broken spirit: a broken and a contrite heart, O God, You will not despise"* (Ps. 51:17).

We learn from these Passages exactly what the Lord looks for. These things are the opposite of pride, as should be obvious! To be frank, inasmuch as few evidence the righteous traits listed in this Eighteenth Verse, the Lord is not near to very many people.

(19) "MANY ARE THE AFFLICTIONS OF THE RIGHTEOUS: BUT THE LORD DELIVERS HIM OUT OF THEM ALL."

Upon reading this Psalm and other Passages, many act upon them presumptuously by claiming that a certain degree of faith will stop all afflictions. In other words, everything, they say, is according to the quantity of faith we have!

But the Scripture does not say this. It rather says the opposite. In other words, tests will come. Great faith must be tested greatly; actually, every *"affliction"* is a test of faith. Will we pass the test, or will we fail?

Most Christians misunderstand the test. Did David fail?

In a sense, he did; however, that which ultimately is the most important did not fail, namely, his faith. Every attack by Satan is to weaken, undermine, and ultimately destroy our faith. Other things, such as failures, may be wrong, but they are incidental. Satan attacks us simply because he wants us to get discouraged and quit. If he can get us to do that, he will have won our soul.

The Lord, despite failures, wants us to get up, renew our vows to Him, beg and plead His forgiveness. Then, from the position of a broken heart and crushed spirit, victory will be ours.

Most of that which presently calls itself *"Church"* little understands this. In today's modern Church, David would be laughed at, ridiculed, and very quickly disfellowshipped; however, the disfellowship would come from man, and not from God. God never disfellowships anyone unless the person insists on continuing in sin. He has given us the Promise of His deliverance.

DELIVERANCE

Regarding the anointing of the Holy Spirit, Jesus said that the Spirit anointed Him *"to preach deliverance to the captives"* (Lk. 4:18). He didn't say, *"to deliver the captives,"* but rather *"to preach deliverance to the captives,"* which is what we are doing in this Volume.

There are many Preachers who call themselves *"deliverance Preachers."*

I'm not doubting their motives or good intentions; however, no Preacher can deliver anyone. Deliverance comes solely from the Lord, and it comes by the individual being taught that his faith must ever rest in the Cross of Christ as its Object. Then the Holy Spirit, Who is God, and Who can do anything, will work mightily within such a life.

When we correctly *"preach deliverance,"* we are correctly telling the people how to be delivered, which is always from Christ as the Source and the Cross as the Means.

No Christian should need deliverance; however, when a Christian does not know God's Way of Victory and does not understand the Cross of Christ as it refers to Sanctification, such a Christian quickly becomes entangled in spiritual bondage. That Christian needs deliverance; however, laying on of hands, as Scriptural as that might be in its own right, will not suffice.

Jesus said:

"You shall know the Truth, and the Truth shall make you free" (Jn. 8:32).

As this Passage plainly says, it's the Truth that sets us free, not some particular act that a Preacher carries out, etc.

Please don't misunderstand! Laying on of hands is Scriptural, but only for the right reasons. Those reasons are blessings and healing (James 5:14). Of course, laying on of hands will definitely help anyone, even those seeking deliverance, provided they know and understand that the laying on of hands is simply an encouragement of faith. It's the Truth of the Cross that sets one free, and nothing else!

(20) "HE KEEPS ALL HIS BONES: NOT ONE OF THEM IS BROKEN."

This Passage tells us that Satan will definitely come against the Child of God, and at times the attack will be powerful; however, the Lord, by using the metaphor of this Twentieth Verse, proclaims the fact that Righteousness ultimately will triumph. The Lord will *"redeem the soul of His servants."* This is not so much speaking of particular wants as it speaks of being redeemed from the clutches of the Evil One.

The gift of this beautiful Psalm at such a crisis in David's life emphasizes the truth that Salvation and Inspiration are both based upon the principle of Grace and never of merit.

Moses, David, Isaiah, Peter, Paul, and others have illustrated this fact. It is when broken, contrite, mortified, and shamed that one is made conscious of one's moral worthlessness. Only then can one be used as a spiritual channel. The modern self-righteous Church does not comprehend this at all!

(21) "EVIL SHALL SLAY THE WICKED:

AND THEY WHO HATE THE RIGHTEOUS SHALL BE DESOLATE."

This Verse points to the fact that the *"evil"* indulged in by the *"wicked"* will fall out ultimately to their destruction. Unrighteousness carries its own desolation, while Righteousness carries its own Blessings.

(22) "THE LORD REDEEMS THE SOUL OF HIS SERVANTS: AND NONE OF THEM WHO TRUST IN HIM SHALL BE DESOLATE."

Those whom God has redeemed, He justifies and saves from all condemnation. We are *"passed from death unto life"* (Jn. 5:24).

PSALM 35

*A Psalm of David:
A Prayer for Deliverance*

(1) "PLEAD MY CAUSE, O LORD, WITH THEM WHO STRIVE WITH ME: FIGHT AGAINST THEM WHO FIGHT AGAINST ME."

As noted, this Psalm was written by David.

CHRIST, THE LAMB OF GOD

This Psalm, more than all, presents Christ, the Lamb of God, and his followers surrounded by the wolves of Satan (Jn. 15:20-25); consequently, this Psalm, which is more a Prophecy than a petition, relates to His rejection and Crucifixion. It reveals the Love of God's heart to man, and the hatred of man's heart to God (Jn. 15:23).

Many think that these Passages and others of similar character should be removed from the Bible. They say that no Christian person should pray so vindictively.

It would certainly be improper for David, or any other sinful man, to present such a petition to God. But in such Psalms, the Petitioner is the Sinless Man, Christ Jesus, and He fittingly calls for the Divine Judgment upon those who hate Him; for in hating Him, they hate God and His people, and also goodness, righteousness, and truth.

Hence, when judging the Pharisees (Mat. 23:13-36), He used language of similar import. In the Thirteenth Chapter of Matthew and related Prophecies, He predicts that He will destroy and cast out of His Kingdom all who hate goodness and practice iniquity.

Some of these petitions for judgment are Personal to Himself and others as they affect His oppressed and hated people. While it is not fitting for us to cry for vengeance upon our tormenters, it is most fitting for Him in our interests to do so.

In this Psalm, the enemies of Christ unjustly accuse Him. He calls on God to vindicate Him and invites His people in expectation of that vindication to join Him in a song of praise.

This and other Scriptures strengthened His faith and comforted His heart prior to and during the trial in the palace of Caiaphas. This is evident from His quotation of Verse 19 as He was on the way to the Garden of Gethsemane (Jn. 15:25).

(2) "TAKE HOLD OF SHIELD AND BUCKLER, AND STAND UP FOR MY HELP."

The *"shield"* and *"buckler"* were two different items. The *"shield"* was a smaller hand weapon. The *"buckler"* covered the whole body. So between the two, the shield protected the soldier from the thrust of his opponent's sword; but, if the sword was able to get past the shield, the soldier's body was protected by the *"buckler."*

We speak here of total protection, which is afforded to all Believers.

(3) "DRAW OUT ALSO THE SPEAR, AND STOP THE WAY AGAINST THEM WHO PERSECUTE ME: SAY UNTO MY SOUL, I AM YOUR SALVATION."

It is believed that the word translated *"stop the way"* really is the name of a weapon; consequently, the Passage should read, *"Bring out also the spear and the battle ax against them who persecute Me."*

The idea of the phrase, *"Say unto My soul, I am Your Salvation,"* refers to the comfort of the soul with the assurance that the Lord is, and ever will be, my Salvation. Even though David prayed these words, more than all they are meant to be a petition given by the Master.

Deliverance from the immediate danger is not all that is meant; but rather support and saving help in all dangers and in all troubles.

(4) "LET THEM BE CONFOUNDED AND PUT TO SHAME WHO SEEK AFTER MY SOUL: LET THEM BE TURNED BACK AND

BROUGHT TO CONFUSION WHO DEVISE MY HURT."

As we have stated, such a petition would not be proper for any human being to utter, other than Christ; however, the Holy Spirit is the One Who is praying these words through the Messiah, and He gives them through the heart and by the tongue of David about a thousand years before the fact.

When Christ prayed this prayer for Himself, it was not for Himself Alone, but actually for the entirety of all Believers. As stated, we could not pray such a prayer; but He could, and He did!

So, in this prayer, understanding that God answered every prayer of His Son, we know that those who oppose the righteous ultimately will be brought to shame and confusion.

(5) "LET THEM BE AS CHAFF BEFORE THE WIND: AND LET THE ANGEL OF THE LORD CHASE THEM."

Chaff is a type of whatever is light, vain, futile, and worthless; chaff driven before the wind represents the confused rout of a beaten army, flying without any resistance before an enemy.

The phrase, *"And let the Angel of the LORD chase them,"* should have been translated *"smite them."* The Angel of the Lord, who protects the righteous (Ps. 34:7), is called on to complete the discomfiture of the wicked ones who are David's enemies, and, above all, the enemies of the Messiah, the Greater Son of David.

(6) "LET THEIR WAY BE DARK AND SLIPPERY: AND LET THE ANGEL OF THE LORD PERSECUTE THEM."

Once again, we emphasize the fact that, although this prayer is prayed by David, it actually is a petition of our Lord, which is given not only on behalf of Himself, but also for the entirety of the Plan of God, and against those who would oppose that Plan.

(7) "FOR WITHOUT CAUSE HAVE THEY HID FOR ME THEIR NET IN A PIT, WHICH WITHOUT CAUSE THEY HAVE DUG FOR MY SOUL."

The phrase, *"Without cause,"* means without provocation on the part of our Lord.

There is no evil like religious evil. This Passage speaks of the Pharisees, Sadducees, and Herodians, who hated the Lord and desired even that He would lose His soul. This is how evil they were!

(8) "LET DESTRUCTION COME UPON HIM AT UNAWARES; AND LET HIS NET THAT HE HAS HID CATCH HIMSELF: INTO THAT VERY DESTRUCTION LET HIM FALL."

This is exactly what happened to these religious leaders of Israel who crucified Christ. Opportunity after opportunity was given to them to repent, but to no avail! So destruction came upon them in A.D. 70, when Titus, who commanded the mighty Roman Tenth Legion, laid siege to Jerusalem, killing over one million Jews and selling another million as slaves at the slave markets of the world. So many Jews were put on the slave markets that the price of slaves dipped to an all-time low.

(9) "AND MY SOUL SHALL BE JOYFUL IN THE LORD: IT SHALL REJOICE IN HIS SALVATION."

The tenor of the petition changes, and the Lord now rejoices, which means that His prayer has been answered. Evil will not triumph!

(10) "ALL MY BONES SHALL SAY, LORD, WHO IS LIKE UNTO YOU, WHICH DELIVERS THE POOR FROM HIM WHO IS TOO STRONG FOR HIM, YEA, THE POOR AND THE NEEDY FROM HIM WHO SPOILS HIM?"

As in Verse 6 of Psalm 34, here likewise are the Messiah, David, and every Believer called *"the poor."* They who are arrayed against us are *"too strong for us."* However, the Lord will help us, and we will praise His Name.

THE PROTECTION OF THE LORD

There is not a Believer who has ever lived, I think, who hasn't felt the oppression of enemies, which, in the natural, have always been far, far too strong for us. Almost all of the time, such opposition comes from inside the Church. That's why we say that religious evil is the most horrible evil of all!

But yet, when we call on the Lord, irrespective of the strength arrayed against us, such strength cannot even begin to compare with that of the Lord. He delivers us, and, to be sure, that's the reason we should ever look to Him. In the natural, we cannot cope. With the Lord, we can do all things!

(11) "FALSE WITNESSES DID RISE UP; THEY LAID TO MY CHARGE THINGS THAT I KNEW NOT."

As David was accused, Christ also was accused, and to a far greater degree. The very name *"Satan"* means *"slanderer."* It should wisely be considered that when one Christian accuses another Christian, they are becoming a tool of Satan.

The *"lie"* is the greatest weapon that one's enemies can use against us. There is no defense against the lie; so, the best thing that a Believer can do when faced with such is simply to turn it over to the Lord.

(12) "THEY REWARDED ME EVIL FOR GOOD TO THE SPOILING OF MY SOUL."

As David had done nothing but good for those who turned out to be his enemies, and for Israel as well, likewise, the Son of David had done nothing but good for the whole of Israel, and even all of mankind, whoever and wherever they might have been.

Among those who slandered David were persons with whom he had sympathized in their troubles, and whom he had tried to help in every capacity. Even Saul admitted to David, *"You are more righteous than I. For you have rewarded me good, whereas I have rewarded you evil"* (I Sam. 24:17).

Of course, our Lord never did evil to anyone, but His enemies were many.

EVIL FOR GOOD

On a personal basis, I too know what it is to help someone (in fact, to help many) on a grand scale, but then, when the opportunity presented itself, these same people rewarded good with evil. As I have said previously, *"When one is down and can do nothing to defend himself, and anyone can do any negative thing to such a person that they so desire, and will not only not be reprimanded, but rather applauded, then one finds out exactly how many good Christians there really are."* Regrettably, there aren't many!

Such anger, jealousy, and envy were in the hearts of these people all along. They just didn't feel it was in their best interests to exhibit such; however, when the opportunity presented itself, such people always take full advantage.

(13) "BUT AS FOR ME, WHEN THEY WERE SICK, MY CLOTHING WAS SACKCLOTH: I HUMBLED MY SOUL WITH FASTING; AND MY PRAYER RETURNED INTO MY OWN BOSOM."

Who this was that David was addressing is not known. But David fasted and sought the Lord earnestly for their healing and deliverance.

The phrase, *"And my prayer returned into my own bosom,"* carries the idea that such prayer did not do these people any good because their hearts were evil; but it did bless David, as all such prayers bless those who petition the Lord in such manner.

(14) "I BEHAVED MYSELF AS THOUGH HE HAD BEEN MY FRIEND OR BROTHER: I BOWED DOWN HEAVILY, AS ONE WHO MOURNS FOR HIS MOTHER."

Possibly David was speaking of Saul; likewise, the Lord Jesus Christ clothed Himself in *"sackcloth"* (the Incarnation) over Israel and a lost world. His *"fasting"* included the denial of all that He previously had known in order that He might *"humble Himself"* for the souls of men.

Even though they in Israel were the enemies of Christ, still, He cried to God for their deliverance. Thankfully, some would be delivered. Most would not, because they would not accept.

(15) "BUT IN MY ADVERSITY THEY REJOICED, AND GATHERED THEMSELVES TOGETHER: YEA, THE ABJECTS GATHERED THEMSELVES TOGETHER AGAINST ME, AND I KNEW IT NOT; THEY DID TEAR ME, AND CEASED NOT."

It is a matter of common experience that when men fall into misfortune from a high position, the base vulgar crowd always turns against them with scoffs, jeers, and every sort of rudeness, insolence, and arrogance.

When this element, i.e., the *"abjects,"* see so-called leaders beating up on someone, they feel free to follow suit, and they always do!

(16) "WITH HYPOCRITICAL MOCKERS IN FEASTS, THEY GNASHED UPON ME WITH THEIR TEETH."

When David needed help, these for whom he had cried to God on their behalf turned against him and rejoiced over his suffering.

They did the same with Christ. As they hurled at David every accusation, even more so they hurled at Christ the venom of the pit.

The short phrase, *"Hypocritical mockers,"* means that they made David the butt of their jests — in fact, their byword. To a far greater degree, they did exactly the same thing with Christ! So what David underwent was a type of that which Christ would undergo.

DAVID

Some may argue that David did terribly wrong, speaking of adultery with Bathsheba and the murder of her husband Uriah in cold blood. Yes! What David did was extremely awful, so awful as to defy description, but none of that gave the people of Israel any room to treat him as they did. They should have done all within their power to help David. They didn't seem to have sense enough to know and realize that all the blessings which had come to them were because of David.

Actually, all of their efforts to hurt David, even to kill him, had actually been in their hearts all along.

(17) "LORD, HOW LONG WILL YOU LOOK ON? RESCUE MY SOUL FROM THEIR DESTRUCTIONS, MY DARLING FROM THE LIONS."

This is a Promise to those who cry to God, and it seems as though He does not answer. The *"lions"* refer to the demon powers of darkness who registered themselves in the lives of the Pharisees and Sadducees who would destroy Him. Even though they thought they had succeeded, in reality they did not. He would deliver man from Satan's terrible bondage by His Death upon the Cross.

(18) "I WILL GIVE YOU THANKS IN THE GREAT CONGREGATION: I WILL PRAISE YOU AMONG MUCH PEOPLE."

This Promise is repeated by David from Verses 9 and 10; but, as before, it is conditional on deliverance being granted, and intended to induce the Lord to grant it, and to grant it speedily.

We learn from all of this that even though David had done seriously wrong, he took the wrong to the Lord. David sought His Grace and His Love! He did not make excuses for his wrongdoing, but he did lay it at the feet of Jehovah; whatever the matter may have been, he took it to the Lord and left it there.

(19) "LET NOT THEM WHO ARE MY ENEMIES WRONGFULLY REJOICE OVER ME: NEITHER LET THEM WINK WITH THE EYE WHO HATE ME WITHOUT A CAUSE."

As this applied to David, it more so applied to the Son of David.

The following Verses proclaim His petition to God that He would not let this terrible travesty of injustice go unnoticed.

The horror is this: Those who did this to Him were not the harlots or the thieves, but those who called themselves religious and righteous; however, they were self-righteous. This was the Church of Jesus' day. It pretty well also characterizes the Church of today.

David's enemies hated him without a cause. To be sure, the enemies of our Lord also hated Him without a cause!

(20) "FOR THEY SPEAK NOT PEACE: BUT THEY DEVISE DECEITFUL MATTERS AGAINST THEM WHO ARE QUIET IN THE LAND."

The phrase, *"For they speak not peace,"* means that irrespective as to what David did, they would not be satisfied until he was dead. They did everything possible to kill him. It was the Lord Who spared him, Who ultimately brought the evil upon their own heads.

The phrase, *"But they devise deceitful matters against them who are quiet in the land,"* refers to the fact that David was not stirring up trouble, and was not doing anything negative against these enemies. But they still wanted him dead!

Everything we read here about David can be multiplied to apply to the Greater Son of David.

(21) "YEA, THEY OPENED THEIR MOUTH WIDE AGAINST ME, AND SAID, AHA, AHA, OUR EYE HAS SEEN IT."

They *"opened their mouth wide"* in scornful derision; they shouted triumphantly, *"Aha, Aha! Our eye has seen his downfall!"*

These very attitudes and actions were derived against Christ when He hung on the Cross! There they mocked Him, saying, *"If You really are the Son of God, come down from the Cross!"*

There is no way that we can fully comprehend the evil that was in the hearts of those who rejected Christ and willed His

Crucifixion! As we have repeatedly stated, there is no evil like religious evil! It has soaked the Earth with blood, causing more bloodshed than anything else ever has.

(22) "THIS YOU HAVE SEEN, O LORD: KEEP NOT SILENCE: O LORD, BE NOT FAR FROM ME."

To be sure, from above the Lord most definitely saw the evil that was in the hearts of those who crucified Christ! He most definitely heard the petition of the Master. And He did not *"keep silence."*

About thirty-three years later, Jerusalem was totally destroyed by the mighty Roman Tenth Legion.

(23) "STIR UP YOURSELF, AND AWAKE TO MY JUDGMENT, EVEN UNTO MY CAUSE, MY GOD AND MY LORD."

David calls on the Lord to *"awake,"* not as though He really is asleep, but as a sort of stirring appeal to Him to arise and manifest Himself.

David asks Him *"to judge my cause — to acquit me, and condemn my enemies."*

All of this proclaims the fact as to how much David looked exclusively to the Lord. He placed no trust in men, but his trust was totally in Jehovah; he knew that the Lord was able to do all things.

The phrase, *"Stir up Yourself, and awake to my judgment,"* carries the idea of impatience. David wanted the Lord to move quickly!

The Lord answered this prayer on both counts — for David and for the Greater Son of David.

(24) "JUDGE ME, O LORD MY GOD, ACCORDING TO YOUR RIGHTEOUSNESS; AND LET THEM NOT REJOICE OVER ME."

David is saying, *"Let Your Law of Righteousness be the rule by which I am judged, and my enemies also. Then the victory will remain with me; and You will not let them rejoice over me."*

David was appealing to the Word of God. This is the appeal which all of us must make!

(25) "LET THEM NOT SAY IN THEIR HEARTS, AH, SO WOULD WE HAVE IT: LET THEM NOT SAY, WE HAVE SWALLOWED HIM UP."

David is asking that when all of this is over, that his enemies would not have triumphed, that they would be able to gloat over him, they would not be able to claim that they had destroyed him, ruined him, and brought him to an evil end.

At the time David was saying these words, it looked like that's what the conclusion would be. In the natural, it didn't look like there was any way that He could come out of this conflict. It looked like His enemies would succeed!

They did not succeed, however, because the Lord most definitely did come to His rescue. This petition prayed by our Lord was answered in totality, in that He was raised from the dead, which tells us that the Cross and the Resurrection struck a blow against evil from which it never will recover.

(26) "LET THEM BE ASHAMED AND BROUGHT TO CONFUSION TOGETHER WHO REJOICE AT MY HURT: LET THEM BE CLOTHED WITH SHAME AND DISHONOR WHO MAGNIFY THEMSELVES AGAINST ME."

The entirety of this petition from Verse 17 through 26 was answered regarding both David and the Messiah. It also will be honored regarding every Child of God.

ANSWERED PRAYER

If David was speaking of Saul, the king was killed on Mount Gilboa by the Philistines. If David was speaking of Absalom and those with him, they too met an untimely end.

The Pharisees and Sadducees of Christ's day were completely destroyed in A.D. 70 by Titus and his armies. Over one million Jews were slaughtered at the siege of Jerusalem. So many were crucified that there was no more room to put crosses. They also were sold, *"clothed with shame,"* as slaves all over the world because they *"magnified themselves against Christ."*

Let it be known: Every single person who magnifies himself against a Child of God by judging and measuring him shall have against him the terrible results of Matthew 7:1-2.

Yes! If Saul had repented, or Absalom had repented, the Lord would have heard, forgiven, and halted the terrible punishment; likewise, if the Israel of Jesus' day had repented, they too would have been spared judgment. The same can be said for anyone. But if there is no repentance and turning away from the terrible opposition against the Lord and His Own, the following will happen:

1. *"They will be ashamed."*
2. *"They will be brought to confusion."*
3. *"They will be clothed with shame and dishonor."*

(27) "LET THEM SHOUT FOR JOY, AND BE GLAD, WHO FAVOR MY RIGHTEOUS CAUSE: YEA, LET THEM SAY CONTINUALLY, LET THE LORD BE MAGNIFIED, WHICH HAS PLEASURE IN THE PROSPERITY OF HIS SERVANT."

This Passage is powerful. It is saying that only those who favor His *"righteous cause"* will *"shout for joy and be glad."* Those who *"have pleasure in the prosperity of Christ"* will be *"magnified."* They will realize that He does no wrong, that the wicked who will not repent must be turned into Hell, plus all the nations which forget God.

Irrespective of the circumstances, the Lord is magnified and has pleasure when His servant prospers. All who will help that servant prosper also will be blessed! Regrettably, it seems that the modern Church understands this not at all. It seems to never learn its lesson.

(28) "AND MY TONGUE SHALL SPEAK OF YOUR RIGHTEOUSNESS AND OF YOUR PRAISE ALL THE DAY LONG."

This Twenty-eighth Verse proclaims the fact that there is no unrighteousness in this type of prayer prayed by the Messiah, and that He is actually righteous in doing such.

David means to promise perpetual gratitude and thankfulness. He will not merely return thanks publicly, once for all, in the great congregation, but will continue to praise God always.

Every Believer should make it a habit to constantly praise the Lord. Some may think they have very little for which to praise Him; however, such thinking is always wrong. If the only thing we have is Salvation, and everything else seems dark and unavailable to us, we still have enough to praise the Lord for a million years over.

Even though the Lord definitely gives us Salvation, this Great Salvation, He also has done so much more for us, and, if we only will look around a little bit, we will see it. And He never will stop doing good things for us. Therefore:

"My tongue shall speak of Your Righteousness and of Your Praise all the day long."

PSALM 36

A Psalm of David:
The Steadfast Love and Faithfulness of God

(1) "THE TRANSGRESSION OF THE WICKED SAYS WITHIN MY HEART, THAT THERE IS NO FEAR OF GOD BEFORE HIS EYES."

As noted, David wrote this Psalm.

A DESCRIPTION OF GOD'S WAY

The Saviour's atoning Work is the theme of this particular Psalm. The structure may be thus exhibited:

1. Description of the sinner — Verses 1-4;
2. Saving Grace of the Saviour — Verses 5-6;
3. Happy state of the forgiven sinner — Verses 7-9; and,
4. Prayer to the Saviour — Verses 10-12.

Transgression to the self-willed man speaks within his heart as an oracle. There is no fear of God before his eyes. The transgression flatters him in his own eyes that his iniquity will never be found out and be punished.

Transgression against God's revealed Law does not merely speak to his heart, but, as an enthroned oracle, speaks within it, and has an accepted dominion over it.

DECEPTION

All of this tells us that the unredeemed man is deceived. In all of this, we must understand that deception is not merely a proposed decision, but, in reality, is a spirit. Demon spirits are behind all deception, giving it power, and deception completely takes over the individual. This is why Paul made the following statement:

"Now the Spirit (Holy Spirit) *speaks expressly* (pointedly), *that in the latter times* (the times in which we now live, the last of the last days, which begin the fulfillment of

Endtime Prophecies) *some shall depart from the Faith* (anytime Paul uses the term *'the Faith,'* in short he is referring to the Cross; so, we are told here that some will depart from the Cross as the means of Salvation and Victory), *giving heed to seducing spirits* (evil spirits, i.e., *'religious spirits,'* making something seem like what it isn't), *and doctrines of devils* (should have been translated, *'doctrines of demons'*; the *'seducing spirits'* entice Believers away from the true Faith, causing them to believe *'doctrines inspired by demon spirits')"* (I Tim. 4:1).

The only thing that can break through the shell of deception is the Holy Spirit. If the Holy Spirit is predominant in the Church, which means that the Cross of Christ is being proclaimed as the Object of Faith, deception will be put down. Otherwise, it won't.

The absence of *"preaching the Cross"* in the last few decades has opened up the Church to the greatest operation of deceiving spirits that it has known since the Reformation. This is the reason that the *"Word of Faith"* doctrine, which, in reality, is no faith at all, at least that God will recognize, has taken such a hold in the Church. This also is the reason for the tremendous popularity of the *"Purpose Driven Life"* scheme.

There has been such a lack of preaching the Cross that anymore the Church doesn't know where it has been, where it is, or where it is going.

Whenever Pope John Paul II died, scores of Preachers in the United States were lauding the Pope, some referring to him as a great man of God, etc. The Cross of Christ has been abandoned; therefore, the modern Church has no foundation.

Let me say again what we've already said several times:

1. The only thing standing between mankind and Hell itself is the Cross of Christ.

2. The only thing standing between the Church and apostasy is the Cross of Christ.

(2) "FOR HE FLATTERS HIMSELF IN HIS OWN EYES, UNTIL HIS INIQUITY BE FOUND TO BE HATEFUL."

Professor Alexander translated this Verse, *"For he flatters himself in his own eyes, as to God's finding his sin and hating it,"* which means that he flatters himself that he will conceal his sin from God, so that God will not discover it to hate it. Once again, we are dealing with deception.

The idea that God doesn't know is ridiculous indeed! But yet the Holy Spirit here through David proclaims the fact that many believe such foolishness. They think they can get by with their sin.

But let it ever be known:

No man gets by with sin. God knows all things, sees all things, and ultimately will judge all things.

(3) "THE WORDS OF HIS MOUTH ARE INIQUITY AND DECEIT: HE HAS LEFT OFF TO BE WISE, AND TO DO GOOD."

The idea is that there was a time when such a man occasionally acted wisely and did what was right. But that time has gone by. Now he is consistently wicked.

THE WAY OF SIN

Sin takes one ever downward. It has no stopping point. It must go ever lower.

This is the reason that the modern ideas of today's Church, such as moral evolution, are so obviously foolish. For example, *"The Purpose Driven Life"* scheme teaches that if one is brought into the Church and associates with *"good people,"* then he will sort of grow into Christianity. The *"born again"* experience, if not altogether denied, is, in fact, altogether ignored. Consequently, the modern Church is being filled with unconverted people.

SIN IS THE PROBLEM

Whether we speak of an unsaved person or a Saved person, sin is the problem. The modern Church can deny that, can claim other things are the problem, can put whatever label it desires on it, but sin is the problem (Rom. 6:1-23).

The Church must come back to the place that it knows and understands that sin is the problem. Then it would no longer suggest the obvious stupidity that we must not mention sin because to do so might offend sinners. Then we would not project the ridiculous *"Word of Faith"* claim that the way to keep people from sinning is to never mention sin.

They state that if we preach about sin, this will develop a sin-consciousness in the hearts of the listener, which will cause them to sin.

What absolute foolishness!

No! The problem is sin! That's the reason that the Holy Spirit mentions sin in the New Testament alone over 260 times. And that count doesn't include the use of expressions such as *"iniquity," "transgression,"* etc.

How foolish can we be to think that if we don't mention sin, then suddenly it will just go away! How ridiculous!

Let me say it again:

Sin is the problem!

THE ONLY ANSWER FOR SIN IS THE CROSS OF CHRIST

Let the Reader meditate on the Heading, *"There is no remedy for sin except the Cross of Jesus Christ."* All of the schemes that man may project (and the modern Church is full of them), all the ideas from the carnal hearts of men which present a way other than the Cross of Christ, all are tantamount to spiritual suicide.

For many years, the Church has tried to project answers for the problem of sin in the life of the Christian other than the Cross! Now it is trying to project another way of Salvation other than the Cross of Christ. The Church has sinned greatly in rejecting the Cross of Christ as the only answer for sin in the life of the Christian, so the next step downward, namely, setting aside the Cross of Christ regarding Salvation, comes easily. As stated, sin is ever downward.

HUMANISTIC PSYCHOLOGY

I was ordained with the Assemblies of God for many years. In the 1960's, this particular Denomination began to lean toward humanistic psychology as the answer for sin in the heart and life of the Christian. Of course, they would not have put it that way, but that's what it amounted to.

During those years, I gave it little thought, because I had very little knowledge regarding psychology. But in the early 1980's, a series of events transpired to help me see that the psychological way was not of God.

Actually, when we began Family Worship Center, which was about 1980, if I remember correctly, my knowledge concerning psychology was so sparse that we even hired a psychologist to serve on the staff of the Church.

During those years, the Ministry owned two Radio Stations, one in Baton Rouge, Louisiana, and one in Bowling Green, Ohio. On our Station in Baton Rouge, I opened up an hour a day for our staff psychologist to deal with people's problems. As stated, I had no knowledge of psychology, and I believed psychologists were people who tried to help others, so that had to be a good thing.

Now, I don't doubt at all that some psychologists are sincerely trying to help people and be of service, but the psychological way is not the way of the Bible, and it will actually help no one. James referred to this way as wisdom that is of this Earth, which, consequently, is *"earthly, sensual, devilish"* (James 3:15).

At any rate, some of the other Preachers on our staff began to come to me and ask me if I had heard what was being taught over the Station by this psychologist. My introduction to Psychology was my listening to the program a couple of times. Instantly I knew it was not Biblical, not from the Lord, and, therefore, would not help anyone.

I had a couple of long discussions with the psychologist and his wife (both were psychologists), all to no avail. After discussing the situation at length with them, we felt we had no alternative but to terminate their employment with this Ministry. Then I began, quite extensively, to study the subject. The more I studied the subject, the more I realized this thing was not of God.

At that time, we had the largest Gospel Television audience in the world. Over our Television Network, I then began to preach and teach that the Church must not be deceived by this error of humanistic psychology. The Church must understand that everything the Believer needs is found in the Word of God (II Pet. 1:3-4).

My stand against psychology did not at all set well with the powers that be in the Denomination with which I then was associated. I was, in fact, hated for my stand, and that's about the best way I know to explain it. That hatred continues unto this hour, and, if possible, it has even intensified.

At that time, I knew that humanistic psychology was not the answer, and I also knew that the Lord was the answer, but I didn't know exactly how the Lord was the answer, except by general understanding, which I found to be woefully insufficient. At that time, I didn't understand that the Cross of Christ was the means of Sanctification for the Believer. And the Devil took full advantage of my ignorance in this area, just as he presently is taking full advantage of the ignorance of untold millions of Christians.

As the Seventh Chapter of the Book of Romans bears out, it is impossible for a Believer to live a victorious life in Christ if such a Believer doesn't understand the Sixth Chapter of Romans, which tells us the way of Sanctification, which is the Way of the Cross.

Unfortunately, the Assemblies of God has gone even deeper into humanistic psychology, that is, if possible, and, as a result, they are now accepting *"The Purpose Driven Life"* scheme, plus other forays into false doctrine, because the way of sin is ever downward.

UNBELIEF

In 1997, when the Lord began to open up to me the great Revelation of the Cross, which is not something new, but actually that which He had already given to the Apostle Paul, it was the most revolutionary thing that had ever happened to me as a Believer.

I remember those beginning days when the Lord began to speak to my heart and say,

"The answer for which you seek is found in the Cross.

"The solution for which you seek is found in the Cross.

"It is the Cross alone in which the answer is found!"

For days, for weeks, even for months, in fact unending, the joy filled and fills my soul to such an extent that I really don't have vocabulary to properly express what took place in my heart. I knew what the Lord was giving me was something very, very special. So I asked Him that that door would ever remain open, that this Revelation would continue to expand. And that's exactly what has happened, what is happening, and ever shall happen. One cannot exhaust the potential of what Jesus did at Calvary's Cross. But the tragedy is that the modern Church knows only a little something about the Cross as it refers to Salvation (and, regrettably, it even seems to be losing much of that), and it knows almost nothing as it regards the Cross concerning Sanctification. As a result, most every Christian is reliving the Seventh Chapter of the Book of Romans all over again.

The conclusion of that is, *"O wretched man that I am! . . ."* (Rom. 7:24).

When the Lord began to open this up to me, I naively thought that if this great Truth could be given to the entirety of the Church, then surely it would accept it eagerly. While a few do eagerly accept the Message of the Cross, I found out that the far greater majority will not.

Why not?

The answer is *"Unbelief"*! They simply do not believe that what Jesus did at Calvary's Cross answers every sin, every perversion, every transgression, every iniquity, etc. So they would rather send poor Believers to humanistic psychologists, who hold no answer whatsoever, and label it *"professional help."*

The majority of the modern Church is ignorant of the Ways of the Lord regarding His Prescribed Order of Victory and, sadder still, it is a willful ignorance. They don't want the Truth. A few do, but most don't!

THE CROSS OF CHRIST, THE DIVIDING LINE

While the Cross of Christ has been the dividing line between the True Church and the apostate Church, even from the very beginning, now it is more pronounced, I believe, than ever. The Lord did not give me this Revelation for me alone, but He meant for it to be given to the entirety of the Church. That's the reason that we are doing everything within our power, through Radio and Television, and through the printed Word, to reach the Church with this all-important Message. Sadly, most Preachers will not heed, and for any variety of reasons. But, as stated, the real reason is *"Unbelief"*!

I listen to some Preachers over Television as they suggest one ploy after another, but never the Cross. One claims that a Believer should take the Lord's Supper every day, and that will guarantee victory over sin. Another claims that the problem is the "family curse," so the Believer should have hands laid on him to rebuke this "family curse." Still another claims that the Believer should memorize two or three Scriptures and quote them over and over throughout the day; this then will move God to action, and victory will be the result. The list is long, and one fad after another is being projected.

"The Purpose Driven Life" claims that its forty days of whatever will give one victory, and "The Government of Twelve" claims that their Encounter Sessions, which include casting demons out of Christians, are the answer.

Let the Reader understand the following:
There is only one answer, and that is "Jesus Christ and Him Crucified" (I Cor. 1:23).

When the Believer places his faith exclusively in Christ and the Cross and maintains his faith exclusively in Christ and the Cross, the Holy Spirit, Who Alone can bring to pass that which must be in our lives, will then begin to work mightily on our behalf (Rom. 6:1-14; 8:1-2, 11; I Cor. 1:17-18, 21, 23; 2:2; Gal. 6:14). This is God's Prescribed Order of Victory, and His only Prescribed Order of Victory.

This line is drawn — the line of the Cross of Christ. Whether it is accepted or rejected will be the indicator to distinguish the True Church from the apostate Church. The Cross of Christ must be accepted, and I mean that everything that Jesus there did must be accepted; if not, it is the apostate Church (Rev. 3:14-22).

(4) "HE DEVISES MISCHIEF UPON HIS BED; HE SETS HIMSELF IN A WAY THAT IS NOT GOOD; HE ABHORS NOT EVIL."

This tells us that the person without God is not merely negatively bad; he determinately chooses a path of life that is evil.

When it says, "He abhors not evil," it means he has no aversion to it, no horror of it, no shrinking from it. Whether a thing is right or wrong is to him a matter of complete indifference, so callous is he, so hardened.

Sin, as stated, is ever downward, and it can only be halted by the believing sinner accepting Christ and what Christ did at the Cross. There is no other way!

(5) "YOUR MERCY, O LORD, IS IN THE HEAVENS; AND YOUR FAITHFULNESS REACHES UNTO THE CLOUDS."

Concerning this, Pulpit says, "Instead of the usual contrast between the wicked man and the Godly one (Ps. 1:1-6; 4:2-3; 5:10-11, etc.), the Psalmist here makes the startling contrast between the wicked man and God!" The character of the wicked man is given in the first four Verses, the portrait of God in the following five Verses.

"God's first and principal characteristic is 'Mercy' — or rather 'Lovingkindness.' This quality is revealed, not on Earth only, but also in Heaven toward the Angels." [11]

Next to Lovingkindness in God comes "faithfulness" — fidelity to every Promise that He has ever made, unswerving attachment to those whom He has once loved, undeviating maintenance of the Truth.

A man who is so described in Verses 1 through 4 would find no compassion on Earth, but the Grace that is born in the Heavens and written upon the clouds, as exhibited in these Passages, can pity and save such a sinner. To those who will come to Him, God is "faithful" to show "mercy." This, in fact, is man's only hope!

(6) "YOUR RIGHTEOUSNESS IS LIKE THE GREAT MOUNTAINS; YOUR JUDGMENTS ARE A GREAT DEEP: O LORD, YOU PRESERVE MAN AND BEAST."

Two great truths are given to us in this Verse.

THE RIGHTEOUSNESS OF GOD

Man has no righteousness, and he cannot obtain any by his own merit, work, or effort. But God has Righteousness that is so abundant it stands like "great mountains."

Irrespective of how many unholy, ungodly, and wicked individuals may come to Him, and irrespective as to the degree of their wickedness, they can never exhaust the Righteousness of God. He stands willing, ready, and able to impute such to "whosoever will" (Jn. 3:16; Rev. 22:17).

HOW RIGHTEOUSNESS IS ACQUIRED

As stated, man can do nothing within himself to earn or merit the Righteousness of God. It cannot be obtained in that manner. It is obtained in only one way:

The individual, whoever he might be,

must place his faith exclusively in Christ. Then the Righteousness of God will immediately be given to such a person.

As well, this *"Righteousness"* is not given in stages, but is given in totality and instantly the moment that faith is evidenced (Rom. 10:9-10, 13; Gen. 15:6; Rom. 4:3).

The ingredient is *"faith"*; however, it must be faith exclusively in Christ. Upon such faith, the Righteousness of God is instantly given.

It doesn't take much to be saved, just simple faith in Christ. The Holy Spirit through Paul said, *"For whosoever shall call upon the Name of Lord shall be saved"* (Rom. 10:13).

However, after one is saved, they are then to begin to understand the Word of God. As they study the Epistles of the Apostle Paul, they will then find out that Christ is the Source of all things (and we speak of Righteousness), and it is the Cross which is the Means by which all of this is done (Rom. 6:1-14; I Cor. 1:17-18, 23; 2:2; Gal., Chpt. 5; Eph. 2:13-18).

Unfortunately, most Christians do not come to this Truth quickly or easily. That's the reason that the Apostle Paul gave so much teaching on the subject. All too often the Believer attempts to live for God by methods which he conceives in his own mind or else others have conceived, i.e., that which is <u>not</u> the Cross of Christ. Such a way is constituted as a way of the flesh, and cannot be blessed by God (Rom. 8:8).

WALKING AFTER THE FLESH, WALKING AFTER THE SPIRIT

Paul said, *"That the Righteousness of the Law might be fulfilled in us, who walk not after the flesh, but after the Spirit"* (Rom. 8:4).

What does *"walking after the flesh"* mean?

The *"flesh,"* as Paul uses the term, refers to the individual's personal ability, strength, power, efforts, etc. Now these things, within themselves, are not necessarily wrong, but we are not to put forth our own plans and schemes as it regards living for God, but rather we are to accept what the Lord has already done for us. To fail to accept what He has done for us, which is Christ and the Cross, constitutes being *"in the flesh."*

The Scripture plainly says, *"So then they who are in the flesh cannot please God"* (Rom. 8:8).

"Walking after the Spirit" pertains to the Holy Spirit, and simply means that the Believer places his faith exclusively in Christ and the Cross, ever making the Cross the Object of his Faith. When this is done, the Holy Spirit will then work mightily within the life of such a Believer, thereby perfecting the Grace of God, which the Holy Spirit Alone can do (Rom. 8:1-2, 11; Gal., Chpt. 5).

It is beyond the strength, the power, and the ability of man, even the most consecrated Believer, to live for God outside of the realm of the Holy Spirit. Every Believer definitely does have the Holy Spirit; but, unless our faith is properly placed, He will little work in one's life, He can little function in one's life, and He also can little develop His Fruit in our lives.

Paul also said, *"For the Law of the Spirit of Life in Christ Jesus has made me free from the Law of Sin and Death"* (Rom. 8:2). This is God's Prescribed Order of Victory, and His only Prescribed Order of Victory.

THE JUDGMENTS OF THE LORD

"Your Judgments" speak of God's Word.

Irrespective of how much man may probe into the depths of the Bible, still, he cannot scale its heights or plummet its depths. Its riches are inexhaustible — and yet man (and even the Church) seldom peruses its noble pages.

Despite the sin and iniquity, which, if not checked, would most certainly destroy man from the face of the Earth, God, through His Love and Mercy, and for His Own reasons, *"preserves man and beast."*

Since the advent of the atomic and hydrogen bombs, men have been fond of speaking of doomsday, when the Earth will be destroyed by thermonuclear war; however, such will not happen. It might certainly be true without the present preservation afforded by God, but God's Plans for this planet are not destruction, but rather blessing.

(7) "HOW EXCELLENT IS YOUR LOVINGKINDNESS, O GOD! THEREFORE THE CHILDREN OF MEN PUT THEIR

TRUST UNDER THE SHADOW OF YOUR WINGS."

God is pictured by Satan as brutal, judgmental, harsh, and destructive. The Holy Spirit tells us that God, in contrast, is *"Lovingkindness."*

THE LOVINGKINDNESS OF GOD

Pure and simple, *"God is good!"*

The way this goodness, this lovingkindness, can be received is for individuals to *"put their trust under the shadow of Your wings."* This is a metaphor for the protection, guidance, leading, and help of the Lord.

The weak, frail, sinful, and wicked sons of Adam, at least those who will believe, should be encouraged by the Promise of the goodness of God; we should take heart and lay aside our natural timidity and turn to the Lord; we should put our trust in Him and gather ourselves under the shadow of His protecting wings, and look to Him, and Him Alone. Then Righteousness will then be granted, the sinfulness and wickedness will be taken away, and safety and defense will be given to all who believe.

What a Promise!

(8) "THEY SHALL BE ABUNDANTLY SATISFIED WITH THE FATNESS OF YOUR HOUSE; AND YOU SHALL MAKE THEM DRINK OF THE RIVER OF YOUR PLEASURES."

Anyone who follows Christ is *"abundantly satisfied."*

Satan makes man believe that if he serves God, his enjoyment of life is over. However, the Holy Spirit tells us through the mouth of David that God's house is a *"fat house"* — meaning an abundance. The pleasures given to the Child of God in following Christ are not only not diminished, but actually increased, becoming a *"river of Your pleasures."*

In truth, man does not really start to live until man accepts Christ.

(9) "FOR WITH YOU IS THE FOUNTAIN OF LIFE: IN YOUR LIGHT SHALL WE SEE LIGHT."

There is no *"life"* outside of God. All else is death. His *"life"* is like a *"fountain"* continually bubbling up (Jn. 4:13-14).

Likewise, there is no true knowledge, wisdom, or understanding other than the illumination of His *"Light."*

Men try to see light from the evil hearts of other men. It is not possible. There is no true *"light"* at Harvard, Yale, Princeton, or the other great universities of this world. There is only *"light"* in His *"Light."*

That's the reason that the Christian should make a lifelong study of the Word of God. In its confines is the *"Light"* (Jn., Chpts. 1-5).

(10) "O CONTINUE YOUR LOVINGKINDNESS UNTO THEM WHO KNOW YOU; AND YOUR RIGHTEOUSNESS TO THE UPRIGHT IN HEART."

A great truth which is all but hidden is found in this Verse.

THE UPRIGHT IN HEART

The idea of this Verse is:

While there might be occasional lapses in the life of the Believer, *"in heart"* that person is sincere. Therefore, *"Lord, please continue to deal justly with those whose heart is right with You."*

The request is that the Lord would continue to deal with His faithful servant, mercifully, graciously, and lovingly.

Every Believer, whoever that Believer might be, is in need of the constant Intercession of Christ. The Bible doesn't teach sinless perfection; this means that no Believer, no matter how close to God such a person might be, can claim such perfection.

We as Believers can believe God that *"sin shall have no dominion over us"* (Rom. 6:14), which, within itself, is a tremendous testimony of faith; however, no Believer can claim sinless perfection.

So the plea is that, despite the occasional lapses, which, incidentally, are never intentional, the Lord will continue to deal with us with Mercy and Grace. And that He always will do!

(11) "LET NOT THE FOOT OF PRIDE COME AGAINST ME, AND LET NOT THE HAND OF THE WICKED REMOVE ME."

This is a prayer of apprehension. It is:

THE FOOT OF PRIDE AND THE HAND OF THE WICKED

By nature, the foot is proud and the hand is wicked. So the prayer is that the Lord would shield the Believer from their power. The Believer also is surrounded by men of proud feet and wicked hands. So we must ask the Lord that we not be influenced by them, for they lead and push men into that deep pit into which evildoers shall fall, out of which they will desire to rise but will not be able, for they shall be eternally thrust down into it. Furthermore their ever-enduring and conscious misery will be sharpened by the knowledge that their own sin and rebellion caused them to be justly shut up in that dark prison house of death. We speak of eternal Hell!

(12) "THERE ARE THE WORKERS OF INIQUITY FALLEN: THEY ARE CAST DOWN, AND SHALL NOT BE ABLE TO RISE."

This Passage clearly and plainly tells us that all who forsake the Lord will be *"cast down"* and *"shall not be able to rise."* This speaks, as stated, of eternal Hell!

Even though most of the world denies the existence of such a place, still, such a place does exist, and, sadly, the far greater majority of the population of the world, and for all time, have gone there and are going there (Mat. 7:13; Lk. 16:19-31; Rev. 20:14-15; 21:8).

PSALM 37

A Psalm of David: The Righteous Vindicated

(1) "FRET NOT YOURSELF BECAUSE OF EVILDOERS, NEITHER BE THOU ENVIOUS AGAINST THE WORKERS OF INIQUITY."

This Psalm is quite long, and contains a tremendous Truth.

TWO PRINCIPLE DIFFICULTIES WHICH CONFUSE AND DISCOURAGE BEGINNERS IN THE CHRISTIAN LIFE

To the redeemed sinner of Psalm 36, cleansed by the Atoning Blood of Psalm 35, the Great Shepherd now says, *"Fret not yourself because of the mysterious prosperity of the wicked, and because of the murderous hatred of the world."* Then He adds that such prosperity will be short-lived, but that ever-enduring prosperity and infinite and eternal love will be enjoyed by the Believer, if he keeps trusting the Shepherd, for He promises to most certainly deliver him and enrich him forever.

Thus, this Psalm anticipates the two principal difficulties which confuse and discourage beginners in the Christian life. We find it unexpected and painful that we should be hated by those in the apostate Church because we have embraced the entirety of the Bible. It also is confounding that evil-doers should prosper. With exquisite tenderness and with perfect understanding of the poor human heart, the Messiah in this Psalm again and again says, *"Don't fret yourself. Keep trusting. Keep delighting. Keep committing. Keep waiting."* And He keeps repeating His Promises as to the speedy disappearance of the wicked.

THE GREAT SHEPHERD

The Great Shepherd, the Lord Jesus Christ, assures the Believer that He will hold us by His Hand; that He will enrich us; and finally, most surely, He will deliver us.

This Psalm is for the heart and bids it contemplate the Great Shepherd, as He loves and guards and vindicates His people.

The lessons taught are to wait on God and to wait for God when perplexed by the prosperity of the evil-doers, and when oppressed by them; not to become heated with vexation; and not to grow angry and retaliate, for the Messiah will vindicate His people when slandered, deliver us when persecuted, and establish us as the rulers of the world. As to the power and prosperity of our enemies, that is only temporary.

The Messiah Himself, in the days of His flesh and when in the midst of His foes, perfectly learned and lived the lessons of this Psalm.

As a Prophecy, it will have its fulfillment during Israel's future *"Time of Trouble,"* when under the oppression of the Antichrist. It has, however, at the same time, counsel and comfort for the people of God in any Dispensation when such people are perplexed and persecuted.

(2) "FOR THEY SHALL SOON BE CUT DOWN LIKE THE GRASS, AND WITHER AS THE GREEN HERB."

If we compare time with eternity, the longest triumph that the wicked ever enjoy is but for a brief space, is soon gone, and endures *"but for a moment."* It has a continuance, however, which to men in this life seems long, often intolerably long; and hence, the disturbance which men's minds suffer on account of it. However, we should think on these things exactly as the Lord does, thereby seeing things from His perspective instead of ours, because our perspective is very limited.

(3) "TRUST IN THE LORD, AND DO GOOD; SO SHALL YOU DWELL IN THE LAND, AND VERILY YOU SHALL BE FED.

(4) "DELIGHT YOURSELF ALSO IN THE LORD: AND HE SHALL GIVE YOU THE DESIRES OF YOUR HEART.

(5) "COMMIT YOUR WAY UNTO THE LORD; TRUST ALSO IN HIM; AND HE SHALL BRING IT TO PASS.

(6) "AND HE SHALL BRING FORTH YOUR RIGHTEOUSNESS AS THE LIGHT, AND YOUR JUDGMENT AS THE NOONDAY.

(7) "REST IN THE LORD, AND WAIT PATIENTLY FOR HIM: FRET NOT YOURSELF BECAUSE OF HIM WHO PROSPERS IN HIS WAY, BECAUSE OF THE MAN WHO BRINGS WICKED DEVICES TO PASS."

In these five Verses, we have a formula given by the Holy Spirit, which, if followed, will bring true peace and prosperity.

THE FORMULA GIVEN BY THE HOLY SPIRIT WHICH BRINGS PEACE AND PROSPERITY

That formula is:

1. TRUST: As previously stated, the one word that characterizes the Psalms is *"trust,"* which, of course, refers to *"trust in the LORD."* If we do such, He has promised us that we will dwell in peace and will be fed both spiritually and physically.

2. DELIGHT: This simply means that our delight must not be in anything in this world, only in the Lord. He Alone can meet every need. He has promised to *"give us the desires of our heart,"* which is a tremendous Promise!

3. COMMIT: We are to trust the Lord, delight in the Lord, and commit our way to Him, which means that we understand that He knows the way (which He most certainly does!) and that which we desire; because our desire is in His Will, *"He shall bring it to pass."*

The Sixth Verse proclaims the fact that we are to desire first of all *"Righteousness"* and also the Lord's *"Judgment,"* which refers to His Word.

4. REST: This proclaims the fact that we have obeyed the Lord in that which He has told us to do, and now we *"rest"* in the assurance that it will come to pass. It may be tomorrow, or it may be years down the road, but come to pass it shall.

He also tells us to not look at the prosperity, so-called, of the wicked, but to keep our eyes on the Lord.

THE CROSS OF CHRIST

This formula still holds true presently, and will ever hold true, but now, due to the fact of the Cross, it is much easier to do. The Cross of Christ has made it possible for the Holy Spirit to come into our hearts and lives, which He does at conversion, and to abide forever. He desires to lead us, guide us, help us, strengthen us, and to do whatever needs to be done in our lives, which He Alone can do. To assure ourselves of this magnificent help on a constant basis, all we have to do is to place our faith constantly in the Cross of Christ, and not allow it to be moved elsewhere (Rom. 6:1-14; 8:1-2, 11).

The Holy Spirit works exclusively within the framework of the Finished Work of Christ (Rom. 8:2). He will not work outside of that framework, inasmuch as the Cross gives Him the legal means to do the things which He Alone can do. As stated, He doesn't require much of us, but He does require that our faith ever be maintained in the Cross of Christ — in other words, that the Cross of Christ ever be the Object of our Faith.

All Believers ought to memorize this little formula and commit ourselves to it, which then gives us a blank check, so to speak.

(8) "CEASE FROM ANGER, AND FORSAKE WRATH: FRET NOT YOURSELF IN ANY WISE TO DO EVIL."

If men dwell unduly on the fact of the prosperity of the wicked, and brood upon it in their hearts, they will be apt, in the first instance, to envy the wicked, which is at once *"to do evil."* Then, from this, they will be naturally tempted to go on to an imitation of their wicked practices, which is to assimilate themselves altogether to the enemies of God, and to be guilty of practical apostasy.

A perfect example of this is found in Psalms 73:2-3. Asaph said:

"But as for me, my feet were almost gone; my steps had well-nigh slipped.

"For I was envious at the foolish, when I saw the prosperity of the wicked."

(9) "FOR EVILDOERS SHALL BE CUT OFF: BUT THOSE WHO WAIT UPON THE LORD, THEY SHALL INHERIT THE EARTH."

What is taking place presently is not where it is or what it is. All of this is going to soon come to an end, and will do so when Jesus Christ comes back, and then the righteous *"shall inherit the earth."*

Especially considering the time when I dictate these notes (July 2005), we don't have long to wait! Jesus is coming very, very soon!

(10) "FOR YET A LITTLE WHILE, AND THE WICKED SHALL NOT BE: YEA, YOU SHALL DILIGENTLY CONSIDER HIS PLACE, AND IT SHALL NOT BE."

This happens constantly at the present time, but in the coming Kingdom Age, which, spiritually speaking, is right around the corner, it will happen totally and completely over the entirety of the Earth. In other words, the *"wicked"* have just about had their day!

(11) "BUT THE MEEK SHALL INHERIT THE EARTH; AND SHALL DELIGHT THEMSELVES IN THE ABUNDANCE OF PEACE."

Jesus quoted the first part of this Verse in Matthew 5:5.

This will take place during the coming Kingdom Age, which will begin at the Second Coming of the Lord. Then the entirety of the world will *"delight ourselves in the abundance of peace."*

(12) "THE WICKED PLOT AGAINST THE JUST, AND GNASH UPON HIM WITH HIS TEETH."

We can expect opposition from the world, the flesh, and the Devil. That opposition will be fierce, i.e., *"and gnash upon him with his teeth."*

NOTES

The Devil uses demon spirits, the world, our own flesh, and the apostate Church in his efforts to steal, kill, and destroy (Jn. 10:10). But in that same Verse from John's Gospel, Jesus has also promised *"more abundant life"* to all who will believe Him, irrespective as to the plots of the wicked.

(13) "THE LORD SHALL LAUGH AT HIM: FOR HE SEES THAT HIS DAY IS COMING."

If the Lord laughs at the wicked, knowing that his prosperity definitely is going to come to an end, then we should do the same. And if we properly understand the Word of God, we will do the same!

(14) "THE WICKED HAVE DRAWN OUT THE SWORD, AND HAVE BENT THEIR BOW, TO CAST DOWN THE POOR AND NEEDY, AND TO SLAY SUCH AS BE OF UPRIGHT CONVERSATION."

This Verse actually pertains to Israel during the latter half of the Great Tribulation; they are here referred to as *"the poor and needy."*

"The wicked" refers to the Antichrist, who has vowed their destruction.

While this is the proper intent of the Verse, still, it holds true even for individual Believers.

(15) "THEIR SWORD SHALL ENTER INTO THEIR OWN HEART, AND THEIR BOWS SHALL BE BROKEN."

If we *"trust," "delight," "commit,"* and *"rest"* in the Lord, we can be assured that the Lord will handle the efforts of *"the wicked."*

FAMILY WORSHIP CENTER CHURCH

Over and over again in the last few years, I have witnessed the enemy, mostly from an apostate Church, but also from the world, attempt to destroy us in every conceivable form. In all of this, we have no way to defend ourselves, which is exactly what the Lord wants and desires. We have to trust the Lord completely and we do continue to trust the Lord completely. I have truly seen the enemy, whoever they may have been, pierced by their own sword, and their bows broken, and none of it has been because of my own efforts — it was all from the Lord.

In its plenary sense, this Fifteenth Verse has to do with the Antichrist during the Battle of Armageddon, when, at the Second

Coming of the Lord, he will be totally defeated, even killed, and *"cast alive* (his soul and his spirit) *into a Lake of Fire burning with brimstone"* (Rev. 19:20).

(16) "A LITTLE THAT A RIGHTEOUS MAN HAS IS BETTER THAN THE RICHES OF MANY WICKED."

This tells us that all the *"righteous"* will not be rich, but it also tells us that what little the righteous man has will be signally blessed by the Lord, which will make it *"far better than the riches of many wicked."*

As the song says:

"Little is much if God be in it!"

(17) "FOR THE ARMS OF THE WICKED SHALL BE BROKEN: BUT THE LORD UPHOLDS THE RIGHTEOUS."

The wicked do not have the protection of the Lord, while the righteous most definitely do have such protection.

(18) "THE LORD KNOWS THE DAYS OF THE UPRIGHT: AND THEIR INHERITANCE SHALL BE FOREVER."

The Lord knows exactly how many days of trouble and trial that the righteous will have to undergo. In other words, the Lord has put a limit on these difficulties. But the Promise is that *"the inheritance"* which will be given to us will be *"forever."*

(19) "THEY SHALL NOT BE ASHAMED IN THE EVIL TIME: AND IN THE DAYS OF FAMINE THEY SHALL BE SATISFIED."

This tells us that the Lord will protect us during times of adversity.

(20) "BUT THE WICKED SHALL PERISH, AND THE ENEMIES OF THE LORD SHALL BE AS THE FAT OF LAMBS: THEY SHALL CONSUME; INTO SMOKE SHALL THEY CONSUME AWAY."

Once again, the prediction is given that *"the wicked shall perish."*

The short phrase, *"The fat of Lambs,"* has to do with the fat of the animal being placed on the Altar and burned, which means it was totally consumed. This is used as an example of what is going to happen to *"the enemies of the LORD."*

(21) "THE WICKED BORROW, AND PAY NOT AGAIN: BUT THE RIGHTEOUS SHOW MERCY, AND GIVE."

The *"wicked"* are ever scheming as to how to get the money of others by fraud. As such,

NOTES

they show no mercy.

The *"righteous"* are the very opposite!

(22) "FOR SUCH AS BE BLESSED OF HIM SHALL INHERIT THE EARTH; AND THEY WHO BE CURSED OF HIM SHALL BE CUT OFF."

In stark clarity, the Lord proclaims the future disposition of both the righteous and the wicked. The former will inherit the Earth, while the latter *"shall be cut off."*

(23) "THE STEPS OF A GOOD MAN ARE ORDERED BY THE LORD: AND HE DELIGHTS IN HIS WAY."

"The steps of a good man are established by the LORD." It means they are *"made firm."*

It is not God's general superintendence of men's steps in goings which is here addressed, but the special strengthening and supporting of the steps of those who believe the Lord.

This is not the ordinary man, but the *"good man."* The Lord *"delights"* in such a man!

(24) "THOUGH HE FALL, HE SHALL NOT BE UTTERLY CAST DOWN: FOR THE LORD UPHOLDS HIM WITH HIS HAND."

This tells us that even *"the steps of a good man,"* which *"are ordered by the LORD,"* are not guaranteed to be without incident.

The good man may be afflicted; he may even fall into some fault, or even into grievous sin (II Sam. 11:4); but as long as he looks to the Lord, God will not suffer him to remain in that spiritually prostrated condition.

Concerning this, Luther said, *"If he falls, God catches him by the hand and raises him up again."*

THE POWER OF THE LORD

Every Christian should do well to help lift someone up who has had the misfortune to fall. Such a person most definitely will be blessed of the Lord.

Regrettably, far too many Christians (Christians?), instead of attempting to raise up someone of this nature, do everything they can to see to it that he stays down. While such actions may hurt, they will not keep the Lord from lifting up such a person. And, as should be obvious, the Lord looks with great disdain at those who would hinder His Work!

(25) "I HAVE BEEN YOUNG, AND NOW AM OLD; YET HAVE I NOT SEEN THE

RIGHTEOUS FORSAKEN, NOR HIS SEED BEGGING BREAD."

This is a tremendous statement! Because it is the Word of God, it constitutes a Promise of unprecedented proportions.

THE BLESSING

David here was speaking of Israel. Still, this great Promise covers the entirety of the Body of Christ for all time. If a Christian (a true Christian) has been reduced to the level of penury, solely and truthfully, it is because such a Christian is not functioning according to the Word of God.

Like many of the Promises of God, this great Promise is conditional. If we function according to the Word of God, we will reap what the Word of God promises. If we go in another direction, the Lord will continue to greatly move upon us and try to bring us back to the right way, but, at that juncture, we begin to forfeit the Blessings.

Let me say it again:

If the Believer adheres to God's Prescribed Order, which is faith in Christ and the Cross, and faith perpetually in Christ and the Cross, such a Believer will most definitely reap the benefits of such a position, which constitutes Blessings of every description. Such a person will never be forsaken by the Lord, and will never be reduced to *"begging bread."*

Why?

The reason is simple. We are serving a miracle-working God. This means that we should learn how to make Him a part of every parcel of our thinking, our doing, and the entirety of our existence. If there is anything that is taught by the great Book of Psalms, that great Truth is taught. We must trust totally and completely in Him; and, for that trust to be proper, it must ever be in Christ and the Cross (Gen. 3:15; 15:6; Mat. 21:22; Mk. 11:24-25; Jn. 14:14; 15:7; Rom. 6:1-14; 8:1-2, 11; Gal., Chpt. 5; 6:14; Eph. 2:13-18; Col. 2:14-15).

(26) "HE IS EVER MERCIFUL, AND LENDS; AND HIS SEED IS BLESSED."

Pulpit says, and rightly so, *"This Psalm contains a good deal of repetition, perhaps intended to emphasize certain portions of its teaching"* (Vss. 1, 7, 8; 3, 27; 11, 22, 29; 7, 34; etc.).[12]

NOTES

The Child of God functions in a manner totally opposite from his counterpart in the world. For instance, the world shows no mercy, while the True Believer does. Also, the True Believer lends, with no thought of gain from that particular loan, while the world does the very opposite. As a result, great Blessings from the Lord follow such an example. They did then, and they do now!

(During the time of Israel, there were no banks to make loans, etc.; therefore, loans had to be derived from individuals. The admonition here is that one not take advantage of those who need help.

Today, it is totally different. Very few loans are made by individuals, and rightly so.)

(27) "DEPART FROM EVIL, AND DO GOOD; AND DWELL FOR EVERMORE."

This is to be understood as a Promise, *"If you will depart from evil, and do good, then you shall dwell in the land forevermore, and do so in a manner of blessing."*

(28) "FOR THE LORD LOVES JUDGMENT, AND FORSAKES NOT HIS SAINTS; THEY ARE PRESERVED FOREVER: BUT THE SEED OF THE WICKED SHALL BE CUT OFF."

"Judgment" is here *"Justice"* and *"Righteousness."*

The idea of the Verse is that the Ways of the Lord, and those who follow those Ways, will be *"preserved forever,"* while the wicked, those who ridicule the Ways of the Lord, *"shall be cut off."* That has not yet happened, but it most definitely will in the coming Kingdom Age, which is very close!

(29) "THE RIGHTEOUS SHALL INHERIT THE LAND, AND DWELL THEREIN FOREVER."

This will come to pass in the coming Kingdom Age!

(30) "THE MOUTH OF THE RIGHTEOUS SPEAKS WISDOM, AND HIS TONGUE TALKS OF JUDGMENT."

The reason that the righteous *"speak wisdom"* is because *"they talk of judgment,"* i.e., *"The Word of God."*

WISDOM

All true wisdom comes from the Lord, and is ensconced in His Word (James 3:17-18), which means that it is imperative that every

Believer make the Bible a lifelong project. It should be studied every day. Because it is the Word of God, it will never grow uninteresting or boring.

According to the Holy Spirit through James, *"the wisdom of this world descends not from above, but is earthly, sensual, devilish"* (James 3:15).

As an example, let's look at the reason that the United States of America is blessed.

First of all, it is probably true that there are more true Born-Again Believers in this country than in any other country in the world. As a result, there is a greater proliferation of the Word of God than anywhere else in the world. So, even though this nation has a long way to go to arrive at the place where it ought to be, still, it bases its direction more so on the Word of God than probably any nation in the world. However, there is here no room for rejoicing, because, sadly, we are departing from that Word, and doing so at an alarming rate.

If the downward trend is not checked, and if Jesus tarries, this nation eventually will destroy itself through sin, which is the result of a departure from the Word of God.

It is truly heartbreaking when it is improper, even illegal, for the Word of God to be read in the public school system, but it is quite satisfactory for the Koran to be read, when the latter book is the cause of almost all the problems in the world today, at least regarding terrorism. That's how far this nation has deteriorated.

THE CORE OF THE DETERIORATION OF THE UNITED STATES

The blame can be laid at the doorsteps of the Church. It has so far departed from the Word of God that, anymore, the far greater majority of people who sit on the pews of Churches are not even Born-Again. They are a member of such-and-such Church, and they may be very religious, but they never really have had a Born-Again experience, as given by the Lord Jesus Christ (Jn. 3:3, 16).

The Church has opted greatly for humanistic psychology, which is a repudiation of the Word of God anyway you look at it. And sadly, humanistic psychology holds no answers whatsoever. By that statement, I mean that this nefarious system holds no positive answers whatsoever! But yet the Church has abandoned the Cross of Christ in favor of the foolish prattle of unredeemed men.

God help us!

(31) "THE LAW OF HIS GOD IS IN HIS HEART; NONE OF HIS STEPS SHALL SLIDE."

Two facts are here given, which are associated as cause and effect.

When a person has the Law of God in his heart (cause), he will neither slide nor go astray (effect).

(32) "THE WICKED WATCHES THE RIGHTEOUS, AND SEEKS TO SLAY HIM."

Let's take a look at the Church as a whole. Those in the Church who advocate a departure from the Word of God, those who actually ridicule the Word of God, will do everything in their power to hinder and hurt those who advocate the Word of God as the answer.

MURDER

The short phrase, *"And seek to slay him,"* refers, in its truest sense, to killing someone; however, it also refers to killing a person's reputation by clandestine gossip, insinuation, or outright slander. Such is grievous in the sight of the Lord, but yet is practiced by too many Christians. The Lord regards such as *"wicked"*; He also regards those who do such as *"the wicked."*

(33) "THE LORD WILL NOT LEAVE HIM IN HIS HAND, NOR CONDEMN HIM WHEN HE IS JUDGED."

This is a general rule which generally applies, but not always.

Sometimes the innocent and righteous are murdered, even as Cain murdered Abel. Furthermore, many have been wrongfully condemned to death and executed, just as Naboth was executed at the instigation of Jezebel.

But in a general sense, this great Promise of God holds true.

The Lord is Omniscient, meaning that He knows all things. So those situations which seem not to be favorable to the Child of God are allowed by the Lord for many and various reasons. We may question ourselves, and we should question ourselves, but we are never to question the Lord!

(34) "WAIT ON THE LORD, AND KEEP HIS WAY, AND HE SHALL EXALT YOU TO INHERIT THE LAND: WHEN THE WICKED ARE CUT OFF, YOU SHALL SEE IT."

Especially as it refers to *"waiting on the LORD,"* the idea of this Verse has to do more so with the Great Plan of God than localized events at localized times.

The Believer is to understand that a day is coming when the wicked will no longer rule, but rather Righteousness will rule. That particular time pertains to the coming Kingdom Age, when the Lord Jesus Christ will Personally rule from Jerusalem and rule the entirety of the world.

This great and glorious time is, so to speak, right around the corner.

(35) "I HAVE SEEN THE WICKED IN GREAT POWER, AND SPREADING HIMSELF LIKE A GREEN BAY TREE."

The wicked may seem to prosper, and actually do so for a while, even as here presented. But the Believer is not to take this seriously. The Believer knows what the end result will be.

(36) "YET HE PASSED AWAY, AND, LO, HE WAS NOT: YEA, I SOUGHT HIM, BUT HE COULD NOT BE FOUND."

This pertains, as stated, to the coming Kingdom Age; however, most every Christian can look back at his own life and will recount this very Scripture being fulfilled. Those who tried to hurt us, who tried to do so with great strength, did not succeed, because the Lord intervened in the situation.

(37) "MARK THE PERFECT MAN, AND BEHOLD THE UPRIGHT: FOR THE END OF THAT MAN IS PEACE."

"Peace" is a tremendous quality. If it is true *"Peace,"* it cannot be found outside of Christ.

THE PEACE OF GOD

Even though this was given in Old Testament times, it also has a New Testament application.

In essence, it is speaking of Sanctifying Peace.

"Justifying Peace" has to do with the peace that comes to the heart of the newly converted. This happens with every new convert because the enmity that is between God and that person has been removed; that *"enmity"* was sin. It was removed by faith, faith expressed in Christ, which is made possible by the Cross. As stated, such peace is referred to as *"Justifying Peace."*

"Sanctifying Peace" is something else altogether. It pertains to the life and living of the Believer. Every Believer has *"Justifying Peace,"* but every Believer, regrettably, does not have *"Sanctifying Peace,"* at least not as they ought to have.

"Sanctifying Peace" is brought about strictly and totally by and through the Cross of Christ. In other words, it is God's Way that Believers ever make Christ and the Cross the Object of their Faith. As we have said any number of times, Christ is the Source, but the Cross is the Means!

If faith is thus applied, and thus maintained, the Holy Spirit, Who works entirely within the framework of the Finished Work of Christ, will then work mightily on our behalf, with the end result being a perpetual *"Sanctifying Peace."* This is the *"more abundant life"* spoken of by Christ (Jn. 10:10). It is available to every Believer, but only on God's terms.

(38) "BUT THE TRANSGRESSORS SHALL BE DESTROYED TOGETHER: THE END OF THE WICKED SHALL BE CUT OFF."

It doesn't matter what individuals say, it doesn't matter what the conventional wisdom may claim, the Word of God plainly and clearly tells us that those who ignore the Lord and His Ways ultimately will be *"cut off."* This refers to the individual dying lost and going to Hell, where they will remain forever and forever.

It also refers to the rule of the wicked being terminated, which it most definitely will in the coming Kingdom Age.

(39) "BUT THE SALVATION OF THE RIGHTEOUS IS OF THE LORD: HE IS THEIR STRENGTH IN THE TIME OF TROUBLE."

The last two Verses sum up the teaching of this Psalm and indicate its special object, which is to encourage and sustain the righteous regarding trials by the assurance that we are under the special protection of God, Who, whenever trouble threatens, will stand forth as our Strength and Defense, and Who ultimately will be our *"Salvation."*

If more people knew this Psalm and understood its implications, there would be less complaining about difficulties and problems. We would know they are temporal, while the Ways of the Lord are eternal!

(40) "AND THE LORD SHALL HELP THEM, AND DELIVER THEM: HE SHALL DELIVER THEM FROM THE WICKED, AND SAVE THEM, BECAUSE THEY TRUST IN HIM."

A tremendous truth is here given.

THE HELP OF THE LORD

The ground of God's favor toward the righteous, the ground of our Righteousness itself, is our trust in Him. Trusting in Him, we take the Word of God as our rule of life and make it our constant endeavor to serve and please Him.

PSALM 38

A Psalm of David:
The Prayer of a Penitent Heart

(1) O LORD, REBUKE ME NOT IN YOUR WRATH: NEITHER CHASTEN ME IN YOUR HOT DISPLEASURE."

This Psalm was written by David; it pictures him pleading to God in regard to his sin and asking for help.

THE THOUGHTS OF JESUS WHILE HE WAS ON THE CROSS

Even in a greater measure, this Psalm pictures the Messiah by revealing the thoughts which filled His heart up to and during the time He was on the Cross. It describes His sympathetic Intercession for His people, who were justly suffering the Wrath of God because of their sin. It records the hatred and ingratitude of those who ought to have loved Him.

"He came unto His Own, and His Own received Him not" (Jn. 1:11).

Himself sinless, He here loads Himself with the Believer's sins; makes full confession of them; admits the justice of the Divine Wrath against them; and utters no reproach against those members of His nation who sought to destroy Him. He does not excuse or belittle sin, nor does He murmur at the Wrath of God against it. He magnifies the Wrath and reposes in the Righteousness of the Judge of all the Earth.

(2) "FOR YOUR ARROWS STICK FAST IN ME, AND YOUR HAND PRESSES ME SORE."

Once again, we remind the Reader that even though David wrote this Psalm, and thereby prayed this prayer on his own behalf, still, it is more so the prayer of the Son of David serving as our Intercessor.

OUR GREAT HIGH PRIEST

What a possession it is to have a Priest Who can perfectly fulfill the Divine requirements, and Who can furnish to His people in all Dispensations a fitting vehicle of language with which to approach God in confession and prayer!

As He takes upon Himself the penalty of the sin of the world (II Cor. 5:21), He knows that the Wrath of God will be directed at Him instead of the ones who rightly deserve it — namely you and me!

Concerning the Intercession of Christ, all on our behalf, the Scripture says, and I quote from THE EXPOSITOR'S STUDY BIBLE:

"But this Man (the Lord Jesus Christ), *because He continues ever* (proclaims the Priesthood of Christ as Eternal, while death was inevitable as it regarded the Aaronic Priests), *has an unchangeable Priesthood.* (This not only refers to that which is Eternal, but to that which also will not change as far as its principle is concerned. The reason is that the Finished Work of the Cross is an *'Everlasting Covenant'* [Heb. 13:20].)

"Wherefore He (the Lord Jesus Christ) *is able also to save them to the uttermost* (proclaims the fact that Christ Alone has made the only true Atonement for sin; He did this at the Cross) *who come unto God by Him* (proclaims the only manner in which man can come to God), *seeing He ever lives to make intercession for them.* (His very Presence by the Right Hand of the Father guarantees such, with nothing else having to be done [Heb. 1:3].)

"For such an High Priest became us (presents the fact that no one less exalted could

have met the necessities of the human race), *Who is Holy, harmless, undefiled, separate from sinners* (describes the spotless, pure, Perfect Character of the Son of God as our Great High Priest; as well, this tells us that Christ did not become a sinner on the Cross, as some claim, but was rather the Sin Offering), *and made higher than the Heavens* (refers to the fact that He is seated at the Right Hand of the Father, which is the most exalted position in Heaven or Earth);

"Who needs not daily (refers to the daily Sacrifices offered by the Priests under the old Jewish economy), *as those High Priests, to offer up Sacrifice, first for His Own sins, and then for the people's* (refers to the work of the Jewish High Priest on the Great Day of Atonement, which specified their unworthiness; Christ did not have to function accordingly): *for this He did once, when He offered up Himself.* (This refers to His Death on the Cross, which atoned for all sin — past, present, and future — making no further Sacrifices necessary)" (Heb. 7:24-27).

(3) "THERE IS NO SOUNDNESS IN MY FLESH BECAUSE OF YOUR ANGER; NEITHER IS THERE ANY REST IN MY BONES BECAUSE OF MY SIN."

It is difficult for the Believer to fully understand the total Intercession of Christ on our behalf, as He literally takes our sin unto Himself — *"My sin."* In order for the great price of Redemption to be paid, our sin must become *"His sin."* Consequently, the *"rebuke,"* the *"chastening,"* and the *"anger"* of God must be directed at Him — the Redeemer.

Every time we as Believers fail the Lord in some respect, and we have to go before Him asking for Mercy and Grace, we should remember the following, and remember it well:

We are allowed that Mercy and Grace, and abundantly so, all because of what He did for us at the Cross. We do not have to suffer the just penalty of sin, for He has already suffered that just penalty. We do not have to take the load of its punishment on ourselves, for He has already suffered that punishment.

While there always are negative results to sin, even terrible negative results, still, we in no way have to suffer the rightful due, because He already has suffered it on our behalf. For us to have to suffer it again would be

NOTES

what is referred to in legal jargon as *"double jeopardy."* And God never will allow such to happen, because to do so would say that what Jesus did at the Cross was insufficient.

That's one of the reasons why it is so wrong, so sinful and so wicked for fellow Christians to try to impose the penalty of sin upon one who has failed. In the first place, they have failed many times themselves. In the second place, even as James said, no human being is worthy to punish another. Whatever is to be done must be left to the domain of the Heavenly Father.

"There is one Lawgiver, Who is able to save and to destroy: who are you who judges another?" (James 4:12).

(4) "FOR MY INIQUITIES ARE GONE OVER MY HEAD: AS AN HEAVY BURDEN THEY ARE TOO HEAVY FOR ME."

In this Passage, we have, at least to a degree, the manner in which Jesus died.

THE DEATH OF CHRIST ON THE CROSS

These sins were *"heavy"* because He bore the sin of the whole world. They were so many that they literally went over His *"Head."* They were so *"heavy"* that, in a sense, they literally killed Him.

While it is true that no man took His Life from Him, that He laid it down of His Own Will (Jn. 10:18), still, I think it can be said that He died of a broken heart — broken because of the weight of sin that He was carrying for the whole world. Hence, John the Baptist said, *"Behold the Lamb of God, which takes away the sin of the world"* (Jn. 1:29).

(5) "MY WOUNDS STINK AND ARE CORRUPT BECAUSE OF MY FOOLISHNESS."

While David prays this prayer because of his own sin, still, once again, these are the Words also of the Son of David.

THE FOOLISHNESS OF SIN

While Christ had no foolishness whatsoever, still, in this one Verse, He takes the penalty for sin, even though, with most, the committing of such was done in foolishness. In other words, even though there was temptation, it was not that severe; but man sins simply because of the sin nature that drives him toward foolish things.

All sin is foolishness, meaning that it makes fools out of men.

There is a certain, strange thrill in the pursuit of sin, but none whatsoever when sin is culminated.

There is only one answer for sin, and that is the Cross of Christ. Sin is so powerful and has such a hold on mankind, that its power cannot be broken outside of faith in Christ and what Christ did at the Cross.

Concerning this, Paul said, *"Knowing this, that our old man is crucified with Him* (all that we were before conversion), *that the body of sin might be destroyed* (the power of sin broken, i.e., 'made ineffective'), *that henceforth we should not serve sin.* (The guilt of sin is removed at conversion, because the sin nature no longer rules within our hearts and lives)" (Rom. 6:6).

IF SIN WAS MADE INEFFECTIVE BY THE SACRIFICE OF CHRIST, WHY ARE BELIEVERS STILL TROUBLED BY SIN?

There are two reasons:

1. Satan is allowed to tempt us in order that our faith might be tested. Satan tempts us in order to get us to fail, while the Lord tests us in order that we might succeed. Such is necessary for the Spiritual Growth of the Believer. We learn from this that our faith is never quite as strong as we think it is.

2. The failure comes about because the Believer has transferred his faith from the Cross of Christ, where it must ever repose, to something else. Improperly placed faith actually is the greatest hindrance to the Body of Christ.

If we place our faith properly in Christ and what He did for us at the Cross, and ever make Christ and the Cross the Object of our Faith, then the Holy Spirit will help us mightily (Rom. 8:1-2, 11) and give us victory over sin. While the Lord does not promise sinless perfection, He most definitely does promise that *"the sin nature shall not have dominion over us"* (Rom. 6:14).

(6) "I AM TROUBLED; I AM BOWED DOWN GREATLY; I GO MOURNING ALL THE DAY LONG."

David is probably speaking here of the terrible sin which he committed against Bathsheba and her husband Uriah.

He is in a terrible physical and spiritual condition, even *"twisted by violent spasms,"* for that's what the phrase, *"I am troubled,"* actually means. It also means *"warped in mind"* and *"driven crazy,"* proclaiming the fact that he also was mentally afflicted because of this sin.

His sin also has *"bowed him down greatly,"* meaning that it was even difficult for him to walk upright.

SIN AND ITS EFFECT ON THE BELIEVER!

If sin doesn't afflict the Believer in this manner, meaning that he cannot stand its impact until it is made right with God, then such a Believer is in terrible spiritual condition.

David was a man who walked close to God; he was one of the greatest men of God who ever lived. But yet, he committed this terrible sin with Bathsheba and then murdered her husband Uriah in cold blood. Yes! This is the same David who wrote over half of the Psalms, the same David who was the greatest king that Israel ever had, and the same David through whose family the Messiah would come, Who, in fact, would be referred to as *"The Son of David."* Therefore, David's terrible sin affects him as he here records, which obviously was before he was approached by Nathan the Prophet.

The Holy Spirit directed Nathan to tell David a little story. It concerned a poor man who had nothing but one little lamb. A rich man, the owner of vast flocks, took this little lamb from the poor man.

When David heard the story related by Nathan, *"his anger was greatly kindled against the man,"* and he pronounced the sentence of death on him.

Then Nathan said to David, *"You are the man"* (II Sam. 12:1-14).

While the Lord forgave David, even as the Fifty-first Psalm reveals, still, there were terrible after-effects of sin, as there always are terrible after-effects of sin.

This is not because God desires to continue to punish such a one, but strictly because sin is so awful! So terrible! So bad! So destructive!

As stated, these were not only the words of David, but they also were the Words of the Greater Son of David, Who proclaimed them all on our behalf. We learn from this a little bit about what He suffered in order that we might be saved.

(7) "FOR MY LOINS ARE FILLED WITH A LOATHSOME DISEASE: AND THERE IS NO SOUNDNESS IN MY FLESH."

The words, *"A loathsome disease,"* should have been translated *"a burning fever"*; for, in the Hebrew, the word *"loathsome"* means *"burning."* As Christ hung on the Cross, a burning fever wracked His Body, even as this Perfect Body was being offered as the Perfect Sacrifice.

(8) "I AM FEEBLE AND SORE BROKEN: I HAVE ROARED BY REASON OF THE DISQUIETNESS OF MY HEART."

Let the Reader see David here, and see him plainly, in the agony of heart, all because of his sin. If we do not feel at least somewhat similar as it regards our own failures, then we need to go back again and study the Word of God, as it relates these horrors of sin and its terrible effects.

WHAT IS SIN?

In short, it is disobedience of the Word of God, whether in thought, word, or deed.

The Law of Moses told the world what sin actually was, and is. Concerning the Law, the Bible says, *"The sting of death is sin* (actually says, *'The sting of the death is the sin'*; the words *'the sin'* refer to the sin nature, which came about at the Fall, and which results in death [Rom. 6:23]); *and the strength of sin is the Law.* (This is the Law of Moses. It defined sin and stressed its penalty, which is death [Col. 2:14-15])" (I Cor. 15:56).

The Law of Moses was given (Ex., Chpt. 20), and sin was then defined in order that man might know exactly what it was, and even what type of sin that it was, hence, The Ten Commandments.

John said, *"Whosoever commits sin transgresses also the Law* (the Greek Text says, *'the sin,'* and refers to Believers placing their faith in that other than the Cross; such constitutes rebellion against God's Prescribed Order, and is labeled as *'sin'*): *for sin is the transgression of the Law.* (This refers to the moral law — The Ten Commandments. Rebelling against God's Order, which is the Cross, opens the door for works of the flesh [Gal. 5:19-21])" (I Jn. 3:4).

Every human being on the face of the Earth, sadly so, has broken the Law of God. Its penalty is death (Rom. 6:23). So where does that leave the person?

JESUS AND THE LAW

The sentence of death hangs over every human being on the face of the Earth because of the broken Law. There is only one recourse for the entirety of the human race, which is the Lord Jesus Christ and what He did for us at the Cross of Calvary.

Concerning Christ, the Scripture says:

"But when the fullness of the time was come, God sent forth His Son, made of a woman, made under the Law,

"To redeem them who were under the Law, that we might receive the adoption of sons" (Gal. 4:4-5).

In other words, Christ came to this world to do for us what we could not do for ourselves. He came as our Substitute, as our Representative Man. He was the Last Adam, the Second Man (I Cor. 15:45-47).

As our Substitute, He kept the Law in every respect, not breaking it one single time. Because He was a Perfect Law-keeper, our faith in Him makes us Law-keepers also. But even though Christ did this for us, there remained the penalty of the broken Law. He addressed that by going to the Cross, suffering its penalty, which was death.

Therefore, when a believing sinner comes to Christ and makes Jesus the Lord of his life, the Law then has no more claim on such a person. Once again, we go back to the words *"double jeopardy."* Jesus lived for us and died for us. He satisfied the Law in every respect. It, therefore, has no more claim on us.

However, the moment the Believer moves his faith from Christ and the Cross to something else, he then comes back under Law. If the Believer remains there, he could suffer destruction.

Concerning this, the Apostle Paul said:

"I do not frustrate the Grace of God: for if Righteousness come by the Law, then

Christ is dead in vain" (Gal. 2:21).

Every person on the face of the Earth who does not accept Christ as Saviour and Lord will answer to the Law at the Great White Throne Judgment (Rev. 20:11-15). If we accept Christ and make Him the Saviour and Lord of our lives, the Law then has been satisfied, and we never will have to answer to it, but rather to Christ, Who was, and is, our Great Substitute in all things.

(9) "LORD, ALL MY DESIRE IS BEFORE YOU; AND MY GROANING IS NOT HID FROM YOU."

We find David here taking his sin totally and completely to the Lord, which is the only place it can be taken.

CATHOLIC PRIESTS

Whether they be Catholic, Episcopalian, or whatever, Scripturally there is no such thing as a Priest, an Office which was fulfilled by Christ at the Cross. While there definitely were Priests in Old Testament times (as it regards Judaism), who served as mediators between God and Israel, when Jesus came, He fulfilled all of those types, being the Great High Priest Himself, which He still is, and which He ever shall be, all on our behalf.

Paul clearly explains this in the Seventh Chapter of Hebrews. Then in the Eighth Chapter, the Apostle says, *"Now of the things of which we have spoken this is the sum: We have such an High Priest, Who is set on the Right Hand of the Throne of the Majesty in the Heavens"* (Heb. 8:1).

As our Great High Priest, He is the Lone Mediator between God and men.

In writing to Timothy, Paul said:

"For there is one God, and one Mediator between God and men, the Man Christ Jesus;

"Who gave Himself a ransom for all, to be testified in due time" (I Tim. 2:5-6).

Therefore, when a person sins and they do not take such to the Lord, but rather to an earthly priest, an office which has been done away with by Christ, such a person does not have their sins forgiven, for no earthly mortal can mediate between God and men. There is only One Who can do that, and that is our Lord Jesus Christ, because of what He did for us at the Cross.

NOTES

(10) "MY HEART PANTS, MY STRENGTH FAILS ME: AS FOR THE LIGHT OF MY EYES, IT ALSO IS GONE FROM ME."

As this applied to David, even more so it applied to the Son of David.

His heart broke; His strength failed. The *"Light"* of His eyes was His Father, and the Lord pulled the blinds on this horrible scene and refused to look at His Only Son — and we speak of the time when Jesus was dying on the Cross. Because He was bearing the sin of the whole world, truly the *"Light would go from Him."* He suffered the pangs of darkness so that you and I would not have to suffer such.

(11) "MY LOVERS AND MY FRIENDS STAND ALOOF FROM MY SORE; AND MY KINSMEN STAND AFAR OFF."

This is a graphic description of what happened to Christ at the Cross, at least as it regards those near Him.

THE RESPONSE OF FRIENDS AND KINSMEN WHILE JESUS WAS ON THE CROSS

At this hour, even the Disciples of the Lord forsook Him. His brothers, even James and Jude, *"stood afar off,"* not accepting Him at this time as the Messiah. They only did so after the Resurrection. No one wanted to be associated with Him.

Why not?

All knew that anyone who hung on a tree was cursed by God (Deut. 21:23); therefore, how could He be the Messiah and be cursed by God at the same time? They simply did not understand the Crucifixion, the mission of Christ, or the price He was paying for lost humanity. So they forsook Him.

Why didn't they know and understand?

Their problem was the same problem we all have: self-will! Not even His closest Disciples understood His Mission and His Purpose. They believed Him to be the Messiah, but rather the conquering Messiah. The suffering Messiah, Who would redeem the world, was something of which they had no knowledge (Isa., Chpt. 53).

Even after the Resurrection and immediately before the Ascension, they asked the question, *"Will You at this time restore again the Kingdom to Israel?"* (Acts 1:6).

They were thinking in terms which were so much smaller than that which He had done. They wanted Israel restored. Instead He restored all of mankind, at least those who will accept Him!

(12) "THEY ALSO WHO SEEK AFTER MY LIFE LAY SNARES FOR ME: AND THEY WHO SEEK MY HURT SPEAK MISCHIEVOUS THINGS, AND IMAGINE DECEITS ALL THE DAY LONG."

The following breaks down this Verse:

THE THREE EFFORTS OF SATAN AGAINST THE CHILD OF GOD

There are three lines, so to speak, in this Verse. They are:

1. Action: *"They lay snares."*
2. Speech: *"They speak mischievous things."*
3. Motive: *"They imagine deceits."*

They do this *"all the day long,"* which speaks of the *"long day of their hatred."*

It should be noted that those who did these things against David, and, above all, against the Greater Son of David, were from within the Church, so to speak. Satan always does his best work from a position of religion.

For instance, the Pharisees and the Sadducees, plus virtually the entire religious hierarchy of Israel, opposed Christ to the extent that they would crucify Him. The Roman world laid no snares for His Life. Neither did they seek His hurt. The *"snares"* and the *"hurt"* came from His Own. God's greatest enemies have always been those who name His Name.

What irony!

Likewise, the true Minister of the Gospel who is called and led by the Holy Spirit will seldom be encouraged by the Church; instead, he will be hindered, discouraged, and even persecuted by those who should be helping him.

(13) "BUT I, AS A DEAF MAN, HEARD NOT; AND I WAS AS A DUMB MAN WHO OPENS NOT HIS MOUTH."

David conducted himself, and so did the Greater Son of David, as though he did not hear their taunts; likewise, he did not open his mouth in his own defense.

What a lesson for us!

NOTES

As it speaks of Christ, it was said, *"Who, when He was reviled, reviled not again"* (I Pet. 2:23).

This is the place where the Holy Spirit desires to bring us.

Why did He take this position that self-will would never take?

The answer is found in the next two Verses.

(14) "THUS I WAS AS A MAN WHO HEARS NOT, AND IN WHOSE MOUTH ARE NO REPROOFS.

(15) "FOR IN YOU, O LORD, DO I HOPE: YOU WILL HEAR, O LORD MY GOD."

Even though these Passages definitely do refer to David, they refer more particularly to the Son of David.

TRUST IN THE LORD

Our Lord would not fight His Own battles. He would let His Father fight for Him. Even though these unholy hypocrites would definitely hinder His Work, still, to hinder was all they could do. They could not stop it, because the Work was the Lord's.

Even though the Messiah conducted Himself as though He did not hear their accusations, you can be sure that the Lord of Glory *"did hear."* He said, *"Vengeance is Mine; I will repay, saith the Lord"* (Rom. 12:19).

Repay, He did!

In A.D. 70, Jerusalem was literally wiped off the face of the Earth. Over one million Jews died in the siege of the city.

Remarkably enough, not one single Believer in Christ died in that siege. They remembered what Jesus told them:

"And when you shall see Jerusalem compassed with armies, then know that the desolation thereof is near.

"Then let them which are in Judaea flee to the mountains; and let them which are in the midst of it depart out; and let not them who are in the countries enter thereinto.

"For these be your days of vengeance, that all things which are written may be fulfilled" (Lk. 21:20-22).

However, it should be noted that the Lord did level against these Pharisees, Sadducees, Herodians, and Scribes certain strong denunciations. To their face, He called them hypocrites (Mat. 15:7). He also called them snakes and vipers, again to their face (Mat.,

Chpt. 23). What He did not do was to use His Power against them!

Regarding the taunts, the sneers, and the jibes which will come, sadly enough, from those who claim to be God's people, the true Believer should ignore them, committing judgment unto the Lord.

(16) "FOR I SAID, HEAR ME, LEST OTHERWISE THEY SHOULD REJOICE OVER ME: WHEN MY FOOT SLIPS, THEY MAGNIFY THEMSELVES AGAINST ME."

David is here saying that his enemies would rejoice when *"his foot slipped,"* meaning that he would fail the Lord in some way. In other ways, they were waiting and watching, hoping to catch him in something that was not right so they could bring accusations against him. The Pharisees, Sadducees, and Scribes did the same identical thing with our Lord. The difference between David and our Lord was as follows:

David did slip, sometimes severely so, even as has every other human being; however, the Feet of our Lord never slipped, not even one time. So the Pharisees and Scribes had to make up out of thin air malicious reports against the Master, which they most definitely did!

RESTORATION

If a Believer fails, the admonition from the Word of God is that we *"restore such an one in the spirit of meekness; considering yourself, lest you also be tempted"* (Gal. 6:1).

How is the Restoration process to be engaged?

The Holy Spirit through Paul limited such to *"you who are spiritual."*

What did He mean by that?

Those who are spiritual are those who adhere strictly to the Word of God, not allowing their own personal thoughts and feelings to enter into the situation, whatever the situation might be.

To *"restore such an one,"* he must first of all be told why he failed.

Every Believer places himself in a position of failure, where the *"works of the flesh"* can manifest themselves in his life, when he places his faith in something other than Christ and the Cross. So the *"spiritual one"* must tell the failing one that the failure was caused by an improper positioning of his faith.

Then he must be encouraged to once again understand that all victory is found exclusively in Christ and the Cross, meaning that Christ and the Cross must ever be the Object of our Faith.

There is only one remedy for sin — not ten, not five, not even two — just one! That one remedy is *"The Cross of Christ"* (Rom. 6:1-14; 8:1-2, 11; I Cor. 1:17-18, 21, 23; 2:2; Gal., Chpt. 5; 6:14; Eph. 2:13-18; Col. 2:14-15).

PUNISHMENT!

Regrettably, most Christians believe that if a Christian fails, he should be punished in some way.

First and foremost, Jesus suffered the punishment on our behalf when He died for our sins on the Cross of Calvary. When anyone thinks that more punishment should be added regarding the individual in question, this is saying, whether the person realizes it or not, that what Jesus suffered was not enough, and something must, therefore, be added to His suffering. This is an insult of the highest order to Christ, as should be extremely obvious!

In the second place, no Believer, no matter who he might be, is without sin. This means that no Believer is qualified to punish another Believer.

James answered this by saying:

"There is one Lawgiver, Who is able to save and to destroy (Who is the Lord)*: who are you who judges another?"* (James 4:12).

In other words, James is saying, *"Who do you think you are, thinking that you are qualified to judge another?"*

Every single Believer on the face of the Earth has had to go before the Lord innumerable times asking forgiveness for sin. Any Believer who tries to claim otherwise, pure and simple, is lying!

Yes! Exactly as David here said, there are many who try their best to catch a Christian in something which is wrong so they can *"magnify themselves against them."* I would seriously doubt the Salvation of such persons!

We must never condone sin; but, at the same time, we must ever love the sinner.

(17) "FOR I AM READY TO HALT,

AND MY SORROW IS CONTINUALLY BEFORE ME."

In essence, David says of himself, *"I am weak and helpless, liable at any moment to stumble and fall."*

And then he said, *"And my sorrow is continually before me,"* meaning that he continually sorrows over his sin, which probably was his sin with Bathsheba, which lies at the root of all his distress. To be sure, his enemies took full advantage of the situation. Instead of trying to help him, they did the very opposite.

Regrettably, this breed of enemies did not die with David. They exist presently, and oftentimes occupy high positions in the world of religion.

(18) "FOR I WILL DECLARE MY INIQUITY; I WILL BE SORRY FOR MY SIN."

As stated, David was probably speaking of the terrible sin with Bathsheba and the murder of her husband Uriah.

But yet, this Passage also portrays Christ in His great Intercessory Work. He literally took our sin as His Own *"sin."*

David here says that he will confess his sin and do so openly; however, he also realizes, even as the next Verse proclaims, that his enemies will take full advantage of the situation.

(19) "BUT MY ENEMIES ARE LIVELY, AND THEY ARE STRONG: AND THEY WHO HATE ME WRONGFULLY ARE MULTIPLIED."

Looking here first of all at Christ, how in the world could anyone be *"an enemy of Christ"*? Why would they *"hate Him"*?

The answer is obvious. Their deeds were evil, and His altogether spotless Life was a rebuke to their hypocrisy and sin.

This must be remembered: those who oppose, resist, and even hate true God-called ones are actually hating the Lord. It is impossible to oppose that which God is doing without opposing God.

Please allow me to make a statement that I've already made in this Volume, but which, I think, bears repeating:

"When one is down, and anything negative that one desires can be done to him, with the knowledge that such action will not be reprimanded, but rather will be applauded, then one very quickly finds out exactly how many good Christians there are."

There aren't many!

(20) "THEY ALSO WHO RENDER EVIL FOR GOOD ARE MY ADVERSARIES; BECAUSE I FOLLOW THE THING THAT GOOD IS."

A tremendous Truth is given us in this Verse.

ISRAEL DURING THE TIME OF DAVID

When David became King of Israel, he was truly God's man for the task. It was God's Will that David be the first King of Israel, and not Saul. Saul was the people's choice, and not God's.

Nevertheless, when David finally became King, the nation was blessed by God as it had never been before. Prosperity was the order of the day; power and strength were obvious on every hand. In other words, the Blessings of the Lord attended Israel in a great way.

That being the case, then why was it that certain powerful individuals in Israel, men whom David, in fact, had made rich, even giving them great positions in government, would rise up against him? Actually, his own son, Absalom, led the rebellion.

They rendered *"evil for good"* simply because they did not know the Lord. They neither knew nor understood the secret of their Blessings. They envied David, thinking they could do better if they only had the reigns of government. They were so spiritually inept that they did not understand that David was the vehicle through which these blessings came. They were totally bereft of that knowledge, unable to see the Truth, even though it was glaringly obvious before their faces. Carnal men cannot see spiritual things!

They were opposed to David because of his touch with God. They didn't have that touch, so they opposed the one who did.

It was the same identical thing during the time of Christ!

It is the same presently!

(21) "FORSAKE ME NOT, O LORD: O MY GOD, BE NOT FAR FROM ME.

(22) "MAKE HASTE TO HELP ME, O LORD MY SALVATION."

Several things are said in these two Verses. They are:

THE LORD'S WAY

Verses 21 and 22 tell us how the Lord will respond to David, and also how He responded to the Messiah:
1. He will not *"forsake Him"*;
2. He will not *"be far from Him"*; and,
3. He will *"make haste to help,"* because the Lord, not man, is His Salvation.

PSALM 39

*A Psalm of David:
Human Frailty*

(1) "I SAID, I WILL TAKE HEED TO MY WAYS, THAT I SIN NOT WITH MY TONGUE: I WILL KEEP MY MOUTH WITH A BRIDLE, WHILE THE WICKED IS BEFORE ME."

The superscription is: *"To the Chief Musician, even to Jeduthun, a Psalm of David."*

THE ACTION OF OUR LORD

This is a Psalm of David and a prayer that was also a song to be sung by the choir led by Ethan. The prayer is from David, but even more so it is from the Son of David.

It must have been a great temptation to pronounce a curse upon the Pharisees, Sadducees, and Scribes, who so bitterly opposed Him. But that He did not do. He literally put a *"bridle on His Mouth."*

Perhaps this is the hardest thing for the Believer to do. There is a tendency to defend oneself; however, the moment we defend ourselves, God cannot defend us. If we allow ourselves to be vilified and we give no negative response, we are following the example of Christ. In effect, the Holy Spirit is telling us, *"Keep your mouth with a bridle, at least as it regards self-defense."*

(2) "I WAS DUMB WITH SILENCE, I HELD MY PEACE, EVEN FROM GOOD; AND MY SORROW WAS STIRRED."

The enemies of our Lord would think that His silence bespoke a lack of intelligence. Little did they realize that His *"silence"* was the Mercy and Grace of God, *"even from good"* — and yet the *"sorrow"* of such would break His heart.

Accordingly, the theme and circumstances of the prior Psalm are here continued. Elect Israel suffers from the Hand of God and from the hand of man: the pressure of the one hand, just; the pressure of the other, unjust. Their Great High Priest prays with them and for them; furnishes their lips with the language they should use in confession, supplication, and deprecation; urges the sinlessness and perfection of His Own Nature as a plea on their behalf as to why they should be heard and delivered; and instructs them as to their feelings and conduct toward their prosperous and persecuting enemies. They are neither to rebuke their foes nor rebel against God. They are to trust Him though He smites them; and, themselves lighter than vanity and but the creatures of a day, yet are they to wait for Him to deliver them from the pride of man.

Thus, the Great Shepherd takes His place at the head of the flock; and He Himself having suffered, He associates Himself with the many sons in their sorrows and sufferings and leads them to Glory.

(3) "MY HEART WAS HOT WITHIN ME, WHILE I WAS MUSING THE FIRE BURNED: THEN SPOKE I WITH MY TONGUE."

David prays, but these also are the Words of the Messiah.

THE LORD JESUS

It is difficult for the Bible Student to imagine the humanity of the Son of God. There was temptation to step outside of the Will of God in respect to His enemies. The anger of righteous indignation burned within His heart; however, to have done so would have been disastrous. Thank God He did not do so. He did speak, however, but what did He say?

(4) "LORD, MAKE ME TO KNOW MY END, AND THE MEASURE OF MY DAYS, WHAT IT IS; THAT I MAY KNOW HOW FRAIL I AM."

There is so much said in this one Passage that it is difficult for us to digest it all.

THE PRAYER OF THE SON OF GOD

David is praying, but, in reality, it is the Son of David Who is praying. In this we see the totality of the Incarnation (God becoming Man). As God, He was unlimited, and, as should be obvious, did not need to pray. As Man, He was very much limited. The "frailty" that He became was in reality weakness, a weakness that Satan would grossly misunderstand.

Paul wrote, *"For though He was crucified through weakness, yet He lives by the Power of God. For we also are weak in Him, but we shall live with Him by the Power of God toward you"* (II Cor. 13:4).

Christ did die in weakness, but it was rather a contrived weakness. This means that He had the power to do otherwise, but He never used that power. Thank God He didn't! Had He done so, had He called on Angels to deliver Him from the Cross, Redemption would have been forfeited. So He died in weakness, meaning that He never used that which was at His disposal. But, to be sure, one day He will use it, and I speak of the Second Coming (Rev., Chpt. 19).

THE FRAILTY OF MAN

David and the Son of Man here speak of *"frailty,"* which refers to spiritual frailty. David wants to know how it will all conclude and what will be *"the measure of his days."*

What did he mean by that?

Knowing how frail he was (and every Believer most definitely should know the same thing), he was somewhat fearful that he would not be able to accomplish that for which the Lord had called him.

These thoughts of David are my thoughts! They should be yours, as well, and, no doubt, are!

Despite the powers of darkness, and despite this *"frailty,"* David did accomplish that which the Lord called him to do.

Through the Power of the Holy Spirit, he made Israel into the greatest nation of the world of its day. Before he died, the Lord gave him in totality the plans for the coming Temple, which would be built by his son, Solomon. The Lord also told him that through his family, the Son of God would come into the world and would be called *"the Son of David"* (II Sam., Chpt. 7).

The Coming of Christ some one thousand years after David proclaimed in stark reality that *"the measure of David's days"* was what it ought to have been, and that despite his *"frailty."*

(5) "BEHOLD, YOU HAVE MADE MY DAYS AS AN HANDBREADTH; AND MY AGE IS AS NOTHING BEFORE YOU: VERILY EVERY MAN AT HIS BEST STATE IS ALTOGETHER VANITY. SELAH."

Beside God, man is nothing!

THE VANITY OF MAN

What a rebuke to the greedy, demanding, preening pride of arrogant man! God says that even the best — the most brilliant, the smartest, the most intelligent, the richest, and the most powerful — are looked at as *"altogether vanity."* Consequently, only that which is done for Christ has any significance.

Man is in this condition because of the Fall. In the Garden of Eden, he fell from a position of total God-consciousness down to the far, far lower level of total self-consciousness. That's the reason for the preening pride and arrogant ostentatiousness of man.

To the few who have good looks, that is soon gone and corrupted because of age. To the few who are rich, they find that riches do not bring satisfaction or true happiness.

Outside of Christ, man cannot really find any reason for being, any purpose in life, or any true reality! Outside of Christ, everything (and I mean everything!) can be constituted, in one way or another, as a *"lie."* Truly, *"man at his best state is altogether vanity."*

(6) "SURELY EVERY MAN WALKS IN A VAIN SHOW: SURELY THEY ARE DISQUIETED IN VAIN: HE HEAPS UP RICHES, AND KNOWS NOT WHO SHALL GATHER THEM."

Outside of Christ, *"every man"* walks in vanity; it is the blight of the human race. It is done so because of pride, which caters to *"self"* and *"the flesh."*

The statement, *"And knows not who shall gather them,"* means that every man's life outside of Christ is a waste. They live, they die, and serve no purpose other than a negative purpose.

(7) "AND NOW, LORD, WHAT WAIT I FOR? MY HOPE IS IN YOU."

This Verse poses the question, *"What is my purpose in life?"*

The question is asked and the answer is given, *"My hope is in You."*

(8) "DELIVER ME FROM ALL MY TRANSGRESSIONS: MAKE ME NOT THE

REPROACH OF THE FOOLISH."

Once again, we see into the heart of the Messiah.

THE INTERCESSORY WORK OF CHRIST

The previous Psalm said, *"The wicked spoke mischievous things"* against Him. They said He was possessed by a demon, a glutton and a drunkard, a boon companion of debauched men, a blasphemer of God and a transgressor of the Law. He calls these *"My transgressions,"* that they heaped upon Him. He, in the wonders of His Grace, took upon Himself the very sin which they committed in thus falsely accusing Him, and He confessed it as His Own!

Although He could have confounded them with a fitting *"good"* reply, yet He remained dumb before them. His heart was stirred with sorrow for them, while, at the same time, it felt the biting flame of their cruel words. But though dumb before men, He was eloquent before God.

As Man, He recalled the brevity of human life and its vanity. He reposed in the knowledge that His Life of shame, sorrow, and rejection had been ordained for Him.

There was only one Man Who could bridle His tongue and Who did not sin with His lips. He was the sinless Son of Man. This sinlessness triumphed even while viewing the prosperity of the wicked when suffering their hatred and false, bitter reproaches.

(9) "I WAS DUMB, I OPENED NOT MY MOUTH; BECAUSE YOU DID IT."

The idea of this Verse is that the Lord allowed the detractors to do what they did, even though He most definitely did not approve of it. In fact, He ultimately would punish them greatly. The reason was the transgression that David committed.

The reason the Lord allowed it against His Son, our Saviour, is because of our transgressions. He was our Substitute; therefore, He had to take the persecution, all on our behalf.

THE LESSON EVERY BELIEVE SHOULD LEARN

The Truth here presented is so far-reaching and so all-inclusive that we should not let it slip. We need to know and understand exactly what the Holy Spirit is here saying.

The Lord never condones wrongdoing in any fashion. It constitutes a grievous sin in God's Eyes for one Believer to try to hurt another, and I speak of trying to hurt them personally. But yet, the Lord, at times, allows such, meaning that He could stop it any time He so desired. He allows it, simply because of our own wrongdoing in some fashion.

Even though the people are wrong, whoever they may be, still, we Believers must understand what is happening and not allow our hearts to be lifted up against these people. We must never try to retaliate.

To be sure, such is hard to do, especially when we know and realize that these people are evil, whoever they might be. But the Godly heart will understand the reason and act accordingly. That's what the Holy Spirit is here saying through David and the Son of David.

(10) "REMOVE YOUR STROKE AWAY FROM ME: I AM CONSUMED BY THE BLOW OF YOUR HAND."

David recognizes that it is the Hand of the Lord which has allowed his many enemies the latitude which they are taking against him. However, in no way do the perpetrators of the evil against David, against the Messiah, or against any true Believer know or understand that it is the Lord Who is allowing such. In no way does the Lord's permission abrogate the sinfulness of their evil conduct. They will pay for it — of that, one can be certain!

Their motives are purely selfish. Above all of that, they are guided by Satan himself.

All of this is for the True Believer to know and understand what is happening to him; consequently, the *"stroke"* that was allowed is said to be from the Lord. It is referred to as *"Your stroke."*

Even though the *"blow"* is given by wicked hands propelled by wicked hearts, still, it is concluded to be *"the blow of Your Hand,"* referring to the Lord.

(11) "WHEN YOU WITH REBUKES DO CORRECT MAN FOR INIQUITY, YOU MAKE HIS BEAUTY TO CONSUME AWAY LIKE A MOTH: SURELY EVERY MAN IS VANITY. SELAH."

The idea of this chastisement is for the true Believer to truly see himself. As such, he is quickly made to realize that all the things he thought were good, even beautiful, are *"consumed away like a moth"* before his very eyes.

The Lord is showing believing man that the reason for his blessing is not at all in his *"beauty,"* which is but *"vanity,"* but is all of the Lord. At least part of the reason for man's failure, which would apply to David and to all of us, is pride.

In chastisement, the Lord strips away from us these things (which lifted us up) that men praised. The Lord lets us quickly know that these things are but *"vanity."* Our trouble is that we very seldom come to this place of proper recognition without chastisement.

(12) "HEAR MY PRAYER, O LORD, AND GIVE EAR UNTO MY CRY; HOLD NOT YOUR PEACE AT MY TEARS: FOR I AM A STRANGER WITH YOU, AND A SOJOURNER, AS ALL MY FATHERS WERE."

This Verse goes ever deeper into the Intercession of Christ.

THE PLEA OF THE MESSIAH

The plea the Messiah makes is the plea that we must make. These same words we often cry to the Father have already been laid at His Feet by His Only Son, Who stands in our place.

We, as Children of God, are *"strangers"* and *"sojourners"* in this life's journey, just as were our *"fathers"* (Abraham, Isaac, Jacob, Moses, Joshua, David, Paul, Peter, John, and all who have served His Great Name). Because we are strangers to this world's system, we are misunderstood, rejected, persecuted, and criticized. This brings *"tears."* We then plead with Him to *"give ear unto my cry."*

(13) "O SPARE ME, THAT I MAY RECOVER STRENGTH, BEFORE I GO HENCE, AND BE NO MORE."

As David pleaded for *"strength,"* likewise the Son of David pleads to the Father for strength for Himself, which, in reality, is for us. Without that *"strength,"* we could not make it.

For us to know *"the measure of our days,"* we must have this *"strength"*!

NOTES

PSALM 40

A Psalm of David:
Praise for Answered Prayer

(1) "I WAITED PATIENTLY FOR THE LORD; AND HE INCLINED UNTO ME, AND HEARD MY CRY."

The superscription is: *"To the Chief Musician, a Psalm of David."*

THE THREEFOLD MINISTRY OF CHRIST

The Tenth Chapter of Hebrews is based upon this Psalm.

1. Jesus Christ is our Redeemer: As our Redeemer, He atoned not only for sin in particular, but for sins in general, having loaded them upon Himself and having confessed them as His Own.

2. Jesus Christ is our Great High Priest: He burdens Himself with our sorrows, encourages us to follow Him in His Life of absolute confidence in God, teaching us to believe in Promises which never fail, and furnishes us with perfect forms of confession, prayer, and praise.

3. Jesus Christ is our Commander: As such, He stands as our Mediator to deliver us from the powers of darkness.

PATIENCE

The word *"patiently"* directs our attention to the thought that God, at times, does not answer immediately; however, the latter portion of the Verse encourages us that ultimately He will answer and *"hear my cry."*

We are enjoined here to do two things. First of all, we are to cry to the Lord and state our needs, doing so with faith. Second, we are to exercise patience with respect to His Answer.

His Answer, according to our petition, involves many things. It takes the Lord no time at all to do anything, but sometimes it does take time to get us ready to receive that for which we are asking. So we must use patience.

(2) "HE BROUGHT ME UP ALSO OUT OF AN HORRIBLE PIT, OUT OF THE MIRY CLAY, AND SET MY FEET UPON A ROCK, AND ESTABLISHED MY GOINGS."

First, the words here are figurative of the

state of sin and death out of which God Alone can save.

Second, *"the miry clay"* refers to man's hatred of the Messiah and the suction of sin which is ever downward. Sin will not, and cannot, remain static. It takes the person ever downward, and there is absolutely no end to the downward spiral until the person is completely destroyed.

The *"horrible pit"* refers to where the *"miry clay"* leads, out of which man cannot extricate himself.

THE MANNER OF DELIVERANCE

It is the Lord Alone Who can deliver from sin. He does so strictly by the virtue of the Cross and what was there accomplished.

It was at the Cross that all sin was atoned and all victory was won.

The very Name of Jesus means *"Saviour."* He also is Saviour by virtue of the Cross, and by virtue of the Cross alone.

His Virgin Birth was absolutely necessary; however, there was no Salvation in that tremendous Miracle of God. His Perfect Life was an absolute necessity, but there was no saving Grace in that either. His Healings and Miracles fall into the same category of necessity, but they contain no Salvation. It is the Cross alone which addressed sin, took away sin, and made it possible for man to be delivered out of this *"horrible pit."*

This is the reason it is so foolish, actually stupid, for the modern Church to embrace humanistic psychology as the answer to man's dilemma. It is impossible to meld humanistic psychology and the Gospel. The very idea of this is an insult to Christ. It states that He didn't accomplish the task at the Cross, and He needs the help of men in order for Deliverance to be effected.

How ridiculous can we be!

UNBELIEF

Pure and simple, the problem is unbelief. Religious leaders simply do not believe that what Jesus did at the Cross answers every sin, every bondage, every transgression, every perversion, and every iota of sin. They may pay lip service to what He did at the Cross; but, if they opt for humanistic psychology or anything else, they actually are screaming, *"Unbelief."*

Jesus Alone can bring us out of the *"horrible pit"* and *"set our feet upon a rock, and establish our goings."*

(3) "AND HE HAS PUT A NEW SONG IN MY MOUTH, EVEN PRAISE UNTO OUR GOD: MANY SHALL SEE IT, AND FEAR, AND SHALL TRUST IN THE LORD."

The *"New Song"* is the Resurrection Song. On that great Resurrection Morn, it will be new in fact but not new in purpose.

CHRIST'S PERFECT OBEDIENCE TO THE WILL OF GOD AS THE SIN-BEARER

The doctrine of this Psalm is Christ's Perfect Obedience to His Father's Will that He be the Sin-bearer of His people, and His Perfect Patience in waiting on God and for God to deliver Him and them out of all afflictions.

The Perfection of His Confidence and Obedience is seen in Him not shirking or shrinking from any trial, however bitter, and in not taking matters out of the Hands of God into His Own Hands — for example, by sending for twelve legions of Angels, or in drinking the stupefying myrrh, or in fearing to face man and preaching to him the Righteousness of God.

He sought no outlet or escape from indignations, sorrows, shame, or wrath. This Psalm points to the reward which crowned this Perfect Obedience.

A NEW SONG

This is the second time that the *"New Song"* is mentioned in the Bible. As with the first time, it has two meanings:

First, it pertains to any person who comes to Christ and makes Him the Saviour and the Lord of his life. When this happens, the Lord puts a *"New Song"* into that person's mouth and heart. It speaks of a completely new way of life, a life that incorporates constant praise to God. The words *"New Song"* refer to absolutely everything being new. It is the *"born again"* experience (Jn. 3:3).

Second, it refers to the coming Kingdom Age, when basically the entirety of the world will sing this *"New Song."* Instead of the world's *"Top 40"* proclaiming praise to evil, there will be, over the entirety of the world, *"praise unto our God."*

Truly, *"many shall see it, and fear, and shall trust in the LORD."*

(4) "BLESSED IS THAT MAN WHO MAKES THE LORD HIS TRUST, AND RESPECTS NOT THE PROUD, NOR SUCH AS TURN ASIDE TO LIES."

As we have stated, *"Trust in the LORD"* is the theme of the entirety of the Psalms.

THE PROUD

The *"proud"* of this Verse are the self-righteous, and those who *"turn aside to lies"* are the idolaters. Their misery contrasts with the happiness and joy of Believers.

This is the age when humanistic psychology has become the mainstay of the modern Church. Psychology is the product of *"the proud."* Such refuses to recognize the total depravity of man and thrusts forth psychology as the answer. God calls it *"lies."* He has promised to *"bless the man who makes the LORD his trust."*

Behavioral science, so-called, the offshoot of flawed, wicked thinking, is far more than psychoanalysis. It is man's new religion that involves itself in every single aspect of modern life. It totally contradicts the Bible. Regrettably and sadly, virtually all of the modern Church has opted for this false way. Behavioral science and atheism go hand in hand. We quickly add that behavioral science was the mainstay of Communism, a failed philosophy.

All of man's failed efforts to attempt to right the wrongs of failed humanity are the result of this lie. To name a few, they include: evolution, affirmative action, self-esteem, multicultural relationships, and homosexuality and lesbianism. All of this spawns its own morality, integrity, forgiveness, salvation, and love; all are man-made, and all are God-rejected.

The modern Church has virtually abandoned the Word of God as the remedy for all the ills of man in favor of humanistic behavioral science, which, in reality, is no science at all.

Even though the morality, integrity, forgiveness, and love, so-called, of the modern Church are somewhat different from that of the world, still they are man-devised, which means they are God-rejected. Whether religious or secular, all of this comes out of a prideful heart. As stated, God calls it *"lies."*

(5) "MANY, O LORD MY GOD, ARE YOUR WONDERFUL WORKS WHICH YOU HAVE DONE, AND YOUR THOUGHTS WHICH ARE TO USWARD: THEY CANNOT BE RECKONED UP IN ORDER UNTO YOU: IF I WOULD DECLARE AND SPEAK OF THEM, THEY ARE MORE THAN CAN BE NUMBERED."

A great truth is given in this Verse.

THE PROMISES OF GOD ARE MORE THAN ENOUGH

It is strange that the modern Church declares that modern man faces problems which are not addressed in the Bible. And yet, the Psalmist says that *"the wonderful works"* of God are so many, that *"His thoughts"* (counsel and cure for our plight) are so numerous, addressing themselves to far more than we ever could need, or that mere mortals could ever begin to enumerate, that only the Messiah can both declare them and speak of them. Worldly man is stupid; religious man is doubly stupid!

THE CROSS OF CHRIST

No matter what problem, sin, transgression, iniquity, or perversion that might plague man, Jesus answered it in totality at the Cross. The Lord addressed every single thing at the Cross that was lost in the Fall. Nothing was left undone; nothing was left unattended! Sin in all of its horror was addressed in totality, and it was atoned for in every respect (Col. 2:14-15).

The amazing thing is that man only has to do one thing in order to receive all the benefits of the Cross, and that is simply to *"believe"* (Rom. 5:1). When he believes properly, the Holy Spirit, Who has the Power, will then perform whatever is needed. That's the reason the Holy Spirit through the Prophet said, *"Not by might* (human might), *nor by power* (human power), *but by My Spirit, saith the LORD of Hosts"* (Zech. 4:6).

(6) "SACRIFICE AND OFFERING YOU DID NOT DESIRE; MY EARS HAVE YOU OPENED: BURNT OFFERING AND SIN

OFFERING HAVE YOU NOT REQUIRED."

Here we are given a glimpse into Old Testament typology.

THE SACRIFICIAL SYSTEM OF OLD

The Divine displeasure with Sacrifice and Offering is defined in the Tenth Chapter of Hebrews as displeasure with them as types and symbols. Even though they were designed by God, and minute instruction given as to how these Sacrifices and Offerings were to be carried out, still, they only were a stopgap measure. They could not take away sins.

Paul plainly said, *"For it is not possible that the blood of bulls and of goats should take away sins"* (Heb. 10:4).

The Sacrifices served as a substitute until the Redeemer would come, but, since their effectiveness lay in animal blood, they were woefully insufficient.

However, what the Holy Spirit here says through David does not conflict with God's infinite delight in the one great Sacrifice of Calvary. On the contrary, the contrast heightens that delight.

There were five great Offerings in the Levitical economy. They were: *"The Whole Burnt Offering," "The Meal Offering," "The Sin Offering," "The Trespass Offering,"* and *"The Peace Offering."* They represent five aspects of Christ's one great Offering of Himself, which is what this Verse and this Psalm intend.

(7) "THEN SAID I, LO, I COME: IN THE VOLUME OF THE BOOK IT IS WRITTEN OF ME."

The words, *"Lo, I come,"* signal His Incarnation; the word *"Book"* is the Bible. Concerning Him, it was *"engraved"* in that *"Book"* that He was to be born as a Man and suffer as a Sacrifice. That was the Will of God!

THE VOLUME OF THE BOOK

The entirety of the Word of God points to Christ and what He would do (and did do) at the Cross. That is the story of the Bible. John the Beloved wrote:

"In the beginning was the Word, and the Word was with God, and the Word was God" (Jn. 1:1).

This again tells us that the entirety of the Word of God points exclusively to the Lord Jesus Christ. This First Chapter of the Gospel according to John also tells us that this *"Word was made flesh and dwelt among us"* (Jn. 1:14). John 1:29 also tells us why He became flesh; it was to go to the Cross, and for that reason alone.

In Isaiah, it is said of Him, *"Therefore have I set My face like a flint, and I know that I shall not be ashamed"* (Isa. 50:7). This means that the Cross was ever His destination!

So, the entirety of the story of the Bible is the Story of Jesus Christ and the price He paid at the Cross in order to redeem fallen humanity. Consequently, all preaching must ever make the Cross the emphasis, and the Cross alone! If that is not the emphasis (I Cor. 1:17), then whatever is being preached is not the Gospel of Jesus Christ, but something else entirely.

(8) "I DELIGHT TO DO YOUR WILL, O MY GOD: YEA, YOUR LAW IS WITHIN MY HEART."

The Incarnation and Atonement were necessary, as predicted of Him and prescribed to Him in the Scriptures. The statement is made that He delighted to obey these prescriptions, for they were not only in the Book, but also in His Heart.

In his letter to the Philippians, Paul addressed this; I quote from THE EXPOSITOR'S STUDY BIBLE:

"Who, being in the form of God (refers to Deity, which Christ always was), *thought it not robbery to be equal with God* (equality with God refers here to our Lord's co-participation with the other members of the Trinity in the expression of the Divine Essence)*:*

"But made Himself of no reputation (instead of asserting His rights to the expression of the Essence of Deity, our Lord waived His rights to that expression), *and took upon Him the form of a servant* (a bondslave), *and was made in the likeness of men* (presents the Lord entering into a new state of Being when He became Man; but His becoming Man did not exclude His position of Deity; while in becoming Man, He laid aside the *'expression'* of Deity, He never lost *'possession'* of Deity)*:*

"And being found in fashion as a man (denotes Christ in men's eyes), *He humbled Himself* (He was brought low, but willingly),

and became obedient unto death (does not mean He became obedient to death; He was always the Master of Death; rather, He subjected Himself to death); *even the death of the Cross.* (This presents the character of His Death as one of disgrace and degradation, which was necessary for men to be redeemed. This type of death alone would pay the terrible sin debt, and do so in totality)" (Phil. 2:6-8).

(9) "I HAVE PREACHED RIGHTEOUSNESS IN THE GREAT CONGREGATION: LO, I HAVE NOT REFRAINED MY LIPS, O LORD, YOU KNOW.

(10) "I HAVE NOT HID YOUR RIGHTEOUSNESS WITHIN MY HEART; I HAVE DECLARED YOUR FAITHFULNESS AND YOUR SALVATION: I HAVE NOT CONCEALED YOUR LOVINGKINDNESS AND YOUR TRUTH FROM THE GREAT CONGREGATION."

Verses 9 and 10 declare how faithfully our Lord, while on Earth, revealed God's Righteousness, Faithfulness, Salvation, Lovingkindness, and Truth to man. The Seventeenth Chapter of the Gospel of John records the fulfillment of this prediction. No other man can even remotely say this as did the Messiah!

A PREACHER OF RIGHTEOUSNESS

The God-called Preacher is to not only preach the Truth, but he also is to point out lies (Vs. 4).

The moment one begins to preach the Cross, which is the Message which must be preached, and which is where the emphasis must ever be, all who are not preaching the Cross will be unhappy with the Message and with the Messenger. I remind the Reader that the spirit of self-righteousness (for that's what it was) is what caused Cain to kill his brother Abel. It also is what caused the Pharisees and Sadducees to murder Christ! They did not subscribe to the Message of the Cross.

Why didn't they?

It's an easy question to answer; but yet, at the same time, it's a very difficult question to answer.

The Message of the Cross is so simple that even a child can properly understand it. For one to gather its benefits, all it requires is to have faith in Christ and what Christ did at the Cross. It's just that simple! (Rom. 5:1; 6:1-14).

Wouldn't it seem that this is exactly what true Believers should want and desire! It might seem that way, but it's not that way!

First, total Faith in Christ and the Cross completely abrogates the human effort in every capacity. Man doesn't like that, and religious man likes that least of all.

Religious man may proclaim to the unredeemed that one cannot earn or merit one's Salvation, but then he will turn right around and try to merit his own Sanctification. In other words, he does the very thing he tells the unredeemed one cannot do.

It's the problem of religious man, who is now saved and possibly even baptized with the Holy Spirit, not wanting to believe that he, as far as receiving from God, is still in the same place as the unredeemed. There is nothing the unredeemed can do to merit God's favor, and there is also nothing the redeemed can to, which means that if we are to receive from the Lord, it must be strictly by faith (Rom. 5:1; 6:1-14).

If Christ and the Cross are faithfully embraced, then every other doctrine, every other nuance, every other proposed manner of victory, and every other religious scheme must go! That is easier said than done.

FALSE DOCTRINE

When a person embraces false doctrine, they embrace it with all of their personality, their faith, and their reputation. Then it becomes very difficult for them to admit they have been wrong. Some few are able to do such, but most aren't!

It also should come as no surprise that there is big money, at times, in false doctrine. There isn't any big money in the Cross.

Preachers propose that they have the only solution, which amounts to their own schemes and fads which they constantly promote. A gullible Christian public embraces the lie, and they pay a lot of money to do so.

Considering that the love of money is the root of all evil, we then begin to see the hold that false doctrine has on most.

For any Preacher or layman to publicly stand and say, *"What I have been believing has been wrong,"* is a very difficult thing to do, which is why most won't do it!

Here in Verse 10, David says, *"I have not hid Your Righteousness within my heart."* There are untold thousands of Preachers presently who know in their hearts that what they are doing is wrong, but they hide it there and will not tell anyone. What they preach is not the Truth, even though it may contain some things which are true.

(11) "WITHHOLD NOT THOU YOUR TENDER MERCIES FROM ME, O LORD: LET YOUR LOVINGKINDNESS AND YOUR TRUTH CONTINUALLY PRESERVE ME."

Sadly, man would show the Messiah no *"mercies"* or *"lovingkindness."* The only thing that preserved Him was *"Your Truth."*

The *"tender mercies"* and the *"lovingkindness"* of the Lord are available to anyone who will humble himself before God. Even though mankind in general showed our Lord no mercy or kindness during His First Advent, He most definitely will show such to all who will trust Him.

(12) "FOR INNUMERABLE EVILS HAVE COMPASSED ME ABOUT: MY INIQUITIES HAVE TAKEN HOLD UPON ME, SO THAT I AM NOT ABLE TO LOOK UP; THEY ARE MORE THAN THE HAIRS OF MY HEAD: THEREFORE MY HEART FAILS ME."

Calamities and afflictions in the sense of *"evils"* and *"iniquities"* result from sin. But these sorrows and troubles did not result from the Messiah's sins, for He had none, but rather from the sins of those whom He came to save.

These griefs so bent Him down that He was not able to look up, and they enfeebled His physical powers so that His heart fainted. He said, *"My soul is exceeding sorrowful, even unto death."* Never was there sorrow in this world comparable to His! (Mk. 14:34).

(13) "BE PLEASED, O LORD, TO DELIVER ME: O LORD, MAKE HASTE TO HELP ME."

Once again, we hear the heart's cry of the Messiah as He prayed to the Father in Heaven.

JESUS WAS FORSAKEN BY ALL EXCEPT HIS FATHER

Man gave Him no help. Even His Own Disciples would not associate themselves with His Suffering or His dying. His Own Kindred forsook Him.

If these Passages do not proclaim the depravity of man, nothing does.

Here is the truth:

The holier and the more righteous the individual, the more is he hated. The One Who was pure Holiness and Righteousness was hated most of all. There was only One Who could deliver Him, only One Who would help Him — His Father in Heaven. No wonder the Holy Spirit through Paul wrote, *"While we were yet sinners, Christ died for us"* (Rom. 5:8).

(14) "LET THEM BE ASHAMED AND CONFOUNDED TOGETHER WHO SEEK AFTER MY SOUL TO DESTROY IT; LET THEM BE DRIVEN BACKWARD AND PUT TO SHAME WHO WISH ME EVIL."

A great lesson is taught in this Verse.

JESUS CHRIST, THE ONLY GOOD MAN WHO EVER LIVED

The religious men of Jesus' day desired that the only truly good Man Who ever lived lose His soul. Let this ever be a lesson to mankind. The true Child of God must ever be wary of the world, and doubly wary of organized religion. It is not of God, and never has been. It seeks to *"destroy"* the soul instead of saving it.

His prayer has been answered. From the day they said, *"His Blood be on us and on our children"* (Mat. 27:25), they have been *"driven backward."* For nearly 2,000, years Israel wandered without a nation and without a home until 1948. Their *"shame"* has known no bounds. The same will come to all who neglect this Great Salvation and its Bearer, the Lord Jesus Christ.

(15) "LET THEM BE DESOLATE FOR A REWARD OF THEIR SHAME WHO SAY UNTO ME, AHA, AHA."

Sinlessness, when compared with the wickedness that rejected the teaching of Verse 10 and which hung the Teacher upon the Tree, justly prays the prayer of Verses 14 and 15. These Verses are a prediction foretelling the doom of the haters of the Messiah, just as Verse 16 predicts the Salvation and felicity of those who love Him.

(16) "LET ALL THOSE WHO SEEK YOU

REJOICE AND BE GLAD IN YOU: LET SUCH AS LOVE YOUR SALVATION SAY CONTINUALLY, THE LORD BE MAGNIFIED."

The contrast here is outstanding! Those who reject Him will be *"driven backward."* Those who seek Him and accept Him will *"rejoice and be glad."*

(17) "BUT I AM POOR AND NEEDY; YET THE LORD THINKS UPON ME: YOU ARE MY HELP AND MY DELIVERER; MAKE NO TARRYING, O MY GOD."

Some are poor and some are needy, but only One, in the fullest sense, was *"poor and needy"* at the same time. The sense of this Verse is that even though the Lord of Glory has taken upon Himself the frailty of man (Immanuel — God with us), still, *"The LORD thinks upon Me."*

He Who was rich became poor for our sakes. He Who had abundance became needy. The mind of man, even while perusing the explanation, will never in his wildest imaginations understand the Sacrifice of the Incarnation. It is beyond our comprehension. It speaks of a goodness and a glory that are beyond fallen or redeemed man.

The words, *"Make no tarrying, O My God,"* refer to the speedy conclusion of the Sacrifice that must be offered, not because of the pain of the *"poor and needy,"* but rather because of the hurried necessity of man.

PSALM 41

A Psalm of David:
A Prayer for Deliverance

(1) "BLESSED IS HE WHO CONSIDERS THE POOR: THE LORD WILL DELIVER HIM IN TIME OF TROUBLE."

This is a Psalm of David and is also a *"Messianic Psalm."* In other words, it portrays the coming Messiah.

PROPHETIC

This Psalm concludes the First Book of Psalms, which is called the Genesis Book. Genesis opens with the First Adam in blessing and closes with his children in affliction; this First Book of Psalms opens with the Second Man in Blessing and closes with His people in affliction.

The Pharaoh of Israel's first affliction (the Book of Exodus) prefigures the Antichrist of Israel's future and last affliction.

This Psalm is prophetic; it has a general application, but it mainly concerns the future sufferings of Israel under the Antichrist — sufferings permitted by God in just punishment for their sins.

Actually, the word *"poor"* in this First Verse actually means *"sick and faint,"* which actually refers to Israel in the coming time of the Great Tribulation. This Psalm was written about 3,000 years ago; now the Great Tribulation is even at the door.

(2) "THE LORD WILL PRESERVE HIM, AND KEEP HIM ALIVE; AND HE SHALL BE BLESSED UPON THE EARTH: AND YOU WILL NOT DELIVER HIM UNTO THE WILL OF HIS ENEMIES."

This Verse has a triple meaning:

1. It speaks of the Lord preserving David when Absalom sought to overthrow him and even kill him.

2. It speaks of Christ in His earthly Ministry, Whom the religious leaders desired to kill even before the Crucifixion.

3. It speaks of Israel being weak and faint during the Great Tribulation.

(3) "THE LORD WILL STRENGTHEN HIM UPON THE BED OF LANGUISHING: YOU WILL MAKE ALL HIS BED IN HIS SICKNESS."

God's future loving sympathy to the fainting elect of Israel is here contrasted with man's duplicity and heartlessness (Vss. 5-8). He promises blessing to anyone who concerns himself with these sick ones.

AMERICA AND ISRAEL

America's fortunes are tied to her treatment of the tiny State of Israel. If America turns her back on Israel, it is certain that our crime problems, drug problems, and economic problems steadily will grow worse. If America blesses Israel, it is certain that somehow these problems will be ameliorated.

Factually, the United States is about the only country in the world which stands with Israel. In truth, we have tried to walk a fine line between the Arab world and the Israelis. For instance, some years ago, we were giving four billion dollars ($4,000,000,000) a year in aid to Israel and four billion dollars a year in aid to Egypt. Whether or not that still holds at the present moment, I am not sure; however, this is an example of that of which I speak.

The Arab world occupies all of the Middle East with the exception of the tiny State of Israel. Even with that tiny State, the West Bank and the Gaza Strip are in Arab hands. Moreover, the land area of the State of Israel equals approximately only one-tenth of one percent (0.1%) of the land area of the entirety of the land area of the Middle East. In other words, the Arabs occupy 99.9 percent of the Middle East. But they want that last 0.1 percent as well! The have invaded Israel several times in the past in an attempt to drive Israel into the sea.

Despite the invasions by the Arabs, Israel has continued to allow the Palestinians (so-called) to remain in Israel; however, if the Arabs had won any one of those invasions, there would not be a single Israeli left alive, at least if they had their way.

The Arabs now are demanding that East Jerusalem be given to them, and that it be established as the Capital of Palestine.

PALESTINIANS?

The name *"Palestinians"* given to the Arabs occupying Israel is a misnomer. There is no such thing as a Palestinian. The name is originally derived from the Philistines, who occupied the Gaza Strip some 3,000 years ago. The Arabs in Israel at the moment are Egyptians, Iraqis, Syrians, Jordanians, etc.

According to the Bible, the entirety of the land area of the State of Israel belongs to Israel. It does not belong to the Arabs. There is plenty of room in Arab countries for those who now occupy Israel; however, the Arabs in the Middle East will not allow the Arabs now occupying part of Israel to resettle in their respective countries. They want to keep them in the State of Israel so they can announce to the world how badly these people are being treated.

THE ANTICHRIST AND ISRAEL

Regrettably, the problems in the Middle East are not going to be solved in the near future. They will be solved, at least for a short period of time, by the Antichrist, when he makes his debut. He will somewhat solve these problems, even allowing Israel to rebuild her Temple on the spot where the Dome of the Rock now sits, so Israel will think that surely he is the Messiah. They will even announce this to the entire world.

This is what Jesus was talking about when He said, *"I am come in My Father's Name, and you receive Me not: if another shall come in his own name, him you will receive"* (Jn. 5:43).

He was speaking of the Antichrist. However, even though Israel will fare quite well during the first half of the Great Tribulation, at the midpoint of that coming time of tragedy, the Antichrist will show his true colors and attack Israel; but for the intervention of the Lord, he would completely destroy her (Dan. 9:27).

At any rate, for the last three and a half years of the Great Tribulation, Israel will suffer as never before. The Prophet Jeremiah referred to this period as *"The Time of Jacob's Trouble"* (Jer. 30:7). Once again, were it not for the intervention of the Lord, these ancient people would be totally and completely annihilated. I speak of the Battle of Armageddon.

Facing what looks like certain annihilation, Israel will begin to cry to the Lord as she has not prayed in many, many years. The Lord will hear and answer that prayer, and the result will be the Second Coming of the Lord Jesus Christ, the most cataclysmic event the world has ever known (Rev., Chpt. 19).

These times of which I speak are very shortly to come to pass. The Church is coming down to the close of its Dispensation. Those who truly know the Lord are soon to be raptured away (I Thess. 4:13-18). At the beginning of the Kingdom Age, Israel will accept Christ not only as her Saviour, but also as her Lord, and she will then be completely and totally restored to her place and position of prominence, exactly as the Prophets predicted so long ago (Acts 1:6-7).

(4) "I SAID, LORD, BE MERCIFUL UNTO ME: HEAL MY SOUL; FOR I HAVE SINNED AGAINST YOU."

As David prays this prayer, he knows that his sins are the reason that God is permitting the terrible difficulties associated with the rebellion of his son Absalom. Likewise, God will permit judgment against Israel by the Antichrist due to Israel's terrible denial of her own Son and Saviour, the Lord Jesus Christ. As the punishment that David receives is just, likewise the punishment that Israel will receive in the Great Tribulation will also be just.

(5) "MY ENEMIES SPEAK EVIL OF ME, WHEN SHALL HE DIE, AND HIS NAME PERISH?"

In this Passage, we see both the Grace of God and the evil heart of man.

THE ENEMIES OF GOD

The Messiah defines the conduct of Israel's enemies as hatred against Himself, which indeed was in its fullness of malignity. Associating them with Himself, Christ prays that God will raise them up from their couch of affliction so that He could execute a just judgment upon their oppressors as He did upon Pharaoh and the Egyptians.

Of course, David first of all prayed this prayer. He did so because his enemies spoke evil of him and desired his death. These enemies, sadly and regrettably, included his son Absalom, his most trusted advisor Ahithophel, and multitudes of others in Israel.

Ironically, Israel sought David's death and refused to forgive him for the sin he had committed with Bathsheba, seemingly never stopping to think that all of their many blessings were due to the Hand of God on David's life.

Which was worse — the sin that David committed, or the sin that the people now committed? The answer is obvious. Their sin was far worse simply because they deigned to lay their hands on God's anointed.

Likewise, Israel spoke such of Christ, desiring His Death and for His Name to perish. They have fought that Name for nearly 2,000 years. That, however, will be the very Name which will come to their rescue in the Battle of Armageddon.

Looking again at David, it's difficult to imagine how the hearts of individuals could be so hard, so calloused, and so evil that they would want to murder David. They did not lack the will, only the way. Such represents the spirit of Cain.

The account in given in the Fourth Chapter of Genesis. Cain was not content to merely disagree with Abel. He had to kill him. It has been the same from then until now. Those who oppose the Cross are not willing to merely disagree. They do everything within their power to stop the voice of the one who is preaching the Cross. They will go to any lengths to do so, the same as did the detractors of David. The spirit of that malignity has not changed, and it cannot change.

The only thing that keeps this Ministry (Jimmy Swaggart Ministries) preaching the Gospel is the law of the land, which, of course, the Lord uses. Were that law not there, the haters of the Cross (and they are many!) would do the same as Cain did to Abel. As stated, that spirit hasn't changed. It simply cannot change.

(6) "AND IF HE COME TO SEE ME, HE SPEAKS VANITY: HIS HEART GATHERS INIQUITY TO ITSELF; WHEN HE GOES ABROAD, HE TELLS IT."

This Passage has a triple meaning:

1. It speaks of David and those who would attempt to destroy him.

2. It speaks of Israel and their terrible opposition to their Messiah, the Lord Jesus Christ.

3. It speaks of the world, and even more so of the apostate Church, which hates both Christ and His people. They desire the destruction of both. They treat them with falsehood, malice, and slander. They speak vanity, that is, they make professions of sympathy, but their hearts are full of malicious falsehoods. They then go forth to publish them. Judas was the embodiment of all such treachery.

(7) "ALL WHO HATE ME WHISPER TOGETHER AGAINST ME: AGAINST ME DO THEY DEVISE MY HURT."

There is a double meaning in this Verse.

AHITHOPHEL AND JUDAS

There is no doubt that these Verses were doubly fulfilled in both David and Christ. Every statement could be understood of both men.

Ahithophel, David's trusted adviser, led the rebellion against David. Judas led such against Christ. Once again, both Ahithophel and Judas enjoyed tremendous honor and blessings under David and Christ, respectively; however, they were not thankful for this. Conditions are always brought about that will show what the heart of man really is.

Why did Ahithophel hate David? Why did Judas hate Christ?

David had never done anything negative to Ahithophel and the others who hated him; and, above all, Christ never did anything negative to Judas or anyone else.

Well, there is a reason!

THE REASON FOR HATRED

Bathsheba was Ahithophel's granddaughter. No doubt, he became incensed as what David did, and David's sin was definitely most awful. However, it was not Ahithophel's place to come against David or to punish him. That prerogative belonged entirely to God. Regrettably, Ahithophel couldn't see this. When his plans went wrong, he committed suicide (II Sam. 17:23).

The problem of Judas was that he rebelled against the Cross.

The great Sixth Chapter of John's Gospel proclaims Christ presenting Himself as the Bread of Life and declaring that all must *"eat His flesh and drink His blood"* (Jn. 6:35, 51, 53). He was speaking of the Cross, the means by which He would die as a Sacrifice. He was saying that every person, that is if they were to have Eternal Life, must accept what He would do at the Cross in totality. Judas had other ideas in mind and did not want to hear that, so he rebelled against the Sacrifice of Christ, and lost his soul in the process (Jn. 6:67-71).

(8) "AN EVIL DISEASE, SAY THEY, CLEAVES FAST UNTO HIM: AND NOW THAT HE LIES HE SHALL RISE UP NO MORE."

Why did Israel wish the worst upon David, when they should have wished the best for him?

THE EVIL HEARTS OF MEN

Multiple tens of thousands in Israel led by Ahithophel and Absalom claimed that David had an evil disease. They attributed all types of malignity to him. They claimed that it would be impossible for David to overcome it, that it was God Who had done this to him because of his great sin.

Then they said, *"He is finished as King of Israel. He shall rise up no more."* How could they come to these conclusions?

These men were full of self-will; their hearts did not suddenly change; they had always been this way. Before they lacked opportunity; now, with each one having his own diabolical ambition, they feel that David can be overthrown and they can rise to even greater glory. God was not in their thoughts, for He is never a party to such.

They painted David in the blackest of terms to the whole of Israel because their own hearts were black. Little did they realize that David would rise again. God gave him many more Psalms which would forever be a great blessing to humanity. As well, He gave him the total plans for the coming Temple. He also outlined to David in exact detail how Israel was to be governed.

It is bad when religious leaders do not recognize God when they see Him, when they find themselves fighting against God. No matter how such may look at the beginning, this is a battle they cannot hope to win!

(9) "YEA, MY OWN FAMILIAR FRIEND, IN WHOM I TRUSTED, WHICH DID EAT OF MY BREAD, HAS LIFTED UP HIS HEEL AGAINST ME."

This speaks of Ahithophel and his betrayal of David. In an even greater sense, it speaks of Judas and shows to what extent he was a familiar friend of Christ. He was a genuine trusted Disciple at one time, but he fell by transgression (Acts 1:25).

One must never condone sin, which should be manifestly obvious. But still, the Lord will never tolerate it when a person tries to hurt one who is His anointed, even as was David. As stated, Ahithophel committed suicide, and so did Judas!

This uprising against David was a type of the manner in which Israel would rise up against Christ. The Lord would not allow Israel to kill David, but He did allow the Israel of Christ's day to kill their Messiah. While all types break down eventually, still, this which happened to David is a perfect type of that which would happen to Christ. The perpetrators, however, did not realize the roles they were playing.

(10) "BUT YOU, O LORD, BE MERCIFUL UNTO ME, AND RAISE ME UP, THAT I MAY REQUITE THEM."

This is the prayer of David that he will be raised up from the deep humiliation and seeming defeat experienced as he was betrayed by Ahithophel and as he fled from Absalom (II Sam. 15:31). As we stated, the Lord did *"raise him up"* and placed him back on his throne. But in an even greater sense, this speaks of the Great Resurrection of the Lord Jesus Christ, when, on the third day, He came out of the tomb.

(11) "BY THIS I KNOW THAT YOU FAVOR ME, BECAUSE MY ENEMY DOES NOT TRIUMPH OVER ME."

Ahithophel, along with treacherous Absalom, did not triumph over David; likewise, Judas and the evil Elders of Israel did not triumph over Christ. Even more so, the *"enemy"* death did not triumph over our Lord. At the Cross, Christ broke the back of sin and death, and He did it once and for all.

(12) "AND AS FOR ME, YOU UPHOLD ME IN MY INTEGRITY, AND SET ME BEFORE YOUR FACE FOREVER."

A great truth is here presented:

INTEGRITY

This Passage could not be understood at all by religious man. How could David speak of his *"integrity,"* especially after his terrible sin with Bathsheba?

He could do so because the *"integrity"* of which he spoke was not man's integrity, but God's. The Lord set David before *"His Face forever"* because David's sin had been forgiven forever. Regrettably, an apostate Church devises its own morality, integrity, and forgiveness; however, it is a man-made morality, integrity, and forgiveness, as such, it can never be accepted by God. Sadly, the integrity that God Alone can give will never be accepted by an apostate Church.

In this Passage, Christ is asserting that because of His sinlessness (integrity), He will be seated upon the Throne of Glory forever. Now that His sinlessness has become our sinlessness, which is God's true *"integrity,"* obtained by our trusting Christ and what

NOTES

Christ has done for us at the Cross, we are seated together with Christ in the Heavenlies (Eph. 2:6) — *"before Your Face."*

(13) "BLESSED BE THE LORD GOD OF ISRAEL FROM EVERLASTING, AND TO EVERLASTING. AMEN, AND AMEN."

Man-made *"integrity"* changes almost daily, as is evidenced in Absalom and Ahithophel. God's *"integrity"* is *"from everlasting, and to everlasting."* All who rise up against the Lord and His Anointed ultimately will be destroyed. All who place their hands in the nail-scarred Hands will live *"from everlasting, and to everlasting."*

This Psalm closes the Genesis Book of the five Books of the Psalms. It closes with a fitting *"Amen, and Amen,"* which signifies that the Word of God is the final authority on everything!

BOOK TWO
(The Exodus Book)
(*Psalms 42-72*)

PSALM 42

Probably Written by David:
An Intense Longing for God

(1) "AS THE HART PANTS AFTER THE WATER BROOKS, SO PANTS MY SOUL AFTER YOU, O GOD.

(2) "MY SOUL THIRSTS FOR GOD, FOR THE LIVING GOD: WHEN SHALL I COME AND APPEAR BEFORE GOD?"

This is the First Psalm of the Exodus Book. As the Book of Exodus opened with an oppressed people longing for deliverance, likewise, this Psalm opens with David being oppressed and longing for deliverance.

A THIRST AFTER GOD

This is the first of some ten Psalms written for the sons of Korah. It doesn't really say that these sons of Korah wrote the Psalms, but more implies that they sang them. Even though it is not stated, David probably wrote this Psalm and maybe some of the others of Korah, as well.

Korah himself died under the Wrath of God several centuries before the time of David

(Num. 16:31), but his children were spared (Num. 26:11). These special Psalms, therefore, sing of redeeming Grace.

This Forty-second Psalm exhibits the perfection of the faith and the warmth of an affection which makes God everything, when, by His just Judgment, nothing remains but poverty, helplessness, and oppression.

This was probably composed when David was fleeing from Absalom. He was cut off from worship at the Tabernacle in Jerusalem, where the Ark of God resided. At this stage, he likely had no knowledge if he would be restored to the Throne or not. As the Psalm begins, we feel the heart's cry of a man who wants God more than anything else.

The little *"hart"* was actually a deer that enjoyed feeding near streams or brooks. Sometimes he would stay in the water for long periods of time, submerged with only his nose protruding out. When he became thirsty, he literally would *"pant,"* with his tongue hanging out, desiring water.

This is the intensity with which David desired God.

Even though he certainly was able to seek after the Lord irrespective of his location, still, in his present situation, he could not go to Jerusalem to offer up Sacrifice. So he asks the question, *"When shall I come and appear before God?"*

Verses 1 and 2 portray a man who has a close walk with God, a man who knows God deeply.

ISRAEL AND HER MESSIAH

The Psalm also gives us a forepicture of Israel when she falls out of Covenant relationship with Jehovah (Lo-ammi; Hos. 1:9) and will suffer the oppression of the Antichrist. At that time, she will cast herself for deliverance upon God as Elohim.

The words also proclaim the Messiah speaking as He takes His place with the oppressed, as Moses did; fitly voices their cry of anguish and of faith; makes God their sufficing portion in the absence of all prosperity; and expresses a thirst and affection for God and a confidence in Him such as Israel ought to express (Williams).[13]

Thus, in all circumstances, whether in the land or in exile from it, whether as Ammi or Lo-ammi, the Messiah is, and always will be, for Israel and before God what He ought to be, so that God perpetually finds in Immanuel's cry for mercy and pardon and in His songs of faith and praise all that His Nature and Heart demand.

It must ever be said that as the Messiah, He cries for Israel, and as the Redeemer, He cries for us.

(3) "MY TEARS HAVE BEEN MY MEAT DAY AND NIGHT, WHILE THEY CONTINUALLY SAY UNTO ME, WHERE IS YOUR GOD?"

Three things are said in this Verse:

DAVID, THE LORD JESUS CHRIST, AND ISRAEL

1. David cries to God because his enemies taunt him at this especially darkened time in his life by saying, *"Where is your God?"*

2. This refers even more so to the Lord Jesus Christ, Who, when on the Cross, was taunted by the religious leaders of Israel. It caused more pain to His heart than even the nails caused to His body. This Third Verse shows that this taunt was leveled at Him during His Ministry as well as during His final agony.

The Pharisees repeated this mocking question when they demanded of Him a sign from Heaven.

3. This very taunt will be addressed to the unhappy sons of Israel by the Antichrist and his minions in the coming *"time of trouble"* (Joel 2:17; Jer. 30:7).

(4) "WHEN I REMEMBER THESE THINGS, I POUR OUT MY SOUL IN ME: FOR I HAD GONE WITH THE MULTITUDE, I WENT WITH THEM TO THE HOUSE OF GOD, WITH THE VOICE OF JOY AND PRAISE, WITH A MULTITUDE WHO KEPT HOLYDAY."

David, not knowing what would happen to him, whether God would restore him to his throne or not, said, *"I remember."*

REMEMBERING WHAT GOD HAS DONE FOR US

David remembered the countless times he had gone to the *"House of God"* with the multitudes in order to *"praise"* the Lord. Sadly, some of this *"multitude"* who had been with David had now turned against him and desired to take his life and his throne. All people do not go to Church with the *"voice of joy and praise."* Many go for other reasons entirely.

When the Children of Israel were in the wilderness, they remembered the leeks and the garlic of Egypt. When David was in the wilderness, he remembered the things of God. Those who remembered Egypt were lost. Those who remembered God were saved!

(5) "WHY ARE YOU CAST DOWN, O MY SOUL? AND WHY ARE YOU DISQUIETED IN ME? HOPE THOU IN GOD: FOR I SHALL YET PRAISE HIM FOR THE HELP OF HIS COUNTENANCE."

David is actually asking himself this question. He is saying that despite the impossible circumstances, there is no need to be discouraged. He is telling himself, *"Hope thou in God."*

By faith, he says that as his thoughts concerned the Tabernacle in Jerusalem and the offering up of Sacrifices, he would yet do this again.

This should be a beautiful encouragement for every Child of God. There are times when most all of us enter into great trouble. Taking a cue from David, faith in God will bring us out.

(6) "O MY GOD, MY SOUL IS CAST DOWN WITHIN ME: THEREFORE WILL I REMEMBER YOU FROM THE LAND OF JORDAN, AND OF THE HERMONITES, FROM THE HILL MIZAR."

David is saying that even though it's a long way from Jerusalem where God resides between the Mercy Seat and the Cherubim, still, *"I will remember You."* He and his men are encamped on *"the hill Mizar."* This is a small hill between Mount Hermon and the Jordan River.

Many Christians, like David, find themselves in places of distress — distress that could be caused, at least in part, by their own failure, as David's. At this time, there is always the tendency to become disillusioned and desire to quit. Yet we must continue to praise the Lord and believe Him for ultimate deliverance. As it came to David, it will come to us. The Lord is no respecter of persons!

(7) "DEEP CALLS UNTO DEEP AT THE NOISE OF YOUR WATERSPOUTS: ALL YOUR WAVES AND YOUR BILLOWS ARE GONE OVER ME."

A great truth is given in this Verse, not only for David, but for all Believers.

DEEP CALLS UNTO DEEP

David is saying by this statement that at times we must be brought into deep distress before we can be brought to the deep things of God. When this deep distress happens, it is as though we have been thrown into a *"water spout,"* with such spewing us up and tumbling us head over heels. It is like giant ocean waves that wash over us, and we are left helpless and unable to defend ourselves or even chart the course of our direction.

This speaks of a most severe trial, as it certainly speaks of David's present circumstances in fleeing from Absalom. At times such as this, one's faith is severely tested, and yet the Holy Spirit has given us this gracious Forty-second Psalm to help guide us during the turbulence.

All of these things that were said of David were said in an even greater sense of the Messiah. Think not that He did not suffer such; He did, and in a way that neither David nor any of us could ever begin to suffer. Actually, only of the Messiah Himself can it fully be said that all the waves and billows of the Divine Wrath went over Him.

Whatever comes over us and to us, we can rest assured that it is always measured by God, meaning that He allows such for our benefit, and will not allow anything to come upon us any harder than we can bear. As He told Paul, *"My Grace is sufficient for you: for My strength is made perfect in weakness"* (II Cor. 12:9).

(8) "YET THE LORD WILL COMMAND HIS LOVINGKINDNESS IN THE DAYTIME, AND IN THE NIGHT HIS SONG SHALL BE WITH ME, AND MY PRAYER UNTO THE GOD OF MY LIFE."

Even though David is in this desolate country so far away from the Tabernacle and the Sacrifices, still the Lord continues to show David His *"lovingkindness in the daytime"* and *"songs in the night."*

Truly He has said, *"I will never leave you, nor forsake you"* (Heb. 13:5).

WE MUST NEVER BLAME GOD!

The temptation during times of great distress is to blame God. The world of humanistic psychology even advises its followers to "*forgive God.*" Such is either blasphemy, or it borders on such! Whether our situation has been caused by our own failure or the failure of others, in either case, God is never at fault. Our attitude must be that of David's. Satan could neither take away the *"lovingkindness"* of the Lord nor David's *"song."* David never stopped praying because he never stopped believing.

(9) "I WILL SAY UNTO GOD MY ROCK, WHY HAVE YOU FORGOTTEN ME? WHY DO I GO MOURNING BECAUSE OF THE OPPRESSION OF THE ENEMY?"

Verse 9 predicts the coming future suffering of Israel under the Antichrist. The suffering will be so severe that they will think that the Promises made by God to Abraham, Isaac, and Jacob are forgotten. David also said that his enemies were claiming that God had forgotten him.

The greatest taunt the enemy can use is to claim that God is no longer with the Believer. Satan and his followers use this type of *"oppression."*

(10) "AS WITH A SWORD IN MY BONES, MY ENEMIES REPROACH ME; WHILE THEY SAY DAILY UNTO ME, WHERE IS YOUR GOD?"

We are given view here into some of Satan's ways.

THE WAYS OF THE EVIL ONE

Absalom and Ahithophel were able to sway Israel against David by claiming that because of David's sin with Bathsheba, God was no longer with him and had forgotten him. Regrettably, Israel believed this lie.

Sadly, much of the modern Church believes the same. It little understands the Grace of God or the Power of God. No doubt Absalom, Ahithophel, and their followers felt justified in their condemnation of David. Self-righteousness always does.

When they claim that God was no longer with David, it was *"a sword in David's bones."*

They would say the same of Christ. The Antichrist will also say the same of Israel during the Great Tribulation, namely, *"Where is your God?"*

(11) "WHY ARE YOU CAST DOWN, O MY SOUL? AND WHY ARE YOU DISQUIETED WITHIN ME? HOPE THOU IN GOD:

NOTES

FOR I SHALL YET PRAISE HIM, WHO IS THE HEALTH OF MY COUNTENANCE, AND MY GOD."

This Verse is basically the same as Verse 5, with one difference. In Verse 5, David states, *"For the help of His Countenance."* In this Verse, he cries, *"Who is the health of my countenance, and my God?"*

The idea is that despite his circumstances, David's countenance has changed because the Spirit of God has moved upon him.

In the Fifth Verse, he thanks the Lord that God is still with him despite what his enemies say. In this Verse, he is saying that as a result of the Lord being with him, he is now restored to *"health."*

Likewise, one day the Lord will bring Israel back to *"health."* This will occur at the Second Coming! He will do the same for all who will trust Him.

PSALM 43

*Probably Written by David:
Prayer for Deliverance from the Ungodly*

(1) "JUDGE ME, O GOD, AND PLEAD MY CAUSE AGAINST AN UNGODLY NATION: O DELIVER ME FROM THE DECEITFUL AND UNJUST MAN."

This Psalm is a continuation of the previous Psalm and was probably also written by David. It, too, has three basic meanings:

THE CRY OF THE SOUL

1. David is pictured as crying to God to be delivered from Absalom. How it must have hurt the sweet singer of Israel to have his own son turn against him and actually try to kill him. There could be no pain like the pain that David then experienced.

2. The Greater Son of David cried to God to be delivered from the evil religious leaders of Israel, which He ultimately was by being raised from the dead.

3. The Messiah will cry to God in Israel's place during the time of the Great Tribulation, when they are threatened with destruction by *"the deceitful and unjust man,"* the Antichrist.

David pleads for God to judge him in

order that the true feelings of his heart may be known. David did not believe (and he was right!) that he had ought against anyone, much less these who were trying to kill him. So he invites the Lord to judge him, that the very recesses of his heart may be known.

When one is asking for deliverance, as David is here doing, it should be obvious that the person must also make certain that he is right with God.

Despite the accusations of Absalom and Ahithophel, and despite the acceptance by Israel of those accusations, still, David knew that his *"cause"* was just. He was asking the Lord to judge him, which God did, and then restored him to his throne.

The *"ungodly nation"* that is spoken of here refers to Israel, which, for a brief time, was following Absalom. Absalom is called a *"deceitful and unjust man"* — a description given by the Holy Spirit.

(2) "FOR YOU ARE THE GOD OF MY STRENGTH: WHY DO YOU CAST ME OFF? WHY GO I MOURNING BECAUSE OF THE OPPRESSION OF THE ENEMY?"

This particular Verse is very similar to Verse 9 of the previous Psalm.

David proclaims the fact that his *"strength"* is God, and not his mighty army or anything else. This would certainly prove to be the case in his defeat of Absalom.

The question, *"Why do You cast me off?"* is more so a plea for the Lord to come to his aid. He knows that without God, he has no chance whatsoever; however, he also knows that with the Lord, he will be vindicated and will be once again placed on the throne. And he was!

(3) "O SEND OUT YOUR LIGHT AND YOUR TRUTH: LET THEM LEAD ME; LET THEM BRING ME UNTO YOUR HOLY HILL, AND TO YOUR TABERNACLES."

All of this portrays the fact that David was very familiar, as should be obvious, with the correct ways of worship, which, of course, included the Sacrifices and all of the functions of the Tabernacle.

THE URIM AND THUMMIM

The *"Light"* and *"Truth,"* as David here uses the terms, are references to the Urim and Thummim. *"Urim"* means *"Lights,"* while *"Thummim"* means *"Perfection."* No one knows exactly what these were. They were carried by the High Priest in a pouch attached to the back of the Breastplate. They were worn near his heart.

Some think they possibly were two stones, with *"Yes"* marked on one and *"No"* marked on the other. That, however, is speculation, at best!

The *"Holy Hill"* referred to here is Zion. So this Psalm was composed when David fled from Absalom and from Zion. Now he prays to be led back to Zion and to the place of worship in the Tabernacle of God.

If David had resorted to human advice and counsel, he would most likely have lost his way. Instead he was led by the Holy Spirit and was completely restored.

The Holy Spirit seldom leads men today simply because men seldom allow the Holy Spirit to lead them. The Holy Spirit will always lead us, so to speak, to the *"Holy Hill and the Tabernacles."* Men will always lead us in the opposite direction.

(4) "THEN WILL I GO UNTO THE ALTAR OF GOD, UNTO GOD MY EXCEEDING JOY: YEA, UPON THE HARP WILL I PRAISE YOU, O GOD MY GOD."

David cries these words, and Israel will also cry them during the deep of the Great Tribulation, when it seems that the Antichrist will prevail.

THE ALTAR OF GOD

The *"Altar of God"* refers to the Brazen Altar, that then probably was at Gibeon. There David would offer up Sacrifices. Then, to celebrate the great things that God would do for him, he would play songs of praise upon his *"harp."*

Despite the terrible distress, David never lost his song.

(5) "WHY ARE YOU CAST DOWN, O MY SOUL? AND WHY ARE YOU DISQUIETED WITHIN ME? HOPE IN GOD: FOR I SHALL YET PRAISE HIM, WHO IS THE HEALTH OF MY COUNTENANCE, AND MY GOD."

This Psalm ends exactly as the previous Psalm. David once again reiterates the fact that God is the *"health of my countenance."* Despite the circumstances, his *"hope is in God."* He is praising Him now, but he will *"yet praise Him"* on the *"Holy Hill"* and *"in the Tabernacles."*

When Israel comes to Christ at the Second Coming, she also will praise the Lord, and do so greatly!

So, as stated, this particular Psalm has a threefold meaning and will be fulfilled in totality.

PSALM 44

Author Unknown, it doesn't Appear to be Davidic: A Cry for Help

(1) "WE HAVE HEARD WITH OUR EARS, O GOD, OUR FATHERS HAVE TOLD US, WHAT WORK YOU DID IN THEIR DAYS, IN THE TIMES OF OLD."

The inscription says: *"To the Chief Musician for the sons of Korah, Maschil."*

THE ACCOUNT OF THE MIRACLES OF OLD

This Psalm was written for the sons of Korah. It doesn't really appear that any of these individuals wrote any of the Psalms, but only that their names were included in the instructions. It just seems that they were to sing the Psalms as they were instructed. As well, the sons of Korah could have been a Worship Group which served for hundreds of years.

Neither does the Psalm appear to be Davidic; therefore, there is no way to know who wrote it, although it is believed by some that Hezekiah could have been the author.

Whoever the writer was, it seems that the Holy Spirit took him back in spirit to God's great Deliverance of Israel under Joshua.

The latter part of the Psalm seems to include Israel under the trying days of the future Antichrist in her cry for deliverance. Many times the Holy Spirit calls attention to the great things done by God *"in the times of old."*

If the Bible is preached faithfully from behind the modern pulpit, the people will know what God did *"in the times of old."* If parents are careful to tell their children these great Bible stories, likewise, they too will know what God did *"in the times of old."*

Inasmuch as the Holy Spirit calls our attention to this fact over and over again, these great and wonderful experiences should be related constantly to the young and old. Knowing what God did in the past gives us faith for what He will do in the present.

(2) "HOW YOU DID DRIVE OUT THE HEATHEN WITH YOUR HAND, AND PLANTED THEM; HOW YOU DID AFFLICT THE PEOPLE, AND CAST THEM OUT."

This is a reference to the Lord casting out the heathen nations (Jebusites, Hivites, and others) out of the Promised Land. It would have been impossible for them to have been driven out by normal means. Only God with His Miracle-working Power could bring such to pass.

Likewise, this is a physical example of the spiritual experience in our own lives, with the Lord driving out the works of the flesh.

THE MEANS OF THE CROSS

There is only one way that the Believer can properly and successfully live for God. There is only one way that he can have victory over the world, the flesh, and the Devil. There is only one way that the Holy Spirit, and not *"works of the flesh,"* will be predominant in our lives. That Way is the *"Way of the Cross."* This is God's Prescribed Order of Victory.

WHAT DO WE MEAN BY THE WAY OF THE CROSS?

As previously stated, we mean that Christ is the Source of all things which come to us from God and the Cross is the Means. The Believer is to understand this and not allow his faith to be moved to other things. In other words, one's faith must ever be in Christ and the Cross, and nothing else. We must understand, believe, and subscribe to the great Truth that what Jesus did at the Cross answers every question, provides every solution, and makes it possible for us to have everything we need. The Holy Spirit, Who Alone can do the things in our lives which need to be done, works only through the parameters of the Finished Work of Christ. He is so stringent regarding this that it is referred to as a *"Law"* (Rom. 8:2).

If the Believer attempts to live for God by any means other than constant faith in Christ and what Christ did at the Cross, he will not be successful in such an effort. Without fail, the works of the flesh will manifest themselves in some way in the life of such a person (Gal. 5:19-21).

What we need to have done in our lives can only be done by the Power of God. All the machinations, efforts, ability, or strength which a human being might evidence cannot bring about what we must be in the Lord. It must entirely be a Work of the Spirit. As we've said several times, the Holy Spirit doesn't require much of us, but He does require (actually He demands) that our faith be exclusively in Christ and what Christ did at the Cross (Rom. 6:1-14; 8:1-2, 11; I Cor. 1:17-18, 21, 23; 2:2; Gal., Chpt. 5; 6:14; Eph. 2:13-18; Col. 2:14-15).

(3) "FOR THEY GOT NOT THE LAND IN POSSESSION BY THEIR OWN SWORD, NEITHER DID THEIR OWN ARM SAVE THEM: BUT YOUR RIGHT HAND, AND YOUR ARM, AND THE LIGHT OF YOUR COUNTENANCE, BECAUSE YOU HAD A FAVOR UNTO THEM."

This one Scripture should tell us that we must function in God's Prescribed Order, or else we will fail!

THE POWER OF GOD

As it was not possible for Israel to gain their inheritance by *"their own sword,"* likewise, it is not possible for us to take our spiritual inheritance by the works of the flesh. *"Heathen"* things, such as jealousy, envy, pride, and malice can only be driven out of our lives by *"Your right Hand, and Your Arm, and the light of Your Countenance,"* which, of course, speak of the Lord and His Power.

Self cannot improve self; consequently, self-esteem is not the answer. Neither are any of the rudiments of psychology the answer. Only by the Power of God can man be changed.

The term *"had a favor unto them"* simply means *"to be pleased with them."*

God is pleased with us when we allow His Power to change us and make us what we ought to be. He is very displeased with us when we try to improve self with self. The Holy Spirit through Paul plainly states, *"So then they who are in the flesh cannot please God"* (Rom. 8:8).

NOTES

HOW CAN WE HAVE THE POWER OF GOD MANIFESTED IN OUR LIVES?

That is the secret to all victory!
Listen again to Paul. He said:
"For the preaching of the Cross is to them who perish foolishness; but unto us who are saved it is the Power of God" (I Cor. 1:18).

How is the preaching of the Cross the Power of God?

As we've already said elsewhere in this Volume, there was no power in the wooden beam called the Cross. Neither is there any power in death, and I speak of the death of Christ. The power is registered completely in the Holy Spirit.

So how is the Holy Spirit connected with the Cross?

He is connected with the Cross in that the Cross gave the Holy Spirit the legal right to work within our lives and to do all the things which He Alone can do (Rom. 8:2). At the Cross, Jesus atoned for all sin — past, present, and future — at least for those who will believe (Jn. 3:16). Inasmuch as all sin was, and is, atoned, which means the sin debt has been forever paid, this makes it possible for the Holy Spirit to come into the heart and life of the individual to abide there forever.

Paul said:

"Know you not that you are the Temple of God, and that the Spirit of God dwells in you?" (I Cor. 3:16). The Power resides in the Holy Spirit, but He is able to dispense this Power to us only because of what Christ has done at the Cross. As we have stated any number of times, He only demands of us that the Cross of Christ ever be the Object of our Faith. Then He is free to function mightily within our lives. Otherwise, He is greatly curtailed!

(4) "YOU ARE MY KING, O GOD: COMMAND DELIVERANCES FOR JACOB."

The simple fact is that humanity needs *"deliverance,"* and we are speaking of deliverance from sin. Jesus said of Himself that He was anointed *"to preach deliverance to the captives"* (Lk. 4:18).

Modern psychology knows nothing about deliverance, and does not believe in such. It feels that it can improve the lot of man. There is no evidence that it ever has succeeded. In fact, it cannot succeed; however, millions can testify to the delivering Power of God.

ALL DELIVERANCE IS FOUND IN THE CROSS OF CHRIST

Let us say it again:

All deliverance, in every capacity and in every form, is found entirely and solely within the parameters of Christ and what He did for us at the Cross. At the Cross, Jesus, in totality, defeated Satan, all fallen angels, and every demon spirit. In other words, the victory that He there won has been heralded throughout the entirety of the spirit world. The Scripture says, and I quote from THE EXPOSITOR'S STUDY BIBLE:

"*Blotting out the handwriting of Ordinances that was against us* (pertains to the Law of Moses, which was God's Standard of Righteousness that man could not reach), *which was contrary to us* (Law is against us, simply because we are unable to keep its precepts, no matter how hard we try), *and took it out of the way* (refers to the penalty of the Law being removed), *nailing it to His Cross* (the Law with its decrees was abolished in Christ's Death, as if crucified with Him);

"*And having spoiled principalities and powers* (Satan and all of his henchmen were defeated at the Cross by Christ atoning for all sin; sin was the legal right Satan had to hold man in captivity; with all sin atoned, he has no more legal right to hold anyone in bondage), *He* (Christ) *made a show of them openly* (what Jesus did at the Cross was in the face of the whole universe), *triumphing over them in it.* (The triumph is complete and it was all done for us, meaning we can walk in power and perpetual victory due to the Cross)" (Col. 2:14-15).

So, deliverance awaits any individual, no matter how bad his situation is, if he will only come to Christ and place his faith strictly in Him.

JACOB

The name *"Jacob"* is used because he is a perfect example of humanity. The very name *"Jacob"* means schemer and fraud. Those words describe humanity. The Lord would deliver *"Jacob"* and change his name to *"Israel"* — Prince with God. Only the *"King,"* the Lord of Glory, could and can do such (Gen. 32:24-28).

(5) "THROUGH YOU WILL WE PUSH DOWN OUR ENEMIES: THROUGH YOUR NAME WILL WE TREAD THEM UNDER WHO RISE UP AGAINST US."

In this Passage, we are told the way!

ENEMIES

In this Passage, we are told how the great Power of God is effected in our hearts and lives.

Who are these *"enemies"*?

In the lives of Christians, they are pride, self-will, envy, strife, etc. It is in the mighty *"Name"* of Jesus that *"we tread them under who rise up against us"* (Mk. 16:17-18). At His *"Name"* every knee shall bow, and every tongue shall confess (Phil. 2:10-11).

(6) "FOR I WILL NOT TRUST IN MY BOW, NEITHER SHALL MY SWORD SAVE ME."

The arm of flesh cannot save us, and yet most of that which is done in the modern Church is through the flesh, *"my bow"* and *"my sword,"* etc.

The Lord has everything mapped out for us in total detail. It is His Word!

If every Believer, no matter who that Believer might be, will ask the Lord to help him understand the Word and not allow him to go astray from the Word, that is a prayer that the Lord will most definitely answer.

There is no way that I can overstress the significance of the Word of God, and our understanding the Word. Nothing is more important than that.

THE EXPOSITOR'S STUDY BIBLE

In about 1995, the Lord began to deal with my heart about putting together a Study Bible that would help Believers to more fully understand the Word of God. At that time, He didn't tell me how to do it or even when to do it, just that ultimately I was to do it.

I will be frank; I shrank back from the task because I realized my gross inadequacy. About that, I was most certainly correct; however, I realized after it was done that anyone, no matter their education or background, would be woefully inadequate for such a task. In other words, if the Lord had not helped me to complete this project, I simply could not have done it.

In about the year 2000, the Lord began to show me how He wanted this project to be done. To be sure, I had spent untold hours thinking about the situation.

Where would I put the notes? At the bottom of the page? At the side of the page? At the back of the book? Almost all Study Bibles are fashioned in one of these ways.

None of those options seemed right, because none of those were what the Lord wanted me to do. The Lord told me to put the expository notes in with the Scripture. In that manner, the Reader will not have to leave his place of reading and go to another part of the page, or even elsewhere in the Bible. The notes were to be embedded within the Text of the Scripture.

And that's exactly what we did.

When I began to put it together, not only had the Lord told me to do such and then showed me how to do it, but He also helped me greatly to get it done.

According to e-mails, letters, and other means of communication, THE EXPOSITOR'S STUDY BIBLE has been, and is, a tremendous value and help to anyone who has a copy; it enables them to more properly understand the Word of God. As stated, there is nothing more important than that.

I personally believe that nothing has ever been placed into the hands of the Christian public to help them understand the Word of God more than THE EXPOSITOR'S STUDY BIBLE. I realize that's quite a statement, but I believe it to be true.

At any rate, whatever help it does afford the Believer is valuable help indeed! As stated, nothing is more important than the Word of God, and nothing is more important than that we properly understand the Word.

(7) "BUT YOU HAVE SAVED US FROM OUR ENEMIES, AND HAVE PUT THEM TO SHAME WHO HATED US."

It is always Satan's boast that he will destroy us. He is constantly proclaiming to the Child of God that we cannot win, that we, in fact, must fail.

Have you ever stopped to think that none of these things that Satan constantly threatens have ever come true? Don't you realize that if Satan could do all the things he claims he is going to do, then he would have done them a long time ago! He hasn't done them because he can't do them.

Despite all of his blow and bluster, you are still here, still shouting *"Glory,"* and prayerfully closer to God than ever, which means that you should not ever listen to Satan.

We have the Promise of the Lord that He will put Satan and all who seek to stop us from gaining our inheritance *"to shame."* In other words, we cannot lose, that is, if we will keep believing!

(8) "IN GOD WE BOAST ALL THE DAY LONG, AND PRAISE YOUR NAME FOREVER. SELAH."

The only thing that it is proper to boast about is the Lord, and we should do so *"all the day long."* We should tell over and over what He has done and what He is doing. We should *"boast"* about His Power to deliver and His Power to save. Along with the boasting, there should be constant *"praise."* The Christian who truly knows God will truly and continually praise.

BOASTING

As it regards *"boasting,"* the Apostle Paul said:

"But God forbid that I should glory (boast), *save in the Cross of our Lord Jesus Christ* (what the opponents of Paul sought to escape at the price of insincerity is the Apostle's only basis of exultation), *by Whom the world is crucified unto me and I unto the world*. (The only way we can overcome the world, and I mean the only way, is by placing our faith exclusively in the Cross of Christ and keeping it there)" (Gal. 6:14).

The Judaizers were coming from Judaea, going into the Churches in Galatia which had been founded by Paul, and were preaching the gospel of circumcision. In other words, they were preaching the Law of Moses. They were telling the Galatians that along with believing in Christ, they also had to keep the Law, of which circumcision was the physical sign of that Covenant.

Paul had taught the Galatians that the Law was completely fulfilled in Christ; therefore, it was no longer binding on Christians. He taught them that they must ever look to

Christ and what Christ did at the Cross, and look to nothing else.

He then said that if there was any boasting involved, it must be *"in the Cross of our Lord Jesus Christ."*

HOW MANY MODERN CHRISTIANS PRESENTLY ARE BOASTING IN THE CROSS?

Regrettably and sadly, almost none! They are boasting in the *"Purpose Driven Life,"* the *"Government of Twelve,"* or the *"Word of Faith,"* etc., but precious few are *"boasting in the Cross of our Lord."*

The Cross of Christ is the only thing in which we should boast. If we boast in anything else, we are doing the same thing the Judaizers were trying to get the Galatians to do, which the Holy Spirit through Paul roundly condemned. The reasons should be obvious!

As we have repeatedly stated, the Cross is where Jesus paid every price, won every victory, and made it possible for us to have all the great things of God. Considering what it is and what it has afforded for you and for me, why shouldn't we boast in the Cross?

(9) "BUT YOU HAVE CAST OFF, AND PUT US TO SHAME; AND GO NOT FORTH WITH OUR ARMIES."

Verses 9 through 16 proclaim a specific time in Israel's history to which the Holy Spirit through the Psalmist addresses Himself. This speaks of Israel's failure and of God's chastisement.

CHASTISEMENT

Prophetically, this Psalm is a forepicture of the affliction of the believing remnant of Israel under the oppression of the Antichrist.

Presently, it speaks of every Christian who, due to failure, suffers, at one time or another, chastisement at the Hand of God. Nevertheless, God's chastisement is never punitive, but rather Redemptive. Anything that God does to His Child or allows to happen to His Child is designed to bring the person to the place of humility and consecration desired by the Holy Spirit.

God's people are afforded a special protection, blessing, and relationship with the Heavenly Father — but only if certain conditions are met. Otherwise, He will *"cast off,"* *"put us to shame,"* and *"will not go forth with our armies."*

The following Verses proclaim to us what God will allow to happen:

1. *"To retreat from the enemy"* (Vs. 10).
2. *"Scattered among the heathen"* (Vs. 11).
3. *"Permit God's people to become slaves to the enemy"* (Vs. 12).
4. *"A reproach, a scorn, and a derision"* (Vs. 13).
5. *"A byword"* (Vs. 14).
6. *"Confusion and shame cover me"* (Vs. 15).
7. *"Given over to the one who reproaches and blasphemes"* (Vs. 16).

ALLOWED BY THE HOLY SPIRIT

All of the above are allowed by the Holy Spirit in order for Israel or even the modern Christian to be brought to the desired place of Repentance.

Regarding Israel, their dispersion has been long and hard. For some 1,900 years, all of that proclaimed in Verses 9 through 16 came to pass in totality. Only since 1948 has God begun to move upon them to bring them to the desired place which ultimately will conclude in Repentance.

Even now, despite God working with them to bring them to the desired place, there is no spiritual renewal whatsoever. The Great Tribulation, which is just ahead, will be the greatest time of trouble for Israel! At the conclusion of this time of *"Jacob's Trouble,"* they will then come back to the Lord Jesus Christ (Jer. 30:7). It will be at the Second Coming (Zech., Chpts. 13-14).

(10) "YOU MAKE US TO TURN BACK FROM THE ENEMY: AND THEY WHICH HATE US SPOIL FOR THEMSELVES."

The writer of this Psalm now complains that the situation of Israel is so acute that the enemy is easily able to put them to flight, and also to seize whatever spoil is there, and Israel cannot stop them.

(11) "YOU HAVE GIVEN US LIKE SHEEP APPOINTED FOR MEAT; AND HAVE SCATTERED US AMONG THE HEATHEN."

Those who were taken captive by these particular *"enemies"* are sold as slaves; consequently, it is easy to see the terrible condition in which God's chosen people find themselves.

(12) "YOU SELL YOUR PEOPLE FOR NAUGHT, AND DO NOT INCREASE YOUR WEALTH BY THEIR PRICE."

Israel is in such a difficult situation. As they see it, God gains nothing in exchange.

That is correct! The Lord gains nothing by His people being subjected to such bondage. So why does He allow these terrible things to take place?

EVERYTHING EITHER IS CAUSED OR ALLOWED BY THE LORD

In a broad sense, the heading applies to the whole of humanity, and it most definitely applies, even in minute detail, to Believers. We are not our own, we are bought with a price, and that price is very, very high! I speak of the Cross of Calvary (I Cor. 6:20). Consequently, everything that happens to us as Believers is minutely allowed by the Lord or even caused by the Lord. The Lord has the Power to keep His people from ever suffering from any type of bondage; however, it is not as simple as that.

When Believers begin to stray, begin to lose their way, begin to go into the world, the Lord loves us so much that He cannot allow us to continue that direction without doing everything short of force to bring us back. So if we suffer, He has allowed such, because He is looking at the long pull, and not merely the short term. He has nothing but good for us, and sometimes He has to take us through difficult places in order that we may finally arrive at that good.

(13) "YOU MAKE US A REPROACH TO OUR NEIGHBORS, A SCORN AND A DERISION TO THEM WHO ARE ROUND ABOUT US."

The idea here is that Israel had come to the place that she was a reproach, not so much that she was cowardly or weak, but rather that she had a weak and powerless God. That's what the heathen said; they claimed that their gods were greater than Jehovah.

Of course, the heathen had absolutely no knowledge of Jehovah or how He worked. The Lord suffers in these situations even more than we do.

(14) "YOU MAKE US A BYWORD AMONG THE HEATHEN, A SHAKING OF THE HEAD AMONG THE PEOPLE."

This is always the case when God's people fall on hard times. And it is all because of sin!

THE WILL OF GOD

It is the Will of God that *"we may prosper* (refers to financial prosperity, which should be the case for every Believer) *and be in health* (speaks of physical prosperity), *even as your soul prospers* (speaks of spiritual prosperity; so we have here the whole Gospel for the whole man)" (III Jn. 2).

The Lord wants us to be all of this and more. Part of the price that Jesus paid at Calvary was that we might have *"more abundant life."* Of course, that refers more than all to Spiritual Life, but it also applies to the physical and material part of man, which also are important.

WHATEVER ONE NEEDS IS IN THE CROSS

One might well say that there is a car in the Cross, if you need one! There is a bigger house in the Cross, if you need one! There is a raise in pay in the Cross, if you need one! There is a better job in the Cross, if you need one!

I think you get the point!

Above all, every spiritual victory is in the Cross.

All that comes from the Lord is received by faith. In other words, the Believer makes Christ and the Cross the Object of his Faith, and then asks the Lord for whatever it is that is needed. He does so with the assurance and understanding that it was all paid for at the Cross.

Considering that our Lord has paid such a price, we should certainly desire everything for which that great price has been paid. I think it is an insult to Him for us to do otherwise!

(15) "MY CONFUSION IS CONTINUALLY BEFORE ME, AND THE SHAME OF MY FACE HAS COVERED ME."

Straying from the Word of God, losing our way spiritually, beginning to believe false doctrine, all lead to the abject situation in which Israel now finds herself. To be sure, untold numbers of Believers presently have found themselves in the same situation.

The way that is not the Way of God always brings confusion.

(16) "FOR THE VOICE OF HIM WHO REPROACHES AND BLASPHEMES; BY REASON OF THE ENEMY AND AVENGER."

Of course, the enemy, if given the opportunity, will reproach God's people and even God Himself. Such an opportunity basically doesn't come unless the Believer loses his way, as Israel here does. Then the blaspheming by the enemy begins!

(17) "ALL THIS IS COME UPON US; YET HAVE WE NOT FORGOTTEN YOU, NEITHER HAVE WE DEALT FALSELY IN YOUR COVENANT."

The idea of this Verse is a little different from what it seems to be on the surface.

Israel is not here saying that she is without sin. What she is saying is this:

"Despite our wayward direction, despite our backsliding, we still need You, and we remember Your Covenant. We may stray from it for a period of time, but we always will come back."

It is not easy to turn out the lights which God has hung up in a man's soul from infancy — and especially when one has once known the Lord.

The lot of the backslider is probably the most miserable of existences. Until that person comes back to the Lord, he will find neither peace of mind nor satisfaction of heart!

(18) "OUR HEART IS NOT TURNED BACK, NEITHER HAVE OUR STEPS DECLINED FROM YOUR WAY."

At this moment (at the conclusion of the Great Tribulation), their hearts truly are crying out to God, and their steps are endeavoring to fit His Way.

All of these Scriptures must be understood in the light of the present situation with Israel, which pertains to the coming Battle of Armageddon. If we look at the entirety of the history of these people, their hearts have been turned back (woefully so!) and their steps have most definitely declined from God's Way. They have also forgotten Him for long periods of time and have also dealt very falsely with His Covenant.

As these Scriptures unfold, what is taking place here pertains to their present condition, which, as stated, will be during the Battle of Armageddon, when they are crying to God for help. To be sure, that help will be forthcoming. If their praying and petitions were lies (in other words, if they were speaking of their entire existence), the Lord could not answer such a prayer. He will most definitely answer this prayer, because it is being prayed in all honesty and integrity.

(19) "THOUGH YOU HAVE SORE BROKEN US IN THE PLACE OF DRAGONS, AND COVERED US WITH THE SHADOW OF DEATH."

Here Israel is admitting that God has rightly broken them because they have for a long period of time forgotten Him and their hearts were turned back from Him.

THE SHADOW OF DEATH

The *"place of dragons"* concerns that terrible time when Israel, even in the very near future, will accept the Antichrist and think that he is the Messiah. Because of this, they will be brought to *"the shadow of death."* The Antichrist will declare war on them in the midst of the Great Tribulation, thereby showing his true colors. At that time, Israel will come close to total annihilation (Jn. 5:43). Were it not for the Second Coming, Israel would be annihilated!

(20) "IF WE HAVE FORGOTTEN THE NAME OF OUR GOD, OR STRETCHED OUT OUR HANDS TO A STRANGE GOD."

They did *"forget the Name of their God,"* and they did *"stretch out their hands to a strange god"* (Dan. 11:39). The one who Israel thought was the Messiah will actually be *"the strange god."*

(21) "SHALL NOT GOD SEARCH THIS OUT? FOR HE KNOWS THE SECRETS OF THE HEART."

They cannot lie to God! They have to be totally clean with Him, because *"He knows the secrets of the heart."* Man may not know even his own heart, but God knows all things!

TRUE REPENTANCE

The Passages in Verses 17 through 22 magnify the fact that man ever tries to minimize his sin and magnify his repentance. God desires the opposite so that we magnify the horror of sin and minimize the glory of our Repentance.

(22) "YEA, FOR YOUR SAKE ARE WE KILLED ALL THE DAY LONG; WE ARE COUNTED AS SHEEP FOR THE SLAUGHTER."

Paul quoted this Passage in Romans 8:36. The Holy Spirit through Paul uses this Passage in the correct sense, basically stating that the things God allows to come upon us are meant to bring us closer to God. Rather than separating us from God, they are designed to bring us into compliance with His Will.

In the Great Tribulation, which is very soon (relative to the present time of year 2005) to come upon this Earth, Israel will truly be *"killed all the day long."* And they will be *"counted as sheep for the slaughter."*

(23) "AWAKE, WHY DO YOU SLEEP, O LORD? ARISE, CAST US NOT OFF FOREVER."

Desperation is in these words!

THE COMING BATTLE OF ARMAGEDDON

In the concluding days of the Great Tribulation and during the Battle of Armageddon, when it looks like Israel will be totally destroyed, they will cry to God. It has been so long since He has moved in their midst that it seems to Israel that He is asleep.

As well, it has been so long since they have prayed and cried to Him for deliverance. Verses 23 through 26 record the beginning of Israel's supplication before God — after a spiritual draught of over 2,500 years.

(24) "WHEREFORE DO YOU HIDE YOUR FACE, AND FORGET OUR AFFLICTION AND OUR OPPRESSION?"

Now when it seems like the Antichrist is going to completely annihilate these ancient people, when he seeks to do what Haman, Herod, and Hitler did not succeed in doing, they will cry to God to let His Face shine upon them once again. Their *"affliction and oppression"* is the most severe that it ever has been. They are now pressed beyond measure, with what seems to be no hope in sight.

(25) "FOR OUR SOUL IS BOWED DOWN TO THE DUST: OUR BELLY CLEAVES UNTO THE EARTH."

This will be the darkest hour of Israel's history, when, as Zechariah prophesied (Zech. 14:1-3), they will come close to total destruction.

(26) "ARISE FOR OUR HELP, AND REDEEM US FOR YOUR MERCIES' SAKE."

Zechariah also says that God will hear their prayer and answer it, for he wrote, *"Then shall the LORD go forth, and fight against those nations, as when He fought in the day of battle"* (Zech. 14:3).

Verses 4 through 7 of the Fourteenth Chapter of Zechariah and the Nineteenth Chapter of Revelation record the Second Coming. At that time, the Lord will truly *"arise."* He will truly *"redeem us for Your Mercies' sake."*

This prayer will be answered after many long years of spiritual declension.

The reason God will answer is because of *"Your Mercies' sake."*

God's Mercy is granted to us only when we realize we don't deserve it.

PSALM 45

Author Unknown:
The King; Messiah's Majesty and Power

(1) "MY HEART IS INDITING A GOOD MATTER: I SPEAK OF THE THINGS WHICH I HAVE MADE TOUCHING THE KING: MY TONGUE IS THE PEN OF A READY WRITER."

The superscription is: *"To the Chief Musician upon Shoshamnin, for the sons of Korah, Mischil, a song of loves."*

THE TONGUE OF THE REDEEMED

The word *"loves"* in the superscription is probably the Hebrew plural of excellency, so that the Title may read: *"A Song of Supreme Love,"* i.e., *"Messiah's love for Jerusalem as a bridegroom for a bride"* (Isa. 62:5).

Even though the author of this Psalm is not known, some Scholars believe that it could have been written by Isaiah on the occasion of the marriage of Hezekiah with Hephzibah (II Ki. 21:1; Isa. 62:4).

The interpretation of the Psalm as Messianic is decided in the First Chapter of Hebrews, where His Godhead also is affirmed.

The Psalm introduces the Deliverer for Whom, in the three prior Psalms, the

Psalmist has prayed. His apparition changes everything and throws a bright ray of sunshine upon the dark background of those Psalms. It is a precious instance of the power of a Divine to occupy itself with such glories when surrounded by such terrors. So, doubtless, Hezekiah and his companions sang this song of conjugal love within the walls of Jerusalem when they were shut in by the Assyrian host.

So will it be in the future. At the moment of Israel's greatest distress (Zech. 14:2-3), the Messiah will appear, will marry Jerusalem, and will destroy her oppressors. The result will be that Israel's future glory will eclipse her past splendors.

The introduction may read thus: *"My heart overflows with a goodly theme. I must speak! The theme concerns the King! My tongue is like the pen of a ready writer."* In other words, I cannot help but speak.

(2) "YOU ARE FAIRER THAN THE CHILDREN OF MEN: GRACE IS POURED INTO YOUR LIPS: THEREFORE GOD HAS BLESSED YOU FOREVER."

This Verse pertains to Israel's restoration, which will take place at the beginning of the Kingdom Age.

ISRAEL AND THE LORD JESUS CHRIST

At the Second Coming and at the beginning of the Kingdom Age, Israel will now see that the Lord Jesus Christ is *"fairer than the children of men."* As He welcomes them home with open arms, they will also see that *"Grace is poured into Your lips."* They finally will learn that the Blessings of God upon Israel were really upon the Lord Jesus Christ. When they rejected Him, the Blessings stopped. When they now accept Him, the Blessings will begin again.

It is the same presently!

The Lord really does not bless us per se, but rather the Lord Jesus Christ within us. Even though all Believers have Christ in them (Jn. 14:20; Rom. 8:10), only those who have their Faith anchored squarely in Christ and the Cross can realize the full potential of what the Lord desires to do in us and to us. Most of the Church lives so far beneath that which the Lord intends.

NOTES

Please allow me to say it again:

It is not possible for the Believer to realize his full potential in Christ unless the Faith of such a Believer is anchored squarely in Christ and the Cross. In other words, he must understand that his Sanctification is wrapped up completely in the Cross of Christ, which demands our Faith at all times (Rom. 6:1-14).

(3) "GIRD YOUR SWORD UPON YOUR THIGH, O MOST MIGHTY, WITH YOUR GLORY AND YOUR MAJESTY."

Verses 3 through 5 speak of Christ's majesty in the Battle of Armageddon, when He defeats the Antichrist and all of Israel's enemies.

Concerning this time, the Prophet Zechariah said, *"Then shall the LORD go forth and fight against those nations, as when He fought in the day of battle"* (Zech. 14:3).

(4) "AND IN YOUR MAJESTY RIDE PROSPEROUSLY BECAUSE OF TRUTH AND MEEKNESS AND RIGHTEOUSNESS; AND YOUR RIGHT HAND SHALL TEACH YOU TERRIBLE THINGS."

This Passage plainly tells us that the Lord will be *"prosperous"* in His attack upon the Antichrist. It will be because our Lord is *"Truth,"* *"Meekness,"* and *"Righteousness."*

In other words, the world will then finally know in the form of Christ what these tremendous qualities can do. None of this, as is obvious, will reside in the Antichrist, even though he claims such. They will reside in Christ.

The *"terrible things"* here mentioned have to do with what Christ will carry out against the Antichrist in the Battle of Armageddon. At that battle, five-sixths of the Antichrist's army will perish at that time, ever how large that army might be (Ezek. 39:2).

(5) "YOUR ARROWS ARE SHARP IN THE HEART OF THE KINGS' ENEMIES; WHEREBY THE PEOPLE FALL UNDER YOU."

These *"enemies"* include the Antichrist and all his armies. The Lord's *"arrows"* will go to the very *"heart"* of these enemies.

"Arrows" represent a metaphor for the manner in which Christ will fight. They speak of the elements which He will use.

Ezekiel said, *"And I plead against him* (the Antichrist) *with pestilence and with blood; and I will rain upon him, and upon his bands, and upon the many people who are with him, an overflowing rain, and great hailstones, fire, and brimstone"* (Ezek. 38:22).

(6) "YOUR THRONE, O GOD, IS FOREVER AND EVER: THE SCEPTER OF YOUR KINGDOM IS A RIGHT SCEPTER."

The Antichrist will announce to the world that his kingdom and his throne will last forever; however, it will actually be very short-lived. By contrast, the Throne of God will last forever. This is proof that Jesus Christ is God, One of the Three Divine Persons in the Trinity.

THE SCEPTER OF POWER

Concerning this *"power,"* Jacob of old prophesied on his deathbed, *"The Scepter shall not depart from Judah, nor a Lawgiver from between his feet, until Shiloh* (Christ) *comes; and unto Him shall the gathering of the people be"* (Gen. 49:10).

As is here obvious, the Scepter of Power belongs exclusively to the Lord Jesus Christ.

Approximately 500 years before Christ, Judah lost her way completely and was taken captive by the Babylonians. The Temple was then destroyed and many in Judah were led away as slaves.

At that time, the scepter of power was transferred from the kings of Judah, David's sons several times removed, and given to the Gentile, Nebuchadnezzar. It has remained in the hands of the Gentiles ever since.

Jesus offered the Kingdom again to Israel, but they would not accept it, because to accept it, they would have to accept Him (Mat. 4:17).

After their rejection of Him, just hours before His Crucifixion, He told His Disciples, *"And they shall fall by the edge of the sword, and shall be led away captive into all nations: and Jerusalem shall be trodden down of the Gentiles, until the times of the Gentiles be fulfilled"* (Lk. 21:24).

WHEN WILL THE TIMES OF THE GENTILES BE FULFILLED?

The *"Times of the Gentiles"* refers to the power, i.e., *"scepter,"* being in the hands of Gentiles, which it has been now for some 2,500 years. In fact, it is presently in the hands of the United States, and has been for most of the Twentieth Century.

NOTES

Next it will be held in the hands of the Antichrist, which shortly will come to pass.

The *"times of the Gentiles"* will not be finished until the Second Coming. At that time, the Scepter of Power will pass from the hands of the Gentiles to the Lord Jesus Christ and He will then give it to Israel, but only after they have fully accepted Him as Saviour and Lord, which they instantly will do (Zech., Chpts. 12-14).

(7) "YOU LOVE RIGHTEOUSNESS, AND HATE WICKEDNESS: THEREFORE GOD, YOUR GOD, HAS ANOINTED YOU WITH THE OIL OF GLADNESS ABOVE YOUR FELLOWS."

The words, *"Your fellows,"* refer to all of the Patriarchs and Prophets of old, as well as all the Disciples, Apostles, and all others. No one can even remotely compare with the Lord Jesus Christ, as would be obvious.

THE OIL OF GLADNESS

Jesus is the Giver of *"more abundant life"* (Jn. 10:10), which He gives to all who follow Him; He does so *"with the oil of gladness."*

All *"gladness"* is in the Lord. This means that all joy, all life, and all happiness are found exclusively in Him.

Satan tries to imitate this *"oil of gladness"* with drugs, alcohol, and other things, but without success.

When Jesus comes into the heart of the Believer, He always does so with *"the oil of gladness."* It is far and away beyond what man can give.

The way we are to enjoy this *"oil of gladness"* is to ever place our faith exclusively in Him and what He has done for us at the Cross.

This is the cure for emotional disturbances, for fear, for much sickness, and for most of the problems which plague humanity. The only answer is Jesus Christ. He Alone has the *"oil of gladness"*!

Paul quoted this Verse in Hebrews 1:9.

(8) "ALL YOUR GARMENTS SMELL OF MYRRH, AND ALOES, AND CASSIA, OUT OF THE IVORY PALACES, WHEREBY THEY HAVE MADE YOU GLAD."

This speaks of the glory, wonder, and beauty of the Messiah in contrast to the evil of the Antichrist. It has a spiritual meaning which only could be said of the Lord of Glory.

The *"and"* before *"cassia"* appears in four manuscripts and in all the ancient Versions. This means that the garments are so impregnated with spices as to seem to be made of them.

Men and women put particular spices or perfumes on themselves in order to smell good. Christ does not have to put anything on Himself, for all of this glory, beauty, wonder, and beautiful aroma all come from within Him.

(9) "KINGS' DAUGHTERS WERE AMONG YOUR HONORABLE WOMEN: UPON YOUR RIGHT HAND DID STAND THE QUEEN IN GOLD OF OPHIR."

In that day, the coming Kingdom Age, Israel will once again be *"honorable."* The *"Right Hand"* refers to God's eternal remembrance of Jerusalem. He said: *"If I forget you, O Jerusalem, let My Right Hand forget her cunning."* So now Jerusalem, safely inhabited by Israel, is at the Messiah's *"Right Hand."*

These Passages describe the Bridegroom, Who is the Lord Jesus Christ. The *"Bride"* will be Israel, portrayed in the following Verses.

THE MARRIAGE SCENE

The marriage scene now begins to open upon us. The Bridegroom has been depicted in all His glorious majesty. The Bride is now to be brought forward. She comes accompanied by a train of attendants — *"honorable women"* or *"noble ladies,"* many of whom are *"king's daughters."*

All of this is symbolism of what will take place between Christ and Israel at the beginning of the Kingdom Age.

(10) "HEARKEN, O DAUGHTER, AND CONSIDER, AND INCLINE YOUR EAR; FORGET ALSO YOUR OWN PEOPLE, AND YOUR FATHER'S HOUSE."

Now Jerusalem is to forget the past and all that has gone before. They are to look to the future. Israel's golden day has now dawned. The time that the Apostles inquired about is now being fulfilled (Acts 1:6-7). The Kingdom has truly been restored to Israel.

The Lord here bids Israel to reflect deeply on the new relation into which she is about to be placed, the new sphere into which she is entering, the new duties which she will have to discharge. She must give herself wholly to her Lord and Spouse; she must have no thought for anyone but Him.

She must break all associations, bonds, and relationships that would separate her and her King, forget the past and come to the present, cease to Judaize and be wholly Christ's.

(11) "SO SHALL THE KING GREATLY DESIRE YOUR BEAUTY: FOR HE IS YOUR LORD; AND WORSHIP THOU HIM."

"The King" is the Lord Jesus Christ. He is the One Who will give Israel and Jerusalem their *"beauty."* Israel is to worship Him, *"for He is your Lord."*

At long last, Israel, exactly as here predicted, will recognize Jesus as their Lord — after some 2,000 years of rejecting Him.

Israel is to have eyes only for Him, and that she shall do!

(12) "AND THE DAUGHTER OF TYRE SHALL BE THERE WITH A GIFT; EVEN THE RICH AMONG THE PEOPLE SHALL INTREAT YOUR FAVOR."

The *"daughter of Tyre"* stands for the Gentile nations which will come with their *"gifts,"* which will be at the beginning of the Kingdom Age. The Lord Jesus Christ is the Source of all Blessings; He is now the President of Planet Earth. At that time, the mightiest in the world will seek the *"favor"* of our Lord!

(13) "THE KINGS' DAUGHTER IS ALL GLORIOUS WITHIN: HER CLOTHING IS OF WROUGHT GOLD."

Both Jerusalem and Israel in general are described in these Passages.

Whenever the nations of the world come to Jerusalem to bring their gifts, they will find a city that is beyond compare. It will be *"glorious"*; as *"gold"* was plentiful in Solomon's day, it will be far more plentiful in the day of *"The King."*

THE BRIDE

In the east, the Bride, in her wedding dress, receives visitors in her father's house. Then, at the appointed time, accompanied by the bridesmaids, her companions, she is conducted to the palace of her husband, who, attended by the most distinguished women of his court, receives her and conducts her alone into the nuptial chamber.

Such is the touching and beautiful figure which here portrays Jerusalem and Israel.

(14) "SHE SHALL BE BROUGHT UNTO THE KING IN RAIMENT OF NEEDLEWORK: THE VIRGINS HER COMPANIONS WHO FOLLOW HER SHALL BE BROUGHT UNTO YOU."

When Jesus came the first time, they spit upon Him, rejected Him, and crucified Him. But now the story will be different. At long last, Israel has accepted Christ as *"The King."* In turn, He will gloriously adorn her. Now *"the virgins her companions"* will no longer be false gods, but instead will be all who worship *"The King,"* i.e., The Lord Jesus Christ.

(15) "WITH GLADNESS AND REJOICING SHALL THEY BE BROUGHT: THEY SHALL ENTER INTO THE KING'S PALACE."

All of this is symbolic of what will take place at the beginning of the coming Kingdom Age, when Israel accepts the Lord Jesus Christ as her Messiah, Saviour, and Lord.

The first time He came, they crucified Him. This time they will receive Him *"with gladness and rejoicing."*

As He enters the Palace, the leaders of Israel in that day will enter with Him. It will be a scene and a time which will undoubtedly be televised all over the world.

Even though much of this is symbolism, still, the principle which is symbolized will most definitely take place. In other words, the Lord Jesus Christ will most definitely take the Throne of Israel, and thereby the world.

(16) "INSTEAD OF YOUR FATHERS SHALL BE YOUR CHILDREN, WHOM YOU MAY MAKE PRINCES IN ALL THE EARTH."

The *"fathers,"* speaking of Israel of the past, for the most part rejected the God of Israel and His Christ; but the *"children,"* speaking of those who will go into the Kingdom Age, will accept Him. In turn, He will give them places of honor and position *"in all the Earth."*

(17) "I WILL MAKE YOUR NAME TO BE REMEMBERED IN ALL GENERATIONS: THEREFORE SHALL THE PEOPLE PRAISE YOU FOREVER AND EVER."

The *"King,"* Who is the Lord Jesus Christ, will be in that day *"remembered in all generations."* He will never again be rejected; consequently, the people shall *"praise Him forever and ever."*

PSALM 46

May Have Been Written by Hezekiah: God is Our Refuge and Strength

(1) "GOD IS OUR REFUGE AND STRENGTH, A VERY PRESENT HELP IN TROUBLE."

The superscription is: *"To the Chief Musician for the sons of Korah. A Song upon Alamoth."*

OUR REFUGE

It is not known exactly who wrote this Psalm or at what particular time; however, there is some evidence that it was written by Isaiah during the siege of Jerusalem by the Assyrians. It is quite possible that the Holy Spirit gave this to the Prophet in order that it be given to Hezekiah at Jerusalem.

If it was written at this time, it would have a double meaning:

1. God addressed Himself to the siege of Jerusalem by Sennacherib.

2. Even more so, it pertains to the siege of Jerusalem by the Antichrist (Zech. 14:1-13), when the Lord will defend Jerusalem and defeat the Antichrist in a great victory.

At that future day and in Hezekiah's day, God will be the only *"refuge."* He will also be *"a very present help."*

TROUBLE

Hezekiah was in trouble, trouble so great as to be compared to the Earth convulsing, to mountains being swept into the midst of the seas, and to raging billows roaring with a force great enough to make the mountains tremble.

Unfortunately, most people, even Believers, call on the Lord only when they are *"in trouble."* To be sure, He is a help at that time, and grandly so; however, if we learn to call upon Him at all times, such will probably avoid the *"trouble."* But all trouble cannot be avoided, and, at that time, the Lord is our *"refuge."*

(2) "THEREFORE WILL NOT WE FEAR, THOUGH THE EARTH BE REMOVED,

AND THOUGH THE MOUNTAINS BE CARRIED INTO THE MIDST OF THE SEA."

This statement inspired by the Holy Spirit is extremely powerful. It addresses itself to *"fear,"* which plagues every Christian at one time or another.

FEAR

Concerning the invasion of Jerusalem by the Assyrians, this particular time was one of the most powerful attacks by Satan against the people of God in all of Israel's history. It was of such import that the Holy Spirit graphically detailed the account three times (II Ki., Chpts. 18-19; II Chron., Chpt. 32; Isa., Chpts. 36-37).

This thrice-told account illustrates the fact of the significance that the Holy Spirit placed on this particular event. Satan meant to destroy Hezekiah, Isaiah, Jerusalem, and the whole of Judah. Without God's direct intervention, the evil one would have succeeded. The attack by Satan was so powerful that it seemed as though the Earth would be removed and the mountains would be *"carried into the midst of the sea."*

The greater the attack by Satan, the greater the victory. The Child of God need not fear.

(3) "THOUGH THE WATERS THEREOF ROAR AND BE TROUBLED, THOUGH THE MOUNTAINS SHAKE WITH THE SWELLING THEREOF. SELAH."

By the use of such descriptive statements, the Holy Spirit outlines just how strong this effort of Satan was; therefore, the Holy Spirit is relating to us as God helped Hezekiah, He will help us irrespective of the strength of Satan's attack. *"God is our Refuge."*

THE BELIEVER'S DEFENSE

The Believer should understand that the forces of darkness arrayed against him are so much greater than he is, so much more powerful, which means that if we face these powers of darkness in the wrong way, we will be defeated.

Of course, Satan's powers, although strong, are nothing compared with our Lord. Satan is a mere creature, while the Lord is the Creator. We Believers must understand how the Lord works — in other words, what is His Prescribed Order of Victory.

NOTES

If we follow that *"Order,"* we will walk in victory without fear. If we do not follow it, the results will be disastrous.

GOD'S PRESCRIBED ORDER OF VICTORY

That Prescribed Order is laid down in the Sixth Chapter of Romans.

There Paul tells us that the problem is sin. He then takes us directly to the Cross (Rom. 6:3-5).

We are to understand explicitly that the Cross of Christ is the place of Refuge. It was there that Satan was totally defeated! It was there that every problem was solved! It was there that every Blessing was made possible! So our faith must ever rest in Christ and the Cross.

Our Lord Jesus Christ has already defeated Satan at the Cross. There every victory was won! There every demon power was defeated! There the bondage of sin was forever broken! There it was made possible that man could be free! The Cross, and the Cross alone, *"is our refuge"* (I Cor. 1:18; Gal. 6:14).

(4) "THERE IS A RIVER, THE STREAMS WHEREOF SHALL MAKE GLAD THE CITY OF GOD, THE HOLY PLACE OF THE TABERNACLES OF THE MOST HIGH."

This is one of the most beautiful Passages in the entirety of the Word of God. Its meaning is twofold:

THE RIVER OF GOD

First, it, no doubt, referred to the underground passage in Jerusalem, which is still there today, which was carved out of solid rock and dug by Hezekiah. It provided a source of water (an underground river) for Jerusalem, which made it somewhat independent of outside sources. During the siege of Jerusalem by Sennacherib, Jerusalem was guaranteed a water supply.

However, the greater meaning of this Passage eclipses the one previously mentioned.

More than all, this statement refers to the river that will flow out from under the Sanctuary in the coming Kingdom Age, which will grow larger as it goes, with one branch going to the Dead Sea (which will provide life to that body of water and see it once again teeming with fish), and the other branch going into the Mediterranean Sea.

A SYMBOL OF THE HOLY SPIRIT

In the Millennial Reign, when this River flows out from the newly-built Temple at Jerusalem, it will serve as a symbol of the Holy Spirit. The Dead Sea in its lifeless state serves as a symbol of barren, wasted lives without God, which produce only death.

The life given to that barren body of water will be a symbol of what Christ can do in the lifeless heart.

Also, in the Perfect Age to come, when God will bring the New Jerusalem down from Heaven, the Scripture says that at that time the river will flow *"out of the Throne of God and of the Lamb"* (Rev. 22:1). The word *"Lamb"* speaks of the Sacrifice that Jesus offered of His Own Body on the Cross. As the River flows out of the Temple, it will flow beside the *"Altar,"* which also is a portrayal in the Kingdom Age of Calvary (Ezek. 47:1).

There is life in this River which flows from *"the Throne of God and of the Lamb."* Actually, it is the only life there is; there is no other. This life cannot be exhausted, for Ezekiel also said, *"A River that could not be passed over"* (Ezek. 47:5).

So, irrespective of the terrible bondage of darkness, this water of life that flows from *"the Lamb"* cannot be exhausted. As it will bring life to the Dead Sea, it also will bring life to the Dead Sea of our lives.

Let us again emphasize that nothing else can do such. Sadly, man has ever tried to substitute other remedies; they have never worked. The Church also has tried to substitute other means. Jeremiah likened them to *"two evils."* He said, *"They have forsaken Me, the Fountain of Living Waters, and hewed them out cisterns, broken cisterns, that can hold no water"* (Jer. 2:13). Only this *"River"* can *"make glad."*

(5) "GOD IS IN THE MIDST OF HER; SHE SHALL NOT BE MOVED: GOD SHALL HELP HER, AND THAT RIGHT EARLY."

Isaiah recorded God's Answer to the Assyrian, *"Behold, I will send a blast upon Him"* (Isa. 37:7).

Jerusalem was God's City. He was in her midst; therefore, she could not be captured. The word *"midst"* in Verse 2 is to be contrasted with *"midst"* in Verse 5. National governments will perish in the tumultuous seas of democracy, but Messiah's Government will forever firmly stand in Zion. Her deliverance will come at *"the dawning of the day,"* i.e., *"right early."*

It is true that Jerusalem was, a little over a hundred years later, taken by the Babylonians; however, due to her sin, the Lord had forsaken her (Ezek. 11:23).

(6) "THE HEATHEN RAGED, THE KINGDOMS WERE MOVED: HE UTTERED HIS VOICE, THE EARTH MELTED."

The Thirty-seventh Chapter of Isaiah records this heathen's rage. In response to his *"rage,"* God will *"utter His Voice,"* and the heathen army will *"melt."* This has an even greater fulfillment concerning the Battle of Armageddon, of which the threat of Sennacherib was a type, when the Lord will utter His Voice before His armies and defeat the raging nations surrounding Jerusalem (Zech., Chpt. 14; Rev. 19:11-21).

(7) "THE LORD OF HOSTS IS WITH US; THE GOD OF JACOB IS OUR REFUGE. SELAH."

The reason for Israel's victory under Hezekiah was *"the LORD of Hosts."* The reason for Israel's victory during the coming Battle of Armageddon will also be *"the LORD of Hosts."*

THE GOD OF JACOB

It is remarkable that the Holy Spirit would choose *"Jacob"* as an example of all that He does for us. And yet it is a tremendous comfort to all who know their Lord.

Jacob was a fraud and a schemer, symbolized by his name, who threw himself on the Mercies of God and requested that the Lord change his life. God did! And as He changed Jacob, He can change any and all of us. He is the Only One Who can.

(8) "COME, BEHOLD THE WORKS OF THE LORD, WHAT DESOLATIONS HE HAS MADE IN THE EARTH."

This Verse has to do with the coming Great Tribulation.

THE GREAT TRIBULATION

The *"desolations"* spoken of here pertain to the *"seven seals,"* the *"seven trumpets,"* and the *"seven vials,"* all typifying judgments which will be poured out on the Earth in the *"Great Day of His Wrath."*

This will only be done after the Earth has gone into such deep sin by continuing to spurn the Mercy and Grace of God, with the Scripture defining its condition as *"ripe"* and *"fully ripe"* (Rev. 14:15, 18).

The words, *"ripe"* and *"fully ripe,"* are symbolic of grapes which had completely dried up until they are of no worth. In other words, God will not pour out great judgment upon the planet (desolations) until there is no other choice.

(9) "HE MAKES WARS TO CEASE UNTO THE END OF THE EARTH; HE BREAKS THE BOW, AND CUTS THE SPEAR IN SUNDER; HE BURNS THE CHARIOT IN THE FIRE."

This will happen at the beginning of the Kingdom Age. Jesus Christ is the Prince of Peace. He Alone can bring peace; consequently, all the efforts made by man, as noble as they may be to stop the wars of planet Earth, can never be realized without the Prince of Peace being the Supreme Head (Isa. 2:2-4).

PEACE

The Lord will destroy all weapons of war during the coming Kingdom Age, literally making war impossible (Isa. 2:2-4; Mic. 4:1-8).

For the last several decades, the nations of the world have spent an average of a little over one million dollars a minute, twenty-four hours a day, seven days a week, on weapons of war. In other words, a great part of the production of the world is going for destruction instead of for construction.

Many nations have spoken of disarmament; however, such is impossible without Christ as the Prince of Peace.

It is a remarkable fact that when Jesus Christ was born, and also throughout the approximate 33-1/2 years of His Life, there was very little war on the Earth at that time. In fact, the great war gates of Janus in Rome were closed at this time, signifying that there were no major conflicts anywhere in the vast Roman Empire. Of course, Rome attributed that to her military might.

NOTES

But the real reason had to do with the Advent of Christ. When Jesus was born, a host of Angels said, *"Glory to God in the highest, and on Earth peace, good-will toward men"* (Lk. 2:14).

When He comes back the second time, which He most definitely will, then peace will forever reign. But not until then!

(10) "BE STILL, AND KNOW THAT I AM GOD: I WILL BE EXALTED AMONG THE HEATHEN, I WILL BE EXALTED IN THE EARTH.

(11) "THE LORD OF HOSTS IS WITH US; THE GOD OF JACOB IS OUR REFUGE. SELAH."

Without actually giving the details, we are told in this Passage what the Lord would do to save Jerusalem regarding the invasion of Sennacherib.

DEPENDENCE ON THE LORD

The phrase, *"Be still, and know that I am God,"* refers to what the Lord would do regarding the defeat of Sennacherib. Jerusalem would have to do nothing. They were exhorted to *"be still."*

In one night, the Lord sent an Angel, who *"smote in the camp of the Assyrians an hundred fourscore and five thousand"* (II Ki. 19:35); consequently, all Jerusalem had to do was simply *"be still."*

One of the hardest things for the Christian to do is to simply *"be still."* The flesh always attempts to do things for God; the flesh always fails. We cannot really *"know that He is God"* until we allow the Holy Spirit to perform the work without the intrusion of the flesh. This is done by the Believer simply exercising his Faith conclusively in Christ and the Cross, which then gives the Holy Spirit latitude to work.

THE EXALTATION OF THE LORD

The phrase, *"I will be exalted among the heathen, I will be exalted in the Earth,"* is exactly what happened when the Lord performed this great Miracle by defeating the Assyrians with just one Angel.

While the Lord is exalted in the lives of all Believers, or most certainly should be, there will come an hour that He will be exalted throughout the entirety of the Earth.

THE GOD OF JACOB

Once again, the Holy Spirit emphasizes that God can only bless us if we come to the realization of our true nature. This is the reason that God used *"Jacob"* as an example.

God cannot be *"the refuge"* of the self-righteous or the prideful. The Pharisees, He will not answer. Those who exalt themselves, He will abase. Those who abase themselves, God will exalt.

How it thrills and humbles us to know that God was not ashamed to align Himself with a man who had been a fraud and a schemer (Jacob), but who finally admitted such and was gloriously changed by the Power of God!

To the self-righteous mind it would seem that God should speak of Himself as *"the God of Israel"* instead of as *"the God of Jacob."* However, *"Jacob"* is what we are; *"Israel"* is what God Alone can make of us.

PSALM 47

It is Believed it may have been Written by Either Hezekiah or Isaiah: God Reigns Over All the Earth

(1) "O CLAP YOUR HANDS, ALL YE PEOPLE; SHOUT UNTO GOD WITH THE VOICE OF TRIUMPH."

The superscription is: *"To the Chief Musician, a Psalm for the sons of Korah."*

REJOICING IN THE LORD

This is the only place in the Bible that commands us to clap our hands respecting praise to God. Other places in the Bible allude to it (II Ki. 11:12; Ps. 98:8; Isa. 55:12).

The author of this Psalm is not exactly known. Quite possibly it was written by either Isaiah or Hezekiah.

It was probably written during the time immediately following the defeat of the Assyrians by one Angel killing 185,000 of their soldiers in one night. The entirety of the body of the Psalm lends credence to this.

Sennacherib's vainglorious record, now lodged in the British Museum, states that after having totally destroyed the Hebrew people in the country and cities, he shut up Hezekiah in Jerusalem *"as a bird in a cage."* Sennacherib did take many of the cities of Judah with every intention of destroying Jerusalem. He did not succeed in the latter.

Hezekiah and the occupants of Judah may have been shut up in that cage for a while, but they eventually got out of that cage in a most remarkable way. It is also remarkable that the Assyrian Monarch does not say that he captured the city, because he actually did not.

In his message to Jerusalem (Isa. 36:4-13), Sennacherib styles himself as *"the great king, the king of Assyria."* But Hezekiah and his handful of followers sang of the Messiah, the Great King, the King of all the Earth. They then looked forward in faith to the promised day when all the mighty Gentile nations and their kings, princes, and rulers would be put by God beneath their feet. And, ultimately, it most definitely shall be so!

This Psalm will most certainly be sung by the Lord Jesus Christ at the defeat of the Antichrist in the Battle of Armageddon.

(2) "FOR THE LORD MOST HIGH IS TERRIBLE; HE IS A GREAT KING OVER ALL THE EARTH."

This Verse may be translated, *"For Jehovah Elyon is to be feared; He is become a Great King over all the Earth"*; or, *"For Jehovah Messiah is the Most High; He is to be feared; He shall become a Great King over all the Earth."*

Sennacherib had made his great boasts that he was the king over all the Earth. The people of God are here proclaiming the very opposite, and rightly so, that Jehovah is King over all the Earth.

The people of God would not, even as they should not, have given allegiance to a poor, frail, earthly mortal.

The fact remains that Jesus Christ is King and Lord of your life, or else some frail mortal is.

(3) "HE SHALL SUBDUE THE PEOPLE UNDER US, AND THE NATIONS UNDER OUR FEET."

After the tremendous victory that Judah experienced with the Angel bringing about the demise of 185,000 of the soldiers of Sennacherib, all in one night, the faith of Hezekiah and others rises to the occasion.

As the Holy Spirit anoints them and inspires them, they now see that not only has the Lord subdued Sennacherib, but He also will subdue all the nations of the Earth. That has not yet taken place, but most definitely will in the coming Kingdom Age.

(4) "HE SHALL CHOOSE OUR INHERITANCE FOR US, THE EXCELLENCY OF JACOB WHOM HE LOVED. SELAH."

Another beautiful story of Grace is here given in this Verse.

THE EXCELLENCY OF JACOB

The *"excellency of Jacob"* refers to the supremacy of Jacob over the nations, which will take place in the coming Kingdom Age. This was involved in the birthright which the Patriarch valued and which Esau despised. He was given this double Promise, the inheritance of Canaan and the Lordship of the nations. To him, therefore, Canaan was more precious than Egypt, hence, his earnest injunction to Joseph to bury him in that Land of Promise.

Once again, the Holy Spirit uses the name *"Jacob"* as an example of what we are and what God desires to make of us, which He Alone can do. Until the Christian comes to the place that he realizes that he is but a *"Jacob"* (a schemer, fraud, deceiver) and that the Holy Spirit Alone is able to make him into an *"Israel"* (Prince of God), he does not know who he is or Who God is. God *"loves"* the man who will admit what he is and what God Alone can make of him.

(5) "GOD IS GONE UP WITH A SHOUT, THE LORD WITH THE SOUND OF A TRUMPET."

This speaks of the victory over the Assyrians; however, it also speaks of the coming victory over the Antichrist. By faith, the *"trumpet"* of victory has already been blown.

VICTORY

As God *"comes down"* when He interposes for the relief or Deliverance of His people, so after the relief or Deliverance is effected, He is viewed as *"going up"* — returning to His glorious Abode, reoccupying His Seat in the Heaven of Heavens, and there remaining until some fresh call is made upon Him.

If the interposition has been one of a striking and unusual character, if the relief has been great, the Deliverance signal, the extraordinary triumph accorded to His people, then He *"goes up with a shout"* — amid the exulting cries and loud jubilations of rescued Israel.

When the occasion is such as to call for a public manifestation of thanksgiving at the House of God, then He *"goes up"* also *"with the sound of the trumpet,"* which was always sounded by the Priests on great occasions of festal joy and gladness (II Sam. 6:15; II Ki. 11:14; I Chron. 13:8; 16:42; II Chron. 5:12; 7:6; 29:27; Ezra 3:10; Neh. 12:35).

All of this proves that this Psalm was sung after the great victory over the Assyrians.

(6) "SING PRAISES TO GOD, SING PRAISES: SING PRAISES UNTO OUR KING, SING PRAISES."

Judah was told here, and so are we, to praise the Lord as both God and King. He definitely is both!

A SONG OF PRAISE

We learn from this Book of Psalms, which really is a book of 150 Songs, just how valuable music and singing are to the Lord, as it regards praises. Because the Holy Spirit has devoted the longest Book in the Bible to this form of praise, this fact teaches us exactly how valuable it is and how the Lord thinks of such.

It is said that there are seven major Religions in the world (including Christianity). Of course, Biblical Christianity is not really a religion, but rather a relationship with a Man, The Man Christ Jesus. At any rate, regarding these major Religions, Christianity is the only one which has a songbook. The reason why should be obvious!

First of all, what in the world does Islam have to sing about? Or Buddhism? Or Shintoism? Or Hinduism?

The redeemed soul alone can sing praises to God!

The reason?

The unredeemed heart has no song of praise to God in its recesses, as should be obvious.

Hezekiah and Isaiah greatly sang praises to the Lord after this great victory, as doubtless did the entirety of Judah and Jerusalem.

The praises sung to God at that time were prophetically the praises that will be sung on that great victory morning when Jesus Christ comes back and defeats the Antichrist, and Israel is then redeemed.

How can we under the New Covenant do less than Judah of old? We have even far more reasons today for which we can sing praises than at any time in history!

(7) "FOR GOD IS THE KING OF ALL THE EARTH: SING YE PRAISES WITH UNDERSTANDING."

The literal translation is, *"Sing a Psalm of instruction."*

THE PRAISE OF UNDERSTANDING

Every song and praise to God, on account of God, on account of His glorious Deeds, contains a rich treasure of instruction and improvement. Here the special instruction is that God is King over the whole Earth, that He reigns over the heathen, and that the heathen shall also sometime or other own His Sovereignty.

The Holy Spirit is saying that we should have *"understanding"* regarding this matter. *"Jesus Christ is King of all the Earth,"* and not the Antichrist. This planet will not succumb to war, pollution, or any other disaster. It will be redeemed by Jesus Christ. He is the *"King of all the Earth."* It belongs to Him, and, to be sure, no matter what the situation, He is closely surveying it moment by moment.

(8) "GOD REIGNS OVER THE HEATHEN: GOD SITS UPON THE THRONE OF HIS HOLINESS."

God had manifested His Kingly power over the heathen at this time by subduing great numbers of them and making them subject to Judah. This is a fore-view of what will take place in the coming Kingdom Age, when truly the Lord will reign not only over Judah, but over the entirety of the world.

HOLINESS

In the coming Kingdom Age when the Lord reigns over the entirety of the Earth, He will do so *"from the Throne of His Holiness."* This is the Throne from which He exercises a just, a righteous, and a Holy rule, which the world has never before seen. As stated, it will be during the coming Kingdom Age.

(9) "THE PRINCES OF THE PEOPLE ARE GATHERED TOGETHER, EVEN THE PEOPLE OF THE GOD OF ABRAHAM: FOR THE SHIELDS OF THE EARTH BELONG UNTO GOD: HE IS GREATLY EXALTED."

This pertains to the great victory of the Lord when He defeats the army of the Assyrians in one night with one Angel. In a greater sense, it speaks of the tremendous victory of the Lord Jesus Christ over the Antichrist, which is yet to come.

THE PRINCES OF THE PEOPLE

The *"Princes of the people"* and *"the people of the God of Abraham"* speak of the Jewish people who will gather around Jesus Christ at His Second Coming. The Antichrist will have then been defeated. Israel will have been saved from annihilation. Even more importantly, they then will recognize Jesus Christ as *"King of kings and Lord of lords."*

SHIELDS OF THE EARTH

The phrase, *"For the shields of the Earth belong unto God,"* refers to the host of Heaven, which help the Lord administer the affairs of the universe.

In his puffed up ego, the Antichrist thought he could defeat God. How did he think so?

He reasoned that if he could destroy the Jewish people, scores of Prophecies in the Bible would thereby be proved false. If even one word of the Word of God fails, then Satan has won. So the Antichrist will use all the forces at his disposal to annihilate Israel, and he will come close to succeeding. Were it not for the Second Coming, he would succeed!

However, the Second Coming will most definitely take place. The Lord will be accompanied by every Saint of God who has ever lived and by the great Angelic Hosts of the Heavens — all arrayed against the Antichrist. In other words, at that time, the Antichrist will find out just how powerful the Lord really is. At that time, the Lord will be *"greatly exalted,"* which means that the Antichrist will not be exalted as he had planned.

PSALM 48

As well, this Psalm Could have been Written by Either Isaiah or Hezekiah: Zion, the City of the Great King

(1) "GREAT IS THE LORD, AND GREATLY TO BE PRAISED IN THE CITY OF OUR GOD, IN THE MOUNTAIN OF HIS HOLINESS."

The superscription is: *"A Song and Psalm for the sons of Korah."*

GREAT IS THE LORD

The author of this Psalm is not known. Possibly it was written, as were a few others, by Isaiah or Hezekiah after the great victory of the Lord over Sennacherib. As the last, it has two meanings:

1. The celebration of great victory over the Assyrian army.

2. The celebration of the coming victory over the army of the Antichrist at the Second Coming of the Lord, of which the previous was a type.

The *"city of our God"* is the city of Jerusalem that Sennacherib vowed to take. The Antichrist will follow suit and also will fail.

THE MOUNTAIN OF HIS HOLINESS

The phrase, *"The mountain of His Holiness,"* was used by faith during the days of Hezekiah. It will be a fact at the Second Coming. Jerusalem has been contested by Satan ever since the day that God chose this city as the place for His Name (I Ki. 11:13, 36). During the Millennial Reign, Jerusalem will truly be *"the mountain of His Holiness."* It will be viewed as such by the entirety of the world, even as the next Verse proclaims!

(2) "BEAUTIFUL FOR SITUATION, THE JOY OF THE WHOLE EARTH, IS MOUNT ZION, ON THE SIDES OF THE NORTH, THE CITY OF THE GREAT KING."

By faith, Hezekiah or Isaiah proclaims what the city of Jerusalem will be during the coming Kingdom Age.

JERUSALEM

Jerusalem is situated in the exact geographical center of the Earth. It has been called *"the navel"* of the Earth. Beautifully so, it is situated where the King will reside.

It will be called *"the joy of the whole Earth"* because Jesus Christ will reign Personally from this great city. It is the Lord Jesus Christ Who will make the city what it actually is. Without Him, it is nothing; with Him, it is everything! It will be His Headquarters city for the entirety of the Earth.

During that time (we continue to speak of the Kingdom Age), ambassadors and kings of the whole Earth will continually come to Jerusalem, and also forever to the *"New Jerusalem"* which will come down out of Heaven from God to dwell on Earth forever (Rev. 21:2-3).

The term, *"The sides of the north,"* refers to Moriah and the Temple site immediately on the north side of Mount Zion.

Sennacherib, the monarch of the Earth of that day, had vowed that Jerusalem would be his; the Antichrist will do the same. Both will fail because it is *"the city of the Great King."*

(3) "GOD IS KNOWN IN HER PALACES FOR A REFUGE."

Many cities of the world that revel in their beauty invite men to observe but can do little else. Jerusalem will then be known as the most beautiful city on the face of the Earth, but her beauty is caused by Something and Someone which no other city has ever had, the Person of the Lord Jesus Christ. His Glory, and His Glory alone, is what will make the city one of splendor and greatness.

The word *"refuge"* is used because this city will dispense justice and fairness to the entirety of the world.

(4) "FOR, LO, THE KINGS WERE ASSEMBLED, THEY PASSED BY TOGETHER."

This speaks of the kings of the Earth during Hezekiah's day who assembled to destroy Jerusalem. They were *"together"* in their will to destroy the city of the people of God. They felt they could not lose, but lose they did!

During the days of the Antichrist, the Antichrist with his kings also will assemble at Jerusalem in order to destroy the city (Rev. 16:12-16). They too will fail!

(5) "THEY SAW IT, AND SO THEY MARVELED; THEY WERE TROUBLED, AND HASTED AWAY."

These kings *"marveled"* at what God did

with one Angel in the destruction of 185,000 Assyrians in one night. They were also *"troubled,"* and, as a result, they *"hasted away."* And rightly so!

The Antichrist will do the same except he will be killed, whereas Sennacherib was later killed by his own sons.

(6) "FEAR TOOK HOLD UPON THEM THERE, AND PAIN, AS OF A WOMAN IN TRAVAIL."

No wonder that *"fear took hold upon them."* With the rising of the sun, they observed 185,000 soldiers dead. The very cream of the Assyrian army had been killed by one Angel in one night (II Ki. 19:32-37).

Fear also will take hold upon the Antichrist and his armies at the Second Coming of the Lord, and rightly so! He will witness Power such as he has never known existed. The pain that he and his armies will experience will be the *"pain of death."*

(7) "YOU BREAK THE SHIPS OF TARSHISH WITH AN EAST WIND."

If Hezekiah did in fact write this Psalm, he probably little understood the full meaning of this statement when the Holy Spirit inspired him to write it. Its greater fulfillment will be at the Battle of Armageddon. No doubt, the Antichrist will use mighty warships, which will be destroyed by the Lord by what is referred to as *"an east wind."*

Some Scholars believe that *"Tarshish"* refers to Spain. If that is correct, the vessels will be great ocean-going vessels, which, no doubt, will coincide with the efforts of the Antichrist to take over the world.

(8) "AS WE HAVE HEARD, SO HAVE WE SEEN IN THE CITY OF THE LORD OF HOSTS, IN THE CITY OF OUR GOD: GOD WILL ESTABLISH IT FOREVER SELAH."

The writer of this Psalm is saying that we have *"heard"* of what God could do, and now we have *"seen"* what the Lord can do. The Lord destroyed the Assyrians and saved Jerusalem, and He will *"establish it forever."* The Palestinians should read this!

This also will be sung by Israel when the Lord Jesus Christ defeats the Antichrist.

(9) "WE HAVE THOUGHT OF YOUR LOVINGKINDNESS, O GOD, IN THE MIDST OF YOUR TEMPLE."

The writer is referring to the times of prayer in *"Your Temple,"* when the enemy was at the gate. Now, God has delivered Jerusalem and His people.

This also will be sung in the *"Temple"* at Jerusalem in the coming Kingdom Age (Ezek., Chpt. 47).

(10) "ACCORDING TO YOUR NAME, O GOD, SO IS YOUR PRAISE UNTO THE ENDS OF THE EARTH: YOUR RIGHT HAND IS FULL OF RIGHTEOUSNESS."

God's action is ever in harmony with His Character; His fame extends, and will extend, to the very ends of the Earth. This is not true of earthly kings. *"Righteousness"* is in His Right Hand in favor of His people as promised and in destruction to their foes as predicted.

(11) "LET MOUNT ZION REJOICE, LET THE DAUGHTERS OF JUDAH BE GLAD, BECAUSE OF YOUR JUDGMENTS."

Even though Jerusalem would rejoice greatly because of the great victory over the Assyrians, and rightly so, still, this has a greater fulfillment at the beginning of the Kingdom Age.

Then the *"daughters of Judah"* will rejoice because of the great victory won by Jesus Christ, victories which have been won because of *"Your Judgments,"* which speak of His Word. As one reads these Passages in Verses 9 through 14, one is reading the eternal future of Jerusalem. It has known much war and bloodshed in the past. When Jesus Christ comes back, it will never again know war or bloodshed, only *"rejoicing."*

(12) "WALK ABOUT ZION, AND GO ROUND ABOUT HER: TELL THE TOWERS THEREOF."

During the Kingdom Age, it will be safe, completely safe, to *"walk about Zion."* One should shout it to the *"towers"* that peace now reigns because the Prince of Peace now reigns.

At the present time (2005), Jerusalem is one of the most dangerous cities in the world. Human bombers have taken many lives and they will probably take many more. This will end for a short time under the Antichrist, but that particular period of peace will be short-lived. Jerusalem will then revert back to a place of great danger, no doubt, greater danger than any city in the world.

But when Jesus comes back (and come back He shall!) this great city will rise to prominence in all the Earth, and be prominent in beauty and splendor as no other city ever has been.

Again we state: It is all because of the Lord Jesus Christ.

(13) "MARK YE WELL HER BULWARKS, CONSIDER HER PALACES; THAT YOU MAY TELL IT TO THE GENERATION FOLLOWING."

This Psalm is sung in testimony to the great victory won by the Lord in the sending of His Angel to defeat the Assyrians. Jerusalem has been spared. No damage has been done to her. The boasts of Sennacherib prove to be empty threats.

Likewise, we should *"tell it to the generation following,"* which is to be taken literally, but more so it refers to the generation of Israelites who will be alive during the Great Tribulation. They are told to read this Psalm and to believe well that just as the Lord delivered Jerusalem from Sennacherib, likewise, He will deliver it from the coming Sennacherib.

During the Battle of Armageddon, half the city will fall (Zech. 14:2), which means that it will be totally destroyed. This given in this Psalm probably envisages the city after its restoration by the Great King, as predicted in Acts 15:16.

(14) "FOR THIS GOD IS OUR GOD FOREVER AND EVER: HE WILL BE OUR GUIDE EVEN UNTO DEATH."

As the writer of this Psalm exclaims over the great victory given to them by the Lord, a vow is made that they will serve God forever. They have vowed that *"He will be our God even unto death."*

This Psalm had its limitations when sung by Hezekiah; it will have no limitations when sung by the people of God at the beginning of the great Kingdom Age. Jesus Christ will then be *"our Guide."* Thank God, there will be no more *"death"* (Rev. 21:4).

PSALM 49

As well, this Psalm may have been Written by Either Isaiah or Hezekiah: Trust in God, Not Riches

(1) "HEAR THIS, ALL YE PEOPLE; GIVE EAR, ALL YE INHABITANTS OF THE WORLD:

(2) "BOTH LOW AND HIGH, RICH AND POOR, TOGETHER."

The superscription is: *"To the Chief Musician, a Psalm for the sons of Korah."*

THE ENTIRETY OF THE WORLD

This Psalm reviews the affliction of the Messiah's people, the foolishness and feebleness of their oppressors, and the glory of Israel's Redeemer. The oppressor is feeble for he has no power against death, to which he is justly doomed because he is a sinner; and he is foolish, for he denies that he is a sinner and ignores the fact of death.

This Psalm will support Israel's faith in her future suffering under the oppression of the false Messiah, just as in the past its truth sustained her when oppressed by the Assyrian. Confronted with the power and wealth of Sennacherib, a type of the Antichrist, she, defenseless and impoverished, could say, *"Why should I fear in the days of evil?"* And her Lord could say to her, *"Be not thou therefore afraid when one is made rich."* Thus, faith can fitly measure man in his folly and impotence, however exalted he may be.

We are not told who wrote this Psalm; however, we do know that the Speaker is the Messiah. In the first four Verses, He proposes an enigma and invites all the nations of the Earth to hear His solution of it.

THE ENIGMA OF MAN

The enigma is this: How can man, who is without understanding and without power, redeem himself from the dominion of death?

The solution is this: It can be done through the Death and Resurrection of a Redeemer.

Thus, this Psalm restates the doctrine of the preceding Psalms as to man's moral ruin and brings forward a Redeemer Whose sufficiency, as such, forms the subject matter, not only of this Psalm, but also of the succeeding group.

Even as the first two Verses proclaim, every individual in the world is included, and for all time. Untold millions around the world are fond of saying that they do not serve Christ, but rather another religion, which means they serve another god; however, that matters not at all. All ultimately will answer to Christ.

There is only one Redeemer, and that is the Lord Jesus Christ. Every single individual who has ever lived, and who ever shall live, will answer to Him either in Redemption or in Judgment, but answer they will!

(3) "MY MOUTH SHALL SPEAK OF WISDOM; AND THE MEDITATION OF MY HEART SHALL BE OF UNDERSTANDING."

We are informed here by the Holy Spirit that the mouth of the Lord Jesus Christ will *"speak wisdom."* Man would do well to heed these words; likewise, the Lord of Glory is the only One Who has *"understanding"* of Death, Hell, and what it takes to redeem man from such.

THE STORY OF THE BIBLE

That's the reason the story of the Bible is *"Jesus Christ and Him Crucified"* (I Cor. 1:23). God has one Redeemer, and that is the Lord Jesus Christ. He has one means of Redemption and that is the Cross of Christ. There is no other, because no other is needed. Pure, plain, and simple: Any Message that does not harmonize completely and totally with the Message of the Cross (I Cor. 1:18) is not Scriptural.

Other than the Cross of Christ, everything else comes from the flesh, which speaks of human nature, which has been corrupted by the Fall. God cannot accept such! In fact, the Holy Spirit through Paul plainly and succinctly says, *"So then they who are in the flesh cannot please God"* (Rom. 8:8). This means that God can never bless that with which He is not pleased!

(4) "I WILL INCLINE MY EAR TO A PARABLE; I WILL OPEN MY DARK SAYING UPON THE HARP."

The sons of Korah sang this Psalm and were accompanied *"upon the harp."* They asked the people to *"give ear to a parable."* It would be a *"parable"* of utmost significance.

A DARK SAYING

The *"dark saying"* referred to that which was not commonly understood.

Many of the Psalms are Prophetic in nature; they deal with things that would be far into the future. To point toward these great Truths, the Holy Spirit would use songs to imprint them upon the heart.

Then music and singing were used to point to that which was to come; now they are used to point to that which already has come. That's the reason that all songs must be perfectly Scriptural for them to be of any use. Regrettably, much of that which passes today for *"Christian"* music and singing is woefully unscriptural.

(5) "WHEREFORE SHOULD I FEAR IN THE DAYS OF EVIL, WHEN THE INIQUITY OF MY HEELS SHALL COMPASS ME ABOUT?"

A great Truth is here given to us.

FEAR

This Passage tells us that there will be *"days of evil"* in the lives of all Christians, referring to trials, tests, difficulties, problems, etc. No matter how much faith one may have, a Believer is not immune to such.

But the Psalmist tells us, as he is inspired by the Holy Spirit, that he has no reason to fear, because he can trust in God's Protection. All of the righteous who trust Him, who look exclusively to Him, are under His Care.

It takes some doing for the Believer to be brought to the place that he has no more fear of man and no more fear of circumstances, no matter how these seem to be on the surface, because he trusts God implicitly. That is the place and position to which the Holy Spirit seeks to bring every Believer.

The phrase, *"When the iniquity of my heels shall compass me about,"* actually says *"my supplanters."* It speaks of those who would trip us up, who would surround us, seeking to harm and hurt. Regrettably, most of such opposition comes from within the Church instead of from without the Church. That is sad but true!

(6) "THEY WHO TRUST IN THEIR WEALTH, AND BOAST THEMSELVES IN THE MULTITUDE OF THEIR RICHES;

(7) "NONE OF THEM CAN BY ANY MEANS REDEEM HIS BROTHER, NOR GIVE TO GOD A RANSOM FOR HIM."

This Truth should be read by all!

RICHES CANNOT REDEEM THE SOUL

What do we learn from these two Verses?

We learn that irrespective of the riches that an individual may possess, such cannot effect the Redemption of the soul. However great his wealth, it cannot redeem.

Peter said, and I quote from THE EXPOSITOR'S STUDY BIBLE:

"Forasmuch as you know that you were not redeemed with corruptible things, as silver and gold (presents the fact that the most precious commodities [silver and gold] could not redeem fallen man), *from your vain conversation* (vain lifestyle) *received by tradition from your fathers* (speaks of original sin that is passed on from father to child at conception);

"But with the Precious Blood of Christ (presents the payment, which proclaims the poured out Life of Christ on behalf of sinners), *as of a Lamb without blemish and without spot* (speaks of the lambs offered as substitutes in the old Jewish economy; the Death of Christ was not an execution or assassination, but rather a Sacrifice; the Offering of Himself presented a Perfect Sacrifice, for He was Perfect in every respect [Ex. 12:5]):

"Who verily was foreordained before the foundation of the world (refers to the fact that God, in His Omniscience, knew He would create man, knew man would fall, and knew man would be redeemed by Christ going to the Cross; this was all done before the Universe was created; this means the Cross of Christ is the Foundation Doctrine of all Doctrine, referring to the fact that all Doctrine must be built upon that Foundation, or else it is specious), *but was manifest in these last times for you* (refers to the invisible God Who, in the Person of the Son, made Himself visible to human eyesight by assuming a human body and human limitations)" (I Pet. 1:18-20).

All of this tells us that our Salvation is a well thought out Plan of the Godhead, which They formulated even before the foundation of the world. This means that God was not at all caught by surprise by the Fall of Adam and Eve.

There is nothing that can redeem the soul but faith in Christ and what Christ did at the Cross, all on our behalf (Jn. 3:16; Rom. 5:1; 10:9-10, 13).

(8) "(FOR THE REDEMPTION OF

NOTES

THEIR SOUL IS PRECIOUS, AND IT CEASES FOREVER:)

(9) "THAT HE SHOULD STILL LIVE FOREVER, AND NOT SEE CORRUPTION."

The great Truth continues!

REDEMPTION

We are told several things in these two Verses. They are:

1. All men need Redemption, both the rich and the poor, the great and the small!

2. This Redemption is so costly that it is impossible to buy such with silver or gold, irrespective of the amount that one might have.

3. This has been true, is true, and will be true forever.

4. Every soul is eternal.

5. *"Corruption"* in its final bearing refers to Hell itself. In other words, money cannot keep a person out of Hell!

Man can be saved from this *"corruption"* only (let me repeat, *"only"*!) by accepting Jesus Christ and what He did at the Cross (Jn. 3:3, 16; 7:37-38; Rev. 22:17).

A DEFINITION OF REDEMPTION

There are several Greek words in the New Testament which define Redemption. The three words used most frequently are:

1. Garazo: This word refers to a slave being bought out of a slave market and being given his freedom.

2. Exgarazo: This word refers to a slave being bought out of a slave market, being given his freedom, never again to be a slave.

3. Lutroo: This word refers to the price paid for the slave and his freedom being so great that neither demons nor angels in eternity future ever will be able to say the price was insufficient.

WHY DOES MAN NEED REDEMPTION?

Redemption means deliverance from some evil by payment of a price; however, it is more than simple deliverance. It means that Christ, through His Death on the Cross of Calvary, not only bought our freedom and paid the price for our Deliverance from sin and all its baggage, but He also bought us. In other words, we now belong to Him.

As it concerns this subject, Paul said,

and I quote from THE EXPOSITOR'S STUDY BIBLE:

"*What?* (By this time, you should know!) *Do you not know that your body is the Temple of the Holy Spirit which is in you* (actually refers to the human body of the Born-Again Believer as being a Sanctuary of the Holy Spirit), *which you have of God* (means that it's all of God and must be treated accordingly), *and you are not your own?* (We belong to the Lord.)

"*For you are bought with a price* (the price was the shed Blood of Christ at Calvary)*: therefore glorify God in your body* (the house of the Spirit), *and in your spirit* (the use of the house), *which are God's* (because we were created by God, and have been purchased at great price)" (I Cor. 6:19-20).

The Christians of the Early Church understood this great Truth. Jesus had taught them that *"everyone who commits sin is a slave to sin"* (Jn. 8:34). In line with this, Paul spoke of himself as *"carnal, sold under sin"* (Rom. 7:14), comparable to being sold under a cruel slave master, which he was before conversion, and would be again, even as a Believer, if he attempted to live for God outside of God's Prescribed Order, which is Faith in Christ and the Cross, Faith in Christ and the Cross alone!

Paul reminded the Romans that in earlier days they had been slaves to sin (Rom. 6:17). This meant that they were under the sentence of death on account of their sin: *"For the wages of sin is death"* (Rom. 6:23). Pure and simple, sinners are slaves. Failing redemption, the slavery would continue, the sentence of death would be carried out. The Cross of Christ is ever seen against this background, for it is the Cross of Christ alone which dealt with sin (Rom. 6:1-14).

THE BLOOD OF CHRIST, THE PRICE OF REDEMPTION

When we read of *"Redemption through His Blood"* (Eph. 1:7), the Blood of Christ is clearly being regarded as the price of Redemption.

Paul further said, *"Being justified freely by His Grace* (made possible by the Cross) *through the Redemption that is in Christ Jesus* (carried out at the Cross)*:*

NOTES

"*Whom God has set forth to be a perfect propitiation* (Atonement or Reconciliation) *through Faith in His Blood* (again, all of this is made possible by the Cross), *to declare His Righteousness for the remission of sins that are past* (refers to all who trusted Christ before He actually came, which covers the entirety of the time from the Garden of Eden to the moment Jesus died on the Cross) *through the forbearance* (tolerance) *of God* (meaning that God tolerated the situation before Calvary, knowing the debt would be fully paid at that time)*;*

"*To declare, I say, at this time His Righteousness* (refers to God's Righteousness, which must be satisfied at all time, and is in Christ and only Christ)*: that He* (God) *might be just* (not overlooking sin in any manner), *and the Justifier of him which believes in Jesus.* (God can justify a believing [although guilty] sinner and His Holiness not be impacted, providing the sinner's faith is exclusively in Christ; only in this manner can God be 'just' and at the same time 'justify' the sinner)" (Rom. 3:24-26).

In Galatians 3:13, what Christ did for us is presented as the price of Redemption; the Scripture says, *"Being made a curse for us,"* which refers to His Substitutionary Work on our behalf. There is no Redemption outside of the Cross.

That's the reason Paul also said, *"Christ sent me not to baptize, but to preach the Gospel, not with wisdom of words, lest the Cross of Christ be made of none effect"* (I Cor. 1:17).

That's the reason Paul also said, *"For the preaching of the Cross is to them who perish foolishness, but to us who are saved it is the Power of God"* (I Cor. 1:18).

And also, *"We preach Christ Crucified"* (I Cor. 1:23).

THAT WHICH CALVARY ACCOMPLISHED

Redemption not only looks back to Calvary, but forward to the freedom in which the redeemed stand.

We must show in our lives that we no longer are caught up in the bondage from which we have been released; we are exhorted to *"stand fast therefore in the liberty wherewith Christ has made us free"* (Gal. 5:1).

How do we do that?

Paul gave this explanation in the Sixth Chapter of Romans. In the first two Verses, he tells us that sin is the problem. Then, in Verses 3 through 5, he tells us that the Cross is the answer for sin, that the Cross is the only answer for sin.

This means the Believer must place his faith entirely in Christ and the Cross and not allow it to be moved to other things. Only then will the Holy Spirit, Who Alone can make us what we ought to be, function in our lives as He should, and as He is sent to do. Without exception, it is all tied to Christ and the Cross.

That's the reason that we so strongly oppose all false doctrine which claims that there is another way of victory. To claim that there is another way of Victory other than the Cross is as bad as claiming that there is another way of Salvation other than the Cross!

Many true Christians would greatly oppose the idea of Salvation outside of Christ and the Cross; but, strangely enough, many good Christians try to find Victory outside of the Cross. It simply cannot be done!

If the Believer desires to live a life for God in which the sin nature no longer dominates his life, he can do so only by placing his faith exclusively in Christ and the Cross. Even though I repeat this over and over and over, I do so because, as simple as the statement is, it is not easy for most Believers to understand it and believe it.

All Salvation is in Christ and the Cross, and all Victory is in Christ and the Cross! The very word *"Salvation"* includes Victory — Victory in every capacity. But regrettably, most Christians have greatly abbreviated the word *"Salvation,"* which means we don't have all that it promises. While any person who is truly Born-Again is truly Saved, that doesn't mean that he truly is walking in victory!

Redemption is for all, because Jesus died for all (Jn. 3:16); however, this great Redemption in all of its great process must be obtained on God's terms, or it cannot be obtained at all!

(10) "FOR HE SEES THAT WISE MEN DIE, LIKEWISE THE FOOL AND THE BRUTISH PERSON PERISH, AND LEAVE THEIR WEALTH TO OTHERS."

All men die, whether rich or poor, whether wise or foolish. Furthermore, whether our estate is great or small, when we die, we leave everything we own to others.

A very rich man in a particular community died. As he was being taken to the graveyard, someone asked, *"How much did he leave?"*

The answer was instant, *"He left it all!"*

If a man lives for wealth (and sadly, most men do, but the far greater majority never achieve it), he is, pure and simple, a *"fool."*

The other day, I saw a sign advertising an insurance company. It said, *"Have you insured your life?"* But it should have read, *"Have you insured your soul?"*

When the poorest of the poor die, they take nothing with them. When the richest of the rich die, they also take nothing with them.

(11) "THEIR INWARD THOUGHT IS, THAT THEIR HOUSES SHALL CONTINUE FOREVER, AND THEIR DWELLING PLACES TO ALL GENERATIONS; THEY CALL THEIR LANDS AFTER THEIR OWN NAMES."

Man's folly is set out in Verse 11. Although he knows that he must die, yet he wants his name perpetuated by naming things after himself. It seems he wishes to persuade himself that he is still alive as long as his lands last. But in spite of all that, he soon is forgotten.

It doesn't matter how rich or how powerful a man has become; if he tries to live his life outside of God, death will still end his life. Then, as our Lord said, *"What shall it profit a man if he gain the whole world and lose his own soul?"* (Mat. 16:26).

(12) "NEVERTHELESS MAN BEING IN HONOR ABIDES NOT: HE IS LIKE THE BEASTS THAT PERISH."

Man cannot perpetuate himself except in the New Birth and by the Lord Jesus Christ. All else is folly. If he thinks otherwise, his thinking is no higher than *"the beasts that perish."*

THE SOUL OF MAN

Man is created an eternal being. This means he will live forever, but the place he ends up living decides it all.

If the person is without God, in other words, he dies without having accepted the Lord Jesus Christ as his personal Saviour, his eternal abode will be Hell. That is a blunt statement, but it is true (Deut. 32:22; Ps. 9:17; Isa. 5:14; Ezek. 32:27; Mat. 5:22, 29; 10:28; 11:23; Mk. 9:43; II Pet. 2:4; Rev. 20:14).

If the person lives for God, Heaven will be their eternal home. In effect, the moment the unredeemed person dies, he instantly goes to Hell. The moment the redeemed person dies, he instantly goes to be with Christ (Phil. 1:23).

WHERE IS HEAVEN?

The only information we have from the Bible about the location of Heaven is found in the short statement of Isaiah 14:13, which says, *"For you* (Lucifer) *have said in your heart, I will ascend into Heaven, I will exalt my throne above the stars of God: I will sit also upon the mount of the congregation, in the sides of the north."* From this we know that Planet Heaven is in the north from Planet Earth. Heaven actually is outside of our universe.

We know from the Word of God that Angels were created by God before this universe was brought into existence, for the Scripture says that they shouted for joy at the beauty of the original creation (Job 38:7). We really do not know how old this universe is.

The science of astronomy tells us that possibly it is millions of years old. What science does not know is the original cause. As a result, they come up with all types of hypotheses about the original creation. We know that God spoke this universe into existence by uttering the Word (Heb. 11:3).

God literally spoke this universe into existence. This is power beyond our comprehension.

It is difficult for some Believers to think of Heaven as a Planet; however, we know there is at least one city there, and we know that this city has streets, walls, and many other things. We can, therefore, reasonably come to the conclusion that Heaven is a Planet.

After the Kingdom Age, which will last a thousand years (Rev., Chpt. 20), the Scriptures tell us that the Lord will transfer His Headquarters from Planet Heaven to Planet Earth. This information is presented in the Twenty-first and Twenty-second Chapters of the Book of Revelation.

We have only touched the surface of what lies in the future for Believers, but it is all so far beyond our comprehension as to defy description. Knowing this, why doesn't the entirety of mankind, and for all time, want to live for God?

The reason is the *"deceitfulness of sin."* This implies unbelief. In other words, most of the human race do not believe there is a literal Hell. Most do believe there is a literal Heaven, at least of some sort, but most have rejected God's Way of making certain of Salvation. As stated, deception and unbelief are the causes of these problems.

(13) "THIS THEIR WAY IS THEIR FOLLY: YET THEIR POSTERITY APPROVE THEIR SAYINGS. SELAH."

Men make great plans to perpetuate their names and memories. Their children attempt to carry out these great plans. About this, the Holy Spirit says, *"Their way is their folly."*

(14) LIKE SHEEP THEY ARE LAID IN THE GRAVE; DEATH SHALL FEED ON THEM; AND THE UPRIGHT SHALL HAVE DOMINION OVER THEM IN THE MORNING; AND THEIR BEAUTY SHALL CONSUME IN THE GRAVE FROM THEIR DWELLING."

The Holy Spirit continues His dialog concerning the foolishness of man.

THE PLIGHT OF THE LOST

Irrespective of how rich and powerful men may be, when they die, they are as defenseless as *"sheep."* Meekly, they are laid in the grave, and all their money, fame, and power (should they have that) can do nothing to stop it. *"Death shall feed on them."*

The statement, *"The upright shall have dominion over them in the morning,"* means that the Godly shall be resurrected and their faith in Christ will give them *"dominion."*

The *"beauty,"* referring to all the riches and power of the wicked, shall be *"consumed in the grave."*

(15) "BUT GOD WILL REDEEM MY SOUL FROM THE POWER OF THE GRAVE: FOR HE SHALL RECEIVE ME. SELAH."

When Jesus died on the Cross, the price was forever paid, thereby lifting the sin debt from man. During the time between His Death and Resurrection, a time frame of some three days and three nights, the Scripture says that Christ went down into Paradise (Eph. 4:8) and liberated all of the souls who were there. This included all who had died in the Faith from the time of Abel to the time of Christ's Crucifixion. In other words, Christ took these liberated souls with Him to Heaven. That is what is meant by the Psalmist saying that the Lord *"redeemed my soul from the power of the grave."*

The phrase, *"For He shall receive me,"* could very well refer to the great Resurrection of Life at the Rapture of the Saints (I Thess. 4:13-18).

(16) "BE NOT THOU AFRAID WHEN ONE IS MADE RICH, WHEN THE GLORY OF HIS HOUSE IS INCREASED."

No matter how much power and riches a person may have on this Earth, and some few have a great deal, all that ends at death. Their wealth will not ransom their souls. They cannot take it with them to another world. In the death world, they will have no advantage because of any wealth they had on Earth.

In fact, their misery in another world will be such as to far outweigh any enjoyment they may have had on Earth.

(17) "FOR WHEN HE DIES HE SHALL CARRY NOTHING AWAY: HIS GLORY SHALL NOT DESCEND AFTER HIM."

Even though these statements pertain to a far wider scope than particular individuals, more than likely Hezekiah would have had Sennacherib in mind when he wrote this Psalm.

Even though this man, when he was alive, was the mightiest man on the face of the Earth, when he died, he *"carried nothing away,"* in spite of his great power and riches on Earth. Likewise, none who trust in riches or power will be helped at the time of death.

(18) "THOUGH WHILE HE LIVED HE BLESSED HIS SOUL: AND MEN WILL PRAISE YOU, WHEN YOU DO WELL TO YOURSELF."

When Sennacherib was on Earth, he (and all like him) was very content with his fame, riches, and power. He was constantly being praised by other men; however, he would find

NOTES

that when he died, none of that followed him.

(19) "HE SHALL GO TO THE GENERATION OF HIS FATHERS; THEY SHALL NEVER SEE LIGHT."

Despite his great riches and power, he died and was cast into outer darkness, a darkness which will last forever (Mat. 8:12; 5:30; Jude, Vs. 13).

(20) "MAN WHO IS IN HONOR, AND UNDERSTANDS NOT, IS LIKE THE BEASTS THAT PERISH."

This Scripture is very similar to Verse 12.

IF MEN DO NOT KNOW THE LORD, THEY DO NOT UNDERSTAND THE SPIRIT WORLD

Because all of this is so very, very important, let us state again what we have said over and over:

No matter how much power, money, riches, wealth, or pride a man might have, if he does not understand the Ways of God and that money and power cannot redeem the soul, then he has no more knowledge than a *"beast"* — and like the beast, he will *"perish."*

The lesson taught is very simple. Man cannot redeem himself, even if he has great might, majesty, or wealth. Christ is the only One Who can redeem the soul, and He does so by and through the fact that He gave Himself as a Sacrifice on the Cross of Calvary, which satisfied the Righteousness of a thrice-Holy God. To receive Salvation, all one has to do is simply give one's heart to Christ and make Him the Saviour of one's soul and the Lord of one's life (Jn. 3:3, 16; Rom. 10:9-10, 13; Rev. 22:17).

Regrettably, the far greater majority of the human race has chosen to disbelieve the Word of the Lord. Instead, and in spite of the never-ceasing failure of all, they believe in frail, poor, flawed man!

PSALM 50

A Psalm of Asaph:
God is the Refuge

(1) "THE MIGHTY GOD, EVEN THE LORD, HAS SPOKEN, AND CALLED THE EARTH FROM THE RISING OF THE SUN

UNTO THE GOING DOWN THEREOF."

As noted, Asaph wrote this Psalm.

As such, and according to Matthew 13:35 and Acts 2:30, both Asaph and David are considered to be Prophets.

The Scriptures attribute twelve Psalms to Asaph, who was one of the great choir directors during David's time in connection with the Ministry of Tabernacle Worship (I Chron. 15:16-19; II Chron. 5:12). It seems that he wrote both the words and music to these Psalms and then presented them in Tabernacle Worship (II Chron. 29:30). The twelve Psalms written by Asaph are: 50, 73, 74, 75, 76, 77, 78, 79, 80, 81, 82, and 83.

GOD OF GODS, EVEN JEHOVAH

The words, *"Mighty God, even the LORD,"* mean *"El Elohim Jehovah,"* which actually says, *"God of Gods, even Jehovah."*

The doctrine of this Verse may be thus explained: The God of Gods, even Jehovah Messiah, summons the Earth to Judgment. The certitude of this Judgment is so sure that it is spoken of as a present fact. The extent of this Judgment, namely, *"from the rising of the sun to its going down,"* is repeated in Matthew 24:27.

This combination of three Names of God, *"El," "Elohim,"* and *"Jehovah,"* is found only here and in Joshua 22:22. There it is translated *"The LORD God of Gods."* Secondly, the three Names seem to mean: *"The Mighty One," "The Many in One,"* or *"The Three in One,"* and *"The Self-Existent One."* He Who is all these, the Psalmist announces, *"has spoken"* (Pulpit).[14]

(2) "OUT OF ZION, THE PERFECTION OF BEAUTY, GOD HAS SHINED."

Immediately prior to the appearance of the Messiah at the Second Coming, Israel will be reduced to the lowest possible depth of misery and well-nigh extinction as a nation. But at that moment, her Deliverer will appear on Mount Zion, as at Sinai, with all the accompaniments of terrific majesty, and He will summon the whole Earth to judgment.

(3) "OUR GOD SHALL COME, AND SHALL NOT KEEP SILENCE: A FIRE SHALL DEVOUR BEFORE HIM, AND IT SHALL BE VERY TEMPESTUOUS ROUND ABOUT HIM."

(4) "HE SHALL CALL TO THE HEAVENS FROM ABOVE, AND TO THE EARTH, THAT HE MAY JUDGE HIS PEOPLE."

This speaks of the Second Coming during the Battle of Armageddon. He came the first time as a Lamb; He will come the second time as a conquering King of kings and Lord of lords.

The Second Coming is going to be the most cataclysmic event that this Earth ever has known. It will be of such moment as to defy all description.

(5) "GATHER MY SAINTS TOGETHER UNTO ME; THOSE WHO HAVE MADE A COVENANT WITH ME BY SACRIFICE."

As always, great Truths are presented in each one of these Verses; some are greater than others, and this Verse falls into that category.

SAINTS

The term, *"My Saints,"* does not refer to the Blood-bought Church that already has been raptured some seven or more years earlier, who will be with the Lord Jesus Christ when He comes (Rev. 19:14; Jude 14-15; Mat. 24:29-31; II Thess. 2:7-10; Zech. 14:5).

The *"Saints"* of whom he here speaks are the Jewish people as designated by their *"Covenant of Sacrifice."* The term *"Saints"* does not express the Believer's moral attitude toward God, but God's Attitude toward the Believer. The Hebrew word might be rendered *"beloved," "engraced"* (Eph. 1:6), or *"benignantly regarded."*

Those whom God so regards and names are those who have entered into Covenant relationships with Him by a Sacrifice for sin. The literal translation of the Hebrew of this Passage is: *"Those ratifying My Covenant over a Sacrifice for sin."* This Covenant made by Sacrifice was typified in Exodus 24:8, explained in Hebrews 9:20, and fulfilled in I Corinthians 5:7.

This implies the death of a victim, the placing on one side and on the other of its divided members, and the ratification of the Covenant between them. The Ordinance pointed forward to Calvary and is illustrated in Genesis 15:9-21.

(6) "AND THE HEAVENS SHALL DECLARE HIS RIGHTEOUSNESS: FOR GOD IS JUDGE HIMSELF. SELAH."

This Passage speaks of a particular Judgment which will take place immediately after the Second Coming. It will be a Judgment of Israel.

THE JUDGMENT OF ISRAEL

In Verse 4, the Holy Spirit plainly says that at this Judgment, it will be the people of Israel who will be judged. The phrase, *"To the Earth,"* from Verse 4 tells us that this Judgment will be on the Earth, not in Heaven.

Israel must give account for the past, but it will only be in the form of recognizing what they did. Every evidence is that all the Jews will, at that time, fully accept Christ in every capacity. So the event, more than anything, is to set the record straight.

The Prophet Zechariah proclaimed this coming time (Zech. 12:10-14; 13:1-6).

There is also evidence that this judgment will include the nations of the world as it regards their treatment of Israel.

(7) "HEAR, O MY PEOPLE, AND I WILL SPEAK; O ISRAEL, AND I WILL TESTIFY AGAINST YOU: I AM GOD, EVEN YOUR GOD."

This is the Messiah, the Lord Jesus Christ, addressing Israel. His *"testimony against them"* will concern their rejection of Him at His First Advent. They rejected Him at that time as the Messiah. Now He is telling them, *"I am God, even your God."*

Even though Israel will have repented at this time, it is obvious here that Israel is going to have to face up to what they did those centuries past when they Crucified the Lord at His First Advent.

(8) "I WILL NOT REPROVE YOU FOR YOUR SACRIFICES OR YOUR BURNT OFFERINGS, TO HAVE BEEN CONTINUALLY BEFORE ME."

The intent of the heart is brought out in this Verse and also should be looked at intently by all Gentiles!

THE CROSS OF CALVARY

The Lord is saying that the reproof which He will give to Israel does not concern the true Sacrifices that they should have offered before Him continually. Rather the reproof will be for the Sacrifices which were offered not for their true and rightful purpose (Atonement), but those which constituted *"works"* alone, as though they were feeding a hungry god.

The method of feeding a hungry god was the method of the heathen. It was not to be the method of God's people.

The true purpose of the Sacrifice always was to point to the coming Redeemer, namely the Lord Jesus Christ, Who would take away their sins, which they should have known. In other words, the Sacrifice was on behalf of the people, and not on behalf of God. God didn't need Sacrifices; it was the people who needed the Sacrifices.

(9) "I WILL TAKE NO BULLOCK OUT OF YOUR HOUSE, NOR HE GOATS OUT OF YOUR FOLDS."

The Lord is saying to Israel, *"I did not need your bullocks or goats."* At the same time, He is saying, *"You are the one who desperately needed the Sacrifices!"* At particular times in Israel's history, the ritual of Sacrifices was carried on with the people having the idea in mind that they could sin all they desired and the Sacrifices would handle it. In other words, they would offer up a Sacrifice, thinking that would atone for the past week, and then proceed with a round of sinning all over again, and then offer up more Sacrifices the next week, etc.

(10) "FOR EVERY BEAST OF THE FOREST IS MINE, AND THE CATTLE UPON A THOUSAND HILLS."

The Lord was saying, *"I do not need your animals; I have plenty of My Own."* As stated, the Sacrificial System was for the people. It certainly was not for God.

Possibly it could be said that it was for Him to the extent that it made it possible for Him to bless those people who made the Sacrifices in the right manner.

(11) "I KNOW ALL THE FOWLS OF THE MOUNTAINS: AND THE WILD BEASTS OF THE FIELD ARE MINE."

The Lord is here saying that He created all of the *"fowls"* and the *"wild beasts."* They are already His, and He doesn't need people giving Him that which already belongs to Him.

(12) "IF I WERE HUNGRY, I WOULD NOT TELL YOU: FOR THE WORLD IS MINE, AND THE FULLNESS THEREOF."

This refers back to the heathen gods to which the pagans offered sacrifices in order to appease their hunger. God is saying, *"Don't put Me in the same class with the heathen gods, or treat Me in the same manner."*

(13) "WILL I EAT THE FLESH OF BULLS, OR DRINK THE BLOOD OF GOATS?"

This also says that Israel, for most of her existence, treated God as the heathen treated their gods. The heathen tried to appease their gods by many sacrifices (even human); likewise, Israel lost the true purpose of what the Sacrifices really meant and conducted themselves as heathen offering up their sacrifices to appease Jehovah.

In worshipping idol gods, Israel took on the spirit of these idols and the people who worshipped them.

(14) "OFFER UNTO GOD THANKSGIVING; AND PAY YOUR VOWS UNTO THE MOST HIGH."

This Psalm most likely was written approximately 700 years before Christ. It was meant as a great warning for Israel of that day, but it also speaks of the judgment which will take place at the Second Coming.

THANKSGIVING

Now the Lord alludes to the correct manner in which the Sacrifices should have been offered. Their method of trying to appease a hungry god was heathenistic. Instead their sacrifices should have been offered in *"thanksgiving"* to God for making a way for His people to have their sins covered and for ultimately sending a Redeemer into the world Who would take away their sin completely. This was their obligation, *"Your vows,"* because they had promised Him that they would do so (Ex. 19:7-8).

(15) "AND CALL UPON ME IN THE DAY OF TROUBLE: I WILL DELIVER YOU, AND YOU SHALL GLORIFY ME."

Another great Truth is given in this Passage.

THE CROSS AND DELIVERANCE

The Lord is telling Israel that if they offered Sacrifices unto God as He commanded them to do, and in the spirit in which they should have offered them, then when trouble came, they could call upon Him and He promised to deliver them, which He always did. This alone, He says, *"shall glorify Me,"* not feeding Him sacrifices as though He were a hungry God.

Let the Reader understand this:

If the Lord would provide deliverance under the Old Covenant, how much more will He do such under the New Covenant, which is a much *"Better Covenant,"* which is *"established upon better Promises"* (Heb. 8:6)?

The type of deliverance of which He speaks refers to any type of trouble which may come.

What a Promise!

As we have said over and over again, Christ is the Source of all Blessings and the Cross is the Means by which these Blessings are given to us. That's the reason the Cross of Christ is so very, very important! (The statement we have just made is actually a very gross understatement! If the Cross is removed, the means of all Blessings is also removed.)

Paul said, and I quote from THE EXPOSITOR'S STUDY BIBLE:

"Behold (mark my words!), *I Paul say unto you* (presents the Apostle's authority regarding the Message he brings), *that if you be circumcised, Christ shall profit you nothing.* (If the Believer goes back into Law, even Law of any kind, what Christ did at the Cross on our behalf will profit us nothing. One cannot have it two ways)" (Gal. 5:2).

The Gentiles in the Churches in Galatia had come to Christ under the Ministry of Paul; but false apostles were now telling these Gentiles that along with accepting Christ, they must also keep the Law of Moses. Circumcision was the physical evidence of that Covenant. Paul is actually telling them that they cannot have it two ways. It's either Christ and the New Covenant, or Circumcision and the Old Covenant. Either one cancels out the other.

CHRIST AND HIM CRUCIFIED

It is the same presently. It really doesn't matter what it is. No matter what avenue we might take, no matter how religious it might be, if it's not Christ and Him Crucified, then *"Christ shall profit you nothing."*

This is why Satan fights the Cross as he does, and he has been amazingly successful.

How many Preachers presently are preaching the Cross?!

Truthfully, not many!

And if they are not preaching the Cross, they really aren't preaching the Gospel (I Cor. 1:17).

(16) "BUT UNTO THE WICKED GOD SAYS, WHAT HAVE YOU TO DO TO DECLARE MY STATUTES, OR THAT YOU SHOULD TAKE MY COVENANT IN YOUR MOUTH?"

This Passage is frightful indeed!

MERE PROFESSORS OF RELIGION

This statement, as given by the Lord, will not only apply to the time it is being given, which is immediately after the Second Coming, but also applies for all time.

The Lord is addressing Himself to professors of religion, even to Preachers — especially to Preachers!

They were familiar with the words of God's Statutes and with the terms of the Covenant. They claimed the right of enforcing them against others (Rom. 2:18-20), but, in their own persons, they set at naught these Statutes.

God declares that they have no right to assume to be teachers of others until they have taught themselves — they are unfit even to *"take His Covenant in their mouth."*

The Lord refers to these individuals, despite the fact of them being very religious, as *"wicked."*

THE CROSS OF CHRIST IS THE DIVIDING LINE BETWEEN THE TRUE CHURCH AND THE APOSTATE CHURCH

It has always been the dividing line; however, it is such now more so than ever. I believe the Lord is going to proclaim the Message of the Cross over the entirety of the world, even to a degree that it never has known before. Those who accept that Message, which is the story of the Bible and which is the Gospel (I Cor. 1:17-18, 21, 23; 2:2; Eph. 2:13-18), are part of the True Church. Those who reject it are part and parcel of the apostate Church.

Paul also said, *"Now the Spirit* (Holy Spirit) *speaks expressly* (pointedly), *that in the latter times* (the times in which we now live, the last of the last days, which begin the fulfillment of Endtime Prophecies) *some shall depart from the Faith* (anytime Paul uses the term, *"the Faith,"* in short he is referring to the Cross; so, we are told here that some will depart from the Cross as the means of Salvation and Victory), *giving heed to seducing spirits* (evil spirits, i.e., *'religious spirits,'* making something seem like what it isn't), *and doctrines of devils* (should have been translated, *'doctrines of demons'*; the *'seducing spirits'* entice Believers away from the true Faith, causing them to believe *'doctrines inspired by demon spirits'*)" (I Tim. 4:1).

(17) "SEEING YOU HATE INSTRUCTION, AND CAST MY WORDS BEHIND YOU."

Why did God call these people *"wicked"*? He did so because they hated His Word, which is the meaning of the word *"instruction."*

INSTRUCTION IN THE WORLD

The Word of God holds the answer to every problem of life. It alone holds the answer.

Peter said, and I quote from THE EXPOSITOR'S STUDY BIBLE:

"According as His Divine Power has given unto us all things (the Lord with large-handed generosity has given us all things) *that pertain unto life and Godliness* (pertains to the fact that the Lord Jesus has given us everything we need regarding life and living), *through the knowledge of Him Who has called us to Glory and Virtue* (the *'knowledge'* addressed here speaks of what Christ did at the Cross, which alone can provide *'Glory'* and *'Virtue'*):

"Whereby are given unto us exceeding great and Precious Promises (pertains to the Word of God, which alone holds the answer to every life problem)*: that by these* (Promises) *you might be partakers of the Divine Nature* (the Divine Nature implanted in the inner being of the believing sinner becomes the source of our new life and action; it comes to everyone at the moment of being *'born-again'*), *having escaped the corruption that is in the world through lust.* (This presents the Salvation experience of the sinner, and the Sanctification experience of the Saint)" (II Pet. 1:3-4).

(18) "WHEN YOU SAW A THIEF, THEN YOU CONSENTED WITH HIM, AND HAVE BEEN PARTAKER WITH ADULTERERS."

The lips of the Israelites were filled with religious language, but their conduct was otherwise.

ADULTERERS

The word *"adulterers,"* refers, of course, to the Seventh Commandment, but also to the First. Most of the time when, through the Prophets, the Holy Spirit mentions *"adultery"* or *"fornication"* in connection with Israel and Judah, He was speaking of idol worship. In other words, Israel was being unfaithful to the Lord, Who Alone was her husband.

SPIRITUAL ADULTERY

Even in the New Covenant, the Holy Spirit continues to use this analogy, and expresses Himself through the Apostle Paul.

In the Seventh Chapter of Romans, in the first four Verses, the Holy Spirit through the Apostle speaks of a woman who is married to a man, who then takes up with another man. Paul says, *"She shall be called an adulteress"* (Rom. 7:3). Then, in Romans 7:4, he tells us that we Believers are *"married to Christ."* Christ is to meet our every need, which He is most capable of doing; in fact, He is the only One Who can do such. We are to look exclusively to Him for all things, knowing that He is ever the Source and the Cross is ever the Means.

If we begin to look to anything else other than Christ and the Cross, if we place our faith in other things, no matter how good those other things may be in their own right, in the Eyes of God, we are being unfaithful to Christ, and He labels us *"spiritual adulterers."* As should be obvious, this is a most grievous sin. But yet, due to the fact that most modern Christians have no understanding of the Cross as it regards our Sanctification, they fall, regrettably and sadly, into this category of *"spiritual adulterers."*

Being in such a position greatly hinders the Holy Spirit from working in our lives as He desires to do. As it regards the Sanctification process, which is the single most important aspect for the Child of God, He can do very little. That being the case, the Spiritual Growth of the Believer advances very little, if at all. Such a person is *"carnally minded,"* which leads to *"death"* (Rom. 8:6).

This terrible sin of *"spiritual adultery"* is what eventually wrecked Israel; it will also do the same for any modern Believer! *"Adultery,"* as we normally think of this sin, as well as all other types of sins, actually are the result of *"spiritual adultery,"* i.e., *"trusting in anything except Christ and the Cross."*

WHY IS THE CROSS OF CHRIST SO IMPORTANT?

It is so important simply because it is the *"Means"* by which the Lord gives us all good things.

The Lord never changes, because He never needs to change. As it pertains to His Nature and Character, He, in fact, cannot change (Mal. 3:6). As we have already said, and as we will continue to say over and over again, *"Christ Jesus is the Source of all good things, but the Cross is the Means."*

That's why Paul said, *"Christ is become of no effect unto you* (this is a chilling statement, and refers to anyone who makes anything other than Christ and the Cross the object of his faith), *whosoever of you are justified by the Law* (seek to be justified by the Law); *you are fallen from Grace* (fallen from the position of Grace, which means the Believer is trusting in something other than the Cross; it actually means 'to apostatize')" (Gal. 5:4).

If we Believers do not understand the significance of the Cross of Christ, then our understanding of the entirety of the Plan of Redemption, i.e., *"Christianity,"* is fatally flawed. And that's the tragedy in the modern Church. It little understands the Cross of Christ as it refers to our Sanctification. Actually, it understands it not at all!

WHAT DOES IT MEAN TO FALL FROM GRACE?

Let's give the explanation immediately.

It means that a Believer has made something other than Christ and the Cross the object of his faith. It doesn't really matter what the other thing or things might be, no matter how good they may be in their own right, if such is done, this stops the Grace of God from flowing to the heart and life of the Believer, meaning that such a Believer has *"fallen from Grace."*

Sometime ago, I listened for a few minutes to a group of Preachers who were discussing this very subject over Television. As they attempted to define what *"falling from Grace"* actually means, they came to the conclusion that it referred to a Believer who had committed some type of grievous sin.

My answer to that is this:

No! Any Believer who commits a grievous sin, as bad as it is, as destructive as it is, is the very one who needs the Grace of God. To be sure, this Believer will have the Grace of God if he properly confesses his sin before the Lord (I Jn. 1:9). Regrettably, the conclusion drawn by these Preachers is essentially the understanding of most of the Church, which is basically wrong. If what these Preachers were saying is true, then every single Believer in the world has *"fallen from Grace."*

Many may read my statement and retort, *"I may have done certain things which are wrong, but I never have committed the most grievous sins, such as. . . ."*

But, in the Eyes of God, any sin, no matter how small it may seem to be in our eyes, constitutes Lawbreaking, and thereby incurs the death penalty (Rom. 6:23). So that means that if we are basing our hopes on the fact that we have not committed certain sins, then our hopes, to be sure, will be dashed on the rocks. Such an attitude stems from self-righteousness, which God cannot tolerate.

(Jesus addressed this in the Eighteenth Chapter of Luke when He gave to us the Parable of the Pharisee and the Publican. If one reads that Parable carefully, one must come to the conclusion that the Lord doesn't favor at all the self-righteous person.)

No! Let me say it again:

Any Believer who places his faith in anything except Christ and the Cross is living in a state of *"spiritual adultery,"* which means the Holy Spirit is greatly hindered in giving to that Believer the good things for which the Lord has paid a terrible price.

The Grace of God is simply the Goodness of God extended to undeserving Saints. If our faith is in anything other than Christ and the Cross, that Goodness stops, which means that we *"fall from Grace,"* i.e., *"stop the flow of Grace to our lives"* (Rom. 6:1-14; I Cor. 1:17-18, 23; 2:2; Eph. 2:13-18; Gal. 6:14; Col. 2:14-15).

ENEMIES OF THE CROSS OF CHRIST

Paul said, and I quote from THE EXPOSITOR'S STUDY BIBLE:

"For many walk (speaks of those attempting to live for God outside of the victory and rudiments of the Cross of Christ), *of whom I have told you often, and now tell you even weeping* (this is a most serious matter), *that they are the enemies of the Cross of Christ* (those who do not look exclusively to the Cross of Christ must be labeled *'enemies'*):

"Whose end is destruction (if the Cross is ignored, and continues to be ignored, the loss of the soul is the only ultimate conclusion), *whose god is their belly* (refers to those who attempt to pervert the Gospel for their own personal gain), *and whose glory is in their shame* (the material things they seek, God labels as *'shame'*), *who mind earthly things.* (This means they have no interest in Heavenly things, which signifies they are using the Lord for their own personal gain)" (Phil. 3:18-19).

When one reads this Verse carefully, one must come to the conclusion, sadly, that virtually the entirety of the modern Church falls into this category. Thank God there are a few exceptions, but, regrettably, there are not many!

Anyone who places one's faith in anything other than Christ and the Cross is labeled *"an enemy of the Cross"* by the Holy Spirit. Sadly, this refers to those who embrace the *"Word of Faith"* doctrine. It refers to those who embrace the *"Purpose Driven Life"* doctrine. It also speaks of those who embrace the *"Government of Twelve"* doctrine. We also could mention *"Denominationalism"* and other things. It refers to anything which is not *"Jesus Christ and Him Crucified"* (I Cor. 1:23).

The Holy Spirit tells us, bluntly and pointedly, that those who are *"enemies of the Cross"* are heading toward *"destruction."* Every person needs to carefully read these words!

(19) "YOU GIVE YOUR MOUTH TO EVIL, AND YOUR TONGUE FRAMES DECEIT."

Many (perhaps most) of the Psalms have a triple meaning. We try to deal with all three aspects, but we major in one. These three are:

1. The Psalm given normally has something to do with the situation at hand, whatever it might have been. In other words, if David gave us a particular Psalm, that Psalm had something to do with his own personal experience at that time.

2. It also has a Prophetic meaning; a great number of the Psalms deal with the coming Great Tribulation, the rise of the Antichrist, the Battle of Armageddon, the Second Coming of the Lord Jesus Christ, and the coming Kingdom Age.

3. It also is applicable for all Saints for all time; consequently, I try to deal with that aspect of each Psalm, at times in great detail.

Let us look at the three directions this Nineteenth Verse gives to us:

THE WORD OF GOD

First, something undoubtedly happened during the time of Asaph which occasioned this Psalm. The Psalm deals with that particular situation.

Second, it pertains presently to any Believer, especially Preachers who preach and teach that which is not the True Gospel, Preachers who espouse a modernist trend, who, above all, are not preaching the Cross of Christ. They *"give their mouth to evil,"* and with their *"tongue, they frame deceit."*

Third, this Psalm has a Prophetic meaning in that it deals with the nations of the world who will oppose Israel, which pertains to this present time in which we now live. As it regards the nations of the world, the Lord is more pointedly addressing the Arab world, which the next Verse will graphically proclaim.

The Lord charges that every nation in the world which opposes Israel does so from a *"mouth of evil"* and a *"tongue that frames deceit."*

(20) "YOU SIT AND SPEAK AGAINST YOUR BROTHER; YOU SLANDER YOUR OWN MOTHER'S SON."

Here the Lord directly speaks to the Arab world. Ishmael was Isaac's brother. The Arabs are slandering their own mother's son. Even though Sarah was Isaac's mother and Hagar was Ishmael's mother, still, Sarah was looked at as the foster mother of Ishmael. Because Hagar was Sarah's servant, she only could bear the son according to Sarah's wishes (Gen. 16:1-6).

(21) "THESE THINGS HAVE YOU DONE, AND I KEPT SILENCE; YOU THOUGHT THAT I WAS ALTOGETHER SUCH AN ONE AS YOURSELF: BUT I WILL REPROVE YOU, AND SET THEM IN ORDER BEFORE YOUR EYES."

The Holy Spirit continues His statement regarding the Arabs.

GOD'S ANSWER TO THE ARAB WORLD

Because of Promises that God made to Hagar and Ishmael (Gen. 17:20-22), and because God always keeps His Promises, the Arab world has thought that He is their God through Ishmael — and that because of His *"silence."* Due to their false religion of Islam, they have thought they are praying to the Lord, and that He is *"one"* with them. Now they will know that they have been wrong.

The Promise was not through Ishmael but through Isaac (Gen. 17:18-19).

Now the Lord *"will reprove"* the Arabs, and will tell them unequivocally that the Promise was through Isaac, not Ishmael — hence, through Christ, not Muhammad.

WHEN WILL THIS REPROOF TAKE PLACE?

It will take place immediately after the Second Coming. At that time, Israel will realize that their Messiah, the One Who has just returned to this Earth, is none other than the Lord Jesus Christ, the One they crucified!

The Prophet Zechariah predicted this coming moment (Zech. 12:10-14; 13:1-9).

Immediately after Israel's acceptance of Christ, the Lord will address the entirety of the nations of the world, primarily as it regards their treatment of Israel (Zech. 14:17-21).

At that time, the Arab world specifically will be addressed. It will be done for many reasons, but basically because of the situation regarding Isaac and Ishmael. In other words, this conflict has raged for approximately 4,000 years. It will be set right at the Second Coming.

The Muslims should read these words; however, they are so spiritually blind, even as most of the world is spiritually blind, that they cannot see what is being said.

All of this means that the United States will not be able to broker a peace agreement between Israel and the Arabs. Quite possibly when the Antichrist makes his debut, he will bring about a false peace for a short period of time. But it will only be a short peace.

The Apostle Paul addressed this when the Holy Spirit through him said, *"For when they shall say, Peace and safety; then sudden destruction comes upon them, as travail upon a woman with child; and they shall not escape"* (I Thess. 5:3). During the first half of the Great Tribulation, when Israel will sign a peace accord with the Arab world and other nations, all brokered by the Antichrist, she will think that the Antichrist is the Messiah, especially considering that he has brought about peace. So she will cry, *"Peace and safety"* to the world; however, at the midpoint of that seven-year peace treaty, the Antichrist will show his true colors by invading Israel, and she will suffer her first defeat since she became a nation in 1948 (Dan. 9:27). Israel will then enter into the most awful tribulation she ever has experienced, even eclipsing the horror of the Holocaust of Nazi Germany in the early 1940's (Mat. 24:21).

Quite possibly, the Arab world will join their forces with the Antichrist; but they too will be sadly disappointed. The man of sin will not tolerate the worship of any god or any supposed god, such as *"Allah,"* because he will claim to be God (Dan. 11:36-39).

During the last half of the Great Tribulation, the power of the Antichrist will be so great that he will be able to impose his will on most nations of the world, and he will seek to control the entire world. He will not succeed in that endeavor (but he will come close), and he will be stopped at the Battle of Armageddon by the Second Coming of the Lord (Rev., Chpt. 19).

All of this means that the times in which we now live are momentous indeed. We are coming down to the very last hours of the Church Age, which means that the Rapture is imminent (I Thess. 4:13-18).

NOTES

Israel is God's Prophetic time clock. When the Lord brought theses ancient people back to their ancient homeland, the Land of Israel, and established them once again as a nation, which took place in 1948, after they had wandered the world as outcasts for nearly 2,000 years, this was a clear fulfillment of Bible Prophecy. At this very moment, Israel is being prepared for the fulfillment of all the Prophecies given by Daniel concerning these ancient people. (For a more in-depth discussion of these Prophecies and events, we recommend THE JIMMY SWAGGART BIBLE COMMENTARY: BOOK OF DANIEL, available through Jimmy Swaggart Ministries.)

Israel will be completely restored; however, before that time comes, which will take place immediately after the Second Coming, Israel will undergo the worst tribulation she ever has encountered in her long history. It is going to take that to finally bring these people out of their rebellion to where they finally will recognize the Lord Jesus Christ. As stated, this will happen at the Second Coming.

At that time, the Lord will reprove all the nations of the world that have sought to hinder Israel, but more specifically the Arab world. Before their very eyes, He will set all things in order that they may know that His Word is the Bible and not the Koran.

(22) "NOW CONSIDER THIS, YOU WHO FORGET GOD, LEST I TEAR YOU IN PIECES, AND THERE BE NONE TO DELIVER."

This is a word of warning to the nations of the world, but especially to the Arab world. They have substituted a false religion in the place of God. They have *"changed the Truth of God into a lie, and worshipped and served the creature more than the Creator, Who is blessed forever"* (Rom. 1:25).

The Holy Spirit continues to say through Paul, *"Who knowing the judgment of God, that they which commit such things are worthy of death, not only do the same, but have pleasure in them who do them"* (Rom. 1:32).

The Holy Spirit here through Asaph plainly says that the nations of the world who have *"forgotten God"* are in danger of being *"torn to pieces,"* with none being able to *"deliver them."*

Specifically, this will happen during the Battle of Armageddon. The Prophet Zechariah said, *"And it shall come to pass in that day, that I will seek to destroy all the nations that come against Jerusalem"* (Zech. 12:9).

(23) "WHOSO OFFERS PRAISE GLORIFIES ME: AND TO HIM WHO ORDERS HIS CONVERSATION ARIGHT WILL I SHOW THE SALVATION OF GOD."

Even though this Passage applies to all people, and for all time, its more specific meaning has to do with the beginning of the Kingdom Age.

THE LORD JESUS CHRIST

Jesus Christ is God's Son; those who praise Him *"glorify Me,"* which speaks of Jehovah. To those who praise Him, He shows them *"the Salvation of God,"* Who is the Lord Jesus Christ.

God is offering the nations of the world an opportunity to repent concerning their treatment of Israel and their rejection of Jesus Christ. This will occur, as stated, at the very beginning of the Kingdom Age. Of course, this invitation will have been given to Israel immediately after the Second Coming, and they will gladly accept. Israel will then become, as the Lord originally intended, the leading nation of the world, all under Christ.

PSALM 51

A Psalm of David:
A Prayer for Forgiveness and Cleansing

(1) "HAVE MERCY UPON ME, O GOD, ACCORDING TO YOUR LOVINGKINDNESS: ACCORDING UNTO THE MULTITUDE OF YOUR TENDER MERCIES BLOT OUT MY TRANSGRESSIONS."

This Psalm is to the Chief Musician, a Psalm of David, when Nathan the Prophet came unto him after he had gone to Bathsheba.

THE CHRONOLOGICAL ORDER

Just as the authorship of the Psalms was inspired by the Holy Spirit, so also was the order of their placement. Several of the preceding Psalms deal with the siege of Jerusalem by Sennacherib and pointed prophetically to the coming Antichrist, who is foreshadowed by Sennacherib.

Psalm 50, written by Asaph, deals with the *"judgment of the nations,"* as well as other things. It is pulled from his collection (Ps. 73-83), which, to the unspiritual eye, is chronologically ill-placed.

However, as we have previously noted, the Holy Spirit knew exactly what He was doing in placing the 50th Psalm where it is. The order fits perfectly.

Psalm 51, which we now will study, does not seem to fit the order of events which transpire in preceding Psalms (the foreshadowing of the Antichrist and the Coming of the Lord); however, I think we will see that it also is placed perfectly.

REPENTANCE

This Psalm was given by the Holy Spirit to David when, his heart broken and contrite because of his sin against God, he pleads for pardon through the atoning Blood of the Lamb of God, foreshadowed in Exodus 12:7. Thus, he was not only fittingly provided with a vehicle of expression in Repentance and Faith, but he was also used as a channel of prophetic communication, which we will see.

David, in his sin, Repentance, and Restoration, is a forepicture of Israel. For as he forsook the Law and was guilty of adultery and murder, so Israel despised the Covenant and turned aside to idolatry (adultery) and murdered their Messiah.

Thus, the scope and structure of the Psalm go far beyond David. They predict the future confession and forgiveness of Israel in the day of the Messiah's Second Coming, when, looking upon Him Whom they pierced, they shall mourn and weep (Zech., Chpts. 12-13).

The first seventeen Verses of this Psalm apply personally to David and prophetically to Israel. The last two are for national Israel alone.

So, as we shall see, the perfect chronological order of these Psalms becomes obvious.

THE INTERCESSORY WORK OF CHRIST

In an even greater way, this Psalm is a vivid portrayal of the Intercessory Work of Christ on behalf of His people. Even though

David prayed this prayer, the Son of David would make David's sin (as well as our sins) His Own and pray through him that which must be said.

There was no Sacrifice provided under the Law for the sins of adultery and murder. David had, therefore, to seek pardon through the Death of the Lamb of God, foreshadowed, as stated, in the Twelfth Chapter of Exodus. That Divine Way of Redemption from death preceded the Law and prefigured Calvary. Taught by the Holy Spirit, David could, however dimly, plead that Sacrifice.

This is the truest prayer of Repentance ever prayed because it symbolizes the Intercessory Work of the Son of David.

David would plead for *"Mercy,"* knowing that he deserved none. He did not approach God from a platform of valuable service rendered to Him or a life used by Him. He approached God as a sinner worthy of death and destruction, pleading for God's *"Mercy."* This is the only type of prayer of Repentance that God will hear.

JUSTIFICATION BY FAITH

David would ask the Lord to *"Blot out my transgressions."* This speaks of *"Justification by Faith,"* meaning the sins are blotted out as though they never existed, declaring one *"not guilty."* The New Testament counterpart is I John 1:9 and Colossians 2:14. The latter says, *"Blotting out the handwriting of Ordinances that was against us, which was contrary to us, and took it out of the way, nailing it to His Cross."*

(2) "WASH ME THOROUGHLY FROM MY INIQUITY, AND CLEANSE ME FROM MY SIN."

In the First Verse, David pleads for the Lovingkindness and Mercy of God. In Verse 2, he addresses his sin.

INIQUITY

"Iniquity" soils the soul. It can only be cleansed by the *"Precious Blood of Jesus Christ"* (I Pet. 1:18-19). There is no earthly cure for sin. Education is not a cure; money is not a cure; culture is not a cure; good works are not a cure; only the *"Precious Blood of Jesus Christ,"* applied to our hearts and lives, is the cure. In other words, it's the Cross!

NOTES

This is the reason that proclaiming the Gospel of Jesus Christ to a lost world is the single most important thing on the face of the Earth. Men must have the opportunity to accept or reject the fact that God has sent His Only Son to bear the sin penalty of the world, and that all who will may *"drink of this Water of Life freely"* (Rev. 22:17).

Irrespective as to race, culture, or creed, the problem with man is sin. The only solution to that problem is the Cross of Christ. That's the reason that the True Gospel Message must not change. Whether given to the educated, the uneducated, or any race of people anywhere in the world, the Gospel must be the same, because the problem is the same, namely sin!

Let us say it again, because it is so very, very important:

"The only solution to that problem is Jesus Christ and what He did at the Cross" (Jn. 3:3, 16; I Jn. 2:1; Rev. 22:17).

SIN

"Sin came into the world" (Rom. 5:12) when Adam succumbed by being tempted by another. The full responsibility for the presence and consequences of sin in the world, nevertheless, fell full weight upon man. Man sinned, and man must die. Death itself silences every attempt to transfer even partially man's guilt upon Satan, in whom sin arose and by whom man was tempted. However, neither sin nor death itself, for all its finality, is the last word about the sinner; for, if *"by a man* (Adam) *came death, by a Man* (the Lord Jesus Christ) *has also come the Resurrection of the dead"* (I Cor. 15:21).

If sin and death were projected through a demonic temptation as a possibility, and through Adam's transgression entered the world as an actuality, sin and death are also cosmically defeated and abolished in man's world and history through God's Man, Jesus the Christ. Through Christ sin is undone and forgiven, death ends in Resurrection, sinners become Saints, and he *"who has the power of death"* is destroyed (Heb. 2:14).

SIN AND FREEDOM

The concept of freedom does not explain sin. While sin is not unrelated to freedom, the latter does not explain the rise of the former. God has authentic freedom and cannot sin. God created man with a freedom that is morally qualified and whose continuance depended on a refraining from sin. Man as created possessed the ability not to sin; the man recreated in Christ, begotten of God, *"does not sin,"* i.e., *"does not habitually sin, does not practice sin"* (I Jn. 5:18).

The ability to sin is not of the essence of freedom. True freedom is constituted by man's created, and later recreated, ability to do the good, not by a morally unqualified faculty to do either the one or the other. In other words, the freedom that God gives is the freedom to live holy and righteous. It does not include a freedom to sin.

Freedom belongs to the essence of man as created by God and as restored by Christ; in neither instance is it a morally neutral and unqualified aspect of humanity. The effect of human sin upon freedom is defined in Biblical thought, therefore, not as another form of freedom, but rather as slavery and bondage (Gal. 5:1). Man as created was no more free to sin than, having sinned and fallen into moral bondage, he is free again to become what he once was, with the latter referring to the total Image of God. Sin constitutes a loss, not an exercise of freedom. Sin is a mystery, immoral and irrational, whose denouement (the outcome of a complex sequence of events) is not found in the concept of human freedom. Freedom as an explanation of sin, in other words, if one is free to sin or not to sin, is false.

SINNING AGAINST GOD

If in freedom man could sin against his Maker, freedom by the same definition would contain the possibility of man's self-propelled return to his Maker.

According to the Genesis account of man's fall into sin, man was not free to sin, but under Divine Command not to sin on threat of death. Adam and Eve were under the restricted Divine Command not to do what they, in fact, did do. Freedom, as authority, is comprised of the components: might plus right. An authority which exercises a might without right is a totalitarian perversion of authority; a freedom which does that which it has no right to do is a perversion of true freedom.

The theological idea that God created man free, that is, with a freedom that was free to sin, is an explanation of sin in terms of sin. If God had endowed man with such freedom, God could not in justice allow man's freedom to suffer that bondage which sin inflicts upon freedom.

SIN, A LOSS OF FREEDOM

In Biblical thought, however, man's act of sin is regarded as a loss of freedom. According to the Genesis account of the Fall, man loses his right to existence in the Garden of Eden, his right to life, and his right to be himself — naked and not ashamed. In the continuing Biblical account, man as sinner is exhibited as no longer free to be himself. He is either a slave to sin and under the power of death, a devotee of idols — who in this devotion to idols becomes sub-human and like his idols, which, regrettably, characterizes most of the human race for all time (Ps. 115:8), or he becomes a captive to Grace and through this captivity again receives his true freedom as a gift from God, a freedom permitting him to enjoy release from, and forgiveness for, his sinful past and the Gift of Grace that justifies his right to live in an open and unending future.

SIN AND THE DIVINE SOVEREIGNTY

Nor is the origin of sin accounted for in a Biblically acceptable manner by the assertion that man is the secondary, and God the primary, ultimate cause of sin. Well-meaning but profoundly misguided defenders of the sovereignty of God have often declared that God Himself is the Source of sin. God is said to have willed sin, to be its primal cause, and even to have created sin. While such assertions are projected in defense of Divine Sovereignty, they are essentially blasphemous.

It is deeply significant that men who make these bold assertions have been known to articulate them in their prayers and worship of God; none, confessing his sins, asserts before God what he claims in his theology, that is, if he has good sense: that God to Whom he prays for the forgiveness of his sins is the primary cause of his sin. Such is ridiculous!

Rejecting both the notion that God willed

sin and that sin is the product of chance, sober Christian thought has never dared say more than that God *"permitted sin."* The clearest expression of the relationship of the Divine Sovereign Will to sin is not discoverable by a search in the area of the origin of sin, but is found at the Cross, where God, at the cost of His Own Son, overcomes and banishes sin.

EXPLANATION?

Every rational analysis of sin reveals that sin presupposes itself, and the history of Christian thought demonstrates that explanations of sin reduce sin into something that carries no guilt and requires no confession.

This is the Truth: *"Sin must be acknowledged and confessed, not explained."*

The Bible no more explains the rise of sin in the world of the Angels and its connection with the origin of sin in man's world than it explains how man, as God's Creation, could sin. There is neither a good moral reason nor a valid rational reason for the reality of sin. There can no more be a truly moral reason for evil than there can be a valid reason for irrationality. Sin is both immoral and irrational.

HISTORY AND THE FALL

Sin is an essentially historical phenomenon. It has an event-character. To become real, it must happen. It is not an event within the Trinitarian activity within the Godhead, an activity both necessary and eternal.

The historical is neither necessary nor eternal; sin, being neither, remains as historical. Being real, sin happened once upon a time. The Fall recorded in Genesis is an historical reality.

The Genesis sequence of Creation-Fall also clearly teaches that sin is neither an item of Creation nor a quality of Creation that, in the process of time, is progressively transformed into emerging good. Sin, on the contrary, is a contradiction to all created and uncreated reality. It is destructive of all good.

The substitution of an evolutionary development of the good for the Biblical historical Fall is a misreading of the good that God in history accomplishes through Jesus Christ. The Biblical account of man's Fall into sin is marked by the complex of contradictions between man and God, husband and wife, and between man and nature, all of which immediately appeared as the consequence of sin.

No Christian can say why he sinned. If he could give a reason for (and thus, an explanation of) his sin, sin would require neither forgiveness nor cancellation, only an explanation; being a justified act, it would have a right to exist. Both the origin of sin and its continuance in the life of every man is and remains an enigma for which there is no apology. Sin has no defense, no right to existence. Every explanation of sin in terms of human freedom turns sin into something that carries neither guilt nor need of Repentance; when explained in terms of the causality or the sovereign Divine Will, sin is naturalized within the being of God Himself.

ORIGINAL SIN

This is a theological, not a temporal, concept; it, therefore, throws no clear light on the origin of sin. Original sin refers neither to the first of all sins, nor to the first sin in human history, but to the first sin of Adam, and only to that, and not to the subsequent sins of Adam. In human history, Eve sinned first; nevertheless, it was by Adam's later sin that *"sin came into the world, and death through sin"* (Rom. 5:12). Original sin is the first sin of Adam, the source of all other sins, including Adam's subsequent sins, and is that power by which death passed upon all men, even though all men have not sinned in the manner of Adam's first sinful act (Rom. 5:14).

TOTAL DEPRAVITY

Original sin provides a clue to the nature of sin and of death. According to the Genesis account, original sin is a proud, loveless, rebellious, thankless, destructive act of self-assertion, first against the God Who gave man his reality, and, simultaneously, against both the self and every other form of created reality. By his initial act of sin, Adam broke that relationship to God, to Eve, and to the natural world, on which, in real though different degrees, his own life and well-being depended.

Adam's sin is a declaration of self-sufficiency; he willed to go it alone. By that original, first sin of Adam, everything is alienated; Adam and Eve each hid from the other by donning clothes, Adam hides from God, Adam blames God and Eve, Eve blames the serpent, and the self is alienated from itself. From the first deprivation of the self, of everything, both the self and the *"not-self,"* there is a corresponding total depravity in which the self is deprived of all those moral and spiritual qualities that constitute the authentic self and its relation to all that is not-self.

Man has lost self-realization; he is his own worst enemy. The self is totally depraved, for the self can do nothing worse or more destructive to God, to his fellows, to his world, and to himself, than sin. Were it not so, death and Hell would be an overkill that exceeded sin's guilt quality. Original sin — and all subsequent sins merely re-emphasize it — so effectively breaks man's relationship to all reality — the self, God, fellowman, and nature — that man cannot reinstate original, authentic relationships. This is disclosed supremely at the Cross, when man kills Him in Whom all reality, Divine and created, is centered.

SIN IS MUCH WORSE THAN MAN REALIZES

Original sin, as that act which breaks all man's created God-relationships, is neither merely moral, intellectual, nor effective, but something deeper than all of these. It is, in essence, religious.

As David said, *"Against You, You only, have I sinned, and done that which is evil in Your sight"* (Ps. 51:4). It is this Divine reference that constitutes the essence of original sin and via this reference becomes also man's sin against himself, his fellowman, and nature. The nature of sin is wholly destructive; sin, therefore, elicits those full realities which the Biblical concepts of death and the infinite Divine Wrath convey.

That sin renders the sinner totally depraved cannot be read from human experience. Although history is saturated with manifold forms of sinful action, a true recognition of sin — as distinct from human error, ignorance, folly, or frailty — does not occur within the field of human observation or experience. No road leads from the experience of sin to the true knowledge of sin. The distinctively religious dimension of sin, as an act which is in the first instance against God, can be disclosed only by God Himself.

Man's moral behavior is often better than total depravity can account for, an ambiguity which derives from God's gracious operations upon man, and a truth that can be known only by Revelation. That every sin against the neighbor or against man's natural environment is also a sin against God is not a humanly attainable knowledge unless imparted by Divine Revelation. Similarly, the knowledge that the sinner's right relationship to God, neighbor, and natural environment cannot be reconstituted except by the Grace of Regeneration can also be known only by means of Revelation.

SIN AND GRACE

Sin is transgression of the Law of God (Ex., Chpt. 20), but it is never merely that. Since the purpose of Law is Grace as indicated by the fact that it was given to Israel within a Covenant situation (Gal. 3:17) and by the Law's own introductory preface, sin is always an act against the Goodness and Grace of God.

This quality of sin, as an act against the Grace of God, emphasizes that sin is never an individual but rather a social matter. Grace is an expression of God's Will to be with and for man in a community in which man is both for God and for his neighbor. This social character of Grace corresponds to the demand of the Law that we love both God and our neighbor. He who loves God cannot hate his neighbor; and he who hates his neighbor cannot love God (I Jn., Chpts. 2-3). Sin, as the rejection of this gracious Divine Will to community is, therefore, not an individualistic act. It is rather a social act — even in its negative, anti-social form. Further, for the reason that sin is a social act, sin is committed not only by the single individual, but by social groups and can be embodied in social structures. A nation can sin no less than an individual; there are national sins and nations, no less than individuals, which are called to repentance and amendment of life. Similarly, the Church can sin and be called to confession and amendment of life, though it must be admitted that rarely do Churches do what they require of their individual members.

THE SOCIAL CHARACTER OF SIN

This communal, social character of sin, which reflects the communal, social character of Divine Grace, helps one to understand why justice is never merely an individual but always an inherently social concept. There is no individual, as distinct from a social, justice. All justice is social justice, because justice is the expression of God's Holiness as it maintains God's gracious Purpose to be with and for man against man's sinful assault against that purpose.

It must also be observed that because of the social character of sin, the distinction between a *"personal"* and a *"social"* effort is grounded in a misunderstanding of the nature of sin. A *"personal"* ethic always turns out to be an ethic of the individual, in contrast to a social ethic. All sin is, indeed, personal, whether that of the individual or of the corporate personality of the Church or nation — as is also all love and right-doing. But there is no individualistic personal effort, as there is no individualistic grace or individualistic justice. The Biblical ideas of Grace, Love, and Justice, as the Biblical teaching that Adam's original sin is also man's sin and Christ's one Act of obedience can be man's righteousness, are in theory surrendered when sin is individualistically defined by reference to a legalistic understanding of the Law, without reference to the social character of God's Grace.

The corporate quality of sin is also clearly seen in the New Testament teachings that one can be forgiven by God only as he forgives others (Mat. 6:14-15), can worship God at the Altar only when in right relationship with his brother (Mat. 5:23-24), and can pray properly only when he addresses God as *"our Father"* and requests daily bread, forgiveness of sins, and deliverance from evil as he prays.

Please note the personal pronouns, *"us"* and *"our."*

SIN AND PUNISHMENT

Sin requires punishment. As an affront against the infinite majesty of God, sin calls for infinite punishment, and that without limit. The Bible, therefore, speaks of the wages of sin being death and of eternal punishment in Hell. Such punishment is the reflex of the Holiness of God whereby He maintains Himself against man's sin. In responding to sin, God's Holiness takes the form of justice expressing itself in infinite wrath and unlimited judgment.

This Divine response, however, takes place in history only at the Cross, where the Son of God becomes the Object of it, and dies. Elsewhere in human history, God's Wrath and punishing justice is always corrective, a form of Wrath for the sake of Grace, a form of judgment which can be turned aside, averted, and repented of by God as men repent and respond favorably to His Grace.

The only Divine Judgment and Wrath God cannot withdraw or repent of in history is that which occurred at the Cross. But that all other manifestations of Divine Judgment upon sin are contingent rather than absolute, corrective rather than final, suggests that all justice which society administers to its criminals should be remedial and corrective, never merely punitive, and never final.

Original sin is the source of all other sins, and these are so manifold as to defy number or name. Yet each of them reflects something of the highly complex nature of sin. In view of this complexity, it is not surprising that the Bible uses many words to denote sin. Sin is, moreover, in Biblical thought many other things — unbelief, distrust, ingratitude, lovelessness, hatred, etc. The greatest sin occurs in reaction to the Cross, where the nature of sin in all its aspects is revealed, and original sin in all its subsequent historical expressions is overcome and forgiven by God's gracious action in Christ. The greatest sin, therefore, is the rejection of Christ Crucified, Who shall judge every man according to the Gospel (Rom. 2:16), which is to say, in reference to God's gracious Will and Purpose.

(The above material on *"Sin"* was derived from the Zondervan Pictorial Encyclopedia of the Bible.)

(3) "FOR I ACKNOWLEDGE MY

TRANSGRESSIONS: AND MY SIN IS EVER BEFORE ME."

The acknowledgment of Verses 3 and 4 is the condition of Divine forgiveness. All sin, in essence, is committed against God; hence, David said, *"I have sinned against Jehovah."* Pharaoh, Saul, and others said, *"I have sinned,"* but they did not add, *"against God."*

God demands that the transgressions be acknowledged, placing the blame where it rightfully belongs, on the perpetrator. He cannot and will not forgive sin that is not acknowledged and for which no responsibility is taken.

Moreover, the unconfessed sin will weigh heavily upon the individual, *"ever before me,"* until it is expunged by the Precious Blood of Christ.

The first step in Repentance is contrition; the second, confession; the third, amendment of life, i.e., *"a change of lifestyle."*

(4) "AGAINST YOU, YOU ONLY, HAVE I SINNED, AND DONE THIS EVIL IN YOUR SIGHT: THAT YOU MIGHT BE JUSTIFIED WHEN YOU SPEAK, AND BE CLEAR WHEN YOU JUDGE."

The second half of Verse 4 is quoted in Romans 3:4. It teaches the doctrine that God is justified in judging sin, and that His statement that all have sinned is true. If, after the words, *"in Your sight,"* the sentence, *"I confess my guilt,"* be supplied, the meaning and argument of the Verse will be clearer. This emphasizes the awfulness of sin in God's Presence.

David's sins were against Bathsheba and her husband Uriah, as well as against all of Israel; however, the ultimate direction of sin, perfected by Satan, is against God.

All sin is a departure from God's Ways to man's ways; every sin that is committed by anyone, in effect, says, *"I can be God better than God can be God."* (Man's ways actually are Satan's ways, and that is the reason that man's ways, even if they come from redeemed man, cannot be used.)

David is here saying that God is always *"justified"* in any Action that He takes, and His *"Judgment"* is always Perfect.

(5) "BEHOLD, I WAS SHAPED IN INIQUITY; AND IN SIN DID MY MOTHER CONCEIVE ME."

NOTES

This Verse proclaims original sin.

ORIGINAL SIN

Verse 5 states that all are born in sin. In other words, no baby is born righteous, but, in fact, is born unrighteous because of Adam's Fall in the Garden of Eden. Some would take exception to the result of sin being passed down on those who have no choice in the matter.

However, millions of innocents have always suffered because of the sins of the guilty. That is a fact of life. The mother uses cocaine; the baby is born addicted. It is innocent, but it still is a victim.

When Adam and Eve were created, in Adam's loins, in effect, was every baby who ever would be born. It is called *"procreation."* Consequently, the first Adam would affect all who came thereafter. But yet, the last Adam, the Lord Jesus Christ, nullified the terrible curse of sin, which is spiritual death, and did so by going to the Cross, which opened up the way for sin to be cleansed and washed.

THE ETERNAL DESTINY OF BABIES

If babies are born in sin (and they are), then are babies lost if they die before they reach the age of accountability?

No!

The age of accountability refers to the ability and power to choose. This age varies with different children according to their upbringing and other factors. Before a baby reaches the age of accountability, it is innocent and does not have the ability to choose; God, therefore, protects it in its innocency until it does have this ability. At that time, the child becomes responsible for his soul's Salvation.

Concerning babies and little children, Jesus said something which answers two questions:

"And Jesus called a little child unto Him, and set him in the midst of them (the single greatest lesson taught by Christ),

"And He said, Verily I say unto you, Except you be converted (born-again), *and become as little children* (a child is totally dependent on its parents, and Believers must be as dependent on Christ), *you shall not enter into the Kingdom of Heaven* (failure of total dependence on Christ and the Cross

will pull one into unbelief, and thereby a lost condition).

"Whosoever (no exceptions to this rule) *therefore shall humble himself as this little child* (requirement for greatness), *the same is greatest in the Kingdom of Heaven* (direct opposite of the standard of the world)" (Mat. 18:2-4).

In this statement, our Lord proclaims the standard of acceptance into the Kingdom of Heaven, which is total trust in Christ; our Lord's statement also proclaims the Divine protection of little children as it regards their soul's Salvation. In other words, there are no little children in Hell!

THE IMMACULATE CONCEPTION

The statement by David given in Verse 5 and other Verses (Gen. 3:15-19; Jn. 8:44; Rom. 2:12-16; Eph. 2:1-3; I Jn. 3:8) disproves the teaching of the Immaculate Conception, i.e., the teaching that Mary was sinless. If Mary indeed was sinless, then her mother and dad also had to be sinless, etc. Mary herself claimed otherwise (Lk. 1:46-47).

This false teaching by the Catholic Church was not conjured to increase the fidelity of the Saviour, but instead to uphold an unscriptural doctrine concerning Mary. Mary's conception was not by Joseph, but by the Holy Spirit (Mat. 1:20); therefore, the seed of man through which the bloodline comes (and, thereby the Fall of man) was not passed on in the Incarnation, which should be obvious.

If Jesus had been born as a result of the union of Joseph and Mary, He would have been born *"in sin"* exactly as David and all the other human beings have been. His conception was Immaculate in the sense that He was not conceived by man, but by God.

(6) "BEHOLD, YOU DESIRE TRUTH IN THE INWARD PARTS: AND IN THE HIDDEN PART YOU SHALL MAKE ME TO KNOW WISDOM."

Religion, which always is man-devised, can only address itself to the externals. The Blood of Jesus Christ applied to our hearts and lives addresses itself to *"the inward parts."* Only God can do this.

All of this tells us that sin is far more than a mere mistake or mendacity. Sin originates in the very vitals of the human being, actually in the heart, i.e., *"the soul and the spirit"* (Mk. 7:21). Consequently, anything that man attempts to do, as it regards sin, only addresses externals, which means that only symptoms are treated, which leaves the problem unattended. As stated, only the Born-Again experience can address itself properly to sin (Jn. 3:3).

THE CROSS OF CHRIST

When Jesus went to the Cross, He not only addressed sins, as it regards acts of sins, but He also addressed the very cause of sin, which is Satan himself.

On the Cross, Jesus Christ atoned for all sin, past, present, and future, at least for all who will believe (Jn. 3:16), which removes Satan's legal right to inflict man with sin (Col. 2:14-15). By atoning for all sin, Jesus addressed the cause of sin. When a believing sinner accepts Christ as his personal and eternal Saviour, all of that individual's sins are washed, cleansed, and taken away (Jn. 1:29).

As sin originates in the heart because of man's fallen condition, now, due to the Born-Again experience, Righteousness can originate in the heart, because the Divine Nature is now a part of the Born-Again person (II Pet. 1:4).

WISDOM

The wisdom the world gives is *"earthly, sensual, devilish"* (James 3:15). As a result, it cannot help anyone, which should be obvious. The *"wisdom"* that comes from above is *"first pure, then peaceable, gentle, and easy to be entreated, full of mercy and good fruits, without partiality, and without hypocrisy"* (James 3:17).

The *"wisdom that comes from above"* is the Word of God. It holds the answer; it alone holds the answer — the answer to every problem as it regards *"Life and Godliness"* which affects the human race (II Pet. 1:3-4).

This means that humanistic psychology holds no answer, simply because it is *"earthly, sensual, and devilish,"* inasmuch as it originates with man and not God.

AN ILLUSTRATION

In the mid-1930's, Socialism was being

touted as the panacea for the ills of America, which then was in an economic depression. A certain Speaker made this statement, *"Socialism can put a new coat on every man in America."* Then he asked, *"Can anything beat that?"*

Among those who were gathered, a man stood up and said, *"You say that Socialism can put a new coat on every man in America. Yes, I know something better. Jesus Christ can put a new man in every coat in America."*

What a statement!

It doesn't matter how involved any effort of man is, it simply cannot take sin away. That's why it is pointless for Preachers to try to deal with the intellect of man. Man's problem is not his intellect. Man's problem is a diseased, evil, wicked heart. Only God can change that.

(7) "PURGE ME WITH HYSSOP, AND I SHALL BE CLEAN: WASH ME, AND I SHALL BE WHITER THAN SNOW."

The petition, *"Purge me with hyssop,"* expresses a figure of speech. *"Purge me with the blood which on that night in Egypt was sprinkled on the doorposts with a bunch of hyssop"* (Ex. 12:13, 22). This portrays David's dependence on *"the Blood of the Lamb."*

THE MOSAIC LAW

As is obvious, David lived in the time of the Mosaic Law. David committed both the sins of adultery and murder, and there was no reprieve for these sins under the Law; it demanded death!

So, what could David do?

Of course, the verdict was up to the Lord, and not David. And yet, the Lord must uphold the Law.

HOW COULD THE LORD UPHOLD THE LAW, AND, AT THE SAME TIME, JUSTIFY DAVID?

The Law must be kept in every respect. As stated, the Law demanded death for the sins of adultery and murder, and David was guilty of both.

The Holy Spirit moved upon David to claim the Promise of the shed blood of the Lamb which occasioned the deliverance of the Children of Israel from Egyptian bondage. They were instructed to kill a lamb, to roast it with fire and then eat it, and, above all, to apply the blood of the Lamb to the doorposts of the houses in Egypt where they resided.

The Scripture was emphatic. It stated:

"And the blood shall be to you for a token upon the houses where you are: and when I see the blood, I will pass over you, and the plague shall not be upon you to destroy you" (Ex. 12:13).

The slain lamb was a *"type"* of the coming Redeemer, Who would die on a Cross, pay the debt of sin that fallen man could not pay, and make it possible for fallen man to be Saved.

It was the same regarding Jesus and the young woman who was brought to Him who was caught in the act of adultery. The Scribes and Pharisees brought this woman to Jesus and demanded that the Law of Moses be carried out and that she be stoned. They thought they had Jesus boxed into a corner.

The Lord's answer to them was short and simple, *"He who is without sin among you, let him first cast the stone at her"* (Jn. 8:7).

And then He said to the woman, *"Neither do I condemn you: go, and sin no more"* (Jn. 8:11).

How could Jesus do this and not break the Law of Moses?

He did it the same way as He did with David and as He has done with all of us.

He satisfied the demands of the broken Law in every respect by going to the Cross and paying the price for us, a price, incidentally, that we never could hope to pay. The Law of God was, thereby, perfectly satisfied; upon Faith in His Finished Work, any and every sinner, no matter how vile, can go free.

Before the Lord, David pled the protection of the shed blood of the Lamb, then only in type, but still as effective then as now.

Let me say it in this way.

THE CROSS OF CHRIST

The only thing that stands between the world and eternal Hell is the Cross of Christ. Now I want the Reader to read those words again. The only remedy is the Cross, not the Church, not good works, not anything else, only the Cross of Christ. Nothing must be added to that or taken from that.

Every single person who walks through that Gate of pearl into the Portals of Glory will be able to do such solely because of the Lord Jesus Christ and what He did at the Cross and our acceptance of His Finished Work (Jn. 3:3, 16; Mat. 11:28-30; Rev. 22:17). In fact, the Bible closes out with the words, *"And the Spirit* (Holy Spirit) *and the Bride* (the Church) *say, Come. And let him who hears say, Come. And let him who is athirst come. And whosoever will, let him take the Water of Life freely"* (Rev. 22:17).

Let us say it again:

"The only thing standing between mankind and eternal Hell is the Cross of Christ."

The following also must be said.

THE ONLY THING STANDING BETWEEN THE CHURCH AND APOSTASY IS THE CROSS OF CHRIST

David could only turn to the slain Lamb in his terrible hour of utmost dilemma. David, in effect, was the Church of that day, or at least its titular head on Earth. He turned to the Cross simply because there was no other place to turn. His life and soul, thereby, were spared.

The Church must understand that the Cross of Christ is the Foundation of the great Plan of God. It was formulated in the Mind of God from even before the foundation of the world.

Listen to the Apostles:

Peter said, *"Forasmuch as you know that you were not redeemed with corruptible things, as silver and gold, from your vain conversation* (lifestyle) *received by tradition from your fathers* (original sin);

"But with the Precious Blood of Christ, as of a Lamb without blemish and without spot:

"Who verily was foreordained before the foundation of the world, but was manifest in these last times for you" (I Pet. 1:18-19).

Paul said, *"According as He has chosen us in Him* (in Christ, because of what He did at the Cross) *before the foundation of the world, that we should be holy and without blame before Him in love"* (Eph. 1:4).

And then John the Beloved said, *"And all who dwell upon the Earth shall worship him* (worship the Antichrist), *whose names are not written in the Book of Life of the Lamb slain from the foundation of the world"* (means that all who are not saved at that time will worship the Antichrist) (Rev. 13:8).

So we see from these Passages that God through foreknowledge knew that He would create man and that man would fall. At that time, the Godhead determined that man would be redeemed by God becoming man and going to the Cross.

We learn from this that the Cross of Christ is the Foundation Doctrine of the entirety of the Plan of God, which is given to us in the Word of God. This means that every single doctrine must be built squarely on the foundation of the Cross of Christ, or else it will be spurious in some way.

Let me say it again:

"The only thing standing between the Church and total apostasy is the Cross of Christ."

(8) "MAKE ME TO HEAR JOY AND GLADNESS; THAT THE BONES WHICH YOU HAVE BROKEN MAY REJOICE."

Forgiveness for the past never exhausts the fullness of pardon for the present and the future. There is provision for all!

FORGIVENESS

When God forgives an individual of sin, the sense of that forgiveness is always felt, and this sense is in itself a deep satisfaction.

But the Psalmist seems to ask for something more. He wants not mere passive peace and rest, but the active thrilling joy which those experience who feel themselves restored to God's favor and bask in the light of His Countenance.

The phrase, *"That the bones which You have broken may rejoice,"* is a figure of speech. It means that the sense of sin is felt even into the bones of the individual, and forgiveness is also felt accordingly. Consequently, the ache and pain cease, and they are replaced by gladness and rejoicing.

One of the great Scriptures in the entirety of the Bible is:

"If we confess our sins, He is faithful and just to forgive us our sins, and to cleanse us from all unrighteousness" (I Jn. 1:9).

HOW DOES THE BELIEVER GO ABOUT ASKING FORGIVENESS?

He goes to the Lord. It is the Lord Whom we have offended, and offended greatly. David took his terrible problem to the Lord by first of all saying, *"Have Mercy upon me, O God"* (Vs. 1). So, first of all, we ask forgiveness and mercy from the Lord.

If we have wronged someone else, we also should go to that person. There even may be an occasion where someone should confess before the entirety of the Body of Christ, at least as far as is possible. But most of the time, the sin should be confessed only to the Lord and to no one else.

It should be done immediately, wherever the person might be. The individual does not have to wait for a Church service, or anything else. The moment one commits any wrong (and, to be sure, the Holy Spirit will make it clear and plain), at that moment, the Believer, even in his heart, should confess his sin to the Lord, confessing that he has sinned and asking for forgiveness. We are promised that all sin instantly will be forgiven (I Jn. 1:7).

ARE THERE DIFFERENT STANDARDS FOR DIFFERENT PEOPLE?

No! The Lord did not require any more of David than he required of other individuals in his kingdom. Now, the sin or sins of some greatly affect more people and do more damage to the great Work of God than others; however, the remedy for one is the same as for the other. It is the Precious Blood of the Lord Jesus Christ, which cleanses from all sin, and does so equally for all (I Jn. 1:7, 9).

When the Lord delivered the Children of Israel from Egyptian bondage, the blood that was applied to the houses in Egypt was the same on all. In other words, Moses had the blood on the doorposts of the house in which he lived the same as all the other people of Israel. There were no exceptions!

When forgiveness is granted by God, as it always will be upon proper Repentance, that forgiveness is total, absolute, and complete. There is no such thing as a partial forgiveness! There is total forgiveness, which the Lord always gives, or there is no forgiveness at all.

All of this means that our Catholic friends are terribly wrong (and any others, for that matter), when they try to have forgiveness of sin by confessing to a man who calls himself a Priest. God will never recognize this! The Scripture plainly and unequivocally tells us:

"For there is one God, and one Mediator between God and men, The Man Christ Jesus;

"Who gave Himself a ransom for all, to be testified in due time" (I Tim. 2:5-6).

There has only been one Priesthood that God has ever recognized, and that was the Levitical Priesthood, ordained by the Law of Moses. This was before the Cross, so those Priests acted as mediators between God and men.

All those Levitical Priests were types of Christ. But when Jesus came to this world and paid the price at Calvary's Cross for the Redemption of man, the Levitical Priesthood was completely abolished.

Why?

It was abolished because the One to Whom that Priesthood pointed, the Lord Jesus Christ, has now come, and has done what no earthly Priest could ever do. The entirety of the Book of Hebrews bears this out.

This means that the Catholic Priesthood is an abomination in the Eyes of God. The same goes for any other so-called Priests!

OUR GREAT HIGH PRIEST

Every Believer now has in Christ the One High Priest that is needed, Who ever lives. The Scripture says:

"Seeing then that we have a Great High Priest, Who is passed into the Heavens, Jesus the Son of God, let us hold fast our profession" (Heb. 4:14).

Then Paul wrote, and I quote from THE EXPOSITOR'S STUDY BIBLE:

"But this Man (the Lord Jesus Christ), *because He continues ever* (proclaims the Priesthood of Christ as eternal, while death was inevitable as it regarded the Aaronic Priests), *has an unchangeable Priesthood.* (This not only refers to that which is eternal, but also to that which will not change as far as its principle is concerned. The reason is the Finished Work of the Cross is an

'Everlasting Covenant' [Heb. 13:20].)

"Wherefore He (the Lord Jesus Christ) *is able also to save them to the uttermost* (proclaims the fact that Christ Alone has made the only True Atonement for sin; He did this at the Cross) *who come unto God by Him* (proclaims the only manner in which man can come to God), *seeing He ever lives to make intercession for them.* (His very Presence by the Right Hand of the Father guarantees such, with nothing else having to be done [Heb. 1:3].)

"For such an High Priest became us (presents the fact that no one less exalted could have met the necessities of the human race), *Who is Holy, harmless, undefiled, separate from sinners* (describes the spotless, pure, Perfect Character of the Son of God as our Great High Priest; as well, this tells us Christ did not become a sinner on the Cross, as some claim, but was rather the Sin Offering), *and made higher than the Heavens* (refers to the fact that He is seated at the Right Hand of the Father, which is the most exalted position in Heaven or Earth)" (Heb. 7:24-26).

Therefore, for some man presently to call himself a *"Priest"* is an insult to Christ of the highest order. In effect, it says that what Christ did at the Cross was insufficient and that He Alone is not qualified to serve as our sole Mediator; in effect, it says that Christ needs help.

What blasphemy!

(9) "HIDE YOUR FACE FROM MY SINS, AND BLOT OUT ALL MY INIQUITIES."

Unforgiven sin stares in the Face of God. This can only be stopped when the sins are put away. They can only be put away by proper Confession and Repentance, with the Blood of Jesus being applied by Faith.

When this is done, the *"iniquities"* are *"blotted out"* as though they never existed. This is *"Justification by Faith."*

JUSTIFICATION BY FAITH

To the great Patriarch Abraham, the all-encompassing doctrine of *"Justification by Faith"* was given. The Scripture says, *"And he* (Abraham) *believed in the LORD; and He* (the Lord) *counted it to him for Righteousness"* (Gen. 15:6).

NOTES

In explaining Justification by Faith, the Apostle Paul used the same Passage (Rom. 4:3).

The term *"Justification by Faith"* actually means *"to be declared not guilty."* And yet, that explanation is somewhat insufficient.

Not only does it mean to be declared not guilty, but it also means to be declared innocent. It means that all sins, iniquities, and infractions are forever done away with as if they never existed. In the Mind of God, in fact, they never did exist. This is *"Justification by Faith."* It declares a person not guilty ever of any sin, even original sin.

HOW IS JUSTIFICATION BY FAITH CARRIED OUT?

It is carried out exactly as it says, *"By Faith."* What does that mean?

First of all, the correct object of faith must be in view. We speak of Jesus Christ and Him Crucified. There is only one sacrifice for sin and that is Jesus Christ and what He did at the Cross. The Scripture says:

"But this Man (this Priest, Christ Jesus), *after He had offered one Sacrifice for sins forever* (speaks of the Cross), *sat down on the Right Hand of God* (refers to the great contrast with the Priests under the Levitical system, who never sat down because their work was never completed; the Work of Christ was a *'Finished Work,'* and needed no repetition)" (Heb. 10:12).

When Jesus paid the price for sin on the Cross, He paid the price for all sin, for all time, at least for all who will believe.

Concerning this, Paul said, *"And you, being dead in your sins and the uncircumcision of your flesh* (speaks of spiritual death [i.e., *'separation from God'*], which sin does!), *has He quickened together with Him* (refers to being made spiritually alive, which is done through being *'born-again'*), *having forgiven you all trespasses* (the Cross made it possible for all manner of sins to be forgiven and taken away);

"Blotting out the handwriting of Ordinances that was against us (pertains to the Law of Moses, which was God's Standard of Righteousness that man could not reach), *which was contrary to us* (Law is against us, simply because we are unable to keep its

precepts, no matter how hard we try), *and took it out of the way* (refers to the penalty of the Law being removed), *nailing it to His Cross*. (The Law with its decrees was abolished in Christ's Death, as if crucified with Him)" (Col. 2:13-14).

All of this tells us that Justification can never be gained by works, only by Faith. We speak of Faith in Christ and what He did for us at the Cross. Anyone who will exhibit Faith in Christ can obtain such Justification, and, once obtained, it is a perfect, a pure, and a complete Justification, in fact, perfect in every respect. Such is freely imputed to all who believe (Jn. 3:16).

(10) "CREATE IN ME A CLEAN HEART, O GOD; AND RENEW A RIGHT SPIRIT WITHIN ME."

David's heart was unclean. Sin makes any heart unclean. The word *"create"* is interesting. It means the old heart is affected by sin, is diseased, and cannot be salvaged. God must, spiritually speaking, *"create a clean heart"* (Ezek. 18:31).

It is impossible for any individual to have a *"right spirit"* if there is unconfessed sin.

A CLEAN HEART

The word *"heart"* denotes the *"inner man,"* the essence of personality, which is the seat and center of all life. The spiritual term or nearest equivalency to the old English word *"heart"* is that of *"ego,"* which represents the *"I, self, person."* It is that term which is formalized, as a logical necessity, to denote that *"center"* to which all of a person's spiritual activities and characteristics refer.

The term was born of logical need for categorical expression, communicative clarity, and practical utility. The *"heart of man"* thus represents that innermost center which is of ultimate importance — that which is basic, central, substantive, and of profound essence.

SCRIPTURAL USAGE

The word *"heart"* (including *"hearts"* and *"hearted"*) is used extensively in the Bible. In fact, the word *"heart"* occurs some 730 times in the Old Testament and 105 times in the New Testament. The word *"hearts"* occurs 112 times in both Testaments combined.

NOTES

"Hearted" is used eight times. Total occurrences of the three forms of the word are found some 955 or more times throughout the Bible, as listed in Strong's Concordance.

CONSISTENCY AND VARIETY OF USAGE

There is a consistency of treatment with all Biblical uses of *"heart."* The term invariably refers to that which is central. Even when the word is used as a figure of speech, expressive of things and situations apart from mankind, it denotes central location, center, or being in the midst; examples include: *"Your borders are in the heart of the seas"* (Ezek. 27:4); *"in the heart of the sea"* (Ps. 46:2); and, *"in the heart of the Earth"* (Mat. 12:40).

The word is employed to express certain important dimensions of man and God's concern in dealings with man.

THE SOUL AND THE SPIRIT

Probably one could say, and not be far wrong, that the word *"heart"* speaks of the *"whole man,"* which refers to one's *"spirit, soul, and body."* But, more specifically, I think, it pertains to the *"soul"* and the *"spirit."*

As the physical heart is the very center of the physical body, and must function right for life to be maintained, likewise, the Holy Spirit uses the word *"heart"* for the spiritual man.

Reaching back up to the Eighth Verse, David uses the phrase, *"Bones which You have broken."* It is a figure of speech that one cannot proceed until things have been made right with God. It is as though a man's leg is broken, and he cannot walk. Unforgiven sin immobilizes the soul the same as a broken bone immobilizes the physical body.

(11) "CAST ME NOT AWAY FROM YOUR PRESENCE; AND TAKE NOT YOUR HOLY SPIRIT FROM ME."

If sin is unconfessed and rebellion persists, God will ultimately *"cast away"* the individual *"from His Presence."* He also will *"take the Holy Spirit"* from the person.

ETERNAL SECURITY

We believe and teach the Doctrine of eternal security, but not unconditional eternal security.

It is Faith which gets a Believer in, and

Faith which keeps a Believer in. If the Believer loses Faith, in other words, no longer trusts Christ for Salvation and Sanctification, such a person forfeits the very thing which got him in and keeps him in — Faith. In fact, this is why the entirety of the Book of Hebrews was written. Jews who had come to Christ were now, for whatever reason, turning their backs on Christ, in effect refuting the Sacrifice of Calvary; they were doing so by going back into Judaism. One cannot have it both ways!

If such is the case, Paul gives the following warning. I quote from THE EXPOSITOR'S STUDY BIBLE.

"For it is impossible for those who were once enlightened (refers to those who have accepted the Light of the Gospel, which means accepting Christ and His Great Sacrifice), *and have tasted of the Heavenly Gift* (pertains to Christ and what He did at the Cross), *and were made partakers of the Holy Spirit* (which takes place when a person comes to Christ),

"And have tasted the good Word of God (is not language that is used of an impenitent sinner, as some claim; the unsaved have no relish whatsoever for the Truth of God, and see no beauty in it), *and the powers of the world to come* (refers to the Work of the Holy Spirit within hearts and lives, which the unsaved cannot have or know),

"If they shall fall away (should have been translated, 'and having fallen away'), *to renew them again unto Repentance* ('again' states that they had once repented, but have now turned their backs on Christ); *seeing they crucify to themselves the Son of God afresh* (means they no longer believe what Christ did at the Cross, actually concluding Him to be an impostor; the only way any person can truly repent is to place his faith in Christ and the Cross; if that is denied, there is no Repentance), *and put Him to an open shame* (means to hold Christ up to public ridicule; Paul wrote this Epistle because some Christian Jews were going back into Judaism, or seriously contemplating doing so)" (Heb. 6:4-6).

All of this totally refutes the doctrine of unconditional eternal security. While it is certainly true that if anyone confesses their sin, God will forgive, cleanse, and wash their sin (I Jn. 1:9); however, if any Christian persists in rebellion, refusing to confess and acknowledge their sin, they, by their own actions, revert themselves to the status of an unbeliever and are thereby lost unless they come back to God in obedience to the Scriptures.

Consequently, eternal security is conditional on the individual adhering to the Word of God, which means to continue to exhibit faith in Christ and what He did for us at the Cross, which refers to him walking in all the light he knows. It always has been that way in the past; it is that way now.

SINLESS PERFECTION?

However, conditional eternal security does not claim, nor can it claim, sinless perfection. That is not the idea. Mercy, Grace, and Pardon instantly await any Believer who will confess his sin before God (I Jn. 1:9). But to the Believer who has sin in his life and will not confess that sin to God, who in fact continues in that sin, at some point he places himself in the status of *"unbeliever,"* and will be *"cast away from God's Presence"* (Gal. 5:19-21).

(12) "RESTORE UNTO ME THE JOY OF YOUR SALVATION; AND UPHOLD ME WITH YOUR FREE SPIRIT."

The Holy Spirit here points to Restoration.

RESTORATION

The business of the Holy Spirit is *"Restoration,"* but only if the individual meets God's conditions as David did, and as we must do. With unconfessed sin, all *"joy"* is lost. With sin confessed, cleansed, and put away, the *"joy of Salvation"* returns. A clean heart, a willing spirit, and a steadfast will are then given by the Holy Spirit.

The Holy Spirit does this only upon the proper conditions being met, which not only include a confession of sin, but also include the Believer's faith being placed exclusively in Christ and the Cross. The Believer loses his way simply because he transfers his faith from Christ and the Cross to something else.

THE OBJECT OF ONE'S FAITH

At the moment of conversion, the person's

faith is exclusively in Christ. While the believing sinner may know very little about Christ, he has expressed faith, and be his faith ever so small, the Holy Spirit will act upon that faith and give that person *"eternal life"* (Jn. 3:16; 10:10; Rom. 10:8-9, 13).

Thereafter however, most likely due to improper teaching or improper example, the person invariably will transfer his faith from Christ and the Cross to his own good works, or some such like thing. Then the Believer encounters trouble.

Why?

He encounters trouble because any faith that is evidenced in anything except Christ and the Cross is constituted by the Lord as *"spiritual adultery"* (Rom. 7:1-4). Christ is to meet our every need; He does so through the Cross. However, if the Believer places his faith in something else, no matter how religious the *"something else"* might be, even if it is right and good in its own way, the Lord constitutes such direction as *"spiritual adultery."* Naturally, the Holy Spirit is seriously hindered in such a situation.

The results?

The person's sin nature springs to life and the person is placed in captivity (Gal. 5:1). Sadly and regrettably, that's where the majority of the modern Church presently is. For the most part, it has abandoned the Cross of Christ; it has devised its own ways and means of victory that God never will honor, which means that the Holy Spirit will not help such a person, which means that the sin nature will rule and reign in such a life, which means that the person has just entered into an unwinnable situation. And until that person brings his faith back to the Christ and the Cross, *"Restoration"* cannot be effected (Gal. 6:1).

(13) "THEN WILL I TEACH TRANSGRESSORS YOUR WAYS; AND SINNERS SHALL BE CONVERTED UNTO YOU."

David was in no condition to proclaim God's truth to *"transgressors"*; consequently, during this time of David's disobedience to God, precious few, if any, sinners were *"converted"* unto the Lord.

The moment the sin was confessed and put away, as heinous as it was, then David was ready to begin teaching the great Word of God to *"transgressors."*

QUALIFICATIONS

Because of a myriad of unscriptural Church rules and regulations, many in the modern Church would never admit that David was now ready to *"teach transgressors Your Ways."* Many Church rules and regulations would demand a period of time, such as a year or more of no preaching, plus psychological counseling, and some would claim that he never should be allowed to teach or preach again.

Such thinking is foolish. Were it correct, no one would be qualified to teach or preach the Gospel.

The reason for this erroneous and unscriptural thinking of the majority in the modern Church is because they do not understand *"Justification by Faith."* By and large, the Church today operates on the principle of *"Justification by Works."* Man loves to add something to what God has already finished. Man would attach man-made rules to God's free pardon of Salvation and Restoration; however, God will have no part of it.

David was now ready to teach and to preach, and the Holy Spirit attested to that.

Man has always conjured up his man-made morality, man-made integrity, and man-made forgiveness. God will not accept such. In the eyes of the modern Church, David would have no morality, integrity, or spirituality. God said otherwise. David had God's morality, God's integrity, and God's spirituality. All else is sinking sand.

This is hard for the self-righteous to accept. Actually, it is impossible for the self-righteous to accept because self-righteousness is a grievous sin within itself. This sin is so bad that it crucified Christ. And, to be sure, were Christ here presently in the flesh, the modern Church would do the same identical thing to Him today as Israel of old then did.

(14) "DELIVER ME FROM BLOODGUILTINESS, O GOD, THOU GOD OF MY SALVATION: AND MY TONGUE SHALL SING ALOUD OF YOUR RIGHTEOUSNESS."

This refers to the terrible sin of having Uriah, the husband of Bathsheba, killed (II Sam. 11:14-21).

THE PARDONED SINNER

Only the consciously pardoned sinner can *"sing aloud of God's Righteousness."* Unpardoned men can speak to His Mercy, but their thoughts about it are unholy thoughts.

THE SIN OF MURDER

The twin sins that David committed, adultery and murder, were heinous, to say the least; however, the murder of Uriah was the worst. It was cold-blooded murder.

It is even worse than a malefactor robbing a store and then, out of sheer malice, pointing a gun at a bystander (whom he does not know and who is doing nothing to him) and blowing him away. That is cold-blooded murder. However, David maliciously and deliberately murdered a friend. He was trying to hide his sin with Uriah's wife, Bathsheba. So, he murdered one of his mighty men, who, even at that very time, was fighting the Lord's battles. It is difficult to imagine any action more despicable, more heinous, or more cold-blooded than that!

HOW COULD DAVID COMMIT SUCH A SIN?

David was anointed by the Lord to be the King of Israel when he was but a boy. David also was a man after God's Own heart. Through David's family would be born the Messiah, Who actually would be called the Son of David. David wrote over half of the Psalms and was used by God as few men have been used. David's name is the first human name in the New Testament and the last human name in the New Testament. When we consider all these things, we again ask the question, *"How could David have done such a thing?"*

There is only answer that can be given!

David shifted his faith from Christ and the Cross to something else. It doesn't really matter what the *"something else"* was. Such a situation opens the person up to be maneuvered by Satan.

The only protection that mankind ever has had, even from the very beginning, is the Cross of Christ.

Let me say it again:

The only thing standing between mankind and eternal Hell is the Cross of Christ. We gain that protection, that Salvation, by simply placing our faith in Christ and what He did at the Cross. If our faith is placed in something else, which David obviously did, all the help which the Cross provides is then forfeited. The Believer is then subjected to the onslaughts of Satan, and has no suitable protection. Such a path will lead to anything, even as it did with David.

THE LESSON WE MUST LEARN

If David, who was one of the greatest men of God who has ever lived, could fall into such a situation, where do you think that leaves us?

No individual can stand against the powers of darkness without functioning in God's Prescribed Order. We should read those words very, very carefully.

I don't care who the man or the woman is. It doesn't matter how much God is using them, even as He was using David. If we step outside of God's Prescribed Order of Victory, which is the Cross of Christ, even as it has always been the Cross of Christ, such a person is slated for failure. It cannot be otherwise!

That's the reason that we at Jimmy Swaggart Ministries are so vehemently opposed to ways and directions which are devised by men; they are not devised by the Lord and they are not in the Word of God. I speak of directions such as *"The Purpose Driven Life," "The Government of Twelve," "The Word of Faith," "Denominationalism,"* or a host of other things that I could name. We know what the end results will be.

Once again, we should allow the example of David to serve as a warning. If it could happen to David (which it most definitely did!), it most definitely will happen to us if we leave God's Way.

Let me say it again:

The Way of the Lord is *"Jesus Christ and Him Crucified"* (I Cor. 1:23). That's why Paul said:

"But God forbid that I should glory (boast), *save in the Cross of our Lord Jesus Christ* (what the opponents of Paul sought to escape at the price of insincerity is the Apostle's only basis of exultation), *by Whom the world*

is crucified unto me, and I unto the world. (The only way we can overcome the world, and I mean the only way, is by placing our faith exclusively in the Cross of Christ and keeping it there)" (Gal. 6:14).

(15) "O LORD, OPEN THOU MY LIPS; AND MY MOUTH SHALL SHOW FORTH YOUR PRAISE."

David's lips now will be opened and he can say, *"My mouth shall show forth God's praise."*

PRAISE

That cannot happen when there is unconfessed sin. That's the reason there is precious little praise in most Churches; or, in many cases, the praise that is offered is hollow and unacceptable to God. God cannot accept *"praise"* from an unclean heart which has unconfessed sin. Men try to offer to God holy worship. God is not looking for such. He is looking for *"holy worshippers"* (Jn. 4:23).

If *"praise"* is not anchored squarely in the Cross of Christ, then it is Praise that God will not accept.

Under the Levitical Law, the Altar of Incense sat immediately in front of the Veil which hid the Holy of Holies. Twice a day the Priests were to bring coals of fire from the Brazen Altar, place those coals on the Altar of Incense, and pour Incense over them, which would fill the Holy Place with a smoke of fragrance. This typified the Intercession rendered by Christ, all on our behalf. It also typified our prayer, praise, and worship.

However, the Intercession of Christ is effective only if our petition, praise, and worship are anchored in the Cross, typified by the coals of fire coming from the Brazen Altar, this latter Altar being a Type of the Cross of Christ.

In fact, when Nadab and Abihu offered up *"strange fire"* on this Altar of Incense, which means that the coals of fire did not originate at the Brazen Altar, they were struck dead on the spot (Lev. 10:1-2).

So, for the Lord to accept our praise and worship, there must not be unconfessed sin in our lives, and our praise and worship also must originate at the Cross.

(16) "FOR YOU DESIRE NOT SACRIFICE; ELSE WOULD I GIVE IT: YOU DELIGHT NOT IN BURNT OFFERING."

This Truth is stated two times: here and in Psalms 40:6.

ANIMAL SACRIFICES

If there had been any animal sacrifices which God desired or required for such offenses as adultery and murder, David willingly would have offered them. But there were none. The Mosaic Law allowed no reconciliation, no sacrifice, for such sins. So David had no recourse in the Levitical Law, which should be a lesson to all of us, as well.

That's the reason the Apostle Paul said, and I quote from THE EXPOSITOR'S STUDY BIBLE:

"For I testify again to every man who is circumcised (some of the Galatian Gentiles were being pressured by false teachers to embrace the Law of Moses, which meant they would have to forsake Christ and the Cross, for it is not possible to wed the two; as well, it's not possible to wed any law to Grace), *that he is debtor to do the whole Law* (which, of course, is impossible; and besides, the Law contained no Salvation).

"Christ is become of no effect unto you (this is a chilling statement, and refers to anyone who makes anything other than Christ and the Cross the object of his faith), *whosoever of you are justified by the Law* (seek to be justified by the Law); *you are fallen from Grace* (fallen from the position of Grace, which means the Believer is trusting in something other than the Cross; it actually means *'to apostatize')"* (Gal. 5:3-4).

Animal sacrifices were woefully insufficient to take away the guilt of sin in any case; therefore, one only enjoyed remission of sin on the basis of that which the animal sacrifices represented, namely, the Coming Redeemer, the Lord Jesus Christ, Who would give His Life on the Cross. That, in fact, is the way David found forgiveness, cleansing, and pardon — in the Sacrifice of Christ, Whose Blood cleanses from all sin, even the worst type of sin, even David's sin (Eph. 2:13-18; I Jn. 1:7).

(17) "THE SACRIFICES OF GOD ARE A BROKEN SPIRIT: A BROKEN AND A CONTRITE HEART, O GOD, YOU WILL NOT DESPISE."

Such a spirit proclaims the fact that the individual is not looking to a ceremony to forgive him of sin; because of his sin, he truly has *"a broken spirit"* and even *"a broken and contrite heart."*

This means that the individual is conscious of his sin, is conscious of the magnitude of his sin, and knows that it is a dread offense against God; these cause him to be brokenhearted. True Repentance always will be accompanied by this of which David speaks.

No penances or sacraments or gifts of costly Churches or men, in expiation of past sins, are desired or accepted by God. Only Repentance, love, and the abandonment of all known sin is accepted by Him, and that on the *"Sacrifices"* of a *"broken spirit"* and a *"broken and contrite heart."*

(18) "DO GOOD IN YOUR GOOD PLEASURE UNTO ZION: BUILD THOU THE WALLS OF JERUSALEM."

Verses 18 and 19 are not, as some think, a meaningless addition to this Psalm by some later writer. Both Verses belong to the structure and prophetic scope of the Psalm.

David's sin, confession, and Restoration illustrate this future Chapter in Israel's history. With their idolatry (adultery) and murder forgiven, they will go forth as messengers of the Gospel to win other nations to wholehearted faith and service in and for Christ. This will take place in the coming Kingdom Age, after Israel has accepted Christ.

Upon Israel's Repentance, the Lord will once again *"build Thou the walls of Jerusalem."*

(19) "THEN SHALL YOU BE PLEASED WITH THE SACRIFICES OF RIGHTEOUSNESS, WITH BURNT OFFERING AND WHOLE BURNT OFFERING: THEN SHALL THEY OFFER BULLOCKS UPON YOUR ALTAR."

This Passage has a double meaning.

SACRIFICES

First of all, the Lord is saying through David that if Repentance is offered from the position of a broken heart, trusting in Christ and what Christ would do at the Cross, typified by the Passover Lamb of the Twelfth Chapter of Exodus, Grace would be given, and then Sacrifices could once again be entered into, which, no doubt, David did.

The second meaning has to do with the coming Kingdom Age. At that time, the Lord Jesus will rule Personally from Jerusalem. He will rule the entirety of the world. At that time, implied in the word *"then,"* animal sacrifices once again will be re-instituted (Ezek., Chpts. 40-48).

Why?

The animal sacrifices during the coming Kingdom Age will be carried out at the Temple in Jerusalem, just as they were during the time of Solomon. However, they will be done only from the basis of a memorial. In other words, the world must never forget the price that was paid by Christ at Calvary, which is what makes the Kingdom Age possible, and all who enter therein.

Our Salvation did not come cheaply. It was purchased at a great price. That price was the Life of our Lord Jesus poured out at Calvary's Cross. So, the re-instituted animal sacrifices, which will take place in the coming thousand-year Kingdom Age, will be strictly as a memorial. Man must never be allowed to forget this price, this great price, that was paid!

PSALM 52

*A Psalm of David:
The Doom of the Wicked*

(1) "WHY DO YOU BOAST YOURSELF IN MISCHIEF, O MIGHTY MAN? THE GOODNESS OF GOD ENDURES CONTINUALLY."

The inscription says: *"To the Chief Musician, Maschil, a Psalm of David, when Doeg the Edomite came and told Saul, and said unto him, David is come to the house of Ahimelech."*

THE BOASTING OF SATAN

This Psalm was written by David at the time when Doeg the Edomite rose up against David, which was when Saul was trying to kill David. As a result of this evil man's actions, many Priests lost their lives.

The setting of the Psalm concerns an event, namely when Saul was attempting to kill David, that took place years before he finally became king of the entire nation of Israel; still, even more so, it concerns the Antichrist who will declare war on Israel at the midpoint of the Great Tribulation; therefore, David in this Psalm is a Type of Christ and Doeg is a type of the Antichrist.

The Holy Spirit uses this occasion to portray not only that which had happened, but also that which would come in the distant future during the Great Tribulation.

As Doeg boasted of himself concerning the destruction of God's Priests, so the Antichrist will *"boast of himself"* by doing the same on an even greater measure.

Doeg hated David as the Antichrist will hate the Lord Jesus Christ.

WHAT THE ANTICHRIST WILL BE LIKE?

The facts set out in this First Verse are:

1. That the Antichrist will be a powerful and merciless tyrant.
2. That he will boast of his success in injuring and destroying the Messiah's people.
3. That he will abuse the Goodness of God which leads men to Repentance.

The doom of this *"mighty man"* of boasting and mischief is predicted in Verse 5.

The Holy Spirit tells us that despite the evil of this man, *"the goodness of God endures continually."* In other words, *"the goodness of God"* ultimately will prevail. This was fulfilled in its totality when David ultimately became king, and the evil followers of Saul were destroyed. Likewise, it will be fulfilled in the Great Tribulation at the Coming of Jesus Christ, when the Antichrist will be killed and the Christ of Glory sets up a Kingdom that ultimately will never end. This will ensure *"the goodness of God."*

All of this tells us that evil ultimately will not triumph; *"goodness"* will be the ultimate victor. Moreover, the only true *"goodness"* is that which is *"of God."* Neither Satan nor any of his followers have any *"goodness."*

The word *"Maschil,"* as it is used in the superscription, means *"instruction."* The three following Psalms are also *"Maschil"* Psalms. They fulfill David's promise in Ps. 51:13 to teach transgressors God's Ways; hence, the Doctrine of these four Psalms (52-55) is that if sin is not confessed and forsaken, then God's Wrath surely will follow.

(2) "THE TONGUE DEVISES MISCHIEFS; LIKE A SHARP RAZOR, WORKING DECEITFULLY."

There are few men in the Bible who were more treacherous or evil than Doeg the Edomite. He falsely accused the High Priest and his family, who were true to David, and, at Saul's command, he willingly slaughtered them. He is, therefore, a type of the Antichrist, and David is a Type of Christ.

THE TONGUE

The *"tongue,"* as James said, *"is full of deadly poison."* James also said, *"The tongue can no man tame."* Only God can do such (James 3:8).

During the latter half of the Great Tribulation, the Antichrist will totally fulfill this Passage. Daniel said, *"He shall speak great words against the Most High"* (Dan. 7:25).

The Antichrist will make a seven-year nonaggression pact with Israel and then break it at the midway point. At that time, he will declare war on Israel and seek to destroy them by *"working deceitfully."*

(3) "YOU LOVE EVIL MORE THAN GOOD; AND LYING RATHER THAN TO SPEAK RIGHTEOUSNESS. SELAH."

This fits Doeg and it also fits the Antichrist. The seven-year period of time in which the Antichrist will set about to rule the world (he will fail!) will be the greatest time of *"evil"* the world has ever known. He will *"love evil"* as all sons of Satan do, but in an even greater measure. Daniel calls him *"a king of fierce countenance"* (Dan. 8:23). He also said, *"He shall destroy the mighty and the holy people"* — Israel (Dan. 8:24).

The name *"Satan"* means *"slander-lying."* Consequently, the sons of Satan also love *"lying."*

Adolf Hitler was another forerunner of the Antichrist. He, as no man to date, magnified the *"lie"* into a tool which served his purpose more than any other man. The Antichrist will take the evil of *"lying"* to an even greater dimension.

(4) "YOU LOVE ALL DEVOURING WORDS, O THOU DECEITFUL TONGUE."

As Doeg loved these things, so also will the Antichrist love these things. Daniel also said, *"And through his policy also he shall cause craft* (deceit) *to prosper in his hand"* (Dan. 8:25).

DECEPTION

The Antichrist will deceive Israel into signing the seven-year nonaggression pact, even though he will have every intention of breaking it, as he will do at the midpoint. Doeg illustrates these four statements respecting the Antichrist:

1. He plotted the destruction of David.
2. He loved evil rather than good.
3. He falsely accused Ahimelech.
4. He rejoiced at Saul's murderous command authorizing him to destroy Ahimelech's entire family.

As stated, all of this is a type, a symbol, a precursor, of what the Antichrist will do regarding Israel in a soon-to-come day.

(5) "GOD SHALL LIKEWISE DESTROY YOU FOREVER, HE SHALL TAKE YOU AWAY, AND PLUCK YOU OUT OF YOUR DWELLING PLACE, AND ROOT YOU OUT OF THE LAND OF THE LIVING. SELAH."

The fourfold judgment of Verse 5 corresponds to the fourfold wickedness of Verses 2 through 4. God shall destroy the Antichrist forever; He shall take him away; He shall pluck him out of his dwellingplace, and He shall root him out of the land of the living.

Concerning the Antichrist, Daniel said, *"But the judgment shall sit, and they shall take away his dominion, to consume and to destroy it unto the end"* (Dan. 7:26).

As the Lord destroyed Doeg the Edomite for his terrible treachery, likewise, He will destroy the Antichrist.

(6) "THE RIGHTEOUS ALSO SHALL SEE, AND FEAR, AND SHALL LAUGH AT HIM."

Even though it looked like Doeg had the upper hand when he was wielding the sword concerning the house of Ahimelech, the Prophecy is that *"the righteous,"* who was David, ultimately would *"see his destruction."* At the time of great victory, David and those who followed him would look back and *"laugh at him* (Doeg)*"* and his threats.

These words were but an indication of the laughter of Israel concerning the Antichrist, when he is destroyed by the Lord Jesus Christ at the Lord's Second Coming. Israel is here called *"the righteous,"* and so they will be when they accept the Lord Jesus Christ as their Saviour, which, as stated, they will do at His Second Advent.

(7) "LO, THIS IS THE MAN WHO MADE NOT GOD HIS STRENGTH; BUT TRUSTED IN THE ABUNDANCE OF HIS RICHES, AND STRENGTHENED HIMSELF IN HIS WICKEDNESS."

Saul, no doubt, made Doeg rich; however, the gold and silver that Saul gave him in no way could protect him from his *"wickedness."* The Lord would have the last say in that.

Likewise, the Antichrist will have great riches. Daniel said, *"But he shall have power over the treasures of gold and of silver"* (Dan. 11:43).

THE OIL RICHES OF THE MIDDLE EAST

The Antichrist, no doubt, will accumulate to himself the oil riches of the Middle East, which will provide him hundreds of billions of dollars with which to pursue his efforts of world conquest.

Men always have believed that great wealth can protect them against almost anything; however, those who trust in *"riches"* instead of trusting in *"God"* ultimately will fail.

David chose to place his trust in God. Doeg chose to place his trust in money. Basically, this is the dividing line for all of mankind. Precious few choose God. Those who do always succeed. Most choose money and ultimately they always lose.

(8) "BUT I AM LIKE A GREEN OLIVE TREE IN THE HOUSE OF GOD: I TRUST IN THE MERCY OF GOD FOREVER AND EVER."

As Verses 8 and 9 portray David at the present time, even more they portray the Messiah in the coming day. As Verse 7 characterizes the Antichrist, Verses 8 and 9 characterize Jesus Christ as a *"green olive tree."* He perfectly and eternally trusts; He perpetually praises; He unalterably and unfalteringly waits.

(9) "I WILL PRAISE YOU FOREVER, BECAUSE YOU HAVE DONE IT: AND I WILL WAIT ON YOUR NAME; FOR IT IS GOOD BEFORE YOUR SAINTS."

David utters these words and praises the Name of the Lord for his victory over the efforts of Satan to destroy him.

THE MESSIAH

In its fuller meaning, this Verse pertains to the Messiah as He praises God in the execution of His Wrath upon the Antichrist. It is this Divine action which is pointed to in the word *"it."*

The last Verse contrasts with the first. The Antichrist boasts of himself (Vs. 1); the Messiah praises God. The Antichrist acclaims the success of his malignity (Vs. 2); the Messiah points to God's Judgment upon it. The Antichrist abuses the Goodness of God; the Messiah rejoices in it.

This Psalm was committed to the Chief Musician in reference to Maschil. It actually means *"the great dancings."* When David slew Goliath, there was dancing. When the Messiah destroys the Antichrist, there will, no doubt, be great dancing.

There was undoubtedly great dancing over David's ultimate victory over Saul and Doeg. As short as this Psalm is, it promises a long day of laughing (Vs. 6), singing (Vs. 9), and dancing.

Hallelujah!

PSALM 53

A Psalm of David:
The Foolishness of Man

(1) "THE FOOL HAS SAID IN HIS HEART, THERE IS NO GOD. CORRUPT ARE THEY, AND HAVE DONE ABOMINABLE INIQUITY: THERE IS NONE WHO DOES GOOD."

This Psalm was written by David and some think it is the same as Psalm 14. That is incorrect.

TWO PSALMS

The Holy Spirit did not make a mistake in including both Psalms, even though they are very similar. He did so for a reason. There are differences, and we hope to bring out at least some of these differences.

1. As Bible Scholars know, the Book of Psalms is really broken into five Sections corresponding with the Pentateuch (Genesis, Exodus, Leviticus, Numbers, and Deuteronomy). Psalm 14 is in the Genesis Book, and this Psalm is in the Exodus Book; consequently, they have different meanings.

2. The first one is for private use and the second is for public use. *"Jehovah"* occurs seven times in the original Text of Psalm 14, and *"Elohim"* occurs seven times in this Psalm. The affliction of the oppressed is the theme of the first and the doom of their oppressors is that of Psalm 53. Psalm 14 views Israel in the power of the oppressor, as in the land of Egypt, and thus, harmonizes with the close of Genesis. The other predicts her triumphant Exodus from affliction and harmonizes with the second Book of the Pentateuch.

The two Psalms are, therefore, quite different. In Psalm 14, the attention of the Reader is directed to the suffering of the Messiah and His servants; it, therefore, is private. The Fifty-third Psalm is given respecting the Judgment of the oppressor (the Antichrist) and the deliverance of the oppressed; it consequently is for public use.

THE FOOL

The *"fool"* who is spoken of here is the Antichrist. It also refers to any individual who falls into this category, but the primary direction of the Holy Spirit is to point out the coming man of sin, *"the fool."*

He is a *"fool"* because he says, *"There is no God."* Daniel said, *"And shall speak marvelous things against the God of gods"* (Dan. 11:36); consequently, despite all the *"good"* that he will promise the world, there will be no *"good"* that is done, but rather evil.

(2) "GOD LOOKED DOWN FROM HEAVEN UPON THE CHILDREN OF MEN, TO SEE IF THERE WERE ANY WHO DID UNDERSTAND, WHO DID SEEK GOD."

This Verse has two meanings:

1. In a sense, this Passage carries the idea of God gazing or literally bowing Himself over to get a better look in His examination of their wicked ways.

God is Omniscient, meaning that He knows all things. So the Passage does not mean that God is lacking in knowledge, but that He minutely scrutinizes what is being done.

2. This also refers to the Great Tribulation,

which signals the rise of the Antichrist. At this time, God will pour out tremendous plagues and judgments upon this Planet; however, He will search Planet Earth to see if such can be avoided, being true to His Nature as a God of Mercy. He will find none who, left on their own, will cry out after God; instead they all refuse to repent (Rev. 9:20-21).

(3) "EVERY ONE OF THEM IS GONE BACK: THEY ARE ALTOGETHER BECOME FILTHY; THERE IS NONE WHO DOES GOOD, NO, NOT ONE."

This Passage has three meanings:

DAVID, MANKIND, THE ANTICHRIST

1. As the Spirit of God spoke through David, He referred to those who followed Saul and made themselves confederate with his opposition to David. Saul was a type of the flesh, and David was a type of the Spirit. Everything of the flesh is *"filthy."*

2. It also refers to the whole of mankind. Paul quoted this in Romans 3:10-18. Jesus said there are no *"good men"* (Mat. 19:16-17). Man is totally depraved. There is nothing in his heart that on its own seeks after God. The Holy Spirit must move upon man by revealing Himself to man and convicting man of his sins before man can be Saved (Jn. 3:16; 16:8-11).

Men continue to think that through their so-called *"goodness"* they can somehow earn Eternal Life. First of all, man cannot earn Eternal Life; second, there is no *"goodness"* in man. The only way that man can have *"goodness"* is by inviting the Lord Jesus Christ into his heart and life. Then man can become *"good,"* but only because Christ lives within.

3. All who follow the Antichrist will be *"filthy,"* and none will be *"good."*

(4) "HAVE THE WORKERS OF INIQUITY NO KNOWLEDGE? WHO EAT UP MY PEOPLE AS THEY EAT BREAD: THEY HAVE NOT CALLED UPON GOD."

These *"workers of iniquity"* included those who followed Saul. At Saul's command, they attempted to kill David. David *"called upon God"*; they did not.

In a greater way, it refers to the followers of the Antichrist who have *"no knowledge"* of God. They will be *"workers of iniquity."* Daniel said, *"And shall destroy the mighty and the holy people"* (Dan. 8:24).

(5) "THERE WERE THEY IN GREAT FEAR, WHERE NO FEAR WAS: FOR GOD HAS SCATTERED THE BONES OF HIM WHO ENCAMPS AGAINST YOU: YOU HAVE PUT THEM TO SHAME, BECAUSE GOD HAS DESPISED THEM."

This Verse directs itself to one particular period.

THE ANTICHRIST

Verse 5 proclaims the destruction of the Antichrist. When the Power of God explodes against the *"man of sin,"* the Antichrist will then be *"in great fear."*

The statement, *"Where no fear was,"* refers to the Antichrist's thinking that God will not take action against him, but now he sees that God has come on the scene and will completely destroy him. This Verse and the last Verse point to the place and predict the time of the destruction of the fool (Antichrist) and his followers. His folly is described in II Thessalonians 2:4 as well as in Verse 1 of this Psalm.

The word *"they"* in Verse 5 refers to his followers. The moral effect of his leadership is fitly expressed in the words *"corrupt," "abominable,"* and *"altogether filthy"* (Vss. 1, 3).

The *"scattering of the bones"* refers to the conclusion of the Battle of Armageddon, when Israel will spend some seven months burying the dead (Ezek. 39:11-12).

The *"shame"* of the defeat of the Antichrist will be obvious to the whole world *"because God has despised them."*

(6) "OH THAT THE SALVATION OF ISRAEL WERE COME OUT OF ZION! WHEN GOD BRINGS BACK THE CAPTIVITY OF HIS PEOPLE, JACOB SHALL REJOICE, AND ISRAEL SHALL BE GLAD."

This will be fulfilled at the Second Advent of Christ. At long last, the *"captivity"* of Israel will be ended.

This *"captivity"* started some 600 years before Christ, has lasted until the present day, and will not end until Christ comes back. Then *"Jacob shall rejoice, and Israel shall be glad"* (Zech. 14:20-21).

PSALM 54

*A Psalm of David:
A Cry for Help*

(1) "SAVE ME, O GOD, BY YOUR NAME, AND JUDGE ME BY YOUR STRENGTH."

This is a Psalm of David, which was written when the Ziphites intended to betray him to Saul. Its account is found in I Samuel, Chapter 23.

A TYPE OF CHRIST

At the time of the writing of this Psalm, David was fleeing from Saul. He heard that the Philistines had invaded the threshingfloors of the city of Keilah.

David *"enquired of the LORD"* if he should go and *"smite these Philistines"* (I Sam. 23:2).

The Lord told him to do so. David fought the Philistines by smiting them with a great slaughter, and the Scripture says, *"David saved the inhabitants of Keilah"* (I Sam. 23:5).

Sadly, David had rescued the citizens of Keilah from the Philistines, but they still sought to betray him *"into the hand of Saul."* The Lord told David that he must leave.

David fights the Philistines but not his own people. He then flees to the *"wilderness of Ziph."* Then, the Ziphites came to Saul to betray David also. On this occasion, as stated, he wrote this Psalm.

David is a Type of Christ. David delivered the Keilahites, but yet they betrayed him. Likewise, Christ has delivered the world, but yet they betray Him. David was a blessing to the Ziphites. Sadly, they too betrayed him. Christ is a great Blessing to humanity; He is, in fact, the only Blessing to humanity. But still, men betray Him and spurn His gracious Kindness.

VENGEANCE BELONGS TO THE LORD

In either case, David does not attempt to avenge himself (Rom. 12:19). He knew that vengeance belongs to God; he knew that when the trusting servant is tried, he should not take matters into his own hands, but rather rely on his Master to rescue him, to vindicate him (Vs. 1), and to punish his tormentors (Vs. 5), thereby verifying the Promise, *"I will recompense, saith the LORD"* (Heb. 10:30).

How so much better off we would be if, as Christians, we would allow the Lord to handle those who mistreat us! To take matters into one's own hands takes matters out of God's Hands. We should humbly submit all injustices to God. Any attempts at vengeance on our part only exacerbate the situation and ultimately will be the ruin of the wounded instead of their blessing.

(2) "HEAR MY PRAYER, O GOD; GIVE EAR TO THE WORDS OF MY MOUTH."

The ways and means are here given.

PRAYER

The answer to any problem that any Believer may have is to *"take it to the Lord in prayer."* How so few of us avail themselves of this grand solution! God answers prayer. His Word pleads with us to bring our needs to Him.

In October of 1991, the Lord instructed me to begin two prayer meetings a day (except for Service nights), which we immediately set out to do.

We kept this regimen for nearly ten years, and, personally, I still adhere to the same principle.

In 1997, the Lord moved greatly upon my heart and life, giving me the Revelation of the Cross, which has altogether revolutionized my life and Ministry. I now preach a complete Message, a Message which will set the captive free and keep the captive free. It is the Cross! The Cross! The Cross!

Regrettably, the modern Church has turned to humanistic psychology. It pays lip service to prayer but little engages in such. Let it be known that there is no help from the broken cisterns of this world. Our only help comes from God, just as David's help came from God.

(3) "FOR STRANGERS ARE RISEN UP AGAINST ME, AND OPPRESSORS SEEK AFTER MY SOUL: THEY HAVE NOT SET GOD BEFORE THEM. SELAH."

The *"strangers"* were the men of Keilah; the *"oppressors,"* were Saul and his henchmen. Why would they seek David's destruction?

They did so because *"they have not set God before them."* God was not their leader or their guide; consequently, they would seek to destroy that which belonged to God.

When it comes to God, men cannot be

neutral. They are either opposed to Him or in favor of Him.

(4) "BEHOLD, GOD IS MY HELPER: THE LORD IS WITH THEM WHO UPHOLD MY SOUL."

Two beautiful statements are made here and sanctioned by the Holy Spirit:

DAVID'S HELPER

God was David's helper. It looked to the whole of Israel that David had no help. It would look the same to the casual observer. Almost everywhere he went, they sought to betray him into Saul's hands; however, David did not depend on men; he depended on God. In the natural, David's situation was hopeless; in the supernatural, Saul's situation was hopeless.

BLESSING FROM THE LORD

The few who did seek to help David would be immeasurably blessed by *"the Lord."* In these times, it's difficult for any individual to help one such as David.

Men sought the favor of Saul since he was the king. David was a hunted fugitive. David looked as though he had no future. In reality, David had the greatest future of all, and Saul had none.

Too often men look on the outward appearance because they have little spirituality. Most do not desire to go against the tide. Therefore, they go with the tide, which always is wrong. The truth is this:

(5) "HE SHALL REWARD EVIL UNTO MY ENEMIES: CUT THEM OFF IN YOUR TRUTH."

This ultimately happened exactly as David said. His *"enemies"* ultimately were *"cut off."* Saul died at the hands of the Philistines. Likewise, those who followed Saul either repented or were *"cut off."*

The reason is obvious. It was because of *"Your Truth."* Men should find out what *"God's Truth"* is and follow it. His *"Truth"* is His Word. His Word will ultimately run out irrespective of what the present situation may seem to be.

(6) "I WILL FREELY SACRIFICE UNTO YOU: I WILL PRAISE YOUR NAME, O LORD; FOR IT IS GOOD."

This *"Sacrifice"* was offered in faith. The *"Praise"* was offered in faith, as well. Despite the difficulties and circumstances, David knew that God ultimately would deliver him.

(7) "FOR HE HAS DELIVERED ME OUT OF ALL TROUBLE: AND MY EYE HAS SEEN HIS DESIRE UPON MY ENEMIES."

Another great Truth is here revealed.

A STATEMENT OF FAITH

Most probably this statement given in Verse 7 was written by faith. David called those things that were not as though they were. The day definitely came when God did *"deliver him out of all trouble."* As well, David ultimately saw *"his desire upon my enemies."*

The *"enemies"* of the Child of God are *"the world,"* *"the flesh,"* and *"the devil."* Within our own strength, we cannot overcome these *"enemies,"* just as David could not overcome in his own strength. God was David's Helper, and God will be our Helper only if we totally rely upon Him.

THE CROSS OF CHRIST

The Lord has a way in which He works. Because it is right, He will not deviate from that way.

That *"Way"* is *"Jesus Christ and Him Crucified"* (I Cor. 1:23).

Every single thing that we receive from the Lord comes to us by the means of Jesus Christ as the Source and the Cross as the Means. The proclamation of *"Jesus Christ and Him Crucified"* is in essence the entirety of the Gospel.

Whatever it is that we receive from the Lord, and I speak of anything and all things, it is the Cross of Christ that has made it all possible. Unfortunately, most Preachers have some knowledge about the Cross as it refers to Salvation, but almost none at all as it refers to our Sanctification; consequently, they try to live for God in all the wrong ways, thereby giving faulty advice to Believers.

At times I will note that which is offered by Preachers over Television. I speak of books, tapes, and other products. Almost all of these efforts pertain to *"works,"* which will not bring the Believer anything. Sadly, even if faith is advanced, it is seldom, if ever, faith in Christ and the Cross. Perhaps Christ will be mentioned, but, if one looks closely at these efforts, one will see that they all center up on *"self,"* i.e., *"the flesh."* And the Scripture plainly tells us:

"So then they who are in the flesh cannot please God" (Rom. 8:8).

Victory is found only in Christ and the Cross. There is no other avenue. God, in fact, is unalterably opposed to every other way and means of supposed Victory. That's why Paul also said:

"God forbid that I should glory (boast), *save in the Cross of our Lord Jesus Christ, by Whom the world is crucified unto me, and I unto the world"* (Gal. 6:14).

A PROPHETIC ANALYSIS OF THIS PSALM

As stated, the setting of this Psalm is aptly described; however, prophetically, it concerns the Messiah and the minority of the Jews who, in the last days, will believe on Him — possibly even the 144,000.

He asks for a just punishment upon their enemies. Being Himself sinless as Man and Righteous as God, He can demand a fitting judgment. He claims a just sentence upon these convicted transgressors.

PSALM 55

A Psalm of David:
Betrayal

(1) "GIVE EAR TO MY PRAYER, O GOD; AND HIDE NOT YOURSELF FROM MY SUPPLICATION."

This Psalm was written by David during the time when his son Absalom and his most trusted advisor, Ahithophel, rebelled against him by seeking to take his throne and turn the hearts of Israel against him. It probably was the most awful time in David's life.

THE LORD JESUS CHRIST

This Psalm also portrays the Lord Jesus Christ, Who was betrayed by His Personal Disciple and chosen Apostle, Judas.

Even though this Psalm concerns David's time, still, it more so concerns the hatred and treachery which the Messiah suffered Personally in the days of his flesh, and which He now suffers and will yet suffer in sympathy with His people (Col. 1:24).

How wonderful it is to be permitted to hear Christ speaking to God! The Gospels record the Words and Acts of Christ; the Psalms reveal His Prayers and Thoughts. What a dignity to be made a partner with Him in the Thoughts and the Notions of His Heart! His is the Voice that is heard in this Psalm; His are the Thoughts; His are the Instructions.

(2) "ATTEND UNTO ME, AND HEAR ME: I MOURN IN MY COMPLAINT, AND MAKE A NOISE."

His cry to God was because of the attitude of Israel against him. He would come unto His Own, and His Own would receive Him not (Jn. 1:11).

(3) "BECAUSE OF THE VOICE OF THE ENEMY, BECAUSE OF THE OPPRESSION OF THE WICKED: FOR THEY CAST INIQUITY UPON ME, AND IN WRATH THEY HATE ME."

This concerns David and those who would take his throne and his life. But in a greater way, it concerns Israel, who *"hated Him"* (Christ). Why did they hate Him?

They did so because their deeds were evil. Unrighteousness cannot abide Righteousness, because Righteousness is a constant rebuke to such.

RIGHTEOUSNESS AND SELF-RIGHTEOUSNESS

Absalom and Ahithophel felt justified in their actions against David. David said, *"They cast iniquity upon me."* Because of David's sin with Bathsheba against Uriah her husband, they felt that they not only could, but should, take his throne. Their knowledge of God's Word was weak, maybe even nonexistent, or they would not have thought this.

In the first place, in God's great Mercy and Forgiveness, David was the same after the sin as he had been before. Self-righteousness can never see this. In their minds, David had forfeited his crown and his place, so they took matters into their own hands. They did not recognize God's Mercy, Grace, or Love. They only saw their own jaded, selfish ambitions. Actually, they were no different now than they had been all along. Ahithophel's heart was just as black before his rebellion as after. The same can be said for Absalom.

They lacked opportunity before; now opportunity presents itself, and they will act.

David had repented of his sin, and God had put it away. As far as God was concerned, David's sin no longer existed. But because Absalom and Ahithophel were self-righteous, as far as they were concerned, it always would exist.

Men would do well to heed the words of this Fifty-fifth Psalm. If they, as Absalom and Ahithophel, deny forgiveness to David, likewise, it will be denied them.

In its greater fulfillment, it speaks of Christ in His earthly Ministry. David had sinned, so his enemies felt they had cause against him. Jesus never sinned, so His enemies would manufacture deceit against Him.

In reality, both David and Christ are identical. And yet, the self-righteous could never accept this comparison.

David had sinned, and sinned greatly, but his sin had been put away by the Lord and would not be remembered against him any more. It is called *"Justification by Faith."* This is proven by the fact that even though his sin is graphically detailed in II Samuel, Chapter 11, it is not even mentioned in I Chronicles, Chapter 20. When this time frame in David's life is accounted, God had wiped it out. As far as God is concerned, it does not exist.

So, David, who is sinful, and Christ, Who is sinless, are one and the same in the Mind of God because of the Shed Blood of Christ and David's faith in it. The same can be said for every individual who has ever put his trust and faith in Christ. We are one with Him (Jn. 14:20).

(4) "MY HEART IS SORE PAINED WITHIN ME: AND THE TERRORS OF DEATH ARE FALLEN UPON ME."

At this critical time in David's life, he felt that possibly he would not survive. *"Death"* seemed imminent. Unless God chose to deliver him, he could not be delivered. In David's mind, he felt that because of his sin no Deliverance was possible (II Sam. 16:10).

The *"sore pain"* in David's heart was there because of the terrible turmoil in Israel due to Absalom's rebellion. But, still, it was there in a greater way because of his own sin and failure. Deep down he knew that he was to blame. (This, however, in no way excused Absalom and Ahithophel.)

NOTES

In the greater fulfillment by the Son of David, He would in no way be at fault; yet He would take all the fault unto Himself, suffering the *"terrors of death"* as though He had sinned.

(5) "FEARFULNESS AND TREMBLING ARE COME UPON ME, AND HORROR HAS OVERWHELMED ME."

It is easy to understand David's feelings when one realizes what he is facing at this time. The plot to take his throne and even his life is so overwhelmingly powerful that in the natural it could not be overcome. Inasmuch as his son Absalom is the perpetrator, this makes the pain and the hurt even more overwhelming. Furthermore, Ahithophel was probably one of the most brilliant human beings on the face of the Earth. The Scripture says of him, *"His advice was as the Counsel of God"* (II Sam. 16:23). Also, Bathsheba was Ahithophel's granddaughter.

FEARFULNESS AND TREMBLING

The fuel of this *"fearfulness and trembling"* was the realization that he had sinned terribly. True, God had put away his sin, but yet the nagging fear was there that perhaps God would allow Absalom and Ahithophel to have their way. At this time, he had no assurance as to what would happen.

Prophetically, Christ would enter into the same argument because He would enter into our place and position. There is little way that we can properly understand this. The Incarnation seems so simple and yet it is beyond the comprehension of any mortal.

Jesus Christ was, and is, fully God and yet fully Man. As God, He was Perfect; likewise, as a Man, He was Perfect — actually the Only Perfect Man Who ever lived. However, His Perfection as Man only referred to His sinlessness. Every other trait of man, with all of its attendant weaknesses and frailties would be incumbent upon Him. Hence, the *"fearfulness and trembling."*

(6) "AND I SAID, OH THAT I HAD WINGS LIKE A DOVE! FOR THEN WOULD I FLY AWAY, AND BE AT REST."

The superscription of this Psalm entitles it *"The Dove of the Distant Oak-Woods."* Verses 2, 6, and 17 illustrate this title.

"Make a noise" (Vs. 2) means *"mourn as*

a dove" as does *"cry aloud."*

Historically, David is symbolized by this dove, but prophetically it means the Messiah.

The unnatural rebellion of Absalom and the treachery of Ahithophel foreshadowed the rebellion of Israel and the betrayal of Judas. The moral condition of Jerusalem when Jesus rode into it is described in Verses 9 through 11, and the pain which the words, actions, and hatred of its citizens caused Him is the subject of Verses 1 through 8. This anguish reached its climax in Gethsemane (Vs. 4-5) when He said, *"My soul is exceeding sorrowful even unto death."* From that stormy wind and tempest, He gladly would have hastened as a dove to a place of refuge in some distant wilderness.

At the more immediate time, David strongly desired to be free of the turmoil and terrible agitation. Perhaps all of us have longed at one time or the other for the same, but it was not to be.

(7) "LO, THEN WOULD I WANDER FAR OFF, AND REMAIN IN THE WILDERNESS. SELAH."

Elijah would try to do the same; so would Jonah. No doubt, every Bible Great faced the same situation at one time or another. There seemed to be no answer to David's dilemma.

It was very difficult for David, as it is for us, to realize that God looked at him exactly as He looked at Christ. In God's Eyes, both were Perfect because of Christ, and that despite the many failures on David's part. Never mind that the far greater majority of Israel would not accept or believe that which God had proclaimed. Nevertheless, the Lord had said through Nathan the Prophet, *"The LORD has put away your sin"* (II Sam. 12:13). Because others will not agree to or even admit this, it is easy for us to succumb to condemnation.

FORGIVENESS

When the Lord forgives, He does not do so partially, but always in totality. In other words, when He forgives, He wipes the slate clean. The person is then looked at by God as if he has never sinned. That's how Paul could say:

"There is therefore now no condemnation (guilt) *to them which are in Christ Jesus* (refers back to Romans 6:3-5 and our being baptized into His Death, which speaks of the Crucifixion), *who walk not after the flesh* (depending on one's own personal strength and ability or great religious efforts in order to overcome sin), *but after the Spirit* (the Holy Spirit works exclusively within the legal confines of the Finished Work of Christ; our faith in that Finished Work, i.e., *'the Cross,'* guarantees the help of the Holy Spirit, which guarantees Victory)" (Rom. 8:1).

If the Believer tries to mix *"Law"* with *"Grace,"* the end result will always be condemnation, because that is all that Law can do.

WHAT IS LAW?

When Paul addressed the subject of *"Law,"* most of the time he was speaking of the Law of Moses; however, in actuality, *"Law"* is anything and everything in which we place our trust other than Jesus Christ and Him Crucified — and I mean anything!

When one looks exclusively to Christ and the Cross, then one opens the door for the Grace of God, which is the Goodness of God, to be administered in an uninterrupted flow to the Saint of God. It only takes faith (Rom. 5:1; 6:11).

To further explain this complicated subject, let us use the two most important aspects of Christian life and living. I speak of prayer and Bible Study. Without these two disciplines, the Christian simply cannot have a proper relationship with the Lord, which should be abundantly obvious.

However, if the Believer doesn't understand that his Victory and Blessing (in other words, all things that pertain to life and living) are derived strictly from what Jesus did at the Cross, but he rather depends on his prayer life and times of Bible Study, he has just turned those two great disciplines into Law.

Now, please don't misunderstand:

In no way does this mean that we are to quit praying or studying the Bible. Away with such a thought! It does mean that we are to engage in these two disciplines in the correct manner, which is to seek leading and guidance from the Lord and to have relationship with Him.

For instance, if prayer, as wonderful as that activity is, guarantees us victory, then how much prayer is needed? Thirty minutes a day? An hour a day? Now, I hope you understand how easy it is to turn something wonderful, beautiful, and necessary, as is prayer, into Law.

No! Our Victory, our Blessing, and everything we receive from the Lord come to us strictly by faith, but yet it must be faith in the correct object, which always is Christ Jesus and Him Crucified (I Cor. 1:23).

THE EMPHASIS

Let's look again at Paul.

The great Apostle said, *"For Christ sent me not to baptize* (presents to us a Cardinal Truth), *but to preach the Gospel* (the manner in which one may be saved from sin)*: not with wisdom of words* (intellectualism is not the Gospel), *lest the Cross of Christ should be made of none effect.* (This tells us in no uncertain terms that the Cross of Christ must always be the emphasis of the Message)" (I Cor. 1:17).

Paul wasn't speaking disparagingly of Water Baptism. Of course not! The Holy Spirit was making the case through him that as wonderful as Water Baptism is (as well as many other things we could name), it is the Cross of Christ which gives us the Victory, and nothing else. Prayer and Bible Study are absolutely indispensable as it regards our relationship with Christ; still, *"Jesus Christ is the Source of all things from God, and the Cross of Christ is the Means by which all of this is done."* Without exception, the object of our faith always must be the *"Cross of Christ."*

(8) "I WOULD HASTEN MY ESCAPE FROM THE WINDY STORM AND TEMPEST."

He *"would"* but he couldn't! Is there an *"escape from the windy storm and tempest"*?

Only in Christ! The answer is found in Verses 16 through 19.

(9) "DESTROY, O LORD, AND DIVIDE THEIR TONGUES: FOR I HAVE SEEN VIOLENCE AND STRIFE IN THE CITY."

David prays that the excellent advice of Ahithophel will be *"divided."* This prayer was answered.

Ahithophel's advice would be ignored, while Hushai's counsel was accepted. Even though Absalom did not know this, Hushai was David's friend. So the Lord answered this prayer in totality.

(10) "DAY AND NIGHT THEY GO ABOUT IT UPON THE WALLS THEREOF;

MISCHIEF ALSO AND SORROW ARE IN THE MIDST OF IT."

This refers to the leaders of the plot to overthrow David and put Absalom on the throne. They went about getting others to join their cause and saved strife among the people. This *"mischief"* would bring great *"sorrow"* to Israel. All rebellion against God brings nothing but *"sorrow."*

(11) "WICKEDNESS IS IN THE MIDST THEREOF: DECEIT AND GUILE DEPART NOT FROM HER STREETS."

This effort by Absalom and Ahithophel was *"wickedness."* It was done so by *"deceit and guile."*

Likewise, the Antichrist will deceive Israel into believing that he is the Messiah (Jn. 5:43).

DECEPTION

"Deception" is Satan's greatest weapon. His ambition is to make people believe that what is of God, isn't, and what is not of God, is! He is amazingly successful.

When the Believer places his faith in something other than Christ and the Cross, which means that he has just abrogated the entirety of the Word of God, he becomes a prime target for deception. In fact, *"deceit"* and *"deception"* are guaranteed to follow.

Many people talk about believing the Word, basing everything on the Word, etc.; however, the entirety of the story of the Bible is *"Jesus Christ and Him Crucified"* (I Cor. 1:23).

Listen to John the Beloved. I quote from THE EXPOSITOR'S STUDY BIBLE:

"In the beginning (does not imply that Christ as God had a beginning, because as God He had no beginning, but rather refers to the time of Creation [Gen. 1:1]) *was the Word* (the Holy Spirit through John describes Jesus as *'The Eternal Logos'*), *and the Word was with God* (*'was in relationship with God,'* and expresses the idea of the Trinity), *and the Word was God* (meaning that He did not cease to be God during the Incarnation; He *'was'* and *'is'* God from eternity past to eternity future)" (Jn. 1:1).

This Passage plainly tells us that Jesus Christ is the Word of God, which means that the entirety of the story of the Bible from Genesis 1:1 through Revelation 22:21 is the

Story of Jesus Christ. He is on every page in the Bible, He is in every sentence, and He is in every Word, because He actually is the Word.

Then John says, *"And the Word was made flesh* (refers to the Incarnation, *'God becoming Man'), and dwelt among us* (refers to Jesus, although Perfect, not holding Himself aloft from all others, but rather living as all men, even a Peasant), *(and we beheld His Glory, the glory as of the Only Begotten of the Father,)* (speaks of His Deity, although hidden from the eyes of the merely curious; while Christ laid aside the expression of His Deity, He never lost the possession of His Deity), *full of Grace and Truth* (as *'flesh'* proclaimed His humanity, *'Grace'* and *'Truth'* proclaimed His Deity)" (Jn. 1:14).

Then John the Beloved tells us exactly why the *"Living Word"* became flesh.

"The next day (refers to the day after John the Baptist had been questioned by the emissaries from the Sanhedrin), *John* (the Baptist) *sees Jesus coming unto him* (is, no doubt, after the Baptism of Jesus and the temptation in the wilderness), *and said, Behold the Lamb of God* (proclaims Jesus as the Sacrifice for sin, in fact, the Sin Offering, Whom all the multiple millions of offered lambs have represented), *which takes away the sin of the world.* (Animal blood could only cover sin. It could not take it away. But Jesus offering Himself as the Perfect Sacrifice took away the sin of the world. He not only cleansed acts of sin, but also addressed the root cause [Col. 2:14-15])" (Jn. 1:29).

So, if one claims to believe the *"Word"* but repudiates or even ignores the Cross, they are only fooling themselves. They are *"deceived."*

(12) "FOR IT WAS NOT AN ENEMY WHO REPROACHED ME; THEN I COULD HAVE BORNE IT: NEITHER WAS IT HE WHO HATED ME WHO DID MAGNIFY HIMSELF AGAINST ME; THEN I WOULD HAVE HID MYSELF FROM HIM."

David is speaking here of the betrayal of Ahithophel. In a greater fulfillment, it speaks of the betrayal of the Messiah by Judas. So, when one reads the words of the Twelfth Verse, one actually is reading the thoughts of Christ concerning Judas.

The phrase, *"Then I would have hid myself from him,"* refers to the fact that Ahithophel was David's closest advisor, so David had opened his heart to this man. He would not have done this with an enemy.

Likewise, the Lord Jesus Christ gave Judas the privilege of being one of His chosen Disciples; Judas, therefore, was one of the most privileged individuals in the world, just as was Ahithophel.

(13) "BUT IT WAS YOU, A MAN MY EQUAL, MY GUIDE, AND MY ACQUAINTANCE."

Once again, David is speaking of Ahithophel, but the Holy Spirit is also speaking of Christ's reference to Judas.

As applied to Judas, the words *"equal," "guide,"* and *"acquaintance"* may be translated, *"My chosen,"* for Jesus elected him an Apostle, *"My fellow tribesman,"* since Judas was the only member of the Twelve who, like the Lord, was of the Tribe of Judah, and *"one who has come to know Me,"* since he accompanied Jesus for three and one half years.

(14) "WE TOOK SWEET COUNSEL TOGETHER, AND WALKED UNTO THE HOUSE OF GOD IN COMPANY."

David is speaking of the times that he went to the place of worship with Ahithophel. So, we ask the question, *"Why would Ahithophel do such a thing?"*

While there are undoubtedly many other reasons, we do know that Ahithophel was the grandfather of Bathsheba. He seemed to harbor a grudge against David because of David's great sin against his granddaughter, and awaited an opportunity to strike. He was not content to put the matter into the hands of God, but tried to take matters into his own hands — a mistake which so many make!

THE FAILURE TO FORGIVE

Ahithophel's advice was as the counsel of God, meaning that he probably was the most brilliant man in the world at that time, but this gift had been given to him by God for the express purpose of helping David. David was the source of all of Ahithophel's Blessings. His status, place, and position were due to David. His riches, power, and wealth likewise were on account of David.

Many individuals in similar circumstances forget the cause and the reason for their

Blessing. It was because of David's anointing and not his. How easy it would have been to forgive David. Then he would have conducted himself like God does. Otherwise, he conducted himself like Satan.

Unforgiveness is a terrible sin; it cuts off all fellowship with God (Mat. 6:14-15). In addition, the only type of forgiveness that God will recognize is the God-kind of forgiveness. To *"forgive"* means *"to unbind,"* which means to discontinue holding someone in a straitjacket. To claim that one has forgiven someone but to continue to hold that person in bondage is no forgiveness at all. God will not recognize such.

Ahithophel would not forgive; he would commit suicide and be eternally lost.

JUDAS

Many down through the centuries have asked the question, *"Why did Judas do what he did?"* Judas was the perpetrator of the most perfidious act in human history.

How could Judas have walked with the Lord for some three and one half years, witnessed all the Miracles and healings which the Lord performed, witnessed the greatest Move of God the world had ever known, been a part of all of it, and yet commit the most awful act in human history?

The answer is found in Judas' rejection of the Cross of Christ.

The Sixth Chapter of John's Gospel proclaims Christ introducing Himself as *"the Bread of Life"* (Jn. 6:35).

The Lord then said that if one is to have this *"Bread of Life,"* one must *"eat the Flesh of the Son of Man, and drink His Blood"* (Jn. 6:53). He was speaking here of the Crucifixion, the manner in which He would die, which was necessary in order that the price be paid for the Redemption of mankind. He was saying that the Believer must become one with Christ in His Crucifixion, Burial, and Resurrection (Rom. 6:3-5). This can be done only by faith (Rom. 5:1-2).

The *"eating of the flesh"* and the *"drinking of the blood"* refer to the fact that the individual must place his all — his past, his present, and his future — in Christ, understanding that everything he has from God has been made possible by Christ and what Christ did at the Cross.

Judas would not accept that. He had no desire for a Cross. Most at that time had no desire for a Cross, even though this was the only manner, faith in that Finished Work, which could bring Salvation to man.

The Scripture says, and I quote from THE EXPOSITOR'S STUDY BIBLE:

"From that time many of His Disciples went back, and walked no more with Him. (The claims of Christ were so profoundly different from what they anticipated that they now refused to accept Him at all!)

"Then said Jesus unto the Twelve, Will you also go away? (The defection of these former Disciples must have deeply pained the Lord's Heart. His question to the original Twelve abrogates the Doctrine of Unconditional Eternal Security. In fact, Judas did go away.)

"Then Simon Peter answered Him, Lord, to whom shall we go? (This presents the Apostle for the second time confessing Who Jesus is, but in more emphatic language.) *You have the words of Eternal Life* (other than Judas, they believed what He said).

"And we believe and are sure that You are that Christ, the Son of the Living God (we have believed, and have come to know [have learned by experience] that You are the Messiah, the Son of the Living God]).

"Jesus answered them, Have not I chosen you Twelve (proclaims far more than random selection, but rather specific direction as given to Him by the Father), *and one of you is a devil?* (Jesus chose Judas, and Judas as well at first chose Christ; however, Judas' choice was turned by unbelief as it has been with millions.)

"He spoke of Judas Iscariot, the son of Simon (means that he was *'a man of Kerioth,'* a place in Judah [Josh. 15:25]; as far as is known, he was the only one of the Twelve who came from Judah, the Tribe of Jesus): *for he it was who should betray Him, being one of the Twelve.* (It is said in this manner because the Holy Spirit will have all know what Judas threw away; it seems that with this Message delivered by Christ, the Message of the Cross, rebellion began in Judas' heart)" (Jn. 6:66-71).

(15) "LET DEATH SEIZE UPON THEM, AND LET THEM GO DOWN QUICK INTO

HELL: FOR WICKEDNESS IS IN THEIR DWELLINGS, AND AMONG THEM."

Even though David was speaking of those who had fomented the rebellion against him, still, the word *"them"* actually refers to *"Ahithophel and Judas."* Sadly, they both went to *"Hell"* when they so easily could have gone to Heaven.

HELL

Regrettably, many Preachers (even most) in this modern age do not even believe there is a place called *"Hell."* Irrespective of their unbelief, there is a *"Hell."* The Bible tells us so.

Hell is the place of unconverted departed spirits. It is the place of eternal punishment and extreme torment. It is a place of consciousness (Lk., Chpt. 16). It is a place for the proud (Mat. 11:23; Lk. 10:15). As well, the fire of Hell is real.

Where the word *"fire"* is used, it is almost always literal. The *"Lake of Fire"* is a part of Hell (Mat. 10:15; Rev. 20:11-15). It is eternal and everlasting. Ahithophel and Judas went to Hell because of their *"wickedness,"* which refers to their rejection of Christ and what He would do for us at the Cross of Calvary.

The entirety of the human race is either on its way to Heaven or to Hell. There is no purgatory or in-between. Likewise, there is no second chance after death. All opportunities for Salvation are on this side of the grave.

Likewise, there is no Salvation other than in Christ. This means that all other religions are false; if one adheres to these false religions, they will lead men to eternal doom.

To be Saved and, thereby, to miss Hell and to make Heaven one's eternal home, one must accept Christ as one's Saviour and one's Lord (Jn. 3:3, 16; Rom. 10:9-10, 13; Rev. 22:17).

(16) "AS FOR ME, I WILL CALL UPON GOD; AND THE LORD SHALL SAVE ME."

Now we go back to the Eighth Verse, where David proclaims the fact that he would try to escape this *"windy storm and tempest."* He would be able to do so only in one way. His avenue of escape was, and is, also our avenue of escape.

In this terrible dilemma, David would resort to the One he knew could save him — God. This is the answer for the entire human race. There is no other. Sadly, the modern Church opts for almost anything other than what is Biblical and truly helpful, which is to *"call upon God."*

It is a simple statement, *"As for me, I will call upon God; and the LORD shall save me."* The Reader should read these words very carefully! He should realize that, as they applied to David (and they most definitely did), they also apply to you and me.

(17) "EVENING, AND MORNING, AND AT NOON, WILL I PRAY, AND CRY ALOUD: AND HE SHALL HEAR MY VOICE."

The modern Church so little resorts to prayer that when it actually does pray, it thinks that God is to appear like a genie out of a bottle. Too many Christians are unaccustomed to prayer and do not seek the Lord as David did, *"evening, and morning, and at noon."*

This tells us that David was a man of prayer. He was accustomed to constantly taking everything to the Lord. His practice is characterized by the phrase, *"Evening, and morning, and at noon."*

Sadly, most Christians little pray except when they offer thanks for their meals.

At a time of utmost crisis in my own personal life and the existence of this Ministry, the Lord spoke to my heart and told me to begin two prayer meetings a day, which we instantly set out to do. That was in October of 1991. For over ten years, a number of us continued this regimen before the Lord. In fact, this Evangelist continues the same regimen unto this day.

At the very beginning (1991), the Lord told me, *"Seek Me not so much for what I can do, but rather for Who I am!"* And that's exactly what we have done, continue to do, and will ever continue to do.

Yes, I constantly state my needs to the Lord, but even more He wants me to have a relationship with Him, and this is what I also desire so very, very much. The key to receiving from the Lord is to have a proper relationship with Him, which cannot be established without a proper prayer life and study of the Word of God.

In 1997, the Lord opened up to me the Revelation of the Cross, which has revolutionized my life and Ministry, and which I believe takes the Church to a deeper depth and higher height than it previously has known.

No! What the Lord gave me did not at all add to the Word of God, nor was it meant to; however, it did shed more light on what the Lord had already given to the Apostles of the Early Church, especially to the Apostle Paul.

When the prayer life of the Believer is linked with proper faith in Christ and the Cross, this becomes an unbeatable combination. To the Believer who would submit himself to such consecration, such a Believer will find it exactly as Simon Peter said, *"Joy unspeakable and full of glory."*

(18) "HE HAS DELIVERED MY SOUL IN PEACE FROM THE BATTLE THAT WAS AGAINST ME: FOR THERE WERE MANY WITH ME."

It seems that this statement refers to the answer to the prayer of Verse 17. God assures David that He will *"deliver his soul."* He has *"peace"* that victory will be his. The *"many"* that David refers to are the Hosts that are with God.

Too often the Christian feels that he is greatly outnumbered. Actually, he is not. The great Hosts who are on his side far outnumber those which Satan can produce. It looked like David was greatly outnumbered, but he really was not!

(19) "GOD SHALL HEAR, AND AFFLICT THEM, EVEN HE WHO ABIDES OF OLD. SELAH. BECAUSE THEY HAVE NO CHANGES, THEREFORE THEY FEAR NOT GOD."

In essence, David is saying that the Lord will fight his battles. And that He did!

The phrase, *"Because they have no changes,"* refers to the fact that those arrayed against David would not change their ways in spite of all the proof that existed in favor of David. They set a course to destroy God's choice man, which means that they had lost all fear of God. Deception does that!

It would prove to be their undoing. They would not be able to defeat David.

(20) "HE HAS PUT FORTH HIS HANDS AGAINST SUCH AS BE AT PEACE WITH HIM: HE HAS BROKEN HIS COVENANT."

Whenever Ahithophel rebelled against David (and, thereby, the Lord), he actually broke a spiritual covenant that he had made to support David and the Work of God. Judas did the same thing.

As predicted in the Eleventh Chapter of Daniel and John 5:43, the majority of the Jews will accept the Antichrist as the Promised Messiah. He will make a Covenant with them, and then, together with them, he will cruelly persecute the believing minority. But after a little time, he will break the Covenant and seek to destroy them all. Even though this Verse obviously applies to David, in its plenary fulfillment, it actually refers to the covenant the Antichrist will make with Israel and then later break.

(21) "THE WORDS OF HIS MOUTH WERE SMOOTHER THAN BUTTER, BUT WAR WAS IN HIS HEART: HIS WORDS WERE SOFTER THAN OIL, YET WERE THEY DRAWN SWORDS."

This refers to both Ahithophel and Judas, and even more so to the Antichrist. He will make Israel believe that he is the Messiah. Sadly, they will accept him to their regret, because *"war was in his heart."* Actually, he will break his seven-year covenant with Israel at the midpoint, declare war on them, and attempt to destroy them (Dan. 9:27).

(22) "CAST YOUR BURDEN UPON THE LORD, AND HE SHALL SUSTAIN YOU: HE SHALL NEVER SUFFER THE RIGHTEOUS TO BE MOVED."

What a Promise!

CAST YOUR BURDEN UPON THE LORD

This Verse refers to David's Salvation and also to the Resurrection of our Lord. It also refers to Israel's deliverance from the Antichrist at the Battle of Armageddon. It also refers to everyone who will *"cast their burden upon the Lord."*

Man is commanded to one thing, then God will do two things. Never is there a Promise without a condition. Christians are in the habit of magnifying the Promises and ignoring the terms of their fulfillment. Then when the Promises are not fulfilled, they murmur and complain.

All of this is brought out explicitly in the case of David, who was sustained and unmoved in all of his trials. Yes, he experienced fear, he experienced testing, and he experienced consternation, as do all men;

however, he learned to take his burdens to the Lord and to leave them there.

The song says:

"If we trust and never doubt,
"He will surely lead us out.
"Take your burdens to the Lord and
leave them there."

(23) "BUT YOU, O GOD, SHALL BRING THEM DOWN INTO THE PIT OF DESTRUCTION: BLOODY AND DECEITFUL MEN SHALL NOT LIVE OUT HALF THEIR DAYS; BUT I WILL TRUST IN YOU."

Ahithophel and Judas were *"brought down into the pit of destruction."* Likewise, the Antichrist will suffer the same fate.

God's Way ultimately will win out. The key is: *"But I will trust in You."* Those who trusted Ahithophel went *"down into the pit of destruction."* Those who trusted Judas did likewise. Those who trust the Antichrist will also be destroyed. But those who trust in the Lord will gain the victory.

PSALM 56

A Psalm of David:
Prayer for Deliverance

(1) "BE MERCIFUL UNTO ME, O GOD: FOR MAN WOULD SWALLOW ME UP; HE FIGHTING DAILY OPPRESSES ME."

This Psalm was written by David, and, as the instructions say, it is a *"Michtam"* Psalm (graven or permanent writing). It was written when Saul was chasing David, and the Philistines took him in Gath (I Sam., Chpts. 21 and 27.)

BEING IN THE WILL OF GOD

It seems that David dwelt in the land of the Philistines *"a full year and four months"* (I Sam. 27:7). From the terminology, it also seems that this was sixteen months that David was out of the Will of God. The terminology of I Samuel, Chapter 27, also suggests the same. Beautifully, in this life's journey, at least with those who really are called of God and are attempting to live for Him to the best of their ability, God uses the weaknesses and failures as much as He uses the victories.

NOTES

To be frank, victories, as wonderful as they are and as much as we want them, teach us little. It seems we learn more from our failures. It's an expensive way to learn, but, regrettably, the human race seems to fall into this pattern — even God's chosen, such as David.

David here is speaking of Saul, who was attempting to kill him. This was a *"daily"* battle with Saul attempting to track David by using any means at his disposal. So, David's difficulties were not occasional; it was a daily struggle.

One could ask the question as to why the Lord didn't take out Saul long before He did? Why did the Lord allow nearly fifteen years of David being pushed to the very brink of death?

All of this time, as difficult as it was, was used by the Lord to build strength and integrity in David. And above all, it built trust in the Lord in David's heart.

Yes, there were failures along the way; however, David overcame those failures, rose to the occasion, and allowed the Lord to lead him to the place and position he ultimately would occupy as King of the great nation of the Israel.

To be sure, him merely being King was not the entirety of the episode. David was being groomed so that his family would be the channel through which the Messiah would come, the *"Greater Son of David."* Much place and position, much education — but education, I'm afraid, that many of us do not like or enjoy — but yet so necessary!

(2) "MY ENEMIES WOULD DAILY SWALLOW ME UP: FOR THEY BE MANY WHO FIGHT AGAINST ME, O THOU MOST HIGH."

This Psalm is occasioned by David's experiences while he was far from his Father's house and in exile among those who hated him. Nevertheless, he was inspired to write it. But its full theme is the experience of the Messiah when He lived in the world among sinners, and especially among the religious aristocracy which hated Him.

All of this was far from the Glory which He had with the Father before the world was. Actually, Christ here is the Speaker; His are the petitions; and His are the expressions of faith and confidence.

WHY WERE DAVID AND OUR LORD HATED?

The words, *"Swallow me up,"* probably would have been better translated *"liers in wait."* In regard to David, they pertained to Saul and his henchmen.

Prophetically, they pertained to the Scribes and Pharisees of Luke 11:54. They literally fought against Christ daily. They despised His Words (Vs. 5); they planned His Death (Vss. 5-6).

The thrice-repeated, *"All the day long,"* means not only all the day, but at any moment of the day.

David, and especially our Lord, had done absolutely nothing to anyone to instigate hatred. In fact, they had done only good. Under David, Israel would rise to the status of one of the greatest nations on the face of the Earth, which brought unprecedented prosperity for all of its people.

And, of course, all who know the Lord know and understand the Grace of our Saviour, Who went about doing good and healing all who were oppressed of the Devil.

David and our Lord were hated not because of anything they had done, but simply because of the evil that was in the hearts of those who manifested such hatred.

Now let me say this:

The world as a whole manifests no love toward the Gospel; still, it does not normally manifest the hatred toward Believers which comes from the apostate Church. I remind the Reader that it was not the drunks, the gamblers, the thieves, etc., who crucified Christ, but rather the Church of that day. It was not the heathen who sought to bring down David, but those who should have been helping him.

THE OFFENSE OF THE CROSS

Concerning this very thing, Paul said, *"And I, Brethren, if I yet preach circumcision, why do I yet suffer persecution?"* (Any message other than the Cross draws little opposition.) *Then is the offense of the Cross ceased.* (The Cross offends the world and most of the Church. So if the Preacher ceases to preach the Cross as the only way of Salvation and Victory, then opposition and persecution will cease. But so will Salvation!)*"* (Gal. 5:11).

The flesh has always opposed the Holy Spirit.

Listen again to Paul:

"For the flesh (in this case, evil desires) *lusts against the Spirit* (is the opposite of the Holy Spirit), *and the Spirit against the flesh* (it is the Holy Spirit Alone Who can subdue the flesh; He does so, as we have repeatedly stated, by our faith being placed exclusively in the Cross): *and these are contrary the one to the other* (these two can never harmonize; as Paul has stated, the old nature must be cast out, which the Holy Spirit Alone can do): *so that you cannot do the things that you would.* (Without the Holy Spirit, Who works by the Cross, the Believer cannot live a Holy Life)*"* (Gal. 5:17).

So, those who do not look to Christ and the Cross exclusively, which means that they are *"walking after the flesh,"* always will greatly oppose those who are attempting to *"walk after the Spirit"* (Rom. 8:1).

That is the center of the problem, *"walking after the Spirit,"* which constitutes one's faith being placed exclusively in Christ and the Cross, which then gives the Holy Spirit latitude to work (Rom. 8:2), versus *"walking after the flesh,"* which pertains to the Believer placing his faith in anything and everything other than the Cross of Christ.

The *"flesh"* always will oppose the *"Spirit,"* i.e., *"Holy Spirit,"* and will do so wherever the flesh manifests itself.

CAIN AND ABEL

The description is perfectly laid out in the Fourth Chapter of Genesis in connection with the First Family. The Lord had given instructions to Adam and Eve as to how fellowship with God could be obtained, plus forgiveness of sins. It would be by the virtue of the slain lamb, which would be a representative of the One Who was to come, namely, the Lord Jesus Christ.

Abel believed what the Lord said and offered up a Sacrifice which was pleasing to the Lord. Abel's brother Cain did not believe the Lord and offered up a sacrifice, but not a slain lamb, rather the fruit and labor of his own hands. God would not accept it!

The Reader must understand:

If the sacrifice is rejected, the one offering the sacrifice is rejected, as well. Conversely, if the Sacrifice is accepted, the one offering the Sacrifice also is accepted.

The Lord will not accept any faith except that which is registered in His Son, the Lord Jesus Christ, and what He did at the Cross for lost humanity in the giving of Himself as a Perfect Sacrifice. That, and that alone, will God accept (Jn. 3:3, 16; Isa., Chpt. 53; Rom. 10:9-10, 13; Rev. 22:17).

Because God accepted Abel but would not accept Cain's sacrifice, Cain murdered his brother in anger. That animosity has continued unto this hour, and comes almost exclusively from the apostate Church, i.e., *"those who refer to themselves as Christians, and who, in fact, are very religious, but do not place their faith exclusively in Christ and the Cross."*

(3) "WHAT TIME I AM AFRAID, I WILL TRUST IN YOU."

David did not deny the presence of fear. He stared death in the face *"daily."* His solution, as given by the Holy Spirit, is very brief, as is all instruction from the Holy Spirit. He said, *"I will trust in You."* This was David's answer; it is ours. Let us look at what actually is being said.

A PERSONAL APPLICATION

The pronoun *"I"* speaks of a personal trust. For a short period of time, God will allow us to lean on the faith of others; however, in the growing process, our personal faith must be developed. Too many Christians depend on the faith of their Pastor or an older Brother or Sister in the Lord.

Yes, we should draw spiritual nourishment and strength from those, still, it is only worthwhile if we allow it to develop our own faith. Faith can only really be developed by the Word of God. And the Word of God can only properly be understood if our faith is anchored squarely in Christ and the Cross.

The reason?

The entirety of the Word of God from Genesis 1:1 through Revelation 22:21 is the Story of Jesus Christ and Him Crucified. That is its entire Story, its complete Story, its complete emphasis (Jn. 1:1, 14, 29).

NOTES

Sadly, the Bible is little understood by most Christians. The reason has just been mentioned; they don't understand the Cross.

Because they don't understand the Cross as it refers to both Salvation and Sanctification, all type of false doctrine permeates the modern Church. Considering that the Cross of Christ is the Foundation of all Doctrine, it's impossible for doctrine not to be false if Believers do not understand the Cross. The Cross actually was formulated in the Mind of the Godhead even from before the foundation of the world (I Pet. 1:18-20).

At the present time, we have a paucity of the understanding of the Word, because we have a paucity of the understanding of the Cross. One could actually say that the two, the *"Word"* and the *"Cross,"* are synonymous. To misunderstand one is to misunderstand the other. To understand one is to understand the other!

There is a greater attack today against the Word of God perhaps than ever before. And yet, Satan is formulating this attack in a different way than he ever has previously. It is not a frontal attack, but rather one that has slipped in almost unnoticed. I speak of the assortment of Bible translations, so-called, which are not in reality translations, but merely paraphrases, which means they are not the Word of God. I speak of Bibles, so-called, such as the *"Message Bible,"* and a host of others similar. If your Bible is not a *"word-for-word"* translation, such as the King James Version, then it really is not the Bible; it's something else entirely.

The Believer must understand that it's not merely the thoughts that are inspired in the Bible, but, in actuality, every *"Word."*

Jesus said, *"Man shall not live by bread alone, but by every Word that proceeds out of the Mouth of God"* (Mat. 4:4). This is so important that I must say it again:

Regarding the Word of God, it's not merely the thought that is inspired, but rather every single Word.

INSPIRATION

The manner of Inspiration, which refers to the Holy Spirit helping the writers to such an extent that there is no error or contradiction in the Bible, carries over even to the exact words.

Let me explain:

The Holy Spirit in essence would search through the vocabulary of each and every Bible writer, choosing the word that would fit what must be said, and then inspiring that writer to use that particular word. Regarding the giving of the Word of God, that's how exact Inspiration is.

When individuals start to paraphrase the Bible, putting it into their own thoughts, what is left is little more than a mockery.

I'm not interested in what other men think. I'm interested in what the Word of God says. And you, the Reader, had better be interested in that capacity, as well.

THE WILL OF MAN

David said, *"I will,"* which speaks of man's power of choice. A person has to *"will"* to live for God, to serve God, and to walk with the Lord before he can do so. The *"will"* is of tremendous significance in the life of the Christian. Salvation depends upon the will. The Holy Spirit through John said, *"Whosoever will . . ."* (Rev. 22:17).

Something else, however, must be said regarding the *"will."* Even though the *"will"* has to be put into motion before the Lord can do anything for the Believer, still, several things must be said about this.

First of all, the Believer does not live for God by means of *"willpower."* In addressing this, the Apostle Paul said, and I quote from THE EXPOSITOR'S STUDY BIBLE, *"For I know that in me (that is, in my flesh) dwells no good thing* (speaks of man's own ability, or rather the lack thereof in comparison to the Holy Spirit, at least when it comes to spiritual things)*: for to will is present with me* (Paul is speaking here of his willpower; regrettably, most modern Christians are trying to live for God by means of willpower, thinking falsely that since they have come to Christ, they are now free to say *'No!'* to sin. That is the wrong way to look at the situation; the Believer cannot live for God by the strength of willpower. While the will definitely is important, it alone is not enough. The Believer must exercise faith in Christ and the Cross, and do so constantly; then he will have the ability and strength to say *'Yes!'* to Christ, which automatically says *'No!'* to the things of the world); *but how to perform that which is good I find not.* (Outside of the Cross, it is impossible to find a way to do good)*"* (Rom. 7:18).

Here Paul plainly and clearly says that he has the will, but, in the same breath, he also states that the will is not enough. And yet, that's how most of modern Christians attempt to live for God — by willpower.

Many think that before they came to Christ, they didn't have the power to say *"No!"* to sin, but now that they have come to Christ, they can say *"No!"* to sin. That's the wrong way to look at the situation. There is only one strength and ability that the Believer has and that is to say *"Yes!"* to Christ. When that is done, everything else is also addressed.

Paul said, *"For all the Promises of God in Him* (in Christ) *are yes, and in Him Amen* (means these Promises will not change), *unto the Glory of God by us* (our preaching the Cross to you will bring Glory to God)*"* (II Cor. 1:20).

God protects the will of all individuals, both redeemed and unredeemed, as far as their ability to say *"Yes!"* to the Lord is concerned. In other words, the worst drunk in the world, who is totally bound by this terrible vice, who cannot quit drinking, can still say *"Yes!"* to Christ, if he so desires. It is the same with the Believer!

Some Believers have the erroneous idea that when a person comes to Christ, they are given some type of superhuman willpower. Not so!

Just as I have already given to you (Rom. 7:18), the idea in the Word of God is that the Believer place his or her faith exclusively in Christ and the Cross, which then will give the Holy Spirit latitude to work in one's life, thereby, bringing about victory. That is God's Prescribed Order. He has no other, because no other is needed! (Rom. 6:1-14; 8:1-2, 11; I Cor. 1:17-18, 23).

TRUST

The word *"trust"* is next.

Virtually all Christians claim their *"trust"* is in God. But when this is analyzed, it is found that most of the time their trust is in man, self, or other things.

It is impossible for the Believer to fully trust God unless the Believer understands the Person of Christ and the Function of Christ.

This means that the Believer must understand that Jesus Christ is Very God and Very Man. He is fully God and fully Man. That is the Incarnation, *"God becoming Man."*

His *"Function"* is the Cross. It was there that He paid every price, met every need, and, above all, satisfied the demands of a thrice-Holy God.

When one fully understands the Cross of Christ, then one fully understands what *"trust"* actually is. And until one understands that, one's *"trust"* is deficient.

Paul said, *"That your faith should not stand in the wisdom of men* (speaks of any proposed way other than the Cross)*, but in the Power of God* (made possible only by the Cross [I Cor. 2:5])*."*

IN YOU

The words, *"In You,"* refer to God. *"God"* was David's Source.

Because of the Lord Jesus Christ and the Cross, we presently have a much better Covenant.

Paul said, *"But now* (since the Cross) *has He* (the Lord Jesus) *obtained a more excellent Ministry* (the New Covenant in Jesus' Blood is superior and takes the place of the Old Covenant in animal blood)*, by how much also He is the Mediator of a Better Covenant* (proclaims the fact that Christ officiates between God and man according to the arrangements of the New Covenant)*, which was established upon better Promises.* (This presents the New Covenant, explicitly based on the cleansing and forgiveness of all sin, which the Old Covenant could not do)*"* (Heb. 8:6).

THE OBJECT OF FAITH

Every person in the world has faith, but only a tiny few have the faith that God will recognize. This means that the object of our faith must be correct, or else our direction is wrong. The Object of Faith must be *"Christ and the Cross,"* and we must never separate Christ from the Cross. Christ is the Source while the Cross is the Means.

Look closely at the following diagram. It will portray God's Prescribed Order:

1. FOCUS: The Lord Jesus Christ (I Tim. 2:5).
2. OBJECT OF FAITH: The Cross of Christ (Rom. 6:3-5).
3. POWER SOURCE: The Holy Spirit (I Cor. 1:18; Rom. 8:2).
4. RESULTS: Victory (Rom. 6:14).

Now let's use the same little diagram and show you the wrong way. This is the way used by most in the modern Church.

1. FOCUS: Works.
2. OBJECT OF FAITH: Performance.
3. POWER SOURCE: Self.
4. RESULTS: Failure!

Paul said, *"For if you live after the flesh* (after your own strength and ability, which is outside of God's Prescribed Order)*, you shall die* (you will not be able to live a victorious, Christian life)*: but if you through the Spirit* (by the Power of the Holy Spirit) *do mortify the deeds of the body* (which the Holy Spirit Alone can do)*, you shall live* (shall walk in victory; but once again, even at the risk of being overly repetitive, we must never forget that the Spirit works totally and completely within the confines of the Cross of Christ; this means that we must ever make the Cross the Object of our Faith, giving Him latitude to work)*"* (Rom. 8:13).

(4) "IN GOD I WILL PRAISE HIS WORD, IN GOD I HAVE PUT MY TRUST; I WILL NOT FEAR WHAT FLESH CAN DO UNTO ME."

Confidence in man and his word never gives occasion for praise. Confidence in God and His Word gives constant occasion for praise.

WHAT DOES IT MEAN TO PUT ONE'S TRUST IN THE LORD?

Before we answer that question, let us say that man-fear is probably the greatest hindrance to doing the Will of God; however, if any God-called man is to do the Will of God, he will find that he has to oppose religious hierarchy, Denominations, relatives, and even close loved ones.

Concerning all of this, Jesus said, *"And I say unto you My friends, Be not afraid of them who kill the body, and after that have no more that they can do* (Believers are not to fear men), *but I will forewarn you Whom you shall fear: Fear Him* (God), *which after He has killed* (life and death are in the Hands of God Alone) *has power to cast into Hell* (the greater fear of God should banish the lesser fear of man; for man can only touch the body, but God can reach the soul and cast it into Hell); *yea, I say unto you, Fear Him* (presents the second time this is stated, and is, therefore, meant to be clearly understood)" (Lk. 12:4-5).

(5) "EVERY DAY THEY WREST MY WORDS: ALL THEIR THOUGHTS ARE AGAINST ME FOR EVIL."

This describes the constant pursuits against David by Saul and his men. As well, this pertains to the Scribes and Pharisees who conducted themselves in the same way against Christ.

Why?

The reason is simple. Their *"thoughts are evil,"* because they are evil. The worst evil in the world is found in the realms of religion.

Religion is a system, any system, devised by men, to help one reach God or to better oneself in some way. It is not of God.

GOD AND MAN

Anything in the realm of religion devised by man cannot be accepted by God. Man is totally incapable of producing anything in this realm that's not already marred and polluted by sin, which is the result of the Fall. So, everything that pertains to Salvation must come exclusively from the Lord, which it has. The Word of God is the foundation of the Way of God. The story of the Bible is the Story of Jesus Christ and Him Crucified (I Cor. 1:23).

When we understand what it took to redeem man, and we speak of the Cross of Calvary, then we begin to understand how bad mankind's condition really is.

Man is not just partially wrong, but totally wrong! Man is not partially poisoned, but totally poisoned! Man is *"dead in trespasses and sins"* (Eph. 2:1).

So anything that pertains to the Salvation of man must be begun entirely by God, which it was, which it has been, and which it is. That's the biggest problem that the Lord has with religious man. Religious man keeps trying to replace the Word of God with something else, which God can never accept.

(6) "THEY GATHER THEMSELVES TOGETHER, THEY HIDE THEMSELVES, THEY MARK MY STEPS, WHEN THEY WAIT FOR MY SOUL."

Saul attempted to seek out David and kill him. The Scribes and Pharisees, likewise, pounced on every word Jesus said, attempting to trap Him in His speech. Incidentally, they never were able to do so.

(7) "SHALL THEY ESCAPE BY INIQUITY? IN YOUR ANGER CAST DOWN THE PEOPLE, O GOD."

David is asking if these brigands will get by with their *"iniquity."* He prays that they will be *"cast down."*

THE ANGER OF GOD

This prayer sets itself against those who would set themselves against God. In this prayer is a Prophecy. The Prophecy has not yet been completely fulfilled.

When Jesus comes back, it then will be completely fulfilled. Saul was cast down; likewise, those who crucified Christ were cast down. However, the prayer must be answered totally to be complete.

When Jesus comes back, thrusts the Antichrist into Hell, and takes over the government of the world, then this prayer will be completely answered.

God's Anger is not the same as the anger of man. His anger originates from a completely different source and has a completely different purpose. God's Anger originates with Righteousness, and its purpose is to stop that which would hinder that Righteousness.

(8) "YOU TELL MY WANDERINGS: PUT THOU MY TEARS INTO YOUR BOTTLE: ARE THEY NOT IN YOUR BOOK?"

The Holy Spirit through David is saying that despite David's *"wanderings"* and his attempts to escape from Saul, God knew at all times exactly where he was. The *"tears"* in the bottle represent an ancient custom that speaks of tremendous pathos and pain. David believed that God has a record of the minutest details of life.

This Passage speaks of tremendous trial. Why?

David had been given a great Call by God.

He also had been given great Faith. Great Faith must be tested greatly. Even under Grace, there is no way for the Spiritual Life to be honed except in this manner (II Cor., Chpt. 12).

(9) "WHEN I CRY UNTO YOU, THEN SHALL MY ENEMIES TURN BACK: THIS I KNOW; FOR GOD IS FOR ME."

The words, *"This I know,"* is a most precious declaration of the Perfect Faith of God's Beloved Son.

True, God was for David, but only because David was for Christ. The only link from God to man is through Christ. Jesus said, *"No man comes unto the Father but by Me"* (Jn. 14:6). This is a prayer of David, but more so it is prayer of Christ.

(10) "IN GOD WILL I PRAISE HIS WORD: IN THE LORD WILL I PRAISE HIS WORD."

Once again, David extols the Word of God. The words are strange to the unspiritual ear, *"Praise His Word."* However, the Word is Christ (Jn. 1:2).

"God's Word" is the only Body of Revealed Truth in the world today and ever has been. Consequently, every Christian should make it his life's work to learn *"The Word."* We also should constantly thank God for His Word.

The double statement in this Verse is not an oversight. The Holy Spirit did this in order that we understand the significance that God places on His Word.

When a person loses his way, it is always and without exception because he has left the Word. The Bible alone holds the answer to every single problem of life and living (II Pet. 1:3-4).

(11) "IN GOD HAVE I PUT MY TRUST: I WILL NOT BE AFRAID WHAT MAN CAN DO UNTO ME."

This Passage is basically the same as Verse 4. Once again, the Holy Spirit is telling us that in order to gain the strength and confidence we must have in life's journey, we must *"put our trust in God."* Then the fear of man leaves.

TRUSTING GOD

Two factors are absolutely essential, that is, if Believers are to fully know and understand what trusting the Lord actually means.

The automatic answer which always speedily comes regarding *"trust"* is that we must anchor our faith in the Word of God. That certainly is true; however, that which says too much concludes by saying precious little.

Many, if not most, Believers do not understand the Word as they should. Admittedly, the Bible is not easy to understand. The Holy Spirit used holy men of God to write it that way in order that the merely curious would turn away, but the truly hungry would dig until they find the nuggets of gold.

For the Word of God to be properly understood, a proper understanding of the Cross must be the order. The story of the Bible is the Story of the Cross, even as the Story of the Cross is the story of the Bible (Jn. 1:1, 14, 29). To have a proper understanding of the Cross is to have a proper understanding of the Word of God.

"Trust" also involves the Baptism with the Holy Spirit. Without the Baptism with the Holy Spirit, which always will be accompanied by the speaking with other tongues (Acts 2:4), there isn't going to be much trust.

A PERSONAL EXPERIENCE

Years ago, I had the privilege of preaching several Campmeetings with one of the great Preachers of that particular time, A. N. Trotter. He had the most powerful anointing of the Holy Spirit on his Ministry of any Preacher I've ever had the privilege to know or hear.

Many times I heard him relate the experiences of his childhood and throughout his Ministry.

He told of his family and the disruption caused when his father abandoned them, which resulted in the family's destitution. His mother came very close to committing suicide.

She certainly was Saved and knew the Lord, but, at that particular time, she knew nothing about the Baptism with the Holy Spirit. As a result, she could register very little faith.

When his mother did receive the Baptism with the Holy Spirit, all of a sudden, things began to change. She started to receive answers to her prayers. Generated by the Holy Spirit, the discouragement and despair left her, and faith took their place. Everything about his family, his home, and his upbringing changed when his mother was baptized with the Spirit.

I maintain that it's not possible for one to

fully trust the Lord, at least as one should, without the Baptism with the Holy Spirit (Rom. 8:1-2, 11).

(12) "YOUR VOWS ARE UPON ME, O GOD: I WILL RENDER PRAISES UNTO YOU."

This is not God making vows, but David vowing to be God's Servant, to give his whole life to Him, and to render praises for His Benefits.

(13) "FOR YOU HAVE DELIVERED MY SOUL FROM DEATH: WILL NOT YOU DELIVER MY FEET FROM FALLING, THAT I MAY WALK BEFORE GOD IN THE LIGHT OF THE LIVING?"

The sense of this statement is:

God surely will deliver the Messiah's Soul out of the death world and His Body out of the grave. The word *"fallen"* has, in the Hebrew Text, no moral significance. It means a thrusting down.

THE LORD JESUS CHRIST

Man proposed to thrust Christ's dishonored Body down into the Earth. God placed it in an honored tomb instead, raised it in Glory, and caused Him to walk in Resurrection Life. In Incarnation, He was an *"ear"* (Perfect Obedience); in Resurrection, He was a *"foot"* (Perfect Power), for His enemies will be made a footstool for His Feet; and, in that day of universal dominion, His Feet shall stand upon the Mount of Olives (Zech., Chpt. 14).

PSALM 57

A Psalm of David:
God Delivers David from King Saul

(1) "BE MERCIFUL UNTO ME, O GOD, BE MERCIFUL UNTO ME: FOR MY SOUL TRUSTS IN YOU: YEA, IN THE SHADOW OF YOUR WINGS WILL I MAKE MY REFUGE, UNTIL THESE CALAMITIES BE OVERPAST."

This is a Psalm of David and it most probably was written when he was being chased by Saul and was in the cave of Engedi. Saul actually entered the very cave where David and his men were hiding; later Saul's life was spared by the generosity of the man (David) whom he sought to kill (I Sam., Chpt. 24).

NOTES

The Rabbins say that God sent a spider to weave a web at the mouth of the cave in which David and his men hid. Saul saw the spider's web and went into the cave with complete confidence that it was empty. We have no way of knowing whether this actually happened or not; but, if it did happen, it would illustrate how God can use the most feeble means to protect His children.

THE MERCY OF GOD

This particular time was one of the most crucial times in David's life. There was absolutely no way that he, with his own ingenuity, could save himself. Therefore, he cried for the *"Mercy of God."* What a beautiful example this Psalm sets for us.

David did not plead his consecration, dedication, or holiness. To have done so would have constituted self-righteousness. In effect, he was saying that he did not deserve to be rescued, so he could not plead any merit. He said, *"Be merciful unto me, O God."*

What a lesson for the self-righteous modern Church! Here was a man *"after God's Own heart,"* but yet he claimed no merit before God. David could not trust in any man to save him. Most that he came into contact with sought to betray him. In the natural there was no way that he could be spared. He knew his only hope was in God, so he said, *"My soul trusts in You."*

What a lesson for us presently! Modern religious man will trust almost anything except God. The mainstay of the modern Church actually is humanistic psychology. In most of the Bible Colleges and Seminaries of the land, the students are by and large taught to trust man instead of God.

Why?

The answer is obvious. The modern Church has all but abandoned the Bible.

Despite the tremendous danger, David felt in his spirit that God was shadowing and protecting him. God was his *"refuge."*

The statement, *"Until these calamities be overpast,"* is a statement of faith. Even though the *"calamities"* were ever-present, David had faith in God that one day they would end. And, indeed, one day they did end!

(2) "I WILL CRY UNTO GOD MOST HIGH: UNTO GOD WHO PERFORMS ALL

THINGS FOR ME."

The words, *"All things,"* are not in the original Hebrew Text; the Verse, therefore, truly is a blank check. Whatever is needed, God will do.

What a tremendous statement!

If men would learn this, then they would *"cry unto God."* His Promise is that He will answer and will *"perform"* what He has promised.

The modern faith movement, which in reality is no faith at all, has so accustomed the Church to instant answers that the Church, by and large, has degenerated into little more than *"McFaith."*

God does not work in this manner. Most of the time, the answers do not come quickly. Perseverance is demanded, and David set an example for us. With David, the *"calamities"* would not be *"overpast"* until several years had expired. David actually would be hounded by Saul for nearly twelve years.

It takes very little faith to ask and receive immediately. It takes much more faith to ask and then to wait and keep believing. Travailing prayer is a foreign language in the modern Church. God does not *"perform"* there very much simply because most do not wait on Him very long!

(3) "HE SHALL SEND FROM HEAVEN, AND SAVE ME FROM THE REPROACH OF HIM WHO WOULD SWALLOW ME UP. SELAH. GOD SHALL SEND FORTH HIS MERCY AND HIS TRUTH."

This is a Psalm of David, but even more so it is a Psalm of the Greater Son, the Lord Jesus Christ. This Verse proclaims Christ's descent into the realm of the dead. It also proclaims His glorious Resurrection from the grave.

Actually, the entire Psalm is the language of the Messiah, with the exception of Verses 5 and 11, which are addressed to Him by the Holy Spirit.

As God saved David, He saved the Messiah.

(4) "MY SOUL IS AMONG LIONS: AND I LIE EVEN AMONG THEM WHO ARE SET ON FIRE, EVEN THE SONS OF MEN, WHOSE TEETH ARE SPEARS AND ARROWS, AND THEIR TONGUE A SHARP SWORD."

These things applied to David. Even more so, they applied to the Greater Son of David.

Mercy and Truth are personified as the Heavenly Messengers sent to rescue the Messiah from Satan, who desired to keep Him swallowed in Sheol. But inasmuch as Satan was totally defeated at the Cross by Jesus' atoning for all sin, which removed Satan's legal right to hold man in captivity, the Evil One had no chance at all to do anything to Christ after His Death on the Cross.

When He died on the Cross, He totally and completely paid the price demanded by a thrice-Holy God, which meant that Satan now was rendered helpless.

THE VICTORY OF THE CROSS

At the Cross, the Victory was totally and completely won. If Jesus had not atoned for all sin, past, present, and future, at least for all who will believe, then He could not have risen from the dead. Inasmuch as the *"wages of sin is death,"* all sin had to be atoned before Resurrection was possible.

Because Jesus did atone for all sin, the Resurrection never was in doubt. Satan harbored no illusions about keeping Jesus in the death world. He knew that was impossible. When Jesus went down into that world, He did not descend as One beaten and whipped, but rather as a Conqueror. By His Death on Calvary's Cross, He had overcome every power of darkness. At the Cross, the total and complete victory was won.

The idea that Jesus became a sinner on the Cross and went to Hell as a sinner, making Him lost and undone without God, even as some teach, is not taught in the Word of God. The idea that Redemption was effected in Hell (of all places!), that Jesus suffered three days and three nights in the flames of fire, that He was tormented by demons, also is not taught in Scripture. The idea that God, after Jesus suffered three days and nights of torture, said to Him, *"It is enough!"* and then He was *"born again,"* the same as any sinner is *"born again,"* and then raised from the dead, is a figment of someone's imagination. It is not the Word of God.

JESUS DID NOT DIE SPIRITUALLY

All of that false teaching comes from the idea that Jesus died spiritually on the Cross, that He, in other words, died as a sinner dies, away from God, even demon-possessed.

Not so!

There is nothing in the Word of God that even remotely supports such foolishness. There is no record that Jesus ever went to the burning side of Hell. The record is clear that He preached to the spirits in prison, which were fallen angels. What He said to them is not revealed.

More than likely, these were the fallen angels who tried to subvert the human race by cohabiting with women. The Sixth Chapter of Genesis proclaims this effort (I Pet. 3:19-20).

Jesus then went into Paradise and delivered all the righteous souls, which included all from the time of Abel to the time of the Crucifixion of Christ, delivering them from that place and taking them with Him to Heaven (Eph. 4:8-9).

Even though the Resurrection, Ascension, and Exaltation of Christ all were of supreme significance, nevertheless it was at the Cross alone where the price was paid, where all victory was won, and nothing needed to be added to what transpired there.

The phrase, *"And their tongue a sharp sword,"* speaks of the hatred of man directed toward the Messiah. There was no distinction or difference in the vehemence of their hatred from the hatred of demons. Actually, the hatred within the Scribes and Pharisees was placed there by demon spirits. Christ met with almost universal hatred.

(5) "BE THOU EXALTED, O GOD, ABOVE THE HEAVENS; LET YOUR GLORY BE ABOVE ALL THE EARTH."

Once again, even in double measure, the Holy Spirit proclaims Jesus Christ as *"God."*

Even though David was lambasted and set upon by Saul, ultimately he was crowned King of Israel. The Greater Son of David was criticized and even hated, but one day He will *"be exalted above the Heavens."* One day soon His *"Glory will be above all the Earth."* This will be fulfilled in the coming Millennial Reign.

(6) "THEY HAVE PREPARED A NET FOR MY STEPS; MY SOUL IS BOWED DOWN: THEY HAVE DUG A PIT BEFORE ME, INTO THE MIDST WHEREOF THEY ARE FALLEN THEMSELVES. SELAH."

(7) "MY HEART IS FIXED, O GOD, MY HEART IS FIXED: I WILL SING AND GIVE PRAISE."

This means that David had long since determined that whatever the price, He would follow the Lord. Despite the great difficulties, he will continue to *"sing and give praise."*

The matter of living for and obeying God is a matter of the *"heart."* It is not a matter of the intellect or strength. Satan succeeds in stopping many Christians because their *"heart"* is not *"fixed."*

This also is said of the Messiah, *"Therefore have I set My face like a flint"* (Isa. 50:7). That glorious Face was set toward Calvary, and nothing must stop the progress in order that mankind would have the opportunity to be redeemed.

(8) "AWAKE UP, MY GLORY; AWAKE, PSALTERY AND HARP: I MYSELF WILL AWAKE EARLY."

Several glorious things are said in this Passage:

1. David did not allow the great difficulties or the constant threat of death to take away his *"song and praise."*

2. It seems that he would *"awake early"* in order to have time with the Lord in communion and fellowship.

3. In this communion and fellowship, it seems that he brought along his harp and would accompany himself while he sang these great Psalms unto the Lord. Hallelujah!

(9) "I WILL PRAISE YOU, O LORD, AMONG THE PEOPLE: I WILL SING UNTO YOU AMONG THE NATIONS."

When David was in the cave of Engedi, which is very close to the Dead Sea, little did he realize just how prophetic this statement was. When the Holy Spirit began to inspire David to write these words and ultimately to sing them, little did he know or realize that what he was writing was the Word of God, and that he was being inspired by the Holy Spirit to do so. It is doubtful he realized that all of these glorious Songs would be put into a Book called *"The Psalms,"* and that they would be read, studied, and sung all over the world — *"among the nations"* — and forever!

(10) "FOR YOUR MERCY IS GREAT UNTO THE HEAVENS, AND YOUR TRUTH UNTO THE CLOUDS."

What would he sing? He would sing of God's *"Mercy"* and His *"Truth."* There could be nothing greater to sing about.

A GREAT EXAMPLE

What an example for us to follow! David is hunted by Saul, and he has no constant dwellingplace. His life is in constant turmoil and imminent danger; yet the joy of the Lord fills his heart and he constantly will *"sing."*

He also probably little realized that the words the Holy Spirit gave him actually would be the words that would pertain in an even greater way to the Coming Greater Son of David.

(11) "BE THOU EXALTED, O GOD, ABOVE THE HEAVENS: LET YOUR GLORY BE ABOVE ALL THE EARTH."

Once again, and even in double measure, the Holy Spirit proclaims Jesus Christ as *"God,"* because it is Christ Who here is being extolled!

Even though David was lambasted and set upon by Saul, he ultimately was crowned King of Israel. The Greater Son of David also was criticized and even hated, but one day He will be *"exalted above the Heavens."* One day soon His Glory will *"be above all the Earth."* This will be fulfilled in the coming Millennial Reign.

PSALM 58

A Psalm of David:
The Depravity of the Wicked

(1) "DO YOU INDEED SPEAK RIGHTEOUSNESS, O CONGREGATION? DO YOU JUDGE UPRIGHTLY, O YOU SONS OF MEN?"

This is a Psalm of David and it basically has four meanings:

1. It speaks of the leaders of Israel during David's day. Many of them had aligned themselves with Saul and tried to destroy David, God's anointed. This sets the occasion for the Psalm.

2. Likewise, the Psalm characterizes the leaders of Israel during Christ's earthly sojourn. They are *"the wicked"* of Verses 3 and 4.

3. The Psalm is the Voice of the Messiah speaking on behalf of Israel in the days of the Great Tribulation when the Antichrist will seek to destroy her.

4. It is a general pronouncement of judgment upon all those throughout all time who fall into the category of *"the wicked"* (Vs. 3). Truly, they will *"melt away as waters"* (Vs. 7).

ISRAEL IN THE LAST DAYS

The First Verse speaks of the unrighteous judgment of Israel by the nations of the world at the Battle of Armageddon. There is, and always has been, a built-in animosity by the nations toward Israel. Many have called them *"Christ killers"* or some other such name. However, that is not the real reason for the animosity.

It is true that Israel was guilty of this crime of all crimes (Acts 2:23). But still, the Roman world, which was representative of the Gentile nations, also was guilty. In the final analysis, every human being who has ever lived put Christ upon the Tree. He went there for the sins of the whole world (Jn. 3:16).

The real reason for the animosity of the nations toward Israel is because these are the people whom God chose from the beginning to bring the Promised Seed into the world. Jesus Christ was that Seed; consequently, *"the god of this world"* has *"blinded the minds of them which believe not,"* which generates a hatred toward Christ and His people, Israel (II Cor. 4:4).

In turn, Israel, which has rejected Christ, also hates Christ and attributes to Him the reason for all their troubles. But He is not the reason. Their troubles are of their own making.

At any rate, the nations of the world, with some few exceptions, have little regard for Israel.

Actually, Israel will be the earthly people to whom the government of this world ultimately will be committed, and who will be responsible to God; therefore, they have been hated by the nations.

The predicted Divine Way of delivering Israel from their oppression will be by the destruction of the Gentile world, which will take place at the Second Coming. Hence, Israel's deliverance and their judgment will synchronize.

During the Battle of Armageddon, Israel will pray for the punishment of these nations which, under the Antichrist, are vowing her destruction. These desires or petitions are voiced for her in the Psalms by her Great High Priest, the Lord Jesus Christ.

(2) "YEA, IN HEART YOU WORK WICKEDNESS; YOU WEIGH THE VIOLENCE OF YOUR HANDS IN THE EARTH."

The hearts of those under Saul who opposed David were *"wicked."* They lived by *"violence."* The same could be said even more so about the oppressors of the Messiah. It also speaks of the evil *"heart"* of the Antichrist and his followers, who will set out to take the world by *"violence."* Despite the judgments of God that will be poured out upon the Earth during the Great Tribulation, still, the Holy Spirit attributes the terrible *"violence"* to the Antichrist.

(3) "THE WICKED ARE ESTRANGED FROM THE WOMB: THEY GO ASTRAY AS SOON AS THEY BE BORN, SPEAKING LIES."

This not only speaks of those under Saul who opposed David and the leadership of Israel who opposed Christ, but even more prophetically it speaks of the Antichrist. The Holy Spirit in this Passage calls him *"the wicked."* Paul called him *"that wicked"* (II Thess. 2:8).

The Antichrist and his followers will *"go astray"* by *"speaking lies"* (I Thess. 5:1, 3).

(4) "THEIR POISON IS LIKE THE POISON OF A SERPENT: THEY ARE LIKE THE DEAF ADDER THAT STOPS HER EAR."

This Passage presents a generalized statement that would apply to anyone who falls into this category, namely, *"the wicked."* It would apply to those who attempted to turn men against David, and even more so to those who *"poison"* people's minds against Christ. Prophetically, it will apply to the Antichrist. He will *"poison"* the world against Israel by *"speaking lies."*

(5) "WHICH WILL NOT HEARKEN TO THE VOICE OF CHARMERS, CHARMING NEVER SO WISELY."

The meaning of Verse 5 is that *"the wicked"* are like the *"deaf adder"* and have no ears to hear the Gospel. Because of their evil instinct, they will not be persuaded into the realm of righteousness. They *"will not hearken to the voice"* and will continue to oppose God and all who stand for Righteousness.

It is interesting to observe the character of Verses 1 through 5, which proclaim the manner in which Satan works. It is sad when so many Christians follow suit.

(6) "BREAK THEIR TEETH, O GOD, IN THEIR MOUTH: BREAK OUT THE GREAT TEETH OF THE YOUNG LIONS, O LORD."

The words, *"lions"* and *"adders,"* actually speak of demon spirits, who were instigating the opposition through *"the wicked."* There are demon spirits behind all false doctrine, error, self-will, and opposition to God's Word.

This speaks of those who opposed David and those who will oppose Israel at the Battle of Armageddon.

(7) "LET THEM MELT AWAY AS WATERS WHICH RUN CONTINUALLY: WHEN HE BENDS HIS BOW TO SHOOT HIS ARROWS, LET THEM BE AS CUT IN PIECES."

This was fulfilled with David and with Christ; prophetically, it will be fulfilled at the Battle of Armageddon, when the Antichrist is defeated by the Coming of the Lord.

(8) "AS A SNAIL WHICH MELTS, LET EVERY ONE OF THEM PASS AWAY: LIKE THE UNTIMELY BIRTH OF A WOMAN, THAT THEY MAY NOT SEE THE SUN."

The six predictions respecting the doom of the wicked are:

1. They shall be helpless (Vs. 6).
2. They shall be powerless (Vs. 7).
3. They shall be weaponless (Vs. 7).
4. They shall be placeless (Vs. 8).
5. They shall be hopeless (Vs. 8); and,
6. They shall be swiftly and thoroughly judged (Vs. 9).

(9) "BEFORE YOUR POTS CAN FEEL THE THORNS, HE SHALL TAKE THEM AWAY AS WITH A WHIRLWIND, BOTH LIVING, AND IN HIS WRATH."

Thorns burn very quickly and very hot. Although the fire kindles easily, it soon expires.

David is saying that when the time of the destruction of the wicked comes, it will be accomplished more quickly and in less time than it takes the heat from the fire of thorns to reach the cooking vessels. This will take place at the Second Coming.

(10) "THE RIGHTEOUS SHALL REJOICE

WHEN HE SEES THE VENGEANCE: HE SHALL WASH HIS FEET IN THE BLOOD OF THE WICKED."

This is a symbolic statement; however, it could literally be fulfilled, meaning that, during the Battle of Armageddon, the Saints actually will walk in the blood of those slain on the battlefield.

(11) "SO THAT A MAN SHALL SAY, VERILY THERE IS A REWARD FOR THE RIGHTEOUS: VERILY HE IS A GOD WHO JUDGES IN THE EARTH."

The meaning of this Verse is that men would see David's life when God ultimately placed him on the throne and proclaimed that there was *"a reward for the righteous."*

PSALM 59

A Psalm of David:
A Prayer for Protection and Punishment

(1) "DELIVER ME FROM MY ENEMIES, O MY GOD: DEFEND ME FROM THEM WHO RISE UP AGAINST ME."

This is another *"Michtam"* Psalm (graven or permanent writing) written by David. The occasion of the writing is found in I Samuel, Chapter 19, when Saul tried to apprehend David and kill him. This was at the early part of David's great trial with Saul.

DELIVERANCE

This Psalm portrays David being delivered from the murderous hatred of his encircling enemies. It also typifies the deliverance of the Messiah from the acute hatred of the religious leaders of Israel as they tried to kill Him before His time in order to prevent Calvary.

It also typifies the deliverance of Israel from the Antichrist during the latter half of the Great Tribulation and at the Battle of Armageddon.

The superscription of the Psalm says that the Prophecy relates to Shushan-Eduth, which refers to the Lily of Testimony. The Song of Solomon compares Israel to a Lily among thorns — one beautiful Lily among many sharp thorns. Such is the double picture in this Prophecy.

When the Messiah was on the Earth, He was a Lily among thorns. He was the Faithful and True Witness. The Psalm also reflects Israel during the latter half of the Great Tribulation as a Lily witnessing in some small measure for her King, but in deadly peril of destruction from the power of the Antichrist and the many thorns which surround her.

(2) "DELIVER ME FROM THE WORKERS OF INIQUITY, AND SAVE ME FROM BLOODY MEN."

This Passage has three meanings:

1. The deliverance of David from Saul and the *"workers of iniquity."*

2. The deliverance of Christ *"from bloody men"* who desired to take His Life before He was scheduled to die on Calvary.

3. The deliverance of Israel from the Antichrist during the Great Tribulation at the Battle of Armageddon.

(3) "FOR, LO, THEY LIE IN WAIT FOR MY SOUL: THE MIGHTY ARE GATHERED AGAINST ME; NOT FOR MY TRANSGRESSION, NOR FOR MY SIN, O LORD."

David cries to the Lord and portrays Saul (the mighty) endeavoring to take his life, not because he committed any *"transgression"* or *"sin"* against Saul, but because of Saul's great evil. It does not mean that David had never sinned; it just means that Saul's anger with him was not because of any sin or transgression on David's part.

In a more perfect way, this speaks of Christ, Who was set upon by the *"mighty,"* that is, the religious leaders of Israel. They also hated Him, not because of any *"transgression"* or *"sin"* on His Part, but because of their own *"transgression"* and *"sin."*

(4) "THEY RUN AND PREPARE THEMSELVES WITHOUT MY FAULT: AWAKE TO HELP ME, AND BEHOLD."

David is picturing Saul going to great lengths to apprehend him, but not because of any *"fault"* on David's part. There also was no *"fault"* on Christ's part, yet the religious leaders of Israel spent all their time seeking to find fault with Him and ultimately to kill Him.

David cries to the Lord to help him. He uses the word *"awake,"* simply because there seemed to be no end to Saul's constant efforts to kill him. From David's perspective, it seemed as though the Lord was asleep and doing little to help him.

Perhaps with all of us, at times, it seems the same way. And yet, the Lord constantly was watching over David, even as He is regarding every Believer, even for all time (Ps. 56:8).

(5) "YOU THEREFORE, O LORD GOD OF HOSTS, THE GOD OF ISRAEL, AWAKE TO VISIT ALL THE HEATHEN: BE NOT MERCIFUL TO ANY WICKED TRANSGRESSORS. SELAH."

This Prophecy relates to the last hours of Jacob's Trouble. Verses 13 and 16 point to this fact. The believing Remnant of Israel is pictured as the last extremity shut up in Jerusalem by the nations and by certain wicked transgressors. The Messiah, in Spirit, takes His Place in their midst, cheers them with the assurance of deliverance, and prays for the destruction of their besiegers. Judgment actually is the keynote of this Psalm.

The *"heathen"* referred to the nations who will surround Jerusalem during the Battle of Armageddon.

(6) "THEY RETURN AT EVENING: THEY MAKE A NOISE LIKE A DOG, AND GO ROUND ABOUT THE CITY."

Verses 6 and 7 morally describe the besiegers as *"dogs,"* a description given by the Holy Spirit, at that!

It also refers to demon spirits which will besiege Jerusalem during the Battle of Armageddon as the Antichrist attempts to take the city. They will encircle the city, that is, *"go round about the city."*

(7) "BEHOLD, THEY BELCH OUT WITH THEIR MOUTH: SWORDS ARE IN THEIR LIPS: FOR WHO, SAY THEY, DOES HEAR?"

During the Battle of Armageddon, the Antichrist will think that he cannot lose this conflict as he besieges Jerusalem. By Television and other means of mass communication, reports will constantly be given of what looks like certain victory — *"Belch out with their mouth."* The Antichrist also will speak of his great destructive power against Jerusalem, *"swords are in their lips."*

At this time, Israel will cry to God for deliverance because they realize that now the Messiah is their only hope. The Antichrist will taunt them by saying, *"Who, say they, does hear?"*

NOTES

(8) "BUT YOU, O LORD, SHALL LAUGH AT THEM; YOU SHALL HAVE ALL THE HEATHEN IN DERISION."

This refers to the Second Coming (Rev., Chpt. 19).

The Lord's disdain for the Antichrist is referred to with a comment, *"Laugh at them."* At that time, the Lord will make short work of *"all the heathen."*

(9) "BECAUSE OF HIS STRENGTH WILL I WAIT UPON YOU: FOR GOD IS MY DEFENSE."

David is saying that whatever the circumstances might be, he will trust God's *"strength."* In response to the taunts of the Antichrist, Israel says, *"God is my defense."*

(10) "THE GOD OF MY MERCY SHALL PREVENT ME: GOD SHALL LET ME SEE MY DESIRE UPON MY ENEMIES."

This was fulfilled in David's life and he did see the defeat of his enemies, namely, Saul and Saul's henchmen. It will have a greater fulfillment regarding Israel in the last days. Israel's *"enemies"* will continue to multiply, but they ultimately shall be defeated by the Lord at the Second Coming, when the Lord will use such a degree of Power that it is beyond the comprehension of mankind (Ezek., Chpts. 38-39).

(11) "SLAY THEM NOT, LEST MY PEOPLE FORGET: SCATTER THEM BY YOUR POWER; AND BRING THEM DOWN, O LORD OUR SHIELD."

This was fulfilled in David's life. It will be fulfilled concerning the Messiah. It also will be fulfilled concerning the destruction of the Antichrist by the Coming of the Lord.

(12) "FOR THE SIN OF THEIR MOUTH AND THE WORDS OF THEIR LIPS LET THEM EVEN BE TAKEN IN THEIR PRIDE: AND FOR CURSING AND LYING WHICH THEY SPEAK."

As the Spirit of God comes upon David in the writing of this Psalm, he is speaking of Saul and those who were seeking to kill him. The reason for their terrible sin was *"pride."*

PRIDE

Prophetically, this speaks of the terrible iniquity of the religious leaders in Christ's day. They were prideful men who, despite the miracles, refused to admit that Jesus was the Messiah. Even though His Lineage was perfect, and He fit the description on all counts, they still would not believe.

He was not of the aristocracy of Israel; He was not among the *"in-crowd."* They, therefore, rejected Him.

This itinerant Peasant was a nobody, at least in their eyes! And yet, they could not deny the miracles — miracles of such power and persuasion as to defy all description, even to the dead being raised. But still, they would not believe.

In fact, miracles seldom have brought about faith. If men will not believe the Word of God (and in Truth, our Lord was the *"Living Word"*), they will not believe anything else.

This Verse also portrays the Antichrist, who will be lifted up in *"pride"* as no man ever has been. The sin of all three — Saul, the religious leaders of Israel in Christ's day, and the Antichrist — is *"pride."*

(13) "CONSUME THEM IN WRATH, CONSUME THEM, THAT THEY MAY NOT BE: AND LET THEM KNOW THAT GOD RULES IN JACOB UNTO THE ENDS OF THE EARTH. SELAH."

In Saul's case, this was fulfilled on Mount Gilboa, where he was killed by the Philistines.

In the case of the Messiah, it was fulfilled with the destruction of Jerusalem in A.D. 70 by the Roman General Titus.

In the Battle of Armageddon, it will be fulfilled with the destruction of the Antichrist. He, along with the rest of the world, will then *"know that God rules in Jacob unto the ends of the Earth."* Once again, *"Jacob"* is held up as an example, not because of what he was, but because of what God made of him.

(14) "AND AT EVENING LET THEM RETURN; AND LET THEM MAKE A NOISE LIKE A DOG, AND GO ROUND ABOUT THE CITY."

The Fourteenth Verse is identical to the Sixth with a slight variation in meaning.

As the Antichrist encircles the city of Jerusalem in order to destroy it, the prophetic prayer asks the Lord to allow this to happen, which then will cause the Antichrist and the demon spirits to believe that the city will fall and Israel will be totally defeated.

(15) "LET THEM WANDER UP AND DOWN FOR MEAT, AND GRUDGE IF THEY BE NOT SATISFIED."

This Verse speaks of the near victory by the Antichrist over Jerusalem. Even though some two-thirds of Israel already will have been destroyed (Zech. 13:8), the Antichrist still will *"grudge"* and *"be not satisfied"* until all of Israel is destroyed. He will be sorely disappointed.

This particular Verse proclaims the present attitude of the modern Palestinians. They aren't satisfied with whatever portion of modern Israel they now possess. They actually want all the Land of Israel, plus every Jew dead. Those are their ultimate goals.

The tiny State of Israel, about the size of the State of Connecticut, actually has only about one-tenth of one percent (0.1%) of the entirety of the land area of the Middle East, which also includes Northern Africa, i.e., Egypt. In other words, the Arabs control the entirety of the Middle East, with the exception of the tiny State of Israel. But, as stated, they also want that tiny piece of land.

There is plenty of room in modern Jordan, for instance, to take care of the Palestinian population. The same could be said for other Arab States. But, in actuality, none of these Arab States will permit a single Palestinian to come into their country, even though they have plenty of room to spare. They want that festering sore in Israel so they can harp to the entirety of the world about how bad the Palestinians are being treated.

Israel has fought some five wars since she became a nation in 1948. Each war was initiated by the Muslims. If Israel had lost any one of these wars, there would be no Israel left today. But Israel won all of these wars. And despite the fact that the Arabs initiated each conflict, Israel has allowed, out of the generosity of their hearts, the Palestinians to remain in the land.

If the tables had been turned, you can bet your bottom dollar that the Muslims never would have allowed the Israelis to remain.

Incidentally, the name *"Palestinian"* is really a misnomer. The word *"Palestinian"* is derived from the ancient Philistines. There is no such thing today as a Palestinian. These people called *"Palestinians"* actually are Syrians, Egyptians, Jordanians, Iraqis, etc.

(16) "BUT I WILL SING OF YOUR POWER; YEA, I WILL SING ALOUD OF YOUR MERCY IN THE MORNING: FOR YOU HAVE BEEN MY DEFENSE AND REFUGE IN THE DAY OF MY TROUBLE."

This speaks of the *"Day of Jacob's Trouble"* (Jer. 30:7).

Yes, despite the power of the Antichrist, the *"Power"* of the Lord will be even greater. Both David and the Messiah will sing of such.

(17) "UNTO YOU, O MY STRENGTH, WILL I SING: FOR GOD IS MY DEFENSE, AND THE GOD OF MY MERCY."

This is a beautiful Passage, signifying the *"strength"* and *"defense"* that God gives, not only to Israel, but to all who love Him and proclaim His Name.

The Holy Spirit through David concludes this Psalm with the word *"Mercy."* This is truly amazing! David and the future Israel (during the coming Great Tribulation) are given this great Blessing, not because of any goodness on their part, but because of goodness on the Lord's Part, which constitutes *"Mercy."*

PSALM 60

A Psalm of David:
A Prayer for Israel's Deliverance

(1) "O GOD, YOU HAVE CAST US OFF, YOU HAVE SCATTERED US, YOU HAVE BEEN DISPLEASED; O TURN YOURSELF TO US AGAIN."

This Psalm was written by David when he strove in Aramnaharaim, which is Mesopotamia. It was situated between the Euphrates and the Tigris Rivers (I Chron. 18:1-5). It also included Aramzobah, where Joab returned and smote some 18,000 in the Valley of Salt (II Sam. 8:3-13). This place is Coelesyria, or Syria.

The first part pertains to David's and Abishai's exploit, which was 22,000. For the most part, it applies to Joab's exploit, which took him some six months to accomplish. It seems that Israel had suffered a military defeat somewhere close to Edom. To deal with the situation, David then sent Joab, who killed 18,000 of the Edomites, which

NOTES

completely subjugated them.

(2) "YOU HAVE MADE THE EARTH TO TREMBLE; YOU HAVE BROKEN IT: HEAL THE BREACHES THEREOF; FOR IT SHAKES."

The greater fulfillment of this prayer and Prophecy will be during the *"Time of Jacob's Trouble"* and his deliverance out of it. This will be during the Great Tribulation that even yet is still to come. At that time, the Earth literally *"will tremble."*

(3) "YOU HAVE SHOWED YOUR PEOPLE HARD THINGS: YOU HAVE MADE US TO DRINK THE WINE OF ASTONISHMENT."

This has a double meaning:

1. It seems to say that Israel had sinned, which resulted in a military defeat that later would be rectified. When David uses the phrase, *"To drink the wine of astonishment,"* it is referring to the surprise experienced in the south when Edom fought Israel. Victory ultimately was won in these conflicts, but not without some difficulty.

2. Its prophetic fulfillment has to do with Israel during the last days under the Antichrist. They will then be reduced to *"astonishment,"* which speaks of the time that the Antichrist will break his seven-year Covenant with them and declare war, which then will threaten their very existence (Dan. 9:27).

(4) "YOU HAVE GIVEN A BANNER TO THEM WHO FEAR YOU, THAT IT MAY BE DISPLAYED BECAUSE OF THE TRUTH. SELAH."

This Passage portrays Israel beneath the banner of Righteousness in the midst of a multitude of foes. Even though Israel has forsaken God and is under Divine chastening because of national apostasy, God still will be true to the Promises He made to the Patriarchs of old.

At this time, the Messiah will be Israel's Jehovah-Nissi (the LORD our Banner). Israel's only hope in the Battle of Armageddon will be this *"Banner."* Little by little, she will draw around this *"Banner,"* and so should God's servants in all times and in all circumstances (Ex. 17:8-16).

Christ Himself will be the *"Banner"* in that coming day!

(5) "THAT YOUR BELOVED MAY BE

DELIVERED; SAVE WITH YOUR RIGHT HAND, AND HEAR ME."

Israel here is referred to as the Lord's *"Beloved."*

The petition as given will be answered and the time will be in the coming Battle of Armageddon. At that time, Israel will be delivered!

(6) "GOD HAS SPOKEN IN HIS HOLINESS; I WILL REJOICE, I WILL DIVIDE SHECHEM, AND METE OUT THE VALLEY OF SUCCOTH."

The phrase, *"God has spoken,"* means that what He says shall be done because it was said *"in His Holiness."*

REJOICING

The phrase, *"I will rejoice,"* refers to the Lord Personally rejoicing. There will be many reasons for this rejoicing.

First of all, it will take place during the time of the Battle of Armageddon. At that time, Israel will cry to Him as possibly she never has cried before. He will hear their cry, which will institute the Second Coming. Then Israel will accept Him and the evidence is they will do so to a man. In other words, not one single Jew will say *"No"* to Christ.

According to the Prophet Zechariah, when they realize Who He is, meaning they realize that He is the One Whom they crucified, *"in that day shall there be a great mourning in Jerusalem"* (Zech. 12:11-14).

DIVISION

The phrase, *"I will divide,"* speaks of the Promise to Israel of the Land of Palestine as her eternal home and of the nations as her servants.

Today there is tremendous dissension between the Arabs and Israel regarding the geography of the Promised Land. The contention will continue until the Antichrist makes his seven-year Covenant with Israel. This will happen in the near future, actually following the Rapture of the Church. At that time, Israel will think that her problems have been solved. Paul said she would cry, *"Peace and safety"* (I Thess. 5:3), but *"then sudden destruction comes upon them."*

The Antichrist will break his Covenant with Israel at this time and attempt to annihilate

NOTES

her. However, God has said something else. The next few Verses tell us what He says.

(7) "GILEAD IS MINE, AND MANASSEH IS MINE; EPHRAIM ALSO IS THE STRENGTH OF MY HEAD; JUDAH IS MY LAWGIVER."

The Lord is saying that He Himself has drawn the boundaries of Israel; consequently, He will give it to whomever He pleases. In this Passage, He says to whom He has given it.

THE LAND OF ISRAEL

"Ephraim" represents the entirety of the Northern Kingdom, and *"Judah"* represents the entirety of the Southern Kingdom. In the Kingdom Age to come, however, Israel no longer will be divided.

The efforts of the Muslims, the Antichrist, or anyone else, to confiscate this property, be it the West Bank, Gaza, Golan Heights, or any other part of Israel, ultimately will fail to be successful. Even if Israel, in some type of treaty, does give some part of *"The Holy Land"* to others, still, at the Coming of the Lord it will revert back to its rightful owner — and that rightful owner is Israel.

(8) "MOAB IS MY WASHPOT; OVER EDOM WILL I CAST OUT MY SHOE: PHILISTIA, TRIUMPH YOU BECAUSE OF ME."

The word *"washpot"* means *"footbath"* or *"ignominious vessel."*

POSSESSION

The phrase, *"Over Edom will I cast out My shoe,"* refers to *"taking possession."* In ancient times, when a piece of property was sold, in order for the previous owner to demonstrate that he had willingly sold and given it up, he would give his shoe to the new purchaser as a sign of possession. It symbolized the right to tread the soil of the property, which now belonged to the new owner.

This means that Edom (Petra) will be reserved and owned by God as a place of refuge for Israel during the Great Tribulation, when the Antichrist abrogates his covenant with them and attacks them.

The phrase, *"Philistia, triumph you because of Me,"* is not truly a proper translation. It should have been translated, *"Over Philistia is My triumph."* In this short sentence, we are told that the Muslim efforts regarding the West Bank and the Gaza Strip will not succeed. Whatever happens at the present has no bearing on the future. When Jesus comes back, the contention over the Land of Israel then will be forever settled.

(9) "WHO WILL BRING ME INTO THE STRONG CITY? WHO WILL LEAD ME INTO EDOM?"

This refers to the Antichrist breaking his covenant with Israel at the approximate three and a half year period. He actually will declare war on her (Dan. 9:27).

Israel then will flee to *"the strong city,"* which is located in ancient *"Edom,"* but is now present-day Jordan, and corresponds to present-day Petra.

PETRA

Petra presently has no population whatsoever, and has been that way for many, many years. It is located in Jordan, approximately 75 miles south of the Dead Sea. At times it is referred to as *"The Rose-Red City of Petra, the City that time forgot."* It can be reached only by a narrow defile which is only a few feet wide, and which is enclosed on both sides by towering cliffs rising straight up for well over one hundred feet. This city would be very vulnerable to air attack, but it is almost impossible to breach by ground assault.

It is believed that Esau, the brother of Jacob, founded this city approximately 1,800 years before Christ (Gen. 33:16). In the Bible, Petra sometimes is referred to as *"Seir"* or *"Sela."*

Having been defeated in battle for the first time since becoming a nation in 1948, Israel then will flee from the Antichrist. This incident will take place at the midpoint of the Great Tribulation. As stated already, Israel's destination will be *"the strong city,"* i.e., *"Petra."*

At that time, the Antichrist easily could annihilate Israel, but his attention will be diverted elsewhere, which will save Israel until a later time. That time will be the Battle of Armageddon (Dan. 9:27; 11:44; Ezek., Chpts. 38-39).

(10) "WILL NOT YOU, O GOD, WHICH HAD CAST US OFF? AND YOU, O GOD, WHICH DID NOT GO OUT WITH OUR ARMIES?"

NOTES

The Tenth Verse actually answers the questions of Verse 9. Because of Israel's terrible spiritual condition (specifically because they crucified their Lord and Messiah), God has, in fact, *"cast them off."* That *"casting off"* has now lasted for approximately 2,000 years.

The Great Tribulation, which will last for seven years, is referred to as *"The Time of Jacob's Trouble"* (Jer. 30:7). According to Christ Himself (Mat. 24:21), this will be the most terrible time the world ever has known, and will be brought about by the Lord for many reasons, but the primary reason is to bring Israel to Himself. That is why it is called *"The Time of Jacob's Trouble."*

During that seven-year period, the Antichrist will make his debut. At the beginning, Israel will think he is the Messiah; they actually will announce such to the entirety of the world. The Antichrist will seem to solve all of Israel's problems.

But the Holy Spirit through the Apostle Paul said, *"For when they shall say, Peace and safety* (refers to Israel, but will as well characterize the world; it pertains to the Antichrist signing the seven-year pact with Israel and other nations [Dan. 9:27])*; then sudden destruction comes upon them* (at the midpoint of the seven-year period, the Antichrist, as stated, will break his pact, actually invading Israel [Rev. 12:1-6])*, as travail upon a woman with child; and they shall not escape* (the Great Tribulation is definitely coming upon this world [Mat. 24:21])*"* (I Thess. 5:3).

Israel will then know that she has made the second greatest mistake in her history, the first being the Crucifixion of Christ. Now she will realize that the Antichrist is not the Messiah, but rather the very opposite. Now will come the hard time, leading up to the Battle of Armageddon.

(11) "GIVE US THE HELP FROM TROUBLE: FOR VAIN IS THE HELP OF MAN."

The *"trouble"* that is spoken of here refers to the seven-year Great Tribulation that Jesus said would be the worst ever (Mat. 24:21). It seems that no nation in the world will come to the help of Israel at that time; therefore, David says, *"Vain is the help of man."*

This also pertains to every single Child of

God. The sad fact of the Church is that it has long since forsaken the help that only God can give, and instead has opted for the *"vain help"* of man. This means that if man does give help, it is for selfish purpose and motive, which really offers no service to the one in need.

THE VAIN HELP OF MAN

It is regrettable, to say the least, that the modern Church has opted for humanistic psychology to meet the needs of mankind. In fact, one of the great statements of the modern Church is, *"You need professional help."*

The modern Church simply does not believe that what Jesus did at the Cross meets every single need that humanity may have. If it pertains to life and living, Jesus addressed it at the Cross (II Pet. 1:3-4).

The problem is unbelief! Pure and simple and to the point, the problem is unbelief! The modern Church does not believe that what Jesus did at the Cross answers the need of humanity. It, therefore, turns to humanistic psychology, and most of the Messages preached from behind modern pulpits consist of this. Preachers are not preaching the Cross; they are preaching something else altogether. But when one analyzes it, it is psychology, which means it certainly is not the Gospel.

THE HELP GIVEN BY THE LORD

Everything that Believers receive from the Lord (and I mean everything!) comes from Christ as the Source and the Cross as the Means. Every single Believer should make the Cross of Christ the exclusive Object of his Faith. When we do this and continue to do this, the Holy Spirit, Who works completely within the parameters of the Finished Work of Christ, will help us in a grand manner (Rom. 6:1-14; 8:1-2, 11; I Cor. 1:17-18; 23; 2:2; Gal., Chpt. 5; 6:14).

Let us say it again:

There is no help from man. If we receive help, it will be from the Lord. We must, however, seek that help in God's Way, which is the Way of the Cross (I Cor. 2:2).

(12) "THROUGH GOD WE SHALL DO VALIANTLY: FOR HE IT IS WHO SHALL TREAD DOWN OUR ENEMIES."

This speaks of the Lord coming to Israel's rescue during the Battle of Armageddon (Rev., Chpt. 19) in order to *"tread down our enemies."* He Alone can do such!

Both Passages (Vss. 11-12) do apply and should be heeded by every Believer. Truly, God is our Refuge, and He Alone can overcome the powers of darkness.

PSALM 61

A Psalm of David:
A Hymn of Trust and Confidence

(1) "HEAR MY CRY, O GOD; ATTEND UNTO MY PRAYER."

This Psalm was written by David and it is a Psalm of trust.

THE GREATER SON OF DAVID

The words are David's, but the Speaker is actually the Messiah. The doctrine of this and similar Psalms is the perfection of the Faith of the Messiah. As Man, He had to undergo every form of hatred, affliction, and adversity. The sharper these became, the more He trusted. His moral glory as the Servant of Jehovah shines through all. He voluntarily took upon Himself this position of dependence and suffering, in union with and on behalf of His people.

Because the Greater Son of David trod this path, we also are cheered and comforted in trial, which causes our faith to be sustained by these communications, for they prove that our King and Shepherd trod these dark paths before us. The Messiah trusted God and was delivered. A similar deliverance is, consequently, assured to us.

(2) "FROM THE END OF THE EARTH WILL I CRY UNTO YOU, WHEN MY HEART IS OVERWHELMED: LEAD ME TO THE ROCK THAT IS HIGHER THAN I."

The petitions of the Messiah are evident in the four Gospels as He, over and over again, resorts to a private place of prayer (Mat. 14:23; 26:36; Mk. 6:46; Lk. 9:28; Jn. 17). The *"Rock"* was the Father. The Lord also is referred to many times as a *"Rock"* (Deut. 32:4, 15, 18, 31; I Sam. 2:2). Irrespective of how high our problems may be, *"The Rock is higher."*

(3) "FOR YOU HAVE BEEN A SHELTER FOR ME, AND A STRONG TOWER FROM THE ENEMY."

The *"Shelter"* for the Messiah was God the Father. He must be our *"Shelter"* as well. As dependent Man, Christ prayed to be led to a Rock-Shelter that was Divine; as sinless Man, He conceived of no higher joy than to perpetually dwell in the Presence of God.

(4) "I WILL ABIDE IN YOUR TABERNACLE FOREVER: I WILL TRUST IN THE COVERT OF YOUR WINGS. SELAH."

As we have stated repeatedly, *"Trust in God"* is the theme of the Book of Psalms. The *"Covert of Your wings"* refers to the *"Shelter for Me."*

TOTAL TRUST

The instigation of the Holy Spirit is to pull the Believer into total *"Trust"* in God. This refers to *"Trust"* for every facet and walk of life. Sadly, most pulpits are silent regarding *"Trust in God."* Religious men trust themselves, other men, government, psychologists, preachers, and many other things, but few *"Trust in God."*

It is impossible for the Believer to fully trust in the Lord, which means to trust explicitly in God's Word, without understanding Christ and the Cross. One must ever understand Who Christ is and What Christ has done. In other words, His Person and His Function.

As it regards His Person, Jesus Christ is Very God and Very Man. This means that He is total God and total Man.

In coming to this world, the Lord laid aside the expression of His Deity, while never losing possession of His Deity. He actually laid aside the expression of that Deity forever. He never ceased to be God, but He will remain a Man forever, thereby with a human body, albeit glorified. That's what John the Beloved was talking about when he said: *"Beloved, now are we the sons of God* (we are just as much a *'son of God'* now as we will be after the Resurrection), *and it does not yet appear what we shall be* (our present state as a *'son of God'* is not at all like what we shall be in the coming Resurrection): *but we know that, when He shall appear* (the Rapture), *we shall be like Him* (speaks of being glorified); *for we shall see Him as He is.* (Physical eyes and a mortal body could not look upon that Glory, only eyes in a glorified body)" (I Jn. 3:2).

Our Lord's function was, and is, the Cross. As we have repeatedly stated, *"Christ is the Source of all things, while the Cross is the Means by which all of these great and glorious things are given to us."* In other words, it is the Cross that made it all possible, because it was there that Jesus Christ atoned for all sin.

Paul said, *"But this Man* (this Priest, Christ Jesus), *after He had offered one Sacrifice for sins forever* (speaks of the Cross), *sat down on the Right Hand of God* (refers to the great contrast with the Priests under the Levitical System, who never sat down because their work was never completed; the work of Christ was a *'Finished Work,'* and needed no repetition);

"From henceforth expecting till His enemies be made His footstool. (These enemies are Satan and all the fallen angels and demon spirits, plus all who follow Satan.)

"For by one Offering He has perfected forever them who are sanctified. (Everything one needs is found in the Cross [Gal. 6:14])" (Heb. 10:12-14).

(5) "FOR YOU, O GOD, HAVE HEARD MY VOWS: YOU HAVE GIVEN ME THE HERITAGE OF THOSE WHO FEAR YOUR NAME."

This exhibits a past experience and a future confidence, both equally perfect.

VOWS

David had made *"vows"* unto the Lord. He failed in some of these vows; however, the Greater Son of David did not fail in His *"vows."* He said, *". . . I do always those things that please Him"* (Jn. 8:29).

Our Lord has not received His *"heritage"* as of yet. It will be forthcoming shortly at the Rapture of the Church and when Israel is gathered to Him at the beginning of the Kingdom Age.

(6) "YOU WILL PROLONG THE KING'S LIFE: AND HIS YEARS AS MANY GENERATIONS."

This was David's prayer, but it was far more sweeping than just referring to David.

David died at 70 years, yet his life was *"prolonged"* through the life of the Messiah, that is, it was unending. *"His years"* through the Messiah and the Eternal Life given by Him will last for many (unending) generations.

(7) "HE SHALL ABIDE BEFORE GOD FOREVER: O PREPARE MERCY AND TRUTH, WHICH MAY PRESERVE HIM."

Today Christ is seated by the Right Hand of the Father and will *"abide before God forever."* Jesus Christ was the *"Mercy and Truth"* prepared for sinful man. What preserved the Messiah will also *"preserve"* us — Mercy and Truth.

(8) "SO WILL I SING PRAISE UNTO YOUR NAME FOREVER, THAT I MAY DAILY PERFORM MY VOWS."

David was the first one we know of who actually and continually sang praises *"unto Your Name forever."* If he did that under the Old Covenant of Law, how could we do less under the New Covenant of Grace.

The statement, *"Daily perform my vows,"* actually means to trust God at all times.

PSALM 62

A Psalm of David:
A Psalm of Longing and Trust

(1) "TRULY MY SOUL WAITS UPON GOD: FROM HIM COMES MY SALVATION."

This Psalm also was written by David and once again, this speaks of David, but even more so it speaks of the Greater Son of David.

PRAYER

One of the secrets of David's great strength and victory with the Lord was his *"waiting upon God."* *"Waiting"* is almost unheard of in the modern Church. Prayer also is almost unheard of. In the modern Church, few look to God for *"Salvation."* They look more so to themselves, or to a particular religious Denomination, or even a psychologist.

The modern Faith Movement basically has taught the very opposite of *"waiting on God."*

The Scriptural Truth is that many things do not come from God easily or quickly. The *"waiting"* also is for our benefit. It is very simple for us to ask, and ask we should. But in the granting of the request, the Lord at times teaches us Trust and Faith by allowing us to *"wait."*

(2) "HE ONLY IS MY ROCK AND MY SALVATION; HE IS MY DEFENSE; I SHALL NOT BE GREATLY MOVED."

Man's hatred of the Messiah occupies the first four Verses of this Psalm. Man's hatred of God's people occurs in the following six.

OUR DEFENSE

In the First Advent, the enemy tried to cast Jesus down from His Excellency (Vs. 1-4), and will try to cast His people down from their excellency immediately prior to His future Coming in Power and great Glory (Vss. 5-10).

These first two Verses reveal the Perfection of the Messiah's Trust while He suffered the hatred described in Verses 3 and 4. David and the Messiah both said that God Alone was their *"Rock."* How many Believers can say the same?

If we take up our own *"defense,"* we will fail. If He is our *"defense,"* we cannot fail.

The term *"greatly moved"* refers to the enemy's attacks and the thought that he has succeeded. We may be *"moved"* a tiny bit, but not *"greatly moved"*!

(3) "HOW LONG WILL YOU IMAGINE MISCHIEF AGAINST A MAN? YOU SHALL BE SLAIN ALL OF YOU: AS A BOWING WALL SHALL YOU BE, AND AS A TOTTERING FENCE."

Matthew 16:27 and Acts 17:31 make it evident that the Messiah is the Man of Verse 3 and the God of Verse 12.

JESUS AND THE RELIGIOUS LEADERS OF ISRAEL

The religious leaders of Israel looked at Jesus as One so feeble that they easily could dispense with Him. They hungered for His Life and their hearts were enflamed with the very hatred of Hell. These were the very men who shouted, *"Crucify Him! Crucify Him!"*

However, the Prophecy is that all of these who *"imagined mischief"* against The Man Christ Jesus *"shall be slain all of you."*

This happened in A.D. 70, when the Roman General Titus laid siege to Jerusalem and over one million Jews were slaughtered.

(4) "THEY ONLY CONSULT TO CAST HIM DOWN FROM HIS EXCELLENCY: THEY DELIGHT IN LIES: THEY BLESS WITH THEIR MOUTH, BUT THEY CURSE INWARDLY. SELAH."

Even if these hypocrites bless Christ with their mouth, their hearts were filled with lies (Mat. 22:16), for they were liars like their father, the Devil (Jn. 8:44-55). They only consulted to cast Him down from His Excellency. He speaks <u>to</u> them in Verse 3 and <u>of</u> them in Verse 4.

(5) "MY SOUL, WAIT THOU ONLY UPON GOD; FOR MY EXPECTATION IS FROM HIM."

When man has been disappointed enough by other men, then he will *"wait only upon God."* One should have no *"expectation"* from other men, because it will not be forthcoming; it only will come from God.

(6) "HE ONLY IS MY ROCK AND MY SALVATION: HE IS MY DEFENSE; I SHALL NOT BE MOVED."

For many Preachers, their Denomination is their *"Rock."* Both David and the Greater Son of David once again use the word *"only"* concerning his *"Rock"* and *"defense."* From this position, he says, *"I shall not be moved."* David set the example; the Greater Son of David verified that example; we are to follow suit.

(7) "IN GOD IS MY SALVATION AND MY GLORY: THE ROCK OF MY STRENGTH, AND MY REFUGE, IS IN GOD."

Over and over again in the Psalms, the Holy Spirit repeats these statements in various forms for our benefit. And yet, too often the modern Church little trusts God for *"Salvation," "Strength,"* and *"Refuge."* But there is no other!

The following Verses will show us how futile is the help of man.

(8) "TRUST IN HIM AT ALL TIMES; YOU PEOPLE, POUR OUT YOUR HEART BEFORE HIM: GOD IS A REFUGE FOR US. SELAH."

Three things are said in this Verse. They are:

1. *"Trust in Him at all times."* This means that we are to trust the Lord for everything, at all times, and in every capacity. We are to believe that He will supply all of our needs, that He will see us through, and that He will give us perpetual victory, all through Christ and the Cross.

2. We here are importuned to *"pour out our heart before the Lord."* This refers to telling Him all of our troubles and all of our needs. When we speak to Him, we are speaking to Someone Who can do all things.

3. Always and at all times, *"God is a Refuge for us."*

The other day I was reading an excellent Message by a particular Preacher as he expounded on the Cross of Christ. He addressed the problem of spiritual failure. What happens if the Believer, whose trust is in Christ and the Cross, fails? His answer, I think, was beautiful.

He said, *"That's why Jesus went to the Cross — for our failures."*

God is our Refuge, not only during the times when our faith is strong, but He also is our Refuge even when we have failed. He is, in fact, the only Refuge!

(9) "SURELY MEN OF LOW DEGREE ARE VANITY, AND MEN OF HIGH DEGREE ARE A LIE: TO BE LAID IN THE BALANCE, THEY ARE ALTOGETHER LIGHTER THAN VANITY."

Four things are here said:

1. *"Men of low degree are vanity,"* meaning that they cannot help. This speaks of those referred to as *"common men."*

2. *"Men of high degree are a lie,"* meaning that they are a fading, false illusion.

3. When all men are weighed in the balances, they are *"found wanting."*

4. To look to man is to look to vanity, which means that there is neither substance nor solidity in them.

(10) "TRUST NOT IN OPPRESSION, AND BECOME NOT VAIN IN ROBBERY: IF RICHES INCREASE, SET NOT YOUR HEART UPON THEM."

We are told here that if riches come by the means of oppression, those riches will be nothing but *"oppressed."*

Even if riches come by honest means, we are not to *"set our heart upon them."* Nothing must be allowed to turn our heart and our eyes away from God. As all of us know, it is very easy to look to money, especially if there is increase.

(11) "GOD HAS SPOKEN ONCE; TWICE

HAVE I HEARD THIS; THAT POWER BELONGS UNTO GOD."

In this Verse we are given a tremendous Truth.

HOW CAN THE POWER OF GOD COME TO THE BELIEVER?

Two things are said in the Word of God about this:

1. *"But you shall receive Power, after that the Holy Spirit is come upon you: and you shall be witnesses unto Me both in Jerusalem, and in all Judaea, and in Samaria, and unto the uttermost part of the Earth"* (Acts 1:8).

2. *"For the preaching of the Cross is to them who perish foolishness: but unto us which are saved it is the Power of God"* (I Cor. 1:18).

How do we link the two, the Holy Spirit and the Preaching of the Cross, which produces the Power?

The Holy Spirit works exclusively within the parameters of the Finished Work of Christ. In other words, it is the Cross that has given the Spirit the legal means to do all that He does (Rom. 8:2).

As a result, it is demanded of us that our faith ever rest in Christ and the Cross. When we do that, and do it perpetually, the Holy Spirit then will work mightily within our hearts and lives, making His Power available to us.

(12) "ALSO UNTO YOU, O LORD, BELONGS MERCY: FOR YOU RENDER TO EVERY MAN ACCORDING TO HIS WORK."

Not only does *"Power"* belong to God, but *"Mercy"* also belongs to Him!

It is futile to look to man for mercy. Unless Christ resides in that man, there will be no mercy.

The Lord minutely inspects the work of every single individual and renders accordingly. We must never forget that!

PSALM 63

A Psalm of David:
The Prayer of a Thirsting Soul

(1) "O GOD, YOU ARE MY GOD; EARLY WILL I SEEK YOU: MY SOUL THIRSTS FOR YOU, MY FLESH LONGS FOR YOU IN A DRY AND THIRSTY LAND, WHERE NO WATER IS."

This Psalm was written by David while he was fleeing from Saul in the wilderness of Judah. This was a dark time in David's life, as this narrative shows.

DEPENDENCE ON THE LORD

The phrase, *"O God, You are my God,"* proclaims the fact that David looked to the Lord exclusively.

The Reader should understand that any trust he places in anything other than the Lord makes that object his *"god."* This is true no matter whether the trust is placed in another person, a system, a Church, or ourselves.

There is only one way to fully trust the Lord, and that is for one to place one's faith exclusively in Christ and the Cross. If we separate Christ from the Cross in any capacity, meaning that we eliminate the Cross or ignore the Cross, then we conclude by *"serving another Jesus,"* which God never can honor (II Cor. 11:4).

The phrase, *"My soul thirsts for You,"* pertains to that which is true of every human being, because God is the Creator of man. That *"thirst"* was placed there by God, and it only can be satisfied by God. Unfortunately, the majority of mankind, and for all time, has tried to slake that thirst with other things, all to no avail. The Lord Alone can slake that thirst.

Concerning this very thing, Jesus said, and I quote from THE EXPOSITOR'S STUDY BIBLE:

"*. . . Whosoever drinks of this water shall thirst again* (presents one of the most simple, common, yet at the same time profound statements ever uttered; the things of the world can never satisfy the human heart and life, irrespective as to how much is acquired)*:*

"But whosoever drinks of the water that I shall give him shall never thirst ('Whosoever' means exactly what it says! Christ accepted is spiritual thirst forever slaked!)*; but the water that I shall give him shall be in him a well of water springing up into Everlasting Life.* (Everything that the world or religion gives pertains to the externals; but this which Jesus gives deals with the very core of one's being, and is a perennial fountain)" (Jn. 4:13-14).

A DRY AND THIRSTY LAND

The phrase, *"My flesh longs for You in a dry and thirsty land, where no water is,"* pertains to this present world. There are many things that Satan proposes, but there is no Water of Life available in the system of this present world. Such comes from the Lord, and only from the Lord.

SEEKING THE LORD

Going back to the beginning of the Verse, the phrase, *"Early will I see You,"* indicates a habit with David (Ps. 57:8-9). David took everything to the Lord each day; he actually started each day with such an approach. This ought to be the habit of every Believer.

I personally come to the office every morning, with the exception of Saturday, at about daylight or before. Our daily Radio Program, *"A Study In The Word,"* begins at 7 a.m. (Central Time). I try to get to the office about one hour before the Radio Program starts so I can spend at least a half hour with the Lord. There are many things I need to bring before Him and I need His Leading and Guidance in all of them.

When I was a child, my grandmother taught me to pray. She taught me that nothing was impossible with God. Over and over again, she would tell me, *"Jimmy, God is a big God. So, when you pray, ask big!"* I have never forgotten those words, and her exhortation to me of so long ago has helped me to touch this world for Christ.

David said, *"Early will I seek You."* As stated, this should be the habit of every single Believer. If a Christian fully develops that habit, his relationship with the Lord develops accordingly. He finds that things go better for him. In spite of attacks by Satan, he finds victory.

It was in prayer and through prayer that the Lord gave me the great Revelation of the Cross. If this Evangelist had not pursued the habit of seeking the Lord, even on a daily basis, I do not believe the Lord would have been able to give me the great Revelation of the Cross. It actually is impossible for a Believer to receive anything from the Lord unless he has a prayer life.

Again, take the advice given by the Holy Spirit through David. Every day make it your habit that *"early will I seek You."* When you do, you will find that things change!

(2) *"TO SEE YOUR POWER AND YOUR GLORY, SO AS I HAVE SEEN YOU IN THE SANCTUARY."*

This Verse shows that David was a frequent worshipper at the Sanctuary, which then was located at a place called *"Nob"* (I Sam. 21:1).

THE SANCTUARY

We must understand that the Old Covenant was a little different than the New. Under the Old Covenant, God did not dwell in men, at least as He does now (I Cor. 3:16). Then, speaking of the time before the Cross, He dwelt between the Mercy Seat and the Cherubim in the Sanctuary. To fully worship God, one, therefore, had to go to the Tabernacle (Sanctuary or Temple).

The times of prayer were at 9 a.m. and 3 p.m. each day other than the Sabbath. A person, of course, also could go at any other time, day or night. If a person had committed sin, he was to take a lamb. Those who were too poor to afford a lamb could bring two pigeons or two turtledoves. For those who were so extremely poor as to not even be able to afford this, they could bring a tenth part of a ephah of fine flour (a little short of a gallon).

Even then, no sin could be forgiven without a blood sacrifice (Heb. 9:22), so Blood Atonement was provided for such paupers by the public through the Priests, as the officiating Priest offered up a lamb each morning and each afternoon.

David certainly could worship God in this wilderness away from the Sanctuary, as is obvious from this and many other Psalms he wrote. God certainly accepted David's worship, because He knew the circumstances. But David longed to once again faithfully attend the worship at the Sanctuary.

THE TEMPLE OF GOD

The Lord no longer dwells in a particular Tabernacle, Church, or Temple. He dwells in Believers (I Cor. 3:16), all made possible by the Cross. The Cross of Christ is the dividing point of history.

The Cross of Christ made available everything that God has for the Believer in a much greater way than under the Old Covenant. That's the reason the Holy Spirit through Paul said, and I quote from THE EXPOSITOR'S STUDY BIBLE:

"*But now* (since the Cross) *has He* (the Lord Jesus) *obtained a more excellent Ministry* (the New Covenant in Jesus' Blood is superior to, and takes the place of, the Old Covenant in animal blood), *by how much also He is the Mediator of a Better Covenant* (proclaims the fact that Christ officiates between God and man according to the arrangements of the New Covenant), *which was established upon better Promises.* (This presents the New Covenant, explicitly based on the cleansing and forgiveness of all sin, which the Old Covenant could not do.)

"*For if that first Covenant had been faultless* (proclaims the fact that the first Covenant definitely was not faultless; as stated, it was based on animal blood, which was vastly inferior to the Precious Blood of Christ), *then should no place have been sought for the Second* (proclaims the necessity of the New Covenant)" (Heb. 8:6-7).

(3) "BECAUSE YOUR LOVINGKINDNESS IS BETTER THAN LIFE, MY LIPS SHALL PRAISE YOU."

Two things are said in this Passage:

A CORRECT ATTITUDE TOWARD THE LORD

1. David easily could have blamed God for his circumstances, like many others do; however, he would attribute nothing to God except *"lovingkindness."* David is saying, *"If I die in this wilderness, I would rather die loving and praising You than to have the fellowship of Saul and be estranged from God."* He was saying that God's Presence and Blessings were *"better than life."*

2. David is also saying that irrespective of his present situation concerning Saul (who is hunting him down like a wild animal, trying to kill him), he will not allow these things to steal his worship of God. Instead, he says, *"My lips shall praise You."* What a lesson for us today!

Anything that can rob us of our praise to God also can take everything else we have. If we cannot be robbed of our praise, ultimately we shall overcome every difficulty. The Reader here sees the secret of David's great victory.

Modern Believers so often blame God for their circumstances. Christian psychologists, so-called, even teach them to *"forgive God."* Such advice borders on blasphemy.

The Lord has never done anything negative to anyone. When one *"forgives God,"* that person is basing their action on a lie. And God can never bless that!

Whatever our circumstances, God is ever *"lovingkindness."* Because God is such and never will cease to be such, *"My lips will praise You."*

(4) "THUS WILL I BLESS YOU WHILE I LIVE: I WILL LIFT UP MY HANDS IN YOUR NAME."

The first ten Verses sing of the First Advent of David's Son and Lord. The Eleventh Verse speaks of His Second Advent (Rev., Chpt. 19).

THE LORD JESUS AND HIS FIRST ADVENT

In our Lord's First Advent, He found this world a wilderness, a dry and weary land without one stream of moral refreshment (Vs. 1), and His Heart longed for the joys He had tasted from all eternity in His Father's Bosom.

But if He found this world to be a thirsty wilderness, yet, by day (Vs. 4) and night (Vs. 6), He found God to be a satisfying Source of perfect happiness. Enriched by His Knowledge of His Heavenly Father, He closely followed Him.

Thus, we have the example set before us as Believers in that we should bless the Lord at all times. We also should *"lift up our hands in His Name."* When we do this, we proclaim victory despite the circumstances and absolve God of all blame regarding our present circumstances, whatever they may be.

(5) "MY SOUL SHALL BE SATISFIED AS WITH MARROW AND FATNESS; AND MY MOUTH SHALL PRAISE YOU WITH JOYFUL LIPS."

What a statement!

God was his life. We speak not only of David, but also of the Greater Son of David. Until we arrive at this place, the place where we know that our Lord satisfies every longing in our heart, we never will know what true Christianity really is!

This can be had only as we place our faith exclusively in Christ and what Christ has done for us at the Cross. Only then will the Holy Spirit work within our lives and give us that which only He can give.

(6) "WHEN I REMEMBER YOU UPON MY BED, AND MEDITATE ON YOU IN THE NIGHT WATCHES."

This speaks of both David and the Messiah (Ps. 119:97-104).

MEDITATION

"Meditation on the Word of God" (both day and night) will cure one of fear and stress, which also will eliminate many sicknesses. To *"meditate"* has the same meaning as a cow chewing her cud. It means to take the morsel and chew it until all the juices are extracted from it. When we do not follow the direction of the Holy Spirit regarding this very Passage on meditation, we receive little from the Word of God, even though the Word holds so very much for us!

Most every night, this Evangelist does the same identical thing as David did. I either will pray or quote Scriptures to myself, and I draw precious sustenance from the Word of God. I do this until I fall asleep. One might say that this is the way the Believer should recharge his spiritual batteries.

(7) "BECAUSE YOU HAVE BEEN MY HELP, THEREFORE IN THE SHADOW OF YOUR WINGS WILL I REJOICE."

David was fond of using this term (Ps. 61:4). He is referring to two things:

1. This speaks of the protection of God, which is symbolized by the wings, which every Believer can enjoy.

2. In the Tabernacle of old, the Cherubim, which were on either end of the Mercy Seat, stretched out their wings over the Mercy Seat, which symbolized the Divine Presence.

(8) "MY SOUL FOLLOWS HARD AFTER YOU: YOUR RIGHT HAND UPHOLDS ME."

This Verse is self-explanatory. Still, it means a degree of relationship and communion that is little known in modern Christendom. It means that we will follow no matter where He leads. Many Christians follow if it is profitable (or if they think it is). But when they face a difficult time, many will cease to follow.

The song says:

"Where He leads me I will follow,
"Where He leads me I will follow,
"Where He leads me I will follow,
"And go with me all the way!"

(9) "BUT THOSE WHO SEEK MY SOUL, TO DESTROY IT, SHALL GO INTO THE LOWER PARTS OF THE EARTH."

David is speaking of Saul and those who would ally themselves with Saul. Actually, David is saying that if they persisted in their actions, they would die lost without God and spend a never-ending eternity in Hell. Sadly, Saul never did repent. He died lost without God.

When one lifts one's hand against God's anointed and does not repent of it, the conclusion is outer darkness.

The people demanded Saul as their king and God allowed it, but Saul, in effect, was a *"work of the flesh."* Still, David would not lift a hand against him.

David was called of God, chosen of God, and anointed by God. As Saul was a *"work of the flesh,"* David was a *"work of the Spirit."* Yet Saul had no fear of opposing David, even to the point of attempting to kill him. Saul lost his soul because of this.

(10) "THEY SHALL FALL BY THE SWORD: THEY SHALL BE A PORTION FOR FOXES."

Both Verses 9 and 10 speak not only of David, but also of the Messiah. Exactly as the Holy Spirit predicted, it was brought to pass.

Saul *"fell by the sword."* In A.D. 70, all of Jerusalem *"fell by the sword."*

(11) "BUT THE KING SHALL REJOICE IN GOD; EVERY ONE WHO SWEARS BY HIM SHALL GLORY: BUT THE MOUTH OF THEM WHO SPEAK LIES SHALL BE STOPPED."

This speaks of David, and it came to pass exactly as stated here. However, it speaks even in greater measure of the Greater Son of David and His Second Coming (Rev., Chpt. 19).

PSALM 64

A Psalm of David:
Prayer for Protection

(1) "HEAR MY VOICE, O GOD, IN MY

PRAYER: PRESERVE MY LIFE FROM FEAR OF THE ENEMY."

This is a Psalm written by David and it speaks of the sweet singer of Israel, but even more so it speaks of the Coming Messiah.

In private the leaders of the Jews composed crafty questions for the Lord in an attempt to entangle Him in His teaching. They wanted to be in a position to accuse Him as a heretic or an insurgent either to the Sanhedrin or to the Roman Government. They wanted him to be condemned to execution.

Finally they succeeded, but not before it was time. In fact, Jesus Himself said, and I quote from THE EXPOSITOR'S STUDY BIBLE:

"Therefore does My Father love Me (proclaims that what Christ was to do held a special value in God's Heart), *because I lay down My Life* (the entirety of the idea of the Incarnation was to purposely *'lay down His Life'*), *that I might take it again* (the Resurrection).

"No man takes it from Me, but I lay it down of Myself (His Death was neither an execution nor an assassination; it was a Sacrifice; He allowed His Death to take place). *I have power to lay it down, and I have power to take it again* (proclaims that what He did, He did voluntarily; He did not step out of the path of obedience, for He died as commanded). *This Commandment have I received of My Father.* (This means that God the Father gave Him the latitude to do what He desired, and His desire was to do the Will of God; so He purposely laid down His Life)" (Jn. 10:17-18).

(2) "HIDE ME FROM THE SECRET COUNSEL OF THE WICKED; FROM THE INSURRECTION OF THE WORKERS OF INIQUITY."

"He came unto His Own, and His Own received Him not" (Jn. 1:11).

THE RELIGIOUS LEADERS OF ISRAEL

These men, the religious leaders of Israel, would go to any lengths to destroy Christ. The greatest *"iniquity"* of all is found in the realm of religion. (Religion is anything that is man-made; Salvation is that which is God-made, and is found only in the Word of God.)

Religion always will persecute true Salvation. (There is no Salvation in religion because religion is man-devised.)

Consequently, the *"wicked"* actually composed the Church of Jesus' day. The Church today, as always, is apostate, with the exception of a remnant that constitutes the True Body of Christ. The greatest hindrance to the Work of God today, as in Christ's day, is not the world, but rather the apostate Church.

(3) "WHO WHET THEIR TONGUE LIKE A SWORD, AND BEND THEIR BOWS TO SHOOT THEIR ARROWS, EVEN BITTER WORDS."

As is recorded in the Twenty-second Chapter of Matthew and the Eleventh Chapter of Luke, these *"wicked"* religious leaders devised their entanglements. Then, in public, they rudely and vehemently proposed their questions to Him.

In this Psalm are found His Comments about their conduct and His Appeal to God about it.

Even though this pertained to David, it pertains even more so to the Greater Son of David.

DAVID AND THE MESSIAH

The reason the Holy Spirit used David to parallel Christ is because it was through David and His lineage that the Messiah would come. The Lord told this to David in II Samuel, Chapter 7. We, therefore, find parallels to Christ in David's life and living.

Of course, we must understand that David was only human and he, therefore, experienced failures, even great failures, in his life, which in no way epitomized Christ, as should be obvious. As we here see, there also were many parallels; and, in such Psalms, we have David speaking, but referring to Christ at the same time.

Someone has said, *"The four Gospels proclaim the acts of Christ, while the Psalms portray His heart and His thoughts."* How wonderful it is to be able to look into the very heart of the Son of God! How wonderful to hear Him pray and petition the Father! This gives us a far greater insight into His Person.

(4) "THAT THEY MAY SHOOT IN SECRET AT THE PERFECT: SUDDENLY DO

THEY SHOOT AT HIM, AND FEAR NOT."

Jesus Christ was *"The Perfect."* He is the Only Perfect Man Who ever has lived.

THE PERFECTION OF CHRIST

Christ was Perfect in His Birth; Perfect in His Life; Perfect in His interpretation of the Word, for, in reality, He was the Living Word (Jn. 1:1); Perfect in His Death; Perfect in the Plan of Redemption, which He brought forth by His Death; Perfect in His Resurrection; Perfect in His Ascension; Perfect in His Exaltation; and Perfect in His Eternal Manhood, although He never ceased to be God.

Tragically enough, the religious leaders of Israel had no fear of God, because self-righteousness produces such a ridiculous position. Sadly, self-righteousness also plagues the majority of the modern Church.

JUSTIFICATION BY FAITH

Because of *"Justification by Faith,"* the word *"perfect"* also could be used of David and every other Believer.

It does not mean that David and the Believer are perfect within themselves; it does mean that God looks at David and the Believer as *"perfect"* because they have placed their trust in the Atoning Sacrifice of the Precious Blood of Jesus Christ, which He offered at Calvary's Cross. Then God looks at David and the Believer exactly as He looks at Christ.

Self-righteous man never can accept God's Righteousness; neither can God accept the self-righteous.

God cannot accept anything less than total and complete perfection. Knowing that such is impossible with man, this great work can be brought out in the Believer's life only in Christ. When the Believer accepts Christ, and puts his faith totally in the Redeemer and what He did for us at the Cross, such a Believer (no matter how much wickedness is in his past) now enters into the Perfection of Christ. That is the only way that God can justify sinful man.

I quote from THE EXPOSITOR'S STUDY BIBLE:

"To declare, I say, at this time, His Righteousness (refers to God's Righteousness, which must be satisfied at all time, and is in Christ and only Christ)*: that He* (God) *might be just* (not overlooking sin in any manner), *and the Justifier of him which believes in Jesus.* (God can justify a believing [although guilty] sinner without His Holiness being impacted, providing the sinner's faith is exclusively in Christ; only in this manner can God be *'just'* and at the same time *'justify'* the sinner)" (Rom. 3:26).

(5) "THEY ENCOURAGE THEMSELVES IN AN EVIL MATTER: THEY COMMUNE OF LAYING SNARES PRIVILY; THEY SAY, WHO SHALL SEE THEM?

(6) "THEY SEARCH OUT INIQUITIES; THEY ACCOMPLISH A DILIGENT SEARCH: BOTH THE INWARD THOUGHT OF EVERY ONE OF THEM, AND THE HEART, IS DEEP."

This pertains to David; but more than all, this Passage pertains to Christ.

THE EVIL OF SELF-RIGHTEOUSNESS

The word *"iniquities"* in this Verse means *"iniquitous questions"* — questions which the religious leaders of Israel hoped would involve Jesus with the Jewish or Roman Governments.

The addition, *"They accomplish a diligent search,"* expresses the satisfaction they felt at planning questions so clever and crafty that they were sure to accomplish their desired purpose.

Christ read their thoughts and knew their hearts. In this Verse, He gives His Judgment on both. He says their hearts were deep, meaning *"deep with iniquity."* In other words, despite the *"front"* they presented to Israel, their hearts were black with sin. We are speaking of the Church of Jesus' day.

Let me say it again:

There is no evil as deep, as bad, as wicked, or as ungodly as that of self-righteous religion. It was not the thieves and the harlots, as wicked as they were, who crucified Christ, but rather the religious leaders of Israel. So deep was their deception that they could kill the Lord in the Name of the Lord!

The situation, to be sure, has not changed at the present. Presently, the biggest hindrance to the Work of God on Earth is the world of organized religion. It seeks to protect its own at whatever price. It cares not at all for the Will of God. It cares only for its own will. And, to be sure, that will is full of iniquity, which means *"hearts deep"* with iniquity.

(7) "BUT GOD SHALL SHOOT AT THEM WITH AN ARROW; SUDDENLY SHALL THEY BE WOUNDED."

With many arrows, the religious leaders of Israel tried in vain to wound the Lord Jesus; but, without fail, God fatally wounded them with only one arrow, which is His Word.

It was not possible for them to overcome Christ. They were murderers at heart, but the Cross is the very reason for which Jesus came. But even though it was the Will of God for Jesus to go to the Cross, it was not the Will of God for the religious leaders of Israel to put Him on the Cross. God judged their hearts as murderous.

Peter said, and I quote from THE EXPOSITOR'S STUDY BIBLE:

"Him, being delivered by the determinate counsel and foreknowledge of God (it was the Plan of God that Jesus would die on the Cross; however, it was not the Plan of God for the religious leaders of Israel to do this thing; that was of their own making and choice), *you have taken, and by wicked hands have crucified and slain* (presents a charge so serious it absolutely defies description! But yet, if they will seek mercy and forgiveness, God will forgive them, even as we shall see)" (Acts 2:23).

The Holy Spirit through Stephen also said:

"You stiffnecked and uncircumcised in heart and ears (presents Stephen using the same language as Moses, when he conveyed God's rebuke to Israel [Deut. 10:16]), *you do always resist the Holy Spirit: as your fathers did, so do you* (everything carried out by God on Earth is through the Person and Office of the Holy Spirit; to resist Him is to resist God, for He is God; they resisted Him by resisting the Plan of God, Who and What was Jesus Christ).

"Which of the Prophets have not your fathers persecuted? (This is very similar to that stated by Christ [Mat. 5:12; 23:30-31, 34-37; Lk. 13:33-34].) *And they have slain them which showed before of the coming of the Just One* (they killed the Prophets who pointed to the One Who was to come, namely Jesus); *of Whom you have been now the betrayers and murderers* (is about as strong as anything that could be said; how different this is from most modern preaching!)" (Acts 7:51-52).

(8) "SO THEY SHALL MAKE THEIR OWN TONGUE TO FALL UPON THEMSELVES: ALL WHO SEE THEM SHALL FLEE AWAY."

The Holy Spirit here through David is saying that when these religious leaders stand before God at the Great White Throne Judgment, the bitter slanders of their tongues against Christ shall rise in judgment against them and cause them to perish.

So fearful will be their doom that, as in the case of Korah, Dathan, and Abiram, all seeing it shall flee.

(9) "AND ALL MEN SHALL FEAR, AND SHALL DECLARE THE WORK OF GOD; FOR THEY SHALL WISELY CONSIDER OF HIS DOING."

At this time, the time of the Great White Throne Judgment, all of Heaven shall fear and shall pronounce the judgment to be from God; they will intelligently ascribe it as His.

(10) "THE RIGHTEOUS SHALL BE GLAD IN THE LORD, AND SHALL TRUST IN HIM; AND ALL THE UPRIGHT IN HEART SHALL GLORY."

At the very time, again the time of the Great White Throne Judgment, when the Judgment of God shall fall upon all of these which fit this description, and for all time, then He Who is both Perfect (Vs. 4) and Righteous shall be glorified together with the upright — He upon His Throne and they round about it, which will include all Believers, for all time.

The account of the Great White Throne Judgment is found in Revelation 20:11-15.

At this Judgment, only unbelievers will be there. No Believers will stand there, simply because our sins have been judged in Christ and what He did for us at the Cross. So humanity can face Christ at the Cross, or face Him at the Great White Throne Judgment. Whether a person believes this or not, every individual who has ever lived will face Christ in one way or the other. Indeed, face Him they shall!

PSALM 65

*A Psalm of David:
Praise and Thanksgiving to God*

(1) "PRAISE WAITS FOR YOU, O GOD, IN SION: AND UNTO YOU SHALL THE VOW BE PERFORMED."

This Psalm was written by David and it involves itself in the Blessings of God that come upon those who will trust the Lord and will stand upon His Promises. Several things are here said:

PRAISE

The phrase, *"Praise waits for You,"* speaks of the constant praise that should come from the hearts of all Believers to God. It might seem to the unspiritual eye that the Passages in Psalms concerning *"praise"* are overly repetitive; however, to the spiritual eye, it is obvious that the Holy Spirit is informing us how important *"praise"* is to our continued victory. It is impossible to praise God too much. It is certainly possible to praise Him too little.

THE LORD OUR GOD

The phrase, *"O God, in Sion,"* refers to the Sanctuary and the Ark of the Covenant, which were in Jerusalem. Under the Old Covenant, completed praise to God had to be at the Sanctuary because that was where God resided between the Mercy Seat and the Cherubim. Now, under the New Covenant, God resides within our hearts (I Cor. 3:16). This was made possible by the Cross!

Consequently, the praise is completed in the heart of the Believer due to the Lord's dwelling within — again, as stated, all made possible by the Cross.

THE VOW

The phrase, *"And unto You shall the vow be performed,"* refers to the Promise of David made to God concerning continuous praise despite situations or circumstances. This should be our *"vow"* as well. Praise waits not in the silence of apprehension, but in confident expectation for the promised moment of Christ's Coming. All praise ultimately points to His Coming.

THE KINGDOM AGE

This Psalm also points to the Coming Kingdom Age, when Jesus Christ will reign over a happy Earth. At that time, Israel will perform her vow of praise, and so will every Believer. Then the converted nations will unite with Israel in the worship of the Messiah. Then the Gentiles will rejoice with His people (Rom. 15:10). He will reign, not only in Zion, but also over the entire Earth; He will fill it with happiness and joy.

(2) "O THOU WHO HEARS PRAYER, UNTO YOU SHALL ALL FLESH COME."

This Verse is freighted with the Promises of God.

PRAYER

The phrase, *"O Thou Who hears prayer,"* presents a Promise to all that God hears our believing petitions. The sadness of the modern Church is that it rarely believes in travailing prayer. We know that because so little of it is done.

Someone has said, *"Prayer changes things."* Really, prayer changes people, and people change things.

As stated elsewhere in this Volume, in October of 1991 we began a regimen of two prayer meetings a day, because I felt that the Lord told me to do such. This was carried on every day except Saturday morning and Sunday. We continued this regimen for over ten years, and I personally continue it myself even unto this day.

Through these prayer meetings, the Lord has revolutionized my Christian experience. When we began in 1991, the Lord spoke to my heart and said, *"Do not seek Me so much for what I can do, but rather for Who I am."* In other words, the Lord wanted a more developed relationship to be put in place, which it was.

Out of that relationship came the great Revelation of the Cross, which took place in 1997, a Revelation which continues growing unto this very hour. I firmly believe that had I not obeyed the Lord regarding the prayer meetings, then the Revelation of the Cross never would have taken place.

A Christian who doesn't have a prayer life

really has no relationship with the Lord; such a Christian can expect precious little from the Lord.

We really should take everything to the Lord in prayer, believing His multitudinous Promises (Jer. 33:3; Mat. 18:18; 21:22; Jn. 15:7; Mk. 11:24).

THE LORD IS NO RESPECTER OF PERSONS

The phrase, *"Unto You shall all flesh come,"* refers to the Lord being no respecter of persons. He will entertain all earnest and honest seekers.

This Passage also speaks of the coming Kingdom Age, when ambassadors from all over the world will come to the Lord Jesus Christ, Who will be governing from Jerusalem, to present their petitions unto Him. He will give them instant answers, which will revolutionize their countries, peoples, and circumstances.

(3) "INIQUITIES PREVAIL AGAINST ME: AS FOR OUR TRANSGRESSIONS, YOU SHALL PURGE THEM AWAY."

David is saying here that iniquitous actions prevail against him by his enemies. But he then says that his heart, made penitent by the Holy Spirit, does not speak further of man's transgressions against him, but only of his own transgressions against God. His faith looks forward for purging to Calvary, as our faith now looks back to Calvary. Faith then said, *"You shall purge"*; faith now says, *"You have purged."*

THE SHED BLOOD OF THE LORD JESUS CHRIST

With all sin being purged by the Precious Blood of Christ, fellowship with God is possible (I Jn. 1:7), and the joys of that fellowship become a conscious experience.

God, in righteous fidelity to His Promises, will answer the prayer of His people for deliverance from their persecutors by terrible deeds of judgment upon these evildoers.

As He executed terrible things in Righteousness upon Pharaoh and his people in the past, so He will upon the Antichrist and his host in the future, and thus ever be to His Saints the God of our Salvation.

The Cross of Christ (and the Cross of Christ alone) made it possible for all sins to be washed away. It was there that Jesus atoned for all sin, past, present, and future, at least for all who will believe; He did so by the giving of Himself as a Sacrifice — a Perfect Sacrifice, we might quickly add — which God the Father accepted in totality.

If our faith is in Christ and what He has done for us at the Cross, then we will be accepted. The Sacrifice accepted means that the person also is accepted; the sacrifice rejected means that the person too is rejected. Only One Sacrifice is accepted by God, and that is the Sacrifice of His Only Son, the Lord Jesus Christ (Jn. 3:16; Heb. 10:12).

(4) "BLESSED IS THE MAN WHOM YOU CHOOSE, AND CAUSE TO APPROACH UNTO YOU, THAT HE MAY DWELL IN YOUR COURTS: WE SHALL BE SATISFIED WITH THE GOODNESS OF YOUR HOUSE, EVEN OF YOUR HOLY TEMPLE."

Whom does God choose and cause to approach unto Himself?

THE LORD JESUS CHRIST

The only One Who meets the criteria laid down here by the Holy Spirit is the Lord Jesus Christ.

Moreover, we are chosen, that is, if we properly abide in Christ. It is only in Christ, through Christ, and by Christ, and what He did for us at the Cross, that we can approach God. Jesus said, *". . . For without Me* (what He did for us at the Cross) *you can do nothing.* (The Believer should read that phrase over and over)" (Jn. 15:5).

Jesus Christ Alone has met all the conditions prescribed by God the Father, and He did it as our Substitute, which means that if our faith is placed in Him and what He did to us at the Cross, we will reap all the benefits for which He died (Rom. 5:1-2).

(5) "BY TERRIBLE THINGS IN RIGHTEOUSNESS WILL YOU ANSWER US, O GOD OF OUR SALVATION; WHO ARE THE CONFIDENCE OF ALL THE ENDS OF THE EARTH, AND OF THEM WHO ARE AFAR OFF UPON THE SEA."

At the time of this writing, and for all the years of the distant past, God has not been *"the Confidence"* of all people; however, He is worthy of such, and this statement proclaims by faith that this will be in the eternal future. One day Jesus will reign supreme upon Planet Earth; then He will be *"the Confidence of all."*

(6) "WHICH BY HIS STRENGTH SETS FAST THE MOUNTAINS; BEING GIRDED WITH POWER."

With *"His strength"* He will still the tumult of the people and so establish universal peace. This will happen in the coming Kingdom Age.

In the past, many Godly men have known the right, but they did not have the might; He not only will know the right, but will have the might to do what needs to be done — *"being girded with power."*

(7) "WHICH STILLS THE NOISE OF THE SEAS, THE NOISE OF THEIR WAVES, AND THE TUMULT OF THE PEOPLE."

There is an unsettling spirit that always has plagued the Earth. This unsettling spirit has been caused by man's estrangement from God. When Jesus reigns, the following will happen:

1. The spirit of the people of the Earth will be settled.

2. The angry *"noise"* of nature, with its cyclones, hurricanes, earthquakes, tidal waves, famines, etc., will be stilled. As stated, this will take place in the coming Kingdom Age, which will last for a thousand years before the Perfect Age begins. (Rev., Chpts. 20-22).

(8) "THEY ALSO WHO DWELL IN THE UTTERMOST PARTS ARE AFRAID AT YOUR TOKENS: YOU MAKE THE OUTGOINGS OF THE MORNING AND EVENING TO REJOICE."

The demonstration of His Power over nature and over man will compel all who dwell in the uttermost parts of the Earth to worship Him.

The Millennial bliss pictured in Verses 8 through 13 is entrancing. The phrase, *"You make the outgoings of the morning and evening to rejoice,"* means *"the entire Earth."* The morning and evening of every day, from one end of Heaven to the other, will witness undiminished joy.

At that time, every Saint of God who has ever lived will rule and reign with Christ and will function in Glorified Bodies; the difference will be comparable to the difference between a little child and a mature adult. In other words, what we then shall have, and what we then shall do, will be so far ahead of what we now have, and what we now do, as to be of no comparison.

(9) "YOU VISIT THE EARTH, AND WATER IT: YOU GREATLY ENRICH IT WITH THE RIVER OF GOD, WHICH IS FULL OF WATER: YOU PREPARE THEM CORN, WHEN YOU HAVE SO PROVIDED FOR IT."

This has reference to several things which follow:

THE BLESSINGS OF GOD

The watering of the Earth has to do not only with great fertility being brought back to the entirety of the planet; it also speaks of the Blessings and Presence of God that will *"visit the Earth."* So these Passages not only speak of fertility gripping the Planet in a manner it has never known, but also speak of the Presence and Power of God which is necessary to bring all of this to pass.

Man has ever tried to bring blessing and prosperity without the Blessings of God. It cannot be done! Before prosperity must come the Presence.

THE RIVER OF GOD

The phrase, *"The River of God,"* refers to the River of the Sanctuary that will flow out from under the threshold of the Temple that will be built at the beginning of the Millennial Reign (Ezek., Chpt. 47). The Holy Spirit through Ezekiel said, *"And every thing shall live whither the River comes"* (Ezek. 47:9).

The phrase, *"Full of water,"* refers to the deserts that then will blossom as a rose (Isa. 35:1).

(10) "YOU WATER THE RIDGES THEREOF ABUNDANTLY: YOU SETTLE THE FURROWS THEREOF: YOU MAKE IT SOFT WITH SHOWERS: YOU BLESS THE SPRINGING THEREOF."

This Passage is so freighted with blessing that it is difficult to put the entirety of the meaning here given by the Holy Spirit into English (or any other language).

THE COMING KINGDOM AGE

All of this means that years, as well as days, will be crowned with goodness. Hill and vale will be covered with golden grain; the pastures will be clothed with flocks; and Earth's happy inhabitants will be constrained to sing aloud and shout for joy. It will be a time of Heaven on Earth.

It is called the *"One-Thousand-Year Millennial Reign"* (Rev., Chpt. 20). Then Jesus Christ will reign supreme from Jerusalem as the Premier of the Earth.

Isaiah said:

"The Government shall be upon His shoulder . . . Of the increase of His Government and Peace there shall be no end" (Isa. 9:6-7).

(11) "YOU CROWN THE YEAR WITH YOUR GOODNESS; AND YOUR PATHS DROP FATNESS."

Men have ever looked to the beginning of each new year with hope and anticipation; they are always disappointed. With the Advent of the Son of Man, however, each year will come forth with Promise, *"Crowned"* with His *"Goodness."* The entirety of each and every year will *"drop fatness,"* which means continual and everlasting prosperity — physically, domestically, materially, and spiritually.

(12) "THEY DROP UPON THE PASTURES OF THE WILDERNESS: AND THE LITTLE HILLS REJOICE ON EVERY SIDE."

This *"fatness"* will extend to the *"wilderness,"* with even the *"little hills* (insignificant places) *rejoicing on every side."*

(13) "THE PASTURES ARE CLOTHED WITH FLOCKS; THE VALLEYS ALSO ARE COVERED OVER WITH CORN; THEY SHOUT FOR JOY, THEY ALSO SING."

The Hebrew Text is very emphatic and actually says, *"They shall most certainly sing."* Nothing then shall take away the song of God's Glory.

THE SONG OF BLESSING

Psalm 65 is one of David's greatest songs of blessing. Later, no doubt, it was sung many times by the great choirs at the Temple in anticipation of the coming Glory. It should be sung by every Child of God today. It will be sung by every Child of God tomorrow.

Please allow us to reiterate:

Every single *"praise"* of God is an exclamation and a proclamation of faith, which, in effect, is saying, *"One day all sin, suffering, and sorrow will cease, and the Glory of God will cover the Earth as the waters cover the sea."*

PSALM 66

The Writer is Unknown:
A Song of Praise and Worship

(1) "MAKE A JOYFUL NOISE UNTO GOD, ALL YE LANDS."

There is no hint as to who wrote this Psalm. David could have written it, but there is no proof.

This Psalm will be sung by Israel and the Messiah at the opening of the Millennium. She will recite His past Action with her enemies and with herself. She will offer the Sacrifices of Praise promised when in trouble (Vss. 13-15); she will invite all who fear God to listen to her testimony as to His Faithfulness and Love and the fulfillment to her of His Promises of Deliverance.

(2) "SING FORTH THE HONOR OF HIS NAME: MAKE HIS PRAISE GLORIOUS."

The *"Name"* of the Lord Jesus Christ has never been honored in the Earth; it never was even honored by Israel, but rather was blasphemed. Now, at long last, at the beginning of the great Kingdom Age, the *"Name"* of the Messiah will be honored all over the world, and all men will sing His praises. The *"Glory of His Name"* will be universal.

(3) "SAY UNTO GOD, HOW TERRIBLE ARE YOU IN YOUR WORKS! THROUGH THE GREATNESS OF YOUR POWER SHALL YOUR ENEMIES SUBMIT THEMSELVES UNTO YOU."

The word *"terrible"* has reference to the *"greatness of Your power."* The Lord is not just mighty; He is Almighty. Due to this *"power,"* all *"enemies"* on the Earth will *"submit themselves unto You."*

For some 6,000 years, God has shown His love to this Planet with only occasional demonstrations of His Power. In the Kingdom Age to come, He will show not only His great Love, but He also will continuously show His great Power. No *"enemy"* will dare seek to circumvent His Will.

(4) "ALL THE EARTH SHALL WORSHIP

YOU, AND SHALL SING UNTO YOU; THEY SHALL SING TO YOUR NAME. SELAH."

This will be the time of universal praise and universal worship. Both the Gentile and the Jew shall likewise *"worship."*

The hit songs of the day no longer will be praise to drugs, immorality, or Satanic influence; rather *"all the Earth . . . shall sing to Your Name."* When this happens, the Earth will yield her increase and prosperity will rule. The Earth presently suffers want and poverty because there is little praise of His Name (Ps. 67:6).

(5) "COME AND SEE THE WORKS OF GOD: HE IS TERRIBLE IN HIS DOING TOWARD THE CHILDREN OF MEN."

At the beginning of the Millennial Reign, through its entirety, and then forever, the constant topic of conversation will be *"the Works of God."*

The word *"terrible"* has the sense of *"works"* being so great and awesome that they literally will cause men to tremble.

(6) "HE TURNED THE SEA INTO DRY LAND: THEY WENT THROUGH THE FLOOD ON FOOT: THERE DID WE REJOICE IN HIM."

The sense of this Verse is that if one doubts what God will do in the future, one should look back at what He has done in the past.

This speaks of the crossing of the Red Sea, when the Children of Israel went across on *"dry land."*

The *"rejoicing"* spoken of refers to the great Campmeeting on the shore of the Red Sea after the terrible army of Pharaoh had drowned (Ex., Chpt. 15).

(7) "HE RULES BY HIS POWER FOREVER; HIS EYES BEHOLD THE NATIONS: LET NOT THE REBELLIOUS EXALT THEMSELVES. SELAH."

Pharaoh thought he could usurp authority over God. He even asked the question, *"Who is the LORD, that I should obey His Voice to let Israel go?"* (Ex. 5:2). Pharaoh would learn that *"God rules."*

The latter portion of the Verse speaks of the seven nations of Canaan that attempted to keep Israel from gaining the Promised Land. They would *"exalt themselves"*; they would be destroyed.

Let every nation realize that God rules in the affairs of men. His Way ultimately will triumph. *"Let not the rebellious"* think they can overcome Him.

(8) "O BLESS OUR GOD, YE PEOPLE, AND MAKE THE VOICE OF HIS PRAISE TO BE HEARD."

In view of what the Lord has done and what He shall do, we should *"Bless our God."*

Oftentimes, the Holy Spirit will refer us to the past in order to give us faith for the future. This Psalm proclaims that.

The Holy Spirit also tells us that *"His praise"* is not to be silent; rather, it is *"to be heard."*

Would this be the case in most modern Churches? I think not!

(9) "WHICH HOLDS OUR SOUL IN LIFE, AND SUFFERS NOT OUR FEET TO BE MOVED."

These Passages speak three things:

1. It has to do with the writer and all those who lived then.

2. It has to do with us and all who live now.

3. It has to do with Israel that ultimately will be restored by God at the beginning of the Kingdom Age.

The Lord Alone can *"hold our soul in life,"* which means to preserve our Salvation.

THE GREAT CONTEST BETWEEN GOD AND SATAN

In the great contest of the ages between God and Satan, Satan says of Job, *"He will curse You* (God) *to Your face"* (Job 1:11). Satan did not succeed, and Job's feet did not move. God will have a people who, no matter the severity of the test or the trial, will be steadfast and unmovable in their faith. God gives us that strength!

(10) "FOR YOU, O GOD, HAVE PROVED US: YOU HAVE TRIED US, AS SILVER IS TRIED."

Great faith must be tested greatly. The modern Faith Message attempts to deny the *"proving."* It is not to be denied.

Even the Messiah *"learned obedience by the things which He suffered"* (Heb. 5:8).

This does not mean that He learned to be obedient; had that been the case, that would imply that He had been disobedient, which He never was. Rather He learned what obedience to God is *"by the things which He suffered."*

(11) "YOU BROUGHT US INTO THE

NET; YOU LAID AFFLICTION UPON OUR LOINS."

The phrase, *"You brought us into the net,"* refers to Israel being delivered from Egyptian bondage, when, immediately before that deliverance, they had been hemmed in by the Red Sea, the Egyptians, and the wilderness (Ex. 14:3-4).

The phrase, *"You laid affliction upon our loins,"* refers to the time of their slavery before deliverance (Ex., Chpt. 1).

(12) "YOU HAVE CAUSED MEN TO RIDE OVER OUR HEADS; WE WENT THROUGH FIRE AND THROUGH WATER: BUT YOU BROUGHT US OUT INTO A WEALTHY PLACE."

The phrase, *"You have caused men to ride over our heads,"* refers to Israel being ruled by the Egyptians for a period of approximately one hundred years.

Why did the Lord allow this?

If Israel had not been forced into servitude, they never would have desired to leave Egypt. So the Lord had to allow them to be brought to a place of such subjugation that they would cry to the Lord for deliverance. And they did! (Ex. 3:7).

The phrase, *"We went through fire and through water,"* speaks of the unceasing efforts of Satan and man to destroy Israel utterly. Satan will do no less to modern Believers!

The phrase, *"But you brought us out into a wealthy place,"* refers to the Promised Land.

In its plenary meaning, it speaks of Israel rejoicing in her position and place regarding the Kingdom Age. Her Twelve Tribes will appear at Mount Zion upon the Millennial Morn and so demonstrate the truth of Verse 9. They will then testify that the chastisements justly laid upon them (Vss. 10-12) were designed in love and executed in wisdom.

(13) "I WILL GO INTO YOUR HOUSE WITH BURNT OFFERINGS: I WILL PAY YOU MY VOWS."

In view of what God has done for Israel, the writer of this Psalm says that he will offer to the Lord *"Burnt Offerings,"* which signifies the price paid at Calvary by the Lord Jesus Christ.

BURNT OFFERINGS

This Passage also refers to the coming Millennial Age, when Israel will once again offer the Sacrifices and will finally be faithful in the paying of their *"vows."* The Sacrifices will then be offered as a memorial of what Christ has done for them in ages past.

Even though this Passage was written by a Jew for the Jewish people, the Text obviously also refers to all that which is held dear by Christendom.

The great deliverance by God of the Children of Israel from Egyptian bondage is symbolic of the great Deliverance effected upon all Believers at Salvation and in our daily walk before God. This deliverance ever will be held up as that example. The *"Burnt Offering"* and the *"Incense of rams"* (Vs. 15) also speak of Calvary, in that Christ was offered up as the Perfect Sacrifice in order that *"whosoever will may come and drink of the water of life freely."* Calvary ever will be the criteria for all praise and worship for the Redemption of man.

(14) "WHICH MY LIPS HAVE UTTERED, AND MY MOUTH HAS SPOKEN, WHEN I WAS IN TROUBLE."

The *"trouble"* here spoken of refers to the terrible bondage of sin that grips the human race, from which Christ Alone can deliver. Our *"lips"* should ever *"utter"* this great Deliverance made possible to all who have accepted the *"Sacrifice"* of Himself that He has offered.

(15) "I WILL OFFER UNTO YOU BURNT SACRIFICES OF FATLINGS, WITH THE INCENSE OF RAMS; I WILL OFFER BULLOCKS WITH GOATS. SELAH."

The writer was so thankful for God's Deliverance that he promised the offering up of these *"Sacrifices"* in thanksgiving.

The Christian also should ever praise the Lord for Calvary.

During the Kingdom Age, such Sacrifices will be offered again, always as a memorial of what Jesus Christ did for us at Calvary's Cross (Ezek., Chpts. 40-48).

(16) "COME AND HEAR, ALL YE WHO FEAR GOD, AND I WILL DECLARE WHAT HE HAS DONE FOR MY SOUL."

The greatest witness in the world occurs when redeemed souls tell others what the Lord has done for them. The great invitation here is:

"Come and hear."

This is the Message that must be taken to the entire world. It actually is the forerunner of the Great Commission (Mk. 16:15).

God requires that we always tell others what He has done for us. This testimony must never be muted. We must ever say, *"Come and hear."*

(17) "I CRIED UNTO HIM WITH MY MOUTH, AND HE WAS EXTOLLED WITH MY TONGUE."

Our *"tongue"* should be used always to praise the Lord. We should praise Him so much that we have no time left for gossip, slander, or foolishness.

(18) "IF I REGARD INIQUITY IN MY HEART, THE LORD WILL NOT HEAR ME."

Two things are said here:

THE TONGUE

Our *"tongue"* constantly should be praising the Lord, leaving no time for *"iniquity."*

Regrettably, the tongue of man, even Believers, is so volatile that it cannot be tamed by man.

Concerning the tongue, James said, and I quote from THE EXPOSITOR'S STUDY BIBLE:

"But the tongue can no man tame (this is the Word of Lord; however, the tongue can most definitely be tamed by the Holy Spirit; the way it is done has to do with the Cross of Christ; the Holy Spirit works within the parameters of the Finished Work of Christ on the Cross; He demands that we ever make the Cross the Object of our Faith, and then He can do mighty things within our lives [Rom. 8:1-2, 11]); *it is an unruly evil, full of deadly poison.* (The Believer must realize this. It means that just because he is Saved, such doesn't necessarily guarantee a change in this problem. As stated, it definitely can be and must be changed, but it can only be so by and through the Cross of Christ)" (James 3:8).

INIQUITY IN THE HEART

If we do not obey the Lord by constantly *"extolling"* the Lord with our praises, then iniquity will fill our hearts. If this happens, it will stop our prayers from being answered.

The reason most prayers are never heard is because individuals will not confess the sin that lurks within their hearts and repent of it. God cannot answer prayer when such exists. Sin must be put away and washed by the Blood of Jesus. It will instantly be done if we abide by the Word (I Jn. 1:9).

(19) "BUT VERILY GOD HAS HEARD ME; HE HAS ATTENDED TO THE VOICE OF MY PRAYER."

The writer is saying that God has heard him, proving that he had not held onto or loved iniquity in his heart.

The writer is speaking of the great Sacrifice of Calvary (Vss. 13-15) that has covered and washed his sin away, thereby opening the path to God.

(20) "BLESSED BE GOD, WHICH HAS NOT TURNED AWAY MY PRAYER, NOR HIS MERCY FROM ME."

Now the writer thanks the Lord for prayer that is answered and praise that is accepted.

Let us warn again:

Prayer can be and will be *"turned away"* if any Believer *"regards iniquity in his heart."*

"Mercy" cannot be extended, nor prayer answered, in such a situation. The channel to God can only be kept open if we depend on Calvary and what Jesus did for us there at the Cross. We must forsake all sin as the Lord lives in us (Gal. 2:20).

Actually, sin and iniquity cannot be overcome unless the Believer places his faith exclusively in Christ and the Cross, which then will give the Holy Spirit latitude to work in our lives. Without Him, none of this can be done.

As we say over and over, *"Christ is the Source, while the Cross is the Means"* (Rom. 6:1-14; 8:1-2, 11; I Cor. 1:17-18, 23; 2:2; Gal., Chpt. 5; 6:14).

PSALM 67

The Writer is Unknown:
Let All the People Praise You

(1) "GOD BE MERCIFUL UNTO US, AND BLESS US; AND CAUSE HIS FACE TO SHINE UPON US; SELAH."

The writer of this Psalm is nameless, and yet it contains one of the greatest Revelations found in the entirety of the Word of God. It really is a continuation of the previous Psalm, but with even greater expectation.

THE WORD OF GOD

According to the Scriptures, God chose Israel as His Agent to lead all nations to Him. To this end, He gave her a sufficient Revelation of Himself and of His Salvation.

Israel refused this high honor; nevertheless, the Divine purpose has not been defeated. Israel will be restored (Rom., Chpts. 9-11). She yet will publish peace to the nations and win all people to the knowledge and Service of God. This will take place during the time of the coming Millennial Reign. It is of this great fact of the future that this Psalm sings. It fitly follows the preceding Psalm. God will bless Israel, and, as a result, all nations will fear Him.

Here appears a deep principle of the Word of God, true in all Dispensations, namely that the spiritual welfare of those far from God is dependent upon Revival and Restoration of the soul among Believers.

THE SHINING OF GOD'S FACE

The phrase, *"Cause His Face to shine upon us,"* is one of the most beautiful Passages found in the Bible. It signifies the Blessings of God upon the person or the people in question. The shining of His *"Face"* speaks of His *"Mercy"* and *"Blessing."* It speaks of God's Approval, and there could be nothing greater than that.

The Face of God shines upon Believers who have placed their faith and their trust exclusively in Christ and the Cross. Concerning this, Paul said, and I quote from THE EXPOSITOR'S STUDY BIBLE:

"But without Faith (in Christ and the Cross; any time Faith is mentioned, always, and without exception, its root meaning is that its Object is Christ and the Cross; otherwise, it is faith God will not accept) *it is impossible to please Him* (faith in anything other than Christ and the Cross greatly displeases the Lord)*: for he who comes to God must believe that He is* (places faith as the foundation and principle of the manner in which God deals with the human race)*, and that He* (God) *is a rewarder of them who diligently seek Him* (seek Him on the premise of Christ and Him Crucified)*"* (Heb. 11:6).

(2) "THAT YOUR WAY MAY BE KNOWN UPON EARTH, YOUR SAVING HEALTH AMONG ALL NATIONS."

The Prophetic Doctrine that the Salvation of the world depends upon the Restoration of Israel (Rom., Chpts. 11-12, 15) is repeated in the last two Verses, as it is affirmed in these first two Verses. This repetition emphasizes its importance.

The great moral lesson is taught here that spiritual prosperity is not to be desired for mere personal enjoyment, but also for the spiritual enrichment of others.

THE KINGDOM NOW PHILOSOPHY

The false doctrine of the *"Kingdom Now"* teaching states the opposite of this Psalm. This teaching states that Christianity ultimately will bring the world into submission to God, which then will signal His Second Coming.

To do this, the proposal is to vote into office political leaders who are favorable toward the Christian philosophy. This doctrine permeates much of the Charismatic world and other segments of Christendom. It is unscriptural; therefore, it is demonic.

The Church is not called on to save society. It is called on to save men out of society. Actually, present day society is doomed. It cannot be salvaged.

Even though the Church is commanded to take the Gospel of Jesus Christ to the world, still, the entirety of the Planet will not be evangelized or brought to the Lord until Jesus Christ comes back in what is referred to as the Second Coming. It is impossible to have a Kingdom Age until you have a King. Jesus Christ Alone is that King.

Only then will Israel be brought back to God and restored to her place of spiritual prominence. She then will go out to the nations of the world to proclaim the Glory of the Lord Jesus Christ. At that time, the Earth truly will serve the Lord (Isa. 66:18-21).

THE RAPTURE OF THE CHURCH

At this present moment, the true Church is waiting for the Trump of God, which will complete God's Salvation process. Believers are now washed, sanctified, and justified (I Cor. 6:11), but not yet glorified. When the Trump of God sounds at the First Resurrection of Life, only then will *"mortality put on immortality"* (I Cor., Chpt. 15). With the Glorifying of the Saints of God, God's Salvation process then will be complete.

After the Rapture, the world will be plunged into the Great Tribulation (II Thess., Chpt. 2). The purpose of this time of *"Jacob's Trouble"* will be to bring Israel back to God. Its theme will be the Second Coming.

These great Psalms portray the Restoration of Israel, which then, in the Kingdom Age, will bring the world to the Feet of Jesus Christ. Then *"all nations"* will know of *"His saving health."*

(3) "LET THE PEOPLE PRAISE YOU, O GOD; LET ALL THE PEOPLE PRAISE YOU."

Again, the Believer is brought back to the tremendous effect of *"praise."*

PRAISE

As we have stated in past Commentary, *"Praise"* is the most powerful prescription for Victory given by God. It is impossible to doubt and praise at the same time. Doubt says that God *"can't"*; *"Praise"* says, that God *"can."* All are commanded to *"praise Him."*

True *"praise"* stems from Calvary (and only from Calvary). This *"praise"* will guarantee victory for the Believer by causing God's *"Face to shine upon us."*

"Praise" says that Satan is defeated and that God ultimately will triumph over all things. Every Believer constantly should *"praise"*; every Church should shout the *"praises"* of God.

The number of people presently who continually praise God is small. However, the day is coming, speaking of the Kingdom Age, when every voice will sound His praises, every song will extol His Greatness, and every headline of every newspaper will proclaim His Power. It is not here now, but it is coming!

(4) "O LET THE NATIONS BE GLAD AND SING FOR JOY: FOR YOU SHALL JUDGE THE PEOPLE RIGHTEOUSLY, AND GOVERN THE NATIONS UPON EARTH. SELAH."

Most of the nations of the world of this day are not glad. They do not *"sing for joy."* Why not?

The reason is obvious. Men judge the people unrighteously. In other words, the great masses of the poor of the world do not get a *"fair shake,"* so to speak. For example:

When there is a catastrophe, such as the December 2004 earthquake in the Indian Ocean, which produced a tsunami that killed over 250,000 people, hundreds of billions of dollars were raised for relief. But the effected people saw precious little of that money. The rest was stolen. The same is true of most charitable efforts.

However, at the Second Coming of Christ, the Lord Jesus will take the government of the world upon His Shoulder, and He will then *"judge the people righteously."* Evil men now *"govern"*; then Jesus Christ will *"govern"* (Isa. 9:6-7).

(5) "LET THE PEOPLE PRAISE YOU, O GOD; LET ALL THE PEOPLE PRAISE YOU."

Verse 5 is a repetition of Verse 3 given by the Holy Spirit in a double manner so that all may know the significance that God places on His people praising Him.

Please understand:

It is not that God is on an *"ego trip."* That is not at all the idea! To even attribute such to God is foolishness.

The Lord desires praise for our benefit, not for His. The Lord doesn't need our praises. There actually is nothing we can do which would add anything to Him.

He desires praise for our benefit. When we praise Him, this shows that we understand Who He is and What He has done for us. It shows our dependence upon Him, and rightly so! It proclaims the fact that we trust Him, and do not give our lives to Satan.

Furthermore, *"Praise"* builds faith in God, trust in His Holy Name, and confidence that He will see us through, which He always does.

Precious few today praise the Lord. But the day is coming shortly when the entirety of the Earth will praise Him continually. That time is the Kingdom Age!

(6) "THEN SHALL THE EARTH YIELD HER INCREASE; AND GOD, EVEN OUR OWN GOD, SHALL BLESS US."

A remarkable Revelation is given to us in this Passage. Much of the world today is plagued by drought, famine, and starvation. Government planners are claiming that the population is too large. Because of the so-called *"overpopulation,"* abortion, which actually is murder, is being lawfully accepted in countries of the world. The proponents of abortion claim it reduces the population.

Let this be clearly understood:

The population is not the problem. The problem is sin. The problem is lack of praise to God, which sin produces. Even in its present state, were it not for war and demonic religion, the world today could feed approximately one hundred billion people.

During the Kingdom Age to come, when the curse is removed, it then will be possible to feed an unlimited number of people.

When the nations of the Earth begin to *"praise the Lord,"* then, and only then, will *"the Earth yield her increase."*

That's the main reason the Holy Spirit implores God's people to continually praise Him.

PROSPERITY

There is a reason that the United States is the bread basket of the world. By that I mean we grow enough foodstuff here in this country to feed ourselves plus several other nations. The reason is the Christians in this nation who truly know the Lord, who truly serve Him, who truly praise His Name.

Regrettably, that number is shrinking almost daily, which presents the greatest disaster this nation ever has known. Of course, the governmental leaders have no knowledge of what I am speaking about, but the Truth is exactly as the Word of God says it is. When people praise the Lord, Blessings follow!

ISLAM

Look at the religion of Islam and the nations of the world which are governed or strongly influenced by that religion. They are economic *"basket cases."* As well, there is precious little freedom in those countries, if any at all.

In some of these Muslim countries, if they had no oil, the people would be living an existence of total poverty, which most now do anyway. Actually, the billions of dollars produced by the oil wealth of those countries do not go the people, but rather to only a few families who are obscenely rich. The majority of the people really get nothing.

The religion of Islam is truly a failed philosophy in every capacity. It has failed economically; it has failed domestically; it has failed socially; and, above all, it has failed spiritually.

There is only one hope for the world, and He is the Lord Jesus Christ. Unfortunately, most of the world doesn't see it that way, and most of the world continues in its poverty, lack of freedom, and terrible spiritual bondage. There is no Salvation outside of Christ! There is no prosperity outside of Christ!

(7) "GOD SHALL BLESS US; AND ALL THE ENDS OF THE EARTH SHALL FEAR HIM."

The great *"Blessing"* of the Kingdom Age will follow the great *"Judgment"* of the Tribulation. God's Judgment poured out upon the Earth during the Great Tribulation will be exhibited only after the world has forgotten Him days without number, and only after the world has spurned His Grace and His Love. God's delight is in *"Blessing."* He wants to *"bless us."* He will do so when two things happen:

1. *"Let all the people praise You"* (Vs. 3).
2. *"And all the ends of the Earth shall fear Him"* (Vs. 7).

PSALM 68

A Psalm of David:
A Song of Triumph

(1) "LET GOD ARISE, LET HIS ENEMIES BE SCATTERED: LET THEM ALSO WHO HATE HIM FLEE BEFORE HIM."

This Psalm describes the bringing up of the Ark to Zion (I Chron., Chpt. 15). It was composed by David and sung as the Ark was being brought into the city. The Ark of God probably was the most important article of furniture in the entire Tabernacle, for God dwelt therein between the Mercy Seat and the Cherubim. (Now He dwells within our hearts [I Cor. 3:16].)

And yet, without the Brazen Altar, which typified Calvary, the High Priest could not even approach the Ark. Even then he only could do so once a year, which occurred on the Great Day of Atonement.

ENEMIES

Who were these enemies?

Then they consisted of heathen nations surrounding Israel who were idol worshippers. Behind these heathen nations were demon spirits promoting the activity against Israel. Israel always considered that her *"enemies"* also were God's *"enemies."* The Presence of God scatters *"enemies."*

Today our enemies are basically the same: the world, the flesh, and the Devil.

These *"enemies"* will not be *"scattered"* unless the Presence of God is obvious. (The Ark of God is the example.)

It is the Cross of Christ which has defeated all the powers of darkness, and Jesus did so by atoning for all sin, past, present, and future, at least for all who will believe (Jn. 3:16). Whenever the Believer places his faith exclusively in Christ and the Cross, he then is guaranteed the help of the Holy Spirit; once again, *"enemies are scattered."*

THE CROSS OF CHRIST

The statement I'm about to make is strong, but yet true.

It is impossible for any Believer to successfully live for God by doing so outside of God's Prescribed Order.

And what is that Prescribed Order?

Even though we've already given the following elsewhere in this Volume, it is so important that we ask the Reader to allow us to say it again:

1. FOCUS: The Lord Jesus Christ (Jn. 1:1, 14, 29; 3:3, 16).
2. OBJECT OF FAITH: The Cross of Christ (Rom. 6:1-14; Col. 2:14-15).
3. POWER SOURCE: The Holy Spirit (Rom. 8:1-2, 11).
4. RESULTS: Victory (Rom. 6:14).

(2) "AS SMOKE IS DRIVEN AWAY, SO DRIVE THEM AWAY: AS WAX MELTS BEFORE THE FIRE, SO LET THE WICKED PERISH AT THE PRESENCE OF GOD."

Satan and all of his powers are no match for the *"Presence of God"*; however, Satan is more than a match for any effort that we

NOTES

may make in the flesh. Sadly, most of the opposition that we bring against Satan is not *"after the Spirit,"* but *"after the flesh."* The most powerful emissaries of Satan tremble and *"melt"* at the *"Presence of God."*

WALKING AFTER THE SPIRIT

In modern terms, to have the *"Presence of God,"* we have to *"walk after the Spirit"* (Rom. 8:1).

How does the Believer do that?

First let's see what it doesn't mean!

Doing spiritual things, as noble and right as they may be in their own perspective, are not what Paul here is addressing. Regrettably, most modern Christians think that the doing of spiritual things constitutes *"walking after the Spirit."* It doesn't!

"Walking after the Spirit" refers, of course, to the Holy Spirit. It refers to the Believer placing his faith exclusively in Christ and the Cross, within which parameters the Holy Spirit works, and within which parameters the Holy Spirit works exclusively.

Paul said, *"For the Law of the Spirit of Life in Christ Jesus has made me free from the Law of Sin and Death"* (Rom. 8:2).

This one Verse tells us exactly how the Holy Spirit works. As stated, He works within the parameters of the Finished Work of Christ, which pertains exclusively to the Cross. That's what the phrase, *"In Christ Jesus,"* actually means.

In fact, whenever Paul uses such a phrase, or even one of its derivatives, such as *"In Him,"* *"In Whom,"* etc., always, and without exception, he is speaking of the Cross of Christ.

Now that we understand how the Holy Spirit works, our faith must be anchored in Christ and the Cross. This the Holy Spirit demands (Gal., Chpt. 5).

WALKING AFTER THE FLESH

Paul uses the term *"walk"* (or *"walking"*) quite a number of times in his writings. It refers to the manner and the way that we as Believers live our life before the world and before God. It is described as a *"walk."*

"Walking after the flesh" occurs when the Believer places his faith in something (or anything) other than Christ and the Cross. The Lord classifies such as *"flesh,"* i.e.,

"trusting in one's self."

Many Believers have it in their minds that *"walking after the flesh"* consists of watching too much television, being too interested in sports, or a hundred and one other similar things. Even though those things may or may not be right, they really have nothing to do with the subject matter at hand.

"Walking after the Spirit" occurs when the Believer places his faith exclusively in Christ and the Cross, while *"walking after the flesh"* occurs when the Believer places his faith anywhere else other than the Cross, be it his Church, a particular religious Denomination, his own good works, etc.

The *"Presence of God"* cannot abide anything that is of the flesh. It can only abide in the realm of that which originates with the Lord. In fact, the *"Presence of God"* is the Holy Spirit in His Function and Operation.

(3) "BUT LET THE RIGHTEOUS BE GLAD; LET THEM REJOICE BEFORE GOD: YEA, LET THEM EXCEEDINGLY REJOICE."

The *"righteous"* need have no fear of Satan, providing the *"Presence of God"* is obvious. Our attitude should be that of *"rejoicing,"* even to *"rejoicing exceedingly."*

The worship described in the Book of Psalms far eclipses even that of modern Pentecostal or Charismatic Churches. This type of worship is hilarious, even to the point where most would consider it fanatical. And now the next Verse will tell us how to worship!

(4) "SING UNTO GOD, SING PRAISES TO HIS NAME: EXTOL HIM WHO RIDES UPON THE HEAVENS BY HIS NAME JAH, AND REJOICE BEFORE HIM."

"JAH" is an abbreviation for Jehovah. He is the One Who is, Who was, and Who is to come. In other words, He is the Self-existent One. Actually, the Name or Title *"JAH"* is only used here.

THE GREATNESS AND GLORY OF GOD

The theme of this Verse is to extol the Greatness and Glory of God. This is commanded by the Holy Spirit for a reason. Satan denies God's Greatness and Glory. As well, the majority of the Earth (the far greater majority) is instead blaspheming God. All of this blasphemy comes up into the spirit world and is heard by both God and Satan. If God's people do not praise the Lord, then all that is heard from Planet Earth in the spirit world is hatred for God and blasphemy. Consequently, whenever the Believer praises the Lord, in effect, he is saying the following:

1. God will handle my problems;
2. Satan is a defeated foe;
3. The Child of God is desiring for the spirit world to know and understand which side he is on. His praises tell all!; and,
4. The praises of the Saints are statements of faith proclaiming that ultimately the entirety of the Earth will praise the Lord.

SINGING

David *"Sang unto God."* Undoubtedly, he accompanied himself on his harp. David also was an excellent singer. But every Believer, no matter the quality of his voice, should *"sing unto God."*

Whenever a Church loses its way with God, the first thing that goes is the praise song. Conversely, when a Church is on fire for God, they truly *"sing praises to His Name."* The spirituality of the Church is mirrored in its singing of praises unto the Lord, or the lack thereof.

We also learn from all of these Passages just how important singing and music are to worship and praise. Because the Lord devoted the longest Book in the Bible, the Psalms (which, in reality, is a Book of Songs), to this form of worship, we know from this just how much He values such. We should not let this lesson be lost on us.

(5) "A FATHER OF THE FATHERLESS, AND A JUDGE OF THE WIDOWS, IS GOD IN HIS HOLY HABITATION."

There are two facts of peculiar sweetness which are here prominent.

First, this Mighty God, in His distant habitation and in the sinless Essence of His Being, is a Father of fatherless and a Guardian of the widow.

Second, He restores and enriches rebellious sinners, at least when they humble themselves, cease their rebellion, and look exclusively to Him.

(6) "GOD SETS THE SOLITARY IN FAMILIES: HE BRINGS OUT THOSE WHICH ARE BOUND WITH CHAINS: BUT THE

REBELLIOUS DWELL IN A DRY LAND."

Several things are said in this beautiful and powerful Verse.

THE SOLITARY

The word *"solitary"* means *"singular"* or *"one."* In the Hebrew, the word is *"yachid,"* which means that the *"one"* will unite.

God oftentimes has one person in a family who is serving Him; consequently, the Salvation of the entire family is dependent upon that one person. Instead of the person lamenting the fact that he is the only one in his family living for God, he rather should thank God for the privilege of being the *"one"* who has accepted Christ, the *"one"* who now has the opportunity to *"bring out those which are bound with chains."*

Actually, all people who do not know Jesus Christ are in bondage to Satan. It is the same as being *"bound with chains."* It is impossible for them to extricate themselves; therefore, the one person, the solitary, the lone Believer, can be used of God to bring others to Christ, which causes their chains to be broken.

Last of all, if the light given by the solitary one is rebuked, the Lord says, *"The rebellious shall dwell in a dry land."* For those who do not heed the Gospel, there is no sustenance. They will continue to *"dwell in a dry land."*

(7) "O GOD, WHEN YOU WENT FORTH BEFORE YOUR PEOPLE, WHEN YOU DID MARCH THROUGH THE WILDERNESS; SELAH."

By inspiration, David is taking the singer (Reader) back to the wilderness experience of Israel. He says that, first of all, God asked the people to go only where He had gone *"before"* them. It was God's Will that His people go through the wilderness, but it was not His Will that they remain in the wilderness as long as they did.

The thirty-eight years of wandering was because of their failure. It was God's Perfect Will that they only remain in this howling wilderness for two years or less.

(8) "THE EARTH SHOOK, THE HEAVENS ALSO DROPPED AT THE PRESENCE OF GOD: EVEN SINAI ITSELF WAS MOVED AT THE PRESENCE OF GOD, THE GOD OF ISRAEL."

NOTES

This Passage is a clear reference to the time when Israel received the Law at Sinai (Ex. 19:16-25).

This Passage also speaks of the terrible *"wilderness"* that Israel will have to go through during the Great Tribulation, the time of Jacob's Trouble.

During the Battle of Armageddon, Jesus Christ will come back. At that time, it will seem as though *"the heavens also dropped at the Presence of God."* Then the term, *"The God of Israel,"* will be known to the whole world.

During the Kingdom Age, Israel, under Christ, will be the greatest nation, actually the leading nation, in all the world. All will be because of Christ. The land area that Israel will then occupy will be that which the Lord originally promised to Abraham. To the north, it will take in all of Lebanon; to the east, it will go to the River Euphrates and take in about half of modern Iraq; to the west, it will extend to the Mediterranean Sea; and, to the south, it will extend to the Suez Canal and also include the Arabian Peninsula.

So, a great part of the Middle East will then be incorporated into the nation of Israel. It will probably be pretty close to one hundred times its present size.

(9) "THOU, O GOD, DID SEND A PLENTIFUL RAIN, WHEREBY YOU DID CONFIRM YOUR INHERITANCE, WHEN IT WAS WEARY."

In the wilderness, the Manna and the Quails *"rained"* upon them from Heaven, and the water flowed for them from the Smitten Rock. Also, this Passage refers to the Coming of Jesus Christ in the Battle of Armageddon (Ezek. 38:22). When He comes back, it will be when Israel is *"weary"* and staring defeat in the face. He will then *"confirm Your inheritance,"* which is Israel.

(10) "YOUR CONGREGATION HAS DWELT THEREIN: YOU, O GOD, HAVE PREPARED OF YOUR GOODNESS FOR THE POOR."

In the wilderness and without God, Israel was poor indeed! But God had *"prepared"* for them. Israel will also be *"the poor"* in the Great Tribulation. The Antichrist will feel that he may have little trouble annihilating these *"poor"* people. Little does he know that *"You, O God, have prepared of Your Goodness for the poor,"* referring to the fact that Israel simply cannot be beaten, no matter what the odds against her are.

(11) "THE LORD GAVE THE WORD: GREAT WAS THE COMPANY OF THOSE WHO PUBLISHED IT."

The *"Word"* that is spoken of here is the Law given on Mount Sinai. It has been *"published"* ever since.

The fuller meaning will be at the Second Coming when the *"Lord will give the Word,"* when *"great will be the company"* of those who oppose the Antichrist, which consists of every Blood-washed Believer who has ever lived.

(12) "KINGS OF ARMIES DID FLEE APACE: AND SHE WHO TARRIED AT HOME DIVIDED THE SPOIL."

This speaks of the conquest of the Promised Land by Joshua. More so it speaks of the Coming of the Lord at the Battle of Armageddon. The Antichrist will attempt to *"flee."* Israel then will *"divide the spoil."* Zechariah said, *"The wealth of all the heathen round about shall be gathered together"* (Zech. 14:14).

(13) "THOUGH YOU HAVE LIEN AMONG THE POTS, YET SHALL YOU BE AS THE WINGS OF A DOVE COVERED WITH SILVER, AND HER FEATHERS WITH YELLOW GOLD."

The idea here is that Israel, who had been living in slavery in Egypt, would come forth as a beautiful dove covered with silver and with feathers tipped in gold.

THE FUTURE RESTORATION

The greater fulfillment regarding Israel will be in the Millennial Reign and her future Restoration as the head, under Christ, of all nations on Earth. She will indeed be glorious to behold at that time. *"Silver"* speaks of Redemption, and *"gold"* speaks of Deity. In other words, this thrown-away *"pot"* will come to Jesus and be saved and finally realize that the One Whom they crucified is, in fact, God (Zech. 13:1, 6).

(14) "WHEN THE ALMIGHTY SCATTERED KINGS IN IT, IT WAS WHITE AS SNOW IN SALMON."

This had to do with Israel's victories under Joshua.

ARMAGEDDON

This Passage more so has to do with Israel's greater victory at Armageddon, when Jesus the Almighty comes back and scatters the kings who are with the Antichrist.

The sense of the terminology is that when God disperses the armies of Israel's enemies during the Battle of Armageddon, it will be like snowflakes driven by a storm against the dark wooded slopes of Mount Salmon near Shechem. In other words, the armies of the Antichrist, despite their large numbers and excellent equipment, will literally not know what hit them.

Concerning this time, and I quote from THE EXPOSITOR'S STUDY BIBLE:

"And I will call for a sword against him (the Antichrist) *throughout all My mountains, saith the Lord GOD: every man's sword shall be against his brother.* (This portrays the fact that the Lord has control over all things!)

"And I will plead against him with pestilence and with blood; and I will rain upon him, and upon his bands, and upon the many people who are with him, an overflowing rain, and great hailstones, fire, and brimstones. (This Verse proclaims the fact that the Lord will use the elements, over which neither the Antichrist nor any other man has any control.)

"Thus will I magnify Myself, and sanctify Myself; and I will be known in the eyes of many nations, and they shall know that I am the LORD. (The phrase, *'Thus will I magnify Myself,'* has reference to anger held in check for a long time, and then exploding with a fury that defies description)" (Ezek. 38:21-23).

(15) "THE HILL OF GOD IS AS THE HILL OF BASHAN; AN HIGH HILL AS THE HILL OF BASHAN."

In this Passage, God is laying claim to Israel, in totality, as His Land. He calls it *"the Hill of God."*

Because of this statement, the battle has raged from the time God gave this land to Abraham. It rages even today with the Palestinians. The Antichrist will attempt to make it his *"hill."* He will fail!

WHY IS ISRAEL SO IMPORTANT?

Israel is very important, which is abundantly obvious in the Bible.

Why?

It was to Abraham, Isaac, and Jacob that great Promises were made regarding the people of Israel who would come from their loins. In the midst of the nations who did not know God, that is, the fallen sons of Adam's lost race, there was no semblance of God and no semblance of faith. So the Lord had to raise up a people for the express purpose of proclaiming His Name, which He did from the loins of Abraham and the womb of his wife Sarah.

These people were the only people on the face of the Earth who knew Jehovah, had relationship with Him, and served Him (at least those who really did). The balance of the world worshipped all type of gods of their own making. Israel was the only monotheistic nation in the world, meaning the only nation that worshipped One God. All the balance of the nations were polytheistic, meaning they worshipped many gods, all fabrications of evil minds and inspired by demon spirits.

So, Israel was the only light of God in the world.

THE ABRAHAMIC COVENANT

I quote from THE EXPOSITOR'S STUDY BIBLE:

"*Now the LORD had said unto Abram* (referring to the Revelation which had been given to the Patriarch a short time before; this Chapter [Genesis, Chapter 12] is very important, for it records the first steps of this great Believer in the path of faith), *Get thee out of your country* (separation), *and from your kindred* (separation), *and from your father's house* (separation), *unto a land that I will show you* (refers to the fact that Abraham had no choice in the matter; he was to receive his orders from the Lord, and go where those orders led him):

"*And I will make of you a great nation* (the nation which God made of Abraham has changed the world and exists even unto this hour; in fact, this nation *'Israel'* still has a great part to play, which will take place in the coming Kingdom Age), *and I will bless you, and make your name great* (according to Scripture, *'to bless'* means *'to increase'*; the builders of the Tower of Babel sought to *'make us a name,'* whereas God took this man, who forsook all, and *'made his name great'*); *and you shall be a blessing:* (Concerns itself with the greatest blessing of all. It is the glory of Abraham's faith. God would give this man the meaning of Salvation, which is *'Justification by Faith,'* which would come about through the Lord Jesus Christ, and what Christ would do on the Cross. Concerning this, Jesus said of Abraham, *'Your father Abraham rejoiced to see My day: and he saw it, and was glad'* [Jn. 8:56].)

"*And I will bless them who bless you* (to bless Israel, or any Believer for that matter, guarantees the Blessings of God), *and curse him who curses you* (to curse Israel, or any Believer, guarantees that one will be cursed by God): *and in you shall all families of the Earth be blessed.* (It speaks of Israel, which sprang from the loins of Abraham and the womb of Sarah, giving the world the Word of God, and, more particularly, bringing the Messiah into the world. Through Christ, every family in the world who desires blessing from God can have that Blessing, i.e., *'Justification by Faith'*)" (Gen. 12:1-3).

That which we have given above is only a small fraction of all that the Lord promised. The idea is that God keeps His Promises. So, Israel is of extreme significance in this respect.

Until Israel is in her proper place, which means that she will have accepted Christ as Saviour and Lord, which she will do immediately after the Second Coming, all the great Promises of God for the world cannot materialize. In other words, Israel is the lynchpin that will set all of this in motion. But for it all to happen, as stated, Israel must first accept Christ, which they most gladly will!

(16) "WHY LEAP YE, YE HIGH HILLS? THIS IS THE HILL WHICH GOD DESIRES TO DWELL IN; YEA, THE LORD WILL DWELL IN IT FOREVER."

As David added these words, he was inspired by the Holy Spirit to serve notice on Satan and his minions that this Israel *"is the Hill which God desires to dwell in."* It has ever been contested by Satan; however, two things are said here:

1. This is where God desires to dwell and ultimately will dwell with Jesus Christ reigning from Jerusalem, which will take place in the coming Kingdom Age. (Incidentally, the terms, *"Kingdom Age"* and *"Millennial Reign,"* mean the same thing, the thousand-year reign of Christ.)

After the Kingdom Age is concluded, the New Jerusalem will come down from God out of Heaven to the eternal, perfect Earth, when God changes His Headquarters from Planet Heaven to Planet Earth.

2. Then he says, *"The LORD will dwell in it forever"* (Rev. 21:10).

(17) "THE CHARIOTS OF GOD ARE TWENTY THOUSAND, EVEN THOUSANDS OF ANGELS: THE LORD IS AMONG THEM, AS IN SINAI, IN THE HOLY PLACE."

This speaks of the Coming of Jesus Christ (Rev., Chpt. 19). If we are to take this Passage literally, it means that there will be over twenty million (20,000,000) *"chariots of God"* occupied by *"Angels."* The Lord will be *"among them,"* i.e., leading them.

The Passage also speaks of His dwelling in Jerusalem during the great Kingdom Age.

(18) "YOU HAVE ASCENDED ON HIGH, YOU HAVE LED CAPTIVITY CAPTIVE: YOU HAVE RECEIVED GIFTS FOR MEN; YEA, FOR THE REBELLIOUS ALSO, THAT THE LORD GOD MIGHT DWELL AMONG THEM."

In essence, Paul quoted a part of this Verse in Ephesians 4:8.

CAPTIVITY MADE CAPTIVE

The phrase, *"You have ascended on high, You have led captivity captive,"* presents a strange thought. It means the following, and I quote from THE EXPOSITOR'S STUDY BIBLE:

"Wherefore He said (Ps. 68:18), *When He ascended up on high* (the Ascension), *He led captivity captive* (liberated the souls in Paradise; before the Cross, despite being Believers, they were still held captive by Satan because the blood of bulls and goats could not take away the sin debt; but when Jesus died on the Cross, the sin debt was paid, and now He makes all these His Captives), *and gave Gifts unto men.* (These *'Gifts'* include all the attributes of Christ, all made possible by the Cross)" (Eph. 4:8).

Before the Cross, when Believers died, they did not go to Heaven, but rather went down into Paradise, which is in the heart of the Earth, actually separated from the burning side of Hell only by a great gulf (Lk. 16:19-31).

Concerning this, and I speak of the time before the Cross, Paul said, *"For it is not possible that the blood of bulls and of goats should take away sins.* (The word *'impossible'* is a strong one. It means there is no way forward through the blood of animals. As well, it applies to all other efforts made by man to address the problem of sin, other than the Cross)" (Heb. 10:4).

Due to the fact that animal blood could not take away sins, the sin debt remained, even over the greatest Believers. Due to the fact that the sin debt remained, these individuals, before the Cross, could not be taken to Heaven, but, as stated, were taken down into Paradise. When Jesus died on the Cross, thereby forever settling the sin debt, at least for all who will believe, then He took these righteous souls with Him to Heaven. The place called *"Paradise"* is now empty. Now (since the Cross) when the Believer dies, his soul and spirit instantly go to be with the Lord Jesus Christ because of what Jesus did at the Cross (Phil. 1:23).

(19) "BLESSED BE THE LORD, WHO DAILY LOADS US WITH BENEFITS, EVEN THE GOD OF OUR SALVATION. SELAH."

Not only does this pertain to everyone who has ever followed the Lord, but, in its fuller meaning, it speaks of the Blessings of the Lord during the Millennial Reign.

The Antichrist will promise the human race *"benefits."* He will not be able to fulfill; however, *"the Lord"* will easily *"load us with benefits,"* even on a *"daily"* basis. The Holy Spirit is saying to the world that the Lord is *"the God of our Salvation,"* not the Antichrist, or anyone else.

In fact, when any Preacher (or anyone, for that matter) proposes a way other than *"Jesus Christ and Him Crucified,"* they actually are functioning in the Antichrist spirit.

Concerning this, John the Beloved said:

"Beloved, believe not every spirit (behind every doctrine there is a *'spirit'*; if it's true Doctrine, the Holy Spirit; if it's false doctrine, evil spirits), *but try the spirits whether they are of God* (the criteria is, *'Is it Scriptural?'*): *because many false prophets are gone out into the world* (and they continue unto this hour).

"Hereby know ye the Spirit of God (as Believers, we are to know what the Spirit of God sanctions)*: Every spirit that confesses that Jesus Christ is come in the flesh is of God* (the Incarnation of Christ speaks of the Cross of Christ, the very reason for which He came; this means the Spirit of God will place His Sanction on the Cross and the Cross alone; anything else is not of God)*:*

"And every spirit that confesses not that Jesus Christ is come in the flesh is not of God (Christ came in the flesh to go to the Cross; this refutes the error of Gnosticism, which claims the flesh of Christ was evil, as much as all matter, they claim, is evil; also, anyone who denigrates or even minimizes the Cross in any way is not of God)*: and this is that spirit of Antichrist* (the spirit that denies the Cross is the spirit of the Antichrist), *whereof you have heard that it should come; and even now already is it in the world.* (The Doctrine of the Cross is essential to the Christian system. He who does not hold it cannot be either regarded as a Christian or recognized as a Christian Teacher)" (I Jn. 4:1-3).

(20) "HE WHO IS OUR GOD IS THE GOD OF SALVATION; AND UNTO GOD THE LORD BELONG THE ISSUES FROM DEATH."

We are here told two things:

1. Only the Lord can save; and,

2. Only the Lord can redeem man from spiritual *"death."*

(21) "BUT GOD SHALL WOUND THE HEAD OF HIS ENEMIES, AND THE HAIRY SCALP OF SUCH AN ONE AS GOES ON STILL IN HIS TRESPASSES."

At the time this was given to David by the Holy Spirit, Calvary was yet in the future. But in the Mind of God, Christ had already wounded the head of Satan (Gen. 3:15). When God gives His Word, irrespective if it's thousands of years into the future when that Word will be fulfilled, in the Mind of God, it is already done, because His Word cannot fail.

Also, this Passage refers to the final defeat of Satan when he will be locked away forever in the Lake of Fire, which will be at the beginning of the Perfect Age (Rom. 16:20; Rev. 20:1-3).

(22) "THE LORD SAID, I WILL BRING AGAIN FROM BASHAN, I WILL BRING MY PEOPLE AGAIN FROM THE DEPTHS OF THE SEA."

This Passage refers to the Second Coming, when Israel will accept Christ to a man. Jews will be brought from all over the world and will make the Land of Israel their home.

The phrase, *"I will bring My people again from the depths of the sea,"* doesn't refer to oceans or other bodies of water, but rather great bodies of people (Rev. 13:1; 17:1, 15).

(23) "THAT YOUR FOOT MAY BE DIPPED IN THE BLOOD OF YOUR ENEMIES, AND THE TONGUE OF YOUR DOGS IN THE SAME."

This speaks of the Battle of Armageddon, when Jesus Christ and the armies of Heaven will come in great power and glory to defeat the Antichrist and his armies. So many of the enemy will die that this Verse undoubtedly will be literally fulfilled. Dogs will lick the blood of the enemy (Ezek., Chpts. 38-39).

(24) "THEY HAVE SEEN YOUR GOINGS, O GOD; EVEN THE GOINGS OF MY GOD, MY KING, IN THE SANCTUARY."

After the Battle of Armageddon, Jesus Christ will set up His government in a newly-built Temple in Jerusalem, as described by Ezekiel (Ezek., Chpts. 40-48). At this time, the whole world will see *"His goings."* The worship of God quickly will spread over the entire Earth. All Men will praise Him; actually, *"everything that has breath will praise the LORD."*

(25) "THE SINGERS WENT BEFORE, THE PLAYERS ON INSTRUMENTS FOLLOWED AFTER; AMONG THEM WERE THE DAMSELS PLAYING WITH TIMBRELS."

When David wrote this Psalm, and when it was sung as the Ark was being brought into Jerusalem, he was referring to the worship of the *"singers"* and the *"musicians"* (I Chron. 15:1-28).

In its greater fulfillment, it refers to the Lord Jesus Christ going into Jerusalem, possibly even through the Eastern Gate. This will be at the beginning of the Millennial Reign. It will be a time of such rejoicing as the world has never seen before. Jesus Christ will then reign supreme.

(26) "BLESS YE GOD IN THE CONGREGATIONS, EVEN THE LORD, FROM THE FOUNTAIN OF ISRAEL."

This simply has reference to Israel's praising God as a nation. They will then finally accept Jesus Christ as Messiah, which will take place at the beginning of the Kingdom Age.

Then *"the fountain of Israel"* will bubble up the praises of the Lord. Then the Promises to Abraham, Isaac, and Jacob will be fulfilled. At long last, Israel will be fully and eternally restored (Rom., Chpts. 9-11).

(27) "THERE IS LITTLE BENJAMIN WITH THEIR RULER, THE PRINCES OF JUDAH AND THEIR COUNCIL, THE PRINCES OF ZEBULUN, AND THE PRINCES OF NAPHTALI."

As David sings this song while watching the Ark of God being carried on the shoulders of the Priests into Jerusalem, his eyes scan the representatives of the various Tribes. He does not name all of them, even though all were there.

The greater fulfillment will be when Jesus Christ, the Greater Son of David, comes into Jerusalem to begin the thousand-year Millennial Reign. The other Tribes also will be there.

Incidentally, Benjamin was the least of the Tribes and the last under the jasper stone of Aaron's breastplate; however, jasper is the first stone in the foundations of the Holy City (Rev. 21:19).

(28) "YOUR GOD HAS COMMANDED YOUR STRENGTH: STRENGTHEN, O GOD, THAT WHICH YOU HAVE WROUGHT FOR US."

When David wrote these words, Israel, as commanded by God, was well on its way to becoming the premier nation on the face of the Earth. Under David, God's Blessings would reign supreme; heretofore, the Tribes had been scattered without leadership and were weak. Even under Saul, because of rebellion, Israel saw little supremacy. Now, under David, and especially under Solomon, Israel would become the premier nation on the face of the Earth.

However, the prophetical meaning of this Passage is the greater blessing of Israel in the Millennial Reign. It says, *"Your God has commanded your strength."*

(29) "BECAUSE OF YOUR TEMPLE AT JERUSALEM SHALL KINGS BRING PRESENTS UNTO YOU."

When David wrote these words under the inspiration of the Holy Spirit, he was looking forward to the Temple that would one day be built in Jerusalem. Under Solomon, *"Gifts"* were brought from all over the world.

The great fulfillment will be when representatives from all nations of the world come to Jerusalem to bring *"presents"* to the Lord Jesus Christ. Solomon was a type of the Greater than Solomon.

(30) "REBUKE THE COMPANY OF SPEARMEN, THE MULTITUDE OF THE BULLS, WITH THE CALVES OF THE PEOPLE, TILL EVERY ONE SUBMIT HIMSELF WITH PIECES OF SILVER: SCATTER THOU THE PEOPLE WHO DELIGHT IN WAR."

The future supremacy of Israel over all earthly monarchs is here compared with these monarchs, which, as in Daniel, are likened to wild beasts, which is predicted in the last stirring stanza of this song (Vss. 28-35). Then, because of the Almighty Power of Jesus Christ, the nations of the world will be *"rebuked."*

(31) "PRINCES SHALL COME OUT OF EGYPT; ETHIOPIA SHALL SOON STRETCH OUT HER HANDS UNTO GOD."

All of this happened in measure during the reign of Solomon. It will happen on a world-wide basis when the Greater than Solomon reigns in Jerusalem.

(32) "SING UNTO GOD, YE KINGDOMS OF THE EARTH; O SING PRAISES UNTO THE LORD; SELAH."

In view of the great happenings that will take place during the Millennial Reign, then all *"kingdoms of the Earth"* will *"sing unto God."* This has not yet been fulfilled, and will not be fulfilled until Jesus Christ comes back.

(33) "TO HIM WHO RIDES UPON THE HEAVENS OF HEAVENS, WHICH WERE OF OLD; LO, HE DOES SEND OUT HIS VOICE, AND THAT A MIGHTY VOICE."

The Holy Spirit through David is extolling

the greatness and the Power of God. The meaning of the Verse is that just as God has reigned supreme in the Heavens, He will then reign supreme upon the Earth. His *"Mighty Voice"* will be heard in every nation of the world.

(34) "ASCRIBE YE STRENGTH UNTO GOD: HIS EXCELLENCY IS OVER ISRAEL, AND HIS STRENGTH IS IN THE CLOUDS."

Looking at the world today, with its evil, rebellion, and war, one may wonder at the capacity of the Lord to bring about these great and glorious times. Concerning that, David is saying the following:

1. *"Ascribe ye strength unto God."* God has the strength to do all that He has promised.
2. He will restore Israel.
3. His *"strength"* will rise up far above the Earth, even *"into the clouds."*

(35) "O GOD, YOU ARE TERRIBLE OUT OF YOUR HOLY PLACES: THE GOD OF ISRAEL IS HE WHO GIVES STRENGTH AND POWER UNTO HIS PEOPLE. BLESSED BE GOD."

The meaning of the Verse is that people think of God as being connected with the Sanctuary, or with the Church, or with some other religious building, shrine, or relic. They do not envision His involving Himself in the economy, science, agriculture, medicine, etc. But then the world (and we speak of the coming Kingdom Age) will see how great and glorious the Lord is in all facets of life and existence. He will be great not only in *"His Holy Places,"* but also great in all other areas of society.

God will enable Israel to finally rise to the heights that He has promised them — *"He gives strength and power unto His people."*

PSALM 69

*A Psalm of David:
The Suffering Servant*

(1) "SAVE ME, O GOD; FOR THE WATERS ARE COME IN UNTO MY SOUL."

David wrote this Psalm, and it is referred to as a *"Messianic Psalm."* And more than likely, every Psalm in this Book would come under that heading.

NOTES

CHRIST, THE TRESPASS OFFERING

Eight quotations from the New Testament establish the relationship of this Psalm to the Messiah. They are:

Matthew 27:34; Mark 15:23; John 2:17, 15:25, and 19:29; Romans 11:9 and 15:3; and, II Corinthians 6:2.

The Voice, therefore, is that of the Man of Sorrows, excepting Verses 22 through 28, which record the Holy Spirit's prediction of temporary wrath upon the nation because of its supreme sin in the Crucifixion of their King and Redeemer (Rom. 11:9-12).

This Psalm throbs with unspeakable agony. It helps the Reader to feel how amazing was, and is, the love that endured such depths of anguish and horror in the interest of people who only hated Him.

At Calvary, Jesus, as the Great Trespass Offering, restored that which He took not away, that is, He perfectly restored to God the love and obedience of which man had robbed God. At the same time, He voluntarily charged Himself with man's foolishness and guiltiness, called them His Own and, thereby, declared Himself to be the guilty Person.

THREE FUNDAMENTAL DOCTRINES OF THE GOSPEL

Founded upon this Divine fact of Jesus as the Great Trespass Offering, three fundamental Doctrines of the Gospel are taught in this Psalm:

1. Sin is the cause of man's misery and of God's wrath toward sin;
2. That Christ's Atoning Sacrifice is the Divinely-appointed Way of Salvation; and,
3. That the Resurrection of Christ is the demonstration of God's acceptance of His Person and of His Work, and a pledge of the future Redemption of the world.

Much of this Psalm also could be applied to David; but, more particularly, it applies to the Messiah.

The word *"waters"* refers to overwhelming troubles that plagued David and the Messiah.

David probably wrote this great Psalm after the terrible situation with Bathsheba and the murder of her husband Uriah.

(2) "I SINK IN DEEP MIRE, WHERE THERE IS NO STANDING: I AM COME

INTO DEEP WATERS, WHERE THE FLOODS OVERFLOW ME."

David is speaking here of the terrible difficulties that his failure has brought upon him. From these Passages, one can surely understand the horror of sin. These words should cause any Christian to want to run as far away from sin as possible. Truly, the words *"deep mire"* perfectly describe sin. There is no way that one, by his own power or ability, can extricate himself from such without the Power of God.

THE CROSS OF CHRIST

There is only one way to deal with sin, not twenty, not ten, not even two, just one, and that one way is the Cross of Christ (Rom. 5:8).

As it regards the Cross, the words of this Verse present the Intercessory Words of the Messiah, Who would put Himself in our place and take our sin as His Own. The only way that we can escape this *"deep mire"* is that He has been there before us and taken our place, even though He Himself never sinned.

If man tries to address sin in any way, shape, form, or fashion outside of the Cross, it is the same thing as Cain offering up his fruit or vegetables on the Altar, which God could not accept (Gen., Chpt. 4).

Please note very carefully the following:

1. The world has ever tried to substitute another god to take the place of the Lord of Glory.

2. The Church has ever tried to substitute another sacrifice to take the place of Calvary.

Both are doomed to failure!

(3) "I AM WEARY OF MY CRYING: MY THROAT IS DRIED: MY EYES FAIL WHILE I WAIT FOR MY GOD."

There is no true Child of God who has not been at this place exactly as David describes it — that is, if we truly love the Lord. No true Christian purposely involves himself in sin. But yet, due to the sin nature and the wiles of Satan, all of us, at one time or another, have failed God. Our concern and attitude certainly should be the same as David's. This speaks of true Repentance.

(4) "THEY WHO HATE ME WITHOUT A CAUSE ARE MORE THAN THE HAIRS OF MY HEAD: THEY WHO WOULD DESTROY ME, BEING MY ENEMIES WRONGFULLY, ARE MIGHTY: THEN I RESTORED THAT WHICH I TOOK NOT AWAY."

This is quoted by Christ in John 15:25. Through His Death on Calvary and Resurrection from the dead, Christ *"restored"* that which man lost by his rebellion against God. Of course, Jesus Himself had nothing to do with the rebellion; yet He took full responsibility for its penalty by paying the total price to settle all accounts.

WHY DO MEN HATE CHRIST?

The answer is obvious: their deeds are evil. He was the only *"Good Man"* Who ever lived; consequently, the evil of man and in man hates His *"good."*

The *"mighty"* here spoken of were the Scribes, Pharisees, Sadducees, Herodians, and Priests — even the High Priest, who made up the ruling aristocracy of Israel.

It was not the left-wing modernists (the Herodians) who crucified Him, but the right-wing fundamentalists (Scribes and Pharisees).

It is true that the Herodians (Herod's party) were opposed to Him, but it was the Scribes and Pharisees who *"hated Him without a cause."*

AMERICA'S GREATEST DANGER!

The left-wing modernists in our society, who deny the Bible, the Virgin Birth of Christ, and other fundamental oracles, do not present the greatest danger today for this nation. That comes rather from the right-wing Fundamentalists, who claim to subscribe totally to the Word of God, but actually twist it, as did the Pharisees of old, to their own self-righteous ends. This is the greatest danger facing the modern Church and the nation as a whole.

The reasons are obvious to the spiritual eye.

The right-wing Fundamentalists, which include great segments of the Pentecostals, Charismatics, Holiness, Baptists, and others, use the same words that the Bible uses regarding morality, integrity, ethics, and holiness; however, too often their version is not what the Bible teaches but is instead a man-made version. This is what makes it so subtle and so deadly.

If the time schedule for God's Redemption for man had been such that Jesus would come now instead of having come some 2,000 years ago, and if the modern Church would be His recipients instead of the Jews of old, then, no doubt, the Fundamentalist Right would be the ones to crucify Him instead of the modernist left.

That is a startling statement, but it is true.

THE BAPTISM WITH THE HOLY SPIRIT

As an example, in the early 1960's, when the Holy Spirit began to fall onto hungry, waiting hearts all over the world, many more of the modernists, who came from Presbyterian, Methodist, or even Catholic Churches, were Baptized with the Mighty Holy Spirit than those who came from Baptist and Holiness Churches, who would have been considered in the ranks of the Fundamentalist Right.

Why?

The modernist left has never pretended to receive great things from God. As a result, their hearts were open. They were spiritually bankrupt and they knew it. On the other side, the Fundamentalist Right, in their self-righteousness, could not even begin to admit that they too were spiritually bankrupt and desperately needed *"Power from on high."* Precious few of those ranks, consequently, at least in relationship to the whole, received from God.

SELF-RIGHTEOUSNESS

The Scribes and Pharisees were identical in their self-righteousness. They were so lifted up in themselves that they could not even begin to conceive that Jesus was the Son of God.

The thoughts of their evil minds went something like this:

"Who is this 'Peasant' Who is trying to tell us, 'God's chosen,' about God?" Therefore, they *"hated Him without a cause."*

They were His *"enemies,"* wrongfully, because of self-righteousness. It destroyed the ancient nation of Israel; it is destroying the modern-day Church.

This Passage also speaks of David, when the *"mighty"* of Israel sought to destroy Him. This could have been written at the time of the rebellion of Absalom.

Concerning self-righteousness in Israel, Paul wrote, and I quote from THE EXPOSITOR'S STUDY BIBLE:

"Brethren, my heart's desire and prayer to God for Israel is, that they might be saved (Israel, as a nation, wasn't saved, despite their history; what an indictment!).

"For I bear them record that they have a zeal of God (should read, *'for God'*; they had a zeal which had to do with God as its object), *but not according to knowledge* (pertains to the right kind of knowledge).

"For they being ignorant of God's Righteousness (spells the story not only of ancient Israel, but almost the entirety of the world, and for all time; *'God's Righteousness'* is that which is afforded by Christ, and received by exercising Faith in Him and what He did at the Cross, all on our behalf; Israel's ignorance was willful!), *and going about to establish their own righteousness* (the case of anyone who attempts to establish righteousness by any method other than Faith in Christ and the Cross), *have not submitted themselves unto the Righteousness of God* (God's Righteousness is ensconced in Christ and what He did at the Cross)" (Rom. 10:1-3).

(5) "O GOD, YOU KNOW MY FOOLISHNESS; AND MY SINS ARE NOT HID FROM YOU."

David does not hide the disgust of his sins. Neither does he do as some, who magnify the repentance, but minimize the sin. His words are guided by the Holy Spirit, so they magnify his sins.

THE INTERCESSORY WORK OF CHRIST

This Passage also refers to Christ in His Intercessory Work in that *"He* (God the Father) *has made Him* (Christ) *to be sin for us* (the Sin Offering [Isa. 53:6, 10; I Pet. 2:24]), *Who knew no sin* (He was not guilty; He was perfectly Holy and Pure); *that we might be made the Righteousness of God in Him* (made so by accepting what He did for us at the Cross)" (II Cor. 5:21).

In His Intercessory Work, Christ takes our sins as His Own and prays to the Father for us as though He is asking for mercy and pardon for His Own sin, when, in fact, He has never sinned. This should greatly humble us. It should take us into the depth of the Love of God that is incomprehensible to mere mortals other than by the Revelation of the Spirit upon our souls.

THE MANNER IN WHICH CHRIST INTERCEDES FOR US

The Psalms give us the Words of Christ regarding His Intercessory Work on our behalf, which pertains to a *"Finished Work."*

In other words, whenever Believers sin, Christ doesn't turn to the Father and pray these Words, or even say anything about our sin. This has already been done by the means of the Written Word, even as we are now studying.

At this moment, Christ is seated at the Right Hand of the Father in Heaven. The Scripture says:

"Who being the brightness of His Glory (the radiance of God's Glory), *and the express Image of His Person* (the exact reproduction), *and upholding all things by the Word of His Power* (carries the meaning of Jesus not only sustaining the weight of the universe, but also maintaining its coherence and carrying on its development), *when He had by Himself purged our sins* (which He did at the Cross, dealing with sin regarding its cause, its power, and its guilt), *sat down on the Right Hand of the Majesty on high* (speaks of the Finished Work of Christ, and that the Sacrifice was accepted by the Father)" (Heb. 1:3).

Furthermore, Paul wrote, *"Wherefore He* (the Lord Jesus Christ) *is able also to save them to the uttermost* (proclaims the fact that Christ Alone has made the only true Atonement for sin; He did this at the Cross) *who come unto God by Him* (proclaims the only manner in which man can come to God), *seeing He ever lives to make Intercession for them"* (His very Presence by the Right Hand of the Father guarantees such, with nothing else having to be done)" (Heb. 7:25).

All of this means that the very Presence of Christ at the Right Hand of the Father guarantees Intercession on our behalf. In other words, God has accepted Christ and what He did at the Cross as full payment. That being done, His Presence before the Father guarantees Intercession on our behalf, without anything else having to be done.

If Jesus had to do anything else to intercede for us, this would mean that Calvary didn't pay it all. But Calvary did pay it all. As one Preacher has so rightly said, *"Were it not for the constant Intercession of Christ, all on our behalf, none of us would last a full day, not even an hour."*

(6) "LET NOT THEM WHO WAIT ON YOU, O LORD GOD OF HOSTS, BE ASHAMED FOR MY SAKE: LET NOT THOSE WHO SEEK YOU BE CONFOUNDED FOR MY SAKE, O GOD OF ISRAEL."

This, of course, applied to David, but it applied much more so to Christ and the Cross. Our Lord was more concerned about those who had followed Him and now did not understand what was happening (we speak of His Own Personal Disciples) than He was about His Own terrible plight.

The meaning of Verses 6 and 7 is that God's abandonment of His Beloved Son at Calvary might upset the faith of those who confide in God for deliverance from human or Satanic hatred. He prayed that they might understand that He, as the Trespass Offering, should be so forsaken.

(7) "BECAUSE FOR YOUR SAKE I HAVE BORNE REPROACH; SHAME HAS COVERED MY FACE."

This Verse pertains to both David and the Messiah. Both suffered terrible reproach. But no one has suffered the reproach that Christ suffered, not even David.

REPROACH

The Hebrew word for *"reproach"* is *"cherpah,"* which means *"to disgrace, to be submitted to acute shame."*

Regarding *"reproach,"* it is obvious why the enemies took advantage of David. The cause was David's great sins in connection with Bathsheba and her husband Uriah. This gave occasion to the enemies of the Lord to greatly reproach the sweet singer of Israel.

While we must never, even for a moment, condone David's terrible sins, we must nevertheless, at the same time, go to the Words of Christ, which He spoke when a woman was caught in the act of adultery:

"He who is without sin among you, let him first cast a stone at her" (Jn. 8:7).

That one statement stops all accusation and all gossip. Regrettably, most Christians do not seem to know this particular Verse of Scripture.

But when it comes to Christ, there was no wrong in Christ, no failure, and no sin, no wickedness. He was, in fact, Perfect.

So how could He be submitted to such reproach? Better yet, why was He submitted to such reproach?

The religious leaders of that hour would have given many excuses for their actions and their hatred concerning Christ, but the real reason was that they were evil. They could not abide His Perfect Goodness.

And there is no evil like religious evil. It pales into insignificance in comparison with anything else one might name. The world has been soaked in human blood, all because of religious self-righteousness.

When President George H. W. Bush was running for a second term of office (1992 election) and was challenged by Governor Bill Clinton of Arkansas, then-President Bush's basic platform against his opponent was:

"My character is better than yours."

I do not think the Lord was pleased with that statement too very much.

If one wants to go in that direction, about the best thing one can say is (and we will use a metaphor):

"Leprosy only covers 92 percent of my body, but it covers 95 percent of yours."

I think the Reader gets my point!

(8) "I AM BECOME A STRANGER UNTO MY BRETHREN, AND AN ALIEN UNTO MY MOTHER'S CHILDREN."

This Prophecy refutes the lie of the Catholic Church that Mary had no other children but Christ. The Gospels are replete with the fact that His Own *"Brethren"* (his half-brothers, so to speak) did not believe in Him (Jn. 7:5).

(9) "FOR THE ZEAL OF YOUR HOUSE HAS EATEN ME UP; AND THE REPROACHES OF THEM WHO REPROACHED YOU ARE FALLEN UPON ME."

This was quoted of Christ in John 2:17. This Passage, given some one thousand years

NOTES

before Christ, nevertheless forecasts the cleansing of the Temple, which Jesus carried out. Christ only had one desire in mind, one goal, one motive, and that was to please God. He desired only to promote God's Glory and the Glory of His Temple. And this He did!

(10) "WHEN I WEPT, AND CHASTENED MY SOUL WITH FASTING, THAT WAS TO MY REPROACH."

David, no doubt, carried out these particular things. But the Passage refers more so to the Greater Son of David. No human being ever suffered the *"reproach"* that Christ suffered.

One can easily find fault with even the Godliest human being; however, there was no fault with Christ! Pontius Pilate, the Governor of Judaea, stated, *"I find no fault in this Man"* (Lk. 23:4). Pilate found no fault, because there was no fault! And yet, they reproached Him in the most vile ways!

(11) "I MADE SACKCLOTH ALSO MY GARMENT; AND I BECAME A PROVERB TO THEM."

Both David and Christ are referred to here.

The term *"sackcloth"* denotes humility. Undoubtedly, this was fulfilled literally in David. There is no record that Christ literally wore *"sackcloth"*; however, this Passage prophesies of that which Christ gave up and became for lost humanity (Phil. 2:5-8).

He laid aside the royal robes of Deity and substituted in their place the *"sackcloth of humanity."* Despite the fact that the Lord Jesus healed untold numbers of sick people, performed miracle after miracle, and even raised the dead, to the religious hierarchy of Israel, He was no more than a joke!

Now we see the most ungodly of the ungodly!

(12) "THEY WHO SIT IN THE GATE SPEAK AGAINST ME; AND I WAS THE SONG OF THE DRUNKARDS."

This speaks of both David and Christ. The phrase, *"Sit in the gate,"* speaks of those who held positions of authority.

The latter part of the Verse probably tells of the ridicule that was heaped upon David because of the incident with Bathsheba. It speaks even more so of the religious leaders of Israel speaking against Christ. They did all within their power to make the Name of

Christ a reproach, until it became *"the song of the drunkards."*

(13) "BUT AS FOR ME, MY PRAYER IS UNTO YOU, O LORD, IN AN ACCEPTABLE TIME: O GOD, IN THE MULTITUDE OF YOUR MERCY HEAR ME, IN THE TRUTH OF YOUR SALVATION."

This speaks of David as a Type of Christ. Both cried to God incessantly. David, as a Type of Christ, knew that God was his only hope. The Greater Son of David would likewise cry to God for leading and guidance.

This should be an example to us. God is the Only One Who can protect us, the Only One Who can change our situation. Sadly, most of the modern Church little seeks the Lord; instead they look to humanistic psychology or some other prattle!

(14) "DELIVER ME OUT OF THE MIRE, AND LET ME NOT SINK: LET ME BE DELIVERED FROM THEM WHO HATE ME, AND OUT OF THE DEEP WATERS."

David is speaking in this Passage of the terrible *"mire"* of sin he has fallen into with Bathsheba, and also of the troubles that his enemies have brought upon him. Among those in Israel who had no desire for God, they all hated David, and they hated him without a cause, exactly as they hated Christ. They would seek any means to destroy him. Thankfully, they did not succeed!

(15) "LET NOT THE WATERFLOOD OVERFLOW ME, NEITHER LET THE DEEP SWALLOW ME UP, AND LET NOT THE PIT SHUT HER MOUTH UPON ME."

This terminology inspired by the Holy Spirit is a perfect picture of the efforts of Satan to destroy an individual. It would apply to both David and Christ. Once again, we are given an introspective look into the sufferings of Christ, which He actually went through to redeem mankind from the slavery of sin. These Passages very well could apply to the horror of Gethsemane. At this place, Satan attempted to kill Christ before He could go to the Cross. Of course, Satan really could not have killed Christ. No one could have killed Him. Previously, He had plainly stated:

"Therefore does My Father love Me, because I lay down My Life, that I might take it again.

NOTES

"No man takes it from Me, but I lay it down of Myself. I have power to lay it down, and I have power to take it again. This Commandment have I received of My Father" (Jn. 10:17-18).

(16) "HEAR ME, O LORD; FOR YOUR LOVINGKINDNESS IS GOOD: TURN UNTO ME ACCORDING TO THE MULTITUDE OF YOUR TENDER MERCIES."

The Hebrew word translated *"lovingkindness"* means *"Grace,"* and as *"tender mercies,"* it signifies the same tender affection that mothers show their offspring.

(17) "AND HIDE NOT YOUR FACE FROM YOUR SERVANT; FOR I AM IN TROUBLE: HEAR ME SPEEDILY."

This refers to David and also to Christ.

Sooner or later, every Believer finds himself *"in trouble."* There is no relief from that *"trouble"* except through Christ. He suffered every type of *"trouble"* that we could ever suffer, and He guaranteed our deliverance if we only will look to Him and believe Him, knowing what He has done for us at the Cross.

As we continue to say, *"Christ is the Source, while the Cross is the Means."*

He has promised to do so *"speedily."*

(18) "DRAW NEAR UNTO MY SOUL, AND REDEEM IT: DELIVER ME BECAUSE OF MY ENEMIES."

The *"enemies"* of both David and Christ were numerous, to say the least. Anyone who is truly called of God will experience the opposition of these *"enemies."* These will come from three sources:

1. The world;
2. The apostate Church; and,
3. Demon spirits.

Of the three, the apostate Church is the worst!

(19) "YOU HAVE KNOWN MY REPROACH, AND MY SHAME, AND MY DISHONOR: MY ADVERSARIES ARE ALL BEFORE YOU."

All of this speaks of David, but much more of Christ. No one knew *"reproach," "shame,"* or *"dishonor"* as did Christ. His *"adversaries"* were many. Mostly, they were made up of the religious leaders of that day.

THE APOSTATE CHURCH

The situation has little changed. The

greatest *"adversaries"* to the Work of God are mainly those who are supposed to promote the Work of God. This speaks of the apostate Church.

The Church, as ancient Israel, is divided into two directions. There is an apostate Church; there was an apostate Israel. In the Church, there is a Remnant that comprises the True Body of Christ; in ancient Israel, there was a Remnant that truly served God.

(20) "REPROACH HAS BROKEN MY HEART; AND I AM FULL OF HEAVINESS: AND I LOOKED FOR SOME TO TAKE PITY, BUT THERE WAS NONE; AND FOR COMFORTERS, BUT I FOUND NONE."

This spoke of David, but far more of Christ. It probably refers to His Trial and the terrible ordeal on the Cross. He actually died of a *"broken heart"* (Jn. 19:34).

At His Trial, there were none who stood by His Side. His Own Disciples forsook Him and fled. The horror of this moment knows no bounds. There were none who stood up for Him.

(21) "THEY GAVE ME ALSO GALL FOR MY MEAT; AND IN MY THIRST THEY GAVE ME VINEGAR TO DRINK."

This was fulfilled at the Crucifixion (Mat. 27:48).

THE EVIL HEARTS OF MEN

It is hard to imagine the cruelty of man upon this occasion. It is even more shocking when we realize that this was done to Him by those who are referred to as the Church of that day. Self-righteousness is cruel — so cruel that it defies description.

It was not the drunks, the thieves, or the harlots who nailed Christ to a Cross. It was instead the religious leaders of that day.

From the beginning until now, that always has been the greatest hindrance to the Work of God. I speak of the religious crowd, i.e., *"the apostate Church."*

(22) "LET THEIR TABLE BECOME A SNARE BEFORE THEM: AND THAT WHICH SHOULD HAVE BEEN FOR THEIR WELFARE, LET IT BECOME A TRAP."

Verses 22 through 28 could, in some small measure, refer to Ahithophel, David's closest advisor and the grandfather of Bathsheba. But they refer far more so to Judas.

THE TABLE

The *"table"* spoken of here refers to that which the Lord prepares for His Own (Ps. 23). Judas did not want the *"table"* that the Lord had prepared; he desired another *"table."* It would become a *"snare."* Along with Judas, this also speaks of the Priests.

The Prophecy given in these Passages is inspired by the Holy Spirit. It should be a warning to those who would seek to oppose God and *"His Anointed."*

Incidentally, Judas did what he did because he did not want any part of the Cross. When Jesus started referring to the Cross, even in an indirect way, Judas determined that was not for him. He rebelled against it, lost his way, and committed suicide.

We learn this from the Sixth Chapter of John's Gospel. This is where Jesus said, *"Except you eat the flesh of the Son of Man, and drink His Blood, you have no life in you.* (This terminology addresses the Cross. Christ would give Himself on the Cross for the Salvation of mankind. To fully believe in Him and what He did for us is what He means here. However, this Verse tells us the degree of believing that is required; it refers to the Cross being the total Object of one's belief. Failing that, there is no life in you)" (Jn. 6:53).

Judas knew that Christ was referring to the Cross. At the close of the Sixth Chapter of John's Gospel, Judas is exposed, at least to Christ; the course was, therefore, set for Judas' terrible, perfidious act. The man who had so much, who had been so privileged, would lose it all and die by suicide. At this very moment, he is in Hell and will remain there forever and forever (Jn. 6:70-71).

(23) "LET THEIR EYES BE DARKENED, THAT THEY SEE NOT; AND MAKE THEIR LOINS CONTINUALLY TO SHAKE."

Even though David uttered these words, they are actually the Words of Christ given to us some one thousand years before the First Advent of the Saviour. Only One Who was totally and completely Perfect could pray such a prayer. And, to be sure, it was fulfilled, and is continuing to be fulfilled, in totality.

All who refuse *"light"* will have *"darkness."* This *"darkness"* will bring a fear that will cause them *"continually to shake."*

(24) "POUR OUT YOUR INDIGNATION UPON THEM, AND LET YOUR WRATHFUL ANGER TAKE HOLD OF THEM."

Judas committed suicide, as did Caiaphas, the High Priest. Both men were instrumental in the Crucifixion of Christ. Some thirty-seven years later, Jerusalem was totally destroyed by Titus and the Roman army.

This did not have to be. But for those who reject the Lord, for those who refuse His Grace and Love, the *"anger of God"* ultimately will *"take hold of them."*

(25) "LET THEIR HABITATION BE DESOLATE; AND LET NONE DWELL IN THEIR TENTS."

This was quoted about Judas in Acts 1:20. It was also quoted in part by Christ concerning Israel and Jerusalem (Lk. 13:34-35). This was fulfilled in both Judas and Jerusalem.

Approximately a thousand years before the fact, God through foreknowledge knew these things would happen and what would be the desolate end of those who would come against Christ.

It has not changed from then until now. It is either Jesus Christ or eternal damnation. These words were uttered not only against Judas and Jerusalem of old, but they are uttered against all who reject Christ and the great price He paid at Calvary's Cross.

(26) "FOR THEY PERSECUTE HIM WHOM YOU HAVE SMITTEN; AND THEY TALK TO THE GRIEF OF THOSE WHOM YOU HAVE WOUNDED."

Jesus was *"smitten of God and afflicted"* while He was on the Cross, but it was not done for sins He Himself had committed, for He had committed none. The Lord Jesus suffered the blow all on our behalf; He became the Sin Bearer of the world, and for all time.

SMITTEN OF GOD

It was absolutely necessary for God to smite Christ on the Cross if man was to be redeemed; but still, it was God Alone Who must do this, and no one else. So, when Judas, along with the Scribes, Pharisees, and leaders of Israel, persecuted Christ, they were grossly out of bounds, and they would suffer the anger and wrath of God for doing so.

The latter part of this Verse refers to *"Your wounded ones,"* which pertains to the followers of the Messiah. They were greatly wounded when they saw Jesus die on the Cross. They did not understand what was happening or why it was happening. Later they would know, but only after the Advent of the Holy Spirit on the Day of Pentecost, when they would receive the Mighty Spirit Baptism (Acts, Chpt. 2).

(27) "ADD INIQUITY UNTO THEIR INIQUITY: AND LET THEM NOT COME INTO YOUR RIGHTEOUSNESS."

This particular Verse presents a chilling statement.

BLASPHEMING THE HOLY SPIRIT

This Verse speaks of Judas and the religious leaders of Israel blaspheming the Holy Spirit. They added this *"iniquity unto their iniquity."* Consequently, they could not come into His *"Righteousness."*

When a person blasphemes the Holy Spirit, for which there is no forgiveness, such a person has no more desire for God, no desire to come to Him, no desire to serve Him. They become so locked in their deception, so depraved in their lostness, that whatever thoughts they have of God are perverted.

There is no hint in Scripture that a person can desire to come to the Lord, can desire to be Saved, and can earnestly seek to be Saved, but cannot because he has blasphemed the Holy Spirit. The very desire of a person to come to God, his desire to be Saved, cannot be brought about by the individual's own accord, but only by the Holy Spirit. If one desires to be Saved, it is the Holy Spirit Who has placed such a desire in the person's heart; and He would never do so if it was impossible for the person to be Saved.

Unfortunately, Satan has caused many to die lost, simply because they, in some manner, thought they couldn't be Saved, even though they desired to be Saved.

Let me say it again:

No matter what a person has done in the past, if that person has the desire to come to Christ, that desire has been placed in the person's heart by the Holy Spirit; and, if the Holy Spirit places such a desire in a person's heart, He most definitely will fulfill that desire, if the individual in question only will believe (Rev. 22:17).

(28) "LET THEM BE BLOTTED OUT OF THE BOOK OF THE LIVING, AND NOT BE WRITTEN WITH THE RIGHTEOUS."

Another great Truth is given to us in this Passage.

NAMES BLOTTED OUT OF THE BOOK OF LIFE

This Verse proves that names can be blotted out of the Book of Life. The same thing also is said in other places of the Bible (Ex. 32:33; Rev. 3:5; 22:19). That this is the Book of Life is clear from the fact that it is the Book wherein the names of the righteous are written. We are given an apt description of this in Hebrews, Chapters 6 and 10.

The entirety of the Book of Hebrews, in fact, was written by the Apostle Paul regarding Christian Jews, who, through discouragement or other reasons, were turning their backs on Christ and going back into Judaism. The Apostle Paul tells them that if they do this, they will lose their souls.

I quote from THE EXPOSITOR'S STUDY BIBLE:

"For it is impossible for those who were once enlightened (refers to those who have accepted the Light of the Gospel, which means accepting Christ and His great Sacrifice), *and have tasted of the Heavenly Gift* (pertains to Christ and what He did at the Cross), *and were made partakers of the Holy Spirit* (which takes place when a person comes to Christ),

"And have tasted the good Word of God (is not language that is used of an impenitent sinner, as some claim; the unsaved have no relish whatsoever for the Truth of God, and see no beauty in it), *and the powers of the world to come* (refers to the Work of the Holy Spirit within hearts and lives, which the unsaved cannot have or know),

"If they shall fall away (should have been translated, 'And having fallen away'), *to renew them again unto Repentance* ('again' states they have once repented, but have now turned their backs on Christ); *seeing they crucify to themselves the Son of God afresh* (means they no longer believe what Christ did at the Cross, actually concluding Him to be an imposter; the only way any person can truly repent is to place his faith in Christ and the Cross; if that is denied, there is no Repentance),

NOTES

and put Him to an open shame (means to hold Christ up to public ridicule; Paul wrote this Epistle because some Christian Jews were going back into Judaism, or seriously contemplating doing so)" (Heb. 6:4-6).

Then Paul said, and I continue to quote from THE EXPOSITOR'S STUDY BIBLE:

"For if we sin willfully (the 'willful sin' is the transference of faith from Christ and Him Crucified to other things) *after that we have received the knowledge of the Truth* (speaks of the Bible Way of Salvation and Victory, which is 'Jesus Christ and Him Crucified' [I Cor. 2:2]), *there remains no more Sacrifice for sins.* (If the Cross of Christ is rejected, there is no other Sacrifice or way God will accept)" (Heb. 10:26).

(29) "BUT I AM POOR AND SORROWFUL: LET YOUR SALVATION, O GOD, SET ME UP ON HIGH."

This speaks of David, but more so of the Son of David. One of the reasons the religious leaders of Israel would not accept Christ as Messiah was because He was *"poor and sorrowful."* They would not *"set Him up on high,"* but God did *"set Him up on high."*

Christ was not of the aristocracy of Israel, but actually was a Peasant. As a result, the religious leaders of Israel looked down on Him, and greatly so!

(30) "I WILL PRAISE THE NAME OF GOD WITH A SONG, AND WILL MAGNIFY HIM WITH THANKSGIVING."

David was noted for praising the Name of the Lord *"with a song."* Jesus and His Disciples also sang a song at the Last Supper (Mat. 26:30).

Even though He was *"poor and sorrowful,"* He nevertheless magnified the Lord with *"thanksgiving."* This is the criteria for Christian Victory. So oftentimes we only thank the Lord whenever things are going well. Here we are taught to *"magnify Him with thanksgiving"* even when things are not going well.

(31) "THIS ALSO SHALL PLEASE THE LORD BETTER THAN AN OX OR BULLOCK THAT HAS HORNS AND HOOFS."

David is saying that praise to the Name of the Lord in song and thanksgiving to God pleases the Lord better than animal sacrifices.

In a greater measure, it speaks of the Greater Sacrifice of Christ on the Cross, which was far better than animal sacrifices.

(32) "THE HUMBLE SHALL SEE THIS, AND BE GLAD: AND YOUR HEART SHALL LIVE THAT SEEK GOD."

Even though the *"humble"* refers to all Believers in general, it speaks even more so of Christ, Who was the most humble of the most humble.

(33) "FOR THE LORD HEARS THE POOR, AND DESPISES NOT HIS PRISONERS."

The word *"poor"* refers to Christ. *"His prisoners"* refer to those who follow Him, *"the poor."*

The Lord will always hear Christ, and those who follow Him will never be *"despised by God."*

It is amazing how the Holy Spirit refers to the Messiah as *"the humble"* and *"the poor."* The only personal thing that the Lord ever said of Himself in His earthly Ministry was, *"For I am meek* (poor) *and lowly in heart"* (Mat. 11:29).

(34) "LET THE HEAVEN AND EARTH PRAISE HIM, THE SEAS, AND EVERY THING THAT MOVES THEREIN."

The One Who is called *"humble"* and *"poor"* ultimately will see the entirety of the Heavens and the Earth praising Him. This will be fulfilled in the coming Millennial Reign and forever.

(35) "FOR GOD WILL SAVE ZION, AND WILL BUILD THE CITIES OF JUDAH: THAT THEY MAY DWELL THERE, AND HAVE IT IN POSSESSION."

This speaks of the coming Kingdom Age. He will *"save Zion"* when He comes back in the Battle of Armageddon. At that time, He will quickly rebuild the cities of Judah that were destroyed by the Antichrist. Then they will *"dwell there"* and not be dispossessed. The Land of Israel is now hotly contested, but the Holy Spirit says that in that great day they will *"have it in possession."*

(36) "THE SEED ALSO OF HIS SERVANTS SHALL INHERIT IT: AND THEY WHO LOVE HIS NAME SHALL DWELL THEREIN."

Here, Jesus is called *"The Seed."* Paul wrote, *"And to your Seed, which is Christ"* (Gal. 3:16).

THE SEED

The sense of this Verse is that Israel really never quite inherited the Promised Land. Under David and Solomon, it could be said that it was completely subjugated; however, there was still rebellion against God.

At the beginning of the Kingdom Age, *"The Seed,"* the Lord Jesus Christ, *"shall inherit it,"* which continues to speak of the Promised Land. Then finally this contested land will be forever possessed. *"And they who love His Name shall dwell therein."* Spiritually, it speaks presently of Believers being in Christ (Rom. 8:1-2, 11).

PSALM 70

A Psalm of David:
A Cry for Help

(1) "MAKE HASTE, O GOD, TO DELIVER ME; MAKE HASTE TO HELP ME, O LORD."

This Psalm was written by David and it has a double meaning:

1. It refers to David's asking the Lord to deliver him from those who hated him.

2. It refers to Israel in the days of the Great Tribulation, when the Antichrist will seek to destroy them.

The majority of this Psalm is almost identical to Verses 13 through 17 of Psalm 40. The theme of the Fortieth Psalm is the Messiah's Personal sufferings in His First Advent; that of this Psalm, His sympathetic sufferings with His people immediately prior to His Second Advent.

As David cried, Israel will cry to God in the last three and a half years of the Great Tribulation.

(2) "LET THEM BE ASHAMED AND CONFOUNDED WHO SEEK AFTER MY SOUL: LET THEM BE TURNED BACKWARD, AND PUT TO CONFUSION, WHO DESIRE MY HURT."

Israel will cry these words in the closing days of the Tribulation (the Time of Jacob's Trouble). In effect, the Son of David will have already prayed this prayer on their behalf. The Second Verse will be fulfilled at the Second Coming.

(3) "LET THEM BE TURNED BACK FOR A REWARD OF THEIR SHAME WHO SAY, AHA, AHA."

During the Battle of Armageddon, the Antichrist will think surely that victory is in his grasp. He will even say, *"Aha, Aha,"* thinking that now Israel is his, and the Jews are destroyed. However, he will be put to *"shame"* at the coming of Jesus Christ.

(4) "LET ALL THOSE WHO SEEK YOU REJOICE AND BE GLAD IN YOU: AND LET SUCH AS LOVE YOUR SALVATION SAY CONTINUALLY, LET GOD BE MAGNIFIED."

This refers in general to anyone who would *"seek God."*

It refers more pointedly to Israel in the last days, when they will at long last *"seek God."*

The word *"magnified"* means that as God is *"magnified,"* there will be rejoicing and gladness.

(5) "BUT I AM POOR AND NEEDY: MAKE HASTE UNTO ME, O GOD: YOU ARE MY HELP AND MY DELIVERER; O LORD, MAKE NO TARRYING."

Christ remained *"poor"* and *"needy"* to the very end, waiting patiently for Jehovah. His people (Israel) will, in a lack of extreme poverty, wait and trust to the end. In Israel's future day of deep suffering, she will nourish her faith by singing this song and by calling to remembrance, as commanded by it, the facts of Psalm 40.

The words, *"Make no tarrying,"* refer to the Battle of Armageddon, when it seems as though all hope was gone. In fact, Israel's only hope at that time will be the coming of the Messiah. He will hear this prayer and answer it.

PSALM 71

David Probably Wrote this Psalm: A Prayer for God's Help in Old Age

(1) "IN YOU, O LORD, DO I PUT MY TRUST: LET ME NEVER BE PUT TO CONFUSION."

There is no proof of the authorship of this Psalm; however, there is a good possibility that the Psalm was given to David for the purpose of refreshing his heart during the dark days of Absalom's rebellion. It must also have refreshed the heart of the Greater Son of David, when He suffered man's hatred. It

NOTES

will feed the faith of Israel in the future and darkest day of her history, which is soon to come in the Great Tribulation (Mat. 24:21).

TRUST IN GOD

This Psalm shows that Israel will come back to Him, believing that He will deliver her from the wicked, unrighteous, and cruel man, the Antichrist. The theme of the entirety of the five Books of the Psalms is *"Trust in the LORD."*

Inasmuch as the Holy Spirit devoted so much attention to this all-important matter, it should be obvious that His intention is for every Believer to do the same.

THE CROSS OF CHRIST, THE DIVIDING LINE OF THE CHURCH

The problem of trust in God versus trust in man has ever been the dividing line of the Church. In other words, do we trust Jesus Christ and what He has done for us at the Cross, which is the story of the Bible, or do we trust other things? This is where Satan makes his greatest push.

Today, the far greater majority of the modern Church places its trust, in one way or another, in humanistic psychology, which really is trust in man. Until the first of the Twentieth Century, psychology was looked upon as another form of witchcraft, which it is. Gradually, it began to make inroads into the thinking of modern, rebellious man. Little by little the world embraced it, because it refused to accept the Bible. Step by step the Church followed suit.

The world of Catholicism embraced humanistic psychology first of all, and then, little by little, the old-line Protestant Churches followed suit. Then, sadly, the Holiness, Pentecostal, and Charismatic world threw in their lot with this ungodly philosophy, as well! Today, there is virtually no part of organized religion that is not completely enmeshed in the world of ungodly, atheistic psychology. It is impossible to trust in God and man at the same time; likewise, it is impossible to trust in the Bible and psychology simultaneously. One or the other must go.

We have God's Promise that if we *"trust in the LORD,"* then we will *"never be put to confusion."*

MODERN SERMONOLOGY

Even though most of the modern Church would deny this, most of the preaching from behind modern pulpits actually is psychology. It has a few Scriptures thrown in to make it seem as if it is Scriptural and legitimate, but it actually is presenting psychological precepts to the public rather than the True Gospel. Virtually, the entirety of the *"Purpose Driven Life"* scheme is psychology. And the Church has bought into it in totality. Further, almost all of the so-called Church Growth methods are based on humanistic psychology. It is subtle, and, as stated, certain Scriptures are selected to make it seem as if it is Scriptural. But what is being preached, proclaimed, and taught is not the Bible, but something else entirely.

In some Churches, the people are told not to bring their Bibles. Instead, certain Scriptures are placed on Big Screens in the Churches, Scriptures from new Versions of the Bible, which are perverted. In other words, the modern Church is being led further and further away from the Bible.

I am not aware of a single popular effort that is being made today in the Church, such as the *"Purpose Driven Life,"* the *"Government of Twelve,"* *"Word of Faith,"* etc., which can be constituted as Scriptural.

And how do I know that?

THE CROSS OF CHRIST

Any Message which eliminates, downplays, repudiates, or even ignores the Cross of Christ is bogus. The Cross of Christ is the only answer for the ills of man.

Listen to Paul:

"But God forbid that I should glory (boast), *save in the Cross of our Lord Jesus Christ* (what the opponents of Paul sought to escape at the price of insincerity is the Apostle's only basis of exultation), *by Whom the world is crucified unto me, and I unto the world.* (The only way we can overcome the world, and I mean the only way, is by placing our faith exclusively in the Cross of Christ and keeping it there)" (Gal. 6:14).

Again, he said: *"In Whom also you are circumcised with the Circumcision made without hands* (that which is brought about by the Cross [Rom. 6:3-5]), *in putting off the body of the sins of the flesh by the Circumcision of Christ* (refers the old carnal nature that is defeated by the Believer placing his faith totally in the Cross, which gives the Holy Spirit latitude to work):

"Buried with Him in Baptism (does not refer to Water Baptism, but rather to the Believer baptized into the death of Christ, which refers to the Crucifixion and Christ as our Substitute [Rom. 6:3-4]), *wherein also you are risen with Him through the Faith of the operation of God, Who has raised Him from the dead.* (This does not refer to our future physical Resurrection, but to that spiritual Resurrection from a sinful state into Divine Life. We died with Him, we are buried with Him, and we rose with Him [Rom. 6:3-5]), and herein lies the secret to all spiritual victory.)

"And you, being dead in your sins and the uncircumcision of your flesh (speaks of spiritual death [i.e., 'separation from God'], which sin does!), *has He quickened together with Him* (refers to being made spiritually alive, which is done through being 'born-again'), *having forgiven you all trespasses* (the Cross made it possible for all manner of sins to be forgiven and taken away);

"Blotting out the handwriting of Ordinances that was against us (pertains to the Law of Moses, which was God's Standard of Righteousness that man could not reach), *which was contrary to us* (Law is against us, simply because we are unable to keep its precepts, no matter how hard we try), *and took it out of the way* (refers to the penalty of the Law being removed), *nailing it to His Cross* (the Law with its decrees was abolished in Christ's Death, as if crucified with Him);

"And having spoiled principalities and powers (Satan and all of his henchmen were defeated at the Cross by Christ atoning for all sin; sin was the legal right Satan had to hold man in captivity; with all sin atoned, he has no more legal right to hold anyone in bondage), *He* (Christ) *made a show of them openly* (what Jesus did at the Cross was in the face of the whole universe), *triumphing over them in it.* (The triumph is complete and it was all done for us, meaning we can walk in power and perpetual victory due to

the Cross)" (Col. 2:11-15).

All of this tells us that if the Preacher is not preaching the Cross (I Cor. 1:23), then whatever it is he is preaching, it's not the Gospel (I Cor. 1:17).

THE REJECTION OF THE CROSS OF CHRIST IS ALWAYS MORAL AND NEVER THEOLOGICAL

What does that heading mean?

It means that if individuals reject the Cross, it is never for theological reasons, meaning that it's difficult to understand. In fact, a child can understand the Cross of Christ. So this means that if the Cross is rejected, it is on moral grounds alone, which constitutes pride, self-will, heresy, etc.

I personally believe that today the Holy Spirit is making the greatest push of all times as it regards the Cross. The Cross of Christ always has been the dividing line between the True Church and the apostate Church. The beginning of this conflict is recorded in the Fourth Chapter of Genesis. It has raged ever since. But due to the fact that we are nearing the end of the Church Age, the Holy Spirit is moving forward with the Message of the Cross in such a way that the Church will have to either openly and blatantly reject it or accept it. Some few accept it; most reject it! Therein lies the dividing line between the True Church and the apostate Church. It is the acceptance or the rejection of the Cross of Christ.

When one turns on that which purports to be Christian Television, one can hear almost every type of so-called means of victory being projected, but almost nothing about the Cross.

The Bible teaches that Jesus answered every single thing at the Cross (Col. 2:14-15). He left out nothing! Everything that was lost at the Fall has been totally and completely addressed. There, all sin was atoned, past, present, and future, at least for all who will believe (Jn. 3:16). It holds the answer for man, and it alone holds the answer for man.

GOD'S PRESCRIBED ORDER OF VICTORY

Whatever it is that man needs, whether unredeemed or redeemed, it can be found only in Christ and what He did for us at the Cross. There is no other answer, no other panacea, no other means, no other way! As we have stated, it is not difficult or complicated at all.

Let me once again give this little diagram, which we've already given in this Volume. Simply because it is so important, I feel it would be proper to state it again.

1. FOCUS: The Lord Jesus Christ (Jn. 1:1, 14, 29).
2. OBJECT OF FAITH: The Cross of Christ (Rom. 6:1-14; Col. 2:14-15).
3. POWER SOURCE: The Holy Spirit (Rom. 8:1-2, 11).
4. RESULTS: Victory (Rom. 6:14; Gal. 6:14).

The Believer must understand that Jesus Christ is the Source of all things which come to us from God. We must also understand that it is the Cross, and the Cross alone, which is the Means by which this is done. This means that the Cross of Christ must ever be the Object of our Faith (Rom. 6:1-14; I Cor. 1:17-18, 21, 23; 2:2).

When the Cross of Christ ever is the Object of our Faith, the Holy Spirit, Who works exclusively within the confines, i.e., the parameters, of the Finished Work of Christ, will then work mightily within our lives, bringing about that which is desired.

THE HOLY SPIRIT

Whatever it is we need, there is no way that we, within ourselves, can bring it about. It can only be done by the Power of the Holy Spirit. That's why the Great Prophet Zechariah said:

"This is the Word of the LORD . . . saying, Not by might, nor by power, but by My Spirit, saith the LORD of Hosts (The phrase, *'Not by* [human] *might, nor by* [human] *power, but by My Spirit,'* presents God's Method of accomplishing His Work. Everything that ever has been done on this Earth, as it regards the Godhead, has been done by the Holy Spirit, with the exception of Christ and His Crucifixion; however, the Holy Spirit even superintended that from the beginning to the end [Lk. 4:18-19])" (Zech. 4:6).

If it is claimed to be for the Lord, whatever is being done must be done by the Moving, Operation, Power, and Person of the

Holy Spirit through Believers. Otherwise, it will not be recognized by God; in fact, it will be constituted as a *"work of the flesh"* (Rom. 8:1).

The phrase, *"Saith the LORD of Hosts,"* presents God's Supreme Personal Power over everything in the material and spiritual universe. All is organized under His Command. As well, the word *"Hosts,"* as used here, is associated with warfare and relates to the word, *"armies."* In other words, He is the *"LORD of Armies"* (Zech. 4:6).

SANCTIFICATION

At the present time, the modern Church is attempting to sanctify itself, that is, if it even knows what the word *"Sanctification"* actually means. Preachers are putting forth every type of proposed plan, with virtually none of these plans being Scriptural, which means the Cross is being ignored.

Let us say it again:

It is the Holy Spirit Alone Who can carry out in our lives that which needs to be, whatever it is (Rom. 8:2). And the Holy Spirit, as stated, works entirely within the framework of the Cross of Christ. So, He demands that our faith be exclusively within the Cross of Christ, and nothing else. If our faith is placed in any other direction, we are labeled by the Lord as *"spiritual adulterers"* (Rom. 7:1-4).

(2) "DELIVER ME IN YOUR RIGHTEOUSNESS, AND CAUSE ME TO ESCAPE: INCLINE YOUR EAR UNTO ME, AND SAVE ME."

This seems to be language that David would have used at the time of Absalom's rebellion. At a later day, it also would refer to the Lord Jesus Christ and to Israel that will face the Antichrist in the last days.

DELIVERANCE

David said, *"Deliver me."* The world of psychology treats men, but only their symptoms. It cannot *"deliver"* men. Only God can *"deliver."* In fact, man does not need treatment; he needs Deliverance.

There is no way that David, the Messiah, Israel, or any Believer, for that matter, can *"escape"* the clutches of darkness except by putting their trust in the Lord Jesus Christ, and what He has done for us at the Cross.

NOTES

When will the modern Church ever learn this?

Prayer is here enjoined as the vehicle that brings God's Help. The words, *"Incline Your ear unto me, and save me,"* speak of travailing prayer. Prayer is the key that unlocks every door, and yet the modern Church little proclaims such from behind its pulpits or believes it in the pew.

(3) "BE THOU MY STRONG HABITATION, WHEREUNTO I MAY CONTINUALLY RESORT: YOU HAVE GIVEN COMMANDMENT TO SAVE ME; FOR YOU ARE MY ROCK AND MY FORTRESS."

The Lord is the One to Whom we can always go, i.e., *"continually resort."* If we will do so, the *"Commandment"* is given to save us. It is a *"Commandment"* that cannot be abrogated by the powers of darkness. The reason is because God is a *"Rock"* and a *"Fortress."* He also is *"my Rock"* and *"my Fortress."*

(4) "DELIVER ME, O MY GOD, OUT OF THE HAND OF THE WICKED, OUT OF THE HAND OF THE UNRIGHTEOUS AND CRUEL MAN."

As David cried these words, they, in a greater way, will fulfill themselves at the Second Coming of the Lord, when He delivers Israel out of the hands of the Antichrist. That is the prophetic meaning of this Passage. It also serves as a foundation for every Believer, and for all time.

(5) "FOR YOU ARE MY HOPE, O LORD GOD: YOU ARE MY TRUST FROM MY YOUTH."

Once again, *"trust in God"* is the theme. Man can either *"hope"* in other men or *"hope"* in God. He cannot place *"hope"* in both.

FAITH IN GOD

From the time that David was old enough to understand, his father Jesse told him of the Ways of the Lord. From the time of his *"youth,"* he learned to trust God. He did so with the *"bear"* and with the *"lion"*; consequently, when he faced Goliath, his faith had already been honed for several years. Actually, when Goliath first saw him, the Scripture says, *"He disdained him: for he was but a youth"* (I Sam. 17:42). But David was a *"youth"* who had long since put his trust in God.

This, and this alone, is the answer to the drug problem in America, the answer to the inner-cities, the answer to rebellion — *"trust in God from my youth."*

(6) "BY YOU HAVE I BEEN HELD UP FROM THE WOMB: YOU ARE HE WHO TOOK ME OUT OF MY MOTHER'S BOWELS: MY PRAISE SHALL BE CONTINUALLY OF YOU."

This speaks of David and of Christ. It also speaks of Israel that was born from Sarah's womb.

ABORTION

The first part of this Verse shows us the horror of murderous abortion. America and any other nation in the world which engage in this horrifying practice will stand one day before God and answer to Him. To be sure, answer they shall! It will not be a pleasant moment for the guilty. Three things are said here:

1. God called David, even from his mother's womb. It was true that the Spirit of God did not come on him until after the anointing by Samuel (I Sam. 16:13). But the Call of God was on David's life even in *"the womb."* The real reason for David's greatness was, *"My praise shall be continually of You."*

2. This Passage speaks also of the Greater Son of David and the Incarnation. There is no way the mind of man can even begin to comprehend the Glory of God becoming man and dwelling among men. Isaiah prophesied that a *"Virgin shall conceive"* (Isa. 7:14). As the secret of David's greatness was praise to God, likewise, the life of the Greater Son of David also was a continuous praise!

3. As stated, this Passage speaks of three (David, Christ, and Israel). Of those three, Israel has little lived up to this Prophetic Promise: however, at the Second Coming, Israel will then begin to praise the Lord and will forever praise Him *"continually."*

(7) "I AM AS A WONDER UNTO MANY; BUT YOU ARE MY STRONG REFUGE."

The meaning of this Verse is that due to David's, the Messiah's, and Israel's many enemies, it was *"a wonder"* that each survived. They did so because God was their *"strong refuge."*

NOTES

(8) "LET MY MOUTH BE FILLED WITH YOUR PRAISE AND WITH YOUR HONOR ALL THE DAY."

David and the Messiah fulfilled this Passage in its entirety. Israel one day will fill her mouth with praise of the Lord Jesus Christ *"all the day."* *"Praise"* is so powerful that we should open it up to the Bible Student somewhat more.

PRAISE

1. It is impossible to *"praise"* and doubt at the same time. *"Praise"* is the key to faith.

2. *"Praise"* of God is a Prophetic Promise that Satan has lost, and God has won.

3. There is little *"praise"* for God that goes up from the Earth at this particular time. By and large, the mouths of men are filled with profanity, cursing, and blasphemy. One day soon that will change. Then, *"everything that has breath will praise the LORD."* Our praises at the time proclaim to the world and Satan that this day will come (Ps. 150:6).

4. Every Believer should subconsciously and consciously praise the Lord constantly. It doesn't have to be loud, but it should be continuous. This is the answer to stress, emotional disturbances, nervous disorders, physical weakness, etc.

5. Praise is the key to Victory. We must never forget that!

(9) "CAST ME NOT OFF IN THE TIME OF OLD AGE; FORSAKE ME NOT WHEN MY STRENGTH FAILS."

This, of course, speaks of David. Even more so, it speaks of Israel. The Holy Spirit reviews God's Love and Care for Israel under her training by Him from birth to old age. She was born of Sarah. She is spoken of at birth (Vs. 6), in her youth (Vs. 5), in her maturity (Vs. 7), and then in *"old age."*

More particularly, this speaks of Israel in the last half of the Great Tribulation, which is soon to come. At that time, her strength will fail. So, she pleads with God to not forsake her. The pleading is that God should not forsake her because of her great sins; therefore, God will not forsake her and will come to her rescue.

ON A PERSONAL NOTE

Personally, I believe the Lord has given

me a mandate to touch this world for Christ. To be sure, we have seen great things in the past, literally hundreds of thousands brought to a saving knowledge of the Lord Jesus Christ, for which we give the Lord all the praise and all the glory.

But in the midst of this, there have been horrifying setbacks. But yet, the burden is still there, the longing is still there, and the cry of the soul is continuous, because the *"course is not yet quite finished."*

As I come into old age, I continually ask the Lord that He give me strength that I might finish that which God has called me to do.

A few months ago (2005), the Lord brought to my mind a Word that He had given to Joshua so long, long ago. He said to the Great Warrior:

"You are old and stricken in years (Joshua, at this time, was probably about 101 years of age), *and there remains yet very much land to be possessed* (the account in this Thirteenth Chapter of Joshua concerns the possession of the land, or the lack thereof, and points to every Believer that which the Lord has prepared for us; however, there are enemies between the Promise and the Possession. God has a Perfect Plan for us, but, regrettably, so few of us press through to that Perfect Plan. We all too often stop short! The words, *'There remains yet very much land to be possessed,'* should strike long, hard, and true to the heart of every Believer)" (Josh. 13:1).

When the Lord gave me this Passage and made it real to my heart, I personally believe He was telling me that even though, spiritually speaking, there was still very much land to possess, still, by the Grace of God, He would help me to possess that land, and thereby *"to finish the course."*

I believe, most assuredly, that the Lord will help me to do this!

(10) "FOR MY ENEMIES SPEAK AGAINST ME; AND THEY WHO LAY WAIT FOR MY SOUL TAKE COUNSEL TOGETHER."

This could be said of David, the Messiah, and of Israel under the Antichrist.

These *"enemies"* of David, the Messiah, and of Israel in the Last Days will be, by and large, religious. Religion, which is man-made, has ever been the nemesis of God. It began with Cain, as recorded in the Fourth Chapter of Genesis.

Absalom, in his rebellion against David, claimed to be serving the Lord (II Sam. 15:8). The High Priest and the ruling religious order of Israel claimed to be serving God when persecuting Christ; likewise, the Antichrist will claim to be God and will demand worship (Rev. 13:4).

As stated, these *"enemies"* constitute the apostate Church, as it has always constituted the apostate Church!

(11) "SAYING, GOD HAS FORSAKEN HIM: PERSECUTE AND TAKE HIM; FOR THERE IS NONE TO DELIVER HIM."

Absalom and his cohorts would say this of David because of the situation with Bathsheba. Most of Israel believed it also. However, God had not forsaken David; in fact, He would not forsake him. God will never forsake anyone who comes to Him in humble contrition and Repentance.

Neither does He change His Call or Plan for the person's life. God called David to be King; that Call had not changed or been abrogated.

THE CALL OF GOD IS WITHOUT REPENTANCE

Consequently, with this type of self-righteous thinking, Absalom and Israel felt free to persecute David. How little it has changed today.

In their self-righteous minds, they felt that God would not deliver David because of his sin with Bathsheba. But, because they lacked understanding of the Grace of God, it would lead to their defeat. God would *"deliver him."*

Israel thought and said the same thing of Christ at His Trial and Crucifixion. Ironically enough, the Antichrist will say the same to Israel during the latter half of the Great Tribulation (Mat. 7:1-2).

Please allow me to make the following statement:

When one is down and cannot defend himself in anyway, and anyone can do any negative thing to him they so desire, and will not be reprimanded, but rather applauded, one then finds out how many true Christians there really are. Regrettably, there aren't many!

But thank God for the few True Believers.

(12) "O GOD, BE NOT FAR FROM ME: O MY GOD, MAKE HASTE FOR MY HELP."

This cry came from David at the most critical time in his life, during Absalom's rebellion. This cry also came from Christ while He was on the Cross.

Prophetically, it will come from Israel during the Battle of Armageddon when it seems that all is lost.

(13) "LET THEM BE CONFOUNDED AND CONSUMED WHO ARE ADVERSARIES TO MY SOUL; LET THEM BE COVERED WITH REPROACH AND DISHONOR WHO SEEK MY HURT."

Several things are said here. They are as follows:

ANSWERED PRAYER

1. As David prays this prayer, it is inspired by the Holy Spirit. Humble contrition and Repentance before God on the part of these *"enemies"* will bring Mercy, Grace, and Deliverance. Otherwise, it will be done exactly as stated.

2. Absalom was killed along with all those *"who sought the hurt"* of David.

3. As this applies to Christ, Judas committed suicide. Furthermore, Caiaphas, the High Priest, who officiated at Jesus' trial (a mock trial) also committed suicide. Also, Jerusalem was totally destroyed by Titus and his armies in A.D. 70.

4. The Antichrist will be totally defeated at the Battle of Armageddon by the Coming of the Lord.

One who opposes God cannot win out. *"If God be for us, who can be against us?"* (Rom. 8:31).

(14) "BUT I WILL HOPE CONTINUALLY, AND WILL YET PRAISE YOU MORE AND MORE."

In Psalms 70 and 71, the word *"continually"* is used three times:

CONTINUALLY

1. *"Say continually, Let God be magnified"* (Ps. 70:4).

2. *"Continually resort to my strong habitation,"* which is God (Ps. 71:3).

3. *"But I will hope continually"* (Ps. 71:14).

NOTES

The word *"hope"* in the Bible is somewhat different from the word *"hope"* in our modern language. The word *"hope"* now basically means *"it may or may not happen."* The word *"hope,"* as used in the Bible, means that it is guaranteed to happen, but it is not known exactly when.

In reference to this *"hope,"* we will *"praise You more and more."*

Verses 14 through 16 present a praise for God that the petitions of the previous Verses will be answered.

At any rate, the word *"continually"* refers to a constant dedication to the Lord, a dedication which is unending.

(15) "MY MOUTH SHALL SHOW FORTH YOUR RIGHTEOUSNESS AND YOUR SALVATION ALL THE DAY; FOR I KNOW NOT THE NUMBERS THEREOF."

The expression, *"I know not the numbers,"* is a figure denoting infinitude (without number).

Once again, the first phrase of this Verse speaks of a constant praise and testimony to the Faithfulness of our Lord.

(16) "I WILL GO IN THE STRENGTH OF THE LORD GOD: I WILL MAKE MENTION OF YOUR RIGHTEOUSNESS, EVEN OF YOURS ONLY."

David said these words, and Israel also will proclaim them in the Millennial Reign. For so many centuries, she has trusted in her own righteousness (Rom. 10:3). Then, she will make mention only of *"Your Righteousness,"* that which speaks of the Lord. This portrays the great battleground between the flesh and the Spirit. The *"strength of the LORD"* is in the Spirit and not in the flesh (Rom. 8:1-2).

WALKING AFTER THE FLESH AND WALKING AFTER THE SPIRIT

Concerning this subject, Paul said, *"There is therefore now no condemnation* (guilt) *to them which are in Christ Jesus* (refers back to Romans 6:3-5 and our being baptized into His Death, which speaks of the Crucifixion), *who walk not after the flesh* (depending on one's personal strength and ability or great religious efforts in order to overcome sin), *but after the Spirit* (the Holy Spirit works exclusively within the legal confines of the

Finished Work of Christ; our Faith in that Finished Work, i.e., *'the Cross,'* guarantees the help of the Holy Spirit, which guarantees Victory)" (Rom. 8:1).

In short, *"walking after the flesh"* constitutes one placing one's faith in anything, no matter what it might be, other than the Cross of Christ.

"Walking after the Spirit" constitutes one placing one's faith exclusively in Christ and the Cross, and in nothing else. In other words, one makes the Cross of Christ the Object of one's Faith, and that exclusively!

(17) "O GOD, YOU HAVE TAUGHT ME FROM MY YOUTH: AND HITHERTO HAVE I DECLARED YOUR WONDROUS WORKS."

This could be said of David, but more so of the Messiah. Both David and the Messiah *"declared"* His *"wondrous works."* Israel also will do the same in the coming Kingdom Age.

Parents should start teaching their children about the Ways of the Lord from the time they are old enough to read, even before. In fact, one cannot start too early. If they would do such, raising them in the way they ought to go, the Scripture plainly tells us, *"When he is old, he will not depart from it"* (Prov. 22:6).

What a Promise! Especially considering the world in which we now live!

(18) "NOW ALSO WHEN I AM OLD AND GREYHEADED, O GOD, FORSAKE ME NOT; UNTIL I HAVE SHOWN YOUR STRENGTH UNTO THIS GENERATION, AND YOUR POWER TO EVERY ONE WHO IS TO COME."

This could be said of David and Israel, as well as every Believer, for that matter.

FINISH THE COURSE AND KEEP THE FAITH

David most certainly said these words of himself, desiring strongly that he finish the work God had called him to do, *"to show Your strength unto this generation"* and to *"every one who is to come."*

It could be said of Christ, although not literally, because He was only thirty-three when He was crucified. However, it could be said figuratively of Him while He was on the Cross, dying for humanity, as He bore the sin of the world.

NOTES

It most certainly will be said of Israel in the latter half of the Great Tribulation, especially during the coming Kingdom Age. Then she will show God's Strength and Power to the whole world forever.

(19) "YOUR RIGHTEOUSNESS ALSO, O GOD, IS VERY HIGH, WHO HAS DONE GREAT THINGS: O GOD, WHO IS LIKE UNTO YOU!"

The righteousness of man is very low. The Righteousness of God *"is very high."* Men keep trying to earn their own righteousness, which is impossible, especially when it's free for the asking from God.

The *"great things"* that He did primarily speak of the Incarnation, when God became flesh and dwelt among men and then paid the price on Calvary's Cross for the Redemption of mankind.

(20) "YOU, WHICH HAVE SHOWN ME GREAT AND SORE TROUBLES, SHALL QUICKEN ME AGAIN, AND SHALL BRING ME UP AGAIN FROM THE DEPTHS OF THE EARTH."

This primarily speaks of the Resurrection of Christ. Because He lives, we shall live also.

(21) "YOU SHALL INCREASE MY GREATNESS, AND COMFORT ME ON EVERY SIDE."

All of this applies to David, Christ, and Israel. It also applies to every Believer, as should be obvious!

(22) "I WILL ALSO PRAISE YOU WITH THE PSALTERY, EVEN YOUR TRUTH, O MY GOD: UNTO YOU WILL I SING WITH THE HARP, O THOU HOLY ONE OF ISRAEL."

This Passage gives further proof that David was the author. Even though there were others who would sing with the harp, still, David strongly alludes to such in other Passages (Ps. 57:8).

MUSIC AND WORSHIP

Music is an integral part of worship. When revival wanes in the local Church, the music becomes stilted and formal, and finally, by and large, disappears altogether, at least in the realm of worship.

This is one of the reasons that Satan has fought so hard as it regards music concerning the worship of the Lord. For instance, that which sometimes is referred to as *"contemporary music,"* which means that it's very much like the world, even like the very worst the world has to offer, is regrettably being used in many Churches. The Holy Spirit, needless to say, cannot function in such.

Music was originated by the Lord. It is made up of three parts, melody, rhythm, and harmony. If any one of these is perverted, the Holy Spirit simply will not function. And, to be sure, contemporary music, or whatever it is called, falls into the category of distorted harmony or melody, or both.

Music, as it refers to the Lord, is not necessarily meant to draw in people, but rather to worship God. While it might accomplish the former, that is not its chief purpose. Therefore, if it fails of true worship, then it fails altogether!

(23) "MY LIPS SHALL GREATLY REJOICE WHEN I SING UNTO YOU; AND MY SOUL, WHICH YOU HAVE REDEEMED."

David says that he would sing of God's great redemptive power. More specifically, he would sing about the Redemption of his own soul. No wonder the Holy Spirit inspired John Newton to write the song, *"Amazing Grace."*

(24) "MY TONGUE ALSO SHALL TALK OF YOUR RIGHTEOUSNESS ALL THE DAY LONG: FOR THEY ARE CONFOUNDED, FOR THEY ARE BROUGHT UNTO SHAME, WHO SEEK MY HURT."

Either David says these words by faith concerning Absalom, or else this latter portion is written after the defeat of Absalom.

Moreover, those who sought the hurt of the Messiah were *"brought to shame."* Those who seek the hurt of Israel will be *"brought to shame"* in the Battle of Armageddon.

PSALM 72

A Psalm of David:
Prayer for Solomon

(1) "GIVE THE KING YOUR JUDGMENTS, O GOD, AND YOUR RIGHTEOUSNESS UNTO THE KING'S SON."

David prays this prayer as it regards his son Solomon, who will occupy the throne after David has passed on. Even though it doesn't plainly say, we know from Verses 1 and 20 that David wrote this Psalm.

THE MILLENNIAL REIGN

Exodus, the second Book of the Pentateuch, opens with a people bound in slavery and closes with the Messiah throned in majesty (Ex. 40:34); likewise, the second Book of the Psalms begins with a people sunk in misery (Ps. 42) and ends with a King reigning in Glory (Ps. 72).

Christ's Millennial Reign and the universal happiness which it will secure is the subject matter of the Psalm. The Speaker is the Holy Spirit, with David being the mouthpiece; the Person spoken to is God, and the Person spoken of is Christ.

The Holy Spirit in Verse 1 asks God to commit the execution of His Judgments on the administration of His Justice unto the true Solomon and confidently states that the result will be the punishment of evil-doers (Vs. 4), the happiness of His people (Vss. 2-4), and their perpetual loyalty to God's Service (Vs. 5).

In these predictions there is no misgiving in the Divine mind as to the perfection of the Messiah's Government, just as in other Prophesies there is no misgiving as to the perfection of His Person and the efficacy of His atoning Work.

(2) "HE SHALL JUDGE YOUR PEOPLE WITH RIGHTEOUSNESS, AND YOUR POOR WITH JUDGMENT."

Now we come to the time of the Kingdom Age and the Government of our Lord, which will be worldwide in scope.

RIGHTEOUS JUDGMENT

The world has never known *"righteous judgment."* In the Millennial Reign it will, for the first time, enjoy such as could only be given by God.

In Psalms 69:29 Jesus is called *"poor and sorrowful."* Now, He Who has suffered poverty will at long last stand as the true champion of the *"poor."* They are even called *"Your poor."*

In the history of the human race, *"the poor"* have received precious little fair treatment. During the coming Kingdom Age, this will change. A few leaders down through history may possibly have had the poor at heart and tried to help them; however, the only real and lasting help they will receive will be at the Hands of the Lord Jesus Christ.

But the greater meaning as it regards the word *"poor,"* has to do with Israel as a people and as a nation.

ISRAEL

For reasons which they themselves do not even understand, the Jews have taken the brunt of sorrow and heartache for many, many centuries, and much of the world has expressed animosity towards them. Admittedly, Israel crucified her Messiah and our Saviour. But still, this is not the reason for the animosity of the world toward Israel. That animosity goes all the way back to the beginning, even to the time of Abraham. They are hated because God raised up these people, called these people, chose these people, and gave the Word of God and the Messiah through these people. These are the causes of the hatred!

It is ironical that Israel hates the Name of Christ, because it is for the Name of Christ that they are hated!

This will all change during the coming Kingdom Age.

(3) "THE MOUNTAINS SHALL BRING PEACE TO THE PEOPLE, AND THE LITTLE HILLS, BY RIGHTEOUSNESS."

The words, *"By Righteousness,"* indicate that as a result of the righteous rule of our Lord, the *"mountains"* and *"hills,"* which pertain to great and small governments, shall, for the first time, see peace which the world has never before known.

(4) "HE SHALL JUDGE THE POOR OF THE PEOPLE, HE SHALL SAVE THE CHILDREN OF THE NEEDY, AND SHALL BREAK IN PIECES THE OPPRESSOR."

The bounty of His Rule in favor of the poor, whether they be the disposed of the world, or Israel per se, is pointed to some eleven times in this Prophecy. This contrasts with the attitude of earthly sovereigns who, as a rule, are binding the oppressed and supporting the oppressor. Here we are plainly told that the Messiah will dispense justice in favor of the poor, not necessarily because they are poor, but because to do so is right.

(5) "THEY SHALL FEAR YOU AS LONG AS THE SUN AND THE MOON ENDURE, THROUGHOUT ALL GENERATIONS."

The idea of this Verse is that never again will sin, wickedness, and unrighteousness rule, beginning with the Kingdom Age, and then going into the Eternal Perfect Age to come!

(6) "HE SHALL COME DOWN LIKE RAIN UPON THE MOWN GRASS: AS SHOWERS THAT WATER THE EARTH."

The blessings beginning with the Kingdom Age, will be worldwide. They will be so abundant, that it will be like spring showers.

BLESSINGS

Our Lord is a fountain of Blessings. In fact, He blesses far more than any of us could ever begin to deserve. And yet, He wants to bless more, and can bless more, that is, if men will only function in the capacity of His Way and not their own way.

If Believers truly live for God, truly try to please Him, and truly look to Christ and the Cross, they can and should expect Blessings of every nature.

(7) "IN HIS DAYS SHALL THE RIGHTEOUS FLOURISH; AND ABUNDANCE OF PEACE SO LONG AS THE MOON ENDURES."

The Solaric Covenant is once again called into focus. It was first addressed in Verse 5. Now, unrighteousness flourishes; then *"the righteous will flourish."* Now there is no peace; then, *"an abundance of peace so long as the moon endures,"* which actually means *"forever."*

All of this tells us that the world is not going to be destroyed by atomic war. As well, it won't be destroyed by the greenhouse effect, by ozone depletion, or any other such like problem.

To be sure, if man is allowed to continue it would very well be destroyed; however, Jesus Christ is coming back, and the Government will then be upon His Shoulder, and of His Kingdom there will be no end, which means that all of these problems will then be gloriously solved, and without difficulty.

(8) "HE SHALL HAVE DOMINION ALSO FROM SEA TO SEA, AND FROM THE RIVER UNTO THE ENDS OF THE EARTH."

This speaks of the entirety of Planet Earth. The prosperity will be evenly divided. There will be no more poverty-stricken nations where only a few are rich; all will be rich. And the reason is because *"He shall have dominion."*

(9) "THEY WHO DWELL IN THE WILDERNESS SHALL BOW BEFORE HIM; AND HIS ENEMIES SHALL LICK THE DUST."

The phrase, *"Shall lick the dust,"* is always a picture of complete submission of enemies.

THE DEFEAT OF ALL ENEMIES

At the present time, only a small portion of the Earth recognizes Jesus Christ as Lord Supreme. Even in so-called Christian nations, the dominion of Christ is spotty at best. Then, in the Kingdom Age, He will be supreme.

There will be no more lifting up of fake luminaries such as Muhammad, Buddha, Karl Marx, or any other poor mortal who has ever lived.

Even in places that have never proclaimed His Dominion (the wilderness), these *"shall bow before Him."*

(10) "THE KINGS OF TARSHISH AND OF THE ISLES SHALL BRING PRESENTS: THE KINGS OF SHEBA AND SEBA SHALL OFFER GIFTS."

The three great families of Shem, Ham, and Japheth will form His Dominion as predicted in Genesis 9:26-27.

This happened in measure with Solomon, who was a Type of Christ; however, the type only pointed toward the future glory that will encompass the entirety of the Earth. When Jesus comes, the reality will cover the Earth.

Christ will hold the answers to every question, the solution to all problems, and men from all over the world will come to Him seeking the solution to their problems; every last one will leave satisfied.

(11) "YEA, ALL KINGS SHALL FALL DOWN BEFORE HIM: ALL NATIONS SHALL SERVE HIM."

As we have repeatedly stated, this will be the time of the Kingdom Age.

At that time, the Lord Jesus Christ will be the Premier of the entirety of the Earth. The Scripture doesn't say that some kings will bow to Him, but rather *"All kings shall fall down before Him."* Every nation on the face of the Earth will then serve Him.

NOTES

At the present time, the nations of the world suffer because of heathenistic religions such as Islam, or Hinduism, etc. In fact, witchcraft rules many nations, which means that they are in part, or altogether, ruled by Satan.

All of this will end at the coming Kingdom Age.

(12) "FOR HE SHALL DELIVER THE NEEDY WHEN HE CRIES; THE POOR ALSO, AND HIM WHO HAS NO HELPER."

Now, the *"needy"* have little recourse. The *"poor"* also fall into the same category, because they *"have no helper."*

All of this will end in the coming Kingdom Age. In fact, the *"needy"* will be needy no longer, and the *"poor"* will be poor no longer.

(13) "HE SHALL SPARE THE POOR AND NEEDY, AND SHALL SAVE THE SOULS OF THE NEEDY."

The word *"spare"* in the Hebrew actually means *"shelter."* How so much the Holy Spirit in the entirety of this Chapter points toward the care that will be given to *"the poor and needy"*!

SALVATION

As well, this Chapter not only points toward the physical and material needs of *"the poor"* being met but also points to the Salvation of their *"souls."*

Unfortunately, in the whole of human history, little care and concern have been shown toward *"the poor."* Too often their *"souls"* are little cared for either. A precedent was set for this in the earthly Ministry of Christ. Mark said, *"The common (poor) people heard Him gladly"* (Mk. 12:37).

This should also be a lesson for our modern Churches. If the *"poor"* are not welcome, then the Gospel of Jesus Christ is not actually being preached.

(14) "HE SHALL REDEEM THEIR SOUL FROM DECEIT AND VIOLENCE: AND PRECIOUS SHALL THEIR BLOOD BE IN HIS SIGHT."

The poor through the ages have been *"deceived"* and have been the subject of *"violence."* Likewise, their *"blood"* has little been *"precious"* in the sight of man. They have born the brunt of wars, starvation, famine, and oppression. This will change, and change completely, under the administration of the Messiah.

Hallelujah!

In modern times, it can easily be observed that where the Gospel of Jesus Christ is preached and practiced (at least somewhat), the *"blood"* of the poor is more *"precious."* Where Jesus Christ is not championed, the poor are looked on as little more than cannon fodder.

(15) "AND HE SHALL LIVE, AND TO HIM SHALL BE GIVEN THE GOLD OF SHEBA: PRAYER ALSO SHALL BE MADE FOR HIM CONTINUALLY; AND DAILY SHALL HE BE PRAISED."

This Prophecy was partially fulfilled when the Queen of Sheba came to Solomon. It will be totally fulfilled in the coming Kingdom Age.

THE LORD JESUS CHRIST

At the time of the Kingdom Age, Jesus Christ will answer every question, solve every problem, heal all the sick, restore man's dominion, and bring spiritual, physical, domestic, and material prosperity. Without being taxed, the nations of the world will bring their *"gold"* to Him. The world will then pray to Him and for Him continually; they will keep praising Him all the day long. In fact, all Believers should have a liberal hand, a praying heart, and a praising tongue.

(16) "THERE SHALL BE A HANDFUL OF CORN IN THE EARTH UPON THE TOP OF THE MOUNTAINS; THE FRUIT THEREOF SHALL SHAKE LIKE LEBANON: AND THEY OF THE CITY SHALL FLOURISH LIKE GRASS OF THE EARTH."

Here is presented the idea that a small amount of seed, planted even in the most unlikely places, will then bring forth an abundant harvest.

Lebanon was noted for its huge cedars. In that time, the crops will be so abundant that, in size, they will be like the great cedars of Lebanon!

At that time, cities will not have a few places devoted to the rich, with the rest being ghettos; all of each city will prosper and be blessed, and will actually *"flourish like grass of the Earth."*

What a day that will be!

NOTES

(17) "HIS NAME SHALL ENDURE FOREVER: HIS NAME SHALL BE CONTINUED AS LONG AS THE SUN: AND MEN SHALL BE BLESSED IN HIM: ALL NATIONS SHALL CALL HIM BLESSED."

This says *"His Name,"* not the name of Buddha, Muhammad, or any other so-called luminary.

Every newspaper in the world will herald His Name. So will every Radio and every Television set, and every other means of communication that may become prominent at that time. In fact, *"all nations shall call Him blessed."*

(18) "BLESSED BE THE LORD GOD, THE GOD OF ISRAEL, WHO ONLY DOES WONDROUS THINGS."

David looked ahead and saw what was coming. It has not even yet come, but come it shall!

In that coming Glad Day, Israel will know that Jesus Christ is God, and will recognize Him as such, and in every capacity.

At that time, the entirety of the Earth will see that the Lord only does wondrous things.

(19) "AND BLESSED BE HIS GLORIOUS NAME FOREVER: AND LET THE WHOLE EARTH BE FILLED WITH HIS GLORY; AMEN, AND AMEN."

Today the Earth is not filled with *"His Glory."* In that day, the entirety of the Earth, with no part excluded, will be filled with the *"Glory"* of Jesus Christ.

A double *"Amen"* is given, which proclaims the certitude of its fulfillment.

(20) "THE PRAYERS OF DAVID THE SON OF JESSE ARE ENDED."

This Twentieth Verse tells us that this is the last Psalm written by David and inspired by the Holy Spirit. Many of the Psalms which follow also were written by David, but undoubtedly they were composed before this one.

When the Book of Psalms was organized, the Holy Spirit inspired the placement of each Psalm. As previously stated, the 150 Psalms (songs) are comprised into five Books corresponding to the Five Books of the Pentateuch. Each Psalm was placed exactly where the Holy Spirit desired it, irrespective of the order in which He inspired them to be written.

BOOK THREE
(The Leviticus Book)
Concerning the Sanctuary
(Psalms 73-89)

PSALM 73

A Psalm of Asaph:
The Prosperity of the Wicked and their End

(1) "TRULY GOD IS GOOD TO ISRAEL, EVEN TO SUCH AS ARE OF A CLEAN HEART."

This Psalm was written by Asaph, who seems to have been the chief of David's music program and the worship of God (I Chron. 16:4-5).

THE SANCTUARY

This is the First Psalm of the Third Book which corresponds to the Leviticus Book of the Pentateuch. As the subject of the First Book was the Blessed Man, (Christ), and that of the Second Book, Israel (His people), the subject of this Third Book is the Sanctuary (His place).

The Divine title of Leviticus is: *"And He called."* Only those whom God chooses to call unto Him can worship Him, and He seeks such worshippers (Jn. 4:23).

Israel, as a worshipper in her future time of trouble, is the subject of the Book, rather than the Messiah and the Remnant, which is that of the first two Books.

Actually, Verse 1 is the conclusion of this Psalm. It accords with Romans 8:1. The similarity appears if both Verses are translated literally: *"Nothing is a condemnation"* and *"Nothing but good is God to Israel."* (Williams).[15]

(2) "BUT AS FOR ME, MY FEET WERE ALMOST GONE; MY STEPS HAD WELL NIGH SLIPPED."

Asaph, perplexed with the problem that the ungodly prosper and the children of the Kingdom at times suffer, learns the lesson that outside of the Sanctuary the mind is distracted and the heart fermented, but that inside all is peace. Looking in confounds, looking out confuses, looking up comforts.

PREOCCUPATION WITH SELF

Asaph's problem was *"self."* Preoccupation with *"self"* always leads to spiritual detraction. Men have ever tried to improve self; men have ever failed. In fact, one of the greatest pastimes in this nation is the improvement of self, or at least the effort to do so. Even the Christian mind fails when endeavoring to improve *"self." "Self"* can only be conquered when it is hidden in Christ. It can be hidden in Christ, only by the Believer placing his faith exclusively in Christ and the Cross. The Cross is the means by which all of this is done (Jn. 14:20; Lk. 9:23-24).

There is not an individual who doesn't need an improvement in self, even the Godliest! But we must understand that it is the Holy Spirit Who Alone can address the need, whatever that need might be. But He will do so only in His Way and Manner, which is always through Christ and the Cross (Rom. 8:1-2, 11).

(3) "FOR I WAS ENVIOUS AT THE FOOLISH, WHEN I SAW THE PROSPERITY OF THE WICKED."

If *"self"* is properly hidden in Christ, there will be no *"envy of the foolish."* Likewise, *"the prosperity of the wicked"* will be properly evaluated in its true spiritual sense, which we will see as this Chapter proceeds.

RELATIONSHIP

Asaph's problem plagues many Christians, even those who occupy high positions as Asaph in the Work of God. This man was in charge of the great worship services in Jerusalem. Under the guidance of the Holy Spirit, he had been appointed by David. Now he is backsliding, and doing so in the very midst of worship. Sadly, it is a common problem.

Judas would lose his way even while walking shoulder to shoulder with the Lord Jesus Christ. Location, geography, environment, and position have little to do with one's spiritual position as far as its possible influence is concerned. Christianity is not a place or a position; it is a relationship with a Person, the Man, Christ Jesus. So, Asaph will come very close to losing his way right in the midst of the greatest Move of God, at least at that time, on the face of the Earth.

THE KEY IS CHRIST

As we've already stated, the *"key"* to

successful and victorious Christian living is never environment, association, or participation. Judas had all of this, as did Asaph. The environment in both cases was excellent. The association was the same, as was the participation.

All of this means that a person can lose their way with God right in the midst of the greatest Move of God that could ever be.

Christ must be the central focus at all times of our life and living. Just as important, we must understand that every single thing that Christ has done for us, is doing for us, and we hope to have done in the future, all, and without exception, comes by the means of the Cross (Lk. 9:23-24).

(4) "FOR THERE ARE NO BANDS IN THEIR DEATH: BUT THEIR STRENGTH IS FIRM."

When one becomes enamored with *"self,"* then one's spiritual judgment becomes flawed. Asaph fell into the age-old trap. First of all, *"prosperity"* is not the purpose of Redemption; Salvation is.

THE DEATH OF THE WICKED

Asaph was wrong about the *"death"* of the wicked. It is anything but positive.

The woman who saw Voltaire die said, *"For all the wealth of Europe, I would not see another infidel die."* (Voltaire was the noted French philosopher and atheist.) His experience would hold true in one way or another for all those who die without God.

Conversely, the death of the righteous is what Asaph erroneously thought was the death of the wicked.

As Toplady, who wrote the song, *"Rock of Ages Cleft for Me,"* was dying, he said, *"What a sunshine, all is light!"*

As the great Evangelist, Dwight L. Moody, was dying, he said, *"If this is death, then death is sweet. This is my coronation day."*

When the great Reformer, Martin Luther, was dying, he said, *"Lord, into your hands I commit my spirit."*

Shortly before the Apostle Paul died, he said, *"I have fought a good fight, I have finished my course, and I have kept the Faith"* (II Tim. 4:7).

Such has been the testimony of multiplied millions. No, there is no *"strength"* in the death of the wicked, only in the death of the righteous.

(5) "THEY ARE NOT IN TROUBLE AS OTHER MEN; NEITHER ARE THEY PLAGUED LIKE OTHER MEN."

Again, Asaph is wrong, but, yet, in some ways he is right.

TROUBLE

The *"trouble"* that is spoken of concerning the righteous has to do with two things:

1. The world's system is not of God but of Satan; consequently, the Child God is constantly *"plagued"* by that system.

2. The Believer, so to speak, is swimming against the tide; consequently, all the debris that comes downstream hits hard against him. But, considering that, still, the life of the follower of Christ is, by far, the most rewarding life there is. If there were no Eternity, living for God would still be the greater choice by far.

(6) "THEREFORE PRIDE COMPASSES THEM ABOUT AS A CHAIN; VIOLENCE COVERS THEM AS A GARMENT."

Asaph is saying that *"the wicked"* constantly engage themselves in *"violence"* with few negative results. As well, they are filled with *"pride,"* and instead of it bringing destruction, it seems to reward them.

(7) "THEIR EYES STAND OUT WITH FATNESS: THEY HAVE MORE THAN HEART COULD WISH."

These statements show that Asaph has given this much thought. Due to his preoccupation with *"self,"* Satan has made great inroads into his soul. One of Satan's greatest weapons is to make the Christian think that by living for God, he is truly missing out; however, Satan is a liar and the father of lies. Truly, the opposite is true.

(8) "THEY ARE CORRUPT, AND SPEAK WICKEDLY CONCERNING OPPRESSION: THEY SPEAK LOFTILY."

The speech of the wicked is lofty concerning how they will oppress people, and no harm seems to come to them, at least so Asaph thinks!

(9) "THEY SET THEIR MOUTH AGAINST THE HEAVENS, AND THEIR TONGUE WALKS THROUGH THE EARTH."

Everything the wicked say is in opposition

to the Word of God. As well, they boast of what they will do, evil as it may be, and they seem to be able to do such without hindrance.

(10) "THEREFORE HIS PEOPLE RETURN HITHER: AND WATERS OF A FULL CUP ARE WRUNG OUT TO THEM."

At times, the wicked cause men who have been converted from a life of covetousness to return to it.

(11) "AND THEY SAY, HOW DOES GOD KNOW? AND IS THERE KNOWLEDGE IN THE MOST HIGH?"

In other words, they laugh at God, thinking they are getting by with their wickedness.

(12) "BEHOLD, THESE ARE THE UNGODLY, WHO PROSPER IN THE WORLD; THEY INCREASE IN RICHES."

In all of this, Asaph seems for the most part to have his eyes on material things. The Bible teaches that prosperity is actually a part of God's Blessings upon His people. However, as we have stated, financial prosperity is not the real reason for Redemption, but rather Salvation. In fact, the Lord wants to bless His people; He will do so in every capacity, if they will only *"seek first the Kingdom of God and His Righteousness"* (Mat. 6:33).

While it is true that some of the ungodly *"prosper financially,"* as a whole it is not true.

(13) "VERILY I HAVE CLEANSED MY HEART IN VAIN, AND WASHED MY HANDS IN INNOCENCY."

A great truth is given to us in this Verse.

FAITH

Every attack that Satan levels against a Believer, irrespective of its direction, is for one purpose: to destroy the faith of the individual. Asaph's faith is wavering. In other words, he is saying that there is no profit in living for God. In these four Verses (13-16) Asaph is doing several things that will rob the joy and even the Salvation of any Believer. They are:

1. He is preoccupied with *"self."* Notice the many times the personal pronoun *"I"* is used!

2. He is forgetting what Salvation really is. Salvation is far more than a few baubles and trinkets. It is Eternal Life in Christ!

3. He has allowed his spiritual vision to be trapped in the short view, when God intends for us to have the long view.

NOTES

In other words, he is saying that his endeavoring to live for God has reaped him no rewards whatsoever. How wrong he is! The rewards of the wicked, such as they are, are fleeting and temporal. The rewards of the righteous are eternal.

(14) "FOR ALL THE DAY LONG HAVE I BEEN PLAGUED, AND CHASTENED EVERY MORNING."

The lesson continues!

COMPLAINING

The Lord is sorely displeased with these types of complaints. This is the opposite of faith and appreciation for what the Lord has done for us, is doing for us, and shall do for us. And yet, so many of us are guilty of this sin.

Whenever we complain, as all of us have at one time or the other, that says that God is not big enough to take care of us. It says that His Word isn't true. It says, in effect, that He has lied to us!

Now, we all know that none of us feel that way, but whenever we complain, this is exactly what we are saying, whether we understand such or not!

It is a sin to complain about anything!

(15) "IF I SAY, I WILL SPEAK THUS; BEHOLD, I SHOULD OFFEND AGAINST THE GENERATION OF YOUR CHILDREN."

Before Asaph voices his thoughts, his mind goes back to the many generations of untold numbers of Believers who have trusted God. The Lord has never failed any of them. So, he is saying that history is against him, which means that his complaints are groundless.

AN ILLUSTRATION

Through discouragement one dear Brother determined in his mind that he was going to cease living for the Lord. He felt that the Lord had not been fair to him, and had not blessed him as he thought he should be blessed. So, he made up his mind that he was going to close the door to the Lord.

But first, he felt that he should at least thank the Lord for all the things which the Lord had done for him in the past, irrespective of the present.

So, he went out into the barn, got on his knees, and began to thank the Lord for all the many things that had transpired in the past years. He recalled when his son was dying, and the Lord miraculously healed him. He recalled the bountiful harvests he had, at times, gathered, which he knew was a direct answer to prayer (he was a farmer).

Occasion after occasion began to come to him, as he endeavored to thank the Lord for all of these things. All of the sudden it hit him. He thought to himself, *"What am I doing?"*

He then said to the Lord, *"Master, You have done so much for me, that if You never do anything else, I owe you so much that I could never turn my back on You."*

(16) "WHEN I THOUGHT TO KNOW THIS, IT WAS TOO PAINFUL FOR ME."

Now, Asaph realizes he is wrong. He knows he is sliding down a path that leads only to destruction. Still, he does not know the answer to his dilemma. And then he says:

(17) "UNTIL I WENT INTO THE SANCTUARY OF GOD; THEN UNDERSTOOD I THEIR END."

How could the Sanctuary give him the answers? Because the Sanctuary is where God dwelt. Now, He no longer sees the alleged prosperity of the wicked, but the Glory of God. Then and only then do the flaws of the wicked become obvious.

As well, when he sees the Lord, he no longer sees himself.

Many Christians attend Churches where the Spirit of the Lord is not present. As well, they spend precious little time in the Bible or on their knees. Then the world and its ways begin to look attractive.

Conversely, the closer that one gets to God, the more he sees the Lord and the less he sees of the world. In fact, the world holds no more attraction. And what little of it he does see is repulsive.

Now, Asaph will portray to us what he sees regarding the world after he has properly seen the Lord.

(18) "SURELY YOU DID SET THEM IN SLIPPERY PLACES: YOU DID CAST THEM DOWN INTO DESTRUCTION."

On the surface, the road of the wicked looks prosperous; however, upon closer inspection it is easy to see that it is *"slippery."* Being so, they will ultimately fall to their own *"destruction."*

(19) "HOW ARE THEY BROUGHT INTO DESOLATION, AS IN A MOMENT! THEY ARE UTTERLY CONSUMED WITH TERRORS."

Now Asaph begins to see what the situation really is. The wicked look as though they are so prosperous, and then all of the sudden they are bankrupt and *"brought into desolation — as in a moment!"*

Now he sees that all of their boasting and clamor against God (Vs. 11) are but bravado. In a moment they are *"utterly consumed with terrors."*

(20) "AS A DREAM WHEN ONE AWAKES; SO, O LORD, WHEN YOU AWAKE, YOU SHALL DESPISE THEIR IMAGE."

At times, it may seem as though the Lord is asleep; however, after a short period the Lord will *"awake."* Then He will intrude into their evil *"dream."*

(21) "THUS MY HEART WAS GRIEVED, AND I WAS PRICKED IN MY REINS."

Now that Asaph has seen the Lord, he has come under Holy Spirit conviction. He is *"grieved"* because of his sin, and to be sure, complaining is a sin. What he has done now dawns upon him, and he is cut to the core of his being.

(22) "SO FOOLISH WAS I, AND IGNORANT: I WAS AS A BEAST BEFORE YOU."

Asaph portrays to us another great truth of the Word of God.

HOLY SPIRIT CONVICTION

One of the major Office Works of the Holy Spirit is to smite with conviction (II Sam. 24:10; Jn. 16:8-11). Sadly, most of the Church world no longer even believes in the convicting Power of the Holy Spirit.

Too often, Preachers attempt to appeal to men by the intellect. It is a wasted effort because intellect is not the problem. The evil heart of unbelief is the problem (Jer. 17:9-10). Only the Holy Spirit can go to the heart of a man and deal with the very seat of the problem. This is what is needed in our Churches, our pulpits, and in the pews possibly more than anything else.

(23) "NEVERTHELESS I AM CONTINUALLY WITH YOU: YOU HAVE HELD ME BY MY RIGHT HAND."

Thank the Lord that He does not cast us

off when we begin to go astray. Rather, He deals with us, speaks to us, and attempts to pull us back in the right direction. He will literally hold us by the hand, so to speak!

(24) "YOU SHALL GUIDE ME WITH YOUR COUNSEL, AND AFTERWARD RECEIVE ME TO GLORY."

Asaph had previously been listening to the *"counsel"* of self-will. Now he tells the Lord, *"I will listen to Your counsel."* God's *"counsel"* is His Word.

It is easy to see that Asaph has had his eyes on the wrong view.

(25) "WHOM HAVE I IN HEAVEN BUT YOU? AND THERE IS NONE UPON EARTH THAT I DESIRE BESIDE YOU."

After seeing the Lord and receiving a fresh touch from Glory, he realizes that his Salvation is not money, place, or position, but Christ. He now knows that Christ satisfies all. His *"desire,"* which had been misplaced, is now on the correct objective, the Lord Jesus Christ and what He has done for us at the Cross.

(26) "MY FLESH AND MY HEART FAILS: BUT GOD IS THE STRENGTH OF MY HEART, AND MY PORTION FOREVER."

Asaph realizes that he has been in the *"flesh"* (Rom. 8:1-6). As well, when he begins to lean on his own strength, which is woefully inadequate, he *"fails."* But now he realizes that *"God is his strength."* Also, he now knows that any and everything he needs can be provided by God — *"my portion forever."*

(27) "FOR, LO, THEY WHO ARE FAR FROM YOU SHALL PERISH: YOU HAVE DESTROYED ALL THEM WHO GO A WHORING FROM YOU."

Asaph now fully sees the position of the wicked. They *"shall perish."*

(28) "BUT IT IS GOOD FOR ME TO DRAW NEAR TO GOD: I HAVE PUT MY TRUST IN THE LORD GOD, THAT I MAY DECLARE ALL YOUR WORKS."

Some bad things have happened, but some *"good"* is coming out of this as well. His perilous situation has caused him to *"draw near to God."* Now his *"trust"* is in the Lord and not in the things that the world has. Asaph vows that he will no longer talk about the prosperity of the wicked but now will *"declare all Your Works."*

NOTES

PSALM 74

A Psalm of Asaph:
The Devastation of Mount Zion

(1) "O GOD, WHY HAVE YOU CAST US OFF FOR EVER? WHY DOES YOUR ANGER SMOKE AGAINST THE SHEEP OF YOUR PASTURE?"

This Psalm was also written by Asaph.

It is thought that this Asaph was the same man who was appointed by David as the chief of his musicians (I Chron. 16:4-6); however, some Scholars feel this could have been another Asaph, or perhaps it could have been even a particular order of musicians and singers named after *"Asaph"* or David. If the latter is the case, then no one knows who wrote the Psalms listed under Asaph's name. Still, it is more than likely that the instructions given and the salutation listing Asaph is referring to the Asaph appointed by David.

THE ENEMY IN THE SANCTUARY

The theme of this Psalm is the enemy in the Sanctuary, even as we shall see in Verse 3.

If it was written by Asaph of old, then the Temple had not yet been built. But still, the prophetic utterance given would refer to the first Temple built by Solomon, which many years later would be destroyed by the Chaldeans. As well, it refers to the second Temple that was destroyed by Titus in A.D. 70. It could possibly also speak of the future Temple that will be built on the Temple site in Jerusalem, and then ultimately taken over by the Antichrist. This Psalm describes the present condition of Zion under the treading down of the Gentiles.

In this First Verse the words, *"Your pasture,"* are used. Similar occurrences are throughout this Psalm — *"Your congregation"* (Vs. 2); *"Your inheritance"* (Vs. 2); *"Your Sanctuary"* (Vs. 7); *"Your turtledove"* (Vs. 19); *"Your poor"* (Vs. 19). These are terms of affection for Israel.

THE ANGER OF GOD

The question is asked by the Psalmist concerning the anger of God against Israel. The *"anger"* was not without cause. Israel had repeatedly gone into deep sin and rebellion. Despite repeated efforts by the Lord of Glory to bring them to the Altar of Repentance, they insisted on their own rebellious ways. Then and only then did God's *"anger smoke against the sheep of His pasture."*

We must remember that God's Anger does not come from personal motives. In other words, His Anger springs from Righteousness, while the anger of man mostly springs from unrighteousness. So, as should be obvious, they are totally different.

(2) "REMEMBER YOUR CONGREGATION, WHICH YOU HAVE PURCHASED OF OLD; THE ROD OF YOUR INHERITANCE, WHICH YOU HAVE REDEEMED; THIS MOUNT ZION, WHEREIN YOU HAVE DWELT."

This Psalm could also refer to the Intercessory Ministry of Christ on behalf of His people.

THE INTERCESSORY MINISTRY OF CHRIST

Little does even the most mature Christian understand the absolute horror of sin. As well, little can the pleadings of the sinner, as sincere as they may be, assuage the terrible wrong that has been done against God. Coupled with contrition and humility must be Christ's Intercessory Work (Heb. 7:25). In effect, everything the Believer receives from God comes through His Son, Christ Jesus. God cannot really bless poor fallen man, even though redeemed. He can only bless Christ within us. Neither can He answer prayer on any merit that we may have, or think we have, consecrated as we may think we are. He can only answer prayer on the merit of Jesus Christ (Jn. 16:23).

As well, any mighty works that we may do are done not at all within the boundaries of our own power. They must be done in His Name (Mk. 16:17). Also, our anointing is really His anointing, that is if we have any anointing at all (Lk. 4:18).

Here, the Intercessor calls to remembrance Israel *"purchased of old"*; consequently, God's *"purchase"* will one day serve Him; likewise, He has *"purchased"* the Church with His Own Blood (Acts 20:28). Therefore, He will have a Church despite the powers of darkness.

UNDERSTANDING THE INTERCESSORY MINISTRY OF CHRIST

Paul wrote: *"Wherefore He* (the Lord Jesus Christ) *is able also to save them to the uttermost* (proclaims the fact that Christ Alone has made the only true Atonement for sin; He did this at the Cross) *who come unto God by Him* (proclaims the only manner in which man can come to God), *seeing He ever lives to make intercession for them.* (His very Presence by the Right Hand of the Father guarantees such, with nothing else having to be done [Heb 1:3])" (Heb. 7:25).

In other words, the very Presence of Christ at the Throne of God, without Him having to say or do anything, guarantees such Intercession. It means that God has accepted the atoning Work that Christ performed on the Cross; thereby, He stands forever as our go-between. That's the reason that Paul also said:

"For there is one God (manifested in Three Persons — God the Father, God the Son, and God the Holy Spirit) *and One Mediator between God and men, The Man Christ Jesus.* (He can only be an adequate Mediator Who has sympathy with and an understanding of both parties, and is understandable by and clear to both; in other words, Jesus is both God and Man, i.e., 'Very God and Very Man')" (I Tim. 2:5).

(3) "LIFT UP YOUR FEET UNTO THE PERPETUAL DESOLATIONS; EVEN ALL THAT THE ENEMY HAS DONE WICKEDLY IN THE SANCTUARY."

The phrase, *"Lift up Your feet,"* refers to a perpetual flow of evil which God would not allow to run over His Feet. It speaks of the evil done in the Sanctuary. There are really four meanings to this Passage:

1. It refers to all the evil that was allowed and was done by the kings of Judah in allowing the Sanctuary to be polluted (II Chron. 33:4).

2. It refers to Nebuchadnezzar destroying Jerusalem and the Temple.

3. It refers to Titus, who destroyed Herod's Temple in A.D. 70.

4. It also refers to *"the abomination of desolation, spoken of by Daniel the Prophet, stand in the Holy Place"* (Mat. 24:15), which

refers to the Antichrist placing his image in the Jewish Temple at Jerusalem for the last three and a half years of the Great Tribulation Period.

(4) "YOUR ENEMIES ROAR IN THE MIDST OF YOUR CONGREGATIONS; THEY SET UP THEIR ENSIGNS FOR SIGNS."

The word *"ensigns"* means *"standard."* It refers to the Antichrist's image that will be set up in the rebuilt Temple at Jerusalem (Dan. 8:9-14; 9:27; 11:45; Rev. 13:1-18; 14:9-11; 20:4-6).

(5) "A MAN WAS FAMOUS ACCORDING AS HE HAD LIFTED UP AXES UPON THE THICK TREES.

(6) "BUT NOW THEY BREAK DOWN THE CARVED WORK THEREOF AT ONCE WITH AXES AND HAMMERS."

Verses 5 and 6 are meant to contrast each other. Verse 5 refers to the building of the Temple. Verse 6 refers to its destruction.

(7) "THEY HAVE CAST FIRE INTO YOUR SANCTUARY, THEY HAVE DEFILED BY CASTING DOWN THE DWELLING PLACE OF YOUR NAME TO THE GROUND."

As the Lord foretold the destruction of the Temple by the Romans, He repeated in substance Verses 7 and 8 of this Psalm. They cast it down to the ground; they did not leave one stone upon another; and history says they burned all of the Synagogues in Israel (Lk. 21:6).

It is said that Titus gave orders that the Temple was to be left standing; however, his soldiers had heard that there was gold between the great stones; therefore, they hooked oxen to these huge stones and pulled them down, but found no gold. The Temple was so completely burned, sacked, and destroyed that it is said that a harrow was run across the ground where the Temple had stood. Such was its destruction, and such was the fulfillment of Prophecy.

(8) "THEY SAID IN THEIR HEARTS, LET US DESTROY THEM TOGETHER: THEY HAVE BURNED UP ALL THE SYNAGOGUES OF GOD IN THE LAND."

We have a first mention in this Verse.

SYNAGOGUES

This is the first mention of *"Synagogues"* in the Old Testament. It was a place that served several functions. Actually, most all of the religious, social, and educational activity of Israel came to be centered in the *"Synagogues."*

Jesus preached extensively in the Synagogues in the first two years of His earthly Ministry. By and large, in the last year of His public Ministry, He was banned from most, if not all, of the Synagogues. Now it becomes somewhat obvious as to why God allowed them to be *"burned,"* which was carried out by the Romans.

(9) "WE SEE NOT OUR SIGNS: THERE IS NO MORE ANY PROPHET: NEITHER IS THERE AMONG US ANY WHO KNOWS HOW LONG."

This refers to the time between Malachi and John the Baptist when there was no Prophet for a period of approximately 400 years.

SIGNS

After the rejection of the Lord Jesus Christ, Who was the True Prophet, actually the fulfillment of all Prophecies of the past, Israel has now gone for about 2,000 years with *"no Prophet"* and *"no signs."*

During Christ's earthly Ministry, Israel asked for a *"sign."* Jesus answered them in this manner, *"There shall no sign be given to it but the sign of the Prophet Jonas (Jonah)"* (Mat. 12:39). This speaks of Christ's Death and Resurrection. Israel rejected this; therefore, no more signs would be given. No greater sign could be given than the Death and Resurrection of Christ.

(10) "O GOD, HOW LONG SHALL THE ADVERSARY REPROACH? SHALL THE ENEMY BLASPHEME YOUR NAME FOR EVER?"

This Passage certainly had meaning concerning the destruction of Judah by Nebuchadnezzar, but much more so it refers to the Great Tribulation, when the Antichrist, as the *"adversary,"* will *"reproach."* He, as no other, will *"blaspheme"* the Name of the Lord.

(11) "WHY DO YOU WITHDRAW YOUR HAND, EVEN YOUR RIGHT HAND? PLUCK IT OUT OF YOUR BOSOM."

This Verse proclaims an idiom that was frequently used in the Israel of that time.

If the hand was in the bosom, it represented no action being taken. But if it was pulled out of the bosom, it was a sign that action was about to be taken.

This prayer will be answered at the Battle of Armageddon when God will take His *"Right Hand"* (the Lord Jesus Christ) out of His *"bosom"* and dethrone the Antichrist.

(12) "FOR GOD IS MY KING OF OLD, WORKING SALVATION IN THE MIDST OF THE EARTH."

In Verses 12 through 17 the Psalmist proclaims the greatness and Glory of God. It is a plea for God to exert Himself and come to the rescue of His people.

(13) "YOU DID DIVIDE THE SEA BY YOUR STRENGTH: YOU BROKE THE HEADS OF THE DRAGONS IN THE WATERS."

This refers to the great deliverance of Israel from Egyptian bondage by the opening of the Red Sea. Here, the majesty of Egypt (*"the dragons"*) was broken.

(14) "YOU BROKE THE HEADS OF LEVIATHAN IN PIECES, AND GAVE HIM TO BE MEAT TO THE PEOPLE INHABITING THE WILDERNESS."

The word *"leviathan"* is a symbol for Satan. The language here is figurative of the defeat of Satanic powers. This speaks of the enemies of God being defeated. As Caleb said, *"For they are bread for us"* (Num. 14:9; Rev. 13:1-3; 17:7-10).

(15) "YOU DID CLEAVE THE FOUNTAIN AND THE FLOOD: YOU DRIED UP MIGHTY RIVERS."

The first part of this Verse seems to refer to the water that came out of the Rock when it was smitten by Moses (Ex. 17:6).

The latter portion refers to the drying up of the Jordan River when Joshua crossed with the Children of Israel into the Promised Land (Josh. 3:13-17).

(16) "THE DAY IS YOURS, THE NIGHT ALSO IS YOURS: YOU HAVE PREPARED THE LIGHT AND THE SUN."

This Passage refers to God as the Creator of all things, and the beauty and wonder of that of which He has created.

All of this debunks the absurdity of evolution. To be frank, evolution is such a crock that no person can honestly believe in this absurdity.

If evolution is true and correct, where are the intermediate species between ape and man? The contended efforts to find *"Big Foot"* become somewhat ridiculous, and even sickening. How ridiculous can we be?

(17) "YOU HAVE SET ALL THE BORDERS OF THE EARTH: YOU HAVE MADE SUMMER AND WINTER."

This could refer to the particular nations of the world containing particular types of people. It also refers to the continents and islands.

The latter portion of the Verse refers to God making the seasons, such as summer and winter, which are eternal (Gen. 1:14-18; 8:22).

(18) "REMEMBER THIS, THAT THE ENEMY HAS REPROACHED, O LORD, AND THAT THE FOOLISH PEOPLE HAVE BLASPHEMED YOUR NAME."

This speaks of those who have opposed the people of God down through the many centuries; however, its greater fulfillment will be when the Antichrist attempts to destroy Israel.

(19) "O DELIVER NOT THE SOUL OF YOUR TURTLEDOVE UNTO THE MULTITUDE OF THE WICKED: FORGET NOT THE CONGREGATION OF YOUR POOR FOREVER."

Both expressions, *"The turtledove"* and *"Your poor,"* refer to Israel. The Intercessor, Who now reverts from His role of Creator (Vss. 12-17) to that of pleading for His people, will ask the Father that they not be turned over to *"the wicked."* Paul called him, *"that wicked"* (II Thess. 2:8) — the Antichrist.

(20) "HAVE RESPECT UNTO THE COVENANT: FOR THE DARK PLACES OF THE EARTH ARE FULL OF THE HABITATIONS OF CRUELTY."

What does the Psalmist mean here by the word *"Covenant?"*

THE COVENANT

The *"Covenant"* that is spoken of here refers to the Promises that were made to the Prophets of old. It is referred to by Christ in the Lord's Prayer, *"Your Kingdom come, Your Will be done, in Earth as it is in Heaven"* (Mat. 6:9-10).

In the last phrase of this Verse, the Psalmist

is referring to the cruelty that is carried on in the world by evil men and women. So, the question is being asked, *"Oh Lord, how long will You tolerate such evil, considering that You have given Promises to Your Prophets?"*

THE CLOSE OF THE CHURCH AGE

This prayer was uttered by Asaph approximately 3,000 years ago. We are now coming to the end of the Church Age, and the great *"Covenant"* given to Isaiah and others, as it regards the coming Kingdom Age, are closer now to being fulfilled than ever. In fact, the Rapture of the Church could take place at any time. The world will then be plunged into some seven years of Great Tribulation, which will be worse than the Planet has ever known before. They will be culminated by the Second Coming, which will be the most cataclysmic event in history. Then will commence the age of Righteousness, when Jesus Christ Personally rules and reigns, which He will do so from Jerusalem for 1,000 years, and then forever, (Rev., Chpts. 21-22).

In other words, all of these Predictions and Promises are very, very close to the beginning of fulfillment!

(21) "O LET NOT THE OPPRESSED RETURN ASHAMED: LET THE POOR AND NEEDY PRAISE YOUR NAME."

This Verse leaps ahead to the coming Great Tribulation, when it looks like Israel will be totally destroyed by the Antichrist.

Israel will then cry to the Lord as never before; to be sure, He will answer. They will then *"praise His Name."*

(22) "ARISE, O GOD, PLEAD YOUR OWN CAUSE: REMEMBER HOW THE FOOLISH MAN REPROACHES YOU DAILY."

There are two points that are made in this Verse; both are beautiful.

1. Israel's Advocate presses this condition of His people as a reason why they should be delivered.

2. He identifies their interest with God. Hence, His Spirit in them calls on God to arise and plead His Own cause.

(23) "FORGET NOT THE VOICE OF YOUR ENEMIES: THE TUMULT OF THOSE WHO RISE UP AGAINST YOU INCREASES CONTINUALLY."

The clamor by the Antichrist will increase in intensity in the Battle of Armageddon. It seems there is no way he can lose. But lose he will, because the Lord will *"arise and plead His Own cause"* (Rev., Chpt. 19).

PSALM 75

*A Song of Asaph:
A Warning to the Wicked*

(1) "UNTO YOU, O GOD, DO WE GIVE THANKS, UNTO YOU DO WE GIVE THANKS: FOR THAT YOUR NAME IS NEAR YOUR WONDROUS WORKS DECLARE."

As noted, Asaph is the writer of this Psalm.

THE SECOND COMING

The speaker of this Verse is the redeemed; the Messiah Himself is the Speaker of the remaining Verses. He is addressed as God.

The phrase, *"Your Name is near,"* refers to the Second Coming. Jesus is the greatest Name of God — God manifest in the flesh.

Israel knew nothing of the Church nor the Rapture of the Church, and these things correspondingly are not mentioned in the Old Testament.

Even though the First Advent of our Lord was graphically portrayed (Isa., Chpt. 53), Israel did not actually read into it all that actually was there. They certainly were looking for the Messiah; but they were looking for a conquering Messiah, and definitely not a suffering Messiah, as Isaiah predicted. They did not at all picture themselves as needing a Redeemer. The Gentile world, yes! But Israel, no! Israel in fact thought that the Gentile world would be made to bow at the feet of Israel upon the appearance of the Messiah.

So when Jesus actually did come, He was not at all the type of Messiah which they were anticipating. So they rejected Him!

(2) "WHEN I SHALL RECEIVE THE CONGREGATION I WILL JUDGE UPRIGHTLY."

This speaks of the Second Coming, when the Lord Jesus will take over the reigns of Government, and will do so for the entirety of the world. It will be the Kingdom Age (Dan. 2:44-45; Rev. 11:15; 22:4-5).

(3) "THE EARTH AND ALL THE INHABITANTS THEREOF ARE DISSOLVED:

I BEAR UP THE PILLARS OF IT. SELAH."

This predicts the termination, confusion, and guilt of man's government, as well as the firm establishment of Messiah's rule, which will take place in the coming Kingdom Age. The latter portion of this Verse speaks of all creation, which is upheld by God through Christ (Heb. 1:3).

(4) "I SAID UNTO THE FOOLS, DEAL NOT FOOLISHLY: AND TO THE WICKED, LIFT NOT UP THE HORN."

Eastern women once wore a protruding ornament on the forehead called *"a horn."* As sons were born to them, their horn was raised, hence, the expression *"to lift up the horn."* It means to become proud. It addressed itself to all who would be lifted up in pride, and specifically addresses the Antichrist.

(5) "LIFT NOT UP YOUR HORN ON HIGH: SPEAK NOT WITH A STIFF NECK."

The coming Antichrist will lift himself up greatly. Paul said, *"And exalts himself above all that is called God, or that is worshipped"* (II Thess. 2:4).

(6) "FOR PROMOTION COMES NEITHER FROM THE EAST, NOR FROM THE WEST, NOR FROM THE SOUTH."

All of these prophetic announcements in Psalms can and do apply to all Believers. Every Christian should understand the following:

PROMOTION

Even though these Psalms were given by the Holy Spirit and pointed to Israel, still they also apply to the Church, at least in the general application; consequently, the pronounced judgments must be attended carefully by the modern Believer. As well, the Blessings promised can be claimed as directed.

The modern Believer, however, must understand that even though the judgments and the Blessings are applicable in measure, still, the intended prophetic fulfillment is to be summed up in Israel.

For instance, *"the horn of the proud"* spoken of in these Verses applies to anyone, but more specifically it applies to the coming Antichrist. Furthermore, the Holy Spirit through the Psalmist mentions all points of the compass except *"the north."*

Why?

NOTES

This tells us that Heaven is north of the Earth. This is confirmed in Isaiah 14:12-14. There it tells us that Lucifer ascended into Heaven from the *"sides of the north."* As a result, we are to understand that, in the Lord's dealings with humanity, promotion comes from *"the north,"* because this is where Heaven is located and where God resides.

(7) "BUT GOD IS THE JUDGE: HE PUTS DOWN ONE, AND SETS UP ANOTHER."

Regrettably, most in the modern Church look to other men for promotion. They little remember that *"God is the Judge."* God is saying that He, not man, is the One Who will *"lift up the horn."* When man does such, it always breeds pride. When God does such, it breeds humility.

In the strict interpretation of this Verse, it means that the Lord will *"put down"* the Antichrist and *"set up"* the Lord Jesus Christ.

(8) "FOR IN THE HAND OF THE LORD THERE IS A CUP, AND THE WINE IS RED; IT IS FULL OF MIXTURE; AND HE POURS OUT OF THE SAME: BUT THE DREGS THEREOF, ALL THE WICKED OF THE EARTH SHALL WRING THEM OUT, AND DRINK THEM."

The Holy Spirit through the Psalmist speaks of a coming day, which pertains to Christ and the entirety of Planet Earth.

THE CUP

The *"cup"* spoken of is a cup of judgment. Jesus spoke of this *"cup"* (Mat. 20:22). It was a cup of sufferings that He would have to drink, as well as His Disciples and all who would follow Him. The world is not in sympathy with the Lord Jesus Christ. The contention is with Christ. The contention is altogether with Christ.

"God" can be looked at in a generic sense, even though that is not correct. Still, the world thinks of God in many connotations, all of them wrong. However, the idea that the Lord Jesus Christ is the only way to the Father is greatly offensive to the world (Jn. 14:6). But, for many reasons, it happens to be true, with the greatest reason of all being that Jesus Christ is the Son of God, Who also paid the price on Calvary's Cross in order for mankind to be saved.

Jesus spoke of the *"cup"* again in the

Garden of Gethsemane (Lk. 22:42). It was filled with sin and death. Jesus drank from the *"cup"* and thereby took upon Himself the Judgment of God that should have come upon us.

Inasmuch as He drank of this cup, all who will not partake of His Great Salvation are called *"the dregs,"* which means the residue that is left over. All who refuse His Salvation will have to drink of *"the dregs,"* which means they will be turned into Hell, reaping what they have sowed (Gal. 6:7-8).

(9) "BUT I WILL DECLARE FOREVER; I WILL SING PRAISES TO THE GOD OF JACOB."

Some twenty-two times in Scripture, the Holy Spirit uses the phrase, *"The God of Jacob."* It refers to the God of Grace, Who met Jacob when He had nothing and deserved nothing but wrath. He promised to bless him and give him everything, which He did (Williams — Gen. 28:12-15).[16]

(10) "ALL THE HORNS OF THE WICKED ALSO WILL I CUT OFF; BUT THE HORNS OF THE RIGHTEOUS SHALL BE EXALTED."

This is a simple statement meaning that everything of man will be *"cut off,"* but everything of *"the righteous* (the Lord Jesus Christ) *shall be exalted."*

PSALM 76

A Psalm of Asaph:
A Song of Deliverance

(1) "IN JUDAH IS GOD KNOWN: HIS NAME IS GREAT IN ISRAEL."

As noted, this Psalm was written by Asaph.

THE GREATNESS OF OUR LORD

At the time of the writing of this Psalm, God was known *"in Judah."* He is not known there now; however, He will be known there in the future. His Name also will be *"great in Israel."*

The names of *"Judah"* and *"Israel"* are given for two reasons:

1. Judah is the Tribe from which Jesus came. As well, the greater part of Jerusalem was situated in the territory of the Tribe of Judah. It was looked at as the ruling Tribe (Gen. 49:10).

2. The name *"Israel"* came from the new name given by the Lord to Jacob (Gen. 32:28). It actually spoke of all of Israel; however, it came to be attached to the Northern portion which broke away from Judah, which resulted in the formation of two nations.

In the coming Kingdom Age, the entirety of the nation will once again be referred to as *"Israel"* (II Sam. 5:1-10).

Williams says, *"Psalm 74 speaks of the enemy in the Sanctuary. Psalm 75 speaks of the Messiah in the Sanctuary. Psalm 76 speaks of Messiah's destruction of the haters of the Sanctuary. Its fulfillment belongs to the days of Micah 4, Zechariah 12 and 14, along with Revelation 19 and other similar Prophecies, when the future kings of the Earth under the Antichrist will, with their armies, encompass Zion and, to their discomfiture, meet the Messiah there Who will judge them and deliver Israel."* [17]

(2) "IN SALEM ALSO IS HIS TABERNACLE, AND HIS DWELLING PLACE IN ZION."

"Salem" is the ancient name given by the Jebusites to Jerusalem (Gen. 14:18; Heb. 7:1-2). The Jebusite stronghold was captured by David when he became King of Israel. David made this city his capital and changed the name to Jerusalem.

"Zion" was the mountain on which the Temple ultimately was built. It also was the place where David stretched the Tabernacle after he took the city of Salem from the Jebusites (II Sam. 5:6-10; 6:1-23; 7:1-2). In a later Psalm, we will find that God Himself chose Zion as His dwellingplace (Ps. 132:13). The time of this choosing was probably when the great plague came upon Israel because of David's sin in numbering the people without giving the required offering of silver for each person, which typified Redemption (II Sam., Chpt. 24).

Then (before the Cross) God dwelt in Zion in the Sanctuary between the Mercy Seat and the Cherubim. Now God dwells no longer in a house made with hands but in the hearts and lives of His Children (I Cor. 3:16).

(3) "THERE BROKE HE THE ARROWS OF THE BOW, THE SHIELD, AND THE

SWORD, AND THE BATTLE. SELAH."

This speaks of the Battle of Armageddon, when the Lord will break in pieces the weapons of the Antichrist. It will take place in the Land of Israel, more particularly in the city of Jerusalem (Ezek. 39:9).

(4) "YOU ARE MORE GLORIOUS AND EXCELLENT THAN THE MOUNTAINS OF PREY."

This Verse goes back to the time when David took the stronghold of Zion, the city of Jebus, which later would be named Jerusalem. The phrase, *"The mountains of prey,"* speaks of this Jebusite stronghold, which was a thorn in Israel's side all the days of Saul. But David took that stronghold and made it his capital.

THE EXPERIENCE OF THE BELIEVER

In the midst of the inheritance that God gives every Believer, all afforded by Christ and dearly paid for at the Cross, Satan desires to erect a stronghold. He will do so without fail, unless we function according to God's Prescribed Order. Satan can be defeated in no other manner.

What is that Prescribed Order?

In short, it is *"Jesus Christ and Him Crucified"* (I Cor. 1:23).

The faith of the Believer must rest supreme in Christ and not at all in himself. The Believer also must understand that everything the Lord gives to us, and in whatever capacity, is all because of the Cross. In other words, while Christ is the Source, the Cross is the Means (Rom. 6:1-14).

When we place our faith in Christ and the Cross and maintain our Faith in Christ and the Cross, when we never allow our Faith to be moved to something else, then the Holy Spirit will work mightily within our lives, tearing down every stronghold of Satan, giving us total and complete victory, even as victory was given to David of old (Rom. 8:1-2, 11).

That is God's Prescribed Order. It is impossible to live victoriously for the Lord without functioning in the manner we have just described. While a person certainly can be Saved without that of which I speak, he definitely cannot grow in Grace and the Knowledge of the Lord except by making the Cross

NOTES

of Christ ever the Object of his Faith (Gal., Chpt. 5; 6:14).

(5) "THE STOUTHEARTED ARE SPOILED, THEY HAVE SLEPT THEIR SLEEP: AND NONE OF THE MEN OF MIGHT HAVE FOUND THEIR HANDS."

This Passage has a double meaning:

VICTORY

First of all, this Passage speaks of the defeat of the Jebusites by God under the leadership of David. The Jebusites were so powerful and so strong that they could not be defeated by natural means. In other words, David had to have supernatural help. That help was forthcoming.

The phrase, *"And none of the men of might have found their hands,"* means that the Lord discomfited them in many and varied ways. In other words, they simply were unable to fight as they should have. The account is given in II Samuel 5:6-10.

As well, this particular Verse speaks prophetically of the Antichrist at the Second Coming of the Lord. At that time, the Antichrist will not be able to *"find his hands,"* which means that his armies will be totally and completely defeated (Rev., Chpt. 19).

(6) "AT YOUR REBUKE, O GOD OF JACOB, BOTH THE CHARIOT AND HORSE ARE CAST INTO A DEAD SLEEP."

This refers to both the Jebusites and the Antichrist; the army of the Jebusites was slaughtered and the armies of the Antichrist also will be slaughtered (Ezek. 39:11-29).

(7) "YOU, EVEN YOU, ARE TO BE FEARED: AND WHO MAY STAND IN YOUR SIGHT WHEN ONCE YOU ARE ANGRY?"

This refers to the Jebusites and prophetically to the Antichrist. It says, *"The Great Day of His* (God's) *Wrath has come; and who shall be able to stand?"* (Rev. 6:17).

(8) "YOU DID CAUSE JUDGMENT TO BE HEARD FROM HEAVEN; THE EARTH FEARED, AND WAS STILL."

This reveals that Israel had some difficulty in taking the stronghold of Zion and might not have done so if God had not helped.

It also refers to the Second Coming of our Lord, when half of Jerusalem will fall to the Antichrist (Zech., Chpt. 14).

(9) "WHEN GOD AROSE TO JUDGMENT,

TO SAVE ALL THE MEEK OF THE EARTH. SELAH."

The *"meek of the Earth"* refers to Israel, at least in this case, when the Antichrist will seek to totally destroy him. At that time, God will *"arise to Judgment."*

"Let God arise and His enemies be scattered" (Ps. 68:1).

(10) "SURELY THE WRATH OF MAN SHALL PRAISE YOU: THE REMAINDER OF WRATH SHALL YOU RESTRAIN."

The *"wrath of man"* refers to the wrath of the Antichrist. The way that it will praise God is the same way that Pharaoh's death praised the Lord (Ex. 10:1-3).

"The remainder of wrath" refers to the Antichrist being halted in his efforts of the destruction of Israel and the dominion of the Earth by the coming of the Lord (Rev., Chpt. 19).

(11) "VOW, AND PAY UNTO THE LORD YOUR GOD: LET ALL THAT BE ROUND ABOUT HIM BRING PRESENTS UNTO HIM WHO OUGHT TO BE FEARED."

Under David and Solomon this was particularly fulfilled (II Chron. 9:13-14). It will be completely fulfilled on a worldwide basis in the coming Millennial Reign, when Christ rules from Jerusalem (Zech. 14:14).

(12) "HE SHALL CUT OFF THE SPIRIT OF PRINCES: HE IS TERRIBLE TO THE KINGS OF THE EARTH."

This means that in the days of the Millennial Reign men will rule only under Christ. If they refuse to carry out His Commands, they will find out that the price they have to pay will be *"terrible"* (Zech. 14:16-19).

In that day, the Lord will not allow sin or evil in any capacity to destroy the peace of the Earth.

PSALM 77

A Psalm of Asaph:
The Greatness of God

(1) "I CRIED UNTO GOD WITH MY VOICE, EVEN UNTO GOD WITH MY VOICE; AND HE GAVE EAR UNTO ME."

The First Verse is the summation of all the following Verses. It is a Psalm written by Asaph.

THE CRY OF THE SOUL

If a person truly comes to the Lord in humility and sincerity, the Lord will surely hear such a cry. He will never turn such away. That was true under the Old Covenant; if it were possible, it is even more true under the New Covenant (Heb. 8:6).

This Psalm pertains to Asaph on a personal basis and to every Believer; it also is a prophetic portrayal of Israel in the last half of the Great Tribulation. It seems she will be totally destroyed by the Antichrist. No doubt, Israel will refer repeatedly to this Psalm during that particular time.

(2) "IN THE DAY OF MY TROUBLE I SOUGHT THE LORD: MY SORE RAN IN THE NIGHT, AND CEASED NOT: MY SOUL REFUSED TO BE COMFORTED."

Several things are said in this Scripture:

In his difficulty, Asaph *"sought the Lord."* Let this be a lesson for the modern Church. If we seek man (for example, the psychologist), we will receive the help man can give, which is none. However, in times of trouble, which ultimately come to all Christians, if we will *"seek the Lord,"* we will receive the help that God can give, which is promised in this Chapter and which will meet our every need.

The phrase, *"My sore ran in the night, and ceased not,"* pertains to the problem that every Believer has. When problems come, they seem to be worse at night and keep the individual awake for hours, even sometimes all night long.

There is only one cure for that and that is prayer and the Word of God. On a personal basis, I always try to pray myself to sleep, or else quote Scriptures in the same capacity. However, at times, I will turn on the light and read several Chapters out of the Word of God, which always strengthens me and gives me peace.

THE CROSS OF CHRIST

Since the Lord in 1997 began to open up to me the great Word of the Cross, showing me what it meant, and I primarily refer to the Cross and our Sanctification, sleepless nights have been few and far between. I can't even remember one, at least one caused by worry, fear, or anxiety.

Unfortunately, precious few in the modern Church understand the Cross as it refers to Sanctification. Most Christians, even though they are sincere, have absolutely no knowledge whatsoever of the Cross in this capacity. They have a smattering of knowledge respecting Salvation; but, when it comes to Sanctification, if one broaches the subject, they will be met with a blank stare. That is tragic, especially considering that almost all of the writings of the Apostle Paul address this all-important subject. Satan has been very successful in pushing the Church away from the Cross to other things. But this fact must be known and understood: The Cross of Christ literally is the foundation of the Great Redemption Plan. It would not be incorrect to state that the Cross of Christ and the Bible are one and the same (Jn. 1:1, 14, 29).

(3) "I REMEMBERED GOD, AND WAS TROUBLED: I COMPLAINED, AND MY SPIRIT WAS OVERWHELMED. SELAH."

The meaning of the Verse is that Asaph felt that God could have prevented him from getting into this trouble; he, therefore, *"complained."* When he did so, his spirit *"was overwhelmed."*

This is the problem with most of us. We tend to want to blame God for our own difficulties. When we do this, our spirit is overwhelmed and the situation worsens. Complaining is never the answer. God will never recognize such.

FORGIVING GOD?

Incorrectly enough, modern Christians are taught by psychologists and even many Preachers that in situations of this nature, they should *"forgive God."* There could be nothing more erroneous than such an idea.

The Lord never has done anything bad or negative to any Believer. He loves us greatly and totally. He gave Himself for us on the Cross. So, for us to blame Him for our problems, and then to add insult to injury by *"forgiving Him,"* is just that — an insult of the highest order.

Such direction will only make a bad matter worse. Whatever problem we are having, we can be doubly certain that it's not the Lord Who has caused the problem. We either caused it ourselves or somebody else did, but it certainly is not the Lord.

So when a Preacher or anyone else tells a Believer that he should *"forgive God,"* that Believer should understand that what they are being told is very close to blasphemy. In fact, any association with such an individual should be severed immediately. As the song says, *"God is good, and He is good all the time."*

(4) "YOU HOLD MY EYES WAKING: I AM SO TROUBLED THAT I CANNOT SPEAK."

Asaph cannot sleep at night and he also does not know what to say to the Lord in prayer. There is a reason for that!

When one's spirit is overwhelmed, as his was, and is that way because of complaining, this doesn't provide very fertile ground for our seeking the Lord.

So we find that he turns from complaining and begins to do that which he should have done in the beginning.

(5) "I HAVE CONSIDERED THE DAYS OF OLD, THE YEARS OF ANCIENT TIMES."

Asaph begins to recall the great Miracles of God in the *"years of ancient times."* He recounts them in his mind. We should also!

During the coming Great Tribulation, which will be Israel's darkest day, Israel will do the same thing. They will remember that God opened the Red Sea and the waters of Jordan. They will remember that He fought their battles and they will hunger for Him to do it again.

(6) "I CALL TO REMEMBRANCE MY SONG IN THE NIGHT: I COMMUNE WITH MY OWN HEART: AND MY SPIRIT MADE DILIGENT SEARCH."

Asaph thinks back to when his nights were not sleepless but rather flavored with song. Then he begins to search his own heart, as every Believer should. Israel will do the same when under the iron fist of the Antichrist on that coming sad day.

(7) "WILL THE LORD CAST OFF FOREVER? AND WILL HE BE FAVORABLE NO MORE?"

Verses 7 through 9 pertain to Asaph; at times, they pertain to us, as well; they also will pertain to Israel during the coming Great Tribulation. The questions asked in these three Verses perhaps are asked by every Christian at one time or another! It seems like God's Face will shine no more upon us.

(8) "IS HIS MERCY CLEAN GONE FOREVER? DOES HIS PROMISE FAIL FOR EVERMORE?"

If God doesn't answer speedily, Satan takes advantage of such, just as He did with Asaph by telling him that God would no longer show *"mercy."* Satan also exclaims that the Promises of God may work for others, but no longer for you.

SATAN'S TACTICS

Let the Believer remember all the times in the past that Satan has fed them one lie or the other:

"You are going to go bankrupt!"

"You have a dread disease which will shortly end your life!"

"All of your children are going to die lost!"

If Satan can get us to believe any lie or even pay it some type of heed, he is going to do it. However, have you ever stopped to think:

If Satan could do all of these things, he would have done them a long, long time ago. He hasn't done them, simply because he cannot do them, which means he is a liar and the father of it.

Instead of his lying suggestions, we should keep our mind totally on the Lord.

(9) "HAS GOD FORGOTTEN TO BE GRACIOUS? HAS HE IN ANGER SHUT UP HIS TENDER MERCIES? SELAH."

What sin Asaph committed is not known. But whatever it was, he seemed to think that he had made God angry. He, therefore, thought that God no longer would show Mercy!

All of the above questions could be answered with a *"No!"* Preoccupation with self only leads to these questions and to doubt.

Whenever an individual comes to this place, doubt has degenerated to despair. God cannot, in fact, forget to be gracious. He also never will cease to be a God of Mercy, even above that of *"tender mercies."*

There is no problem which the Lord will not solve for us if we hold our faith steadfast in His Name, understanding that He has addressed every problem at the Cross. That is the key! Keep your faith anchored in Christ and the Cross, which is the same thing as anchoring your faith in the Word.

(10) "AND I SAID, THIS IS MY INFIRMITY: BUT I WILL REMEMBER THE YEARS OF THE RIGHT HAND OF THE MOST HIGH."

Here the Psalmist ceases his dejected self-occupation and becomes occupied with God; consequently, his despondency vanishes. This is the only cure for misery and despair. Despite his *"infirmity,"* he is saying he will do the following:

"I will remember."

Remember what?

"The years of past Blessings. I will account of them, and speak of them in my mind."

This is the greatest manner in which to defeat the suggestions of Satan. We should remember what the Lord has done in our own lives and think about it over and over, and also remember that the Lord does not change. What He did yesterday, He will do today. We must continue to believe.

(11) "I WILL REMEMBER THE WORKS OF THE LORD: SURELY I WILL REMEMBER YOUR WONDERS OF OLD."

"Remembering the Works of the LORD" have to do with that which is given in His Word and with all the great and wonderful things He has done for us. We should never forget them, meaning that we remember them constantly.

The phrase, *"Surely I will remember Your wonders of old,"* refers to all the Miracles recorded in the Word of God. Yes! It also refers to the Miracles the Lord has performed for us. They are more numerous than we realize!

(12) "I WILL MEDITATE ALSO OF ALL YOUR WORK, AND TALK OF YOUR DOINGS."

The phrase, *"I will meditate also of all your Work,"* means that we are constantly thinking of that which the Lord has done, which builds faith for the present and also for the future.

On a personal basis, I have learned to pray constantly. In other words, every waking moment, at least when my mind is not on certain things that I'm doing, I am thanking the Lord for what He has done and also for what He will do. I continuously present to Him my needs, because His Word tells me to do so (Jn. 15:7; Mat. 21:22, etc.).

We also are constantly to *"talk of His doings."*

God's Word and Ways are timeless. As it worked for Asaph, it will work for anyone who will embark on that which was tendered by the Holy Spirit. We are not only to remember these things done by God, but we are to meditate on them and talk of them.

What Great Promises!

In these very Verses, we see the cure for worry, anxiety, and fear, as well as the prescription for the building of faith. Any time we meditate upon the Lord and talk of His wondrous works, such always builds faith.

When we murmur and complain, the very opposite is the result. Our faith is torn down, and the door opens for fear and anxiety to set in, which is exactly what Satan wants and desires. Obey the Word and the Word will obey you.

(13) "YOUR WAY, O GOD, IS IN THE SANCTUARY: WHO IS SO GREAT A GOD AS OUR GOD?"

Williams says, *"Occupation of heart with others outside the Sanctuary and occupation of heart with self inside the Sanctuary both produce misery, but occupation of heart with God inside the Sanctuary gives comfort and victory."* [18]

THE SANCTUARY

Anything outside of the Sanctuary is out of fellowship with God; likewise, even though we are inside the Sanctuary, like Asaph, if we are preoccupied with self, we are out of fellowship with God, which will produce the *"trouble"* of Verse 1. What the *"self"* problem produced is not clear, and it really does not matter. Asaph's problem was self, which caused his wrongdoing, or disconcertment of heart. It would be the same for us.

Why was God's Way *"in the Sanctuary"*? Simply because that's where God dwelt. Whenever one leaves the Sanctuary (the place of God), one tends to think of other things as *"great."* They never are! Only God is *"great."*

THE NEW COVENANT

Under the New Covenant, we have a much greater way, a much better way, all based on Better Promises. Now the Lord literally lives within our hearts and lives (I Cor. 3:16). This means that we do not have to go to some particular building in some particular place, but that the Lord always is with us. This makes it much easier to meditate upon Him and to declare His wondrous works; the Holy Spirit, Who abides within us on a permanent basis, which Old Testament Saints did not have, is always ready to comply with any of our petitions.

(14) "YOU ARE THE GOD WHO DOES WONDERS: YOU HAVE DECLARED YOUR STRENGTH AMONG THE PEOPLE."

Now Asaph will begin to *"talk"* of God's *"doings,"* exactly as he has spoken in Verse 12. He says this:

1. *"God does wonders"*: If He has done wonders in the past, He will do wonders now, because the statement is in the present tense.

2. He has declared each person enough *"strength"* to overcome Satan and maintain victory.

3. Our Victory, as always, is in Christ and the Cross; this, we must never forget (Rom. 6:1-14; 8:1-2, 11; I Cor. 1:17-18, 21, 23; 2:2; Gal. 6:14).

(15) "YOU HAVE WITH YOUR ARM REDEEMED YOUR PEOPLE, THE SONS OF JACOB AND JOSEPH. SELAH."

God's Way in the Sanctuary secured the Salvation of the sons of Jacob and Joseph.

"Jacob" is used because of his scheming nature, while *"Joseph"* is used because he was hated. God is saying this:

He was able to change Jacob and to preserve Joseph. As He did it for these, He will do it for all others, at least for those who will believe Him.

(16) "THE WATERS SAW YOU, O GOD, THE WATERS SAW YOU; THEY WERE AFRAID: THE DEPTHS ALSO WERE TROUBLED."

Verses 16 through 19 portray the Ways of God in symbolic manner. Verse 14 pertains to *"Jacob"* and *"Joseph."* He did *"wonders"* with them and gave them enough *"strength"* to make them what He wanted them to be.

GOD'S WILL AND GOD'S ACTION

The Will of God is God's Action on Earth. The nature of His Will is expressed in the word *"Sanctuary,"* which means *"Holiness."*

There must, therefore, always be a Divine harmony between His Will and His Action. Those who would have fellowship with Him must subject themselves to the action of His Holy Nature. Man must suit himself to it.

Only by the means of the New Birth and the desire to consecrate to Him all of one's heart, strength, and soul will make this possible (Williams).[19]

Whenever God through *"Moses"* spoke to the waters, His Word went even to the *"depths."*

(17) "THE CLOUDS POURED OUT WATER: THE SKIES SENT OUT A SOUND: YOUR ARROWS ALSO WENT ABROAD."

This Passage could prophetically speak of the Battle of Armageddon, when God will speak to the elements which will be used against the Antichrist (Ezek. 38:22).

(18) "THE VOICE OF YOUR THUNDER WAS IN THE HEAVEN: THE LIGHTNINGS LIGHTENED THE WORLD: THE EARTH TREMBLED AND SHOOK."

This also refers to the Battle of Armageddon, just as the Seventeenth Verse. Even though Prophecy, as this, may speak of events thousands of years into the future, with God it is the same as the present, because in the Mind of God it already has happened.

(19) "YOUR WAY IS IN THE SEA, AND YOUR PATH IN THE GREAT WATERS, AND YOUR FOOTSTEPS ARE NOT KNOWN."

The sense of the Passage is that as *"footsteps"* (footprints) are not left in the sea, neither is the *"Way"* of God so easily tracked.

God's *"Way"* is His Word. It is not man's way. Man does not understand it; in fact, within himself, man cannot understand it.

Paul said, *"His Ways are past finding out"* (Rom. 11:33).

(20) "YOU LED YOUR PEOPLE LIKE A FLOCK BY THE HAND OF MOSES AND AARON."

The names, *"Jacob," "Joseph," "Moses,"* and *"Aaron"* are significant. Moses and Aaron typify Christ as King and Priest. A flock thus doubly led is surely led. Jacob and Joseph express how doubly precious to God is the flock itself, because the sheep are the sons of these fathers so beloved of God (Williams).[20]

NOTES

PSALM 78

Written by Asaph:
God's Dealings with His People Israel

(1) "GIVE EAR, O MY PEOPLE, TO MY LAW: INCLINE YOUR EARS TO THE WORDS OF MY MOUTH."

This Psalm was written by Asaph; Jesus referred to him as a Prophet (Mat. 13:35). In fact, all who wrote the Psalms could be placed in that category.

THE LAW

This is an Old Testament command to obey the Law of Moses. The statement, *"Give ear to My Law,"* is found some 32 times in the Old Testament, but not once in the New.

The latter portion of the Verse means to stretch out, or put forth, every effort to obey the Law.

The Law of God was Holy (Rom. 7:12); however, it could not save anyone. In fact, it was not meant to save anyone. God gave the Law for several reasons:

1. This was the only Law on the face of the Earth that was from God; consequently, it far exceeded all other laws which were man-made.

2. The Law of Moses addressed itself to every part and parcel of life. It was a pattern for living. It addressed itself to God, to one's fellowman, and to one's self (Ex. 25:8-9).

3. It was not designed by God for the purpose of saving the soul. In fact, the keeping of it could not save the soul (Gal. 2:16; 3:11).

4. The Law was given that sin and failure might be portrayed as such, that is, that one would know what sin is. Actually, the Law defined sin (Rom. 3:20; 7:7, 13).

5. The Law was God's Standard of morality and Righteousness. It was what God expected and demanded of fallen man.

6. Due to the Fall, man was unable to keep the Law, no matter how hard he tried. So the Law was like a mirror that showed man what he was, but gave him no power to change himself.

7. The Law contained a curse, as all law contains a curse. Knowing that man could not keep the Law, because the flesh was too

weak to do so, God planned that man would fall back on the coming Saviour, of which the Sacrificial System was a Type.

However, even faith evidenced in the Sacrifices, which were a part of the Law, could not save, because the blood of bulls and goats could not redeem man from sin; however, faith in what they represented, namely Christ, could save man from sin. Actually, man has always been Saved in the same manner.

In the Old Testament, man was Saved by looking forward to the coming Sacrifice of Christ; after the Sacrifice of Christ, man looked backward to the same (Rom. 3:10, 19-20; 4:3; 7:7, 13; 8:1-2).

(2) "I WILL OPEN MY MOUTH IN A PARABLE: I WILL UTTER DARK SAYINGS OF OLD."

This was quoted by Matthew concerning Christ (Mat. 13:35).

THE PARABLE

The puzzle here is not in the expression of mystery or in words hard to understand, but in great wonderment of how these many miraculous things happened to Israel.

The Psalm narrates how Jehovah, Who is Israel's Sanctuary in Egypt, in the desert, and in the Land of Israel, was dishonored in all three periods of the nation's history. It predicts His election of Mount Zion for His future Sanctuary. The first part of this Psalm tells how the fathers turned away from Him in the desert; the second part records similar action by the children in the Land.

The expression in the First Verse, *"The Words of My Mouth,"* actually refers to Jesus Christ, and would continue on to His First Advent. The *"Mouth"* of Verses 1 and 2 is His Mouth.

Jesus is Jehovah. He not only gave the Law through Moses, but also ministered the Great Gospel of Grace in His First Advent (Jn. 1:17).

(3) "WHICH WE HAVE HEARD AND KNOWN, AND OUR FATHERS HAVE TOLD US."

Moses was the first to write down the Word of God under the Inspiration of the Holy Spirit (Lk. 24:27). It is most probable that the first Book Moses wrote was the Book of Job. He may even have written it in collaboration with Job himself. Job actually was contemporary with Moses for a number of years.

If Moses actually did write the Book of Job, then that Book is the oldest Book in the world.

Next, Moses would have written the Book of Genesis, possibly even while he was tending sheep on the backside of the desert. Then came Exodus, Leviticus, Numbers, and Deuteronomy — and in that order. Moses would have written Exodus through Deuteronomy in the wilderness. Joshua actually was the first one to have the Word of God in hand. It was given to him by Moses (Josh. 1:8).

(4) "WE WILL NOT HIDE THEM FROM THEIR CHILDREN, SHOWING TO THE GENERATION TO COME THE PRAISES OF THE LORD, AND HIS STRENGTH, AND HIS WONDERFUL WORKS THAT HE HAS DONE."

The Holy Spirit is saying here that it is extremely important for parents to recount the *"wonderful works"* of God to *"their children."*

CHILDREN AND THE WORD OF GOD

It is imperative that children learn the Word of God. Considering that the Bible is the only revealed Truth in the world, and ever has been, this makes it absolutely imperative that all learn and understand its contents. Man continues to try to solve his own problems, and he always fails. He fails because his wisdom comes from man and not from God. Only the Bible holds the answer to every problem that faces humanity. The children must learn it; the Holy Spirit said so, and the only way they can learn it is for the parents to teach it to them.

MY PERSONAL EXPERIENCE

I personally started studying the Bible when I was eight years old. Even at that tender age, I carried a Bible with me everywhere I went. (It was a small one with very fine print.) My parents greatly encouraged me to study its contents. It is truly my *"Lamp"* and my *"Light"* (Ps. 119:105).

In my personal study, I almost never skip around in the Bible. It has been my habit to begin with Genesis and go straight through to Revelation. For many years, I read the Bible completely through once about every six weeks. I did this for years, but now, because of my constant writing, my method has somewhat changed.

Because the Bible is the Word of God and never can be exhausted, my interest in it has not only not decreased, but rather it actually becomes more interesting to me with each passing day.

THE GREATEST CRISIS

Every single problem that a Believer has is the result of the Believer, in some way, not knowing or understanding the part of the Word of God that deals with that problem. That doesn't mean that if we properly understand the Word of God, we can avoid all problems and difficulties in life. The Bible doesn't teach such; experience also proves otherwise. Satan is going to try to hinder, and he will use many and varied means to do so. That is a given.

Peter said, and I quote from THE EXPOSITOR'S STUDY BIBLE:

"Beloved, think it not strange concerning the fiery trial which is to try you (trials do not merely happen; they are designed by wisdom and operated by love; Job proved this), *as though some strange thing happened unto you* (your trial, whatever it is, is not unique; many others are experiencing the same thing!)*:*

"But rejoice (despite the trial), *inasmuch as you are partakers of Christ's sufferings* (refers to suffering for Righteousness' sake)*; that, when His Glory shall be revealed* (refers to His Second Coming), *you may be glad also with exceeding joy.* (There will be great joy in the heart of every Saint when we come back with the Lord at the Second Coming)" (I Pet. 4:12-13).

That having been said, however, many problems can be avoided if we understand the Word of God as we should.

On one of the blackest days of my life and in the history of this Ministry, I laid my Bible on the table in front of me and said, *"I don't know the answer to victory over the world, the flesh, and the Devil; however, I know that the answer is found in the Word of God, and by the Grace of God, I'm going to find that answer."*

Other than the time that the Lord Jesus Christ Saved my soul, that was the greatest decision I've ever made.

Out of that came the great Revelation of the Cross, which has revolutionized my life and Ministry. I have every confidence this also is the Message of the Holy Spirit to the Church in these last of the last days.

(5) "FOR HE ESTABLISHED A TESTIMONY IN JACOB, AND APPOINTED A LAW IN ISRAEL, WHICH HE COMMANDED OUR FATHERS, THAT THEY SHOULD MAKE THEM KNOWN TO THEIR CHILDREN."

The *"Testimony in Jacob"* was His Personal dealings with the Patriarch. He would change him from Jacob the schemer to Israel the Prince with God.

THE LAW IN ISRAEL

The *"Law in Israel"* was that which was given by God to Moses. The nation now was supposed to be a Prince with God. Sadly, they failed miserably — as man will fail in every position of trust in which he is placed. But, still, God loves us.

That the children should be taught by the fathers was not a suggestion; it was a *"Command."*

If all parents would take this *"Command"* seriously, the drug problem, alcohol problem, and crime problem would be solved. The only effective solution to these problems is found in the Bible, which demands an acceptance of Jesus Christ as the Saviour of one's soul and the Lord of one's life.

For the first time in history, during the coming Kingdom Age, the world will be Paradise on Earth, because Jesus Christ will be here and the Word of God will be adhered to strictly. The answer now is Jesus Christ and the Word of God; the answer then will be Jesus Christ and the Word of God.

(6) "THAT THE GENERATION TO COME MIGHT KNOW THEM, EVEN THE CHILDREN WHICH SHOULD BE BORN; WHO SHOULD ARISE AND DECLARE THEM TO THEIR CHILDREN."

The Move of God is actually limited to its present generation unless that generation proclaims the Truth to the coming generation.

A COMMAND OF THE LORD

Actually, each generation must have its own Revival and its own Moving of the Holy

Spirit. The Work of God that transpired in the generations past will not suffice for the present generation; consequently, most Church Denominations generally begin with a Move of God and then gradually begin to die as the following generations fail to have their own Revival. Part of the blame must go to the present generation that does not sufficiently *"declare them to their children."*

(7) "THAT THEY MIGHT SET THEIR HOPE IN GOD, AND NOT FORGET THE WORKS OF GOD, BUT KEEP HIS COMMANDMENTS:

(8) "AND MIGHT NOT BE AS THEIR FATHERS, A STUBBORN AND REBELLIOUS GENERATION; A GENERATION THAT SET NOT THEIR HEART ARIGHT, AND WHOSE SPIRIT WAS NOT STEADFAST WITH GOD."

Let us say it again:

EVERY GENERATION MUST HAVE ITS OWN REVIVAL

If any generation doesn't properly live for God before the children and doesn't properly prepare its children by teaching them the Word of God, the end result will be a generation that doesn't know God. That's exactly what has happened to this present generation in which we now live (2005).

Despite the fact that we don't desire to come to such a conclusion, we must, however, conclude that the previous generation, which includes most of us reading these words, did not do a very good job in training and raising up our children. In other words, the home was deficient and the Church also was deficient! It still is.

If that were not the case, the Church would not presently be following a plethora of false doctrines, which it is.

Observing the Pentecostal Denominations, with which I once was associated, the spiritual deterioration is so acute and accelerating so rapidly that these big, bloated, fat Denominations are now but a shell, spiritually, of what they once were. In fact, if no Revival is forthcoming and if Jesus tarries, these same Denominations shortly will be ordaining homosexuals to preach.

Regrettably, this present generation is a *"generation that set not their heart aright, and whose spirit is not steadfast with God."* It is sad, but true!

(9) "THE CHILDREN OF EPHRAIM, BEING ARMED, AND CARRYING BOWS, TURNED BACK IN THE DAY OF BATTLE."

It is not known if Asaph is speaking of *"Ephraim"* as a Tribe or of the Northern Kingdom of Israel, which used *"Ephraim"* as one of its names. It also is not clear what battle Asaph is speaking of, or what timeframe.

Hosea said this: *"Ephraim is joined to idols; let him alone"* (Hos. 4:17).

This much is known. When the Northern Kingdom of Israel broke away from Judah, they went into gross idol worship (I Ki. 12:28-30). The following is sure:

(10) "THEY KEPT NOT THE COVENANT OF GOD, AND REFUSED TO WALK IN HIS LAW;

(11) "AND FORGOT HIS WORKS, AND HIS WONDERS THAT HE HAD SHOWN THEM."

It seems that Ephraim was defeated because God allowed it. The reasons were fourfold:

1. They refused to keep the Covenant of God.

2. They refused to walk in His Law.

3. They forgot all the glorious things which He had done in the past.

4. They also forgot the Miracles that He performed on their behalf.

(12) "MARVELOUS THINGS DID HE IN THE SIGHT OF THEIR FATHERS, IN THE LAND OF EGYPT, IN THE FIELD OF ZOAN."

The Holy Spirit is saying here that the Children of Israel must not forget the great Miracle that God performed for them in the deliverance of their fathers from the slavery of Egypt. They were to tell this repeatedly and to talk of it constantly.

(13) "HE DIVIDED THE SEA, AND CAUSED THEM TO PASS THROUGH; AND HE MADE THE WATERS TO STAND AS AN HEAP."

The opening of the Red Sea by the Power of God was the greatest Miracle performed for mankind at that particular time. They must ever remind their children of this great happening.

(14) "IN THE DAYTIME ALSO HE LED THEM WITH A CLOUD, AND ALL THE

NIGHT WITH A LIGHT OF FIRE."

If this great experience had been told to their children, there is no doubt the children would have listened with intense interest and never would have forgotten it. Evidently, Israel forgot these great Miracles!

(15) "HE CLAVE THE ROCKS IN THE WILDERNESS, AND GAVE THEM DRINK AS OUT OF THE GREAT DEPTHS."

The Lord brought so much water out of the Rock that it slaked the thirst of nearly three million Israelites plus all their sheep and cattle, which presents a Miracle of unprecedented proportions. It also was meant to portray the smiting of Jesus Christ on the Cross of Calvary, which would issue forth a veritable river of life to all who would drink thereof and believe (Jn. 7:37-39).

(16) "HE BROUGHT STREAMS ALSO OUT OF THE ROCK, AND CAUSED WATERS TO RUN DOWN LIKE RIVERS."

This means that the force of the water coming out of the smitten Rock was not merely a trickle, but could be classified as a small river — enough to slake the thirst of millions of Israelites in that howling wilderness. Likewise, what Jesus did at Calvary's Cross is enough to slake the spiritual thirst of every soul, no matter how many may come.

As the songwriter said:

"There is room at the Cross for you."

(17) "AND THEY SINNED YET MORE AGAINST HIM BY PROVOKING THE MOST HIGH IN THE WILDERNESS."

Even though the Children of Israel had witnessed an astounding number of miracles, they *"sinned yet more against Him."*

MIRACLES AND UNBELIEF

God is a God of Miracles. He also still performs miracles today. The Church should believe God for miracles. But within themselves, miracles have never caused people to live right. Israel is a prime example. If men will not adhere to the Word of God, miracles will not serve as a great inducement.

Why did they sin?

Unbelief is the basis of sin and is the cause of all judgment (Rom. 11:20-32; Heb. 3:12, 19; Jude 5; Rev. 21:8). They sinned because they had no faith. Miracles do not produce faith. Only the Word of God can produce

NOTES

faith (Rom. 10:17).

(18) "AND THEY TEMPTED GOD IN THEIR HEART BY ASKING MEAT FOR THEIR LUST."

How did this tempt God?

TEMPTING GOD

First of all, Israel was not thankful and did not appreciate the Manna that God had provided for their sustenance.

Second, they murmured and complained concerning His Provision, and then they demanded meat. Because the Manna was a Type of Christ, they were, in effect, saying, *"We don't want Christ."*

Every Christian should realize that when we murmur and complain against God, we are, in effect, tempting Him, which means to provoke Him. This is something no sane person desires to do.

The Lord, thankfully, is gracious and kind. However, just because judgment does not come immediately, as it did with Israel, we should not think that our sin goes unnoticed. To be sure, such an attitude hinders and hurts. Then we wonder why God doesn't answer prayer!

(19) "YEA, THEY SPOKE AGAINST GOD; THEY SAID, CAN GOD FURNISH A TABLE IN THE WILDERNESS?"

First they tempted Him, and now they speak against Him. They were saying that God was going to take them out into the wilderness and there let them die. They questioned His Leading! They questioned His Authority! And they questioned His Provision!

FURNISHING A TABLE IN THE WILDERNESS

In the natural, there did not seem to be any way that God could furnish food for these people in the wilderness. There was no game in the wilderness or any other way that provision could be provided, especially considering that there were three million people who needed to be fed each and every day.

But God did furnish a table in the wilderness, because He is able to do all things. True, the people were not happy with what He furnished, but that wasn't God's fault. He gave them *"Angel food,"* but they quickly tired of that and started to demand meat.

(20) "BEHOLD, HE SMOTE THE ROCK, THAT THE WATERS GUSHED OUT, AND THE STREAMS OVERFLOWED; CAN HE GIVE BREAD ALSO? CAN HE PROVIDE FLESH FOR HIS PEOPLE?"

Even though these people saw the Miracle of bringing water out of the Rock, which actually was a type of the great Eternal Life that Christ would provide at Calvary for the whole world, these faithless people not only did not understand its meaning, but they also held it with contempt.

They taunted God by saying, *"He gave us streams in the desert; can He also give Bread? Better yet, can He provide flesh for His people?"*

Their attitude shows that they held God in contempt. They were functioning in the same evil attitude as Herod when he demanded to see a Miracle of Christ (Lk. 23:8).

(21) "THEREFORE THE LORD HEARD THIS, AND WAS WROTH: SO A FIRE WAS KINDLED AGAINST JACOB, AND ANGER ALSO CAME UP AGAINST ISRAEL."

The names used by the Holy Spirit, *"Jacob"* and *"Israel,"* are not without meaning. The Holy Spirit is saying that the Lord created a great nation from Jacob's loins. Before God changed *"Jacob,"* he was a schemer and a fraud. Jacob's name was changed to *"Israel, the Prince of God."* However, *"Israel"* the nation is now reverting back to a scheming, fraudulent *"Jacob."* Instead of blessing, God now will bring Judgment.

Let it ever be known and understood:

God cannot condone sin in His Chosen any more than He can in those who do not profess His Name.

(22) "BECAUSE THEY BELIEVED NOT IN GOD, AND TRUSTED NOT IN HIS SALVATION."

Once again, we face the sin of unbelief!

UNBELIEF

Their sin was unbelief. This also is the sin of the modern Church. The Bible is an unread Book by most Christians. Most who call themselves *"Believers"* rarely believe. Instead the Church has opted for secular, humanistic psychology. The Church cannot believe in God and, at the same time, believe in man. One or the other must go.

THE CROSS AND UNBELIEF

The type of unbelief registered some 3,600 years ago is no different than the type of unbelief being registered presently.

Then, Israel had to believe that God could furnish a table in the wilderness. Now, the modern Christian must place his faith exclusively in the Lord Jesus Christ and what Christ did at the Cross. Either way it is God's Salvation.

Basically, it is much easier presently for one to express faith in the Cross of Christ than it was several thousands of years ago, that is, for Israel to believe that God could sustain them in the wilderness. And yet, it should not have been too difficult then, considering all the miracles they previously had seen.

Presently, we have the Bible, the Word of God, before us, which is the Story of the Cross of Christ. So there is really no excuse! But yet the major problem regarding Christ and the Cross is not ignorance, but rather unbelief.

(23) "THOUGH HE HAD COMMANDED THE CLOUDS FROM ABOVE, AND OPENED THE DOORS OF HEAVEN."

The quotations here are poetical. They actually mean that God had opened the windows of Heaven, which represents open-ended blessings, that is, if Israel only would believe Him.

(24) "AND HAD RAINED DOWN MANNA UPON THEM TO EAT, AND HAD GIVEN THEM OF THE CORN OF HEAVEN."

(25) "MAN DID EAT ANGELS' FOOD: HE SENT THEM MEAT TO THE FULL."

Even though both of these Scriptures are also poetical, they still say what actually happened.

Concerning this, Pulpit says, *"The quotation 'Angels' Food' may mean either the actual food on which Angels subsist, or food supplied by the Ministration of Angels, and derived from their dwelling-place."* [21]

I don't think it would be correct to state dogmatically that Angels require no food. So what was given the Israelites was special indeed!

(26) "HE CAUSED AN EAST WIND TO BLOW IN THE HEAVEN: AND BY

HIS POWER HE BROUGHT IN THE SOUTH WIND.

(27) "HE RAINED FLESH ALSO UPON THEM AS DUST, AND FEATHERED FOWLS LIKE AS THE SAND OF THE SEA:

(28) "AND HE LET IT FALL IN THE MIDST OF THEIR CAMP, ROUND ABOUT THEIR HABITATIONS.

(29) "SO THEY DID EAT, AND WERE WELL FILLED: FOR HE GAVE THEM THEIR OWN DESIRE."

As usual, a great Truth is given here to us.

UNGODLY DESIRE

It was *"their desire"* and not God's. One of the great Works of the Holy Spirit in the human heart is to bring our desires in conformity with the Word of God. It is not an easy task. Man, too often, even Christian man, wants his own way instead of God's Way.

The desire on the part of Israel was evil, as is every desire fomented in the heart of man, even Christian man. *"Their own desire"* would have disastrous results.

The people were dissatisfied with the Manna. They wanted meat to eat, or so they said! So the Lord sent in millions of quails, which most definitely satisfied their desire for this type of sustenance; however, the Lord was greatly displeased with their desire, because it found fault with what He already was doing on their behalf.

THE WILL OF GOD

Even those Believers who are totally consecrated to the Lord must ever understand that the Will of God must be supreme within our hearts and lives. We must ardently seek God's Will and be satisfied with nothing except His Will. At the very moment our own personal will enters into the picture, trouble will loom on the horizon, and it will wreak disastrous results.

Every Believer should desire only the Will of God — nothing less and nothing more! If we ardently desire the Will of God, the Lord will see that this is what we get, which will be altogether to our good.

Any time a man, even a Believer, thinks he knows more than God, that's when real trouble begins. This attitude is one of man's greatest problems.

NOTES

(30) "THEY WERE NOT ESTRANGED FROM THEIR LUST. BUT WHILE THEIR MEAT WAS YET IN THEIR MOUTHS,

(31) "THE WRATH OF GOD CAME UPON THEM, AND SLEW THE FATTEST OF THEM, AND SMOTE DOWN THE CHOSEN MEN OF ISRAEL."

Israel's lust and complaints angered God, so His Wrath fell on them. The expression, *"chosen men of Israel,"* seems to mean that these individuals led Israel into this sin. Evidently, these *"chosen men"* would not listen to Moses (Num. 11:31-35). The foment ultimately would develop into full-fledged rebellion, which caused the destruction of all who were above twenty years of age.

(32) "FOR ALL THIS THEY SINNED STILL, AND BELIEVED NOT FOR HIS WONDROUS WORKS.

(33) "THEREFORE THEIR DAYS DID HE CONSUME IN VANITY, AND THEIR YEARS IN TROUBLE."

Ultimately, they died in the wilderness; they never did see the Promised Land. All of this was because of unbelief. After pride, the greatest sin is unbelief. Pride always generates self-righteousness and unbelief. This prideful sin actually says that it can do a better job than God can do. They did not believe God, but rather they believed in themselves, which is the bane of the human race, even the Church!

God's Word is His Will. However, we must understand that Word before we start claiming things.

The Lord promised to meet Israel's needs while they were in the wilderness, but He never promised to bless their murmuring and complaining. He never promised to bless their wrong direction or their sin, which God can never bless.

So when we talk about obeying His Word, we better know that of which we speak.

(34) "WHEN HE SLEW THEM, THEN THEY SOUGHT HIM: AND THEY RETURNED AND ENQUIRED EARLY AFTER GOD."

This Scripture and the next few Passages speak of a half-hearted repentance.

REPENTANCE

Pulpit says, *"The repentance* (Ex. 32:28,

35; 33:4, 10; Num. 11:33; 16:48) *is not always noticed in the Mosaic narrative, being, as it was, short-lived, if not even feigned. But no doubt after each outpouring of Divine Vengeance, there was at least some show of repentance, as noted in Exodus 33."* [22]

Their repentance was, as we shall see, what one might call *"a forced repentance."* In other words, they only wanted the judgment to stop; their hearts were not necessarily changed.

(35) "AND THEY REMEMBERED THAT GOD WAS THEIR ROCK, AND THE HIGH GOD THEIR REDEEMER."

They knew that God could save them and deliver them from their enemies. Still, their attitude was to *"use God"* rather than to *"serve God."*

(36) "NEVERTHELESS THEY DID FLATTER HIM WITH THEIR MOUTH, AND THEY LIED UNTO HIM WITH THEIR TONGUES."

Their repentance was not actually real. What they were saying with their mouths was not what they actually believed or felt in their hearts. They were not sorry for their sin. They only were sorry because of the judgment of God that it brought upon them.

When the Lord would begin to apply pressure regarding judgment, they then would seek His Face in order that the judgment cease. But there was no real change of heart!

(37) "FOR THEIR HEART WAS NOT RIGHT WITH HIM, NEITHER WERE THEY STEADFAST IN HIS COVENANT."

As stated, their problem was a *"heart"* problem. They did not lack understanding or knowledge. They had *"an evil heart of unbelief."*

The problem with man is not that he doesn't know what is right, but that he doesn't want to do what is right. The Holy Spirit, as usual, goes to the *"heart"* of the problem.

(38) "BUT HE BEING FULL OF COMPASSION, FORGAVE THEIR INIQUITY, AND DESTROYED THEM NOT: YEA, MANY A TIME TURNED HE HIS ANGER AWAY, AND DID NOT STIR UP ALL HIS WRATH."

In this Passage, we are given a most beautiful description of the Love of God. It is as follows:

NOTES

THE LOVE OF GOD

1. The Lord is full of *"compassion."* The word *"compassion"* means that He feels our hurt and infirmity down into the depths of His very Being.

2. God forgives our *"iniquity,"* even though our repentance oftentimes is half-hearted. If we take one step toward Him, He will take a thousand steps toward us.

3. He *"destroys us not,"* when we actually deserve destruction. He also blesses us when we do not deserve blessing, but rather deserve the opposite.

4. He *"turns His anger away,"* when we have not met all of His conditions for such. He is eager to save and eager to show His Love and Blessing.

5. Due to our great sin, He may show us a little of His Wrath, but only a small part. The Wrath of God that has been turned on us because of our sin represents only a small portion of what we rightly deserve.

(39) "FOR HE REMEMBERED THAT THEY WERE BUT FLESH; A WIND THAT PASSES AWAY, AND COMES NOT AGAIN."

The Lord knows the frailty of the flesh. Due to the Fall of man, the constant pressure of the sin nature is ever-present. Accordingly, He shows us Mercy, Grace, and Pardon far more than we ever could begin to deserve.

The expression, *"He remembered,"* is a beautiful statement. The Lord remembers that *"the flesh is weak,"* meaning that it is frail in us. It means that *"in our flesh dwells no good thing"* (Rom. 7:17). It is God Who made us to be flesh, so He has compassion on the weakness of that flesh, but He never condones sin.

God is *"Spirit,"* while man is *"flesh."* There is a vast difference between the two. *"Spirit"* is eternal, while *"flesh"* is of fleeting duration.

THE FLESH

Before the Cross, Israel was given very little information regarding the flesh, simply because, at that time, the Holy Spirit was limited to what He could do. But Christ's Perfect Sacrifice on the Cross satisfied the terrible sin debt that man owed to God and made it possible for the Holy Spirit to abide permanently within the hearts and lives of Believers. Then it was possible for us to receive the correct teaching, which the Holy Spirit gave to the Apostle Paul, who then imparted it to the Church (Rom. 6:1-14).

Paul told us that we must not *"walk after the flesh,"* which refers to depending on our own ability, strength, power, or efforts (Rom. 8:1).

The Holy Spirit through Paul bluntly states, *"So then they who are in the flesh cannot please God"* (Rom. 8:8). This refers to the Believer attempting to live his Christian life by means other than faith in Christ and the Cross.

As should be obvious, when Paul speaks of *"the flesh,"* he is not speaking of the meat on our bones, but rather is using the expression as a metaphor to explain human effort and ability. All human effort and ability, even when it comes from the Godliest, simply will not work. Anything that God does for us is always generated by Him, carried out by Him, and done through Him. Trusting in Christ and what Christ has done for us at the Cross is the Means by which we *"walk after the Spirit,"* which all Believers are commanded to do (Rom. 8:1-2).

The struggle between the *"flesh"* and the *"Spirit"* represents the great struggle for the Believer. The flesh is ever trying to gain the ascendancy; the flesh is very deceptive, especially if it is religious flesh.

The Word of God presents only one Way for the Believer to function, and that is through faith (Rom. 5:1-2). However, it must be faith in the correct object, and that correct Object always is the Cross of Christ (Rom. 6:1-14; I Cor. 1:17-18, 21, 23; 2:2; Gal. 6:14).

It is absolutely impossible for any Believer to *"walk after the Spirit"* (which means to not *"walk after the flesh"*) unless faith is fully expressed in Christ and what He has done for us at the Cross. We must never forget: Christ is the Source, while the Cross is the Means.

(40) "HOW OFT DID THEY PROVOKE HIM IN THE WILDERNESS, AND GRIEVE HIM IN THE DESERT!"

Actually, Israel provoked the Lord some ten times in approximately two years (Num. 14:22).

(41) "YEA, THEY TURNED BACK AND TEMPTED GOD, AND LIMITED THE HOLY ONE OF ISRAEL."

How is it possible for one to limit God?

LIMITING GOD

It is possible to limit God because of unbelief; when we limit God, He cannot do for us what He desires to do. Every Believer has limited God in some way. One might even say that *"limiting God"* is the crowning sin of the Church.

Israel limited Him many times. One of the most outstanding of these times is recorded in Numbers, Chapters 13 through 15. Israel lacked the faith to enter the Promised Land.

Think of it! All of Heaven was ready for Israel to enter into the Land that God had prepared for them. Every provision had been made. The very Angels of Heaven had been alerted to help them as they went in, but Israel would not do so! Because of unbelief, they limited God!

How guilty is the modern Church of doing the same thing today? God wants to bless us. He wants to help us. He wants to do great things for us, but He cannot do so because of our sin of unbelief. In effect, we *"limit Him."*

THE CROSS OF CHRIST AND LIMITING GOD

Unless one properly understands the Cross of Christ (and I refer to the Cross as it pertains to our Sanctification), then such a Believer is guaranteed to *"limit God."* It cannot be otherwise!

Paul said, and I quote from THE EXPOSITOR'S STUDY BIBLE:

"Examine yourselves, whether you be in the Faith (the words, *'the Faith,'* refer to *'Christ and Him Crucified,'* with the Cross ever being the Object of our Faith)*; prove your own selves.* (Make certain your Faith actually is in the Cross, and not other things.) *Know you not your own selves, how that Jesus Christ is in you* (which He can only be by our faith expressed in His Sacrifice), *except you be reprobates?"* (Rejected)*"* (II Cor. 13:5).

John the Beloved said: *"For whatsoever is born of God overcomes the world* (if we follow God's Prescribed Order, we will overcome the world)*: and this is the victory that overcomes the world, even our Faith.* (John is speaking here of Faith in Christ and the Cross, which then gives the Holy Spirit latitude to work within our lives)" (I Jn. 5:4).

So, if one doesn't want to limit God, it is imperative that the Believer understands the Cross of Christ as it refers to Sanctification.

(42) "THEY REMEMBERED NOT HIS HAND, NOR THE DAY WHEN HE DELIVERED THEM FROM THE ENEMY."

The Holy Spirit is telling us that Israel had no faith because they forgot the great miracles the Lord had performed for them in the past. Over and over again, the Holy Spirit admonishes us to mediate about and talk about constantly the things He has done for us in the past (Ps. 77:10-12). This is His Word; it builds faith.

(43) "HOW HE HAD WROUGHT HIS SIGNS IN EGYPT, AND HIS WONDERS IN THE FIELD OF ZOAN."

Verses 43 through 58 proclaim the great miracles and wonders of God performed in Egypt and in the Promised Land. These are mighty things done by God, which, it seems, were little appreciated by Israel.

MIGHTY THINGS DONE BY GOD

The modern Christian may well wish that God would do for him what He did for Israel of old; however, God has done as much for us, and even more. The physical miracles that God performed in those days so long ago were types of the Spiritual Miracles that He has given, and continues to give, to us presently.

The miracles that God performed in Egypt were all destructive, and yet they were a form of mercy. The Children of Israel belonged to God. He had the right to demand their release. If Pharaoh had cooperated with God, Egypt would have been greatly blessed.

As it was, Pharaoh rebelled against God, and the Lord applied enough pressure that Pharaoh finally relented. The choice was Pharaoh's and not God's. The judgments would have stopped when Pharaoh stopped. Pharaoh would not stop his rebellion; therefore, when Pharaoh finally relented, Egypt was a wreck. The fault was Pharaoh's and not God's.

(44) "AND HAD TURNED THEIR RIVERS INTO BLOOD; AND THEIR FLOODS, THAT THEY COULD NOT DRINK."

This refers to the great Nile River and all of its tributaries.

This means that for a period of time there was no water to drink (Ex. 7:19-21).

(45) "HE SENT DIVERS SORTS OF FLIES AMONG THEM, WHICH DEVOURED THEM; AND FROGS, WHICH DESTROYED THEM."

Pulpit says, *"This was a particular sort of fly or beetle, rather than many different sorts."* [23] These particular flies sucked the lifeblood out of human beings and animals. The *"frogs"* also had some type of biting power which brought destruction. The implication is that many Egyptians died from these plagues.

(46) "HE GAVE ALSO THEIR INCREASE UNTO THE CATERPILLAR, AND THEIR LABOR UNTO THE LOCUST."

This means their crops were destroyed.

THE INCREASE

Even though Asaph is speaking here of the miracles the Lord performed in ancient Egypt, still, we today should also take careful notice of the truths here given.

Bringing it up to the present time, that for which we labor and work, and I speak of our *"increase,"* can be blessed by the Lord or can be destroyed by the Lord. And yet, under the New Covenant, the situation is somewhat different than it was during the time mentioned in this Psalm.

Since the Cross, great and wonderful things are promised to every Believer, but only on the Lord's terms.

What are those terms?

Satan cannot steal our *"increase"* if our Faith is anchored exclusively in Christ and the Cross. We have the guaranteed help of the Holy Spirit in all circumstances (Rom. 8:1-2, 11). But, as we've already stated, if the Believer has made something other than the Cross the object of his or her faith, this greatly limits the Holy Spirit in what He can do to help us. In those situations, Satan does take most of the increase, a situation which applies, regrettably, to most of the modern Church.

WHAT TYPE OF INCREASE?

In the last few years, when one thinks of *"increase,"* unfortunately, most think of material things; however, the *"increase"* of which the Word of God in the New Covenant speaks pertains to that which is spiritual. To be sure, if the spiritual is affected, everything else will be affected, whether positive or negative.

As stated, the Believer must keep his faith in Christ and the Cross, which then will stop the Evil One from taking that which rightly belongs to the Child of God.

(47) "HE DESTROYED THEIR VINES WITH HAIL, AND THEIR SYCAMORE TREES WITH FROST.

(48) "HE GAVE UP THEIR CATTLE ALSO TO THE HAIL, AND THEIR FLOCKS TO HOT THUNDERBOLTS."

The Lord created the elements and He has total control over all that He has created. So He used the elements in order to carry out that which He desired in connection with Egypt. He can do the same presently, if He so desires.

(49) "HE CAST UPON THEM THE FIERCENESS OF HIS ANGER, WRATH, AND INDIGNATION, AND TROUBLE, BY SENDING EVIL ANGELS AMONG THEM."

The term *"evil angels,"* is not explained. It could mean one of two things:

EVIL ANGELS

1. Fallen angels under the domain of Satan but still answerable to God, as everything is. If they are ordered to carry out certain particulars, they must obey (I Ki. 22:19-23).

2. They could be righteous Angels who carried out the intended results of God's *"anger, wrath, and indignation, and trouble,"* with the word *"evil"* referring to the actions they carried out.

(50) "HE MADE A WAY TO HIS ANGER; HE SPARED NOT THEIR SOUL FROM DEATH, BUT GAVE THEIR LIFE OVER TO THE PESTILENCE;

(51) "AND SMOTE ALL THE FIRSTBORN IN EGYPT; THE CHIEF OF THEIR STRENGTH IN THE TABERNACLES OF HAM."

From all of this we learn that the Lord says what He means and means what He says.

THE ANGER OF GOD

The Lord grew angry, even exceedingly angry, with Pharaoh, who ignored warning after warning — more so than any other human being in history. The reason Egypt was destroyed was not the fault of God but rather the fault of Pharaoh.

The Children of Israel did not belong to Pharaoh and did not belong to Egypt. They were slaves in Egypt, but it was Pharaoh who had made them that way. These people actually belonged to God and not to this despot. So the Lord had every right to demand their release, which He did. He also had every right to exert whatever force was needed in order for this release to be effected.

We are not told, except in this Passage, whatever it was that took the firstborn of every household and of every beast. It is referred to as *"the pestilence."*

The Hebrew doesn't actually tell us what the word *"pestilence"* means. In the Hebrew, it merely reads *"the plague which destroys."*

(52) "BUT MADE HIS OWN PEOPLE TO GO FORTH LIKE SHEEP, AND GUIDED THEM IN THE WILDERNESS LIKE A FLOCK."

The Holy Spirit through Asaph outlines the tender leading of Israel by Jehovah. In fact, He became their Shepherd.

Pulpit says, *"The guidance began from Succoth, and was effected by means of the Pillar of the Cloud and the Pillar of Fire"* (Ex. 13:20-22).[24]

(53) "AND HE LED THEM ON SAFELY, SO THAT THEY FEARED NOT: BUT THE SEA OVERWHELMED THEIR ENEMIES."

They were *"sore afraid"* at *"Pi-hahiroth."*

*"And Moses said unto the people, Fear ye not, stand still, and see the Salvation of the LORD, which He will show to you today: for the Egyptians whom you have seen today, you shall see them again no more forever.

"The LORD shall fight for you, and you shall hold your peace"* (Ex. 14:13-14).

(54) "AND HE BROUGHT THEM TO THE BORDER OF HIS SANCTUARY, EVEN TO THIS MOUNTAIN, WHICH HIS RIGHT HAND HAD PURCHASED."

In this Passage, the whole of Israel is called *"His Sanctuary."* It actually was the place of His Headquarters on Earth among men.

"This mountain" probably refers to Mount Zion, where the Temple was to be built, where God would reside between the Mercy Seat and the Cherubim.

This land, which presently is much contested by the Arabs and the Jews, still belongs to God; consequently, neither the United Nations nor any country in the world will have the final say! God will!

(55) "HE CAST OUT THE HEATHEN ALSO BEFORE THEM, AND DIVIDED THEM AN INHERITANCE BY LINE, AND MADE THE TRIBES OF ISRAEL TO DWELL IN THEIR TENTS."

This Passage means that the Holy Spirit drew the boundaries in this land for each particular Tribe. The Holy Spirit actually designed everything.

The Shepherd of Israel, Who divided the land for Israel's inheritance, is likewise our Shepherd, Who is the Lord Jesus Christ. As He guided Israel so long ago, He desires to do the same with us today, and even on a greater scale. Now we have the Holy Spirit abiding within us constantly, which Israel of old did not have (I Cor. 3:16).

(56) "YET THEY TEMPTED AND PROVOKED THE MOST HIGH GOD, AND KEPT NOT HIS TESTIMONIES."

Despite all the Lord had done for Israel, despite all the miracles, and despite His Leading, Guidance, and Provision for them in every capacity, still, they refused to believe Him; they even *"tempted and provoked"* Him.

Considering all that has been given to us under the New Covenant, are we presently doing any better, or even as well?

(57) "BUT TURNED BACK, AND DEALT UNFAITHFULLY LIKE THEIR FATHERS: THEY WERE TURNED ASIDE LIKE A DECEITFUL BOW."

A *"deceitful bow"* is one which is not dependable, that is, one which has lost its strength, or one which does not shoot straight. The Children of Israel could be depended on to do the wrong thing almost every time!

(58) "FOR THEY PROVOKED HIM TO ANGER WITH THEIR HIGH PLACES, AND MOVED HIM TO JEALOUSY WITH THEIR GRAVEN IMAGES."

IDOLS AND IMAGES

Upon arriving in the Promised Land, Israel quickly took upon herself the practices of the heathen round about her. They began to make idols and images and worshipped them as God instead of Jehovah.

Today in the modern Church, we believe we no longer are troubled by such.

But John the Beloved wrote: *"Little children, keep yourselves from idols"* (I Jn. 5:21).

Was the Church of John's day making idols (images) and worshipping them in the manner of Israel of old?

No! However, the *"idols"* the Holy Spirit was speaking of through John were the type of idols that we today can and do have within our hearts. This refers to anything that takes the place of God.

(59) "WHEN GOD HEARD THIS, HE WAS WROTH, AND GREATLY ABHORRED ISRAEL."

Concerning this, Williams says, *"The Divine Title in Verse 21 is 'Jehovah,' in Verse 59, 'Elohim.' As in the first Book of the Bible, so here, and throughout the Scriptures, these changes of Title are designed. 'Jehovah' expresses Covenant relationship; 'Elohim,' Creation relationship. He did not forsake them in the wilderness* (Neh. 9:17), *but He did forsake them in the Land* (Vs. 60); *and accordingly the Titles are used in harmony with the facts."* [25]

(60) "SO THAT HE FORSOOK THE TABERNACLE OF SHILOH, THE TENT WHICH HE PLACED AMONG MEN."

THE TABERNACLE

The Tabernacle here addressed was that which was built by Moses as directed by God and set up under Joshua at Shiloh, which was a city in the area occupied by the Tribe of Ephraim (Josh., Chpt. 18). It remained there throughout the period of the Judges, which lasted for several hundreds of years (Judg. 18:31; 21:19; I Sam. 1:3, 24; 2:14; 3:21; 4:4).

Due to the gross disobedience of Israel, the Lord *"forsook"* this Sanctuary when He allowed the Ark of the Covenant to be taken by the Philistines (the Ark of the Covenant was the place where God dwelt between the

Mercy Seat and the Cherubim [I Sam. 4:11-22]).

(61) "AND DELIVERED HIS STRENGTH INTO CAPTIVITY, AND HIS GLORY INTO THE ENEMY'S HAND."

This pertains to the Ark of the Covenant being captured by the Philistines and remaining in that area for a particular period of time (I Sam., Chpts. 4-6).

(62) "HE GAVE HIS PEOPLE OVER ALSO UNTO THE SWORD; AND WAS WROTH WITH HIS INHERITANCE."

Some thirty thousand (30,000) soldiers of Israel died in the battle in which the Ark of the Covenant was taken by the Philistines (I Sam. 4:10).

(63) "THE FIRE CONSUMED THEIR YOUNG MEN; AND THEIR MAIDENS WERE NOT GIVEN TO MARRIAGE."

So many of the young men of Israel were consumed in this particular war that there was an extreme shortage of potential husbands for many of the young women; as a result, many never did marry.

(64) "THEIR PRIESTS FELL BY THE SWORD; AND THEIR WIDOWS MADE NO LAMENTATION."

Because the Priests did not follow the Commandments of the Lord, they were given over to the enemy, and many of them were killed in this particular battle. The Priests carried the Ark of the Covenant into the battle thinking it would guarantee their victory. Because of their great sin, it did not!

(65) "THEN THE LORD AWAKED AS ONE OUT OF SLEEP, AND LIKE A MIGHTY MAN WHO SHOUTS BY REASON OF WINE.

(66) "AND HE SMOTE HIS ENEMIES IN THE HINDER PARTS: HE PUT THEM TO A PERPETUAL REPROACH."

When Israel had suffered the judgments of Verses 62 through 64 and was brought to Repentance, the Lord smote their enemies and manifested His mighty Power.

(67) "MOREOVER HE REFUSED THE TABERNACLE OF JOSEPH, AND CHOSE NOT THE TRIBE OF EPHRAIM:

(68) "BUT CHOSE THE TRIBE OF JUDAH, THE MOUNT ZION WHICH HE LOVED."

When a permanent site was chosen by the Lord for the Tabernacle and the Ark of the Covenant, the Lord chose Judah over all the other Tribes of Israel. The capital of Judah was Jerusalem, or at least David made this city the capital when he defeated the Jebusites (II Sam., Chpt. 5).

(69) "AND HE BUILT HIS SANCTUARY LIKE HIGH PALACES, LIKE THE EARTH WHICH HE HAS ESTABLISHED FOREVER."

THE TEMPLE

The plans for the Temple, down to the finest details, were given to David. Nothing was left to man's imagination. It was all of God.

Solomon, David's son, actually built the Temple. If the Temple and the manner in which it was built would be replicated today (2005), it would cost approximately a trillion dollars ($1,000,000,000,000).

(70) "HE CHOSE DAVID ALSO HIS SERVANT, AND TOOK HIM FROM THE SHEEPFOLDS:

(71) "FROM FOLLOWING THE EWES GREAT WITH YOUNG HE BROUGHT HIM TO FEED JACOB HIS PEOPLE, AND ISRAEL HIS INHERITANCE.

(72) "SO HE FED THEM ACCORDING TO THE INTEGRITY OF HIS HEART; AND GUIDED THEM BY THE SKILLFULNESS OF HIS HANDS."

DAVID

Saul was man's choice! David was God's choice! It was God's perfect Will that David be the first king of Israel.

God took David from humble beginnings and promoted him to be the king of His chosen people. But more importantly, the family of David was chosen to be the one through which the Messiah ultimately would come (II Sam., Chpt. 7).

Notice the two different names presented here:

1. *"Jacob"*: the natural seed of Abraham.
2. *"Israel"*: the spiritual seed of Abraham (Gen. 32:28; 45:25-28).

The Lord through David *"fed"* Israel because David had *"integrity of heart."* However, the *"integrity"* that David had was God's integrity and not man's.

It's only those who have God's *"integrity"* who will be shepherds that God desires, who will guide God's sheep *"by the skillfulness of His Hands — the Holy Spirit."*

PSALM 79

*A Psalm of Asaph:
A Prayer for the Destruction of
Heathen Enemies*

(1) "O GOD, THE HEATHEN ARE COME INTO YOUR INHERITANCE; YOUR HOLY TEMPLE HAVE THEY DEFILED; THEY HAVE LAID JERUSALEM ON HEAPS."

As noted, this Psalm was written by Asaph.

THE DESTRUCTION OF THE TEMPLE

First of all, this Psalm would have to be put in the category of being completely prophetic. In other words, it was written before the Temple was even built.

Two Temples in Jerusalem were destroyed; the first one was destroyed under Nebuchadnezzar, and the second was destroyed under Titus the Roman General in A.D. 70.

The Temple that yet is to be built in Jerusalem will be defiled by the Antichrist at the midpoint of the Great Tribulation.

The word *"defiled,"* as the Holy Spirit here uses it, could have one of two meanings: *"destroyed"* or *"blasphemed."*

When the Antichrist takes over the Temple in Jerusalem, he will not actually destroy the Temple, but he will defile it. Daniel gives the account (Dan. 8:9-13). Paul said that the Antichrist will claim to be God and will sit in the Temple of God (II Thess. 2:4). The Apostle John also said that the Antichrist would blaspheme God's Tabernacle (Rev. 13:6).

But more than likely, this Prophecy refers to the destruction of the Temple and Jerusalem by the Babylonians, which took place in 590 B.C.

(2) "THE DEAD BODIES OF YOUR SERVANTS HAVE THEY GIVEN TO BE MEAT UNTO THE FOWLS OF THE HEAVEN, THE FLESH OF YOUR SAINTS UNTO THE BEASTS OF THE EARTH."

So many Jews died in the siege of Jerusalem by Nebuchadnezzar that the bodies remained unburied and were consumed by vultures, hyenas, and jackals.

ISRAEL

The nation of Israel was meant by God to be the strongest and most powerful nation on the face of the Earth. Not so much because of a mighty army or other natural endowments, but rather because of the Blessings of God. Despite repeated warnings, they forfeited all of this; hundreds of thousands were slaughtered and other hundreds of thousands were sold into slavery. The great city of Jerusalem and its Temple were completely destroyed.

Sin will take one further than one wants to go, and the price always will be higher than one can afford to pay.

(3) "THEIR BLOOD HAVE THEY SHED LIKE WATER ROUND ABOUT JERUSALEM; AND THERE WAS NONE TO BURY THEM."

The siege of Jerusalem, engineered by Nebuchadnezzar, lasted for eighteen months. As stated, many Israelites died from warfare, but many more from starvation and sickness; so many died that the survivors didn't even try to bury the dead (Jer. 14:16).

(4) "WE ARE BECOME A REPROACH TO OUR NEIGHBORS, A SCORN AND DERISION TO THEM WHO ARE ROUND ABOUT US."

When Jerusalem was destroyed by Nebuchadnezzar, Jeremiah made this statement:

"All who pass by clap their hands at you; they hiss and wag their head at the daughter of Jerusalem, saying, Is this the city that men call The perfection of beauty, The joy of the whole Earth?

"All your enemies have opened their mouth against you: they hiss and gnash the teeth: they say, We have swallowed her up . . ." (Lam. 2:15-16).

(5) "HOW LONG, LORD? WILL YOU BE ANGRY FOREVER? SHALL YOUR JEALOUSY BURN LIKE FIRE?"

These questions were asked when both Nebuchadnezzar and Titus destroyed Jerusalem; however, they will ask with even greater intensity during the latter half of the Great Tribulation. The Holy Spirit calls this time *"The time of Jacob's trouble"* (Jer. 30:7). Israel will then cry to God as she never has before.

(6) "POUR OUT YOUR WRATH UPON THE HEATHEN WHO HAVE NOT KNOWN YOU, AND UPON THE KINGDOMS THAT HAVE NOT CALLED UPON YOUR NAME."

This also has been said in the past, but it will be said even more so in that future day of Israel's terrible Tribulation, which is very soon to come to pass.

At that time, Israel will begin to plead her case with God. The United States and all the other countries of the world will have forsaken her. God is her only hope; she calls upon Him to remember that she had once called upon His Name, and now she is calling upon His Name again.

(7) "FOR THEY HAVE DEVOURED JACOB, AND LAID WASTE HIS DWELLING PLACE."

The expression *"dwelling place"* means *"pasture."* Jacob is likened to sheep being devoured by wild beasts (the nations). These wild beasts trample upon and waste the pastures.

(8) "O REMEMBER NOT AGAINST US FORMER INIQUITIES: LET YOUR TENDER MERCIES SPEEDILY PREVENT US: FOR WE ARE BROUGHT VERY LOW."

All of this happened in the past; but, more than likely, it will have its greater fulfillment during the latter half of the coming Great Tribulation. At that time, some two-thirds of the population of Israel will be killed (Zech. 13:8). In fact, it will look as though they will be totally annihilated.

They realize that they have sinned greatly in the past. They are now pleading with the Lord not to remember their *"former iniquities."* They are asking that God's *"tender mercies speedily"* come to meet them.

This is a true prayer of Repentance that Israel seldom has prayed. It is a prayer that will be heard and answered.

(9) "HELP US, O GOD OF OUR SALVATION, FOR THE GLORY OF YOUR NAME: AND DELIVER US, AND PURGE AWAY OUR SINS, FOR YOUR NAME'S SAKE."

"Five" is the number of Grace in the Bible. Israel's petitions are here five in number:
1. *"Remember not our former iniquities"*;
2. *"Speedily come to meet us"*;
3. *"Help us, O God"*;
4. *"Deliver us"*; and,
5. *"Purge away our sins."*

This moment, even though futuristic, is so holy that one is brought to tears even while reading the words.

As this will be the prayer of Israel during the Battle of Armageddon, likewise, it should be the prayer of the entirety of the modern Church. It is a prayer of true Repentance; it is most definitely a prayer that God will hear and answer.

(10) "WHEREFORE SHOULD THE HEATHEN SAY, WHERE IS THEIR GOD? LET HIM BE KNOWN AMONG THE HEATHEN IN OUR SIGHT BY THE REVENGING OF THE BLOOD OF YOUR SERVANTS WHICH IS SHED."

These words have, no doubt, been said by the heathen in the past. They will be said even more so by the heathen in the future. As Israel cries to God, the Antichrist will taunt her by asking, *"Where is your God?"* (Ezek. 38:18-23).

(11) "LET THE SIGHING OF THE PRISONER COME BEFORE YOU; ACCORDING TO THE GREATNESS OF YOUR POWER PRESERVE THOU THOSE WHO ARE APPOINTED TO DIE."

The Holy Spirit through the Prophet Zechariah said, *"For I will gather all nations against Jerusalem to battle; and the city shall be taken, and the houses rifled, and the women ravished; and half of the city shall go forth into captivity, and the residue of the people shall not be cut off from the city"* (Zech. 14:2).

The Lord will answer the prayers of Israel, for Zechariah also prophesies, *"Then shall the LORD go forth, and fight against those nations, as when He fought in the day of battle"* (Zech. 14:3).

(12) "AND RENDER UNTO OUR NEIGHBORS SEVENFOLD INTO THEIR BOSOM THEIR REPROACH, WHEREWITH THEY HAVE REPROACHED YOU, O LORD."

Ezekiel said, *"And it shall come to pass at the same time when Gog shall come against the Land of Israel, saith the Lord GOD, that My fury shall come up in My Face"* (Ezek. 38:18).

(13) "SO WE YOUR PEOPLE AND SHEEP OF YOUR PASTURE WILL GIVE YOU THANKS FOREVER: WE WILL SHOW FORTH YOUR PRAISE TO ALL GENERATIONS."

This Passage lets us know that the Prophecy given in this Psalm pertains more to the coming Great Tribulation. Then Israel will truly give the Lord *"thanks forever."* They truly *"will show forth His praise to all generations."* They never have done that in the past. They will do so in the future, in the coming Kingdom Age.

PSALM 80

*A Psalm of Asaph:
A Prayer for Restoration*

(1) "GIVE EAR, O SHEPHERD OF ISRAEL, YOU WHO LEAD JOSEPH LIKE A FLOCK; YOU WHO DWELL BETWEEN THE CHERUBIMS, SHINE FORTH."

The title, *"Shepherd of Israel,"* is a new one.

THE SHEPHERD OF ISRAEL

In the blessing of Joseph (Gen. 49:22-26), figures are used of the Shepherd and the Vine with fruitful branches running over the wall. Hence, the nation here is called Joseph, and the Messiah is addressed as its Shepherd.

This Psalm, as the previous, delineates Israel's history and future.

It deals with God bringing them out of Egypt and blessing them greatly, and then, in the First and Second Advents of *"The Son of Man,"* bringing judgment because of sin.

(2) "BEFORE EPHRAIM AND BENJAMIN AND MANASSEH STIR UP YOUR STRENGTH, AND COME AND SAVE US."

When the cloud was taken up from Israel in the wilderness, the Tribes journeyed. Immediately after the Kohathites, who were bearing the Sanctuary and the Ark, came Ephraim, Benjamin, and Manasseh. At that time, Moses cried, *"Rise up, O Jehovah, and let Your enemies be scattered, and let them who hate You flee before You"* (Num. 10:11-36).

Accordingly, in this Psalm, they occupied this position in relation to the Ark. These Tribes were the children of Rachel.

(3) "TURN US AGAIN, O GOD, AND CAUSE YOUR FACE TO SHINE; AND WE SHALL BE SAVED."

In Ezekiel, we are told of the Glory of God departing from Jerusalem and the Temple (Ezek. 11:22-23). Ezekiel also saw the Glory of God returning (Ezek. 43:1-5).

NOTES

This will be during the opening days of the Millennial Reign.

The awe-striking flame, called the Shekinah, when flashed between the Cherubim upon the Mercy Seat in the Sanctuary (Vs. 1), was the Glory of God and symbolized His Presence. This Psalm prays for that Glory to return. It will return when the Messiah returns. And the Messiah will cause His people to return, *"Turn us again, O God."* He will shine forth from the Sanctuary to their relief and to the discomfiture of their oppressors. Thus, He will recover and replant His Vine called *"Israel"* (Williams).[26]

(4) "O LORD GOD OF HOSTS, HOW LONG WILL YOU BE ANGRY AGAINST THE PRAYER OF YOUR PEOPLE?"

The anger of God against His people because they killed the Messiah has lasted now for nearly 2,000 years.

(5) "YOU FEED THEM WITH THE BREAD OF TEARS; AND GIVE THEM TEARS TO DRINK IN GREAT MEASURE."

No people on Earth have shed tears as long as has Israel.

THE TEARS OF ISRAEL

These Passages speak of great sorrow. The tears literally have been mingled with their blood.

In World War II, Adolf Hitler tried to annihilate every one of the twelve million Jews on the face of Planet Earth. He succeeded in exterminating some six million. The German death camps of World War II always will be a reminder of the savagery of Satan's hatred for these people whom God loves so much.

At the Crucifixion of Christ, Israel plainly stated that they desired *"His Blood to be upon them and upon their children"* (Mat. 27:25). Sadly, what they asked for, they received exactly. In A.D. 70, Titus the Roman General sacked and burned Jerusalem. Over one million Jews died in that carnage. It is said that so many crosses with Jews hanging on them were put in the ground that there simply was no more room to put crosses.

From that time until this, these people have suffered as few have suffered — and for nearly 2,000 years.

No! God is not the One Who did this. He simply allowed them to have what they asked for, which was the Blood of Christ upon themselves and their children. Without God to restrain him, Satan then began his siege of death. Satan's onslaughts of tyranny against these beleaguered people will not come to an end until the Battle of Armageddon, when Jesus Christ comes back. They will have to accept Christ as their Saviour before the carnage concludes (Zech. 13:6).

(6) "YOU MAKE US A STRIFE UNTO OUR NEIGHBORS: AND OUR ENEMIES LAUGH AMONG THEMSELVES."

This has happened many times in Israel's history; it is happening even now with Israel's neighbors, Saudi Arabia, Jordan, Syria, Egypt, Iran, and others.

During the last half of the *"Time of Jacob's Trouble"* (Jer. 30:7), when it looks like Israel will be totally destroyed by the Antichrist, her enemies will *"laugh among themselves."*

(7) "TURN US AGAIN, O GOD OF HOSTS, AND CAUSE YOUR FACE TO SHINE; AND WE SHALL BE SAVED."

The prayer, *"Cause us to return,"* is a petition for Israel to be restored to nationhood and that the Temple be rebuilt so the worship of God may once again begin in the Sanctuary.

THE DIVINE TITLES

The Divine Titles, *"O God"* (Vs. 3), *"O God of Hosts"* (Vs. 7), and *"O LORD God of Hosts"* (Vs. 19), teach the importance of seeking to learn the lesson which the Holy Spirit designs in such variations. The expression, *"Cause Your Face to shine,"* was used frequently by ancient Israel. It means that God would give Blessings.

When the Face of God shines upon anyone or anything, that signals His Approval, which also signals all type of Blessings. There is not a human being on the face of the Earth, at least if they are sane, who wouldn't want the Face of the Lord to shine upon them. That is what I want more than anything else in the world.

Even as I dictate these notes, I sense the Presence of God. My prayer is:

"O Lord, as Israel of old cried to You, we do the same. In the Name of Jesus Christ, Your Son and our Saviour, because of what He did for us at the Cross and our faith in that Finished Work, please let Your Face shine upon us, and let it never cease to shine. This we ask, and for this we plead. We do so not because of any good within ourselves, but because our Sponsor, the Lord Jesus Christ, is good. Thank You for hearing us. Again, we ask all of this in the Most Glorious Name of the Lord Jesus Christ."

(8) "YOU HAVE BROUGHT A VINE OUT OF EGYPT: YOU HAVE CAST OUT THE HEATHEN, AND PLANTED IT."

That *"Vine"* was Israel. To be sure, the Lord expected that Vine to grow and to bring forth fruit.

Jesus addressed this very thing in John's Gospel. He said, and I quote from THE EXPOSITOR'S STUDY BIBLE:

THE TRUE VINE

"I Am the True Vine (the True Israel, as He is the True Church and the True Man; more specifically, He Alone is the Source of Life), *and My Father is the Husbandman* (refers to God the Father not simply as the Vinedresser, but also the Owner, so to speak).

"Every branch (Believer) *in Me* (to have Salvation, we must be *'in Christ,'* which refers to trusting in what He did at the Cross) *that bears not fruit* (the Holy Spirit Alone can bring forth fruit within our lives, and He does such through the Finished Work of Christ, which demands that the Cross ever be the Object of our Faith) *He takes away* (if the Believer refuses the Cross, ultimately he will be taken out of the Body of Christ)*: and every branch that bears fruit* (has some understanding of Christ and the Cross), *He purges it* (uses whatever means necessary to make the Cross the total Object of one's Faith), *that it may bring forth more fruit* (only when the Cross becomes the total Object of one's Faith can the Holy Spirit perform His Work of bringing forth proper fruit [Rom. 8:1-2, 11])" (Jn. 15:1-2).

In actuality, Israel has brought forth precious little fruit; however, that will change in the coming Kingdom Age.

THE HISTORY OF ISRAEL

The history of Israel as a nation begins with the Exodus. The nation was transplanted from Egypt by the Loving Hand of

God into a soil better fitted for it, in order that it might have ample room to grow up and develop itself freely. God *"brought it out of Egypt,"* not merely in the exercise of His ordinary providence over humanity, but by an active exertion of His Almighty Power, and a long series of miraculous manifestations, without which the transfer could not have been effected.

God had to *"cast out the heathen"* (Hivites, Hittites, Gergashites, Amorites, Canaanites, Perizzites, and Jebusites) in order to plant Israel; Once these heathen nations had been driven out, He *"planted"* His Own people in that land — Pulpit.[27]

(9) "YOU PREPARED ROOM BEFORE IT, AND DID CAUSE IT TO TAKE DEEP ROOT, AND IT FILLED THE LAND."

Israel did possess the Land, but not all at once. They took it little by little. Its farthest limits were taken during David's time (I Ki. 4:21, 24).

During the coming Kingdom Age, Israel will once again occupy all that was promised originally to Abraham. To the north, the boundary will extend all the way to Lebanon, and probably will include Lebanon. To the east, it will go to the River Euphrates, which means that Israel will then occupy at least half of Iraq, all of modern Syria, plus Jordan, and even the Arabian Peninsula. To the south, it will go to the Suez Canal. To the west, it will go to the Mediterranean Sea.

During the coming Kingdom Age, after Israel possesses all of this land, she probably will be at least fifty times larger than her present size.

(10) "THE HILLS WERE COVERED WITH THE SHADOW OF IT, AND THE BOUGHS THEREOF WERE LIKE THE GOODLY CEDARS."

The cedars of Lebanon are intended; at that time, they represented the largest trees in the entire world. They marked the boundary line on the north.

The Land of Israel was the only nation on the face of the Earth that served the True God. Every other nation served idols, that is, demon spirits.

(11) "SHE SENT OUT HER BOUGHS UNTO THE SEA, AND HER BRANCHES UNTO THE RIVER."

NOTES

The *"Sea"* here refers to the Mediterranean Sea. The *"River"* refers to the Euphrates River (Gen. 15:18; I Ki. 4:21, 24).

(12) "WHY HAVE YOU THEN BROKEN DOWN HER HEDGES, SO THAT ALL THEY WHICH PASS BY THE WAY DO PLUCK HER?"

Israel lost her way because of sin. It is always sin which causes the difficulties, the problems, the dying, and the death. Sin is the cause of all heartache in the world today; it has ever been that way!

(13) "THE BOAR OUT OF THE WOOD DOES WASTE IT, AND THE WILD BEAST OF THE FIELD DOES DEVOUR IT."

The heathen nations which surrounded Israel are referred to by the Holy Spirit as *"beasts,"* which is what they actually were.

When Israel was trusting and serving the Lord, no nation or group of nations in the world could defeat her. When they forsook the Lord, they were ripe for the plucking, and the surrounding nations took full advantage.

(14) "RETURN, WE BESEECH YOU, O GOD OF HOSTS: LOOK DOWN FROM HEAVEN, AND BEHOLD, AND VISIT THIS VINE."

The words, *"Once more,"* should be supplied in these petitions because the meaning is found in the Hebrew Text.

It means, *"Once more look down from Heaven! Once more behold! Once more visit this Vine!"*

This prayer began to be answered with the formation of Israel as a nation in 1948. It will continue to be answered through the Great Tribulation until Israel finally accepts Christ at the beginning of the Kingdom Age (Zech. 13:1).

(15) "AND THE VINEYARD WHICH YOUR RIGHT HAND HAS PLANTED, AND THE BRANCH THAT YOU MADE STRONG FOR YOURSELF."

Israel is God's *"Vineyard,"* and He will once again make it *"strong."*

Some of the modern Kingdom Age teaching states that Israel is no more, has been abandoned by God, and never will be brought back. Such is a lie. This *"Vineyard"* will be restored. The Holy Spirit said so (Rom. 11:12, 23, 26).

(16) "IT IS BURNED WITH FIRE, IT IS

CUT DOWN: THEY PERISH AT THE REBUKE OF YOUR COUNTENANCE."

Because of sin, the Lord has frowned upon Israel, and rightly so! The prayer is that His Face would once again begin to shine upon His people. If it does (and it will, because even now it is beginning to do so), such will rebuke and destroy their foes. This Verse should read: *"They* (the destroyers of the Vine) *shall perish at the rebuke of Your Countenance."*

(17) "LET YOUR HAND BE UPON THE MAN OF YOUR RIGHT HAND, UPON THE SON OF MAN WHOM YOU MADE STRONG FOR YOURSELF."

The Chaldee reads, *"King Messiah, the Man upon God's Right Hand"* (Heb. 1:3).

When the Lord claimed for Himself the Title, *"Son of Man,"* He possibly was referring to this Verse and this Prophecy.

The Hebrew Name *"Benjamin"* means *"the son of the Right Hand."* Jacob laid his right hand upon Ephraim, thus symbolizing the bestowment of privilege, power, and authority. Christ is the True Benjamin and the True Ephraim. He is the Son of the Father's Right Hand, Whom God has made strong for Himself.

It is Christ Who has totally and completely defeated the powers of darkness, which include Satan, every fallen angel, and every demon spirit. He did so at the Cross (Col. 2:14-15). This *"Son of Man,"* Who is *"made strong for God,"* has done it all for us. We never dare forget that!

(18) "SO WILL NOT WE GO BACK FROM YOU: QUICKEN US, AND WE WILL CALL UPON YOUR NAME."

The moral results of the Messiah's entrance into the Sanctuary is seen in this Verse. Whenever Jesus enters into the Millennial Temple, Israel will never again turn their back on Him. They guarantee their continuance and loyalty. The Holy Spirit superintends this Prophecy; on that coming Glad Day, Israel will keep her promise, but only because they then will accept the Lord Jesus Christ. This, as we have repeatedly stated, will take place during the coming Kingdom Age!

(19) "TURN US AGAIN, O LORD GOD OF HOSTS, CAUSE YOUR FACE TO SHINE; AND WE SHALL BE SAVED."

NOTES

For the soul into which He shines, there is no going back. Whomever He quickens, He eternally attaches to His Name. With Him Alone is there Salvation.

Let us say it again:

"O LORD, let Your Face shine upon us, and we shall be Saved."

PSALM 81

Written by Asaph:
God's Goodness and Man's Waywardness

(1) "SING ALOUD UNTO GOD OUR STRENGTH: MAKE A JOYFUL NOISE UNTO THE GOD OF JACOB."

This Psalm is presented to the Chief Musician upon Tittith, a Psalm of Asaph.

THE GOD OF JACOB

The expression, *"God of Jacob,"* means the *"God of all Grace."* These are His Old Testament and New Testament Titles. Israel's Messiah is the Speaker in this Psalm. In it are the tender thoughts and loving purposes of His Heart for His Sheep. Matthew 23:37 and Luke 19:42 portray Christ as Israel's Shepherd.

In regard to this, Williams says, *"In this Psalm we find that as man immediately fell from Creation blessing, so Israel immediately fell from Redemption blessing. Both Covenants were conditional; the one upon abstinence from the knowledge of evil, the other upon abstinence from the worship of idols. Both Covenants failed because of human imperfection. But Grace, acting in Divine Perfection, avails, and will avail, to recover, and even more than recover, all that was lost."* [28]

THE GOD OF OUR STRENGTH

The expression, *"Unto God our strength,"* is the secret of the victorious life. Sadly, Israel began to imagine that the *"strength"* she possessed was of her own making and was not from God; consequently, she refused to recognize her moral weakness, she went about to establish her own righteousness and miserably failed, as fail she must (Rom. 10:3).

This also is the most difficult problem the modern Church faces. We tend to forget that

God is our *"strength."* We think somehow that past and present blessings are indicative of our righteousness or moral worth. They are not! They are indicative of His Righteousness and moral worth.

The Holy Spirit, Who is God, is the One Who supplies the *"strength of God"* to us. This Almighty Strength is made possible to us all because of what Jesus did at the Cross, and only because of what Jesus did for us at the Cross. Even as we've already said any number of times in this Volume, the Holy Spirit works entirely within the parameters of the Finished Work of Christ (Rom. 8:2). Actually, He will not vary from those parameters.

He doesn't require much of us, but He does require that the Cross of Christ ever be the Object of our Faith. The great Sixth Chapter of Romans proclaims to us the manner in which the Believer is to live for God.

ROMANS, CHAPTER SIX

The first two Verses proclaim to us that the problem is *"sin."* Call it what you may, label it what you like, but the problem is sin!

In Verses 3, 4, and 5, we then are told that the only answer for sin (and I mean the only answer!) is the Cross of Christ. There we were baptized into His Death, buried with Him by baptism into death and raised with Him in newness of life. He was our Substitute, and our identification with Him guarantees us all for which He has paid such a price.

In the Mind of God, when we came to Christ, the Lord literally placed us in Christ, and in every capacity. He, in fact, placed us in His Death, Burial, and Resurrection. Paul also said, *"I am crucified with Christ, nevertheless I live . . ."* (Gal. 2:20).

Upon faith, we are literally placed into Christ, regarding His Death, His Burial, and His Resurrection. Our faith is to remain in that great Sacrifice which He afforded and we are not to allow it to be moved to anything else.

THE GOOD FIGHT OF FAITH

Now this is where the struggle begins. Satan will do everything within his hellish power to move our faith from Christ and the Cross to something else. And he doesn't care too very much what the *"something else"* is.

NOTES

It always will be a very religious *"something else."* Because it is religious, it deceives us.

If we are to walk in victory on a daily basis, meaning that the sin nature does not control us or dominate us in any way, we only can do so by exhibiting faith in Christ and the Cross, and in nothing else. That is our ticket to victory; that is our victory; that is our only victory!

Christ is the Source of all things from God, and the Cross is the Means by which all of these things are given to us. It is the Holy Spirit Who superintends all that Christ is and all that Christ has done. Upon proper Faith, which always pertains to the Cross of Christ being its Object, the Holy Spirit will guarantee us all the Blessings for which Christ has paid such a price. Then God becomes our *"strength"* in a way that we never could begin to imagine!

(2) "TAKE A PSALM, AND BRING HITHER THE TIMBREL, THE PLEASANT HARP WITH THE PSALTERY."

This, as do many other Passages, proclaims not only the approval, but actually the creation of musical instruments for the worship of God. Such was done at the time, is being done now, and actually will be done forever in eternity in praise to God (Rev. 5:8-9).

SINGING AND MUSICAL INSTRUMENTS IN PRAISE TO GOD

The *"timbrel"* was a tom-tom or drum. The *"harp"* and *"psaltery"* were stringed instruments. The *"trumpet"* of Verse 3 is a wind instrument. So all types of musical instruments were used.

During the early days of the Latter Rain Outpouring of the Holy Spirit (early 1900's), some Pentecostal and Holiness Churches would not allow a stringed instrument to be in the Church building. Their reasoning was the such was used in nightclubs and other such places, so they would not be proper in Church. Their reasoning was unscriptural and faulty.

First of all, just because something is used in an ungodly place does not mean that it is wrong to use it in Church. If so, it would be wrong to use a chair, electricity, or even a building.

The individuals who make such self-righteous rulings clearly don't know their Bibles very well! Long before there were such places of evil intent, the Holy Spirit designed musical instruments to be used in worship of God. So it was the nightclubs that borrowed the things of God, and not the opposite.

THE WORLD AND THE CHURCH

When we use the word *"Church,"* we aren't speaking of institutionalized religion, but rather the Mystical Body of Christ, whoever that might be and wherever they might be.

As long as the world borrows that which is ordained of God, it presents no problem to the Church; however, when the Church begins to borrow things from the world, things which have no validity in Scripture, things which are not God's Ways, and attempts to incorporate them into the Church, then the Church has great difficulties.

For instance, most Church Government is not based on the Bible, but rather on secular governments — hence, most Church elections and the unscriptural position of most deacon boards. Actually, most of that which incorporates itself in the modern Church is of man's doings and has no validity in the Word of God; therefore, no lives are changed, no broken hearts are mended, no bondages are broken, and no souls are Saved. It is only when the Spirit of God can move, which always will be according to the Word of God, that these wonderful attributes are brought about.

God help us to stay with the Word!

(3) "BLOW UP THE TRUMPET IN THE NEW MOON, IN THE TIME APPOINTED, ON OUR SOLEMN FEAST DAY."

THE LAW OF MOSES

The terms, *"New moon"* and *"Solemn feast day,"* both have to do with the Law of Moses, which has no bearing whatsoever on the New Covenant.

These were commands given concerning the worship of God at these particular times. Under the New Covenant, true worship of the Lord has nothing to do with ceremonies or rituals, but rather is *"in Spirit and in Truth,"* which should be conducted at any and all times (Jn. 4:24).

In attempting to explain the worship of God, one might say that *"worship is what we are, while praise is what we do."* In other words, everything the Believer does should be so constructed as to be the worship of the Lord. This is what the Holy Spirit intends. This is how the Patriarch Abraham, as he ascended the mountain in order to offer up his son Isaac as a Burnt Offering, which the Lord had demanded, could say, *"I and the lad will go yonder and worship, and come again to you"* (Gen. 22:5).

(4) "FOR THIS WAS A STATUTE FOR ISRAEL, AND A LAW OF THE GOD OF JACOB."

Under the Old Covenant, Israel was the only nation on Earth that had the *"Law of God"*; consequently, for any Gentile to be Saved, they had to become a proselyte Jew. Some few did! (Ruth 1:16-17).

ISRAEL

It was God's intention that He would send the Messiah, Who would come through Israel, and Who would perfectly keep the Law, all in order that not only Jews, but the entirety of the world, might come to Repentance — without all the rudiments of the Law; however, Israel rejected her Messiah and abrogated her place and position. So the Lord built the Church instead (Mat. 16:18). Israel, one might say, was to be the leader of the Church, but they refused it (Mat. 23:37-39). Now the True Church of Jesus Christ is open to *"whosoever will,"* including Jews (Rev. 22:17).

Still, the Prophecies are given that God will bring Israel back from her rebellious state and she will yet become a part of the Great Plan of God (Rev., Chpts. 6-19; Rom. 11:25-32). Israel's purpose under God actually was threefold:

1. To give the world the Word of God. She succeeded in doing that. All Bible Books were written by Jews.

The Scripture says:

"He showed His Word unto Jacob, His Statutes and His Judgments unto Israel.

"He has not dealt so with any nation: and as for His Judgments, they have not known them. Praise ye the LORD!" (Ps. 147:19-20).

(It is believed that Luke may have been Gentile; however, quite probably he was one of the seventy chosen by Christ, thereby a Jew.)

2. Israel was to serve as the womb of the Messiah. That also was accomplished, with Christ being born of the Virgin Mary.

3. They also were to evangelize the world; in this they failed, because they rejected Jesus Christ. The world today is being evangelized by the Church; however, Israel will yet carry out this role (Isa. 66:19). This will take place in the coming Kingdom Age.

(5) "THIS HE ORDAINED IN JOSEPH FOR A TESTIMONY, WHEN HE WENT OUT THROUGH THE LAND OF EGYPT: WHERE I HEARD A LANGUAGE THAT I UNDERSTOOD NOT."

The appellatives, *"Jacob,"* *"Israel,"* and *"Joseph,"* express Grace, Glory, and Affection.

SEPARATION

This Scripture doesn't mean that the Great Shepherd did not understand the Egyptian language, but that He did not acknowledge the Egyptians as His sheep. Instead of the word *"understood,"* the Hebrew verb should have been translated *"acknowledged,"* as in Psalms 32:5.

He makes this statement in order to emphasize the separateness of Israel, His flock. They knew His Voice, and He knew theirs, but He stood in no such relationship to the Egyptians, nor they to Him.

This definite separation is what He, in the Psalm, presses upon them to recognize, for their spiritual glory consisted of their recognition of it and their obedience to it; however, Israel refused to recognize it and to practice it, and so does the Christian Church today. The result is the same with the Church as it was with Israel: faithlessness and defeat — Williams.[29]

(6) "I REMOVED HIS SHOULDER FROM THE BURDEN: HIS HANDS WERE DELIVERED FROM THE POTS."

This refers to Israel's deliverance as slaves under Egyptian bondage.

THROUGH CHRIST BY THE MEANS OF THE CROSS

The deliverance of Israel from Egyptian bondage presents a physical illustration of our Spiritual Redemption. As Israel was delivered, you and I, through Christ, also have been delivered from Satanic bondage. The Deliverance was effected, both for Israel and for Believers presently, by Christ through the Means of the Cross.

Deliverance is effected in no other manner. Every other effort, no matter what the source, no matter how religious it might be, falls to the ground. It is at the Cross alone where every sin was atoned and every power of darkness defeated (Col. 2:14-15). Simple faith in Christ and what He did for us at the Cross will bring Deliverance, no matter how severe the bondage may be.

(7) "YOU CALLED IN TROUBLE, AND I DELIVERED YOU; I ANSWERED YOU IN THE SECRET PLACE OF THUNDER: I PROVED YOU AT THE WATERS OF MERIBAH. SELAH."

The *"trouble"* of Verse 7 is a covering term expressive of the trials of the wilderness. They were designed by the Lord as tests of faith, for when faith is tested, it grows exceedingly (I Pet. 1:7; II Thess. 1:3).

The *"secret place of thunder"* refers to Mount Sinai. The *"waters of Meribah"* were a test (waters of murmuring and strife [Ex. 17:7]).

THE WILDERNESS

This was a wilderness experience for Israel, which presents itself as a type of the world. As the wilderness had no sustenance, likewise, the world has no sustenance. There was no water for the people to drink. The *"water"* in this instance stood for Eternal Life. In other words, the world cannot produce or give Eternal Life.

As the wilderness was bereft of *"water,"* likewise the world is bereft of Salvation. Moses was told by the Lord to smite the Rock. The Rock was a Type of Christ. Out of the Rock flowed a river of *"water,"* which was symbolic of Eternal Life, that all may come and drink, all made possible by the Cross, for it was there where Jesus was smitten.

God's proving them was to see if they fully appreciated the *"water"* they were drinking, which had been supplied miraculously. Sadly, they did not appreciate it and ultimately they were lost. Regrettably, much of the modern Church falls into the same category.

(8) "HEAR, O MY PEOPLE, AND I WILL TESTIFY UNTO YOU: O ISRAEL, IF YOU WILL HEARKEN UNTO ME."

Verses 8 through 10 may be understood as having been addressed to Israel as they left Egypt. The love which invites the total fulfillment of Verse 10 is grieved if anything else is turned to for assistance. As Israel did not *"hearken"* unto the Lord, sadly the modern Church little hearkens, at least unto God. Instead the Church hearkens frequently to man-devised philosophies.

(9) "THERE SHALL NO STRANGE GOD BE IN YOU; NEITHER SHALL YOU WORSHIP ANY STRANGE GOD."

How many strange gods are prevalent in the modern Church?

STRANGE GODS

The *"strange god"* expressed here refers to heathenistic idols that actually were representations of demon spirits. The modern Church prides itself in the fact that this no longer exists; however, John the Beloved says, *"Little children, keep yourselves from idols"* (I Jn. 5:21).

He did so because *"strange gods"* abide plentifully in the modern Church. Modern psychology is a *"strange god."* So is *"philosophy,"* which is *"vain deceit"* (Col. 2:8).

When we worship anything, or look to anything, or depend upon anything, other than Jesus Christ and the Cross, this then comes under the heading of a *"strange god."* Paul referred to such as *"another Jesus"* (II Cor. 11:4).

(10) "I AM THE LORD YOUR GOD, WHICH BROUGHT YOU OUT OF THE LAND OF EGYPT: OPEN YOUR MOUTH WIDE, AND I WILL FILL IT."

This meant that every desire and need of Israel would be fulfilled if they only would have believed God. Likewise, the modern Church is given the same Promise. But the modern Church, regrettably, turns too often to other things.

A BLANK CHECK

This Verse proclaims the fact that the Lord is a *"miracle-working God."* He performed Miracles yesterday, He is performing them now, and He will perform them always.

NOTES

The last phrase of this Verse, *"Open your mouth wide, and I will fill it,"* virtually gives the Believer a blank check. It's not what He can give, but rather how wide can we open our mouth?

(11) "BUT MY PEOPLE WOULD NOT HEARKEN TO MY VOICE; AND ISRAEL WOULD NONE OF ME."

As Israel, time and again, forsook the Law of God, likewise, the modern Church seems to follow suit. Israel rejected her Messiah when He finally did come; likewise the modern Church rejects Jesus Christ and what He did for us at the Cross. Ultimately the Apostate Church, together with Israel, will accept the Antichrist when he comes (II Thess. 2:3-12).

At that time, the True Church will have been raptured away (I Thess. 4:16-17).

(12) "SO I GAVE THEM UP UNTO THEIR OWN HEARTS' LUST: AND THEY WALKED IN THEIR OWN COUNSELS."

This does not refer to the unconverted world, but Israel as God's Own people. It also could be speaking of the Church.

THE COUNSELS OF GOD

If we do not desire God's *"Counsels,"* then He will allow us to walk in our own *"counsels."* That spells disaster! This means to forsake the Word of God. In the modern Church, the Bible is, by and large, an unread and unfollowed Book. The Bible is the *"Counsel"* of the Lord!

(13) "OH THAT MY PEOPLE HAD HEARKENED UNTO ME, AND ISRAEL HAD WALKED IN MY WAYS!"

In Verses 13 through 16, the Lord tells Israel what He would have done for them if they only had obeyed. Israel did not walk in God's *"Ways."* They rather walked in their own ways. This also is the fault of too many modern Christians. We too often walk in man's ways instead of God's *"Ways."*

THE WAYS OF GOD

The Ministry of the Holy Spirit is to straighten out man's walk. We too easily leave the Word of God for empty and foolish philosophies devised by men.

What is God's Ways?

Once again, His Ways are His Word.

When the Lord first began to open up to me the Message of the Cross, it revolutionized my life. It also has revolutionized the life of every single person who has ever lived who has placed their faith and trust in that which the Lord has provided.

Knowing that the majority of the Preachers in the modern Church little understood the Cross as it regards Sanctification, I thought, at least at the time, that if they only could hear, then they would accept and receive. To my dismay, I found out that, while Scriptural ignorance was a problem, it really was not the problem. The problem was, and is, unbelief. In other words, most Preachers simply do not believe that what Jesus did at the Cross affords unparalleled victory, and that this alone affords unparalleled victory. Some may pay lip service to what I've just said, but then they make a mockery of their confession by placing their faith in other things.

Victory is found in the Cross alone!

(14) "I SHOULD SOON HAVE SUBDUED THEIR ENEMIES, AND TURNED MY HAND AGAINST THEIR ADVERSARIES."

The *"adversaries"* came whenever Israel turned to her own ways instead of God's. We have the Promise of this Passage that if we will walk in God's *"Ways,"* He will *"subdue our enemies."* What a Promise!

What and who are these enemies?

They are many and varied.

In Israel's day, the enemies were foreign nations. Pertaining to the Church, they are Preachers, so-called, who promote *"another Jesus,"* which means they have no confidence in the Cross (II Cor. 11:4).

(15) "THE HATERS OF THE LORD SHOULD HAVE SUBMITTED THEMSELVES UNTO HIM: BUT THEIR TIME SHOULD HAVE ENDURED FOREVER."

The Lord is saying that He would have subdued these *"haters"* if only Israel would have *"submitted themselves unto Him."* If they had done so, Israel would never have been defeated; Israel, in fact, would have *"endured forever."* Again, what a Promise!

To be sure, the modern Christian has the same Promise, that is, if we only will believe this which the Lord has said.

(16) "HE SHOULD HAVE FED THEM ALSO WITH THE FINEST OF THE WHEAT: AND WITH HONEY OUT OF THE ROCK SHOULD I HAVE SATISFIED YOU."

These are affectionate terms, with *"wheat"* speaking of prosperity and *"honey out of the rock"* speaking of God's special additional Blessings.

PROSPERITY

The honey which the bees lodge in the rocks of Palestine is esteemed most delicious. Only God can *"satisfy"* the hunger and the thirst of the human heart.

Back in Verse 10, the expression, *"Open your mouth, and I will fill it,"* refers to asking big. In other words, one cannot ask too big of God. Whatever we are able to ask, He is able to do, and more! It means we should not ask small, but big.

I was Saved and baptized with the Holy Spirit when I was eight years old. During those formative years (8-12), my Grandmother was my Bible College and my Seminary. Of all the things she said to me, I can remember one thing so vividly. She said, *"Jimmy, God is a big God, so ask big!"*

I have never forgotten that. It has helped me to touch this world for the Lord Jesus Christ.

PSALM 82

A Psalm of Asaph:
God the Righteous Judge

(1) "GOD STANDS IN THE CONGREGATION OF THE MIGHTY; HE JUDGES AMONG THE GODS."

As noted, this Psalm was written by Asaph.

MAGISTRATES AND RULERS

The first four Verses of this Psalm are an account of the Lord Jesus standing in the Temple in the midst of what was the Congregation of God and judging the rulers of the people. He fulfilled the first four Verses of this Psalm (Mat., Chpts. 21-23; Jn., Chpts. 8-10). As God, He stood in the Congregation of God and judged among the gods (judges, magistrates, or rulers). Sadly, they rejected His Judgment.

These religious leaders willed not to know or to understand. They chose to continue to walk in darkness; accordingly, He told them that they were the blind leading the blind. As a result of their rejection of foundational truth, the whole land was moved away from righteous judgment — Williams.[30]

(The word *"gods"* in the Hebrew is the same as *"judges."*)

(2) "HOW LONG WILL YOU JUDGE UNJUSTLY, AND ACCEPT THE PERSONS OF THE WICKED? SELAH."

Israel was designed by God to be His Representative in the Earth and the Judge of the nations. Hence, her Magistrates were termed *"gods"* — Representatives of God. To them, the Word of God was committed in order that they should communicate it to the nations (Ex. 7:1; Jn. 10:34-35; Acts 23:5).

Israel failed to fulfill this Divine Purpose; therefore, the prediction of this Psalm is that the Messiah would take up this Divine Purpose and perfectly fulfill it as Judge of Israel and of all nations — through His Body, the Church (Eph. 1:20-23).

(3) "DEFEND THE POOR AND FATHERLESS: DO JUSTICE TO THE AFFLICTED AND NEEDY.

(4) "DELIVER THE POOR AND NEEDY: RID THEM OUT OF THE HAND OF THE WICKED."

When religious leaders leave the Way of God and devise their own ways, the people then become pawns. True and righteous judgment demands that true Servants of God serve the people (Jn. 13:12-17). When religion prevails, the Way of God is turned upside down, with the people washing the feet of religious leaders rather than the opposite.

(5) "THEY KNOW NOT, NEITHER WILL THEY UNDERSTAND; THEY WALK ON IN DARKNESS: ALL THE FOUNDATIONS OF THE EARTH ARE OUT OF COURSE."

These wicked religious leaders would not hear Christ; therefore, they continued in darkness until the nation finally was destroyed.

Israel was the only nation on the face of the Earth that had the Gospel. They refused to live it or give it; therefore, the Gospel was pulled out of their hands and given to the Gentiles (Acts 13:46).

(6) "I HAVE SAID, YOU ARE GODS; AND ALL OF YOU ARE CHILDREN OF THE MOST HIGH."

The statement means that God had appointed Israel as judges (gods) simply because they were chosen of God and were the Children of God; however, Israel failed to fulfill this purpose, and ultimately they were destroyed.

To whom much is given, much is required. Jesus quoted the above Scripture in John 10:34. The following is what He said concerning these unfaithful judges:

(7) "BUT YOU SHALL DIE LIKE MEN, AND FALL LIKE ONE OF THE PRINCES."

Israel was so lifted up in herself that she felt she merited righteousness. The Lord's pronouncements told them they would die, and die lost (Mat., Chpt. 23). Even though they were called *"princes,"* that is, Representatives of God, still they would *"fall."* And fall they did!

(8) "ARISE, O GOD, JUDGE THE EARTH: FOR YOU SHALL INHERIT ALL NATIONS."

For some four hundred years, Israel went without a Prophet (from Malachi to John the Baptist). They rejected John the Baptist, and they rejected their own Messiah. For a little over thirty-five years, God did nothing. But in A.D. 70, He did *"arise."* At that time, He did *"judge."* Jerusalem and the Temple were completely destroyed. Over one million Jews were slaughtered by the Romans.

Israel failed, but Jesus Christ will never fail. The Messiah has taken up this Divine Purpose, and He will perfectly fulfill it as Judge of Israel and of all nations. Being at the same time the Representative of God and God Himself, He will administer just judgment to all. In this Eighth Verse, Jesus Christ is addressed as *"God"* and the *"Judge of all the Earth."* And so He is!

PSALM 83

A Psalm of Asaph:
A Prayer for the Destruction of
Israel's Enemies

(1) "KEEP NOT YOUR SILENCE, O GOD: HOLD NOT YOUR PEACE, AND BE NOT STILL, O GOD."

As noted, this Psalm was written by Asaph.

THE LORD AND ISRAEL

As the previous Psalm proclaimed the Messiah's destruction of Israel, which was caused by their terrible rebellion, this Psalm reflects the efforts of the Antichrist to completely annihilate Israel. He thinks that God has forsaken them and they, therefore, are ripe for his plunder, but he is mistaken. Though God has judged Israel, He has not forsaken her.

The timeframe pertains to the Great Tribulation, but more particularly to the last three and a half years, and even more particularly to the Battle of Armageddon.

God is here importuned to take up Israel's cause. It is interesting to note His Titles in this Psalm. The titles *"Elohim"* (Vss. 1, 12, 13), *"El"* (Vs. 1), *"Jehovah"* (Vss. 16, 18), and *"Most High"* (Vs. 18) express the Messiah's relationships toward Israel, toward the Millennium, and toward the nations.

This Psalm opens with a description of Israel's peril.

(2) "FOR, LO, YOUR ENEMIES MAKE A TUMULT: AND THEY WHO HATE YOU HAVE LIFTED UP THE HEAD."

The following proclaims the nations which have tried to destroy Israel, or will in the future.

THE LAST HEAD

Actually, seven heads have been lifted up (Rev., Chpts. 13, 17). The heads were and are:
1. Egypt;
2. Assyria;
3. Babylon;
4. Medo-Persia;
5. Greece;
6. Rome; and,
7. Revised Rome.

Actually, it is the *"last head"* that is spoken of here (Revised Rome). This one will persecute Israel greatly in the Great Tribulation. This *"head,"* representing ten nations, as outlined in Daniel 7:7 and Revelation 13:1, will join with the Antichrist in opposing Israel. This will take place in the last three and a half years of the Great Tribulation.

(3) "THEY HAVE TAKEN CRAFTY COUNSEL AGAINST YOUR PEOPLE, AND CONSULTED AGAINST YOUR HIDDEN ONES."

CRAFTY COUNSEL

Daniel said that the Antichrist will cause *"craft to prosper"* (Dan. 8:25). The word *"craft"* actually means *"deceit."* It means that the seven-year pact that the Antichrist will make with Israel will be broken by *"deceit"* at the midpoint.

The term, *"Hidden ones,"* means the Antichrist will think that God no longer cares for Israel; however, God does care for Israel. That care has been somewhat *"hidden,"* but now it will come to full bloom, as the Antichrist will graphically behold.

(4) "THEY HAVE SAID, COME, AND LET US CUT THEM OFF FROM BEING A NATION; THAT THE NAME OF ISRAEL MAY BE NO MORE IN REMEMBRANCE."

The phrase, *"They have said,"* presents many having said many things; however, it is God Who decides the bottom line.

THE NAME OF ISRAEL

For all time the general object of Israel's enemies has been to cut them off from being a nation; however, the greatest effort of all will be in the coming Great Tribulation, when Satan will infuse into the Antichrist the greatest power ever invested in any man for evil.

Because Israel crucified her Messiah, God then scattered them all over the world, and they actually ceased to be a nation for nearly 2,000 years. Even though they were regathered in 1948 and once again became a nation, still, the Antichrist will think that God no longer cares. To be sure, he will believe that God exists and can do mighty things, but he will believe that the Lord no longer will function on behalf of Israel. The Antichrist thinks this because of the silence of Heaven toward these people for nearly 2,000 years.

But yet the Word of God is filled with predictions of Israel's Restoration (Isa. 2:1-4; 4:1-6; 11:1-16; 12:1-6; 14:1-3; 18:7; 26:1-9; Jer. 23:3-8; 30:8-22; 31:1-40; Rom. 11:25-32; etc.). Evidently, the Antichrist will not believe these great predictions given by the Lord. Regrettably, most in the modern

Church also do not believe that Israel will be restored. But let all know the following:

RESTORATION

The re-gathering of Israel from all over the world to once again form a nation in 1948, plus all that has taken place since then, is not merely a political accident. All of this has been ordained by God. To be sure, Israel still has some hard days to go. In fact, the hardest days of all are just ahead.

They will once again be played for a fool; they will accept the Antichrist as the Messiah. At that time, they will cry, *"Peace and safety."* But Paul said, *"Then sudden destruction comes upon them, as travail upon a woman with child; and they shall not escape"* (I Thess. 5:3).

At that time, the Antichrist will show his true colors and attack Israel. She will suffer her first military defeat since she became a nation in 1948. Then she will face the hardest time of all. It will take place during the last half of the Great Tribulation, a timeframe of approximately three and a half years. During that time, the Antichrist will set out to completely destroy her, that is, to annihilate Israel from the face of the Earth. He will not succeed, but it will not be for lack of trying.

This is the *"evil thought"* of Ezekiel 38:10.

(5) "FOR THEY HAVE CONSULTED TOGETHER WITH ONE CONSENT: THEY ARE CONFEDERATE AGAINST YOU."

The timeframe of this Verse is the last half of the Great Tribulation. These who are *"confederate"* are the ten horns of Daniel 7:7. John said these kings would be confederates with the Antichrist, i.e., *"the Beast"* (Rev. 17:12).

(6) "THE TABERNACLES OF EDOM, AND THE ISHMAELITES; OF MOAB, AND THE HAGARENES;

(7) "GEBAL, AND AMMON, AND AMALEK; THE PHILISTINES WITH THE INHABITANTS OF TYRE;

(8) "ASSUR ALSO IS JOINED WITH THEM: THEY HAVE HELPED THE CHILDREN OF LOT. SELAH."

Verses 6 through 8 symbolically portray the ten kings, who will arise against Israel in the second half of the Great Tribulation. These symbols are not meant to portray a location, or even the correct names, because Daniel said these kings would come out of the old Roman Empire territory (Dan. 7:7).

Even though the ten mentioned in these three Verses do come from the old Roman Empire territory, they do not come from the exact locations. As stated, they are meant to serve as a symbol of what will come in the last days.

(9) "DO UNTO THEM AS UNTO THE MIDIANITES; AS TO SISERA, AS TO JABIN, AT THE BROOK OF KISON:

(10) "WHICH PERISHED AT ENDOR: THEY BECAME AS DUNG FOR THE EARTH.

(11) "MAKE THEIR NOBLES LIKE OREB, AND LIKE ZEEB: YEA, ALL THEIR PRINCES AS ZEBAH, AND AS ZALMUNNA."

Verses 9 through 11 represent the *"seven heads"* which greatly opposed Israel down through the ages (Rev. 13:1). These named are not the *"heads,"* but are symbolic of the opposition against Israel down through the ages. Those seven heads were: Egypt, Assyria, Babylon, Medo-Persia, Greece, Rome, and, finally, the ten kings, which are yet to arise.

The *"seven heads"* are portrayed by the seven names in the three Verses above.

(12) "WHO SAID, LET US TAKE TO OURSELVES THE HOUSES OF GOD IN POSSESSION."

THE ANTICHRIST AND THE TEMPLE

This Passage speaks of the Antichrist, who will take over the rebuilt Temple (Houses of God) at the midpoint of his seven-year pact with Israel. He will do this by setting up his own statue in the *"House of God,"* and will demand worship (II Thess. 2:4).

(13) "O MY GOD, MAKE THEM LIKE A WHEEL; AS THE STUBBLE BEFORE THE WIND."

Ezekiel said this would come to pass. He called it *"a great shaking in the Land of Israel"* (Ezek. 38:19). It will take place during the Battle of Armageddon, which will be the time of the Second Coming.

(14) "AS THE FIRE BURNS A WOOD, AND AS THE FLAME SETS THE MOUNTAINS ON FIRE;

(15) "SO PERSECUTE THEM WITH YOUR TEMPEST, AND MAKE THEM

AFRAID WITH YOUR STORM.

(16) "FILL THEIR FACES WITH SHAME; THAT THEY MAY SEEK YOUR NAME, O LORD.

(17) "LET THEM BE CONFOUNDED AND TROUBLED FOREVER; YEA, LET THEM BE PUT TO SHAME, AND PERISH."

The Fourteenth Verse talks about *"fire."* Ezekiel said that God would rain *"fire and brimstone"* on the Antichrist (Ezek. 38:22).

The Fifteenth Verse speaks of *"Your tempest"* and *"Your storm."* Ezekiel 38:22 portrays the same.

Likewise, the Thirty-eighth and Thirty-ninth Chapters of Ezekiel describe the fulfillment of Verses 16 and 17.

(18) "THAT MEN MAY KNOW THAT YOU, WHOSE NAME ALONE IS JEHOVAH, ARE THE MOST HIGH OVER ALL THE EARTH."

Concerning God's Deliverance of Israel in the Battle of Armageddon, Ezekiel also said, *"The heathen shall know that I am the LORD, the Holy One in Israel"* (Ezek. 39:7).

PSALM 84

*Author Unknown:
The Blessing*

(1) "HOW AMIABLE ARE YOUR TABERNACLES, O LORD OF HOSTS!"

This Psalm, or Song, is to be presented to the Chief Musician upon Gittith, a Psalm for the sons of Korah.

THE SANCTUARY

The word *"Tabernacles"* in the Hebrew is *"Mishkam."* It means *"dwelling place"* or *"where God dwells."* The word also is the plural of *"majesty,"* which expresses the greatness and glory of the Sanctuary.

The word *"amiable"* means *"lovable"* or *"desirable."* This actually refers to every part of the Temple or *"Tabernacle."* God dwelt between the Mercy Seat and the Cherubim. All the other parts of the Tabernacle, such as the Brazen Altar, the Brazen Laver, the Table of Shewbread, the Golden Lampstand, and the Altar of Worship (Incense) were Types of Christ. Every single part of the Tabernacle and Temple was, in some way, a Type of Christ, expressive of His Atoning, Mediatorial, or Intercessory Work.

This Psalm was written for the sons of Korah. This does not really indicate who exactly wrote the Psalm.

Williams says, *"The doctrine of the Psalm is that the Sanctuary is a home of pure and satisfying bliss, and that the road to it is a highway of happiness though it passes through a valley of weeping.*

"This Psalm portrays the joys of God's dwelling place and restoration to it, which occupies the heart. Yet, it is not the Sanctuary apart from God that is longed for. As well, the road thither is only a way of sunshine and safety if trodden with Him." [31]

This Song expresses the cry of the heart that every modern Believer in the Lord Jesus Christ must have. For that which was only in shadow is now a fact, which should elicit greater worship, if possible.

(2) "MY SOUL LONGS, YEA, EVEN FAINTS FOR THE COURTS OF THE LORD: MY HEART AND MY FLESH CRIES OUT FOR THE LIVING GOD."

This must be the cry of every *"soul."* Only those who have the longing of Verse 2 will reap the blessing of Verse 11. Jesus Christ is either Lord of all or not Lord at all!

Nothing can satisfy the soul of man except the Lord. In addition to being created a physical being, man also was created by God as a spiritual being. As such, the soul of man can find solace and fulfillment only in the Lord. Satan may attempt to meet the need in many and varied ways, but he never succeeds, because it is impossible for him to succeed.

As someone has well said, *"The soul of man is so big that only God can fill it up."*

(3) "YEA, THE SPARROW HAS FOUND AN HOUSE, AND THE SWALLOW A NEST FOR HERSELF, WHERE SHE MAY LAY HER YOUNG, EVEN YOUR ALTARS, O LORD OF HOSTS, MY KING, AND MY GOD."

THE DWELLING PLACE OF GOD

The Psalmist is saying that as the *"sparrow"* and the *"swallow"* have a house and a nest, likewise, until man finds God and God's dwelling place, man will have no home.

The meaning of the Verse is that as the sparrow and the swallow find love and rest in their midst, so the Believer finds love and rest in the Sanctuary.

THE ALTARS

The *"Altars"* pointed to are the Brazen and the Golden Altars. These two Altars foreshadow Christ in His Atoning Death for the sinner and in His Risen Life for the Believer. The soul finds its home in a Crucified and Risen Saviour. Under the Old Covenant, the Believer came to the Sanctuary to find Christ. Now Christ comes to the Believer and makes the Believer His Sanctuary (I Cor. 3:16).

(4) "BLESSED ARE THEY WHO DWELL IN YOUR HOUSE: THEY WILL BE STILL PRAISING YOU. SELAH."

Unceasing praise (I Chron. 9:33) fills the hearts and clothes the lips of those who dwell with God. This is not always so in respect to earthly Princes. They may appear attractive at first, but the longer they are observed, the more their attraction wears off.

It is the opposite with Christ. The more we carefully inspect Him, the more Perfect He becomes!

PRAISE

The expression, *"They will be still praising You,"* refers to continuous praise that never ends even though the difficulties of Verse 6 may be faced.

The Church has been taught much concerning praise for God in regard to alleged blessings. It knows little about praising God in times of adversity.

(5) "BLESSED IS THE MAN WHOSE STRENGTH IS IN YOU; IN WHOSE HEART ARE THE WAYS OF THEM."

Over and over again, the Ways of God are contrasted with the ways of man. *"Blessed is the man"* who follows the Ways of God (His Way is His Word). There is no blessing to the man who follows the ways of man.

The road that leads to the Sanctuary is trod only by the feet of those whose hearts are in that road.

(6) "WHO PASSING THROUGH THE VALLEY OF BACA MAKE IT A WELL; THE RAIN ALSO FILLS THE POOLS."

The *"Valley of Baca"* actually means the *"valley of weeping."* It produces a well of tears. The meaning of the Verse is this:

THE VALLEY OF BACA

Some modern faith teaching claims that, with proper confession, all *"Valleys of Baca"* can be eliminated. This, in reality, is no faith at all, and is totally contrary to Scripture. In every Christian life, there are one or more *"Valleys of Baca."* They are placed there by the *"LORD of Hosts,"* as portrayed in Verse 1, for our Spiritual Enrichment. It is the intention of the Holy Spirit to teach us the lesson He desires to teach, which He does in the *"Valley of Baca,"* and then to turn it into a *"well."*

The Holy Spirit also tells us that it is not His intention that we remain there. We are only *"passing through."*

At this stage, the Christian facing the *"Valley of Baca"* can do one of two things:

1. The Christian can lose heart and faith, blame God or others for his position, and lose his way to the Sanctuary. Sadly, millions have done this.

2. The Christian can turn this *"Valley of Baca,"* this hardship, this difficulty, into a *"well."* If this happens, the Promise of the Holy Spirit is that the Believer will be refreshed by rain and pools of Spiritual Water (Isa. 43:2; 44:3; Zech. 10:1).

If the spirit of the Believer is carnal, this valley will only be a valley of weeping. But to the Spiritual Heart, it will be a new nature and an unfailing reservoir of strength and refreshment.

It is all gained by the Believer making certain that the Cross of Christ is ever the Object of his Faith. Most of the times, a *"Valley of Baca"* is put in our path in order that we may come to the end of ourselves and realize that Christ is our Source for everything, while the Cross is the Means.

As someone has well said, and rightly so, *"All Revelation is preceded by desperation."*

(7) "THEY GO FROM STRENGTH TO STRENGTH, EVERY ONE OF THEM IN ZION APPEARS BEFORE GOD."

If we determine, by the Grace of God, to make this *"Valley of Baca"* into a *"well,"* this Passage promises us *"strength"* for the journey.

STRENGTH TO STRENGTH

The expression, *"strength to strength,"* refers to enough *"strength"* for the day, but not the morrow. There will be a fresh supply of *"strength"* awaiting at that time. This teaches us trust as we go *"from strength to strength."*

As we trust God for the necessary *"strength"* for each day, we will be led to *"Zion"*; there we will appear before God. The companionship of the Messiah on the homeward road guarantees all needed supplies for the way.

(8) "O LORD GOD OF HOSTS, HEAR MY PRAYER: GIVE EAR, O GOD OF JACOB. SELAH."

Now that the weary traveler has come through the *"Valley of Baca"* and has made it a *"well,"* thereby going *"from strength to strength,"* he finally stands before the *"God of Jacob."*

THE GOD OF JACOB

Over and over again in the Psalms, the appellative *"God of Jacob"* is used. It speaks of the *"God of all Grace."*

God took Jacob, who merited nothing but wrath, and heaped upon him untold Blessings and changed him for time and eternity.

The Psalmist is asking the Lord to do for him the same as He did for Jacob. He believes that God is no respecter of persons. This also should be the prayer of every Believer.

(9) "BEHOLD, O GOD OUR SHIELD, AND LOOK UPON THE FACE OF YOUR ANOINTED."

The Lord is here referred to as *"our Shield,"* meaning that He has protected us on this trying journey.

YOUR ANOINTED, THE LORD JESUS CHRIST

The first one to refer to the coming Messiah as *"The Anointed"* was Hannah, the mother of the great Prophet Samuel. She said, and I quote from THE EXPOSITOR'S STUDY BIBLE:

"The adversaries of the LORD shall be broken to pieces (whoever it be who contends with Him); *out of Heaven shall He thunder upon them* (the Lord is the Supreme Judge): *the LORD shall judge the ends of the Earth* (the whole Earth up to its remotest quarters); *and He shall give strength unto His King* (is a distinct Prophecy of David's kingdom), *and exalt the Horn of His Anointed.* (This looks onward to the Messiah, David's Greater Son. This is the first time that the term 'His Anointed' is used, as it refers to the Messiah. It is even more special in that Hannah used it. From this point on, others take up the theme of God's Anointed One — the Messiah [Ps. 2:2; 45:7; Isa. 61:1; Dan. 9:25-26]. And so the song of Hannah ends here, but actually continues on in the hearts and lives of untold millions)" (I Sam. 2:10).

The Anointed One, the Lord Jesus Christ, is the only Mediator between God and man (I Tim. 2:5). Now that we have this Mediator, we are given assurance of our audience with God, that is, *"to look upon the face of Your Anointed."*

(10) "FOR A DAY IN YOUR COURTS IS BETTER THAN A THOUSAND. I HAD RATHER BE A DOORKEEPER IN THE HOUSE OF MY GOD, THAN TO DWELL IN THE TENTS OF WICKEDNESS."

Now that the Sanctuary has been reached and we are able to stand before the Lord and see His *"Face,"* the conclusion is easily reached.

THE PRESENCE OF GOD

A few moments in the Presence of God is greater than anything Satan or the world would have to offer a thousand times over. The most menial position in the great Work of God is far better than the best or the greatest that the world may offer.

The writer is saying that he would gladly go through a *"thousand Valleys of Baca"* to have this short time in the Presence of God.

(11) "FOR THE LORD GOD IS A SUN AND SHIELD: THE LORD WILL GIVE GRACE AND GLORY: NO GOOD THING WILL HE WITHHOLD FROM THEM WHO WALK UPRIGHTLY."

Several things are said in this Passage:

1. *"For the LORD God is a Sun and Shield."* This means that God illuminates, invigorates, warms, and sustains life like the Sun. He also protects and defends all who trust in Him as a shield in the hands of a mighty man.

2. *"The LORD will give Grace and Glory."*

This means that the Lord will give us *"Grace"* to go through the *"Valleys of Baca,"* and then *"Glory"* once we reach the Sanctuary.

3. *"No good thing will He withhold from them who walk uprightly."* We must not make the mistake of assuming that we know what the good things are. We must allow Him to give us the *"good things"* that He desires to give, because He knows what we need.

(12) "O LORD OF HOSTS, BLESSED IS THE MAN WHO TRUSTS IN YOU."

This Passage directs itself in two meanings:

1. We trust Him to give us the good things that He knows we ought to have instead of us making the decisions ourselves.

2. The man who places his trust in God will always be *"blessed."*

The Divine Titles of this Chapter are significant. They are:

DIVINE TITLES

1. Jehovah Sabaoth (Vs. 1) — *"The LORD of Hosts."*

2. Jehovah (Vs. 2) — *"The Eternal and Immutable One."*

3. El (Vs. 2) — *"Strong One."*

4. Elohim (Vs. 3) — *"The Self-Existent and Eternal Creator."*

5. Jehovah Elohim (Vs. 8) — *"The Eternal, Immutable Covenant One in Relationship with His people."*

6. The God of Jacob (Vs. 8) — *"The God of all Grace."*

PSALM 85

Author Unknown:
God's Anger Removed from Israel

(1) "LORD, YOU HAVE BEEN FAVORABLE UNTO YOUR LAND: YOU HAVE BROUGHT BACK THE CAPTIVITY OF JACOB."

This Psalm was presented to the Chief Musician; it was a Psalm for the sons of Korah.

THE GRACE OF GOD

This Psalm was written for the sons of Korah. The title of the Psalm does not say it was written *"by"* or *"of"* Korah, but *"for"* Korah. If, in fact, a descendant of the rebel Korah (Num., Chpt. 16) wrote this Psalm, it proclaims to us the great Grace that gave these words of life and hope. It is the Grace that saves sinners who are dead in sins.

It also could have been written by David at the time that Absalom's rebellion had been put down and David had been restored to the throne.

Some have thought this Psalm pertains to Israel's return from Babylonian captivity. However, there is no indication of such except in prophetic spirit. Also it very well could speak of the Great Intercessor, Christ, pleading for Israel in the Last Days.

We will deal with it from the viewpoint of David, with the understanding that it well could have reference to Israel during the coming Great Tribulation and the beginning of the Millennial Reign.

(2) "YOU HAVE FORGIVEN THE INIQUITY OF YOUR PEOPLE, YOU HAVE COVERED ALL THEIR SIN. SELAH."

Israel had greatly sinned in David's day by throwing in their lot with the rebellion of Absalom. They now receive forgiveness for their iniquity. Israel is *"Your people,"* and God has *"covered all their sin."*

Because of David's great sin with Bathsheba, Israel thought surely they were justified in their rebellion. They were not justified. Actually, they sinned greatly, and, if possible, their sin was worse than David's. David was God's anointed; consequently, no person or people had the right to dispossess or harm him. If they had destroyed him, they would have destroyed themselves. Their sin was great because their attempt at destruction was great. They were totally out of the Will of God.

This Passage also could speak (and undoubtedly does speak) of Israel's rejection of the *"Son of David."* At the conclusion of the Battle of Armageddon, when Jesus Christ comes back, Israel will then pray the great prayer of David's Repentance (Psalm 51). God will then forgive their sins, and renew and restore them.

(3) "YOU HAVE TAKEN AWAY ALL YOUR WRATH: YOU HAVE TURNED YOURSELF FROM THE FIERCENESS OF YOUR ANGER."

As God turned away His Anger from Israel

for attempting to destroy David, likewise, He will turn His Wrath away from them in a future day. This wrath has burned so fiercely over these centuries because of their Crucifixion of Christ. This will happen at the beginning of the Millennial Reign (Zech. 12:10-14; 13:1).

(4) "TURN US, O GOD OF OUR SALVATION, AND CAUSE YOUR ANGER TOWARD US TO CEASE."

The expression, *"Turn us,"* actually speaks of Repentance. God's *"anger"* must cease and then Salvation be granted to them who engage in true Repentance. At the beginning of the Millennial Reign, Israel will truly repent.

(5) "WILL YOU BE ANGRY WITH US FOREVER? WILL YOU DRAW OUT YOUR ANGER TO ALL GENERATIONS?"

The *"generations"* spoken of here refer to the long period of time that has passed between the First Advent of Christ to the moment of reconciliation — now approximately 2,000 years.

During this time, God's *"anger"* has burned toward Israel; consequently, the Jewish people have suffered greatly. God has done exactly what He has told them He would do (Deut. 28:37; I Ki. 9:7; II Chron. 7:20; Ps. 44:14). The fault is Israel's and not God's — as the fault is always ours, and never God's!

(6) "WILL YOU NOT REVIVE US AGAIN: THAT YOUR PEOPLE MAY REJOICE IN YOU?"

This prayer very well could have been prayed by David after Absalom's rebellion. It definitely will be prayed by Israel in the second half of the Great Tribulation. Israel then will realize that the Antichrist has made a fool of her. As she sees the nations gather against her with total annihilation in mind (Ezek., Chpt. 38), she will know that her only hope is in God. After many generations, she once again wants her people to *"rejoice in You."*

(7) "SHOW US YOUR MERCY, O LORD, AND GRANT US YOUR SALVATION."

The Greater Son of David will, in His Intercessory role, pray this prayer on behalf of Israel. They never could be accepted otherwise. Israel does not ask for justice, but rather for *"Mercy"* — and even more so, for *"Your Mercy."* Then they can be granted *"Salvation."*

NOTES

Then they will be saved from the Antichrist.

(8) "I WILL HEAR WHAT GOD THE LORD WILL SPEAK: FOR HE WILL SPEAK PEACE UNTO HIS PEOPLE, AND TO HIS SAINTS: BUT LET THEM NOT TURN AGAIN TO FOLLY."

If David prayed this prayer regarding Israel's sin in joining Absalom's rebellion, the Lord will answer by telling them not to *"turn again to folly."* Sadly, they did not heed the Lord the first time. In the Latter Day, they will heed Him and never again *"turn to folly."*

Upon proper Repentance, the Holy Spirit tells us to listen carefully to what *"the LORD will speak."* The answer is glorious and comforting! *"He will speak peace unto His people, and to His Saints."*

The Reader also should note that these Passages clearly refute the unscriptural doctrine of *"Unconditional Eternal Security."*

(9) "SURELY HIS SALVATION IS NIGH THEM WHO FEAR HIM; THAT GLORY MAY DWELL IN OUR LAND."

This was fulfilled partially in David's day; it will be fulfilled totally in the Millennial Reign. When Jesus Christ dwells in Jerusalem, *"Glory will dwell in our Land."*

"His Salvation" is actually twofold:

1. To save Israel from the clutches of the Antichrist in the Battle of Armageddon.

2. To save Israel from sin, which, by far, is her greatest need!

(10) "MERCY AND TRUTH ARE MET TOGETHER; RIGHTEOUSNESS AND PEACE HAVE KISSED EACH OTHER."

This is one of the most powerful and beautiful Passages in the entirety of the Word of God. It brings together the unsatisfied Law of God with the Mercy of God. Under the Law, Mercy and Truth could not meet. *"Righteousness and Peace"* could not *"kiss"* or greet each other. However, in Christ, the two will meet.

RIGHTEOUSNESS AND PEACE

In the Tabernacle and Temple, a Veil hid the Holy of Holies, which was where God resided. On the Veil were inscribed Cherubims, which denote the Holiness of God. No man could enter except the High Priest, and then only once a year on the Great Day of Atonement.

The Great Day of Atonement signifies the cleansing of Israel at the beginning of the Millennial Reign — it is yet unfulfilled as far as Israel is concerned.

There was no Mercy in the Law. The writer of Hebrews said, *"He who despised Moses' Law died without mercy under two or three witnesses"* (Heb. 10:28).

For instance, when Achan stole the forbidden silver, gold, and garments from Jericho, he died without mercy and was stoned to death (Josh. 7:22-26). Whether he repented or not is not known. The whole world was under the same type of Law; there was no mercy, at least from the precept of Law. The Veil which hid the Holy of Holies was ever a reminder of that.

MERCY AND TRUTH

When Jesus died on Calvary, the Veil was rent from top to bottom (Mat. 27:51), meaning that God Himself pulled aside the Veil in order that *"whosoever will may come and drink of the Water of Life freely"* (Rev. 22:17). In other words, Mercy and Truth *"met together,"* because Truth was forever satisfied when every demand of the Law was met. Jesus fully met those demands by giving His Life as a Perfect Sacrifice; this Perfect Sacrifice Alone could satisfy the demands of a thrice-Holy God.

Now that *"Truth"* was fully satisfied, *"Mercy"* could be extended to *"whosoever will."*

The beautiful wonder of all of this is that Jesus Christ is both *"Mercy"* and *"Truth."* He actually is *"Mercy," "Truth," "Righteousness,"* and *"Peace."* Now He has paid the price for man's Redemption. As the *"Last Adam"* and the *"Second Man,"* Jesus Christ attained the great *"Truth"* and *"Righteousness"* which man could never attain. He did so as our Substitute and as our Representative Man (I Cor. 15:45, 47).

Based on the fact that the *"Truth"* of the Law has been forever satisfied, *"Mercy"* can now be extended to all. In Christ, *"Righteousness and Peace have kissed each other."*

(11) "TRUTH SHALL SPRING OUT OF THE EARTH; AND RIGHTEOUSNESS SHALL LOOK DOWN FROM HEAVEN."

This Passage means that only a Heaven-born Righteousness could undertake the justification of guilty men. The foundation of this Salvation was laid at Golgotha, where, in the Cross of Jesus, Verse 10 was fulfilled. There Truth and Righteousness judged sin in the Person of Christ. That one and only question between God and man being settled, Mercy and Peace flowed freely to sinners, making it possible for the pardon and prosperity of Verses 1 through 3 to be realized and enjoyed.

THE CROSS OF CHRIST

Mercy fulfills the Promises given by Truth; therefore, in the Psalms, Mercy necessarily always precedes Truth, for man has forfeited every title to Divine favor and Promise.

Righteousness through the Atoning Death of the Lamb of God furnishes this Great Salvation, and Mercy bestows it. Thus, Christ becomes the Believer's Righteousness, so the judgment that would have been our ruin has, in Grace, become our Peace.

"Righteousness and Peace kiss each other." This Righteousness was not wrought by man on Earth — that was impossible — it descended from Heaven, and hence, is ever-enduring. As a result, Truth springs out of the Earth, Glory dwells in the Land and yields its increase, and Righteousness reigns. Jehovah becomes *"merciful to His Land and to His People"* (Deut. 32:43) — Williams.[32]

(12) "YEA, THE LORD SHALL GIVE THAT WHICH IS GOOD; AND OUR LAND SHALL YIELD HER INCREASE."

Once again, this points in an even greater way to the coming Millennial Reign. Israel will at long last make her peace with God and see the Blessing that the Lord has promised her if only she would do so.

Before, because of Israel's sin, God expressed anger; but now, because of Israel's Repentance, God *"gives that which is good."*

(13) "RIGHTEOUSNESS SHALL GO BEFORE HIM; AND SHALL SET US IN THE WAY OF HIS STEPS."

Two thousand years ago, Jesus Christ asked Israel to *"follow Me."* They refused to do so. Now, at long last, they shall follow *"the way of His steps."*

RIGHTEOUSNESS

Actually, Christ is *"Righteousness."*

Consequently, it will accompany Him and follow Him wherever He goes. He will leave a trail beautiful with the lovely fruit of *"Righteousness."* In this respect, He will contract effectively with the past and present rulers of the Earth.

Those of us in whom His Spirit dwells will express the moral glory of this same *"Righteousness"* in our daily lives among our fellowmen.

PSALM 86

A Psalm of David:
A Psalm of Petition, Penitence, and Praise

(1) "BOW DOWN YOUR EAR, O LORD, HEAR ME; FOR I AM POOR AND NEEDY."

The title of this Psalm is *"A Prayer of David,"* so we conclude that David is its author. But more so it is an Intercession by the Messiah on behalf of His people. Therefore, He will take their place and pray the prayer they need to pray by saying, *"I am poor and needy."*

These Psalms and the account of Christ's Intercessory Work on our behalf are given that we may in turn say the same of ourselves as He says of us.

The occasion of the Psalm was probably when David was forgiven of his great sin with Bathsheba, was delivered from Absalom's rebellion, and was restored to his throne.

(2) "PRESERVE MY SOUL; FOR I AM HOLY: O THOU MY GOD, SAVE YOUR SERVANT WHO TRUSTS IN YOU."

The Virgin Mary, in Verse 16, emphasizes the fact that Christ truly became Man; otherwise, He could not be an Advocate for men. It was necessary that, as Man, He should be tempted in all points (Heb. 4:15). It was equally necessary that, as an Intercessor, He should be sinless; hence, He, the True David, could say what David himself never could say, *"I am holy."*

(3) "BE MERCIFUL UNTO ME, O LORD: FOR I CRY UNTO YOU DAILY."

As David cried *"daily"* for Deliverance from the powers of darkness that sought to destroy him, likewise, our Heavenly Intercessor, the Lord Jesus Christ, intercedes on our behalf *"daily."* He pleads for mercy, which all of us must have, that is, if we are to survive spiritually!

(4) "REJOICE THE SOUL OF YOUR SERVANT: FOR UNTO YOU, O LORD, DO I LIFT UP MY SOUL."

God, by His mighty Power, rescued David from those who sought his life and from the dominion of the lowest Hell. God also will deliver all those who trust Christ, no matter what dilemma they find themselves in.

David appeals to Jehovah's Ear. In his distress, he finds in God all his joy, comfort, and hope of Deliverance. He finds the Lord a Sufficiency, and he expresses his faith, love, and confidence — so infinitely perfect in his own case that he could be said to be the advocate of his people.

THE INTERCESSION OF CHRIST

This prayer, as prayed by David, is also prayed by our Heavenly David. The faith, love, and confidence that we should confess, He confesses for us and makes us true and acceptable worshippers.

Personally, He was poor, needy, holy, and believing (Vss. 1-2), but as our Intercessor, He pleads for sympathy (Vss. 1, 6), deliverance (Vs. 2), compassion (Vs. 3), refreshment (Vs. 4), and forgiveness for us (Vs. 5) — Williams.[33]

Truly He makes Intercession for us, does it on a constant basis, and does so simply by being in the Presence of God. This means that God has accepted Christ and what He did at the Cross as payment in full, all on our behalf (Heb. 7:25-26).

(5) "FOR YOU, LORD, ARE GOOD, AND READY TO FORGIVE; AND PLENTEOUS IN MERCY UNTO ALL THEM WHO CALL UPON YOU."

What a blessing this Verse is! Look at what it says.

A PORTRAYAL OF OUR LORD

1. The Lord is good. He does not sit before us as an austere Judge, but rather as a merciful Benefactor. He loves you; He loves you so much that He went to the Cross, all on your behalf. No mere man, within himself, is good; but our Lord definitely is good, because He is *"Lord."*

The word *"Lord"* means *"Covenant God,"* meaning that He has made a Covenant with the human race. According to that Covenant, if they will accept Him, to all who do so, He will show all His Goodness, which is unending.

2. He is ready to forgive. All one has to do in order to have forgiveness from the Lord is simply to ask. The Holy Spirit through John the Beloved said, and I quote from THE EXPOSITOR'S STUDY BIBLE:

"If we confess our sins (pertains to acts of sin, whatever they might be; the sinner is to believe [Jn. 3:16]; the Saint is to confess), *He* (the Lord) *is faithful and just to forgive us our sins* (God will always be true to His Own Nature and Promises, keeping Faith with Himself and with man), *and to cleanse us from all unrighteousness.* ('*All*' not some. All sin was remitted, paid for, and put away on the basis of the satisfaction offered for the demands of God's Holy Law, which sinners broke when the Lord Jesus died on the Cross)" (I Jn. 1:9).

3. Our Lord is plentiful in Mercy. It is the Holy Spirit through David saying these words, and not merely my own thoughts.

The Mercy of God is the outward manifestation of pity; it assumes need on the part of him who receives it, and resources adequate to meet the need on the part of him who shows it.

"Mercy" is the act of God, while *"Peace"* is the resulting experience in the heart of man. Grace describes God's Attitude toward the Lawbreaker and the rebel; Mercy is His Attitude toward those who are in distress.

In the order of the manifestation of God's purposes of Salvation, Grace must go before Mercy . . . only the forgiven may be blessed. From this it follows that in each of the Apostolic salutations where these words occur, Grace always precedes Mercy (I Tim. 1:2; II Tim. 1:2; Tit. 1:4).

God is the *"Father of Mercies"* (II Cor. 1:3).

GOD'S ATTITUDE TOWARD MAN

Though man is alienated from God, God is not alienated from man. John 3:16 bears this out. His Attitude toward the sinner does not need to be changed by His Efforts. With regard to man's sin, an expiation (forgiveness) is necessary, consistent with God's Holiness and for His Righteousness' sake, and that expiation His Grace and Love have provided in the Atoning Sacrifice of His Son; man, of himself, and a sinner, justly exposed to God's Wrath (Jn. 3:36), could never, within himself, find an expiation.

As Lightfoot says, *"When the New Testament writers speak at length on the subject of Divine Wrath, the hostility is represented, not as on the part of God, but of men."* Through that which God has accomplished in Christ, by His Death on the Cross, man, on becoming regenerate, escapes the merited Wrath of God. The making of this expiation (forgiveness), with its effect in the Mercy of God, is what is expressed in the word *"Mercy."*

However, in all of this, we must ever understand that man is in no way worthy of the Mercy of God, nor can he do anything to make himself worthy. Mercy from God is received by unworthy man simply by man understanding that he is not worthy and that he is a sinner deserving wrath; on the confession that he is a sinner, who deserves wrath, but who places his faith and trust in Christ, Mercy is extended to him in totality.

When God grants mercy, He never grants partial mercy, but only mercy in total. The sin is washed, cleansed, and forgiven, as though it never took place.

4. We must call on Him. We have sinned against the Lord, so it is to the Lord to Whom we must appeal. If we appeal in the right attitude, He always will grant mercy.

The Lord is ready to do all of these things upon proper confession of sin; however, the Church generally is not.

Why not?

When Believers leave the Bible, they invent their own righteousness, salvation, forgiveness, mercy, justification, integrity, and morality. The words used are the same; but, regrettably, the meanings given by most in the modern Church have little relationship to the Bible meanings. This always has been Satan's trump card; sadly, he has succeeded very well.

Man can either accept what God says (His Word), or what man says. One cannot accept both.

(6) "GIVE EAR, O LORD, UNTO MY PRAYER; AND ATTEND TO THE VOICE OF MY SUPPLICATIONS."

Now we come to the subject of prayer.

PRAYER

"Prayer" is the great bulwark of the Christian. Sadly, few engage in its blessed Promises. James said, *"Is any among you afflicted? Let him pray"* (James 5:13). Regrettably, the modern Church little prays, which shows they don't believe too very much in prayer.

That God's Ear is always attent to the prayers of His people does not make it superfluous for us to entreat His Attention. He will listen more favorably when besought to listen.

We should seek the Lord avidly, not only for what He can do, but also for Who He is. Without a proper prayer life, it is impossible for any Believer to establish any type of relationship with the Lord.

HOW TO PRAY

First of all, when a Believer begins to pray, he should first of all thank the Lord for all that He is doing for us. The Psalmist said, *"Enter into His gates with thanksgiving, and into His courts with praise: be thankful unto Him, and bless His Name"* (Ps. 100:4).

When the Psalmist wrote this, he was, of course, speaking of the earthly Temple in Jerusalem, which was where the Lord then dwelt. However, due to the fact that, since the Cross, all Believers have instant access to the very Throne of God, I think one could say, and be Scripturally correct, *"Enter into His Throne with thanksgiving, and into His Presence with praise."*

We should petition the Lord (supplicate Him) to meet our needs only after we have properly thanked Him for what He has done and is doing for us.

My Grandmother taught me something about prayer a long, long time ago. She said this to me many times:

"Jimmy, God is a big God, so ask big!"

I have never forgotten that and it has helped me to touch the world for Christ.

(7) "IN THE DAY OF MY TROUBLE I WILL CALL UPON YOU: FOR YOU WILL ANSWER ME."

NOTES

Three things are here said. They are very simple, but, oh, so appropriate!
1. Trouble will come.
2. When it comes, call on God.
3. God has promised to answer.

(8) "AMONG THE GODS THERE IS NONE LIKE UNTO YOU, O LORD; NEITHER ARE THERE ANY WORKS LIKE UNTO YOUR WORKS."

The title *"gods"* refers to heathenistic *"gods,"* which actually are demon spirits, which promise all sorts of things to their worshippers. In comparison to these *"gods,"* *"none are like unto You, O Lord."*

Every other god, so-called, of all the religions of the world, is no god at all; they are merely figments of men's imaginations. In fact, all of these religions, be it Islam, Buddhism, Hinduism, etc., do not worship the True God, but rather a god of their own manufacture. It is the God of the Bible Alone Who is God. Through the Prophet Isaiah, He said: *"You are My witnesses, saith the LORD, and My servant whom I have chosen, that you may know and believe Me, and understand that I am He: before Me there was no God formed, neither shall there be after Me.*

"I, even I, am the LORD; and beside Me there is no Saviour" (Isa. 43:10-11).

(9) "ALL NATIONS WHOM YOU HAVE MADE SHALL COME AND WORSHIP BEFORE YOU, O LORD; AND SHALL GLORIFY YOUR NAME."

This is yet unfulfilled. It will be totally fulfilled in the coming Millennial Reign. Jesus will then reign supreme in Jerusalem. The nations of the world will send ambassadors, presidents, and rulers to Him to *"worship before You, O LORD."*

(10) "FOR YOU ARE GREAT, AND DO WONDROUS THINGS: YOU ARE GOD ALONE."

Three things are said here:

YOU ARE GOD ALONE

1. The Greatness of God knows no bounds. He will be able to do what needs to be done to make this Planet what He wants it to be.

2. In the coming Kingdom Age, when the nations of the world send their ambassadors to Him, He will give them the answers to all

of their problems of every nature: economic, agricultural, social, and, above all, spiritual. He truly will *"do wondrous things."*

Presently, in fact, He has done such and is doing such for those who dare to believe Him.

3. On the entirety of the Planet, He then will be *"God Alone."* Muhammad will be no more; Buddha will be no more; all other pretenders likewise will vanish into oblivion. Satan also will be locked away. All the nations of the world will worship *"God Alone."*

(11) "TEACH ME YOUR WAY, O LORD; I WILL WALK IN YOUR TRUTH: UNITE MY HEART TO FEAR YOUR NAME."

David prays these words, as we should. More so, the Messiah, as the Intercessor, will pray them on behalf of Israel. As our Intercessor, He does the same for us presently, which He will do for any who come to Him and believe Him.

Three things are here said:

1. *"Teach me Your Way, O LORD."* Man's problem is that he goes in the way of other men or his own way. Both are destructive. Only *"Your Way"* will lead us to God.

2. *"I will walk in Your Truth."*

What is *"Truth"*?

Truth is not a philosophy. Philosophies change; the *"Truth"* does not change. The *"Truth"* is threefold, corresponding with the Trinity:

A. Jesus Christ is *"Truth"* (Jn. 14:6).

B. The Holy Spirit is *"Truth"* (I Jn. 5:6).

C. God's Word is *"Truth"* (Jn. 1:17).

Some claim that *"all truth is God's Truth."* That statement is true if one understands what it actually says; however, most people confuse the word *"true"* with the word *"Truth."* They are different things altogether. Some have mistaken assembled facts for *"Truth."* Actually, all *"Truth"* can be summed up in Jesus Christ, that is, *"The Word of God."*

3. *"Unite my heart to fear Your Name."* The heart all too often is divided. David prays that every faction of his heart be united in order that he may properly *"fear Your Name."* The world does not fear God; most of the Church does not fear God. If we properly fear Him, which means to truly respect Him and His Word, He will teach us and give us *"Truth,"* and we will walk therein.

(12) "I WILL PRAISE YOU, O LORD MY GOD, WITH ALL MY HEART: AND I WILL GLORIFY YOUR NAME FOREVERMORE."

David implores the Lord to unite his heart and then he could properly praise the Lord. Only a united heart can praise the Lord with *"all my heart."* Only this *"will glorify Your Name forevermore."*

Jesus prayed this prayer in John, Chapter 17. Five times in this one prayer, He prayed for the Church (His Heart) not to be divided, *"That they may be one, as We are"* (Jn. 17:11).

As David prays this prayer, the Greater Son of David is praying, *"Father, the hour is come; glorify Your Son, that Your Son also may glorify You"* (Jn. 17:1).

(13) "FOR GREAT IS YOUR MERCY TOWARD ME: AND YOU HAVE DELIVERED MY SOUL FROM THE LOWEST HELL."

There is a Hell!

HELL

As many have said, *"There is a Heaven to gain, and a Hell to lose."* As surely as there is a place called *"Heaven"* (Rev., Chpts. 21-22), there also is a place called *"Hell"* (Lk. 16:19-31).

Only the Lord can save the soul from Hell, which He does through Christ and what He did for us at the Cross, which demands our faith in that Finished Work.

(14) "O GOD, THE PROUD ARE RISEN AGAINST ME, AND THE ASSEMBLIES OF VIOLENT MEN HAVE SOUGHT AFTER MY SOUL; AND HAVE NOT SET YOU BEFORE THEM."

As David prays this prayer, and as it regards those who had risen up against Him, it also speaks of the Greater Son of David.

As our Lord prayed this prayer, *"the proud"* spoken of here refers to the Scribes, Pharisees, and Sadducees, that is, the religious leaders of Israel.

"The assemblies of violent men" are the Sanhedrin.

At the trial of Jesus, God had no part in their proceedings. Hence, David said, *"And have not set You before them."* In other words, while these *"violent men"* claimed to be doing the Work of God, they truly were doing the work of Satan.

Tragically, all too often the modern Church follows the same course as *"the proud"* of old!

(15) "BUT YOU, O LORD, ARE A GOD FULL OF COMPASSION, AND GRACIOUS, LONGSUFFERING, AND PLENTEOUS IN MERCY AND TRUTH."

The world says that the God of the Bible is *"cruel"* and *"judgmental."* The Holy Spirit through the Messiah says that He is *"full of compassion"* and *"gracious, longsuffering, and plenteous in Mercy and Truth."* Satan deceives the world in making them believe that God is the opposite of what He really is.

WHAT IS GOD REALLY LIKE?

If one wants to know Who God is, What God is, and How God is, one need only look at the Lord Jesus Christ. I quote from THE EXPOSITOR'S STUDY BIBLE:

"Philip said unto Him, Lord, show us the Father, and it suffices us (like Philip, all, at least for the most part, want to see God, but the far greater majority reject the only manner and way to see Him, which is through Jesus).

"Jesus said unto him, Have I been so long with you, and yet have you not known Me, Philip? (Reynolds says, *'There is no right understanding of Jesus Christ until the Father is actually seen in Him.'*) *He who has seen Me has seen the Father* (presents the very embodiment of Who and What the Messiah would be; if we want to know what God is like, we need only look at the Son)" (Jn. 14:8-9).

This Fifteenth Verse also has reference to the Restoration of Israel, when God forgives them of the terrible crime they committed against His Son, Who was, and is, their Messiah and their Saviour, as well as the Saviour of the entire world, at least for all who will believe (Jn. 3:16).

(16) "O TURN UNTO ME, AND HAVE MERCY UPON ME; GIVE YOUR STRENGTH UNTO YOUR SERVANT, AND SAVE THE SON OF YOUR HANDMAID."

Even though David prayed this prayer, still, the Greater Son of David is praying it for Himself, for Israel, and for you and me.

The *"Mercy"* for which he asks, which says, *"upon me,"* is an Intercessory prayer for Israel and for all Believers. As stated, Christ is our Intercessor. The Lord will take upon Himself Israel's sin and then request *"Mercy"* for them, which He also does for us!

Israel would not save the *"Son"* of the Virgin Mary, *"Your handmaid"*; God did save *"His Son"* from the powers of darkness when He went to the Cross. God turned the situation around and made the Cross the Means by which Satan and all of his cohorts of darkness were defeated (Col. 2:14-15). Through the Cross, the Lord Jesus Christ saves all who come to Him. He will save Israel when they, at long last, come to Him. This will occur at the Second Coming (Zech. 13:1).

(17) "SHOW ME A TOKEN FOR GOOD; THAT THEY WHICH HATE ME MAY SEE IT, AND BE ASHAMED: BECAUSE YOU, LORD, HAVE HELPED ME, AND COMFORTED ME."

The *"token for good"* of which David here speaks probably was the restoration to his throne, which Absalom and many of the leaders of Israel tried to take. They had claimed that the Lord would not now help David because of his great sin with Bathsheba. In their minds, now was their time to strike (Ps. 3:1-2).

The *"token for good"* also speaks of Christ. His Resurrection was shown to Him. Those who hated Him also saw it. Whenever they stand before Him at the Second Coming, when He has defeated the Antichrist at the Battle of Armageddon, when He has delivered Israel, then they will be *"ashamed."*

As the Lord helped David and comforted him, and as He helped Christ and comforted Him, likewise He will help Israel and comfort her on that coming Glad Day!

PSALM 87

Author Unknown:
The Glories of Zion

(1) "HIS FOUNDATION IS IN THE HOLY MOUNTAINS."

This Psalm or Song was written for the sons of Korah. It very well could have been penned by David.

HIS FOUNDATION

"Mountains" may be the plural of Majesty for Mount Zion, or it may mean the hill country of Judaea, which was the birthplace of the Messiah.

Or it could refer to the New Jerusalem, which actually will be built on a great mountain, believe it or not, some 1,500 miles high (Rev. 21:14-16).

This Psalm probably was given by the Spirit on the occasion of the bringing up of the Ark to Jerusalem (II Sam., Chpt. 6).

(2) "THE LORD LOVES THE GATES OF ZION MORE THAN ALL THE DWELLINGS OF JACOB."

This means that the Lord has chosen Zion (the Mount on which the Temple was built) as His chief habitation in Israel (Isa. 8:18; Ps. 48:2; 50:2; 78:68).

THE PRESENCE OF EMMANUEL

The theme of this Psalm is the Birth of the Messiah in the hill country of Judaea (Bethlehem) and the subsequent establishment of His Throne and Sanctuary on Mount Zion. The plans for the Temple had been given to David, but it was built by David's son, Solomon.

The glory of Zion will not then be her beauty, wealth, or military strength, but the Presence of Emmanuel. The consequent supremacy of Zion and of Israel over all other nations is here declared.

Many modern-day religionists make the grand mistake of believing that God has abandoned Jerusalem and Israel because of her rejection of the Messiah. It certainly is true that God has allowed Satan to persecute Israel greatly for the last twenty centuries because of their rejection of Christ. But still, according to His Word and the events that now are transpiring, God has in no way abandoned her.

Actually, the greatest Restoration any nation ever has known is about to take place.

The nations of the world are somewhat touched upon in this Chapter; however, Israel ultimately will have the chief place in that history, because, in her and through her, the Messiah was born.

(3) "GLORIOUS THINGS ARE SPOKEN OF YOU, O CITY OF GOD. SELAH."

NOTES

Jerusalem is here portrayed!

JERUSALEM

Jerusalem and Babylon are the two prominent cities of the Bible. Babylon was established first and represents man's rebellion against God. It was built by Nimrod; it was *"the beginning of his kingdom,"* that is, *"the beginning of his kingdom of rebellion"* (Gen. 10:10).

Jerusalem was previously known as *"Salem"* at a time when Melchizedek was its king. It became a city of Righteousness. Melchizedek was a Type of Christ and guaranteed this. He was so honored by God that Abraham paid tithes to him (Gen. 14:18-20). Since the lesser generally pays tithes to the greater, and considering who Abraham was, the fact that the Holy Spirit placed Melchizedek in an even greater position than Abraham tells us just how great this king of Salem actually was. He was a Type of Christ, especially of the Priesthood of Christ.

So the first mention we have of Jerusalem was in connection with Melchizedek.

However, there came a point in time when Satan exerted dominion over Salem (Jerusalem). It came to be inhabited by the Jebusites and then was called *"Jebus"* (Judg. 19:10). The Jebusites ultimately made the city a stronghold right in the midst of Israel. In other words, Satan had established a stronghold in the very midst of God's Inheritance for His people.

This is a perfect example of what the Evil One attempts to do, spiritually speaking, in the heart and life of every Believer. In one way or another, he desires to erect a stronghold. If the Believer doesn't understand the Cross and what Jesus there did in connection with our Sanctification, he will succeed (Rom. 6:1-14).

When David became the King of Israel, the first thing he did was to take this *"stronghold"* and defeat the Jebusites. David then made the city his capital and called it *"Jerusalem"* (II Sam. 5:6-10). On Zion's hill in Jerusalem, the Temple would be built. As already stated, the plans for the Temple were given to David, but Solomon, David's son, actually built it.

Satan's city Babylon was destroyed many

centuries ago; however, the Babylon spirit exists throughout the entirety of the world. The Eighteenth Chapter of the Book of Revelation proclaims the rebuilding of the city of Babylon.

Since present-day Iraq is the site of ancient Babylon, the excursion of the United States into Iraq and other events in that part of the world all figure into the fulfillment of the rebuilding of the city of Babylon.

Ancient Babylon ceased to exist about 2,000 years ago, while Jerusalem, although continuing to exist throughout this entire period, has been contested almost from the very beginning. At the present time, Jerusalem is the *"sore spot"* in the world. The Palestinians demand it as their capital, and Israel also demands it for her capital, with the latter being rightly so.

The problem will not be settled until Jesus Christ returns, which He shortly will.

(4) "I WILL MAKE MENTION OF RAHAB AND BABYLON TO THEM WHO KNOW ME: BEHOLD PHILISTIA, AND TYRE, WITH ETHIOPIA; THIS MAN WAS BORN THERE."

The name *"Rahab,"* as used here, has nothing to do with Rahab the harlot addressed in the Book of Joshua. It rather is a poetic name for Egypt and means *"boaster"* (Isa. 51:9).

JEHOVAH'S SERVANTS

Psalms 22:7 possibly will help explain Verse 4. The two names given here by the Holy Spirit, *"Rahab"* (meaning Egypt) and *"Babylon,"* in Hebrew are expressed as *"arrogance"* (boastful) and *"confusion."* These two terms fitly portray the nature of human government.

The three great families into which Noah's Prophecy divides humanity (Gen. 9:25-27) are brought together in Verse 4. Shem, Ham, and Japheth are represented by Israel, Egypt, and Assyria. All nations ultimately are comprised in these (Isa. 19:25). Furthermore, all ultimately shall become Jehovah's servants.

Concerning Jerusalem, when Jehovah recorded the history of the nations, He wrote, *"This Man* (Christ) *was born there."* Actually, Bethlehem is a suburb of Jerusalem. This Prophecy could have been known by the Wise Men from the East who came to Jerusalem asking, *"Where is He Who is born King of the Jews?"* (Mat. 2:1-2).

All of these nations, no matter how powerful they once were, ultimately will give place and way unto the Lord Jesus Christ.

(5) "AND OF ZION IT SHALL BE SAID, THIS AND THAT MAN WAS BORN IN HER: AND THE HIGHEST HIMSELF SHALL ESTABLISH HER."

After the Second Coming of Christ, Jerusalem will be the premier city on the face of the Earth, and untold millions of people will desire to visit her. In fact, at that time the entire world will desire to be connected with Jerusalem, and many will claim to have been born there.

But the Scripture says, *"The Highest Himself shall establish her."* This speaks of Christ, Who will make Jerusalem His Capital over the entirety of the world.

At His First Coming, He was known as the Miracle Worker, and even His most strident enemies did not deny such. In the coming Kingdom Age, He also will be known as the Miracle Worker, but this time over the entirety of the world.

(6) "THE LORD SHALL COUNT, WHEN HE WRITES UP THE PEOPLE, THAT THIS MAN WAS BORN THERE. SELAH."

When the history of the nations is reckoned during the Millennial Reign, the majesty, money, power, and prestige of all other cities shall pale into insignificance when compared with *"Zion."*

Why?

CHRIST AND JERUSALEM

In the Mind of God, the greatest event that ever has occurred on Planet Earth is that *"This Man* (Christ) *was born there."* As stated, Bethlehem is a suburb of Jerusalem.

Combined with Calvary and the Resurrection, no other event supersedes this. And yet, Zion's greatness is attributed to the Birth of Christ and not to His Crucifixion. The Crucifixion also took place in *"Zion,"* but it was the most foul deed ever carried out by wicked hearts.

Inasmuch as this great event of Psalm 87 takes place in the Millennial Reign, the terrible sin committed by the people of Zion no longer will be remembered by God. It will be blotted out, which speaks only of the sin of the people who carried out this atrocious deed. That which Calvary accomplished will not be blotted out — it has made, is making, and will make everything possible.

So, in God's Mind, the Birth of Christ in *"Zion"* is forever captured, which ensures its Glory forever. At that time, Israel will have come back to God and repented of the terrible deeds of the past.

THE CROSS OF CHRIST

We always must remember that every single thing that God has done for us — His great Salvation, the Baptism with the Holy Spirit, Justification by Faith, and everything else — all, and without exception, have been made possible by the Cross. Without specifically referring to the tragedy of the Crucifixion, in this Eighty-seventh Psalm, the Holy Spirit portrays that Israel committed a horrible deed, but it is now all forgiven, cleansed, and forgotten. It (the Crucifixion) will never be remembered anymore against Israel, while the results of what Jesus did at the Cross will be forever remembered. Actually, the Crucifixion of the Lord will be commemorated on a daily basis as Sacrifices are once again offered in Jerusalem, but strictly as a memorial (Ezek., Chpts. 40-48).

(7) "AS WELL THE SINGERS AS THE PLAYERS ON INSTRUMENTS SHALL BE THERE: ALL MY SPRINGS ARE IN YOU."

In that coming Day of the Kingdom Age, all blessings will flow out of Zion, which will ensure the blessings of the entirety of the world (Isa. 2:2-4).

This last Verse of the Eighty-seventh Psalm tells us that Jerusalem will be a city of music in that coming Glad Day. It will all be in praise to the Lord.

PSALM 88

Author Unknown:
The Cry of a Desperate Man

(1) "O LORD GOD OF MY SALVATION, I HAVE CRIED DAY AND NIGHT BEFORE YOU."

This is a Song or Psalm for the sons of Korah. Exactly who wrote it is not known. It is entitled, *"To the Chief Musician upon Mahalath-Leannoth,"* which means *"shoutings and dancings."*

The Title, *"shoutings and dancings,"* is peculiar inasmuch as the Psalm does not end in a burst of sunshine, as usual, but in deepest night. It does not record suffering from the hand of man, but from the Hand of God. There is faith and hope in the Psalm, but no comfort.

It is a *"Maschil"* Psalm. It instructs as to the mystery of Christ's experiences when under the Wrath of God during His Crucifixion, Death, and Burial. We must quickly add, however, that the Wrath of God was upon Him not because of any sins that He committed, for He committed none whatsoever, but for our sins. He was our Substitute, and He Alone could be our Substitute.

SHOUTINGS AND DANCINGS

Concerning *"shoutings and dancings,"* there were two such in Israel — the great dancing that celebrated David killing Goliath (I Sam. 18:6) and the great dancing that accompanied the establishment of the Ark in Zion (II Sam. 6:12-19). David was the central figure in each. David also was a Type of Christ, and the killing of Goliath was a portrayal of Satan's defeat at Calvary's Cross. The establishment of the Ark in Zion was a Type of the Second Coming of Christ in Glory and Power.

Even though this Psalm contains no sunshine, still, the instructions given by the Holy Spirit proclaim to us Christ's Victory over death, Hell, and the grave. That is what made David's victory over Goliath an occasion for such joy. The *"shoutings and dancings"* proclaim not only what had then taken place but also that which they represented, which Israel would not have understood at that time. Then, it was future; now, it is past.

In a sense, Israel was shouting and dancing not only for that which had happened, but for that which would happen in the distant future, which would be the greatest victory of all. If Israel could shout and dance at the future prospect of such, we who now are recipients of the Great Victory of the Lord Jesus Christ over Death, Hell, and the

Grave should also shout and dance, and even far more!

JONAH, THE GREAT SIGN

As Jonah was three days and three nights in the belly of the whale (the power of death), shut up in this dark prison of the sea, so was the Greater than Jonah three days and three nights under the dominion of death and shut up in the darkness of the abyss (Mat. 12:40-41). As Jonah trusted, prayed, and believed for deliverance, this Psalm proclaims the Messiah also doing so.

The Holy Spirit has given to the world the words of Jonah's prayer (Jonah, Chpt. 2), and He also has given in this Psalm the words of the Messiah's prayer.

How amazing that the Spirit of Truth should here invite men to contemplate the Eternal Son of God when He was in that abyss and communicate to us the very words of the prayer which He from thence addressed to God!

(2) "LET MY PRAYER COME BEFORE YOU: INCLINE YOUR EAR UNTO MY CRY."

Just as our Lord trusted God during His Lifetime, and when hanging upon the Cross, so He trusted Him when He was imprisoned in Sheol. He truly believed that God would deliver Him; and, as is obvious, God did!

PRAYER

We also should take everything to the Lord in prayer. We should seek His constant Guidance, His constant help, and we should believe that He will hear us and will answer. In the Word of God, we are importuned over and over again to bring everything to the Lord and to expect an answer (Jer. 33:3; Mat. 21:22; Mk. 11:24-25; Jn. 14:14; 15:7, etc.).

Regrettably, the modern Church is not a praying Church. For the most part, the reason it is not a praying Church is because it has abandoned the Cross, which is where all victory was won. If the Believer doesn't understand the Cross as it regards Sanctification (and most don't), then such a Believer, pure and simple, will not really know how to live for God.

Without a proper understanding of the Cross, our relationship with Christ is sorely impaired.

Let us say it again:

The maturity of the Believer is predicated solely upon the Believer's proper understanding of the Cross of Christ. Without a proper understanding of the Cross, there can be no maturity; and, tragically, a lack of Spiritual Maturity will negatively impact all aspects of our life and living.

(3) "FOR MY SOUL IS FULL OF TROUBLES: AND MY LIFE DRAWS NEAR UNTO THE GRAVE."

This Psalm could well be a part of the prayer that Jesus prayed in the Garden of Gethsemane.

Our Lord admitted to His Soul being *"full of troubles."* In today's modern climate, the Word of Faith people would claim that such is a bad confession. This, in reality, is no faith at all. According to these people, there never can be any trouble for a Child of God.

Here before us, however, we have the Word of God, actually the very prayer of our Saviour, contrasted with the false teaching of these modern false apostles.

Which one will you believe?

(4) "I AM COUNTED WITH THEM WHO GO DOWN INTO THE PIT: I AM AS A MAN WHO HAS NO STRENGTH."

He had much *"strength"* to deliver others. He had no *"strength"* to deliver Himself. If He had delivered Himself, He could not have delivered others.

The *"pit"* refers to the Paradise part of Hell, where all the righteous souls, from Abel to the Resurrection of Christ, were held captive. Jesus had to go down into that *"pit"* and *"lead captivity captive,"* which He did (Eph. 4:8).

I remind the Reader that when Calvary was completed, our Lord did not go down into that *"pit"* as a defeated victim, but rather as the Conquering Lord. Satan was totally and completely defeated at the Cross. The Word of God is clear on that fact.

It says, and I quote from THE EXPOSITOR'S STUDY BIBLE:

"Blotting out the handwriting of Ordinances that was against us (pertains to the Law of Moses, which was God's Standard of Righteousness that man could not reach), *which was contrary to us* (Law is against us, simply because we are unable to keep its

precepts, no matter how hard we try), *and took it out of the way* (refers to the penalty of the Law being removed), *nailing it to His Cross* (the Law with its decrees was abolished in Christ's Death, as if Crucified with Him);

"And having spoiled principalities and powers (Satan and all of his henchmen were defeated at the Cross by Christ atoning for all sin; sin was the legal right Satan had to hold man in captivity; with all sin atoned, he has no more legal right to hold anyone in bondage), *He* (Christ) *made a show of them openly* (what Jesus did at the Cross was in the face of the whole universe), *triumphing over them in it.* (The triumph is complete and it was all done for us, meaning we can walk in power and perpetual victory due to the Cross)" (Col. 2:14-15).

I think it is obvious from these Passages that all victory was won at the Cross. The idea, as some teach, that Jesus won our victory by dying as a sinner on the Cross and then went to Hell, as all sinners go to Hell, and was tortured for three days and nights, and then was Born-Again and raised from the dead, holds no validity whatsoever in Scripture. Such teaching is a figment of men's imagination. It never happened!

Jesus defeated Satan and every power of darkness at Calvary's Cross. Because *"The wages of sin is death"* (Rom. 6:23), Jesus could not have risen from the dead if even one sin remained unatoned at the Cross. The mere fact that He was raised from the dead proves that all sin — past, present, and future — was atoned, at least for all who will believe (Jn. 3:16; I Jn. 2:1).

(5) "FREE AMONG THE DEAD, LIKE THE SLAIN WHO LIE IN THE GRAVE, WHOM YOU REMEMBER NO MORE: AND THEY ARE CUT OFF FROM YOUR HAND."

When Jesus died on Calvary, no one, even His most ardent Disciples, believed He would rise from the dead (Lk., Chpt. 24). He was put in the *"grave"* (the tomb) to be *"remembered no more."*

SMITTEN OF GOD AND AFFLICTED

The phrase, *"And they are cut off from Your Hand,"* refers to Jesus' being *"smitten of God and afflicted"* (Isa. 53:4). The Disciples could not understand how He could be *"cut off"* and be the Messiah at the same time! They lacked understanding because they lacked knowledge of the Word (Lk. 24:25-27). At that time, they did not realize that His being *"cut off"* meant that we would not be *"cut off."*

(6) "YOU HAVE LAID ME IN THE LOWEST PIT, IN DARKNESS, IN THE DEEPS."

We, as sinners, should have suffered this terrible judgment. Instead, Christ suffered it for us.

THE PRICE THAT WAS PAID

Indeed, there is a monumental difference between you and I dying and Christ dying!

We, being sinners, never could have escaped this *"lowest pit."* Satan had a just claim upon all of mankind. But Satan had no just claim upon Christ, because Christ was not born of the seed of man and had never sinned. The Holy Spirit, therefore, could rightly, justly, and legally bring Him from the dead, especially considering that He atoned for all sin. Satan could not do anything about this.

Sin provides the legal right that Satan has to hold man in bondage. Considering that Jesus had no sin Himself (none whatsoever! He never sinned in any capacity), and that He atoned for all sin, this removed Satan's legal right to hold man in bondage, at least for all who will believe (Col. 2:14-15).

As a result of what Christ did at the Cross, He could liberate all the righteous dead who had gone before and had trusted in Him. He has breached this *"lowest pit"* and *"darkness in the deeps"* so that we need have no fear. The First Adam caused the darkness; the Last Adam conquered the darkness.

THE CROSS OF CHRIST, THE ONLY THING BETWEEN MAN AND ETERNAL HELL

Every Believer needs to read that heading very carefully. Without the Cross of Christ, all of mankind would be destined to eternal Hell; man, without exception, would go to Hell, if Christ had not died on the Cross! The Cross of Christ stopped that, and the Cross of Christ alone stopped that!

As we say over and over again, *"Christ is the Source, and the Cross is the Means."*

It is very disconcerting that the modern Church preaches the Cross almost none at all. The Word of Faith people, which is no faith at all, repudiate the Cross. The *"Purpose Driven Life"* scheme does not mention the Cross, because that, they say, might offend people!

As stated, the Cross is little preached, if at all! What little it is preached regards Salvation, and that alone; it regards Sanctification not at all. Anymore, the Cross is very little being preached, even for Salvation. So that means that most of the people coming to modern Churches really aren't even Born-Again. The few who are Born-Again are given every direction in the world as it regards living for God, except the only way that truly works, which is the Cross.

Paul gave us this in the Sixth Chapter of Romans. In that Chapter, the Believer is taught how to walk free of the dominion of the sin nature. It is all by and through the Cross of Christ, which means that we must ever make the Cross of Christ the Object of our Faith. Only then can the Holy Spirit, Who Alone can make our lives what they ought to be, work effectively within us (Rom. 8:2, 11).

(7) "YOUR WRATH LIES HARD UPON ME, AND YOU HAVE AFFLICTED ME WITH ALL YOUR WAVES. SELAH."

The *"wrath"* of God, which we rightly deserved, should have been poured out on us, or it could have been poured out on Him instead. He took the *"wrath"* that I justly should have received. In taking this *"wrath,"* He had to be *"afflicted"* by God (Isa. 53:4).

(8) "YOU HAVE PUT AWAY MY ACQUAINTANCE FAR FROM ME; YOU HAVE MADE ME AN ABOMINATION UNTO THEM: I AM SHUT UP, AND I CANNOT COME FORTH."

Coming from Christ, this type of terminology seems strange to the unknowing heart. This is because most do not really understand the Incarnation.

THE INCARNATION OF CHRIST

Jesus was Very God and never ceased to be God; but, still, He also was Very Man. But even though He never ceased to be fully God, He never would use any of His attributes of Deity. Everything He did was as a Man, *"The Man Christ Jesus."* He went through His sufferings as a Man. He faced Calvary as a Man. He faced Death as a Man. If He had not done so, His Sacrifice would have been worthless!

Since man was born in original sin, man could not redeem himself. Angels could not redeem man, because they are of a another creation. Because God is Spirit, He cannot die. So in order for man to be redeemed, God would have to become Man, which He did!

As our Lord faced Death and all of its horrors, especially when one considers the fact that demon powers swarmed all around Him at this time (Ps. 22:12-14), His Death was unspeakably horrible — more horrible than any death has ever been. Yet, He faced this terrible sojourn with faith — the same type of faith we have (Vs. 1).

The *"acquaintance"* that He speaks of here pertains to all concerned, that is, His Disciples, His Own Relatives, even God and the Holy Angels. Truly, He was *"made an abomination unto them,"* because He was bearing the penalty for the sins of the world (II Cor. 5:21).

This is the reason He cried in Gethsemane, *"Father, if You be willing, remove this cup from Me"* (Lk. 22:42).

In the tomb, He was truly *"shut up,"* and, within Himself, He could not *"come forth."* Jesus, within Himself, could not have been raised from the dead. His Father would have to raise Him from the dead, which He did (Rom. 8:11).

(9) "MY EYE MOURNS BY REASON OF AFFLICTION: LORD, I HAVE CALLED DAILY UPON YOU, I HAVE STRETCHED OUT MY HANDS UNTO YOU."

This Passage proves the truth of Christ's Personal helplessness. He cried to God, His Father, for help, guidance, leading, direction, and power, even exactly as we do. He suffered *"affliction"* exactly as we do, even far greater. The secret of His total Victory was His *"calling daily upon You."* It is the secret of our victory, as well.

The *"stretching out of the hands unto God"* refers to a total dependence upon God. This we must emulate, as well (Jn. 8:28-29).

(10) "WILL YOU SHOW WONDERS TO THE DEAD? SHALL THE DEAD ARISE AND PRAISE YOU? SELAH."

There are many unbelievers who claim

Christ did not really die, that He only swooned, revived in the tomb, and then escaped. This is absurd and ridiculous, to say the least!

THE RESURRECTION OF THE LORD JESUS CHRIST

The Roman soldiers who attended the Crucifixion were unbiased. Before the crucified were taken down from the Cross, it was the business of the soldiers to see to it that the person was dead (Jn. 19:31-34). He did not swoon; He died. Truly, God would *"show wonders to the dead"* (Christ) and raise Him from the dead. Truly, He would *"arise and praise You."*

The Resurrection sets Christianity apart from every other faith. The instigators of all others, such as Islam, Confucianism, Buddhism, Marxism, and Hinduism, are all dead. Christ is not dead. The Lord raised Him from the dead. An unbelieving world would ask, *"How do you know?"*

After Napoleon Bonaparte, the Emperor of France, had been banished to the island of St. Helena, he was asked this question, *"Do you believe that Jesus Christ really rose from the dead?"*

For a long time, Napoleon stood looking over the ocean, which was not far from where he stood. Finally he answered, saying:

"You can go to the poorest of the poor and mention the Name of Jesus. Instantly recognition and respect will be obvious. You also can go the Crowned Heads of Europe and mention the Name of Jesus. Likewise, respect and reverence instantly will be given. Men lay down their lives for Him. Mighty armies will march by His authority.

"Sir, no dead man could command that type of respect."

I have to shout, *"Hallelujah!"*

No! There were too many people of impeccable testimony who saw Him alive after His Resurrection. According to the Apostle Paul, there were over 500 people who saw Christ after His Resurrection (I Cor. 15:3-8).

(11) "SHALL YOUR LOVINGKINDNESS BE DECLARED IN THE GRAVE? OR YOUR FAITHFULNESS IN DESTRUCTION?"

Truly, God's *"lovingkindness"* was *"declared in the grave,"* when He raised Christ from the dead.

NOTES

Even though Christ's Body was destroyed, still, God's *"faithfulness"* in raising Him from the dead overcame Satan's power of death.

These Passages are some of the most miraculous and wonderful in Scripture. They speak of the great victory won by Jesus Christ, and we speak of victory over the world, the flesh, and the Devil, and, above all, over sin, death, and the grave. His Victory is our victory. All that He did was done for us!

(12) "SHALL YOUR WONDERS BE KNOWN IN THE DARK? AND YOUR RIGHTEOUSNESS IN THE LAND OF FORGETFULNESS?"

The meaning of this Verse is that death will bring darkness and the one who dies will be forgotten.

THE TORMENTS OF SATAN REGARDING THE DEATH OF CHRIST

The modern Believer little understands that Christ was taunted by Satan exactly as we are, actually far, far more! Jesus had performed mighty Miracles by the Power of the Holy Spirit, but the Evil One was telling Him that at death it would all be over and that God would not raise Him from the dead, that when He died, no more *"wonders* (Miracles) *would be known,"* and that all of His *"Righteousness"* would be forgotten in this land of darkness.

However, when Satan did this (and he must have done it constantly), this next Verse tells us how the Lord responded.

(13) "BUT UNTO YOU HAVE I CRIED, O LORD; AND IN THE MORNING SHALL MY PRAYER PREVENT YOU."

The Messiah took these accusations of Satan to the Father. He is saying that on the third *"morning,"* He will be resurrected.

The word *"prevent"* in the Hebrew is *"kawdam,"* which means *"to precede or to anticipate."* The use of the word *"prevent"* tells us that the Father answered Him and told Him that He would be raised from the dead.

(14) "LORD, WHY DO YOU CAST OFF MY SOUL? WHY DO YOU HIDE YOUR FACE FROM ME?"

Evidently, His Father had revealed to Him that His Death on the Cross of Calvary would occasion His dying alone! At that time, the

Father would not even be able to look upon Him, much less answer His Prayers and Petitions, at least for this period of time (from 12 noon until 3 p.m.).

God would do this because there was no other choice. The Saviour was bearing the curse of sin for the whole world. This was the fulfillment of the Prophecy of John the Baptist, *"Behold the Lamb of God, which takes away the sin of the world"* (Jn. 1:29). In this state, God would have to hide His *"Face from Me."*

Isaiah prophesied these words, *"And we hid as it were our faces from Him"* (Isa. 53:3). No one actually saw Jesus die. From 12 noon until 3 p.m., darkness covered that part of the world and hid the death of the Son of God from all inquisitive eyes (Lk. 23:44).

As already stated, God turned His Face away from His Beloved Son, because the Son was bearing the penalty for sin for the entirety of mankind, and for all time. God could not look upon sin, even though it was being borne by His Only Son.

(15) "I AM AFFLICTED AND READY TO DIE FROM MY YOUTH UP: WHILE I SUFFER YOUR TERRORS I AM DISTRACTED."

Christ's mission on Earth was to die at Calvary. This was why He came *"from My youth up."* When He was twelve years old, He said these words, *"Wist ye not that I must be about My Father's business?"* (Lk. 2:49).

What was His Father's business?

It was many things, but the primary one was for Him to die on Calvary.

The last words He spoke before He died were, *"It is finished! Father, into Your Hands I commend My Spirit"* (Jn. 19:30; Lk. 23:46).

The *"terrors"* spoken of here refer to God hiding His Face from Him.

(16) "YOUR FIERCE WRATH GOES OVER ME; YOUR TERRORS HAVE CUT ME OFF."

God's *"wrath"* had to be poured out on Him or us. He took our place. God cannot abide sin in any form, even on His Only Son, even though His Son had never sinned.

Christ became one with our sin and failure and took the full penalty upon Himself. That penalty was the Wrath of God. The end result was the Death that He died, because *"the wages of sin is death"* (Rom. 6:23).

NOTES

(17) "THEY CAME ROUND ABOUT ME DAILY LIKE WATER; THEY COMPASSED ME ABOUT TOGETHER."

The meaning of this Verse is that the enemies of Christ constantly swarmed around Him and attempted to catch Him in His speech, or even to kill Him, before He would go to Calvary. As water runs over someone when it is poured out, so likewise did these enemies do the same.

(18) "LOVER AND FRIEND HAVE YOU PUT FAR FROM ME, AND MY ACQUAINTANCE INTO DARKNESS."

When Jesus went to Calvary, He was forsaken both by those who loved Him and those who were considered friends. The Scripture says, *"All forsook Him, and fled"* (Mat. 26:56).

The meaning of the second portion of this Verse is that He went into darkness bearing the sin of the world, and they could not follow.

THE SUFFERINGS OF CHRIST

The depth of suffering disclosed in this Psalm is beyond the power of human reasoning to fathom; it pierces the heart with a sense of the sinfulness of sin; it melts with a consciousness of the amazing love of Him Who voluntarily suffered its judgment in order to redeem those justly doomed to its eternal punishment.

The last line of this Psalm may also mean that darkness was His only Companion as He descended into that region of horror.

The writer of Hebrews summed up this Psalm in these words:

"Who in the days of His flesh, when He had offered up prayers and supplications with strong crying and tears unto Him Who was able to save Him from death, and was heard in that He feared;

"Though He were a Son, yet learned He obedience by the things which He suffered" (Heb. 5:7-8).

PSALM 89

*Probably Written by Ethan:
Praise for the Lord*

(1) "I WILL SING OF THE MERCIES

OF THE LORD FOREVER: WITH MY MOUTH WILL I MAKE KNOWN YOUR FAITHFULNESS TO ALL GENERATIONS."

This is a *"Messianic"* Psalm, of which there are nineteen; however, it is my contention that the entirety of the Psalms (all 150) fall into the same category. They all portray Christ in one of His Atoning, Intercessory, Mediatorial, or High Priestly roles. Because most Believers do not understand these various roles, they do not understand that many of the Psalms apply to Him.

Most do not understand that those Psalms in which sin is being confessed portray Christ in His Intercessory role. When Christ is confessing sin, it is all on our behalf, and not at all on His behalf, for He has committed no sin. He already has made the Intercession which all of us need; it is recorded in the Psalms, which means that presently His very Presence at the Throne of God guarantees Intercession for all who trust Him (Heb. 7:25-27).

Because it is so important, let me say it again:

As it regards Intercession on our behalf, whatever words need to be said have already been said. They are recorded here in the Psalms.

The instructions of the Psalm are given to Ethan the Ezrahite, who was a choir leader. It does not necessarily mean that he wrote the Psalm, although he probably did.

FAITHFULNESS OF THE MESSIAH

Concerning this, Williams says, *"The Messiah, in the confidence of Coronation and of the fulfillment of the sure Promises made to Him as David* (Acts 13:34), *recites these Promises, voices the lament of His people at their seeming breach, and then closes the Psalm as He began it, with praise to Jehovah.*

"Thus, during His life of sorrow, His death of shame, and His arrest in Sheol, nothing is seen in Him but perfection — a perfection of Faith toward God and of love toward man." [34]

In Verses 1 through 4, He claims the Throne as His by Divine appointment. The *"faithfulness"* of God that is known *"to all generations"* is made known by the Messiah. Everything we know about God is through His written Word and His Living Word, both of which are Christ Jesus (Jn. 1:1-5).

(2) "FOR I HAVE SAID, MERCY SHALL BE BUILT UP FOREVER: YOUR FAITHFULNESS SHALL YOU ESTABLISH IN THE VERY HEAVENS."

The Law came by Moses, but Grace and Truth came by Jesus Christ (Jn. 1:17). *"Mercy"* is a product of Grace; both Grace and Mercy are made possible by the Cross! God's *"faithfulness"* to this Promise (Covenant) is guaranteed by Jesus Christ in the *"very heavens."*

This pertains to the coming Kingdom Age; it speaks of the time immediately following the Second Coming. Then Israel will bow at the Feet of Christ and accept Him as Saviour and Lord. Then, because of Israel's repentant condition, Mercy will be extended and will last forever.

The Word here is that this Promise is established in the faithfulness of Christ and is recorded in Heaven.

(3) "I HAVE MADE A COVENANT WITH MY CHOSEN, I HAVE SWORN UNTO DAVID MY SERVANT.

(4) "YOUR SEED WILL I ESTABLISH FOREVER, AND BUILD UP YOUR THRONE TO ALL GENERATIONS. SELAH."

The Seventh Chapter of II Samuel records the Davidic Covenant, which promised David an Eternal Seed and Throne. Chapters 12, 15, and 17 of Genesis record the Abrahamic Covenant, which promised an Eternal Seed and Land. Both Covenants were unconditional in the sense that God will bring them to pass. Both Covenants are yet to be fulfilled in totality, but they most definitely will be fulfilled in the coming Kingdom Age.

THE COVENANTS

It must be understood that Covenants made and upheld by God do not excuse sin, failure, or wickedness. Actually, God plainly said to David concerning his sons and those who would follow thereafter, *"If he commit iniquity, I will chastise him with the rod of men."* This is what happened. David's sons and all Israel committed iniquity, and they are now in the process of being chastened.

Still, the Covenants ultimately will be fulfilled in totality. Israel will get the Land, and David will get the Throne. The Lord said,

"To all generations," which means forever.

The Lord proclaimed that if His Covenant concerning day and night (the Solaric Covenant) could be broken, *"then may also My Covenant be broken with David, My servant, that he should not have a son to reign upon his throne"* (Jer. 33:21). In other words, the Covenant given to David by God is as eternal as the Solaric Covenant (Gen. 1:14-19).

Jesus Christ is the Root of David and will reign supremely forever. That was the intention of the Davidic Covenant; its total fulfillment will commence with the Second Coming.

(5) "AND THE HEAVENS SHALL PRAISE YOUR WONDERS, O LORD: YOUR FAITHFULNESS ALSO IN THE CONGREGATION OF THE SAINTS."

Once again, we are given here great Promises. To be sure, they will be fulfilled.

FAITHFULNESS

This Chapter is replete with the *"faithfulness"* of God. The word occurs seven times (Vss. 1, 2, 5, 8, 24, 33, and 49). The word *"lovingkindness"* in Verse 49 could have been translated *"faithfulness."*

Verses 5 through 14 extol the greatness of the Messiah. Even though, by and large, Earth does not now *"praise Your wonders,"* still, in the not-too-distant future, Earth and Heaven will *"praise Your wonders, O LORD."* This terrible contest between good and evil, and between Jesus and Satan, is about over. There never has been any doubt about the outcome. Jesus Christ will be praised forever!

(6) "FOR WHO IN THE HEAVEN CAN BE COMPARED UNTO THE LORD? WHO AMONG THE SONS OF THE MIGHTY CAN BE LIKENED UNTO THE LORD?"

These *"sons of the mighty"* are Angels. Here it is stated that no Angel *"in the Heaven can be compared unto the LORD."* So, on both Earth and in Heaven, there is nothing to compare with the Lord Jesus Christ.

(7) "GOD IS GREATLY TO BE FEARED IN THE ASSEMBLY OF THE SAINTS, AND TO BE HAD IN REVERENCE OF ALL THEM WHO ARE ABOUT HIM."

Sadly, there is not much *"reverence"* for Jesus Christ in this present world. Shortly this will change. After the Battle of Armageddon, when the Wrath of God is poured out upon this Planet, then Jesus will come back with such Power and force as to defy all description. Then, He will be *"greatly to be feared."*

(8) "O LORD GOD OF HOSTS, WHO IS A STRONG LORD LIKE UNTO YOU? OR TO YOUR FAITHFULNESS ROUND ABOUT YOU?"

Quite possibly Jesus had this Scripture in mind when He spoke about the Stronger Man (Himself) overcoming Satan, who also refers to himself as a *"strong man."* Jesus will *"spoil"* Satan's house, which refers to the fact that the Evil One will be defeated in totality, and in every capacity (Mat. 12:29). It was all done at the Cross (Col. 2:14-15).

Verses 8 through 14 proclaim how *"strong"* our Lord really is.

(9) "YOU RULE THE RAGING OF THE SEA: WHEN THE WAVES THEREOF ARISE, YOU STILL THEM."

The spirit world of darkness is likened to *"the raging of the sea."* Only Jesus can *"still them."* How foolish it is for poor, fallen man to think that pitiful humanistic psychology, or such like, can still these *"waves"*! Only Jesus can do this. He does it through the Means of the Cross, that is, it is the Cross which makes everything possible!

(10) "YOU HAVE BROKEN RAHAB IN PIECES, AS ONE WHO IS SLAIN; YOU HAVE SCATTERED YOUR ENEMIES WITH YOUR STRONG ARM."

"Rahab" is a poetic name for Egypt; it means *"boastful."* When the Lord delivered the Children of Israel from Egyptian bondage, He *"broke Rahab."* With His Might and Power, He *"scattered His Enemies with His strong Arm."* He is the Author of our Salvation.

The defeat of Pharaoh was a prelude to what Jesus would do to Satan at the Cross of Calvary. It is recorded in Colossians, Chapter 2. To be sure, the deliverance of the Children of Israel from Egypt, by the Means of the Blood being applied to the doorposts (Ex., Chpt. 12), was a sign, symbol, or prelude to what would take place at Calvary's Cross. There Satan and all of his cohorts of darkness were totally and completely defeated. Always, it is the Cross!

The Cross! The Cross!

(11) "THE HEAVENS ARE YOURS, THE EARTH ALSO IS YOURS; AS FOR THE WORLD AND THE FULLNESS THEREOF, YOU HAVE FOUNDED THEM."

Two things are said in this Verse:

1. This declares that the heavens and Earth and all in them are the Creation of God, not a product of evolution.

2. No part of the heavens is in a state of rebellion against God; however, Earth most definitely is in a state of rebellion. This Passage says, *"The Earth also is Yours."* This battle between good and evil for supremacy of this Planet has long raged. In this Passage, which is connected with the Davidic Covenant, notice is served on Satan that this rebellion will be put down, and *"the world and all its fullness"* shall be ruled by the Messiah. This will take place at the Second Coming.

(12) "THE NORTH AND THE SOUTH YOU HAVE CREATED THEM: TABOR AND HERMON SHALL REJOICE IN YOUR NAME."

As Verse 11 refers to the entirety of the Earth, Verse 12 refers to Israel. As the battle has raged for the world in general, it has raged far more regarding Israel. In the Abrahamic Covenant, God promised the Land to Abraham's descendant, Isaac. Instead, Ishmael, a product of the flesh, has attempted to wrest this Land from Isaac. The contest rages even today, and addresses itself to both the Jews and the Palestinians.

There is a statement in this Verse which says that Isaac will be the recipient of this Land according to the Covenant; however, it will not take place until the Second Coming. Up until that time, the battle will continue to rage, even growing hotter; it will be hottest of all in the soon-to-come Great Tribulation.

(13) "YOU HAVE A MIGHTY ARM: STRONG IS YOUR HAND, AND HIGH IS YOUR RIGHT HAND."

In the Twelfth Verse, the Promise was made that Satan would not secure the Land of Israel; in the Thirteenth Verse, the statement is made that God has a *"mighty Arm"* and a *"strong Hand"* to carry out that which He has promised. When it talks about the height of *"Your Right Hand,"* it means that there is no one stronger.

(14) "JUSTICE AND JUDGMENT ARE THE HABITATION OF YOUR THRONE: MERCY AND TRUTH SHALL GO BEFORE YOUR FACE."

The Messiah is strong because of four qualities: (a) *"Justice"*; (b) *"Judgment"*; (c) *"Mercy"*; and, (d) *"Truth"*.

All of these qualities are made evident presently in the heart of Believers, at least all who will function according to God's Prescribed Order; but they will not come into total fruition until the coming Kingdom Age. Then these qualities, or attributes, will shine forth like the noonday sun; the Messiah will be their Source, and the entirety of the world will be their parish.

(15) "BLESSED IS THE PEOPLE WHO KNOW THE JOYFUL SOUND: THEY SHALL WALK, O LORD, IN THE LIGHT OF YOUR COUNTENANCE."

The *"joyful sound"* in this instance concerns the people who will live in the Millennium, who will, therefore, *"hear"* the *"joyful sound"* of the trumpet on the morning of Jubilee. That *"sound"* will proclaim Deliverance to the captives and Restoration of their forfeited estates. Then the Davidic Covenant will be fulfilled in all of its totality. Israel will be the supreme nation on the face of the Earth. Its people will be *"blessed."*

Because Israel is in her rightful place, the entirety of the world will then know blessing as it never has known previously. The balance of the world will know that the Source of their blessing is Israel, with Christ, of course, at the Head, and Israel will then be given its rightful place in the hearts and minds of all men.

THE GOVERNMENT OF THE WORLD

At that time, the Government of the world will be on the Shoulder of Christ (Isa. 9:6-7), and Israel will rule the nations of the world under Him. The Glorified Saints, with Glorified Bodies (the same as Christ after the Resurrection), will help Christ administer the Spiritual Affairs of Planet Earth. It will be a time of Heaven on Earth.

At the conclusion of this one-thousand-year Millennial Reign, Planet Earth will then be restored. John said, *"There will be *no more sea"* (Rev. 21:1). Then the New Jerusalem will come down from God out of Heaven (Rev. 21:2-3), with God changing His Headquarters from Heaven to Earth. This will truly be a *"joyful sound."*

(16) "IN YOUR NAME SHALL THEY REJOICE ALL THE DAY: AND IN YOUR RIGHTEOUSNESS SHALL THEY BE EXALTED."

The following are the varied names given to the Lord in the Old Testament:

OLD TESTAMENT NAMES GIVEN TO THE LORD AND THEIR MEANING

1. Jehovah-Elohim — The Eternal Creator (Gen. 2:4-25).
2. Adonai-Jehovah — The Lord our Sovereign: Master Jehovah (Gen. 15:2, 8).
3. Jehovah-Jireh — The Lord will see or provide (Gen. 22:3-14).
4. Jehovah-Nissi — The Lord our Banner (Ex. 17:15).
5. Jehovah-Ropheka — The Lord our Healer (Ex. 15:26).
6. Jehovah-Shalom — The Lord of Peace (Judg. 6:24).
7. Jehovah-Tsidkeenu — The Lord our Righteousness (Jer. 23:6; 33:16).
8. Jehovah-Mekaddishkem — The Lord our Sanctifier (Ex. 31:13; Lev. 21:8; 22:8-9; Ezek. 20:12).
9. Jehovah-Sabaoth — The Lord of Hosts (I Sam. 1:3).
10. Jehovah-Shammah — The Lord is present (Ezek. 48:35).
11. Jehovah-Elyon — The Lord Most High (Ps. 7:17; 47:2; 97:9).
12. Jehovah-Rohi — The Lord my Shepherd (Ps. 23:1).
13. Jehovah-Hoseenu — The Lord our Maker.
14. Jehovah-Eloheenu — The Lord our God (Ps. 99:5, 8-9).
15. Jehovah-Eloheka — The Lord your God (Ex. 20:2, 5, 7).
16. Jehovah-Elohay — The Lord my God (Zech. 14:5).

The Greatest Name, however, ever given to Him was that which was spoken by the Angel Gabriel, *"You shall call His Name JESUS: for He shall save His people from their sins"* (Mat. 1:21).

(17) "FOR YOU ARE THE GLORY OF THEIR STRENGTH: AND IN YOUR FAVOR OUR HORN SHALL BE EXALTED."

This speaks of the coming Kingdom Age. The *"glory of the strength"* of Israel will be the Lord Jesus Christ.

In Scripture, the word *"horn"* refers to dominion. In that coming Day, the Lord Jesus Christ will exalt Israel, which refers to giving them dominion over the entirety of the Earth. In other words, every nation on the face of the Earth will be subservient to Israel, which is what God intended at the beginning (Gen. 12:1-3).

However, in that day Israel's dominion will not be one of force, but rather will be one of Love. Every nation on the face of the Earth will gladly submit to Israel, simply because their prosperity and blessings, which come solely from the Lord Jesus Christ, will be dependent upon that subservience. But, for all the obvious reasons, it will be a subservience that will gladly be rendered.

(18) "FOR THE LORD IS OUR DEFENSE; AND THE HOLY ONE OF ISRAEL IS OUR KING."

In Old Testament times, when Israel looked exclusively to the Lord, when she functioned correctly, He proved, without fail and in every capacity, to be her defense. No nation or group of nations could defeat her when she stood in this posture. But when she started looking to other nations, or to herself, for her defense, then she easily was defeated.

The analogy holds true for modern Believers presently. When we look to Christ and the Cross exclusively, when we ever make the Cross of Christ the Object of our Faith, the Holy Spirit will guarantee our protection and victory. But if we place our faith in anything except Christ and the Cross, the results are disaster — and every time!

During the coming Kingdom Age, Israel will properly worship and trust the Lord. The Lord will be their *"King"* and rule the entirety of the Earth from Jerusalem (Isa. 9:6).

(19) "THEN YOU SPOKE IN VISION TO YOUR HOLY ONE, AND SAID, I HAVE LAID HELP UPON ONE WHO IS MIGHTY; I HAVE EXALTED ONE CHOSEN OUT OF THE PEOPLE."

Verses 19 through 37 refer to the Davidic

Covenant. It speaks of David, but it also speaks of the Greater Son of David.

The *"Vision"* here addressed concerns the many Prophecies, starting with Genesis 3:15, that are given concerning the coming of the Redeemer. Jesus spoke of these in Luke 24:27.

David was *"chosen out of the people"* by God. In too much of the modern Church, the Ministry is a profession instead of a Calling. Only those who are *"chosen"* by God will be anointed by God.

(20) "I HAVE FOUND DAVID MY SERVANT; WITH MY HOLY OIL HAVE I ANOINTED HIM."

This refers to Samuel anointing David with oil as the future king of Israel, even while Saul was then king (I Sam., Chpt. 16). Even though Saul was the first king of Israel, he was not chosen by God; he was chosen by the people. Saul was a work of the flesh.

Conversely, David was a work of the Spirit, who, therefore, would be contested mightily in his struggles to obey God and take the throne. Righteousness, however, ultimately would prevail. The reason is found in the next Verse.

(21) "WITH WHOM MY HAND SHALL BE ESTABLISHED: MY ARM ALSO SHALL STRENGTHEN HIM."

This speaks of tremendous opposition by the powers of darkness which would work through Saul. But the Lord would give David *"His Hand"* to *"establish"* him and *"His Arm"* to *"strengthen"* him. Only by this could David overcome; without this, David could not have overcome. Despite the difficulties, David now cannot fail.

THE MODERN BELIEVER AND THE CROSS

The first phrase of the Twenty-first Verse could be translated, *"With whom by My Hand he* (David) *shall be established."*

Every single Promise made here in these predictions is also made to the modern Child of God. We can have every single Promise exactly as it was tendered toward David; we can have even more because we are living under the New Covenant, which is established on Better Promises.

For the modern Christian, however, there is a way and a manner in which all of this

NOTES

must be done. It is the Way of the Cross. This means that every Believer must make the Cross of Christ the Object of his Faith. And the Cross of Christ alone must be the Object of his Faith.

When the Believer does that and continues doing that, the Holy Spirit, Who is God and Who Alone can do what is needed, will work mightily on our behalf. The great problem with the modern Christian is that he tries to do for himself what only the Holy Spirit can do. The reason modern Christians do this is because they little know or understand how the Holy Spirit works.

(Please see our Study Guide on THE CROSS OF CHRIST, How The Holy Spirit Works.)

HOW THE HOLY SPIRIT WORKS

Even though we can give here only a very brief synopsis of this all-important subject, suffice it to say, the Holy Spirit works exclusively within the parameters of the Finished Work of Christ (Rom. 8:2). He, in fact, will work after no other fashion. To be frank, the Holy Spirit looks at every other direction than the Cross of Christ as *"spiritual adultery"* (Rom. 7:1-4). To be sure, He will remain in the heart and life of the Believer who is living in a state of spiritual adultery, but His Help, as should be understood, will be greatly limited.

The only way to have the full help and Power of the Holy Spirit Working and Operating within our lives is that our Faith ever be established in Christ and what Christ has done for us at the Cross. This, the Holy Spirit demands (Rom. 6:1-14; 8:1-2, 11; Gal., Chpt. 5; 6:14).

Only then will we be firmly established, and only then will the Arm of the Lord work on our behalf!

(22) "THE ENEMY SHALL NOT EXACT UPON HIM; NOR THE SON OF WICKEDNESS AFFLICT HIM."

But, oh, how they would try! Saul continuously tried to kill David. Here he is called *"the enemy."* But God said, *"shall not"*!

If everybody says *"Yes"* and God says *"No,"* it should be obvious as to Who will win. Saul was this *"son of wickedness"*; he could not kill, or even cripple David because of the

Power of God that protected David.

THE LORD JESUS CHRIST

This Verse also pertains to Christ. The guarantee is here given that Satan will not take best.

Some would argue that Satan afflicted Christ on the Cross. But while Christ definitely was afflicted on the Cross, it was not by Satan; it was by God (Isa. 53:4). Referring to the terrible death He would die, God had to afflict Him, because this was the requirement if man was to be redeemed.

The word *"exact"* means *"to dun for debt."* Jesus owed Satan nothing, which means that the enemy had no claim whatsoever on Him!

The word *"afflict"* means *"to abase," "to defile," "to weaken."* The religious leaders of Israel attempted to accomplish such, but they did not succeed, even despite all of their vile actions. In the Eyes of the Father, Whose Eyes Alone count, Jesus was not abased or weakened in any capacity.

(23) "AND I WILL BEAT DOWN HIS FOES BEFORE HIS FACE, AND PLAGUE THEM WHO HATE HIM."

This struggle against David lasted for about 15 years. Ultimately, Saul was killed on Mount Gilboa. Saul's mission to destroy David, inspired by Satan, was a fruitless effort because God was on David's side.

All of this tells us that the Believer must be very careful that he does not find himself fighting against God. To oppose that which is of God and belongs to God is the same as opposing God! Unfortunately, millions of Christians follow wrong advice or follow the erroneous direction of ungodly religious leaders, so-called, and thereby find themselves in a very perilous situation.

Most in such a situation never do find out the truth, because they are following man instead of God, that is, they are not being led by the Spirit. They do not know the reason that they have precious little, if any, of the Blessings of God! They do not know the reason for the calamities which so often befall such.

As this was said of David, it also pertains to Christ. In fact, it pertains more so to Christ than all!

We must always remember that the Lord says He will *"plague them who hate Him"* (Christ).

Let us say it again:

If we oppose those who truly are of God, no matter the circumstances, we are opposing God. In one form or another, the *"plague"* is upon those who follow such a direction.

(24) "BUT MY FAITHFULNESS AND MY MERCY SHALL BE WITH HIM: AND IN MY NAME SHALL HIS HORN BE EXALTED."

His Horn refers to the Messiah, Who would come through David, that is, *"his lineage"* (II Sam. 7:8-17; Rev. 22:16).

These words are spoken of David, but more particularly they are spoken of Christ. He has been exalted because of what He has done for us at Calvary's Cross.

(25) "I WILL SET HIS HAND ALSO IN THE SEA, AND HIS RIGHT HAND IN THE RIVERS."

The immediate meaning of this Verse is that David would conquer all from the Mediterranean to the Euphrates. Powerful armies opposed him; none were successful in their opposition.

As it refers to Christ, it simply refers to His dominion over the entirety of the Earth.

(26) "HE SHALL CRY UNTO ME, YOU ARE MY FATHER, MY GOD, AND THE ROCK OF MY SALVATION."

David referred to God in three ways:

1. *"My Father,"* which proves sonship by adoption and other redemptive acts.

2. *"My God,"* which indicates true relationship through Redemption.

3. *"The Rock of my Salvation."*

David could say these things only in a partial sense. The Messiah could say them in a total sense, meaning He could say them as no other!

(27) "ALSO I WILL MAKE HIM MY FIRSTBORN, HIGHER THAN THE KINGS OF THE EARTH."

Another great Truth is here given!

THE FIRSTBORN

After the statements of the previous Verse, the next prediction is that David's Son, the Messiah, shall also be a Son of the Heavenly Father — the Firstborn and only truly Begotten Son of God, Whom God will exalt higher than all kings of the Earth (Rev. 11:15).

All other so-called *"firstborns,"* such as *"Israel"* (Ex. 4:22), *"Ephraim"* (Jer. 31:9), and *"David,"* are, in some way or another, reflections or representatives of the real and only True *"Firstborn."*

Today, most people in the world do not recognize the Lord Jesus Christ. They do not believe that He is the Son of God, even as Israel did not, and does not, believe that He is their Messiah. But in the coming Kingdom Age, immediately after the Second Coming, when Jesus Christ comes in great Power and Glory and quickly finishes off the Antichrist (all of which will be observed throughout the world via Television and other means of mass communication), there will be no doubt about Who Jesus is or What Jesus is!

(28) "MY MERCY WILL I KEEP FOR HIM FOR EVERMORE, AND MY COVENANT SHALL STAND FAST WITH HIM."

The Davidic Covenant was unconditional, because it really was not anchored in David, but rather in the Greater Son of David.

A CHILD OF GOD

When the believing sinner accepts Christ, he instantly is taken into this *"Covenant,"* which actually is the *"New Covenant."* It is gained by faith, and by faith alone (Rom. 5:1-3; Eph. 2:8-9).

This Covenant is everlasting, even as the Apostle Paul proclaims in Hebrews 13:20. The terminology is: *"My Covenant shall stand fast with Him."*

THE NEW COVENANT CANNOT FAIL

Every other Covenant that ever was made between God and man has failed; however, failure never was on the part of God, but always on the part of man.

The New Covenant also is between God and man, but it cannot fail.

Why not?

Jesus Christ is our Representative Man, that is, *"the Last Adam"* and *"the Second Man"* (I Cor. 15:45, 47). In other words, Jesus Christ represents the entirety of the human race, at least all who will believe in Him.

Jesus Christ is also God. He is both God and Man, *"Very God and Very Man."* Inasmuch as the Covenant is totally in Him, this means it cannot fail.

I might fail, or you might fail, but Christ will never fail! This Covenant *"stands fast with Him,"* meaning it never will be broken.

(29) "HIS SEED ALSO WILL I MAKE TO ENDURE FOREVER, AND HIS THRONE AS THE DAYS OF HEAVEN."

All of these Verses apply both to David and the Messiah.

In this Passage, the Lord proclaims once again His prediction concerning David and the Davidic Covenant.

In this Covenant, God meant exactly what He said. The throne of David will exist forever. Even though Israel lost her way, which put everything on hold for now some 2,000 years, God will bring her back and restore her, and the Throne of David will once again become supreme and last forever.

The culminating meaning of *"His Seed"* refers to Christ. Paul said so (Gal. 3:16). Jesus Christ will *"endure forever."* *"His Throne"* (will endure) *as the days of Heaven,"* meaning it will have no end.

(30) "IF HIS CHILDREN FORSAKE MY LAW, AND WALK NOT IN MY JUDGMENTS."

In the Twenty-eighth Verse, the Lord said that His *"Mercy"* would remain with David and his descendants forever, and the Covenant also would stand fast. That in no way, however, means that God condones or overlooks sin in any fashion. God can no more overlook sin in David or his descendants than He can in the most rank heathen. He plays no favorites.

(31) "IF THEY BREAK MY STATUTES, AND KEEP NOT MY COMMANDMENTS."

Pulpit says, *"If they profane My Statutes; i.e., make light of them, either in their words or in their lives."* [35] All Believers must learn that God says what He means and means what He says. Many of us have found that out the hard way! That's the reason that the Bible must be the criteria for all that we do. It has the final word on everything.

As the Prophet said, *"To the Law and to the Testimony"* (Isa. 8:20).

(32) "THEN WILL I VISIT THEIR TRANSGRESSION WITH THE ROD, AND THEIR INIQUITY WITH STRIPES."

This particular Scripture proclaims a Truth that must not be overlooked.

CHASTISEMENT

God will chastise those He loves. His chastisement actually is a form of His Love.

There are many who call themselves Christian who sin with impunity; yet they suffer no chastisement from God whatsoever. I suggest that they really are not sons, but rather bastards (Heb. 12:8).

If a person truly is a Child of God, that individual is going to experience chastisement at one time or another (Heb. 12:5-11).

(33) "NEVERTHELESS MY LOVINGKINDNESS WILL I NOT UTTERLY TAKE FROM HIM, NOR SUFFER MY FAITHFULNESS TO FAIL."

Even though David or some of his descendants would sin, and the Lord would have to visit their transgression with the rod, still He would follow through the lineage all the way to Christ, which He did. God's *"faithfulness did not fail."* Christ was born of the Virgin Mary despite Israel's terrible spiritual declension.

As stated, the Davidic Covenant was unconditional, simply because it was altogether in the Lord. The next few Verses proclaim this.

(34) "MY COVENANT WILL I NOT BREAK, NOR ALTER THE THING THAT IS GONE OUT OF MY LIPS."

This was the Promise that was given approximately one thousand years before Christ. Satan did everything within Hell's power to break this *"Covenant."* At one time, the only person in the lineage left was the baby Joash; all the others in the lineage had been killed by the wicked Queen Athaliah.

The Scripture says, *"She arose and destroyed all the seed royal of the house of Judah"* (II Chron. 22:10).

But she only thought she destroyed *"all the seed royal."*

Baby Joash was not killed because Jehoshabeath, the daughter of the king, stole him from among the king's sons who were slain (II Chron. 22:11). He was hidden in the Temple so that the royal line of David might be continued to fulfill the Davidic Covenant, which promised a king on the Throne of Judah as long as they had a kingdom with any possibility of Righteousness.

NOTES

This was Satan's third attempt to destroy the royal line of David so that God's Word could not be fulfilled (II Chron. 21:4, 17; 22:1, 10).

However, this little baby boy (Joash) survived and became the king of Judah, and the lineage continued until the Birth of Christ.

(35) "ONCE HAVE I SWORN BY MY HOLINESS THAT I WILL NOT LIE UNTO DAVID."

This Passage concerns the events that transpired in II Samuel, Chapter 7. God's Promises are sure.

God cannot lie! What He says He will do, that He will do!

(36) "HIS SEED SHALL ENDURE FOREVER, AND HIS THRONE AS THE SUN BEFORE ME."

God guarantees this Covenant with David, just as He guarantees the Solaric Covenant. This refers to the Sun, Moon, and Stars. It means forever!

(37) "IT SHALL BE ESTABLISHED FOREVER AS THE MOON, AND AS A FAITHFUL WITNESS IN HEAVEN. SELAH."

This means that at the Second Coming of Christ, David and every Saint of God who has ever lived will come back to reign on Earth forever. At that time, David will once again be established as king over Israel. David, along with all the Glorified Saints, of course, will serve under Christ. This will be during the one-thousand-year Millennial Reign, and then in the new heavens and new Earth forever.

(38) "BUT YOU HAVE CAST OFF AND ABHORRED, YOU HAVE BEEN WROTH WITH YOUR ANOINTED."

Verses 38 through 46 refer back to Verses 31 and 32.

David sinned greatly (Bathsheba and Uriah), as well as Solomon and all of his kingly descendants. Regarding chastisement, God did exactly what He said He would do (Vs. 32).

(39) "YOU HAVE MADE VOID THE COVENANT OF YOUR SERVANT: YOU HAVE PROFANED HIS CROWN BY CASTING IT TO THE GROUND."

If Ethan the Ezrahite actually wrote this Psalm, then his statement here is prophetic because it refers to the dispersion of Israel to

Babylon, and then even to the final dispersion after Titus the Roman General destroyed Jerusalem in A.D. 70.

THE COVENANT

The statement, *"Made void the Covenant of Your servant,"* is not a contradiction of the Thirty-fourth Verse, which says, *"My Covenant will I not break."* It does mean this:

Even though Israel was totally dispersed in A.D. 70, actually ceasing to be a nation now for nearly 2,000 years, still, the Covenant will be brought back to fruition at the conclusion of the Great Tribulation. For this length of time, it has been *"made void"*; however, it has not been broken and will be re-established at the Second Coming of Christ (Zech., Chpts. 12-13; Rom. 11:25-27).

(40) "YOU HAVE BROKEN DOWN ALL HIS HEDGES; YOU HAVE BROUGHT HIS STRONGHOLDS TO RUIN."

Once again, this refers to the Babylonian dispersion as well as to the total destruction in A.D. 70. The *"stronghold"* spoken of here could mean Masada, where many Jews died, and many others committed suicide. This followed the fall of Jerusalem in A.D. 70. The Lord did exactly what He said He would do. He *"visited their transgression with the rod, and their iniquity with stripes"* (Vs. 32).

(41) "ALL WHO PASS BY THE WAY SPOIL HIM: HE IS A REPROACH TO HIS NEIGHBORS."

During the dispersion to Babylon, the Prophet Ezekiel mentioned these nations that would *"spoil"* Israel. They were Ammon, Edom, Moab, Philistia, Tyre, and others (Ezek., Chpts. 25-26).

(42) "YOU HAVE SET UP THE RIGHT HAND OF HIS ADVERSARIES; YOU HAVE MADE ALL HIS ENEMIES TO REJOICE."

Whereas God had fought <u>for</u> Israel so many times in the past, now He fights <u>against</u> Israel. In other words, God will use Nebuchadnezzar as one of His instruments of destruction, plus other nations. As stated, God cannot abide sin in His chosen any more than He can in the ungodly.

(43) "YOU HAVE ALSO TURNED THE EDGE OF HIS SWORD, AND HAVE NOT MADE HIM TO STAND IN THE BATTLE."

When God was with Israel, she won battle after battle with little or no loss whatsoever in her own ranks. But now God fights against her instead of for her — all because of sin on her part.

(44) "YOU HAVE MADE HIS GLORY TO CEASE, AND CAST HIS THRONE DOWN TO THE GROUND."

Jeremiah refers to this in his Lamentations (Lam., Chpt. 1). He even says, *"The LORD has done that which He had devised; He has fulfilled His Word that He had commanded in the days of old: He has thrown down, and has not pitied: and He has caused your enemy to rejoice over you, He has set up the horn of your adversaries"* (Lam. 2:17).

(45) "THE DAYS OF HIS YOUTH HAVE YOU SHORTENED: YOU HAVE COVERED HIM WITH SHAME. SELAH."

The meaning of this Verse is that Judah's glory as a nation was cut short in comparison to what it could have been. They lost their way because of sin; consequently, they were *"covered with shame."* To be sure, shame will cover all who engage in sin of any nature. Ultimately, such will come!

(46) "HOW LONG, LORD? WILL YOU HIDE YOURSELF FOREVER? SHALL YOUR WRATH BURN LIKE FIRE?"

Three questions are asked in this Passage.

THE GREAT QUESTIONS

These are questions which will be asked in the second half of the Great Tribulation, more specifically during the Battle of Armageddon, when it looks like Israel will be totally destroyed.

Destroyed by Titus in A.D. 70, the Jews wandered the world as outcasts for nearly 2,000 years. During this time, the Lord has hidden His Face from Israel, and they have suffered untold agony. For example, six million were slaughtered in World War II by demon-possessed Hitler.

The Jews rejected their Messiah, the King of Glory, and accepted the worldly king, Caesar. The Scripture says, *"The Chief Priests answered, We have no king but Caesar"* (Jn. 19:15). Caesar has proven to be a very hard taskmaster!

God's *"Wrath"* will burn even hotter during the Great Tribulation. Of this time, Jesus said, *"For then shall be Great Tribulation,* such as was not since the beginning of the world to this time, no, nor ever shall be" (Mat. 24:21). It also is called *"The Time of Jacob's Trouble"* (Jer. 30:7).

(47) "REMEMBER HOW SHORT MY TIME IS: WHEREFORE HAVE YOU MADE ALL MEN IN VAIN?"

The Psalmist now laments the present status of Israel. Regrettably, even in this Passage very little responsibility is taken for the terrible sin committed. In other words, man is little concerned, it seems, with God's Glory and Will.

These questions rather concern how much trouble man is in, how much longer he must suffer, and how he can be freed from it. God's interests generally are last. This is why the First Commandment was given, that is, *"Love the Lord your God with all your heart...."* Conversion means an entire right-about-face experience and a wholehearted surrender to God to love Him supremely (Mat. 22:37). True Repentance little laments our plight, but instead our terrible sin against God and how we have defrauded Him.

(48) "WHAT MAN IS HE WHO LIVES, AND SHALL NOT SEE DEATH? SHALL HE DELIVER HIS SOUL FROM THE HAND OF THE GRAVE? SELAH."

This Passage refers to both physical death and Spiritual Death. Because of the Fall in the Garden of Eden, all men are subject to physical death. Due to the Fall, man is born dead spiritually and eternally. This is why the New Birth is necessary — to make man alive spiritually and to cancel the eternal death penalty (Jn. 3:15-17; Eph. 2:1-10).

The Psalmist seems to be asking this question: *"In view of the fact that men sin and die, how is it that God can keep His Covenant with David?"*

He further asks the following:

(49) "LORD, WHERE ARE YOUR FORMER LOVINGKINDNESSES, WHICH YOU SWORE UNTO DAVID IN YOUR TRUTH?"

The plea is for the Lord to bring Israel back to her place of greatness. These words possibly will be spoken in the latter half of the Great Tribulation, when the Antichrist is vowing Israel's total destruction. Israel then will recall God's great Covenant with David.

NOTES

The words, *"In Your Truth,"* mean that it cannot fail — and yet, it looks like it will fail; however, at their most crucial time, Jesus Christ will come back to once again re-establish the Davidic Covenant. As stated, it will take place at the Second Coming.

(50) "REMEMBER, LORD, THE REPROACH OF YOUR SERVANTS; HOW I DO BEAR IN MY BOSOM THE REPROACH OF ALL THE MIGHTY PEOPLE."

The reproach that Israel has suffered (and they have suffered much) is because of their sin. It was not God's fault; it was their fault, as all sin is the fault of the sinner.

Many bear the reproach of Christ, but Israel said she did not want to bear His reproach; Israel rather desired Caesar. She has found to her dismay that Christ's reproach would have been much lighter (Mat. 11:28-30).

A PERSONAL EXPERIENCE

Some time ago, I received a letter from a Jewish gentleman who was very upset with me. If I remember correctly, he was the head of some particular Jewish Defamation Chapter. I don't remember the city.

He was upset because I had made the statement over our Telecast that the Jews had suffered greatly because of their rejection of Jesus Christ.

"Is that the kind of God you serve?", he asked! Actually, it was more of a statement than a question.

From my statements, he had gathered (incorrectly, I might add) that I was claiming that God had brought great judgment upon Israel for what they did regarding the Lord Jesus.

My answer to him was as follows:

I related to him that when Israel crucified Christ, they had taken themselves out from under the protecting Hand of God. When they stated they wanted Caesar instead of Jesus, they placed themselves in another category altogether.

No! It was not God Who has brought the untold suffering on the Jews in the last 2,000 years, especially the Holocaust of Nazi Germany of the 1930's and 1940's. It was Satan who did these things, because Satan hates the Jews supremely!

Whenever Israel did what they did, and when millions of people down through the ages have done the same thing, God lifts His Hand of protection, which leaves them at the mercy of Satan and the world. Please believe me, there is no mercy from those quarters.

No! I wasn't saying that God did such a thing, but I was saying that Israel brought it upon herself, as all who sin bring it upon themselves, no matter what or who it might be.

(51) "WHEREWITH YOUR ENEMIES HAVE REPROACHED, O LORD; WHEREWITH THEY HAVE REPROACHED THE FOOTSTEPS OF YOUR ANOINTED."

Due to God's great Promises to Israel, the Holy Spirit still refers to them as *"Your Anointed."* They have been away from God for a long time, but the Scripture says they are coming home. And come home they shall! (Rom. 11:25-29).

(52) "BLESSED BE THE LORD FOREVERMORE. AMEN, AND AMEN."

This closes the Leviticus Book of Psalms. The Holy Spirit says that no matter how the situation looks, the Lord is *"Blessed."*

The sufferings spoken of in Verses 50 and 51 are those suffered by Christ as High Priest in sympathy with the sufferings of His people. This is an effective picture of the identification of a true Advocate with the miseries and sorrows of those He represents (Williams.)[36]

BOOK FOUR
(The Numbers Book)
Concerning Israel and the Gentiles
(Psalms 90-106)

PSALM 90

The Author is Moses:
The Everlasting God

(1) "LORD, YOU HAVE BEEN OUR DWELLING PLACE IN ALL GENERATIONS."

Moses wrote this Ninetieth Psalm, and some even think he also wrote the Ninety-first. It is supposed that he wrote it at the beginning of the forty years in the wilderness, the wanderings of which are the subject of the fourth Book of Psalms (Numbers).

DEPENDENCE ON GOD

Moses pinpoints the basic problem in the Work of God from the very beginning up until the present. It is this:

Moses is saying that the Lord is our *"dwelling place in all generations."* This is the same as *"in Him we live, and move, and have our being"* (Acts 17:28). In other words, we look to God for everything.

Satan, however, seeks to pull men away from total dependence on God, and he has been very successful. He desires that men look to a religious denomination or organization, a Preacher or a Priest, a dogma or a doctrine. If Satan can succeed in doing such (and he has succeeded with the far greater majority), then he has succeeded in severely crippling the Christian.

Most Christians look to God plus something else. This constitutes a little leaven, which ultimately will consume the whole. In other words, after a while, the people are no longer looking to God at all, but to their Church, Denomination, Preacher, or to other things. Consequently, their *"dwelling place"* is the Baptist Church, the Pentecostal Church, the Holiness Church, the Catholic Church, or wherever!

Our *"dwelling place"* cannot be both. It must be God, and God Alone. No, it is not wrong to associate with a Church, a Denomination, or to love a Preacher. But we must always understand that while these things may or may not contribute to our Spiritual Growth, it is God and God's Word to which we always must look.

The Word of God must be the criteria for all things, and not some Church or Preacher or other thing.

The Holy Spirit emphasized the fact that this was not to be just for Moses' day, but *"in all generations."*

(2) "BEFORE THE MOUNTAINS WERE BROUGHT FORTH, OR EVER YOU HAD FORMED THE EARTH AND THE WORLD, EVEN FROM EVERLASTING TO EVERLASTING, YOU ARE GOD."

The phrase, *"Even from everlasting to everlasting, You are God,"* proclaims the fact that God is unformed, unmade, and uncreated, meaning that He always was, always is, and always shall be. Admittedly, it is impossible for us as human beings to understand such terminology. With humans, we have to have a beginning and an ending, but God has neither. As far as fully comprehending such, however, it is impossible for man to do so. If we could comprehend it, that would mean that God is no bigger and no wiser than we are.

And that's the problem with man. Man is ever attempting to pull God down to his level instead of allowing God to pull man up to His level. God did come down to man's level on one occasion, and that's when God became Man, which we refer to as the Incarnation. But He did so for one particular purpose, and that was to redeem man in order that man might be brought back to God.

Men come and go, Denominations do the same, and religious orders may be strong today and weak tomorrow. But if we put our trust totally and completely in the *"Lord,"* we know that He will not change.

Williams says, *"Those who pass through life depending on their own strength find it a way of labor and sorrow; those who lean on the Hand of Adonai find it a way of joy and rejoicing — even in the wilderness."* [37]

(3) "YOU TURN MAN TO DESTRUCTION; AND SAY, RETURN, YOU CHILDREN OF MEN."

The Second Verse speaks of Creation, and the Third Verse speaks of the Fall.

God placed a tree in the Garden called *"The Tree of the Knowledge of Good and Evil"* (Gen. 2:17). Adam and Eve were told not to partake of the fruit of that tree.

They disobeyed, and the results were awful, to say the least!

A CHOICE?

Some would think, and even teach, that man has a choice. He can either sin or not sin.

No! God has not given man any choice regarding sin.

The choice God gives to man is to obey God. When man disobeys God, he sets in motion a series of events of destruction that beggar description. That's what makes sin so bad.

Whenever a parent teaches a child about a high voltage electrical line, he doesn't give the child a choice. To do so might result in the death of the child. He tells the child in no uncertain terms, *"Don't touch that line, or even get anywhere near it!"* He knows that disobedience will bring death to the child. So the child doesn't have a choice, because of the severity of the situation.

It is the same with sin! Man has never been given a choice by God whether or not to sin. Man was told in the beginning, and he continues to be told at present, to forsake all sin, and to do so immediately.

The latter part of this Verse presents an appeal for man to return to God. Until man does return to God, there is no relief from sin and its penalty. Sin is so awful, so bad, so terrible, so destructive, and so death-dealing that it took the Cross to satisfy and address this terrible horror. It took the death of God's Only Son (Jn. 3:16).

(4) "FOR A THOUSAND YEARS IN YOUR SIGHT ARE BUT AS YESTERDAY WHEN IT IS PAST, AND AS A WATCH IN THE NIGHT."

The meaning of this Verse is:

GOD AND ETERNITY

1. Man should look at eternity as God looks at eternity. In other words, we should base our actions on the eternal instead of the temporal. Sadly, the majority of the world sells out for the temporal.

2. Man only has a short time on this Planet to make his mark for God; consequently, he must *"redeem the time"* (Eph. 5:16).

3. Considering the Fall and the price that God has paid in order for man to be redeemed, God expects us to take full advantage of His Redemption Plan. The decision a person makes, as it regards God's Redemption Plan, will affect him for time and eternity, which means forever and forever.

(5) "YOU CARRY THEM AWAY AS WITH A FLOOD; THEY ARE AS A SLEEP: IN THE MORNING THEY ARE LIKE GRASS WHICH GROWS UP."

As Verse 2 speaks of Creation, and Verse 3 speaks of the Fall, likewise, Verse 5 speaks of the brevity of life in this mortal coil, especially as it relates to eternity. In other words, we must make the most of what God gives us.

(6) "IN THE MORNING IT FLOURISHES, AND GROWS UP; IN THE EVENING IT IS CUT DOWN, AND WITHERS."

This is the way that man's life is described:

THE LIFE OF A MAN

There is so little distance between the cradle and the coffin, between the baby's cry and the death rattle in the throat; there is so little time between our good morning and our good night.

Someone has said that life is like a spark that flies upward from the flames of the fire, flickers and dies; like a snowflake that falls in all of its beauty from the heavens, and then quickly melts; like the stay of the postman at the door. And yet, the decision we make in this life as it regards Jesus Christ decides where we will spend eternity, and that decision alone decides where we will spend eternity.

(7) "FOR WE ARE CONSUMED BY YOUR ANGER, AND BY YOUR WRATH ARE WE TROUBLED."

In this Verse, we are given a glimpse as to what Jesus did as it regards the Redemption of fallen humanity.

THE ANGER AND WRATH OF GOD

The *"anger"* and *"wrath"* mentioned here speak of the curse that God placed upon the human race because of the Fall. As far as is known, the human race (as well as fallen angels) is the only part of God's Creation that is in rebellion against Him. In other words, the human race is at war with God; consequently, it is in league with Satan, at least all who aren't Born-Again, and is attempting to overthrow God's Kingdom. Jesus said as much to the religious leaders of Israel, *"You are of your father the Devil, and the lusts of your father you will do"* (Jn. 8:44).

THE CROSS OF CHRIST

The Incarnation refers to the Lord coming to this Earth and God becoming Man. He came for one purpose and that was to satisfy the terrible sin debt owed by man to God, which man could not pay, and thereby to satisfy the Righteousness of a thrice-Holy God.

Since God is Almighty, He can do anything. He could have redeemed the human race without having to send His Son to Calvary. He had the Power to do that! On the other hand, however, God cannot do anything that is an affront to His Nature and His Character. He cannot do anything that is contrary to His Righteousness. So, even though He had the Power to redeem man without Calvary, such would be opposed to His Nature, which cannot overlook sin in any manner. The terrible debt of sin has to be paid.

It was paid at the Cross, and paid in totality. In other words, all sin was atoned — past, present, and future — at least for all who will believe (Jn. 3:16). Man could not atone for sin by his own machinations; if sin was to be atoned, it would have to be done outside of man, but yet by man.

So God became Man in order to accomplish this task. It is rightly referred to as *"The Greatest Story Ever Told."*

At Calvary, the *"anger"* and *"wrath"* of God were poured out on His Only Son, Who took the full brunt of the blow in that He gave up His Life, which satisfied the demands of God.

In order to be Saved, all man has to do is simply believe in Christ, which means to believe that He is the Son of God, and that He died on the Cross in order that we might be Saved. Simple faith in Him and what He did for us guarantees a perfect Salvation (Rev. 22:17).

THE CROSS PAID IT ALL

If Jesus had not gone to the Cross, man could not have been Saved. This means that all those who died in the faith before the Cross, all those who were held in Paradise, would have been taken over by Satan, and would have been lost forever. But when that event became a reality, that event in which they had faith even before its actual occurrence, they were taken out of Paradise and transported by our Lord to Heaven (Eph. 4:8-10).

Now when a Believer dies, he instantly goes to be with the Lord Jesus Christ in Heaven (Phil. 1:23).

THE CROSS AND SANCTIFICATION

The Cross of Christ not only assured Salvation, but also assures Sanctification. All the Believer has to do in order to live a Godly, holy, sanctified life, victorious over the world, the flesh, and the Devil, is to place his faith exclusively in Christ and the Cross, and not allow it to be moved elsewhere, which then will give the Holy Spirit the latitude to develop His Fruit within our lives — in other words, to make us more Christlike. This is the only way it can be done.

A full ninety-nine percent of the Bible is given over to living for God, and only about one percent is given over to being Saved. Actually, the first percentage is probably even higher than what I've just stated.

That's the reason we are so strong as it regards the Cross. There is no other way for the Christian to live a Godly life except by evidencing faith in Christ and the Cross. As we have said over and over again, Christ is the Source of all things which come from God, and the Cross is the Means by which all things are given to us.

That's the reason we are so hard on these religious schemes and fads which seem to take the Church by storm; they actually are worthless!

THE PURPOSE DRIVEN LIFE SCHEME

In 2004 and 2005, the book, *"The Purpose Driven Life,"* took the Church world by storm. A staggering number were sold, somewhere between twenty and thirty million copies.

The very fact that millions in the Church world opted for this manner of living, so-called, tells us that whatever it is they had previously, and I speak of the spiritual sense, did not satisfy them. So they opted for this new scheme.

Let me say it quickly:

If a Believer truly knows Christ, and truly has his Faith in Christ and the Cross, this then gives the Holy Spirit latitude to then work within the Believer's life and brings about the desired results. There will be no need for anything else, and there will be no desire for anything else.

So when Christians, so-called, run after this new wave, it just reveals the fact that whatever it is they previously possessed, it was not meeting their need.

Truly, whatever they previously had was not meeting their need. The modern Church has strayed so far away from Christ and the Cross that anymore it hardly knows where it has been, where it is, or where it is going. Sadly, *"The Purpose Driven Life"* scheme will serve them no better at all than what they previously had embraced.

Not long after the book came out, Frances handed me a copy and said, *"Read this and tell me what you think."*

I read seven or eight pages and quickly ascertained they were not *"preaching the Cross,"* so I knew that whatever it is they are preaching and teaching is not the Gospel. As it regards the Gospel of Jesus Christ, the Holy Spirit through Paul tells us exactly what that Gospel is.

He said:

"For Christ sent me not to baptize (presents to us a cardinal Truth), *but to preach the Gospel* (the manner in which one may be saved from sin and sanctified unto Holiness)*: not with wisdom of words* (intellectualism is not the Gospel), *lest the Cross of Christ should be made of none effect.* (This tells us in no uncertain terms that the Cross of Christ must always be the emphasis of the Message)" (I Cor. 1:17).

Paul tells us here that if we preach anything else other than the Cross of Christ, we simply aren't preaching the Gospel. As a result, whatever it is that is being preached will serve no purpose.

I handed the book back to Frances. She asked, *"You're not going to read it all?"*

This was my reply: *"I don't have to read it all. They are not preaching the Cross, not at all, as it regards their 'Purpose,' so I know automatically that whatever it is they are pitching, it's not the Gospel of Jesus Christ. As a result, it will serve no one any good purpose whatsoever."*

I continued: *"In fact, not only will it not help the people involved, but the end result will be destruction."*

Concerning this, Paul said the following:

ENEMIES OF THE CROSS

"Brethren, be followers together of me (be *'fellow-imitators'*) *and mark them which walk so as you have us for an example* (observe intently).

"*For many walk* (speaks of those attempting to live for God outside of the victory and rudiments of the Cross of Christ), *of whom I have told you often, and now tell you even weeping* (this is a most serious matter), *that they are the enemies of the Cross of Christ* (those who do not look exclusively to the Cross of Christ must be labeled *'enemies'*):

"*Whose end is destruction* (if the Cross is ignored, and continues to be ignored, the loss of the soul is the only ultimate conclusion), *whose God is their belly* (refers to those who attempt to pervert the Gospel for their own personal gain), *and whose glory is in their shame* (the material things they seek, God labels as *'shame'*), *who mind earthly things.* (This means they have no interest in Heavenly things, which signifies they are using the Lord for their own personal gain)" (Phil. 3:17-19).

All of this tells us that no Believer, Preachers included, can be ambivalent toward the Cross. This means that it's not possible to claim to believe in the Cross and, at the same time, promote these religious schemes and fads devised by men. One or the other must go.

Jesus said, "*If any man will come after Me* (the criteria for Discipleship), *let him deny himself* (not asceticism, as many think, but rather that one denies one's own willpower, self-will, strength, and ability, depending totally on Christ), *and take up his Cross* (the benefits of the Cross, looking exclusively to what Jesus did there to meet our every need) *daily* (this is so important, our looking to the Cross, that we must renew our faith in what Christ has done for us, even on a daily basis, for Satan will ever try to move us away from the Cross as the Object of our Faith, which always spells disaster), *and follow Me* (Christ can be followed only by the Believer looking to the Cross, understanding what it accomplished, and by that means alone [Rom. 6:1-14; 8:1-2, 11; I Cor. 1:17-18, 21, 23; 2:2; Gal. 6:14; Eph. 2:13-18; Col. 2:14-15])" (Lk. 9:23).

He then said, "*And whosoever does not bear his Cross* (this doesn't speak of suffering, as most think, but rather ever making the Cross of Christ the Object of our Faith; we are saved and we are victorious, not by suffering, although that sometimes will happen, or any other similar things, but rather by our Faith, but always with the Cross of Christ as the Object of that Faith), *and come after Me* (one can follow Christ only by Faith in what He has done for us at the Cross; He recognizes nothing else), *cannot be My Disciple.* (The statement is emphatic! If it's not Faith in the Cross of Christ, then it's faith that God will not recognize, which means that such people are refused. In other words, they ultimately lose their soul)" (Lk. 14:27).

Now I think we see just how important the Message of the Cross actually is!

(8) "YOU HAVE SET OUR INIQUITIES BEFORE YOU, OUR SECRET SINS IN THE LIGHT OF YOUR COUNTENANCE."

This Passage means that God will judge sins, both secret and open.

SECRET SINS

The term, *"secret sins,"* applies to most all of the human race. The majority of humanity, and most of the Church, function on the basis of *"iniquities before You,"* that is, sins which are open and known to others. The Church applauds millions but yet who have *"secret sins"* in their hearts and lives.

In this Passage, God is saying that He does not judge as man judges, but that the *"secret sins"* are also called to account. Sadly, this refers to the far greater majority of mankind.

Self-righteousness loves to exalt itself while hiding its *"secret sins."* The truly righteous will not exalt itself at all, realizing that there are many things in their hearts and lives that others may not know about, but yet God knows. As a result, there is no room for self-exaltation.

SINS OF IGNORANCE

Due to the lack of preaching and teaching on the subject of the Cross as it regards Sanctification, few Believers understand this topic at all. And when a Believer doesn't understand how the Cross figures in to the Sanctification process, he will fail, and without fail! In other words, the sin nature somehow will rule in such a person's life, and the Believer will commit sins and then attempt to keep them secret.

No matter how consecrated such a person

might be, no matter what type of prayer life they have, no matter how much Bible Study they do, no matter how many souls to whom they witness, no matter how much money they give to the Work of God, if such a Believer doesn't understand the Cross as it regards Sanctification, it will be impossible for such a Believer to live a victorious life, no matter how hard they try.

No! These individuals are not hypocrites. They love God. And they are innumerable!

Listen to what Paul said, and I continue to quote from THE EXPOSITOR'S STUDY BIBLE:

A LACK OF UNDERSTANDING

"For that which I do (the failure) *I allow not* (should have been translated, *'I understand not'*; these are not the words of an unsaved man, as some claim, but rather a Believer who is trying and failing)*: for what I would, that do I not* (refers to the obedience he wants to render to Christ, but rather fails. Why? As Paul explained, the Believer is married to Christ, but is being unfaithful to Christ by spiritually cohabiting with the Law, which frustrates the Grace of God; that means the Holy Spirit will not help such a person, which guarantees failure [Gal. 2:21]); *but what I hate, that do I* (refers to sin in his life, which he doesn't want to do, and in fact hates, but finds himself unable to stop; unfortunately, due to the fact of not understanding the Cross as it refers to Sanctification, this is the plight of most modern Christians)" (Rom. 7:15).

Erroneously enough, some Preachers have taught that the Seventh Chapter of Romans applies to Paul before He was Saved. Nothing could be further from the Truth.

In this Fifteenth Verse of the Seventh Chapter of Romans, Paul said that he hated sin, and no unbeliever hates sin. In fact, unbelievers love sin. So, the Seventh Chapter of Romans proclaims a man — in this case, Paul — trying to live for God after his great Damascus Road experience. The man was Saved, baptized with the Holy Spirit (Acts 9:10-18), and called to be an Apostle; actually, during this time, he was an Apostle. But still He did not know how to live for the Lord.

To Paul's credit, no one else at that time did either. The great meaning of the Cross had not yet been given to anyone. In fact, the Lord would give the meaning of the New Covenant, which is the meaning of the Cross, to the Apostle Paul, and he would give it to us. The Message of the Cross really characterizes all of Paul's writings.

Before the great Truth of the Message of the Cross was revealed to the Apostle Paul, he did not understand how to properly live for God, and he lived a life of spiritual failure, exactly as does every Believer who does not understand the Cross as it regards Sanctification. A Believer can only live a life of Victory if he places his Faith entirely in Christ and the Cross, which then gives the Holy Spirit latitude to work in his life.

People who don't understand how the Cross effects our Sanctification will commit sin and keep committing sin, whatever it might be, and the situation will get worse and worse, no matter how hard they try otherwise. If they go to a Preacher, most of the time the Preacher is in worse condition than they are. If he tells them anything, he probably will merely state, *"You've got to try harder."* Or else he might tell them, *"You need professional help."* Both avenues have absolutely no value!

So, in such cases, which involve almost all of the modern Church, we have *"secret sins,"* which are multitudinous.

Let me say it again:

The only way that victory over these *"secret sins"* can be obtained is for the Believer to understand that his victory is totally and completely in the Cross. Consequently, he must place his Faith entirely in Christ and the Cross, not allowing anything else to be its object, only the Cross. If that is done and is maintained, the Holy Spirit, Who Alone can give us what we need and make of us what we need to be, will then work mightily within our lives.

As we've said over and over, the Holy Spirit works entirely within the parameters of the Finished Work of Christ. He will work in no other capacity.

(9) "FOR ALL OUR DAYS ARE PASSED AWAY IN YOUR WRATH: WE SPEND OUR YEARS AS A TALE THAT IS TOLD."

Williams says, *"The Ninth Verse speaks of the pride of man's heart being broken, its self-sufficiency banished, and its energies governed by wisdom."* [38]

THE TALE THAT IS TOLD

If we do not know the Lord, our days are spent under His Wrath because God cannot abide sin. If we do not allow the Lord Jesus to assuage that wrath, then our years are no more than a short *"tale"* that can be quickly told and then forgotten.

What a sad commentary on the rich, brilliant, intellectual, and powerful, who think somehow these attributes will have some eternal consequence. They won't! Only a life lived in God's Service will make any difference at all.

(10) "THE DAYS OF OUR YEARS ARE THREESCORE YEARS AND TEN; AND IF BY REASON OF STRENGTH THEY BE FOURSCORE YEARS, YET IS THEIR STRENGTH LABOR AND SORROW; FOR IT IS SOON CUT OFF, AND WE FLY AWAY."

Williams says, *"As the Second Verse speaks of Creation, the Third speaks of the Fall, and the Fifth of the Flood; the Tenth Verse speaks of the wilderness experience."* [39]

THE SELF-RELIANT

The *"strength"* of this Verse means the pride of self-reliance — of independency of God — as contrasted with the action of the dependency of faith.

The carnal will draw on their own resources of strength, fortitude, courage, and wisdom. The result is labor and sorrow. Faith finds its resources in God and proves Him to be an inexhaustible treasury of goodness, gladness, song, and victory.

In this Verse, we have the fact that the median age is about 70 years old — the length of life. Many definitely live longer than that, but considering all the nations of the world where the life span is much shorter than in the United States, the average life span comes out to about 70 years.

The idea here is not how long one lives, but what one does with his life during the time given to us on this Earth by God.

(11) "WHO KNOWS THE POWER OF YOUR ANGER? EVEN ACCORDING TO YOUR FEAR, SO IS YOUR WRATH."

For the most part, men do not fear God. Many do not even believe there is a God. Nevertheless, there is a God, and He will do exactly as He has said in His Word. His Power is absolute but not arbitrary.

THE WRATH OF GOD

There can be no true Revival until there is a true conviction of sin, which requires Scriptural preaching against sin and its results. The *"Wrath of God"* must also be preached and understood for there to be a true Revival. Without any fear of contradiction, I think one can say that every Revival in history has been accompanied by these two principles — conviction of sin, and the fear of the Wrath of God.

And yet, these two subjects rarely are mentioned anymore in the modern pulpits. According to *"The Purpose Driven Life"* scheme, if the Preacher mentions sin, or even the Cross, that might be offensive to people, so nothing like that is ever spoken of. As a result, precious few, if any, at least in that scheme, are Born-Again.

(12) "SO TEACH US TO NUMBER OUR DAYS, THAT WE MAY APPLY OUR HEARTS UNTO WISDOM."

In view of man's prayerless condition and the short life span, Moses pleads with the Lord to *"teach us."* This Verse should sum up the cry of the human heart, but regrettably it little does. Several things are said here:

REQUIREMENTS FOR RIGHTEOUS LIVING

1. We should desire that God *"teach us."* And by His Word, He is teaching us! This means that men should labor to study and learn the Bible. Sadly, so few do!

2. *"Number our days."* We do not have forever, only an allotted period of time. Instead of wasting our days, we should make them count.

3. *"Apply our hearts unto wisdom."* Sadly, the wisdom the world seeks after is, by and large, *"earthly, sensual, and devilish"* (James 3:15). James also said, *"The wisdom that is from above is first pure, then peaceable, gentle, and easy to be entreated, full of mercy and good fruits, without partiality,*

and without hypocrisy" (James 3:17).

Likewise, let no man say that this *"wisdom"* is unattainable. James also said, *"If any of you lack wisdom, let him ask of God, Who gives to all men liberally, and upbraids not; and it shall be given him"* (James 1:5).

(13) "RETURN, O LORD, HOW LONG? AND LET IT REPENT YOU CONCERNING YOUR SERVANTS."

Williams says, *"The dark background of Verses 3 through 12 makes the doctrine of Verses 13 through 17 more precious to faith. The doctrine is that the only hope for the Earth and its inhabitants is in the coming of the Messiah. His Advent will compensate for all the calamities of the wilderness, so to speak, in this night of misery and pain, and He will endow man with a new moral nature so that the works of man's hands will be only good."* [40]

(14) "O SATISFY US EARLY WITH YOUR MERCY; THAT WE MAY REJOICE AND BE GLAD ALL OUR DAYS."

The sense of this Verse is that there is no satisfaction other than the *"mercy"* of God. Only when we are recipients of such may we *"rejoice and be glad all our days."* Sadly, few take advantage of this.

(15) "MAKE US GLAD ACCORDING TO THE DAYS WHEREIN YOU HAVE AFFLICTED US, AND THE YEARS WHEREIN WE HAVE SEEN EVIL."

This should be the cry of every man, even the most consecrated Christian. Moses is asking that the days of affliction be no more than the days of gladness. How so much every one of us should cry these words! Our stumblings are many; consequently, the affliction, cast upon us by God, and rightly so, in order to bring us to the end of ourselves, we pray will not be longer than the days of rejoicing.

(16) "LET YOUR WORK APPEAR UNTO YOUR SERVANTS, AND YOUR GLORY UNTO THEIR CHILDREN."

Moses pleads that the sin of the Children of Israel will not stop *"Your Work"* from appearing to God's people. Likewise, he asks that God's Glory would not die with the failure of the wilderness, but would continue to abide in the children of these who had lost their way.

The sense of this Verse is that it is far greater reaching than we at first realize. It is as far as:

1. That our failures not stop *"Your Work."*
2. That the next generation would know *"Your Glory."*

It is stated that religious Denominations rarely get past the third generation, at least as far as spirituality is concerned. In other words, they lose their way. Without proper leadership, any generation will be lost.

(17) "AND LET THE BEAUTY OF THE LORD OUR GOD BE UPON US: AND ESTABLISH THOU THE WORK OF OUR HANDS UPON US; YEA, THE WORK OF OUR HANDS ESTABLISH THOU IT."

The sense of this Verse is that there is no *"beauty"* on the Earth other than that which is given by the Lord. The *"work of our hands"* is nothing unless it is established by God.

The Holy Spirit signals us the significance of this Passage by giving it a double statement. Man longs for his work to be established and remain. The only work of our hands that will be established is that which is His Work; consequently, everything else ultimately will perish.

PSALM 91

*Probably Written By Moses:
God is a Refuge and a Fortress*

(1) "HE WHO DWELLS IN THE SECRET PLACE OF THE MOST HIGH SHALL ABIDE UNDER THE SHADOW OF THE ALMIGHTY."

The absence of a superscription suggests that this Psalm was written by Moses, for the previous one was written by him. If this be so, then all the Scriptures quoted in the temptation in the dessert (Mat., Chpt. 4) were Mosaic.

That the Messiah is the great figure of this Psalm is decided by Matthew 4:6.

THE SECRET PLACE OF THE MOST HIGH

Williams says, *"The previous Psalm introduced the wilderness and contrasted the misery and happiness of travelers in it who trust self or God. This Psalm points to the*

One Man Who passed through it undefiled, unhurt, and trusting and loving God in perfection." [41]

As Psalm 90 spoke of the difficulties of man in traveling through this wilderness of life, likewise, this Psalm portrays Christ treading the same path of wilderness experience before us and overcoming all. He is given here as our example that we are to follow.

As Verse 1 of Psalm 90 speaks of the *"dwelling place,"* likewise, Verse 1 in this Psalm speaks of dwelling in the *"secret place of the Most High."* The heart cries out for this *"secret place."* What is it?

The *"secret place"* is Christ. Jesus said as much: *"At that day you shall know that I am in My Father, and you in Me, and I in you"* (Jn. 14:20).

(2) "I WILL SAY OF THE LORD, HE IS MY REFUGE AND MY FORTRESS: MY GOD; IN HIM WILL I TRUST."

As Christ enters the *"secret place of the Most High,"* the Holy Spirit assures Him that companionship with God will be a safe refuge from Satan's power and from all the dangers of the way.

THE REFUGE

The Church must realize that it is facing the combined forces of darkness; consequently, man's pitiful efforts of psychology, psychotherapy, or any other such effort, all provide no safety. The only *"refuge and fortress"* is *"God."*

If man's problem only were man, possibly the world of psychology would be of some value. However, man's opposition comes from the world of darkness, for which man is no match. Our efforts, therefore, are futile.

The Messiah said, *"In Him will I trust."* One cannot trust God and man at the same time. The Messiah also said, *"No man can serve two masters"* (Mat. 6:24).

(3) "SURELY HE SHALL DELIVER YOU FROM THE SNARE OF THE FOWLER, AND FROM THE NOISOME PESTILENCE."

This Verse is very dear to me on a personal basis. Perhaps the following will shed some light on that subject.

THE SNARE OF THE FOWLER

The *"snare of the fowler"* was the demon forces of darkness that opposed Christ, either through the evil religious leaders of Jesus' day or in their own capacity. They came in such quantity that there were called the *"noisome pestilence,"* which means a *"rushing calamity"*: one that sweeps everything before it. Christ had the promise of the Holy Spirit that He would be delivered.

The only assurance of victory that we as Christians have in this wilderness of life is by entering into His Victory. He became our Substitute, and we identify with Him.

The powers arrayed against us are so deadly that even with all the attributes of God, still, without Christ, our position is hopeless.

Paul said, *"It is not I, but Christ Who lives in me"* (Gal. 2:20).

A PERSONAL EXPERIENCE

One night in prayer meeting, during a particularly trying time for this Ministry, the Spirit of the Lord moved upon my heart and gave me this particular Verse. If the Reader will notice, this Verse says, *"Surely He shall deliver you from the snare of the fowler, and from the noisome pestilence."* Not *"Maybe so,"* or *"Hope so,"* or *"If conditions are right,"* but *"Surely."*

I never will forget that night. Waves of the Glory of God rolled over my soul. I had a Promise from the Lord and I knew that God always keeps His Promises. He was telling me that the Devil would not take best.

In glorious illumination, I saw that Promise come to pass in my heart and life, even in a far greater way than I ever would have imagined.

First the Lord took me to the Cross and explained to me the problem, which is the sin nature. Then He told me the solution to that problem, which is the Cross, and the Cross alone. Finally, He taught me how the Holy Spirit works within our lives. I knew beyond a shadow of a doubt that this was the fulfillment of that Promise.

The answer to every spiritual problem we might have is found in the Word of God. I think one can say, without any fear of contradiction, that every question we might have about any topic or subject, no matter what it might be, is found in the Bible. If the Bible doesn't address the subject, it most assuredly will address us to our Lord, Who definitely will show us where to find the answer, no matter what the question might be — providing we are faithful to Him.

As I dictate these notes, I look at this Scripture before me, and I rejoice in my heart with a joy that is beyond explanation. The Lord said, *"Surely,"* and that's exactly what He did!

(4) "HE SHALL COVER YOU WITH HIS FEATHERS, AND UNDER HIS WINGS SHALL YOU TRUST: HIS TRUTH SHALL BE YOUR SHIELD AND BUCKLER."

Boaz spoke these same words to Ruth, *"Under Whose wings you are come to trust"* (Ruth 2:12). Boaz undoubtedly derived that Word from this very Verse.

THE HOLY OF HOLIES

This Passage has to do with the Holy of Holies. It speaks of where God dwelt between the Cherubim and the Mercy Seat. He invited Christ to dwell there with Him. In turn, Christ paid the price for us that we also may dwell there with Him.

"His Truth" is threefold:

1. Christ: *"I am the Way, the Truth, and the Life"* (Jn. 14:6).
2. *"Your Word is Truth"* (Jn. 17:17).
3. *"Your Spirit is Truth"* (I Jn. 5:6).

These, and these alone, will be *"Our shield and buckler."*

(5) "YOU SHALL NOT BE AFRAID FOR THE TERROR BY NIGHT; NOR FOR THE ARROW THAT FLIES BY DAY."

The sense of this Verse is:

THE TERROR BY NIGHT

The *"terror by night"* speaks of the spiritual darkness of Satan. Ezekiel said of him, *"You shall be a terror, and never shall you be any more"* (Ezek. 28:19). The first part of this Fifth Verse promises Satan's defeat.

The idea of the phrase, *"Terror by night,"* is that Satan always brings spiritual darkness. He is the cause of all of the pain, suffering, poverty, ignorance, superstition, sickness, war, man's inhumanity to man, and death and dying which are in the world today and which have been for all time.

Satan was defeated totally at Calvary's Cross. That being the case, why does the following play into our lives?

IF SATAN IS DEFEATED, WHY IS HE STILL CAUSING SO MANY PROBLEMS?

First, let's establish the fact from the Word of God that Satan has been totally and completely defeated. This took place at Calvary's Cross.

Paul said, and I quote from THE EXPOSITOR'S STUDY BIBLE:

"And having spoiled principalities and powers (Satan and all of his henchmen were defeated at the Cross by Christ atoning for all sin; sin was the legal right Satan had to hold man in captivity; with all sin atoned, he has no more legal right to hold anyone in bondage), *He* (Christ) *made a show of them openly* (what Jesus did at the Cross was in the face of the whole universe), *triumphing over them in it.* (The triumph is complete and it was all done for us, meaning we can walk in power and perpetual victory due to the Cross)" (Col. 2:15). Men are held in bondage, whether redeemed or otherwise, simply because they will not trust in what Christ did at the Cross for them, a Work He actually did for the entirety of mankind, and for all time.

Regarding the unsaved, it is obvious; however, the problem is almost as bad among the ranks of Believers. To walk in perpetual victory, which God means for the Child of God to do, the Believer has to place his Faith exclusively in Christ and the Cross and keep it there (Rom. 6:1-14; I Cor. 1:17-18, 23; 2:2). Then the Holy Spirit can work in our lives, bringing about all of that for which Jesus paid such a price at Calvary's Cross.

GOD'S PRESCRIBED ORDER OF VICTORY

The Lord has His Way of Victory, and it is *"Jesus Christ and Him Crucified"* (I Cor. 1:23). The only answer for sin (and sin is the problem!) is the Cross of Christ. There is no other, as there need be no other (Heb. 10:12-13). If the Believer will trust in Christ and the Cross, and trust in Christ and the Cross exclusively, he will walk in perpetual victory, meaning that sin will not have dominion over him (Rom. 6:14).

THE ARROW THAT FLIES BY DAY

The short phrase, *"The arrow that flies by day,"* refers to the deliberate effort by Satan to destroy the soul. Satan devises a temptation, oppression, or trap for the Believer, and shoots it like an *"arrow."* The only thing that can stop it is the *"shield and buckler"* of Verse 4, which every Believer has if his faith is properly placed in Christ and the Cross.

(6) "NOR FOR THE PESTILENCE THAT WALKS IN DARKNESS; NOR FOR THE DESTRUCTION THAT WASTES AT NOONDAY."

The meaning of this Verse is:

PESTILENCE AND DESTRUCTION

"The pestilence that walks in darkness" pertains to every disease, sickness, scourge, or plague which comes from the world of Satanic darkness. When the Child of God is protected by *"Your shield and buckler,"* he need have no fear.

The *"destruction that wastes at noonday"* refers to Satan's destroying great multitudes, yet not touching the Child of God who is dwelling in the *"secret place of the Most High."* Regarding the world of darkness, the Child of God is facing powers which we never can hope to conquer if we try to do it by means of the flesh. Regrettably, that is where most Christians presently are. And that is the reason for all the failures. Many actually lose hope and give up.

There is a way that every power of darkness can be totally and completely decimated within our hearts and lives. It is God's Way. It is the Way of the Cross. That's what Paul taught us in the Sixth Chapter of Romans. If we ignore that Sixth Chapter of Romans, we are ignoring one of the single most important aspects of the Word of God. The end result will be wreckage.

That's the reason I grieve when I see Christians by the untold thousands ignore the Cross, or else even repudiate the Cross. I know that they are opening themselves up to the powers of darkness, which is a battle they cannot hope to win — at least they can't win it in that manner.

(7) "A THOUSAND SHALL FALL AT YOUR SIDE, AND TEN THOUSAND AT YOUR RIGHT HAND; BUT IT SHALL NOT COME NEAR YOU."

This refers to the great number of people who are being destroyed by the powers of darkness. They are destroyed because they put their trust in other things. With multiple tens of thousands, it is alcohol, drugs, lust, greed, or the love of money. Satan's ways to destroy people are almost infinite. The majority of the Planet succumbs to his wiles. But the Believer who puts his trust in God has a Promise: *"It shall not come near you."* Hallelujah!

THE CROSS OF CHRIST

But let us say it again:

All protection is found in the Cross, and in the Cross alone! Anything and everything else, no matter how religious it might be, pertains to the flesh, which God will never honor. This Promise does not apply to those who pursue this direction.

The Cross of Christ is *"the secret place of the Most High."* It is *"the shadow of the Almighty."* It is *"my refuge and my fortress."* It is *"our shield and buckler."* The Cross is our everything. To ignore or deny the Cross places one in the position of facing these powers of darkness by one's own strength, which guarantees failure.

(8) "ONLY WITH YOUR EYES SHALL YOU BEHOLD AND SEE THE REWARD OF THE WICKED."

The *"reward of the wicked"* is twofold:

THE REWARD OF THE WICKED

1. A life lived without the Peace of God, with Satan constantly *"stealing, killing, and destroying"* (Jn. 10:10).

2. Eternal Hell without God, which is more horrible than one ever could begin to contemplate (Rev. 21:8).

(9) "BECAUSE YOU HAVE MADE THE LORD, WHICH IS MY REFUGE, EVEN THE MOST HIGH, YOUR HABITATION."

All of this concerns the Messiah; every Believer is allowed to enter into His Victory.

The Holy Spirit here is the Speaker. The Messiah is assured victory by the Holy Spirit only because He *"has made the LORD His refuge."* There is no other safety.

Let us say it again:

That safety is the Cross of Christ, and the Cross of Christ alone!

(10) "THERE SHALL NO EVIL BEFALL YOU, NEITHER SHALL ANY PLAGUE COME NEAR YOUR DWELLING."

Because His *"dwelling"* is the *"secret place of the Most High,"* it is impossible for *"evil to befall You."* Every effort (plague) by Satan is stopped.

Verses 11 and 12 were quoted by Satan. His quoting them showed his intelligence in recognizing that the Psalm applied to Jesus (Mat. 4:6).

(11) "FOR HE SHALL GIVE HIS ANGELS CHARGE OVER YOU, TO KEEP YOU IN ALL YOUR WAYS."

This shows how much Satan knows the Bible. Nevertheless, he still thinks he can circumvent the Word of God. Angels did constantly help Christ (Mat. 4:11; Lk. 4:10-11).

A CORRUPTION OF THE WORD OF GOD

Satan corrupted this Scripture by omitting the phrase, *"In all Your Ways,"* and inserting in its place the phrase, *"At any time."*

The Messiah's path through the desert of the wilderness was one of dependence upon God. Satan's effort in the temptation was to move Him to independence, but he failed. Christ walked a path of perfect submission, obedience, and dependence; likewise, all those who walk after Him in like dependence and Faith can be assured of His Victory.

(12) "THEY SHALL BEAR YOU UP IN THEIR HANDS, LEST YOU DASH YOUR FOOT AGAINST A STONE."

Thus, Satan attempted to use the Word of God against Christ. Satan's efforts were several-fold.

THE SIN OF PRESUMPTION

First of all, Satan desired to pull Christ from God's Will to his will (Satan's will). This is his constant effort with each and every Believer.

Next, he twisted the Word of God, as millions today twist the Word of God and enter thereby into Satan's deception.

Finally, he attempted to get Christ to commit the sin of presumption, which is the sin of so many in the Ministry. It means to twist the Word of God in order that it means something that God did not intend.

NOTES

(13) "YOU SHALL TREAD UPON THE LION AND ADDER: THE YOUNG LION AND THE DRAGON SHALL YOU TRAMPLE UNDER FEET."

Satan quoted Verses 11 and 12, but he did not dare quote Verse 13, because it promised his defeat. This Verse has to do with Genesis 3:15 and the great Promise given by God: *"It shall bruise your head, and you shall bruise His heel."*

SATAN'S DEFEAT

The *"lion and adder and dragon"* all speak of Satan. It says that Christ shall trample in victory this *"dragon."*

Paul said, *"And has put all things under His feet, and gave Him to be the Head over all things to the Church, which is His Body, the fullness of Him Who fills all in all"* (Eph. 1:22-23). Christ is the Head; the True Church is His Body. As is obvious, the feet are on the Body; the Church (the True Church), therefore, can trample underfoot the powers of darkness — but only in Christ, and only as long as He is the Head.

(14) "BECAUSE HE HAS SET HIS LOVE UPON ME, THEREFORE WILL I DELIVER HIM: I WILL SET HIM ON HIGH, BECAUSE HE HAS KNOWN MY NAME."

These are the Words of the Heavenly Father. How amazing that sinful men should be permitted to hear the sweet converse of the Three Persons of the Trinity!

Paul may have had this Passage in mind when he said, *"And has raised us up together, and made us sit together in Heavenly Places in Christ Jesus"* (Eph. 2:6).

The Lord came to manifest the Father's Name. So at the close of His pilgrimage, He could say, *"I have manifested Your Name unto the men whom You gave Me"* (Jn. 17:6).

(15) "HE SHALL CALL UPON ME, AND I WILL ANSWER HIM: I WILL BE WITH HIM IN TROUBLE; I WILL DELIVER HIM, AND HONOR HIM."

Here is the *"honor"* that God has given Him: *"Wherefore God also has highly exalted Him, and given Him a Name which is above every name"* (Phil. 2:9).

(16) "WITH LONG LIFE WILL I SATISFY HIM, AND SHOW HIM MY SALVATION."

In the opening Verses the Messiah enters

the wilderness and defeats all that Satan throws at Him. In the closing Verses, He ascends the Throne.

VICTORY

Considering the terrible wilderness of Psalm 90, the sense of this last Verse is that if we will enter into the Victory that Christ won in His earthly sojourn of Ministry, Calvary, and the Resurrection, we will be given *"long life"* (Eternal Life), and we will find total satisfaction.

The Lord has promised to show us *"My Salvation,"* which consists of victory over the powers of the enemy, which can only be found in Christ. And Christ can only be found in the Cross. Because Christ without the Cross is *"another Jesus"* (II Cor. 11:4; Lk. 9:23).

PSALM 92

Author Unknown:
A Song for the Sabbath Day

(1) "IT IS A GOOD THING TO GIVE THANKS UNTO THE LORD, AND TO SING PRAISES UNTO YOUR NAME, O MOST HIGH."

As noted, the author of this Psalm is unknown.

This is a wilderness Psalm which proclaims the Sabbath as God's Rest for His people. Israel will be the singer on the morning of the Sabbath Day of Hebrews, Chapter 4. That is the Sabbath intended in the superscription.

Williams says, *"Israel here sings of Him and addresses Him as 'Jehovah' (the Lord) and 'Elyon' (Most High)."* [42]

Consistently, the Holy Spirit proclaims the *"good thing"* of thanking and praising the Lord. We should *"give thanks"* and *"sing praises."*

There is a perfect type of the Salvation experience given in the Book of Exodus that corresponds with Psalms 90 through 94 and takes us step-by-step into that which is afforded by Christ. It is as follows:

THE WAYS OF THE LORD

1. The deliverance of the Children of Israel from Egypt is presented in the Fourteenth Chapter of Exodus. This Exodus Deliverance is a type of the Believer being delivered from the clutches and bondage of sin, and Egypt is a type of the world; it corresponds with Psalm 90. This particular Psalm portrays man's helplessness without God — as Israel was helpless in Egypt and could not be delivered without the help of God.

2. The giving of the Manna is portrayed in the Sixteenth Chapter of Exodus. The Manna is a Type of Christ. This corresponds with Psalm 91, which pictures Christ winning total victory over Satan and allowing us to enter into His glorious accomplishments. He becomes the Manna, which characterizes all that we need.

3. The Sabbath portrays the Rest that comes to the Child of God upon acceptance of Christ (rest from one's works), and is characterized in the Sixteenth Chapter of Exodus. Likewise, the Ninety-second Psalm corresponds with the *"Sabbath"* in providing Rest for the people of God.

4. The Water out of the Rock, as characterized in the Seventeenth Chapter of Exodus, which typifies the Mighty Outpouring of the Holy Spirit, corresponds with Psalm 93, which also speaks of the *"floods"* of the Holy Spirit that fill our soul.

5. The Seventeenth Chapter of Exodus also portrays the coming of *"Amalek,"* who is a type of the flesh, who fought with Israel and with whom every Christian also battles. This corresponds with Psalm 94, which characterizes both the flesh and the Antichrist.

(2) "TO SHOW FORTH YOUR LOVINGKINDNESS IN THE MORNING, AND YOUR FAITHFULNESS EVERY NIGHT."

This proclaims constant praises both *"morning"* and *"night."* The Lord is portrayed in *"lovingkindness"* and *"faithfulness."*

PRAISING THE LORD

When one considers that within most Churches a *"Hallelujah!"* has never been heard, then one realizes how utterly spiritually destitute most of the Church world actually is. If the Holy Spirit, under the Old Covenant, instructed the people to praise the Lord in this manner, how can we, under the New Covenant, do less? And yet, to most

Christians, praise is foreign and strange.

Why?

The only answer that can be given is that these individuals have only embraced a philosophy of Christianity and have never actually met Christ. In other words, they are not Saved.

(3) "UPON AN INSTRUMENT OF TEN STRINGS, AND UPON THE PSALTERY; UPON THE HARP WITH A SOLEMN SOUND."

A tremendous truth is here given concerning praise to the Lord.

MUSIC AS USED BY THE LORD IN PRAISE AND WORSHIP

The Book of Psalms is Earth's First Songbook, at least of which we are aware. The striking thing about this Book is that every Song was given by the Lord.

It was through David that the Holy Spirit orchestrated the worship of God through musical instruments, choirs, songs, and singers; therefore, all true worship of God in any and all Churches comes from the Root of David.

Of the major religions in the world, Christianity is the only one that has a Songbook; correspondingly, it is the only manner of worship that has anything to sing about. (Christianity actually is not a religion, but a relationship with a Person, The Man Christ Jesus.)

The less spiritual, the less vibrant the musical worship. The more spiritual, the more vibrant the musical worship.

Music was created by God in three parts: *"Melody," "Harmony,"* and *"Rhythm."* If any one of these three parts is distorted, as in so-called contemporary Christian music, it is impossible to worship the Lord with such a musical arrangement.

The Book of Psalms is the longest Book in the Bible. This demonstrates to us the emphasis placed by the Holy Spirit on worship using music and singing. Probably one could say the no worship is higher than that instituted by the Psalms.

When I was eight years old, I asked the Lord to give me the talent to play the piano. To make the story brief, He heard my prayer, gave me that talent, and also gave me an understanding of what the Holy Spirit desires for music which is to be used in the worship of the Lord.

In the last several decades, I have watched Satan make a great attack against music used in the worship of the Lord; this attack is so great that I would classify it second only to the perversion of the Word of God.

This attack is masqueraded under the guise of emulating the music of the world in order to attract young people.

In the first place, our music doesn't draw anyone. It is the Spirit of God which draws people, and nothing else! As well, worship has to do with the Saints of God and not the unsaved. In trying to become like the world, we become totally unlike God, which means that there is no reason for our existence.

To be sure, Satan understands music. There is evidence that he was in charge of the great choirs of Heaven which performed at the great dedication of the Universe when it was created by God. The Lord said to Job, and I quote from THE EXPOSITOR'S STUDY BIBLE:

"Where were you when I laid the foundations of the Earth? Declare, if you have understanding. (The truth that God made all things is obvious according to the creation. A creation must have a Creator. Therefore, the alleged theory of evolution is a farce. Evolution cannot honestly even be called a *'theory,'* because a theory has to have at least some rudiments of fact to buttress its claims. Evolution has no facts whatsoever.)

"Who has laid the measures thereof, if you know? Or who has stretched the line upon it? (The idea is that God has planned and created the Universe down to the most fine detail.)

"Whereupon are the foundations thereof fastened? Or who laid the corner stone thereof? (In fact, the worlds are held up by the Word of God [Heb. 11:3])*;*

"When the morning stars sang together, and all the sons of God shouted for joy? (The Lord is speaking here of the completion of the Earth and the Universe, and of the celebration that followed by the Angels of Heaven.

"Lucifer, before his Fall, was called the *'son of the morning'* [Isa. 14:12].

"There is a possibility that these *'morning stars'* who *'sang together'* were led in their worship and celebration by Lucifer, the *'son of the morning'*)" (Job. 38:4-7.)

Satan, therefore, has great understanding of music, knows its significance to the worship of the Lord, and has tried his very best to pervert it. Sadly, he has succeeded in most cases.

(4) "FOR YOU, LORD, HAVE MADE ME GLAD THROUGH YOUR WORK: I WILL TRIUMPH IN THE WORKS OF YOUR HANDS.

(5) "O LORD, HOW GREAT ARE YOUR WORKS! AND YOUR THOUGHTS ARE VERY DEEP."

Praises are rendered to God for what the Lord has done for Israel. It uses expressions such as *"Your Work," "Works of Your Hands,"* and *"Your thoughts."* The Holy Spirit is proclaiming the fact that God has done much for Israel; they, as a result, should constantly praise Him.

How can the Church do less?

When we revert back to the helplessness of man in Psalm 90 and realize what God has done for us, then how can we help but praise Him!

(6) "A BRUTISH MAN KNOWS NOT; NEITHER DOES A FOOL UNDERSTAND THIS."

God labels as *"fools"* those who do not understand the worship of God. This would extend not only to the man of the world, but also to religious man. The expression, *"brutish man,"* speaks of man being more like an animal than a responsible human being.

At the Fall, man did descend toward the animal kingdom. At the New Birth, he is made a New Creature and becomes more like God. Those who do not know or understand the worship of God are little more than brute beasts.

(7) "WHEN THE WICKED SPRING AS THE GRASS, AND WHEN ALL THE WORKERS OF INIQUITY DO FLOURISH; IT IS THAT THEY SHALL BE DESTROYED FOREVER."

The sense of this Verse is that even though the wicked may seem to be flourishing, still, unless they turn to God, they ultimately will be destroyed.

CONTRASTS?

One of the most difficult things for the Believer is to observe what seems to be a contrast. At times, it seems like the Believer is not blessed, but the wicked are. Many Believers have allowed this to hinder their walk with God. The intention of the Spirit is this:

Ultimately, the righteous will be blessed, and ultimately the wicked will be destroyed. The wicked are described as fuel, that is, *"grass"* (Vs. 7), and the righteous as fruit, that is, *"palms"* (Vs. 12).

Someone has well said, *"The worst day a person ever has had with the Lord is a thousand times better than the best day one ever has had with the Devil."* Truthfully, there really are no bad days with the Lord, and there really are no good days with the Devil. But the Evil One is a master at making people believe that good is bad, bad is good, up is down, and down is up, and he often succeeds!

(8) "BUT YOU, LORD, ARE MOST HIGH FOR EVERMORE."

The sense of this Verse is that unconverted men refuse to recognize the wrath that awaits them and the glory that awaits the righteous.

THE ETERNITY OF THE GOVERNMENT OF GOD

This Eighth Verse actually means that Jehovah will be enthroned forever. This statement, preceded and followed by declarations as to the destruction of the wicked, makes it terribly clear that the eternity of His Government necessitates the eternity of their misery; for as long as His Government lasts, a rebellion and recovery by the unredeemed, along with Satan and his hordes, will be impossible.

(9) "FOR, LO, YOUR ENEMIES, O LORD, FOR, LO, YOUR ENEMIES SHALL PERISH; ALL THE WORKERS OF INIQUITY SHALL BE SCATTERED."

Israel looked at her enemies as God's enemies. And so they were! They both had the same enemies. Relationship with Him involves this.

(10) "BUT MY HORN SHALL YOU EXALT LIKE THE HORN OF AN UNICORN: I SHALL BE ANOINTED WITH FRESH OIL."

The word *"horn"* refers to Israel's future exaltation and dominion as the premier nation of the world, which will take place in the coming Kingdom Age. At that time, she will be brought back to God, will accept Jesus Christ, and will *"be anointed with fresh oil."*

ANOINTED WITH FRESH OIL

Even as I use that term, *"Anointed with fresh oil,"* I sense the Presence of God. That's what the modern Church desperately needs — *"a fresh enduement of Power from on High."*

I need this fresh anointing! You need this fresh anointing! This is the key to the entirety of the Work of God.

Unfortunately, it is about as scarce as the proverbial hen's teeth. But yet, it is still available, and the results will be the same today as they were in yesteryear.

(11) "MY EYE ALSO SHALL SEE MY DESIRE ON MY ENEMIES, AND MY EARS SHALL HEAR MY DESIRE OF THE WICKED WHO RISE UP AGAINST ME."

This not only refers to a constant ongoing blessing and determination by the Lord upon His people, but also speaks of Israel ultimately accepting Jesus Christ as her Saviour and seeing the Antichrist totally defeated.

PROMISES OF GOD

Also this Verse certainly applies to the Believer under the New Covenant. All the Promises that are given here to Israel can be accepted and enjoyed by the modern Believer, except those Promises which are dispensational and, thereby, affect Israel only.

The Word of God is so powerful, so far-reaching, and so all-encompassing that it will stretch to any need. It is that powerful!

(12) "THE RIGHTEOUS SHALL FLOURISH LIKE THE PALM TREE: HE SHALL GROW LIKE A CEDAR IN LEBANON."

The Christian is comparable to a palm and to a cedar. The one grows in a sandy plain, the other on a rugged mountain. The one has a taproot that draws nourishment from the meat, the other is refreshed from above. The one is beautiful, the other strong. The Christian has a secret source of life; he receives blessings from beneath and from above, and he is morally beautiful and strong.

But above all, this speaks of Christ. And yet, when we place our faith and trust in Christ, everything He is also is credited to us.

(13) "THOSE THAT BE PLANTED IN THE HOUSE OF THE LORD SHALL FLOURISH IN THE COURTS OF OUR GOD."

Israel sings here of Elohim, *"Our God."*

The implication in this Verse is that *"the wicked"* of Verse 7 may flourish for a while, but then they will be cut off; nevertheless, those who are *"planted"* in God's Grace will eternally *"flourish."*

We have the Promise of the Lord on this!

(14) "THEY SHALL STILL BRING FORTH FRUIT IN OLD AGE; THEY SHALL BE FAT AND FLOURISHING."

This speaks of the Child of God who never will stop bearing fruit, even in old age.

It also speaks of Israel in her *"old age."* She has been away from God for so long, but she finally is brought back to Him. Then she will begin to *"bring forth fruit."* During the Millennial Reign, she *"shall be fat and flourishing."*

(15) "TO SHOW THAT THE LORD IS UPRIGHT: HE IS MY ROCK, AND THERE IS NO UNRIGHTEOUSNESS IN HIM."

Williams says, *"The Fruit and Strength of the Spirit exhibited in the Christian life is an effective testimony to the moral glory of the Lord Jesus Christ. Recognizing that moral glory, Israel shouts with exultation, "He is my Rock — there is no unrighteousness in Him!"* [43]

PSALM 93

Author Unknown:
The Lord is Clothed with Majesty

(1) "THE LORD REIGNS, HE IS CLOTHED WITH MAJESTY; THE LORD IS CLOTHED WITH STRENGTH, WHEREWITH HE HAS GIRDED HIMSELF: THE WORLD ALSO IS STABLISHED, THAT IT CANNOT BE MOVED."

It is not known who wrote this Psalm. No doubt David wrote some which have no title, but we really cannot tell which ones.

THE LORD REIGNS

This Psalm corresponds somewhat with the Water coming out of the *"Rock"* in the Seventeenth Chapter of Exodus, and the previous Psalm corresponds with the giving of the *"Sabbath,"* which signifies the *"Rest"* we find only in Christ. The *"Sabbath"* is portrayed in the Sixteenth Chapter of Exodus.

When Jesus Christ died on Calvary and then was raised from the dead with a Glorified Body, then the Holy Spirit could be given (Jn. 7:39). Now that Christ has been glorified and has ascended back to Heaven, it can be said that *"The LORD reigns"* and *"He is clothed with Majesty"* (Phil. 2:9-11).

With the great price paid at Calvary's Cross, the Holy Spirit can now abide in the hearts of believing, Born-Again Saints. It can now be said that *"the world also is stablished."* Now that this great price has been paid and the *"lion, adder, and the dragon"* defeated (Ps. 91:13), there is no doubt of the outcome. *"It cannot be moved."*

(2) "YOUR THRONE IS ESTABLISHED OF OLD: YOU ARE FROM EVERLASTING."

Israel will, no doubt, sing this Psalm upon the Millennial Morn at the close of her weary wilderness journey, which has lasted now for some 2,000 years.

The sense of this Passage is that the outcome is not in doubt. Every word of every Prophecy will be fulfilled.

All human history and its final settlement is comprised in the brief compass of this Psalm. It sets out the Majesty of the King's Person, the stability of His Kingdom, the antiquity of His Throne, and the eternity of His Being.

(3) "THE FLOODS HAVE LIFTED UP, O LORD, THE FLOODS HAVE LIFTED UP THEIR VOICE; THE FLOODS LIFT UP THEIR WAVES."

In some small measure, this could refer to the Water that came out of the Rock when it was smitten by Moses, typifying what Jesus did at the Cross, which made possible the Mighty Baptism with the Holy Spirit; however, the probable meaning is that it refers to the nations of the world.

It presents a picture of Millennial Glory. The angry nations (Rev. 11:18), likened to the raging waves of the storm-tossed ocean, are subdued, and the Messiah, mightier than they, is seen seated upon His Throne.

(4) "THE LORD ON HIGH IS MIGHTIER THAN THE NOISE OF MANY WATERS, YEA, THAN THE MIGHTY WAVES OF THE SEA."

This is likened to Christ's stilling the raging of the Galilean Sea (Jn. 6:16). He will still the future raging of the hostile nations and will establish universal peace.

(5) "YOUR TESTIMONIES ARE VERY SURE: HOLINESS BECOMES YOUR HOUSE, O LORD, FOREVER."

This Passage make several statements:

1. *"Your Testimonies"* refer to God's Word and its various Revelations of Truth.

2. The words, *"Very sure,"* refer to the absolute fulfillment of all that God has said.

3. The Foundation of God's House is *"Holiness,"* as the foundation of man's house is unholiness.

4. The foundation of *"Holiness"* will never change; it will remain *"forever."*

5. The Believer can obtain *"Holiness"* only if he ever makes the Cross of Christ the Object of his Faith. We aren't holy because of what we have done, but we are holy because of what He has done. With proper Faith in Him and what He did for us at the Cross, Holiness is freely imputed to the Believer.

Regarding the attainment of this great attribute of God, the Believer can do nothing except exhibit faith; but there are many things the Believer can do which quickly will make him unholy.

The answer for Victory is the Cross! The answer for Deliverance from sin is the Cross! Only the Cross!

PSALM 94

Author Unknown:
The Lord is Clothed with Majesty

(1) "O LORD GOD, TO WHOM VENGEANCE BELONGS; O GOD, TO WHOM VENGEANCE BELONGS, SHOW YOURSELF."

As noted, the author of this Psalm is unknown.

THE TIME OF JACOB'S TROUBLE

This Psalm corresponds with *"The Time of Jacob's Trouble"* (Jer. 30:7), which will introduce the Antichrist, who will be the greatest *"work of the flesh"* ever devised by Satan. This will conclude Israel's wilderness journey. It is pictured here with the two Messiahs (the false and the True) and their thrones confronted.

In the latter half of the Great Tribulation, Israel will cry to God as never before. She will plead with the Lord when it seems she is facing annihilation, *"Show Yourself."*

(2) **"LIFT UP YOURSELF, YOU JUDGE OF THE EARTH: RENDER A REWARD TO THE PROUD."**

When Israel realizes that no nation in the world is lifting a hand to save her, she will cry for the Messiah to come. He is her only hope. The *"proud"* spoken of here pertains to the man of sin, the Antichrist.

(3) **"LORD, HOW LONG SHALL THE WICKED, HOW LONG SHALL THE WICKED TRIUMPH?"**

When one considers Israel's pressed condition during the Antichrist's seven-year reign of blasphemy, she will cry to the Lord, *"How long?"*

(4) **"HOW LONG SHALL THEY UTTER AND SPEAK HARD THINGS? AND ALL THE WORKERS OF INIQUITY BOAST THEMSELVES."**

Daniel said, *"He shall destroy the mighty and the holy people"* (Dan. 8:24). He also wrote, *"And shall speak marvelous things against the God of gods"* (Dan. 11:36).

(5) **"THEY BREAK IN PIECES YOUR PEOPLE, O LORD, AND AFFLICT YOUR HERITAGE."**

This concerns the Antichrist breaking his seven-year Covenant with Israel at the midpoint. He will then set out to systematically destroy *"Your heritage."*

(6) **"THEY SLAY THE WIDOW AND THE STRANGER, AND MURDER THE FATHERLESS."**

The Antichrist will attempt to do what Hitler failed to do. He will have no mercy on any. He will hate Israel with a passion, and the reason is this:

THE RAPTURE OF THE CHURCH

Several years before the Great Tribulation begins, the Church will be raptured away (I Thess. 4:16-17). Even though many Believers do not believe in the Rapture of the Church, it also is true that most do not understand the Rapture.

In the first place, the *"Rapture"* and the *"Resurrection"* refer to the same event. We are told of this event in the Fourth Chapter of I Thessalonians. In the Fifteenth Chapter of I Corinthians, we are told what will happen when it takes place. So if anyone says they don't believe in the Rapture, they should be asked if they believe in the Resurrection. Of course they do, which means they also believe in the Rapture, whether or not they will admit it.

One may argue over the time of the Rapture (even though there should be no argument over that either), but one cannot Scripturally argue against the fact of the Rapture. Believe it or not, the Rapture most definitely is going to take place.

THE ANTICHRIST

Sometime after the Rapture, the Antichrist will make his debut. The Bible doesn't say how long it will be between the Rapture and the beginning of the Great Tribulation. We do know that the Antichrist will not be revealed until after the Rapture of the Church. Paul said so (II Thess. 2:5-12). So immediately after the Rapture, the Antichrist will begin to exert himself.

His very first accomplishment will be to solve the great problem between Israel and the descendants of Ishmael which has raged for many, many centuries. Today, this great problem manifests itself in the antagonism between the Muslim nations and Israel.

The brightest minds in the United States and elsewhere have not been able to solve this thorny problem. Many thought that the death of Yasser Arafat would solve or reduce the problem; however, it wasn't solved, and it wasn't even reduced.

The Antichrist will be endued with the powers of darkness as no other man before him. His first great triumph will be to bring peace to Israel and the Muslims. He will broker a seven-year non-aggression pact with Israel and other nations (Dan. 9:27) — the *"one week"* means a week of years, or seven years. At that time, Israel will applaud him as their Messiah. He will undoubtedly be an apostate Jew.

This is the time when Israel will announce to the world that this is the one for whom they have been looking for so long. At the same time, they also will greatly renounce the Lord Jesus Christ and proclaim to the entire world that all along He was an impostor. The peace accord that the Antichrist has just brokered will prove to Israel and the world that he actually is the long awaited Messiah, because no one before had been successful in doing this, although many attempts had been made for many, many years.

At that time, Israel will cry *"Peace and safety,"* which will be the first three and a half years of the Great Tribulation. At the midpoint of that dark period of time, the Antichrist suddenly will show his true colors, break his pact with Israel and invade her. Israel will suffer her first military defeat since she became a nation again in 1948. Were it not for the help of the Lord, she would be totally and completely destroyed.

But the Lord will intervene by causing tidings to come to the Antichrist from the east and from the north (Dan. 11:44). The Antichrist will interrupt his attack against Israel and go north and east to fight other great battles and to further consolidate his empire. His ambition will be to take over the entirety of the world. Were it not for the Second Coming, he would most definitely succeed.

When the Antichrist attacks Israel, they will stop saying, *"Peace and safety,"* for the Scripture says, *"Then sudden destruction comes upon them as travail upon a woman with child; and they shall not escape"* (I Thess. 5:3).

Even as Paul proclaims in the Second Chapter of II Thessalonians, the Antichrist at this time will take over the Temple in Jerusalem, which has just been constructed and of which the Jews are so proud, and will set himself up as God and demand worship (II Thess. 2:4). He also will declare war on anything that pertains to the God of Heaven and His Son, the Lord Jesus Christ.

The Scripture says, *"These shall make war with the Lamb* (Jesus Christ)*"* (Rev. 17:14). The Antichrist will banish the Bible in every nation where he has authority. During this time, innumerable people will die for their testimony of Jesus Christ (Rev. 6:9-11).

ISRAEL

The Antichrist will vent his anger not only on the Tribulation martyrs, but also on all Israel. Ironically, Israel has hated Jesus Christ, Whom they denied as their Messiah, but the Antichrist will declare unconditional war upon them because of his hatred for Jesus Christ.

Right after the terrible chaos of September 11, 2001 (9/11/01), Benjamin Netanyahu, the former Israeli Prime Minister, said the Muslims hate the United States as much as they hate Israel. They hate us because of our proclamation of Jesus Christ.

He is correct!

The Muslim world refers to Israel as the *"little Satan"* and America as the *"great Satan."* They hate us with a passion. If the Muslims had the power, they would force everyone in the United States to become Muslim, or else be slaughtered, or made into a slave. They do not lack the will, only the way!

When the Antichrist attacks Israel, the Muslim world will think, at least at the very beginning, that he is their Saviour. The Antichrist will appear to succeed in doing what they (the Muslims) have not been able to do, and I speak of destroying Israel.

But because the Antichrist will brook no worship other than of himself, he shortly will turn against the Muslims. He will put down every vestige of every religion in the world, at least in the places where he has control. He will demand worship for himself, thereby destroying the religion of Islam, along with every other religion (II Thess., Chpt. 2).

And yet, during the second half of the Great Tribulation, Israel will begin to turn toward the Lord Jesus Christ.

The Prophet Malachi said:

"Behold, I will send you Elijah the Prophet before the coming of the great and dreadful day of the LORD:

"And he shall turn the heart of the fathers to the children, and the heart of the children to their fathers, lest I come and smite the Earth with a curse" (Mal. 4:5-6).

During the Battle of Armageddon, Israel will cry to God as never before. The Lord is their only hope. He will not disappoint them. Their petitions and their cries and their pleadings will result in the Second Coming, which will be the most cataclysmic event the world has ever known.

(7) "YET THEY SAY, THE LORD SHALL

NOT SEE, NEITHER SHALL THE GOD OF JACOB REGARD IT."

This Prophecy continues to leap ahead to the coming Great Tribulation.

THE BLASPHEMY OF THE ANTICHRIST

The Antichrist will blaspheme the Lord of Glory, proclaiming that God can do nothing to stop him. He also will blaspheme the Old Testament, claiming the *"God of Jacob"* does not regard it. What he does not know is that the very words he is using, that is, *"God of Jacob,"* have a special meaning. They specifically refer to God Who met Jacob when he had nothing and deserved nothing and then gave him Grace and the Promise of every known blessing of Life (Gen., Chpt. 28).

Likewise, this same God will once again come to the rescue of *"Jacob"* (Israel) when she has nothing and deserves nothing; He will give her Grace and certain victory over the man of sin.

(8) "UNDERSTAND, YE BRUTISH AMONG THE PEOPLE: AND YE FOOLS, WHEN WILL YOU BE WISE?"

In this Passage, the Holy Spirit calls the Antichrist a *"fool"* and those who follow him, *"brutes."* The question, *"When will you be wise?"*, refers to the certain demise of those who think they can circumvent the Bible. They also are *"fools."*

(9) "HE WHO PLANTED THE EAR, SHALL HE NOT HEAR? HE WHO FORMED THE EYE, SHALL HE NOT SEE?"

The Holy Spirit is here informing the Antichrist that God hears all and sees all.

Concerning this all-important Verse, Pulpit says, *"This argument for a real, personal, intelligent God appears here for the first time. It is of irresistible force. 'Can it be possible that God, Who planned and made the curious mechanism of hearing and vision, is Himself without those faculties, or something analogous to them? Must He not hear those cries, and see those outrages, which men, who are His creatures, see and hear? Is it conceivable that He can be an unobservant and apathetic God?'"* [44]

Beautifully enough, the words, *"planted"* and *"formed,"* as applied respectively to the Ear and to the Eye by the Holy Spirit, are found by modern science to be exactly appropriate to the marvelous structure of these organs.

(10) "HE WHO CHASTISES THE HEATHEN, SHALL NOT HE CORRECT? HE WHO TEACHES MAN KNOWLEDGE, SHALL NOT HE KNOW?"

The Holy Spirit is saying that as the Lord chastised the heathen of the past, He will likewise chastise the heathen of the present, meaning the Antichrist.

God doesn't change! His Word proclaims to us Who He is and What He is. So there is no reason for anyone to be ignorant of God and what He will do. As stated, the Word of God is filled with untold numbers of examples.

(11) "THE LORD KNOWS THE THOUGHTS OF MAN, THAT THEY ARE VANITY."

The great thoughts of the Antichrist to conquer the world, even at a time when it looks like he will succeed, will conclude as being *"vanity."* So are all who set themselves against God.

Incidentally, the word *"vanity"* means *"empty nothings."*

This speaks of the unredeemed. After the believing sinner comes to Christ, he becomes a *"new creation"* — old things pass away, and all things become new (II Cor. 5:17). It is called the *"born-again"* experience (Jn. 3:3).

Then the Believer is to have a *"renewing of the mind,"* inasmuch as he is no longer *"conformed to this world,"* but rather *"transformed"* (Rom. 12:1-2).

(12) "BLESSED IS THE MAN WHOM YOU CHASTEN, O LORD, AND TEACH HIM OUT OF YOUR LAW."

The sense of this Verse is that the Great Tribulation is Israel's chastening. Through this chastening, she will be brought back to *"Your Law"* (Jer. 30:7).

Even though chastening of this nature will not purify one, the idea is that the person, in this case the nation, so chastened will turn to God. Israel will do that!

THE GREAT TRIBULATION

Jesus said that the Great Tribulation will be worse than anything the world has ever seen (Mat. 24:21). The Lord will bring this terrible period on the world for many reasons, and the greatest reason of all will be to bring Israel to her spiritual senses. In order to do this, a number of things must be done.

For the first time in history, the Judgment of God will be poured out on this Earth in an unprecedented way. It is the *"Great Day of His Wrath, and who shall be able to stand?"* (Rev. 6:17).

The Church will already have been taken out, and the Lord will pour out His Wrath on a world that has forgotten Him days without number. But despite the great judgments coming upon the Earth, symbolized by the *"seals," "trumpets,"* and *"vials,"* the world still will not repent. In fact, their epithet will continue to read, *"And they repented not"* (Rev. 2:21; 9:20-21; 16:9, 11).

During the second half of the Great Tribulation, after the Antichrist has revealed his true colors, not a single nation in the world will come to the aid of Israel. They do not want to incur the wrath of the Antichrist. At best, they will remain neutral. Israel will stand alone except for God!

(13) "THAT YOU MAY GIVE HIM REST FROM THE DAYS OF ADVERSITY, UNTIL THE PIT BE DIGGED FOR THE WICKED."

The twofold purpose for the Great Tribulation is here presented in this Thirteenth Verse:

THE PURPOSE OF THE GREAT TRIBULATION

1. These *"days of adversity"* (seven years) will serve to bring Israel back to God, whereby the Lord Jesus Christ will give her *"rest."*

2. This period also will bring to a head all of man's efforts from the very beginning in his rebellion against God. Satan will play the high stakes at this time. *"The wicked"* (II Thess. 2:8) is the Antichrist, who will fall into the *"pit."*

(14) "FOR THE LORD WILL NOT CAST OFF HIS PEOPLE, NEITHER WILL HE FORSAKE HIS INHERITANCE."

Another great Truth is here borne out.

MODERN DOMINION TEACHING

The modern-day Dominion Teaching, which proclaims that the Church is now Israel, and that modern Israel has no place in the Plan or Promises of God, is grossly unscriptural, which makes it completely false! The Church is spiritual Israel, meaning that *"Japheth now dwells in the tents of Shem"* (Gen. 9:27). However, the Promises of God are multitudinous that National Israel will be restored. This Passage is but one of those many.

If God has said it (and He most certainly has!), then it shall be done. The beginning of this Restoration occurred in 1948, when Israel once again finally became a nation, after wandering all over the world for approximately 2,000 years.

(15) "BUT JUDGMENT SHALL RETURN UNTO RIGHTEOUSNESS: AND ALL THE UPRIGHT IN HEART SHALL FOLLOW IT."

Judgment divorced from righteousness entails oppression. When the Son of Man returns to judge the Earth, then judgment will return to righteousness and all the upright in heart will gladly follow in its train. Judgment was in Pilate; Righteousness was in Christ. There was divorce and opposition; as a consequence, the crime of crimes — the Crucifixion of the Prince of Life.

(16) "WHO WILL RISE UP FOR ME AGAINST THE EVILDOERS? OR WHO WILL STAND UP FOR ME AGAINST THE WORKERS OF INIQUITY?"

The confession of Verses 16 through 19 is that the Messiah Alone can and will protect defenseless Israel.

(17) "UNLESS THE LORD HAD BEEN MY HELP, MY SOUL HAD ALMOST DWELT IN SILENCE."

At that time (the Battle of Armageddon), it will seem that no nation on Earth will come to Israel's rescue.

THE UNITED STATES AND ISRAEL

America has poured many billions of dollars into Israel since her formation as a State in 1948. In the last several years, however, it seems that America's support is weakening. If that truly is the case, it will spell nothing but trouble for the U.S.A. In the last days, America will not come to Israel's rescue, nor will any other nation; consequently, unless the Lord answers Israel's cry, her plea will be met with *"silence."*

(18) "WHEN I SAID, MY FOOT SLIPS; YOUR MERCY, O LORD, HELD ME UP."

The meaning of this Verse is that at the

most critical time during the Battle of Armageddon, when it looks like sure victory for the Antichrist, when half of Jerusalem has fallen (Zech. 14:1-3), then Israel will cry, *"Have mercy, O LORD, hold me up."*

Hold her up, He will! Of this time, the Prophet Zechariah said, *"He will come back and fight against those nations, as when He fought in the day of battle. And His Feet shall stand in that day upon the Mount of Olives"* (Zech. 14:3-4).

(19) "IN THE MULTITUDE OF MY THOUGHTS WITHIN ME YOUR COMFORTS DELIGHT MY SOUL."

This means that at this critical juncture in Israel's long history, the only *"comforts"* she will have are the Promises of God that are given, which *"delight My soul."* Really, the only *"comforts"* that any Believer has are the Promises of God. But, to be sure, that is all that is needed!

(20) "SHALL THE THRONE OF INIQUITY HAVE FELLOWSHIP WITH YOU, WHICH FRAMES MISCHIEF BY A LAW?"

In this Passage, Israel contrasts the Earth under the Antichrist with the Earth under Christ. Daniel said that the Antichrist would *"think to change times and laws"* (Dan. 7:25). In other words, God's Law cannot exist in conjunction with the aberrant law of the Antichrist.

This has ever been man's problem. He continues to try to change God's Laws into his own man-made laws; this always brings *"mischief."*

(21) "THEY GATHER THEMSELVES TOGETHER AGAINST THE SOUL OF THE RIGHTEOUS, AND CONDEMN THE INNOCENT BLOOD."

Israel here is called *"the righteous,"* because they are the ancient people of the Book. The Antichrist will *"condemn"* them to death. Instead, <u>he</u> will die.

(22) "BUT THE LORD IS MY DEFENSE; AND MY GOD IS THE ROCK OF MY REFUGE."

After so many years in the wilderness, now nearly 2,000 years, Israel is finally coming home. She now realizes that neither her own strength nor the strength of any other nation can save her; furthermore, no other nation is coming to her aid anyway. Now she knows that God is her *"Rock."*

(23) "AND HE SHALL BRING UPON THEM THEIR OWN INIQUITY, AND SHALL CUT THEM OFF IN THEIR OWN WICKEDNESS; YEA, THE LORD OUR GOD SHALL CUT THEM OFF."

The Thirty-eighth and Thirty-ninth Chapters of Ezekiel proclaim exactly how the Lord will do this.

PSALM 95

A Psalm of David:
A Psalm of Praise to God

(1) "O COME, LET US SING UNTO THE LORD: LET US MAKE A JOYFUL NOISE TO THE ROCK OF OUR SALVATION."

God is not only a Rock of Defense, but also the Rock of Salvation, which means that He is a strong Defense, and His Salvation is all-powerful (Heb. 7:25).

The *"joyful noise"* that we are to make is the singing of hymns, with all giving Glory to God (Ps. 96:1-3).

THE RESTORATION OF ISRAEL

This Psalm was written by David. The next five have no titles, so the authors are not known. There is a good possibility that David was the author of some, if not all, of the next five Psalms.

Psalm 94 portrays the wilderness journey. Now the first fingers of dawn are about to break upon the Millennial Morn. The long night of weeping for Israel is about to come to an end. Israel has seen the Earth under the Antichrist. Now she will see the Earth under Christ.

Thus, this Psalm and the following five are priceless illustrations of the victorious power of a Divinely-given faith that will enable the lovers of the Messiah in that dark night of shame, torture, and death to sing praise to His Glorious Appearing and Kingdom.

It will happen! The Word of God says so!

(2) "LET US COME BEFORE HIS PRESENCE WITH THANKSGIVING, AND MAKE A JOYFUL NOISE UNTO HIM WITH PSALMS."

We are here given a wonderful directive by the Holy Spirit concerning the approach of the Believer to the Lord.

THANKSGIVING

We are always to come into the Presence of the Lord *"with thanksgiving."* Especially when we consider that we deserve nothing good, but yet He has given us everything, we should all the more desire to constantly praise Him. No Christian should enter into prayer without a time of thanksgiving unto the Lord before making our petitions to Him. This should be a practice and a habit.

In the course of our worship, there should be the singing of hymns, that is, the *"joyful noise."*

For some ten years, we conducted two prayer meetings a day at Family Worship Center. I was present at all of them, except for the times that Frances and I were out of town. A group of our faithful people would gather with Frances and me every morning and every night. I personally, to a degree, still maintain this regimen.

In October of 1991, the Lord told me to do this, and I did my best to obey Him faithfully. Even though it took a number of years, He rewarded this most glorious time with the great Revelation of the Cross. At times during these prayer meetings, it would be hard to pray; at other times, the Glory of God would fill the hearts and lives of all who were present.

Little by little, the Holy Spirit brought me to the place where I could be given this great Revelation, which has changed my life and Ministry, and has been the change agent of every person in the world who has ever truly known the Lord. It is the Cross of Christ where every question is answered, every enemy defeated, and a door is opened that the Holy Spirit may do great things, which He has (Acts, Chpt. 2).

(3) "FOR THE LORD IS A GREAT GOD, AND A GREAT KING ABOVE ALL GODS."

The Holy Spirit is really the Author of this Psalm, all of the Psalms, and, in fact, the entirety of the Word of God (Heb. 3:7; II Pet. 1:21).

Here, the Holy Spirit calls upon Israel to worship the Messiah as God of the whole Earth. His Doctrine is that faith admits one into the future Sabbath Rest of the Kingdom, and unbelief excludes one from it. The Kingdom Age will be Earth's great Sabbath of Rest.

Creation Rest, Redemption Rest, and Millennial Rest are all based upon the Person and Work of Christ. Faith brings us into these *"Rests"*; unbelief excludes us.

In this one Verse, the Holy Spirit addresses God by three Names:
1. Jehovah — The Lord;
2. El — the Great God; and,
3. Elohim — God.

(4) "IN HIS HAND ARE THE DEEP PLACES OF THE EARTH: THE STRENGTH OF THE HILLS IS HIS ALSO."

The idea of this Passage is that God created all things, and, in essence, controls all things.

"The deep places of the Earth" have to do with the underworld prisons, where some fallen angels are locked away, and also Hell itself (Lk. 16:19-31; I Pet. 3:19-20).

(5) "THE SEA IS HIS, AND HE MADE IT: AND HIS HANDS FORMED THE DRY LAND."

Over and over again, the Holy Spirit refutes the lie of evolution. God is the Creator of all and deserves worship by all.

(6) "O COME, LET US WORSHIP AND BOW DOWN: LET US KNEEL BEFORE THE LORD OUR MAKER."

This Verse is the great invitation to come to Jesus. He is God's Rest — an indescribable Rest. How wonderful is the Grace that invites sinners to share God's Rest! This is a Rest that never can be disturbed. Its wonders are developed by the God of Glory (Heb., Chpts. 3-4).

(7) "FOR HE IS OUR GOD; AND WE ARE THE PEOPLE OF HIS PASTURE, AND THE SHEEP OF HIS HAND. TODAY IF YOU WILL HEAR HIS VOICE."

This Passage is quoted in Hebrews 3:7-11 and 4:7.

THE PEOPLE OF HIS PASTURE

The heathen believed that there was a god for the mountains, another for the plains, and another for the sea with its sands and shoals. But these Passages witness that there is but One God, and that the sea and the deepest and highest portions of the Earth are His.

His Sheep are to praise Him in anticipation because He is great and good.

What a privilege to say, *"He is our God"* and *"We are the people of His pasture."* And what a pasture it is!

The expression, *"The Sheep of His Hand,"* refers to our being made by Him. It has a far greater meaning than if a shepherd purchased sheep. In this instance, it means that God created the Sheep — *"the Sheep of His Hand."*

Accordingly, we are admonished to *"hear His Voice,"* the Voice of the Shepherd.

Considering that He has made us, we would be foolish not to *"hear His Voice."* Sadly, however, the majority of the world, and for all time, must be labeled as very foolish. Most have no desire to hear Him. In fact, they deny Him!

(8) "HARDEN NOT YOUR HEART, AS IN THE PROVOCATION, AND AS IN THE DAY OF TEMPTATION IN THE WILDERNESS:

(9) "WHEN YOUR FATHERS TEMPTED ME, PROVED ME, AND SAW MY WORK."

In order to feel the force and anguish of the appeal of this translation of Verses 8 and 9, it is suggested:

"O that you would hear His Voice today! O that you would not harden your heart as at Meribah, and as at Massah in the wilderness, when your fathers tempted Me and put Me to the proof! And yet they saw My mighty works!"

(10) "FORTY YEARS LONG WAS I GRIEVED WITH THIS GENERATION, AND SAID, IT IS A PEOPLE WHO DO ERR IN THEIR HEART, AND THEY HAVE NOT KNOWN MY WAYS."

"I was grieved with that generation that they should not enter into My rest."

THE WAYS OF GOD

Regarding this, Williams says, *"Such is man's heart. He wills not to recognize God's Ways in severity and goodness. Those who believe the Scriptures and who have some little knowledge of their own hearts have no difficulty in believing that the very people who witnessed and profited by the marvelous miracles of the wilderness challenged God to provide a table for them in the desert, and when it was provided, declared that Pharaoh's was better, so they desired to appoint a captain to return into Egypt!"* (Num. 14:3-4).[45]

Is it any wonder that God would not allow that generation, the one delivered from Egypt, at least all who were twenty years old and older, to enter into the Promised Land?

(11) "UNTO WHOM I SWORE IN MY WRATH THAT THEY SHOULD NOT ENTER INTO MY REST."

A tremendous Truth is given in these Scriptures, which is just as appropriate for the present time as it was then.

UNBELIEF

The greatest sin of all just may be the sin of faithlessness. The entire fabric of the Plan of God demands Faith. Men forsake God because they don't believe God. Others claim to believe Him, but yet show by their actions that their faith is weak. In the wilderness, Israel showed unbelief. They died because of that unbelief and *"could not enter into God's Rest."*

GOD'S WORD BUILDS FAITH

Why is it that Israel did not know God's Ways? They saw His Miracles, and they knew His Acts, but they did not know His Ways. As wonderful as miracles are, and as wonderful as we want and need them, they do not build faith. God's Word builds Faith, God's Word alone (Rom. 10:17).

Even though Israel in the wilderness had very little access to the Word of God (because Moses had thus far only written the Books of Job, Genesis, and maybe Leviticus and Numbers; Deuteronomy was not written until the very conclusion of the wilderness experience), still, Israel definitely had access to the Word of God in that the Lord conveyed to Moses what He desired and Moses conveyed it to the people. All the people had to do was believe what the Man of God said. But this they refused to do.

UNBELIEF COMES IN MANY WAYS

Unbelief is not all the time a flat denial of the Word of God. Most of the time it is a failure to believe what the Word actually says, by twisting or perverting it to make it mean something else.

For instance, the Cross of Christ is the Foundation of the Faith. It is the Story of the Bible all the way from Genesis 1:1 through Revelation 22:21. But yet, Satan is very successful at steering the faith of the Believer away from the Cross of Christ to other things.

Many actually claim to believe in the Cross, but actually do not. The extent of their faith in the Cross is *"Jesus died for me."* Now that is one of the greatest statements ever made, and it is very, very true. But still it only pertains to the Salvation experience, which means that virtually the entirety of the modern Church has almost no knowledge whatsoever as it regards Sanctification and the Cross. As a result, it keeps trying to live for God by the means of one kind of law or another, which always brings about disaster.

And yet, when they hear the Message of the Cross, or they have the opportunity to hear it, most will ignore it, turn it aside, or flatly state that they do not believe it. It is a problem of unbelief.

Paul said, *"For the preaching of the Cross is to them who perish foolishness; but unto us which are saved it is the Power of God"* (I Cor. 1:18).

The Greek word translated *"preaching"* is *"logos,"* which actually means *"word"* or *"message."* So the Verse should have been translated accordingly.

The *"Word of the Cross"* or the *"Message of the Cross"* is actually the Message of the Bible. On that foundation everything is built (I Pet. 1:18-20).

PSALM 96

Possibly Written by David:
A New Song of Praise to the Lord

(1) "O SING UNTO THE LORD A NEW SONG: SING UNTO THE LORD, ALL THE EARTH."

This Psalm has no title. The author is unknown, but there is a possibility that the writer was David.

NOTES

THE CHURCH

Beginning with Psalm 90, the Salvation and historical experiences of Israel are given to us in each of the Psalms leading up to the great Kingdom Age. Even though Israel is the subject, still, the Church will have a great part in all these things.

The Church is not actually mentioned in these Psalms; however, the Fifteenth Chapter of I Corinthians proclaims to us what will take place at the First Resurrection. The Twentieth Chapter of Revelation gives a little more detail.

In the coming Kingdom Age, every Born-Again Saint who has ever lived, both Jews and Gentiles (Eph. 2:13-18), will be given Glorified Bodies. This will include all Believers up to the end of the Great Tribulation. All of these Saints will help the Lord administer the affairs of this Earth and the entirety of His Creation during the entirety of the Kingdom Age, and then on into the Perfect Age, which is forever and forever (Rev., Chpts. 21-22).

The Church was never in God's Perfect Plan. He planned for Israel to accept Him at His First Advent, and then to evangelize the world, which, of course, would have included the Gentiles. The entire world always was in the great Plan of God. But Israel rejected Him, and so the Plan had to be modified somewhat.

While the Resurrection remains the same, the power and authority of the Move of God on Earth now resides in the Church, and we speak of the True Church, with Israel left out. At the Second Coming, Israel will be restored.

THE NEW SONG

The setting of the New Song seems to be at the beginning of the great Millennial Reign. Israel, having sung the previous Psalm, now invites the nations to join her in a *"New Song."* Psalm 97 will be that *"New Song."* The reason why the nations should sing this New Song are given in Verses 4 through 6 and 13. This *"New Song"* belongs to the day when the kingdoms of the world shall become the Kingdom of Jehovah and of His Christ (Rev. 11:15; 12:10).

(2) "SING UNTO THE LORD, BLESS HIS NAME; SHOW FORTH HIS SALVATION FROM DAY TO DAY."

The doctrine of this Psalm is that the Advent of the Messiah into the world will make it a Paradise and that His rule alone can eliminate dissension, war, misery, and injustice, and establish society in an enduring brotherhood — *"His Salvation."*

(3) "DECLARE HIS GLORY AMONG THE HEATHEN, HIS WONDERS AMONG ALL PEOPLE."

Men may test the reality and credibility of this Prophecy by surrendering their sinful hearts to the government of Immanuel. They then will experience a love, a peace, and a moral power to which their hearts were strangers previous to conversion.

THE GLORY OF GOD

Despite the present efforts to take the Gospel of Jesus Christ to the *"heathen,"* there still are major parts of the world that know little of *"His Glory"* and *"His Wonders."* Much of the world is steeped in demonic Islam, Hinduism, spiritism, and other works of darkness. During the great Kingdom Age to come, however, the whole world finally will know, beyond the shadow of a doubt, of *"His Glory"*!

(4) "FOR THE LORD IS GREAT, AND GREATLY TO BE PRAISED: HE IS TO BE FEARED ABOVE ALL GODS."

Satan's great contest with God has always been to make himself God instead of Jehovah. He has sought to do this through demon spirits, idol worship, false religions, and a myriad of false ways of Salvation.

FALSE DOCTRINE

Paul addressed himself to this in the Eleventh Chapter of II Corinthians. At this time, he was dealing with the apostasy within Christianity instead of idols and other things. He calls the promoters of these false doctrines, *"false apostles, deceitful workers, and Satan's ministers"* (II Cor. 11:13, 15). These were in the ranks of Christianity, and were works of Satan to be ranked in the same category as idols and false religions.

In the coming Kingdom Age, all of these false religions will be put down and done away with.

(5) "FOR ALL THE GODS OF THE NATIONS ARE IDOLS: BUT THE LORD MADE THE HEAVENS."

In the Hebrew, the word *"idols"* is *"elililim,"* which means *"nothings, vanities, emptiness and things of naught."* So the definition of *"idols"* could be summed up in one word, they are *"nothing."* Regrettably, the far greater majority of the world serves these *"nothings"* instead of the Lord Who created all things.

IDOLS

Idolatry is vigorously condemned both in the Old Testament and New Testament because it degrades both God and man. It denies the existence of the True God Who created the world and mankind, Whose Glory cannot be adequately comprehended in any tangible form. It is absurd that a person could carve an idol with his own hands and then be afraid of what he has made.

Some religions claim that an image is an aid to worship, though not an object of worship. The danger of such reasoning is that two people may have a different idea of what the image signifies. One person may look upon it as a representation and void of value or power in itself. But another may regard it as the abode of the god and fraught with power, and he, therefore, will worship the image.

A visible representation of the deity tends to restrict a person's concept of God, for he will base his concept of God, consciously or unconsciously, upon the image or picture.

Finally, man becomes like that which he worships (Hos. 9:10). If his god is lifeless and cold, it can bring him no real hope or comfort. Only the True and Living God can fulfill the hope of Eternal Life.

IDOLATRY IN THE NEW TESTAMENT

Idolatry is not mentioned as frequently in the New Testament as in the Old Testament. In the New Testament, idolatry includes the worship of any gods other than the Living and True God. The Christian Church arose in a world given to idolatry, but also out of a Jewish background that maintained a stubborn protest against image worship.

Paul pictures the widespread idolatry of the pagan world (Rom. 1:18-25). He observes that their idol worship was so multifarious that the Athenians had even erected an altar to an unknown god (Acts 17:23). He never implies an interpretation widely held today that idolatry represents a primitive phase of religious development. Paul considered it a perversion, a turning away from the knowledge of the True God. Paul called idolatry a work of the flesh (Gal. 5:20), and warned the Christians to shun the worship of idols (I Cor. 10:14).

Church members who lived in heathen communities had to be careful not to compromise themselves with idolatry (Acts 15:29). One problem for early Christians was the eating of meat that had been offered to idols. Paul said that idols had no real existence, so eating meat offered to them would not be wrong, but he added that a Christian should do nothing that would cause a weaker brother to stumble (I Cor. 8:1-13; 10:14-33). Paul warned that one may abhor idols but commit other sins (Rom. 2:22). He emphatically denied that idols have any real existence (I Cor. 12:2; Gal. 4:8; I Thess. 1:9). His protest against idolatry was so effective in Ephesus that it hurt the business of those engaged in making silver images of Diana (Acts 19:23-27). Idolatry is used figuratively by Paul to include covetousness (Eph. 5:5; Col. 3:5) and gluttony (Phil. 3:19).

MYSTERY RELIGIONS

Mystery religions, in which the individual or the community sought to appropriate the experiences of dying or rising nature gods, such as Osiris, were widespread in the Greco-Roman world of Paul's time. Emperor worship was also an accepted practice. Herod the Great established the cult of Augustus at Samaria. Caligula (A.D. 37-41) ordered his image to be set up in the Temple at Jerusalem. Christians suffered severely at the hands of Domitian (A.D. 81-96), who insisted that he be worshipped as *"God"* and *"Lord."*

The Book of Revelation appeared at such a time with its warning against the danger of idolatry (Rev. 2:14, 20). It also affirms the powerlessness of idols (Rev. 9:20) and warns against worshipping an image of the beast (Rev. 13:14-15; 14:9-11), and promises the exaltation of those who refuse to worship the beast or its image (Rev. 20:4).

(The above material on idols and idolatry was gleaned from the material of F. B. Huey, Jr. We are grateful for his contribution.)

(6) "HONOR AND MAJESTY ARE BEFORE HIM: STRENGTH AND BEAUTY ARE IN HIS SANCTUARY."

The emphasis is on the pronoun *"His."* There are many other sanctuaries today in the world, but they are false. As just stated, they are *"nothings."* The only *"strength"* and *"beauty"* in the world are in *"His Sanctuary."*

Since the Cross, which atoned for all sin and, thereby, made it possible for the Holy Spirit to live permanently in the hearts and lives of Believers, Believers have become His Temple (I Cor. 3:16).

(7) "GIVE UNTO THE LORD, O YE KINDREDS OF THE PEOPLE, GIVE UNTO THE LORD GLORY AND STRENGTH."

The nations of the world are invited to share in this *"strength"* and *"beauty."* They are invited to give the *"LORD"* the *"Glory"* due His Name instead of wasting it on *"idols."*

(8) "GIVE UNTO THE LORD THE GLORY DUE UNTO HIS NAME: BRING AN OFFERING, AND COME INTO HIS COURTS."

Since the very beginning of time, *"Glory"* which has been *"due unto His Name"* has been dissipated on *"nothings"* or *"idols."* The Lord has never received that Glory; in the coming Kingdom Age, He most definitely will.

FEAST OF TABERNACLES

The second half of Verse 8, which concerns the bringing of offerings, refers to the Prophecies of Zechariah. Then the nations of the world will come to Jerusalem to keep the *"Feast of Tabernacles"* (Zech. 14:16-19).

During the coming Kingdom Age, these great Feasts will once again be introduced. At that time, the nations of the world (representatives) will be required to go up to Jerusalem to worship the King, the Lord of Hosts.

Israel never quite knew the meaning of these glorious Feasts, even when she was keeping them; consequently, their true significance was gradually diluted until these Feasts became merely *"Feasts of the Jews"* (Jn. 5:1).

All of these Feasts portrayed and glorified Christ. In the coming Millennium, their true worth and value will be known and will serve as a memorial unto Christ forever.

(9) "O WORSHIP THE LORD IN THE BEAUTY OF HOLINESS: FEAR BEFORE HIM, ALL THE EARTH."

This Passage also corresponds with the Fourteenth Chapter of Zechariah, when in that great coming Kingdom Day, *"There shall be upon the bells of the horses, 'HOLINESS UNTO THE LORD.'"* In other words, Christ's Kingdom will be absolute Holiness. It, however, will be God's Holiness, and not man's holiness.

(10) "SAY AMONG THE HEATHEN THAT THE LORD REIGNS: THE WORLD ALSO SHALL BE ESTABLISHED THAT IT SHALL NOT BE MOVED: HE SHALL JUDGE THE PEOPLE RIGHTEOUSLY."

For the first time, the world and its entirety will know government that is not corrupt, because *"The LORD reigns."* It will not be moved away from this righteous Government. Isaiah said, *"The Government shall be upon His Shoulder"* (Isa. 9:6).

(11) "LET THE HEAVENS REJOICE, AND LET THE EARTH BE GLAD; LET THE SEA ROAR, AND THE FULLNESS THEREOF."

When Jesus Christ reigns over the entirety of Planet Earth in this glorious Kingdom Age, then the heavens can rejoice and the Earth can be glad. The sea will roar, not with anger, but with praises unto the Lord.

THE NATIONS OF THE WORLD

All the nations of the world will then be called to give God the glory that is due Him and to come with proper offerings into the courts of the Lord, the place of universal worship.

Originally, God intended all nations to worship Him in His Temple at Jerusalem (Mk. 11:17), but Israel failed to evangelize the nations, or even consider these other nations having a part with them in God's Blessings. The question consequently may be asked, *"How was Abraham's Seed to be a blessing to all nations of the Earth if true worship was to be limited to the Jews only?"* (Gen. 12:1-3; Gal. 3:8).

Paul quotes freely from the Prophets, proving that God's Plan was to save the Gentiles also (Rom. 9:14-33). So another similar question presents itself: *"How could all the Earth be commanded to fear and give Glory to God if only the Jews were to be blessed?"*

Israel's exclusivity, which was caused by her self-righteousness, eliminated all but their select ones and brought about their rejection of Jesus Christ. Self-righteousness always excludes everyone else who does not join its group or subscribe to its man-made standards.

(12) "LET THE FIELD BE JOYFUL, AND ALL THAT IS THEREIN: THEN SHALL ALL THE TREES OF THE WOOD REJOICE."

As the next Psalm shows, the nations will respond to a renewed invitation from Israel. Creation itself will unite in this song (Rom. 8:18-23).

The terminology given here concerning the *"heavens"* and the *"Earth"* (which includes the *"sea"* and the *"fields"* and even the *"trees"*) delineates the entirety of Planet Earth and the heavens. For the first time since the Fall, this Planet will be in union with God, because Jesus Christ reigns.

(13) "BEFORE THE LORD: FOR HE COMES, FOR HE COMES TO JUDGE THE EARTH: HE SHALL JUDGE THE WORLD WITH RIGHTEOUSNESS, AND THE PEOPLE WITH HIS TRUTH."

This Judgment will take place at the beginning of the Kingdom Age, when Christ will judge the nations of the world as to how they treated Israel (Isa. 1:25-31; 11:3-9; Dan. 7:13-14; Rev. 1:5-8; 5:10; 20:4-6). This *"Judgment"* has nothing to do with the coming *"Great White Throne Judgment,"* which will take place at the conclusion of the Kingdom Age (Rev. 20:11-15). Neither does it have anything to do with the *"Judgment Seat of Christ,"* which will take place in Heaven after the First Resurrection of Life (Rom. 14:10; II Cor. 5:10).

PSALM 97

Author Unknown:
The Lord Reigns: Rejoice

(1) "THE LORD REIGNS; LET THE

EARTH REJOICE; LET THE MULTITUDE OF ISLES BE GLAD THEREOF."

As the previous Psalm gave the invitation, this Psalm proclaims its fulfillment. This is the *"New Song"* that is spoken of in 96:1. It is new for Earth, but not for Heaven. It sings of a new day for humanity — a day of righteousness, peace, and brotherhood. It will dawn when God causes His First Begotten to return to the Earth on that Great Millennial Morn and commands all the Angels to worship Him (Heb. 1:6).

Gladness will the hallmark of this Government because *"The LORD reigns."*

THE LORD REIGNS

Man has ever tried to bring about this Utopia on the Earth, especially during the last half of the Twentieth Century, even at the present. President Franklin D. Roosevelt had his *"New Deal,"* President John F. Kennedy had the *"New Frontier,"* and President George H. W. Bush had his *"Thousand Points of Light."*

While I applaud these men for attempting to alleviate some of Earth's problems, which are many, still, it simply cannot be done without the Lord Jesus Christ. Man has been trying to rebuild the Garden of Eden without the Tree of Life. Man has ever failed, as man ever will fail.

Hunger, war, disease and pestilence, elements which seem to be warped, and man's inhumanity to man: none will be addressed until Jesus comes back, which will take place at the Second Coming. Then, and then only, can the *"New Song"* be sung in all the Earth. To be sure, that day most definitely is coming! It will be because *"The LORD reigns."* Now man reigns, which results in all the problems. Then *"the LORD will reign,"* and He Alone, which will bring about the *"New Song."* Then the world will have something to sing about.

(2) "CLOUDS AND DARKNESS ARE ROUND ABOUT HIM: RIGHTEOUSNESS AND JUDGMENT ARE THE HABITATION OF HIS THRONE."

There will be a reason for the great *"gladness"* on Planet Earth at that time. It will be because *"righteousness and judgment are the habitation of His Throne."*

CLOUDS AND DARKNESS

The implication of this Verse is as follows: During the entirety of the thousand-year reign of Christ on this Earth during the Kingdom Age, *"clouds and darkness"* at times will surround His Throne. The world will see Him on a constant basis, but at times His Glory will be so paramount and so obvious that it must be shielded from ordinary mortals for all the obvious reasons.

John the Beloved gives us an idea of what Jesus then will look like in the First Chapter of the Book of Revelation. He describes the Saviour, and then says, *"When I saw Him, I fell at His feet as dead. And He laid His Right Hand upon me, saying unto me, Fear not; I am the First and the Last"* (Rev. 1:12-18).

(3) "A FIRE GOES BEFORE HIM, AND BURNS UP HIS ENEMIES ROUND ABOUT."

This speaks of the Second Coming.

THE SECOND COMING AND THE BATTLE OF ARMAGEDDON

The Apostle Paul said, *"When the Lord Jesus shall be revealed from Heaven with His mighty Angels, in flaming fire, taking vengeance on them who know not God"* (II Thess. 1:7-8). Thus, Christ will appear to His Adversaries whom He will destroy. This will be during the Battle of Armageddon.

At that time, the Lord, even as He has done in the past, will use the elements of the heavens to destroy the Antichrist and his armies. The Prophet Ezekiel described it by saying, *"And I will plead against him* (against the Antichrist) *with pestilence and with blood; and I will rain upon him, and upon his bands, and upon the many people who are with him, an overflowing rain, and great hailstones, fire, and brimstone"* (Ezek. 38:22).

(4) "HIS LIGHTNINGS ENLIGHTENED THE WORLD: THE EARTH SAW, AND TREMBLED."

The Second Coming will be, without a doubt, the most cataclysmic event the world ever has known. If the world thinks it has seen power in the detonation of an atomic bomb (and God created the atom!), it hasn't seen anything by comparison to the Power and the Glory of the Son of God. Jesus Himself mentioned this coming time:

"For as the lightning comes out of the east, and shines even unto the west; so shall also the coming of the Son of Man be . . ."

"Immediately after the Tribulation of those days shall the sun be darkened, and the moon shall not give her light, and the stars shall fall from Heaven, and the powers of the Heavens shall be shaken:"

"And then shall appear the sign of the Son of Man in Heaven" (Mat. 24:27-30).

(5) "THE HILLS MELTED LIKE WAX AT THE PRESENCE OF THE LORD, AT THE PRESENCE OF THE LORD OF THE WHOLE EARTH."

Again, this speaks of the Second Coming.

THE BATTLE OF ARMAGEDDON

At this time, the Antichrist will bear down upon Israel; his efforts are described in Ezekiel, Chapters 38 and 39. He will think that there is nothing that will be able to stand in his path. No nation in the world at that time will come to Israel's rescue. So, in the mind of the Antichrist, he will be on the verge of taking over Planet Earth.

There are three reasons the Antichrist hates Israel:

1. She is the people through whom God chose to reveal His Word and His Son to the entire world. Even though they rejected Him, they still are His people.

2. In the second half of the Great Tribulation, Israel will begin to come back to God. Some will begin to accept Jesus Christ as their Saviour. So the hatred that fills the heart of the man of sin will be inspired by Satan, as he seeks to stop this Restoration.

3. Satan, who is working through the Antichrist, knows that if he can defeat Israel, then hundreds of Prophecies concerning these ancient people will fall to the ground. If that happens, then he has won. In other words, the Lord is defeated, and Earth now belongs to Satan, and, above all, the very Throne of God now belongs to him.

Everything hinges on the Word of God. If even one part of it falls down, then Satan has won. The Scripture tells us, *"For You have magnified Your Word above all Your Name"* (Ps. 138:2). There is nothing in the world more important than the Word of God. Nothing else even comes close!

THE WORD OF GOD

That's the reason that every Believer should avail himself of the opportunity to make the Word of God a lifelong study. The very reason, I believe, the Lord instructed me to develop THE EXPOSITOR'S STUDY BIBLE is that it might be an aid and a help in order that all could learn the Word of God to a greater degree. As stated, nothing is more important than that!

As far as a learning tool regarding the Word of God, I don't believe there is anything that ever has been placed in the hands of the Christian public that will help achieve this task anymore than this *"tool of instruction."* If you haven't availed yourself of getting a copy, I would encourage you to do so.

The Word of the Lord will not fail. The Lord Jesus Christ will come back to this Earth and will rescue Israel, defeat the Antichrist, and set up a Kingdom which will never end.

(6) "THE HEAVENS DECLARE HIS RIGHTEOUSNESS, AND ALL THE PEOPLE SEE HIS GLORY."

This will take place in the coming Kingdom Age. At that time, all the nations of the Earth will behold the Glory of the Lord. There will be no doubt regarding His Power or His ability to remake the Earth, which He most definitely will do.

(7) "CONFOUNDED BE ALL THEY WHO SERVE GRAVEN IMAGES, WHO BOAST THEMSELVES OF IDOLS: WORSHIP HIM, ALL YE GODS."

This Passage proclaims to us that the world has ever been bathed in idolatry.

IDOLATRY

When God originally made man, He made him in His Image; consequently, there is something birthed in man that desires to worship. Sadly, precious few desire to worship God. The majority of the world worship idols. In the U.S.A. and Canada, the idols are Hollywood, sports activities, education, money, fame, intellect, and countless other things.

But the most fervent worship of all is in the realm of religion. Men may worship a Denomination, a Ministry, a Preacher, a Creed, or a Doctrine. Others worship the philosophy of Christianity without really knowing

Christ. Thus is the world full of idolatry.

THE CROSS OF CHRIST

All worship which does not have as its foundation the Lord Jesus Christ and what He did for us at the Cross must be labeled as *"idolatry."*

In Old Testament times, whenever the Priests went into the Holy Place twice a day, at 9 a.m. and 3 p.m., their instructions were to bring coals of fire from the Brazen Altar, which was a Type of the Cross of Christ, and apply those coals to the Altar of Incense. Then they were to pour Incense over these coals, which would fill the Holy Place with fragrance, which typified the Intercession of Christ, all on our behalf. When the correct order was followed, it meant the Lord would accept our prayers, our petitions, our praise, and our worship.

But the coals of fire had to come from the Brazen Altar. If they came from any other ignition, the Priests could be stricken dead on the spot. Two Priests were! They were two of Aaron's sons: Nadab and Abihu. These two offered up *"strange fire"* on the Altar, which *"the LORD commanded them not"* (Lev. 10:1-2). As stated, they died on the spot!

All of this portrays the fact that God can give nothing to man except it comes through Christ by means of the Cross. God also can accept no worship from man, unless it also comes to Him through Christ and the Cross. This means that anything which pertains to Christianity, but which is not based squarely on Christ and the Cross, is looked at by God as a form of idolatry.

Most of what today passes for *"Christianity"* actually is idolatry. I speak of the *"Purpose Driven Life"* scheme, the *"Government of Twelve"* scheme, the *"Word of Faith"* scheme, *"Denominationalism,"* and a hundred and one other things that could be mentioned.

Because it is so important, let us say it again:

If it is not based squarely on Christ and the Cross, then it is unacceptable to God and is put in the same position as Cain's sacrifice, recorded in the Fourth Chapter of Genesis.

(8) "ZION HEARD, AND WAS GLAD; AND THE DAUGHTERS OF JUDAH REJOICED BECAUSE OF YOUR JUDGMENTS, O LORD."

Israel herself succumbed to idolatry many centuries past. Even when she was restored to her land, she made the Law into idolatry. They rejected Christ, which plunged them into a spiritual abyss, which scattered them over the face of the globe and resulted in untold suffering and sorrow. At the Second Coming, they will be restored. At that time, *"Zion will hear and be glad."*

(9) "FOR YOU, LORD, ARE HIGH ABOVE ALL THE EARTH: YOU ARE EXALTED FAR ABOVE ALL GODS."

With purpose, the Holy Spirit continues to repeat a variation of the statement, *"Exalted far above all gods."*

GOD ALONE MUST BE WORSHIPPED

It is not without design that the statement, *"Exalted far above all gods,"* is given repeatedly. The great contest between good and evil, which has raged from the very beginning, even before the creation of man, is wrapped up in this statement.

The great effort of Satan always has been for men to worship him instead of Jehovah. The Holy Spirit here tells us that, at long last, all false worship will be ended. This will take place in the coming Kingdom Age, when Satan is locked away in the bottomless pit, where he will remain for the entirety of the one thousand years (Rev. 20:1-3).

In the Kingdom Age, all false worship will, at long last, be ended. The statement of Christ made so long ago to the woman at the well will finally be fulfilled: *"God is a Spirit: and they who worship Him must worship Him in spirit and in truth"* (Jn. 4:24).

(10) "YOU WHO LOVE THE LORD, HATE EVIL: HE PRESERVES THE SOULS OF HIS SAINTS; HE DELIVERS THEM OUT OF THE HAND OF THE WICKED."

This statement certainly can be taken literally by any Believer; however, the pointed direction made by the Holy Spirit refers to the Battle of Armageddon, the Antichrist, and God's great Deliverance of His people.

THE ANTICHRIST

The *"evil"* spoken of here pertains to the

Antichrist. Israel will be deceived at the beginning by thinking that the man of sin is the Messiah. They will sign a seven-year non-aggression pact with him. Paul said they will at that time say, *"Peace and safety."* However, their *"peace and safety"* will not last long: *"Then sudden destruction comes upon them, as travail upon a woman with child; and they shall not escape"* (I Thess. 5:3). Israel will then realize that she has been duped. She will realize the one they think is righteous really is *"evil."*

The preservation spoken of here will be twofold:

1. At this time (midway through the Tribulation) the Antichrist will attack Israel. Many will be killed. Israel will vacate Jerusalem for the time being and will flee into the wilderness, *"where she has a place prepared of God"* (Rev. 12:6). That place is *"Petra,"* located where modern Jordan now is. It is about fifty miles south of the Dead Sea.

2. The Second Coming of the Lord, which will take place during the Battle of Armageddon.

At this time, the Lord will *"deliver them out of the hand of the wicked,"* that is, the Antichrist.

(11) "LIGHT IS SOWN FOR THE RIGHTEOUS, AND GLADNESS FOR THE UPRIGHT IN HEART."

By and large, the world has known nothing but darkness. Now it will know *"light."* The Coming of the Lord will bring *"gladness"* to the entirety of the Planet.

(12) "REJOICE IN THE LORD, YE RIGHTEOUS; AND GIVE THANKS AT THE REMEMBRANCE OF HIS HOLINESS."

At long last, God's *"Holiness"* will be the foundation of His Kingdom.

HOLINESS

The word *"Holiness"* really means that everything will be set apart for His Service. Every single thing done will be at His Direction. Satan will be locked away in the bottomless pit, along with all his demon spirits and minions of darkness. It will be a time of *"light"* and *"gladness"* such as the world never has known — Heaven on Earth. The whole world will *"rejoice in the LORD and give thanks."*

NOTES

PSALM 98

Author Unknown:
Praise to God for His Salvation

(1) "O SING UNTO THE LORD A NEW SONG; FOR HE HAS DONE MARVELOUS THINGS: HIS RIGHT HAND, AND HIS HOLY ARM, HAS GOTTEN HIM THE VICTORY."

As noted, the author of this Psalm is unknown.

THE NEW SONG

This glorious *"New Song"* will salute Jehovah Messiah on that Millennial Morn and will have three voices:

1. Israel: This nation of old, God's chosen people, will sing a *"New Song"* concerning the *"marvelous things"* the Lord has done. After over 2,000 years of rebellion, Israel at long last will come home to her God and her Messiah.

2. The Gentiles: The Messiah will govern the Earth with Righteousness and the nations with Equity. Well may men sing at the prospect of such a rule! Previously they never have enjoyed a government which has exhibited righteousness and equity.

3. Nature: Paul wrote, *"For we know that the whole Creation groans and travails in pain together until now"* (Rom. 8:22). It groans because of the Fall (Gen., Chpt. 3). At the beginning of the Millennial Reign, nature no longer will be convulsed; for the first time, it will respond to its Creator in harmony.

THE CROSS AND ELEMENT JUDGMENTS

As I dictate these notes, it is November 7, 2005. In the last year or so, the world has seen a convulsion of the elements as it seldom has seen or known in the past. The tsunami of December 2004 saw upwards of 250,000 people instantly killed. For the first time in modern American history, an entire city, New Orleans, Louisiana, was completely destroyed by a hurricane. A few days ago, an earthquake struck the subcontinent of Asia and killed nearly 75,000 people. And then a couple of nights ago, a tornado ripped through the State of Indiana, laying waste entire sections of the countryside and killing a number of people. What was striking about this tornado was that the tornado season ended last June.

What is happening to the elements?

Of course, history records these happenings from the very beginning, and some have been much worse even than those just mentioned. However, I think the pattern we presently are seeing is a little different than what has been seen or known in the past. For example, there were more major hurricanes in the 2005 hurricane season than ever before since records started being maintained.

TWO REASONS FOR THE GREAT
DISTURBANCE OF THE ELEMENTS

First of all, our Lord Himself predicted that toward the end, *"There shall be famines, and pestilences, and earthquakes, in divers places. All these are the beginnings of sorrows"* (Mat. 24: 7-8).

Despite that fact that these things have existed from the beginning, the Lord's Words imply that there will be an increase in the last of the last days — the days in which we now live. We are seeing that come to pass.

Among other things, this tells us that we are living in the very closing days of the Church Age. The great Prophecies of the Prophets and Apostles of the past, such as the Rapture, the rise of the Antichrist, the Great Tribulation, the Battle of Armageddon, and the Second Coming are about ready to come to pass. In other words, we are living on the very eve of the fulfillment of these things.

If that is correct, the elemental disturbances will not only not diminish, but they will increase and intensify.

Second, the only thing that stands between mankind and eternal Hell, or one might say, the total Judgment of God, is the Cross of Christ. God is unalterably opposed to sin in every form and description. Sin is the ruination of the universe, the ruination of all that is good. And the only answer for sin is the Cross of Calvary.

I firmly believe that one of the major reasons for the increase of the disturbance in the elements is because the Cross of Christ

NOTES

is no longer, or very little, preached. The Cross alone holds back judgment; however, if it is ignored or denied, this removes the only protective device for the world.

To be sure, the proper preaching of the Cross would not stop all elemental disturbance; however, I definitely do believe it would slow it down. But tragically, the Cross is little being preached!

VICTORY

The *"victory"* that is spoken of in Verse 1 of this Psalm is victory over the Antichrist, the world, the flesh, and the Devil.

"His Right Hand, and His Holy Arm" refer to our Lord's almighty Power. Basically, the same phrase was used in the Song of Moses whenever the Lord delivered Israel from Egypt (Ex. 15:6).

The Holy Spirit is comparing Israel's great Deliverance from the Antichrist to Israel's Deliverance from Egypt. The Victory also can be stretched to include Victory over every power of darkness by modern Believers. It can be done only through Christ and the Cross.

Jesus said: *"You shall know the Truth, and the Truth will make you free"* (Jn. 8:32).

John the Beloved wrote and said, *"And this is the victory that overcomes the world, even our Faith"* (I Jn. 5:4).

The *"faith"* of which John here writes pertains to Faith in Christ and what Christ did for us at the Cross. Belief in the Finished Work of Christ gives the Holy Spirit, Who Alone can bring about the desired victory, latitude to work in our lives to achieve it (Rom. 8:2).

This *"victory"* is available to every single Believer. All one has to do is to understand that every single thing we receive from God comes to us from Christ as the Source and the Cross as the Means. The Lord cannot give anything to Believers, or anyone, for that matter, except by and through the Cross. It is the Cross which has made it all possible.

JESUS CHRIST AND THE CROSS

Christ had to be the Son of God; this was absolutely necessary. But as significant a fact as that obviously is, that alone brings no Redemption. In fact, our Lord has always been the Son of God, meaning that He always has been God. However, even though He was, and is, the Son of God, that alone effected no Deliverance for anyone. For Deliverance to be effected, the full payment for sin had to be offered, and that was the Sacrifice of Himself (Heb. 10:5-15). If man was to be redeemed, the Cross had to be.

It was at the Cross that all sin was atoned and all victory was won. The Cross opened the door for God to give all things to His people.

To be sure, before the Cross, which includes all of Old Testament times, God definitely did give things to individuals during those times. But He did it, one might say, on credit. In other words, it all was done with the Cross ever in view, because there the debt would be paid (Gen. 3:15; 15:6).

The Believer must understand that every single thing that comes to us (and I mean every single thing!) from God is made possible (always, and without exception!) by the Cross (I Cor. 1:17-18, 23; 2:2; Gal., Chpt. 5; 6:14; Col. 2:14-15).

(2) "THE LORD HAS MADE KNOWN HIS SALVATION: HIS RIGHTEOUSNESS HAS HE OPENLY SHOWED IN THE SIGHT OF THE HEATHEN."

The word *"Salvation"* has a far greater meaning that even most Christians realize.

SALVATION

Salvation actually means *"deliverance"* from the powers of sin, Satan, and darkness, all made possible by the Cross of Christ, and made possible only by the Cross of Christ. That's the reason that all of man's efforts to save himself are little more than putting a Band-Aid over a cancer.

Man is hopelessly bound up by the powers of darkness; he can in no way be set free by his own strength, power, education, or intellect. Only Jesus Christ and His mighty Power can set the captive free (Lk. 4:18). Consequently, the Church, with all of its ceremony, has not one iota of Salvation in it. Neither does education, power, or money. There is no Salvation in this present world. All Salvation comes from God and was bought, purchased, and brought about in its entirety by the Death, Resurrection, and

NOTES

Victory of our Lord and Saviour, Jesus Christ.

Every person who ever has been Saved has always been Saved in the same manner. In the Old Testament, men were Saved by looking forward to Calvary. Now men are Saved by looking backward to Calvary. It was at Calvary where Jesus Christ won the victory. He paid the price there for man's Redemption. He satisfied all claims that God had against man. What Christ did at the Cross appeased God's Anger against man, which was there because of sin. With all sin atoned, that anger was lifted, and rightly so! Now *"whosoever will, let him take the Water of Life freely"* (Rev. 22:17).

RIGHTEOUSNESS

The *"Righteousness"* addressed in this Second Verse of this Psalm concerns the tremendous Victory that will be won by the Lord Jesus Christ in His defeat of the Antichrist at the Battle of Armageddon. This will be obvious *"in the sight of the heathen,"* that is, *"all nations."*

(3) "HE HAS REMEMBERED HIS MERCY AND HIS TRUTH TOWARD THE HOUSE OF ISRAEL: ALL THE ENDS OF THE EARTH HAVE SEEN THE SALVATION OF OUR GOD."

As the nations of the world in olden times witnessed with wonder the birth of the Twelve Tribes, so will they see with astonishment their Restoration. These are the marvelous things, the Victory, the Salvation, the Righteousness, the Mercy, and the Truth which are celebrated in Verses 1 through 3. All the nations of the world will be summoned to sing in unison with nature as they witness the *"Salvation of our God."*

(4) "MAKE A JOYFUL NOISE UNTO THE LORD, ALL THE EARTH: MAKE A LOUD NOISE, AND REJOICE, AND SING PRAISE."

The world has ever attempted its celebrations; however, they ring with a hollow sound. At long last, there is a true *"joyful noise"* because the Lord Himself is the Author of this celebration.

THE JOYFUL NOISE

Not only will this *"noise"* be *"joyful,"* but it also will be *"loud"* because it will be worldwide in worship, scope, and adoration.

For the very first time in the sordid history of the world's rebellion against God, in the coming Kingdom Age, the world will now truly have something to *"rejoice"* about. Moreover, all will *"sing praise"* unto the Lord. For over six millennia, the world has sung praise unto Satan. Now Satan is totally defeated and locked away in the bottomless pit. The praise now will go to its Rightful Owner, the Lord Jesus Christ.

What a happy day it will be, when the entirety of Planet Earth is singing praises unto the Lord! Hallelujah!

No wonder she will sing praises. There will be no more poverty, sin, sickness, and suffering. Death will have been defeated. All that man has striven mightily to do, but has failed so miserably in his efforts, will, at long last, be brought to fruition — and all by the Lord Jesus Christ and what He did for us at Calvary's Cross.

(5) "SING UNTO THE LORD WITH THE HARP; WITH THE HARP, AND THE VOICE OF A PSALM.

(6) "WITH TRUMPETS AND SOUND OF CORNETS MAKE A JOYFUL NOISE BEFORE THE LORD, THE KING."

The world then will be filled with music — but music unto God.

MUSIC

The very structure of music has within it the incorporation of the Divine Trinity. The sound of music is combined under three headings, all given by God:

1. Melody: This speaks of an ordered structure of sound that is referred to as the *"tune"* or *"melody."*

2. Harmony: This has to do with the accompanying voices or instruments regarding the different parts of music, such as lead, alto, bass, or tenor. It is interesting to note that before the Death and Resurrection of Christ, most music was written in the minor keys. All of the Psalms, for example, were written before Christ and basically were written in minor keys.

After His Death and Resurrection, the writing of music gradually shifted from the minor keys to the major keys. It was as though the Holy Spirit was making a statement through this all-important aspect of worship called music. Since the Cross and the Resurrection, man has a far greater opportunity to be in harmony with God.

3. Rhythm: This has to do with the measured beats, of which many of the Psalms, and with which most music is written today. For example, if a song is written in 4/4 time, it means there are four beats to each measure. If it is written in eights, it means there are eight beats to each measure.

All of this, if used properly, is of God and is accepted by Him as a part of our worship. Greatly so, we might quickly add!

In the 1970's, and especially in the 1980's, modern contemporary Christian music, so-called, became a part of the *"Christian"* scene. (The word *"contemporary"* means that it corresponds with its counterpart in non-Christian music.) In other words, it was borrowed from the world, brought into the Church, and made a part of what is referred to as *"worship."* However, it was not worship of God, but rather of Satan.

Satan does borrow from God, but God never borrows from Satan. It is, therefore, virtually impossible to worship God by or with contemporary music. There are two reasons for this, which have nothing to do with taste or style, which are as follows:

CONTEMPORARY CHRISTIAN MUSIC

First of all, this type of music was borrowed from Satan. It can, therefore, have no part in the worship of God.

Many of the so-called artists who feature this type of music consider the rock groups of this age as their heroes. These are the musicians they choose to emulate. It should be overly obvious, I think, that this cannot be of God.

How can that which is obviously of the Devil be ordained of God?

Concerning such, the Apostle Paul said, and I quote from THE EXPOSITOR'S STUDY BIBLE:

"You cannot drink the Cup of the Lord, and the cup of devils (if we are going to associate with demons, the Lord will not remain)*: you cannot be partakers of the Lord's table* (the Lord's Supper), *and of the table of devils* (that which the world offers)" (I Cor. 10:21).

Second, in contemporary music, the ordered structure of melody, harmony, and rhythm instituted by the Holy Spirit has been altered or distorted, which means it is no longer the same as that which was originally ordained by God.

In contemporary Christian music, so-called, the melody has been tampered with until it no longer follows a prescribed pattern. The harmony also has been disturbed. Consequently, the ordered, structured spirit of man recreated by the Holy Spirit cannot favorably respond to such disorder, and true Biblical worship is not possible.

Some have presented the argument that contemporary Christian music is only a tool to reach the youth, but that argument has no validity. That would be the same as using alcohol to try to reach the drunk, or using gambling to reach the gambler, or using drugs to reach the drug addict. That is really just another one of man's ridiculous ways, and not a very clever one, at that! It only will lead to death (Prov. 16:25).

(7) "LET THE SEA ROAR, AND THE FULLNESS THEREOF; THE WORLD, AND THEY WHO DWELL THEREIN.

(8) "LET THE FLOODS CLAP THEIR HANDS: LET THE HILLS BE JOYFUL TOGETHER."

These two Verses proclaim ordered Nature for the first time in human history.

NATURE

For the first time in history, in the coming Kingdom Age, Nature will be at one with God.

The harmony of Nature was interrupted at the Fall (Gen., Chpt. 3; Psalm 8). From that time until now, it has not functioned properly. As a result, the world has been overwhelmed with drought, earthquakes, famines, storms, hurricanes, and tidal waves. Nature, as created by God, was not created in this manner. It became this way at the Fall, and now actually answers to Satan.

Even though God uses Nature, and has, at times, changed Nature according to believing prayer, still, the world never has known what God's ordered, structured Nature really is. In the Millennial Reign, God's Nature (and we speak of the elements) will, for the first time, function properly.

(9) "BEFORE THE LORD; FOR HE COMES TO JUDGE THE EARTH: WITH RIGHTEOUSNESS SHALL HE JUDGE THE WORLD, AND THE PEOPLE WITH EQUITY."

This Verse tells us that during the coming Kingdom Age, all class struggle will be eliminated.

CLASS STRUGGLE

God's *"Judgment"* will be a fair judgment — with all the people of the world being judged equally. In today's climate, even under the best of circumstances, and with the best intentions of human judges, there still is little justice and little true judgment. When the Righteous Judge comes back, the world will know true, honest, and equal judgment for the first time. Then there will be no tiny few amassing the riches of the world while the far greater majority live in poverty and don't even have enough to eat. All caste systems will be done away with.

Communism, which actually is a religion inspired by Satan, claimed to eliminate the *"class struggle."* It not only did not eliminate it, it actually nurtured and increased it. Christ truly will do away with all *"class struggles."*

Democracy claims to address itself to those evils that always have plagued man, and democracy has come closer to achieving this goal than any other philosophy. But even in the very heart of democracy, bias, prejudice, and racism are all rampant.

Even though Congress passes legislation which endeavors to address these ills, and even though the Judicial Branch attempts to carry out the legislation, still the problem is very little ameliorated. The reason is simple; these age-old problems of man cannot be solved by legislation. It is not a problem of good laws or bad laws, but a problem of bad hearts — and only God can change a person's heart. The answer is not the laws which Congress can produce, or the interpretations of the laws by the Judicial Branch, and neither is it education, of which man thinks so highly. The answer alone is the Lord Jesus Christ, Who Alone can change men. With Him Alone can there be *"equity."*

PSALM 99

*Author Unknown:
Admonitions to Fear, Praise,
and Worship God*

(1) "THE LORD REIGNS; LET THE PEOPLE TREMBLE: HE SITS BETWEEN THE CHERUBIMS; LET THE EARTH BE MOVED."

It is not known who wrote Psalm 98 or Psalm 99. David very well could have, but there is nothing in the title or instructions to give any clues.

THE LORD REIGNS

The song of the previous Psalm is made possible because of the proclamation of Psalm 97 and Psalm 99, *"The LORD reigns."* This simply means that the Lord reigns in Zion and that He has established justice, judgment, and righteousness in Jacob. This pertains to the beginning of the great Millennial Morn.

This Psalm concerns Jehovah Messiah, Who bears in His Hand the title deed of the Earth (Rev. 5:5). At this time, He will ascend His Throne, to which are attached the Cherubim uttering their cry of *"Holy, Holy, Holy."* Then men and Angels in the Creation will fall and worship at His Feet. This Psalm corresponds with Revelation, Chapters 4 and 5. All of this pertains to the coming Kingdom Age!

(2) "THE LORD IS GREAT IN ZION; AND HE IS HIGH ABOVE ALL THE PEOPLE."

Animated by this great vision, the pilgrim company joyfully shouts, *"Jehovah takes the Kingdom."*

THE DEITY OF THE MESSIAH

The meaning of the statement, *"High above all the people,"* refers to the Deity of the Messiah. Although He is Very Man, still, He also is Very God. Man has ever tried to assuage his own problems. He has never succeeded. Only the One Who is *"high"* can do so. No wonder Gabriel, the mighty Angel Who stands in the Presence of God, proclaimed, *"You shall call His Name JESUS: for He shall save His people from their sins"* (Mat. 1:21).

Of all the glorious names given to God in the Bible, the Name *"Jesus"* is the most glorious of all. All of His other Names speak of His attributes. The Name of *"Jesus"* speaks of His Finished Work as the Saviour of man. No wonder it is said, *"The LORD is great."*

(3) "LET THEM PRAISE YOUR GREAT AND TERRIBLE NAME; FOR IT IS HOLY."

This Verse speaks of worship.

WORSHIP

The Cherubim in the Fourth Chapter of Revelation announce the Kingdom and its Judgments with a thrice-repeated *"Holy."* This triple *"Holy"* marks the three stanzas of the Psalm. The first (Vs. 3) states the reason why the nations should praise the Messiah; the second (Vs. 5) shows why Israel should praise Him; and the third (Vs. 9) repeats the motive why all nations should praise Israel's God and Lord.

Williams says, *"In the first three Verses, Israel invites the nations to come to Zion and worship the King; in the following five Verses, she invites her own Twelve Tribes to worship at His footstool; and in the last Verse she repeats the invitation of the nations and emphasizes the important command that the place of worship is to be Zion's Holy Hill."* [46]

(4) "THE KING'S STRENGTH ALSO LOVES JUDGMENT; YOU DO ESTABLISH EQUITY, YOU EXECUTE JUDGMENT AND RIGHTEOUSNESS IN JACOB."

This Verse proclaims how the Lord can change people and situations.

EQUITY

The power of the King shall be employed, as portrayed in this Verse, on behalf of judgment, equity, and righteousness. This is not true of earthly governments and monarchs.

The word *"equity"* is used repeatedly by the Holy Spirit in these Psalms, meaning that the Lord of Glory will at long last bring equality to this Earth.

THE LORD CAN CHANGE MEN AND SITUATIONS

The name *"Jacob"* was oftentimes used by the Holy Spirit in place of the name *"Israel."* The meaning is clear; as the Lord changed *"Jacob"* from a schemer to a Prince with God, likewise He will change National Israel.

As the Lord changed Jacob of old, He can likewise change any man or any situation, that is, if men will believe Him.

Part of the great rejoicing of the previous Chapter will be from the Glorified Saints who were changed by the Power of the Living God. They could not change themselves, but God changed them. He is the only One Who can turn hate into love, selfishness into unselfishness, Hell into Heaven, poverty into plenty, sin into Salvation, and death into life. He truly is the Deliverer; He is the only Deliverer, and it is all done by and through the Cross.

(5) "EXALT YE THE LORD OUR GOD, AND WORSHIP AT HIS FOOTSTOOL; FOR HE IS HOLY."

In the Third Verse it says, *"His Name is Holy,"* and in this Verse it says, *"He is Holy."* All the nations of the world are given the invitation to worship the Holy One. For the first time in history, the nations of the world will then respond favorably.

(6) "MOSES AND AARON AMONG HIS PRIESTS, AND SAMUEL AMONG THEM WHO CALL UPON HIS NAME; THEY CALLED UPON THE LORD, AND HE ANSWERED THEM."

There is a great lesson in this Verse portrayed by the Holy Spirit. We would do well to exercise the great Truth here given.

TWO DIVINE PRINCIPLES

Moses actually exercised the office of Priest before Aaron (Ex. 24:6-8). He even consecrated Aaron (Ex., Chpt. 28), so both of them were among His Priests.

Samuel represents the Prophets. This is very touching and very important. The Holy Spirit recognizes and brings forward those who in the past were true to His Communications despite national and ecclesiastical apostasy.

These men figure together all who loved and trusted the Messiah in the past, and who were faithful to His Word. These three, of course, died thousands of years ago; but, true to His Promise, they will appear with Him in the Glory of His Kingdom, and along with them, all whom they represent and who exercised the faith they exercised. This is consolation to all who at any time trust the Promises of God. The consolation is the greater when one notices that Verse 8 declares these great Saints had been sinners, that is, weak and erring sinful men, not sinless men.

Williams says, *"Therefore, two great Divine principles appear in these Verses. One, that God forgives confessed sin; the other, that He judges its action. Sin may be forgiven, but its consequences must be reaped. However, the consequences are ordained by God, and not by man."* [47]

(7) "HE SPOKE UNTO THEM IN THE CLOUDY PILLAR: THEY KEPT HIS TESTIMONIES, AND THE ORDINANCE THAT HE GAVE THEM."

Another great Truth is here given.

ORDINANCES AND TESTIMONIES

All of these men in some way broke the *"Testimonies"* and the *"Ordinances."* However, their hearts were not tuned to rebellion, but to God; consequently, the Holy Spirit judged them in the light of Justification by Faith and called them righteous when they had no righteousness. So it could be said of them that as Christ kept these *"Testimonies"* and *"Ordinances,"* they entered into His Victory and were accorded the same by the Holy Spirit.

(8) "YOU ANSWERED THEM, O LORD OUR GOD: YOU WERE A GOD WHO FORGAVE THEM, THOUGH YOU TOOK VENGEANCE OF THEIR INVENTIONS."

God always forgives sin upon proper Confession and Repentance. He also forgets that which has been done in the past and wipes the slate clean as though it never had been done. But still, sin is never to be looked at with impunity. Its consequences must always be reaped.

Verses 6, 7, and 8 have a special message for the heart. They reveal that the new-born Israel of the future will be identified with the faithful Israel of the past. The child of Ruth will be hailed as a son born to Naomi. When it was hard for Naomi to speak by faith, she called herself *"Mara,"* which means *"bitter"* (Ruth 1:20). Now this will be forgotten because Naomi has come home.

(9) "EXALT THE LORD OUR GOD, AND WORSHIP AT HIS HOLY HILL; FOR THE

LORD OUR GOD IS HOLY."

This Passage is basically the same as Verse 5. *"His footstool"* is *"His Holy Hill."* Still, the Holy Spirit is not engaging in vain repetition. The Fifth Verse extols Israel to worship Him; the Ninth Verse extols the nations of the world to praise Israel's God and Lord.

As we repeatedly have stated, Israel's purpose was threefold:

1. To give the world the Word of God, which they did.

2. To be the womb of the Messiah, which they were, though with great difficulty.

3. To evangelize the world: In this they failed, but they will fulfill this Purpose and Plan at long last when they invite the nations of the world to come and worship their God, which will take place in the coming Kingdom Age.

PSALM 100

Author Unknown:
A Call to Praise the Lord

(1) "MAKE A JOYFUL NOISE UNTO THE LORD, ALL YE LANDS."

Seven times in the Psalms, men are commanded to make a joyful noise unto God (66:1; 81:1; 95:1-2; 98:4-6; 100:1).

IN THE KINGDOM AGE, THE WORLD WILL BE ONE

"Seven" is God's number; it speaks of totality, completion, perfection, fulfillment, and universality. This speaks of Christ reigning supreme in the coming great Kingdom Age.

Every country in the world will then serve Him. There will be no such thing as one country or area being Muslim, and another part being Hindu, and another part something else. All will be followers of Christ. When He comes, the whole Earth will make a joyful noise unto Him. Because He has not yet come, a dreadful noise of weeping, quarreling, and mutual slaughter ascends continually to Heaven. His Advent will put an end to the reign of sin and its visible fruit.

(2) "SERVE THE LORD WITH GLADNESS: COME BEFORE HIS PRESENCE WITH SINGING."

Then the themes of the world will be *"gladness"* and *"singing."* What a change from the present!

In the Kingdom Age, Christ will reign from Jerusalem. Emissaries from all over the world will be constantly coming to this great City. By the thousands, they will enter into His Presence with singing. It will be a never-ending *"joyful noise"* — and rightly so!

A PERSONAL EXPERIENCE

Some time ago, I was in Washington D.C. If I remember correctly, we were there to meet with the President about a certain situation, which we did. At any rate, I happened to be in the Old Executive Office Building, which is near the White House.

A man walked up to me and asked if I would come into one of the side rooms and address a Jewish conclave that then was taking place. I agreed to do so.

A friend and I walked into a very large room, which was completely packed with people. There must have been 500-600 Jewish leaders from all over the nation present on that particular day. I don't know exactly why they were there, but they asked me to speak to them for a few minutes.

What I am about to say was not my idea, but actually was an idea given to me by my friend who accompanied me into the room. He was a Jewish Christian and a Preacher of the Gospel.

Because everyone present knew me through the Telecast, when I was introduced, the response was a mixture of approval and disapproval. Many knew of my strong support for Israel, but they also knew of my stand for the Lord Jesus Christ, which doesn't go over in a great way with Jews.

At any rate, I greeted this group of very influential Jewish Rabbis and businessmen. Then I made the following statement, given to me by my friend:

"Here we are, gathered together in Washington, D.C., the city of freedom for the entire world." I elaborated on that for a few minutes, and then continued, *"But there is coming a day shortly when the entire world no longer will look to Washington, D.C. as*

the citadel or fortress of freedom, but rather will look to Jerusalem, D.C."

Most of the Jews in that large room look puzzled when I used the term *"Jerusalem, D.C."* They evidently never had heard it used in this manner.

Seeing the consternation on their faces, after a short pause, I said, *"Jerusalem, D.C., David's Capital."*

I won't forget that moment. There was a hush that settled over the entire congregation. You could have heard the proverbial pin drop. Those in the front row were close enough for me to see that they had tears in their eyes. Then they broke into applause.

And that is true. In the coming Kingdom Age, the entire world will look to *"Jerusalem, D.C., David's Capital."* But there will be a great change that the Jewish people now do not recognize. Then, the Lord Jesus Christ, Jehovah Messiah, will be the ruling Master, not only of this City, but also of all of Planet Earth. Israel, in totality, will accept Him as Messiah, Saviour, and Lord.

(3) "KNOW YE THAT THE LORD HE IS GOD: IT IS HE WHO HAS MADE US, AND NOT WE OURSELVES; WE ARE HIS PEOPLE, AND THE SHEEP OF HIS PASTURE."

Many things are said in this Psalm that will yet be sung on the Millennial Morn. They are as follows:

1. Jesus Christ is God, not Buddha, Muhammad, or any other foolish man-made or Satan-made fake deity.

2. We are the product of His Hand, and not a product of senseless, mindless evolution.

3. He saved us; we could not save ourselves.

4. We are His people. We belong to no other.

5. We who constitute the sheep will forage in His Pasture. This will be a pasture which He has provided, which He Alone can provide, and which was made possible by the Cross.

(4) "ENTER INTO HIS GATES WITH THANKSGIVING, AND INTO HIS COURTS WITH PRAISE; BE THANKFUL UNTO HIM, AND BLESS HIS NAME."

As the song continues, Israel was to carry out this command, singing the song in the old economy of God. They almost never succeeded in doing so.

NOTES

ISRAEL'S GREAT FEAST DAYS

Israel of old was commanded by God to send representatives from each household and from each Tribe to Jerusalem on three occasions during the year.

The first occasion incorporated three Feasts: Passover, Unleavened Bread, and Firstfruits. It took place during our March or April, and covered about eight days. It was the time of the barley harvest.

The second gathering took place in either the latter part of May or the early part of June, some fifty days after Passover. At this occasion, the Feast of Pentecost was celebrated. It was the time of the wheat harvest.

The third gathering included Atonement, Trumpets, and Tabernacles; it lasted for approximately twenty-one days. It took place in our months of September or October. It was the time of the fruit harvest.

In all, there were seven great Feasts, each typical of Christ and a great Work that He would carry out. Four of these Feasts, in type, have been fulfilled; three have not.

They are as follows:

THE PROPHETICAL MEANING OF THE FEASTS

1. Passover: This was fulfilled with Christ's Death on Calvary.

2. Unleavened Bread: This was a Type of Christ's Perfect Body given in Sacrifice, hence, the word *"unleavened."*

3. Firstfruits: This was a Type of Christ's Resurrection, which guarantees the Resurrection of all Believers.

4. Pentecost: This was a Type of the Outpouring of the Holy Spirit on the Day of Pentecost, with Christ as the Baptizer (Mat. 3:11).

5. Trumpets: This is a type of the Rapture, when Christ will come back for His Saints. The Trumpet blast also will signal the beginning of the Restoration of Israel (I Thess. 4:16-17).

6. Atonement: This is a type of the cleansing of Israel, which will take place at the beginning of the Kingdom Age, which will take place immediately after the Second Coming of Christ. In actuality, Atonement was fulfilled at Calvary, but will not be complete until Israel is cleansed, which they will be at the beginning of the Kingdom Age.

7. Tabernacles: This is a type of coming Millennial Reign, when Christ will reign supreme over the entirety of the world.

The last three Feasts are yet unfulfilled, a fact which is obvious!

At these Feasts, or whenever anyone came to Jerusalem into the Temple to offer up Sacrifice to the Lord, they were to enter into the *"gates"* of Jerusalem with *"thanksgiving."* And then whenever they entered the *"courts"* of the Lord, which were very close to the Brazen Altar and the Brazen Laver, they were to enter with constant *"praises."*

As stated, Israel little kept these Commandments of the Lord; however, on that Millennial Morn, they will at long last and forever carry out that which was ordained so long ago by the Holy Spirit.

(5) "FOR THE LORD IS GOOD; HIS MERCY IS EVERLASTING; AND HIS TRUTH ENDURES TO ALL GENERATIONS."

Three things are said in this Passage:

A DESCRIPTION OF THE LORD

1. *"For the LORD is good"*: Now He is pictured as anything but good. Satan has very cleverly and skillfully deceived the world into believing that God is not good. At the beginning of the Kingdom Age, when the Lord reigns, then the world will know that He is *"good."*

2. *"His Mercy is everlasting"*: What a beautiful statement! Mercy is a product of Grace. There will be no restraints, time limits, or portions allotted to *"Mercy."* It is *"everlasting."*

3. *"His Truth endures to all generations"*: Christ is Truth; consequently, as He reigns, His Truth will never be abrogated. It will endure to all generations and henceforth forever. Hallelujah!

PSALM 101

*A Psalm of David:
The King's Manifesto*

(1) "I WILL SING OF MERCY AND JUDGMENT: UNTO YOU, O LORD, WILL I SING."

As noted, David wrote this Psalm.

THE PERSONAL PERFECTION OF CHRIST

This Psalm plus the following Psalms through 106 complete the fourth Book (the Numbers Book). They portray the Character and Capacity of the King to Whom is to be given the Kingdom. These Psalms show how He was to be tested by suffering, whether Personal or sympathetic.

David, who wrote this Psalm and was a Type of Him, was also tested by suffering. The Messiah's fitness for the Throne, His sympathy with all who fear God, and His opposition to evil and evildoers are set out in this third group. The King pledges Himself in this first Psalm of the group to reign with Mercy for the righteous (Vs. 6) and with Judgment for the wicked (Vss. 3-5 and 7-8). These activities will characterize His Government (Williams).[48]

His Personal Perfection is the subject of the first two Verses of this Psalm. His Love for Jehovah, His loyalty to Mercy and Judgment, His intelligent course of Conduct with a Perfect Heart and a Perfect Way, in which Abraham was commanded to walk and be Perfect (Gen. 17:1), prove His Personal suitability to exercise the government of the whole Earth.

As David says these words, the Son of David, in effect, is saying them.

(2) "I WILL BEHAVE MYSELF WISELY IN A PERFECT WAY. O WHEN WILL YOU COME UNTO ME? I WILL WALK WITHIN MY HOUSE WITH A PERFECT HEART."

David could only desire these things; Christ was these things.

WISE BEHAVIOR

The expression, *"Behave myself wisely,"* was said of David several times while Saul was attempting to kill him (I Sam. 18:5, 14-15).

David was a Type of Christ. Saul was a type of the evil Pharisees and Sadducees who attempted to kill Christ. As David behaved himself wisely, Christ, the Greater Son of David, behaved Himself wisely. David's way was not perfect; however, the Way of the Son of Man was *"A Perfect Way."* He also had *"A Perfect Heart."* David could only desire these things; Christ <u>was</u> these things, *"The Perfect Way and Perfect Heart."*

David, by faith, could say this of himself because he would enter into the great victory won by Christ, as any Born-Again Believer can do and must do. God can settle for nothing less than perfection. And perfection is found only in Christ!

(3) "I WILL SET NO WICKED THING BEFORE MY EYES: I HATE THE WORK OF THEM WHO TURN ASIDE; IT SHALL NOT CLEAVE TO ME."

This was the heart of David, although not always his actions. It must be the heart of every Believer.

Man looks on the outward; God looks on the heart (I Sam. 16:7). This was the cry of David and the action of the Messiah.

TURNING ASIDE FROM THE WORD OF GOD

The *"turning aside"* has to do with deviating from the Word of God, which is the action of the modern Church.

The Sadducees denied the Word of God. The Pharisees twisted the Word of God and also added to it. Christ said that He hated their work.

The besetting sin of the modern Church is this: *"Turning aside from the Word of God."*

The Bible must be the criteria, the bottom line, so to speak, for all things. If it is not Scriptural, then it's not legitimate, and it must be discarded.

For example, despite the fact that almost every Church in the U.S.A. and Canada is embracing the *"Purpose Driven Life"* scheme, it simply is not Scriptural. The same can be said for the *"Government of Twelve"* and the *"Word of Faith."* *"Denominationalism"* falls into the same category, which speaks of those who put their trust in a Denomination instead of the Word of God.

(4) "A FROWARD HEART SHALL DEPART FROM ME: I WILL NOT KNOW A WICKED PERSON."

The word *"froward"* means *"perverse"* or *"wicked."*

FALSE APOSTLES

The sense of this Verse is that Christ would never agree to or place approval upon the perverseness of the Scribes, Sadducees, and Pharisees. Those who *"turned aside"* with a *"froward heart"* were, therefore, classified in the Mind of Christ as a *"wicked person."* His every Action and His every Message were in constant opposition to the Pharisees and their ilk. They hated Him for it and they determined to kill Him.

Presently, true Preachers of the Gospel must be opposed to everything that is unscriptural. The reasons should be obvious.

The end result of such direction will not be a mere mendacity, but rather destruction.

The Holy Spirit laid down the pattern for Preachers when He told the Prophet Ezekiel that he must warn both the unrighteous and the righteous. If they heard his Message and ignored it, at least the Prophet would have delivered his soul. If he did not warn them, they still would die in their sins; but the Holy Spirit also made the awful pronouncement, *"But his blood will I require at your hand"* (Ezek. 3:18).

Prophets generally fill this role, even in this modern age. To be sure, they seldom are liked and appreciated, but mostly criticized, caricatured, and cut off from the balance of so-called Ministry. To be sure, there is not much Scriptural evidence in the Bible of Prophets predicting blessings and positive things. Generally, it is the opposite. That's the reason they are hated!

Moreover, the calling to account must not be left only to the Prophets, but really is the responsibility of every single Preacher, at least if he is to be true to his calling. The Preacher must call to account with as much diplomacy and kindness as he can muster, but he still must be crystal-clear about what he is saying. No one should have any doubt about what he is talking about or whom he is talking about. The souls of men are at stake, so the Message must be crystal-clear.

(5) "WHOSO PRIVILY SLANDERS HIS NEIGHBOR, HIM WILL I CUT OFF: HIM WHO HAS A HIGH LOOK AND A PROUD HEART WILL NOT I SUFFER."

This could apply to anyone, but its greater fulfillment pertains to the action of the Scribes, Sadducees, and Pharisees who slandered Christ.

SLANDER

In this one Verse, we find the entirety of

the foundation of Satan's work. First of all, the very meaning of the word *"Satan"* means *"slanderer."* He lost his high position as one of God's choice Angels (the most beautiful) because of pride. All of his followers, who certainly included the Scribes, Sadducees, and Pharisees, will suffer Satan's fate. This also would include all those who are self-righteous and self-willed.

The word *"slander"* means to use the tongue to defame, abuse, scandalize, belittle, or blacken the character of another. The religious leaders of Israel slandered Christ constantly. It is one of Satan's favorite weapons.

There are commands in the Bible against slander (Ex. 23:1; Deut. 22:13-18; James 4:11; I Pet. 2:1).

The three causes of slander are:
1. An evil heart (Lk. 6:45);
2. Hatred (Ps. 109:3); and,
3. Idleness (I Tim. 5:13).

(6) "MY EYES SHALL BE UPON THE FAITHFUL OF THE LAND, THAT THEY MAY DWELL WITH ME: HE WHO WALKS IN A PERFECT WAY, HE SHALL SERVE ME."

As always, a great Truth is given to us in this Verse.

THOSE WHOM THE LORD CHOOSES

Christ said He would put His Eyes on the *"faithful of the land"* and not upon the ruling religious hierarchy. Those who were faithful could *"dwell"* with Him. Those who walked in His *"perfect way"* would serve Him. In selecting His Disciples, He completely ignored the ruling religious hierarchy of Priests, Pharisees, Scribes, and Sadducees. He rather chose men with humble occupations, men such as Simon Peter, and even a hated tax-collector and publican by the name of Matthew.

The same can be said regarding those whom He chooses at present. Christianity is broken up into various beliefs constituting various Denominations. These Denominations constantly lay their hands on individuals to signify their approval. These seldom are recognized by God because they are man-chosen and not God-chosen.

Conversely, those whom God lays His Hand on are seldom, if ever, recognized by institutionalized religion. The same opposition that Christ received from the religious hierarchy of His Day will be brought against God's chosen by the religious hierarchy of today.

(7) "HE WHO WORKS DECEIT SHALL NOT DWELL WITHIN MY HOUSE: HE WHO TELLS LIES SHALL NOT TARRY IN MY SIGHT."

Regrettably, most organized religion works from a foundation of *"deceit."* It functions as its master, Satan, by *"telling lies."*

This definitely applies to anyone; but, more specifically, it is pointed toward the religious hierarchy of those who opposed Christ in His earthly Ministry.

RELIGIOUS LEADERS

The religious leaders of Jesus' day would have been given the highest marks regarding reputation and integrity; however, they murdered the Lord of Glory. How could this be?

Their reputation and integrity were all man-made and man-bestowed. It was not a reputation or integrity that was recognized by God.

This is possibly Satan's greatest effort. He attempts to substitute something of his own making for that of God's making. Too often he succeeds. In the modern Church, most of that which goes under the guise of morality, integrity, honesty, salvation, sanctification, and justification are, sadly, of the man-made variety, which are not recognizable by God. The clues are obvious.

That which is recognized by man is seldom recognized by God; conversely, man, even religious organizations, generally will not recognize that which God does.

The modern Christian must be very careful that what he is supporting is not man-devised and unacceptable to God. Those who *"work deceit"* and *"tell lies"* are those who have *"turned aside"* (Vs. 3) from the Word of God.

Much more pointedly, this Seventh Verse points forward to the Antichrist, who will attempt to dwell in the House of God, working his deceit (II Thess. 2:4, 9).

(8) "I WILL EARLY DESTROY ALL THE WICKED OF THE LAND; THAT I MAY CUT OFF ALL WICKED DOERS FROM THE CITY OF THE LORD."

At the very beginning of the Millennial

Reign, Christ will put down the *"wicked of the land."* All doers of wickedness shall not be allowed in *"the City of the LORD."*

JUDGMENT AND JUSTICE

Because man's definition of wickedness so often deviates from the Word of God, this statement, if uttered by man, would be extremely dangerous. Nevertheless, the Lord of Glory utters these Words; He does so with a *"Perfect Way"* and a *"Perfect Heart"* (Vs. 2).

Judgment and justice without bias, favoritism, or prejudice will assure all the rightness of His Commandments. This never has been done on Planet Earth. As a matter of fact, it could not be done. But the Lord of Glory will carry it out.

It is ironic that the Pharisees called Him wicked and attempted to destroy Him. In reality, they were the wicked, and they were destroyed. Their destruction by Titus the Roman General in A.D. 70 was a fore-glimpse of the coming destruction of *"the wicked"* (Antichrist) in the Battle of Armageddon.

PSALM 102

*Author Unknown:
A Prayer of Penitence*

(1) "HEAR MY PRAYER, O LORD, AND LET MY CRY COME UNTO YOU."

It is not known who wrote this Psalm. It has no title.

THE REJECTED SAVIOUR

The subject of this Psalm is twofold. The glories of Christ as the Great King are contrasted with His Sufferings as the rejected Man. Here, as in so many other Scriptures, His Sufferings and glories, always in that order, are brought together.

It was necessary that He should be both the Man of Sorrows and the Mighty God. As the One, He is equipped with Mercy; as the other, with Judgment. He is the Afflicted One of the superscription.

(2) "HIDE NOT YOUR FACE FROM ME IN THE DAY WHEN I AM IN TROUBLE; INCLINE YOUR EAR UNTO ME: IN THE DAY WHEN I CALL ANSWER ME SPEEDILY."

NOTES

Both Verses 1 and 2 pertain to Christ as Very Man, the Perfect Sacrifice, although He never ceased to be Very God. He spent the entirety of His earthly Ministry as Very Man, The Man Christ Jesus. As such, He cried to His Heavenly Father for help from His many sufferings.

This is difficult for the unspiritual ear to hear. The writer of Hebrews, however, said, *"To make the Captain of their Salvation perfect through sufferings"* (Heb. 2:10). When He became Man, He did not take upon Himself the *"nature of Angels,"* but He took upon Himself *"the Seed of Abraham"* (Heb. 2:16).

(3) "FOR MY DAYS ARE CONSUMED LIKE SMOKE, AND MY BONES ARE BURNED AS AN HEARTH."

Williams says, *"The sufferings experienced by the Messiah, as evidenced in Verses 1 through 11, introduce His Glories as Redeemer, while those of Verses 23 and 24 show His Glories as Creator."* [49]

The sufferings He endured from the opposition of virtually all of Israel, especially the religious hierarchy, literally consumed Him. He felt their rejection down to His *"bones."* It was said of Him, *"The world was made by Him, and the world knew Him not"* (Jn. 1:10).

(4) "MY HEART IS SMITTEN, AND WITHERED LIKE GRASS; SO THAT I FORGET TO EAT MY BREAD."

As Christ dealt with a lost world and was destitute over their spiritual condition, the Scripture says, *"In the mean while His Disciples prayed Him, saying, Master, eat"* (Jn. 4:31).

(5) "BY REASON OF THE VOICE OF MY GROANING MY BONES CLEAVE TO MY SKIN."

In the Garden of Gethsemane, the Word says, *"And began to be sorrowful and very heavy"* (Mat. 26:37). The writer of Hebrews says, *"Who in the days of His flesh, when He had offered up prayers and supplications with strong crying and tears unto Him Who was able to save Him from death, and was heard in that He feared"* (Heb. 5:7). This tells us that the entirety of His earthly Ministry was filled with such consternation because of the terrible sin of the people, especially the religious leaders.

(6) "I AM LIKE A PELICAN OF THE WILDERNESS: I AM LIKE AN OWL OF THE DESERT."

What is meant by this statement?

SELF-RIGHTEOUSNESS

Both the *"pelican"* and the *"owl"* were unclean fowls; they were, therefore, unacceptable. The idea of this Passage is that Christ was treated by the religious hierarchy like an unclean fowl.

How could religious men who claimed to keep the Law of Moses, and who were, in fact, the religious leaders of Israel, be so mistaken about the very Lord of Glory?

Their problem was self-righteousness, and it is the problem of the modern Church. They who should have known the truth were without excuse.

In studying the Prophecies of Daniel, they knew that the Messiah was to be born at approximately this time. In their mind's eye, however, they could not conceive of a peasant being the Messiah. He did not fit their stereotype — in other words, He was not one of them.

RELIGION

Religion is a cruel business. Religion is always man-made and never can be accepted by God. The Pharisees who claimed to be the spiritual leadership of Israel had twisted the Word of God and added to it, so that it little resembled what had originally been given by God. Today, likewise, religious leaders love to make rules and regulations that have no foundation in the Word of God whatsoever. They also enjoy forcing men to obey these rules. This spirit even characterized the Disciples in the last days of Jesus' earthly Ministry (Lk. 22:24).

(7) "I WATCH, AND AM AS A SPARROW ALONE UPON THE HOUSE TOP."

A little sparrow would seldom be seen alone unless its mate had been killed or its nest and young destroyed.

Basically, Christ was alone. Even though He was surrounded by Disciples and others, still, they little knew His Mission until after the Crucifixion and Resurrection. When He suffered on Calvary, all His Disciples forsook Him and fled (Mat. 26:56).

NOTES

(8) "MY ENEMIES REPROACH ME ALL THE DAY; AND THEY WHO ARE MAD AGAINST ME ARE SWORN AGAINST ME."

The Scribes and Pharisees, as is evident from this Verse, bound themselves by an oath to destroy Him.

THE GREATEST OPPOSITION TO THE WORK OF GOD

How could these religious leaders seek to kill the One Who had done nothing but preach the Gospel to the poor, heal the brokenhearted, preach Deliverance to the captives, recover the sight of the blind, and set at liberty them who are bruised? (Lk. 4:18). They did it because their hearts were evil — grossly evil!

It will come as a shock to most, but the greatest sin and opposition to the God of Glory and His Work are not in the bars, houses of ill fame, or from those who live in obvious and open sin. The greatest opposition to God and His Work comes from that which calls itself the Church. Actually, Satan's best work is done through the apostate Church. In fact, most of that which calls itself *"Church"* really is apostate.

No! God neither condones nor looks favorably on any sin. But still, Jesus said, *"The publicans and the harlots go into the Kingdom of God before you"* (Mat. 21:31). The *"you"* which He was talking about were the Pharisees.

Was Jesus condoning the sins of the publicans and harlots? No! He was not!

His point was that these individuals knew they were sinners. Some of them would repent. The self-righteous Pharisees never admitted they were sinners. In their minds, they did not need to repent. Jesus said of them, *"When you had seen it, repented not afterward, that you might believe him"* (Mat. 21:32).

How many Church leaders have you ever seen repent? There have been a few, but not many. Actually, the modern Church cannot even abide repentance. Why not?

REPENTANCE

Repentance is an ugly business. One must admit he is a sinner and is in desperate need of a Redeemer. Self-righteousness does not know what to do with such because it brings shame and reproach to its self-righteous ranks.

Jesus said that when one repents, his Ministry begins (Rev. 2:5). A self-righteous Church says if one repents, his Ministry ends.

What a contrast!

(9) "FOR I HAVE EATEN ASHES LIKE BREAD, AND MINGLED MY DRINK WITH WEEPING."

Someone has said that the saddest words ever uttered are, *"And you will not come to Me, that you might have Life"* (Jn. 5:40).

THE TWOFOLD SORROW OF CHRIST

The great sorrow of our Lord was twofold: first, Israel's rejection of Him; and second, what it would mean to them. By their rejection of Him, they would bring upon themselves swift and horrible destruction. Luke said He beheld Jerusalem and wept over it (Lk. 19:41). He wept because of the great destruction that He predicted, a great destruction that was coming due to their rejection of Him, the Lord of Glory.

This destruction would be the sack of Jerusalem by the Roman General Titus in A.D. 70, which would result in over one million Jews dying in that siege, and other hundreds of thousands being sold as slaves all over the world. The suffering was incalculable, as would be overly obvious. That's why He wept!

Let it be understood: All enemies of the Cross also face destruction. Sadly and regrettably, this pertains to almost the entirety of the modern Church (Phil. 3:18-19).

(10) "BECAUSE OF YOUR INDIGNATION AND YOUR WRATH: FOR YOU HAVE LIFTED ME UP, AND CAST ME DOWN."

On the Mount of Transfiguration, He was *"lifted up,"* for the Voice said, *"This is My Beloved Son."* And on the Mount of Condemnation (Calvary), He was *"cast down,"* for He cried, *"Why have You forsaken Me?"*

(11) "MY DAYS ARE LIKE A SHADOW THAT DECLINES; AND I AM WITHERED LIKE GRASS."

He did not come to live; He came to die. But in His Death, He brought Eternal Life.

THE REASON JESUS CAME

It would be very difficult for the modern Faith Message to understand, or even believe, Verses 1 through 11 concerning Christ.

One religious leader has said that Christ headed up a huge business conglomerate, and all His Disciples were rich.

How does that fit with Verses 1 through 11?

Another religious leader said that Jesus died to *"glorify His self-esteem"*! When we turn aside from the Word of God, false doctrines abound.

(12) "BUT YOU, O LORD, SHALL ENDURE FOREVER; AND YOUR REMEMBRANCE UNTO ALL GENERATIONS."

Whereas Verses 1 through 11 spoke of His First Advent, Verses 12 through 22 speak of His Second Advent. As the First was in suffering and sorrow, the Second will be in glory and victory.

Verse 12 is in response to Verse 11. The Holy Spirit says, *"But You, O Jehovah, shall sit enthroned as King forever."* He then goes on to foretell the Restoration of Israel.

(13) "YOU SHALL ARISE, AND HAVE MERCY UPON ZION: FOR THE TIME TO FAVOR HER, YEA, THE SET TIME, IS COME."

The *"set time"* for Israel's Restoration began in 1948. She was then finally restored again as a nation. It will come to fruition in the Battle of Armageddon. It will seem like Jerusalem and Israel will be completely destroyed. At that time, Israel will cry out to God for her Messiah. He then *"will arise"* and *"have mercy upon Zion"* (Rev., Chpt. 19).

(14) "FOR YOUR SERVANTS TAKE PLEASURE IN HER STONES, AND FAVOR THE DUST THEREOF."

The great love of Israel for their beloved Zion is expressed here.

JERUSALEM

This Passage is even carried over today in the fact that modern Israel desires the world to look at Jerusalem as her capital. But the United States and many other nations do not do this for fear of offending the Arabs. Regrettably, America does not understand Israel's concern for Jerusalem regarding her past, her present, or her future.

(15) "SO THE HEATHEN SHALL FEAR THE NAME OF THE LORD, AND ALL THE KINGS OF THE EARTH YOUR GLORY."

This will take place in the coming

Kingdom Age, and will continue forever and forever (Isa. 2:2-4; Dan. 2:44-45; Zech., Chpt. 14; Rev. 11:15; 22:4-5).

(16) "WHEN THE LORD SHALL BUILD UP ZION, HE SHALL APPEAR IN HIS GLORY."

This Passage is presently being fulfilled before our very eyes.

THE BUILDUP OF ZION

In 1948, Israel became a nation again, after nearly 2,000 years of wandering as outcasts all over the world. Hitler's efforts to exterminate the Jews in World War II were Satan's great effort to stop this fulfillment of Prophecy. He did not succeed, but it was not for lack of trying.

Despite almost every nation in the world being opposed to modern Israel, with the new President of Iran even stating, *"Israel must be wiped off the face of the map,"* this tiny country, about the size of the State of Connecticut, continues to grow. As stated, all of it is in fulfillment of Bible Prophecy.

Israel is God's prophetic time clock. The status of Israel pretty well tells the Church the timeframe of the Prophecies concerning the Endtime. Jesus likened Israel to a *"fig tree."* He said, *"When his branch is yet tender, and puts forth leaves, you know that summer is near"* (Mat. 24:32).

Israel is now putting forth leaves, so we know that we are living in the last of the last days.

These are the last days of the Church Age. All events and signs point to the Restoration of Israel, which actually will not take place until the Second Coming. From this, we know the Rapture is going to take place very, very soon! (I Thess. 4:13-18).

(17) "HE WILL REGARD THE PRAYER OF THE DESTITUTE, AND NOT DESPISE THEIR PRAYER."

The *"destitute"* spoken of here pertains to Israel in the Battle of Armageddon. God will hear their prayer at that time and will answer it. The answer will be the Second Coming!

(18) "THIS SHALL BE WRITTEN FOR THE GENERATION TO COME: AND THE PEOPLE WHICH SHALL BE CREATED SHALL PRAISE THE LORD."

This Verse has to do with the coming Kingdom Age. All the babies that will be born during that time will be raised to praise the Lord. What a difference between now and then!

Beginning with the Kingdom Age and continuing with the Perfect Age, as described in the final two Chapters of the Book of Revelation, this world finally will function as God intended for it to function in the very beginning. Satan and all of his minions of darkness, which include all fallen angels and demon spirits, will be locked away in the bottomless pit during the Millennial Reign, and then transferred to the Lake of Fire in the Perfect Age, which will last forever and forever (Rev. 20:1-3, 10).

(19) "FOR HE HAS LOOKED DOWN FROM THE HEIGHT OF HIS SANCTUARY; FROM HEAVEN DID THE LORD BEHOLD THE EARTH."

The sense of this Verse is twofold:

1. The very mission of Christ to Calvary was to set the captive free that *"whosoever will may drink of the Water of Life freely."*

2. This specific meaning of this Passage through Verse 22 is that God will see Israel's plight in the latter half of the Great Tribulation, especially in the Battle of Armageddon, when He will come to their rescue.

(20) "TO HEAR THE GROANING OF THE PRISONER; TO LOOSE THOSE WHO ARE APPOINTED TO DEATH."

This pertains to the efforts by the Antichrist to completely annihilate Israel. He will attempt to do what Hitler called the *"final solution."* At that time (the Battle of Armageddon), Israel will literally be *"appointed to death."* It is called *"The Time of Jacob's Trouble"* (Jer. 30:7). But, in that same Passage, Jeremiah also said, *"He shall be saved out of it."*

The Antichrist will reckon, but without God. Instead of Israel being *"appointed to death,"* the Antichrist will be *"appointed to death."*

(21) "TO DECLARE THE NAME OF THE LORD IN ZION, AND HIS PRAISE IN JERUSALEM."

The purpose of the Lord will be threefold:

THE RESTORATION OF ISRAEL

1. *"To loose those who are appointed to death."*

2. *"To declare the Name of the LORD in Zion."*

3. *"And His praise in Jerusalem."*

When Israel rejected Christ in His First Advent, the Lord withdrew His visible Protection of Israel. They actually said they didn't want that protection. They said, *"We have no king but Caesar"* (Jn. 19:15). Caesar has proven to be a hard taskmaster!

(22) "WHEN THE PEOPLE ARE GATHERED TOGETHER, AND THE KINGDOMS, TO SERVE THE LORD."

The sense of this Verse is the Glory of the Millennial Morn. Satan's day is over. He is locked away in the bottomless pit. The demon spirits of darkness that have clouded Planet Earth for so long also are locked away. Now the purpose of the nations will be *"to serve the LORD."*

(23) "HE WEAKENED MY STRENGTH IN THE WAY; HE SHORTENED MY DAYS.

(24) "I SAID, O MY GOD, TAKE ME NOT AWAY IN THE MIDST OF MY DAYS: YOUR YEARS ARE THROUGHOUT ALL GENERATIONS."

This Passage has two meanings:

1. It refers first of all to the Messiah in His earthly Ministry and the price He paid for the Deliverance of humanity. He was about thirty-three years old when the Lord delivered Him (Rom. 8:32), so He was taken away in the *"midst of His days."*

2. It also refers to Israel as referred to in Verses 12 through 22. Israel's days were shortened because of sin. Israel was meant to be a light *"throughout all generations,"* but she herself extinguished that light. Jesus Himself said to the Church, *"Repent, and do the first works; or else I will come unto you quickly, and will remove your candlestick out of his place, except you repent"* (Rev. 2:5).

He removed Israel's candlestick, exactly as He has removed, and will continue to remove, the candlestick of many Churches.

(25) "OF OLD HAVE YOU LAID THE FOUNDATION OF THE EARTH: AND THE HEAVENS ARE THE WORK OF YOUR HANDS."

We aren't told here when all this was done. Whenever Genesis 1:1 says, *"In the beginning, God created the heavens and the Earth,"* this does not tell us exactly when that *"beginning"* was. If science honestly can prove that the Earth is a billion years old, or a trillion years old, this will not contradict the Word of God.

Whenever the beginning was, the Lord devised it and did it. We speak of all that was needed to create this Earth and all of the heavens. All of this tells us that this Creation is not the product of mindless evolution. One of the greatest sins in this modern age is the sin of unbelievers in fostering the ungodly lie of the evolutionary fabrication. On the surface, it is a joke. When examined even in a cursory fashion, it becomes even more ridiculous.

They may talk about the *"missing link,"* but the truth is, the whole chain is missing. If evolution is true, where are the intermediary specimens? The idea that it takes billions of years to bring about all of these things still does not negate the fact that if evolution is a true science, there would be beings of different stages. There are none. There never have been any. And there never will be any.

Most biologists and scientists know that evolution is a lie. However, if they come out and say so, it could cost them their jobs. So they say nothing!

(26) "THEY SHALL PERISH, BUT YOU SHALL ENDURE: YEA, ALL OF THEM SHALL WAX OLD LIKE A GARMENT; AS A VESTURE SHALL YOU CHANGE THEM, AND THEY SHALL BE CHANGED."

This Passage tells us something about Planet Earth.

A FACT OF CREATION

The word *"old"* in the Hebrew is *"balah."* It means *"to fail, decay, to waste away."* The meaning of *"balah"* is never *"annihilation,"* but *"a gradual change because of wear and tear."*

The heavens and Earth are made of materials that wax old and decay. The idea here is that they are being affected by sin and the bondage of corruption. They will be renewed and liberated from this corrupt state to a new and eternal state and will be kept eternally new when all sin is put down (I Cor. 15:24-28) and everything is restored as before the curse. There will be no more curse or bondage of corruption after this (Rom. 8:21-24; Heb. 1:10-12; Rev. 21:1; 22:3).

(27) "BUT YOU ARE THE SAME, AND YOUR YEARS SHALL HAVE NO END."

The material creations that have been cursed and brought under the bondage of corruption to wax old will, of necessity, be renewed and changed to the state of eternal newness. God, however, will never wax old. He will never need to be renewed. He is eternally the same.

These events, that is, the material creations being *"made new,"* occur at the beginning of the Perfect Age. Peter addressed it (II Pet. 3:10-13).

(28) "THE CHILDREN OF YOUR SERVANTS SHALL CONTINUE, AND THEIR SEED SHALL BE ESTABLISHED BEFORE YOU."

This has a twofold meaning:
1. It refers to Israel that will be restored and will worship God forever.
2. It refers to all Believers, which includes Israel and the True Church.

It means that eternal generations of natural people shall continue upon Planet Earth forever and will be established. The Plan of God for the human race was not cancelled by the Fall (Gen., Chpt. 3), but only was delayed. That which God formerly intended will be carried out in its totality. God has never lost a battle. In truth, He cannot lose!

PSALM 103

David is the Author:
Thanksgiving to the Lord

(1) "BLESS THE LORD, O MY SOUL: AND ALL THAT IS WITHIN ME, BLESS HIS HOLY NAME.

(2) "BLESS THE LORD, O MY SOUL, AND FORGET NOT ALL HIS BENEFITS."

David penned the words of this Psalm, but the Author is the Holy Spirit. He composes the words for the hearts and tongues of lovers of Immanuel by framing the language so as to be a personal and fitting expression of worship and praise. The title also declares the relationship of the Psalm to the Messiah.

REDEMPTION

The Messiah's benefits to sinful and sorrowing men occupy the first place in the Psalm — they are six in number (Vss. 1-5).

The subject of this Psalm is Redemption. It begins with a thanksgiving unto the Lord for all that He has done. The word *"bless"* in the Hebrew is *"barak."* It means *"to kneel, to bless as an act of adoration to God or man."* It begins with a cry from the very soul, *"all that is within me,"* giving praise to *"His Holy Name."*

We are admonished to *"forget not all His benefits."* These benefits are many. They are listed in the next three Verses, and are as follows:

1. *"Who forgives all your iniquities."*
2. *"Who heals all your diseases."*
3. *"Who redeems your life from destruction."*
4. *"Who crowns you with lovingkindness and tender mercies."*
5. *"Who satisfies your mouth with good things."*
6. *"So that your youth is renewed like the eagles."*

Let's look at them one by one:

(3) "WHO FORGIVES ALL YOUR INIQUITIES; WHO HEALS ALL YOUR DISEASES."

There are two great Promises in this particular Verse.

THE FORGIVENESS OF SIN

The forgiveness of sin is placed at the top of the list, and rightly so. Man's greatest problem is sin and its guilt. God's greatest gift to man is redeeming him from sin. This was done at the Cross, and is what makes the Cross the very foundation of Christianity. Without the Cross, there is no forgiveness, no cleansing from sin. Without the Cross, the sin debt never would have been paid, and this spiritual sword of Damocles would have forever hung over the heads of humanity.

Unfortunately, much of the modern Church is ignoring the Cross and trying to face sin in other ways. They try to address the subject by simply not addressing it. In other words, they ignore the factor of sin as though it does not exist.

Others claim that preaching on sin will

create a sin-consciousness, so sin should never be mentioned. Others claim that if sin is mentioned, it might offend the unsaved people, so better not even mention it.

In spite of these ridiculous and absurd directions which most of the modern Church take, sin is still the factor that is *"stealing, killing, and destroying."* It is the greatest problem for the human race, and it also is the greatest problem for the Christian.

Other than God cleansing and washing sin away upon proper confession and Repentance, which He does by and through the Means of Christ and the Cross, there is no panacea for sin.

The Catholic Church openly states that *"the Church saves,"* which means that if one keeps all the ceremonies, rules, regulations, dogmas, and creeds of the Catholic Church, he will be saved. This is blatantly unscriptural and spurious. The Protestant world, however, is little different.

Millions of Baptists believe that their association with the Baptist Church saves. Yes, they teach the acceptance of Jesus Christ; but, at the same time, they add to it the necessary association with their particular organization. In other words, it is Jesus *"plus"*! Many Pentecostals fall into the same category.

THE CHURCH

Some time back, I overheard a Preacher who was ordained with one of the small Pentecostal Denominations. He repeatedly used the phrase, *"The Church."* By the phrase, *"The Church,"* he was referring to his own Denomination.

I did not question him about it, so I have no idea what his true thoughts were. Nevertheless, by the use of the phrase, *"The Church,"* to speak of his own particular Denomination, he was implying that this earthly institution carried some type of spiritual connotation. It doesn't, and neither does any Church body. However, the far greater majority of those who call themselves *"Christians"* think that by associating themselves with some particular Denomination, this constitutes, in some way, a part of their Salvation. It does not! Actually, if that truly is their thought (and, in the hearts of many, it is!), then it actually has the opposite effect.

NOTES

Paul addressed himself to this in the Epistle to the Galatians. He said, *"Christ is become of no effect unto you, whosoever of you are Justified by the Law; you are fallen from Grace"* (Gal. 5:4).

Many would argue that their attitudes and beliefs regarding particular Church Denominations have nothing to do with the *"Law of Moses."* However, while it doesn't in principle, it does in spirit.

Anyone who is placing any dependence whatsoever on anything other than Jesus Christ and what He has done for us at the Cross is *"fallen from Grace."* It is a sobering statement, but it is true.

FALLEN FROM GRACE

Most people have an erroneous idea of what *"fallen from Grace"* actually means.

Some time back, I heard two Preachers on Television discussing this very subject. They came to the conclusion that committing certain types of sin constituted falling from Grace. Those Preachers were dead wrong!

Falling from Grace means to fall from the position to where the Grace of God can be extended to us, and on an unending basis. The position by which Grace is extended to any Believer is one's faith in Christ and what Christ has done for us at the Cross. When we maintain Faith in Christ and the Cross, then this maintains a constant, uninterrupted flow of Grace to our hearts and lives.

The Galatians to whom Paul wrote were turning their faith from Christ and the Cross to something else. (He wrote scathingly, I might quickly add.) They were being encouraged by false teachers to do so. The great Apostle tells the Galatians (plus you and me) that if we place our faith in anything other than Christ and the Cross, the result will be catastrophic; in that event, the Grace of God, without which we cannot live this Christian experience, will be stopped within our lives!

No! Committing certain types of sins, other than rebellion against Christ and what He has done for us at the Cross, does not constitute falling from Grace. Actually, such a person is the very person who needs the Grace of God. As stated, falling from Grace occurs when one places his faith in something (anything) other than exclusively in

Christ and the Cross.

Every Believer must understand that every single thing we receive from God comes to us through Christ as the Source and the Cross as the Means.

THE LAW

The Pharisees of Jesus' day believed that their strict adherence to the *"Law"* guaranteed them Salvation. To be sure, they were far more meticulous about and faithful to their religious structure than most modern Church members. But, still, it did not save them whatsoever. Every one of them who depended on such died lost.

While most modern Christians are not entangled with the Law of Moses as were the Pharisees, still, *"Law"* continues to be the problem. It may not be the Law of Moses, but it is *"Law"* — law that we make up ourselves, or our Church devises, or our religious Denomination, or other Preachers, etc.

Let's say it another way:

The Lord considers anything and everything that's not faith in Christ and what Christ did at the Cross as *"Law."* Regrettably, that's where most modern Christians are. Such a position constitutes spiritual wreckage. The Believer simply cannot live for God in this fashion, at least not successfully.

But yet, most Christians never think of the little rules and regulations which they themselves devise as being *"Law,"* and as being off-base. But they are!

These particular things might actually be good within themselves. However, when we place our faith in them, whatever they might be, this means that we are not keeping our faith in Christ and the Cross, but rather something else, which the Lord can never accept. It is either *"Law"* or *"Grace."* It cannot be both!

IS IT WRONG TO ASSOCIATE ONESELF WITH A CHURCH DENOMINATION?

No, it is not wrong, as long as one understands that any and all Church Denominations are strictly man-made and carry no spiritual qualifications whatsoever. Ideally, all Church Denominations (organized religion) merely are tools, and should function only in an administrative capacity. If all adherents involved in organized religion understand this, there is no harm. In this case, one can associate with, or disassociate from, any particular religious Denomination with no spiritual harm.

Satan is very subtle. He desires that people not believe the Word of God at all. However, if people insist on believing it, he desires and attempts to get them to twist the Word or accept some false belief or doctrine that will damn their soul. He succeeds tremendously well.

Only God can forgive sins; neither men, Preachers, Priests, Churches, Denominations, nor religious orders have absolutely anything to do with it.

Any unsaved person at any time or any place can accept Jesus Christ as his own personal Saviour, and God instantly will pardon, cleanse, wash, and forgive any and all sin (Rom. 10:9-10, 13). Likewise, any Christian can at any moment and at any place ask the Lord to forgive him of any sin he has committed, and instantly it will be done (I Jn. 1:9).

DIVINE HEALING

Concerning the latter portion of the Third Verse, *"Who heals all your diseases,"* the question must be asked, *"Did Christ bear our sicknesses, as well as our sins, on the Cross?"*

The Fifty-third Chapter of the Book of Isaiah carries the account of what Christ did for mankind at Calvary:

"He bore our griefs." The word *"griefs"* actually means *"sicknesses."*

Some have argued that this does not mean sicknesses; however, the quotation and fulfillment of this Prophecy in Matthew 8:16-17 proves that the bearing of sicknesses and infirmities was physical and not spiritual healing only.

At the Atonement, Jesus truly addressed every single thing that man lost at the Fall. Nothing was left out and nothing was eliminated. Everything was included.

Our Lord not only addressed everything that Adam lost, His Sacrifice at Calvary also addressed Satan and all his cohorts of darkness, actually going to the very cause of all sin in mankind.

Paul said:

"And having spoiled principalities and

powers, *He made a show of them openly, triumphing over them in it"* (Col. 2:15).

The great Apostle also said: *"That in the dispensation of the fullness of times, He might gather together in one all things in Christ, both which are in Heaven, and which are on Earth, even in Him"* (Eph. 1:10).

When Jesus died on the Cross, He addressed not only the need of man, what man lost at the Fall, and everything that man lost at the Fall, but He also addressed Satan's revolution. The Atonement of Christ was so thorough, so complete, so absolute, and so perfect that the Holy Spirit through Paul referred to it as *"The Everlasting Covenant"* (Heb. 13:20). This means the Atonement will never have to be changed, amended, or replaced. It is *"everlasting."*

At this moment, we do not yet have all for which He paid such a price; we only have the *"firstfruits"* (Rom. 8:23). The balance will come at the Resurrection. But now, we do have enough to live the life we ought to live and to experience blessings unparalleled. If we do not partake of that for which the Lord Jesus Christ has paid such a price, it is our fault, and not the fault of the Lord.

Considering the price that Christ paid, don't you think He wants us to have all for which He has paid this great price?

THE CROSS OF CHRIST

The way all of this is obtained, that is, everything He did for us in the Atonement, is that our faith must rest securely within Christ and the Cross. This is absolutely imperative. The modern Church, unfortunately, is not preaching the Cross. It is preaching anything and everything but the Cross! As a result, most of that today which passes for *"Church"* is man-conceived, man-devised, man-led, and man-operated. As a result, the Holy Spirit has very little to do with what presently is taking place.

And, to be sure, the worst thing that can happen to a Church, any Church, is that it can function pretty well without the Holy Spirit.

God help us! That is the plight of the modern Church. It functions pretty well without the Holy Spirit. Never mind that lives aren't changed. The machinery functions at an unprecedented pace, that is, it looks like great things are happening, but, in reality, nothing is happening.

(4) "WHO REDEEMS YOUR LIFE FROM DESTRUCTION; WHO CROWNS YOU WITH LOVINGKINDNESS AND TENDER MERCIES."

Another great Truth is here presented.

REDEEMING THE LIFE

The word *"redeem"* means to purchase something back that has been lost through debt, default, or failure to pay. It has the same idea as man *"hocking"* a valuable item for a specified sum of money and then going back at a later time to redeem the item by paying the specified sum.

In the Garden of Eden, man *"hocked"* his soul to Satan for a specified promise. Satan promised man Eternal Life (Gen. 3:4-5), but Satan lied! Instead he gave man eternal death (Gen. 2:17). Actually, Adam and Eve already had Eternal Life by virtue of the Tree of Life, which grew in the midst of the Garden, and which was a Type of Christ.

Then man attempted to redeem what he had lost and found that the price was far higher than he ever could hope to pay (Gen. 3:7). Sadly, man has been trying to pay for his own Redemption ever since. He ever fails, but he keeps trying.

Even at the beginning, God promised that He would redeem man from his terrible fallen state (Gen. 3:16). That Promise was the Coming of Christ; man was saved by believing the Promise of the Coming Lord. Then, upon the fulfillment of time, God sent His Son, Christ Jesus, Who paid the price for fallen humanity (Jn. 3:16). This means that in the Mind of God, every single human being who ever has lived was redeemed at Calvary — that is, if they will believe it and accept it. Some few believe; most don't! Those who believe are redeemed instantly from destruction.

By rights, we should receive just punishment for the many sins we have committed. But instead Christ took the punishment upon Himself and then He crowns us with *"lovingkindness and tender mercies."* This is so great and wonderful that it defies description.

(5) "WHO SATISFIES YOUR MOUTH

WITH GOOD THINGS; SO THAT YOUR YOUTH IS RENEWED LIKE THE EAGLE'S."

Then, and only then, is the craving in man's heart finally *"satisfied."* Someone has said, *"The soul of man is so big that only God can fill it up."* Then the renewal of our youth takes place. This does not mean that the individual will not grow old or that time will roll back. It has the following two meanings:

THE EAGLE

1. The Holy Spirit uses the *"eagle"* as an example. Once a year, eagles cast off their old feathers and receive new ones; therefore, despite their age, they have a continual look of youthfulness. Likewise, when an individual accepts Christ and becomes a new creature, the guilt of sin is removed, and the redeemed one always has a youthful spirit!

2. Now that Eternal Life has come, in spite of the aging process, the Child of God looks forward to the moment when *"mortality puts on immortality."* This will come at the First Resurrection of Life (I Thess. 4:16-17).

So, in Verses 3 through 5 the Lord *"forgives, heals, redeems, crowns, satisfies, and renews"* all who come to Him. What a Blessing!

(6) "THE LORD EXECUTES RIGHTEOUSNESS AND JUDGMENT FOR ALL WHO ARE OPPRESSED."

All who are without God are *"oppressed."* The word *"oppressed"* has to do with Satan's heavy hand upon the human race. In other words, the way is hard, very hard; however, whenever one comes to Jehovah, the Covenant God, the Lord sets about to deliver the *"oppressed one."* He does two things:

DELIVERANCE

1. The Lord executes Righteousness. This means that whereas individuals had no righteousness of their own and could in no way obtain such, yet the Lord freely imputes *"Righteousness"* to the one who has been *"oppressed"* (Rom. 4:22-25).

2. Our Lord executes Judgment. The Judgment is twofold:

In the first place, God judged His Own Son, Jesus Christ, in order that we would not have to be judged. Fallen man had already been judged, and the penalty was death.

NOTES

In the second place, Satan was judged in that he has no more hold on redeemed man. Therefore, the *"oppressed"* go free.

THE CROSS OF CHRIST IS THE MEANS OF DELIVERANCE

Sin is the means by which Satan holds mankind in bondage. In other words, he has the legal right to do what he does because of man's sin. However, when Jesus went to the Cross, he went there to atone for all sin, past, present, and future, at least for all who will believe (Jn. 3:16).

In the offering up of Himself, He satisfied the claims of a thrice-Holy God, which means that Satan lost the legal right he had, as it regards captivity and bondage, due to the fact that all sin has now been atoned. This left him totally and completely defeated, plus all of his minions of darkness, be they fallen angels, demon spirits, or both!

That being the case, why is it that many Christians, even though they are truly Born-Again and Spirit-filled, are held in bondage to the powers of darkness? If Jesus has atoned for all sin, which removed Satan's legal right to hold man in bondage, how can man continue to be in bondage?

WHY CHRISTIANS ARE IN BONDAGE?

Satan is able to keep Christians in bondage because, in effect, he has their consent. It is not consent as we normally think of consent, but rather that these Christians have neglected or ignored God's Prescribed Order of Victory.

That Prescribed Order of Victory is *"Jesus Christ and Him Crucified"* (I Cor. 1:23). Some would read these words and say, *"You people act like the Cross is the answer to every problem!"*

Whoever would think that is now beginning to get the Message. That's exactly right! The Cross, and the Cross alone, is the answer to every single problem.

If the Believer understands that it is the Cross (and the Cross alone) which contains his victory, he now is on the right path. He will then place his faith in the Cross and not allow it to be moved, which then will give the Holy Spirit latitude to work in his life. Considering that the Holy Spirit is God, he quickly will begin to find what victory is all about.

This is God's only Way.

It is the *"Cross"*! The *"Cross"*! The *"Cross"*!

(7) "HE MADE KNOWN HIS WAYS UNTO MOSES, HIS ACTS UNTO THE CHILDREN OF ISRAEL."

Natural intelligence can recognize Divine *"Acts,"* but only to the spiritual mind does God make known His *"Ways."*

GOD'S WAYS AND GOD'S ACTS

The Church too often settles for God's *"Acts"* instead of finding out His *"Ways."* Paul said, *"That I may know Him"* (Phil. 3:10).

Most seek God for what He can do, that is, if they seek Him at all! However, the ever constant effort of the Holy Spirit is to bring the Believer to the place where he seeks God for Who He is — in other words, *"relationship."*

When Jacob left Canaan to go into Syria, he met God at a particular place and called it *"Bethel,"* which means *"The House of God"* (Gen. 28:19). Here he was learning what God could do. Some twenty years later, Jacob came back to the same place. Once again, there was a visitation from the Lord. Now, Jacob calls the place *"El-Bethel"* (Gen. 35:7), which means *"The God of the House of God."*

Twenty years before, Jacob was aware of God's *"Acts."* Now, some twenty years later, he is beginning to be aware of God's *"Ways."* He had learned what God could do, and now he learns Who God is.

(8) "THE LORD IS MERCIFUL AND GRACIOUS, SLOW TO ANGER, AND PLENTEOUS IN MERCY."

In this and the following Verses, God outlines His Dealings with Israel in the wilderness and even in the Land. His Dealings also are thus with us. This Verse says He is four things:

GOD'S WAYS

1. *"Merciful"* — withholding punishment we rightly deserve for our wrongs.

2. *"Gracious"* — showing Grace, meaning unmerited favor.

3. *"Slow to anger"* — when our repeated failures should make Him angry, they do not.

4. *"Plenteous in mercy"* — mercy that never is exhausted.

(9) "HE WILL NOT ALWAYS CHIDE: NEITHER WILL HE KEEP HIS ANGER FOREVER."

No matter what has happened, if the Believer will humble himself and confess his wrongdoing, the Lord will discontinue His admonishment and cool His Anger. God does not hold grudges.

(10) "HE HAS NOT DEALT WITH US AFTER OUR SINS; NOR REWARDED US ACCORDING TO OUR INIQUITIES."

All of this means that the Lord has not dealt with us according to what we deserve. I speak of chastisement that fits the wrongdoing. While He definitely does chastise us, it is not nearly to the degree to what we ought to experience. Instead, any time we repent, and do so sincerely, He gives us what we do not merit, which is forgiveness (Titus 3:5-7).

This is one of the reasons God takes such a stern attitude toward Believers who will not show mercy or be quick to forgive. He expects us to conduct ourselves toward others as He has conducted Himself toward us. Regrettably, few do.

(11) "FOR AS THE HEAVEN IS HIGH ABOVE THE EARTH, SO GREAT IS HIS MERCY TOWARD THEM WHO FEAR HIM."

This refers to unlimited Mercy, but with a condition. The condition is that we *"fear Him."* What type of fear is being spoken of here?

THE FEAR OF THE LORD

The type of fear that the Lord wants us to have, as it regards His Person, is that we understand perfectly that He says what He means and means what He says. If we disobey, we should fear not to address that disobedience in the right fashion.

Sin always brings with it a terrible penalty. Nevertheless, if we take our sin to the Lord, properly confess it before Him, and ask Him to forgive us from straying from the Cross (for that is what causes the sin in the first place), He will be quick to forgive and to cleanse from all unrighteousness. His Word says so! (I Jn. 1:9).

If we fail to do this which His Word demands, we should fear what His Reaction will be.

The type of *"fear"* of which the Psalmist here speaks is not the *"spirit of fear"* that Paul mentioned in II Timothy 1:7, nor is it the fear that Adam voiced after his Fall (Gen. 3:10). The type of fear that the Holy Spirit is speaking of means that we are to Respect, Reverence, and Honor God, and do so to the extent that we obey His Word.

(12) "AS FAR AS THE EAST IS FROM THE WEST, SO FAR HAS HE REMOVED OUR TRANSGRESSIONS FROM US."

This is equivalent to *"blotting out our sins"* (Acts 3:19; Isa. 43:25; 44:22).

THE REMOVAL OF OUR TRANSGRESSIONS

As it is impossible to bring the east and the west together, so it is impossible to bring the forgiven sinner and his forgiven sins together. The Divine fact stated in this Verse gives a peace which nothing can destroy to those who believe it. The Holy Spirit used the designation of *"east"* and *"west"* for a reason. Regarding *"north"* and *"south,"* both have *"poles,"* which represent starting and stopping points. In other words, if one sets out on a northward passage and travels long enough, finally he will reach the North Pole. Then he will begin to go south, even though he continues in the same direction.

"East" and *"west"* have no poles; consequently, when one starts out traveling eastward, even if he would travel forever, he still would be traveling east. The same could be said for traveling *"west."*

When sins and transgressions are properly confessed before the Lord, and if there is true Repentance, this guarantees the removal of all sins and also guarantees that they never again will be brought before us.

It's a shame that at times Christians enjoy dragging up something that happened in the past, but God never does and never will. As far as God is concerned, it never has existed. It is called *"Justification by Faith."*

(13) "LIKE AS A FATHER PITIES HIS CHILDREN, SO THE LORD PITIES THEM WHO FEAR HIM."

The word *"pity"* in the Hebrew is *"rawkham,"* which means *"to love, to have compassion, to show mercy."*

Why does He pity us?

NOTES

The next Verse tells us why.

(14) "FOR HE KNOWS OUR FRAME; HE REMEMBERS THAT WE ARE DUST."

There is a vast difference between *"flesh"* (fallen flesh, at that!) and *"Spirit,"* which is God (Jn. 4:24).

As it regards what the Lord remembers, it must be said that He remembers what man forgets, that is, our infirmities, while man remembers what God forgets, that is, our sins.

(15) "AS FOR MAN, HIS DAYS ARE AS GRASS: AS A FLOWER OF THE FIELD, SO HE FLOURISHES."

As a flower is beautiful for a short time, so is man. But then...!

(16) "FOR THE WIND PASSES OVER IT, AND IT IS GONE; AND THE PLACE THEREOF SHALL KNOW IT NO MORE."

As the flower shortly is gone, so man passes away. One cannot tell where the flower had been; and no matter how great a man may have been, one also can little tell where he has been!

(17) "BUT THE MERCY OF THE LORD IS FROM EVERLASTING TO EVERLASTING UPON THEM WHO FEAR HIM, AND HIS RIGHTEOUSNESS UNTO CHILDREN'S CHILDREN."

The sense of this Verse has to do with the previous Verses.

MAN

There is no dependability in man, but there is great dependability in *"The Mercy of the LORD."* Man never needs to fear that God's Mercy will run short. We have the Promise of the Holy Spirit that it is *"from everlasting to everlasting,"* which means unfailing and incapable of failure. Once again, by design the Holy Spirit emphasizes the fact that this Mercy is given only to those *"who fear Him."*

Even though the man of Verses 15 and 16 is not here for long, he has the Promise that the same Mercy that has been extended to him will be extended to his children and their children forever. And now a further condition is given:

(18) "TO SUCH AS KEEP HIS COVENANT, AND TO THOSE WHO REMEMBER HIS COMMANDMENTS TO DO THEM."

There are three requirements to be a recipient of the *"Mercy of the LORD"*:

1. *"Fear Him"*;
2. *"Keep His Covenant"*; and,
3. *"Remember His Commandments, to do them."*

God will not and cannot show His Mercy to those who flout His Word. What He has asked of us must be done, but yet even the best of us cannot properly meet these requirements. Due to the Fall, no matter how sincere a person might be, even if he is Born-Again and baptized with the Holy Spirit, he still will fall short (Rom. 3:23).

So what is the solution?

The solution is our trust in Christ and what He did for us at the Cross. As the *"Last Adam,"* He did for us what we could not do for ourselves. He lived this life perfectly and perfectly kept the Law in every respect, all as our Substitute. He then went to the Cross in order to satisfy the claims of the broken Law, which was death. The key to all of this is that our faith in Christ and what He did for us at the Cross puts us down as *"law-keepers"* in every respect and gives us the Perfection of Christ. That's what Christ was all about. He did for us what we could do for ourselves.

(19) "THE LORD HAS PREPARED HIS THRONE IN THE HEAVENS; AND HIS KINGDOM RULES OVER ALL."

Unfortunately, the Lord at present does not rule over all. So this Scripture pertains to the future. It will be fulfilled in the Kingdom Age. *"His Throne"* is prepared in *"the Heavens."* The term *"Heavens"* also includes the Earth.

The sense here is that the one Throne then will govern both Heaven and Earth and thus fulfill the Lord's Prayer, *"Your Will be done on Earth as it is in Heaven."* This ultimately will be answered and fulfilled.

(20) "BLESS THE LORD, YE HIS ANGELS, THAT EXCEL IN STRENGTH, THAT DO HIS COMMANDMENTS, HEARKENING UNTO THE VOICE OF HIS WORD."

The short phrase, *"His Angels,"* is here used. Actually one-third of the Angels fell with Satan and now serve their master in the kingdom of darkness (Rev. 12:4). These, of course, do not praise God; however, the two-thirds of the Angels that remained in their place of submission to their Creator do praise Him and *"excel in strength."* In other words, they are careful to do His Will.

(21) "BLESS YE THE LORD, ALL YE HIS HOSTS; YE MINISTERS OF HIS, THAT DO HIS PLEASURE."

Angels are here called *"Ministers,"* which means they carry out God's Will according to *"His pleasure."*

(22) "BLESS THE LORD, ALL HIS WORKS IN ALL PLACES OF HIS DOMINION: BLESS THE LORD, O MY SOUL."

The Psalm ends as it begins with an admonishment for us to ever kneel in reverence and respect to the Lord of Glory, Who has given us all good things, despite the fact that we are poor, frail, flawed, and fallen human beings made of dust.

GOD AND MAN

Man is quite insignificant in comparison to God and all the great things that God has created. But, still, God has taken extraordinary measures and gone to unheard of lengths to redeem man from his terrible, pitiful state. When we consider these things, we must ever stand in awe of Him and continue to bow the knee to the Lord of Glory, which means that we bless Him.

When we consider what the Lord has done in order to redeem man, that is, actually becoming Man Himself, then our respect and reverence should know no bounds.

PSALM 104

*Author Unknown:
Praise to God the Creator*

(1) "BLESS THE LORD, O MY SOUL. O LORD MY GOD, YOU ARE VERY GREAT; YOU ARE CLOTHED WITH HONOR AND MAJESTY."

In the title, there is no evidence as to who wrote this Psalm.

It concerns the Creation of this Earth as well as all living creatures. Since God is the Creator, He is the most suitable Monarch to govern it and them. His Glory as Creator is the Doctrine of the Psalm.

The great and mighty Works of God and His Providence over all Creation make Him a Person of great Honor and Majesty among all His Subjects.

This Psalm will show that the conception of Deity and of creative power is not human but Divine; the language is that of pure science. None of the great religions of the world, either ancient or modern, approach this portrayal in sublimity or accuracy (Williams).[50]

(2) "WHO COVERS YOURSELF WITH LIGHT AS WITH A GARMENT: WHO STRETCHES OUT THE HEAVENS LIKE A CURTAIN."

This refers to the great Light in which God dwells that no man can approach unto and man neither has seen nor can see in his sinful state (I Tim. 6:16).

CREATION

In this Passage, as in the First Chapter of Genesis, light appears as the first attribute and evidence of the Creator. The word *"curtain"* means *"tabernacle,"* and should have been so translated in this Passage.

The Heavens are presented scientifically in Verse 2 as a vast tent curtaining from view the Angelic Hosts and their glorious Creator.

The first Act of God in the recreation of Earth was to bring forth light (Gen. 1:3). Satan always brings darkness (Gen. 1:2), and God always brings light.

LIGHT

There is some evidence that, before the Fall, Adam and Eve also were encased in an enswathement of light. They lost that light at the Fall.

There is also further evidence that every Glorified Saint also will have clothing of light, so to speak.

During the Transfiguration, the Bible says, *"And His Face did shine as the sun, and His raiment was white as the light"* (Mat. 17:2).

The Greek word for *"light"* as here used is *"stilbo,"* which actually means *"living light."* In other words, this *"light"* came from within Christ and covered Him as He stood that day on the Mount of Transfiguration.

John the Beloved wrote, *"And it does not yet appear what we shall be: but we know that, when He shall appear, we shall be like Him"* (I Jn. 3:2).

As stated, this indicates that all Glorified Saints will wear a garment of light.

(3) "WHO LAYS THE BEAMS OF HIS CHAMBERS IN THE WATERS: WHO MAKES THE CLOUDS HIS CHARIOT: WHO WALKS UPON THE WINGS OF THE WIND."

The sense of this Verse is that Creation serves the Creator.

(4) "WHO MAKES HIS ANGELS SPIRITS; HIS MINISTERS A FLAMING FIRE."

As the previous two Verses show the wisdom of the Creator of the Heavens, this Verse shows His supremacy over the Angels. Of course it does! He is their Creator!

(5) "WHO LAID THE FOUNDATIONS OF THE EARTH, THAT IT SHOULD NOT BE REMOVED FOREVER."

The foundations of the Earth were laid and accompanied by the singing and celebration of Angels, of which it seems that Lucifer was the leader (Job 38:4-7; Prov. 8:29).

THE CONTEST BETWEEN GOD AND SATAN

At some point in time regarding eternity past, Lucifer, one of God's wisest and most beautiful Angels, led a revolution against God, in which he was joined by approximately one-third of the Heavenly Hosts. From then until now, he has waged war against God. Much of this war has been over the supremacy of the Earth.

Due to the Fall of man in the Garden of Eden, at the present time Satan is the *"god of this present world"* and *"the prince of the powers of the air"* (II Cor. 4:4; Eph. 2:2). This is the cause of all death, war, greed, murder, hate, pain, sickness, and suffering. This, however, will end soon. Jesus Christ is coming back to rid the Earth of that which has caused its destruction (Rev., Chpt. 19).

(6) "YOU COVER IT WITH THE DEEP AS WITH A GARMENT: THE WATERS STOOD ABOVE THE MOUNTAINS."

This refers to the first universal flood, as described in Genesis 1:2. It was at the time of the Lucifer's rebellion. It does not refer to Noah's flood.

The word *"deep"* in the Hebrew is *"tehom,"*

which means *"an abyss of a surging mass of water."*

(7) "AT YOUR REBUKE THEY FLED; AT THE VOICE OF YOUR THUNDER THEY HASTED AWAY."

This Verse probably refers to Genesis 1:2, which was the time that God brought the Earth back to a habitable state.

The word *"thunder"* used in this Seventh Verse could mean that God used electric power (lightning) to separate the waters.

(8) "THEY GO UP BY THE MOUNTAINS; THEY GO DOWN BY THE VALLEYS UNTO THE PLACE WHICH YOU HAVE FOUNDED FOR THEM.

(9) "YOU HAVE SET A BOUND THAT THEY MAY NOT PASS OVER; THAT THEY TURN NOT AGAIN TO COVER THE EARTH."

The sense of these Passages is that the waters (flood) would not cover the Earth unless the Lord commanded them to do so. This has to do with the re-creation. It is not a contradiction concerning Noah's flood.

In Genesis 1:2, the waters covered the entirety of the Earth. Verses 7 through 9 simply mean that God appointed the waters certain places and the dry land certain places.

(10) "HE SENDS THE SPRINGS INTO THE VALLEYS, WHICH RUN AMONG THE HILLS."

In the re-creation of the Earth, given to us in the First Chapter of Genesis, this Verse merely pertains to the fact that God traced out the places for the rivers, streams, lakes, etc.

(11) "THEY GIVE DRINK TO EVERY BEAST OF THE FIELD: THE WILD ASSES QUENCH THEIR THIRST.

(12) "BY THEM SHALL THE FOWLS OF THE HEAVEN HAVE THEIR HABITATION, WHICH SING AMONG THE BRANCHES."

At the re-creation of the Earth, rivers, streams, lakes, etc., covered the entirety of the Earth; however, rebellion against God down through the centuries has made a great part of the Earth into a desert.

Through the satellites it is possible to see the courses of rivers that once ran in the desert but now no longer do. When Jesus comes back the second time without sin unto Salvation, the *"deserts"* will once again *"blossom as the rose,"* because the whole Earth will once again know that which the Lord originally intended, as it regards rivers, lakes, streams, etc.

(13) "HE WATERS THE HILLS FROM HIS CHAMBERS: THE EARTH IS SATISFIED WITH THE FRUIT OF YOUR WORKS.

(14) "HE CAUSES THE GRASS TO GROW FOR THE CATTLE, AND HERB FOR THE SERVICE OF MAN: THAT HE MAY BRING FORTH FOOD OUT OF THE EARTH;

(15) "AND WINE THAT MAKES GLAD THE HEART OF MAN, AND OIL TO MAKE HIS FACE TO SHINE, AND BREAD WHICH STRENGTHENS MAN'S HEART.

(16) "THE TREES OF THE LORD ARE FULL OF SAP; THE CEDARS OF LEBANON, WHICH HE HAS PLANTED;

(17) "WHERE THE BIRDS MAKE THEIR NESTS: AS FOR THE STORK, THE FIR TREES ARE HER HOUSE.

(18) "THE HIGH HILLS ARE A REFUGE FOR THE WILD GOATS; AND THE ROCKS FOR THE CONIES."

These Passages proclaim God as the Creator of all things. It should easily be understood that Creation demands a Creator. It is a ridiculous idea, to say the least, that all of this could take place by the method of blind chance.

The teachers of evolution have no idea about what is the first cause of all things, so they come up with every type of weird hypotheses which the deluded brain of man can produce. God is the First Cause, and the Only Cause.

(19) "HE APPOINTED THE MOON FOR SEASONS: THE SUN KNOWS HIS GOING DOWN.

(20) "YOU MAKE DARKNESS, AND IT IS NIGHT: WHEREIN ALL THE BEASTS OF THE FOREST DO CREEP FORTH.

(21) "THE YOUNG LIONS ROAR AFTER THEIR PREY, AND SEEK THEIR MEAT FROM GOD.

(22) "THE SUN ARISES, THEY GATHER THEMSELVES TOGETHER, AND LAY THEM DOWN IN THEIR DENS."

Concerning all of this, Williams says, *"Since Messiah is Jehovah Elohim, then is He fitted to be King over all the Earth, for having made* it and man and the living creatures, He is the most suitable Monarch to govern it and them. His Glory as Creator is the doctrine of this Psalm; and it harmonizes with Genesis 1 and 2." [51]

(23) "MAN GOES FORTH UNTO HIS WORK AND TO HIS LABOR UNTIL THE EVENING.

(24) "O LORD, HOW MANIFOLD ARE YOUR WORKS! IN WISDOM HAVE YOU MADE THEM ALL: THE EARTH IS FULL OF YOUR RICHES."

When one considers all that has been done in the Creation, one is forced to exclaim the Truth of Romans 11:33, *"O the depth of the riches both of the wisdom and knowledge of God! how unsearchable are His Judgments, and His Ways past finding out!"*

THE CREATION OF PLANET EARTH

It is said that the Earth, even in its present form and with a curse upon it (Gen. 3:17), has the capacity to feed approximately one hundred billion (100,000,000,000) people. (The population in 2005 is nearly seven billion.) The reason for the present day difficulties in feeding much of the world is not because of the deficiency of Planet Earth, but because of demonic religion, hate, war, greed, pride, and man's inhumanity to man. In short, it is because of sin.

When God originally created this Planet, it was created with the capacity to sustain life and provide riches to a magnitude that man cannot comprehend. The reason for the problems of this Earth is not God or His Creation, but man and his sin.

In his twisted way, man tries to *"save"* Planet Earth. While we should admire and abet every correct method, the present efforts are like putting a Band-Aid over cancer. Planet Earth truly is about to be cleaned up, but that will be at the Second Coming of Christ. Paul said it now *"groans"* for that Deliverance, which most surely will come (Rom. 8:22).

(25) "SO IS THIS GREAT AND WIDE SEA, WHEREIN ARE THINGS CREEPING INNUMERABLE, BOTH SMALL AND GREAT BEASTS."

The Continents of this Planet have been minutely inspected for precious metals, as least as far as modern technology allows.

NOTES

However, the riches of the great oceans have little been tapped. That awaits the Coming of the Lord.

(26) "THERE GO THE SHIPS: THERE IS THAT LEVIATHAN, WHOM YOU HAVE MADE TO PLAY THEREIN."

The word *"leviathan"* in the Hebrew is *"livyathan,"* which means *"a great sea serpent."* It is a symbol of Satan. The language expressed here could have one of two meanings:

1. Giant sea creatures, such as whales.
2. A symbol of Satan. If, in this instance, it does refer to Satan, it means that he has somewhat to do with the mighty oceans. If this is the case, this could possibly explain some of the mysteries of the Bermuda Triangle and other oceanic phenomena.

(27) "THESE WAIT ALL UPON YOU; THAT YOU MAY GIVE THEM THEIR MEAT IN DUE SEASON."

Creation is dependent upon the Creator. Most of the animate creation, however, such as man, does not look to God at all, but rather to other men or his own ingenuity, which explains why much of the world goes to bed hungry each night.

(28) "THAT YOU GIVE THEM THEY GATHER: YOU OPEN YOUR HAND, THEY ARE FILLED WITH GOOD."

If man will look to God, depend upon Him, earnestly seek His Face, and believe Him for His Blessings, the Lord will *"fill our open hand."* He has promised to do this, and He will do it!

(29) "YOU HIDE YOUR FACE, THEY ARE TROUBLED: YOU TAKE AWAY THEIR BREATH, THEY DIE, AND RETURN TO THEIR DUST."

Once again, we find here that man is totally dependent on His Creator. But yet, he doesn't seem to realize that. Man keeps trying to chart his own course.

We wonder why there is so much *"trouble."* It is because God *"hides His Face."*

Why?

It is because of man's sin and man's unbelief!

(30) "YOU SEND FORTH YOUR SPIRIT, THEY ARE CREATED: AND YOU RENEW THE FACE OF THE EARTH."

The sense of this Verse is that God upholds this Planet in all of His Creation by

"His Spirit."

THE SPIRIT OF GOD

The Spirit of God originally moved upon the face of the waters (Gen. 1:2). From that time, He continues to move in order to ensure God's Creation. Thus, the prognostications by some that this Earth will be destroyed by the *"greenhouse effect," "ozone depletion,"* or other similar theories hold no Scriptural or literal reality.

Actually, this Planet never will be destroyed, although it will be refurbished and made new at the conclusion of the great Millennial Reign of Christ (II Pet. 3:12-13).

(31) "THE GLORY OF THE LORD SHALL ENDURE FOR EVER: THE LORD SHALL REJOICE IN HIS WORKS."

Even though this Planet, because of man's sin, has suffered terrible abuse in the last six thousand or more years, it will *"endure forever"* because *"the Glory of the LORD shall endure forever."* The Lord rejoices in *"His Works."* He does not rejoice over destruction unless it furthers His Work.

(32) "HE LOOKS ON THE EARTH, AND IT TREMBLES: HE TOUCHES THE HILLS, AND THEY SMOKE."

The sense of this Verse is that God has such awesome Power that He is able to do with His Creation what He desires.

THE RESHAPING OF THE EARTH

The Scripture says, *"And unto Eber were born two sons: the name of the one was Peleg; because in his days the Earth was divided"* (I Chron. 1:19).

Peleg lived not long before Abraham. It seems that in his time there was a tremendous upheaval on Earth. In other words, at that time, it seems that the Continents of the Earth were divided.

Today there is mounting evidence that our Continents were at one time joined together. It is said that the Continents can be fitted together like a jigsaw puzzle. The east coast of South America matches the west coast of Africa, where the rounded corner of Brazil fits into the gulf of Guinea. Facing coasts of the United States and Europe also can be fitted together. At last, scientists are waking up to the fact of something the Bible recorded as Truth about 4,000 years ago. This upheaval took place in the days of Peleg, Noah's great-great-grandson.

The breaking apart of the Continents would explain the presence of the American Indians and inhabitants of numerous islands before the discoveries of the explorers of the old world.

(33) "I WILL SING UNTO THE LORD AS LONG AS I LIVE: I WILL SING PRAISE TO MY GOD WHILE I HAVE MY BEING.

(34) "MY MEDITATION OF HIM SHALL BE SWEET: I WILL BE GLAD IN THE LORD."

In these two Verses we find a great Truth:

MEDITATION

The word *"meditation"* is used quite extensively regarding communion with the Lord.

The word probably can be best explained by comparing it to a cow chewing her cud. She chews it until there is absolutely no juice left in it; she thereby derives all the pleasure, nutriments, and sustenance that is possible. Likewise, if we would constantly do the same with the Word of God, this would solve most of the nervous breakdowns and emotional problems, plus a host of other type of problems. There is a healing virtue about the Word of God.

The Psalmist said he would do four things:

1. *"I will sing unto the LORD as long as I live."*

2. *"I will sing praise to my God while I have my being."*

3. *"I will have sweet meditation of God."*

4. *"I will be glad in the LORD."*

(35) "LET THE SINNERS BE CONSUMED OUT OF THE EARTH, AND LET THE WICKED BE NO MORE. BLESS THOU THE LORD, O MY SOUL. PRAISE YE THE LORD."

The word *"Hallelujah"* first occurs here in the Bible. The word *"Praise"* should have been translated *"Hallelujah."*

It is connected not with the Salvation, but with the destruction, of men.

The first Hallelujah in the New Testament also celebrates the destruction of sinners (Rev. 19:1-2).

This Verse is a prediction and a prayer. Both are expressed in the form of the Hebrew verb which reads: *"Sinners shall be consumed out of the Earth"* and *"Let sinners be consumed out of the Earth."*

The language of the New Testament is similar, which proclaims the coming destruction of the wicked (Mat. 13:41-42; II Thess. 1:8-9; Gal. 1:8-9; I Cor. 16:22).

Because some men have continued to express an obstinacy toward God, even after they have been given repeated opportunities to repent, God must ultimately destroy such men for the betterment of society and the continuation of the human family. The Scripture here says God shall do it!

When God does this, and He shall do it (Rev., Chpt. 19), the Holy Spirit will shout *"Hallelujah!"* We should also!

PSALM 105

Author Unknown:
God's Wondrous Works on Behalf of Israel

(1) "O GIVE THANKS UNTO THE LORD; CALL UPON HIS NAME: MAKE KNOWN HIS DEEDS AMONG THE PEOPLE."

It is not known who wrote this Psalm.

It reviews the Grace and Faithfulness of the Messiah toward the Patriarchs and to Israel, demonstrating His Ability to rule the whole Earth, and suggesting the argument that as He was able to deliver and maintain them, so is He competent to bless and govern all men.

The Psalm opens with an exhortation to praise the Messiah, the King, and closes with a *"Hallelujah"* in Verse 45.

The action of the Messiah with Israel is a Picture and a Promise of His future action with the world. The Covenant consummated at Calvary will be the basis of His Millennial rule; the Promises of that Covenant then will be performed and fulfilled.

(2) "SING UNTO HIM, SING PSALMS UNTO HIM: TALK YE OF ALL HIS WONDROUS WORKS."

Because it is the Holy Spirit Who is the Speaker in this Psalm, we must realize how absolutely significant are these words. Every Believer should *"sing"* of all the wondrous works of the Lord, and do so constantly. We also must constantly *"talk"* of all these great works. This builds faith!

MUSIC AS IT REGARDS WORSHIP AND PRAISE

All 150 of the Psalms are Songs; they were written by the Holy Spirit. Even though David and others were the instruments used by God, still, it was the Holy Spirit Who gave the words, and undoubtedly also the melody.

Since the Book of Psalms is the longest Book in the Bible, we should realize from this just how important is Praise and Worship. This is Praise and Worship regarding music and singing and the accompaniment with musical instruments.

No wonder that Satan has done everything within his power to pollute and pervert sacred music. Regrettably and sadly, he has succeeded in most cases.

One could say, without any fear of Scriptural contradiction, that the spiritual temperature of the Church can be measured by the music.

(3) "GLORY YE IN HIS HOLY NAME: LET THE HEART OF THEM REJOICE WHO SEEK THE LORD."

For those who glory in the Holy Name of the Lord, for such who seek the Lord, and do so habitually, *"their heart will rejoice."*

Here we see the cure for demonic oppression.

(4) "SEEK THE LORD, AND HIS STRENGTH: SEEK HIS FACE EVERMORE."

Every Believer has many reasons for seeking the Lord. If we do so, we are assured of *"His Strength."* Because we need that strength constantly, we must *"seek His Face evermore."*

How many Christians follow this regimen? I'm afraid that number is few!

(5) "REMEMBER HIS MARVELOUS WORKS THAT HE HAS DONE; HIS WONDERS AND THE JUDGMENTS OF HIS MOUTH."

We should recall all the wonderful Works of the Bible which the Lord has performed, and we also must recall all the wonderful Works He has done for us personally. This we should do constantly.

All of this is meant to strengthen our faith and also that we understand that all of our help comes from the Lord. If we look to man, we get the help that man can give, which is nothing. If we look to the Lord, we get the help which He can give, which is everything.

(6) "O YE SEED OF ABRAHAM HIS SERVANT, YE CHILDREN OF JACOB HIS CHOSEN."

This statement, as is obvious, is directed toward Israel of old; however, it now could read, *"O ye seed of Abraham His servant, ye Children of the Lord, His chosen."* In other words, as Israel was very special in God's sight at that time, likewise, the True Church is special presently.

(7) "HE IS THE LORD OUR GOD: HIS JUDGMENTS ARE IN ALL THE EARTH."

The actual Hebrew translation is, *"He, Jehovah, is our God."*

Pulpit says, *"The Psalmist now commences the praise of Jehovah in his own person, acting as spokesman for his people; and first of all declares the Godhead; next, the Lord's universal dominion."*

The phrase, *"His Judgments are in all the Earth,"* means that *"His sentences, decrees, laws, and His Word in every respect, have a universal range, and command the obedience of all men."* [52]

(8) "HE HAS REMEMBERED HIS COVENANT FOREVER, THE WORD WHICH HE COMMANDED TO A THOUSAND GENERATIONS."

The Psalmist now praises God's Faithfulness. The Lord entered into a Covenant with Israel, and that Covenant still holds good. He has not forgotten it and will never forget it.

The Covenant will be consummated and fulfilled at the Second Coming, when Israel then accepts the Lord Jesus Christ as her Saviour, her Lord, and her Messiah. To all those who claim that Israel is no more, they should read this particular Verse, plus scores of others which promise the same thing.

God most certainly will do that which He says He will do!

(9) "WHICH COVENANT HE MADE WITH ABRAHAM, AND HIS OATH UNTO ISAAC."

This Covenant could be constituted in the following:

THE COVENANT

1. A Promise was first of all given by God to Abraham (Gen. 12:1-3).

2. The Promise was enlarged into a Covenant (Gen. 15:18).

3. In this Covenant, an *"oath"* was originally sworn to Abraham (Gen. 22:16); but a further Promise to *"perform the oath"* was given to Isaac (Gen. 26:3).

(10) "AND CONFIRMED THE SAME UNTO JACOB FOR A LAW, AND TO ISRAEL FOR AN EVERLASTING COVENANT."

The Lord told Jacob, *"I am the LORD God of Abraham your father, and the God of Isaac: the land whereon you lie, to you will I give it, and to your seed"* (Gen. 28:13).

After the Lord had changed the name of Jacob to *"Israel,"* he then reaffirmed the Promise and the Covenant by saying to the Patriarch, *"And the land which I gave Abraham and Isaac, to you I will give it, and to your seed after you will I give the land"* (Gen. 35:12).

THE CONFLICT OVER THE LAND OF ISRAEL

Due to these Promises, Satan has fought tenaciously that anyone and everyone might have the Land of Israel except the very ones to whom it was promised by the Lord. Those ones are the *"Israelites."* However, in spite of Satan's efforts, the Palestinians, the Arabs, and the Muslims should realize that when God makes Promises, He keeps His Promises.

The Land of Israel doesn't belong to the Muslims; it belongs to Israel. And when I say, the *"Land,"* I speak of all that which God promised, and not just some of it.

In giving the Palestinians part of Israel, Israel has violated the Word of God.

I am told that before President George W. Bush completes his second term, he is going to pressure Israel to give half of Jerusalem to the Muslims. I am not sure if the President himself has made this statement. However, if he has, and if he tries to carry it through, such very well could invite the Judgment of God. Jerusalem and the entirety of the Land of Israel belong to the Jews, and to no one else.

(11) SAYING, UNTO YOU WILL I GIVE THE LAND OF CANAAN, THE LOT OF YOUR INHERITANCE."

First of all, we should note the strength by which the Holy Spirit calls to attention this *"Covenant."*

THE CONFLICT

Even now God is in the process of bringing the Covenant to fruition. He said that He would give unto Abraham's natural seed the Land of Canaan for an everlasting possession (Gen. 17:8).

The conflict over the Land of Canaan has raged since the time of Abraham and Sarah. The offspring of Ishmael, Abraham's son by the Egyptian Hagar, also have claimed this land almost from that particular time. Isaac, the true son of Abraham and Sarah, was promised the land by God. The Lord said, *"You shall call his name Isaac: and I will establish My Covenant with him, for an Everlasting Covenant, and with his seed after him"* (Gen. 17:19).

The Lord also promised to make of Ishmael a great nation, which He has done (Gen. 17:20). In fact, the sons of Ishmael have almost the entirety of the Middle East, with the exception of Iran, which is Persian. But yet the Lord continued to say, *"My Covenant will I establish with Isaac"* (Gen. 17:21).

Almost every day news reports from Israel are carried across the news networks of the United States and around the world. Invariably, these news reports deal with this conflict.

SATAN AND HIS OPPOSITION

Even from the very beginning, Satan has done all within his power to abrogate this Promise given to Abraham so long, long ago. He has not succeeded, and he will not succeed, but it will not be for a lack of trying.

The formation of Israel as a nation in 1948, after some 2,000 years of these beleaguered people wandering as vagabonds all over the world, presents the first visible fulfillment of this great Prophecy. But yet, trouble has raged between Israel and the Muslims from that very time in 1948. It has been unabated, with the Arab League trying several times to dislodge Israel, that is, to completely destroy her. They have not been successful. As stated, their lack of success has not been due to a lack of trying.

Satan will continue to make every effort possible to stop this Covenant from being fulfilled. He will not succeed, although, for a time, it will look as though he will.

THE SPIRIT AND THE FLESH

Abraham tried to *"help"* the Lord bring to fruition the promised son. Ishmael was the result! Isaac was a Work of the Holy Spirit, meaning that God had to miraculously bring forth Isaac, which He did! Abraham was 100 years old and Sarah was 90. As would be overly obvious, Abraham no longer could father children, and neither could Sarah conceive. The Lord, however, renewed the youth of both Abraham and Sarah and made it possible for this miracle child to come into the world. All hope of the flesh had to be exhausted before the Lord would do this.

Ishmael, the work of the flesh, has caused the world untold problems. Through this *"work of the flesh,"* Satan originated the Muslim religion, which is the cause of virtually all the terrorist activity in the world today.

The Muslims hate Israel and call her *"little Satan."* They also hate the United States of America and call us the *"great Satan."* If they had their way, they would slaughter or make slaves of every person in this nation who would not accept the religion of Islam. They do not lack the will; they only lack the way.

Our government foolishly claims that the Koran is a book of love and peace. Nothing could be further from the truth. In fact, the Koran is the cause of all terrorist activity. Pure and simple, it is the religion of Islam that causes all of these problems. It is foolish indeed for us to think that we can democratize Iraq or any Muslim nation! The two, democracy and Islam, are not even on the same planet.

Every nation in the world controlled by Islam is a basket case in every respect. Socially, it is at the bottom of the ladder; economically, it is at the bottom of the ladder; freedom-wise, it is at the bottom of the ladder.

We should learn from all of this that works of the flesh never can bring forth proper fruit. Such is impossible!

Whatever is of the Lord will bring forth eternal blessings, but that which is of the flesh, that is, Satan, will bring anything but blessings.

THE ANTICHRIST

In the not-too-distant future, Israel will

accept the Antichrist as their Messiah. It will be the second greatest mistake they ever have made. They rejected Christ, their True Messiah, when He first came. They now will accept the false messiah when he comes (Jn. 5:43).

The Antichrist will sign a seven-year non-aggression pact with Israel and other nations. This will be the beginning of the *"Great Tribulation,"* which the Prophet Jeremiah referred to as *"The Time of Jacob's Trouble"* (Jer. 30:7). At this time, Israel will cry, *"Peace and safety"* (I Thess. 5:3), thinking they have ensured their security. However, they will be anything but secure. It will be Satan's great effort to abrogate this eternal Covenant, for the Bible says, *"Then sudden destruction comes upon them"* (I Thess. 5:3).

At that time, the Antichrist will show his true colors by declaring war on Israel. She then will enter into the most difficult time of her long history. Threatened with total annihilation and suffering her first defeat since becoming a nation in 1948, she will at long last begin to cry to God. The Lord will hear that cry, and Jesus Christ will come back (Rev., Chpt. 19), for He Alone can ensure the perpetuity of this Covenant.

In reading these Passages (Vss. 8-11), the falseness of the *"Kingdom Now"* teaching becomes obvious. This teaching claims that Israel is no more and has been done away with. Sadly, the Church is full of false doctrine and false apostles, of which this false doctrine is but a part.

(12) "WHEN THEY WERE BUT A FEW MEN IN NUMBER; YEA, VERY FEW, AND STRANGERS IN IT."

When God made this Covenant with Abraham and confirmed the same with Jacob, truly they were *"but a few men in number."* In fact, for approximately 215 years, there was only a handful of people who were called of God in the *"Promised Land."* Truly, they were *"strangers in it"* and were surrounded by a host of enemies.

Unless God had been the One Who made the Covenant, it would have been impossible for such to have been carried out.

(13) "WHEN THEY WENT FROM ONE NATION TO ANOTHER, FROM ONE KINGDOM TO ANOTHER PEOPLE."

NOTES

This small group sojourned among the Philistines for a short period of time (Gen., Chpt. 20) and the Egyptians for quite a period of time (Gen., Chpts. 13, 45; Ex., Chpt. 12).

Even when they were able to come into the Promised Land proper, they were surrounded by some ten hostile nations (Gen. 15:18-21).

(14) "HE SUFFERED NO MAN TO DO THEM WRONG: YEA, HE REPROVED KINGS FOR THEIR SAKES."

Pharaoh and Abimelech were threatened with death if they touched them (Gen. 12:17; 20:3; 26:11).

(15) "SAYING, TOUCH NOT MY ANOINTED, AND DO MY PROPHETS NO HARM."

At times, God has preserved His Prophets for His Own Reasons; but, at other times, He has allowed His Prophets to be maltreated and even killed (Mat. 23:37).

By and large, as it regards God's True Prophets, the treatment by the world, and also by the Church, has been extremely negative. True Prophets are a rebuke to the world and an embarrassment to an apostate Church. As a result, few have regarded God's Command, *"Touch not My anointed."*

TRUE PROPHETS

Some, on the other hand, have used this Verse to claim that Preachers should not be questioned about anything. But no one, Prophet or otherwise, is above the Word of God. If a Preacher maliciously violates the Word of God, no matter what such a man may call himself, he must be *"marked"* (Rom. 16:17). This 15th Verse means that no one should inflict any bodily harm to any Prophet of the Lord, which ought to be obvious.

Even when a Prophet fails, which happens at times, with Abraham (Gen. 12:14-19) and David (II Sam. 12:1-9) being examples, still, that gives no one the right to do such a person harm. While we never should condone sin, still, no Believer has the right to punish another. That remains exclusively in God's domain.

(16) "MOREOVER HE CALLED FOR A FAMINE UPON THE LAND: HE BROKE THE WHOLE STAFF OF BREAD."

This happened several times (Gen.,

Chpts. 13, 26, 41-47).

The following Verses proclaim the exceptional lengths to which God will go to ensure His Covenant with His people. This should make us realize that His every Word will come to pass exactly as He has spoken them.

(17) "HE SENT A MAN BEFORE THEM, EVEN JOSEPH, WHO WAS SOLD FOR A SERVANT."

God, of course, had nothing to do with the hatred and ungodliness of Joseph's brothers. But the Lord will use such a situation to bring about His intended results. Since God is Omniscient (all-knowing) and Omnipotent (all-powerful), He is able to use the events at hand, whatever they may be, to bring about His desired Will. If Joseph's brothers had not done what they did, the Lord would have found another way.

The brand of modern gospel that presently is dished up to a gullible Christian public hardly understands the True Gospel that would so treat Joseph.

(18) "WHOSE FEET THEY HURT WITH FETTERS: HE WAS LAID IN IRON."

The Thirty-ninth Chapter of Genesis gives this account. Joseph is lied about and committed to prison; yet the Bible says, *"But the LORD was with Joseph"* (Gen. 39:21).

According to much of what passes presently for Gospel, if Joseph had had faith, none of these things would have happened to him! However, even with an elementary knowledge of the Bible, we know this to be untrue. It was God's Will that Joseph be put in prison. It was God's Will that *"he was laid in iron."*

Why?

(19) "UNTIL THE TIME THAT HIS WORD CAME: THE WORD OF THE LORD TRIED HIM."

God had a mission for Joseph, and Joseph was not even aware of it at the time. But Joseph would have to be put to the test.

THE TESTING OF FAITH

Someone has well said, *"Faith must be tested, and great faith must be tested greatly."*

Joseph little realized the Plans God had for him or what the Lord was doing. We look at these things after the fact, but Joseph lived them. As far as he knew, he would spend the rest of his life in this prison.

But yet, all of this taught him faith, trust, and dependence on God. At this time, he little knew that for which he was being trained, but God knew, because God always knows.

The Lord minutely knows at all times where His Children are and what they are doing. He knows everything to such an extent that the Scripture says He *"numbers the very hairs of our head."* He also notes every sparrow's fall to the ground, wherever it might be (Mat. 10:29-30).

This proclaims such a minute inspection that it defies description.

Yes, the Lord knows exactly where we are at all times, and is directing events; however, His Direction depends a lot upon our faith or the lack thereof, our obedience or the lack thereof, etc.

Joseph stayed in prison for several years, possibly even as long as seven years. During this time, he must have asked himself many questions. But he never stopped believing, and he never stopped trusting. As stated, great faith must be tested greatly.

(20) "THE KING SENT AND LOOSED HIM; EVEN THE RULER OF THE PEOPLE, AND LET HIM GO FREE."

In the Fortieth Chapter of Genesis, Joseph interpreted dreams that two of his fellow prisoners had. One man was the king's butler, and the second was the king's baker. The interpretation of the butler's dream said he would be released from prison and restored to his former position. Joseph asked the butler to speak a word on his behalf, but the Scripture says, *"Yet did not the chief butler remember Joseph, but forgot him"* (Gen. 40:23).

Even though it was cruel on the butler's part to do such a thing, still, God used it to the advantage of Joseph. If Joseph had been released from prison at that time, he would have been little more than an out of work slave. It is important for us to learn that God's Timing is also a part of His Will. At God's Time, the king sent for Joseph and loosed him.

(21) "HE MADE HIM LORD OF HIS HOUSE, AND RULER OF ALL HIS SUBSTANCE."

This was God's intention all along. The hardships that God planned for Joseph, the hardships Joseph had to go through, prepared him for this time.

(22) "TO BIND HIS PRINCES AT HIS PLEASURE; AND TEACH HIS SENATORS WISDOM."

In this Scripture, we learn who actually is the greatest!

EGYPT

At this time, Egypt was the most powerful nation on the face of the Earth; consequently, the advisors to Pharaoh, here called *"Senators,"* would now be taught by an ex-convict. Only the Lord could work out such a thing. Only an obedient, trusting, and faithful servant such as Joseph could be molded to fit this position.

Many of us would greatly enjoy being the *"ruler"* of all of Pharaoh's substance. We would love to *"teach his Senators wisdom."* But many of us do not want to pay the price which must be paid in order for God to make us what He wants us to be.

(23) "ISRAEL ALSO CAME INTO EGYPT; AND JACOB SOJOURNED IN THE LAND OF HAM."

The word *"Ham"* is another word for Egypt. It pertains to the people of Egypt descending from *"Ham,"* Noah's son (Gen. 9:18-19).

This *"sojourn"* lasted for 430 years (Ex. 12:41).

From the time of Abraham to Jacob going into Egypt was approximately 215 years. The Children of Israel also spent 215 years in Egypt. The two periods of times totaled 430 years.

(24) "AND HE INCREASED HIS PEOPLE GREATLY; AND MADE THEM STRONGER THAN THEIR ENEMIES."

Jacob's seed increased greatly in Egypt. They were *"stronger"* because God was with them.

ISRAEL

These people called *"His people"* (the Jews), who came from the loins of Abraham and the womb of Sarah, were God's People for a purpose and a reason:

1. They were to give the world the Word of God. This they did, for all the Books of the Bible, both Old and New Testaments, were written by Jews. (Some think that Luke may have been a Gentile, but others think he was one of the *"seventy,"* or possibly a proselyte.)

2. To be the womb for the Messiah, which they were. Jesus was born of the Virgin Mary of the Tribe of Judah. This was the greatest event in human history other than the Death and Resurrection of Christ.

3. Israel was to evangelize the world and take the great message of Redemption to lost humanity. In this they failed. They also rejected their own Messiah and were sent into spiritual and physical dispersion. By and large, they alienated themselves from God's continued program of the Church.

(25) "HE TURNED THEIR HEART TO HATE HIS PEOPLE, TO DEAL SUBTILLY WITH HIS SERVANTS."

This does not mean that God forced Egypt to hate the Israelites. It does mean that God provided the opportunity for them to do so; however, this was done by their own free will.

ISRAEL AND EGYPT

If the Pharaoh who now occupied the throne had been kind to the Israelites, even as the Pharaoh under Joseph had been those years earlier, Israel would not have desired to leave Egypt. In fact, they would not have left. So the Lord allowed this Pharaoh to do what he desired to do, which was to make slaves of the Israelites; this He did, and it brought tremendous hardships.

In that time of great adversity, the Israelites then began to cry to God for deliverance. Then the Lord said, *"I have surely seen the affliction of My people which are in Egypt, and have heard their cry by reason of their taskmasters; for I know their sorrows;*

"And I am come down to deliver them out of the hand of the Egyptians, and to bring them up out of that land unto a good land and a large, unto a land flowing with milk and honey" (Ex. 3:7-8).

Regrettably, most Believers, even as Israel of old, will not do what the Lord wants them to do unless they think it is in their best interest to do so. Of course, anything the Lord wants us to do is always in our best interest; however, much of the time it is hard for us to see that. Most of the time we see the very opposite, which means we are charting our own course instead of allowing the Lord to do such.

As an example, David was anointed three times before Israel finally accepted him as king. In fact, they did not accept him as king until they felt and believed it was in their best interest to do so. It is the same with modern Believers! The Lord oftentimes has to allow adversity to come our way, even severe adversity at times, before we will desire to do His Will. Without the adversity, we would have continued our direction of self-will rather than God's Will.

(26) "HE SENT MOSES HIS SERVANT; AND AARON WHOM HE HAD CHOSEN."

The pronoun *"he"* refers to Moses choosing Aaron, which means that Aaron was not really chosen by God. Moses was God's choice. He was sent by God to deliver Israel from the mightiest nation on the face of the Earth. This obviously would be quite a formidable task!

(27) "THEY SHOWED HIS SIGNS AMONG THEM, AND WONDERS IN THE LAND OF HAM."

Ham was one of the three sons of Noah, from whom the entirety of the human race has descended (Gen. 9:18-19). The descendants of Ham settled in Egypt, parts of Africa, and the Middle East.

Through Moses, God did *"show His signs"* throughout the Land of Egypt.

(28) "HE SENT DARKNESS, AND MADE IT DARK; AND THEY REBELLED NOT AGAINST HIS WORD."

When the Holy Spirit repeats facts, He frequently does so in moral rather than chronological order. So is it here and in other parts of the Scripture. The Holy Spirit, with design, also may omit parts of the history. Thus, only eight of the ten plagues in Egypt are here reviewed.

THE DARKNESS

The close connection between the plague of darkness and the compelled submission of the Egyptians is very striking. God sent the darkness and the Egyptians let the Hebrews go.

This alludes possibly to the ninth plague; but as a substantive statement, the word *"darkness"* is to be understood as a covering term expressive of the entire period of the Divine punitive action upon Pharaoh. It was indeed a time of darkness, and it lasted several months.

According to some of the best manuscripts, the phrase, *"And they rebelled not against His Word,"* should have been translated, *"And they rebelled against His Word."* This means that the word *"not"* should not have been inserted. As is obvious, Pharaoh and the leadership of Egypt rebelled against the Word of God.

(29) "HE TURNED THEIR WATERS INTO BLOOD, AND SLEW THEIR FISH.

(30) "THEIR LAND BROUGHT FORTH FROGS IN ABUNDANCE, IN THE CHAMBERS OF THEIR KINGS.

(31) "HE SPOKE, AND THERE CAME DIVERS SORTS OF FLIES, AND LICE IN ALL THEIR COASTS.

(32) "HE GAVE THEM HAIL FOR RAIN, AND FLAMING FIRE IN THEIR LAND.

(33) "HE SMOTE THEIR VINES ALSO AND THEIR FIG TREES; AND BROKE THE TREES OF THEIR COASTS.

(34) "HE SPOKE, AND THE LOCUSTS CAME, AND CATERPILLARS, AND THAT WITHOUT NUMBER,

(35) "AND DID EAT UP ALL THE HERBS IN THEIR LAND, AND DEVOURED THE FRUIT OF THEIR GROUND.

(36) "HE SMOTE ALSO ALL THE FIRSTBORN IN THEIR LAND, THE CHIEF OF ALL THEIR STRENGTH."

The above Scriptures make it obvious that the Creator is in charge of His Creation, whether it be insects or the elements. He would use all of these things as it regarded Egypt, which is a precursor of what He will do in a wholesale way during the coming Great Tribulation. It is outlined in Chapters 6 through 19 of the Book of Revelation. Then, in the Battle of Armageddon, the Lord will once again use the elements; He will do it in a fashion and degree as never before (Ezek. 38:22).

(37) "HE BROUGHT THEM FORTH ALSO WITH SILVER AND GOLD: AND THERE WAS NOT ONE FEEBLE PERSON AMONG THEIR TRIBES."

Two great truths are brought forth here.

WEALTH AND HEALTH

The *"silver"* and *"gold"* here mentioned was payment for the many years of slavery.

It may seem to some that God is not keeping account; however, when His payday does come (and it will come!), it will be done as only He can do.

After the Death Angel passed through the land of Egypt and killed the firstborn of every home, at least those who did not have the blood on the doorpost, which included virtually the entirety of the Egyptians (Ex. 12:13), the Egyptians wanted the Israelites to leave immediately. In essence, they paid them to leave by giving them copious amounts of silver and gold. The Egyptians just wanted the Israelites to leave; but, as stated, this was payment for their many years of slavery, even though the Egyptians did not understand that.

Furthermore, the Scripture seems to indicate that the Lord healed every sick person among the Israelites and then gave strength even unto the most aged so that *"there was not one feeble person among their Tribes."*

JOSEPH

The great deliverance of the Children of Israel from Egyptian bondage had much to do with Joseph's faithfulness. Looking back to Verse 19, during the two years that elapsed before Joseph gave the interpretation of Pharaoh's dreams, the Word of God was training him. That is, Joseph kept trusting the fidelity of that Word, which was the source of his interpretations.

Concerning this, Williams says, *"It was a very real and lengthened testing of his faith and patience, that he, the interpreter, should remain in a prison, and the subject of the interpretation, the butler, dwelt luxuriously in a palace."* [53]

However, Joseph did not question God. He remained faithful, and the result, years later, was the deliverance of God's people.

(38) "EGYPT WAS GLAD WHEN THEY DEPARTED: FOR THE FEAR OF THEM FELL UPON THEM."

Many may ask the question, *"Why did God allow these people whom He loved so much to be subjected to slavery for so many years in Egypt?"*

THE PLAN OF GOD

It is now obvious that God had plans for Israel. If the situation in Egypt had been favorable, the Israelites would not have desired to leave; therefore, He allowed such to be grievous in order to make them cry to Him for deliverance, which they did!

God has a plan for every single Believer. Yes, the plan can be abrogated by our faithlessness. But if we believe God and remain faithful even though there are great difficulties along the way, the Holy Spirit ultimately will bring us out to God's intended design and purpose (Eph. 3:20).

Had it been too easy in Egypt, Israel would not have desired to depart. It was not easy, so they strongly desired to leave; however, Egypt did not want to let them go. God, therefore, sent the plagues that left Egypt a devastated wreck.

Egypt could have acquiesced at any time, and their nation would have been spared. The Israelites were God's people. He had the right to demand their release. Egypt had no right to demand that they be kept as slaves. So, whenever enough pressure was applied, Egypt strongly desired that they depart, which they did!

(39) "HE SPREAD A CLOUD FOR A COVERING; AND FIRE TO GIVE LIGHT IN THE NIGHT."

With such tenderness, God oversaw the departure of His people. His Spirit was evident in the *"cloud"* by day and the *"fire"* by night. Some erroneously think that this was a greater presence of leading that we have under the New Covenant, but this is not so. Then the Holy Spirit was <u>with</u> them; now He is <u>in</u> us (Jn. 14:17; 15:26). As a result, today we have a far greater leading than did the Children of Israel when they were led out of Egypt — and all because of the Cross!

(40) "THE PEOPLE ASKED, AND HE BROUGHT QUAILS, AND SATISFIED THEM WITH THE BREAD OF HEAVEN."

The experience of the previous Scriptures is found in Exodus 13:21-22, the account of the quails is found in Exodus 16:1-13 and Numbers 11:4-35, and the account of the Manna is found in Exodus 16:14-22.

(41) "HE OPENED THE ROCK, AND THE WATERS GUSHED OUT; THEY RAN IN THE DRY PLACES LIKE A RIVER."

The account of this miracle is found in Exodus 17:5-7.

THE ROCK

The *"Rock"* was a Type of Christ. The *"waters"* that *"gushed out"* were a type of the Eternal Life given according to the price that Jesus paid at Calvary.

The *"dry places"* are symbolic of this world and the barrenness of its spiritual obligation. The *"River"* symbolizes the magnitude of the great Gift of God. It was not a trickle of water that came out this Rock, but a veritable *"River"* — enough to satisfy some five million Israelites, plus all their cattle, sheep, and other livestock. There is also enough to satisfy the hunger and the thirst of every heart that comes to this life-giving stream, which is a Type of the Holy Spirit (Jn. 7:37-39).

(42) "FOR HE REMEMBERED HIS HOLY PROMISE, AND ABRAHAM HIS SERVANT."

These were the Promises that God gave to Abraham (Gen. 12:1-3; 13:14-18; 15:18-21; 17:1-8). God remembers every Promise He has ever made. He calls them *"Holy Promises."* Hallelujah!

(43) "AND HE BROUGHT FORTH HIS PEOPLE WITH JOY, AND HIS CHOSEN WITH GLADNESS."

What *"joy"* they had as they watched the mighty Red Sea open before them at the Command of God! How they rejoiced on the shores of the Red Sea at the things that God had done!

We also should ever rejoice and praise His Holy Name, realizing that He has delivered us from the terrible bondages of darkness. What *"joy"* we should have! What *"gladness"* should characterize our hearts and lives!

(44) "AND GAVE THEM THE LANDS OF THE HEATHEN: AND THEY INHERITED THE LABOR OF THE PEOPLE."

The great inheritance that God has given us is carved out of that which Satan intended for the destruction of our lives. Every single soul has been slated for destruction by Satan, but as the song says:

"He brought me out of the miry clay,
"He set my feet on the Rock to stay,
"He put a song in my soul today,
"A song of praise, Hallelujah!"

(45) "THAT THEY MIGHT OBSERVE HIS STATUTES, AND KEEP HIS LAWS. PRAISE YE THE LORD."

Once again, this Psalm closes with a *"Hallelujah!"* (The word *"praise"* in the Hebrew is *"Hallelujah!"*)

As He Saved Israel for a purpose and a reason — to observe His Statues and keep His Laws — He has likewise Saved us for a purpose and a reason — that we might be a shining light in the midst of a darkened world. Hallelujah!

PSALM 106

Author Unknown:
Israel's Sins and God's Mercy

(1) "PRAISE YE THE LORD. O GIVE THANKS UNTO THE LORD; FOR HE IS GOOD: FOR HIS MERCY ENDURES FOREVER."

This is the last Psalm of that which commonly is called *"The Numbers Book"* — Psalms 90 through 106.

THE MESSIAH

Williams says, *"The claim is made by the Holy Spirit on behalf of the Messiah, Who so lovingly, skillfully, and powerfully shepherded such a wholly unlovable, unbelieving, treacherous, idolatrous, immoral, and ungrateful people such as the Israelites. He is the only One fitted to successfully govern corrupt and sinful humanity.*

"The conduct of Israel is a humiliating proof of the hopeless corruption of human nature and an overwhelming demonstration of man's need of a new birth in order to fit him for the Kingdom of Heaven." [54]

The Scriptures predict with confidence that Christ will establish a just understanding and a gracious government over man, and that He will change the Earth, at present a wilderness, into a Paradise.

In view of this, this Psalm begins with *"Hallelujah"* (*"Praise"*).

(2) "WHO CAN UTTER THE MIGHTY ACTS OF THE LORD? WHO CAN SHOW FORTH ALL HIS PRAISE?"

It is not known who wrote this Psalm.

The answer is that no one can exhaustively analyze, understand, or show the meaning and purpose of Divine actions or adequately praise such actions. But the Messiah can and will show forth all God's praises.

(3) "BLESSED ARE THEY WHO KEEP JUDGMENT, AND HE WHO DOES RIGHTEOUSNESS AT ALL TIMES."

This Passage shows us that spiritual intelligence will always recognize Divine actions and bow and worship because of such action.

Spiritual intelligence also results only from the subjection of the mind to the Scriptures and from an unvarying life of righteous conduct.

(4) "REMEMBER ME, O LORD, WITH THE FAVOR THAT YOU BEAR UNTO YOUR PEOPLE: O VISIT ME WITH YOUR SALVATION."

As stated, even though the writer of this Psalm is unknown, still, the author requested of the Lord that he be remembered with two things:

FAVOR AND SALVATION

1. *"Favor"*: God shows favor to those who *"keep judgment and do righteousness at all times."*

2. *"Salvation"*: This is a conscious *"Salvation"* that only can come from the Lord. Most of that which presently is called *"Salvation"* by the world, and even by the Church, has no relationship to God's *"Salvation"* because it comes from man. The bitter fruit of Satan's deception is *"man's salvation."* Regrettably and sadly, the majority of the so-called Christian world does not have God's Salvation, which comes only from Christ as the Source, and the Cross as the Means, but rather that of man.

(5) "THAT I MAY SEE THE GOOD OF YOUR CHOSEN, THAT I MAY REJOICE IN THE GLADNESS OF YOUR NATION, THAT I MAY GLORY WITH YOUR INHERITANCE."

Love delights in possession, hence, the terms, *"Your people," "Your chosen," "Your nation"* and *"Your inheritance."*

(6) "WE HAVE SINNED WITH OUR FATHERS, WE HAVE COMMITTED INIQUITY, WE HAVE DONE WICKEDLY."

The nature of evil is seen in the terms, *"sin," "iniquity,"* and *"wickedness."*

The problem is *"sin."* Whether it is unbelievers or Believers, still, the problem is sin.

NOTES

There is only one remedy for sin, and that is the Cross of the Lord Jesus Christ. This is the reason why the Cross of Christ is so very, very important! This is the reason the Apostle Paul said, *"But though we, or an Angel from Heaven, preach any other gospel unto you than that which we have preached unto you, let him be accursed"* (Gal. 1:8).

If the Church is not preaching the Cross, pure and simple, it's not preaching the Gospel (I Cor. 1:17-18, 23; 2:2).

(7) "OUR FATHERS UNDERSTOOD NOT YOUR WONDERS IN EGYPT; THEY REMEMBERED NOT THE MULTITUDE OF YOUR MERCIES; BUT PROVOKED HIM AT THE SEA, EVEN AT THE RED SEA."

Israel did not wish to understand or take the trouble to study the ten plagues or wish to remember the countless mercies of their Great Shepherd. Forty hours took Israel out of Egypt, but forty years did not take Egypt out of Israel.

(8) "NEVERTHELESS HE SAVED THEM FOR HIS NAME'S SAKE, THAT HE MIGHT MAKE HIS MIGHTY POWER TO BE KNOWN."

God did not save Israel because of their righteousness or morality, but for *"His Name's sake."* Likewise, the virtue of Salvation comes to the believing sinner and forgiveness to the repentant Christian not because of any personal righteousness, but always for *"His Name's sake."*

MIGHTY POWER

It took *"mighty power"* to save Israel from Egyptian bondage; likewise, it takes *"mighty power"* to save man from the bondage of sin's darkness. Consequently, psychology, education, money, philanthropy, and even the Church cannot save.

In all the myriad of religions over the world, Christianity (which really is not a religion, but a relationship) is the only one that affords a changed life, because Christ is the only One Who can truly change men. Buddha cannot, and neither can Joseph Smith, nor Confucius, nor Muhammad, nor any other mortal!

As the unredeemed person trusts Christ for Salvation, the Believer, in order to live a righteous life, must continue to trust Christ and the Cross for Sanctification. Most Believers neither know nor understand this.

Even though every Believer understands somewhat the part the Cross plays in connection with our Salvation, they really don't have a clue as it regards our Sanctification. As a result, most Christians simply do not know how to live for God.

THE CROSS OF CHRIST

It is to the Apostle Paul that this great truth was given (Gal. 1:11-12). While the Cross of Christ is more or less the subject in all of Paul's Epistles, still, it is the Sixth Chapter of Romans which gives us the details of God's Prescribed Order of Victory.

In this Chapter, the first two Verses proclaim the fact that sin is the problem. Then Verses 3 through 5 tell us that the Cross of Christ is the only cure for sin. And we must remember that Paul is addressing all of this to Believers, which tells Believers how to live for God.

The balance of the Sixth Chapter proclaims the fact that if the Believer continues to exhibit faith in the Cross of Christ, and ever makes the Cross of Christ the Object of our Faith, then he is promised that *"sin* (the sin nature) *shall not have dominion over us"* (Rom. 6:14).

The Sixth Chapter of Romans has been described as a presentation of the *"mechanics of the Holy Spirit,"* which tells us how the Holy Spirit works, which is by and through the Cross. The Eighth Chapter of Romans has been described as a presentation of the *"dynamics of the Holy Spirit,"* which tells us *"what"* the Holy Spirit can do in our lives once we understand *"how"* He works.

Due to a scarcity of teaching on this all-important subject, most Believers have precious little knowledge of what the Sixth Chapter of Romans actually means.

This *"mighty power"* is available to us, but only on God's terms. Those terms are the Cross of Christ, and the Cross of Christ exclusively! In other words, the Cross of Christ must ever be the Object of the Believer's Faith. Only then can the Believer walk in victory (Rom. 6:1-14; 8:1-2, 11; I Cor. 1:17-18, 23; 2:2).

(9) "HE REBUKED THE RED SEA ALSO, AND IT WAS DRIED UP: SO HE LED THEM THROUGH THE DEPTHS, AS THROUGH THE WILDERNESS."

NOTES

The opening of the Red Sea was one of the greatest miracles that God has ever performed. It certainly typifies the Born-Again experience; but, more than all, it typifies the victory of the Believer over the world, the flesh, and the Devil.

The waters that stood up like two walls on both sides of the Children of Israel were symbolic of the great weight of sin which binds the sinner, and which can crush the Believer, that is, if the Believer does not understand the Cross as it refers to Sanctification, which, regrettably, most don't!

When Jesus Christ died on Calvary, He opened a path through that great *"depth"* of sin so that all who will, may come. All of this means that the sinner little knows how lost he is, and the Christian little knows how Saved he is.

The word *"depths"* lays to rest the claim that the waters here only were a few inches deep. Factually, at this juncture, the Red Sea probably was one hundred or more feet deep.

(10) "AND HE SAVED THEM FROM THE HAND OF HIM WHO HATED THEM, AND REDEEMED THEM FROM THE HAND OF THE ENEMY."

The enemy in this case was Egypt, whose sponsor was Satan. Israel could only have been extricated by God. No military force in the world could have carried this out; only God could, and He did!

SATAN

Satan hates the human race, even those who serve him diligently. He hates us because originally we were created in the Image of God (Gen. 1:27).

Satan especially hates the Child of God. The hatred is so severe that he will go to any lengths to bring down the Christian. This is the reason that leaning on the arm of flesh only can bring disaster. Paul spoke of this:

"For the Law of the Spirit of Life in Christ Jesus has made me free from the Law of Sin and Death" (Rom. 8:2).

WHAT IS THE LAW OF THE SPIRIT OF LIFE IN CHRIST JESUS?

This one statement proclaims to us the fact of the most powerful Law in the world, the only Law that can make one *"free from the Law of Sin and Death,"* which is the second most powerful Law in the world. This is a *"Law"* that was devised by the Godhead sometime in eternity past.

The *"Spirit"* pertains to the Holy Spirit. The short phrase, *"Of Life,"* refers to the fact that the Holy Spirit is the Superintendent of the Life which comes exclusively through Christ.

The short phrase, *"In Christ Jesus,"* probably more closely proclaims the meaning of the New Covenant than anything else. Paul uses the phrase, or one of its derivatives, nearly 100 times in his fourteen Epistles.

The phrase, ever how it is used, always refers to what Christ did at the Crucifixion. It concerns the benefits of the Cross, that is, what He there did accomplish, as it regards the greatest victory in human history. This is *"the Law of the Spirit of Life in Christ Jesus."* As stated, this is the only Law in the universe that can make one *"free from the Law of Sin and Death."*

HOW DOES THIS LAW OPERATE WITHIN OUR LIVES?

It operates by faith!

First of all, the Believer is to understand that every single thing he receives from the Lord comes to him exclusively from Jesus Christ as the Source and the Cross as the Means.

God has not changed; and God cannot change. However, before the Cross the Lord was very limited as to what He could give man. Pertaining to every single thing that was given, it was done, one might say, on credit — by that, we speak of looking forward to what the Cross would bring about. The Cross of Christ is the foundation of the Word of God. It is the story of the Word of God, all the way from Genesis 1:1 through Revelation 22:21.

If one takes the Cross out of Christianity, we are left with *"another Jesus,"* which means it is not the Jesus of the Bible (II Cor. 11:4).

One is to ever make the Cross of Christ the object of his faith. When that is done, the Holy Spirit, Who works exclusively within the parameters of the Finished Work of Christ, will work mightily on our behalf (Rom. 8:11; Gal. 2:20-21). If we do not look exclusively to Christ and the Cross, the end result is that we *"frustrate the Grace of God,"* which means that we stop the flow of the Grace of God, which translates into abject failure — continued failure, at that!

If one will keep one's faith anchored solely in the Cross of Christ, the *"Law of the Spirit of Life in Christ Jesus,"* will without fail *"make us free from the Law of Sin and Death"* (Rom. 8:2).

(11) "AND THE WATERS COVERED THEIR ENEMIES: THERE WAS NOT ONE OF THEM LEFT."

This great truth continues!

TOTAL AND COMPLETE VICTORY

When the Children of Israel came out on yonder shore, the entirety of the army of the Egyptians had been drowned beneath the briny waves of the Red Sea. The evidence is that Pharaoh also was among the Egyptian dead. As the Scripture says, *"There was not one of them left."*

It is the Will of God that every enemy in the life of the Believer be totally and completely defeated. As long as there is one enemy raising his ugly head in our life and dominating us in some way, we are not experiencing the full victory that Christ paid for at the Cross of Calvary.

The Bible does not teach sinless perfection, but it definitely does teach that *"sin shall not have dominion over you"* (Rom. 6:14).

Jesus didn't die on the Cross that <u>some</u> of these enemies be defeated, but that <u>every last one</u> of these enemies be defeated!

THE SEVENFOLD VICTORY

There is a beautiful illustration in the Fifth Chapter of Revelation which describes this.

In John the Beloved's Vision of the Throne of God, he said, *"And I beheld, and, lo, in the midst of the Throne and of the four Beasts* (living creatures), *and in the midst of the Elders, stood a Lamb as it had been slain, having seven horns and seven eyes which are the Seven Spirits of God sent forth into all the Earth"* (Rev. 5:6).

This is a most strange apparition. What does it all mean?

What John saw really was a symbolism, which is meant to explain something. The

"*Lamb as it had been slain*" refers to Christ and what He did at the Cross. The "*seven horns*" speak of dominion — total dominion, in fact. "*Seven*" is God's number of totality, universality, and perfection. So it speaks of a perfect dominion.

We must remember that what Jesus did at the Cross was exclusively for us. So whatever we here see has to do with us and our relationship with the Lord.

The "*seven horns*" pertain to the fact that the Believer is to have total and complete dominion over every sin, every fault, and every weakness within his life. In other words, his victory is to be a perfect victory, a total victory, an absolute victory.

The "*seven eyes*" speak of a perfect illumination. If the Believer looks exclusively to the Cross of Christ, ever making that the Object of his Faith, which is symbolized by the "*Slain Lamb,*" he can be guaranteed perfect illumination, which means he will not be taken over or deceived by false doctrine, and he also will have total dominion over sin in every capacity.

This does not, as stated, teach sinless perfection. But it does teach that sin will not have dominion over the Believer (Rom. 6:14).

Just as there was not one Egyptian left, there should also not be any sin left!

(12) "THEN BELIEVED THEY HIS WORDS; THEY SANG HIS PRAISE."

After they have experienced His deliverance, how many millions "*sing His praises*"?

There are millions who only have embraced a philosophy of Christianity, and not Christ Himself; consequently, there are no "*praises.*" To be sure, whenever there is true Deliverance, there are true praises. And true Deliverance can only come about by the Believer evidencing faith in Christ and the Cross. With the Cross of Christ as the Object of one's Faith, the Holy Spirit will then work mightily; however, when that is lacking, virtually everything stops. In the modern Church, there is regrettably little understanding of the Cross, which results in little acceptance of the Cross as it regards Victory in one's life. As a result, there is very little true praise given to God.

(13) "THEY SOON FORGOT HIS WORKS; THEY WAITED NOT FOR HIS COUNSEL."

NOTES

How so much this describes the modern Church.

FORGETTING WHAT GOD HAS DONE

It has been said that at the beginning of every Move of God, great praises go to Him because of His great delivering Power. But then another generation comes along that is born physically, but not spiritually. Not only do they "*forget His Works,*" but they never really have experienced His Works. As a result, "*they no longer wait for His Counsel,*" but rather seek the counsel of man.

Verse 13 characterizes the majority of the present-day Church. Little by little, it has abandoned the Word of God and has accepted the counsel of men, even going so far as to claim that the Bible doesn't address itself to modern man, who thereby needs the help of humanistic psychology.

Such borders on the very edge of acute blasphemy.

In truth, the Word of God holds the answer for every single problem that man might have (II Pet. 1:3-4).

A man gave a child a puzzle. He expected her to take several hours to put the puzzle together. To his surprise, she finished it in a few minutes.

Considering that she was very young, he asked her, "*How did you do that?*"

She responded, "*I looked on the back of the box, which gave the front of the puzzle and the back of the puzzle. When the puzzle is completed, the back of the puzzle shows a man.*

"*When you get the man right, everything else is right.*"

The man can get right only by accepting the Lord Jesus Christ.

(14) "BUT LUSTED EXCEEDINGLY IN THE WILDERNESS, AND TEMPTED GOD IN THE DESERT."

Israel so soon forgot; likewise, we so soon forget. Verse 14 characterizes the plight of the modern Christian.

LUST

Within itself, the word "*lust*" does not always denote evil, especially when it refers to desiring things of the Spirit; however, that of which this Verse speaks is that which is evil.

Israel lusted after the flesh, and for the flesh; sadly, so do many of us (Ex. 16:6-8; Num. 11:4-6).

In its base form, *"lust"* is a desire for that which is over and above that which God has given us. Israel was not satisfied with the Manna, which was a Type of Christ. They wanted *"flesh."* And then they tempted God, saying, *"Is the LORD among us or not?"* (Ex. 17:7). Doubt never can see God, even when He is in the very midst; Faith always sees God.

(15) "AND HE GAVE THEM THEIR REQUEST; BUT SENT LEANNESS INTO THEIR SOUL."

This Passage is amazing! It also closely portrays the modern Church.

THE MODERN CHURCH

The last few years have seen the Church clamoring for money, position, earthly power, and numerous other things. Oftentimes, God has granted the request, but the price has been high — leanness into the soul.

Israel wanted things, but not Christ. The modern Church wants things, but not Christ.

But we must understand that everything other than Christ brings *"leanness."*

Pulpit says, *"By 'leanness' is meant dissatisfaction or disgust. After eating freely of the quails for a full month, the food became 'loathsome' to them* (Num. 11:20). *Whether it actually produced the pestilence which followed* (Num. 11:33), *or whether that was a separate and distinct affliction, it is impossible to determine."* [55]

I personally think that the attitude of the Israelites brought about this judgment from the Lord.

As a Believer, we must be very careful concerning our requests to the Lord. We must desire first of all His Will, and His Will alone! Regrettably, all too often, we desire our own will and not His. Such a direction always brings *"leanness into the soul,"* that is, *"Judgment."*

(16) "THEY ENVIED MOSES ALSO IN THE CAMP, AND AARON THE SAINT OF THE LORD."

The example is found in Numbers, Chapters 12, 16, and 17.

JUSTIFICATION BY FAITH

It is interesting that in the Sixteenth Verse Aaron is called *"The Saint of the LORD,"* and then, in the Nineteenth Verse, reference is made to the Golden Calf that he made.

Many have difficulty understanding this. It portrays the life experience of all Christians. Such could be said only by *"Justification by Faith."* Sanctification *"makes"* one not guilty; Justification *"declares"* one not guilty.

In this case, the Righteousness of Christ was imputed to Aaron, just as the Righteousness of Christ is imputed unto us. Then, through Christ, the Golden Calf is forgotten, and the Saint is remembered — all because of Christ and the Cross.

"Justification by Faith" is gained solely by the believing sinner evidencing Faith in Christ. Christ paid the penalty which we could not pay; our faith in Him thereby grants unto us a total, pure, and perfect Justification by God. It is based solely and totally upon the Sacrifice of Christ and our faith in that Finished Work.

THE CROSS OF CHRIST

That's the reason the Cross of Christ is so very important! In fact, it is the heartbeat of Christianity; one might say it is the very engine of the soul. Without the Cross, there is no Justification and there is no Sanctification. Without the Cross of Christ, there is nothing. That's the reason we constantly state, *"Christ is the Source, and the Cross is the Means."*

When the Church ignores the Cross, or worse yet, repudiates the Cross, this presents the greatest sin of all. There is no greater sin, because such typifies gross unbelief. And regrettably, most of the modern Church is doing just that — either ignoring the Cross or openly repudiating the Cross.

(17) THE EARTH OPENED AND SWALLOWED UP DATHAN AND COVERED THE COMPANY OF ABIRAM."

The Sixteenth Chapter of Numbers gives the account of this episode. The warning is clear.

DEATH

God called Moses and Aaron to perform a task. Satan attempted to hinder that call. His greatest method of operation is to use fellow Believers. The great majority of the

Church is led by man and not by God.

In this case, Satan used powerful religious leaders in the camp. His methods have not changed today. The far greater hindrance to the Work of God is religious leaders (so-called) attempting to usurp authority over those whom God has called. It brought death then, and it will bring death now. The Church as a whole has almost no moving of the Holy Spirit within it. Of course, some few definitely do have such a Move of the Holy Spirit, but only a few.

That which is outlined in Verses 16 and 17 of this Chapter proclaims the reason why there is such little moving of the Holy Spirit. Religious men little desire to follow God. They love to wield authority themselves, but their authority is not God-given, but rather man-given. Such always brings death to the Church.

Those whom God truly has called have ever been hindered by those whom God has not called, those who have called themselves. Bible Government has been diluted and man's government has taken its place — and all because of usurping authority over that which is truly of God.

(18) "AND A FIRE WAS KINDLED IN THEIR COMPANY; THE FLAME BURNED UP THE WICKED."

Men will have Holy Spirit fire or else they will have the fire of God's Judgment. Sadly, there is precious little Holy Spirit fire in the modern Church. Because we are living in the Day of Grace, some erroneously believe that God does not bring Judgment on modern Dathans and Abirams. While we truly are living in the Day of Grace, still, if there is no Repentance, ultimately the Judgment of God will come upon rebellion now, just as it did then.

THE JUDGMENT OF GOD

While this Judgment from the Lord is not always as obvious as it was with these here mentioned, still, the spiritual death is very obvious, or else it should be. It is obvious to those who truly know the Word of God, those who truly are seeking to follow that which the Lord has laid down.

In this Day of Grace, the Lord actually is less lenient that He was under Law. The Scripture plainly says, and I quote from THE EXPOSITOR'S STUDY BIBLE, *"And the times of this ignorance God winked at* (does not reflect that such ignorance was Salvation, for it was not! Before the Cross, there was very little Light in the world, so God withheld Judgment); *but now commands all men everywhere to repent* (but since the Cross, the *"Way"* is open to all; it's up to us Believers to make that *"Way"* known to all men [Acts 17:30]).

(19) "THEY MADE A CALF IN HOREB, AND WORSHIPPED THE MOLTEN IMAGE."

The sacred name of Horeb is given to Sinai so to heighten the sin of representing the God of Glory by an animal that ate grass.

(20) "THUS THEY CHANGED THEIR GLORY INTO THE SIMILITUDE OF AN OX THAT EATS GRASS."

This Passage shows that the idol worship of Egypt was still ingrained in the Israelites. As stated, it took very little time to get the Children of Israel out of Egypt, but it took much time to get Egypt out of the Children of Israel.

These people continued to *"worship."* In other words, their action continued to be very religious. How so like the modern Church! How many Golden Calves abound today in the form of vain philosophies, modern psychology, false doctrines, and man-made religion?

(21) "THEY FORGOT GOD THEIR SAVIOUR, WHICH HAD DONE GREAT THINGS IN EGYPT."

This is speaking of the mighty plagues that God brought upon the Egyptians. They forgot that He, not man, was their Saviour!

How far have we gone down the same road today, in forgetting God our Saviour? Most of the modern Church looks to humanistic psychology, which originated with man, thereby with Satan.

God help us!

(22) "WONDROUS WORKS IN THE LAND OF HAM, AND TERRIBLE THINGS BY THE RED SEA."

Egypt is here referred to as the descendants of Noah's son, Ham. These Passages show the incurable evil of the human heart. In the midst of the mightiest move of God the world ever had known, these people lost their way. As wonderful as miracles are, they little will direct the human heart toward God. For any person to stand spiritually strong, there must be a strong adherence to the Word of God. Tragically, the Bible is an unread Book in the modern Church.

(23) "THEREFORE HE SAID THAT HE WOULD DESTROY THEM, HAD NOT MOSES HIS CHOSEN STOOD BEFORE HIM IN THE BREACH, TO TURN AWAY HIS WRATH, LEST HE SHOULD DESTROY THEM."

This says two things to us:

1. Irrespective of our past experiences in God, none of us would be here were it not for our Heavenly Moses, the Lord Jesus Christ. He turns away the Wrath of God from us in His Intercessory role — and all on our behalf (Heb. 7:25-26).

2. This Passage also portrays to us the significance of any Godly intercessor. Samuel said, *"God forbid that I should sin against the LORD in ceasing to pray for you"* (I Sam. 12:23). Paul basically prayed the same way concerning those who had forsaken him, *"I pray God that it may not be laid to their charge"* (II Tim. 4:16).

For those who are in sin, their only hope is in the prayers of Godly loved-ones. When these Godly loved-ones no longer are there. . . .

(24) "YEA, THEY DESPISED THE PLEASANT LAND, THEY BELIEVED NOT HIS WORD."

The cause of all error, sin, failure, wrong direction, incorrect leading, and straying from God is because of failure to believe the Bible.

This Passage pertains to Numbers, Chapters 13 and 14. The people sent in twelve spies. Ten of the twelve were faithless. Only Caleb and Joshua maintained their faith. The ten said, *"We cannot take the land,"* while the two (Caleb and Joshua) said, *"Let us go up at once and possess it, for we are well able to overcome it."* However, unbelief prevailed and an entire generation died in the wilderness as a result of that unbelief.

(25) "BUT MURMURED IN THEIR TENTS, AND HEARKENED NOT UNTO THE VOICE OF THE LORD."

Murmuring and complaining have to be two of the greatest sins in the life of any Believer. Such action always marks faithlessness.

NOTES

And yet, I suspect that every single Christian has committed these sins at one time or another.

We should be warned that the Lord looks very dimly on such attitude and action. When we do such, we actually are registering a complaint against the Lord. The problem may be ours or others, but it certainly is not the fault of the Lord.

(26) "THEREFORE HE LIFTED UP HIS HAND AGAINST THEM, TO OVERTHROW THEM IN THE WILDERNESS."

God considered the unbelief of the Children of Israel an even greater sin than the making of the Golden Calf. That is a startling statement, but true! The greatest sin then, and the greatest sin now, is failure to believe the Bible.

UNBELIEF

To make it more pointed, unbelief registered toward the Cross is the greatest sin of this present age; it, no doubt, has been the greatest sin of every age.

Without fear of contradiction, I think it can be said that all unbelief centers up in a failure to believe that what Jesus did for us at the Cross answers every question and meets every need. Tragically and sadly, the modern Church simply does not believe that the answer is in the Cross; therefore, they recommend humanistic psychology, or a hundred and one other directions. But in spite of all of that, the problem continues to be unbelief as it regards the Cross of Christ.

The sin of the Golden Calf was grievous indeed; however, when we consider that the sin of unbelief is even greater than that sin, we come to realize just how bad unbelief actually is. Now that we have defined it, meaning that it is centered up in a failure to believe what Jesus did at the Cross, such unbelief becomes even more marked and more obvious.

(27) "TO OVERTHROW THEIR SEED ALSO AMONG THE NATIONS, AND TO SCATTER THEM IN THE LANDS."

This was done twice:

1. During the time of Jeremiah, when God overthrew Judah, after having overthrown the Northern Kingdom of Israel some 133 years earlier: The people were taken captives to

Babylon and remained there some seventy years and then were reinstated in the land.

2. The second dispersion, when Titus the Roman General surrounded Jerusalem, sacked and burned the city: Over one million Jews were killed in this horrible siege. At this time, Israel ceased, by and large, to exist as a nation. They wandered among the nations of the world for nearly 2,000 years before they finally were formed again as a nation in 1948.

So, this prediction was given by the Lord through the Psalmist quite a few centuries before the actual happening, especially the second dispersion.

(28) "THEY JOINED THEMSELVES ALSO UNTO BAAL-PEOR, AND ATE THE SACRIFICES OF THE DEAD."

The Hebrew noun *"Ba-al"* means *"master,"* *"possessor,"* or *"husband."* At times, it is used with suffixes, like Baal-peor or Baal-berith. The word may have retained something of its original sense; but, in general, Baal is a proper name and refers to a specific deity, Hadad, the Semitic storm-god, the most important deity, so-called, in the Canaanite pantheon.

BAAL

The Baal cult affected and challenged the worship of Yahweh throughout Israelite history. Little by little, Israel switched her allegiance from the God of Heaven, Who was her *"Master"* and *"Husband,"* to Baal by calling him her *"master"* and *"husband."*

Baal was a principal name for many, if not all, of the heathen gods. He was, in effect, the king of the gods.

With the same *"name"* being given to Baal as to the God of Heaven (Master or Husband), in times of great spiritual declension, it was easy for Israel to gradually move her worship over to an idol she could see with her eyes instead of to the God of Heaven, Whom she could not see with her eyes.

SACRIFICES OF THE DEAD

The *"sacrifices of the dead"* have to do with communicating with the dead. This cannot be done, and all such efforts are in the realm of witchcraft. Hence, the modern *"channeling"* and the *"teaching of reincarnation"* are false and pertain to witchcraft; they are, therefore, demonic. All pretended traffic with the dead is forbidden in the Word of God (Deut. 18:11; I Sam., Chpt. 28; I Chron. 10:13; Isa. 8:19).

All of this has to do with witchcraft, and is forbidden in the Word of God. This means that Believers are to have nothing to do with *"psychics,"* *"fortune tellers,"* *"palm readers,"* or those who claim to have access to the spirit world. They may definitely have access to the spirit world; but most definitely it is not the spirit world of Light, but rather of darkness. As such, nothing can come from such actions but demon spirits.

(29) "THUS THEY PROVOKED HIM TO ANGER WITH THEIR INVENTIONS: AND THE PLAGUE BROKE IN UPON THEM."

The word *"inventions"* has to do with new ways of committing sin. All sin ultimately invites and will entertain *"plague."* America and Canada are today *"plagued"* because of sin. These *"plagues"* consist of alcoholism, drug addiction, gambling, diseases such as AIDS, homosexuality, etc., all resulting in untold heartache, suffering, and sorrow for the people.

(30) "THEN STOOD UP PHINEHAS, AND EXECUTED JUDGMENT: AND SO THE PLAGUE WAS STAYED."

Men are ever seeking to stop the *"plague"* by human means. It is not possible to do so. It is like putting a Band-Aid on cancer. Only two things can stop the *"plague"*:

1. The Blood of Jesus Christ, which pertains to the Cross.

2. Fidelity to the Bible.

(31) "AND THAT WAS COUNTED UNTO HIM FOR RIGHTEOUSNESS UNTO ALL GENERATIONS FOREVERMORE."

Phinehas became the third High Priest. God gave him an everlasting Priesthood because of his zeal for righteousness in slaying the rebels. He will be an everlasting Priest like all the Redeemed who are made Kings and Priests to reign on Earth (Rev. 1:5-6; 5:10; 20:4-6; 22:4-5).

(32) "THEY ANGERED HIM ALSO AT THE WATERS OF STRIFE, SO THAT IT WENT ILL WITH MOSES FOR THEIR SAKES."

The *"waters of strife"* were at *"Meribah"* (Num. 20:13).

MAN'S COMPLAINTS ARE SENSELESS

The Children of Israel who did this thing were the group who were to go into the Promised Land. The old unbelieving generation had now died off; so the evil heart of unbelief that resided in their fathers also resided in them. They complained, they murmured, and they blamed their plight on Moses.

Man's complaints, like these, are usually senseless.

If the nation had obeyed God in the first place, they would have been through the wilderness and out of it now for some 38 years. They themselves were responsible for their being in such an evil place. So their complaints against Moses and against God were groundless.

Perhaps this sin of murmuring and complaining about conditions which are, in fact, our own fault is the greatest weakness of any Christian. None of this was God's or Moses' doings. They had only themselves to blame. Sadly, Moses would handle himself poorly in this instance and would himself sin greatly.

(33) "BECAUSE THEY PROVOKED HIS SPIRIT, SO THAT HE SPOKE UNADVISEDLY WITH HIS LIPS."

The sin that he committed was in striking the Rock the second time, when God had told him rather to speak to it. The Rock was a Type of Christ (I Cor. 10:4). It already had been smitten once previously, which was a Type of Christ's dying on Calvary (Ex. 17:5-7).

THE SMITING OF THE ROCK

Israel is back at the same place (Meribah). When we are out of the Will of God, about the best we can do is to travel in circles.

There was no water and the people were thirsty, so the Lord told Moses to speak to the Rock and the water would come out. When Moses smote the Rock the second time, which was disobedience to the Lord, he was saying, by symbolism, that the first smiting of the Rock, which symbolized Jesus' dying on Calvary, did not suffice for the sins of man. In other words, Christ needed to be crucified again. His smiting the Rock the second time, therefore, was a grievous sin in the Mind of God.

The way that Moses spoke unadvisedly with his lips was that he said, *"Must we fetch you water out of this Rock?"* (Num. 20:10). First of all, Moses spoke harshly to Israel and not to the Rock as commanded. Further, he called attention to *"we"* — himself and Aaron — as the source of supply, and not Jehovah.

Moses would be denied the privilege of going into the Promised Land because of this sin. He did not lose his soul, but he most definitely lost that which was so very dear to him – entering the Promised Land.

(34) "THEY DID NOT DESTROY THE NATIONS, CONCERNING WHOM THE LORD COMMANDED THEM."

The nations that occupied the Promised Land, and we speak of the time before the entrance of the Children of Israel, were the Jebusites, the Hivites, the Canaanites, and others. These are symbols of enemies that are within our lives, such as jealousy, pride, envy, etc. As God ordered Israel to destroy her enemies, He orders us to do the same with spiritual enemies.

THE CROSS OF CHRIST

But let it be understood: There is only one way these spiritual enemies can be defeated by the modern Christian. Actually, these enemies have already been defeated at the Cross of Calvary. None were excluded; all were defeated in totality.

The Believer is to exhibit faith in Christ and the Cross and not allow his faith to be moved elsewhere, which then will give the Holy Spirit great latitude to work within our lives and to bring about the intended results.

The problem with many modern Christians, and I speak of those who truly love the Lord, is that we are attempting to fight battles which the Lord already has fought and won. I don't think the Lord takes kindly to that. In a sense, our doing such is the same as Moses striking the Rock the second time, when, as it regarded that second time, all he had to do was to speak to it.

Considering that Jesus already has paid the price at Calvary's Cross and defeated every enemy, all we have to do is simply speak to these problems in the Name of Jesus, making certain that our faith is maintained in Christ and the Cross. Then Victory is ours.

But let me say it even again, because it is so very, very important. The Lord does not look kindly on our attempts to fight battles which our Lord already has fought and won, battles which we cannot hope to win in any case. Without the Lord, we are no match for Satan; however, it seems we take quite a long time to come to that conclusion.

(35) "BUT WERE MINGLED AMONG THE HEATHEN, AND LEARNED THEIR WORKS."

As Israel could not come to terms with these idol worshippers, likewise, we cannot come to terms with any sin within our lives. If we do not defeat it, then it will defeat us.

This Verse proclaims the blight, not only of Israel of old, but also of the modern Church.

THE WAYS OF THE WORLD

It is perfectly acceptable for the world to adopt the ways of the True Church; however, when the Church adopts the ways of the world, it brings nothing but disaster. And that's exactly what the modern Church is now doing.

It has adopted, and is adopting, the advertising methods of the world. All the means of so-called Church Growth are based on business and advertising models of the world.

There is nothing in the New Testament concerning Church Growth. There is plenty in the New Testament regarding Christian Growth, but not Church Growth.

The truth is, we are filling our Churches with people who really have never been Born-Again, simply because we have adopted the ways of the world. The methods of the world will add absolutely nothing to the Work of God. Not only will nothing be added, but much will be taken away. Our *"mingling among the heathen"* and *"learning their works"* will never come out to any good, but always to harm.

The Holy Spirit will not and cannot bless anything that He Himself has not conceived. But such a lesson seems so difficult for us to learn.

(36) "AND THEY SERVED THEIR IDOLS: WHICH WERE A SNARE UNTO THEM."

These people did not become acclimated to Israel's God, but rather Israel became acclimated to their gods (idols).

THE LAW OF REGRESSION

If one rotten apple is placed in a barrel of good apples, the rotten apple does not become healthy like the good apples. The opposite happens. The good apples also become infected, until the whole barrel is rotten.

Paul said, *"A little leaven leavens the whole lump"* (I Cor. 5:6).

If sins of the flesh or spirit are allowed to remain in our lives, they ultimately will affect the whole.

It is the same with false doctrine. If it is not actually abandoned and repented of, ultimately the individual, or even an entire Denomination, will become nothing but the false doctrine.

(37) "YEA, THEY SACRIFICED THEIR SONS AND THEIR DAUGHTERS UNTO DEVILS,

(38) "AND SHED INNOCENT BLOOD, EVEN THE BLOOD OF THEIR SONS AND OF THEIR DAUGHTERS, WHOM THEY SACRIFICED UNTO THE IDOLS OF CANAAN: AND THE LAND WAS POLLUTED WITH BLOOD."

Israel sank to the lowest depths of sinful bondage. They actually began to engage in human sacrifice; they offered their sons and daughters to these idol gods (devils).

HUMAN SACRIFICE

The Children of Israel were the only people on the face of the Earth who truly knew God. For such a people to sink to the level of offering up little boys and girls as sacrifices to heathen gods is abominable beyond compare. And yet, that's what Israel did! Now we certainly should understand why the Lord had to take the measures that He took. Even then, He sent Prophet after Prophet to try to turn them — but all to no avail!

It is said that one of these hideous images had outstretched arms on which the choicest of little boys and girls would be placed. These children would be tied to the idol's arms and a fire would be built in the idol's body. Little by little the idol grew red hot. Evil priests beat drums to drown out the screams of the dying children, who slowly were burned to death — and this was done by God's chosen people.

DEMON SPIRITS

The word *"devils"* actually is used for demons. There actually is only one chief Devil, Lucifer, but there are many demons. They are given several names: unclean spirits, familiar spirits, evil spirits, and others. Demon spirits greatly influence all unsaved people and even possess some of them. As well, they seek to hinder, hurt, harm, and influence Believers. They are to be resisted by the Name of Jesus, the Word of God, and the Blood of our Saviour.

A Christian cannot be demon-possessed, but definitely can be demon-influenced or demon-oppressed. Demon possession comes from within, while demon oppression comes from without.

The resources of the Child of God against demon spirits are prayer, bodily control, and the whole armor of God, all wrapped up in one's faith in Christ and the Cross (Mat. 17:21; Eph. 6:10-18).

There are demon spirits for every sickness, unholy trait, and doctrinal error known among men. They must be cast out or resisted in order to experience relief from them. Disease germs, which are closely allied with unclean spirits, really are living forms of corruption which come into the bodies of men and bring them to death. Just as refuse breeds maggots, so man in his fallen state of corruption breeds germs through unclean living and contact with corruption in the fallen world. They are agents of Satan which corrupt the bodies of his victims.

Traffic with demon spirits (such as witchcraft, communication with the dead, horoscopes, ouija boards, astrological charts, and other similar things) is forbidden in the Bible (Ex. 22:18; Gal. 5:19-21; Rev. 9:21; Num. 22:7; Isa. 8:19; II Chron. 33:6; Jer. 10:2).

(39) "THUS WERE THEY DEFILED WITH THEIR OWN WORKS, AND WENT A WHORING WITH THEIR OWN INVENTIONS."

The word *"inventions,"* as here used, refers to new ways of sinning. In other words, Israel not only learned of the evil direction of their heathen neighbors, but added to that evil direction. That is, they did the heathen one better!

(40) "THEREFORE WAS THE WRATH OF THE LORD KINDLED AGAINST HIS PEOPLE, INSOMUCH THAT HE ABHORRED HIS OWN INHERITANCE."

This Passage, plus many more of similar substance, completely invalidates the erroneous doctrine of Unconditional Eternal Security. God cannot abide sin in the lives of His chosen any more than He can in the heathen.

When one understands the previous Verses concerning Israel, who entered into Satan worship to such an extent that they sacrificed their own children to these heathenistic gods, then one can understand how God would come to *"abhor His Own inheritance."*

(41) "AND HE GAVE THEM INTO THE HAND OF THE HEATHEN; AND THEY WHO HATED THEM RULED OVER THEM."

The Lord did not do this, however, until all avenues of Mercy and Grace were exhausted. This is what He said through the Prophet Jeremiah:

"Since the day that your fathers came forth out of the land of Egypt unto this day I have even sent unto you all My servants the Prophets, daily rising up early and sending them:

"Yet they hearkened not unto Me, nor inclined their ear, but hardened their neck: they did worse than their fathers" (Jer. 7:25-26).

They still would not repent!

(42) "THEIR ENEMIES ALSO OPPRESSED THEM, AND THEY WERE BROUGHT INTO SUBJECTION UNDER THEIR HAND."

When Israel was living for God, her enemies could make no headway against her whatsoever, which shows that God helped and blessed them. However, when Israel turned away from God, then God allowed her enemies to *"oppress them."* Israel's blessings were totally tied to God; likewise, sin could and did deter and stop these Blessings.

(43) "MANY TIMES DID HE DELIVER THEM; BUT THEY PROVOKED HIM WITH THEIR COUNSEL, AND WERE BROUGHT LOW FOR THEIR INIQUITY."

This Passage, as well as countless others in the Word of God, proclaims the fact that sin is the cause of the problems of man. And there is only one way that sin can be addressed properly, which is by the individual evidencing faith in Christ and the Cross.

Despite the fact that Israel broke her promises with God over and over, still, *"He continued to deliver them."* Despite that, they continued to go deeper and deeper into sin, until finally there was no recourse other than for God to take them into captivity.

The Lord's Ways will not change; in fact, His Ways cannot change. Every Believer should understand that as the Lord dealt with Israel and Judah of old, He also will deal with us. We should not forget that!

(44) "NEVERTHELESS HE REGARDED THEIR AFFLICTION, WHEN HE HEARD THEIR CRY."

Even though Israel sinned greatly, still, when they were in great *"affliction"* and *"cried unto the LORD,"* He always heard them and responded accordingly — except when they rejected His only Son and their only Saviour, the Lord Jesus Christ.

When Solomon dedicated the Temple, this very petition was ensconced in his prayer (II Chron. 6:36-39).

God's answer to Solomon was the same as it had been to all people. It remains the same presently:

"If My people, which are called by My Name, shall humble themselves, and pray, and seek My Face, and turn from their wicked ways; then will I hear from Heaven, and will forgive their sin, and will heal their land" (II Chron. 7:14).

(45) "AND HE REMEMBERED FOR THEM HIS COVENANT, AND REPENTED ACCORDING TO THE MULTITUDE OF HIS MERCIES."

God constantly kept in mind His Covenant with the very people who provoked Him to abhor them. He always was ready to repent (change His Mind) toward Israel and to forgive and deliver them if they would meet His righteous terms of the Covenant (II Chron. 7:14).

(46) "HE MADE THEM ALSO TO BE PITIED OF ALL THOSE WHO CARRIED THEM CAPTIVES."

God gave Israel favor in the eyes of her captors (II Ki., Chpt. 25; Dan. 1:19-6:2).

(47) "SAVE US, O LORD OUR GOD, AND GATHER US FROM AMONG THE HEATHEN, TO GIVE THANKS UNTO YOUR HOLY NAME, AND TO TRIUMPH IN YOUR PRAISE."

This request and prayer was answered in regards to the dispersion at Babylon. It has not been answered concerning their dispersion in A.D. 70.

However, a part of this petition is in the process of being answered now, *"Gather us from among the heathen."*

The world has just witnessed the emigration of hundreds of thousands of Jews from the former Soviet Union to the Holy Land. The emigration will continue, not only from Russia, but also from other countries of the world.

The latter part of the petition has not yet been answered, and will not be answered until the Lord comes back in the midst of the Battle of Armageddon. Then Israel truly will *"give thanks unto Your Holy Name."* Then they truly will *"triumph in Your praise."*

(48) "BLESSED BE THE LORD GOD OF ISRAEL FROM EVERLASTING TO EVERLASTING: AND LET ALL THE PEOPLE SAY, AMEN. PRAISE YE THE LORD."

This Book (Numbers) closes with the expected *"Amen,"* but the repeated *"Amen"* is here changed to *"Hallelujah!"* This harmonizes with the theme of the Book. *"Amen"* expresses the desire that the wilderness journey should end and the Kingdom should be established; *"Hallelujah"* joyfully announces the gratification of both desires.

It is, therefore, fitting that the end of the dark night of the wilderness and the dawn of the bright day of the Kingdom should be greeted with a double *"Hallelujah!"* — one at the commencement of the Psalm (Vs. 1), and the other at its close.

BOOK FIVE
(The Deuteronomy Book)
(*Psalms 107-150*)

PSALM 107

*Author Unknown:
Praise to God for Deliverance*

(1) "O GIVE THANKS UNTO THE LORD,

FOR HE IS GOOD: FOR HIS MERCY ENDURES FOREVER."

As noted, the author of this Psalm is unknown.

THE DEUTERONOMY BOOK

This is the First Psalm of the fifth Book of the Psalms, which corresponds to the Fifth Book of the Pentateuch (Deuteronomy). The Divine title for that Book is *"These are the Words."* Israel was about to take possession of Canaan and was promised prosperity if they would be obedient to the Word of God, but slavery, affliction, and banishment were promised for disobedience. The Message of Book Five of the Psalms is similar, but the circumstances are different.

PROSPERITY

Williams says, *"Prosperity is shown to be dependent upon acceptance of the Word of God as the rule of life. But the Message is not now directed to a new and untried people, but instead to a tested, rebellious, and fallen people."* 56

In other words, the Book of Deuteronomy was directed toward a people who were about to possess the Promised Land; however, this last and fifth Book of the Psalms is directed toward fallen Israel, which ultimately will be brought back to God and to total possession of the Promised Land. This Message is accompanied by Grace. The observer learns that the Messiah is both loving and kind, and kind and loving.

This fifth Book, even as the First Verse proclaims, presents the beauteous picture of the Messiah coming as the Word of God with healing and help to those who, by disobedience to that Word, had brought themselves to ruin.

The First Psalm of each Book gives the keynote of the Book. So it is here.

Let the Reader know and understand that *"the LORD is good."* We must also ever understand that *"His Mercy endures forever."* And thank God for that!

If we meet His conditions, His Mercy will always be extended to us, no matter what sin we have committed.

THE CONDITIONS FOR MERCY

I have used the word *"conditions"* for effect, but the truth is, there is only one condition. Mercy will always be extended to the seeking soul, no matter what the sin, or disobedience, or the transgression has been, providing that soul looks exclusively to Christ and what Christ did for us at the Cross. That is the only requirement.

The old song says:

"Kneel at the Cross,
"Christ will meet you there,
"Come while He waits for you;
"List' to His Voice,
"Leave with Him your care,
"And begin life anew."

It is only at the Cross that the Lord will meet the seeking soul. He will meet the individual, whoever he might be, no place else! If we try to come any other way, we are judged as *"a thief and a robber"* (Jn. 10:1).

Furthermore, Jesus speaks of a *"Door,"* which, in reality, proclaims the way to Himself as the *"Door"* (Jn. 10:1-2).

We must, however, remember that this *"Door"* is a blood-splattered door. The symbolism harks back to the original Passover, when the blood was applied to the doorposts on each side and on the header of the door to each house (Ex. 12:7).

Let us say it again:

Christ will meet the seeking soul at the Cross, and at the Cross alone. If we attempt to come to Him any way other than the Cross, the Holy Spirit will bar all access (Eph. 2:13-18).

(2) "LET THE REDEEMED OF THE LORD SAY SO, WHOM HE HAS REDEEMED FROM THE HAND OF THE ENEMY."

The redeemed are urged to proclaim the Grace that redeemed them.

REDEMPTION

Every person who has been redeemed, and we speak of the time all the way from Abel to this particular moment, which, no doubt, refers to millions, all and without exception were redeemed by and through Christ and what He did for us at the Cross. The Cross of Christ is the means of Redemption, and the only means, we might quickly add.

So, whenever the Preacher preaches anything other than *"Jesus Christ and Him*

Crucified," he is preaching a gospel that will set no one free, that will cleanse no sin, that will redeem no soul. It is only the Message of the Cross which will accomplish such (Rom. 6:1-14; I Cor. 1:17-18, 23; 2:2; Gal. 6:14; Eph. 2:13-18; Col. 2:14-15).

THE ENEMY

The *"enemy"* here addressed presents a twofold meaning.

First and foremost, it speaks of every soul which has been redeemed, and the fact that every soul was redeemed from the powers of darkness, that is, *"the Devil."*

Paul said: *"Who gave Himself for our sins* (the Cross), *that He might deliver us from this present evil world* (the Cross alone can set the captive free), *according to the Will of God and our Father* (the standard of the entire process of Redemption):

"To Whom be Glory forever and ever (Divine Glory). *Amen"* (Gal. 1:4-5).

The second meaning has to do with the Antichrist and the future Glad Day when he will be defeated by the Lord at the Second Coming, which will redeem Israel. Then, *"the redeemed of the LORD shall say so."*

(3) "AND GATHERED THEM OUT OF THE LANDS, FROM THE EAST, AND FROM THE WEST, FROM THE NORTH, AND FROM THE SOUTH."

This speaks of the terrible dispersion that is referred to in the previous Psalm (106:41).

FOUR COMPANIES

They are grouped into four companies: wanderers, prisoners, fools, and homeless.

Concerning this, Williams says, *"These four companies that will be gathered from all points furnish a four-square picture of the rejecter of God's Word. He is homeless, enslaved, infirm, and restless. But in Christ as the Word of God there is Redemption for the self-ruined rebels. His Grace and Power avail to recover them and to restore nature."* [57]

This Third Verse is in the process of being fulfilled even now. When it is completely fulfilled, which will take place immediately after the Second Coming, Israel will then *"give thanks unto the LORD."*

(4) "THEY WANDERED IN THE WILDERNESS IN A SOLITARY WAY; THEY FOUND NO CITY TO DWELL IN.

(5) "HUNGRY AND THIRSTY, THEIR SOUL FAINTED IN THEM."

These two Verses pertain to Israel's rejection of Christ, and even their crucifying of Him, with the subsequent destruction which followed. Titus, commanding the mighty Roman Tenth, completely destroyed Jerusalem, razing the Temple to the ground, thereby destroying all Jewish national life. Over one million Jews were slaughtered in that carnage, with other hundreds of thousands sold as slaves all over the world, completely glutting the slave markets.

From that time, A.D. 70, Israel has done exactly what this Passage says, *"They wandered in the wilderness."* In other words, they found the entirety of the world a wilderness, which has now lasted for some 2,000 years.

The words, *"Solitary way,"* refer to a dispersion or wandering such as no people or nation ever has experienced.

As soon as they would find one city that they felt would welcome them, something would happen to drive them to another.

Because of their great rebellion against God, these, God's chosen people, who were to experience the great Blessings of God, instead have wandered the world *"hungry and thirsty"* for nearly 2,000 years.

After the horrible holocaust of World War II, where some six million Jews were slaughtered by demon-possessed Hitler, they then demanded a homeland — their ancient homeland, the Land which once had been known as *"Israel."* Miraculously, that became a reality in 1948. And yet, Israel has another judgment and tribulation to face. It will be the latter half of the Great Tribulation, which Jesus said would be worse than anything the world has ever known, or that Israel has ever known — even worse than the Holocaust of World War II (Mat. 24:21).

At that time, it will seem as though they are bound and destined for total annihilation. In other words, the Antichrist will attempt to do what Haman, Herod, and Hitler failed to do. He will come close to succeeding.

(6) "THEN THEY CRIED UNTO THE LORD IN THEIR TROUBLE, AND HE DELIVERED THEM OUT OF THEIR DISTRESSES."

This Verse gives us Israel's solution.

CRYING TO THE LORD

In a few simple words, this Verse proclaims the Coming of the Lord. It will be during the Battle of Armageddon. At this time, Israel will cry unto the Lord as they never have cried to Him before. As stated, they will be on the verge of total annihilation, with the Antichrist bearing down in a military campaign that appears to him to be total victory. The Lord will then deliver them, for He is the only One Who can deliver them.

The Holy Spirit will allow them to be maneuvered into a position where no nation on the face of the Earth (even the U.S.A.) will lift a hand to help them. The Antichrist will think surely that He can carry out the *"final solution."* He thinks he will wipe them from the face of the Earth, exactly as the new President of Iran said must be done.

As Israel then cries to the Lord, He will hear them, with this very Passage proclaiming the guarantee of that Promise. The Lord will come to their rescue, and do so as never before.

The Coming of the Lord will be without a doubt the greatest single phenomenon ever experienced on Planet Earth. At that time, Israel will be totally and completely delivered, with a victory so sure and so final as to be total in every respect. It all will be because of the Lord Jesus Christ, the very One Whom they crucified.

(7) "AND HE LED THEM FORTH BY THE RIGHT WAY, THAT THEY MIGHT GO TO A CITY OF HABITATION."

This speaks of the Lord's great victory at Armageddon (Ezek., Chpts. 38-39).

The *"city of habitation"* is Jerusalem. Now at long last it will be safely inhabited.

(8) "OH THAT MEN WOULD PRAISE THE LORD FOR HIS GOODNESS, AND FOR HIS WONDERFUL WORKS TO THE CHILDREN OF MEN!"

The entirety of this Psalm is a paean of praise to God for the great Deliverance He has brought which speaks of the defeat of the Antichrist at the Battle of Armageddon.

And yet, every Believer should praise the Lord, and do so constantly, for the great Redemption which He has afforded us. We have

NOTES

no less to be thankful for; we actually have even more reason to praise His Name.

These *"wonderful works"* include the Virgin Birth, His spotless Life, Calvary — above all, Calvary — and then the Resurrection, the Ascension, and also the Exaltation of Christ, which means that this great Plan of Salvation has been afforded for all, that is, for all who will believe (Jn. 3:16).

(9) "FOR HE SATISFIES THE LONGING SOUL, AND FILLS THE HUNGRY SOUL WITH GOODNESS."

There are some twenty millions alcoholics in the United States presently. There are over thirty million compulsive gamblers. There are over thirty million drug addicts, whether on prescription drugs or street drugs. And these are but a part of the bondages which bind humanity.

All of this proclaims a searching — a searching for something that will satisfy.

This Ninth Verse tells us in no uncertain terms that it is the Lord Alone Who can *"satisfy the longing soul."* He Alone can *"fill the hungry soul with goodness."* Satan tries to accomplish this task with the vices just mentioned; however, whatever method Satan uses, the soul is left empty and famished, because the Lord Alone can meet this need.

(10) "SUCH AS SIT IN DARKNESS AND IN THE SHADOW OF DEATH, BEING BOUND IN AFFLICTION AND IRON."

This Passage has two meanings:

BOUND IN AFFLICTION AND IRON

First of all, this Verse pointedly refers to Israel and the great Redemption from the terrible bondage which came upon them because of their rejection of God's Word, that is, *"their Messiah, and our Saviour, the Lord Jesus Christ."*

It also refers to every single person who has been brought from darkness to light by the Grace and Mercy of the Lord. All who do not know Christ *"sit in darkness,"* no matter who they are and what they do. The *"shadow of death"* constantly hangs over them. Their affliction is so severe that it is the same as being bound by iron.

This is the reason that man's foolishness dissolves into futility in trying to save himself.

This Scripture is referred to twice, once

in each Testament. Isaiah spoke of it (Isa. 9:2), and he is again quoted in Matthew (Mat. 4:16).

Matthew spoke of the Coming of Christ (the First Advent) as the fulfillment of Isaiah's Prophecy. Jesus Christ is the only Light. There is no other; therefore, when Israel rejected Christ, they rejected the only Light they could ever have.

Likewise, today the great universities of the world provide no light other than the solitary copy of the Bible that hopefully is found in their libraries. Likewise, Buddha is no light, neither is Muhammad, Confucius, nor any other so-called luminary. The only way out of the darkness is Christ, and, more particularly, what He did for us at the Cross.

Christ is the Source of all things that come to us from God, and the Cross is the Means of these things being made available.

(11) "BECAUSE THEY REBELLED AGAINST THE WORDS OF GOD, AND CONTEMNED THE COUNSEL OF THE MOST HIGH."

This pertains to the rejection of Jesus Christ by Israel, which brought on terrible judgment.

This also is a comment on the Words of the Holy Spirit through Solomon, *"But you have set at naught all My counsel, and would none of My reproof"* (Prov. 1:25).

The *"counsel"* was Christ; His Message was the *"reproof."*

(12) "THEREFORE HE BROUGHT DOWN THEIR HEART WITH LABOR; THEY FELL DOWN, AND THERE WAS NONE TO HELP."

When Israel rejected Jesus Christ, there remained no more remedy for them. Because of this rejection, God could no longer help them. Therefore, *"There was none to help."*

This pertains to the terrible destruction of Jerusalem by Titus in A.D. 70.

That which brought on this horrible carnage, which literally dissolved Israel as a nation and scattered them all over the world, was brought on by Israel purposely taking herself out from under the protective hand of God.

When Jesus was introduced as their King, they, clearly and with determination, said, *"We have no king but Caesar"* (Jn. 19:15).

NOTES

They were offered the choice between Jesus Christ and Jesus Barabbas. They chose Barabbas, who was a *"robber"* (Jn. 18:39-40).

As a result, they have found out two things: First of all, Caesar has proven to be a hard taskmaster. Second, they have been robbed ever since.

(13) "THEN THEY CRIED UNTO THE LORD IN THEIR TROUBLE, AND HE SAVED THEM OUT OF THEIR DISTRESSES."

By design, this Verse is almost identical to Verse 6.

Verse 6 proclaims the reason for their trouble, and Verse 13 proclaims their deliverance by the Lord from their trouble.

All of this tells us that such trouble, that is, trouble brought on because the Lord cannot help us, is because of our own disobedience. It also tells us that if we will purposely cry to the Lord and come to Him in deep Contrition and Repentance, then He will hear us and will save us and deliver us.

Once again, this Verse speaks of the glorious and phenomenal Second Coming (Rev., Chpt. 19), when Israel will be saved from the hand of the Antichrist, and will likewise accept Christ as her Messiah, Lord, and Saviour.

(14) "HE BROUGHT THEM OUT OF DARKNESS AND THE SHADOW OF DEATH, AND BROKE THEIR BANDS IN SUNDER."

Truly, for some 2,000 years, Israel has walked in darkness as well as in *"the shadow of death."* They were in this saddened condition when Jesus came the first time. They refused Him. Consequently, they have remained in this benighted state for some 2,000 years. At the Second Coming, He will *"break their bands asunder"* (Ps. 2:3). He will do so simply because they will accept Him.

This invitation is open not only to Israel, but to all of mankind.

(15) "OH THAT MEN WOULD PRAISE THE LORD FOR HIS GOODNESS, AND FOR HIS WONDERFUL WORKS TO THE CHILDREN OF MEN!"

This same Verse is repeated some four times (Vss. 8, 15, 21, 31). To be sure, the Holy Spirit did this for a purpose.

THE PURPOSE OF THE HOLY SPIRIT

When one considers the terrible rejection by Israel of her Messiah and the great Mercy of God in bringing them back to a place of Repentance and fulfillment, then we understand the insistence of the Holy Spirit in requesting that men should praise the Lord!

As well, how can we, under the New Covenant, do any less? He has been so *"good"* to us and has performed such *"wonderful works"* within our lives. We truly have been brought from darkness to light — and we could in no way extricate ourselves from this darkness!

So we should praise the Lord constantly for what He has done for us, and do so without fail!

(16) "FOR HE HAS BROKEN THE GATES OF BRASS, AND CUT THE BARS OF IRON IN SUNDER."

The terrible bondages that Satan binds us with are spoken of as the strength of *"brass"* and *"iron."* The foolishness of man in thinking that such can be broken by religion, good works, philanthropy, psychology, or various philosophies, or even the Church, is foolishness indeed! The Seventeenth Verse calls such *"fools."* Only Jesus Christ can *"set the captive free."* That's the reason Israel has walked in such darkness all of these centuries. They rejected the only One Who could deliver them from their bondage, that is, Christ; likewise, He is the only One Who can deliver anyone from any bondage.

This is what Calvary was all about. It took the Cross to set the captive free, because it was there that Jesus atoned for all sin, past, present, and future, at least for all who will believe; He did so by giving Himself as a Perfect Sacrifice, which, in the shedding of His Blood and the pouring out of His Life, satisfied the demands of a thrice-Holy God. There the price was paid, and paid forever! (Col. 2:14-15).

(17) "FOOLS BECAUSE OF THEIR TRANSGRESSION, AND BECAUSE OF THEIR INIQUITIES, ARE AFFLICTED."

As with all of these Verses, tremendous truths are brought forth.

FOOLS

The word *"fools,"* as here used, pertains to those who are perverse, those depending upon their own wisdom, which is foolishness to God (I Cor. 1:20-25).

Sadly, the far greater majority of the Church world depends upon the wisdom of man. Those who do not trust Him truly are *"fools."*

The Foundation of Christianity is the Cross of Christ. In fact, the Cross was predicted by God Almighty shortly after the Fall (Gen. 3:15). It runs like a theme throughout the entirety of the Bible.

The Lord will meet no one, will answer no one, will respond to no one, other than at the foot of the Cross. It is the Cross, and the Cross alone, which makes it possible for the Lord to give us Salvation and anything and everything that comes to us from God.

The Holy Spirit here labels as *"fools"* all Christian men, so-called, who devise their schemes which eliminate the Cross, as most of the modern fads do. I might quickly add that destruction will be the end result of all those who follow such teaching which abandons, ignores, or even repudiates the Cross. The Holy Spirit through Paul referred to such purveyors of false teaching as *"Enemies of the Cross"* (Phil. 3:17-19).

(18) "THEIR SOUL ABHORS ALL MANNER OF MEAT; AND THEY DRAW NEAR UNTO THE GATES OF DEATH."

The *"meat"* addressed here refers to the *"meat"* of the Word of God (I Cor. 3:2; 10:3; Heb. 5:12, 14).

Israel did not want the *"meat of the Word"*; therefore, they went into spiritual death.

The same can be said for the modern Church. The Bible presently is an unread Book. Either psychology or the latest fad is preached from behind too many pulpits. It is not *"meat"* and it will set no captive free.

(19) "THEN THEY CRY UNTO THE LORD IN THEIR TROUBLE, AND HE SAVES THEM OUT OF THEIR DISTRESSES."

This is the very nature of the Lord. Poor man stumbles after his own foolish wisdom; with his back to the wall, he cries to the Lord. Then with Mercy and Grace God answers and *"saves them out of their distresses."* All of us have knelt at this Altar of Grace.

It also refers to Israel which will cry to Him in the Last Days, and He will hear.

This Verse is repeated four times in this Psalm (Vss. 6, 13, 19, 28). Correspondingly, inasmuch as this is a portrayal of God's great delivering Power, the Holy Spirit four times in this Chapter implores us to *"Praise the*

Lord for His Goodness." How could we do less?

(20) "HE SENT HIS WORD, AND HEALED THEM, AND DELIVERED THEM FROM THEIR DESTRUCTIONS."

The Holy Spirit directs our attention to *"His Word."* This is the *"meat"* of the 18th Verse. Jesus Christ is the Living Word (Jn. 1:1-5). Only *"His Word"* can heal. He also *"delivered them."*

DELIVERANCE

When the modern Church thinks of Deliverance, it thinks of the drug addict or the alcoholic. Truly, these need Deliverance, but the Church itself needs Deliverance even more. It needs Deliverance from its self-righteousness, its pride, and its self-made goodness, which is the cause of its self-righteousness. These things require *"deliverance"* exactly as the drug addict or the alcoholic. However, it is very hard for religious man to be delivered because he is deceived and cannot see. His evil comes from the *"good"* side of the *"Tree of the Knowledge of Good and Evil"* (Gen. 2:17).

(21) "OH THAT MEN WOULD PRAISE THE LORD FOR HIS GOODNESS, AND FOR HIS WONDERFUL WORKS TO THE CHILDREN OF MEN!"

When we consider His healing Power that not only heals the body, but, above all, the soul, and His delivering Power, which comes to us by virtue of the Cross, which is the only Power that can deliver from sin, then we begin to realize why the Holy Spirit was repetitious in His insistence that we *"praise the Lord for His Goodness,"* and praise Him continually.

(22) "AND LET THEM SACRIFICE THE SACRIFICES OF THANKSGIVING, AND DECLARE HIS WORKS WITH REJOICING."

The word *"Sacrifice"* has reference to offering up something of value. This Passage basically has the same meaning as Hebrews 13:15, *"The Sacrifice of Praise."*

It refers to praise offered up to the Lord based on the fundamental work of Calvary, hence, the word *"Sacrifice."*

Let it be understood: Whenever the word *"Sacrifice"* is used in the Bible in connection with the Lord, always and without exception it refers to what Jesus would do, or

NOTES

has done, at the Cross of Calvary.

THE SACRIFICE OF PRAISE

All Believers should praise the Lord in times of distress, and our *"thanksgiving"* and our *"praises"* should be based on our giving up something of value. But if it stops there, we miss the point altogether. All praise, all worship, all thanksgiving, and all prayer must be based on the rudiments of Calvary, and Calvary alone.

A beautiful type is found in the Old Testament. Twice a day the Priests went into the Holy Place of the Tabernacle and applied Incense to the Altar of Incense. They did so only after coals of fire had been brought from the Brazen Altar and placed on the Altar of Incense. The Incense was poured over these burning coals; these burning coals from the Brazen Altar typified the Cross.

The Altar of Incense typified the Intercession of Christ, all on our behalf, which enables us to praise the Lord, to offer Him thanksgiving, to worship Him, and also to offer up our petitions of prayer, whatever the need might be. Were it not for this Intercession, all made possible by the Cross, the Lord could not accept our worship, our praying, etc. It is the Cross, and the Cross alone, which makes all of this possible.

(23) "THEY THAT GO DOWN TO THE SEA IN SHIPS, WHO DO BUSINESS IN GREAT WATERS."

Verses 23 through 30 have reference to the ships that traffic in commerce on the great oceans; however, they could refer to any activity of legitimate commerce, irrespective of place or location. In these Passages, we are told of the dangers of such and the protection afforded by the Lord to those who believe in Him.

(24) "THESE SEE THE WORKS OF THE LORD, AND HIS WONDERS IN THE DEEP."

In these Passages, the Holy Spirit shifts the emphasis from the spiritual to the material, showing us that the Lord is mightily concerned about all the activity of His children.

Here we are admonished to *"see the Works of the LORD,"* referring to nature, and its power, which was created by God.

(25) "FOR HE COMMANDS, AND RAISES THE STORMY WIND, WHICH

LIFTS UP THE WAVES THEREOF."

This Verse, and several of the following Verses, could well be a prophetic example of the storm that came upon the Sea of Galilee, when Jesus spoke to it, saying, *"Peace, be still"* (Mk. 4:35-41).

In this Passage in Psalms, it seems as though the Lord is the One Who *"raises the stormy wind"*; however, we know from the account given in Mark that it is Satan who caused that particular storm.

Is there a contradiction?

No, there is no contradiction. Satan is the one who steals, kills, and destroys (Jn. 10:10); however, he only can do what God allows him to do. So, even though Satan may be the cause of such, he has to receive permission from the Lord to do so; even then, the Lord gauges the degree of whatever is to be done (Job, Chpts. 1-2).

(26) "THEY MOUNT UP TO THE HEAVEN, THEY GO DOWN AGAIN TO THE DEPTHS: THEIR SOUL IS MELTED BECAUSE OF TROUBLE."

Man always has felt that he is master of his fate. Today, with our vaunted technology, man has raised himself to the position of a little god. Still, in spite of modern technology, God can use the power of nature to make man realize in just a few moments time just how absolutely helpless he really is. This should be very obvious as it regards the hurricanes, tsunamis, earthquakes, and other violent acts of nature.

(27) "THEY REEL TO AND FRO, AND STAGGER LIKE A DRUNKEN MAN, AND ARE AT THEIR WIT'S END."

In a few moments time, with earthquakes, hurricanes, and storms of many varieties, man soon finds himself helpless, even with all his ability and technology, that is, *"at their wit's end."*

(28) "THEN THEY CRY UNTO THE LORD IN THEIR TROUBLE, AND HE BRINGS THEM OUT OF THEIR DISTRESSES."

We are admonished to ask God for help exactly as the Disciples asked the Lord for help in the storm that threatened them on the Sea of Galilee. He has promised to help!

(29) "HE MAKES THE STORM A CALM, SO THAT THE WAVES THEREOF ARE STILL."

NOTES

In the account given by Mark, it says, *"There was a great calm"* (Mk. 4:39). Two things are said here:

1. It is God's Power that governs nature, and Satan has to have His Permission to bring about storms and all other such phenomena.

2. We are admonished to call upon the Lord in time of trouble, irrespective of its location, and ask for His Deliverance. He has promised to help; He, in fact, is the only One Who can help.

(30) "THEN ARE THEY GLAD BECAUSE THEY BE QUIET; SO HE BRINGS THEM UNTO THEIR DESIRED HAVEN."

Almost every Believer has experienced the gladness that is spoken of here because of the Deliverance of the Lord in times of great trouble.

We are warned to remember that it is the Lord Who brings us to our desired destination, and not our own ingenuity, ability, or technological helps.

(31) OH THAT MEN WOULD PRAISE THE LORD FOR HIS GOODNESS, AND FOR HIS WONDERFUL WORKS TO THE CHILDREN OF MEN!"

This is the fourth repetition of this Passage by the Holy Spirit. As stated, it was done by design.

He wishes to impress upon us our absolute helplessness and His absolute Power, and that we continually should praise Him for His Goodness *"to the children of men."*

(32) "LET THEM EXALT HIM ALSO IN THE CONGREGATION OF THE PEOPLE, AND PRAISE HIM IN THE ASSEMBLY OF THE ELDERS."

This speaks of the formal worship of God in the Tabernacle, Temple, or Church.

The following Passages proclaim to us why we should *"exalt Him."*

(33) "HE TURNS RIVERS INTO A WILDERNESS, AND THE WATERSPRINGS INTO DRY GROUND;

(34) "A FRUITFUL LAND INTO BARRENNESS, FOR THE WICKEDNESS OF THEM WHO DWELL THEREIN."

In these two Scriptures, we are given the reason for the hunger, starvation, famine, want, and poverty in all countries of the world. It is because of *"the wickedness of them who dwell therein."*

SIN, THE CAUSE OF ALL PROBLEMS

Places in the Earth's deserts where mighty rivers once flowed have been photographed by Satellites flying thousands of miles above the Earth's surface. This means that the area once was fruitful and productive, but now is barren.

Why?

These two Passages characterize so much of the world. Even in the United States, which is so very fruitful, the warning signs already are upon us. Sadly, the intellectual types think they can solve the problem by addressing themselves to the symptoms instead of to the cause. Pollution certainly is a detriment; but, still, the main culprit is *"sin,"* which fosters greed, selfishness, and man's inhumanity to man.

Man, for the most part, however, refuses to agree that the cause is sin. Even the Church today is eliminating the word *"sin"* from its vocabulary. The modern Church does not know the problem, which is sin, and does not know the solution, which is Jesus Christ and Him Crucified. As such, the Church is of no value. That's the reason these Words of Our Lord apply directly to the modern Church:

"I know your works, that you are neither cold nor hot: I would you were cold or hot.

"So then because you are lukewarm, and neither cold nor hot, I will spew (vomit) *you out of My mouth"* (Rev. 3:15-16).

When the Lord tells us that this modern Church (which is the Laodicean Church) makes Him sick to His stomach, that's really bad! However, as distasteful as it is, it must be said!

(35) "HE TURNS THE WILDERNESS INTO A STANDING WATER, AND DRY GROUND INTO WATERSPRINGS."

Conversely, the Holy Spirit informs us that God, upon Repentance, can reverse a desperate situation. He can make the wilderness to rejoice and blossom as the rose.

Disobedience to God's Word not only banished man from Paradise, but also changed Eden into a stormy desert, for such is that fair Garden today; however, the Eighth Chapter of Romans predicts Redemption for the Earth as well as for man.

NOTES

In the Millennial Reign, the entirety of Planet Earth will once again bloom.

Even now, the Lord has promised that if we will do certain things, He will *"heal our land"* (II Chron. 7:14).

(36) "AND THERE HE MAKES THE HUNGRY TO DWELL, THAT THEY MAY PREPARE A CITY FOR HABITATION."

Much of the world at this present time goes to bed hungry each night. Each day thousands of little children through weakness sink to the earth and are simply unable to rise. They die where they are fallen. It is called *"the silent death."*

Only God has the answer to these problems. I wish it were possible to say that man will repent and that the present problems will be rectified. It is possible, but highly improbable.

Still, the Lord has promised us that He is coming back to right the wrongs and to rectify this cursed situation; therefore, the only answer to these problems is *"The Coming of the Lord."*

(37) "AND SOW THE FIELDS, AND PLANT VINEYARDS, WHICH MAY YIELD FRUITS OF INCREASE."

This will happen in the Millennial Reign, when Christ reigns supreme. The curse will then be lifted, sin will then be put down, Satan will be locked away with all of his demon spirits, and then *"the fields will yield fruits of increase"* in such copious abundance as to defy all description!

(38) "HE BLESSES THEM ALSO, SO THAT THEY ARE MULTIPLIED GREATLY; AND SUFFERS NOT THEIR CATTLE TO DECREASE."

We must not leave the impression that this only can come about during the coming Kingdom Age. In fact, it has come to pass millions of times in the past and present for those who will dare to live for God and believe His great Promises.

That which belongs to the Child of God should be an oasis in the midst of a desert. With faith in God and in His Word, it can be even now.

(39) "AGAIN, THEY ARE MINISHED AND BROUGHT LOW THROUGH OPPRESSION, AFFLICTION, AND SORROW."

Once again, the Holy Spirit calls our

attention to the wages of sin.

Person after person, area after area, even nation after nation is *"brought low"* by sin. The Holy Spirit emphatically portrays to us the picture of God's Blessings upon righteousness and His curse upon sin. We would do well to heed what He is telling us.

(40) "HE POURS CONTEMPT UPON PRINCES, AND CAUSES THEM TO WANDER IN THE WILDERNESS, WHERE THERE IS NO WAY."

These Verses emphasize the ruin to nature and to man that results from disobedience to God's Law.

Princes and governmental leaders who despise that Word are clothed with contempt; despite their vaunted position, they ultimately meet a dead end.

(41) "YET SETS HE THE POOR ON HIGH FROM AFFLICTION, AND MAKES HIM FAMILIES LIKE A FLOCK."

This is God's Message to *"the poor"* of the world. Whenever they seek help for changes in government, sadly, precious little help is forthcoming. Here they are exhorted to seek the Lord for their prosperity. He has promised to hear and to answer. He has already done so multiplied millions of times!

(42) "THE RIGHTEOUS SHALL SEE IT, AND REJOICE: AND ALL INIQUITY SHALL STOP HER MOUTH."

The Holy Spirit emphasizes to us that if we will but follow the Word of the Lord, the Lord will set His people on high, above the reach of calamity. Consequently, we should *"rejoice."*

The Blessings of the Lord and the profit in living for God will be obvious, even to the unbeliever. Actually, one of the greatest testimonies intended by the Holy Spirit is that the unbeliever will see the Blessings of God upon the Believer and be drawn and attracted to the Goodness of God as a result of what he has witnessed.

(43) "WHOSO IS WISE, AND WILL OBSERVE THESE THINGS, EVEN THEY SHALL UNDERSTAND THE LOVINGKINDNESS OF THE LORD."

Now the cap is placed on this Psalm.

THE WISE WILL UNDERSTAND

The Holy Spirit has so carefully laid out the path to ruin and the path to Redemption and the paths of both poverty and plenty. He is telling us to be *"wise"* and heed what He is saying, that is, *"Observe these things."*

If we will do so, we then will understand that in the midst of all the suffering and pain, the *"lovingkindness of the LORD"* is evident. He truly blesses His people with good things, not only in the spiritual sense, but also physically, materially, domestically, financially, and in every other way.

The Believer is to trust the Lord for all things. He is to place his faith exclusively in Christ and the Cross, which is the same thing as placing his faith in the Word of God, for they both are synonymous. Faith properly placed will guarantee the Blessings of God. The Believer is to expect such Blessings; he is to expect God to do great things; he is to expect miracles! The Believer's faith always will be rewarded if he does so! But his faith always must be in the proper object, and that Object is *"Jesus Christ and Him Crucified."*

PSALM 108

*A Psalm of David:
Israel Looks to God for Help*

(1) "O GOD, MY HEART IS FIXED; I WILL SING AND GIVE PRAISE, EVEN WITH MY GLORY."

This is a Song or Psalm of David.

ALL BLESSINGS COME FROM CHRIST

This Psalm is composed of portions of Psalms 57 and 60. It is not haphazard borrowing from these two Psalms to make a third, as some think who are unskilled in the Word of Righteousness (Heb. 5:13), but is a beautiful medley of Songs, arranged by the Holy Spirit, which harmonizes with the Deuteronomy Book of the Psalms; for just as the Fifth Book of the Pentateuch recalls and repeats Divine lessons and facts taught and recorded in the prior Books, so it is here. Hence, the dominant note in this Song is sounded in the words, *"God has spoken,"* as recorded in Verse 7 (Williams).[58]

By the union of these two Psalms, the fundamental truth is repeated and emphasized that all blessings for Israel, for the nations, and for the Earth, are based upon the Messiah as the Word of God.

The Speaker is the Messiah. His heart is *"fixed"* in order to obtain the Will of God regarding the Salvation of mankind, the Restoration of Israel, and the Restoration of all things. Even though not yet an accomplished fact, in the heart of God it is nevertheless thought of as such; therefore, the Messiah *"will sing and give praise"* as though it is already accomplished. He will do it even with *"My Glory,"* signifying that the Glory of God rests upon the fulfillment of these Divine Promises.

(2) "AWAKE, PSALTERY AND HARP: I MYSELF WILL AWAKE EARLY."

We have here the discipline of the sweet singer of Israel, David.

DAVID'S DISCIPLINE

David is saying here that he would rise early in order to spend time alone with God. During these times of meditation, prayer, worship, and praise, the Spirit of God would begin to move upon him relative to these Psalms. He would, no doubt, take the *"psaltery and harp"* and accompany himself as he sang these Songs or Psalms of praise.

What a lesson for us today! (Actually, most, if not all, of the worship of God enjoyed today in the realm of music, choirs, singing, and musical instrumentation came as God the Holy Spirit moved upon David relative to this tremendous expression of faith.)

It is obvious here that David had a proper prayer life. It is impossible for any Believer to have the relationship with the Lord that one should have unless each Believer has a similar prayer life.

Regrettably and sadly, not only is this not a Bible-reading generation, neither is it a praying generation; hence, the modern Church is in worse spiritual condition than at any time, I believe, since the Reformation.

My prayer is that God will bring us back to His Word.

(3) "I WILL PRAISE YOU, O LORD, AMONG THE PEOPLE: AND I WILL SING PRAISES UNTO YOU AMONG THE NATIONS."

As David said these words, the Greater Son of David will say them even more.

NOTES

Little did David realize that the Psalms God had given him actually would be sung *"among the nations."*

However, its greater fulfillment will be in the days of the Millennial Reign, when David truly will sing these Psalms in every nation of the world. What a delightful thought!

(4) "FOR YOUR MERCY IS GREAT ABOVE THE HEAVENS: AND YOUR TRUTH REACHES UNTO THE CLOUDS."

Here *"Your Mercy"* is linked to *"Your Truth."* These are the two great attributes of God and speak of the Messiah. He is *"Mercy"* in living form; He also is *"Truth"* in visible proclamation (Jn. 1:1-5).

(5) "BE THOU EXALTED, O GOD, ABOVE THE HEAVENS: AND YOUR GLORY ABOVE ALL THE EARTH."

This is a prayer that is a Prophecy. God has never been so exalted; however, at the Advent of the soon-coming Kingdom Age, that is, *"The Millennial Reign,"* He then will be exalted throughout the entirety of Planet Earth. Now His Glory does not cover this Earth; then, it shall.

(6) "THAT YOUR BELOVED MAY BE DELIVERED: SAVE WITH YOUR RIGHT HAND, AND ANSWER ME."

Our Lord continues to speak.

THE MESSIAH

"Your Beloved" speaks of the Messiah. The petition, as spoken through David one thousand years before the Incarnation, was that He may be able to accomplish His task and be delivered from the powers of darkness. The petition for Salvation by the *"Right Hand"* of God was made, and the answer was given. It is recorded in Verse 7.

It is difficult for the unspiritual heart to understand the Messiah's pleading for such deliverance. Most think that, inasmuch as He is God, such prayers would not become Him; however, they become Him perfectly.

While He is Very God, He also is Very Man. Even though He is Very God, He never used His attributes of Deity. If He had done so, He could not have delivered man. He must face the Evil One on the same ground that we, as poor, dejected humanity, face Satan. He did so and won the victory and was delivered. Consequently, we are able to enter into

His Deliverance, which effected our deliverance, which all was made possible by the Cross. Praise the Lord!

(7) "GOD HAS SPOKEN IN HIS HOLINESS; I WILL REJOICE, I WILL DIVIDE SHECHEM, AND METE OUT THE VALLEY OF SUCCOTH."

To the petition of Verse 6 the answer is forthcoming, *"God has spoken in His Holiness."* Therefore, the Messiah *"will rejoice."* This is not fulfilled yet, but will be fulfilled during the future Tribulation and at the Second Advent of Christ.

ISRAEL BELONGS TO GOD

The Antichrist will think to make the Land of Israel his own. But the Lord here lays down the gauntlet. He says that He, and not the Antichrist, *"will divide Shechem, and mete out the Valley of Succoth."* In other words, the Lord will *"say the saying"* and *"do the doing"*!

(8) "GILEAD IS MINE; MANASSEH IS MINE; EPHRAIM ALSO IS THE STRENGTH OF MY HEAD; JUDAH IS MY LAWGIVER."

In no uncertain terms, the Lord claims these districts of Israel as *"Mine."*

At this moment, the Palestinians are claiming parts of Israel, and even Jerusalem as their capital. It is the age-old conflict. This means it didn't begin yesterday; in reality, it began with Abraham.

To be blunt, the Land of Israel belongs to the Jews. It does not belong to the Muslims, the Arabs, the Palestinians, or any other group. It belongs to the Jews!

The Arabs and the Muslims now control all of the Middle East with the exception of the tiny State of Israel. But they also want that, and are doing everything within their power to obtain this Land.

Why?

THE AGE-OLD CONFLICT

There is no oil under the sands of Israel; all the oil is under the sands of the Arabs. There are very little or no precious metals. So why does this conflict rage today greater than ever?

The problem is spiritual, even though most of the participants do not really understand that.

Satan is behind the efforts of the Palestinians and the Arabs to take the Land of Israel. The truth is, the name *"Palestinians"* is a misnomer! In other words, such really doesn't exist.

The name *"Palestinian"* comes from the ancient name *"Philistines,"* and there are no more Philistines.

Those who refer to themselves as *"Palestinians"* actually are Syrians, Jordanians, Egyptians, etc. In other words, they belong in these respective countries, and not in Israel.

The world falsely believes that the cause of this conflict is that the Palestinians want a State of their own. Israel has offered that repeatedly but with no success. Despite the concessions made by Israel, the human bombs keep exploding.

The real truth of the matter is that the Muslim world wants every Jew dead and for the Arab world, that is, the Muslims, to take possession of the entirety of the Land of Israel. That is their goal, and is so stated in their manifesto.

The only friend that Israel has in the world at the present time is the United States of America. And that friendship exists only because of the millions of Born-Again Believers in this country. That is the only reason! After the Rapture of the Church, Israel will have no one, not even the U.S.A., to help her. She will be on her own — but for the Lord!

Incidentally, Judah is called the *"Lawgiver"* because it was from the Tribe of Judah that Christ came.

(9) "MOAB IS MY WASHPOT; OVER EDOM WILL I CAST OUT MY SHOE; OVER PHILISTIA WILL I TRIUMPH."

In these Passages, the Messiah predicts the future supremacy of Israel and the subjugation of the Gentiles.

THE FULFILLMENT OF BIBLE PROPHECY

Moab and Edom constitute modern Jordan.

The phrase, *"Moab is My washpot,"* presents a term of extreme contempt.

The phrase, *"Over Edom will I cast out My shoe,"* refers to this area being reduced to a state of total subjugation to Israel. This will take place in the coming Kingdom Age.

The phrase, *"Over Philistia will I triumph,"* refers to this area, presently occupied by the Palestinians, being one of the greatest enemies of Israel.

The prediction here is that God finally will triumph over Philistia; the implication is that before He does, this part of the Promised Land will give God and the Jews more trouble even than it presently is doing.

(10) "WHO WILL BRING ME INTO THE STRONG CITY? WHO WILL LEAD ME INTO EDOM?"

The *"strong city"* is referring to *"Sela"* or *"Petra."*

Petra was the rock-hewn stronghold capital of Edom of old (II Ki. 14:7; Isa. 16:1).

Petra sometimes is known as Sela. It is situated about midway between the Dead Sea and the Gulf of Aquaba.

Before the advent of modern weaponry, it was practically impregnable. It is over a mile in length, and is surrounded by towering mountains. It is about three-fourths of a mile in width.

The only entrance is through a magnificent gorge with high and frequent nearly-touching walls. The gorge is over a mile in length, which provides an excellent defense for the city.

It is believed by some that Esau may have been the founder of this city. It was very prominent from the Fourth Century B.C. to A.D. 105, when it was incorporated into Roman territory. When Rome fell, the city was abandoned, and it is empty at the present time.

This is the city or area to which Israel will flee when she is attacked by the Antichrist at the midpoint of the Great Tribulation. Before this time, Israel will think that the Antichrist is the Messiah, but she will quickly be brought to her senses whenever the Antichrist shows his true colors and proceeds with attempts to completely destroy her. Israel will at that time suffer her first military defeat since she became a nation in 1948.

Hundreds of thousands of Jews will flee at this time to this particular area (Sela or Petra), and many will remain there for the entire second half of the Great Tribulation.

With modern weaponry, the Antichrist could easily destroy Israel, even in this place; however, according to Daniel 11:44, the

NOTES

Antichrist will have bigger fish to fry, and will save Israel for a later time; the later time will occur at the Battle of Armageddon, when he will be defeated by the Coming of the Lord.

As the Antichrist is fighting great battles in the east and the north, hundreds of thousands of Jews undoubtedly will drift back into the Land of Israel and Jerusalem proper, where they will prepare a defense, which will meet the Antichrist when he comes down to destroy them. Ezekiel predicts the outcome in the Thirty-eighth and Thirty-ninth Chapters of his Book.

(11) "WILL NOT YOU, O GOD, WHO HAS CAST US OFF? AND WILL NOT YOU, O GOD, GO FORTH WITH OUR HOSTS?"

Both Verses 10 and 11 are almost identical to Verses 9 and 10 of Psalm 60.

The last two questions of Verse 11 answer the first two of Verse 10:

"Who will bring Me into the strong city? Who will lead Me into Edom?"

"God will, Who has predicted the flight of Israel to Petra and Edom — God Who will not protect Israel in their Land from the Antichrist, but Who will protect them in Edom for 1,260 days [Mat. 24:15-22; Rev. 12:6, 14]" (Ps. 108:10-11).

God's purpose in this is to bring Israel back to Himself (Ezek. 20:33-44).

(12) "GIVE US HELP FROM TROUBLE: FOR VAIN IS THE HELP OF MAN.

(13) "THROUGH GOD WE SHALL DO VALIANTLY: FOR HE IT IS WHO SHALL TREAD DOWN OUR ENEMIES."

The *"trouble"* addressed here is the full-scale attack by the Antichrist in order to destroy Israel. At that time, it seems that no nation on the Earth (even the U.S.A.) will come to her help; therefore, she says, *"For vain is the help of man."*

The question may be asked, *"How can Israel stand up at all under the onslaught of the Antichrist, with all his vaunted power?"*

The Prophet Zechariah gives the answer:

"And he who is feeble among them at that day shall be as David; and the House of David shall be as God, as the Angel of the LORD before them" (Zech. 12:8).

And then the Lord Himself will come back and He will *"tread down our enemies"* (Rev., Chpt. 19).

PSALM 109

The Author is David:
A Psalm of Vengeance on Enemies

(1) "HOLD NOT YOUR PEACE, O GOD OF MY PRAISE."

The Holy Spirit is the Author of this Psalm (Acts 1:16-22). The Speaker is the Messiah. The instrument is David.

CHRIST AND JUDAS

Here the Messiah appears as the Word of God. As such, He personifies Love, Goodness, and Righteousness, and is the Representative Head of all who love Him as the Truth. For these He prays, and they are assured of happiness and victory.

On the other hand, Judas, unnamed, is here the head and representative of all who rebel against the Messiah as the Word of God, and who, consequently, hate all who are pure and lovely. For these there must, therefore, be the bitter fruit of rebellion. They bring this doom not only upon themselves, but also upon those connected with them.

In effect, this Psalm has a double fulfillment, and we speak of the betrayal of David as well as the betrayal of our Lord.

Ahithophel was the culprit in David's betrayal and Judas was the culprit in the betrayal of the Lord.

The Psalm refers to both!

The request of the Messiah that God not hold His peace means that the heart of God is to be given concerning Judas.

(2) "FOR THE MOUTH OF THE WICKED AND THE MOUTH OF THE DECEITFUL ARE OPENED AGAINST ME: THEY HAVE SPOKEN AGAINST ME WITH A LYING TONGUE."

A tremendous truth is given in this Verse.

AHITHOPHEL AND JUDAS

This speaks of the mouths of both Ahithophel and Judas. They lie because there was nothing derogatory that could truthfully be said about David or the Messiah.

It is easy for the unspiritual heart to understand such about Christ; but considering David's great sins with Bathsheba and against her husband Uriah, it is difficult for the unspiritual heart to understand these words when applied to David.

However, they do apply, because these sins had been forgiven and washed by the Blood of Christ; therefore, in the Mind of God, they no longer existed against David; in fact, as far as God was concerned, David never committed these terrible sins. This is the great doctrine of *"Justification by Faith,"* which is applicable to all Saints of God. Where would any of us be without it?

(3) "THEY COMPASSED ME ABOUT ALSO WITH WORDS OF HATRED; AND FOUGHT AGAINST ME WITHOUT A CAUSE."

The Holy Spirit continues to emphasize this perfidious deed!

WITHOUT A CAUSE

The Holy Spirit emphasizes the words, *"Without a cause."* Ahithophel owed all of his blessing, prosperity, and position to David. Even though Bathsheba was Ahithophel's granddaughter, and David's actions with her, no doubt, served as fuel for her grandfather's evil heart, still, there really was no valid reason — just an excuse.

Likewise, Judas was treated with all kindness and respect. Just as was Ahithophel, Judas was given one of the greatest positions on the face of the Earth as a Disciple of Christ. Why and how was there hatred in the hearts of both?

Regarding Ahithophel, quite possibly there was envy, jealousy, and disdain for direction. Ahithophel may have looked down on David because of his humble upbringing. When David sinned greatly with his granddaughter, Bathsheba, this brought out the evil that already was in his heart.

Richard Nixon was asked after Watergate, *"How many friends do you have left?"* His wise reply was, *"Oftentimes a person is your friend simply because of what you can do for them or to them."*

Judas wanted no part of the Cross. The entire Sixth Chapter of John the Beloved's Gospel is given over to the Cross of Christ. It is veiled in metaphors, but nevertheless it speaks of the Cross. The last few Verses of that Chapter tell us that Judas wanted no part of the Cross, which means that he would not accept the real reason for which Jesus actually came. So he committed the most perfidious deed in human history, the betrayal of the Son of the Living God.

(4) "FOR MY LOVE THEY ARE MY ADVERSARIES: BUT I GIVE MYSELF UNTO PRAYER."

The meaning of this Verse is that both David and the Messiah gave their love to both Ahithophel and Judas. Sadly, both became adversaries.

The worst sin of all is the sin against love. There is no evil that can compare with such.

Neither David nor Christ lifted his hands against these adversaries. Instead they took it to the Lord in prayer. What a lesson for us today!

(5) "AND THEY HAVE REWARDED ME EVIL FOR GOOD, AND HATRED FOR MY LOVE."

The Holy Spirit once again emphasizes the gravity of this sin. Nothing but good was given to both Ahithophel and Judas. Nothing but love was extended to them. Both David and Christ were rewarded with hatred. This is sin against light, which constitutes the worst sin of all. The judgment pronounced in Verses 6 through 20, therefore, presents a just judgment.

(6) "SET THOU A WICKED MAN OVER HIM: AND LET SATAN STAND AT HIS RIGHT HAND."

Accordingly, the language of this Psalm is judicial and prophetic. Enemies of the Messiah, the Word of God, will be judged and the righteousness of their punishment and the grounds for it are set out in Verses 6 through 20.

Satan stood at the right hand of Judas and then entered into him (Lk. 22:3).

If men will evil, then further evil is willed to them.

(7) "WHEN HE SHALL BE JUDGED, LET HIM BE CONDEMNED: AND LET HIS PRAYER BECOME SIN."

The judgment pronounced may seem harsh to the unspiritual ear; yet it is a just judgment. Judas and Ahithophel were shown nothing but love and good. They not only sinned against the love and good, but tried with all their strength to destroy the bearer of both. They were not satisfied to indulge

NOTES

in their wrongdoing; their desire was to kill both David and Christ.

PRIDE

This is the sin of pride. It is far greater than the sin of passion. Ahithophel was not satisfied just to rebel against David; he must kill David. His failure was not for lack of trying.

Likewise, Judas was not satisfied with resigning his position as a chosen Apostle. Judas also went to great lengths to insure the death of the only One Who ever has lived Who really could be called Good.

This is characteristic of religious sin. In the world of religion, when men are wrong, they are not satisfied to oppose; they also must attempt to destroy the individual. For example, the Catholic Church slaughtered hundreds of thousands in the Middle Ages. Many segments of Protestantism also have been guilty of the same.

The Messiah recognizes that the hatred shown to His people is shown to them because they belong to Him. The hatred really is directed against Him. In return for the love which He and they show to men, evil and religious men recompense hatred (for both Ahithophel and Judas were religious). The fact that man so treated Him and so treats those who love Him is an unanswerable proof of the unfathomable corruption of man's moral nature.

Shortly after September 11, 2001, Benjamin Netanyahu, the former Prime Minister of Israel, said, *"The Muslims hate us* (Israel) *because of the age-old conflict. They hate you* (the U.S.A.) *because of Jesus Christ."* This assessment by the former Prime Minister of Israel was correct!

(8) "LET HIS DAYS BE FEW; AND LET ANOTHER TAKE HIS OFFICE."

The days of Judas were few. He was probably in his early thirties when he committed suicide. Another took his office (Acts 1:23-26).

(9) "LET HIS CHILDREN BE FATHERLESS, AND HIS WIFE A WIDOW."

Sometime back while we were visiting Jerusalem, I was taken to the supposed spot where Judas committed suicide. There is a cliff there, which, if I remember correctly, is 10 to 12 feet high. It was from this cliff that he hanged himself (Mat. 27:5). When Luke wrote the Book of Acts, he wrote that Judas fell from where he hanged himself onto the rocks below and *"all his bowels gushed out"* (Acts 1:18).

JUDAS

The historian Lightfoot says that the Devil, after strangling Judas, lifted him up in the air and dashed his body on the ground.

As I stood there surveying the scene, I noticed that a couple of yards away from my feet was a ditch with raw sewage running through it. As I stood there, I realized that the horror of the sin of Judas was still being symbolized by the Holy Spirit. Regarding his death, even some 2,000 years later, raw sewage is a fitting symbol of the end of his life.

(10) "LET HIS CHILDREN BE CONTINUALLY VAGABONDS, AND BEG: LET THEM SEEK THEIR BREAD ALSO OUT OF THEIR DESOLATE PLACES."

There is some hint in these Passages that the wife and children of Judas were either active co-conspirators of Judas' sinful actions or passively gave their tacit approval to it.

(11) "LET THE EXTORTIONER CATCH ALL THAT HE HAS; AND LET THE STRANGERS SPOIL HIS LABOR."

This Passage, at least in part, was fulfilled when the Priests refused to take back the blood money (thirty pieces of silver) and thereafter desired no part of Judas (Mat., Chpt. 27).

(12) "LET THERE BE NONE TO EXTEND MERCY UNTO HIM: NEITHER LET THERE BE ANY TO FAVOR HIS FATHERLESS CHILDREN."

The question begs to be asked, *"If Judas' wife or children had repented and thrown themselves on the Grace of God, would God have forgiven them?"*

Every Scripture from Genesis 1:1 through Revelation 22:21 says, *"Yes!"* The evidence is that they desired no forgiveness. They persisted in their rebellion and hatred. If possible, they continued to go deeper into their sin. Due to their own actions, they denied themselves mercy and cut themselves off from all that would do them favor.

(13) "LET HIS POSTERITY BE CUT OFF; AND IN THE GENERATION FOLLOWING LET THEIR NAME BE BLOTTED OUT."

NOTES

Every evidence is that this is exactly what happened!

The Septuagint and the Vulgate read *"his name"* instead of *"their name,"* meaning that due to the fact that his children died before marriage, there was no posterity to carry on the name of Judas. It was blotted out.

(14) "LET THE INIQUITY OF HIS FATHERS BE REMEMBERED WITH THE LORD; AND LET NOT THE SIN OF HIS MOTHER BE BLOTTED OUT."

Is it possible that even Judas' father and mother were co-conspirators in his terrible crime? It seems they could have been.

It is spoken of as *"the sin."* If possible, it seems they continued even deeper into their hatred of Christ and rebellion against God; consequently, their sins and iniquities could not be forgiven.

(15) "LET THEM BE BEFORE THE LORD CONTINUALLY, THAT HE MAY CUT OFF THE MEMORY OF THEM FROM THE EARTH."

The memory of them being cut off possibly refers to Verse 13. It would seem that the children of Judas were cut off in death before marriage, thereby leaving no posterity. There is, therefore, no memory because they do not exist.

(16) "BECAUSE THAT HE REMEMBERED NOT TO SHOW MERCY, BUT PERSECUTED THE POOR AND NEEDY MAN, THAT HE MIGHT EVEN SLAY THE BROKEN IN HEART."

The Holy Spirit would attribute the death of Jesus to both Judas and the Priests (Acts 3:14-15).

Christ was the Poor and Needy Man. His was the wounded heart.

(17) "AS HE LOVED CURSING, SO LET IT COME UNTO HIM: AS HE DELIGHTED NOT IN BLESSING, SO LET IT BE FAR FROM HIM."

The cursing spoken of here has little, if anything, to do with profanity. It is speaking of the terrible curse of sin. Judas delighted not in the Blessings that Christ would bring as the Giver of Eternal Life. He had no desire for it. He loved sin and desired to continue therein.

This Passage, as well as Verse 18, not only pertains to Judas and Ahithophel, but likewise to all who spurn the clarion call of the Lord Jesus Christ.

(18) "AS HE CLOTHED HIMSELF WITH CURSING LIKE AS WITH HIS GARMENT, SO LET IT COME INTO HIS BOWELS LIKE WATER, AND LIKE OIL INTO HIS BONES."

Sin is not an external matter only; it penetrates the very heart and vitals of the sinner. The *"bowels"* speak of the inner being of man. Sin goes to the very core, even *"like oil into his bones."*

That is the reason that sin cannot be assuaged by *"New Year's Resolutions,"* or *"turning over a new leaf,"* or by any other earthly means. Even the Church, with all of its religious ceremony, cannot set one captive free. Only the shed Blood of Christ being applied to a person's heart and life can assuage the guilt and remove the sin (Jn. 3:16).

(19) "LET IT BE UNTO HIM AS THE GARMENT WHICH COVERS HIM, AND FOR A GIRDLE WHEREWITH HE IS GIRDED CONTINUALLY."

At the moment, Judas Iscariot is in Hell. That is a somber thought, but true. He could have been an Apostle of the Lord Jesus Christ forever, ruling and reigning with Him. His name could have been inscribed on the foundations of that city built foursquare (Rev. 21:14). But instead he is in Hell, and the garment of sin covers him. It will squeeze him like a girdle and do so forever.

Judas must endure all of this — the torture, the Hell, the horror, and the eternity of it all — simply because he would not accept the Cross of Christ!

(20) "LET THIS BE THE REWARD OF MY ADVERSARIES FROM THE LORD, AND OF THEM WHO SPEAK EVIL AGAINST MY SOUL."

This was not only the fate of Judas and Ahithophel, but is also the fate of all who spurn, refuse, and reject the Mercy, Grace, and extended Love of the Lord Jesus Christ.

(21) "BUT DO THOU FOR ME, O GOD THE LORD, FOR YOUR NAME'S SAKE: BECAUSE YOUR MERCY IS GOOD, DELIVER THOU ME."

The efforts of both Judas and Ahithophel were to murder Christ and David. The plea here is for deliverance from their evil actions.

NOTES

The prayer was answered. David was delivered from Absalom and Ahithophel, and Christ was gloriously raised from the dead.

(22) "FOR I AM POOR AND NEEDY, AND MY HEART IS WOUNDED WITHIN ME."

There is no hurt like the hurt of a broken heart. Both David and Christ were in no position to defend themselves. Actually, it was not the Will of God that they even attempt to do so. Hence, they are described as *"poor and needy."*

It is a great sin to hurt those who cannot defend themselves. The hearts of both were wounded and crushed by those they had loved, befriended, and directed to Salvation, who turned on them with murderous hatred. There is no hurt like the hurt of being betrayed by a friend.

(23) "I AM GONE LIKE THE SHADOW WHEN IT DECLINES: I AM TOSSED UP AND DOWN AS THE LOCUST."

These are the words of David when set upon by his son, Absalom, and his most trusted advisor, Ahithophel.

They also are the words of Christ, Who used none of His great Power to defend Himself against the traitor, Judas Iscariot.

(24) "MY KNEES ARE WEAK THROUGH FASTING; AND MY FLESH FAILS OF FATNESS."

These were the words of David in seeking God regarding the great rebellion that had been brought against him by both Absalom and Ahithophel.

There is no record that Christ fasted while in His earthly Ministry other than the temptation in the wilderness. And yet, in His last days, He could have suffered so because of the terrible hurt at seeing what His people would do to Him, that it could be called *"fasting."*

(25) "I BECAME ALSO A REPROACH UNTO THEM: WHEN THEY LOOKED UPON ME THEY SHOOK THEIR HEADS."

Matthew said, *"They who passed by reviled Him, wagging their heads"* (Mat. 27:39).

THE CRUCIFIXION

This Passage speaks of the Crucifixion. The Holy Spirit here will portray the sin not only of Judas and Ahithophel, but also of the leaders of Israel who threw in their lot with Absalom and Ahithophel, and the religious leaders who conspired with Judas to kill the Lord of Glory.

The pronoun *"them"* proclaims an irony in that it refers to those who were very religious. It was not the drunks, drug addicts, or harlots who crucified Christ; tragically and sadly, it was the Church of that day. In fact, there is no evil like *"religious evil."*

It has not changed unto this hour. The greatest hindrance to the Work of God on this Earth is not ensconced in these vices which we have named, as wicked and evil as they might be, but rather *"The Church."* Of course, the True Church doesn't fall into that category; however, the True Church is infinitesimally smaller than the apostate Church.

Most of organized religion is included in the apostate Church. This doesn't mean it's wrong to be organized, or that every single Church in such falls into that category. They all do not; however, most do!

In fact, most so-called *"independents"* fall into the same category. Religious apostasy has nothing to do with organization or anything of that nature. It has to do with doctrine — more specifically, the manner in which the Cross is rejected or accepted.

Through the Apostle Paul, the Holy Spirit tells us that the Gospel of Jesus Christ is the Cross of Christ. He said:

"For Christ sent me not to baptize, but to preach the Gospel: not with wisdom of words, lest the Cross of Christ should be made of none effect" (I Cor. 1:17).

So, in this one Verse, we plainly are told that the Gospel is *"the Cross of Christ,"* referring to what Jesus there did for us.

The great Apostle then said, *"But though we, or an Angel from Heaven, preach any other gospel unto you than that which we have preached unto you, let him be accursed"* (Gal. 1:8).

So it becomes very obvious as to what the Gospel is, and the penalty attached for disobedience.

(26) "HELP ME, O LORD MY GOD: O SAVE ME ACCORDING TO YOUR MERCY."

There was no one who either David or Christ could turn to but God. There was no man to help.

(27) "THAT THEY MAY KNOW THAT THIS IS YOUR HAND; THAT YOU, LORD, HAVE DONE IT."

The prayer of both David and the Messiah was that God would act so mercifully and powerfully on their behalf that there would be no doubt as to Who had accomplished their deliverance. Even their worst enemies would have to know that it was God.

David was delivered, and Jesus was raised from the dead. So this prayer was answered in all of its totality.

(28) "LET THEM CURSE, BUT BLESS YOU: WHEN THEY ARISE, LET THEM BE ASHAMED; BUT LET YOUR SERVANT REJOICE."

The sense of this Verse is that, despite the curse that was willed upon them by their adversaries, it would not and could not stop the Blessings of the Lord.

The Prophecy had been given by Balaam long ago, *"Surely there is no enchantment against Jacob, neither is there any divination against Israel: according to this time it shall be said of Jacob and of Israel, What has God wrought!"* (Num. 23:23).

As the curse then would not work against Israel, likewise, the curse would not work against the Prince of Israel, for Jesus was the True Israel.

Despite their *"curse"* and efforts of destruction, God brought them through, and both David and Christ rejoiced.

(29) "LET MY ADVERSARIES BE CLOTHED WITH SHAME, AND LET THEM COVER THEMSELVES WITH THEIR OWN CONFUSION, AS WITH A MANTLE."

I think it is obvious that now these *"adversaries"* have been *"clothed with shame,"* which proclaims the fact that this prayer ultimately was answered. Their end has been *"confusion."*

What was in the hearts of Judas and Ahithophel?

How did they think they could destroy the Lord's Anointed?

Sin and rebellion confuse men. They no longer know or understand what is right or wrong, because they no longer seek the Will of God, but their own will instead. Hence, *"confusion covers them as with a mantle."*

Let it be clearly understood: All who follow in their train will come to the same ignominious, shameful, and disgraceful end!

(30) "I WILL GREATLY PRAISE THE LORD WITH MY MOUTH; YEA, I WILL PRAISE HIM AMONG THE MULTITUDE."

David, by faith, cries to God, and, by faith, he praises God. It is a praise of victory, although, at that time, victory has not yet come. But victory would come, as victory did come!

VICTORY!

In effect, David is saying that Absalom and Ahithophel will not be successful in their efforts; they will fail, and David will stand *"among the multitude"* praising God at the Tabernacle in Jerusalem. That he did!

As well, some one thousand years before the Incarnation, the Messiah would praise the Lord for victory over the Evil One. Now He sits at the Right Hand of the Father, making Intercession for the multitudes who constantly are praising Him.

(31) "FOR HE SHALL STAND AT THE RIGHT HAND OF THE POOR, TO SAVE HIM FROM THOSE WHO CONDEMN HIS SOUL."

In Psalm 109, Jehovah stands at the Right Hand of the Poor Man. In Psalm 110, the Poor Man sits at the Right Hand of Jehovah. He was poor in spirit as well as in circumstances, but God would not be ashamed to stand at the *"Right Hand"* of this Poor Man — the Lord Jesus Christ. He became poor that we might become rich (II Cor. 6:10; 8:9).

PSALM 110

David is the Author:
The Eternal King and Priest

(1) "THE LORD SAID UNTO MY LORD, YOU SIT AT MY RIGHT HAND, UNTIL I MAKE YOUR ENEMIES YOUR FOOTSTOOL."

This Passage is unfulfilled at present except for the Messiah's sitting on the Right Hand of the Father.

Some seven quotations in the New Testament confirm the application of this Psalm to the Messiah (Mat. 22:44; Mk. 12:36; Lk. 20:42; Acts 2:34; I Cor. 15:25; Heb. 1:13; 10:13).

The Speaker is the Holy Spirit. The human instrument is David. The Person spoken of and spoken to is the Messiah. The verb *"said"* in this First Verse is a special Hebrew word almost always used of Divine Personal utterance.

THE TRINITY

The first Hebrew word in the first phrase translated *"LORD"* is *"Jehovah."* The second word translated *"Lord"* is *"Adonai."*

This means there are two Divine Persons called Jehovah recorded here. In fact, there are three, simply because the Holy Spirit is inspiring David to write these Words.

And yet, there aren't three Gods, only One, but manifested in Three Persons, *"God the Father," "God the Son,"* and *"God the Holy Spirit."*

So we have in this Passage God the Father speaking to God the Son, telling Him to *"sit at My Right Hand."*

THE ENEMIES OF OUR LORD

To place the foot upon the neck or body of defeated enemies was a common practice of Oriental conquerors. This part of this Verse has not yet been fulfilled. It will be fulfilled at the Second Coming, when the Lord will place Satan and all of his minions of darkness into the bottomless pit. Then the Lord Jesus Christ will be Lord of all, and over the entire Earth!

(2) "THE LORD SHALL SEND THE ROD OF YOUR STRENGTH OUT OF ZION: RULE THOU IN THE MIDST OF YOUR ENEMIES."

This Verse pictures His enthronement in Zion and the committal to His Hand of the scepter of strength, emblem of His worldwide dominion. This is speaking of the coming Kingdom Age.

Incidentally, the *"Millennial Reign"* and the *"Kingdom Age"* are one and the same. The word *"Millennial"* actually means one thousand, because one thousand years will be the length of the Kingdom Age.

(3) "YOUR PEOPLE SHALL BE WILLING IN THE DAY OF YOUR POWER, IN THE BEAUTIES OF HOLINESS FROM THE WOMB OF THE MORNING: YOU HAVE THE DEW OF YOUR YOUTH."

This Verse could be translated, *"Your people shall be a free people and willing to follow You in the day of Your power, arrayed in garments of Holiness and as youthful and fresh as the dewdrops from the breast of the dawn."*

The phrase, *"From the womb of the morning,"* corresponds to *"From the brook in the way"* (Vs. 7). Both statements refer to the Resurrection — the one to its occasion, the other to its continuance.

(4) "THE LORD HAS SWORN, AND WILL NOT REPENT, YOU ARE A PRIEST FOREVER AFTER THE ORDER OF MELCHIZEDEK."

This is spoken of in Hebrews 5:6 and 6:20.

THE ORDER OF MELCHIZEDEK

The *"Order of Melchizedek"* was different from the Levitical or the Aaronic Priesthood. The Melchizedek Order was eternal, whereas the Aaronic Order was temporary.

Who was Melchizedek?

1. He was the king of Salem, which was ancient Jerusalem. Therefore, he was a Gentile (Gen. 14:18).

2. He was a Priest of God in Abraham's day, which was long before the Levitical or Aaronic Priesthood was instituted (Gen. 14:18).

3. He met Abraham returning from his military victory, and Abraham gave him a tenth of the spoils (Gen. 14:16-24). He was called the King of Righteousness and the King of Salem, which means *"Peace"* (Heb. 7:2).

4. He had no descent (recorded pedigree), which means he was without a recorded father and mother, and without recorded beginning of days or end of life. He did have a father, mother, birth, and death, but these were not recorded so that he could be a Type of Christ, Who was an Eternal Being without beginning or ending (Mic. 5:2; Isa. 9:6-7; Heb. 1:8).

5. He was made a Type of Christ so that Christ could be made a Priest after his order. He was an ordinary man, but he was even greater than Abraham, hence, Abraham paying him tithe.

Christ would take His Eternal Priesthood, as a result of the Incarnation, after the order of Melchizedek, Who was a Gentile, in order that He (Christ) might be the Great High Priest for all people, both Jew and Gentile. The statement, *"The LORD has sworn, and will not repent,"* means that this never will change.

Under the Mosaic Law, it was not lawful for a Gentile to come before a Jewish Priest with a sacrifice unless the Gentile became a proselyte Jew. Actually, there was a *"wall of partition"* that separated the Court of the Gentiles from the place of actual sacrificial offerings. If a Gentile crossed this wall of partition, he could be killed.

Therefore, Christ became a Great High Priest after the *"Order of Melchizedek,"* who was a Gentile, that all people, both Jew and Gentile, may come unto Him.

(5) "THE LORD AT YOUR RIGHT HAND SHALL STRIKE THROUGH KINGS IN THE DAY OF HIS WRATH.

(6) "HE SHALL JUDGE AMONG THE HEATHEN, HE SHALL FILL THE PLACES WITH THE DEAD BODIES; HE SHALL WOUND THE HEADS OVER MANY COUNTRIES."

Both of these Verses predict a great victory!

THE VICTORY OF THE MESSIAH OVER THE ANTICHRIST

Both of these Verses predict Messiah's triumph over the Antichrist and his followers. The Antichrist will be the great head over many countries, and his followers will be the dead bodies of Verse 6.

This speaks of the Battle of Armageddon (Ezek. 38:19), when the Lord of Glory shall come back and take vengeance on the enemies of Righteousness. All the kings, presidents, and world leaders who throw in their lot with the Antichrist will experience the Wrath of God. Christ will *"wound these heads."*

All of this will take place at the Second Coming (Rev., Chpt. 19).

(7) "HE SHALL DRINK OF THE BROOK IN THE WAY: THEREFORE SHALL HE LIFT UP THE HEAD."

This means that Christ shall be refreshed and satisfied in His conquests of the nations (Isa. 53:1-5; Joel, Chpt. 3; Zech., Chpt. 14; Rev. 19:11-21).

To *"lift up the head"* means that He will be exalted over the nations of the world; as the only Head, He will rule in Righteousness, Holiness, and Judgment (Isa. 2:2-4; Dan. 2:44-45; Zech., Chpt. 14; Rev. 20:4-6).

PSALM 111

*Author Unknown:
Praise to the Lord*

(1) "PRAISE YE THE LORD. I WILL PRAISE THE LORD WITH MY WHOLE HEART, IN THE ASSEMBLY OF THE UPRIGHT, AND IN THE CONGREGATION."

This and the two following Psalms are the three Hallelujah Psalms, which Israel will sing to the Messiah on the day of His enthronement in Zion. Psalm 111 claims the Perfection of His Works; Psalm 112, the Perfection of His Ways; Psalm 113, the Perfection of His Person. This triple anthem will praise Him as the Word of God because of His fidelity to the Word of God (Rev. 19:13). The first two Psalms commence with *"Hallelujah"* (*"Praise"* is the meaning of Hallelujah), and the last Psalm commences and closes with *"Hallelujah."*

The Antichrist has now been defeated. Satan and all of his minions of darkness have been locked away. Righteousness rules and reigns, for Christ is Righteousness. Therefore, on that great Millennial Morn, Israel, along with all of humanity, will *"praise the LORD with the whole heart."*

(2) "THE WORKS OF THE LORD ARE GREAT, SOUGHT OUT OF ALL THEM WHO HAVE PLEASURE THEREIN."

The latter portion of the Verse means that the Great Works of God are studied with great pleasure by those who love and fear Him.

What are these *"Works of the LORD"*?

THE WORKS OF THE LORD

1. The Promise of a Redeemer to salvage the human race (Gen. 3:15).

2. The sending of the flood to destroy the evil that was about to destroy the world (Gen., Chpts. 6-7).

3. The call of Abraham, through whom the Messiah ultimately would come, and to whom was given the great Message of *"Justification by Faith"* (Gen. 12:1-3; 15:6).

4. The birth of Isaac, the miracle child, when both his parents were past age, through whom the Seed (Christ) would come (Gen., Chpt. 21).

5. The protection of the sons of Jacob (Children of Israel) in Egypt until they became a strong nation (Gen., Chpt. 46).

6. The Deliverance of the Children of Israel from Egypt (a type of the world) through Moses by the Passover (Ex. 12:14).

7. The Promise to David that through him and his family the Messiah would come (II Sam., Chpt. 7).

8. The Promise that the Messiah would be born through a Virgin (Isa., Chpt. 7).

9. The Coming of the Seed, the Messiah, Virgin-born, the Incarnation — God becoming Man, God with us (Lk., Chpt. 2).

10. The Ministry, Message, Miracles, and Perfect, spotless, sinless Life of the Messiah (the four Gospels).

11. The Death of Christ on Calvary, as the Perfect, Sacrificial, Vicarious, Substitutionary Offering of Himself, which paid the price for humanity's Redemption (Mat., Chpt. 27). The Cross of Christ is, in fact, the very reason that God became Man and gave Himself on the Cross. This, and this alone, would satisfy the righteous demands of a thrice-Holy God. The Cross of Christ is the central pivot of the Great Plan of God, having been ordained by the Godhead in eternity past, even before the foundation of the world (I Pet. 1:18-20).

12. The Resurrection (Mat., Chpt. 28).

13. The Ascension (Acts, Chpt. 1).

14. The sending of the Holy Spirit (Acts, Chpt. 2).

15. The building of the Church (Mat. 16:18).

16. The Rapture of the Church (I Thess. 4:13-18).

17. The Great Tribulation (Rev., Chpts. 4-19).

18. The Battle of Armageddon (Ezek., Chpts. 38-39).

19. The Second Coming (Rev., Chpt. 19).

20. The putting down of all enemies and the Millennial Reign (Rev., Chpt. 20).

21. The making of the New Heavens and the New Earth (Rev., Chpt. 21).

22. The Holy City, New Jerusalem, coming down from God out of Heaven, transferring the Headquarters of God from Heaven to Earth (Rev., Chpt. 21).

(3) "HIS WORK IS HONORABLE AND

GLORIOUS: AND HIS RIGHTEOUSNESS ENDURES FOREVER."

The work of Satan is dishonorable, and so is the work of his followers. The only work that is honorable is that which is done for God and which is of God. Because it is honorable and righteous, it will endure forever.

(4) "HE HAS MADE HIS WONDERFUL WORKS TO BE REMEMBERED: THE LORD IS GRACIOUS AND FULL OF COMPASSION."

Verses 2 through 4 extol the glory of His Works. Mere words never could plumb the depths or scale the heights of that which He has done.

THE WORKS OF THE LORD

The Lord's Works are always redemptive, glorious, fair, just, equitable, merciful, righteous, and good. They, therefore, will endure forever.

Moreover, all that He has done has been solely for us and not for Him. This truly is Love that is pure and undefiled; consequently, God's Works always will be remembered and sought out.

And yet, the greatest Work of all is that which Jesus performed on the Cross of Calvary. There He satisfied the demands of a thrice-Holy God. There He atoned for all sin, past, present, and future, at least for all who will believe (Jn. 3:16). There He defeated Satan and all of his minions of darkness; He did so by removing the legal right, namely sin, that Satan had to hold man in captivity (Col. 2:14-15). There the work was so complete and the price was so fully paid that, upon His Death, the Way to the very Throne of God was opened for seeking man (Mat. 27:51).

(5) "HE HAS GIVEN MEAT UNTO THEM WHO FEAR HIM: HE WILL EVER BE MINDFUL OF HIS COVENANT."

Two things are here said:
1. God constantly provides food and sustenance for those who fear Him.
2. He constantly seeks to carry out His Covenant responsibility.

There always has been a breakdown on man's side of the Covenant. For everywhere that man is placed, man fails. Nevertheless, the viability of the Covenant is in Christ and not man; consequently, there is no fear or even possibility of this Covenant ever being broken.

Hallelujah!

(6) "HE HAS SHOWN HIS PEOPLE THE POWER OF HIS WORKS, THAT HE MAY GIVE THEM THE HERITAGE OF THE HEATHEN."

The Messiah's providential Care of His people in the past in Egypt (Vs. 4), in the wilderness (Vs. 5), and in Canaan (Vs. 6), is recalled and celebrated, and His Performance of His Word is acknowledged in Verses 6 and 7.

(7) "THE WORKS OF HIS HANDS ARE VERITY AND JUDGMENT; ALL HIS COMMANDMENTS ARE SURE."

The word *"verity"* means *"Truth."*

TRUTH

All of this is given in contrast to man's works and laws, which are flawed, faulty, and which soon perish. Sadly, the far greater majority of the human family put their trust in that provided by man; these will find the opposite of truth and judgment. Man's commandments are for sale to the highest bidder; conversely, the Messiah's *"Commandments are sure."*

Someone has said:
"One life will soon be past,
"Only what's done for Christ will last."

(8) "THEY STAND FAST FOREVER AND EVER, AND ARE DONE IN TRUTH AND UPRIGHTNESS."

All the talk of the present concerns the *"ozone depletion"* or the *"greenhouse effect"* or such similar terminology, and claims are made that these will bring about the destruction of the Earth. Man certainly has wreaked havoc on this Planet, but still the Earth belongs to God, because He is Earth's Creator. As such, this Earth, plus all of God's Creation, will *"stand fast forever and ever."*

There is coming a day when the Lord will renovate the heavens and the Earth with fire, but this only means that they will be transformed from one state to another and not that they will be annihilated (II Pet. 3:7-13).

(9) "HE SENT REDEMPTION UNTO HIS PEOPLE: HE HAS COMMANDED HIS COVENANT FOREVER: HOLY AND REVEREND IS HIS NAME."

The word *"Reverend"* simply means that

His Name is to be reverenced.

Regrettably and sadly, His Name is not too very much reverenced in the world at present; however, that is soon to change, which will take place at the Second Coming.

(10) "THE FEAR OF THE LORD IS THE BEGINNING OF WISDOM: A GOOD UNDERSTANDING HAVE ALL THEY WHO DO HIS COMMANDMENTS: HIS PRAISE ENDURES FOREVER."

When men lose *"the fear of the LORD,"* they lose wisdom; consequently, the diverse and sometimes foolish directions taken by political leaders in America (or any other country in the world) are because of a loss of the *"fear of the LORD."*

There is a sensible and wise *"understanding"* of all things, spiritual, political, physical, and material, concerning those who *"do His Commandments."* This is not speaking of education pertaining to facts, figures, or knowledge of the same. It is speaking of the ability to use all such information to the betterment of all, and not the greedy grasping of personal desires.

PSALM 112

Author Unknown:
Blessed is the Man who Fears the Lord

(1) "PRAISE YE THE LORD. BLESSED IS THE MAN WHO FEARS THE LORD, WHO DELIGHTS GREATLY IN HIS COMMANDMENTS.

(2) "HIS SEED SHALL BE MIGHTY UPON EARTH: THE GENERATION OF THE UPRIGHT SHALL BE BLESSED."

It is not known who wrote this Psalm or the previous one.

PRAISE THE LORD

This Song is an expansion of the last Verse of the previous Psalm. It praises the Messiah because of His Ways upon Earth, and because He molds men into His Own moral image. It celebrates and illustrates the fact that everyone who surrenders himself into the hands of this Mighty God and obeys Him speedily becomes like Him. So, the first three Verses apply to the Messiah. He is the Blessed Man of Verse 1 and the Upright Man of Verse 2.

(3) "WEALTH AND RICHES SHALL BE IN HIS HOUSE: AND HIS RIGHTEOUSNESS ENDURES FOREVER."

The pronoun *"His"* refers to the Messiah. It is into *"His House"* that we are invited, where wealth and riches abide. This is an eagerly sought-after prize. Admittance into *"His House"* is by the route of *"His Righteousness."*

He freely imputes *"His Righteousness"* unto all who believe, which is all made possible by the Cross; conversely, He will withhold *"His Righteousness"* from those who attempt to earn such. It must be freely received in order to be freely given.

(4) "UNTO THE UPRIGHT THERE ARISES LIGHT IN THE DARKNESS: HE IS GRACIOUS, AND FULL OF COMPASSION, AND RIGHTEOUS."

Two great truths are given in this Verse.

THE MESSIAH IS UPRIGHT

The word *"Upright"* in Verse 2 is singular in the Hebrew and thereby applies to the Messiah. The word *"upright"* in this Verse is plural in the Hebrew Text and thereby applies to His servants. Thus is the argument illustrated that He can make His servants like Himself, just as David molded the timid fugitives of Adullam's cave into the mighty men of Hebron's throne (I Sam. 22:2; II Sam. 23:8).

CHRIST IS THE LIGHT IN THE DARKNESS

Isaiah spoke of this and was quoted by Matthew (Mat. 4:16; Isa. 9:2).

There is no Light but Christ. This is so important that we must repeat it: *"There is no Light but Christ."*

The fake luminaries of the world, such as Buddha, Muhammad, Joseph Smith, Confucius, or the graduates of prized institutions, such as Harvard, Yale, Cambridge, or Oxford, have no light unless they have Christ. Many have knowledge, but no Light; consequently, knowledge without Light only brings confusion.

The *"upright"* (followers of Christ) emulate their Master in graciousness and compassion.

As well, their righteousness comes from Christ.

(5) "A GOOD MAN SHOWS FAVOR, AND LENDS: HE WILL GUIDE HIS AFFAIRS WITH DISCRETION."

The word *"lends"* signifies all kinds of generous actions, because to lend is a very rare Grace.

(6) "SURELY HE SHALL NOT BE MOVED FOREVER: THE RIGHTEOUS SHALL BE IN EVERLASTING REMEMBRANCE."

Prosperity comes even to the unrighteous, but is fleeting and ultimately goes away. The contrasts given by the Holy Spirit concerning the righteous show that their prosperity shall last forever because it is anchored in Christ. The *"seed"* and *"generation"* of Verse 2 signify the spiritual sons of the Messiah.

(7) "HE SHALL NOT BE AFRAID OF EVIL TIDINGS: HIS HEART IS FIXED, TRUSTING IN THE LORD.

(8) "HIS HEART IS ESTABLISHED, HE SHALL NOT BE AFRAID, UNTIL HE SEE HIS DESIRE UPON HIS ENEMIES."

Evil tidings shall not put the Believer in fear, for he shall see God's Judgment upon his enemies.

The word *"until"* in Verse 8 expresses the steadfastness of his faith during the entire period between the reception of the news (evil tidings) and the destruction of his foes.

(9) "HE HAS DISPERSED, HE HAS GIVEN TO THE POOR; HIS RIGHTEOUSNESS ENDURES FOREVER; HIS HORN SHALL BE EXALTED WITH HONOR."

The true and false Messiahs and their followers are contrasted in the last two Verses of this Psalm. Three statements are made respecting the Messiah (for this Verse speaks of Him).

He enriches, His Beneficence never ends, and He Triumphs.

(10) "THE WICKED SHALL SEE IT, AND BE GRIEVED; HE SHALL GNASH WITH HIS TEETH, AND MELT AWAY: THE DESIRE OF THE WICKED SHALL PERISH."

"Wicked" in the first line of this Verse is singular in the Hebrew Text. It means the lawless one of Daniel 11:36 and II Thessalonians 2:8.

"Wicked" in the last line of this Verse is plural in the Hebrew Text, and means the lawless ones, that is, the followers of the lawless one, the Antichrist.

Thus, the great picture is drawn. The Antichrist and those who hope in him will perish, while those whose expectation is based on Christ will triumph.

PSALM 113

*Author Unknown:
Praise to God*

(1) "PRAISE YE THE LORD. PRAISE, O YE SERVANTS OF THE LORD, PRAISE THE NAME OF THE LORD."

As noted, it is not known who wrote this Psalm.

PRAISE THE LORD

This is the last of the three Hallelujah Psalms. It differs from the two previous ones in that it begins and closes with *"Hallelujah."*

It also is the first of six Hallel Psalms (113-118). These Israel sang then and now sings at the Paschal Supper. At that Supper, four cups of wine are drunk.

The first three were and are sung after the second cup; the remaining three Psalms are sung after the fourth cup. They are sung in Matthew 26:30. The Greek Text here reads: *"And having sung* (the last Hallel, Psalm 118), *they went forth to the Mount of Olives."*

It brings these Psalms very near to the heart when one remembers that they were sung by the Lord Himself on the night of His betrayal. Considering the atmosphere of that last Supper, they have an added preciousness for the Believer.

This Psalm (113), sung in that night of weakness and to be sung in the coming day of power, links together the Messiah's sufferings and the glories that are to follow. It invites the servants of Jehovah to praise Him (Williams).[59]

Only those can worship God who are the servants of God. *"To praise the Lord"* is to bless Him for what He is in His Being and Essence. *"To praise the Name of the Lord"* is to bless Him for His Perfections and Excellencies manifested in His Actions.

What the Messiah Personally is, as already

stated, is the theme of this Psalm.

(2) "BLESSED BE THE NAME OF THE LORD FROM THIS TIME FORTH AND FOREVERMORE."

The words, *"From this time forth,"* relate to the occasion of His future enthronement in Zion. The duration of that Kingdom is foretold in this Verse, *"forevermore."*

(3) "FROM THE RISING OF THE SUN UNTO THE GOING DOWN OF THE SAME THE LORD's NAME IS TO BE PRAISED."

Concerning the world, the extent of His Kingdom is here predicted — worldwide.

Regrettably and sadly, at this present time there is precious little praise going up to the Lord from the hearts of men. Tragically enough, the spirit world is filled with profanity, vulgarity, and blasphemy. That is soon to change!

When Jesus Christ reigns supreme and brings all under His submission, then praises to the Lord's Name will come forth from every place the Sun shines.

(4) "THE LORD IS HIGH ABOVE ALL NATIONS, AND HIS GLORY ABOVE THE HEAVENS."

As Verse 3 proclaimed the extent of His reign, Verse 4 proclaims its universality.

He is not an earthly king produced by political manipulation; He is from Heaven and thereby from another source; He is not tainted with the terrible Fall of man. His Glory is even above the heavens.

(5) "WHO IS LIKE UNTO THE LORD OUR GOD, WHO DWELLS ON HIGH."

The sense of the words, *"Who dwells on high,"* in the Hebrew Text, is *"Who has enthroned Himself on high,"* for example, over the highest heavens from when He looks down upon both Heaven and Earth. God enthrones Himself, for there is none greater than He.

(6) "WHO HUMBLES HIMSELF TO BEHOLD THE THINGS THAT ARE IN HEAVEN, AND IN THE EARTH!"

To interest Himself in the heavens is wonderful condescension, but to descend in His affections still lower to the Earth is Amazing Grace (Gen. 1:1).

The Hebrew word for *"humbles"* is *"shapel,"* which means *"to lower oneself."*

This the Lord did when He came to this Earth in order to die on Calvary. The Scripture says, and I quote from THE EXPOSITOR'S STUDY BIBLE:

"Who, being in the form of God (refers to Deity, which Christ always was), *thought it not robbery to be equal with God* (equality with God refers here to our Lord's co-participation with the other Members of the Trinity in the expression of the Divine Essence)*:*

"But made Himself of no reputation (instead of asserting His Rights to the expression of the Essence of Deity, our Lord waived His Rights to that expression), *and took upon Him the form of a servant* (a bondslave), *and was made in the likeness of men* (presents the Lord entering into a new state of Being when He became Man; but Him becoming Man did not exclude His Position of Deity; while, in becoming Man, He laid aside the *'expression'* of Deity, He never lost *'possession'* of Deity)*:*

"And being found in fashion as a man (denotes Christ in men's eyes), *He humbled Himself* (He was brought low, but willingly), *and became obedient unto death* (does not mean He became obedient to death; He was always the Master of Death; rather, He subjected Himself to death), *even the death of the Cross*. (This presents the character of His Death as one of disgrace and degradation, which was necessary for men to be redeemed. This type of death alone would pay the terrible sin debt and do so in totality)" (Phil. 2:6-8).

(7) "HE RAISES UP THE POOR OUT OF THE DUST, AND LIFTS THE NEEDY OUT OF THE DUNGHILL."

That He Who is so great can interest Himself in that which is so poor can only be explained by undiluted love.

(8) "THAT HE MAY SET HIM WITH PRINCES, EVEN WITH THE PRINCES OF HIS PEOPLE."

This Verse could possibly be best explained by the words of the following song:

"He brought me out of the miry clay,
"He set my feet on the Rock to stay,
"He put a song in my soul today,
"A song of praise, Hallelujah!"

(9) "HE MAKES THE BARREN WOMAN TO KEEP HOUSE, AND TO BE A JOYFUL

MOTHER OF CHILDREN. PRAISE YE THE LORD."

As the Psalm begins with *"Hallelujah"* (Praise), it ends with *"Hallelujah."*

The *"barren woman"* speaks of Israel and her glorious Restoration. He predicts that she will do two things:

1. Ultimately she will be a joyful mother of children of the Lord.

2. She will then sing forever praises to the Lord, *"Praise ye the LORD."*

PSALM 114

Author Unknown:
God's Power Demonstrated in the Exodus

(1) "WHEN ISRAEL WENT OUT OF EGYPT, THE HOUSE OF JACOB FROM A PEOPLE OF STRANGE LANGUAGE."

As noted, the writer of this Psalm is unknown.

JACOB

Concerning this, Williams says, *"The sublime poetry of this Song is felt by the dullest and delighted in by the noblest minds. It links the Messiah's intervention on behalf of His people Israel at the commencement of their national history* (Vss. 1-6) *with His future intervention on their behalf at the close of the present period of their exile"* (Vss. 7-8).[60]

The First Verse commemorates the powerful, even the all-powerful, Deliverance of Israel from Egyptian bondage. The name *"Jacob"* is used here and in Verse 7 to emphasize that Grace, not merit, forms the basis of past and future Deliverance for Israel, as well as for ourselves.

(2) "JUDAH WAS HIS SANCTUARY, AND ISRAEL HIS DOMINION."

Then, Judah and Israel were His Sanctuary; now, the Church is His Sanctuary (the Body of Christ), the individual Believer (I Cor. 3:16).

After the reign of Solomon, due to differences, the kingdom was divided, with the Northern Kingdom at times called Samaria, or Ephraim, or Israel. The Southern Kingdom, where Jerusalem was located, was referred to as Judah.

While the separation is recognized in the Bible, this does not mean that the Lord looked at any of these individuals occupying either the Northern or the Southern portions as anything other than Jews.

(3) "THE SEA SAW IT, AND FLED: JORDAN WAS DRIVEN BACK.

(4) "THE MOUNTAINS SKIPPED LIKE RAMS, AND THE LITTLE HILLS LIKE LAMBS."

The argument of the Psalm, as to the past, is: If nature, represented by the Red Sea, Sinai, and Jordan, trembled at the manifestation of God, how much more should the sinners of Canaan tremble before Him!

That they did so, the Second and Fifth Chapters of Joshua record; as to the future, the physical convulsions of nature accompanying the Second Advent of our Lord, as predicted in Revelation, should and will make Israel's future adversaries tremble.

(5) "WHAT AILED YOU, O THOU SEA, THAT YOU FLED? THOU JORDAN, THAT YOU WERE DRIVEN BACK?

(6) "YOU MOUNTAINS, THAT YOU SKIPPED LIKE RAMS; AND YOU LITTLE HILLS, LIKE LAMBS?"

The Holy Spirit draws our attention to the great Power of God, to which even nature must respond accordingly. There is no power in the world like that!

(7) "TREMBLE, THOU EARTH, AT THE PRESENCE OF THE LORD, AT THE PRESENCE OF THE GOD OF JACOB."

The *"Presence of the Lord"* means His *Parousia* or Revelation — that is, His future Coming in Power and Great Glory. The word *"Lord"* in this Verse is *"Adon."*

THE POWER OF GOD

The following question begs to be asked: *"Why should men tremble before a God so kind as to deliver a multitude of slaves from their oppressor, making them His dwelling place and Kingdom, Who moves seas, mountains, and rivers for their advantage, and, finally, Who turns flinty rocks to water for their thirst?*

The answer is that this kindness shows affection for His ancient people and is so much evidenced that a fearful doom will fall upon all who ill treat them (Mat. 25:31-46).

The Holy Spirit tells us that nature trembled, not at these feeble fugitives, but at Him Who led them.

(8) "WHICH TURNED THE ROCK INTO A STANDING WATER, THE FLINT INTO A FOUNTAIN OF WATERS."

The sense of this Verse is that the Rock was Christ (I Cor. 10:4). It refers to the waters from the Smitten Rock, which typified Calvary (Ex. 17:6; Num. 20:11).

"The flint" stands for the stony heart of men that is melted by the Grace of God and turned into *"a fountain of waters"* (Jn. 4:13-14).

PSALM 115

Author Unknown:
Praise to God Who is Our Help and Shield

(1) "NOT UNTO US, O LORD, NOT UNTO US, BUT UNTO YOUR NAME GIVE GLORY, FOR YOUR MERCY, AND FOR YOUR TRUTH'S SAKE."

It is not known who wrote this Psalm, as no name is given in the title or instructions.

THE KINGDOM AGE

This Song has to do with the beginning of the Millennial Reign. On the happy morning of Israel's Restoration, she will ascribe to the Messiah the Glory of the Deliverance sung of in the previous Psalm. His Mercy to her throughout her entire history and His Truth to her in fulfilling the Promises of her Restoration will be the theme of her Song.

Now that Israel has accepted Christ as their Messiah, Saviour, and Lord, the very One they crucified, they will now be restored to her rightful place of dominion over the nations of the world, which God intended at the very beginning.

Israel lost so much by failing the Lord, and we also lose so much by following in the same train.

(2) "WHEREFORE SHOULD THE HEATHEN SAY, WHERE IS NOW THEIR GOD?"

Reviewing her history, Israel will exultingly say in that day, *"Why should the nations at any time have said, and how can they now say, 'Where then is their God?'"* As stated, this will be during the time of the Kingdom Age!

(3) "BUT OUR GOD IS IN THE HEAVENS: HE HAS DONE WHATSOEVER HE HAS PLEASED."

This always has been the case, but God can be depended upon to do right in everything He does.

In this Passage, Israel is saying that her God is in the heavens and is, therefore, invisible and not a visible god of wood or stone in the Earth. In olden times, all the nations in the world, except Israel, worshipped such false gods of wood or stone. Israel alone knew the God of the heavens, the Creator of the Universe.

(4) "THEIR IDOLS ARE SILVER AND GOLD, THE WORK OF MEN'S HANDS."

Israel will declare that all of God's dealings with her were the acts of His Grace and Truth. She will joyfully contrast this activity of Love and Holiness with the helplessness of idols and with the worthlessness and folly of idolatry.

(5) "THEY HAVE MOUTHS, BUT THEY SPEAK NOT: EYES HAVE THEY, BUT THEY SEE NOT:

(6) "THEY HAVE EARS, BUT THEY HEAR NOT: NOSES HAVE THEY, BUT THEY SMELL NOT:

(7) "THEY HAVE HANDS, BUT THEY HANDLE NOT: FEET HAVE THEY, BUT THEY WALK NOT: NEITHER SPEAK THEY THROUGH THEIR THROAT."

The Holy Spirit is here speaking of objects made by the hands of men, which, therefore, are dead. In our cultured, educated age, most think this is a thing of the past, a sin that no longer is applicable; however, spiritual and Scriptural introspection will prove otherwise. Idolatry is rampant, even more widely disseminated than ever before.

IDOLATRY

John the Beloved wrote, *"Little children, keep yourselves from idols"* (I Jn. 5:21). These words were not uselessly given by the Holy Spirit.

The idols of today, however, are far more subtle and deadlier than the idols of the past.

As the idols of old could not hear, speak, smell, or touch, the idols of today can do all of these things and more.

Please note:

Anything that enters into our lifestyle along with Christ becomes an idol. Christ is to be all in all. He is not to be a part of our lifestyle, but all of our lifestyle (Mat. 11:28-29). Israel's problem of old was that they worshipped idols along with the Lord. Samuel the Prophet emphatically told them, *"Serve the LORD only"* (I Sam. 7:3).

The sin of Israel of old is also the sin of the modern Church. Christ is just a part of our worship.

Along with Christ we worship Hollywood, sports, education, money, and a wide variety of other things; however, the greatest idol of all is religion. As someone has well said, *"The doing of religion is the most powerful narcotic there is."* This *"idol"* of religion has taken untold millions to Hell, and is continuing to take other millions there even unto this very moment.

Millions have made an idol out of their Denomination, their respective local Church, or even a Preacher. Others make an idol out of a particular doctrine which has been taken out of context and turned into heresy.

It certainly is not wrong to love our Church or our Pastor, etc., but it is wrong to place them in a spiritual position. Some of these things are not wrong within themselves, but we make idols of them by our attention and servitude.

Christ must be all in all and, thereby, all of all!

(8) "THEY WHO MAKE THEM ARE LIKE UNTO THEM; SO IS EVERY ONE WHO TRUSTS IN THEM."

A great truth is here presented, and we should pay careful attention.

WORSHIPPERS OF IDOLS BECOME LIKE THE IDOLS THEY WORSHIP

The heading is so important that I want to say it again:

"Worshippers of idols become like the idols they worship — senseless, cruel, and impure."

At the present time, multitudes worship idols made with their own hands, or made up within their own minds. An idol is an idol, whether it be made manually or mentally. To worship God under the similitude of metal, stone, wood, bread, or mind is idolatry — such as are many religious activities in both Catholic and Protestant Churches.

If an individual is truly following Christ, that person will exhibit a Christlike spirit. If they are following other things of religion, which so many are, they will have a contentious spirit, an unkind spirit, a cruel spirit, a destructive spirit — they have become like that which they worship!

(9) "O ISRAEL, TRUST THOU IN THE LORD: HE IS THEIR HELP AND THEIR SHIELD."

As Israel of old could not trust in the Lord and idols at the same time, likewise the modern Church cannot trust in psychology, education, therapy, or counseling and the Lord at the same time. The Lord will not be a *"help and shield"* to those who place their trust partially in Him and partially in man. The sadness of it all is that there is no help whatsoever in that which man produces, namely the world of psychology and psychotherapy.

THE CROSS OF CHRIST

Without fear of much contradiction, I think I can say the following:

If the Believer has anchored his faith in something other than Christ and the Cross; if, in other words, he doesn't understand that the Source of all things is Christ and the Cross is the Means, and that the Holy Spirit works exclusively within the framework of the Finished Work of Christ; then, because of his lack of understanding of these all-important truths, such a Believer has made an idol out of something.

Again, without fear of contradiction, I think I can say that the Cross of Christ and our Faith there properly placed is the only defense against idols. The Cross of Christ is, in fact, the story of the Bible. It runs all the way from Genesis 1:1 through Revelation 22:21. This means that if the Believer doesn't properly understand Christ and the Cross, then he doesn't properly understand the Bible. To properly understand one is to understand the other. To misunderstand or deny one is to misunderstand or deny the other!

(10) "O HOUSE OF AARON, TRUST IN THE LORD: HE IS THEIR HELP AND THEIR SHIELD."

The *"House of Aaron"* pertains to the Ministry. If the Priesthood placed their trust in the Lord, basically the majority of the people would follow suit. The same holds true with Ministry today.

If the pulpit proclaims that which is right, much of the time the pew will follow suit; regrettably, in the far-greater majority of cases, the pulpit little stands on the Word of God (Jn. 1:1, 14, 29; Rom. 6:1-14; 8:1-2, 11; I Cor. 1:17-18, 23; 2:2; Gal., Chpt. 5; 6:14; Eph. 2:13-18; Col. 2:14-15).

(11) "YE WHO FEAR THE LORD, TRUST IN THE LORD: HE IS THEIR HELP AND THEIR SHIELD."

These three Verses (9-11) point to every aspect of society:

1. Israel: This pertained to the nation as a whole trusting in the Lord; it also will apply to any nation.

2. Aaron: This pertained, as stated, to the Ministry of that day and also of today.

3. The individual: No matter what the nation or the Ministry does, the Christian is to *"trust in the LORD."* The Holy Spirit pinpoints the admonition even down to the specific individual. He could not be more clear or plain.

(12) "THE LORD HAS BEEN MINDFUL OF US: HE WILL BLESS US; HE WILL BLESS THE HOUSE OF ISRAEL; HE WILL BLESS THE HOUSE OF AARON.

(13) "HE WILL BLESS THEM WHO FEAR THE LORD, BOTH SMALL AND GREAT."

A tremendous Promise is given here.

TO BE BLESSED IS TO PROSPER

In these two Verses, the Holy Spirit covers not only Israel, but all who *"fear the LORD, both small and great."* In other words, these great Promises are meant for every human being on the face of the Earth, if they only will *"fear the LORD."*

The type of fear mentioned here is not the type of fear that a slave has for a master. It is the type of fear that tenders respect, appreciation, gratitude, and love. At the same time, it knows that God says what He means and means what He says! Proper love actually cannot be tendered toward God unless proper fear also is tendered toward Him.

(14) "THE LORD SHALL INCREASE YOU MORE AND MORE, YOU AND YOUR CHILDREN."

As stated, blessing means *"increase,"* and in every capacity.

Believers should expect the Lord to bless them. To be sure, they should obey Him, seek His Face, desire His Will in all things, and then expect Him to bless them, which His Word promises that He will do, exactly as we are here studying.

(15) "YOU ARE BLESSED OF THE LORD WHICH MADE HEAVEN AND EARTH."

Over and over again in the Bible, we are reminded that *"God made Heaven and Earth."*

CREATION AND THE CREATOR

It is as though the Holy Spirit anticipated the erroneous fabrication of evolution, which is one of the most ridiculous heresies ever fostered upon an unbelieving, gullible public. Regrettably, this lie is taught as fact (therefore truth) in the public school systems of America and Canada and in the majority of the world.

Because the value of human life is lessened, evolution paves the way for abortion, infanticide, suicide, and euthanasia.

And why not?

It's only a tissue or a blob, or at most a higher form of animal life. Evolution teaches that man has no soul or spirit and that man has no eternal future. It is impossible to believe in evolution and God at the same time.

For all the teaching of evolution, it still cannot agree on the first cause. The Bible is clear on the subject. God is the First Cause of all things (Jn. 1:1-3).

Those who believe in the Lord and His Word are blessed by Him.

(16) "THE HEAVEN, EVEN THE HEAVENS, ARE THE LORD's: BUT THE EARTH HAS HE GIVEN TO THE CHILDREN OF MEN."

Exploration into space (or near space) will only have limited success at the present time. No doubt, after the Second Coming, the frontiers of space will be pushed out considerably concerning the Glorified Saints and the vast Creation of God.

In the Garden of Eden, God gave dominion of Planet Earth to Adam (Gen. 1:26). It is obvious as to the results. Man fell and changed lords, in that he, by and large, now worships Satan as lord instead of Jehovah. The results have been misery, pain, sickness, suffering, heartache, murder, war, and sorrow.

Very shortly, the Lord is going to take the total control of this Earth unto Himself. This will occur at the Second Coming.

(17) "THE DEAD PRAISE NOT THE LORD, NEITHER ANY WHO GO DOWN INTO SILENCE."

The argument of this Verse is that only living men can witness in the Earth to God's Love and Holiness and Power. They only can vindicate before men His Name, that is, His Character, by their testimony to the Perfection of His Ways with them.

As would be obvious, after a person dies, this no longer can be done.

This Verse is not teaching *"soul sleep"* as some claim. This particular doctrine claims that when the Believer dies, his soul and his spirit sleep in the grave until the coming Resurrection. There is nothing in the Word of God that substantiates such a claim. The moment the Believer dies, he (or she) instantly goes to be with Christ. Paul said so (Phil. 1:21).

(18) "BUT WE WILL BLESS THE LORD FROM THIS TIME FORTH AND FOREVERMORE. PRAISE THE LORD."

Williams says, *"'From this time forth' means, historically, from the commencement of the Millennial Reign."* 61

This Verse expresses Israel's confidence in the Glory and success of the Messiah's Government.

Faith can make spiritually and morally true future Divine Promises and can sing of them.

PSALM 116

*David is the Author:
Praise to God for Deliverance*

(1) "I LOVE THE LORD, BECAUSE HE HAS HEARD MY VOICE AND MY SUPPLICATIONS."

As noted, this Psalm was written by David.

THE RESURRECTION

There are six Hallel Psalms, of which this is the fourth. The comforting Message to faith in this Song is that the Resurrection of Christ is a pledge and assurance of the Resurrection of His people, and that as God carried Him victoriously through the sorrows of life and of death, so will He triumphantly carry those who by faith are united to Him; hence, our Resurrection is based upon and connected with His Resurrection.

(2) "BECAUSE HE HAS INCLINED HIS EAR UNTO ME, THEREFORE WILL I CALL UPON HIM AS LONG AS I LIVE."

This Psalm, sung by Christ and His small band of Disciples on the eve of His Crucifixion, will be sung again by Him in the midst of the great congregation on the morn of His Coronation, which will take place very shortly after His Second Coming.

The idea of both Verses 1 and 2 is that the Messiah called upon God at the time of His Death and was delivered out of the death world.

(3) "THE SORROWS OF DEATH COMPASSED ME, AND THE PAINS OF HELL GOT HOLD UPON ME: I FOUND TROUBLE AND SORROW."

The first part of this Psalm (Vss. 3-11) presents the Messiah's recalling of His First Advent while in weakness and Atonement. In Verses 12 through 19, He anticipates His Second Advent in Power and Glory, and He praises and worships Jehovah in respect to both.

This double theme appears in the introduction. He offers praise because of His Deliverance out of the death world and because of the promised fulfillment of the Covenant granting Him the Kingdom (Vss. 14-19; Williams).62

(4) "THEN CALLED I UPON THE NAME OF THE LORD; O LORD, I BESEECH YOU, DELIVER MY SOUL."

Death is a grievous enemy. The Messiah's sorrows in the death world and His Prayer when there, are the subject of Verses 3 through 6. His joyful testimony on the morning of His Resurrection is the theme of Verses 7 through 11.

(5) "GRACIOUS IS THE LORD, AND RIGHTEOUS; YEA, OUR GOD IS MERCIFUL."

Considering what the Lord had done, the Messiah, as well as David, would praise Him. The Messiah spoke more of His Petitions,

Supplications, Prayers, and Victories through David than through any other Psalmist. This was because it was through David's lineage that the Messiah would come; hence, for many reasons, there was a great spiritual bond.

(6) "THE LORD PRESERVES THE SIMPLE: I WAS BROUGHT LOW, AND HE HELPED ME."

The word *"simple"* refers to *"sinless."* Because He was such, He was guarded safely when He was in the death world.

(7) "RETURN UNTO YOUR REST, O MY SOUL; FOR THE LORD HAS DEALT BOUNTIFULLY WITH YOU."

The *"rest"* intended in this Verse is that of John 17:4-5. The Messiah, having accomplished Redemption, returned to the ineffable repose of the Father's bosom, so to speak.

The word *"soul"* in Verses 4 and 7 demonstrates that the Person Who prayed in Sheol is the very same Person Who praised in Resurrection Life and Power (Acts 2:27). He was *"this same Jesus"* (Acts 1:11).

(8) "FOR YOU HAVE DELIVERED MY SOUL FROM DEATH, MY EYES FROM TEARS, AND MY FEET FROM FALLING."

The word *"falling"* has no moral significance. The Hebrew word means *"a thrusting down."* The sense of the Verse is that He was delivered from being perpetually thrust down, for Sheol is bottomless; and so He was raised up (resurrected).

(9) "I WILL WALK BEFORE THE LORD IN THE LAND OF THE LIVING."

A thousand years before the First Advent of Christ, the Holy Spirit through David predicts the Resurrection of the Lord.

Some may ask the questions: *"Doesn't Satan have the ability to read these Passages which predict his defeat? And if he does read them, how could Satan think he could overcome God?"*

I personally have no doubt that Satan read these very words a short time after they were written, but he simply does not believe them. Despite every single prediction in the Word of God that already has been fulfilled, Satan simply does not believe the other predictions in the Word of God concerning his total defeat and destruction. He is the great deceiver, and he himself is thereby deceived. He actually thinks that ultimately he will win.

NOTES

Of course, we know that he won't!

(10) "I BELIEVED, THEREFORE HAVE I SPOKEN: I WAS GREATLY AFFLICTED."

The first line of Verse 10 means that because the Messiah believed the Resurrection Promise made to Him, He, therefore, uttered this testimony respecting His Sorrows and Brokenness.

Faith in the Lord and in His Word opens the mouth and always has her tribute of praise to offer. This faith of Verse 10 is most striking, for it was exercised in the face of death, and is now exercised by Him in Resurrection. It also energizes His Song by anticipating His future Reign of Power and Majesty.

(11) "I SAID IN MY HASTE, ALL MEN ARE LIARS."

The word *"haste"* in the Hebrew does not mean *"hastily,"* but *"hasting on."* The Lord went through that which He had to go through, as it regards the Cross, as speedily as possible. He hasted through it as a pilgrim making speed to the Father's House. As He hasted, His true and deliberate Judgment toward man because of the Fall was that all men are untrustworthy.

The Holy Spirit repeats this testimony in Romans 3:4, *"God forbid: yea, let God be true, but every man a liar."*

There is only One Who has been totally trustworthy, totally truthful, only One Who never has told a lie, and that is our Lord and Saviour, Jesus Christ.

(12) "WHAT SHALL I RENDER UNTO THE LORD FOR ALL HIS BENEFITS TOWARD ME?"

As David asked this question, likewise, the Son of David asks the same.

If it is impossible for the Lord of Glory, God's only Son, to render unto Jehovah just recompense for *"all His benefits,"* how so very impossible is it for us!

This is one reason why we are instructed to constantly praise the Lord for all of these benefits. Praise in no way pays for, or is meant to pay for, all that God has done for us. The main purpose of the Holy Spirit is that we understand these benefits did not accrue from our own hand or the hand of any man, but from God.

(13) "I WILL TAKE THE CUP OF

SALVATION, AND CALL UPON THE NAME OF THE LORD."

The sense of this Verse is that contained in the *"Cup of Salvation,"* is the privilege of being able to *"call upon the Name of the LORD,"* with the expectancy of His hearing us and answering our petition, providing it is in His Will (I Jn. 5:14).

(14) "I WILL PAY MY VOWS UNTO THE LORD NOW IN THE PRESENCE OF ALL HIS PEOPLE."

The sense of this Verse is found in Psalm 40: *"Then said I, Lo, I come: in the volume of the Book it is written of Me, I delight to do Your Will, O My God: yea, Your Law is within My heart"* (Ps. 40:7-8).

THE GREAT VICTORY OF CHRIST IS OBVIOUS TO ALL

What Christ did in the Redemption of man was done *"in the presence of all."* He was born of the Virgin Mary, which was obvious to all who cared to investigate. He lived a Perfect, sinless Life; He died on Calvary in full view of observers; His Resurrection was carried out in the Presence of the Roman Government, the whole of Israel, and also His Own Disciples.

As Paul stated, *"This thing was not done in a corner"* (Acts 26:26).

So, why is it that most in the world reject Him?

UNBELIEF

Pure and simple, as the Heading states, the problem is *"unbelief."*

Unbelief creates its own peculiar set of circumstances. In the face of incontestable evidence, in the face of that which is obvious, still, if the person does not desire to believe, they will reject that which is so very obvious.

To reject Christ, to disbelieve Him, puts the person in the place and position of rejecting Him in the face of undeniable evidence. When unbelief takes over a person, they cannot see the obvious! They become blind! That's the reason that Jesus said to the Church at Laodicea, *"Because you say, I am rich, and increased with goods, and have need of nothing; and knowest not that you are wretched, and miserable, and poor, and blind, and naked"* (Rev. 3:17).

It's impossible to show a blind person anything! The only thing that can break through that blindness of unbelief is the Power of God. Even then, many still refuse to *"see."*

(15) "PRECIOUS IN THE SIGHT OF THE LORD IS THE DEATH OF HIS SAINTS."

This Verse has several meanings:

DEATH

1. This Verse refers to the preciousness in the sight of the Lord of the death on Calvary of His Glorious Son and our Saviour, Jesus Christ. (The word *"precious"* means *"costly."*)

2. It is costly to the Work of God upon the passing of any of His Saints. The only light in the world is the Light of Christ, which reposes in the lives of the Saints.

3. Death is an enemy, because it cuts short so many things — above all, the lives of those who truly are stanchions of righteousness. The Scripture says, *"For He* (Jesus) *must reign* (refers to the one-thousand-year Reign of Christ on Earth after He returns), *till He has put all enemies under His Feet* (the subjugation of all evil powers, which will take place at the conclusion of the Millennial Reign [Rev., Chpt. 20]).

"The last enemy that shall be destroyed (abolished) *is death.* (Death is the result of sin [Rom. 6:23], and the Cross addressed all sin. After the Resurrection, when all Saints are given Glorified Bodies, it will be impossible to sin. Even during the Millennial Reign, sin will still be in the world, but not in the Glorified Saints. It will be eradicated when Satan and all his fallen angels and demon spirits, plus all the people who followed him, are cast into the Lake of Fire, where they will remain forever [Rev., Chpt. 20]. Death will then be no more)" (I Cor. 15:25-26).

(16) "O LORD, TRULY I AM YOUR SERVANT; I AM YOUR SERVANT, AND THE SON OF YOUR HANDMAID: YOU HAVE LOOSED MY BONDS."

The sense of this Verse is twofold — it speaks of both David and the Messiah. Its Message is humility.

The word *"handmaid"* likewise has a double meaning. It refers to both Mary and

Israel, for Jesus was born of both the Virgin and of Israel.

As the *"Son of the handmaid,"* represented by the Incarnation, Jesus died and was buried. Jehovah *"loosed His bonds"* and raised Him from the dead.

(17) "I WILL OFFER TO YOU THE SACRIFICE OF THANKSGIVING, AND WILL CALL UPON THE NAME OF THE LORD."

The Holy Spirit proclaims to us the fact that Christ, as well as David, would not call upon the Name of the Lord except in thanksgiving. At times, needs were acute, with God's Face seemingly hidden; still, thanksgiving would be offered, and would be called *"The Sacrifice of Thanksgiving."*

Anytime the word *"Sacrifice"* is used, as it regards prayer, even as given here, always and without exception, it refers to the fact that all of our worship, all of our petitions, all of our thanksgiving, and all of our praise, must be based solely upon the Cross of Christ, which is the Great Sacrifice. If we try to approach the Lord in any manner or way other than by and through the Cross of Christ, the Holy Spirit will close the door to such efforts (Eph. 2:18).

The tragedy is, Satan has been so successful at pushing the Church away from the Cross, that anymore the Cross plays little or no part at all in one's alleged walk with the Lord. As such, there is a woeful ignorance as it regards the Cross of Christ, which means that the Lord classifies the efforts made by most Christians as unacceptable.

Let us say it again:

We must meet the Lord at the Cross, and do so unfailingly, or we cannot meet Him at all.

(18) "I WILL PAY MY VOWS UNTO THE LORD NOW IN THE PRESENCE OF ALL HIS PEOPLE."

This is the second time this Verse is given to us verbatim, but not without cause. Once again, it refers to the tremendous victories won by the Lord Jesus Christ on behalf of a world that was altogether unlovely, and yet supremely loved by Him.

(19) "IN THE COURTS OF THE LORD'S HOUSE, IN THE MIDST OF YOU, O JERUSALEM. PRAISE YE THE LORD."

In David's reign, Tabernacle worship was located in Jerusalem. More importantly, this speaks of the beginning of the Kingdom Age, with Christ reigning in Jerusalem and worshipping *"in the Courts of the LORD's House."*

This will be at the beginning of and throughout the great Kingdom Age. At this time, the great victories bought and paid for by the Lord Jesus Christ at Calvary's Cross will be heralded continually all over the world *"in the presence of all His people."* No wonder the world at that time will say, *"Praise ye the LORD."*

PSALM 117

Author Unknown:
Praise the Lord

(1) "O PRAISE THE LORD, ALL YE NATIONS: PRAISE HIM, ALL YE PEOPLE."

It is not known who wrote this short Psalm.

The Apostle Paul quotes this Verse in Romans 15:11.

PRAISE THE LORD

This Song proclaims the beginning of the great Millennial Reign. Israel now invites the nations of the world to unite with her in praising the Messiah, and the reason is set out in the Second Verse. Israel used the word *"nations"*; Paul used the word *"Gentiles."* It always was God's Plan for the entirety of the world, both Jew and Gentile, to *"praise the LORD."*

At the beginning, Israel was commanded to be separate from the other nations; but she turned this separation into isolation. She refused to take the Gospel to the world; consequently, Christ said of her, *"Woe unto you, Scribes and Pharisees, hypocrites! For you compass sea and land to make one proselyte, and when he is made, you make him twofold more the child of Hell than yourselves"* (Mat. 23:15).

Now, at long last, Israel will obey the Lord. She will encourage the nations of the world to join her in accepting the Lord and praising His great Name.

(2) "FOR HIS MERCIFUL KINDNESS IS GREAT TOWARD US: AND THE TRUTH

OF THE LORD ENDURES FOREVER. PRAISE YE THE LORD."

The reason for such praise is hereby given. It is because of His Grace and fidelity toward Israel. (The words, *"is great toward,"* should read, *"has prevailed over."*)

Two statements are made here:
1. His Grace abounded.
2. His fidelity endured.

ISRAEL AND THE LORD JESUS CHRIST

In His enduring fidelity, our Lord will fulfill to Israel the Promise of the Kingdom, and in His abounding Grace, which will prevail over all their misconduct, He will forgive their sins.

From the day that Israel was redeemed out of Egypt to the present moment, she has done, and will in the future yet do, everything possible to prevent the fulfillment of the Promises made to her. Idolatry, apostasy, hypocrisy, ingratitude, the murder of Prophets and of the Messiah (above all, the murder of her Messiah!), centuries of hatred regarding His Name and people, and her future acceptance of the Antichrist in preference to Him (Jn. 5:43) — all will be forgiven. She will invite the nations of the world to join with her in the praising of Grace that as to sin forgives everything and as to Promise forgets nothing.

Thus the nations will learn through His dealings with her what a Glorious God and Saviour is the Messiah!

PSALM 118

Author Unknown:
Thanksgiving for the Lord's Salvation

(1) "O GIVE THANKS UNTO THE LORD; FOR HE IS GOOD: BECAUSE HIS MERCY ENDURES FOREVER."

There is no record as to who wrote this Psalm. Some thirty times the Messiah is named in these Twenty-nine Verses as *"JAH," "Elohim,"* and *"Jehovah."*

THE LAST SONG

This was the last Song sung at the Paschal Supper, as stated by Hebrew historians. It gives it an added preciousness to the heart who knows the Lord to picture Him singing it immediately before setting out for Gethsemane. As the True Israel, He could perfectly sing it, and as the High Priest of His people thus express His faith in her faith and make real and bring near the joys of the morning, which are predicted to follow the sorrows of that dark night and the afflictions of Jacob's long exile.

As well, this Song will be sung by Israel on the happy morning of her renewed espousal. As stated in the previous Psalm, she will invite the nations of the world to trust Jehovah and to praise Him. She will testify that the Messiah is her one and efficient Saviour.

The phase, *"His Mercy endures forever,"* is often used by the Holy Spirit and by Israel for good purpose.

(2) "LET ISRAEL NOW SAY, THAT HIS MERCY ENDURES FOREVER."

The short phrase, *"Now say,"* refers to the coming Kingdom Age, when Israel will repeatedly proclaim the fact that the Mercy of the Lord endures forever. She will say this because of the constant failure that checkers her past through her present; therefore, they realize that it only is by the Mercy of God that they have been spared.

(3) "LET THE HOUSE OF AARON NOW SAY, THAT HIS MERCY ENDURES FOREVER."

The Priesthood of Israel also constantly failed and failed constantly; therefore, the act of Grace that will be extended toward them by the Messiah in the coming Kingdom Age will be and can be attributed only to *"His Mercy."*

(4) "LET THEM NOW WHO FEAR THE LORD SAY, THAT HIS MERCY ENDURES FOREVER."

Likewise, these three Passages concerning Israel, Aaron, and those who fear the Lord are likewise portrayed in Verses 9 through 11 of Psalm 115. There Israel, Aaron, and all who fear the Lord were importuned to *"trust in the LORD."* Here these three are importuned to understand that it strictly is by the Mercy of God that they have been brought to this great place of glory and victory.

GRACE AND MERCY

Mercy is an attribute of God; it is a product of Grace.

Somewhere in the distant past God made a conscious decision to deal with the fallen human family with Grace. (Grace had to be a conscious decision by God, or else it could not be Grace.)

Once God had made the decision to deal with the human family by Grace, then Mercy became its guaranteed product. God had a choice regarding Grace; He has no choice regarding Mercy. If He chose the avenue of Grace (and He did), then He has no choice but to extend Mercy, because Mercy is the natural product of Grace.

These great attributes of Mercy and Grace not only extend themselves to Israel but also to *"whosoever will,"* hence, the invitation, *"them now who fear the LORD."*

(5) "I CALLED UPON THE LORD IN DISTRESS: THE LORD ANSWERED ME, AND SET ME IN A LARGE PLACE."

Even though it is not specifically known, David probably wrote this Psalm.

A LARGE PLACE

David could have uttered these words which pertain to his great deliverance from Saul, and so forth. However, more importantly, these are the words that Israel will use in recalling the great victory the Lord will give her when the Antichrist is in the process of overwhelming her. As Israel utters these words, it is past tense. As we read them, it is yet future tense.

In that day, she will call on the Lord, and He will answer her. It is remarkable in the fact that He has not answered her in over 2,000 years. If Grace will respond to a pathetic plea and Mercy will come to her rescue and set her *"in a large place,"* this *"large place"* will constitute the tremendous position of authority and blessing that Israel will enjoy under Christ during the Kingdom Age — and forever.

(6) "THE LORD IS ON MY SIDE; I WILL NOT FEAR: WHAT CAN MAN DO UNTO ME?"

Once she realizes that God has heard her and is coming to her rescue, which pertains to the Second Coming, then all fear is dispelled. Zechariah proclaims that Jehovah will fight in that day as when He fought in the day of battle. Consequently, what can the Antichrist do? (Zech. 14:3).

(7) "THE LORD TAKES MY PART WITH THEM WHO HELP ME: THEREFORE SHALL I SEE MY DESIRE UPON THEM WHO HATE ME."

At long last, Israel realizes that to have the Lord on her side and take her part is better than all men and their riches. I wonder if the Church will ever learn this!

(8) "IT IS BETTER TO TRUST IN THE LORD THAN TO PUT CONFIDENCE IN MAN."

One of Israel's great problems of the past was putting confidence in man and not in God. It is our problem, as well. Men look to other men and receive the help that men can give, which is little or none. If we put our trust in God, we will not fail because God cannot fail.

(9) "IT IS BETTER TO TRUST IN THE LORD THAN TO PUT CONFIDENCE IN PRINCES."

During the Battle of Armageddon, Israel, it seems, will not have the help of any nation. Those she thought surely would come to her rescue, such as America, will not respond to her cry, but God will.

Some seven years before, she put confidence in the Antichrist, and then some three and a half years later realized that she had been played for a fool.

The Holy Spirit calls this terrible time *"Jacob's Trouble"* (Jer. 30:7). Israel will be maneuvered into a place where she must trust God and not man. Sometimes the Lord maneuvers us in the same way.

THE CROSS OF CHRIST

What Jesus did at the Cross answers every type of spiritual problem, which deals with emotional stability, etc. The answer to all sin, all failure, all bondage, all perversion, and all transgression of any type is *"Jesus Christ and Him Crucified"* (I Cor. 1:23). But regrettably, the greater part of the modern Church doesn't believe that, but rather turns to humanistic psychology. They do so simply because they do not understand what

Jesus did at the Cross, or else they do not believe that what He did there at the Cross truly meets our every need.

The truth is, humanistic psychology holds no answer whatsoever. It holds none for the unredeemed, and neither does it hold any for the redeemed. And yet, one of the great watchwords of the modern Church is, *"You need professional help."* There is no help from that source! And it should be obvious to those who truly know the Lord.

If anyone will put their faith exclusively in Christ and the Cross, victory ultimately will be theirs. This holds no matter who the person is and no matter what the situation is. This does not mean that there never will be another problem, and neither does it mean that there never will be another failure. It does mean, however, that the person is on the right road and ultimately *"sin will no longer dominate that person"* (Rom. 6:14).

Now, one either believes the Bible or one doesn't believe the Bible. We cannot have it both ways.

I believe God!

(10) "ALL NATIONS COMPASSED ME ABOUT: BUT IN THE NAME OF THE LORD WILL I DESTROY THEM."

This speaks of the nations of the world that will gather at the Battle of Armageddon. They actually will be brought there by demon spirits (Rev. 16:12-16). Amazingly enough, the Prophecy concerning the destruction of the Antichrist was given at least some 3,000 years before the fact. If the Antichrist only would read and believe the Bible, he would know of his doom. Likewise, if all would read and believe the Bible, they also would know and understand the eternal consequences of their actions.

(11) "THEY COMPASSED ME ABOUT; YEA, THEY COMPASSED ME ABOUT: BUT IN THE NAME OF THE LORD I WILL DESTROY THEM."

The sense of this Verse is similar to the previous Verse. It is so designed by the Holy Spirit in order that we may understand the complexion of the opposition against Israel at that great day. Many nations of the world will throw in their lot with the Antichrist. They will feel that victory is theirs with no chance of defeat. And yet, the Holy Spirit ensures their destruction.

(12) "THEY COMPASSED ME ABOUT LIKE BEES; THEY ARE QUENCHED AS THE FIRE OF THORNS: FOR IN THE NAME OF THE LORD I WILL DESTROY THEM."

The hundreds of thousands, or even millions, of men who will gather at Armageddon are compared by the Holy Spirit — *"like bees."*

The word *"quenched"* refers to the nations being defeated as fire is quenched.

This statement of confidence in the Name of the Lord is repeated three times for emphasis (Vss. 10-12).

(13) "YOU HAVE THRUST SORE AT ME THAT I MIGHT FALL: BUT THE LORD HELPED ME."

The word *"you"* is important because it refers to Satan. He energized the enemies of Verses 7 through 12. It is he who excites the nations of the world to respond to the admonition of the Antichrist to destroy Israel.

SATAN

Job illustrates this section of the Psalm. Satan was the unseen power behind the Sabeans, the Chaldeans, the tempests, the sore sickness, and all the calamities that afflicted the Patriarch.

God permitted Satan to so chastise Job, but forbade him to touch Job's life (Job 1:12). So it is here: Satan is permitted to chastise Israel sore, but not to destroy her.

The moral effect of this Divine Action will be the same with Israel as it was with Job. She will enter the gates of Righteousness and will praise the Messiah. And she will confess that she certainly would have fallen beneath the strokes of the adversary had not her faithful Lord and Redeemer supported her.

(14) "THE LORD IS MY STRENGTH AND SONG, AND IS BECOME MY SALVATION."

Israel here confesses that her Restoration apart from the once-rejected Messiah is impossible.

(15) "THE VOICE OF REJOICING AND SALVATION IS IN THE TABERNACLES OF THE RIGHTEOUS: THE RIGHT HAND OF THE LORD DOES VALIANTLY."

As a result of the great Redemption and Restoration, there is *"the voice of rejoicing."* Israel rejoices because she is saved, and because of the powerful *"Right Hand of the LORD."*

(16) "THE RIGHT HAND OF THE LORD IS EXALTED: THE RIGHT HAND OF THE LORD DOES VALIANTLY."

The Right Hand of Jehovah is symbolic of His Power (Ex. 15:6; Ps. 17:7; 20:6; 44:3).

(17) "I SHALL NOT DIE, BUT LIVE, AND DECLARE THE WORKS OF THE LORD."

It looked for a time as though Israel would surely die. They have survived all of these many centuries; but, with the onslaught of the Antichrist, who has annihilation in mind, it seems impossible to survive. The words, *"But live,"* speak of Israel's Resurrection, and that by the Power of God. Now, Israel promises to *"declare the Works of the LORD"* forever.

(18) "THE LORD HAS CHASTENED ME SORE: BUT HE HAS NOT GIVEN ME OVER UNTO DEATH."

Israel now acknowledges the wisdom and love which permitted her sufferings at the hands of man. She approves these moral lessons. When the Believer comes to this place, he can expect the same type of deliverance that God gave unto Israel.

(19) "OPEN TO ME THE GATES OF RIGHTEOUSNESS: I WILL GO INTO THEM, AND I WILL PRAISE THE LORD."

The *"gates of Righteousness"* were opened to Israel upon the First Advent of Christ. She refused to walk through those gates of Righteousness. Now the Lord has given her a second opportunity. Now she proclaims for all to hear and see, *"I will go into them."* Not only will she go into them, but she will do so *"praising the LORD."*

(20) "THIS GATE OF THE LORD, INTO WHICH THE RIGHTEOUS SHALL ENTER."

On her own, Israel could never claim Righteousness; neither can we!

RIGHTEOUSNESS

Israel now accepts the Righteousness that the Lord freely gives unto her, which she rejected so long ago in favor of her own righteousness (Rom. 10:3). Israel will now forsake her own bankrupt righteousness, which was no righteousness at all, and accept the Righteousness freely given by the Lord Jesus Christ.

We cannot receive God's imputed Righteousness until we first admit that we are not worthy of it and never can be worthy of it. Only then will God grant it.

This *"gate"* was called by Christ *"a strait gate, and a narrow way"* (Mat. 7:14). Extra baggage cannot pass through it.

(21) "I WILL PRAISE YOU: FOR YOU HAVE HEARD ME, AND ARE BECOME MY SALVATION."

Now Israel proclaims that the once-rejected Saviour is her God and her Redeemer.

(22) "THE STONE WHICH THE BUILDERS REFUSED IS BECOME THE HEAD STONE OF THE CORNER."

This was quoted and referred to in Matthew 21:42, Mark 12:10-11, Luke 20:17, Acts 4:11, and I Peter 2:4-8.

THE STONE

This *"Stone"* is Jesus Christ. He is the One Who was refused, even though He was, and is, *"The Head Stone of the Corner."*

Without Him, Israel has no place, no position, and no status; without him, Israel has nothing! Jesus Christ is the True Israel, as He is the True Man and the True Church (Isa. 28:16; Mat. 16:18; Eph. 2:20; I Pet. 2:7-8).

(23) "THIS IS THE LORD'S DOING; IT IS MARVELOUS IN OUR EYES."

The whole of Salvation is from the Lord. None of it pertains to man in the realm of its origin; all pertains to God. This is the reason that God will not accept our self-righteousness. Man has no part to play in this afforded Salvation except to receive it upon believing faith (Jn. 3:3, 16).

(24) "THIS IS THE DAY WHICH THE LORD HAS MADE; WE WILL REJOICE AND BE GLAD IN IT."

This refers to Israel's great day of Restoration, which will take place at the Second Coming. She will then acknowledge that it is all of the Lord and none of her; consequently, it will be a day of rejoicing and gladness.

It is a glorious day when any believing sinner comes to Christ; and then every day thereafter should also be a day of *"rejoicing and gladness."*

(25) "SAVE NOW, I BESEECH YOU, O LORD: O LORD, I BESEECH YOU, SEND NOW PROSPERITY."

Prophetically, this Verse pertains to Israel's

glad day, when, at the Feast of Tabernacles, which is at the beginning of the Kingdom Age, she not only will ask the Lord for prosperity, but also will rejoice in a prosperity already sent — because Jesus Christ is that prosperity.

These words were sung by the Jews at all Feasts of Tabernacles. They did so while carrying green branches in their hands.

(26) "BLESSED BE HE WHO COMES IN THE NAME OF THE LORD: WE HAVE BLESSED YOU OUT OF THE HOUSE OF THE LORD."

This whole Song will be sung by the Messiah and Israel on the future glad morning of their espousals. The Psalm voices His Oneness with them.

THE BLESSED SONG

Israel cried these words upon Christ's First Advent (Mat. 21:9). When He made His first entrance into Jerusalem, the whole city asked, *"Who is this?"* The answer was forthcoming, *"This is Jesus the Prophet of Nazareth of Galilee"* (Mat. 21:10-11).

Five days later they crucified Him. They did not know Who He was. Almost all the world today does not know Who He is.

Hours before they crucified Him, He said, *"You shall not see Me henceforth, till you shall say, Blessed is He Who comes in the Name of the Lord"* (Mat. 23:39).

He, in effect, was saying, *"You will see Me again, and you will be glad to accept Me as your Messiah"* (Zech. 12:10-13:1; Isa. 66:7-8; Rom. 11:25-29).

At the beginning of the Kingdom Age, Christ will once again come into Jerusalem and Israel will shout these words all over again. The difference then will be that now Israel is a redeemed Israel, and they now will know Who He is.

(27) "GOD IS THE LORD, WHICH HAS SHOWED US LIGHT: BIND THE SACRIFICE WITH CORDS, EVEN UNTO THE HORNS OF THE ALTAR."

Now, Israel will exclaim: *"Jehovah Messiah is God."* They now see the Light, and Jesus is that Light.

They now will proclaim to the world that they understand the meaning of the Sacrifices of old. When the Sacrifice was bound with cords to the Altar, likewise, Jesus Christ died on Calvary for Israel and also for all of humanity.

(28) "YOU ARE MY GOD, AND I WILL PRAISE YOU: YOU ARE MY GOD, I WILL EXALT YOU."

Here, after some 2,000 years, they will exalt Him. They will proclaim to the whole world, *"Messiah is my God."* This will undoubtedly be the greatest Revival in history. It will take place at the conclusion of the Battle of Armageddon at the Second Coming. He came the first time as a babe in a manger. He grew up as a Peasant. This time He will come as King of kings and Lord of lords (Rev., Chpt. 19).

(29) "O GIVE THANKS UNTO THE LORD; FOR HE IS GOOD: FOR HIS MERCY ENDURES FOREVER."

Thus, Israel closes this grand and great Psalm as it was opened. It was opened with Mercy; it closes with Mercy. Israel then will proclaim to the whole world that *"God is good."*

How can we who have been washed in His Precious Blood proclaim less?

PSALM 119

*Author Unknown:
Blessings of the Word of God*

There are some preliminary remarks that must be made before we begin commentary on the 119th Psalm.

THE AUTHORITY AND SUFFICIENCY OF THE BIBLE AS THE RULE OF LIFE

This Psalm is the longest in the great Book of Psalms; it also is the longest Chapter in the Bible. The entire Psalm extols the greatness, glory, beauty, power, and wonder of the Word of God. It is beautiful and glorious that the Holy Spirit designed it in this manner.

The Psalm contemplates the celestial pilgrim's walking through a squalid place on a dangerous road in the dark night, completely dependent upon a Lamp to light his way and guide his feet (II Pet. 1:19).

The lesson of the Psalm is that the Lamp

may be completely trusted and that whoever follows its Light will be preserved from the squalors of the way, saved from the dangers of the path, and surely led to its desired end. This Lamp is the Bible.

The Messiah's testimony to the authority and sufficiency of the Bible as the rule of life is the theme of this Psalm.

THE WORD OF GOD, HIDDEN IN THE HEART AND OBEYED IN THE LIFE

The Messiah is the Blessed Man Who fully satisfies its language, for He Himself is the Word of God (Jn. 1:1-3). Like Him, only those who are subject to His Word are blessed.

The theme of this Psalm is the Word of God that is hidden in the heart and obeyed in the life.

The argument of the Bible, of which this Psalm is representative, is that it is an infallible counselor in every possible need and circumstance of the heart and life.

There are twenty-two letters in the Hebrew alphabet. There also are twenty-two stanzas in this Psalm. Each stanza contains eight Verses. There are, therefore, one hundred seventy-six Verses in all.

All the first words in the eight Verses of the first stanza begin with the letter *"A."* All the first words of the eight Verses of the second stanza begin with the letter *"B."* And so on to the end of the Psalm. The beginning of each one of these twenty-two stanzas is headed up by a letter of the Hebrew alphabet.

THE TEN WORDS

In this great Psalm, the Bible is given ten titles corresponding to the Ten Commandments. These titles (or words) are used throughout the Psalm. They are as follows: *"Way," "Testimonies," "Precepts," "Commandments," "Law," "Judgments," "Righteousness," "Statutes," "Word,"* and *"Paths."*

Each Verse in all of the one hundred seventy-six Verses contains one of these words, with the exception of four Verses: 90, 121, 122, and 132.

It is not known who wrote this Psalm, but there is strong evidence that David could have been the author. The following is the case for David's authorship.

NOTES

DAVID, THE AUTHOR OF THE 119TH PSALM?

1. The description of the Blessed Man (Vss. 1-3) is similar to David's picture of a righteous man in Psalm 15.

2. The term, *"Your servant,"* is used thirteen times in this Psalm (Vss. 17, 23, 38, 49, 65, 76, 84, 122, 124, 125, 135, 140, 176). The term is used by David thirty-four times in Scripture, and not once by Hezekiah, Ethan, Nathan, Ezra, or others to whom some ascribe the authorship. It is used only fifteen times in Psalms other than in Psalm 119; and, in every such case, it refers to David. Hence, its use in Psalm 119 most probably pertains to him. David also is called *"My servant"* by God twenty-two times; *"His servant,"* four times; and, *"the servant of the LORD"* (Ps. 18 Heading).

3. The term, *"whole heart,"* is used six times in Psalm 119, and is used only by David in two other Psalms (9:1; 111:1).

4. The thirty vows of the Psalmist are purely Davidic, as can be seen by comparing them with vows in other Psalms of David.

5. The sixty-nine requests of the Psalmist are purely Davidic, as can be seen by comparing them to other requests by David.

6. Many points of the testimonies of the Psalmist could not be applied to any other man we know of as they could to David.

7. Many of the experiences of the Psalmist are true of David only as is shown by comparing them with the record of David.

8. There are twenty-five statements of distress in this Psalm, and they are purely Davidic, as is shown by comparison with similar statements of David elsewhere. The author of Psalm 119 speaks of God's Word to Kings (Vs. 46), he makes it the subject of his Songs (Vs. 54), he is afflicted while going astray (Vs. 67; Psalm 38), he is persecuted by princes (Vs. 161), he sojourns along his pilgrimage (Vs. 54; I Sam., Chpts. 19-30), he is surrounded by bands of robbers (Vs. 61; I Sam., Chpts. 22-24 and 26-30), the proud deal perversely with him (Vs. 78; II Sam., Chpts. 15-18), his soul faints and pants for God (Vs. 81; 131; Ps. 38:10; 42:1), and he goes astray like a lost sheep (Vs. 176); these and many other details of Psalm 119 remind

us of David and fit his life more than any other person in Scripture.

ALEPH (1-8)
(The First Chorus)

(1) "BLESSED ARE THE UNDEFILED IN THE WAY, WHO WALK IN THE LAW OF THE LORD."

The word *"undefiled"* (or perfect) can only be said of the Messiah. He Alone walked perfectly in the Law of the Lord.

THE KEEPING OF THE LAW

Regrettably, there was no one who ever perfectly kept the Law but Christ. And yet the demand was given by God that the Law be kept. If not, there was a terrible curse attached to it (Deut., Chpt. 28). There also was a great blessing attached to the Law regarding all those who would *"observe and do all His Commandments"* (Deut. 28:1). It did not say *"some of the Commandments,"* but *"all of the Commandments."*

God gave the Law, and it was holy; however, He gave no power enabling man to keep it; consequently and sadly, all broke the Law, even Moses.

It was God's Plan that man realize his helplessness in effecting his own Salvation and thereby run to the Redeemer Who was to come (Gen. 3:15). That Redeemer was Christ Jesus. He kept the Law perfectly (the word *"undefiled"* also means *"without blemish"*).

The moment that one in Grace begins to believe and trust in the Undefiled One (Christ Jesus), then all the victory won by Christ becomes the victory of the Believer, including the keeping of the Law, which Christ kept perfectly. In other words, because of one's faith in Christ and what Christ did at the Cross, God looks at the Believer as though he accomplished and carried out all the things that Christ did. Christ's victory becomes our victory.

THE APOSTLE PAUL

This is the great struggle that the Apostle Paul had in the Seventh Chapter of Romans. Even after his conversion, he kept trying to keep the Law himself and kept failing (Rom. 7:15); however, the moment he accepted Christ's Finished Work on the Cross of Calvary (Rom. 8:1), then Christ's victory became his victory.

This is the reason that most Church rules are an affront to Christ. In man's efforts to keep them, the breeding ground for self-righteousness is developed. Actually, all the rules that Churches make for the purpose of ensuring holiness only end up by ensuring unholiness. The reason is that they are reverting back to Law, which man could not keep then, and man certainly can not keep now.

No, the idea is not that we can keep sinning, but that we enter into Christ's victory. One's faith placed in the Cross of Christ is the only way that the Believer can overcome sin (Rom. 6:1-14). This is the only way that the Law can be kept.

GOD'S PRESCRIBED ORDER OF VICTORY

When the Holy Spirit through the Apostle Paul was ready to tell Believers how to live for God, that is, how to perpetually walk in victory, He gave us this information in the Sixth Chapter of Romans. The Holy Spirit starts with the problem of sin, for that is the cause, the problem, and the difficulty that plagues the Believer (Rom. 6:1-2). The Holy Spirit is giving this information for Believers, not unbelievers!

Immediately after telling us that the problem is sin, then Verses 3 through 5 (Rom., Chpt. 6) proclaim the solution for the sin problem, which is the Cross of Christ.

To abbreviate the statement, *"We are baptized into His Death, buried with Him by Baptism into Death, and raised with Him in newness of life."*

In other words, it was at the Cross where all sin was atoned and thereby addressed, even the cause of sin. It was there that Satan and all of his cohorts of darkness were totally and completely defeated (Col. 2:14-15).

We also must remember that Paul is dealing with the *"sin nature"* in this Sixth Chapter of Romans. In the original Greek Text, Paul uses the word *"sin"* some seventeen times. Before fourteen of these times, he uses what is referred to as *"the definite article,"* which means the English translation would read *"the sin."*

This means the Holy Spirit is not dealing with particular acts of sin, but rather the sin principle, or the cause of sin, the sin nature. He is telling us how to have victory over the sin nature.

WHAT IS THE SIN NATURE?

The *"sin nature"* is the result of the Fall in the Garden of Eden.

Due to the Fall, Adam and Eve lost the Divine Nature. In its place came the *"sin nature."* This simply means that the nature of Adam and Eve totally and completely changed until their every bent and direction was toward sin. As a result of the manner of procreation, this means that every single human being which would thereafter be born would be born in original sin, that is, *"born with a sin nature."*

The moment the believing sinner comes to Christ, the sin nature is made dormant, that is, *"ineffective"* (Rom. 6:6).

Providing the faith of the individual remains in Christ and the Cross, that is, he ever makes the Cross of Christ the Object of his Faith, the sin nature will remain ineffective; however, tragically, most Christians don't understand the Cross as it refers to our Sanctification, which is taught in the Sixth Chapter of Romans, and they transfer their faith to something else.

And it really doesn't matter what the *"something else"* is, if it's not Christ and the Cross, then the Holy Spirit will be seriously hindered in His helping us. The result will be a revival of the sin nature. Virtually the entire modern Church is struggling with the sin nature, and they really don't even know what the problem is, let alone the cure.

They are not subscribing to God's Prescribed Order of Victory, which is faith in Christ and the Cross; rather they are trying to live for God by some other means.

THE HOLY SPIRIT

Everything we receive in our hearts and lives from the Lord is given to us by the Holy Spirit. He Alone can make us Christlike; He Alone can develop His Fruit, Righteousness, and Holiness within our lives. We cannot do these things ourselves, no matter how hard we try.

But the great questions are:

"Does He do this automatically? Or is there something we have to do?"

First of all, He doesn't do it automatically. If He did, every Christian would be perfectly mature, and there never would be another failure. We know that isn't correct, so we know that He doesn't carry out these tasks automatically.

In a sense, there really is nothing we can do, with the exception of one thing, and that is to evidence faith; however, it is the object of faith that is so very, very important. That Object must be Christ and the Cross, for the Holy Spirit always works totally and completely within the parameters of the Finished Work of Christ. In other words, it was the Cross that gave the Holy Spirit the legal right to do all the things which He does.

With our faith placed properly in Christ and the Cross, the Holy Spirit will then begin to work mightily within our lives to carry out that which only He can do, which will give us victory over the world, the flesh, and the Devil (Rom. 8:1-2, 11).

Four things are at work here. They are:

1. The Lord Jesus Christ;
2. The Cross of Christ;
3. The Holy Spirit; and,
4. Our Faith, which must always make the Cross of Christ its Object.

THE CROSS

The Reader should carefully note the following:

1. The only way to God is through the Lord Jesus Christ (Jn. 14:6).
2. The only way to Jesus Christ is through the Cross (Lk. 9:23).
3. The only way to the Cross is a denial of self (Lk. 9:23).

The Believer must never separate Christ from the Cross. That's why Paul said, *"We preach Christ Crucified"* (I Cor. 1:23).

This doesn't mean that we are putting Christ back on the Cross, or that we are getting on some type of Cross ourselves, but rather that we are to experience the benefits of the Cross. We are to ever understand that the Lord Jesus Christ is the Source of all things, while the Cross is the Means. We never dare forget that! This is the key to all

Blessings from the Lord (Gal. 6:14).

If the Believer will place his faith properly, which always is in Christ and the Cross, the Holy Spirit will then, as stated, begin to work mightily within one's life to help such a Believer to grow in Grace and the Knowledge of the Lord, and also to have Victory, and we speak of total Victory over the world, the flesh, and the Devil. The Cross of Christ is the answer and the solution — the only answer and the only solution. There is no other, even as there need be no other!

(2) "BLESSED ARE THEY WHO KEEP THE TESTIMONIES, AND WHO SEEK HIM WITH THE WHOLE HEART."

We are to *"keep His Testimonies"*; if we do, we shall be *"blessed."* The only way this can be done is to *"seek Him with the whole heart,"* that is, *"place one's faith exclusively in Christ and what Christ has done for us at the Cross"* (Rom. 6:1-14; Gal. 6:14).

Two things are here said:

1. Through Him Alone can these *"Testimonies"* be kept (Mat. 11:28).

2. *"With the whole heart"* and not a divided heart. Someone has said, *"We should make a list of all the things that are dear to us, and then make sure that the only name on that list is Christ Jesus."* The *"whole heart"* will find Him; the divided heart will not.

(3) "THEY ALSO DO NO INIQUITY: THEY WALK IN HIS WAYS."

The cry of the soul in the consecrated Christian is to *"do no iniquity."* The absolute only way this can be done is to *"walk in His Ways."*

THE WAYS OF THE LORD

As we've already stated, this *"Way"* is given to us in the Sixth Chapter of Romans. If we walk in that *"Way,"* we will gain the victory this *"Way"* promises. If we devise a way of our own, the results will be disaster. Regrettably, that's what most of the modern Church is presently doing.

Satan will do all within Hell's power to divert the Christian from God's Ways. The four words, *"Walk in His Ways,"* are the key to Victory. For instance, false doctrine, apostasy, psychology, philosophies, humanism, and religion all are man's ways; they all will breed iniquity. His Way is His Word, and His Word is the Cross of Christ (Jn. 1:1-3, 14, 29).

(4) "YOU HAVE COMMANDED US TO KEEP YOUR PRECEPTS DILIGENTLY."

As stated, the command is for His Precepts to be kept, but no power in the Law was given to do such. Why would God have designed it this way?

THE LAW OF GOD

To the unspiritual, it may seem cruel for God to demand that someone do something which within themselves they cannot do (Rom., Chpt. 7).

No, the manner in which God gave the Law was not cruel; it was rather merciful.

Man's problem always has been pride. If God had given the Law and then also the power for man to keep that Law, then man would have only been lifted up further in his own pride and propelled deeper into his own self-righteousness.

The manner in which God designed His Salvation Plan is that man would be shown what is right and what is wrong (the Law), and then commanded to keep such. It was not possible for man to do so; therefore, he was to throw himself on God and seek Him in order that the Lord might do for him what he could not do for himself. In other words, if God had given man the power to keep the Law, it would have caused man to run from God instead of to God. By not giving him power to keep the Law, ideally man would run to God, admit that he was not able to live the life that God demanded, and thereby seek the help that only God can give. This manner defeats pride in man because he sees his helplessness and builds trust in God.

Sadly, Israel perverted the Law of God by adding many more laws, and made the Word of God of none effect (Mat. 15:6). They then went about to establish their own righteousness, which denied the Righteousness of God. They murdered the Lord of Glory, and did so in the Name of the Lord (Rom. 10:3).

(5) "O THAT MY WAYS WERE DIRECTED TO KEEP YOUR STATUTES!"

The ways of man (*"my ways"*) are so corrupt because of the fallen nature that there is no ingrained desire to keep God's *"Statutes."* This desire has to be given by God, and it is, in fact, given the moment the person accepts Christ as one's Saviour.

(6) "THEN SHALL I NOT BE ASHAMED, WHEN I HAVE RESPECT UNTO ALL YOUR COMMANDMENTS."

Unless we respect *"all"* of God's Commandments, there will be shame within our hearts, and rightly so!

In man's self-righteous efforts to keep the Commandments in his own strength, he soon finds that he can keep some but not others. Self-righteous man takes delight in the ones he can keep (or thinks he can keep) and tries to hide the ones he cannot keep.

And then James says, *"If we offend in one point, we are guilty of all"* (James 2:10); consequently, the only way that *"all the Commandments"* can be kept is for us to enter into the Victory that Christ has already won in His keeping of all the Commandments.

THE LORD JESUS CHRIST AND THE LAW OF GOD

Christ came to this world as our Substitute. In effect, He was the *"Last Adam"* and the *"Second Man"* (I Cor. 15:45, 47). Incidentally, the short phrase, *"Last Adam,"* tells us that there never will be a need for another.

Jesus Christ came to do what the First Adam did not do, which was to keep the Law of God perfectly, and to not do what the First Adam did do, which was to break that Law.

Even though our Saviour never ceased to be God, it was not as God that He perfectly kept the Law; He perfectly kept the Law of God as a Man, *"The Man Christ Jesus."* He was Very God and Very Man, but He performed no miracles and carried out no great works by the means of Deity, but only as a Man anointed by the Holy Spirit (Acts 10:38).

God needs no anointing to do anything. The Man Christ Jesus did need the anointing of the Holy Spirit to do what He did, because He did all of these things as our Substitute — in effect, our Substitute Man (Lk. 4:18-19).

Throughout His entire Life, our Saviour kept the Law perfectly in every respect, that is, in thought, in word, and in deed. He did all of this for us, and not at all for Himself. We are the ones who needed this perfection, not Him.

To satisfy the problem of the broken Law, however, Christ would have to go to the Cross, which was the very reason He came. On the Cross, He atoned for all sin, past, present, and future, thereby satisfying the demands of a thrice-Holy God. By the shedding of His Precious Blood and the giving of His Life, He paid the price for all our sins.

It was on the Cross where all victory was won, every Satanic power was defeated, and all sin was atoned. The moment that Jesus died, the giant Veil which separated the Holy of Holies from the Holy Place in the Temple was ripped from top to bottom, as if two giant hands split it open, which, no doubt, is exactly what happened — the Hands of God.

This opened up the way to the very Throne of God; now, because of what Jesus did at the Cross and our faith in that Finished Work, it is possible for man to enter. The great clarion call now is, *"And the Spirit and the Bride say, Come.* (This presents the cry of the Holy Spirit to a hurting, lost and dying world. What the Holy Spirit says also should be said by all Believers.) *And let him who hears say, Come.* (It means if one can *'hear,'* then one can *'come.'*) *And let him who is athirst come.* (This speaks of Spiritual Thirst, the cry for God in the soul of man.) *And whosoever will, let him take the Water of Life freely.* (This opens the door to every single individual in the world. Jesus died for all and, therefore, all can be saved, if they only will come)" (Rev. 22:17).

It is said that the Veil was sixty feet tall, weighed approximately two thousand pounds, was four inches thick, and that four yoke of oxen could not pull it apart. But God did, because, due to what Christ did at the Cross, the way to the very Throne of God was now wide open (Mat. 27:51).

Now with the Law totally and completely satisfied in every capacity, and we speak of the Perfect Life of Christ and the Perfect Redemption afforded by the Death of Christ on the Cross, simple faith in Christ and what He has done for us takes us from the position of law-breaker, which demands death (Rom. 6:23), to the position of law-keeper, all made possible by Christ.

The only way that any Believer can keep all the Commandments of God is by doing so through and in Christ. Christ already has kept them all, and our faith in Him makes us perfect as regards to the Commandments, in spite of what our past may have been. It is called *"Justification by Faith."*

(7) "I WILL PRAISE YOU WITH UPRIGHTNESS OF HEART, WHEN I SHALL HAVE LEARNED YOUR RIGHTEOUS JUDGMENTS."

The moral condition of the heart is decided by obedience to the Word of God; consequently, true worship depends upon knowledge of the Word. We might quickly add that all Spiritual Maturity is dependent on one's knowledge of the Cross of Christ. Little knowledge of the Cross, little maturity; much knowledge of the Cross, much maturity!

(8) "I WILL KEEP YOUR STATUTES: O FORSAKE ME NOT UTTERLY."

The sense of this Verse is:

"Do not in any case take away this Lamp in which I am trusting, else I shall stumble in the darkness and fall."

BETH (9-16)
(The Second Chorus)

(9) "WHEREWITHAL SHALL A YOUNG MAN CLEANSE HIS WAY? BY TAKING HEED THERETO ACCORDING TO YOUR WORD."

There has been only one Person on Earth Who could truthfully use the words of this Psalm. He was the Messiah. He is the only One Who kept every Commandment, Statute, Judgment, Word, Testimony, Law, Precept, Way, Righteousness, and Promise.

In this Passage, He gives us that which kept Him as a young Man from the snares of the enemy; it will consequently keep any and all young men and women who will abide by the Bible.

THE BIBLE, THE ONLY REVEALED TRUTH

The Bible should be studied constantly. It is the only revealed Truth in the world today, and ever has been. It holds the treasures of the ages, for it is the Word of God.

The reading and studying of it effects a cleansing in the heart and life of the Believer today, just as the Brazen Laver of old, which was its type, afforded cleansing for the Priests (Eph. 5:26).

From 1960 through 2005, the Federal Government of the United States of America has spent approximately a quarter of a trillion dollars ($250,000,000,000) trying to assuage the terrible drug problem. Regrettably, despite the expenditure of this massive sum of money, they are no closer today than when they began.

And yet, between the covers of the Bible, there is an answer to the drug problem, the alcohol problem, immorality, and every other problem that plagues humanity. It not only contains the answer, but it holds the only answer. Sadly and regrettably, not only has government forsaken the Word of God, but the Church, by and large, has followed suit.

WORLD EVANGELISM BIBLE COLLEGE AND SEMINARY

At World Evangelism Bible College and Seminary here in Baton Rouge, Louisiana, which is a part of Jimmy Swaggart Ministries, the curriculum is Bible, and Bible only. When students who feel a Call of God on their lives come here for Ministry, or those who just love the Word of God, it is Bible they learn, and nothing else. No psychology, sociology, anthropology, or any other type of man-made solutions are offered — just the Bible.

When we study doctrine, we do so directly from its source: The Book of Romans and the other Epistles. When we study eschatology, we do so from the Books of Daniel, Revelation, II Thessalonians, and others. When we study missions, we use the Book of Acts. When we study preaching, we study the Epistles and the Gospels.

We offer a one-year, a two-year, a three-year, and a four-year degree in Bible. Strangely enough, in most other Bible Colleges today, a degree in Bible is no longer offered.

The Apostle Paul said: *"That the man of God may be perfect, thoroughly furnished unto all good works"* (II Tim. 3:17).

THE CROSS OF CHRIST

In all of this teaching, the major theme of this Bible College is the Cross of Christ. We believe that the Cross is the Story of the Bible, as the Bible is the story of the Cross (Jn. 1:1, 14, 29).

One cannot really understand the Word of God unless one understands the Cross of Christ. So when students, young or old, come to this Bible College, or when people come to our Church, or when they obtain our materials, they will be taught the Cross of Christ, that is, the Word of God.

(10) "WITH MY WHOLE HEART HAVE I SOUGHT YOU: O LET ME NOT WANDER FROM YOUR COMMANDMENTS."

The Messiah is the only One Who could ever say that He always sought the Lord with His whole heart and never did wander from the Commandments of the Lord.

HIS VICTORY IS OURS

The prayer of Verse 10 was His Prayer, because the Word of God was the dearest of all to Him. Is it the dearest of all to you?

There are two foundation principles of the Spiritual Life that appear in these Passages; first, that the Bible associates its Reader with God; second, that its teachings make the life clean and the heart happy. The moral result of subjection to the authority of the Holy Scriptures is health of soul, holiness of life, and happiness of heart. Nothing else can claim such!

When the Believer evidences his faith exclusively in Christ and the Cross, which is not as easy as it sounds, such a Believer enters into the Victory of our Lord, which is intended. Then the Believer is seeking the Lord with his *"whole heart"*; such a Believer will have the Promise of the Lord that the Holy Spirit will not allow us to *"wander from the Lord's Commandments."* For this to happen, however, it is imperative that one's faith remain in Christ and the Cross (Gal., Chpt. 5).

The reason that we say this is not easy is because Satan will fight such a Believer with every weapon at his disposal. That's why, regarding this very thing, Paul told us, *"Fight the good fight of Faith, lay hold on Eternal Life, whereunto you are also Called, and have professed a good profession before many witnesses"* (I Tim. 6:12).

Even though it is a *"fight,"* it is a *"good fight"* at the same time, because it is the *"right fight."*

All of this means that Satan will attempt to pull you away from the Cross of Christ to other things. You will have to fight to keep your faith where it ought to stay. Sadly, Satan will use Preachers to pull you away; however, please remember the following:

The *"Source"* of everything you receive from God is Christ. The *"Means"* by which He gives us all of these things is His *"Cross."*

(11) "YOUR WORD HAVE I HID IN MY HEART, THAT I MIGHT NOT SIN AGAINST YOU."

Before the lips can fitly declare the teachings of the Scriptures, the heart must be home to the Scriptures. Its Words form the rule of faith, and subjection to its Judgments is the secret of a life of victory.

THE SECRET OF ALL VICTORY

The secret of victory, joy, and power is the heart being filled with the Word of God. Regrettably, the hearts of too many Christians are filled with baseball, basketball, or football statistics, stock market reports, or other meaningless trivia. Jesus filled His Heart with the Word. These Passages portray to us His Example that we might follow.

The foremost reason for false doctrine and the success of false apostles stems from the fact that the Church as a whole has little Bible fidelity.

I personally have read the Bible completely through over fifty times. It is truly a *"Lamp unto my feet, and a Light unto my path"* (Ps. 119:105).

THE EXPOSITOR'S STUDY BIBLE

Somewhere in the time frame around 1995, the Lord began to deal earnestly with my heart about developing a Study Bible that would help Believers to more properly understand the Scriptures. At first, I dismissed this prompting. But the Holy Spirit then pushed even harder!

When I knew the Lord truly was speaking to me, my thoughts settled upon my inadequacy to undertake such a momentous task. And of that, namely, my inadequacy, I was totally correct! But still, the Holy Spirit did not let up; rather He intensified His Efforts.

For approximately five years, the project stayed on my mind, even growing more and more intense with the passing of time. I looked at quite a number of Study Bibles, some of which had excellent helps. The manner in which they were put together, however, sometimes made it difficult for the Reader to properly find and understand the supplied study aids. Most of the time, the commentary was at the bottom of the page, or at the side of the page. Some had the commentary at the back of the book.

As one man told me, *"I have a number of good Study Bibles, but at times it is so difficult to find the notes, that by the time I do locate them, I've lost my train of thought. But THE EXPOSITOR'S STUDY BIBLE is totally different in that the commentary notes are placed right with the Scripture, even in the midst of the Text at times, which makes it very easy to find and understand."*

It must have been about the year 2000 when the Lord began to show me exactly how He wanted this Study Bible to be designed. It was a method I had never seen before, and to me was totally unique; and, as far as I'm concerned, it is unique regarding any Study Bible in the world presently.

The Lord showed me that my expository notes explaining the Scripture should immediately follow the Scripture, even at times being embedded in the Scripture. The person, therefore, does not have to go to the back of the Bible, or even to the bottom or side of the page, to seek the information on the particular Passage. It's right there before the Reader's eyes.

I even believe the Lord instructed us to make the Text jet black and the notes in red, because this makes it very easy to read the Text without the notes, if that's what the Reader desires to do.

When I began to do the actual work of developing this Study Bible, I can say, without any fear of contradiction, that the Lord most graciously helped me as I carried out the work, just as He had told me to do the project and then showed me how to do it.

After THE EXPOSITOR'S STUDY BIBLE was finished, I went back and read it in its entirety. I marvel at the help that it provides. I look at it and realize that I could not have done this by my own understanding and ability. The Lord most surely helped me to develop this product, which has been published to help Believers more properly understand the Word of God.

The excuse that untold numbers of Christians use for not properly studying the Bible is, *"I just don't understand it."* Now, truthfully, some parts of the Bible are easy to understand, but other parts are quite difficult. I would pray that we have helped lessen the impact of this problem.

This I do know: The reports we have received from untold numbers of Christians have been that THE EXPOSITOR'S STUDY BIBLE has helped them immeasurably. We give the Lord all the Praise and Glory for that.

(12) "BLESSED ARE YOU, O LORD: TEACH ME YOUR STATUTES."

The word *"blessed"* means *"happy."* So, in these Passages, we are told what makes God happy. Actually, the entirety of this 119th Psalm, with its twenty-two choruses, tells us what makes God happy.

THE MESSIAH

The Messiah was Very God and Very Man. As Very Man, He laid aside Deity and all of its accoutrements (Phil. 2:5-8), while never losing its possession. In other words, Christ laid aside the expression of His Deity, while never losing the possession of His Deity.

As a Man, He had to learn the Word of God exactly as we do now; consequently, He would ask the Father to teach Him the Word of God. There is no doubt that Jesus did this from the time He was a child old enough to understand (Lk. 2:38-50). He did this as our example, and we are to follow suit by asking the Lord to *"teach us"* as well!

(13) "WITH MY LIPS HAVE I DECLARED ALL THE JUDGMENTS OF YOUR MOUTH."

This is the obligation of every Preacher and every single Believer. Regrettably, many Christians declare some of God's Judgments, but not all of them. The Messiah declared them all, even though it aroused great anger in the hearts of the religious hierarchy.

(14) "I HAVE REJOICED IN THE WAY OF YOUR TESTIMONIES, AS MUCH AS IN ALL RICHES."

When one considers that the Bible is to be placed in our interests on the same level (and above) as our employment, profits from business, education, automobiles, houses, and all the other items of life, then we realize the degree of significance that God places in such.

And why not?

The Word of God is the greatest Treasure on the face of the Earth. But yet, how many Christians place the Bible on the same level as did the Messiah?

(15) "I WILL MEDITATE IN YOUR PRECEPTS, AND HAVE RESPECT UNTO YOUR WAYS."

The word *"meditate"* is the secret of life.

MEDITATION

The Messiah meditated day and night, as we will see upon further investigation of this Psalm. This is the cure for depression, nervous breakdowns, emotional disturbances, worry, fear, or any other disability — meditation on the Word.

Few men today have respect for God's Ways. Man's ways are eagerly sought after, even by the Church; most of the time, God's Ways are largely ignored.

(16) "I WILL DELIGHT MYSELF IN YOUR STATUTES: I WILL NOT FORGET YOUR WORD."

The Messiah delighted Himself in the Word of God. (This was a constant, daily affair.) In other words, this was His Delight.

What is your delight?

Too many Christians pay too little tribute to the Bible, if any at all. From this Psalm, we learn to what degree and level the Holy Spirit places the Word of God in our lives.

If we delight in the Word of God, then we will not forget such, but it will be a constant source of strength at every capacity of life.

GIMEL (17-24)
(The Third Chorus)

(17) "DEAL BOUNTIFULLY WITH YOUR SERVANT, THAT I MAY LIVE, AND KEEP YOUR WORD."

The Reader will find that the first four Verses of this stanza express the activities of the heart toward God excited by the study of and the obedience to His Word, and the second four express the contempt and hatred that an obedient person receives from man.

NOTES

THE ROAD MAP FOR LIFE IS THE BIBLE

Man lives by every Word which proceeds out of the Mouth of God. He who would live a full life must, therefore, love and obey the Bible. Regrettably, the far greater majority of the human race attempts to live by physical bread alone. By doing so, they neglect and even deny the spirituality of man. One does not truly *"live"* until one truly *"keeps Your Word."*

The Bible, which actually is Christ the Living Word, is the Source, one might say, of all Life (Jn. 1:1). There remains no other source; consequently, those who ignore the Bible are dead while they live.

(18) "OPEN THOU MY EYES, THAT I MAY BEHOLD WONDROUS THINGS OUT OF YOUR LAW."

There are wondrous things in the Word, but the eyes must be unveiled in order to see them. To see them, the Reader must sit where Mary of Bethany sat (Lk. 10:38-42). What Martha did was important; however, what Mary did is that which the Holy Spirit desires to bring to us, namely, to learn Christ.

(19) "I AM A STRANGER IN THE EARTH: HIDE NOT YOUR COMMANDMENTS FROM ME."

The Bible makes its lover a stranger to this world, but it is a satisfying companion for the lonely exile. The Bible lover will find no companionship among those who deny its contents.

The sense of the second part of this Verse is not that God attempts to conceal His Word, but that the seeker is encouraged to request of the Lord His Personal attention as Teacher. What a privilege to have the Holy Spirit Himself teach us! (Jn. 16:13).

(20) "MY SOUL BREAKS FOR THE LONGING THAT IT HAS UNTO YOUR JUDGMENTS AT ALL TIMES."

This is an expression used of deep passion or intense longing, and shows to what extent the Psalmist hungered for Righteousness (Mat. 5:6). How many Christians have this type of hunger for the Word of God? This is the secret of the fulfilled life.

Regrettably, many Christians never have read the Bible through once, much less made it a part of their everyday lives. The Bible should be just as much a part of our everyday existence as the three meals a day of which we partake for our physical nourishment.

Is it such in your life?

(21) "YOU HAVE REBUKED THE PROUD WHO ARE CURSED, WHICH DO ERR FROM YOUR COMMANDMENTS."

Those who are too proud to subject their wills to the teaching of the Scriptures bring a curse and not a blessing upon themselves and become the bitter persecutors of those who make the Scriptures their delight.

Here we are shown by the Holy Spirit that pride is the reason for neglect of the Word. It was pride that caused Adam and Eve in the Garden of Eden to *"err from Your Commandments"* (Gen., Chpt. 3). It is pride that causes the majority of the Church to drift from the Bible toward humanistic psychology.

The word *"rebuke"* in this Passage is seemingly mild; however, the end results are staggering.

(22) "REMOVE FROM ME REPROACH AND CONTEMPT; FOR I HAVE KEPT YOUR TESTIMONIES."

The sense of this Verse is for the lover of the Bible not to allow reproach and contempt to weaken his love for the Word of God. Unfortunately, the Bible lover is regarded by the populace with hostility and by the cultured with contempt; but this does not embitter his spirit. Unaffected by their contempt and hostility, he keeps on reading, loving, and delighting in the Book.

(23) "PRINCES ALSO DID SIT AND SPEAK AGAINST ME: BUT YOUR SERVANT DID MEDITATE IN YOUR STATUTES."

All of these Passages speak of Christ as our example. The mightiest in Israel spoke against Christ, but His Solace was *"Your Statutes."* In these, He did meditate.

This is the answer for criticism, reproach, contempt, emotional disturbances, nervous breakdowns, and all other negative attacks. Over and over, the Holy Spirit draws our attention to the word *"meditate."* There is healing, strength, encouragement, joy, power, and Deliverance in the Believer's meditating on the Word of God. We must not forget that!

(24) "YOUR TESTIMONIES ALSO ARE MY DELIGHT AND MY COUNSELORS."

NOTES

The Word of God must be our Counselor.

THE COUNSELOR

What a rebuke to a worldly Church that seeks the counsel of man from a man-made philosophy, with its man-made answers! The Word of God should be our Counselor — and the Word of God alone!

Yes, we should avidly seek the counsel of Godly men and women; but if, at any time, their counsel opposes the Word of God, it should be instantly ignored.

It is sad that many in the modern Church say we today face problems that are not addressed in the Bible, and that in order for a solution to be found, psychology must be added to the Scriptures. Such constitutes blasphemy!

This is a denial of the Author of the Book, Who is God, and His Inspiration of the same. The idea that the Creator did not address all the needs of His Creation in His Word is ignorance at best and blasphemy at worst.

DALETH (25-32)
(The Fourth Chorus)

(25) "MY SOUL CLEAVES UNTO THE DUST: QUICKEN THOU ME ACCORDING TO YOUR WORD."

The Messiah's love for the Bible and His Perfect Obedience to its teachings alone illustrate the statements of this stanza.

THE PROTECTION IS IN THE WORD

The idea of this Verse is that the soul will fall into the dust (defeat) unless it is quickened by the Word of God. There is another interpretation to the Verse as well.

Even though greatly weakened by trial, even fainting, the true servant of Jehovah keeps cleaving to God's Testimonies. This stanza presents the Bible as a restorative, the only restorative.

A great part of the Church in what is referred to as the *"Faith Message"* has attempted to bypass tests and trials. It is not to be done. Great Faith must always be tested greatly. The only thing that sustains during these times, or any other time, is *"Your Word."*

(26) "I HAVE DECLARED MY WAYS,

AND YOU HEARD ME: TEACH ME YOUR STATUTES."

The cry of the Psalmist here is to lay the heart bare before God and to enumerate the areas of weakness that cause us to be bowed to the *"dust"* of the previous Verse.

THE WORD OF GOD WILL POINT OUT WEAKNESSES WITHIN OUR LIFE

Such a heart attempts to hide nothing from God. This has little to do with petitions in the sense of material things. The cry is that the Lord will point out to us the weaknesses which have caused us so much problem, in order that we may overcome them. This is a part of the convicting Power of the Holy Spirit.

Part of the great task of the Holy Spirit, Who always directs us to the Word, is to smite with conviction (Jn. 16:7-11); unfortunately, much of the modern Church does not even believe in the convicting Power of the Holy Spirit; they call it *"condemnation."* Consequently, there is precious little Spiritual Growth in such ranks.

The idea of this Passage is that the Holy Spirit will call our attention to certain portions of the Word of God which spotlight areas of weakness in our lives, which we are then to declare before God. He has promised to hear us and to further teach us from His Word (Statutes), showing us how to obtain victory. If we closely follow the Word, we will find that it always points us ultimately to the Cross of Christ (Rom. 6:1-14; 8:1-2, 11; I Cor. 1:17-18, 23; 2:2).

The Word of God is to be a mirror *"declaring our ways"* and instruction for victory over these deficiencies.

(27) "MAKE ME TO UNDERSTAND THE WAY OF YOUR PRECEPTS: SO SHALL I TALK OF YOUR WONDROUS WORKS."

The Word is Living Water. It gives life and keeps alive. It is Heavenly Bread and so strengthens man's heart. To experience and enjoy these truths, a teachable will with active moral affections is necessary.

THE SEARCHLIGHT OF THE HOLY SCRIPTURES

The entire life, inward and outward, must be subjected to the searchlight of the Holy Scriptures. The continuance of such criticism must be desired and must be accepted as the infallible judge of Truth and error. Not the judgment of the conscience, nor of the Church, nor of society, but that of God's Word should be desired, sought for, and accepted.

The sense of this Passage is that we are to request the Holy Spirit to be our Teacher, as He has promised to do (Jn. 16:13). While it is true that the Ministry Gift of *"Teacher"* is given by Christ to the Church (Eph. 4:11), still, we are also to request Personal Instruction by the Spirit of God. Too much of the Body of Christ little knows the Word of God; they rely solely on others for instruction. The Holy Spirit is displeased with such and requests that we also ask for His Personal Instruction, even though we enjoy the help given by any and every God-called Teacher.

(28) "MY SOUL MELTS FOR HEAVINESS: STRENGTHEN THOU ME ACCORDING UNTO YOUR WORD."

Once again, as in Verse 25, the Holy Spirit calls our attention to the difficulties of the way, and that *"strength"* can come only through *"Your Word."*

Sadly, precious few take advantage of such. At any given time, tens of thousands of Christians are in psychological group therapy, which offers no help whatsoever; rather it will tender harm. Others spend countless hours with Preachers who use psychological counseling, which also will tender only harm and no healing. Any Preacher who points anyone to anything other than the Word of God has betrayed his calling, that is, if he ever was truly called of God. This not only grieves the Holy Spirit, but it also subjects hurting souls to little more than witchcraft. Anything the seeking soul needs is in the Word of God (II Pet. 1:3-4).

(29) "REMOVE FROM ME THE WAY OF LYING: AND GRANT ME YOUR LAW GRACIOUSLY."

This is a request by the Messiah; it also should be our request: That all falsity, prevarication, and everything that is contrary to Truth or that is the opposite of the Way of Truth should be removed from us.

THE WAY OF PSYCHOLOGY IS THE WAY OF LYING

It truly is a tragic situation when one considers that almost all of the Christian bookstores are filled with books on psychology, psychoanalysis, and psychological counseling. Furthermore, the far greater majority of sermons preached behind Christian pulpits are psychologically laced, which means they represent *"the way of lying."* It is impossible to mix the Bible Way with the psychological way.

A short time ago, I picked up an academic catalog which listed the various Seminaries in America and the courses they offered. Almost all were psychology or psychologically oriented. There was almost no Bible. In most Bible Colleges and Seminaries, one can receive many and varied degrees, but not a degree in Bible. That is tantamount to a student going to a Law School and not being able to receive a degree in Law.

In most religious circles, the Bible is relegated to second position, that is, if it is given any position at all.

Let it ever be known that the Bible is the Word of God, and it addresses itself to every need that man may have. All else is the word of man and is the *"way of lying."*

WHY THE PSYCHOLOGICAL WAY?

Almost *en masse*, and irrespective of Denominational attachments or affiliations, the Church has opted for the psychological way.

The question must be asked, *"Why?"*

Briefly, psychology, in its basic sense, claims to be a cure for the soul. I maintain that it has no cure; it is not even a science; it is a fallacy, pure and simple. It stems from humanism and evolution.

Words such as *"rehabilitation"* and *"psychological therapy"* have absolutely no place in the Word of God. Actually, such terms insinuate that man can heal man, that sickness can cure sickness, that sin can cleanse sin, and that bondage can deliver bondage. But a little common Bible sense would expose the fallacy of such thinking!

Psychology neither accepts nor believes that man has a *"sin nature"* (I Jn. 1:8), which, in reality, is the contributor of man's spiritual and moral problems. Most of its humanistic teachings claim that problems originate in childhood, or even in the mother's womb. Consequently, if these hang-ups can be addressed, then the problem can be solved.

It may take many months, even years, and many thousands of dollars before one even proposes to be helped; actually no one ever is cured by this route. And, to their credit, most psychologists don't even claim that their patients are cured.

PSYCHOLOGY, A ROMAN CIRCUS

Someone has said that much of the advice given by modern-day psychology is worthy of a Roman circus. Its absurdities only lead to more absurdities. The techniques and methods are constantly changing, with the newest fad becoming even more absurd than the fad that preceded it.

The landscape is littered with marriages that not only have not been helped by the psychological way, but have actually been destroyed by it. The messed-up lives which have resorted to this shamanism are kept undercover only by the dangling carrot that promises help — but never delivers!

If demon spirits are the founders of all error (and I know they are), then demon spirits are undoubtedly the authors of the psychological way — just as demon spirits instigate witchcraft.

The obvious question is: *"Why has the Church fallen for this shamanism?"*

The answer really is very simple:

THE CROSS OF CHRIST

First of all, the Church scarcely believes in the Cross of Christ anymore, which means they don't really believe in the Word of God. The Church scarcely believes that Jesus saves, redeems, and sets the captive free, all done by and through the Cross. Actually, the Church hardly even believes in sin any more. It is only a *"psychological maladjustment"* which can be cured by *"group therapy"* or some other psychological mishmash, they say!

The fact is, it is impossible to believe in the psychological way (the lying way) and the Bible at the same time. One or the other will have to go, and one or the other will go!

The Word is seldom preached from behind most pulpits any more. The Bible may be presented as *"window dressing,"* but, in reality, the latest psychological fad (which passes for Gospel) is propagated much of the time. Many good things are said, but it is not the Gospel of Jesus Christ. Yet this is the only Gospel that sets the captive free.

Sadly, this includes all types of Churches — of whatever name, stripe, or orientation. Yes, there are a few who still believe in the Power of God, but not many! There are a few Preachers who still preach the Gospel, but not many! The Holy Spirit through the Apostle Paul outlined it perfectly:

"Having a form of Godliness, but denying the power thereof: from such turn away" (II Tim. 3:5).

CHRISTIAN PSYCHOLOGY?

Sadly, many Church leaders are openly stating that mankind is facing problems today that are not addressed in the Bible, and that psychology must be wedded with the Bible in order to solve these problems.

The Church has tried to salve its conscience by papering over its psychological jargon with a Scripture here and there. It is called *"Christian Psychology."*

Let the seeker for help beware: There is no such thing. All psychology (and I mean all!) was birthed in the minds of humanistic thinkers who have no regard for the Bible, who have little belief in God whatsoever. Psychology does not know the cause and neither does it have any cure. It only can catalog symptoms.

The Bible is God's Way; it either holds the answers to man's spiritual and moral problems, or else it is a lie. Simon Peter said:

"According as His Divine Power has given unto us all things that pertain unto life and Godliness, through the knowledge of Him Who has called us to Glory and Virtue" (II Pet. 1:3).

Either God, through His Word, did give us *"all things that pertain unto life and Godliness"* or He didn't. I believe He did. You would do yourself well to believe it too. All else is *"the way of lying."*

(30) "I HAVE CHOSEN THE WAY OF TRUTH: YOUR JUDGMENTS HAVE I LAID BEFORE ME."

The Holy Spirit takes us even deeper into the Word respecting this Scripture.

THE WAY OF TRUTH

In Verse 29, we have the warning of the *"way of lying"* and the request to be removed from such. In this Verse, we have *"the way of Truth."* This *"Way"* is the Bible. How so clear and plain it is! In today's Church society, you can have the *"Judgments"* (Bible) laid before you, or you can take the psychological way. The choice is yours!

In the last few years, the subtle lie has been proposed in the psychological way that *"all truth is God's Truth."* It sounds good, but it is in fact a *"lying way."* The proponents of such claim that God gave the great truth of psychology to Freud and others of such ilk. Even a scant knowledge of the Bible, however, proclaims the fallacy of such. God does not give His Truth to enquiring minds. He only gives it to searching and seeking hearts (Jer. 29:13).

The Scripture plainly tells us, *"But the natural man receives not the things of the Spirit of God* (speaks of the individual who is not Born-Again)*: for they are foolishness unto him* (a lack of understanding)*: neither can he know them* (fallen man cannot understand Spiritual Truths)*, because they are spiritually discerned.* (Only the regenerated spirit of man can understand the things of the Spirit)*"* (I Cor. 2:14).

Actually, Truth is not a philosophy, it is a Person, and that Person is Jesus Christ. The Bible says the following:

1. *"I* (Jesus) *am the Way, the Truth, and the Life"* (Jn. 14:6).
2. *"Your Word is Truth"* (Jn. 17:17).
3. *"The Spirit is Truth"* (I Jn. 5:6).

Consequently, only those who are led by the Spirit, which always leads to Christ and His Word, find Truth.

(31) "I HAVE STUCK UNTO YOUR TESTIMONIES: O LORD, PUT ME NOT TO SHAME."

The word *"stuck"* actually means *"I have been glued to."*

EMBRACING THE WORD

Let it be known that being glued to *"Your Testimonies"* is not one way of victory, but the only way.

The sense of the Passage, *"Put me not to shame,"* does not merely mean that there is a possibility of such, but that the only thing that will keep us from being put to shame is

"Your Testimonies," and that if we do not *"stick to Your Testimonies,"* we will be *"put to shame."* The *"lying way"* of Verse 29 always ultimately brings shame.

(32) "I WILL RUN THE WAY OF YOUR COMMANDMENTS, WHEN YOU SHALL ENLARGE MY HEART."

The idea of this Verse is:

"When You shall have removed from me the 'way of lying' and put me in the 'way of Truth,' I will run the 'Way of Your Commandments' without any stumblingblock in my way. My heart will be enlarged, will throw out all 'way of lying,' and will fill itself with 'Your Testimonies,' which are 'The Ways of Truth.'

To enlarge the heart means *"to arouse its moral affections."* To understand and profit by the Scriptures, contrition of heart, rather than cleverness of head, is necessary.

HE (33-40)
(The Fifth Chorus)

(33) "TEACH ME, O LORD, THE WAY OF YOUR STATUTES; AND I SHALL KEEP IT UNTO THE END."

Allow us to remind the Bible Student that these petitions are the heartthrob and cry of the Messiah. If they are of Him, they should be of us, as well!

TEACH US, O LORD

Once again, as in the previous stanza (Vs. 27), the request is tendered toward God that the Holy Spirit *"teach Me."*

The Believer should glean all that is possible from those in the God-given Office of the Teacher (Eph. 4:11), but also should constantly petition the Heavenly Father to instruct. The following is a guardian against false teachers.

John said:

"But the Anointing which you have received of Him abides in you, and you need not that any man teach you: but as the same Anointing teaches you of all things, and is Truth, and is no lie, and even as it has taught you, you shall abide in Him" (I Jn. 2:27).

John is not teaching that Saints have no further need of Gospel Ministers or Teachers, for God has set them in the Church to teach.

NOTES

He does mean that what is taught should be subjected to Scripture, and that the anointing of the Holy Spirit will help us to judge all teaching, whether it be Biblically correct or not (Mat. 7:15-20).

Far too many Christians accept whatever is taught if it sounds pleasing to the ear, irrespective of its Scriptural validity. The safeguards given below will prevent such.

1. Personal knowledge of the Word of God.
2. The Holy Spirit leading us Himself into all Truth (Jn. 16:13).

(34) "GIVE ME UNDERSTANDING, AND I SHALL KEEP YOUR LAW; YEA, I SHALL OBSERVE IT WITH MY WHOLE HEART."

The Word cannot be understood apart from a personal knowledge of its Author.

THE BIBLE AND ITS AUTHOR

Please allow me to emphasize again the necessity of reaping from God-given Teachers (Eph. 4:11), but most of all to impress upon the Reader the absolute necessity of petitioning the Lord that He Personally give us understanding of His Word. The enquiring heart may wonder at the necessity of having to ask the Lord, especially since He knows our need of such. Yes, He does know; however, He desires that we hunger and thirst after Righteousness. He only will respond to a heartfelt hunger. He does not respond to curiosity.

This stanza teaches that if a Bible Student disassociates the Book from its Author, his eyes will be unopened (Vss. 33-37), his mind uninstructed (Vss. 34, 38), his heart unaffected (Vss. 34, 36), and his feet unled (Vs. 35). The eyes, the mind, the heart, and the feet must be governed by the Word of God (Williams).[63]

The *"understanding,"* which pertains to our mind, can only be enlightened as it begins in the heart, and a *"whole heart"* at that! Many have tried to learn the Word of God with the mind (intellect) only. They never have succeeded. They finish with a lack of understanding, just as they began.

Please allow me to say it again:

The Word cannot be understood apart from a personal knowledge of its Author.

(35) "MAKE ME TO GO IN THE PATH OF YOUR COMMANDMENTS; FOR

THEREIN DO I DELIGHT."

The words, *"Teach Me,"* in Verse 33 actually mean *"make Me to see."* It corresponds with the *"make Me to go"* in this Verse. Too many have tried to go when they have not yet seen.

The sense of the Verse is that the human heart is so turned away from the paths of God that the Holy Spirit must use power to bring us back to the correct path, and will do so only upon the petitioning cry of the searching heart. If there is little delight in the Word of God, there will be little petition for *"the path of Your Commandments."*

(36) "INCLINE MY HEART UNTO YOUR TESTIMONIES, AND NOT TO COVETOUSNESS."

The Bible is more precious than gold. It can fill the broken heart with hope and strength that money cannot do.

One of the sins of the modern Church is the using of the Bible to get gain. While it certainly is true that God blesses, and blesses abundantly, still, *"the path"* taken by the Holy Spirit places a far greater value on a knowledge of the Giver than on the Gift.

(37) "TURN AWAY MY EYES FROM BEHOLDING VANITY; AND QUICKEN THOU ME IN YOUR WAY."

Any teaching that does not harmonize with the Bible is *"vanity."* How so easy it is for the eyes to be diverted to *"vanity"*! Satan has a way of making it appear appetizing, even religious. Such is the modern Church. By and large, its eyes are fastened onto *"vanity"* instead of *"Your Way."*

(38) "STABLISH YOUR WORD UNTO YOUR SERVANT, WHO IS DEVOTED TO YOUR FEAR."

The words, *"Devoted to Your fear,"* that is, the Scriptures, teach the true way of worshipping God. There is little devotion to the Word of God when there is little devotion to the *"fear of God."*

(39) "TURN AWAY MY REPROACH WHICH I FEAR: FOR YOUR JUDGMENTS ARE GOOD."

The sense of the Passage is that it seems the writer (whether David or someone else) had committed a secret evil for which he is sorry. If it becomes known to the public, it will be a heavy reproach.

NOTES

PERFECT WISDOM AND INFINITE LOVE

The second meaning of this Verse pertains to the deliverance of Israel from Egypt. The entrance into the Promised Land put an end to the reproach by Egypt that Israel was trusting a God Who was not able to perform His Promises.

The true heart dreads such a reproach, but rests in the conviction that the Divine Judgments as to the fitting time and way of making good the Promises are animated by Perfect Wisdom and infinite Love.

(40) "BEHOLD, I HAVE LONGED AFTER YOUR PRECEPTS: QUICKEN ME IN YOUR RIGHTEOUSNESS."

If we long after His Word (Precepts), we will long after His Righteousness.

RIGHTEOUSNESS

The *"Righteousness"* spoken of is God's Righteousness, *"Your Righteousness."* It is imputed Righteousness, which is the only type that God will recognize; it refers to the fact that it is Righteousness that is freely given to the Saint who expresses faith in Christ and what Christ did at the Cross.

Most righteousness in the world and in the Church is self-righteousness, which God will not and cannot recognize. Man has no personal righteousness; moreover, man can do nothing to attain righteousness. Therefore, he is totally dependent upon God to provide His Righteousness. Consequently, God is angered when man attempts to substitute a false and fake self-righteousness for His Righteousness.

The word *"quicken"* actually means *"to make alive."* God's Righteousness gives life, while self-righteousness brings death.

VAU (41-48)
(The Sixth Chorus)

(41) "LET YOUR MERCIES COME ALSO UNTO ME, O LORD, EVEN YOUR SALVATION, ACCORDING TO YOUR WORD."

Salvation which is not according to God's Word is a false salvation. It can neither silence mockers nor influence kings.

MERCIES

The word *"Mercies"* establishes the

foundation upon which all gifts from God are bestowed. It all comes from Christ and through the Cross. To be frank, Christ and the Finished Work of the Cross must never be separated. The benefits of what He did at the Cross will flow from that Finished Work forever and forever. So much so that Paul referred to it as *"The Everlasting Covenant"* (Heb. 13:20), meaning that the New Covenant, which was consummated at the Cross, will never have to be amended or replaced.

Man, even the most righteous of Believers, merits nothing good. Everything is received from God, even by the most ardent seeker, solely because of God's Grace and Mercy — again we say, through what Jesus did at the Cross. Any petitioner who comes from any other basis will be turned away (Isa. 66:2; Eph. 2:13-18).

Even though the Words are spoken by the Messiah Himself, the accomplishments of the Petitioner are not even mentioned, but rather are ignored. The Word of God is extolled by the Holy Spirit with such a consistent pattern that it is impossible to misunderstand its application.

(42) "SO SHALL I HAVE WHEREWITH TO ANSWER HIM WHO REPROACHES ME: FOR I TRUST IN YOUR WORD."

It is a reproach from the world today to trust solely in the Word of God, as it was a reproach then.

THE VALIDITY OF THE WORD OF GOD

The Bible proclaims a Salvation (Vs. 41) that closes the mouth of the skeptic (Vs. 42); fills the mouth of the Believer (Vs. 43); energizes a life of obedience (Vs. 44); gives breath of view (Vs. 45); dignity of conduct (Vs. 46); satisfaction to the emotions (Vs. 47); resolution of character (Vs. 48); and provides inexhaustible food for the highest intellect and noblest mind. Thus, the Scripture is competent to perfectly furnish all who turn to it for moral teaching, actually for everything that pertains to Life and Godliness (II Tim. 3:17).

Concerning this very thing, Simon Peter said, and I quote from THE EXPOSITOR'S STUDY BIBLE:

"According as His Divine Power has given unto us all things (the Lord with large-handed generosity has given us all things) *that pertain unto Life and Godliness* (pertains to the fact that the Lord Jesus has given us everything we need regarding life and living), *through the knowledge of Him Who has called us to Glory and Virtue* ('knowledge' addressed here speaks of what Christ did at the Cross, which alone can provide 'Glory and Virtue'):

"Whereby are given unto us exceeding great and precious Promises (pertains to the Word of God, which alone holds the answer to every life problem)*: that by these* (Promises) *you might be partakers of the Divine Nature* (the Divine Nature implanted in the inner being of the believing sinner becomes the source of our new life and actions; it comes to everyone at the moment of being 'born-again'), *having escaped the corruption that is in the world through lust.* (This presents the Salvation experience of the sinner, and the Sanctification experience of the Saint)" (II Pet. 1:3-4).

THE UNITY BETWEEN THE BIBLE AND ITS AUTHOR

The terms, *"Your Mercies," "Your Salvation," "Your Word," "Your Judgments," "Your Law," "Your Testimonies," "Your Precepts," "Your Commandments,"* and *"Your Statutes,"* mark the unity existing between the Bible and its Author. To belittle the One is to belittle the Other.

To the humblest life, the Scriptures, if loved and obeyed, impart a refinement, a dignity, a grace, a power, and an intelligence that secures perfection of conduct under all circumstances and in all circles. Evil will be rebuked and courage and righteousness will be praised.

(43) "AND TAKE NOT THE WORD OF TRUTH UTTERLY OUT OF MY MOUTH; FOR I HAVE HOPED IN YOUR JUDGMENTS."

The Psalmist actually is saying that the Word of God is his only hope; and likewise it is our only hope.

The word *"utterly"* is an interesting term in Hebrew and is not easy to translate. Its first occurrences are in Genesis 1:31 and 7:19. It suggests a mouth overflowing with Words of Divine Truth.

(44) "SO SHALL I KEEP YOUR LAW CONTINUALLY FOREVER AND EVER."

Only the Messiah could say such. And yet, if our trust is in Christ and what He has done for us at the Cross, then His Perfect Record becomes our perfect record. By the great Grace of Justification by Faith, we too can say the same.

(45) "AND I WILL WALK AT LIBERTY: FOR I SEEK YOUR PRECEPTS."

Jesus said He came to *"set at liberty them who are bruised"* (Lk. 4:18). He did so by directing people to the Bible.

LIBERTY

Jesus Christ was the Living and Incarnate Word. The Bible brings liberty; all else brings slavery. Humanity is bruised by Satan and the powers of darkness. This creates a prison. The Word of God, and the Word of God alone, occasions liberty from this prison.

Psychology teaches that child abuse in any form institutes a prison and perversion of actions and mind. In that, they are correct! Even though psychology is excellent at cataloging symptoms, still, it knows neither the cause nor the cure.

Jesus Christ was anointed by the Holy Spirit to *"set at liberty them who are bruised."* He Alone, in accordance with His Word, can heal the bruised and set them at liberty. As stated, He does this through the great Work which He carried out at Calvary's Cross. All Salvation is in the Cross! All healing is in the Cross! All deliverance is in the Cross! All power is in the Cross! (Rom. 6:1-14; 8:1-2, 11; I Cor. 1:17-18, 23; 2:2; Col. 2:14-15).

(46) "I WILL SPEAK OF YOUR TESTIMONIES ALSO BEFORE KINGS, AND WILL NOT BE ASHAMED."

Multiple millions believe that a life shut in-between the covers of the Bible must necessarily be a narrow one. The opposite is found by experience to be the truth.

TRUST IN THE WORD

This Verse has two meanings:

1. A Christian needs little Grace or courage to speak for the Bible to those who are beneath him socially, but to so speak to his equals or superiors and not be shamed is quite another matter, and is dependent upon a life of close fellowship with God.

2. Even though in this world system there is a stigma and a reproach (Vs. 42) carried by those who *"trust in Your Word,"* still, dependence on that Word will give us boldness that will not flinch even when before great men.

A PERSONAL EXPERIENCE

I remember once standing before the President of the United States, Ronald Reagan. I said to him, *"Mr. President, I want you to know I am praying for you, and do so constantly."*

That was all that I said. Then I proceeded to break the handshake and go my way, for that was what protocol demanded; however, the President did not let go of my hand. I immediately halted the process and looked at him. He said to me, and with deliberation, *"Reverend Swaggart, You will never know how much I appreciate what you have just said."*

I knew that he meant what he said and it was not merely a political statement.

(47) "AND I WILL DELIGHT MYSELF IN YOUR COMMANDMENTS, WHICH I HAVE LOVED."

This Verse is very similar to Verse 35. The love and delight of the Psalmist comes from *"Your Commandments,"* and not the things of the world. How many Christians can say the same? The love and delight are there because the heart is there (Vs. 34). Regrettably, the delight of too many Christians is in sports, entertainment, money, and other such things. Such never will lead to the victory of the heart and the soul, which only the Word of God can give.

(48) "MY HANDS ALSO WILL I LIFT UP UNTO YOUR COMMANDMENTS, WHICH I HAVE LOVED; AND I WILL MEDITATE IN YOUR STATUTES."

Over and over, the Holy Spirit draws our attention to the words, *"meditate"* and *"Your Statutes."* This is the answer for stress, nervous disorders, emotional disturbances, and all other such problems.

The expression, *"To lift up the hands,"* expresses a resolute engagement and a prayerful desire. It also denotes a total submission to the Word of God.

ZAIN (49-56)
(The Seventh Chorus)

(49) "REMEMBER THE WORD UNTO YOUR SERVANT, UPON WHICH YOU HAVE CAUSED ME TO HOPE."

The theme of this section is the Bible as the sustainer of the life and the comforter of the heart. It pictures the child of Heaven amid the sorrows of Earth, sustained and comforted by the Words of Life.

TOTAL DEPENDENCE ON THE WORD

In this Verse, the Messiah expresses to Jehovah the fact of His total dependence being placed on the Word. He also sings of what the Bible, with its Promises and Records, were to Him during His earthly pilgrimage. Thus, during His life of sorrow, trial, and hatred, He did not throw the Bible aside in favor of other methods, but clung to it all the closer.

Such is the experience also of those in whom He dwells. Like our Lord, the more we read and love the Bible, the more we want to read and love it.

(50) "THIS IS MY COMFORT IN MY AFFLICTION: FOR YOUR WORD HAS QUICKENED ME."

The Messiah does not deny affliction, nor does He offer any direction that guarantees no affliction, but He does offer Hope (Vs. 49) in the Word of God, which *"quickens Me."*

(51) "THE PROUD HAVE HAD ME GREATLY IN DERISION: YET HAVE I NOT DECLINED FROM YOUR LAW."

Christ says that despite the derision, He still holds firm to *"Your Law."*

THE PROUD

The proud deride the Promises of the Bible, but the humble rest upon them and hold fast to them. They prove that, in the absence of all natural joys, the Scriptures can fill the life with sweetness, sunshine, and strength.

In this Passage, the Pharisees, whom *"the proud"* symbolize, claim, ironically, to be sticklers for the Law. The Truth fragmented their claims. Actually, they had so inserted their traditions that they had *"made the Commandment of God of none effect"* (Mat. 15:6). Christ adhered strictly to the Word of God and was held *"greatly in derision"* by the Pharisees.

(The Bible of Jesus' day consisted of Genesis through Malachi.)

Little has changed today. Those who adhere strictly to the Bible are held in derision, not only by the world, but also by the Church — and all because of pride.

(52) "I REMEMBERED YOUR JUDGMENTS OF OLD, O LORD; AND HAVE COMFORTED MYSELF."

The comfort that every soul needs can only be derived from the Bible. It gives assurance, strength, leading, direction, and power. Actually, true and lasting comfort can only be derived from the Word of God.

This is brought about by remembering the great accomplishments that God has performed for His people in the past, which will comfort His people in the present. Every situation of life is addressed between the covers of the Bible. The Believer should constantly avail himself of the opportunity of meditating on its accounts.

(53) "HORROR HAS TAKEN HOLD UPON ME BECAUSE OF THE WICKED WHO FORSAKE YOUR LAW."

This Verse could read, *"Hot indignation has taken hold upon Me because of the lawless who forsake Your Law."*

INDIGNATION

The Messiah felt hot indignation when the Word of God was perverted (Mk. 3:5; 7:6-13; Lk. 7:30-35; 11:39-54).

A holy anger and a just indignation become the true witness for God and for His Truth. Men who take little interest in the authority and inspiration of the Scriptures rarely become heated when discussing them. But the more they are loved, the hotter will be the indignation of those who love them against those who corrupt or deny them.

(54) "YOUR STATUTES HAVE BEEN MY SONGS IN THE HOUSE OF MY PILGRIMAGE."

The word *"songs"* is another indication that David may have been the author of this Psalm. One or more of the Psalms indicate that David, especially in exile (*"my pilgrimage"*), would arise early in order to get alone with God. He oftentimes would accompany his singing, probably some of these very Psalms, with his harp (Ps. 57). We should quote the Word, meditate on the Word, and sing the Word, exactly as did David!

(55) "I HAVE REMEMBERED YOUR NAME, O LORD, IN THE NIGHT, AND HAVE KEPT YOUR LAW."

This speaks of meditation on the Word and *"Your Name in the night."* This particular time is Satan's most fertile field. Problems and difficulties loom larger. The only defense against this is to meditate on the Word (Ps. 1:2) and to remember the power of *"Your Name."*

(56) "THIS I HAD, BECAUSE I KEPT YOUR PRECEPTS."

This Passage states something peculiar, unique, and characteristic of the Messiah. Although all other servants of God without exception failed in perfectly believing and obeying the Bible, He, in fact, perfectly loved and followed its Precepts. Thus, He Alone satisfies the language of this section, as He Alone illustrates the faith, loyalty, and love of all the other sections of this Psalm (Williams).[64]

The only way that we can say that we have kept all *"Your Precepts"* at all times is by entering in by faith into the Perfect Life of our Perfect Master, which is made possible to us by what He did at the Cross, and only by what He did at the Cross. Only then will the Father accredit such to us.

CHETH (57-64)
(The Eighth Chorus)

(57) "YOU ARE MY PORTION, O LORD: I HAVE SAID THAT I WOULD KEEP YOUR WORDS."

Anyone who believes that the Scriptures are not necessary in a life of intimate fellowship with God is contradicted by the teaching of this Verse. In fact, the entire Bible contradicts this erroneous idea.

PORTIONS

The bane of the modern Church is that *"portions"* devised by man attempt to usurp authority over the *"portions"* given by God. Either God is our *"Portion"* or He isn't. There can be no mixing of the two. *"Portions"* of the world weaken the soul, while *"portions"* solely of God strengthen and gladden the heart. The basic reason for the problems of the Christian is that God is not totally and completely *"my Portion."*

Jehovah was to be Levi's Portion (Josh. 13:33), but he failed to realize his wealth and walk worthy of it. Messiah was the True Levi.

These Verses exhibit Him as such, and reveal the loyalty and affection of His Heart to the Scriptures. God was the Portion of His Soul; the Bible, the treasure of His Heart. His Knowledge of and union with God did not make Him independent of the Scriptures; but, on the contrary, because Jehovah was His Portion, therefore, He said that He would keep and hold fast to His Word.

And so He did, totally and completely; and so must we, as well!

(58) "I INTREATED YOUR FAVOR WITH MY WHOLE HEART: BE MERCIFUL UNTO ME ACCORDING TO YOUR WORD."

As Man, our Lord judged His Ways by the Word of God, and always set His Feet in the paths pointed out by the Scriptures, and not in the paths suggested by His Own Will.

FAVOR

Concerning this, Williams says, *"Favor means the conscious Presence of God. Messiah's whole heart desired such communion and also a practical experience of the good things promised by faith in the inspired Word. He only desired such things as the Bible spoke of. He, as Man, had an independent Will; hence, He could say, 'Not My Will, but Thine be done.' He always acquiesced to the Will of God."* [65]

(59) "I THOUGHT ON MY WAYS, AND TURNED MY FEET UNTO YOUR TESTIMONIES."

As we previously have stated, all of the Psalms present Christ in one of His Atoning, Mediatorial, or Intercessory roles. Some of the Psalms seem to be the opposite of what Christ would do or think. However, we must remember that when such is the case, it is presenting the Intercessory role of Christ, when He puts Himself totally in our place.

THE WAYS OF THE LORD

Our Lord here proclaims the fact that He

looked at His Own Personal Ways, and realized that within Himself, as a Man, He was woefully insufficient. He, therefore, determined to address His Life in every capacity according to the Word of God. That must also be our example!

And yet, the following question must be asked.

"If one does not know the Bible, how can one guide his steps by the Bible?"

Of course, the answer to that is obvious. One cannot subscribe to that which one does not know. Tragically, most of the modern Church is Biblically illiterate.

How many modern Believers set aside a little time each and every day for the study of the Word of God? Even most Preachers don't do such, much less the laity. Consequently, most little know what the Word of God actually says; as a result, their lives are not guided by the Truth of the Word, but rather by other things, and such a situation always brings trouble. In fact, all trouble, in one way or the other, can be traced to an ignorance of the Word of God.

(60) "I MADE HASTE, AND DELAYED NOT TO KEEP YOUR COMMANDMENTS."

Abraham (Gen. 22:3) hasted and delayed not to keep the Commandments given to him; yet his obedience was not always perfect. In effect, Jesus is the True Abraham.

The sense of this Verse is that the most important thing in the world to the Messiah was to *"keep Your Commandments."* Therefore, He would make haste in applying Himself to the Scriptures and the Scriptures to Himself.

(61) "THE BANDS OF THE WICKED HAVE ROBBED ME: BUT I HAVE NOT FORGOTTEN YOUR LAW."

This is another Passage that could refer to wicked men seeking the life of David (I Sam., Chpts. 21-28; II Sam., Chpts. 15-18).

The perfect keeping of the perfect Law did not keep the bands of the wicked away, nor from their insidious activity, but it did give a comfort that nothing else could give (Ps. 119:52).

The idea that enough faith and confession of the Word will stifle all Satanic activity is not Scriptural. Actually, great Faith must be tested greatly. The test is whether we will remain faithful to the Word or not!

NOTES

The *"wicked,"* which included the Pharisees, Sadducees, and Herodians, robbed Christ of everything imaginable. I speak of His rightful Place and Position, His Honor, Character, and Reputation. Nevertheless, He trusted in the Word to bring Him out. And so it did!

(62) "AT MIDNIGHT I WILL RISE TO GIVE THANKS UNTO YOU BECAUSE OF YOUR RIGHTEOUS JUDGMENTS."

The sense of this Psalm and this Passage is that neither suffering nor ease could weaken the affection of the heart of our Lord for the Scriptures.

Paul and Silas at Philippi illustrate these two Verses (Vss. 61-62). They were cruelly scourged by the wicked and painfully confined in the stock. But this treatment did not affect their belief in, nor chill their attachment to, the Scriptures of Truth. For at midnight they prayed and sang praises to God. Faith declared these sufferings to be righteous, while reason felt them to be pitiless (Acts 16:25-26).

(63) "I AM A COMPANION OF ALL THEM WHO FEAR YOU, AND OF THEM WHO KEEP YOUR PRECEPTS."

The criteria is *"Your Precepts,"* not man-made rules and regulations or traditions.

ACCEPTED BY GOD

The companions of the Messiah were not the religious leaders of His day. His friends were fishermen, tax collectors, and those whom He had delivered from the powers of darkness. They had simple love for the Word of God and for Him.

As then, so today, those who adhere to the Word of God will have little companionship with those of the religious hierarchy, whoever they may be. This only heightens the reproach (Ps. 119:39) because the world thinks and says that the only integrity it recognizes is that which accompanies religious leaders selected by man. Far better to have the acceptance of God and be rejected by the world (as well as an apostate Church) than be accepted by the world and the Church and be rejected by God.

(64) "THE EARTH, O LORD, IS FULL OF YOUR MERCY: TEACH ME YOUR STATUTES."

Once again, the petition is given by the Messiah to be taught the Bible by the Holy Spirit. Some 300 years later, Isaiah would prophesy, *"He wakens morning by morning, He wakens My ear to hear as the learned"* (Isa. 50:4).

Concerning this, Williams says, *"As the adversity of Verse 61 failed to turn our Lord away from the Bible, so the prosperity of Verse 64 did not weaken His fidelity to it either. On the contrary, the abundance of the Mercies experienced by Him intensified His love for God's Statutes. How often it is otherwise with men! Adversity on the one hand and prosperity on the other sap loyalty to the Sacred Book."* 66

TETH (65-72)
(The Ninth Chorus)

(65) "YOU HAVE DEALT WELL WITH YOUR SERVANT, O LORD, ACCORDING UNTO YOUR WORD."

The author of this Psalm refers to himself as *"Your servant,"* which is a familiar term of David.

GOD-BREATHED SCRIPTURES

Fidelity to *"Your Word"* ensures blessings from the Lord. He honors nothing else.

This stanza emphasizes the argument of the Psalm that God-breathed Scriptures make men wise unto Salvation, to teach, reprove, correct, discipline, perfect, and furnish them thoroughly unto every good work (II Tim. 3:16-17). The Scriptures, which are morally perfect, produce moral perfection when perfectly obeyed.

The Speaker here, as always, is the Messiah. He speaks, as we shall see, for Himself and for His people.

(66) "TEACH ME GOOD JUDGMENT AND KNOWLEDGE: FOR I HAVE BELIEVED YOUR COMMANDMENTS."

This Passage illustrates another petition to the Holy Spirit that we be taught by Him Personally.

UNDERSTANDING THE WORD

According to the Bible, immediately upon conversion, intelligence instantly increases. Upon fellowship with God, and after enjoying Spiritual Growth, which only can come by fidelity to the Word, *"Good Judgment and Knowledge"* are vastly increased. The more study and understanding of *"Your Commandments,"* the more *"Judgment and Knowledge."* Therefore, a constant perusal, study, and meditation on the Word should be our occupation.

As stated, every Believer should set aside a few minutes each day for the study of the Word. There is no more profitable occupation.

(67) "BEFORE I WAS AFFLICTED I WENT ASTRAY: BUT NOW HAVE I KEPT YOUR WORD."

Some lack understanding in applying this Passage, and other similar Scriptures, to the Messiah, because He never *"went astray."* But yet, it does apply to Him.

Once again, He speaks for Himself and for His people. This appears especially in Verses 67 and 71.

TRUE PRIEST AND ADVOCATE

These two Verses illustrate our Lord's Offices as the Sin Offering and the Peace Offering (Lev., Chpts. 4-8).

He takes the sins of His people upon Himself and transfers to them the perfection which belonged to Himself Alone. Thus, He makes their (and our) defections from God's Law His Own. As a True Priest and Advocate, He presents Himself as the guilty One, and, at the same time, credits us with the perfection of the obedience which only He Personally rendered to the Word of God.

One might say that, in the Whole Burnt Offering, Christ gives His Perfection to us. In the Sin Offering, He takes our sin unto Himself, and suffers its penalty. When that is done, Peace with God is once again established, and thereby celebrated by the Peace Offering, which all Believers were required to enjoy as a Feast. The Sin Offering has removed the sin, communion with God is re-established, and such presents a reason for rejoicing. And rightly so!

The word *"afflicted"* in this Verse means *"oppressed."* The words, *"Went astray,"* in the same Verse mean *"a straying one."*

Prior to Restoration, Israel is here described as continually erring from God's Law. But now they are pictured as observing *"Your*

Word" ("*I kept Your Word*").

This can be done only through Christ, Who kept the Word perfectly. This will be done by Israel in the coming Kingdom Age, but not before then!

(68) "YOU ARE GOOD, AND DO GOOD, TEACH ME YOUR STATUTES."

Again, the Holy Spirit is implored to *"teach Me."* That which He teaches will be *"Your Statutes."*

THE STATUTES OF GOD

The Statutes of God fill the Earth with goodness. He does good, and is Good (Acts 10:38); consequently, His Word is good. His Actions accord with the Promises and engagements of His Word; obedience to His Government, as revealed in His Commands, secures intelligence and a right judgment in the duties and responsibilities of life.

(69) "THE PROUD HAVE FORGED A LIE AGAINST ME: BUT I WILL KEEP YOUR PRECEPTS WITH MY WHOLE HEART."

The hatred of the proud against the lover of the Bible makes the Bible more precious to the meek.

KEEPING THE PRECEPTS

The Pharisees accused the Lord of breaking the Commandments, because He healed on the Sabbath Day. They forged that lie on the Devil's anvil. However, they were disqualified as judges because they neither knew nor understood His Word.

Religious Pharisees enjoy condemning others when, if they knew the Word, they would not condemn at all (Mat. 7:1-5).

(70) "THEIR HEART IS AS FAT AS GREASE; BUT I DELIGHT IN YOUR LAW."

The phrase, *"As fat as grease,"* pertains to that which is insensible and stupid. Such a heart is incompetent to judge the Commandments of God. It means that the Pharisees, and others similar, had filled their hearts with that which was other than the Word of God. The Messiah could say, that far from breaking the Law, He delighted in keeping the Law, which He always did, not failing even once.

(71) "IT IS GOOD FOR ME THAT I HAVE BEEN AFFLICTED; THAT I MIGHT LEARN YOUR STATUTES."

NOTES

The writer of Hebrews says, *"Yet learned He obedience by the things which He suffered"* (Heb. 5:8).

This does not mean that He learned to be obedient. For had that been the case, that would mean that He had been disobedient, which He never was. It simply means that He learned the principle of obedience; and He learned it through chastening and discipline. Such are helpful Bible teachers.

(72) "THE LAW OF YOUR MOUTH IS BETTER UNTO ME THAN THOUSANDS OF GOLD AND SILVER."

The possession and understanding of the Scriptures proclaim greater wealth than all the treasure the world contains. This powerful Truth, as illustrated in this Verse, is little understood, or even believed, by the majority of those who call themselves *"Christians."* Nevertheless, it is true!

JOD (73-80)
(The Tenth Chorus)

(73) "YOUR HANDS HAVE MADE ME AND FASHIONED ME: GIVE ME UNDERSTANDING, THAT I MAY LEARN YOUR COMMANDMENTS."

The words given in this Psalm certainly could apply to the writer, whether David or another. However, the True Speaker is the Greater Son of David, and the words apply to Him in perfection, as they apply to others of necessity only in part.

THE LEARNING OF THE COMMANDMENTS

Christ's human life of dependence on God and affection for His Word shines forth in every Verse of this stanza. He returns thanks for the Body that God prepared Him (Heb. 10:5), a Body, incidentally, which was prepared for Sacrifice; and, as Man, He expresses His dependence on God to interpret the Scriptures. His thanks to God concerning such pertains to the Incarnation.

This 119th Psalm is the longest Chapter in the Bible. It is given over entirely to expressing the glory, the wonder, the magnificence, and the fidelity of the Word of God. That the Holy Spirit would devote the longest Chapter in the Bible exclusively to the

Word of God lets us know the value that God places on His Word. We must not allow that to be lost on us.

That's the reason that we say that every Believer should make the Bible a lifelong study. The Bible is the road map for life. There is no other.

TRANSLATIONS

I believe Satan presently is making his greatest attack ever against the Word of God. However, he is doing it in a different way than ever before.

Instead of attacking the Word of God frontally, as he oftentimes has in the past, he is simply attacking it today by perverting it. I speak of the paraphrases which claim to be Bibles, but really aren't, such as The Message Bible.

Let the Reader understand the following:

If the Bible from which you study is not a word-for-word translation, such as the King James Version, and a few others similar, then what you are studying is not a Bible, but only some religious thoughts. In other words, if it's not a word-for-word translation, then it's not the Word of God.

Due to the fact that no original Texts of the Word of God remain, every single Bible which is truly a Bible actually is a translation.

The Bible originally was written in Hebrew (Old Testament) and Greek (New Testament). Despite the fact that there are no original Texts in existence today, there are tens of thousands of copies of the Word of God which come down to us presently, some going back not too very far removed from the original Texts. I speak of the Dead Sea Scrolls, and other such copies.

Scholarship states that if but ten copies of the original are available, then such copies are judged to be authentic. As stated, there are tens of thousands of copies of the various Books of the Bible available presently.

At any rate, the Believer should make doubly certain that his Bible is a word-for-word translation, such as the King James Version.

(74) "THEY WHO FEAR YOU WILL BE GLAD WHEN THEY SEE ME; BECAUSE I HAVE HOPED IN YOUR WORD."

This is the same Truth as stated in Matthew 10:40, *"He who receives you receives Me, and he who receives Me receives Him Who sent Me."*

THE TRUSTWORTHINESS OF THE SCRIPTURES

Our Lord's affection for and reliance on the Word of God and the consequent and resultant blessings cause those who worship God to rejoice when they look upon Him. His experience of the trustworthiness of the Scriptures heartens His Disciples; and when, by and by, we see Him by sight, we will indeed be glad! We will then witness the glories which will be given to Him because He perfectly loved and obeyed the Law of God.

(75) "I KNOW, O LORD, THAT YOUR JUDGMENTS ARE RIGHT, AND THAT YOU IN FAITHFULNESS HAVE AFFLICTED ME."

In the most strict interpretation, this Passage applies to Christ in His Incarnation.

AFFLICTION

The word *"afflicted"* has relation to His First Advent in His great Humility. He was poor and needy and acquainted with grief; but, far from murmuring at this design of His Father's Will or chilled in His Affection for His Scriptures, He clung to them the more as being faithful to Him, and He admired the righteousness of their Judgments.

This also is the place and position to which the Holy Spirit strives to bring us. Christ is our Example.

It is hard for the modern Believer in the present spiritual climate to understand the need for *"affliction"* and the need for what is thought of as severe Judgments; however, such is needed in the lives of all Christians. Such produces *"gold tried in the fire"* (Rev. 3:18).

(76) "LET, I PRAY YOU, YOUR MERCIFUL KINDNESS BE FOR MY COMFORT, ACCORDING TO YOUR WORD UNTO YOUR SERVANT."

The Messiah does not pray for the removal of these afflictions, but instead for the enjoyment of compensating comforts, but only such comforts as accord with God's Word. Many Christians are praying for certain *"afflictions"* to be removed, when, in fact, they either were placed or allowed by the Holy

Spirit, and, as such, cannot be moved.

Paul said that he *"besought the Lord thrice, that it might depart from me."* The Lord did not do such, but gave *"Grace sufficient"* (II Cor. 12:8-9).

(77) "LET YOUR TENDER MERCIES COME UNTO ME, THAT I MAY LIVE: FOR YOUR LAW IS MY DELIGHT."

God's tender mercies and the delights of His Law were life itself to our Saviour. *"Delight"* in the Hebrew Text stands in the plural number and, therefore, means *"many delights"* or *"supreme delight."*

The sense of the Verse is, that with the *"affliction"* (Vs. 75), God will send *"comfort"* which consists of *"tender mercies."*

(78) "LET THE PROUD BE ASHAMED; FOR THEY DEALT PERVERSELY WITH ME WITHOUT A CAUSE: BUT I WILL MEDITATE IN YOUR PRECEPTS."

His enemies accused Him and hated Him *"without a cause"* (Jn. 15:25), but He, in His Love, Saved sinners *"without a cause"* (Rom. 3:24).

THE PROUD WILL BE PUT TO SHAME

This Verse plus the next may be read in the future tense, as in Hebrew. They predict that the proud shall be put to shame; that those who worship God shall turn to the Messiah in order to learn the Divine Testimonies, and that Christ shall never be put to shame because His Heart was sound in the Statutes of Jehovah.

The unjust and contemptuous conduct of the proud Pharisees toward Him did not embitter His Spirit. The only effect was to dispose Him more than ever to meditation in the Scriptures. In such action, His people should imitate Him!

What a comfort and joy for us from Christ, our Example. His defense against these proud religious leaders was meditation in *"Your Precepts."*

The *"proud"* who *"dealt perversely with Him without a cause"* were not removed. They were allowed to remain in their perfidious slander. His shelter from their constant attacks was in the Word, just as our shelter is in the Word.

(79) "LET THOSE WHO FEAR YOU

NOTES

TURN UNTO ME, AND THOSE WHO HAVE KNOWN YOUR TESTIMONIES."

As then, so now, the decision has to be made either to follow *"the proud"* or *"turn unto Me"* — Christ.

THE TRUE CHURCH AND THE APOSTATE CHURCH

In Verses 78 and 79, we have the specter of institutionalized religion versus the pureness of the Word ensconced in Christ. The Word is even placed above the Name of the Messiah (Ps. 138:2). Those who feared God turned to the Messiah; those who did not fear God turned to *"the proud"* (Pharisees).

It is amazing how the Holy Spirit places both institutionalized religion and Christ in a juxtaposition (He contrasts them). Ideally, they were to have been the same, as most people think of the Church and Christ. While it is correct that the True Body of Christ is the same as Christ, still, the great majority of that which is called *"Church"* is apostate, and actually is the enemy of Christ.

So the Believer has to accept one or the other. He cannot accept both!

(80) "LET MY HEART BE SOUND IN YOUR STATUTES; THAT I BE NOT ASHAMED."

The initial acrostic letter in this stanza (*"Jod"*) is the smallest in the Hebrew alphabet. The Messiah Himself mentions it in Matthew 5:18. A *"tittle"* is an ornamental mark set over a Hebrew letter.

The plea of this Verse is that we not stray from the Word of the Lord, and that our heart will be sound only as it is properly grounded in the Word.

CAPH (81-88)
(The Eleventh Chorus)

(81) "MY SOUL FAINTS FOR YOUR SALVATION: BUT I HOPE IN YOUR WORD."

No man who longs for and faints for Salvation from God will go unheard (Mat. 5:6).

TESTING

This chorus of eight Verses serves as sharp tests to weaken the Messiah's affection for and confidence in the Scriptures. The tests fail to weaken Him and help make His Faith more manifest in them, and also serve to teach Him to trust in their Author.

The first four Verses of this stanza concern testing at the Hands of God; the second four, testing at the hands of man.

The Messiah is saying, *"My Soul faints for Your Salvation from trouble"* and *"My Eyes faint with desire for Your Word"* — in other words, the fulfillment of its Promises.

In times of great tests, it often seems as though such will never end, and God has hidden His Face. At these times, the Great Promises of God seem to be placed on hold, so the Messiah will cry for the Word of God to hasten its fulfillment in victory.

The phrase, *"I hope in Your Word,"* means *"I have hoped, I am hoping, and I will ever hope in Your Word"* — that is, *"I will persist in believing in the reality and certitude of its Promises."*

(82) "MY EYES FAIL FOR YOUR WORD, SAYING, WHEN WILL YOU COMFORT ME?"

The first part of this Scripture says, *"I will not stop looking for the fulfillment of Your Word and, in fact, I will, if necessary, look until I go blind."* This expresses the type of faith and trust that the Messiah had in the Word of God. It is the type of trust that we should have, as well.

The question concerning *"comfort"* is not asked from the position of futility, but from the position of total trust, knowing that *"comfort"* will come, but not knowing exactly when.

(83) "FOR I AM BECOME LIKE A BOTTLE IN THE SMOKE; YET DO I NOT FORGET YOUR STATUTES."

Our Lord was under a constant burden of sorrow that perpetually rested on Him. This was prefigured by the outermost covering of the Tabernacle in the wilderness. It had no beauty that it should be desired, but it veiled beauties unspeakable and full of glory.

THE STATUTES OF THE LORD

The phrase, *"For I am become like a bottle in the smoke,"* pertains to Israel's rejection of Christ and the constant persecution heaped upon Him by the Pharisees. His only strength, hope, defense, and that which He could totally depend on was *"Your Statutes."*

What a lesson for us today! As the Word was Christ's stay, it is our stay as well. But tragically, the far greater majority of the Church opts for humanistic psychology, psychoanalysis, pastoral counseling (most of which is psychology), all man-devised, and consequently of no help whatsoever, actually harmful.

The bottles of ancient times actually were made out of skins. They were placed over a fire and the smoke soon parched them until the skin was hard and shriveled. This represented what Christ was going through concerning His mental state, regarding the spiritual opposition by both Satan and the Pharisees.

(84) "HOW MANY ARE THE DAYS OF YOUR SERVANT? WHEN WILL YOU EXECUTE JUDGMENT ON THEM WHO PERSECUTE ME?"

The words, *"How many,"* are a form of speech meaning *"few are."*

Christ, as Lord, could at any moment have destroyed His persecutors, but, as Man, He would not take vengeance into His Own Hands, for vengeance belongs unto God (Rom. 12:19).

Likewise, no Christian should lift a hand to wreak vengeance on tormentors or persecutors even if the occasion presents itself. Since Christ is our Example, we must leave it to God.

(85) "THE PROUD HAVE DUG PITS FOR ME, WHICH ARE NOT AFTER YOUR LAW."

The closer one is to the Word, there is more humility; the further away from the Word, more self-righteousness.

PRIDE

The *"proud"* are the self-righteous Pharisees. The Fifteenth Chapter of Matthew records some of the pits that the proud dug for Him. They professed zeal for God's Law, but He, knowing their hearts, could truthfully say, *"They are not after Your Law."* That is, their questions were not in harmony with the Scriptures and, in fact, showed their ignorance of the Scriptures.

All self-righteousness, which is a product of pride, is caused by a departure from the Bible; consequently, Church rules and regulations not in harmony with the Word of God breed self-righteousness. So do all philosophies, doctrines, and teachings that do not line up with the Word of God, hence, the problem with most of modern Christianity.

(86) "ALL YOUR COMMANDMENTS ARE FAITHFUL: THEY PERSECUTE ME WRONGFULLY; HELP THOU ME."

The sense of the first part of this Passage is that even though God did not deem it desirable to lift the persecution, still, the Word of God (Commandments) would see Him through.

PERSECUTION

The constant claim of the Pharisees was that Jesus broke the Law. While He did break their man-made laws, He never broke the Law of God, of which He actually was the Author, but rather He fulfilled it.

The four words, *"They persecute Me wrongfully,"* have caused the spilling of more blood than possibly any four words in history. Religious men are fond of making laws, edicts, rules, regulations, by-laws, and stipulations which have no foundation in the Word of God. They also are very fond of forcing men to obey these man-made laws. If men do not do so, persecution always arises. As the self-righteous persecuted Christ, they have always done the same to True Believers through the centuries, and do the same today.

Denominations are fond of making rules that have no foundation in Scripture. They are fond of creating a man-made morality, integrity, and holiness. It appears good to the world and to the majority of the Church, but it is that which God will not recognize because it adds to or takes away from His Word. Godly men are to resist even to the death.

As previously stated, the Lord would not lift a hand to use His Mighty Power against His persecutors, but would look to the Word and cry to the Father, *"Help Thou Me."* That is our Example!

(87) "THEY HAD ALMOST CONSUMED ME UPON EARTH; BUT I FORSOOK NOT YOUR PRECEPTS."

"Almost" means *"quickly."* The sense of the Verse is: *"They wish to quickly make an end of Me."*

THE PROUD

The persecution by *"the proud"* (Pharisees) demanded that Christ conform to their ways. They would continue their relentless attacks trying to force Him to do so. Trumpeting loudly their claims of upholding the Law of God, they, in fact, had long since forsaken such, instituting their own man-made law. The Messiah, despite their persecution and torment, would not deviate one iota from *"Your Precepts."*

The faith of the Saint in anchored in the Word. Satan's relentless attack is to move us away from the Word, and He oftentimes (actually most of the time) uses religious, self-righteous men to carry out his aims. As Christ held tenaciously to *"Your Precepts,"* we also, and at all costs, are to do the same.

(88) "QUICKEN ME AFTER YOUR LOVINGKINDNESS; SO SHALL I KEEP THE TESTIMONY OF YOUR MOUTH."

The word *"quicken"* means *"make alive."*

CHRIST, OUR EXAMPLE

The sense of this Verse is that the Messiah is asking the Father to keep Him alive as *"the proud"* attempted to kill Him. The Father answered His Prayer despite the relentless efforts of the Pharisees until the appointed time of Calvary.

It also means that despite the persecution, and during the persecution, the Lord continued to show *"lovingkindness"* to the Messiah, thereby making Him alive spiritually at all times. This was done because the Messiah did not depart from *"the Testimony of Your Mouth."*

Let the Bible lover ever understand: As Christ handled such things, we are to do likewise. As Christ received the benefits of the Word despite the heavy persecution that was not lifted, we too shall receive *"Your Lovingkindness"* only if we too cling to the Word.

CHRIST AS THE MAN

It is difficult for the Reader to grasp the fact that Christ sought the Will of God and prayed to His Heavenly Father, exactly as we do. The reason this is strange to us is because it is difficult for us to separate the Man Christ Jesus from Christ Jesus as Deity.

We must understand that even though Christ relinquished the expression of His Deity, He never lost possession of His Deity, meaning He never ceased to be God. However, He never used His Powers of Deity, not even one time, to do anything; He did everything as a Man anointed and helped by the Holy Spirit (Lk. 4:18-19).

As God, our Lord needed no anointing to do anything; however, as Man, The Man Christ Jesus, He most definitely needed the anointing, exactly as we do.

We also must understand that Christ was not half-Man and half-God. He was Very Man and Very God, meaning totally Man and totally God.

When He came to this Earth, however, He came as a Man, functioned as a Man, thought as a Man, and suffered as a Man. This had to be if He was to be the *"Last Adam"* and the *"Second Man"* (I Cor. 15:45, 47). He had to hurt as we hurt, seek as we seek, ask as we ask, trust as we trust. That's the reason for these prayers that He prayed.

LAMED (89-96)
(The Twelfth Chorus)

(89) "FOREVER, O LORD, YOUR WORD IS SETTLED IN HEAVEN."

God's Word is eternal. Its plan for man is eternal. It is already settled in Heaven and will be carried out on Earth to the letter. This is why we may know in infinite detail the program of God from eternity past into all eternity future (Acts 15:18; Eph. 2:7; 3:11).

The word *"settled"* means that it stands fast without change, as the Plan of God is declared to be (Mat. 24:35; Mk. 13:31; I Pet. 1:23-25).

THE GUARANTEE OF THE WORD

In this Eighty-ninth Verse, the Messiah sings of the unshakeable Rock, the Word of God, to which He clung, and from which all the tests of the previous stanza failed to detach Him. He declares that Rock to be firm, infinite, and eternal.

This Verse could very well read, *"O Jehovah, You are forever; Your Word is settled in Heaven."*

Amid the changes and trials of Earth, the eternal and unchanging Word of God is a priceless possession. The Messiah Himself said that Heaven and Earth would pass away, but His Word would never pass away, for it is settled in Heaven where nothing can reach or shake it. Hence, the unceasing efforts of its enemies to corrupt or destroy it have failed, and will fail.

The Devil's hammers beat upon the anvil of God's Word; the hammers break; the anvil remains.

As an incidental, the field of archaeology has an unwritten rule, or at least they once did. It is as follows:

"If any objects are unearthed in excavations that seem to contradict the Bible, they are to be laid aside with no comment, because every time in the past that such has happened, future excavations have always proved the Bible to be true."

(Many years ago, archaeologists made premature announcements concerning things that seemed to contradict the Bible. Every time future excavations proved such to be wrong. Consequently, the unwritten rule quoted above was instituted.)

(90) "YOUR FAITHFULNESS IS UNTO ALL GENERATIONS: YOU HAVE ESTABLISHED THE EARTH, AND IT ABIDES."

In the Eighty-sixth Verse it says, *"All Your Commandments are faithful."* In this Passage, this *"faithfulness"* extends forever.

GOD UPHOLDS HIS WORD

All man-made religious laws, rules, and regulations are constantly changing. In other words, they *"wiggle"* (that is, the same laws apply to some and not to others). God's Word does not change!

The sense of this Verse is that as God establishes and upholds His Creation (the Earth and the Universe), likewise, He upholds His Word. Actually, it is His Word that upholds His Creation, which makes His Word far greater than His Creation.

Concerning Creation, the Scripture says, *"Through Faith we understand that the worlds were framed by the Word of God, so that things which are seen were not made of things which do appear"* (Heb. 11:3).

This means that God began with nothing, thereby speaking into existence the things needed to create the universe.

(91) "THEY CONTINUE THIS DAY ACCORDING TO YOUR ORDINANCES: FOR ALL ARE YOUR SERVANTS."

It is God's Word that spoke all things into existence, and it is God's Word that thereby upholds all things. This shows us how great His Word actually is. The Scripture says, *"And God said, Let there be Light: and there was Light"* (Gen. 1:3).

Astronomers tell us that light continues to expand at the rate of 186,000 miles a second, which is the speed of light. This means that it has continued to expand out into the universe at this particular rate from the moment that God spoke it into existence.

The Bible does not merely <u>contain</u> the Word of God; the Bible <u>is</u> the Word of God. Knowing and understanding this, we should make the Bible a lifelong study in order that we may learn its contents.

Sadly and regrettably, the world pays it no attention at all. Sadder still, most Believers little pay attention to the Bible as they should.

Every Believer should read the Bible through at least once every year, and, if the truth be known, even more often. If the Believer truly wants to understand the Word, the Lord will see that such a desire is fulfilled.

(I strongly recommend that the Reader secure THE EXPOSITOR'S STUDY BIBLE. I personally feel that this Bible [King James Version] will open up the Scriptures to you as nothing that has ever been placed in your hands. There is not another Study Bible in the world today, we think, that can even remotely compare with this Bible and the study tools it provides.)

(92) "UNLESS YOUR LAW HAD BEEN MY DELIGHTS, I SHOULD THEN HAVE PERISHED IN MY AFFLICTION."

"So then Faith comes by hearing (it is the publication of the Gospel which produces Faith in it), *and hearing by the Word of God.* (Faith does not come by simply hearing just anything, but rather by hearing God's Word and believing that Word)" (Rom. 10:17).

THE DELIGHT OF THE WORD OF GOD

God's Law was the Messiah's *"delights,"* meaning the supreme joy of His Heart.

The verb *"to perish"* has many meanings in Hebrew. Here it suggests that the Messiah's sinless Body would have sunk underneath the pressure of severe suffering — for example, in the Garden of Gethsemane — but He was kept alive by resting on the Words of Scripture.

(93) "I WILL NEVER FORGET YOUR PRECEPTS: FOR WITH THEM YOU HAVE QUICKENED ME."

The Messiah gives all the credit to the Bible for victory, sustenance, power, and for keeping Him alive — *"quickened Me."*

If David wrote this Psalm (or whoever), his feelings were the same. Ours should be the same as well.

(94) "I AM YOURS, SAVE ME; FOR I HAVE SOUGHT YOUR PRECEPTS."

The word *"save"* signifies preservation through trial and opposition.

"I have sought" includes *"I am seeking and will continue to seek."*

This refers to seeking answers to questions, or seeking the fulfillment of Promises.

(95) "THE WICKED HAVE WAITED FOR ME TO DESTROY ME: BUT I WILL CONSIDER YOUR TESTIMONIES."

As in the previous stanza, so here man's hatred fails to awaken in His Heart any doubt as to the faithfulness of God's Word and the value of its Promises.

THE PROTECTION OF THE WORD

"The wicked" in the Messiah's day referred to the Pharisees. Regrettably, *"Phariseeism"* did not die with the death of these particular Pharisees. The breed abounds today and is ensconced as *"spiritual wickedness in high places."* The Believer's greatest danger always will come from this source.

Contrary to popular belief, Satan's greatest attacks do not come from *"sins of passion,"* such as alcohol, drugs, or immorality, as vile as those sins might be, but rather from *"sins of pride"* (Vs. 78).

Down through the ages, the far greater majority of the human family has died lost because *"the wicked"* destroyed them. *"The wicked"* are *"false apostles, deceitful workers, and Satan's ministers"* (II Cor. 11:12-15).

(96) "I HAVE SEEN AN END OF ALL PERFECTION: BUT YOUR COMMANDMENT IS EXCEEDING BROAD."

This Verse means that there is an end or boundary to the extent of God's Work in

Creation, but no boundary to His Word in Revelation — it is infinite and eternal. There is no end to that Commandment. The last line may read: *"Exceedingly spacious is Your Commandment."* As spacious as are the heavens and the Earth — and even an elemental study of astronomy overwhelms the mind with the vast distances in space — yet the Bible exceeds it all in dimension.

MEM (97-104)
(The Thirteenth Chorus)

(97) "O HOW I LOVE YOUR LAW! IT IS MY MEDITATION ALL THE DAY."

Even though all the Passages in this Psalm refer to the Messiah and His Love for God's Word, still, the Holy Spirit lifts the Greater Son of David to a higher exclamation in this thirteenth Chorus than all previously given. Once again we are drawn to His constant *"meditation."*

MEDITATION

There is a hill that is shaped like a horseshoe that somewhat surrounds Nazareth, the boyhood home of Christ. (A part of this hill presently has been removed due to mining operations.)

I personally have stood on the extreme northwestern summit of this hill (the place where the city fathers determined to kill Christ [Lk. 4:28-30]). As one stands there with his back to Nazareth and looks across the valley of Megiddo, one can see Mount Gilboa where Saul and Jonathan were killed by the Philistines. In the far distance, it is even possible to see Mount Carmel, where Elijah called fire down from Heaven. Immediately beside this hill is the Mount that is thought to be the Mount of Transfiguration.

Christ, as a boy, must have stood many times at that very place overlooking these places of Biblical interest. It would have been a place of privacy and solitude. In those days, His Bible would have been scrolls of the Pentateuch, the Prophets, and the Wisdom Books, such as the Psalms (Genesis — Malachi).

With some imagination, it is not difficult to see Him as a Boy holding one or more of the Scrolls in His hands, memorizing its Texts, as well as meditating on its Precepts.

NOTES

I wonder how old He was when He looked at the words of this very Verse and realized that the pronoun *"I"* actually was Himself! How many hours did He spend in this and other secluded spots to meditate daily and even nightly on the Word of God? (Ps. 1:1-2).

JESUS AS A BOY

As a boy, He helped His foster father Joseph as a carpenter. In His late teens and throughout his twenties, He, no doubt, had hewn much of the material that had gone into some of the furniture and houses in the immediate vicinity. In fact, Josephus, the great Jewish historian, said that Jesus, as a carpenter, made many things, but His specialty was plow-yokes.

Nazareth could hardly grasp the fact that the One they called the carpenter's son, and a peasant at that, could be the Messiah. But He was!

There was no excuse whatsoever for the religious hierarchy of Israel not to know that He was the Messiah. Daniel had prophesied the approximate time that He would come (Dan. 9:24-26). As well, the genealogy of every family in Israel was kept in the Temple in Jerusalem. It would have been very simple for these religious leaders to follow the lineage of David through whom the Messiah would come (II Sam. 7:7).

They easily could follow the lineage to Joseph, who would have been king had the Davidic lineage continued. Jesus was Joseph's firstborn, although not fathered by Him, but decreed by the Holy Spirit (Lk. 1:26-33). Isaiah had prophesied His Birth by the Virgin (Isa. 7:14), and the Prophet Micah had foretold that He would be born in Bethlehem (Mic. 5:2). So there was no excuse for Israel not knowing Who He was!

(98) "YOU THROUGH YOUR COMMANDMENTS HAVE MADE ME WISER THAN MY ENEMIES: FOR THEY ARE EVER WITH ME."

How could our Lord have *"enemies"*?

His Perfect Life was a rebuke to their imperfect lives. His fidelity to the Bible was a rebuke to their man-made rules and regulations. They hated Him because He kept God's Commandments and they did not, even though they loudly professed that they did.

He also was wiser than they were because God's Law was with Him, but not with them. So they hated Him without a cause.

(99) "I HAVE MORE UNDERSTANDING THAN ALL MY TEACHERS: FOR YOUR TESTIMONIES ARE MY MEDITATION."

In Jesus' day, the synagogue was the center of all teaching, instruction, and training. The Law and the Prophets were the textbooks (the Scrolls).

THE BIBLE

Considering His constant meditation on the Word, what must the reaction have been of His teachers? He would testify Himself that even as a child He knew more than they (Lk. 2:40-49).

Every servant of God should love the Bible to the extent of meditating on it all the day, but only One Servant of Jehovah ever lived Who could truthfully make the declaration of these Verses.

In Jesus' time, all little boys, beginning at the age of eight, had to commit to memory large portions of the Law of Moses. In some cases, the Book of Leviticus was completely memorized. How much Jesus committed to memory (and thereby had instant recall) is not known; however, His familiarity with the entire Bible (Genesis — Malachi) excelled all others by far!

(100) "I UNDERSTAND MORE THAN THE ANCIENTS, BECAUSE I KEEP YOUR PRECEPTS."

The claim is made, accurately so, that He understood more about God and His Word than even Moses, David, Isaiah, Jeremiah, Ezekiel, or Daniel — all because of the knowledge of and the keeping of *"Your Precepts."*

All of these great men kept the Law of God sometimes; our Lord kept each and every Word of the Bible perfectly at all times.

(101) "I HAVE REFRAINED MY FEET FROM EVERY EVIL WAY, THAT I MIGHT KEEP YOUR WORD."

If David wrote these words, he would have been moved upon by the Holy Spirit to do so. It would pertain solely to the Messiah, but also would include David and all others who trust in Christ as their Saviour. No human being, even the most holy, other than Christ can say that he has kept his feet *"from every evil way."* And yet such glorious accomplishment is attributed to all who trust that Great Name.

How?

Christ entered into our failure, took our place, and became our Substitute so that we may enter into His Perfection; therefore, by Faith, we can say such, knowing that God, because of believing Faith, will without fail attribute such to us, all because of Christ and what He did for us at the Cross.

The Word of God will expunge *"every evil way."*

(102) "I HAVE NOT DEPARTED FROM YOUR JUDGMENTS: FOR YOU HAVE TAUGHT ME."

In previous Choruses of this One hundred and Nineteenth Psalm, we have witnessed the petition for the Holy Spirit to serve as Teacher. We have here the explanation that the petition was heard and granted, *"For You have taught Me."*

(103) "HOW SWEET ARE YOUR WORDS UNTO MY TASTE! YEA, SWEETER THAN HONEY TO MY MOUTH!"

Our Lord declares that the Word instructed Him about the moral character of every course of conduct and taught Him so effectively that He did not swerve from any path approved by the Divine Judgment.

THE SWEETNESS OF THE WORD OF GOD

In the previous stanza, the Messiah sang of the strength of God's Word; here He sings of its sweetness. As well, He testifies that this sweetness is filled with witness. Thus is the lesson taught about the nature and effect of Inspiration. Its nature is sweetness; its effect, wisdom. The Messiah here joyfully exclaims how sweet to His Palate and how precious to His Heart is the Law of God.

(104) "THROUGH YOUR PRECEPTS I GET UNDERSTANDING: THEREFORE I HATE EVERY FALSE WAY."

The True Word always leads to God.

FALSE WAYS

This stanza closes with the statement that the wisdom that flows from the Scriptures destroys all desire for false teaching; however, we must ever remember that the Word of God and the Cross of Christ are basically one and the same. In fact, the story of the Bible is the Story of *"Jesus Christ and Him Crucified"* (I Cor. 1:23).

The Believer, therefore, must understand the Cross; by that, we refer to the understanding that everything we receive from the Lord is all made possible by Christ as the Source and the Cross as the Means. Once that is understood and our faith is placed firmly and squarely in the Cross of Christ, and we do not allow it to be moved, every *"false way"* will become obvious and apparent. In fact, the only way that the Believer can escape false doctrine, which is Satan's greatest effort, is for the Believer to deny Himself, which speaks of denying his own strength and ability, and then to take up the Cross daily and follow Christ (Lk. 9:23).

Once the Cross is properly understood, there will be an inbred hatred for false teaching, which equally filled the Messiah's heart along with His great Love for the pure Word. Likewise, His followers must follow in His path.

As stated, the True Word leads to God. False ways lead to eternal darkness and to an eternal hatred for God and His Word. Be he Preacher or otherwise, the Believer who does not hate every false way truly does not love *"Your Word."*

NUN (105-112)
(The Fourteenth Chorus)

(105) "YOUR WORD IS A LAMP UNTO MY FEET, AND A LIGHT UNTO MY PATH."

The only *"Lamp"* in the world that produces *"Light"* is the Bible. In the first two Verses, the Messiah speaks of the Bible as a Light and declares His Purpose to follow it. In the last two Verses (111-112), He speaks of it as a heritage, in reality, a treasure, and professes His determination to obey it.

THE LAMP AND THE LIGHT

I have made the following statement repeatedly:

"The Bible is the only revealed Truth in the world today, and ever has been."

That is quite startling to most people, even Christians. The statement means that all else is darkness and produces no light.

NOTES

Two things are emphasized in this Verse, *"feet"* and *"path."* The pilgrim's feet are pictured on a path which alone can find its way through the pitfalls, traps, ensnarements, and obstacles that line the way. However, even though the path is there, still, it cannot be safely trod unless the *"Lamp" "lights"* the *"Path."* The *"Lamp"* is the Bible.

It is Satan's business to substitute other lamps. He is amazingly successful. The Church is fraught with such. Preachers by the tens of thousands espouse things that seem good to the carnal ear, but they are not Gospel and consequently provide no Light. It is the business of the Preacher of the Gospel to hold up the *"Lamp"* and nothing else.

(106) "I HAVE SWORN, AND I WILL PERFORM IT, THAT I WILL KEEP YOUR RIGHTEOUS JUDGMENTS."

The Messiah swore to uphold God's Word.

FIDELITY TO THE WORD

The Messiah's Fidelity was to the Bible, which guarantees the wrath not only of Satan, but also of man, and especially of an apostate Church. His Fidelity was to the Bible, and not to the myriad rules and regulations made up by the Pharisees.

The Messiah had sworn His Fidelity to the Word, and by no less than Himself. In other words, everything hinges on the Word of God. It never will be deviated from. (The word *"swear"* means to take an oath — Hebrews 6:13, 17.) The great source of contention in Christianity is whether we should or should not abide by the Bible. That always has been the dividing line.

(107) "I AM AFFLICTED VERY MUCH: QUICKEN ME, O LORD, ACCORDING UNTO YOUR WORD."

The very purpose of afflictions is to drive us to the Word.

AFFLICTIONS

Even though the Path did lighten and gladden, still, it was a Path of affliction from God. Some modern doctrines have attempted to make the Path golden. It is not! It is a Path that is freighted with tests. The tests are from God. They are called *"afflictions."* They teach us trust, obedience, dependence, and thus, increase Spiritual Strength.

In this Passage, the Messiah also proclaims the Truth that the Lord will give Him Grace *"according unto Your Word."* So the afflictions are sent by the Lord, but victory and security are promised according to His Word.

(108) "ACCEPT, I BESEECH YOU, THE FREEWILL OFFERINGS OF MY MOUTH, O LORD, AND TEACH ME YOUR JUDGMENTS."

The *"freewill offerings"* spoken of here refer to *"The Sacrifice of Praise"* (Heb. 13:15).

This means that we are to offer praise even when the Path of Verse 105 seems difficult. The Lord has promised that if we do such, He will *"teach us His Judgments."*

Being repetitive, everything, irrespective of its course, is intended by God to pull us to the Word, ever to the Word. Once again the Messiah implores the Holy Spirit to *"teach Me Your Judgments."* The abundant repetition of this request should be a lesson to us as well!

(109) "MY SOUL IS CONTINUALLY IN MY HAND: YET DO I NOT FORGET YOUR LAW."

This Verse tells us that the Messiah's Strength, Security, and Protection was *"Your Law,"* that is, *"Your Word."*

SPIRITUAL WICKEDNESS IN HIGH PLACES

To have *"the life in the hand"* means to be in deadly danger. This danger was from the Pharisees, the religious hierarchy in Israel at that time. The danger for the Child of God is twofold:

1. From demon spirits in the world of spiritual darkness.

2. From the religious hierarchy of the apostate Church, which makes up the far greater majority of that which is called *"Christianity."*

Allow me to remind the Reader that it was not the drunks, gamblers, thieves, or harlots, as vile as their sins were, who nailed Christ to the tree, but it was the *"Church"* of that day. *"Spiritual wickedness in high places"* concerns itself with a powerful section of the world of Satanic darkness. A part of its function is *"religious hierarchy"* (Eph. 6:12), which almost all the time opposes that which is truly of the Lord.

(110) "THE WICKED HAVE LAID A SNARE FOR ME: YET I ERRED NOT FROM YOUR PRECEPTS."

These *"snares"* were laid by the Pharisees.

THE SNARE

The Pharisees attempted to ensnare Christ in His Speech that they might be able to accuse Him and, thereby, diminish His Popularity among the people. Their ultimate goal was to kill Him (Mat. 26:3-4). God permitted such in order that the Messiah might run to the Word for defense and protection. The Holy Spirit states through Him that He did not even one time err *"from Your Precepts."*

What an example!

This Passage also tells us that it is quite possible to err from the Word; actually the only One Who ever could say that He never erred from the Word was the Messiah. All others have erred many times; however, it is ever the task of the Holy Spirit to bring us back to the Word. If we allow the Holy Spirit to have His Way in our lives, He will accomplish this task (Jn. 16:13).

(111) "YOUR TESTIMONIES HAVE I TAKEN AS AN HERITAGE FOREVER: FOR THEY ARE THE REJOICING OF MY HEART."

Several things are said here by the Messiah:

1. The Bible was His Strength, Power, Security, Defense, and also His Offense.

2. The Bible was not only His present help, but, because it never changes, stands as His security forever.

3. In the midst of great tests, danger, and opposition by *"the wicked,"* the Word produced a *"rejoicing"* in His heart.

As such was the Messiah, such will be to us if we only will give fidelity to the Word as He did.

(112) "I HAVE INCLINED MY HEART TO PERFORM YOUR STATUTES ALWAYS, EVEN UNTO THE END."

A lamp is useless unless it is used; a treasure, valueless unless drawn upon. The heart rather than the head is to be exercised in Bible Study, and the sure result will be obedient action.

Jesus said, *"If a man love Me, he will keep My Words"* (Jn. 14:23). Such a man will find that Word to be a Lamp and a Light, a Treasure and a Joy in and on life's pathway.

SAMECH (113-120)
(The Fifteenth Chorus)

(113) "I HATE VAIN THOUGHTS: BUT YOUR LAW DO I LOVE."

This Chorus concerns false teachers and false doctrine.

FALSE TEACHING

The statement, *"I have vain thoughts,"* means *"I hate false teaching."* Satan's greatest effort is to twist the Word in the mouth of false teachers, thereby causing their followers to be pulled away from the Truth and the correct interpretation of the Bible. (The word *"vain"* means *"empty nothings."*)

The question constantly is asked, *"How can such be detected, inasmuch as all claim their interpretation to be true?"* Jesus alluded to these false teachers:

"Beware of false prophets, which come to you in sheep's clothing, but inwardly they are ravening wolves. Wherefore by their fruits you shall know them" (Mat. 7:15, 20).

Sadly, most Churches have no Moving, stirring, or Operation of the Holy Spirit in their services. This should let us know that He is not there. If He is not there, it is a sure sign that false teaching is being propagated from the pulpit.

Another sign of *"evil fruit"* is a lack of worship, or else false worship, of which much abounds. If God is worshipped, He must be worshipped in Spirit and in Truth (Jn. 4:24).

BIBLE WORSHIP

The Altar of Incense situated in the Tabernacle of old gives us an idea as to the worship which God will accept.

Two times a day, at the time of the morning Sacrifice (9 a.m.) and the evening Sacrifice (3 p.m.), coals of fire were brought from the Brazen Altar and placed on the Altar of Incense, with Incense poured over these coals, which produced a fragrance and smoke which filled the Holy Place.

The Altar of Incense is a type of the Intercession of Christ, all carried out presently, and all on our behalf (Heb. 7:25). In this Intercession also rests our petitions, our praying, our praise, and our worship.

As we have stated, these coals of fire came from the Brazen Altar, which was a type of the Crucifixion of Christ. The Priests were not allowed to bring coals of fire from any ignition other than the Brazen Altar, even under the penalty of death (Lev. 10:1-2).

All of this meant that all praise, petitions, and worship are totally dependent upon the Brazen Altar, which is a type of the Cross. In other words, if our praise and our worship are not centered directly in the Cross of Christ, then it is praise and worship that God never will accept. Regrettably, most praise and worship falls outside of the category of the Cross. In other words, it is not anchored in the Cross, which means it is not acceptable to God.

FALSE DOCTRINE AND THE CROSS

To be frank, the only protection against false doctrine is the Word of God, which refers to the Believer knowing and understanding the Word. If the Believer properly understands the Word, the Believer will properly understand the Cross at the same time (Jn. 1:1-3, 14, 29).

If the Cross of Christ is ridiculed or even ignored, the end result always will be false doctrine.

DOUBLE THOUGHTS

The word *"thoughts"* means *"double thoughts"* (James 1:8). The reference is doubtless to associating another god with Jehovah and thus setting up a double worship as in the past: for example, Jehovah and the golden calf; later, Jehovah and tradition; today, Jesus and Mary, or Jesus and Denominationalism, which includes anything that is added to Christ. But to Messiah as Man, as Abraham's Seed and the True Israel, the Law of God was supremely loveable.

(114) "YOU ARE MY HIDING PLACE AND MY SHIELD: I HOPE IN YOUR WORD."

The Law inspired His Confidence and its Author was His hiding Place and Shield.

Actually, it is impossible to separate the Word from the Giver of the Word. One cannot know the Word without knowing the Giver of the Word. Likewise, if one truly knows the Giver of the Word, he will make the Word his *"hiding place and shield."*

The word *"hope"* has a different connotation in the Bible than in its present use. Now it means *"maybe."* In the Bible, it means *"certainty,"* but without knowing the exact time of fruition.

(115) "DEPART FROM ME, YE EVILDOERS: FOR I WILL KEEP THE COMMANDMENTS OF MY GOD."

The choice then and the choice now is either man's ways or God's Ways. The Messiah labeled as *"evildoers"* all those who refused God's Ways. He was speaking of the Pharisees, but it also refers to all in all ages and times. False teaching leads into sin; consequently, false teachers are evildoers. Their efforts, however, only result in attaching the Messiah, if it were possible, more resolutely to the Commandments of God, as it should us.

(116) "UPHOLD ME ACCORDING UNTO YOUR WORD, THAT I MAY LIVE: AND LET ME NOT BE ASHAMED OF MY HOPE.

(117) "HOLD THOU ME UP, AND I SHALL BE SAFE: AND I WILL HAVE RESPECT UNTO YOUR STATUTES CONTINUALLY."

"Uphold Me" and *"hold Me up"* are noteworthy verbs in the Hebrew Text. They represent God's supporting the Believer from both above and from beneath — carried, and at the same time, held by the hand.

The absolute dependence on God and His Word characterizes Paul's statement, *"It is not I, but Christ, which lives in me"* (Gal. 2:20).

(118) "YOU HAVE TRODDEN DOWN ALL THEM WHO ERR FROM YOUR STATUTES: FOR THEIR DECEIT IS FALSEHOOD."

This Verse could be paraphrased: *"You have set at naught all them who err from Your Statutes, for their cunning efforts to turn Me from them have been in vain."*

Thus, the Messiah gives the Glory to God for the failure of these false teachers to detach Him from the Bible.

(119) "YOU PUT AWAY ALL THE WICKED OF THE EARTH LIKE DROSS: THEREFORE I LOVE YOUR TESTIMONIES.

(120) "MY FLESH TREMBLES FOR FEAR OF YOU; AND I AM AFRAID OF YOUR JUDGMENTS."

The appalling doom awaiting these false teachers causes the Messiah's Heart to love the sacred Book which predicts their destruction, while, at the same time, His sinless flesh shudders at the nature of that Judgment.

The statement is clear: All false teachers and false teaching ultimately will be doomed. Let this be a warning to all those in the Church who have substituted other things in place of the Bible, or who have twisted its Word for their own perfidious gain (I Tim. 6:5).

AIN (121-128)
(The Sixteenth Chorus)

(121) "I HAVE DONE JUDGMENT AND JUSTICE: LEAVE ME NOT TO MY OPPRESSORS."

Christ, being Perfect, affirms in this stanza the moral Perfection of the Bible and declares it to be His rule of life. Only the sinless Son of David could say that He practiced Judgment and Righteousness, and did so continuously. Consequently, the *"oppressors"* (Pharisees) could attack Him verbally and physically and ultimately kill Him, but could not in the least weaken His Faith in the Bible or His hold on God.

What an Example He is to us!

(122) "BE SURETY FOR YOUR SERVANT FOR GOOD: LET NOT THE PROUD OPPRESS ME."

God had only One Perfect Servant upon Earth. He had many servants, and thus He said, *"My servant Abraham," "My servant Moses,"* etc.; but of the Messiah, He said, *"My Servant."* It was not necessary to add the name Jesus; therefore, He says, *"Behold My Servant Whom I uphold."*

THE GUARANTEE

Here our Lord prays for deliverance from His detractors and bases His claim to be delivered from them on His integrity, as is outlined in the previous Verse, on His relationship to God, and on His loyalty to the Scriptures.

The word *"surety"* means *"a guarantee."* The guarantee of the Word was what the Messiah had, and it is what we also have.

"The proud" who oppressed Him were the Pharisees and religious leaders who had forsaken the Word of God. Christ's Perfect Life, based on the Perfect Word, was a constant rebuke to them, hence, the oppression.

Jehovah was the intervening surety between His Beloved Son and the proud oppressors. As Man, Christ was defenseless, hence, His prayer to God to become His Security and Guarantee.

(123) "MY EYES FAIL FOR YOUR SALVATION, AND FOR THE WORD OF YOUR RIGHTEOUSNESS."

As it is here used, the word *"fail"* does not mean to fail God, but rather expresses *"longing desire."* In other words, our Lord said, *"My eyes have a longing desire for Your Salvation. . . ."*

Christ was Righteousness, which means that He did not merely possess Righteousness. Therefore, He loved the Word of Righteousness (Jn. 16:10).

(124) "DEAL WITH YOUR SERVANT ACCORDING UNTO YOUR MERCY, AND TEACH ME YOUR STATUTES."

(125) "I AM YOUR SERVANT; GIVE ME UNDERSTANDING, THAT I MAY KNOW YOUR TESTIMONIES."

As the Incarnate One, He would use the words, *"Your Servant,"* setting an example for us regarding attitude. Yet He was His Son, as we are also, but by adoption (Rom. 8:15; Eph. 1:5).

THE LORD WILL TEACH US THE WORD

Twice in these two Verses the Messiah implores the Holy Spirit to teach Him the Word of God. In the Incarnate state, that is, as Man, He had to learn exactly as we do; He would, therefore, implore the Holy Spirit to teach Him. As Man, He would ask for *"Mercy,"* because He was the Second Man and the Last Adam, therefore, our Substitute (I Cor. 15:45, 47).

(126) "IT IS TIME FOR YOU, LORD, TO WORK: FOR THEY HAVE MADE VOID YOUR LAW."

The words, *"To work,"* mean *"to intervene."*

IT IS TIME FOR YOU, LORD, TO WORK

Concerning the Pharisees, Jesus said, *"Thus have you made the Commandment of God of none effect by your tradition."*

He called them *"hypocrites,"* and said, *"In vain they do worship Me, teaching for doctrines the commandments of men"* (Mat. 15:6-9).

Regrettably and sadly, America and Canada, as well as all the nations of the world, are *"making void Your Law."* In other words, they are forsaking the Bible.

The Bible is the only standard on which correct morality can be based. All else is vain. Sadder still, the Church has largely abandoned the Bible, and the nation has followed suit.

The Church is always a barometer. If it loses its moorings, so does the nation; therefore, the strength of this nation and any nation is *"God-called Preachers of the Gospel proclaiming the uncompromised Word."* Instead, most modern Preachers have only a *"form of Godliness, denying the power thereof"* (II Tim. 3:5). They spue forth psychology, philosophy, and other foolishness derived by man. But even in this very bleak atmosphere, Grace can abound if God's True Church (and there is a True Church!) will only believe and cry for revival. The Lord works best when the situation seems hopeless.

I realize that the Reader may conclude that this prayer of the Messiah was not answered. Quite the contrary! Even though religion nailed Him to the Tree, still, the Lord did work mightily. By His Death and Resurrection, man's eternal Redemption was purchased and consummated. Further, the Holy Spirit was sent to fill the hearts of men, which He now can do, because Christ atoned for all sin at the Cross of Calvary, and the terrible sin debt which hung over the heads of the human race thereby was lifted (Acts 2:4); that sin debt is removed for all who will believe (Jn. 3:16).

Thus began the greatest Move of God the world has ever known, which continues unto this hour.

Hallelujah!

God delighted in delivering Israel when such was hopelessly locked up in Pharaoh's prison. Likewise, He delighted in delivering the Hebrew children from the fiery furnace and Daniel from the lions' den. He delights in sending a Move of the Holy Spirit when the possibility of such seems hopeless. God is a God of the impossible! He still says, *"If My people which are called by My Name . . ."* (II Chron. 7:14).

(127) "THEREFORE I LOVE YOUR COMMANDMENTS ABOVE GOLD; YEA, ABOVE FINE GOLD."

He Who was Himself the Incarnate Word

of God here reveals His Affection for the Written Word of God.

THE WORD OF GOD IS TO BE LOVED ABOVE GOLD

How many Believers put their love for the Bible above gold?

Most Christians put their employment and monetary gain first and hope there may be a good Church nearby — if a good Church is of any concern at all! Very few Christians put the Bible first, which demands a good Church, and then seek employment nearby or else drive a distance in order to be close to *"Your Word."*

(128) "THEREFORE I ESTEEM ALL YOUR PRECEPTS CONCERNING ALL THINGS TO BE RIGHT; AND I HATE EVERY FALSE WAY."

In this Verse, the Messiah testifies to the inspiration, moral perfection, inerrancy, and authority of the Bible, and declares that its effect as a moral teacher is to beget hostility to evil. He says that all of its Precepts concerning all things are right (Williams).[67]

Once again, He proclaims His hatred for all false ways of Salvation, which are in reality no Salvation at all. So should every Minister of the Gospel!

PE (129-136)
(The Seventeenth Chorus)

(129) "YOUR TESTIMONIES ARE WONDERFUL: THEREFORE DOES MY SOUL KEEP THEM."

Immanuel's love for the Scriptures and His grief because men ignore them are the keynotes of this stanza. How many Believers can say, *"Your Testimonies are wonderful,"* not only as a matter of fact, but as a matter of experience?

THE TESTIMONIES OF THE LORD

The keeping of the Scriptures brings the soul into conscious touch with the Author. This experience is what the Bible aims at and secures if it is to be submitted to as the rule of life and faith.

It testifies to wonders both physical and moral. The excellence of its moral wonders proves the Volume to be Divine; the accuracy of its physical marvels demonstrates it to be supernatural. Because its testimonies are wonderful, the Messiah cherished them.

(130) "THE ENTRANCE OF YOUR WORDS GIVES LIGHT; IT GIVES UNDERSTANDING UNTO THE SIMPLE."

As the thirsty traveler in the hot desert longs for water and drinks eagerly of it, so Jesus felt toward the Scriptures.

THE ENTRANCE OF THE WORD GIVES LIGHT

"Entrance" signifies a doorway. An Eastern peasant's house had few, if any, windows. Light entered through the door; hence, to open the Scriptures means to explain them. The Messiah opened the Scriptures to His Disciples after His Resurrection (Lk. 24:45); the Apostle Paul opened them to the Thessalonians (Acts 17:3), and prayed that they might be opened to the Ephesians (Eph. 1:18).

The only *"Light"* in the world is the Bible. The Koran provides no light; the Book of Mormon provides no light; no other so-called sacred books provide any light either; however, a closed Bible also provides no light. It must eagerly be pursued and imbibed into our heart. We must become inebriated on it. This means constant study, perusal, meditation, and searching. Such will provide the greatest treasure, fulfillment, and development because it alone satisfies the hunger and slakes the thirst.

The word *"simple,"* as here used, means *"sincere."* To the sincere heart, God will reveal Himself; hence, Christ spoke in parables in order that the merely inquisitive would be turned aside and the truly sincere would press further on (Lk. 8:10).

(131) "I OPENED MY MOUTH, AND PANTED: FOR I LONGED FOR YOUR COMMANDMENTS."

This Passage exemplifies the absolute thirst for the Word of God by the Messiah. Why?

THE COMMANDMENTS OF THE LORD

The Word of God was the Strength of the Messiah, as well as His comfort, Protection, Fulfillment, Sustenance, Power, Leading, Guidance, Direction, understanding, Knowledge, Judgment and the fulfillment of every legitimate Desire. It, and it alone, will do the same for any who will search its pages, meditate on its Words, and seek its counsel, thereby knowing its Author. Sadly, precious few take advantage of its treasure trove.

(132) "LOOK THOU UPON ME, AND BE MERCIFUL UNTO ME, AS YOU USED TO DO UNTO THOSE WHO LOVE YOUR NAME."

This Verse is said to be one of the Verses in which not one of the ten words describing the Word of God is found. However, the phrase, *"Used to do,"* should be *"as You give Judgment to those who love Your Name."* The Hebrew word translated *"used to do"* is translated *"Judgment"* eighteen times in this Psalm.

INVESTIGATING THE BIBLE

In this Verse, we find that love for the Author, Word, and Name are synonymous.

Many have attempted to investigate the Bible for scientific or other purposes without knowing the Author or the wonder and glory of His Name. Such cannot be done.

The Bible was not written for the carnal mind, but for the searching heart. Men learn it with their hearts rather than with their heads; consequently, their lives are changed by its moral teachings because its purpose is not to provide clever sayings, but Spiritual Direction.

Paul said, *"But the natural man receives not the things of the Spirit of God: for they are foolishness unto him: neither can he know them, because they are spiritually discerned"* (I Cor. 2:14).

(133) "ORDER MY STEPS IN YOUR WORD: AND LET NOT ANY INIQUITY HAVE DOMINION OVER ME."

This Verse may be translated: *"Guide My steps by Your Word, cause My conduct to harmonize with the Bible, and let not any iniquitous action of man have power against Me."*

OBEDIENCE TO THE BIBLE

Verses 132 through 136 constitute a prayer. It is a prayer for deliverance from man's evil actions, which proves this is the force of the word *"iniquity."* It has no moral relation to the Messiah.

As previously stated, the religious hierarchy would attempt to push Jesus from the Word of God. His complete Obedience to such was a rebuke to their man-made laws, rules, and regulations. They were ordering His Steps in their word, while He was asking the Father to order His Steps in *"Your Word."* He asked for the Father's help that their strong efforts would in no way have any dominion over Him. The prayer was answered, and yet the answering of it only increased the anger, wrath, and hatred of the Pharisees for the Messiah.

(134) "DELIVER ME FROM THE OPPRESSION OF MAN: SO WILL I KEEP YOUR PRECEPTS."

The efforts of Satan have ever been to push believing man from the path of the Word. Mostly he uses religious man to do such.

DELIVERANCE FROM OPPRESSION

Our Lord's Prayer for deliverance from oppression was not in order that He might have leisure to enjoy Himself, but rather liberty to practice the teachings of the Bible. Persecution aims at preventing the reading of that Holy Book, and seeks the destruction of those who do read, practice, and seek to obey it.

Reading, loving, practicing, and obeying God's Law bring the soul into God's Presence and into the conscious enjoyment of fellowship with Him.

This only can be done in one way, and that is by the Believer placing his faith exclusively in Christ as the Source of all things from God and the Cross as the Means by which these things are given unto us. When this is done, and continues to be done, and never ceases to be done, the Holy Spirit will guarantee to us all the benefits of the Cross. We then enter into Christ's Victory; and this is the only way that one can enter into His Victory.

(135) "MAKE YOUR FACE TO SHINE UPON YOUR SERVANT; AND TEACH ME YOUR STATUTES."

The phrase, *"Make Your Face to shine,"* means, *"Give Me Your favor or Grace."* It is a favorite and beautiful statement in the Psalms. God's Face cannot shine upon anything but His pure and unsullied Word. It will not shine on error, unbelief, doubt, or any vacillation from Scripture.

Again, the Messiah implores the Holy

Spirit to *"teach Me Your Statutes."*

(136) "RIVERS OF WATERS RUN DOWN MY EYES, BECAUSE THEY KEEP NOT YOUR LAW."

"Floods of tears" is the corresponding English idiom for *"rivers of waters."* In a previous stanza (Vs. 126), the Messiah mourned because men made void His Father's Law; here He weeps because they did not prize and obey it.

TZADDI (137-144)
(The Eighteenth Chorus)

(137) "RIGHTEOUS ARE YOU, O LORD, AND UPRIGHT ARE YOUR JUDGMENTS."

In these Verses, the Messiah sets out in order the excellencies of God's Word as righteous, pure, true, and everlasting.

THE EMPHASIS PLACED ON THE BIBLE BY THE HOLY SPIRIT

The extolling of the Word of God in these Passages is a wonder to behold, and by the Messiah, at that! The emphasis that the Holy Spirit places on the Bible concerning this all-important Psalm should draw our total attention to the following:

1. The longest Psalm (Chapter) in the entirety of the Bible, consisting of 176 Verses, is dedicated to the Grace, Glory, Power, and Majesty of the Bible. From this, we certainly should understand what the Holy Spirit is telling us.

2. Even though the writer may have been David or someone else, still, the Messiah is the Speaker, which underscores its significance.

3. The Messiah emphasizes His Love for the Bible above all else in this world. He gives it the total credit for Sustenance, comfort, Power, and Illumination, thereby guaranteeing victory over Satan. As it was for Him, so it is with us.

(138) "YOUR TESTIMONIES THAT YOU HAVE COMMANDED ARE RIGHTEOUS AND VERY FAITHFUL."

These are the only true Testimonies in the world today, and ever have been. All other testimonies, be they religious or intellectual, are conceived by man, much of the time are inspired by Satan, and are thereby specious.

The great conflict that plagues the Planet has always been the battle between the Word of God and the word of man. Even though the Word of God is always faithful and man's word never is faithful, still, unrighteous men with hearts of evil plus even the majority of the Church opt for man's word instead of God's Word.

(139) "MY ZEAL HAS CONSUMED ME, BECAUSE MY ENEMIES HAVE FORGOTTEN YOUR WORDS."

The Messiah had a consuming zeal to the fidelity of the Word. So should every Christian, be they Preacher or otherwise.

THE WORD OF GOD, THE ONLY TRUE MAP

Here the Messiah pours out His Grief because men forget God's Word. As well, they became His enemies because they *"have forgotten Your Words."* Those who do not abide by the Word are always the enemies of those who do. Here the conflict rages.

During the times of the Early Church, Paul's greatest enemies were those who were within the Church but were trying to add to the Word or take away from the Word. Let it be understood that these detractors were not those who would have been considered cults; but, for the most part, they were from the Mother Church in Jerusalem (Gal. 2:11-14). Satan, in fact, carries on his greatest work from inside the Church. It always has been that way!

(140) "YOUR WORD IS VERY PURE: THEREFORE YOUR SERVANT LOVES IT."

Only the Word of God is pure; man's word never is pure. Because of its purity, the Messiah loved it.

Sadly, men make void the teaching of the Book, then they cease to obey its Law, and finally they forget it altogether.

(141) "I AM SMALL AND DESPISED: YET DO NOT I FORGET YOUR PRECEPTS."

In this one Verse, we learn some things about the Humanity of Christ.

THE LORD JESUS CHRIST

The word *"small"* means *"insignificant."* One of the reasons why the Lord Jesus was despised was because He loved and believed the Bible. All who similarly love and believe it must expect to be despised as well. Almost all of this wrath will come not from the world, but from the Church. Christ's greatest enemies were the religious leaders of His day; likewise, with few exceptions, the greatest enemies to the Word of God today are religious leaders.

Many would blanch at the Lord of Glory calling Himself *"small"* (*"insignificant"*), but that He was.

1. He was born in a manger (a smelly stable), simply because there was no money for commodious accommodations.

2. He was a peasant and, therefore, of humble surroundings.

3. He had no connection whatsoever with the ruling and wealthy aristocracy of Israel.

4. There is no record that He ever attended any of their rabbinical schools or institutions of higher learning or associated with such.

5. He was a carpenter's son; and even though this was an honest and upright profession, still, it was far beneath the ruling class.

6. He was raised in Nazareth, which had a reputation of *"low class"* (Jn. 1:46).

7. All His Life, He carried with Him the stigma of His Mother Mary's becoming pregnant before her marriage to Joseph. Those in Israel who knew anything of such considered Him to be a *"bastard."* Isaiah prophesied that He would be *"despised and rejected of men"* (Isa. 53:3).

(142) "YOUR RIGHTEOUSNESS IS AN EVERLASTING RIGHTEOUSNESS, AND YOUR LAW IS THE TRUTH."

Williams says, *"The Righteousness of the Divine Essence and the Righteousness of His Testimonies, Commandments, Precepts, and Statutes is one and the same Righteousness."* [68] As a consequence, the Statements and Doctrines of the Bible are dependable and free from error.

As the Messiah said, *"Your Law is the Truth,"* likewise the Master said, *"Your Word is Truth"* (Jn. 17:17). It, and it alone, is the Truth, as it regards literary form. There is no other.

(143) "TROUBLE AND ANGUISH HAVE TAKEN HOLD ON ME: YET YOUR COMMANDMENTS ARE MY DELIGHTS."

The sense of the Verse is, *"I have trouble and anguish, but they do not cause Me to turn from You or Your Word."*

NOTES

THE WORD OF GOD IS DESIGNED TO CHANGE THE HEARTS AND LIVES OF MEN

In recent years, the propagators of that which commonly is referred to as *"The Faith Message"* have attempted to remove all *"trouble"* and *"anguish"* by repeated confession of the Word. Such is sin!

The Bible is not a talisman, amulet, or charm that, if spoken, will bring certain things into being. Its purpose, as designed by the Holy Spirit, is to change the hearts and lives of men, and not necessarily things, although, at times, this does happen.

God permits *"trouble"* and *"anguish"* for a good reason. They are intended to drive us to the Word, where we will find that His Commandments *"are My delights."* That Word is a fountain of happiness and a source of wisdom that keeps the heart cheerful and alive in times of trial.

(144) "THE RIGHTEOUSNESS OF YOUR TESTIMONIES IS EVERLASTING: GIVE ME UNDERSTANDING, AND I SHALL LIVE."

This Passage says several things:

1. The only *"Righteousness"* is found in the Word of God, which denies all man-made righteousness.

2. It is a *"Righteousness"* that is *"everlasting"*; consequently, it will be the same tomorrow as it is today.

3. The plea of the Messiah is that the Holy Spirit give Him understanding regarding *"Your Testimonies."* This must be our prayer as well.

4. The word *"live"* means *"to overcome in victory and to overcome continuously."* It is a continuous action. Nothing but the Bible can provide this type of overcoming life; this is the Testimony of this Chorus.

KOPH (145-152)
(The Nineteenth Chorus)

(145) "I CRIED WITH MY WHOLE HEART; HEAR ME, O LORD: I WILL KEEP YOUR STATUTES.

(146) "I CRIED UNTO YOU; SAVE ME, AND I SHALL KEEP YOUR TESTIMONIES."

Our Lord's cry to God to help Him in His

Fidelity to the Word ensured the keeping of that Word. The word *"cried"* refers to a heart-longing desire akin to physical hunger or thirst.

DEDICATION TO PRAYER AND TO THE BIBLE

The portrayal in this stanza of the Messiah's dedication to prayer and the Bible surely sets an example for us. And yet, precious few Christians take advantage of it.

The Messiah will show here how that, in times of danger and opposition, prayer and the Bible are the only true sources of strength.

Intelligence, verity, and fullness in prayer result from daily meditation in the Word of God. If the Bible is neglected, prayer is impoverished. It is a cherished treasure for the heart and a ruler of the conduct; the Messiah's eager prayer for deliverance from His enemies was not that He might have exemption from opposition, but that He might have liberty to enjoy and obey the Word of God.

(147) "I PREVENTED THE DAWNING OF THE MORNING, AND CRIED; I HOPE IN YOUR WORD.

(148) "MY EYES PREVENT THE NIGHT WATCHES, THAT I MIGHT MEDITATE IN YOUR WORD."

Once again, we are given insight into the heart of our Lord.

THE HABITS OF THE MASTER

At least in His formative years, it seems the early morning hour was the Lord's time of prayer. We would do well to follow His example. How so wonderful to start the day in this way!

At night, His Mind would absorb the Scriptures as He meditated on them. No doubt, when He awoke after going to sleep, He always would meditate on the Word. If He did this (and He certainly did!), then we should do the same. Only similar fidelity will ensure to our heart the benefit of the Scriptures as it did His.

On a personal note, I memorize Scripture, and during the night before going to sleep, and each time I awaken, I will begin to meditate on those Scriptures — actually to quote them in my mind and spirit. There could be nothing greater to ease the mind and to feed the soul.

(149) "HEAR MY VOICE ACCORDING UNTO YOUR LOVINGKINDNESS: O LORD, QUICKEN ME ACCORDING TO YOUR JUDGMENT."

We would do well to read carefully these Scriptures and then apply them to our lives.

THE PRAYER OF OUR LORD

Jesus prayed that the answer to His Petition should be measured by God's lovingkindness and that His Heart should be refreshed, revived, maintained, and kept sensitive to the Judgments of the Divine Law. He desired that the Scriptures be the instrument and channel of refreshment and vivification to His Mind and Faith. He prayed to be kept in-between the banks of that channel.

Such is the force of the term, *"According to."* This term occurs twice in the Verse. It first measures the boundlessness of God's Love and then the boundaries of His Judgment. Answers to prayer measured by that love and limited by that Judgment strengthen faith, instruct the understanding, and animate the heart.

(150) "THEY DRAW NEAR WHO FOLLOW AFTER MISCHIEF: THEY ARE FAR FROM YOUR LAW."

How strange it was that the Pharisees were so near to Him, yet did not know Him! This occurred because they did not know God's Word.

We cannot know Christ unless we know the Word!

(151) "YOU ARE NEAR, O LORD; AND ALL YOUR COMMANDMENTS ARE TRUTH."

The Pharisees were near to Christ, but, as stated, did not know Christ. They did not know Who He was; and if they did, they wouldn't admit it. But yet, at the same time, Jehovah was near the Master, and He knew and loved Him well.

This Passage tells us that God hovers near all who are true to His Word. He was the Messiah's friend and the Pharisees enemy. And so He will be to all who oppose His Word.

(152) "CONCERNING YOUR TESTIMONIES, I HAVE KNOWN OF OLD THAT YOU HAVE FOUNDED THEM FOREVER."

The last Verse of this Chorus proclaims

the Messiah testifying to the inspiration and antiquity of the Sacred Scriptures. He declares God to be their Author and predicts that they will endure forever (Mat. 24:35).

Also in this Passage, He refers to His Preincarnation. He was, in fact, the Living Word (Jn. 1:1-3).

RESH (153-160)
(The Twentieth Chorus)

(153) "CONSIDER MY AFFLICTION, AND DELIVER ME: FOR I DO NOT FORGET YOUR LAW."

The word *"deliver"* in the Hebrew is *"halaz,"* which means *"to rescue with a gentle hand."* (Actually, there are twenty-five different Hebrew words translated *"deliver."*)

DELIVERANCE

These are requests for deliverance from trouble. The Messiah mentions His afflictions several times and repeatedly prays for help from God. His trouble seems to be more from enemies than anything else.

Neither suffering nor fear could weaken the Messiah's affection for the Bible, nor cause Him to swerve from its teaching. On the contrary, He prayed that it might continually be the source of refreshment and strength to Him.

Affliction, affection, subjection, and dependence appear in the petitions of the first two Verses. Sadly, affliction has caused many of God's servants to forget His Law, but it was not so with the Messiah — it only deepened His Affection for it.

Even David in his affliction forgot the Promises of that Law and said, *"I shall one day perish by the hand of Saul"* (I Sam. 27:1). Regrettably, all of us, with the exception of Christ, have veered from the Word of God, which always brings trouble, sometimes great trouble.

Only a sinless heart could say, *"I do not forget Your Law"* (Vs. 153), *"I do not decline* (swerve) *from Your Testimonies"* (Vs. 157), and *"Consider how I love Your Precepts"* (Vs. 159). On David's lips, or ours, such words would be untrue, self-righteous, proud, and Pharisaic, but, on the lips of the Messiah, were not so.

NOTES

(154) "PLEAD MY CAUSE, AND DELIVER ME: QUICKEN ME ACCORDING TO YOUR WORD."

Several things are said in this Passage. They are as follows:

DELIVERANCE THROUGH THE WORD OF GOD

1. *"Plead My cause."* When suffering injustice, most men defend themselves, but the Messiah resigned Himself to God, pleading for His Deliverance.

2. *"Deliver Me."* The word *"deliver"* in this Passage is different from the same word in the previous Verse. The word in the Hebrew is *"ga'al."* It means *"to redeem."* The Messiah was asking that God would deliver Him from those who were *"the wicked"* (Ps. 119:155). The word has to do with the price that is paid to purchase something. It has the idea of God paying any price to redeem one who is trusting His Word, a price, I might quickly add, that was paid at the Cross.

3. *"Quicken Me."* The prayer for *"quickening,"* which means *"to make alive,"* is repeated nine times in this Psalm — three times in this stanza alone. It expresses the Messiah's continual dependence upon God and His Word.

A PERSONAL EXPERIENCE

It was early summer in 1988. Frances and I, our entire family, and the Church and Ministry had undergone tremendous difficulties. Some were because of my own failure, and some because of the failure of others.

One Friday afternoon, we received word of a most vile effort to be carried out by *"persecutors and enemies"* (Ps. 119:157). The attack not only would be vile, but it would be without mercy, and on a worldwide basis. In no uncertain terms, it was designed to *"steal, kill, and destroy"* (Jn. 10:10). The accusations, which were totally false, were so vile that I will not repeat them here. They came from the leadership of a major Pentecostal Denomination.

My immediate reaction was to defend myself. I called the Ministry lawyers as well as our Television Studio. I thought, *"I will go on the air and tell the world of this perfidious action."* Needless to say, Frances and I slept very little that night. The time I was not lying awake in the bed, I was outside the house walking up and down the drive praying, importuning the Lord as to what we should do.

A little bit before daylight, the Spirit of the Lord moved on my heart in a powerful way, but without giving direction. It must have been about 9 a.m. the next morning, which was Saturday, when our two grandsons, Gabriel and Matthew, came over to our house. I was sitting outside with them. Frances was inside. All of sudden, she came out the door. There was a look of joy and relief on her face. She held the Bible in her hand. She thrust it toward me and said, *"I was reading and this is what the Lord gave me!"*

I looked at the Scripture to which she referred. The moment I read it, the Spirit of the Lord came all over me, and I began to weep. I knew the Lord had spoken, and this was His Answer:

"The LORD shall fight for you, and you shall hold your peace" (Ex. 14:14).

Instantly, I abandoned the other plans I foolishly and hastily had made. I called the Ministry lawyer and told him to forget the situation. I also called our Television Studio and informed them that we had changed our plans.

This is the ideal for every Christian. We are not to plead our cause; He is to plead our cause!

This is not to say that the efforts of these individuals didn't hurt us, because, in fact, they hurt us badly. However, I had the satisfaction of knowing that I had obeyed the Lord, and that's all that really matters.

Today the Ministry is on Television over a good part of the world. We also are filling the nation with Radio Stations in order to preach the great Message of the Cross. I fully expect that what we now are seeing will grow to unprecedented proportions, even to a greater degree than ever. Had I taken matters into my own hands on that Saturday morning in 1988, there is a good possibility that the Ministry would no longer exist today.

But it still exists, even greater than ever, and we give the Lord all the praise and all the glory, due to the faithfulness of His Word.

(155) "SALVATION IS FAR FROM THE WICKED: FOR THEY SEEK NOT YOUR STATUTES."

Deliverance was near to this dependent Man, because He loved the Bible, but was far from the self-reliant, because they despised it. It would be as close to them as the righteous if they would seek God and follow His Ways. The Word is near all men (Rom. 10:8), but it does not profit unbelievers (Heb. 4:2).

(156) "GREAT ARE YOUR TENDER MERCIES, O LORD: QUICKEN ME ACCORDING TO YOUR JUDGMENTS."

The Messiah, as Man, prayed exactly as we pray; He requested God's *"tender mercies."*

The very Name, *"LORD,"* refers to *"Covenant,"* and promises such. God cannot deal with man in justice, only in mercy. All men are guilty; therefore, all men need mercy. Even though the Messiah was not guilty, He would take our guilt upon Himself and bring to fulfillment the greatest Mercy of all.

(157) "MANY ARE MY PERSECUTORS AND MY ENEMIES; YET DO I NOT DECLINE FROM YOUR TESTIMONIES."

This speaks of the Pharisees, Sadducees, and Scribes. Considering that He never did anything unkind to them (or to anyone else, for that matter), why were they His enemies, and why did they persecute Him?

Fidelity to the Word always arouses great anger in the hearts of the self-righteous. Self-righteousness was the crowning sin of Jesus' day; it is the crowning sin of the modern Church today, as well!

Their effort was to push Him away from the Bible. Instead it drew Him closer.

(158) "I BEHELD THE TRANSGRESSORS, AND WAS GRIEVED; BECAUSE THEY KEPT NOT YOUR WORD."

This Passage could be translated, *"I looked upon the traitors and loathed them because they kept not Your Word."* So ardent was His Affection for the Scriptures, that He thus regarded His Persecutors, the Scribes, and Pharisees. He knew where their direction would lead them and all who followed them. It would lead to destruction! It happened in A.D. 70, when Titus, the Roman General, completely leveled Jerusalem and the Temple, which resulted in the deaths of over one millions Jews, with many of those who survived being sold into slavery.

His Grief was not for Himself, but for the Word. The Holy Spirit treats the cause instead of the symptom. The cause was their lack of fidelity to the Word.

(159) "CONSIDER HOW I LOVE YOUR PRECEPTS: QUICKEN ME, O LORD, ACCORDING TO YOUR LOVINGKINDNESS."

In contrast to the treachery of the Pharisees to that Holy Law, the Messiah truthfully could exclaim, *"Consider how I love it."*

(160) "YOUR WORD IS TRUE FROM THE BEGINNING: AND EVERY ONE OF YOUR RIGHTEOUS JUDGMENTS ENDURES FOREVER."

In this Verse, our Lord repeats the testimony of Verse 152, but especially urges the inerrancy of the Sacred Volume. In essence, He says, *"Your Word is true from the first Chapter of Genesis; all its statements are righteous and shall stand eternally."*

Thus, He testified to the truthfulness of the Bible as a whole and to the truthfulness of all its parts. It is true as the Word of God, and its Words are the Words of God.

The word *"beginning"* in the Hebrew is *"Rosh."* From this, we derive that our Lord is going back all the way to the Book of Genesis. It is the Book of Beginnings. It is followed by the balance of the Pentateuch, the historical Books, and the great Books of the Prophets. Every Word of it is true, and in every respect. There is no error of any nature.

SCHIN (161-168)
(The Twenty-first Chorus)

(161) "PRINCES HAVE PERSECUTED ME WITHOUT A CAUSE: BUT MY HEART STANDS IN AWE OF YOUR WORD."

The Hebrews inscribed upon the first page of the Bible the words, *"How dreadful is this place! This is none other than the House of God, and this is the Gate of Heaven."*

WITHOUT A CAUSE

If David wrote this, he was referring to the many leaders of Israel who rebelled with Absalom (II Sam., Chpts. 15-18). If this does refer to Absalom, he had no cause for rebelling against his father. Those who followed him had even less cause. Hence, God brought them all to justice.

More pointedly, it refers to the persecution of the Greater Son of David by the rulers and leaders of Israel. Luke 11:53 and 12:11 illustrate this Verse. Our Lord's Heart did not tremble at the threats of the rulers (Lk. 11:54), but His Heart did tremble at the Word of God (Lk. 12:5). A soul is dead indeed that neither trembles nor rejoices when reading the Bible.

Only once was there a Man on Earth Whose heart continually maintained a right attitude toward the Bible. His pure Soul trembled with Holy fear at its Words and rejoiced at its teaching. As Jehovah's Servant, He fulfilled the conditions of Isaiah 66:2 and Deuteronomy 6:6, for not only did He love God's Holy Law, but He loved it exceedingly.

All opposition to Christ and His Word is always and without exception *"without a cause."* The opposition is caused by an evil heart of unbelief, which denotes a lack of fidelity to the Bible; consequently, when men stand before God there will be no excuse.

THE OFFENSE OF THE CROSS

Paul said, *"And I, Brethren, if I yet preach circumcision, why do I yet suffer persecution?* (Any Message other than the Cross draws little opposition.) *Then is the offense of the Cross ceased.* (The Cross offends the world and most of the Church. So, if the Preacher ceases to preach the Cross as the only way of Salvation and Victory, then opposition and persecution will cease. But so will Salvation and Victory!)" (Gal. 5:11).

HOW COULD THERE BE AN OFFENSE IN THE CROSS?

For several reasons, the Cross of Christ is an offense to both the unbeliever and the Believer. The unbelievers refuse to admit that their situation is so perilous, so terminal, so wicked that it took God becoming Man, coming down to this mortal coil, and dying on a cruel Cross in order for man to be saved. Unbelieving man is loath to admit that his situation is that bad!

It was to Believers, however, that the Apostle Paul addressed his statement about the Cross being an offense, which it is because it strips away every rudiment of the flesh. When Paul used the word *"flesh,"* he was speaking of one's own strength, ability, efforts, ingenuity, etc. It is hard for man, even Believers, to admit that what we must have, what we must be, and what we must do, can be brought about by ourselves not at all, but must be done entirely by the Holy Spirit (Rom. 8:1-2, 11; Gal. 5:16-18).

And then we learn that the Holy Spirit works exclusively within the parameters of the Finished Work of Christ (Rom. 8:2). This demands that our faith be exclusively in Christ and the Cross, not allowing it to be placed anywhere else (Rom. 6:1-14).

The Cross demands surrender; we speak of surrender of self in all of its alleged qualities. This means looking exclusively to Christ, and thereby understanding that everything He gives us comes to us exclusively through the Cross, and by no other means. It is hard for Believers to accept that. We want to think that it's our strength, our ability, our efforts, etc. The Cross of Christ strips all of that away (Gal. 2:20-21).

But for everything it strips away, it gives us in turn something that is *"joy unspeakable and full of glory."* It provides for us the working of *"more abundant life"* in our life and living (Jn. 10:10). This is True Christianity, and anything else is less than it can be.

(162) "I REJOICE AT YOUR WORD, AS ONE WHO FINDS GREAT SPOIL."

When men find treasure, there is great rejoicing. The Messiah says that even greater treasure is found in *"Your Word,"* which will produce exhilarating rejoicing. The question could be asked, *"Does the modern Christian rejoice over the contents of the Book as much as he rejoices over the results of a sporting event, an increase in the stock market, or any other activity of life?"* Sadly, for the most part, the answer is an obvious *"No!"*

For one to *"rejoice at Your Word,"* one must first know the Word. And knowledge of the Word can only be arrived at by persistent study of the Word. Furthermore, the Believer must experience the Word.

How is that done?

EXPERIENCING THE WORD

Down through my Christian experience, the Lord has shown me many things. Every single time, He has taken me to His Word. When, in 1997, He gave me the Revelation of the Cross, the Lord took me directly to the Word.

He showed me first of all what the sin nature was, and how it functioned, and pointed me to the example given in the Sixth Chapter of Romans. The Holy Spirit literally explained it to me.

Then He told me that the solution for the sin nature, the only solution, is the Cross of Christ. This occurred several days later, but again He took me to the Word, more specifically to Romans 6:3-5. And then some weeks later, the Lord showed me the part the Holy Spirit plays in all of this, which is considerable indeed. The Lord took me to Romans 8:2, and explained that to me. As stated, everything the Lord has given me always has been exactly according to His Word; and every time He has shown me the answer to my dilemma in His Word, whatever the dilemma has been.

When one truly seeks the Lord, such an one will experience Revelation, but that Revelation will always come from the Bible. If it doesn't, it is not a Revelation from God, but rather from an angel of light (II Cor. 11:13-15).

(163) "I HATE AND ABHOR LYING: BUT YOUR LAW DO I LOVE."

The sense of this Verse is that the persecutors of Christ were liars, as are all those who vacillate from God's Word. The more one loves the teaching of the Bible, the more one hates and abhors all falsehood.

Someone has said, *"The hardest thing for a Christian to do after coming to Christ is to 'quit lying,'"* because the entire fabric of fallen humanity is made of *"the lie."* Satan is a liar and the father of it (Jn. 8:44).

The only Truth is God's Word. All else is a lie.

(164) "SEVEN TIMES A DAY DO I PRAISE YOU BECAUSE OF YOUR RIGHTEOUS JUDGMENTS."

Another great Truth is given in this Verse.

SEVEN TIMES A DAY

The number *"seven"* signifies completion, fulfillment, totality, and perfection. It means that the *"praise"* of the Messiah was Perfect and unceasing. How wonderful it must have been to be in His Presence! Still, constant praise, according to His Word, will propel us into His Presence.

This means that all day long He kept praising God for the Bible. He loved it exceedingly, and found nothing in it to offend Him, as so many do today. He laid bare all His conduct to its scrutiny.

How can we do less?

(165) "GREAT PEACE HAVE THEY WHICH LOVE YOUR LAW: AND NOTHING SHALL OFFEND THEM."

"Great peace" follows fidelity to and love of *"Your Law."* A heart governed by the Sacred Writings is filled with peace. It is not disturbed by difficulties or doubts as to their inspiration or to supposed moral defects in them.

(166) "LORD, I HAVE HOPED FOR YOUR SALVATION, AND DONE YOUR COMMANDMENTS.

(167) "MY SOUL HAS KEPT YOUR TESTIMONIES; AND I LOVE THEM EXCEEDINGLY.

(168) "I HAVE KEPT YOUR PRECEPTS AND YOUR TESTIMONIES: FOR ALL MY WAYS ARE BEFORE YOU."

Only a perfect Believer could make the statements of these last three Verses. Such a Believer was Jesus of Nazareth.

But these Verses set up the stand which His followers should aim at; works of obedience should follow upon faith for Salvation, and love for the Scriptures with subjection of the entire life to their teachings should characterize all who profess to believe upon Him.

THE PERFECTION OF THE SCRIPTURES

This Testimony to the inspiration, authority, infallibility, sufficiency, and moral perfection of the Scriptures in the mouth of the most deeply consecrated Christian as a personal testimony of affection and obedience would only reveal spiritual blindness, religious pride, self-righteousness, and ignorance. If the Reader will once again carefully read these last three Verses, I think he will agree with what I have just stated.

But on the lips of the Lord Jesus, it is the very perfection of Truth.

NOTES

TAU (169-176)
(The Twenty-second Chorus)

(169) "LET MY CRY COME NEAR BEFORE YOU, O LORD: GIVE ME UNDERSTANDING ACCORDING TO YOUR WORD."

This is the twenty-second and final stanza. If possible, it increases in intensity the Messiah's extolling the Word of God. It opens with a *"cry"* for the *"understanding"* of the Bible.

UNDERSTANDING OF THE WORD

Religious man cries not at all for such. Even the most consecrated Christian has little intensity of hunger for the Bible as expressed here. In these Passages, we learn the secrets of victory, power, overcoming strength, and all that God has for us — His Word.

Millions, including Christians, are crying for many and varied things, but precious few exhibit this type of longing for the Word of God.

This last stanza completes the Messiah's testimony to the authority and sufficiency of the Holy Scriptures.

(170) "LET MY SUPPLICATION COME BEFORE YOU: DELIVER ME ACCORDING TO YOUR WORD."

This word *"deliver"* in the Hebrew is *"nazal,"* which means *"to pluck out of the hands of the enemy; to recover."* It is a different word from that found in Verses 134, 153, and 154.

DELIVERANCE

The supplication is that deliverance would come, *"according to Your Word."* The Bible teaches *"deliverance,"* while psychology teaches *"treatment."* Psychology is a fallacy. Sin does not respond to treatment, and neither do the powers of darkness. Only the Power of God can deliver and *"set the captive free"* (Lk. 4:18).

Too much of that which passes for *"deliverance"* in modern Christendom is no deliverance at all. It is not *"according to Your Word."*

Humanism has taken, and is taking, its deadly toll in the ranks of humanity; likewise, religious humanism follows suit. Religious men are proposing to save society by political means, by religious means, and by social and other means. This is no different than Satanic humanism with a religious face. There is humanism which looks to man and denies God and there is humanism with looks to man and espouses God, but in either case, they have no solutions.

The answer to the ills of mankind is not an improved political party, a religious parade, or a new set of rules and regulations, but Deliverance which only can be brought about by the Power of God through the Lord Jesus Christ. That's the reason that Paul, with all his vaunted education and knowledge, said, *"For I determined not to know any thing among you, save Jesus Christ, and Him Crucified"* (I Cor. 2:2).

What did Paul mean by that statement?

JESUS CHRIST AND HIM CRUCIFIED

Jesus Christ, as a good Man, or as a great Prophet, could deliver no one from sin. Jesus Christ, dying on Calvary and thereby paying the price for lost humanity, bruised Satan's head and broke the back of the powers of darkness. He did so by atoning for all sin, which guarantees freedom from sin for all who will believe Him (Gal. 2:20-21).

The Cross of Christ is the only thing standing between man and eternal Hell. It is the only means by which the sinner can be free from the bondage of his sin. It is the only means by which the Believer can walk in victory, which speaks of continued and perpetual victory over sin. It all comes by the means of the Cross. Christ is the Source, and the Cross is the Means.

When Jesus atoned for all sin, which He did by the giving of Himself as a Perfect Sacrifice on the Cross of Calvary, this removed the legal right that Satan has to hold man in bondage. Sin is that right; but, with all sin atoned, that legal right is forever removed.

If the Believer will place his faith exclusively in Christ and the Cross, and keep his faith there, the Holy Spirit will work mightily within his life, bringing about Victory, even on a daily basis (Lk. 9:23-24).

Jesus said, *"You shall know the Truth and the Truth shall make you free"* (Jn. 8:32). The *"Truth"* is *"Jesus Christ and Him Crucified"* (I Cor. 1:23).

THE CROSS OF CHRIST AND PSYCHOLOGY

This is the reason it is so wrong for Preachers to steer the Believers, no matter how difficult or vile their problems might be, to anything other than Christ and the Cross. There is no hope in humanistic psychology. It holds no answers, and it never has held any answers. The only answer is in Jesus Christ and Him Crucified. That's the reason the Apostle Paul said what he did regarding the Church at Corinth (I Cor. 2:2).

One can place one's faith exclusively in Christ and the Cross and guarantee thereby the help of the Holy Spirit, Who can do anything; or else one can place his faith in humanistic psychology. He cannot do both. Unfortunately, most of the modern trends, such as *"The Purpose Driven Life,"* are psychology-driven, which means they are not Scripture-driven.

If the Preacher is not preaching the Cross, he is not preaching the Gospel. He might be preaching some things about the Gospel, but he is really not preaching the Gospel.

That's why the Apostle Paul said:

"Christ sent me not to baptize, but to preach the Gospel, not with wisdom of words, lest the Cross of Christ should be made of none effect" (I Cor. 1:17).

(171) "MY LIPS SHALL UTTER PRAISE, WHEN YOU HAVE TAUGHT ME YOUR STATUTES."

The word *"utter"* means *"to bubble over with."* The effect of Heaven's legislation is to make earthly lips overflow with praise, because all the teaching of the Bible is Righteousness. The instructed tongue sings of its perfection. So sang the Messiah. This was His Testimony.

(172) "MY TONGUE SHALL SPEAK OF YOUR WORD: FOR ALL YOUR COMMANDMENTS ARE RIGHTEOUSNESS."

In these two Verses, we have *"praise"* and *"testimony."* Our Lord's utterance to God was *"praise."* His utterance to man was *"testimony"* of *"Your Word."*

THE INSPIRATION OF THE BIBLE

The idea of modern foolish thinking that some parts of the Bible possibly may be inspired while other parts are fable is complete and utter nonsense. All — from Genesis through Revelation — is Righteousness. If one does not believe all of the Bible, one cannot believe any of the Bible. If one tiny part of it is untrue, then all of it is untrue, because Inspiration claims all of it.

One does not have to perfectly understand all the Word, for the Messiah constantly asks for help regarding its instruction; but one must believe all the Word of God, whether we understand it all or not. Only Christ perfectly understood it all, because only Christ perfectly obeyed it all. However, many believe all of it, while not fully understanding all of it. Nevertheless, the example set before us of the Messiah constantly asking for instructional help from the Holy Spirit is a constant reminder to us that we can do the same and receive the same — understanding.

Even in the most ardent devotees of the Bible, Biblical ignorance persists, simply because of lack of attention.

(173) "LET YOUR HAND HELP ME; FOR I HAVE CHOSEN YOUR PRECEPTS."

Jesus desired neither deliverance by man's hand nor the prosperity of his ways, but He did ardently desire God's Salvation and His Word.

Too many Christians constantly seek the help of men. The Messiah's example shows us that there is little help from that source. The *"help"* comes from His *"Hand."* He only will help if we *"have chosen His Precepts."*

(174) "I HAVE LONGED FOR YOUR SALVATION, O LORD; AND YOUR LAW IS MY DELIGHT."

The word *"Salvation"* is hinged with God's Covenant. *"O LORD"* guarantees total Deliverance, Victory, Development, and Fulfillment.

SALVATION

"Salvation" is more than many have been led to believe. The modern Church has stripped Salvation so much that today it is little more than a creed, dogma, or formula. True Bible Salvation involves a complete new lifestyle with a totally new direction, which only can involve itself in a *"new creation"* (II Cor. 5:17).

This glorious Covenant, which the Messiah Himself brought to the fore, is the fulfillment of *"Your Law."* It brings *"My delight."* There is no other lasting delight on the face of Planet Earth than that which the Lord can give.

(175) "LET MY SOUL LIVE, AND IT SHALL PRAISE YOU; AND LET YOUR JUDGMENTS HELP ME."

Jesus said, *"Man shall not live by bread alone, but by every Word that proceeds out of the Mouth of God"* (Mat. 4:4). Most have never learned this, and they attempt to live only by bread.

(176) "I HAVE GONE ASTRAY LIKE A LOST SHEEP; SEEK YOUR SERVANT; FOR I DO NOT FORGET YOUR COMMANDMENTS."

The correct rendering of this Verse is, *"I have wandered about as a lost sheep, but I have not forgotten Your Commandments."*

THE GUARANTEE OF THE WORD

These statements are not contradictory, but complementary. To wander as a lost sheep here expresses defenselessness and loneliness, not moral defection. This is plain from the Messiah's declaration that, even under adverse circumstances, He had not, and did not, forget God's Commandments.

When man, however, wanders as a lost sheep, it is because he has willfully chosen his own way (Isa. 53:6).

The request by the Messiah, *"Seek Your Servant,"* is a rare request in Scripture. Many times, God commands, exhorts, and calls upon man to seek Him as the condition for blessing (Deut. 4:29; I Chron. 4:39; Isa. 55:6; Mat. 6:33; Col. 3:1; Heb. 11:6), but here the request is that God seek us!

This prayer is answered in two ways:

1. Those who constantly abide by the Word are ever guarded, solicited, protected, and cared for.

2. The total fulfillment of this request that came from the heart of the Messiah was answered when God came through Christ seeking the lost sheep (Lk. 15:1-7; 19:10).

The Holy Spirit began this great Psalm by stating the Blessing of the Messiah, the Undefiled Man Who ever perfectly walked in the Law of the Lord. The Holy Spirit ends it by inspiring the Greater Son of David to give credit for such to the Word of God, and then to proclaim that He would never forget *"Your Commandments."*

PSALM 120

*Author Unknown:
Prayer of Distress*

(1) "IN MY DISTRESS I CRIED UNTO THE LORD, AND HE HEARD ME."

Who wrote this Psalm is not known, but the Speaker is the Messiah. It concerns His Sufferings and the companionship of the ungodly.

SONGS OF DEGREES

In the great One Hundred and Nineteenth Psalm, with its twenty-two stanzas, the Messiah sang of the Lamp (the Bible) that lightens the celestial way.

In the next fifteen Psalms, which are called the *"Songs of Degrees"* or *"Ascents,"* He will sing of that way, for it is an ascending way — it leads up to God.

These Songs, as stated, are fifteen in number and form five groups of three each. Each triplet has as its theme, *"trouble," "trust,"* and *"triumph"*:

1. A cry of distress (trouble);
2. A declaration of trust; and,
3. A song of triumph.

Thus, in each group of three, there is ascent of trouble through trust to triumph.

The central Psalm of the fifteen is entitled, *"For Solomon,"* which relates to the Greater than Solomon. Seven Psalms precede and seven follow this central Psalm.

Many interpretations, thoughts, or opinions have been given regarding the meaning of these *"Ascents," "Degrees,"* and *"Steps."* Some have thought they had reference to the steps leading to the Temple, or the going up of the Tribes to Jerusalem at the three annual Feasts. Some even have thought that they were connected with Hezekiah's added fifteen years, coupled with the degrees on the sun dial of Ahaz. But all these are mere suppositions.

Probably that which seems to be obvious, *"the Ascent which leads up to God,"* is the intention of the Holy Spirit.

DISTRESS

This Verse pertains to Israel in the coming Great Tribulation, when she is distressed by the Antichrist; and it also can apply to the modern Believer. In these Psalms of Degrees, we will look at all three, *"The Messiah," "Israel,"* and *"the modern Believer."*

As we have repeatedly discussed in Psalm 119, Christ, in His distress because of the religious leaders of Israel, sought no help from man, but rather sought help only from the Lord. His petition was always heard because it always was centered in God's Word.

Israel, in her coming day of distress, when it looks as though the Antichrist will destroy her completely, will cry unto the Lord. It will be the first time in nearly 2,000 years. And He will hear her!

As it regards the modern Believer who is in distress, the modern Church advocates almost anything except the Lord. The reason is because the modern Church has abandoned the Cross of Christ. Consequently, there is no victory, for all victory is in the Cross (Rom. 6:1-14).

The only *"cry unto the LORD"* which will be heard and answered is the cry that is based strictly upon the Cross of Christ. A cry based on anything else, no matter what the other things might be, no matter how good they may be in their own right, still, will receive no answer. If our petition is outside the Cross, there will be no answer. The Lord will not hear such a petition. Regrettably, this means that the Lord does not hear many prayers.

THE CROSS AND THE ALTAR OF INCENSE

We already have given the following at least twice in this Volume. But because of its tremendous significance, please grant us the liberty to address it even again.

The ritual of the Altar of Incense is a perfect example of this of which we speak.

Twice a day, at the time of the morning sacrifice (9 a.m.) and the evening sacrifice (3 p.m.), the Priests would go into the Holy Place, take coals of fire from the Brazen Altar with them, and deposit those coals on the Altar of Incense, which sat immediately in front of the Veil which hid the Holy of Holies. After the coals of fire were placed on the Altar, Incense would then be poured over those coals, which filled the Holy Place with fragrance and smoke.

The Altar of Incense typifies the Intercessory Work of Christ, all on our behalf. His Intercession guarantees our praise and our petitions (Heb. 7:25-26). The Brazen Altar, which sat immediately in front of the Tabernacle and typified the Cross of Christ, is what produced the coals of fire. This means that the Intercession of our Lord, which is taking place at this very moment, and which is made possible by the Cross, is predicated on our Faith in Christ and what He did for us at the Cross. If coals of fire had been brought from some ignition other than the Brazen Altar, it could occasion death, which it actually did. Nadab and Abihu, sons of Aaron, were stricken dead on the spot because they offered up *"strange fire,"* meaning they secured those coals of fire from some place other than the Brazen Altar. They died as a result (Lev. 10:1-2).

This portrays to us the fact that God will accept nothing unless it comes through the Cross. As it held true then, it holds true now! Everything must be based on our Faith in Christ and what He did for us at the Cross. The Faith of the Believer must never change from that particular Object to anything else (Lk. 9:23; 14:27; Rom. 6:1-14; 8:1-2, 11; I Cor. 1:17-18, 23; 2:2; Gal. 2:20-21; Chpt. 5; 6:14; Eph. 2:13-18; Col. 2:14-15).

(2) "DELIVER MY SOUL, O LORD, FROM LYING LIPS, AND FROM A DECEITFUL TONGUE."

The slanderous tongues of the Pharisees attested to the innocency of the Messiah. These hypocrites, in their self-righteousness, loudly trumpeted their devotion to the Bible, while all the time opposing it. They read into it what they wanted it to say, instead of what God had said. *"Lying"* and *"deceit"* constantly were on their lips and tongues.

Likewise, much of the modern Church, because of its acute self-righteousness, which stems from abandonment of the Bible, has never before engaged in so much *"lying"* and *"deceit"* as at the present.

The Antichrist also will engage in *"lying"* and *"deceit"* as no person before him ever has. His promoter will be Satan. Daniel said he would cause *"craft* (lying and deceit) *to prosper"* (Dan. 8:25). Israel, at the first, will

NOTES

believe these lies and accept him as the Messiah (Jn. 5:43). At the midpoint of the Great Tribulation, Israel will see the *"lying lips and deceitful tongue"* of the Antichrist and cry unto the Lord, *"Deliver my soul."*

(3) "WHAT SHALL BE GIVEN UNTO YOU? OR WHAT SHALL BE DONE UNTO YOU, YOU FALSE TONGUE?"

The sense of this Verse is that the Pharisees were called *"you false tongue."* They were totally destroyed when Jerusalem was sacked and burned by Titus, the Roman General. Over one million Jews were crucified during this horrible siege.

Conversely, at the time of the end, and we speak of the coming Great Tribulation, Israel will cry to God instead of against God. The Antichrist then will be defeated and destroyed by the coming of Christ. The following Verse tells us how!

(4) "SHARP ARROWS OF THE MIGHTY, WITH COALS OF JUNIPER."

The Judgment of the Lord against the Pharisees was exceedingly dreadful! It will be the same against the coming Antichrist. Ezekiel said this concerning his coming destruction, *"An overflowing rain, and great hailstones, fire, and brimstone"* (Ezek. 38:22).

This will take place at the Second Coming!

(5) "WOE IS ME, THAT I SOJOURN IN MESECH, THAT I DWELL IN THE TENTS OF KEDAR!"

Mesech and Kedar were sons of Ishmael. They represent the Scribes and Pharisees, who indeed were of the seed of Abraham, but born after the flesh, exactly as was Ishmael. Then the Messiah said, *"Woe is Me."* There is nothing worse than self-righteousness, which is a work of the flesh, which characterized the Scribes and Pharisees. Christ, the Perfect Righteousness, was set down in the midst of this vortex of evil — for there is no evil like religious evil.

(6) "MY SOUL HAS LONG DWELT WITH HIM WHO HATES PEACE."

The Lord's earthly life was a short one, yet it was so filled with sorrows that, measured by suffering, it truthfully could be recorded as a long one.

HATRED FOR CHRIST

In His early life the Messiah had to pitch

his tent, so to speak, among men who hated peace. They were animated by the spirit of the Antichrist.

This spirit that characterized the Scribes and Pharisees also will cause Israel to accept the Antichrist as the Messiah not so long after the Rapture of the Church (II Thess. 2:6-8). The Antichrist will promise peace, and, with this promise, he will destroy many (Dan. 8:25). The Sixth Chapter of Revelation portrays the man of sin riding a white horse, which is symbolic of peace. It all is a charade. Actually, he hates peace, which will result in the red horse of war quickly following (Rev. 6:4).

(7) "I AM FOR PEACE: BUT WHEN I SPEAK, THEY ARE FOR WAR."

The True Messiah was peace personified; He was rejected by Israel. The false messiah will promise peace, but will bring war.

In Christ's earthly sojourn, He spoke of peace, but was rejected, condemned, and crucified. Israel literally declared war on Him. Therefore, the false messiah will declare war on them (Dan. 9:27).

I might quickly add that self-righteousness is the cause of the *"war."* In one way or another, such always is the case!

PSALM 121

Author Unknown:
A Song of Degrees, God's Sustaining Power

(1) "I WILL LIFT UP MY EYES UNTO THE HILLS, FROM WHENCE COMES MY HELP."

Even though we explained the following in the previous Psalm, still, I think it would be helpful, concerning these fifteen Songs of Degrees, if we said the same thing in another way, hopefully shedding a little more light on this very important segment given by the Holy Spirit.

The author of this Psalm is unknown.

UNDERSTANDING THE SONGS OF DEGREES

These fifteen Psalms, constituting *"Songs of Degrees"* according to their structure, are divided into five groups of three Psalms each.

NOTES

The First Psalm of each group speaks of *"distress and trouble"* (120, 123, 126, 129, 132); the Second Psalm of each group speaks of *"trust and deliverance"* by God (121, 124, 127, 130, 133); the Third Psalm of each group speaks of *"blessing and triumph"* upon Zion (122, 125, 128, 131, 134).

This is the Second Psalm of the first triplet; consequently, its keynote is Trust. The first two Verses are spoken by the Messiah. In them, He expresses His Determination to look for deliverance from the trouble described in the previous Psalm.

There has been much discussion as to the exact meaning of this First Verse. Some think that inasmuch as God's Tabernacle at this time was on the mountains of Jerusalem, it is this to which the Psalmist was referring. However, I don't think that is the case. I think the next Verse will throw more light on the subject.

(2) "MY HELP COMES FROM THE LORD, WHICH MADE HEAVEN AND EARTH."

The Psalmist, and also the Messiah, did not say that His help came from the hills, but that He would lift up His Eyes and look upon the hills, and then say, *"My help comes from the LORD,"* Who not only made these hills, but Heaven as well!

OUR HELP COMES FROM THE LORD

The intention of the Holy Spirit is to direct our attention to the fact that our help comes from the Lord, and not from man. It is rare to even find a Christian who perfectly understands such. The thinking of most Christians is to seek the help of man.

We are told emphatically in the Scriptures that man provides no help. It is God Who provides the help. While it is true that God uses men, still, it is God Who institutes the leading and the direction. It is far better to trust Him and receive the help that only He can give.

Verses 3 through 8 proclaim to us what Jehovah will not do and what He will do. What He will not do is set out in Verses 3 and 4; what He will do is given in Verse 5. Again, what He will not permit is stated in Verse 6, and then what He will perform is given in Verses 7 and 8. What He will not do is just as great as what He will do.

What He will not do or permit is as follows:

(3) "HE WILL NOT SUFFER YOUR FOOT TO BE MOVED: HE WHO KEEPS YOU WILL NOT SLUMBER."

This is the first thing the Lord will not do.

SECURITY

As long as our foot is anchored on the path of His Word, our Lord will see to it that nothing can move it off. He will protect us from everything except ourselves. The lover of the Word is never robbed of his free moral agency; consequently, the will of the person can make the decision to stay with Christ or to leave Christ. God never tampers with that. However, He does guarantee protection from all outside forces.

In the Eighth Chapter of Romans, the Apostle Paul enumerates all the things that shall not be able to separate us from the love of Christ. He mentions many things, but in no place does the Holy Spirit claim that we are protected from ourselves (Rom. 8:34-39). In other words, the Holy Spirit will warn a Believer against false doctrine, and will even throw many roadblocks across his path to keep him from the false way, but if the Believer insists in accepting false doctrine, the Holy Spirit will not stop such an one and will allow him to do what he desires to do. It will result in wreckage!

The Scripture says, *"Whosoever will...."* As long as we *"will"* to do God's Will, He will watch over us constantly and forever. He never sleeps!

(4) "BEHOLD, HE WHO KEEPS ISRAEL SHALL NEITHER SLUMBER NOR SLEEP."

The idea of Verse 4 is the same as of Verse 3, with one exception. Verse 3 pertains to the individual, and Verse 4 pertains to the entirety of the Nation of Israel.

THE PROTECTION OF JEHOVAH

The sense of this Verse is that the God of Israel, contrary to the many gods of the heathen, never slept and constantly watched over His people.

Much of the worship of these heathenistic gods by the surrounding tribes, such as the Canaanites, Jebusites, and others, was structured to arouse or to awaken these gods that were said to be sleeping! The Messiah is saying that Israel's God never slept.

(5) "THE LORD IS YOUR KEEPER: THE LORD IS YOUR SHADE UPON YOUR RIGHT HAND."

"Your shade" means *"Your protection,"* that is, *"Your defense."*

Protection was especially needed on the right hand, as the side which was guarded by no shield. Therefore, the Holy Spirit is saying that Jehovah would be Israel's Shield.

This Verse and all following for the balance of this Chapter proclaim what the Lord will do for Israel and for the Believer.

(6) "THE SUN SHALL NOT SMITE YOU BY DAY, NOR THE MOON BY NIGHT."

The Lord would not allow the elements, which He created, to be any type of hurt to Israel.

What a Promise!

(7) "THE LORD SHALL PRESERVE YOU FROM ALL EVIL: HE SHALL PRESERVE YOUR SOUL."

The preservation of our soul is strictly from God. He has promised to do such. Satan is a master liar. No doubt, he has told you, the Reader, that you will not make it and you will lose your soul. He probably has told you that many times. There are a couple of things which should be here considered:

First of all, if Satan could do all the things he claims he's going to do, he would have long since done so. He hasn't done so, which means that you are still here, simply because he cannot do so.

THE CROSS OF CHRIST

These Promises given by God were just as real then as they are now. But then, due to the fact that the Cross was still in the future, the possession of the Promise was not as easy to obtain as now.

Since the Cross, the Holy Spirit can now live in the heart and life of the Believer, and do so permanently (I Cor. 3:16). The Lord doesn't require much of us, but He does require one thing, and that is faith. But it must be Faith in Christ and the Cross. In other words, the Cross of Christ must ever be the Object of our Faith, and it must be so on a permanent basis.

Once we do this, the Holy Spirit will use His Almighty Power on our behalf. To be sure, whatever might be hard for us is absolutely nothing for Him. But He will not work outside of the Cross. It is the Cross of Christ that gives Him the legal means to do what He does. We are given this great Truth in Romans 8:2.

If the Believer maintains his Faith in Christ and the Cross, and doesn't allow it to be moved elsewhere, *"the LORD shall preserve you from all evil."*

(8) **"THE LORD SHALL PRESERVE YOUR GOING OUT AND YOUR COMING IN FROM THIS TIME FORTH, AND EVEN FOREVERMORE."**

As the Psalm speaks of trust, likewise, it emphasizes the fact that the Lord not only protects, but has promised certain and guaranteed protection from any and all attacks by Satan, not only in the present, but on into the future, and *"even forevermore."* This is an ironclad contract that requires only *"trust in the Lord."*

PSALM 122

The Author is David:
Pray for the Peace of Jerusalem

(1) **"I WAS GLAD WHEN THEY SAID UNTO ME, LET US GO INTO THE HOUSE OF THE LORD."**

As noted, this Psalm was written by David.

THE SPIRITUAL JOURNEY OF EVERY BELIEVER

These Songs of Degrees express themselves, as previously stated, in three directions:

1. Israel's tragedy, her eventual trust, and ultimate triumph.
2. The Messiah's great distress regarding Israel's rejection of Him, as symbolized by the First Psalm of each triplet, which always is a distress Psalm; then the great trust that Christ had in the Word, as symbolized by the 119th Psalm, which is the Second Psalm of each set of three; His ultimate triumph, as He becomes the King of Israel in the coming Millennial Reign, which is symbolized by the Third Psalm in each set of triplets.
3. These Songs of Degrees, which are compacted in five sets of three, also symbolize the spiritual journey of every Believer. In our living for God, the great struggle between the Spirit and the flesh commences. Truly, it is a time of distress, as pictured in the First Psalm in each one of these sets. Gradually, the Believer begins to learn trust, which is symbolized by the second Psalm. The Messiah, Israel, and the Believer all eagerly await the day of triumph, when corruption will put on incorruption and mortality will put on immortality (I Cor. 15:53-54). This is symbolized by the Third Psalm of each set of three. The 122nd Psalm is the first of the *"triumph"* Psalms.

The Messiah's heart, saddened by the long centuries of Israel's unbelief, is now gladdened by their cry, *"Let us go into the House of Jehovah."*

(2) **"OUR FEET SHALL STAND WITHIN YOUR GATES, O JERUSALEM."**

This speaks of the time when Israel will stand triumphant, victorious, and redeemed in the great City of Jerusalem. So is it ever! Assurance of Salvation quickly follows upon true Repentance.

The Vision belongs to the future, but faith makes present what Grace promises. So the Messiah exclaims that His Feet and Israel's feet are already standing within the gates of Zion. So sure is it that it already has been announced.

(3) **"JERUSALEM IS BUILT AS A CITY THAT IS COMPACT TOGETHER."**

The Messiah is the Speaker in Verses 1, 2, 8, and 9. The Holy Spirit speaks in Verses 3 through 7.

JERUSALEM

In this Passage, Jerusalem is pictured by the Holy Spirit as a city that is built as He desires. In abbreviated form, this statement exclaims the fact of Jerusalem's tremendous troubles of the past that now are over. The battle has been fought and won! Israel, the Messiah, and the Glorified Saints all worship the Lord in triumph. Jerusalem has seen her last conflict and now will resound with eternal shouts!

(4) **"WHITHER THE TRIBES GO UP, THE TRIBES OF THE LORD, UNTO THE TESTIMONY OF ISRAEL, TO GIVE THANKS UNTO THE NAME OF THE LORD."**

They are here called the *"Tribes of the LORD,"* with this name in the Hebrew meaning *"JAH"* and not *"Jehovah."*

THE TWELVE TRIBES

At this time, Israel's Twelve Tribes, redeemed and with new hearts, which will take place immediately after the Second Coming, are presented as worshippers. Restored Jerusalem will be indwelt by a united people. All Israel will testify for Christ by ascending thither to the Messiah's Throne, which will be placed there.

Incidentally, the word *"compact"* in Verse 3 means united. Men have ever tried to unite on other than the Bible. They always have failed. Now because the Bible is the foundation, because the Holy Spirit is leading and guiding, and because the Messiah is reigning supreme, at long last Godly unity truly will prevail.

At this time, Israel will testify for Christ as she ought to have done in the past, but did not.

(5) "FOR THERE ARE SET THRONES OF JUDGMENT, THE THRONES OF THE HOUSE OF DAVID."

The term, *"Thrones of Judgment,"* means the Great Throne for Judgment, the Throne of the House of David, the Messiah's Throne (Mat., Chpt. 25). The plural is used to express greatness and majesty. This Throne will be placed in Jerusalem. This signifies the government of the world that will be upon the Shoulder of the Messiah (Isa. 9:6).

(6) "PRAY FOR THE PEACE OF JERUSALEM: THEY SHALL PROSPER WHO LOVE YOU."

This Command by the Holy Spirit should be obeyed even by modern Christians. Prosperity is promised to all who do obey it. This speaks of the great Promise that God gave to Abraham, *"I will bless them who bless you, and curse him who curses you"* (Gen. 12:3).

(7) "PEACE BE WITHIN YOUR WALLS, AND PROSPERITY WITHIN YOUR PALACES."

The Holy Spirit in Verse 6 not only tells us to pray for the peace of Jerusalem, but also gives us the prayer that we ought to pray. It is this Seventh Verse.

JERUSALEM AND PROSPERITY

The Holy Spirit sought their prosperity by enriching them at Pentecost, not because they were so admirable, but because they were the dwelling place of God. Even though it was given, sadly Israel rejected it. Because they rejected what the Holy Spirit offered, war instead took its place. In A.D. 70, Titus the Roman General destroyed the city and killed over one million Jews. Now, at long last, the peace given by the Holy Spirit will be accepted with joy and gladness. It will bring prosperity to Jerusalem, to Israel, and to the entire world.

(8) "FOR MY BRETHREN AND COMPANIONS' SAKES, I WILL NOW SAY, PEACE BE WITHIN YOU."

Two perfections of the Messiah's Heart appear in the last two Verses — its sensitivity to the Voice of the Holy Spirit and its Affection for the people of God's choice. Directly the Spirit invites the nations to say, *"Peace be within you,"* immediately the Messiah exclaims, *"I will now say, 'Peace be within you.'"* His Affection is expressed in the words, *"Brethren"* and *"companions."*

In the Twentieth Chapter of John's Gospel, the Lord anticipated the day here predicted in calling them His *"Brethren."* He said, *"Peace be unto you"* (Jn. 20:17-21).

(9) "BECAUSE OF THE HOUSE OF THE LORD OUR GOD I WILL SEEK YOUR GOOD."

This Song is for David and it relates to David, that is, to the True David, the Messiah.

PSALM 123

Author Unknown:
Prayer for Mercy

(1) "UNTO YOU LIFT I UP MY EYES, O YOU WHO DWELL IN THE HEAVENS."
Who wrote this Psalm is not known!

THE KING OF THE HEAVENS

This is the First Psalm of the second triplet; it, therefore, speaks of distress and trouble.

The word *"dwell"* would probably have been better translated by *"sit enthroned."* The contrast is thus shown between the great

King of the heavens and the proud but puny king of the nations.

In times of trouble, which this Psalm portrays, Israel was enjoined to look to God, and, as well, the Messiah. Once again, the Holy Spirit exhorts the modern Believer also to do this in times of acute trouble and otherwise.

(2) "BEHOLD, AS THE EYES OF THE SERVANTS LOOK UNTO THE HAND OF THEIR MASTERS, AND AS THE EYES OF A MAIDEN UNTO THE HAND OF HER MISTRESS; SO OUR EYES WAIT UPON THE LORD OUR GOD, UNTIL THAT HE HAVE MERCY UPON US."

In ancient times in the East, masters directed their servants with the hand rather than with the voice. Servants would, therefore, watch the hand of their master. Likewise, God's Hand directs, supplies, protects, comforts, caresses, corrects, and rewards His servants.

The lesson is carried out even further with the Holy Spirit directing man to place his total trust in God.

In the First Verse, the Messiah speaks Personally. In the following three Verses, He speaks on behalf of His people — hence, the *"I"* of Verse 1 and the *"our"* and *"us"* of Verses 2 through 4. He credits them (us) with His Own Faith and burdens Himself with their (our) fear.

(3) "HAVE MERCY UPON US, O LORD, HAVE MERCY UPON US: FOR WE ARE EXCEEDINGLY FILLED WITH CONTEMPT."

The meaning is twofold:

MERCY

1. The Messiah and those who followed Him were held with scorn and contempt by the Pharisees and the religious elite of Israel. As the Intercessor, Christ cried on behalf of His Disciples and those who followed Him. He asks for Mercy *"upon us."* How gladdening and delightful to the heart to see the manner in which Christ places Himself on equal basis with our fear, distress, trouble, and difficulties!

2. During the days of the Great Tribulation, when Israel seems at the point of annihilation, Christ will intercede for them. He, Whom they scorned and rejected, will cry for Mercy on their behalf. Men wonder how God could extend Mercy to a people who with murderous intent killed His Only Son. He will extend Mercy because the One they murdered will now plead on their behalf. God will not and cannot reject the plea of His Son, Christ Jesus. His Hand will beckon and not reject.

Hallelujah!

In reality, this is the only reason that any of us can claim His great Salvation. Christ intercedes on our behalf and God cannot deny His Son.

(4) "OUR SOUL IS EXCEEDINGLY FILLED WITH THE SCORNING OF THOSE WHO ARE AT EASE, AND WITH THE CONTEMPT OF THE PROUD."

The Messiah and His Disciples suffered the contempt and the scoffing of the proud and careless Pharisees.

Israel will suffer the same contempt during the second half of the Great Tribulation. The one called *"the proud"* will be the Antichrist. He will be *"at ease,"* thinking surely that victory is his and that Israel will fall like a ripe plum. The prayer by the Messiah on behalf of the Israel of the Third Verse will prove how wrong he is.

PSALM 124

The Author is David:
Praise for Deliverance

(1) "IF IT HAD NOT BEEN THE LORD WHO WAS ON OUR SIDE, NOW MAY ISRAEL SAY."

David wrote this Psalm and it is the Second Psalm in the second triplet; it is, therefore, a Psalm imploring trust.

TRUST

This Song, no doubt, related to David and to all who named the Name of the Lord. David was the writer, but the Messiah was the Speaker. So, it pertains to the Believer, Israel, and the Messiah, but it is more probable that the Holy Spirit had Hezekiah in mind when this was written.

Hezekiah was a symbol of Israel being shut up in Jerusalem with Sennacherib vowing Israel's destruction and also is symbolic of the Antichrist during the Battle of Armageddon. As the Lord sent an Angel in that day of so long ago, likewise, He will send Christ Jesus during this future time of Israel's distress.

God's Plan, whether it be through Israel or through the Church, has formidable forces arrayed against it. Satan vows destruction. For this reason, total trust must be placed in God or else no victory will be ours. As this statement was made of Israel, likewise it is made of the Believer. It is folly indeed to seek the trembling hand of man! Satan cannot be defeated except by the Power of God.

(2) "IF IT HAD NOT BEEN THE LORD WHO WAS ON OUR SIDE, WHEN MEN ROSE UP AGAINST US."

Men rose up against Israel of old, against the Messiah, and, as well, also rises up against the modern Believer. Satan uses men; almost always they are men of religion. They do the work of their father, Satan (Jn. 8:44).

(3) "THEN THEY HAD SWALLOWED US UP QUICK, WHEN THEIR WRATH WAS KINDLED AGAINST US."

The efforts by Satan seem to be overwhelming; therefore, the Messiah, when calling to remembrance past victories, animates Israel to trust for present ones. As faith makes actual the escape trusted for, so is it here regarded as an accomplished fact.

(4) "THEN THE WATERS HAD OVERWHELMED US, THE STREAM HAD GONE OVER OUR SOUL.

(5) "THEN THE PROUD WATERS HAD GONE OVER OUR SOUL."

The enemy is here compared to a raging flood, to wild beasts, and to a fowler. The term, *"Proud waters,"* expresses arrogancy. *"Waters"* would be better translated, *"flood."*

(6) "BLESSED BE THE LORD, WHO HAS NOT GIVEN US AS A PREY TO THEIR TEETH.

(7) "OUR SOUL IS ESCAPED AS A BIRD OUT OF THE SNARE OF THE FOWLERS: THE SNARE IS BROKEN, AND WE ARE ESCAPED."

As stated, Hezekiah illustrates this Psalm, but still, its message belongs to the future. In a vainglorious cylinder of Sennacherib's, previously shown in the British Museum, the proud monarch records that he shut up Hezekiah in Jerusalem *"as a bird in a cage."* But the Scriptures of Truth relate that the snare of the fowler was broken and the bird escaped! (II Chron. 32).

(8) "OUR HELP IS IN THE NAME OF THE LORD, WHO MADE HEAVEN AND EARTH."

If all men would realize this as much as Israel was forced to see and believe this Truth, there would be many Deliverances from sin, sickness, and suffering (Mat. 8:17; Jn. 10:10; I Pet. 2:24).

How so much the Holy Spirit implores us to look to the Lord, and not man. How so hard it is to come to this place of trust, and how so rewarding when finally our eyes begin to truly see and our ears begin to truly hear, and, thereby, we truly trust!

TRUST AND THE CROSS

About all that Believers could do before the Cross, was to express a desire to truly follow the Lord, and to truly trust Him. Do to the fact that the Holy Spirit did not then reside in the hearts and lives of Believers, while He still helped, still, it was nowhere like it is presently. In other words, it was much harder for the Believers then to obey.

Since the Cross, and due to the fact that the Holy Spirit now resides permanently within our hearts and lives (I Cor. 3:16), if we follow the directions of Scripture, the Holy Spirit will grandly help us, and trust in the Lord will be easy to follow. But the trouble is, most modern Believers do not know God's Prescribed Order of Victory.

GOD'S PRESCRIBED ORDER OF VICTORY

All Victory is in the Cross! And when we speak of *"victory,"* we are speaking of victory over sin, over Satan, and all the powers of darkness. We are given the description in Romans, Chapter 6.

In the first two Verses, we are told that the problem is *"sin."* In the next three verses (3-5), we are taken to the Cross. And one must remember, Paul is addressing his statement solely to Believers.

In taking us to the Cross this proclaims to us the Victory of the Cross. It simply means that our faith must ever be registered in Christ and what He did for us at the Cross. That is God's Prescribed Order of Victory.

When the Believer's Faith is properly anchored, the Holy Spirit, Who works exclusively within the framework of the Finished Work of Christ, will then gladly and grandly exhibit His Power on our behalf.

However, due to the fact that this is God's manner of Victory, Satan will do everything within his power to move our faith to something else, and most of the time, will use Preachers to do so. That's why Paul told us that we must *"fight the good fight of Faith"* (I Tim. 6:12). As we've said elsewhere in this Volume, while it is a *"fight,"* it is a *"good fight,"* because it is the *"right fight."* In fact, it is the only fight we can win. If we try to fight any other type of fight, we will lose, simply because we are on the wrong battlefield and fighting the wrong fight, a fight that God never intended for us to fight, simply because Christ has already fought this fight and won.

The Believer must ever understand that all victory is in the Cross, and only in the Cross! Any other direction, while it might look good on the surface, is simply not of God (Lk. 9:23; 14:27; Rom. 6:1-14; 8:1-2, 11; I Cor. 1:17-18, 23; 2:2).

PSALM 125

Author Unknown:
God Surrounds and Protects His People

(1) "THEY WHO TRUST IN THE LORD SHALL BE AS MOUNT ZION, WHCH CANNOT BE REMOVED, BUT ABIDES FOREVER."

It is not known who wrote this Psalm. As well, it is the Third Psalm in the second triplet and, thereby, a Psalm of Triumph. It celebrates the destruction of the Antichrist's kingdom and the establishment of the Messiah's Government.

This verse is broken down into three basic promises. They are:

TRUST IN THE LORD

Repeatedly, the Holy Spirit draws our attention to His demand and constant reminder of continued *"trust in the Lord."* Satan's greatest area of attack is to move us away from this foundation, the foundation we might quickly add, which is the Cross.

Likewise, when the Church begins to drift away from God, it, as well, starts demanding of its adherents that trust be placed in religious leaders instead of God. Such is seldom said so bluntly, but the implication is there. Sadly, the greatest area of testing that the modern Believer will face will little come from the world, but more from *"the Church."*

Sooner or later most denominations place in their constitutions and bylaws demands upon their followers that necessitate transferal of allegiance from God to man. The modern faithless Church, thereby, becomes a tool of Satan by demanding the opposite of the Holy Spirit. The Early Church instituted by the Holy Spirit had to face this same problem with the apostate Church (the Nation of Israel). It was either obey God or men (Acts 5:29). The modern Christian faces the same dilemma.

UNMOVEABLE

Despite Satan's repeated attacks, God has promised that Zion will always remain. He speaks of Jerusalem. No city has ever been contested more than this city. This Passage, plus others of similar content, is the reason why. Satan ever tries to abrogate the Word of God.

The modern conflict over Jerusalem is between Judaism and Islam. The Muslims claim a great part, or all, of the city. Israel claims it all, as well. Even though both presently are spiritually bankrupt, still, the Lord has said, *"In Isaac shall your seed be called"* (Gen. 21:12).

(Israel is the descendent of Isaac; the Arabs are the descendents of Ishmael.)

This conflict will intensify during the Great Tribulation. At first the Antichrist will seem to solve the problems presently existing between Israel and the Muslims, but then his true colors will be shown. He will break his seven-year covenant with Israel and other nations and declare war on Israel, with her suffering her first military defeat since becoming a nation in 1948.

During the Battle of Armageddon (Ezek.

Chpts. 38-39), it will look as though Israel will be annihilated with Jerusalem completely destroyed (Zech. 14:2).

Satan will then think that he has surely abrogated the Great Word of God. He will be sadly disappointed because Zechariah said, *"Then shall the LORD go forth, and fight against those nations as when He fought in the day of battle"* (Zech. 14:3). Israel and, thereby, Jerusalem will triumph because Israel at long last will finally put her *"trust in the LORD."*

ABIDES FOREVER

Trust in man may seem to be fruitful for a season, but, ultimately, man fails as all men must; consequently, those who trust in man fail as well. Those who trust in the Antichrist will fail. Those who trust in God will abide forever. What a Promise!

(2) "AS THE MOUNTAINS ARE ROUND ABOUT JERUSALEM, SO THE LORD IS ROUND ABOUT HIS PEOPLE FROM HENCEFORTH EVEN FOREVER."

The word *"henceforth"* defines the time of the fulfillment of this Prophecy. It will be the morn of Christ's Millennial Reign.

The abiding forever of *"Mount Zion"* is likened unto the eternal future of the *"mountains round about Jerusalem."* In other words, as long as those mountains exist, the Lord will be *"round about His people."* It also is quite a Promise!

(3) "FOR THE ROD OF THE WICKED SHALL NOT REST UPON THE LOT OF THE RIGHTEOUS; LEST THE RIGHTEOUS PUT FORTH THEIR HANDS UNTO INIQUITY."

This Passage would have been better translated, *"The Scepter of the lawless one* (Dan. 11:36; II Thess. 2:8) *shall not remain upon the lot of the Righteous."*

The *"Righteous"* is Christ and all who follow Him, and the place is Israel. This Verse predicts the close of the Antichrist's reign and of his possession of God's pleasant Land.

The latter portion of this Third Verse refers to the people of God whose hands are manacled to iniquitous oppression. This points to the liberation of Israel from the tyranny of the Antichrist which will take place at the Second Coming.

NOTES

THE RIGHTEOUS

The first *"Righteous"* used in this Verse pertains to Christ. The second *"Righteous"* pertains to Believers.

If the *"Righteous"* walk away from the Lord, and *"put forth their hands unto iniquity,"* the situation will deteriorate speedily.

Sin is the problem, and the only way to overcome sin, is by one's faith being placed exclusively in Christ and the Cross, even as we have repeatedly stated.

Trusting in something other than what the Lord has done for us at the Cross, constitutes the greatest sin of all. This is the *"iniquity"* here addressed. When this sin is committed, and we speak of one's faith being moved from the Cross to something else, then acts of sin will begin to show themselves, with the situation now deteriorating even faster. Sin is the problem, and the Cross of Christ is the solution, and the only solution.

(4) "DO GOOD, O LORD, UNTO THOSE WHO BE GOOD, AND TO THEM WHO ARE UPRIGHT IN THEIR HEARTS.

(5) "AS FOR SUCH AS TURN ASIDE UNTO THEIR CROOKED WAYS, THE LORD SHALL LEAD THEM FORTH WITH THE WORKERS OF INIQUITY: BUT PEACE SHALL BE UPON ISRAEL."

The Messiah's Goodness and Severity appear in these two Verses. Verse Four says that He will do good to those who follow Him, namely Israel, and to all those in the Kingdom Age who follow His Ways. Actually, it will be a time of goodness such as the world has never known before.

The Fifth Verse proclaims the fact, and picking up on the latter half of Verse Three, those who profess to be His citizens but compromise with evil will share the doom of the sons of Israel who compromise with the Antichrist. Those of Israel who do such will be eternally associated with the workers of iniquity. A path is either straight or crooked. If it is not after the Lord then it is crooked.

During the Kingdom Age Christ will not allow these *"workers of iniquity"* to take peace from Israel, or anywhere in the world for that matter! Peace will reign supreme because the Prince of Peace, the Lord Jesus Christ, will enforce it.

PSALM 126

*Author Unknown:
Deliverance from Captivity*

(1) "WHEN THE LORD TURNED AGAIN THE CAPTIVITY OF ZION, WE WERE LIKE THEM THAT DREAM."

Who wrote this Psalm is not known. As well, it is the First Psalm in the third triplet and, thereby, a Song of Distress or Trouble.

TURNING THE CAPTIVITY

There is a possibility that Hezekiah wrote this Psalm. It portrays the great victory won by the people of God over the Assyrians.

The deliverance of Jerusalem from mighty Sennacherib was so glorious that all of it seemed like a dream. Defeat for Israel was certain in as much as they had no defense against the mighty monarch. In Israel's mind they could see no way that victory could come. In fact, the Assyrian Monarch had already taken the northern kingdom of Israel into captivity. As well, he had taken basically all of Judah, with the exception of Jerusalem, and he was knocking on its door.

They had nothing to depend on but the Promises of God (II Ki. 19:20-34). And then it happened, *"The Angel of the LORD went out, and smote the Assyrians"* (II Ki. 19:35).

This, the great victory over Sennacherib, is a prelude to what will happen to the Antichrist at the Second Coming of the Lord, when it looks like there is no hope for Israel and Jerusalem.

LIKE A DREAM

The mighty army of Sennacherib was camped some miles from Jerusalem, with emissaries being constantly sent to that city demanding surrender. The Lord had spoken to the Prophet Isaiah that the great Assyrian monarch would not win this conflict; however, the siege lasted for nearly two years, which as should be understood, caused tremendous consternation among the people. No doubt, the questions ran thick and fast, as to how Jerusalem could be spared. A short time before the northern kingdom of Israel had been taken captive, and as well, the

NOTES

entirety of the country of Judah had been overrun by the Assyrians. Jerusalem was the only hold out. But then it happened, and without warning.

The people in Jerusalem went to bed one particular night, with the sword of Damocles, so to speak, continuing to hang over their heads; however, the morning would bring a totally different perspective. It could have happened in the following manner.

A runner comes from Sennacherib's army. The watchman on the wall announces his coming, not knowing who he is.

No doubt, when the man came into the city that early morning hour, having run the entire distance, he was in a hurry to proclaim the most excellent news to the citizenry of Jerusalem.

The news spread like wildfire. The entirety of the mighty army of Sennacherib was decimated. 185,000 soldiers who went to sleep the night before, did not awaken the next morning. What had caused it?

Sennacherib did not know, and neither did his wise men; however, the Lord informed Isaiah, and possibly Hezekiah, as to what had happened. One angel had decimated the entire army, and had done so in one night.

That's why the people then said, *"When the LORD turned again the captivity of Zion, we were like them who dream."*

They gave the Lord the credit; however, it had happened so fast, and with such magnitude, that it was almost like a dream.

(2) "THEN WAS OUR MOUTH FILLED WITH LAUGHTER, AND OUR TONGUE WITH SINGING: THEN SAID THEY AMONG THE HEATHEN, THE LORD HAS DONE GREAT THINGS FOR THEM.

(3) "THE LORD HATH DONE GREAT THINGS FOR US; WHEREOF WE ARE GLAD."

The Messiah reminds Israel of the great joy she experienced when the Lord gave great victory over Sennacherib. The city of Jerusalem became a campmeeting of joy. Every mouth was filled with laughter and every tongue with singing. Israel announced to all the surrounding nations what the Lord had done for them. They called it, *"great things,"* and *"great things"* it definitely was!

Such will be to all those who put their

trust in the Lord.

(4) "TURN AGAIN OUR CAPTIVITY, O LORD, AS THE STREAMS IN THE SOUTH."

The Messiah, as Israel's Great High Priest, cries to God on her behalf. He will not only remind Israel of the great victories won in the past but will insure by His petition the great victory they must have against the Antichrist.

OUR GREAT INTERCESSOR

The Lord Jesus Christ, our Great Intercessor, by using the word *"our"* makes Himself One with Israel's captivity and, thereby, insures her deliverance, *"for He has made Him to be sin for us, Who knew no sin; that we might be made the Righteousness of God in Him"* (II Cor. 5:21).

As well, Christ Jesus, our Great Intercessor, becomes One with us in our sin and captivity, and so does by taking the penalty of that sin upon Himself, that we might become One with Him in His Victory and Deliverance. Very easily the Heavenly Father could turn a deaf ear to our cry as well as to Israel's cry as, in fact, He would have to do. But to His Son and our Saviour, He will not and, in fact, cannot turn a deaf ear to Him. He will always hear His Petition and answer His Plea. This is the Intercession of Christ, all on our behalf (Heb. 7:25).

TURN AGAIN OUR CAPTIVITY

The phrase, *"To turn again our captivity,"* is a figure of speech for the restoration of prosperity.

The sense of this Verse is, *"Restore, O Jehovah, prosperity to us as the streams restore prosperity to the southern desert."*

This desert depends upon the streams of the springtime for its prosperity. Suffering burdens that land if these streams fail. Such is the vivid picture given here of Israel's future time of suffering.

(5) "THEY WHO SOW IN TEARS SHALL REAP IN JOY.

(6) "HE WHO GOES FORTH AND WEEPS, BEARING PRECIOUS SEED, SHALL DOUBTLESS COME AGAIN WITH REJOICING, BRINGING HIS SHEAVES WITH HIM."

More specifically this refers to Israel in the terrible day of the last half of the Great Tribulation. More pointedly, it refers to the Battle of Armageddon when it seems that Israel will be lost. At that time, the tears will copiously fall.

The *"precious seed"* that she has will be her last and only seed and represents her crying to God for deliverance. The Holy Spirit has promised that this seed will bring forth much fruit. As Israel's captivity was turned to rejoicing in the days of the Assyrian (Sennacherib), likewise, her tears will be turned to rejoicing in the days of the Assyrian (the Antichrist).

"This Seed is Christ," Paul said (Gal. 3:16).

"The Sheaves" a symbol like of the harvest which come at long last, is Righteousness.

During this time of great trouble, Israel will be delivered by the Coming of the Lord.

PSALM 127

*Written by Solomon:
Trusting God is Fruitful*

(1) "EXCEPT THE LORD BUILD THE HOUSE, THEY LABOR IN VAIN WHO BUILD IT: EXCEPT THE LORD KEEP THE CITY, THE WATCHMAN WAKES BUT IN VAIN."

The subscription says, *"A Song of degrees for Solomon."*

THE CENTRAL SONG OF DEGREES

While the subscription suggests that this Psalm was given by the Spirit to Solomon, still, it relates to an even greater degree to the *"Greater than Solomon."* It is the central Psalm of the Songs of Degrees. It is preceded and followed by seven Songs.

The sense of this Verse is that Faith contrasts the sufficiency of God with the insufficiency of man. Man's efforts to build a house, to defend it, and to furnish and enrich it are vain. This is the Second Psalm of the third triplet and, thereby, a Song of trust.

(2) "IT IS VAIN FOR YOU TO RISE UP EARLY, TO SIT UP LATE, TO EAT THE BREAD OF SORROWS: FOR SO HE GIVES HIS BELOVED SLEEP."

As usual, these Verses, being the Word of

God, unfold great Truths.

TREASURES

The argument of this Verse is that God gives to His loved one, while asleep, treasures that men toil for early and late in vain. Williams says, *"Thus He gave to Adam, while sleeping, a bride; to Abraham, a Covenant; to Jacob, a Promise; to Solomon, wisdom; and to Daniel, the substance and interpretation of the dream which the Chaldean magicians toiled in vain to discover."* [69]

"His Beloved" is singular in the Hebrew Text. Solomon's name was Jedediah (Beloved of Jehovah).

Consequently, this Psalm is *"for Solomon,"* relating to Solomon, that is, the True Solomon, the Messiah. He (the Messiah) is God's Beloved One, crucified on Calvary, buried in a tomb, raised from the Dead. He now sits beside God the Father. The next Verse explains what God gave to *"His Beloved"* in the sleep of death on Calvary's Cross that resulted in the Salvation of *"whosoever will"* (Rev. 22:17).

(3) "LO, CHILDREN ARE AN HERITAGE OF THE LORD: AND THE FRUIT OF THE WOMB IS HIS REWARD."

The *"house"* that is spoken of in Verse One, which is built by the Lord, will be full of children. This house is built of Living Stones — a multitude of redeemed sinners that no man can number (I Pet. 2:5; Rev. 7:9).

(4) "AS ARROWS ARE IN THE HAND OF A MIGHTY MAN; SO ARE CHILDREN OF THE YOUTH."

God is building a spiritual house of sons. The *"Mighty Man"* is Jesus Christ. These sons, loved and energized by Him, become more than conquerors. *"The Youth"* speaks of Christ dying at thirty-three years old and, thereby, bringing many sons (arrows) into *"the house."*

(5) "HAPPY IS THE MAN THAT HAS HIS QUIVER FULL OF THEM: THEY SHALL NOT BE ASHAMED, BUT THEY SHALL SPEAK WITH THE ENEMIES IN THE GATE."

"The Man" is Jesus Christ.

CALVARY

The great price paid at Calvary was not in vain. Millions have flocked and will flock to His banner, *"His quiver full of them."*

Our Lord said, *"And they shall come from the east, and from the west, and from the north, and from the south, and shall sit down in the Kingdom of God"* (Lk. 13:29). The fruit of the great price paid at Calvary is the souls of men brought to Jesus, which, thereby, makes *"the Man,"* Christ Jesus, *"happy."*

The Promise is given here by the Holy Spirit that none will ever be ashamed that they followed Him.

ENEMIES

"The enemies in the gate" speak of the *"gates of Hell."* Jesus said, "And upon this Rock I will build My Church *(House);* and the gates of Hell shall no prevail against it" (Mat. 16:18). Every *"enemy"* in the gate will be destroyed by those who name the Great Name of Jesus (Mk. 16:15-18).

(It is quite true that God often gives sleep to a sleepless patient in answer to prayer, but that is not the doctrine of the second Verse of this Psalm. Its teaching is that God gives gifts to His obedient children while sleeping, gifts which human energy can never win, gifts which are rewarded because of one's faith in Christ and what Christ has done for us at the Cross.)

PSALM 128

*Writer Unknown:
The Rewards of Faithfulness*

(1) "BLESSED IS EVERY ONE WHO FEARS THE LORD; WHO WALKS IN HIS WAYS."

As noted, the writer of this Psalm is not known.

THE COMING KINGDOM AGE

This Psalm is the closing Song of the third triplet and, therefore, a Song of Triumph. It triumphantly pictures the happiness which Israel and humanity will enjoy when the Messiah is seated as King in Zion. This Psalm looks forward to that great and glorious day, consequently, expressing the exclamated joy of those who participate in it.

In that day (the coming Kingdom Age) all will fear the Lord and walk in His Ways and will, therefore, be *"blessed"* (happy). It is all a vivid picture of the future Millennial Kingdom.

(2) "FOR YOU SHALL EAT THE LABOR OF YOUR HANDS: HAPPY SHALL YOU BE, AND IT SHALL BE WELL WITH YOU."

At that time, the coming Kingdom Age, the Messiah will be seated as King. From Him will go out streams of Blessings and rivers of Joy. They will flow to the ends of the Earth. The Earth will be productive, and Israel and Jerusalem will be peaceful and prosperous.

In the present spiritual climate most do not *"eat the labor of their hands."* It is wasted through drought, famine, pestilence, war, and grief. In that great coming day, these evils will no longer rule as they now do; consequently, happiness and well-being will be the norm. This will not be brought about by a change of philosophy, political party, advancement, or science, but by a Person, the Man Christ Jesus.

(3) "YOUR WIFE SHALL BE AS A FRUITFUL VINE BY THE SIDES OF YOUR HOUSE: YOUR CHILDREN LIKE OLIVE PLANTS ROUND ABOUT YOUR TABLE.

(4) "BEHOLD, THAT THUS SHALL THE MAN BE BLESSED WHO FEARS THE LORD."

The words, *"Your wife,"* referred to Israel that is no longer the *"wife of whoredoms"* of Hosea (Hos. 1:2). As well, the *"children"* will not be *"children of whoredoms"* who come from the wayward wife. But this *"wife,"* a fully restored Israel, shall be a *"fruitful vine"* and will now become a part of *"Your House." "Your children"* will be like *"olive plants"* and will have their backslidings healed. Hosea said, *"His beauty shall be as the olive tree"* (Hos. 14). Restored Israel will be given a place at the table.

Concerning this great and glorious time, the coming Kingdom Age, every man on the face of the Earth who fears the Lord will be *"blessed."*

(5) "THE LORD SHALL BLESS YOU OUT OF ZION: AND YOU SHALL SEE THE GOOD OF JERUSALEM ALL THE DAYS OF YOUR LIFE.

(6) "YEA, YOU SHALL SEE YOUR CHILDREN'S CHILDREN, AND PEACE UPON ISRAEL."

There is a charge of untruthfulness made by unbelievers regarding this Psalm. It pertains to this Fifth Verse. It is objected that its statements are not true, for many excellent Christian people have unproductive lands or trades, sickly wives, and childless homes.

THE PROMISE

That is true now because Christ is still neglected and disowned by the world. Man prefers to govern himself; the result is misery. Christian people have to share this misery and sympathize with their fellow creatures. But when the Messiah is crowned in Jerusalem, the statements in this Psalm will become true, and its truth will be recognized.

In Deuteronomy 28 Israel is warned that if they turned away from the Bible they would not enjoy the labor of their own hands but others would eat the crops produced by their toil. This has come to pass; it is true today and it will remain true until Israel repents and turns to the Lord.

As well, this principle affects all people and all nations. All that is promised in this Psalm emphasizes the reality of the promised happiness under the future government of the Messiah and the dependence of both the happiness and the prosperity upon relationship to Him.

As well, in this present time and for all Believers, faith can spiritualize the material blessings of this Song and make them real and present. Thus, homes can be filled with spiritual and personal children, as well as lands clothed with spiritual and literal harvest, and hearts filled with Millennial Peace that will cause Believers to taste the happiness of Verse One and experience the prosperity of Verse Four.

A PERSONAL EXPERIENCE

On our Ministry grounds is a building named after the great Pentecostal Missionary, H.B. Garlock. I had the privilege of meeting him just once and his wife several times. He was a great man of God who saw parts of West Africa opened up to the Gospel. During the Forties and Fifties, the miracles that God gave to him in Africa were like a

Chapter out of the Book of Acts. He tells of one such experience and it relates to this particular Psalm.

While in Africa, brother Garlock had contracted black water fever, which was by and large a sentence of death. There seemed to be no hope. Preparations for his funeral were already being made.

He recalled the moment when the pronouncement of death came and with his body wracked with fever, he began to implore the Lord. He asked that his life be spared and that God would touch him and give him healing.

The Spirit of God drew his attention to the Bible on his bed. He opened it at random, and the Holy Spirit drew his attention to this Verse, *"Yea, you shall see your children's children."* Healing came in a matter of minutes.

In the early 1980's, I was in Central America. I had the occasion to meet the great grandson-in-law of Brother Garlock. He told me how that brother Garlock had performed the wedding ceremony for him and his wife, brother Garlock's great granddaughter.

He said on this occasion Brother Garlock told of this great experience that had taken place so long ago in West Africa and how God had promised him that he would see his grandchildren. And so it was.

Brother Garlock went home to be with the Lord some years ago while in his mid eighties. His lovely wife Ruth, followed some years later. The Promises of God will never fail.

PSALM 129

Author Unknown:
A Prayer for Judgment for Those
Who Afflict Israel

(1) "MANY A TIME HAVE THEY AFFLICTED ME FROM MY YOUTH, MAY ISRAEL NOW SAY."

The author of this Psalm is unknown and it is the First Song of the fourth triplet, and, as in correspondence with the other groups, its theme is trouble. The first three Verses recall past trials; the last four, future trouble; the central Verse justifies God's Actions in both periods (Vs. 4).

The Speaker here is the Messiah.

NOTES

ISRAEL

Our Lord here recalls Israel's struggles in her beginnings as a nation. In fact, the word *"youth"* refers to this particular time (Jer. 2:2; Ezek. 16:4; Hos. 2:15). Her *"afflictions"* were without and within. From the time of God's call of Abraham (Gen. 12:1), she suffered tremendous animosity from the surrounding nations, which included Egypt, the Syrians, the Assyrians, plus the hostile tribes such as the Canaanites, and others who were ensconced in the Promised Land. The cause of *"affliction"* was three fold:

1. Israel was called by God to give the world the Bible.
2. Israel, as well, was to be the womb of the Messiah.
3. Israel was to evangelize the World.

She succeeded in the first two and failed in the last but will yet fulfill God's Call of World Evangelism in the coming Kingdom Age (Isa. 66:18-21).

Consequently, the opposition by Satan is obvious. But despite that opposition, the Lord said, *"Shall I bring to the birth, and not cause to bring forth? Saith the LORD: shall I cause to bring forth, and shut the womb? Saith your God"* (Isa. 66:9).

In fact, all who follow the Lord will suffer the same *"affliction."*

(2) "MANY A TIME HAVE THEY AFFLICTED ME FROM MY YOUTH: YET THEY HAVE NOT PREVAILED AGAINST ME."

The meaning of this Verse is threefold:

ISRAEL'S COMING VICTORY

First of all, the statement, *"Have not prevailed against me,"* may seem strange to the unspiritual ear, especially considering Israel's destruction by Titus the Roman General in A.D. 70 and their subsequent dispersion throughout the nations of the world now for nearly two thousand years; however, man has the failing of surveying a situation only in part. God looks at the whole. Ultimately, Israel will reign supreme over this obvious trouble and tragedy. The Holy Spirit said this:

"Who has heard such a thing? Who has seen such things? Shall the Earth be made to bring forth in one day? Or shall a nation be

born at once? For as soon as Zion travailed, she brought forth her children"* (Isa. 66:8).

THE MESSIAH

The affliction against the Messiah was horrendous to say the least. But Satan and his minions did not prevail and, in fact, could not prevail.

The opposition of the Pharisees and Sadducees, who were, along with the Scribes, Israel's religious elite and were used by Satan, nevertheless, they did not prevail. The Messiah, even though not recognized then by Israel as such and despite the great opposition, went to Calvary and redeemed humanity by the shedding of His Precious Blood; likewise, on the Third Day He rose from the dead. Now He sits by the Right Hand of the Father victorious over all powers of darkness (Eph. 1:20-23).

Likewise, He is coming again. Satan will energize the Antichrist as no man has ever been helped by the evil one. But the Antichrist will not prevail. Jesus Christ will come again. In this Verse we have His Promise (Rev., Chpt. 19).

BELIEVERS

Every Child of God will be greatly contested by the powers of darkness. And even though the *"affliction"* may be severe, still, we have this Promise that they will not prevail against us because they did not prevail against Christ. The Christian has no past, while Satan has no future.

(3) "THE PLOWERS PLOWED UPON MY BACK: THEY MADE LONG THEIR FURROWS."

This refers to the scourging of the backs of the people of God while in Egyptian slavery. As well, it refers to the literal pulling of plow yokes that Israelites were forced to wear as beasts of burden. The latter perhaps is the true meaning, for in Verse Four it states that God cut them loose from such cords of slavery.

PERSECUTION

As well, it definitely includes the Midonites, the Syrians, and others. The power that energized them was Satan. He also moved the High Priests and the Romans to scourge the Messiah, the True Israel. The anguish of that form of torture is vividly expressed here by the terms, *"They plowed,"* and *"they made long their furrows."*

But the affliction that yet awaits Israel will far exceed what has already been suffered, and the faith of the remnant will then be sustained by the teaching of this Song. Just as the enemy failed in the past, so he will fail in the future. His failure in the past is stated in Verses 1 through 3; his failure in the future is predicted in Verses 5 through 8.

(4) "THE LORD IS RIGHTEOUS: HE HAS CUT ASUNDER THE CORDS OF THE WICKED."

The statement, *"Jehovah is righteous,"* is placed in the center of this Psalm.

THE WAYS OF THE LORD

This Verse vindicates the actions of the Lord in permitting the past and future afflictions of His people. However sharp and prolong the trial may be, faith always justifies God and is satisfied that there is a righteous reason why such suffering should be permitted.

As in the case of Job, so in every similar trial the end glorifies God and secures blessing to man; wisdom is justified of her children; God in His moral Government vindicates Himself and disciplines His people. The fruit of trial, therefore, secures vindication for God and benefaction for man.

The meaning is clear, even though the Lord will allow great opposition and at times seeming defeat, still, He has promised that He will *"cut asunder the cords of the wicked."* Satan will not prevail as long as we trust the Righteousness of the Lord and not our own righteousness.

(5) "LET THEM ALL BE CONFOUNDED AND TURNED BACK WHO HATE ZION."

This prayer was prayed by the Messiah and is, therefore, guaranteed of fulfillment. This should be a warning to the people and nations of the world who *"hate Zion."*

THE ARABS

In present circumstances, the Arab people, over one hundred million strong and glutted with hundreds of billions of dollars of oil money, repeatedly express their hatred of

"Zion." In late 2005, the new President of Iran stated that *"Israel should be blotted from the face of the earth."* He has made several other statements in this same capacity since then. In fact, Israel, at this time, is pretty much friendless except for America, who's favor, however, seems to be weakening.

The stage is already being set for the advent of the Antichrist. Israel has come close to annihilation many times in the past. This future day of the Antichrist's aggression will seem like the death knell. But the Messiah has said that the Antichrist will be confounded as well as all who follow him. This is a Prayer, a Promise, and a Prediction that should well be heeded by all.

(6) "LET THEM BE AS THE GRASS UPON THE HOUSETOPS, WHICH WITHERS AFORE IT GROWS UP."

Housetops in the Middle East, for the most part, are flat; consequently, at times, grass will grow on top of the houses, because of seed that is blown on the tops of these houses by dust, etc. Having no soil, the grass soon withers.

The Antichrist and all who oppose Israel will likewise *"wither."* The doom of the enemy is here predicted and desired.

The destruction of the firstborn in Egypt and of the Assyrian host in the days of Hezekiah were but foreglimpses of what the Righteous Lord will do. Jehovah, in a judgment that was righteous, punished in these instances the oppressor and delivered the oppressed. Such will Jehovah do in that coming day.

(7) "WHEREWITH THE MOWER FILLED NOT HIS HAND; NOR HE WHO BINDS SHEAVES HIS BOSOM."

In this passage the Antichrist is likened to *"the mower."* He will not fill his hand nor gather profit from his invasion of Israel, but will rather suffer the very opposite!

(8) "NEITHER DO THEY WHICH GO BY SAY, THE BLESSING OF THE LORD BE UPON YOU: WE BLESS YOU IN THE NAME OF THE LORD."

The sense of this Verse is:

WHAT GOD HAS BLESSED CANNOT BE CURSED

Even though Israel has long strayed from God, even though the curse has rested upon her (Deut. 28), even though the Antichrist will think that God has deserted His ancient People, still, he will find to his utter dismay that God has not deserted them and that their oppressor will have no blessing from the Lord.

Let it ever be known that what God has blessed cannot be cursed. While it is true that God may allow a curse that comes from His Hand, nevertheless, woe be unto anyone else who lifts his hand against *"God's Anointed."*

Millions have called Israel *"Christ killers."* They have erroneously thought, as Adolf Hitler did, that they would have the blessing of God in persecuting these ancient people. Let it here be said that there can never be any blessing from the Lord upon those who would persecute Israel or lift a hand against any that God has called. The words of the Holy Spirit are, *"Touch not My anointed, and do My Prophets no harm"* (Ps. 105:15).

PSALM 130

*Author Unknown:
My Soul Waits for the Lord*

(1) "OUT OF THE DEPTHS HAVE I CRIED UNTO YOU, O LORD."

"The depths" relate to the depth of the affliction which Israel will suffer under the False Messiah, which will be the just punishment for her rejection of the True Messiah.

As well, it refers to the cause of these *"depths,"* which is sin.

Who wrote this Psalm is not known. It is the Second Psalm in the fourth triplet and, thereby, a song of trust.

INTERCESSION

The first four Verses are a cry for forgiveness from the *"guilt"* of sin; the last four for deliverance from the *"misery"* of sin. The last line of this Psalm is to be understood as a prayer for deliverance from the iniquities which the righteous suffer from evil men.

The Singer of this glorious refrain is the Messiah. The First Verse proclaims His Sob of Anguish. He will, as Israel's High Priest in the day of her future sufferings, confess her sins, plead for forgiveness from them, and animate her to set her hope upon Jehovah, Who will surely redeem her out of the hand of her enemies.

As well, and with the same intensity of petition does the Lord intercede on behalf of all who name His Great Name. The wonder of all His Intercession is beyond the comprehension of frail mortals. Even though we have stated it several times in the past and will, no doubt, do so in the future, still, due to its significance, allow us to state it again.

CHRIST OUR SUBSTITUTE

Christ became our Substitute in all things. Mere mortals could not go to Calvary for their own sins because the Sacrifice would have been tainted. The Redeemer went on our behalf, becoming our Substitute. We are to identify with that in order to be Saved. As we do so, and have faith in what was done, the Father accepts the Sacrifice of His Only Son on our behalf and accredits us with such as though we had offered the same perfect Sacrifice. His Resurrection is accredited to us accordingly (Rom. 6:3-5). As our Substitute, He even allows us to be seated with Him, in Spirit, in Heavenly Places (Eph. 2:6).

It is the great and glorious doctrine of *"Substitution and Identification."* He became my Substitute and I identify with Him, which speaks of what He did at the Cross, always the Cross (I Cor. 1:17-18, 21, 23; 2:2).

As well, he became my Substitute in the all-important aspect of Intercession (Heb. 7:25). The following Verses will shed even more light on this subject.

(2) "LORD, HEAR MY VOICE: LET YOUR EARS BE ATTENTIVE TO THE VOICE OF MY SUPPLICATIONS.

(3) "IF YOU, LORD, SHOULD MARK INIQUITIES, O LORD, WHO SHALL STAND?"

The depravity of all men is declared in this Verse. All have failed and failed repeatedly; consequently, no man, irrespective of his so-called good works, can stand before God. The utter lostness of man has never been understood by the human race and little by the Church, hence, the abounding of self-righteousness. The only One Who can stand Righteous in the Presence of Jehovah is Christ.

Consequently, we can have His Righteousness, which we obtain by simple faith in Him and what He did for us at the Cross, or else we can try to obtain righteousness by good works, or some other method, which amounts to self-righteousness, which God can never accept. Those are the two choices! But let it ever be understood:

God will accept the Righteousness of Christ and the Righteousness of Christ alone. He will accept nothing else.

As well, we must remember that the Righteousness of Christ is afforded us strictly through the Cross, and by no other means. Consequently, it requires Faith in Christ and what He did for us at the Cross for this Righteousness to be obtained (Rom. 6:3-5, 11).

(4) "BUT THERE IS FORGIVENESS WITH YOU, THAT YOU MAY BE FEARED."

The first word in Verse Four in the Hebrew Text is *"for"* and corresponds with the *"for"* of Verse Seven, and the double argument then clearly appears that a cry for forgiveness of sins is to be addressed to God, for only He can forgive. A cry for Deliverance from oppression is to be made to Him, for He is mighty to save. A double lesson is at the same time taught: First, Divine forgiveness aims for holiness as a consequence; second, that suffering is the certain companion of Sanctification because evil hates goodness.

This Psalm, therefore, recognizes the fact of suffering but attaches more importance to the forgiveness of sin which causes suffering than to the deliverance from suffering itself. Men are always very willing to ask God to relieve them from suffering but are very unwilling to ask Him to save them from sinning.

A better translation of Verse Four may be thus rendered, *"for with You is forgiveness to the end that You may be reverenced."*

SIN AND THE CROSS

Man's problem is sin! This refers to the following:

Man is not condemned near as much for what he does, as bad as that might be, as for who and what he is. He is a sinner, and we speak of original sin, and as such, there is no way that he can untangle himself from the roots of this dread malady. He is hopelessly bound, with it taking its deadly toll. It is clearly understood that the world little knows or understands the terrible bondage of sin, but worse still, the Church seems to little understand it also.

At the present time, the word *"sin"* is little used behind most pulpits, and the word *"sinner"* almost never! The use of such, it is stated, might offend the listener. What does the Bible say about the sinner, i.e., mankind in general?

"As it is written (Ps. 14:1-3), *there is none righteous, no, not one* (addresses the complaint of the Jews and clinches the argument with the Scriptures, which the Jews could not deny):

"There is none who understands (proclaims total depravity), *there is none who seek after God* (man left on his own will not seek God and, in fact, cannot seek God; he is spiritually dead).

"They are all gone out of the Way (speaks of the lost condition of all men; the 'Way' is God's Way), *they are together become unprofitable* (refers to the terrible loss in every capacity of wayward man); *there is none who does good, no, not one* (the Greek Text says, 'useless!').

"Their throat is an open sepulcher (the idea is of an open grave, with the rotting remains sending forth a putrid stench); *with their tongues they have used deceit* (speaks of guile, deception, hypocrisy, etc.); *the poison of asps is under their lips* (man cannot be trusted in anything he says):

"Whose mouth is full of cursing (wishes someone evil or hurt) *and bitterness* (bitter and reproachful language):

"Their feet are swift to shed blood (the world is filled with murder, killing, and violence):

"Destruction and misery are in their ways (all brought about by sin):

"And the way of peace have they not known (and cannot know until Christ returns):

"There is no fear of God before their eyes (there is no fear of God, because unbelieving man does not know God)" (Rom. 3:10-18).

There is only one solution for this terrible dilemma, and that is the Cross of Christ! Not ten solutions, not five, not even two, only one!

NOTES

Considering that the Cross of Christ is the only solution, what is the Church doing about this? Is it preaching the Cross? Is it proclaiming the Cross? Is it lifting up Jesus as it regards the Cross? Is it preaching the Cross as the only answer for man's dilemma?

No, it is doing none of these things, but rather is offering its platitudes of self-made hypocrisy — and hypocrisy it is. Consequently, no souls are Saved, no lives are changed, no bondages are broken, and because the real problem is not addressed, not at all! Let us say it again:

The problem is sin, and the only solution is the Cross of Christ.

(5) "I WAIT FOR THE LORD, MY SOUL DOES WAIT, AND IN HIS WORD DO I HOPE.

(6) "MY SOUL WAITS FOR THE LORD MORE THAN THEY WHO WATCH FOR THE MORNING: I SAY, MORE THAN THEY WHO WATCH FOR THE MORNING."

This is faith that waits on God and that waits for God. Saul was willing to wait on God but not to wait for God, and so he lost the Kingdom (I Sam. 10:8; 13:8-14).

(7) "LET ISRAEL HOPE IN THE LORD: FOR WITH THE LORD THERE IS MERCY, AND WITH HIM IS PLENTEOUS REDEMPTION.

(8) "AND HE SHALL REDEEM ISRAEL FROM ALL HIS INIQUITIES."

Once again, a great Truth is given to us.

THE SONG OF TRUST

This Song of Trust gives abundant hope not only for Israel, but for all who would take advantage of God's great Salvation Plan; likewise, the type of forgiveness that God extends is the only type of forgiveness God will recognize in the hearts of His Children. The penalty for unforgiveness is extremely harsh and rightly so. The penalty is that if we do not forgive as God forgives, the Lord will not forgive us (Mat. 6:14-15).

Men are fond of devising their own types of forgiveness, which God will not recognize and, therefore, voids. The penalty remains; consequently, the pulpit and the pew in thousands of Churches are barren, lifeless, and void. They have refused to forgive, and, therefore, God refuses to forgive them. Sins pile up that are unforgiven, unwashed, and uncleansed. All fellowship with God is abrogated; communion instantly stops, with the person being treated of necessity by Jehovah as a heathen (Mat. 18:17).

The truth is that even the most consecrated Christian is constantly needing forgiveness (Rom. 3:23; I Jn. 1:7). This is what the Intercession of Christ is all about (Heb. 7:25).

If this is not known and understood, it is a sure sign of acute self-righteousness, which speaks of hypocrisy (Mat. 7:5).

PSALM 131

*The Author is David:
Humility Before the Lord*

(1) "LORD, MY HEART IS NOT HAUGHTY, NOR MY EYES LOFTY: NEITHER DO I EXERCISE MYSELF IN GREAT MATTERS, OR IN THINGS TOO HIGH FOR ME."

David wrote this Psalm, and it is the Third Song in the fourth triplet and is, thereby, a Song of Triumph; however, the Triumph that is recorded here will be little understood by the unspiritual ear. It speaks of humility which is, in fact, the greatest Triumph of all. Even though David wrote the Words, the Messiah was the Speaker and, thereby, the Subject of this Song.

THE HEAVENLY MONARCH

The Holy Spirit, basing His Appeal upon the truth of these Passages, invites Israel to reposeful confidence in such a Monarch as the Messiah and to enter and enjoy the Kingdom promised in the last Verse of the previous Psalm.

Earthly Monarchs are mostly proud, selfish, ignorant, self-confident, unjust, and cruel. The Messiah offers a contrast to all this. The Spirit paints Him in beautiful colors: neither haughty nor proud, neither self-confident nor willful, but gentle, submissive, and resigned. He is subject to God's Will and Government as a weaned child accepts and submits to the wise and loving action of its mother in changing its food.

It is difficult for the unspiritual heart to understand the God of Glory submitting Himself to such and, in fact, becoming such.

The Holy Spirit through the Apostle Paul said, *"Let this mind be in you, which was also in Christ Jesus"* (Phil. 2:5).

(2) "SURELY I HAVE BEHAVED AND QUIETED MYSELF, AS A CHILD THAT IS WEANED OF HIS MOTHER: MY SOUL IS EVEN AS A WEANED CHILD."

The Messiah is saying that He recognizes His Place under others as a subject of training and discipline. Luke said, *"And the Child grew, and waxed strong in spirit, filled with wisdom: and the Grace of God was upon Him"* (Lk. 2:40).

A CHILD

The child is used as an example primarily because it is totally helpless regarding its own defense and, therefore, must depend totally upon others.

Likewise, Christ said, *"Whosoever therefore shall humble himself as this little child, the same is greatest in the Kingdom of Heaven"* (Mat. 18:4).

We are commanded to defend the faith (Jude, Vs. 3) but never to defend ourselves; likewise, Christ would not defend Himself but would consign all such to the Father. We are to do the same!

The sense of this Verse is that as a weaned child submits its will to that of its mother, so will the Messiah, as God's Perfect King be wholly subject to God and by ruling in His Fear, this will form a contrast to self-willed human kings. Thus, He will rule the world in the coming time of the Kingdom Age. As stated, what a contrast to present day potentates.

(3) "LET ISRAEL HOPE IN THE LORD FROM HENCEFORTH AND FOREVER."

In effect, the Psalmist, i.e., *"Christ"* is saying, *"Let Israel follow My example of satisfaction and hope, as a weaned child, forever."*

She is to do this because the Character of the King being such, a Perfect Government will, therefore, be enjoyed by His Subjects, and Israel will dwell in peace.

In the previous Psalm (Ps. 130:7), the nation is encouraged to set her hope on Jehovah because He was about to redeem her (Ps. 130:8). In this Psalm (131:3) she is invited to continue setting her hope upon

Him *"from henceforth and forever"* because the promised Redemption shall have then become a reality.

PSALM 132

*The Author is David:
Worship and Blessings with
the Return of the Ark*

(1) "LORD, REMEMBER DAVID, AND ALL HIS AFFLICTIONS."

The authorship of this Psalm is not certain, but it is almost sure that it was written by David. Some have felt that Hezekiah might have been the author. While it is true that Hezekiah is shadowed, as we will refer to later, still, there is not the slightest bit of evidence regarding his authorship or even Solomon's, as some also have suggested.

David's name is mentioned four times in this Psalm. The fact that the Psalmist does not once refer to himself as being someone other than David but, rather, says everything about David is ample proof that David himself wrote the Psalm.

As well, only David would know all the details of his own trials and his own afflictions as referred to in Verses 1 through 5.

It seems to be obvious that the author was brought up in Bethlehem Ephratah, which was the home of David, and lends credence to identifying the author as David. As well, the author addresses God as *"Your servant David"* and *"Your Anointed"* which are Davidic terms.

AFFLICTIONS

David had many afflictions (troubles), which he prayed about many times. This is the First Psalm in the fifth and last triplet, and it, as the rest of the First Psalm in each set, denotes trouble. These Ascent Psalms speak of Promise, Presence, and Provision, as well as of Trouble, Trust, and Triumph.

The first recalls blessing promised to the Messiah; the second, blessing pictured with the Messiah; the third, blessing predicted from the Messiah. Until He comes there will only be distress of nations (Lk. 21:25), which spells *"afflictions"* which teach trust (Williams).[70]

However, when He comes, there will be universal concord, and Zion His City and Throne, will be an inexhaustible source of happiness to Israel and to all the world. In other words, the terrible tension evidenced in Israel proper and Jerusalem in particular at this present time, will be no more.

This Psalm contains a Prayer and Promise, and, as always, the Promise exceeds the prayer in Grace.

(2) "HOW HE SWORE UNTO THE LORD, AND VOWED UNTO THE MIGHTY GOD OF JACOB."

We see in this particular Verse as well the strength of the Modern Church.

THE ARK OF THE COVENANT

The *"vow"* that David makes concerns the bringing of the Ark of the Covenant to Jerusalem. The Ark was where God resided between the Mercy Seat and the Cherubim. It was the source of Israel's Strength and Grace. It represented the Power of God; likewise, the strength of the modern Church is not its buildings, educational institutions, ministerial degrees, numbers of people, or the finery of its appointments; the strength of the Church is the Glory of God, of which the Ark is a Type.

Everything in Israel revolved around the Tabernacle which housed the Ark where the Glory of God resided; likewise, if everything in the Church does not revolve around the Power, Presence, and Provision of the Holy Spirit, the Church will be little more than any other secular institution. If the Glory of God is present, then it is *"Church."* If the Glory of God is not present, it is just another gathering of people.

As David pined for the Ark, likewise, the Preacher must pine for the Glory of God. As David went to any length in order to bring the Ark into Jerusalem, likewise, the Preacher of the Gospel and all others for that matter, should seek God incessantly for the anointing of the Holy Spirit to rest upon the pulpit and the pew.

With the Glory of God, broken hearts will be mended; Deliverance will be preached to the captives; blinded eyes will be opened; the bruised will be set at liberty, and the acceptable year of the Lord proclaimed (Lk. 4:18-19). Without the Glory of God, all are man-made and, therefore, tainted, flawed, and worthless.

THE MIGHTY GOD OF JACOB

It is interesting that the Holy Spirit through David used the term, *"Mighty God of Jacob."* It is done for a reason. No finer example is given in the Bible than Jacob, who deserved nothing good from God but, in turn, was given everything and, above all, was changed from a fraud to a Prince — Israel.

The Holy Spirit designed it thusly in order that we may have hope as well. For every man is a Jacob, which implies fraud, schemer, cheat, and scoundrel (self-righteousness blanches at this), and only God can changes such into Purity, Holiness, Sanctification, Grace, Godliness, and Glory.

(3) "SURELY I WILL NOT COME INTO THE TABERNACLE OF MY HOUSE, NOR GO UP INTO MY BED;

(4) "I WILL NOT GIVE SLEEP TO MY EYES, OR SLUMBER TO MY EYELIDS,

(5) "UNTIL I FIND OUT A PLACE FOR THE LORD, AN HABITATION FOR THE MIGHTY GOD OF JACOB."

It is obvious that David has placed the business of Israel and his own occupation aside, with his total attention being given to the bringing of the Ark to Jerusalem.

This is the type of zeal that brings Revival. As well, it shows David's conscious knowledge of the importance of this act. He is being urged and prompted by the Holy Spirit.

A PLACE FOR THE LORD

If the Preachers of this nation (or any nation), or anyone else for that matter, would have the same hunger for Revival as David evidenced here, then as the Ark came, Revival will come as well!

David made a *"place"* for the Lord. Sadly, in most Christian lives the Lord has no *"place."*

The last Message that Christ gave to the Church is found in Revelation Three, *"Behold, I stand at the door, and knock: if any man hear My Voice, and open the door, I will come into him, and will sup with him, and he with Me"* (Rev. 3:20). That particular Church had no place for Him. Tragically, the far greater majority of Churches in America and around the world, likewise, have no *"place"* for Him. Only a few do.

David was one of the few kings of Israel who made a *"place"* for the Ark. What kind of *"place"* does God occupy in your heart?

Then, the Lord occupied a Tabernacle; later a Temple; now, the heart and life of the Believer (I Cor. 3:16).

(6) "LO, WE HEARD OF IT AT EPHRATAH: WE FOUND IT IN THE FIELDS OF THE WOOD."

If this is to be taken literally, the implications are woeful and give us an indication of the terrible spiritual plight of Israel under Saul.

THE SPIRITUALITY OF ISRAEL

Approximately seventy years earlier, the Ark, after being brought back from the land of the Philistines, was taken to Kirjath-Jearim. This was shortly after the death of Eli the High Priest (I Sam. 6:21). Why it was not taken to Shiloh where the Tabernacle was is not known. It remained there until Saul, a time of about twenty years, and throughout his reign, which was forty years. It seems that the time of which we now address, was about ten years into David's rule (seven years over Judah and three over combined Judah and Israel). The total is approximately seventy years.

During these seventy years, there is no evidence that Israel abided by the Law of Moses or conducted the Feasts. The Great Day of Atonement where the Great High Priest would go in once a year and offer up blood on the Mercy Seat was obviously ignored. Saul's bloody reign with his murderous intent toward David is the result.

When the Ark (the Presence of the Lord) is ignored in the modern Church, the results vary not at all. The flesh will ever attempt to kill the Spirit.

SPIRITUAL DETERIORATION

If this Scripture is to be taken literally, the terrible deterioration becomes painfully obvious. The Ark was taken *"into the house of Abinadab"* (I Sam. 7:1). Surely these were of the tribe of Levi, and maybe his son *"Eleazar"* was a Priest; nevertheless, this was not where the Ark belonged. It should have been with the other holy vessels at Shiloh

— unless the Philistines had taken Shiloh, of which there is no evidence.

Worse yet, it seems the Ark was little attended, being situated near a grove of trees, that is if we are to take David's statement literally.

The shame, even horror of this beggars description. This was the place where Jehovah resided. This is a perfect lesson, teaching us that if the leadership (Saul) has no concern for the Presence of God, likewise, the people will have no concern or little understand its significance and value. How so like the modern Church.

Most of the Churches under the guise of Christendom little know or even understand the Presence of God. Most, sadly, not only do not understand it but want no part of it. The terrible neglect and unconcern in that day of so long ago too perfectly pictures the present.

However, and thank God, Israel now has a King Who places God above any and all.

(7) "WE WILL GO INTO HIS TABERNACLES: WE WILL WORSHIP AT HIS FOOTSTOOL."

This is the indication that God has chosen Jerusalem as the appointed place for His Name. This is the first time the Ark will reside in Zion at Jerusalem. It is the beginning of that which is to come.

A SHORT HISTORY OF THE ARK OF GOD

After the death of David, Solomon will build the Temple as a House for the Ark and the other Holy Instruments of God.

About four hundred years later, the Babylonians would destroy the city and the Temple because of Israel's spiritual degradation. Many of the Holy Vessels were taken to Babylon, but no mention was made of the Ark. Tradition says that Jeremiah may have hid it in a cave. At any rate, there is no record that it was retrieved and placed in the second Temple built by Zerubbabel.

Also, when Herod's Temple was built near the time of the Birth of Christ, there was no Ark of the Covenant placed in the Holy of Holies. It is said that when the army of Titus the Roman General burned the city and destroyed the Temple, when they entered the Holy of Holies, it was found empty. The Glory of God was gone and, in fact, had never been there, and we speak of Herod's Temple. Actually, the Glory of God left the Temple shortly before its destruction by Nebuchadnezzar (Ezek. 11:22-23).

The Glory of God left Israel some five hundred years before Christ, and it has not yet returned; in fact, it will not return until the beginning of the Millennial Reign. Ezekiel, in his Vision, saw it leave, and during his visions of the coming Kingdom Age, saw it return (Ezek. 43:1-2).

Ezekiel described the Temple that will be built as the Headquarters of Christ during the Millennial Reign. It will be on the old Temple site at Jerusalem. Even though many Sacrifices will be offered continually during the Kingdom Age as a memorial of what Christ did at Calvary, still, there will be no Great Day of Atonement, which of old was a type of the coming Calvary. Now, Calvary is past and needs no type of its cleansing of sin, hence, no Ark in the Millennial Temple.

THE NEW JERUSALEM

All of this in its beauteous glory, however, will be done away with at the end of the Great Millennial Reign. At that time, there will be a New Heaven and a New Earth, and it is said, *"I John saw the Holy City, New Jerusalem, coming down from God out of Heaven, prepared as a bride adorned for her husband"* (Rev. 21:2).

At long last, that which God originally intended and of which the Ark that David brought into Jerusalem was a type, will now be a reality, for John also said, *"And I heard a great Voice out of Heaven saying, Behold, the Tabernacle of God is with men, and He will dwell with them, and they shall be His people, and God Himself shall be with them and be their God"* (Rev. 21:3).

So, as the Holy Spirit gives us the beginning, He also gives us the eternal future, glory beyond compare, with God eternally dwelling among men.

David longed for the time when he along with all others could go to the Tabernacle at Jerusalem where the Ark would be ensconced, and there worship God. The Glory then was great; however, it was only symbolic of that which ultimately will come, which will be Glory beyond compare. As David worshiped at *"His footstool,"* likewise, David will worship, along with every Blood-washed Saint who has ever lived, in the New Jerusalem that is yet to come. No wonder when John saw it, he closed out the great Book of Revelation by saying, *"Even so, come, Lord Jesus"* (Rev. 22:20).

And as well, the only entrance into that City and to the Throne of God is by *"the Grace of our Lord Jesus Christ."* And then He said, *"may it be with you all"* (Rev. 22:21).

(8) "ARISE, O LORD, INTO YOUR REST; THOU, AND THE ARK OF YOUR STRENGTH."

David, no doubt, was referring to the great Prophecy of Moses as given in Numbers 10:35-36. Moses said, *"Rise up, Lord, and let Your enemies be scattered; and let them who hate You flee before You. And when it rested, he said, return, O Lord, unto the many thousands of Israel."*

(9) "LET YOUR PRIESTS BE CLOTHED WITH RIGHTEOUSNESS; AND LET YOUR SAINTS SHOUT FOR JOY."

In reality, the *"Priests"* and *"Saints"* were not such and, in fact, could not be without the Presence of the Ark. This carries over today as well. Without the Presence of God, it is *"another Jesus," "another Spirit,"* and *"another Gospel"* (II Cor. 11:4).

There can be tremendous activity without the presence of the Ark, but there can be no *"joy."* Only His Presence provides such. The joyful shouting which accompanied its entrance into Zion foreshadowed the shouting aloud for joy which will signal the Messiah's future entrance into His beloved City.

(10) "FOR YOUR SERVANT DAVID'S SAKE TURN NOT AWAY THE FACE OF YOUR ANOINTED."

David requested such because of God's Promise made to him concerning the Coming of *"Your Anointed."* David knew that he was not worthy of such and, in fact, never could be worthy.

Three men were prominently associated with the Ark of Israel: Eli the Priest; Samuel the Prophet; and, David the King. They all sinned and failed, but in Him Whom they typified, there is not, nor can be, sin or failure.

NOTES

(11) "THE LORD HAS SWORN IN TRUTH UNTO DAVID; HE WILL NOT TURN FROM IT; OF THE FRUIT OF YOUR BODY WILL I SET UPON YOUR THRONE.
(12) "IF YOUR CHILDREN WILL KEEP MY COVENANT AND MY TESTIMONY THAT I SHALL TEACH THEM, THEIR CHILDREN SHALL ALSO SIT UPON YOUR THRONE FOR EVERMORE."

These particular two Verses present a tremendous Promise.

HEZEKIAH

Very probably, Hezekiah when shut up by the Assyrians in Jerusalem, read these two Verses over and over. It was a time of trouble, distress, and disunion. The mighty Assyrian army was the most powerful in the world. Furthermore, this terrible time of testing lasted for about two years (II Kings 19:29). And if this were not enough, God sent the Prophet Isaiah unto Hezekiah with a solemn message, *"Set your house in order; for you shall die, and not live"* (II Kings 20:1). At this time, the king was childless, helpless, and hopeless. God's Promises to David of sonship and glory had seemingly failed. It was a trial sharp enough to confound Hezekiah and Isaiah and their companions. Isaiah had given the Prophecy some thirty years earlier, *"A virgin shall conceive, and bear a Son, and shall call His Name Immanuel"* (Isa. 7:14). If Hezekiah died childless as it looked like he would do, there would be no heir to continue the lineage that God had promised to David (II Sam. 7:12-16) in order to bring the Messiah into the world. (For the Prophecies to be fulfilled, the lineage had to continue unbroken, whether king or not, until the appointed time when the Virgin would conceive and bring forth the Promised Son.)

However, in the face of seeming impossibilities, they trusted, were delivered, and they were assured that the Virgin would surely give birth to the Son promised to David, and that to Him would be given His Father's Throne in perpetuity and power. He is the true Ark of Jehovah; as Priest, Prophet, and King, naught can be found in Him but perfection.

The deliverance that God afforded Hezekiah and Isaiah by the sending of the Angel was so profound and miraculous that the Psalmist said it was like a *"dream"* (Ps. 126:1). What a test of faith this must have been! Still, the greater the test, the greater the victory!

(13) "FOR THE LORD HAS CHOSEN ZION; HE HAS DESIRED IT FOR HIS HABITATION.

(14) "THIS IS MY REST FOREVER: HERE WILL I DWELL; FOR I HAVE DESIRED IT."

Satan has ever contested this Promise of God concerning Zion and Jerusalem; consequently, this city has had the very opposite concerning the *"rest"* that God has promised. Its ground has been soaked countless times with blood. The battle rages even today. The Arabs claim the city for Muhammad. The Jews claim it for the Promises, of which this is but one. While the contest may be fierce, nevertheless, the following Verses will be fulfilled.

(15) "I WILL ABUNDANTLY BLESS HER PROVISION: I WILL SATISFY HER POOR WITH BREAD."

In this Passage He has promised that His Government will prosper. This will take place during the coming Great Kingdom Age when Christ rules in Zion.

(16) "I WILL ALSO CLOTHE HER PRIESTS WITH SALVATION: AND HER SAINTS SHALL SHOUT ALOUD FOR JOY."

In Verse Fifteen we have the Promise of material and financial prosperity concerning the coming days of Jerusalem. In this Verse we have the Promise of coming Holy Spirit Revival. That which Israel rejected on the Day of Pentecost they will now accept.

(17) "THERE WILL I MAKE THE HORN OF DAVID TO BUD: I HAVE ORDAINED A LAMP FOR MY ANOINTED."

The word *"Horn"* represents Power and Authority that will be held by Jesus Christ.

"My Anointed" refers directly to Christ. So, Christ will be the reason for the tremendous abundance and the outpouring of the Holy Spirit. Let it ever be known that as Christ will be then, He is now, at least for all who believe Him.

(18) "HIS ENEMIES WILL I CLOTHE WITH SHAME: BUT UPON HIMSELF SHALL HIS CROWN FLOURISH."

We are told here that the prosperity will be forever, and His Dominion will be likewise.

NOTES

Daniel said, *"And the Stone that smote the image became a great mountain, and filled the whole Earth"* (Dan. 2:35).

PSALM 133

The Author is David:
The Joy of Brotherhood and Harmony

(1) "BEHOLD, HOW GOOD AND HOW PLEASANT IT IS FOR BRETHREN TO DWELL TOGETHER IN UNITY!"

David wrote this Psalm and it is the second Psalm in the last set of three and is, therefore, a Song of Trust.

UNITY

First of all let me state that there can be no unity in the Lord outside of His Word. In other words, all unity must be based strictly on the Word of God, and if it's based on anything else, then it's false.

In this Psalm the Holy Spirit takes David to a spiritual high of prophecy, with David probably at that time, not understanding its full implications.

The Holy Spirit looks ahead with Divine Omniscience, knowing that after Solomon's death, Israel will be divided into two kingdoms, Israel and Judah. The subject of the Holy Spirit is the healing of this terrible breach which will not really be brought about until the coming Millennial Reign, and He states that He, the Holy Spirit, will be the catalyst in that grand time Who will bring such to pass.

There are two types of unity, the man-made variety and that which can only be given by God, and as stated, with the latter always being based strictly on the Word of God.

That which is devised by man characterizes the majority of what calls itself *"Church."* The great push for unity in the modern Church, which began years ago with the National Counsel of Churches and grew into the World Counsel of Churches, can only be described as satanic. It is satanic because it is not Scriptural. Sadly, in the last few years, the Pentecostal and Charismatic branches of the Church have tried as well to effect unity, which, in fact, is no unity at all, at least that which God recognizes. As would be obvious, it is man-devised.

THE CATHOLIC CHURCH

In the Sixties and on through the Eighties, many Catholics began to be brought into a saving knowledge of Jesus Christ, with many, consequently, being baptized with the Holy Spirit as well! In fact, our Ministry (Jimmy Swaggart Ministries) was instrumental in seeing a great move of God brought about among the Catholics. It was done simply by the Word of God being preached, which brought about conviction in the hearts and lives of these people, as well as untold thousands of others, resulting in Salvation. At that time, we were one of the few telling these Catholics who had come to Christ, that they must leave the Catholic Church. In other words, they could not stay in the midst of false doctrine. One or the other, they or the false doctrine, had to go. Regrettably, they were being encouraged by many others to remain in the erroneous teaching of the Catholic Church. Much of the latter was under the guise of *"unity."*

COMPROMISE

Unity in such fashion can only be brought about by compromise of Scripture, which affects the very foundations of the faith. Amos asked, *"Can two walk together, except they be agreed?"* (Amos 3:3). There is no way that one who believes in *"Salvation by Grace through Faith"* can walk together with one who believes and teaches *"Salvation by works."* The Catholic Church pure and simple, teaches *"Salvation by works."* Regrettably, so do many Protestants. Such a direction is totally unscriptural, and, thereby, proclaims a false way of Salvation. Nothing can be worse (Eph. 2:9)!

The danger of unscriptural *"unity"* is perhaps the greatest danger facing the Church presently. The tremendous push that is now being made in almost all organized religion toward this unscriptural position is a sign of the last days and will, no doubt, lead up to the advent of the man of sin, the Antichrist. The apostate Church, which has existed since the dawn of time, will steadily grow stronger in these last days. The situation at this moment is far more critical than most realize.

NOTES

The old-line denominations have, by and large, denied the faith, while most of those who call themselves *"fundamentalists"* have drifted into legalism.

Likewise, great segments of the Pentecostal and Charismatic Churches have opted for the *"health and wealth"* message, which, at its very roots, is heresy. (The fundamental basis of this erroneous doctrine is the emphasis that is placed on materialism instead of Christ and Him Crucified).

THE REMNANT

I realize that the tenor of my words is negative; however, the situation is far worse than most realize. True, there is a Remnant constituting the true Body of Christ; it is not always easily recognized, and in some cases it is even associated in some ways with the apostate Church (Mat. 13:24-30).

It must be understood that Satan is a master at getting people to believe what is of God, isn't, and what is not of God, is.

The Holy Spirit is now in the beginning stages of separating the true Body of Christ from the apostate. It may not be totally discernable to all, but it will be discernable to those who know their Lord.

The dividing line between the True Church and the apostate Church is the Cross of Christ. In fact, it has always been this way, but will be this way in these last days, I believe, more than ever (I Cor. 1:17-18, 21, 23; 2:2; Gal., Chpt. 5; 6:14).

The Antichrist's spirit is increasing almost daily in the apostate Church; however, the Moving and Operation of the Holy Spirit is about to begin strongly in the true Body of Christ. The apostate Church will have its unity, which has Satan as its foundation. The true Body of Christ will have its unity, which is the Word of God.

(2) "IT IS LIKE THE PRECIOUS OINTMENT UPON THE HEAD, THAT RAN DOWN UPON THE BEARD, EVEN AARON'S BEARD: THAT WENT DOWN TO THE SKIRTS OF HIS GARMENTS;

(3) "AS THE DEW OF HERMON, AND AS THE DEW THAT DESCENDED UPON THE MOUNTAINS OF ZION: FOR THERE THE LORD COMMANDED THE BLESSINGS, EVEN LIFE FOR EVERMORE."

Faith can sing in days of sorrow, *"all will be well,"* and most probably this Psalm was sung by Hezekiah and the people of Jerusalem in their day of disunion and distress.

UNITY ACCORDING TO THE HOLY SPIRIT

The unity predicted in this Prophecy will be the creation of the Holy Spirit. He is here compared to the oil descending upon Aaron and to the dew descending upon Zion. The oil was precious, and that dew was Hermonic. It was a sea mist precipitated upon the mountains of Hermon, and it was of all forms of dew the most valuable.

The oil united Aaron and his garment, and the dew united Hermon and Zion. Hermon on the north figures Ephraim; Zion on the south, Judah. Thus, Ephraim and Judah in the great Kingdom Age will enjoy the Baptism with the Holy Spirit, for that Baptism establishes unity (Eph. 4:5). The uniformity of the flesh is not the unity of the Spirit. The one is originated by man and fails; the other is created by God and is eternal.

The words, *"It is like,"* of Verse Two, should have been translated so at the beginning of Verse Three. The same dew that descended upon Hermon descended upon Zion, and the same oil that descended upon Aaron descended upon his garment. The double figure emphasizes unity, with both the *"oil"* and the *"dew"* symbolizing the Holy Spirit, all made possible by the Cross.

THE LAST DAYS

This *"unity,"* even though effective by the Holy Spirit, and thereby after a fashion coming into being at present, still, will not and, in fact, cannot be brought about totally until the Coming of the Lord.

As previously stated, lack of unity is because of lack of fidelity to the Bible. The first serious breach that is recorded in the early Church came about at Corinth. Paul said, *"And that there be no divisions among you."* He then went on to say, *"but that you be perfectly joined together in the same mind and in the same judgment"* (I Cor. 1:10). The only way this can be is by agreement with and on the Word of God.

The reason this was brought about was because of individuals getting their eyes off of Christ and onto man. Paul asked, *"Is Christ divided?"* (I Cor. 1:12-13).

The answer is obvious, *"No, Christ is not divided, but, tragically, men are."* Therefore, all the different doctrines, denominations, groups, and splinters of Christianity are not Scriptural. As is obvious, all are not in one mind and one judgment as commanded by the Holy Spirit.

There are many reasons for this. One is that Christ Who is the Head of the Church is treated by most as a passive Head instead of the active Head, which He is (Eph. 1:20-23). When He returns, as He will, He will then enforce the unity, which will be brought about by the Holy Spirit with the Word of God as its foundation. Until then, the only true unity that Christians can have is love; therefore, we are commanded to love one another (I Jn. 3:14). Tragically, there is not much of that, because the Church, at least for all practical purposes, has abandoned the Cross of Christ. Anything that is done outside of the Cross, will prove to be specious in some way. Conversely, everything that is built squarely on the foundation of the Cross of Christ, will prove to be Scripturally correct (I Pet. 1:18-20).

PSALM 134

*David is Probably the Author:
An Exhortation to Praise*

(1) "BEHOLD, BLESS YE THE LORD, ALL YE SERVANTS OF THE LORD, WHICH BY NIGHT STAND IN THE HOUSE OF THE LORD."

This is the last of the Songs of Degrees or Ascents and is, therefore, a Song of Triumph. All is sunshine and blessing. It is a scene of Millennial peace and glory, for Christ now reigns in Jerusalem. The Holy Spirit now invites the servants of Jehovah to praise Jehovah in the House of Jehovah.

The phrase, *"By night,"* means one of two things:

THE EVENING SACRIFICE

First of all, it could pertain to the evening

Sacrifice, which will, no doubt, be a time of great and glorious blessing each and every day of the Millennial Age when representatives from all over the world will, with gladdened hearts, rejoice at this happy time. For long periods of time during Israel's history, the Sacrifices commanded by God were ignored because of sin. Even when they were correctly kept, still, the motivation oftentimes was selfish and, therefore, rejected by God. Now, all of that is past. Israel and all of the world will now rejoice in the Sacrifices which will serve as a memorial of what Christ did at Calvary.

CONTINUOUS PRAISE AND WORSHIP

If it does not refer to the evening Sacrifice, it could refer to the continuous praise that will be offered up to the Lord of Glory, which will, no doubt, be so voluminous that it will never stop, continuing day and night.

At present, most of that which comes up from Planet Earth is blasphemy, profanity, and filth. At the dawn of the Millennial Kingdom, those days of darkness will forever end, and now there is continuous praise.

(2) "LIFT UP YOUR HANDS IN THE SANCTUARY, AND BLESS THE LORD."

Truly, men will then know and understand that all Blessings, Prosperity, Salvation, Peace, and Power come from Jesus Christ Who is the Source, while the Cross is the Means; consequently, from all over the world men will then look toward Zion, expecting the supply of all their needs to be met. They will not be disappointed.

It is difficult for us to imagine at the present time the praise and worship that will characterize Jerusalem in that day, especially at the Temple site.

Likewise, all over the world and in every country men will look toward Jerusalem, constantly breathing a prayer, knowing as Ezekiel said, *"The LORD is there"* (Ezek. 48:35).

(3) "THE LORD THAT MADE HEAVEN AND EARTH BLESS YOU OUT OF ZION."

As the first two Verses invited the servants of Jehovah to praise Him, Verse Three is the response to the invitation. In the Millennial Day, men will bless Him, and He will bless men.

THE CERTITUDE OF BLESSING

The word *"you"* of this Verse may emphasize the certitude of Millennial Blessing to every subject of the Kingdom, irrespective of age, status, or sex. As well, it portends the Messiah Who will affirm the Divine Promises made to Him as the center of blessing to Israel and to the world. The Hebrew Text reads: *"Jehovah will bless you out of Zion."*

Now, men the world over will recognize Christ as the Creator of the heavens and the Earth and not attribute such to the foolishness of mindless evolution.

Thus, these fifteen Songs of Ascents, grouped into five triplets, mount in each triplet from Trouble through Trust to Triumph and lead into the Peace, the Glory, the Blessing, and the Happiness of the Messiah's future Kingdom.

It is also a picture of the progress of every Child of God. Upon conversion and due to the constant war between the Spirit and the flesh, trouble immediately appears. Little by little the Christian learns Trust and then, ultimately, Triumph, which will look forward to the moment the Trump shall sound, and then we will know the glorious Triumph of being forever with Him.

The author of this Psalm is unknown, but the Syriac attributes it to David.

PSALM 135

Probably Written by David: Praise to God for His Greatness

(1) "PRAISE YE THE LORD. PRAISE YE THE NAME OF THE LORD; PRAISE HIM, O YE SERVANTS OF THE LORD."

There is no indication in the instructions of this Psalm as to who wrote it; however, if David did truly write the previous Psalm, then he wrote this one as well. The first two Verses are almost identical to the first two Verses of the previous. (Some think Hezekiah could have written it.)

HALLELUJAH!

The word *"praise"* in the Hebrew actually means *"Hallelujah!"* Therefore, this Psalm begins with *"Hallelujah"* and closes with *"Hallelujah."*

It is startling as to the admonishment of the Holy Spirit regarding praise to the Lord. Actually, the entirety of this Psalm is given over to praising the Lord for the many things He has done, and even for the things He will do.

Yet, the far greater majority of Churches in Christendom have never heard the sound of even one *"Hallelujah"* or any type of praise whatsoever.

Why?

The answer is obvious. They do not know the One of Whom we are speaking. They have some head knowledge of Him but no heart knowledge whatsoever; therefore, there is no praise.

Verse One pertains to those who do the work of the Lord such as Levites and the Priests. Familiarity, at times, stifles praises because it has a tendency to breed contempt, but only if the relationship begins to weaken. When this happens, worship deteriorates into ceremony, which makes up the majority of modern Christianity. Ceremony as ritual, contains no worship, and certainly contains no Salvation, but yet makes up most of that in most modern Churches, and is erroneously thought to be worship.

(2) "YE WHO STAND IN THE HOUSE OF THE LORD, IN THE COURTS OF THE HOUSE OF OUR GOD."

Due to the Courts of the House of the Lord being mentioned in this Verse, presents some indication that David did not write this Psalm, and because the Temple was built after he had passed on.

THE COURTS OF THE HOUSE OF THE LORD

In front of the Temple were three Courts. The first Court, which was nearest to the Temple proper, was referred to as the *"Court of Men,"* or sometimes as the *"Court of Israel."*

The Court immediately behind this court was the *"Court of Women."*

There was a third Court referred to as the *"Court of the Gentiles."* Between that Court and the Court of Women, there was a barrier erected, which most believe to have been approximately four feet tall. Gentiles were not allowed to cross this barrier under penalty of death.

This latter court, the Court of the Gentiles, was the only part of the Temple where Gentiles could come and worship God. It was in the Court of the Gentiles where Jesus ran out the moneychangers, etc. (Jn. 2:13-17).

In the coming Kingdom Age, to be sure, the newly built Millennial Temple will be used exclusively for worship of the Lord, and for nothing else!

(3) "PRAISE THE LORD; FOR THE LORD IS GOOD: SING PRAISES UNTO HIS NAME; FOR IT IS PLEASANT."

We are told to praise Him because *"the LORD is good."* Surprisingly, the majority of the world thinks of the Lord as anything but good. The reasons are obvious.

Most of the world is evil and, therefore, desires a God that would condone its evil. Because He doesn't and, in fact, cannot, but rather, greatly opposes its evil, those of evil hearts condemn and accuse Him.

In these praises, singing is to be included; consequently, the Christian should be careful regarding the songs that he sings. All Christian songs must never violate the Word of God. His Name should be extolled because *"it is pleasant."* Isaiah said, *"And His Name shall be called Wonderful, Counselor, The Mighty God, The Everlasting Father, The Prince of Peace"* (Isa. 9:6).

(4) "FOR THE LORD HAS CHOSEN JACOB UNTO HIMSELF, AND ISRAEL FOR HIS PECULIAR TREASURE."

This Psalm, no doubt, has been sung many times in the past; however, it really points toward the time that the Messiah will dwell in Jerusalem (Vs. 21). The Song will then be sung by redeemed Israel at the Coronation of the Great King in Zion.

JACOB AND ISRAEL

Deuteronomy 32 predicts Israel's apostasy to idolatry, her rejection of the Messiah, and the Divine indignation that would justly follow. It also proclaims her final restoration and pardon which this Psalm portrays.

It is strange and yet beautiful that the Holy Spirit would use both the name *"Jacob"* and *"Israel"* in this Passage, the reason being that God must portray what Jacob was before the Lord made him to be Israel, *"His peculiar treasure."* In this one Verse is wrapped up the entirety of the human race. Man is morally bankrupt, depraved, perverted, and unable to extricate himself out of the mire into which he has sunk. But, irrespective of what man is, Jesus Christ can extricate him and change him from a deceiver (Jacob) to a Prince (Israel).

Likewise, there was no moral goodness in Jacob that caused the Lord to choose him. But there was moral Goodness in God, and, therefore, from this basis He chose Jacob; likewise, God chooses no man because of the residual of moral goodness; man has none. All Grace comes from the good Heart of God. Man is spiritually bankrupt, and even Christian man within himself contains no good thing. All is dependent upon God.

(5) "FOR I KNOW THAT THE LORD IS GREAT, AND THAT OUR LORD IS ABOVE ALL GODS."

That which speaks of idols, as this does, seems strange to the modern ear. Modern man thinks this ancient text has little, if any, meaning for modern society. He is wrong!

Even though the idols may not be made of wood, stone, or metal, still, they are idols. And to be frank, religion is the greatest idol of all. John the Beloved said as much, *"Little children, keep yourselves from idols"* (I Jn. 5:21).

(6) "WHATSOEVER THE LORD PLEASED, THAT DID HE IN HEAVEN, AND IN EARTH, IN THE SEAS, AND ALL DEEP PLACES."

This Passage extols the Lord as Creator of the heavens and the Earth and all that is therein. It leaves no place for the prattle of evolution.

(7) "HE CAUSES THE VAPORS TO ASCEND FROM THE ENDS OF THE EARTH; HE MAKES LIGHTNINGS FOR THE RAIN; HE BRINGS THE WIND OUT OF HIS TREASURIES."

The heathen worshiped idols in order to secure good weather for their crops, and for various other reasons. They worshiped the sun, the moon, and things made with their hands. We are told here that God controls the weather, and not some dumb idol!

In Israel of old, drought was a sign of the displeasure of God caused by sin (Ruth 1).

NOTES

In this day of Grace, there is some evidence that God also uses the weather in this fashion. There is some evidence, as well, that Satan uses the weather to steal, kill, and destroy (Jn. 10:10; Mk. 4:35-41).

And yet, as it regards the Child of God, Satan, weather or not, can do nothing to the Believer unless it is allowed by the Lord. Every Believer should take comfort in that (Rom. 8:35).

(8) "WHO SMOTE THE FIRST BORN OF EGYPT, BOTH OF MAN AND BEAST."

The great deliverance of Israel from Egyptian bondage is ever portrayed by the Holy Spirit as an example of the Power of God. As well, it is symbolic of man's Salvation, with Egypt symbolic of the world.

But more so, it is symbolic of the Believer being delivered from the clutches of Satan; unfortunately, most Christians, and because of not understanding the Cross as it refers to Sanctification, simply do not know how to live for God. As a result, the sin nature rules them, at least in some way, which institutes bondage, as would be obvious (Gal. 5:1). As a result, they are under the jackbooted heel of Satan, just as much as the Children of Israel were in Egypt. And, as well, as Israel was delivered by virtue of the slain lamb, likewise, Christ and Him Crucified is the Source of the Believer's Victory as well, and the only Source.

THE BELIEVER AND THE CROSS

The Believer is to understand, everything we receive from the Lord, comes to us exclusively through Christ and by the means of the Cross. In other words, it is the Cross of Christ that has made it possible for the sinner to be Saved, and the Believer to be Sanctified. There is no other means or way, as there needs to be no other means or way (Rom. 6:3-5).

Consequently, the Believer is to place his faith exclusively in Christ and the Cross, not allowing it to be placed in anything else. This is not easy, and simply because it places self in a position of total incompetence, which doesn't set well with most; nevertheless, that is the manner of the Cross. It strips the Believer of everything in which one might place one's faith, making the Cross of Christ the exclusive Object of all true Faith.

THE HOLY SPIRIT

When the Believer evidences faith in Christ and the Cross, and doesn't allow his faith to be moved to other things, the Holy Spirit Who works exclusively within the parameters of the Finished Work of Christ, meaning that the Cross is a legal Work, then He will begin to help the Believer, will begin to exert His mighty Power on the Believer's behalf, making the Believer what the Believer ought to be.

To be sure, the Holy Spirit doesn't require much of us, but He most definitely does require that our Faith be exclusively in Christ and the Cross, and nothing else (Rom. 6:3-5, 11; 8:1-2, 11).

Then and only then can the Believer walk in victory, and we speak of perpetual Victory. Any other avenue of approach, stops the Work of the Holy Spirit, which guarantees the defeat of the Christian. Our Victory is exclusively in Christ and the Cross and in nothing else.

(9) "WHO SENT TOKENS AND WONDERS INTO THE MIDST OF YOU, O EGYPT, UPON PHARAOH, AND UPON ALL HIS SERVANTS."

In the Eyes of God, Pharaoh is placed no higher than his servants. All answer to God! All alike partake of either His Grace or His Judgment.

Egypt in that day was the mightiest nation on the face of the Earth. In a matter of weeks, by the Power of God, it was reduced to wreckage; likewise, Christ, upon His Death at Calvary, reduced Satan's kingdom to wreckage. The wreckage of Egypt was beautifully symbolic of the wreckage of Satan at Calvary. Calvary was the fulfillment of the Promise made in the Garden of Eden so long ago (Gen. 3:15).

Jesus addressed this when He said, *"Or else how can one enter into a strong man's house, and spoil his goods, except he first bind the strong man? And then he will spoil his house"* (Mat. 12:29).

In this Passage Jesus tells us that He is infinitely stronger than Satan, and as well, that he made wreckage of Satan's empire of darkness at Calvary's Cross.

(10) "WHO SMOTE GREAT NATIONS, AND SLEW MIGHTY KINGS;

(11) "SIHON KING OF THE AMORITES, AND OG KING OF BASHAN, AND ALL THE KINGDOMS OF CANAAN."

The reader must understand that these kings and kingdoms were emissaries of Satan, resplendent with his power. They were placed there and energized by Satan for the very purpose of hindering the Children of Israel from taking their inheritance.

As Egypt was a type of the world from which we are delivered at Salvation, and as well, a type of bondage from which the Believer is delivered unto Sanctification, upon one's continued faith in Christ and the Cross, likewise, the Promised Land is symbolic of the mighty Baptism with the Holy Spirit. Satan does not want the Child of God to be filled with the Holy Spirit; consequently, mighty hindrances are set up to hinder our spiritual progress.

In today's vernacular, *"Sihon"* and *"Og"* represent false doctrine, doubt, unbelief, and other negatives.

We can listen to *"Sihon"* and *"Og,"* or we can listen to the Holy Spirit. We cannot listen to both!

(12) "AND GAVE THEIR LAND FOR AN HERITAGE, AN HERITAGE UNTO ISRAEL HIS PEOPLE."

The Promised Land, which constitutes and is symbolic of the Holy Spirit, with all of its great heritage is promised to *"His People."* Settle for nothing less; believe God. As He *"slew"* and *"smote"* in days of old, He will do the same for those who will dare to believe Him today.

Satan occupies the Promised Land. He is there for the very purpose of hindering the Child of God. Don't allow it, for we are told how to have victory, which Victory is found exclusively in the Cross of Christ (Rom. 6:1-14).

(13) "YOUR NAME, O LORD, ENDURES FOREVER; AND YOUR MEMORIAL, O LORD, THROUGHOUT ALL GENERATIONS."

Satan does not fear us as such, but he does fear *"the Name of the LORD."* In this Passage God has said that His Name would stand as a *"memorial throughout all generations."* In other words, it will never lose its Power.

Too often, this modern Christian generation looks back on the great miracles that God performed so long ago and wishes for a display of His Power accordingly. The Holy Spirit is telling us here that if we will believe Him, then this modern generation can see exactly what generations of old saw. God does not change. He has lost none of His Power.

(14) "FOR THE LORD WILL JUDGE HIS PEOPLE, AND HE WILL REPENT HIMSELF CONCERNING HIS SERVANTS."

The sense of this Verse is that the Lord will judge the righteous after the Rapture, which pertains to *"the Judgment Seat of Christ"* (I Cor. 3:11-15). This pertains to *"works"* and not *"sins,"* of which the latter were already judged at Calvary.

The Lord *"will repent Himself,"* simply means that He will have compassion on all His servants (Eph. 1:10; 2:7; 3:11; Rev. 22:4-5).

(15) "THE IDOLS OF THE HEATHEN ARE SILVER AND GOLD, THE WORK OF MEN'S HANDS."

The Holy Spirit here continues to pull us from men to God, a lesson that it seems we are slow to learn.

THE WORK OF MEN'S HANDS

The term, *"The work of men's hands,"* has to do with any religious work which is not of God, which means that it is something other than that laid down in the Word, which particularly speaking, pertains to the Cross and the Sacrifice there offered.

Actually, the very meaning of the word *"religion"* in its strictest spiritual sense is that it is man-made and not God-made.

Cultured, educated men look back on the Millennia of the past, congratulating themselves on their educational advancement; however, the world is still full of religiosity, which is *"the work of men's hands,"* and not God's. Anything that adds to or takes away from the Word of God, which in essence, is the Message of the Cross, is man-made and, thereby, not acceptable by the Lord of Glory. In fact, Paul said, and I quote from THE EXPOSITOR'S STUDY BIBLE, *"Behold ('mark my words!'), I Paul say unto you* (presents the Apostle's authority regarding the Message he brings), *that if you be circumcised, Christ shall profit you nothing* (if the Believer goes back into Law, and Law of any kind, what Christ did at the Cross on our behalf will profit us nothing. One cannot have it two ways)" (Gal. 5:2).

He then reinforces his statement by saying, *"Christ is become of no effect unto you* (this is a chilling statement, and refers to anyone who makes anything other than Christ and the Cross the Object of his Faith), *whosoever of you are justified by the Law* (seek to be justified by the Law); *you are fallen from Grace* (fallen from the position of Grace, which means the Believer is trusting in something other than the Cross; it actually means, *'to apostasize'*)" (Gal. 5:4).

The idea of all of this is, if we trust in anything other than Christ and the Cross, and we mean anything, all that Jesus did at the Cross will be of no value to us. That being the case, spiritual wreckage and the loss of the soul will be the end result (Phil. 3:18-19).

(16) "THEY HAVE MOUTHS, BUT THEY SPEAK NOT; EYES HAVE THEY, BUT THEY SEE NOT;

(17) "THEY HAVE EARS, BUT THEY HEAR NOT; NEITHER IS THERE ANY BREATH IN THEIR MOUTHS."

The Word of God has *"Life."* As well, it has *"Light."* All made by man, irrespective of its religious content, has no *"Life"* or *"Light."*

IDOLS AT THE PRESENT

If we read these words as given by the Psalmist so long ago, and think that it speaks only of heathenistic idols, then we miss the point. John the Beloved said, *"Little children, keep yourselves from idols. Amen."*

The statement as given by John does not refer to the heathen worship of idol gods, but of the heretical substitutes for the Christian conception of God, or anything that pulls us away from Christ and the Cross. We must never forget that!

In fact, religion is the greatest idol of all. The truth is, untold millions the world over have made their own particular Church an idol, or their religious denomination, or particular dogma's or creeds. If our faith is in anything, and I mean anything, other than Christ and the Cross, then whatever the other thing might be, we have turned such into an idol.

(18) "THEY WHO MAKE THEM ARE LIKE UNTO THEM: SO IS EVERY ONE WHO TRUSTS IN THEM."

The worshippers of idols of old took upon themselves the character of those idols, and so do the present worshippers of such.

Going back to those days of so long ago, how could such be if these idols had no *"Life"* or *"Light?"*

Even though these idols were lifeless, still they represented demon spirits that worked in and through them; likewise, all false doctrine, which incidentally is instigated by demon spirits, as well, ingrains itself in its false apostles. Such has no *"Life"* or *"Light."*

Paul said, and I quote from THE EXPOSITOR'S STUDY BIBLE, *"Now the Spirit* (Holy Spirit) *speaks expressly* (pointedly), *that in the latter times* (the times in which we now live, the last of the last days, which begin the fulfillment of Endtime Prophecies) *some shall depart from the Faith* (anytime Paul uses the term *'the Faith,'* in short he is referring to the Cross; so, we are told here that some will depart from the Cross as the means of Salvation and Victory), *giving heed to seducing spirits* (evil spirits, i.e., *'religious spirits,'* making something seem like what it isn't), *and doctrines of Devils* (should have been translated, *'Doctrines of Demons'*; the *'seducing spirits'* entice Believers away from the true Faith, causing them to Believe *'Doctrines inspired by Demon spirits'*)" (I Tim. 4:1).

Let us say it again, *"Worshippers of idols take upon themselves the character of these idols, be they idols of old, or be they false doctrine of the present."*

(19) "BLESS THE LORD, O HOUSE OF ISRAEL: BLESS THE LORD, O HOUSE OF AARON."

The impotency of idols and of everyone who trusts in them is contrasted with the Almightiness of the Messiah and the happiness of those who trust in Him.

Israel, now restored, will at long last fulfill that which she was ordained by God to do so very long ago. They will no longer worship idols but will *"bless the Lord."*

(20) "BLESS THE LORD, O HOUSE OF LEVI: YE WHO FEAR THE LORD, BLESS THE LORD."

Whenever men abrogate the Word of God, likewise, they lose their *"fear of God."*

BLESS THE LORD

As Verse Nineteen admonishes the whole of Israel to *"bless the Lord,"* likewise, the priestly order of Israel, the Levites, will function in their capacity, and we speak of the coming Kingdom Age, as originally intended by God. In other words, they will build the House of the Lord instead of their own house. At that time, they will be a blessing to the entirety of the Earth. They will function in the realm of the Sacrifices and all the other duties of the Temple. Aaron will once again be the Great High Priest. David, at that time, and forever, will be King. Jesus Christ will rule over all.

(21) "BLESSED BE THE LORD OUT OF ZION, WHICH DWELLS AT JERUSALEM. PRAISE YE THE LORD."

As previously stated, this Psalm is prophetic with its fulfillment pointing towards the coming Kingdom Age. Then Jesus Christ will dwell at Jerusalem. He was rejected and refused at the First Advent. He will be accepted at the Second Advent.

Israel will now be the premier nation on the face of the Earth with Jerusalem as the capital city, not only at Israel proper, but also for the entirety of the world.

So when we look at Israel presently, we must not look at them as they now are, but as the Lord will ultimately make them, which pertains to the coming Kingdom Age. To be sure, that will not be long in coming.

PSALM 136

Author Unknown:
Praise and Thanksgiving to God

(1) "O GIVE THANKS UNTO THE LORD; FOR HE IS GOOD: FOR HIS MERCY ENDURES FOREVER."

The author of this Psalm is not known. It is Israel's response to the call of the prior Psalm to worship and praise the Messiah. It could well have been sung by Hezekiah and his companions and also by the returned captives from Babylon. But it will yet be sung by the Tribes of Israel in the future day of their deliverance when the Messiah will appear in majesty to destroy all their adversaries, which will be the Second Coming.

MERCY

The Holy Spirit so constructed the Psalm that it would extol the Glory of His Power and the virture of His Mercy, which is the product of His Grace. It is beautifully amazing at the attention the Holy Spirit gives to the Mercy of God, and rightly so.

This Verse tells us to give thanks unto Him because *"He is good."* His Goodness is an exclamation that *"His Mercy endures forever."*

First of all, we note that it is *"His Mercy."* Man has no mercy outside of God. It is interesting that the Holy Spirit begins this beauteous Psalm by extolling the goodness of God. Why not!

God became flesh and dwelt among men, taking upon Himself the frailties of the human family. All that man could not do for himself, God did for him, even though He was unloved by man. This is goodness that is incomprehensible to the unspiritual heart.

(2) "O GIVE THANKS UNTO THE GOD OF GODS: FOR HIS MERCY ENDURES FOREVER."

The First Verse spoke of the goodness of God, while this Verse speaks of the supremacy of God.

THE TRINITY

The Hebrew for *"God of gods"* is *"Elohim of the Elohim."* This does not mean that there are other gods (not counting idols) than Elohim. For the Lord through Isaiah said, *"I am the First, and I am the Last; and beside Me there is no God"* (Isa. 44:6). He is speaking here of the Trinity of which all are equal. In the Trinity, *"His Mercy endures forever."*

(3) "O GIVE THANKS TO THE LORD OF LORDS: FOR HIS MERCY ENDURES FOREVER."

The Hebrew is, *"Adonim of the Adonim,"* which means, *"Sovereign of the Sovereigns; Master of the Masters; and Ruler of the Rulers."*

This Verse speaks of the *"sovereignty"* of God!

(4) "TO HIM WHO ALONE DOES GREAT WONDERS: FOR HIS MERCY ENDURES FOREVER."

This Verse speaks of the Miracle Working Power of God, and in essence states that He Alone can perform Miracles.

THE MIRACLE WORKING GOD

God is the only One Who can perform true Miracles. The Scripture here plainly says, *"Who Alone does."* It is ironical that the Holy Spirit uses the same terminology regarding the false prophet who will make his appearance in the Great Tribulation. It says of him as well, *"he does great wonders"* (Rev. 13:13); however, the *"wonders"* performed by the false prophet will not have the expected results but, in fact, will have the opposite of that which God Alone can bring about. Everything that God does tends towards life; everything that Satan does tends towards death. God's great Wonders are always brought about from the position of Mercy.

(5) "TO HIM WHO BY WISDOM MADE THE HEAVENS: FOR HIS MERCY ENDURES FOREVER."

This Verse extols the Wisdom of God as it regards creation.

THE WISDOM OF GOD

This Verse ascribes to God all the planetary systems as well as His Own residence as described in Revelation, Chapters 21 and 22. John wrote that it was Jesus Christ Who made all things (Jn. 1:3). The Work of the Trinity in Creation could be crudely described as God the Father serving as the Owner, the Lord Jesus Christ serving as the Architect, with the Holy Spirit serving as the actual Builder (Gen. 1:1-2).

(6) "TO HIM WHO STRETCHED OUT THE EARTH ABOVE THE WATERS: FOR HIS MERCY ENDURES FOREVER."

We find in this Verse God extolled as the Restorer of all things.

THE RESTORATION

We find in Genesis 1:2 that waters cover the Earth; however, Verse Six of our study proclaims the fact that the *"Earth is above the waters."*

The Sixth Verse proclaims God's original creation. At sometime after that creation,

Lucifer, who ruled the Earth at that time under God, rebelled against the Lord, which caused God to flood the entirety of the Earth with water, which some refer to as the first flood. This was not the flood of Noah but rather, that of Lucifer (Ps. 104:5-9; Isa. 14:12-14; Jer. 4:23-26; II Pet. 3:5-8). Genesis 1:6-7 records God dispelling Lucifer's flood, and bringing the Earth back to a habitable state.

(7) "TO HIM WHO MADE GREAT LIGHTS: FOR HIS MERCY ENDURES FOREVER."

The word *"made"* as here used, proclaims the Lord bringing the sun, the moon, and the stars back to their original creation as light givers.

In Genesis 1:16 it says, *"And God made two great lights* (the sun and the moon)*; the greater light to rule the day* (the sun)*, and the lesser light to rule the night."*

This is not speaking of the time God created these orbs, that having taken place in eternity past. In other words, with Lucifer's rebellion, these light bearers ceased to function as they should with the result being that *"darkness was upon the face of the deep"* (Gen. 1:2).

So when the Lord brought the Earth back to a habitable state, He once again regulated the sun, the moon, and the stars that had already been created sometime in the past, that they would now function as they should, which they have.

(8) "THE SUN TO RULE BY DAY: FOR HIS MERCY ENDURES FOREVER.

(9) "THE MOON AND STARS TO RULE BY NIGHT: FOR HIS MERCY ENDURES FOREVER."

As stated in the notes, as it regards Verse Seven, the sun, moon, and stars were created by God along with the Earth and other planetary bodies sometime in the distant past. When the Scripture says, *"In the beginning God created the heavens and the Earth,"* that doesn't tell us exactly when that was. So, if science can prove beyond a doubt that the Earth is millions of years old, etc., this would not disprove the Bible in any way. In fact, the Word of God dispels the notion, that the Earth is only about six thousand years old as some claim. The facts are, we do not know exactly how old it is, because the Lord did not see fit to tell us.

When God set about to bring this Earth back to a habitable state, it was not necessary to recreate the planetary bodies, but only to bring them back to a serviceable state, which He did. The Holy Spirit is telling us here that all of this has to do with Mercy.

(10) "TO HIM WHO SMOTE EGYPT IN THEIR FIRSTBORN: FOR HIS MERCY ENDURES FOREVER."

To the unspiritual heart one cannot equate the destruction of all of Egypt's firstborn with Mercy; nevertheless, everything that God did in Egypt was an act of Mercy.

GOD'S JUDGMENT IS ALSO AN ACT OF MERCY

As it regards Egypt and their enslavement of the Children of Israel, it must be remembered, that the Children of Israel belonged to God, not to Pharaoh; therefore, the Lord had the right to demand their release. Pharaoh, despite the miracles, hardened his heart and would not let Israel go; consequently, God intensified the pressure.

Each act that God performed was an act of Mercy. God could easily have destroyed Egypt in the beginning, but He did not do so. He first of all politely requested the release of His people and then performed the necessary miracles to bring about that release. While it was true that at the conclusion Egypt was totally wrecked, still, the fault was Pharaoh's hardened heart, not God's action.

(11) "AND BROUGHT OUT ISRAEL FROM AMONG THEM: FOR HIS MERCY ENDURES FOREVER."

To bring Israel out was not only an act of Mercy for Israel, but for Egypt as well. For God to do with Israel what He desired, which was to bring a Redeemer into the world, it would necessitate a land of their own without interference from other occupants. Regrettably, Israel did not drive out the occupants of the Promised Land, which was commanded by God, and this was ever a thorn in their side.

(12) "WITH A STRONG HAND, AND WITH A STRETCHED OUT ARM: FOR HIS MERCY ENDURES FOREVER."

This indicates that Israel under no stretch of the imagination could have delivered themselves. It took the mighty Power of God. As well, this was to serve always as a symbol of the Salvation experience, and as well, of victory for the Child of God.

No person can save himself anymore than Israel could have delivered themselves. As well, Believers cannot walk in victory unless they do so according to God's Prescribed Order, which is Faith exclusively in the Cross of Christ, which then gives the Holy Spirit latitude to work within our lives, Who Alone can bring about the Victory so desired.

As Pharaoh held Israel in slavery, likewise, Satan, of whom Pharaoh was a type, holds men in slavery, and as well, even most Believers.

The foolish idea that men can save themselves is foolish indeed! It takes a *"strong hand"* and a *"stretched out arm"* for God to deliver man, which He does by and through the Cross, even as the Twelfth Chapter of Exodus proclaims. All is done because of *"Mercy."*

(13) "TO HIM WHICH DIVIDED THE RED SEA INTO PARTS: FOR HIS MERCY ENDURES FOREVER."

Critics of the Bible claim that the Red Sea, at least where the Children of Israel crossed, was only a few inches deep. The truth is, it was actually from seventy-five to one hundred feet deep and about twelve miles wide.

When the Lord opened this body of water with one of the greatest Miracles ever performed, walls of water stood up on either side from seventy-five to one hundred feet high. The path through this body of water was probably a mile or more wide through which nearly three million people could cross, along with all of their cattle and stock. As stated, this was truly one of the greatest Miracles that God ever performed.

As well, the Red Sea is symbolic of the prison system where Satan keeps men bound. Only God's Power as registered that day of so long ago, which was Almighty Power, can set the captive free. In other words, the same Power that it took to open that body of water, is the same Power it takes to liberate man from the bondage of Satan. That's the reason that man's pitiful and pathetic efforts to address this situation, such as humanistic psychology, is pitiful indeed! When will the Church learn this?

NOTES

(14) "AND MADE ISRAEL TO PASS THROUGH THE MIDST OF IT: FOR HIS MERCY ENDURES FOREVER."

The magnitude of this Miracle is beyond comprehension. It took faith for Israel to pass through. They had to believe that God Who had made this path through the Red Sea would, as well, continue to defy the laws of gravity by holding the water up like two walls on either side.

UNBELIEF

A short time ago over CBS Television, a documentary was aired concerning some of the great miracles of the Bible. Both sides were presented; those who did not believe that such miracles ever took place, and those who claimed to believe; however, even those who claimed to believe the Biblical account of the miracles, still, tried to explain them by natural means. The end results were that the unbelief of the Believers was about as bad as the unbelief of the unbelievers.

The Believers, so-called, attempted to explain the fiery furnace of the Hebrew children, as there being a *"cold spot"* in the midst of it, in which the three Hebrew children stood.

How ridiculous can one be. The fire was so hot, that the soldiers who cast in the young men were killed. No, there was no *"cold spot,"* it was the Power of God, and the Power of God alone which spared those young men.

Concerning the Red Sea the Scripture says, *"The Lord caused the Sea to go back by a strong east wind all that night, and made the Sea dry land, and the waters were divided"* (Ex. 14:21).

Still, this was a Divine Miracle, not something accomplished by the mere forces of nature. Not only was the opening of the Red Sea done by Divine Power, but as well, it was undone by the same Power. As well, we must remember, a wind blowing strong enough to make a path through the sea which was about twelve miles wide, and then to hold the waters up like a wall seventy-five to one hundred feet high, without any other miraculous force at work would have been strong enough to blow all the Israelites and the Egyptians away. So, God would have to perform another miracle by channeling the wind, which He did. Therefore, such cannot be explained away as mere phenomena. Miracles cannot be explained by natural means, if they can, they aren't miracles.

(15) "BUT OVERTHREW PHARAOH AND HIS HOST IN THE RED SEA: FOR HIS MERCY ENDURES FOREVER."

We can be certain, that whatever the Word of God says, is exactly the way it happened.

THE POWER OF GOD

By the command of God the same sea that was divided now comes back to its original position while Pharaoh and his hosts were in the seabed, coming after Israel. Thus, this evil monarch and all his hosts met their doom. At any time he could have accepted Israel's God and, thereby, experienced Israel's Redemption. God dealt with him over a period of many weeks by demonstrating His mighty Power, but Pharaoh would not listen; therefore, he was without excuse. This Act of God in destroying him and his army was an act of Mercy.

EGYPT

Some argue that there is no record in Egypt's historical archives of such happenings, and, therefore, this proves, they say, the Biblical account of this Miracle as untrue.

While it is true that there is no record in Egypt's history of such, still, Egypt made it a practice of not recording her defeats, only her victories.

Likewise, there is no record in Egypt's history of Joseph's serving as the Viceroy, second only to Pharaoh (Gen. 41:37-44). The reason that Egypt would have omitted such from her historical narratives is because the Pharaoh who occupied the throne of Egypt at this time was not really an Egyptian but was actually one of the shepherd kings who ruled Egypt. His name was *"Apepi."* It seems that he may have even ruled jointly with his father and grandfather for a period of time.

When Joseph stood before him, he was standing before a man who was not an Egyptian but was probably from somewhere east of Egypt.

Later, this dynasty would be overthrown, beginning a fresh or new dynasty. The founder was the Assyrian of Isaiah 52:4, who

NOTES

conquered Egypt; perhaps Rameses II, whose son, Meneptah, was the Pharaoh of the Exodus, the subject of this Fifteenth Verse.

(16) "TO HIM WHICH LED HIS PEOPLE THROUGH THE WILDERNESS: FOR HIS MERCY ENDURES FOREVER."

God intended for the stay of the Children of Israel in wilderness to be of short duration — a few months to two years at the most. The forty years was because of Israel's unbelief and rebellion. Still, God took care of them by constantly performing great miracles, despite their unbelief. All of this was because of His Mercy.

(17) "TO HIM WHICH SMOTE GREAT KINGS: FOR HIS MERCY ENDURES FOREVER."

This speaks of Pharaoh as well as the kings mentioned in following Verses. This should be an example to all who would attempt to resist God and His Plan. The mightiest of nations and empires have crumbled when they set themselves against God. The greatest earthly king of all will be smitten by Him and that will be the coming future Antichrist. As Sihon and Og did not learn, he will not learn either.

(18) "AND SLEW FAMOUS KINGS: FOR HIS MERCY ENDURES FOREVER:

(19) "SIHON KING OF THE AMORITES: FOR HIS MERCY ENDURES FOREVER:

(20) "AND OG THE KING OF BASHAN: FOR HIS MERCY ENDURES FOREVER."

Tradition says that Sihon was the brother of King Og. Both were Amorites. They were giants of the race of the Rephaim at the time of the conquest of Palestine. Og's kingdom was a powerful one, having sixty cities fortified with high walls, gates, and bars (Deut. 3:4-5). These included two royal cities, Ashtaroth and Edrei. At the latter, the Israelites defeated and slew him.

Sihon's capital was *"Heshbon."* Moses sent an embassage to Sihon asking permission for the Israelites to pass through his kingdom. When Sihon refused, the Israelites defeated and killed him at Jahaz and occupied his territory.

These kings were powerful and could have in no way been defeated by Israel except for God's help.

(21) "AND GAVE THEIR LAND FOR

AN HERITAGE: FOR HIS MERCY ENDURES FOREVER."

Og's territory was given to the half tribe of Manasseh (Deut. 3:13).

Sihon's territory was given to the tribes of Reuben and Gad (Num. 32:23-38; Josh. 13:10).

(22) "EVEN AN HERITAGE UNTO ISRAEL HIS SERVANT: FOR HIS MERCY ENDURES FOREVER."

It was *"an heritage"* that Israel did not deserve and, in fact, could not deserve. It was strictly a gift from the Lord; likewise, the heritage that every Child of God has in no way is given because of personal merit, but only because of *"His Mercy."*

(23) "WHO REMEMBERED US IN OUR LOW ESTATE: FOR HIS MERCY ENDURES FOREVER."

The *"low estate"* that is spoken of concerned our terrible lost condition from which we could in no way extricate ourselves. In this Passage it refers to Israel's deliverance from Egyptian bondage, which was symbolic of our deliverance by the Power of the shed Blood of Jesus Christ.

God delivered Israel and delivers us because He cannot forget the Promises that He has made (Gen. 3:15).

God remembers His Mercy and Grace and forgets our sins. Regrettably, man forgets God's Mercy and Grace and remembers our sins.

(24) "AND HAS REDEEMED US FROM OUR ENEMIES: FOR HIS MERCY ENDURES FOREVER."

The word *"redeemed"* means to rescue and to break the power of the one who has us bound, namely Satan. This Redemption is so powerful that it not only redeemed *"us,"* but also it destroyed *"our enemies."* The *"enemies"* here represent Egypt which was a type of Satan's domain. As Egypt was completely destroyed by the Power of God, likewise, Satan's domain of darkness was completely destroyed by Jesus Christ at Calvary.

(25) "WHO GIVES FOOD TO ALL FLESH: FOR HIS MERCY ENDURES FOREVER."

The *"food"* that is spoken of here pertains not only to spiritual food but also to natural food. Jesus said, *"Man does not live by bread alone but by every word that proceeds out of the Mouth of God"* (Mat. 4:4). Only God can provide both spiritual and natural food.

(26) "O GIVE THANKS UNTO THE GOD OF HEAVEN: FOR HIS MERCY ENDURES FOREVER."

Considering all that He has done for us, how could we help but give thanks. One is left humbled after reading the account of all that God has done, is doing, and shall do.

As *"His mercy endures forever,"* likewise, our *"thanks"* unto Him should endure forever.

PSALM 137

Author Unknown:
The Mourning of the Exiles in Babylon

(1) "BY THE RIVERS OF BABYLON, THERE WE SAT DOWN, YEA, WE WEPT, WHEN WE REMEMBERED ZION."

Who wrote this Psalm is not known, nor is it clear as to exactly when it was written. As is obvious, it refers to Israel's captivity under the Babylonians, as they are the only captives referred to in this Psalm.

CAPTIVITY

The captives of Israel, such as Daniel, Ezekiel, Nehemiah, Esther, Mordecai, Ezra, and their companions, must have often wept by the waters of Babylonia as they remembered Zion. Their hearts were not in captivity to the wealth and honors and pleasures of Babylon but were, instead, true to the broken walls and burned gates of distant Jerusalem.

In this one Psalm we find the gist of the tremendous spiritual struggle that has prevailed from the very beginning. It is centered in Babylon, which typifies man and all of his efforts (actually, stimulated by Satan), and Jerusalem, which represents the things of God.

JERUSALEM AND BABYLON

From its foundation in Genesis 10:11 to its fall in Revelation, Chapter 18, Babylon continually appears as the hater and oppressor of Jerusalem.

The two cities are opposed. The one is God's city; the other, man's. The one figures truth; the other, falsehood. The one represents the Kingdom of Light; the other, that of darkness. These cities exist today as principles.

They will exist in the future as principles and as facts. Jerusalem, as a material city, will, with the spiritual principles attaching to it, become the City of the Messiah, the Great King, while Babylon, as a material city, will, with the principles of evil attaching to it, forever perish.

The city-state of Babylon represents the head of gold and Nebuchadnezzar's dream (Dan. 2:31-38).

Babylon, we believe according to Bible prophecy (Rev. 18), will be rebuilt and become a great center of commerce as well as of religious activity in the Last Days. It will be destroyed by the Lord just before His Second Coming by a great earthquake (Rev. 16:17-21).

(2) "WE HANGED OUR HARPS UPON THE WILLOWS IN THE MIDST THEREOF."

This particular Verse proclaims the condition of Believers out of the Will of God, which hinders the righteous as much as those who are rebellious. Daniel, Ezekiel, Nehemiah, etc., were not out of the Will of God, but had to suffer as a result of those who were. We read here their accounts.

CAPTIVES OF SATAN

Captivity to the world paralyzes both hand and tongue so that it is impossible in such an atmosphere to sing the Lord's Song. Jehovah's servants may bring their harps down with them into Babylon in the belief that they will be able to sing there, but they find it impossible. The hand that should awaken on the harp-string the Sacred Song is the very hand that must hang the harp upon the willows; likewise, the tongue that was wont to sing of Messiah and of Zion only has sufficient energy to lament. Babylon robs the Christian of his song and his testimony; directly, he is enslaved by it. Tears instead of songs must be his bitter experience.

THE CROSS OF CHRIST

Regrettably, there are millions of good Christians presently, who are captive to Satan, and simply because they do not know or understand that victory is found in the Cross of Christ, and the Cross of Christ alone. They have some knowledge of the Cross as it refers to Salvation, but none at all as it regards Sanctification; as a result, they attempt to live for God by means which aren't Scriptural. Even though they are sincere, and their motives are right, still, having something else other than the Cross as the object of ones faith, guarantees the resurrection of the sin nature, which will begin to control the Believer, and irrespective as to whom that Believer might be. And regrettably, that is the state of most modern Christians. They do not understand the Cross as it regards Sanctification; consequently, they have their faith in other things, which means the Holy Spirit will not help them, and simply because they are actually living in a state of *"spiritual adultery"* (Rom. 7:1-4).

It should be overly obvious, that the Holy Spirit, although remaining, still will not and, in fact, cannot help such a Believer in such a state. So the Believer is left on his own, which guarantees failure, i.e., *"the rule of the sin nature"* (Rom. 6:12-13). That being the case, faith improperly placed, guarantees that *"Christ will be of no effect unto you"* (Gal. 5:4).

The result of all of this is, in one way or the other, captivity by Satan, which makes for a miserable existence for the Christian, and despite his dedication and sincerity. We must never forget the following:

As the Cross of Christ is the means by which every person is saved, likewise, it is the means by which every Believer walks in victory. It only requires the understanding that every single thing we receive from the Lord, comes to us from Christ as the Source and the Cross as the Means. We must never forget that, thereby ever making the Cross of Christ the Object of our Faith (Rom. 6:1-14; 8:1-2, 11; I Cor. 1:17-18, 21, 23; 2:2).

(3) "FOR THERE THEY WHO CARRIED US AWAY CAPTIVE REQUIRED OF US A SONG; AND THEY WHO WASTED US REQUIRED OF US MIRTH, SAYING, SING US ONE OF THE SONGS OF ZION."

The word *"there"* emphasizes this hostile environment.

(4) "HOW SHALL WE SING THE LORD'S SONG IN A STRANGE LAND?"

There were several reasons they could not sing.

1. They were in a strange land against their

will, being held captive by the Babylonians.

2. They were there because of their failure and their sin, except certain ones who had not sinned.

3. Jerusalem was wasted and burned with fire, along with the Temple.

4. Under these conditions and because of their situation, there was no joy.

As well as typifying the historical narrative of an actual event, this portrays the Christian as well, who has lost his way. He still belongs to God but is held captive by Satan. The Lord's Song simply cannot be sung in a strange land (spiritually speaking). Many Christians have fooled themselves by believing such is possible, but soon there is no song at all. Sadly, many Christians fall into these same circumstances.

(5) "IF I FORGET YOU, O JERUSALEM, LET MY RIGHT HAND FORGET HER CUNNING."

The right hand of the musicians strum the harp. As any musician knows, once the skill is perfected, it is not easily forgotten. So, the Psalmist is saying that even though he is not playing his harp, he has not forgotten how to play. And even though he is not in Jerusalem, he will not forget her glory and her joys.

This statement is also a testimony of faith to the coming Restoration.

(6) "IF I DO NOT REMEMBER YOU, LET MY TONGUE CLEAVE TO THE ROOF OF MY MOUTH; IF I PREFER NOT JERUSALEM ABOVE MY CHIEF JOY."

The meaning of this Verse as well as Verse Five is that even though the Psalmist cannot see Jerusalem and realizes that it is in a serious state, still, his only hope of Restoration and coming victory is that he will not forget Jerusalem and what it represents, namely God. He realizes what he has lost and what he must regain. He has faith that it will be regained.

(7) "REMEMBER, O LORD, THE CHILDREN OF EDOM IN THE DAY OF JERUSALEM; WHO SAID, RASE IT, RASE IT, EVEN TO THE FOUNDATION THEREOF."

Edom was a small country that bordered Moab and Judah. It was located at the extreme southern end of the Dead Sea. Petra is located in Edom. The Edomites were the

NOTES

descendants of Esau (Gen. 36:1).

ESAU AND JACOB

Esau and Jacob were symbolic of the struggle between the flesh and the Spirit (Gen. 25:22-23); therefore, as this Psalm typifies the age-old struggle between good (Jerusalem) and evil (Babylon), likewise it portrays Edom as symbolic of the flesh, precipitating the struggle.

In as much as Edom rejoiced in the day of Jerusalem's defeat, probably the lament of this Psalm refers to Nebuchadnezzar's destruction of Jerusalem.

This prayer of the Psalmist was answered in the prophecy given by Ezekiel (Ezek. 25:12-14).

This should be a lesson to all; even though Jerusalem and Judah had grievously sinned, still, the Lord took great exception to the attitude of surrounding nations and their opposition against Israel during this time. Judgment by God was pronounced upon all of the countries concerned (Egypt, Babylon, the Philistines, Ammon, Moab, Edom, and others). Judah and Jerusalem were God's property. He would administer the punishment that was necessary. As well, He would use whom He desired, Babylon in this case; however, He took great exception to Babylon, even though they were His Instrument of chastisement, simply because they took too much delight in what they did (Jer. 51:34-35).

While it is certainly true that God will chastise those He loves for their failures and sins, however, He reserves that right for Himself and takes great exception when another Christian, or anyone else for that matter, attempts to carry out their own punishment. God gives that right to no man (Rom. 12:19; Heb. 12:5-6).

(8) "O DAUGHTER OF BABYLON, WHO IS TO BE DESTROYED; HAPPY SHALL HE BE, WHO REWARDS YOU AS YOU HAVE SERVED US."

It seems this Prophecy was given before Babylon was destroyed and promised its destruction. There is a possibility that the Psalmist already had the Prophecies of Ezekiel and Jeremiah in hand. Babylon had punished Israel with great delight, now Babylon would, in turn, receive just kind. The Medes and the Persians would be God's instruments of destruction (Dan. 5). This Prophecy contains the same spirit as the edict uttered by Christ (Mat. 7:1-2).

(9) "HAPPY SHALL HE BE, WHO TAKES AND DASHES YOUR LITTLE ONES AGAINST THE STONES."

These last two Verses are an offense to many.

THE EXECUTING OF GOD'S WRATH

To connect the happiness of the man who dashes little children against stones with a happiness of the forgiven sinner of Psalm 32:1 is impossible to them. And yet, the language is exactly similar in the Hebrew Text.

The word *"happy"* is from a Hebrew root meaning to be upright. The happiness of a true moral relationship to God is a right happiness, whether it results from receiving God's pardon or executing God's wrath. The former happiness belongs to the present day of Grace — the latter to the future day of Judgment. God's Actions, whether in Grace or Judgment, are Perfect and in harmony with His Being and Nature and awakens praise in every Spirit-taught heart.

That a tyrant should suffer the same misery that he inflicted on others is not injustice but justice. There is, therefore, nothing unrighteous in Verses Eight and Nine.

However, at the same time, the language is probably figurative. Babylon represents idolatry; her children are the idol images beloved by her. To destroy these is indeed happiness to the servants of Truth.

THE FIGURATIVE LANGUAGE OF THE HOLY SPIRIT

Three figures appear in this Psalm:

1. The woman, represented by the word *"your"* in Verse Nine. The woman represents Babylon: *"You say in your heart, I am, and none else beside me; I shall not sit as a widow, neither shall I know the loss of children"* (Isa. 47:8).

2. Children: *"But these two things shall come to you in a moment in one day, the loss of children, and widowhood"* (Isa. 47:9). The children represent idols personified by sorceries and enchantments.

3. The Stone: *"And the Stone that smote the image became a great mountain, and filled the whole Earth"* (Dan. 2:35). The Stone is the Messiah. Babylon represents idolatry and its fruit. Idolatry and the Messiah are in conflict. The issue must be His Triumph and their destruction.

PSALM 138

The Author is David:
I Will Praise You with my Whole Heart

(1) "I WILL PRAISE YOU WITH MY WHOLE HEART: BEFORE THE GODS WILL I SING PRAISE UNTO YOU."

David wrote this Psalm and as David is the harp, likewise, the Speaker or the One Who makes the music is the Messiah. As Israel's High Priest He sings the song for and with His people.

THE TRUSTWORTHINESS OF THE WORD OF GOD

The praise of the first three Verses, the predictions of the next three, and the persuasion of the last two are based upon the trustworthiness of the Word of God.

The first six Verses will have their fulfillment in the future day of the Messiah's Glory, and the last two express His faith while waiting for that Glory.

The predictions in Verses 4 through 6 relate to the time when all the kings of the Earth — the gods of Verse One — will become subject to the Words of the Messiah's mouth.

(2) "I WILL WORSHIP TOWARDS YOUR HOLY TEMPLE, AND PRAISE YOUR NAME FOR YOUR LOVINGKINDNESS AND FOR YOUR TRUTH: FOR YOU HAVE MAGNIFIED YOUR WORD ABOVE ALL YOUR NAME."

The reason for the praise and the worship is because God has magnified His Word above His Name.

MAGNIFYING GOD'S WORD ABOVE HIS NAME

The Lord's Name means His Reputation and Character for Faithfulness and Goodness. His Word is His Promise. In that future day, His Performance will exceed His Promise, proclaiming the veracity of His Word.

It shall be as if a penniless man owing one thousand dollars of a ten thousand dollar note, turned for help to a rich man having a reputation for benevolence. The rich man promises to pay the note, and on the day when it is due, hands the debtor a check not just for one thousand dollars, but rather for ten thousand dollars. Thus, the rich man would magnify His Word above all His Name.

(3) "IN THE DAY WHEN I CRIED YOU ANSWERED ME, AND STRENGTHENED ME WITH STRENGTH IN MY SOUL."

On the Millennial Morn Israel will proclaim in song that all her expectations founded upon the Promises of God will be surpassed by their performance.

(4) "ALL THE KINGS OF THE EARTH SHALL PRAISE YOU, O LORD, WHEN THEY HEAR THE WORDS OF YOUR MOUTH.

(5) "YEA, THEY SHALL SING IN THE WAYS OF THE LORD: FOR GREAT IS THE GLORY OF THE LORD."

The kings of the Earth in that great Millennial Day will become subject to the words of the Messiah's Mouth. They will applaud His Ways, and great will be His Glory.

THE COMING KINGDOM AGE

At this time and for all Millennia past, very few kings have praised the Lord, or desired to hear the Words of His Mouth, or to *"sing in the ways of the Lord;"* consequently, the Earth has suffered pain, sorrow, heartache, war, grief, sickness, and disease: all the fruit of sin. In the coming Kingdom Age, the world will know prosperity, joy, and happiness throughout every nation simply because *"the Words of His Mouth"* shall be heeded, subsequently bringing forth praise and singing. That praise which is presently foreign will, at that time, be common.

(6) "THOUGH THE LORD BE HIGH, YET HAS HE RESPECT UNTO THE LOWLY: BUT THE PROUD HE KNOWS AFAR OFF."

The Lord, as the Self-humbled One (Phil. 2:8), will be enthroned; the proud one (the Antichrist) (Isa. 10:13; Dan. 11:36) will be afar off in the Lake of Fire (Rev. 19:20). The followers of the lowly One will share His Glory; the followers of the proud one will become the companions of his doom.

NOTES

(7) "THOUGH I WALK IN THE MIDST OF TROUBLE, YOU WILL REVIVE ME: YOU SHALL STRETCH FORTH YOUR HAND AGAINST THE WRATH OF MY ENEMIES, AND YOUR RIGHT HAND SHALL SAVE ME.

(8) "THE LORD WILL PERFECT THAT WHICH CONCERNS ME: YOUR MERCY, O LORD, ENDURES FOREVER: FORSAKE NOT THE WORKS OF YOUR OWN HANDS."

Great Promises are given to us in these two Verses. Every Believer should read them and the notes carefully.

TRUSTWORTHINESS OF THE PROMISES

The confidence of the Messiah and His people and the trustworthiness of the Promises of God are expressed in these last two Verses. He and His people are one; hence, He walks with us in the midst of trouble. Our enemies are His enemies, and as His people are revived and delivered, He accounts that as true for Himself.

He is persuaded of a perfect fulfillment of the Divine purposes relating to Himself and to us.

The most Perfect Work of God's Hands was the sinless Body which He prepared for His Beloved Son. He glorified that Body on the Mount of Transfiguration and on the day of Ascension. He did not forsake and never will forsake that supreme Work of His Hands, as the next Psalm reveals.

SUBSTITUTION AND IDENTIFICATION

This is the reason that identification with Christ as our Substitute is the only way to Salvation. That which we are, He became; that which we could not become, He did; that which He is, we might be, and all because we identify with Him. That's the reason that God justified Abraham by faith and, in fact, could justify him in no other manner (Gen. 15:6).

Every Believer must understand, that irrespective of Satan's attacks, irrespective of our failures, we must ever know and realize that our Lord will never *"forsake the works of His Own hands."*

Why?

His Mercy endures forever!

Even though these two Verses pertain to Israel of old, and the coming glad day when the Lord will once again restore them. Still, it also pertains to every single Believer on this road of life. The promise to Israel is, likewise, the Promise to us as well!

PSALM 139

The Author is David:
The Presence and Power of God

(1) "O LORD, YOU HAVE SEARCHED ME, AND KNOWN ME."

As noted, David wrote this Psalm.

THE SEARCHING OF GOD

Williams says, *"The closing words of the prior Psalm introduce, as already noticed, the sinless tabernacle of clay prepared by God for His Beloved Son. This Psalm developed the subject, and sets out the moral and physical perfections of that perfect human body. The Singer is the Messiah.*

"He here exposes His whole Nature, emotional and physical, as man, together with His Action, His inaction, His Thoughts, His Words and His Ways to the scrutiny of God's Eye, and nothing but Perfection is found." [71]

And all of this means, that there is here absolute harmony between the incarnate Word of God and the written Word of God (Jn. 1:1). All of this reveals the Perfect Submission and Obedience of Christ's human Nature to the Word of God.

When the Scripture speaks of God searching certain things (Ps. 44:20-23; 139:23-24; Jer. 17:10; I Chron. 28:9; Rom. 8:27; Rev. 2:23; I Cor. 2:10), it doesn't mean that God lacks in knowledge. God is omniscient, meaning that He knows all things, past, present, and future. He searches our heart, or whatever, that we might know, and not that He might know, for He already knows!

The searching here as portrayed in Verse One proclaims the fact that God, as stated, searched the Messiah, and in every capacity, and found nothing but perfection. This had to be in order that Christ could be the Perfect Sacrifice, for God could accept nothing less than perfection.

NOTES

(2) "YOU KNOW MY DOWNSITTING AND MY UPRISING, YOU UNDERSTAND MY THOUGHT AFAR OFF."

All of this continues to apply to the Messiah.

THE INCARNATION

Never was a Plan of Salvation so perfected as that which God brought to dying humanity through His dearly beloved Son. God knew that every action of His Son, as well as every thought, would spell only perfection. He knew from eternity past, *"afar off,"* because He planned such before the foundation of the world (Isa. 40:21; Heb. 9:26; I Pet. 1:18-20).

(3) "YOU COMPASS MY PATH AND MY LYING DOWN, AND ARE ACQUAINTED WITH ALL MY WAYS."

The word *"compass"* means *"scrutinize."* Therefore, God scrutinized the path of the Messiah and inspected all His Ways. He found nothing but Perfection. There is no one ever that this perfection could be spoken of except Christ. Man has always been *"found wanting."* Christ lacked nothing and was, therefore, Perfect and could, thereby, stand as the Second and Last Adam Who never failed in contrast to the first Adam who did fail.

(4) "FOR THERE IS NOT A WORD IN MY TONGUE, BUT, LO, O LORD, YOU KNOW IT ALTOGETHER."

God knew all about the words of the Messiah, His Ways, and even His Thoughts while they were being formed. He found every Word to be perfect. All who search the Gospels will have to likewise admit that in Him there was no guile (I Pet. 2:22; 3:10).

(5) "YOU HAVE BESET ME BEHIND AND BEFORE, AND LAID YOUR HAND UPON ME."

The words, *"To lay,"* signify to lay protectingly, while *"beset"* means to guard.

Beautifully we are promised the same protection if we will but follow in His Steps (Eph. 6:11-17).

(6) "SUCH KNOWLEDGE IS TOO WONDERFUL FOR ME; IT IS HIGH, I CANNOT ATTAIN UNTO IT."

The sense of this Verse is that the Messiah admired God's infinite Intelligence and Love and rejoiced that it was impossible to get outside them. He lived and moved and had

His Being in God.

THE INCARNATION

This Passage, as well, speaks of the Incarnation. At this time, Christ laid aside His expression of Deity, while never losing His possession of Deity (Phil. 2:5-8). He purposely laid aside the knowledge that could only be ensconced in Deity (Omniscience) as well as His exalted Position; however, because of His Obedience in going to His Death on the Cross, *"God also has highly exalted Him and given Him a Name which is above every name"* (Phil. 2:8-9).

(7) "WHERE SHALL I GO FROM YOUR SPIRIT? OR WHERE SHALL I FLEE FROM YOUR PRESENCE?"

The Messiah exulted in the knowledge that the greatest distance could not separate Him from God, nor the darkest night hide Him from His loving Eye.

The fact that God's Spirit is everywhere and that His Presence is, likewise, causes some to misunderstand His Purpose. *"If this is so,"* they say, *"why does He allow all the pain and suffering that goes on in the world, especially among innocent victims such as children?"*

This is an age-old question that has been asked by many; hopefully, the following may shed some light on these questions.

THE MANNER OF GOD'S CREATION

God's Creation concerning man was different than His Creation of Angels. When the Angels were created is not known; however, it seems that when they were created, they were all created at one time. In other words, all Angels are the same age, even though they all aren't of the same rank. As well, there has never been any such thing as baby Angels, proving that God did not give Angels the power of procreation (the ability among themselves to bring other Angels into being); however, when God created humankind, He made only a pair, Adam and Eve. He gave them the ability and power of procreation. They could bring forth children into the world, with their children bringing forth children and on down the line, thereby, populating the Earth. To do this God placed within man (Adam) the seed of procreation (Gen. 9:9). Actually, the woman has no seed other than one exception, the Lord Jesus Christ (Gen. 3:15).

The consequence of this manner of creation is that in Adam's loins, in effect, was every single child who would ever be born; therefore, when Adam sinned, which brought about the Fall, he not only fell, but, as well, all after him would be born fallen because their seed was in his loins (Gen. 5:3).

THE SON OF GOD

Jesus Christ, born of the Virgin Mary, came as the Second Man and the Last Adam (I Cor. 15:45-47), and as the first Adam's defeat brought death to the whole of humanity, likewise, the Last Adam's (Christ Jesus) victory brought life to the entirety of the human race — at least to those who would believe (Jn. 3:16).

When Angels fell, God segregated the fallen from the nonfallen, but there was no way the fallen man at the time could be separated from the nonfallen because due to the manner of Creation, all were fallen. In effect, this meant that Adam and Eve changed lords. God had been their Lord, and now Satan becomes their lord. Sin caused the Fall, and the fruit of sin is suffering, pain, heartache, death, sickness, war, grief, demon possession, poverty, and so on — therefore, the condition of the world.

THE FREE MORAL AGENCY OF MAN

Man was created by God to have the power of choice. There is no hint anywhere in the Bible that God tampers with man's choice. He will deal with man, move upon man, speak to man, but will never force man; therefore, the decisions that are made by man bring Eternal Life and all the blessings of such providing man accepts the Lord, or if in rebellion, brings eternal damnation with all the baggage of sin, suffering, pain, and sorrow. So, the condition of this world is man's choice and not God's. Of course, the question of the skeptic is, *"Why doesn't God, with all of His Omnipotence and Omniscience, do something about the situation?"*

CALVARY

The answer is, God has done something

about it and is doing something about it.

Jesus went to Calvary some two thousand years ago in order to redeem fallen man. Every so-called good thing that man has done throughout all of human history cannot even begin to remotely compare with what Jesus Christ did at Calvary.

We must not forget that the Fall of man was far more pronounced than anyone realizes. Man didn't fall part of the way, he fell all the way; therefore, to bring man back to a redemptive state, would take a work of Redemption of which there was no compare.

And now, to complete this great Redemptive process, the First Resurrection of Life is soon to take place, and then our Lord is coming back to this Earth again, in which He will set up a Kingdom, that will be totally unlike anything the world has ever known. Satan and all his cohorts of darkness will be locked away in the bottomless pit, and the Law of God will prevail over the entirety of the world, with this Planet then knowing a prosperity and peace such as it has never known before. So, the Lord most definitely has done something, and is doing something about the situation. In fact, the condition of this world hurts Him far more than it does any of us.

(8) "IF I ASCEND UP INTO HEAVEN, YOU ARE THERE: IF I MAKE MY BED IN HELL, BEHOLD, YOU ARE THERE."

This portrays the Omnipresence of God. As well, it states His total control not only over the Kingdom of Heaven, but over the kingdom of darkness as well. In fact, Jesus Christ has already ascended into Heaven and is now seated by the Right Hand of the Father (Eph. 2:4-7), and He also descended into Hell where he preached to the spirits in prison, which took place immediately after His Death on Calvary's Cross (I Pet. 3:19). After accomplishing this task, He then liberated all of the souls that were in Paradise, took them with Him to Heaven, all made possible by the Cross.

THE SIN DEBT PAID

Before the Cross, and due to the fact that the sin debt was not paid, and because animal blood was insufficient (Heb. 10:4), when Believers died, they did not go to Heaven, but rather were taken down into Paradise. Admittedly, there was a great gulf that separated them from the burning side of hell, still, they were held captive by Satan. They were comforted, but at the same time, it was the Cross alone that could free them from this place (Lk. 16:19-31). Everything depended on the Cross.

When Jesus died, thereby paying the terrible sin debt, and doing so in totality, Satan now had no more hold on these righteous souls. Which included all of the Old Testament Saints; therefore, Jesus liberated them from this place (Eph. 4:8). Now, when Saints die (since the Cross), they immediately go to Heaven to be with Jesus (Phil. 1:23).

Even though the Fall of man was dire indeed, far worse than anyone realizes, still, what Jesus did at the Cross, was far greater for the good than the Fall was for the bad.

REDEMPTION

Perhaps the Greek words which define Redemption, will give us a greater understanding. They are:

1. Garazo: This Greek word means that Jesus has purchased believing sinners out of the slave market.

2. Exgarazo: This Greek word means that we were purchased, never to be put up for auction again.

3. Lutroo: This Greek word means that such a price was paid, that no one in eternity future, be it angels or demons, can ever question if enough was paid.

(9) "IF I TAKE THE WINGS OF THE MORNING, AND DWELL IN THE UTTERMOST PARTS OF THE SEA;

(10) "EVEN THERE SHALL YOUR HAND LEAD ME, AND YOUR RIGHT HAND SHALL HOLD ME."

The Messiah exulted in the knowledge that neither the greatest distance could separate Him from God, nor the darkest night hide Him from the loving Eye.

As is understood, He became our Substitute in all of these things and guaranteed the Father's help to us exactly as it was and is to Him, for we are joint-heirs with Him (Rom. 8:17), meaning that the Father gives us the same credence as He does His Only Son.

(11) "IF I SAY, SURELY THE DARKNESS

SHALL COVER ME; EVEN THE NIGHT SHALL BE LIGHT ABOUT ME.

(12) "YEA, THE DARKNESS HIDES NOT FROM YOU; BUT THE NIGHT SHINES AS THE DAY: THE DARKNESS AND THE LIGHT ARE BOTH ALIKE TO YOU."

The meaning of these two Verses is that all is open before God. The mark of evil is concealment, undercover, covered, hidden. God's Ways are the opposite. Nothing is hidden from His Eyes, nor can it be hidden from His Eyes.

As well, it speaks of God's certain Eye constantly watching over His Beloved Son, even during the darkest times, with Satan attacking fiercely. He has promised the same Divine Protection for us, and all because of Christ and what He did at the Cross.

(13) "FOR YOU HAVE POSSESSED MY REINS: YOU HAVE COVERED ME IN MY MOTHER'S WOMB."

This Passage pertains to the Incarnation of Christ.

THE INCARNATION

The words *"possess"* and *"covered"* here mean to collect and to knit together, and *"reins"* is a comprehensive term embracing the human body both physically and emotionally. The Verse may be illustrated by the action of an able manufacturer in first assembling the parts of a machine and then putting them together. The mystery of the Incarnation is, therefore, the subject of Verses 13 through 16. The members of Christ's sinless Body existed continually in the secrecy of the Divine Wisdom, and when the time came, they were woven together in the body of the Lord's mother, and done so by decree of the Holy Spirit (Mat. 1:18).

THE WICKED SIN OF ABORTION

The terrible decision arrived at by the United States Supreme Court in the Roe vs. Wade case legitimizing abortion in America will forever stand as one of the most bloodiest, most wicked decisions in American history or any other history for that matter.

From the moment of conception, the child is a living soul; consequently, if its life is taken, in the Eyes of God this is constituted as murder. That would be the same in any circumstance whether it is rape, child abuse, or any other situation. The manner in which the child was conceived has absolutely no bearing on the eternal worth of the child; therefore, if the baby is purposely aborted anytime after conception, the person that consents to such and the person who carries it out are guilty of murder and will be held accountable for such by God, except in some rare cases.

Is there forgiveness for such? Yes, just as there is forgiveness for any sin other than blaspheming the Holy Spirit (I Jn. 1:9); therefore, any doctor or nurse who participates in abortion or any mother who would consent to one can be forgiven. They need not live in condemnation (Rom. 8:1); however, once forgiveness is requested and granted and Restoration is enjoyed, one certainly should not involve oneself in such again, nor should they desire to do so.

ABORTION AND EVOLUTION

Abortion is the outgrowth of evolution which denies God and His Creation. As such, man is constantly cheapened and the worth of life constantly lessened. Evolution claims that man is just a higher form of animal and has no soul or spirit. According to this absurdity, man lives and dies and that's it. There is no Heaven, Hell, or any future accounting to be given; therefore, the proponents of such reason that abortion as well as infanticide and euthanasia are not only legitimate, but at times desirable. God's Word says the opposite:

1. Man was created by God (Gen. 1:26).
2. Man is a living human being from the time of conception (Ps. 139:13-14).
3. Man was not only created by God, but also was created in God's Image (Gen. 1:27).
4. Man is a living soul, hence, an eternal soul (Gen. 2:7).
5. Man is responsible to God (Gen. 2:15-17).
6. Man will one day stand before God and be judged for his actions (Heb. 9:27).

THE COMING JUDGMENT

The world as a whole doesn't believe in a coming judgment. It doesn't believe that man will give account to God. In fact, it doesn't even believe that man is responsible.

The world has been so psychologized, which means that its thinking is the very opposite of the Bible, it believes and teaches that if man goes wrong, its because of environment, or something someone else has done. So, in the thinking of the world, and according to humanistic psychology, man is not responsible.

God says the very opposite!

Every unredeemed person who has ever lived, will have to stand one day at the Great White Throne Judgment, where they will give account. There the books will be opened, with every deed, every action, and even every thought recorded by God. In other words, man cannot lie about his life on Earth, everything that he has done is recorded in the proverbial black and white (Rev. 20:11-15).

All who stand there that day will be eternally lost, and the truth is, none will have any recourse. In other words, they will not be able to say that they aren't guilty, because the books will show the exact truth.

THE CROSS OF CHRIST

But there is an alternative to the Great White Throne Judgment. God became man, came to this world, and came for the express purpose of going to the Cross of Calvary, where He would there take the wrath of God upon Himself, all to atone for our sins. So, the truth is, man can accept Jesus Christ today as his Saviour, or he will face Him tomorrow as his Judge. It's either Christ and the Cross or eternal Hell! That's a blunt statement, but it is true (Rev. 20).

Christ took the Wrath of God for us, because the Wrath of God is always evidenced against sin. We can accept Christ and what He did for us at the Cross, or we will stand at the Great White Throne Judgment.

The world doesn't want to believe that, and most of the Church follows suit; nevertheless, that's what the Bible says, and that's exactly what will happen. Man will give account one way or the other.

(14) "I WILL PRAISE YOU; FOR I AM FEARFULLY AND WONDERFULLY MADE: MARVELLOUS ARE YOUR WORKS; AND THAT MY SOUL KNOWS RIGHT WELL."

As this Passage certainly refers to every human being, more particularly it refers to the Messiah. The miraculous nature of His Birth and His full Testimony to it formed the subjects for praise. *"Fearfully"* signifies *"miraculously."*

(15) "MY SUBSTANCE WAS NOT HID FROM YOU, WHEN I WAS MADE IN SECRET, AND CURIOUSLY WROUGHT IN THE LOWEST PARTS OF THE EARTH."

This means that His human Body was skillfully made from the dust of the ground. Even though the conception of Christ in the womb of Mary was decreed by the Holy Spirit, still, it had to be of the same substance as every other man. He came to this world as the *"Second Man,"* and the *"Last Adam"* (I Cor. 15:45-47).

The only thing different about Christ and every other man as it regards His physical Body, was the fact that God was his Father, and not mortal man, with the latter bringing about all of the problems of original sin. Jesus was not conceived by man, therefore, did not have a sin nature, as all other human beings do, due to Adam's Fall.

The Incarnation, God becoming Man, one might say, was the most miraculous event in human history. It was prophesied by Isaiah some seven hundred and fifty years before it took place (Isa. 7:14). I cannot help but wonder what others of Isaiah's day thought concerning the prophecy that a *"Virgin would conceive!"*

CHRIST AND SIN

Some argue that Christ, and because He was God, could not sin; however, that begs the issue.

First of all, God cannot grow hungry, cannot get tired, etc., but Jesus experienced all of these things.

No, Jesus was the *"Second Man,"* and the *"Last Adam,"* and as such, He had to have the capacity to sin. Had that not been the case, His Incarnation would have been without meaning. He had to face everything the original Adam faced, but on a much grander scale. In other words, Satan would hurl against Christ manifold temptations, and in reality, Adam was not tempted at all, but rather Eve. If Jesus could not sin, then His coming as the *"Second Man"* and the *"Last Adam"* would have been meaningless. As well, Satan tempting him in the wilderness would have been meaningless also.

Yes, He was tempted! Yes, He had the capacity to sin! Yes, however, he never failed in one single point, not in word, thought or deed. He kept the Law perfectly in every respect. In fact, had He failed even one time, there would have been no Salvation. He had to do what the original Adam did not do, which was to walk perfectly before God, and He could not do what the original Adam did do, which was to fail God.

Please note, that the Holy Spirit referred to Him as the *"Last Adam,"* meaning that there will never be the need for another one. His Mission to Earth was clear and simple. He must keep the Law perfectly and in every respect which he did, and to do so as our Substitute. As well, to satisfy the broken law, which characterized every human being, He would have to go to the Cross, which He did, there giving Himself as a Perfect Sacrifice, thereby satisfying the demands of a thrice-Holy God. Him satisfying those demands, removed the penalty of the broken law from everyone who makes Christ his Saviour. It is called the *"born again"* experience (Jn. 3:3).

(16) "YOUR EYES DID SEE MY SUBSTANCE, YET BEING UNPERFECT; AND IN YOUR BOOK ALL OF MY MEMBERS WERE WRITTEN, WHICH IN CONTINUANCE WERE FASHIONED, WHEN AS YET THERE WAS NONE OF THEM."

This Passage has two meanings. First of all, it pertains to the perfect Body created for the Son of God. The members of that sinless Body were not imperfect but unperfect, which means unformed, in fact, but all its parts were inscribed from eternity.

As well, it pertains to the moment of conception of the baby in the mother's body and throughout its development.

ABORTION

As well, in this one Passage we have the mystery of the conception of the human being in the womb of the mother.

This Verse refers to the embryo stage of growth from the fertilized egg until organs have developed so that it can live independently. Even though this was spoken of Christ, still, it tells us as well that all the human members of every human being are contained or written in the Book of God. In fact, it tells us that the very hairs of the head are numbered and recorded (Mat. 10:30).

So, whenever a baby is aborted, it is a human being that is murdered, not merely an unformed glob or mass. In other words, the characteristics of that child are seen by God from the moment of conception, and at times even before conception. God knows exactly what it will be like, its characteristics, even down to the most minute detail.

America will pay for the gruesome crime that it commits everyday by the aborting of thousands of babies. To be sure, God will not look favorably upon such, and will ultimately visit such with judgment! If we fully understand this, then we fully understand the horror of abortion.

(17) "HOW PRECIOUS ALSO ARE YOUR THOUGHTS UNTO ME, O GOD! HOW GREAT IS THE SUM OF THEM!"

These truths were very precious to the Messiah as relating to His Incarnation. In effect, Verse Fifteen states that He was made of the same material as the first Adam, which emphasizes the fact that His Body was human and not Angelic. His human Body was the supreme Work of God's Own Hands (Heb. 10:5).

(18) "IF I SHOULD COUNT THEM, THEY ARE MORE IN NUMBER THAN THE SAND: WHEN I AWAKE, I AM STILL WITH YOU."

This speaks of the preciousness of the Incarnation of Christ. All is remarkable when we realize how much He gave up to become such.

THE INCARNATION

This Verse speaks of His Death and Resurrection and of the continual preciousness of the Incarnation even during these horrible times, and we speak of the Cross.

When He awoke (the Resurrection) and returned once more to the glory which He had with the Father before the world was, He would continue and forever relate this preciousness in His thoughts exactly as His Father. We must never forget, that the Incarnation, God becoming man, was altogether for us. More particularly, it was altogether for sinners.

THE CHURCH

These mysteries relating to His physical Body are also true of His Mystical Body, the Church, for just as the members of Christ's human Body were registered in God's Book from eternity and had a continuous existence, so all the members of His Mystical Body have had a corresponding existence. Just as the Divine Love and Care for everyone of the precious members of Christ's human Body existed from everlasting, so they are ever enduring for every member of His Mystical Body, the Church.

(19) "SURELY YOU WILL SLAY THE WICKED, O GOD: DEPART FROM ME THEREFORE, YOU BLOODY MEN.

(20) "FOR THEY SPEAK AGAINST YOU WICKEDLY, AND YOUR ENEMIES TAKE YOUR NAME IN VAIN."

These Passages speak of the absolute sinless Perfection of this human Body that was developed by God for the Incarnation and, therefore, for the Redemption of man, by providing a Perfect Sacrifice. It was never tainted by sin and, in fact, could not be tainted by sin if it were to serve the purpose for which it was originally formed; therefore, neither God nor His Son can abide evil in any form.

THE EVIL OF RELIGION

These *"bloody men"* had to do with those who would defile that Perfect sinless Body by demanding its Crucifixion. These were the religious leaders of Jesus' day.

They did not realize that when they were speaking against Christ, they were actually speaking against God. As well, when they blasphemed Christ, they were taking God's Name in vain.

Taking it further still, any wicked thing spoken against any of God's children, especially His anointed, is, in effect, speaking wickedly against God.

The word *"bloody"* means that they would be guilty of His Blood, a curse which they have suffered unto this very day. In fact, they said, *"His Blood be on us, and on our children"* (Mat. 27:25).

It has come to pass, over and over again, even without stopping, from that time until now. And, in fact, the most horrifying time for the Jews is even yet to come, which will be even worse than the Holocaust of the 1940's.

(21) "DO NOT I HATE THEM, O LORD, WHO HATE YOU? AND AM NOT I GRIEVED WITH THOSE WHO RISE UP AGAINST YOU?

(22) "I HATE THEM WITH PERFECT HATRED: I COUNT THEM MY ENEMIES."

These two Verses speak of the Messiah's rejoicing when wicked and bloodthirsty men are destroyed by God. He gives a satisfactory reason for the justice of their doom; He abhors them; He hates them with a perfect hatred — not a sinful hatred, but with a perfect hatred. This demands a sinless nature which Christians do not have.

We must understand, that these individuals of which the Holy Spirit here speaks, are those who would dethrone God if they had the power to do so. They would make this world and all that is in it a cesspool of iniquity, bringing untold heartache and sorrow upon every human being. They are the enemies of all that is good.

While we Believers understand, at least to a degree, this situation, we are not allowed to take vengeance in our own hands, not at all! That's the reason the Scripture plainly says, and as it regards vengeance upon those who would hinder the Work of God, and would harm God's people, *"Dearly beloved, avenge not yourselves, but rather give place unto wrath; for it is written, Vengeance is Mine; I will repay, saith the Lord"* (Rom. 12:19).

(23) "SEARCH ME, O GOD, AND KNOW MY HEART: TRY ME, AND KNOW MY THOUGHTS:

(24) "AND SEE IF THERE BE ANY WICKED WAY IN ME, AND LEAD ME IN THE WAY EVERLASTING."

David requested this just as he should because of his total desire to be what God wanted him to be. How many Christians earnestly desire for God to minutely inspect their thoughts even to the depths of their hearts, to search for any wickedness that may lurk there?

SINLESS PERFECTION?

This request by David does not pertain to sinless perfection, for no human other than

Christ has ever attained to such. Neither does it mean a perfect heart because, regrettably, such is not, even in the most consecrated (Jer. 17:9-10); however, on David's part it did show a willingness and even a consuming desire to be what God wanted him to be. This should ever be our prayer and goal.

SINLESS PERFECTION!

The greater sense of these two Verses pertain to the Messiah. This Perfect One was to be searched by God in a manner that no human heart has ever been searched, and when it was done, and most definitely it was, nothing but perfection was found. It had to be so for two major reasons:

1. He was to be the Perfect Sacrifice of which all the sacrifices that had gone before were mere types. As such, God could only accept perfection — both in body and spirit.

2. Also, since the first Adam was imperfect, the Last Adam, as stated, had to be Perfect. As the first Adam became the role model, sadly so, for fallen humanity, the Last Adam, the Lord Jesus Christ, had to walk perfectly in order that we might enter into His Perfection. He not only had to be Perfect in life, but as well, He had to be Perfect in death, and so He was!

PSALM 140

The Author is David:
Prayer for Deliverance from One's Enemies

(1) "DELIVER ME, O LORD, FROM THE EVIL MAN: PRESERVE ME FROM THE VIOLENT MAN."

David is the author of this Psalm, but the Messiah is the Speaker.

OPPOSITION

This Psalm applies to David and all others for all time who are called by the Lord. More particularly, the Psalm applies to the Messiah and the tremendous opposition that came against Him in the First Advent and, as well, portrays the great opposition by the Antichrist who will come before the Second Advent.

The *"evil man"* and *"the violent man"* pertain to the Pharisees, the Sadducees, the Scribes and the Herodians with their snares, nets, and gins as in Matthew 22.

It is strange but yet true, that most of the opposition against the Child of God comes from the religious sector. While the world is not at all in sympathy with the message of Jesus Christ, still, for the most part, it stays its distance. However, the apostate Church is something else altogether.

It feels that it not only must oppose the true Message of Jesus Christ and Him Crucified, but as well, must stop the Messenger, and must do so by any means, in order that the Message not be delivered. Such opposition had its beginning with Cain killing Abel, as recorded in Genesis 4. That antagonistic spirit has not stopped from then until now.

(2) "WHICH IMAGINE MISCHIEFS IN THEIR HEART; CONTINUALLY ARE THEY GATHERED TOGETHER FOR WAR."

The Gospels record the mischiefs, the hostility, the stinging slanders, the cruelty, and the snares planned in secret and skillfully set in public in order to cause Christ to swerve from the Law of Moses. They never succeeded, but it was not for lack of trying.

Again we state, all of this came from the religious leaders of Israel.

If the truth be known, the greatest hindrance to the Work of God on Earth, is not the distilleries, the drug lords, the casinos, etc., as wrong and evil as those things are, but rather institutionalized religion. Most may find that hard to believe; however, I remind the reader, that it was not the drunks and the harlots, as wicked and sinful as they were, who crucified Christ, but rather the Church of its day. The next Verse tells us what they were and what they are.

(3) "THEY HAVE SHARPENED THEIR TONGUES LIKE A SERPENT; ADDERS' POISON IS UNDER THEIR LIPS. SELAH."

It is remarkable that all of these statements made concern the religious elite of the Israel of Jesus' day. There are several types of religion, all man-made, all evil and wicked, and, thereby, opposed to God, although claiming to serve Him, and as well, opposed by God.

RELIGION

Religion is that which is devised entirely

by man in order to reach God, or to better oneself in some way. Christianity is not a religion, but rather a relationship, and with a Man, the Man Christ Jesus. Of course, we speak of Bible Christianity, and not that which has been corrupted by religion.

Buddhism, Islam, Confucianism, Hinduism, Mormonism, Catholicism, and a host of similar which we have not named, all are under the heading of religion. This means that they actually were instigated by Satan, and are energized by demon spirits. A great part of Christianity falls into the same category.

To easily explain religion, and to make it possible to be easily recognized, the following should be noted.

RELIGION AND THE CROSS OF CHRIST

Any way proposed other than Jesus Christ and Him Crucified, as the way to Salvation, and the way to total and complete victory in this life lived for the Lord, pure and simple, is religion. It doesn't matter in what Denomination it might be ensconced, or who is preaching it, if the Message is not, *"Jesus Christ and Him Crucified,"* then whatever it is its not the Gospel. Paul also said, and I quote from the EXPOSITOR'S STUDY BIBLE: *"For Christ sent me not to baptize* (presents to us a Cardinal Truth), *but to preach the Gospel* (the manner in which one may be saved from sin)*: not with wisdom of words* (intellectualism is not the Gospel), *lest the Cross of Christ should be made of none effect* (this tells us in no uncertain terms that the Cross of Christ must always be the emphasis of the Message)" (I Cor. 1:17).

The great Apostle also stated, *"For the Preaching* (Word) *of the Cross is to them who perish foolishness* (Spiritual things cannot be discerned by unredeemed people, but that doesn't matter; the Cross must be preached just the same, even as we shall see)*; but unto us which are saved it is the Power of God* (the Cross is the Power of God simply because it was there that the total sin debt was paid, giving the Holy Spirit, in Whom the Power resides, latitude to work mightily within our lives)" (I Cor. 1:18).

He said to the Church at Corinth, and to all other Churches and believers as well, *"And*

NOTES

I, Brethren, when I came to you, came not with excellency of speech or of wisdom (means that he depended not on oratorical abilities, nor did he delve into philosophy, which was all the rage of that particular day), *declaring unto you the Testimony of God* (which is Christ and Him Crucified). *For I have determined not to know anything among you* (with purpose and design, Paul did not resort to the knowledge or philosophy of the world regarding the preaching of the Gospel), *save Jesus Christ and Him Crucified* (that and that alone is the Message which will save the sinner, set the captive free, and give the Believer perpetual victory)" (I Cor. 2:1-2).

And finally, the Apostle said, *"But God forbid that I should Glory* (boast), *save in the Cross of our Lord Jesus Christ* (what the opponents of Paul sought to escape at the price of insincerity is the Apostle's only basis of exultation), *by Whom the world in crucified unto me, and I unto the world* (the only way we can overcome the world, and I mean the only way, is by placing our Faith exclusively in the Cross of Christ and keeping it there)" (Gal. 6:14).

In fact, the great Apostle gave us God's Prescribed Order of Victory, which is the Cross of Christ, and our total and complete faith in that Finished Work, and all of his fourteen Epistles. The Scriptures I've given, are just those which are highlighted. For more information read the Fifth Chapter of Galatians, which will go into detail concerning Christ or other things. In fact, the Apostle tells us in Galatians 5:4, that if we resort to anything other than the Cross of Christ, we fall from Grace.

So, any message, no matter how cleverly prepared and delivered, no matter how pleasing to the ear, if its not the Message of the Cross, which refers to the fact that the Cross of Christ is the only means by which God can deal with the human race, then whatever the message might be, it must be labeled as *"religion,"* which means that its not of God.

PAUL

The false gospel of Paul's day deceived many people because it was so closely similar to the true Gospel; likewise, the Bible was used as the foundation of all this specious teaching. All the same words were used and great Sanctification and Holiness were claimed. Those who were not as acquainted with the Scripture as they should have been became unwitting pawns (Gal. 3:1).

God's Salvation is all of Him and none of man. And, yet, man keeps trying to insert something else into God's already Perfect Plan. Those who do so in any capacity will always greatly oppose the true Gospel. They are called *"serpents"* with *"adders' poison under their lips"* (Mat. 23).

(4) "KEEP ME, O LORD, FROM THE HANDS OF THE WICKED; PRESERVE ME FROM THE VIOLENT MAN; WHO HAVE PURPOSED TO OVERTHROW MY GOINGS."

Every intention of *"these wicked"* was to stop the mission of Christ. His people are called to suffer similarly, but we have the strength and consolation derived from the knowledge that He makes our afflictions His Own; that He understands them; that He engages to supply sufficient faith and fortitude for us to endure them.

Back to Verse Three, the Holy Spirit quotes this Verse in Romans 3:13 as a proof of the total depravity of fallen man's nature.

(5) "THE PROUD HAVE HID A SNARE FOR ME, AND CORDS; THEY HAVE SPREAD A NET BY THE WAYSIDE; THEY HAVE SET GINS FOR ME. SELAH."

The Pharisees and Sadducees and their followers are called *"the proud."* All religion has as its foundation, pride. This pride always produces self-righteousness.

SELF-RIGHTEOUSNESS

These individuals, although the religious leaders of Israel, hated Christ, as is overly obvious. They did everything they could to hinder Him, and to be sure, were it not for His mighty Power to heal the sick and perform miracles, they would have done away with Him much sooner. They didn't do so simply because the crowds would have rebelled against them.

But finally it still became so bad, that anyone who followed Christ was threatened with excommunication from the Synagogue. This meant they were deprived of all means to make a living, were ostracized by their families, in other words, treated as one dead.

NOTES

That's how much that the religious leaders of Israel hated Christ — so much, that they would unlawfully, and illegally, crucify Him.

It is unthinkable that the highest religious order of Israel would do such to Christ; sadly, it has not changed. The majority of that which calls itself *"Church"* actually expends all of its energy fighting that which is truly of Christ.

(6) "I SAID UNTO THE LORD, YOU ARE MY GOD: HEAR THE VOICE OF MY SUPPLICATIONS, O LORD."

The Messiah's defense was His Heavenly Father, as our defense must be our Heavenly Father. What an example for us to follow! When He was reviled, He reviled not again (I Pet. 2:23).

This is even more amazing when we consider that Christ had amazing Power and could have caused great difficulties for His oppressors. There are two reasons He did not do so:

1. First of all, He used His Powers as though it were the Father's Power and not His; consequently, He did nothing but what the Father told Him to do so (Jn. 14:24).

2. He did not come to destroy men's lives, irrespective as to who they were, or what they did, but rather to save them (Lk. 9:56).

(7) "O GOD THE LORD, THE STRENGTH OF MY SALVATION, YOU HAVE COVERED MY HEAD IN THE DAY OF BATTLE."

The Divine Protection sheltering the Messiah's Head contrasts with the mischief that is to overwhelm the head of His enemies (Vs. 9).

He attributed to His Father the source of all His Strength. As well, during the horror of Calvary, His Head was covered and protected by the Father, while the head of the enemy was uncovered and, thereby, bruised (Gen. 3:15).

(8) "GRANT NOT, O LORD, THE DESIRES OF THE WICKED: FURTHER NOT HIS WICKED DEVICE; LEST THEY EXALT THEMSELVES. SELAH."

Verses 1 through 5 address themselves to the Pharisees and Sadducees, and others of that day and pertain to the First Advent. Verses 8 through 11 pertain to the Antichrist (the wicked) and the False Prophet (his wicked device). The desire of the Antichrist will be to take over the world. His efforts will be multifold: social, militarial, economic, and above all, spiritual. The False Prophet will perform miracles which will quickly entice the apostate Church. This wicked duo will seek to *"exalt themselves"* (Rev. 19:20).

(9) "AS FOR THE HEAD OF THOSE WHO COMPASS ME ABOUT, LET THE MISCHIEF OF THEIR OWN LIPS COVER THEM."

There is a possibility that David was speaking of Absalom regarding his rebellion. If so, this Passage was fulfilled. It was also fulfilled in the Pharisees and Sadducees who persecuted Christ. It will be fulfilled in the Antichrist and the False Prophet at the Second Coming. The next Verse tells us what will happen.

(10) "LET BURNING COALS FALL UPON THEM: LET THEM BE CAST INTO THE FIRE; INTO DEEP PITS, THAT THEY RISE NOT UP AGAIN."

The eternal destiny of both these heads and their followers is contrasted in Verse 10 with the eternal felicity of the Messiah and His followers in Verse Thirteen.

We are told in this Passage concerning the Antichrist and his followers that *"they rise not up again."*

As we have previously mentioned, this certainly does pertain to all who seek to oppose God and His Plan, but more directly it pertains to the Antichrist and his followers. We are told here that this will be the end of the last uprising; there will be no more; rebellion is now put down.

(11) "LET NOT AN EVIL SPEAKER BE ESTABLISHED IN THE EARTH: EVIL SHALL HUNT THE VIOLENT MAN TO OVERTHROW HIM."

The *"evil speaker"* could have referred to Absalom as well as Judah and all who oppose God. But more particularly it concerns the Antichrist. Daniel said he will have a mouth speaking great things (Dan. 7:8).

"The violent man" refers to many but even more so the Antichrist. His *"evil"* shall bring him to a violent end (Ezek., Chpts. 38-39).

(12) "I KNOW THAT THE LORD WILL MAINTAIN THE CAUSE OF THE AFFLICTED, AND THE RIGHT OF THE POOR.

(13) "SURELY THE RIGHTEOUS SHALL GIVE THANKS UNTO YOUR NAME: THE UPRIGHT SHALL DWELL IN YOUR PRESENCE."

The words, *"afflicted," "poor," "righteous,"* and *"upright"* all refer to the Messiah. God will maintain no cause except that of the Messiah. Hence, Jesus said, *"follow Me"* (Mat. 4:19).

There are myriad causes in the world, but only one that God will maintain; therefore, the Christian must make certain that his cause is God's Cause.

If the Messiah gives *"thanks unto your Name,"* then we are to give thanks unto His Name. If we follow Him and offer Him praise, then we *"shall dwell in His Presence"* because *"the upright"* (the Messiah) will dwell in His Presence.

PSALM 141

The Author is David:
Prayer to be Kept from Sin and Temptation

(1) "LORD, I CRY UNTO YOU: MAKE HASTE UNTO ME; GIVE EAR UNTO MY VOICE, WHEN I CRY UNTO YOU."

This is a Psalm of David and, yet, the Voice of the Messiah. The tenor of this Verse tells us that the Father was the Messiah's total dependence. He sought help only from Him.

THE FINAL AUTHORITY

In the Church we should certainly seek the counsel of Godly brethren. We should eagerly want and desire their input providing it is Scriptural; however, the final authority is always the Word of God, which alone the Holy Spirit will sanction.

In the modern Church there is far too much of men answering to men instead of answering to God. Spiritual deterioration always promotes men and demotes God. The following will give the reader an idea of how far this deterioration has gone.

DENOMINATIONALISM

Denominationalism has pretty much taken over the major denominations.

First of all, let us state that associating with a denomination is not wrong; however, denominationalism is wrong. The latter demands fidelity to its rules and regulations over the Bible.

A leader in a Pentecostal denomination called one of their Pastors demanding that he do certain things. The brother related to the denominational leader that what was being demanded was not Scriptural. The answer was immediately forthcoming, *"Your responsibility is not the Scriptures but to me. Whatever I demand you are to obey. If it is wrong, I will answer and not you."*

Those words or words similar have sent hundreds of millions of people to Hell. In the first place, every single individual, Preacher and layman alike, is responsible first and foremost to the Scriptures. The idea that some poor, frail, mortal could demand that someone else do something wrong, and they would incur no Scriptural or spiritual responsibility, is a lie at best, an outright blasphemy at worst. Regrettably, this pervades the majority of, if not all, Pentecostal denominations and is rife in most Charismatic Churches. Men love to lord it over other men, and religious men love to lord it over other men more than all. Jesus warned of this (Mk. 10:42-45). There is a strong possibility that the day is near when those who desire to follow Christ will be forced out of institutionalized religion. To obey God or men is the criteria and has actually always been the criteria.

(2) "LET MY PRAYER BE SET FORTH BEFORE YOU AS INCENSE; AND THE LIFTING UP OF MY HANDS AS THE EVENING SACRIFICE."

In the old sacrificial system, Incense was to burn before the Lord from the Altar of Incense twice a day, at both the morning and evening sacrifices (Ex. 29:39; Num. 28:4). These rituals were to be carried out without fail.

The sacrifices were symbolic of what Christ would do at Calvary's Cross. The burning of the incense typified the intercessory Work of Christ, which made it possible for Believers to seek the Face of the Lord, and to praise Him, meaning that such petitions, prayer, and praise would then be accepted.

Understanding this, we must come to the conclusion that there was a perpetual prayer coming from the heart of the Messiah to God. It did not mean constant vocal prayer, but it did mean a state of prayer, which should be our example. How precious the Incense of the Messiah's Prayer and how acceptable the lifting up of His Hands were to God surpasses human comprehension.

(3) "SET A WATCH, O LORD, BEFORE MY MOUTH; KEEP THE DOOR OF MY LIPS."

The Scripture says, *"Out of the abundance of the heart the mouth speaks"* (Mat. 12:34). The Messiah is the only One of Whom it can be said that His Heart was Perfect before God and, consequently, everything that came from His Lips was edifying and Holy.

SOME OF THE GREATEST PROBLEMS OF THE CHRISTIAN

1. Slander: speaking evil of a brother in the Lord, or anyone else for that matter, is roundly condemned in the Word of God (James 3:1-6; 4:11-12). Paul placed *"whisperers"* in the category of *"haters of God."* The Greek word is *"psithuristes,"* which means secret detractors who pretend secrecy and carry out accusations against men, whether true or false, blasting their reputation by clandestine gossip.

2. Judging: Jesus called all who judge *"hypocrites"* (Mat. 7:1-5).

3. Doubt: the speaking of words of doubt regarding God and His Divine provision, especially in times of trial, is one of the greatest temptations to any Christian. It, in effect, calls God a liar and places doubt about His Ability to perform what He has promised. A generation of Israelites lost their ticket to the Promised Land because of speaking words of doubt (Num., Chpts. 13-14). Through Paul, the Holy Spirit said, *"Faithful is He Who calls you, Who also will do it"* (I Thess. 5:24). God considers it a great sin to question His Word (Rom. 14:23).

(4) "INCLINE NOT MY HEART TO ANY EVIL THING, TO PRACTICE WICKED WORKS WITH MEN WHO WORK INIQUITY: AND LET ME NOT EAT OF THEIR DAINTIES."

The separation of evil, which characterized Christ when on Earth, characterizes those in whom He dwells, also.

THE EXAMPLE OF CHRIST

The subjection of Christ and His dependence

solely upon His Heavenly Father as a man, and His shrinking from evil are foretold in the petitions of both Verses Three and Four. The words *"incline not,"* mean *"permit not to incline."*

In this case, the men who practice wicked works were the Pharisees, Sadducees, and Scribes. They were the religious leaders of Israel. It was possible for Him to have their blessing and the fruit of such (dainties), but if so, He would not have the Blessing of God; consequently, He wanted nothing they offered, either good or bad. The reader must, as well, understand that Christ's Example is our path to follow.

The iniquities of Verse Four are to be understood as Doctrinal and not moral. These religious leaders demanded that He follow them instead of God. His answer is given in this Psalm.

(5) "LET THE RIGHTEOUS SMITE ME; IT SHALL BE A KINDNESS: AND LET HIM REPROVE ME; IT SHALL BE AN EXCELLENT OIL, WHICH SHALL NOT BREAK MY HEAD: FOR YET MY PRAYER ALSO SHALL BE IN THEIR CALAMITIES."

That for which David prayed is exactly that for which the Messiah prayed as well. *"The Righteous"* could only refer to the Heavenly Father and in both cases concern David and the Messiah. In the first place, He uses the pronoun *"Him"* which refers to one person.

THE OIL OF HEALING

God does not allow fellow Christians to smite each other. Vengeance belongs to Him and to no one else (Ps. 94:1; Heb. 10:30).

When David spoke of the *"oil"* which anointed the *"head,"* he was referring back to the Twenty-third Psalm, *"You anoint my head with oil"* (Ps. 23:5).

The sheep, during the day as they attempted to forage for food, would, at times, get burrs entangled in the wool on the forehead, also sometimes getting bruised. At the end of the day, the Shepherd would remove all entanglements from the wool on the head and gently massage it with oil.

The pronoun *"their"* refers to the same individuals in Verse Six — *"their judges,"* which refers to the Pharisees and other religious leaders.

The Messiah was praying that all direction would come from the Father and none from the Pharisees. Anything they did was considered *"calamities."* He wanted no part of it.

The Pharisaical spirit of the self-righteous has not changed even today. They are not righteous and, therefore, have no kindness and will, if permitted to do so, break the head of the Child of God. No wonder David said, *"Let us fall now into the hand of the LORD; for His mercies are great: and let me not fall into the hand of man"* (II Sam. 24:14).

(6) "WHEN THEIR JUDGES ARE OVERTHROWN IN STONY PLACES, THEY SHALL HEAR MY WORDS; FOR THEY ARE SWEET."

The words, *"In stony places,"* in the Hebrew actually read *"the hands of the rock,"* and correspond to *"the hands of the snare"* of Verse Nine.

The snare for the foot had two *"hands"* which sprang up and seized their prey. The judges of Verse Six were the Scribes and Pharisees. The *"stony places"* or *"the rocks"* refer to the Messiah. The Lord of Glory paid no heed to these evil religious leaders but, in effect, overthrew their stranglehold on the people. And then Mark said that the common people heard Him gladly (Mk. 12:37).

The words the common people heard were *"sweet words,"* for it is said, *"Never a man spake like this Man"* (Jn. 7:46).

(7) "OUR BONES ARE SCATTERED AT THE GRAVE'S MOUTH, AS WHEN ONE CUTS AND CLEAVES WOOD UPON THE EARTH."

A great truth is here presented.

THE HATRED FOR CHRIST

This Passage shows the hatred of man's heart to the Messiah and His Followers.

The sense of this Verse is that if these *"judges"* (Pharisees, Sadducees, and Scribes) had their way, they would have killed the Messiah before His time. As well, modern counterparts will do the same to all true followers of the Lord and, in fact, have always done so. The battle between religion (man's way) and righteousness (God's Way) has raged ever since Cain killed Abel. It rages no less today.

The religious crowd which comprises almost all of that which calls itself *"Christianity,"* including many Fundamentalists, Pentecostals and Charismatics, were it not for the laws of the land would quickly kill anyone who is of the Spirit, and of course, we speak of the Holy Spirit. They would do it in the Name of God exactly as the Pharisees killed Christ in the Name of God.

(8) "BUT MY EYES ARE UNTO YOU, O GOD THE LORD: IN YOU IS MY TRUST; LEAVE NOT MY SOUL DESTITUTE."

Protection from these *"judges"* (self-righteous Pharisees) can be given only by God; consequently, David and the Messiah looked to God for protection and help. The implication is that if God did not give it, there would be no protection, and the soul would be left destitute.

(9) "KEEP ME FROM THE SNARES WHICH THEY HAVE LAID FOR ME, AND THE GINS OF THE WORKERS OF INIQUITY."

So the *"hands"* of the *"rock"* of Verse Six overthrew those who had planned that the *"hands"* of the snares should overthrow Him. The Hebrew word used here shows that the Rock is an immovable Rock (Mat. 16:18).

OPPOSITION

The opposition by the Pharisaical crowd is vicious. They laid many *"snares"* for the *"righteous;"* however, these *"workers of iniquity"* would not succeed. Down through history, it has looked like they have succeeded many times. Much blood has been spilled; however, the implication is that if the Believer will place his trust in God (Vs. 8), these *"wicked"* shall not be successful until God has finished with the individual, whether it be David, or the Messiah, or all who follow Christ.

(10) "LET THE WICKED FALL INTO THEIR OWN NETS, WHILE THAT I WITHAL ESCAPE."

The doom of the wicked is predicted in this Verse. The future tense should be used here as in the Hebrew Text. The sense of the Verse is that the Pharisees, the Sadducees, and the Herodians were caught in their own snares, but the Messiah passed safely through and over them.

PSALM 142

The Author is David:
David's Prayer in the Cave of Adullam

(1) "I CRIED UNTO THE LORD WITH MY VOICE; WITH MY VOICE UNTO THE LORD DID I MAKE MY SUPPLICATION."

This Psalm was written by David and even though it portrays his heart, more so it portrays the Messiah when He was shut up in the prison house of Sheol. The Pharisees constantly laid a snare for Him, with ultimately all, even His closest Disciples, deserting Him.

To cry *"with a voice"* expresses deep anguish, and the repetition of the expression implies the deepest anguish, as is recorded in this First Verse. In this cry there was no rebellion, only affection and confidence.

(2) "I POURED OUT MY COMPLAINT BEFORE HIM; I SHOWED BEFORE HIM MY TROUBLE."

As David poured out his complaints to God and his Greater Son poured out His to the Father, likewise, we are given an example that we are to follow. Sadly and regrettably, the modern Church has for the most part turned away from God to the psychologists and such like. There is no help from that source, but there is help from God.

Scripturally, the only One to Whom we ever have the right to complain is the Lord. We are to never complain to others (Num. 11:1-3).

There is no record that the Messiah ever complained to any man, but He did relate to the Father the injustices and cruelties practiced upon Him by His Oppressors. How very wonderful that men should be invited to look upon Him in Sheol. How amazing that we should be told what He said and felt when in that region.

(3) "WHEN MY SPIRIT WAS OVERWHELMED WITHIN ME, THEN YOU KNEW MY PATH, IN THE WAY WHEREIN I WALKED HAVE THEY PRIVILY LAID A SNARE FOR ME."

The sense of this Verse is that when His Spirit was overwhelmed within Him, then He was supported by the remembrance that God knew His Life of sorrow. This implies conscious sinlessness, and of course, we are continuing to speak of the Messiah.

He invited God to scrutinize His Conduct from the cradle to the Cross. It was a life of constant and bitter trial, but it was a sinless Life. He was tested daily by snares privily laid for Him, but He never sinned. Men hated Him, but He was unspeakably precious to God.

Verses Three and Six correspond. The one sings of comfort in affliction; the other, of deliverance from affliction.

(4) "I LOOKED ON MY RIGHT HAND, AND BEHELD, BUT THERE WAS NO MAN WHO WOULD KNOW ME: REFUGE FAILED ME; NO MAN CARED FOR MY SOUL.

(5) "I CRIED UNTO YOU, O LORD: I SAID, YOU ARE MY REFUGE AND MY PORTION IN THE LAND OF THE LIVING."

The absolute abandonment and loneliness of the Messiah, especially when in the hands of the High Priests and of Pilate when nailed to the Cross, are obvious in these two Verses.

THE ABANDONMENT OF CHRIST

It is ironical and even impossible to comprehend that the One Who came to die for wayward and lost humanity would hang on the Cross, and there was not one single man, even His closest Disciples, who would admit they knew Him! Not one soul stepped forward to help Him or to even say one kind word on His behalf.

The phrase, *"No man cared for My soul,"* has reference to His dying on the Cross and, thereby, being made a curse for us (Deut. 21:23; Gal. 3:13). Israel reasoned that if He was crucified on a Cross, this meant that He was not the Messiah and was, therefore, doomed!

In reality, He was made a curse for us, but not because of His sin, for He had none, but because of our sin. The sadness of it is His detractors desired that His soul go to Hell, and, yet, He dies for them. Such love man has never seen and, in fact, does not even understand (Gal. 3:13-14).

Of course, wishing His soul to go to Hell did not include His Disciples, or the many who knew Him and, in fact, had been healed by Him. We speak here of the religious leaders of Israel.

The phrase, *"On My right hand,"* refers to

NOTES

the position of those who should stand on behalf of the One in question, in this case, Christ. Sadly, there was no man there.

Even though no man would stand with Him, still, the Lord would be His refuge. His unfailing faith in and dependence upon God up to the last moment is expressed in the words, *"In the land of the living."*

He suffered the rage and cruelty of His persecutors, but He took His complaint to His Father. God was *"His portion"* and no one else.

(6) "ATTEND UNTO MY CRY; FOR I AM BROUGHT VERY LOW: DELIVER ME FROM MY PERSECUTORS; FOR THEY ARE STRONGER THAN I."

Shut up in the prison house of Sheol, and to which He descended from Golgotha, He trusts, prays, and believes. He cries for deliverance and, in fact, this cry had come up some one thousand years even before the actual fact of the Cross. In the next Verse He predicts the triumph which His Resurrection will bring to the righteous.

(7) "BRING MY SOUL OUT OF PRISON, THAT I MAY PRAISE YOUR NAME: THE RIGHTEOUS SHALL COMPASS ME ABOUT; FOR YOU SHALL DEAL BOUNTIFULLY WITH ME."

Here, the Messiah prays that He will be delivered out of the death world. He knows that His Prayer will be answered and the subsequent joy that His Resurrection will bring to His people.

THE FACT OF THE RESURRECTION

Only a small percentage of the world now believes that Christ was really resurrected from the dead; however, soon the fact of the Resurrection shall be manifested to all of the world; then there will be a crowning day both for Him and those who believe.

On the fact of the Resurrection stands the foundation of Christianity. If Christ were not really raised from the dead, Christianity is a hoax; however, the fact that He was raised from the dead is the most scrutinized fact in history. The following are just a few of these proofs:

HIS CLOSEST DISCIPLES

No one, not even His closest Disciples,

understood His statements about dying and being brought from the dead. Actually, they did not even believe it (Lk., Chpt. 24). So, there was no collaboration from even His closest concerning a hoax or anything that resembles such.

A HOAX?

The idea that His friends stole His Body out of the tomb, consequently perpetrating the hoax, is facetious indeed! If such had happened, one can be sure that the authorities would have spared no effort or expense in the attempt to find the body. No body was ever found because no dead body existed.

THE ROMAN ARMY

The Roman army itself testifies to the fact that Jesus was resurrected from the dead (Mat. 28:11-12). Pilate himself gave the order that *"a watch"* should be placed at the tomb (a watch was four soldiers, changed every three hours). It is not possible for someone to have stolen away the Body of Christ under the very eyes of four Roman soldiers, who were under the penalty of death if they forsook their post.

The argument that these soldiers were asleep is silly, especially since so many guards were under a death penalty for failure to stay awake. For all to fall asleep and not hear all the noise and the removal of the giant stone and the taking of the body is facetious indeed (Mat. 27:62-66).

The Scripture says, *"There was a great earthquake: for the Angel of the Lord descended from Heaven, and came and rolled back the stone from the door, and sat upon it"* (Mat. 28:2). The Scripture says those soldiers *"became as dead men"* (Mat. 28:4). The soldiers then went into the city and told the Chief Priests what had happened. Money was given to them, and they were told to say that the Disciples had stolen the body of Christ by night (Mat. 28:11-15). If, in fact, the soldiers had gone to sleep, they would have been court-martialed and put to death.

THE APPEARANCES OF CHRIST AFTER THE RESURRECTION

Some say there were ten appearances of Christ after the Resurrection, and some say there were twelve. It seems there may have been twelve. They are as follows:

1. Mary Magdalene (Mk. 16:9; Jn. 20:15-16).
2. Women at the tomb (Mat. 28:9).
3. Two Disciples on the road to Emmaus (Lk. 24:13-31).
4. To Peter (Lk. 24:34; I Cor. 15:5).
5. The ten (Jn. 20:19).
6. The eleven (Jn. 20:26).
7. The seven (Jn. 21:1-22). This was after the second Sunday.
8. The eleven on a certain mountain in Galilee (Mat. 28:16).
9. The twelve, including Matthias (Acts 1:26; I Cor. 15:5).
10. Five hundred Brethren (I Cor. 15:6).
11. James the Lord's brother (I Cor. 15:7; Gal. 1:19).
12. All of the Apostles (Mk. 16:19-20; Lk. 24:50-53; Acts 1:3-12, 26; I Cor. 15:7).

PSALM 143

David is the Author:
A Prayer in the Hour of
Darkness and Distress

(1) "HEAR MY PRAYER, O LORD, GIVE EAR TO MY SUPPLICATIONS: IN YOUR FAITHFULNESS ANSWER ME, AND IN YOUR RIGHTEOUSNESS."

As noted, David wrote this Psalm. In David's heart and while he prayed, he asked for help regarding Saul who had driven him away from his inheritance, his family, his place of worship, and everything else that was dear to him. Saul made him dwell in darkness (in dark places of hiding) as though he were dead. David's spirit was overwhelmed and made desolate by being driven away from his inheritance.

The sweet singer of Israel set a true example for all men in distress. He did not give up on God or lose faith but trusted fully in Him to bring him out of his troubles, and to be sure, the Lord did exactly what David requested.

THE MESSIAH AND REDEMPTION

The greater fulfillment of this Psalm has

to do with the Greater Son of David. As David prayed for deliverance, likewise, the Messiah prays out of the depths and darkness of Sheol. The Holy Spirit by allowing us to see inside this dark moment opens up to us the stupendous degree of the quality and the quantity of the price that was paid for our Redemption. The Incarnation is little understood even by the greatest lovers of the Bible. The following are some of the things that were obvious in the earthly life of our Lord.

1. His total lack of defending Himself.
2. His total trust in God to defend Him, as is obvious in this First Verse and many others.
3. His Petitions and Prayers were prayed exactly as we should pray. In other words, He was and is our Perfect Example.
4. The hatred that He faced from the religious world was shocking even to the most calloused observer.
5. The far-greater majority of His statements were made against the religious world (Mat. 23), not against those who are commonly referred to as *"sinners."*
6. His great compassion was for the lost, burdened, hurting, dispossessed, sick, sore, and suffering of which there were so many because of sin. He never chided them, condemned them or scolded them; rather, He healed and set them free.
7. His choice of the most common of men to be His Disciples, and His not choosing even one of the religious elite.
8. His total consecration to God and to the Word, and His never experiencing even one failure, yet, taking upon Himself all of our failures so that we may take upon ourselves all of His victory. He never had to apologize or say, *"I'm sorry"* or ask forgiveness because of error on His Part. He did all of this not as God, but as a Man, *"The Man Christ Jesus"* (I Tim. 2:5).

(2) "AND ENTER NOT INTO JUDGMENT WITH YOUR SERVANT: FOR IN YOUR SIGHT SHALL NO MAN LIVING BE JUSTIFIED."

In this Verse David and the Greater Son of David declared the Righteousness of God and the unrighteousness of man, and as Jehovah's atoning Servant, He occupies the center of the Verse as the Mediator or the Daysman. Thus, the commencement of the Verse points to the righteous Judge, the closing of the Verse to the unrighteous sinner, and the middle of the Verse between the Judge and the accused — to the mediating Saviour.

JUSTIFICATION

Verse Two, instituted by the Holy Spirit, is a powerful statement. That man cannot justify himself and that God will freely justify man upon believing faith is the foundation of the great Christian faith — and, yet, man and most of all religious man continues to try and justify himself. Almost every man in the world when asked about his relationship with God will answer thusly:

Most will automatically begin to justify themselves. They will point to bad things they haven't done, or the many good things they claim to have done.

Others will proudly trumpet their religion and their religious activity — attempting to justify themselves. The rich man will often talk about his giving to charities. The criminal will boast that he is not as bad as other criminals. Many will speak of their hard work and providing for their families. The list is endless.

A WORKS SALVATION

The truth is, the world understands Justification by Faith not at all, and sadly, most of the Church falls into the same category. Most of that which comes from behind modern pulpits is a *"Salvation by works,"* and to be sure, *"Sanctification by works,"* which God will not accept and, in fact, cannot accept (Gal., Chpt. 5).

It comes as a shock to the unspiritual ear and to those who are not scripturally knowledgeable that bad men and good men alike must present themselves in the same manner before God for Salvation. The good man must repent as well as the bad man. While good things that are accomplished certainly merit commendation and gratitude, still, they merit no Salvation. The Bible says:

"But we are all as an unclean thing, and all our righteousnesses are as filthy rags" (Isa. 64:6).

It is very difficult for those who think of themselves as *"good"* to accept God's statement about themselves. It is especially hard for religious man to accept such. The main reason that the religious elite of Jesus' day hated Him so much was because of their self-righteousness.

SELF-RIGHTEOUSNESS

Self-righteousness hates God's Righteousness, which, in effect, means that the majority of that which is called *"Church"* hates God's way of Salvation because they are trying to earn it by their own good works, Church membership, religious activity, and codes of ethics that have been devised by man. God will have none of it.

The Scriptural Truth is that all may come and, in fact, all must come in the manner in which God has prescribed, which is to admit that we are all undeserving sinners with no way to extricate ourselves from this morass, and we must throw ourselves on the Mercy of God and believe and accept the provision that He made for us in the Death and Resurrection of His Son and our Saviour, the Lord Jesus Christ. Anyone who does this will be Saved (justified) instantly. And without this, no one will be justified (Rom. 10:9-10).

(3) "FOR THE ENEMY HAS PERSECUTED MY SOUL; HE HAS SMITTEN MY LIFE DOWN TO THE GROUND; HE HAS MADE ME TO DWELL IN DARKNESS, AS THOSE WHO HAVE BEEN LONG DEAD."

The *"enemy"* of both Verses Three and Four is death — the last enemy that is to be destroyed. He that had the power of death is Satan. In these two Verses are foretold the Messiah's Death on the Cross: *"His life smitten down to the ground"* — and His sojourn in Sheol: *"Made to dwell in darkness."* This is the death He suffered so that you and I might not have to suffer such.

(4) "THEREFORE IS MY SPIRIT OVERWHELMED WITHIN ME; MY HEART WITHIN ME IS DESOLATE."

The extremity of horror which our Lord suffered in the death world is revealed in the statements that He dwelt in darkness, that to His Consciousness His imprisonment was prolonged, and that His Spirit was overwhelmed and His Heart desolate.

(5) "I REMEMBER THE DAYS OF OLD; I MEDITATE ON ALL YOUR WORKS; I MUSE ON THE WORKS OF YOUR HANDS."

The depth of this anguish was deepened by the remembrance of the Glory which our Lord had with the Father before and at Creation.

(6) "I STRETCH FORTH MY HANDS UNTO YOU: MY SOUL THIRSTS AFTER YOU, AS A THIRSTY LAND, SELAH."

The language of intense suffering, of full subjection of will, and of confident expectation of the Promised Resurrection are all expressed in Verses 6 through 11. Our Lord is pictured in the darkness of the abyss, stretching out His Hands in His distress; His Soul thirsts for God; for the first time ever He was separated from the Father. God did not and, in fact, could not for a period of time look upon His Son or heed His Prayer, and we speak of the last three hours He was on the Cross, because He was bearing the sin penalty of the world.

The Prophet Habakkuk said, *"You are of purer eyes than to behold evil, and cannot not look on iniquity"* (Hab. 1:13). Even though Jesus never sinned, still, He was bearing the penalty for our sin, thereby, becoming a Sin-Offering, which God could not look upon except in judgment.

(7) "HEAR ME SPEEDILY, O LORD: MY SPIRIT FAILS: HIDE NOT YOUR FACE FROM ME, LEST I BE LIKE UNTO THEM WHO GO DOWN INTO THE PIT."

Our Lord cries out, *"Do not continue to hide Your Face from Me, for I am become like the eternal prisoner of death."*

The statement, *"Go down into the pit,"* refers to Hell itself. There is no Scriptural record that Jesus went into the burning side of Hell (Lk. 16:23-25); however, He did go into the Paradise part of the abyss (Eph. 4:8-9). He also preached to the spirits in prison, which were fallen angels and not men (I Pet. 3:19).

THE JESUS DIED
SPIRITUALLY DOCTRINE

The false doctrine of the *"Jesus died spiritually teaching"* is found nowhere in Scripture. Such teaches that the soul of Christ was damned by God, with Him dying exactly as a sinner dies, thereby, going to Hell. This teaching claims that God Almighty, after observing His Son being tormented in the burning side of Hell for three days and nights, then said at the end of that period of time, *"It is enough,"* and then Jesus was *"born again,"* exactly as any sinner is Born-Again. This means, according to that teaching, that Salvation was effected in Hell of all places and not at the Cross.

Such might sound plausible to those who do not know their Bibles; however, there is not a shred of such evidence in Scripture. This false doctrine strikes at the very heart of the Atonement and, in effect, claims that Jesus' Death on Calvary did not set the captive free but, actually, needed Hell itself added to Calvary to accomplish this task. Such is fiction and holds no validity in Scripture.

The atonement was finished and complete at Calvary's Cross. When our Lord said *"it is finished,"* this refers to the Plan of Redemption. At the moment the giant Veil in the Temple, which hid the Holy of Holies, was rent from top to bottom, this signified that it was done by God, and also signified that Redemption was now complete (Mat. 27:51).

Due to the fact that all sin was atoned at the Cross, the Resurrection was never actually in doubt. In fact, if there had been one sin left unatoned, Jesus could not have risen from the dead, because the wages of sin is death (Rom. 6:23).

While the Resurrection, the Ascension, and the Exaltation of Christ were of immense significance, as should be obvious, they were the result of the Atonement at Calvary's Cross, and not the cause. Paul said, *"We preach Christ crucified,"* not *"Christ resurrected,"* etc.

Again, I state, everything that Christ did, was of immense significance, and especially the Resurrection; however, whatever is done, we must never take away from what was done at the Cross. There, Redemption was begun, and there it was completed, and completed in totality. In other words, it needed absolutely nothing to finish the task. The Resurrection came about, as important as it was, because of the Finished Work of Calvary, and again I state, not as the cause of it.

(8) "CAUSE ME TO HEAR YOUR LOVINGKINDNESS IN THE MORNING; FOR IN YOU DO I TRUST: CAUSE ME TO KNOW THE WAY WHEREIN I SHOULD WALK; FOR I LIFT UP MY SOUL UNTO YOU."

NOTES

Christ prayed for the Father to raise Him in the morning, *"For I trust in You for this — Your Name and Righteousness are pledged thereto."* He made no attempt to deliver Himself from the horrors that overwhelmed Him but prayed that the Holy Spirit might show Him the way out of this prison. Men in pain welcome death as a relief from suffering. It was not so with the Lamb of God. His Atonement finished, He descended into the horrors of the abyss, but what His anguish was, will possibly never be known by man. The fact that He did suffer there is declared in many passages of the Scriptures — the abyss of death.

And yet, His sojourn there, was that of a conqueror, and not a victim. He was a conqueror in every respect, because His Sacrifice at Calvary's Cross was accepted in totality by the Father.

God's true servants in all dispensations may with David use the words of this Psalm as a vehicle of prayer and faith in times of deep trial, but only One could fully suffer the sorrows revealed here.

(9) "DELIVER ME, O LORD, FROM MY ENEMIES: I FLEE UNTO YOU TO HIDE ME."

Now, with the price of Redemption paid, the Father will answer this prayer and deliver Christ from the enemy of death.

(10) "TEACH ME TO DO YOUR WILL; FOR YOU ARE MY GOD: YOUR SPIRIT IS GOOD: LEAD ME INTO THE LAND OF UPRIGHTNESS."

The *"land of uprightness"* refers to the Resurrection. In the Garden or Gethsemane Christ said, *"Not My will, but Yours, be done"* (Lk. 22:42). Even in the abyss He will ask for nothing but *"Your will."* He found no fault in God's Redemption Plan that required a suffering on His part that tongue could never tell. He said, *"Your Spirit is good."*

As well, David, in a terrible time of sorrow and heartache said the same, not blaming God for his plight. What a lesson for us today!

(11) "QUICKEN ME, O LORD, FOR YOUR NAME'S SAKE: FOR YOUR RIGHTEOUSNESS' SAKE BRING MY SOUL OUT OF TROUBLE."

The words, *"Quicken Me,"* actually mean

"make Me alive," which refers to the Resurrection. This prayer was answered, and for *"Your Name's sake."*

(12) "AND OF YOUR MERCY CUT OFF MY ENEMIES, AND DESTROY ALL THEM WHO AFFLICT MY SOUL: FOR I AM YOUR SERVANT."

At the Cross, Satan, who had the power of death, was defeated (Heb. 2:14). And then at long last at the end of the Millennial Reign when Christ shall have delivered up the Kingdom to God, then death itself will be finally and totally destroyed, once again, all made possible by the Cross (I Cor. 15:24-26). Consequently, the Body of Christ looks forward to that great time when all these enemies will be *"cut off."* At that time, Satan and all his minions will be cast into the Lake of Fire (Rev. 20:10). Death and Hell, as well, will be cast into the same place (Rev. 20:14). Then, there will be no more Satan, sin, or death with all of its attendant horrors. These enemies will be forever *"cut off."* All of this will be brought about because of the following:

CALVARY

At Calvary, the Messiah bruised the head of Satan, meaning that he took away the right of Satan to hold man in bondage, which right is sin. Jesus atoned for all sin, past, present, and future, at least for all who will believe (Jn. 3:16).

Christ as God's Son was God's Servant as no man had ever been God's Servant. Men can be called *"servants of God"* only because they identify with their Perfect Substitute, the Lord Jesus Christ, Who was God's Perfect Servant. As God's Perfect Servant He could become what we are in order that we may become what He is, a Perfect Servant.

At Calvary the stranglehold that Satan had on man was forever broken. The only authority that Satan now has is a pseudo authority over men who willfully remain in sin or over Christians who do not know their scriptural rights purchased for them by Christ at Calvary.

The prayer of Verse Twelve has been answered partially; it will be totally at the conclusion of the Kingdom Age, and of that you can be sure.

NOTES

PSALM 144

The Author is David:
I will Sing a New Song

(1) "BLESSED BE THE LORD MY STRENGTH, WHICH TEACHES MY HANDS TO WAR, AND MY FINGERS TO FIGHT."

As noted, this Psalm was written by David.

The time of its writing would have been after the putting down of the rebellion of Absalom (II Sam., Chpt. 18). This was the only time in David's life that his people rebelled against him. As it pertained to David, it pertains even more so to the Greater Son of David.

TRIUMPH AND SUNSHINE OF THE RESURRECTION AND MILLENNIAL MORNINGS

The two previous Psalms which preserved the prayer of the Messiah when in the darkness of the tomb are followed in this Psalm by the triumph and sunshine of the Resurrection and Millennial mornings. These glorious mornings are brought together here, as they are in so many passages in the Bible.

The multiplication of the expressions of what God was to both David and the Messiah, because both are in view here, makes both Verses One and Two throb with exultation and emotion.

Here, David describes his great victory over Goliath, as well as all other victories, to the Gracious God of Glory; likewise did the Messiah. Even though Verse One has to do with fighting in the natural, still, it speaks even more of fighting in the spiritual.

SPIRITUAL WARFARE

The Church is at war. It is a spiritual conflict, but war nevertheless. John said, *"For this purpose the Son of God was manifested, that He might destroy the works of the Devil"* (I Jn. 3:8). Even though this was done by Christ at Calvary, still, it remains to the Church, the Body of Christ, to proclaim and herald this great victory. Incidentally, it was accomplished at the Cross.

The stranglehold that Satan had over mankind has been destroyed. That's the reason that Paul said, *"I determined not to know anything among you, save Jesus Christ, and Him crucified"* (I Cor. 2:2). This is the message that must be proclaimed because it was at Calvary that Christ defeated Satan and defeated him totally, and did so by atoning for all sin, which removed Satan's legal right which he had, which enabled him to hold man in bondage.

Tragically, the modern Church little preaches or proclaims this Message. Instead, it trumpets the message of humanistic psychology.

In the last few years much has been said about *"spiritual warfare."* Believers have been encouraged to dress up in combat boots, military fatigues, and do other such things. Even though such is desired to serve only as symbolism, still, true spiritual warfare has little resemblance to the majority of modern teaching. Sadly, the modern Church looks more like *"Club Med"* than a battlefield.

WHAT IS SPIRITUAL WARFARE?

Of course the answer to that is obvious, it is warfare against the spiritual forces of darkness, which includes all demon spirits, headed up by Satan himself. Every true Believer faces this conflict.

So the great question really isn't as to its identification, but rather as to how it is fought.

Sometime ago I was reading a book by some Preacher whose name I now forget. He was well educated, but seemingly not too very much in things of the Spirit, although he claimed such as his strong suit.

His definition as to how spiritual warfare was to be engaged was that every Believer upon arising each morning, should go through the physical motions of putting on the *"whole armor of God."*

First of all, he said, the Believer must gird his loins with Truth, and should go through the motions of putting on this particular *"girdle."* Then he should put on the breastplate of righteousness, literally going through the motions once again of donning this particular garment, etc.

He went throughout the entirety of the litany as Paul gave us in Ephesians 6, claiming that this would ward off the powers of darkness and give the Believer victory through the day.

NOTES

He was insistent that this be done each and every morning, etc.

The truth is, this would be funny if it wasn't so serious. Such admonition constitutes nothing more than foolishness.

I have seen many Preachers explain all of this over Television, and they would use a Roman soldier as their example.

Let it be understood, that Paul used a Roman soldier, because that was what was obvious at the time. In fact, the Roman guard has absolutely nothing to do with what Paul was speaking, other than to serve as some type of example, which Paul used (Eph. 6:10-17).

If one analyzes Paul's statements carefully, one will find that every single passage in Ephesians as it relates to this subject, points to the Cross of Christ.

For instance, Paul said, *"Stand therefore, having your loins girt about with Truth"* (Eph. 6:14).

What did he mean by that?

First of all, the *"Truth"* of which he speaks, concerns Christ and the Cross. The great Apostle himself said, *"We preach Christ crucified"* (I Cor. 1:23).

Jesus said, *"You shall know the Truth, and the Truth shall make you free"* (Jn. 8:32).

Again that's what Paul was talking about when he said to the Corinthians, and every other Believer as well, and for all time, *"For I determined not to know anything among you, save Jesus Christ, and Him crucified"* (I Cor. 2:2). That and that alone is the *"Truth."*

One can look at every other example used by Paul in Ephesians 6 and all will lead to the Cross, that is if the Believer understands the Cross as it regards our Sanctification.

MANNER OF SPIRITUAL WARFARE

So, the manner in which the Believer engages in spiritual warfare, is for one to place one's faith exclusively in Christ and the Cross, not allowing it to be moved or deviated to other things. Now this is where the real spiritual warfare comes in. Paul also said, *"Fight the good fight of Faith, lay hold on Eternal Life, whereunto you are also Called, and have professed a good profession before many witnesses"* (I Tim. 6:12).

The *"warfare"* is all centered up in this *"good fight of faith."*

Satan will do everything within his power to move our faith from Christ and the Cross to other things. He doesn't too much care what the other things are, how good they may be in their own right, just so our faith is not in Christ and the Cross. We must ever remember that Christ is the Source while the Cross is the Means.

God hasn't changed. He's the same as He always was, and in fact, always will be. The problem was and is, concerns God getting the things which man needs to him, considering that man is woefully sinful and wicked, and as such, God cannot, in effect, have any contact with man, at least in the manner in which man desperately needs. God cannot condone sin, cannot honor sin, cannot have anything to do with sin. So this is where the Cross comes in.

It was at the Cross that all sin was atoned, the price totally and completely paid, making is possible upon simple faith registered by mankind in Christ and what Christ did at the Cross, for God to give man whatever he needs. It is called *"Grace,"* which simply means the Goodness of God extended to undeserving man.

So, Satan doesn't want Believers to know and understand the Cross as it regards Sanctification, or how the Christian grows in grace, and brings forth fruit unto the Lord; therefore, he will do everything within his hellish power to subvert the Message of the Cross, to sidetrack the Message of the Cross, or to cause the Church to even repudiate the Cross, which a great part of it has, in fact, done.

Let the readers understand, that the only thing that stands between the world and eternal Hell is the Cross of Christ. That is it in a nutshell. One could also state that the only thing standing between the Church and apostasy is the Cross of Christ.

Satan fears nothing but the Cross of Christ. He doesn't fear our education, our personal ability and strength, our money, etc. He fears only what Jesus did at the Cross, because it was there that he was totally and completely defeated (Col. 2:1-2; Gal., Chpt. 5).

(2) "MY GOODNESS, AND MY FORTRESS; MY HIGH TOWER, AND MY DELIVERER: MY SHIELD, AND HE IN WHOM I TRUST; WHO SUBDUES MY PEOPLE UNDER ME."

David used the words, *"My goodness,"* and they are also used by the Messiah. About one thousand years later Jesus said, *"There is none good but One, that is, God"* (Mat. 19:17). There is no contradiction.

Within man there is no goodness and no way within oneself to have goodness; however, the moment Christ comes into the heart, goodness comes in; consequently, David, along with every other Saint, can claim, and without reservation, the Goodness of God.

PROTECTION

If one will notice, David, as well as the Messiah, claim God as their *"Fortress."* This speaks of protection from demon spirits and the powers of darkness. This is the reason that the world of psychology has no success whatsoever in dealing with the problems of humanity. All problems of a spiritual nature have, either directly or indirectly, demon spirits as their cause. Every weapon against them is futile unless supplied by the Lord (Eph. 6:11-17).

Some would maintain that while this may be true, God uses the psychologists to help the people! Paul answered this. He said, and I quote from THE EXPOSITOR'S STUDY BIBLE: *"Now we have received, not the spirit of the world* (which is of Satan), *but the Spirit which is of God* (upon conversion, the Believer receives the Spirit of God); *that we might know the things that are freely given to us of God* (the only way we can truly know).

"Which things also we speak, not in the words which man's wisdom teaches (corrupted wisdom), *but which the Holy Spirit teaches* (which is an understanding of the Word of God); *comparing spiritual things with spiritual* (communicating Spiritual Truths to spiritual men by the Spirit).

"But the natural man receives not the things of the Spirit of God (speaks of the individual who is not Born-Again): *for they are foolishness unto him* (a lack of understanding): *neither can he know them* (fallen man cannot understand spiritual Truths), *because they are spiritually discerned"* (only the regenerated spirit of man can understand the things of the Spirit)*"* (I Cor. 2:12-14).

As is here obvious, God does not use the

wisdom of this world to deliver His people. He does use the following:
1. His Word (Mat. 4:4).
2. Prayer (Mk. 11:22-24).
3. The Name of Jesus (Mk. 16:17-18).

THE LORD JESUS CHRIST, THE CROSS, AND THE HOLY SPIRIT

In Verse One David emphasizes the fact that the Lord is his strength. This is the key to victory. No man within himself is a match for the powers of darkness; therefore, the secret is in allowing the Holy Spirit to be our strength.

Such at times is not easy to do. Oftentimes we think we are opposing the powers of darkness in the strength of the Lord when, in reality, we are opposing Satan with our own strength. On these occasions we fail, as fail we must.

This is the reason that Jesus told us the following: *"If any man will come after Me* (the criteria for Discipleship), *let him deny himself* (not asceticism as many think, but rather that one denies one's own willpower, self-will, strength, and ability, depending totally on Christ), *and take up his cross* (the benefits of the Cross, looking exclusively to what Jesus did there to meet our every need) *daily* (this is so important, our looking to the Cross; that we must renew our Faith in what Christ has done for us, even on a daily basis, for Satan will ever try to move us away from the Cross as the Object of our Faith, which always spells disaster), *and follow Me* (Christ can be followed only by the Believer looking to the Cross, understanding what it accomplished, and by that means alone [Rom. 6:3-5, 11, 14; 8:1-2, 11; I Cor. 1:17-18, 21, 23; 2:2; Gal. 6:14; Eph. 2:13-18; Col. 2:14-15])" (Lk. 9:23).

Jesus then said, and along these same lines, *"And whosoever does not bear his cross* (this doesn't speak of suffering as most think, but rather ever making the Cross of Christ the Object of our Faith; we are Saved and we are victorious not by suffering, although that sometimes will happen, or any other similar things, but rather by our Faith, but always with the Cross of Christ as the Object of that Faith), *and come after Me* (one can follow Christ only by Faith in what He has done for us at the Cross; He recognizes nothing else), *cannot be My Disciple* (this statement is emphatic! If it's not Faith in the Cross of Christ, then it's faith that God will not recognize, which means that such people are refused)" (Lk. 14:27).

Because it's so important, let us say it again:

If a person does not *"bear his cross,"* in their coming after the Lord, which refers to looking to what the Cross provides, which is everything, then plainly, purely, and simply, Jesus emphatically stated, that such a person *"cannot be My Disciple."* Looking exclusively to Christ and the Cross is the secret of all Divine protection from demon spirits, and every power of darkness. It is the secret of all victorious, overcoming Christian living, victory over the world, the flesh, and the devil.

(3) "LORD, WHAT IS MAN, THAT YOU TAKE KNOWLEDGE OF HIM! OR THE SON OF MAN, THAT YOU MAKE ACCOUNT OF HIM!

(4) "MAN IS LIKE TO VANITY: HIS DAYS ARE AS A SHADOW THAT PASSES AWAY."

That the Mighty God, Whose Glory and Power nature reveals, should so concern Himself with man, who is as a breath and a shadow, as to send His Beloved Son to redeem him, fills the heart with wonder and praise.

Concerning this, Pulpit says, *"It enhances our estimate of God's goodness to consider the insignificance and unworthiness of the creatures on whom He bestows His Grace."* [72]

(5) "BOW YOUR HEAVENS, O LORD, AND COME DOWN: TOUCH THE MOUNTAINS, AND THEY SHALL SMOKE.

(6) "CAST FORTH LIGHTNING, AND SCATTER THEM: SHOOT OUT YOUR ARROWS, AND DESTROY THEM."

David is referring here to the Might and Majesty of God relative to His Appearance on Mount Sinai (Ex. 19:16-19). David reasons that if God could do such that He could also deliver him. Of course, God did deliver him.

The Greater Son of David prayed thusly as well. David was asking to be delivered from his enemies. The Messiah was asking to be delivered from the most strident forces of darkness that had determined to foil His Resurrection.

LEAVING VENGEANCE TO GOD

Every Believer has the Scriptural right to

pray that God would stop those who are attempting to stop the Work of God. The Christian has the right to pray in this way. At the same time, we must be very careful what we do to defend ourselves.

David did not defend himself against Saul. He only did so against Absalom when there was no other choice. Christ used His Power to destroy the powers of Satan, but not to destroy men, even wicked and evil men. He left that to the Father, even as we must leave such to the Father (Rom. 12:18-19).

(7) "SEND YOUR HAND FROM ABOVE; RID ME, AND DELIVER ME OUT OF GREAT WATERS, FROM THE HAND OF STRANGE CHILDREN;

(8) "WHOSE MOUTH SPEAKS VANITY, AND THEIR RIGHT HAND IS A RIGHT HAND OF FALSEHOOD."

David was delivered, and the Messiah was delivered. This speaks of David being placed on the throne and Christ being resurrected. In the Resurrection His foes were defeated, and He was delivered from *"them"* (Vs. 6), for example, and the *"strangers"* of Verse Seven.

There is no meaningless repetition in Verses Eight and Eleven. The fundamental doctrine of man's incurable corruption is declared to be the same at the time of Christ's Future Coming as it was at the time of His First Coming. Both Advents foretell man's unchanged moral condition, notwithstanding two thousand intervening years of so-called culture.

(9) "I WILL SING A NEW SONG UNTO YOU, O GOD: UPON A PSALTERY AND AN INSTRUMENT OF TEN STRINGS WILL I SING PRAISES UNTO YOU.

(10) "IT IS HE WHO GIVES SALVATION UNTO KINGS: WHO DELIVERED DAVID HIS SERVANT FROM THE HURTFUL SWORD."

In all this David was a Type of the Messiah Who, having been raised from the dead, promises to sing a new song on mounting His Millennial Throne, which most definitely will take place at the beginning of the Kingdom Age.

(11) "RID ME, AND DELIVER ME FROM THE HAND OF STRANGE CHILDREN, WHOSE MOUTH SPEAKS VANITY, AND THEIR RIGHT HAND IS A RIGHT HAND OF FALSEHOOD."

The word *"strange"* in both Verses Seven and Eleven is derived from a Hebrew root signifying *"to know and not to know,"* for example, estrangement and hostility. The Messiah's enemies in His First Advent knew Him and, yet, refused to know Him (Jn. 7:28), and His future appearance will be preceded by similar conduct (II Pet. 3:1-7). Man is by nature a stranger to Grace and to God — estranged from Him and hostile to Him.

(12) "THAT OUR SONS MAY BE AS PLANTS GROWN UP IN THEIR YOUTH; THAT OUR DAUGHTERS MAY BE AS CORNER STONES, POLISHED AFTER THE SIMILITUDE OF A PALACE:

(13) "THAT OUR GARNERS MAY BE FULL, AFFORDING ALL MANNER OF STORE: THAT OUR SHEEP MAY BRING FORTH THOUSANDS AND TEN THOUSANDS IN OUR STREETS:

(14) "THAT OUR OXEN MAY BE STRONG TO LABOUR; THAT THERE BE NO BREAKING IN, NOR GOING OUT; THAT THERE BE NO COMPLAINING IN OUR STREETS."

This prayer was prayed by David and similarly by the Messiah. It has never been fulfilled in totality, only in part. Those who trust the Lord have been the recipients of His great Blessings, but still, the happy time that is pleaded cannot be fully brought about until Jesus reigns in Jerusalem; consequently, this speaks of the glorious Kingdom Age that is yet to come.

KINGDOM NOW?

The hearts of men long for such. But as ever, they try to bring it about by human means. Such is not possible. When the King comes, the Kingdom will come as well.

Regrettably, the modern teaching of *"Kingdom Now"* is but another effort of man cloaked in religious phraseology that will be no more successful than the efforts of the most wicked. Men continue to try to improve self. Even religious man with religious efforts tries to improve self, all fail. Self must be hidden in Christ. When Christ comes back, and come back He will, the prayer that David prayed so long ago will finally materialize and be the happy result of Emmanuel's Government.

Again we state, self cannot bring in the coming Kingdom Age, irrespective of the motivation. It will only be done when Jesus comes back the second time, which He most definitely will. Then and only then will the Kingdom Age commence. Otherwise, all of these modern efforts, are foolish to say the least!

(15) "HAPPY IS THAT PEOPLE, WHO IS IN SUCH A CASE: YEA, HAPPY IS THAT PEOPLE, WHOSE GOD IS THE LORD."

We find in these Verses, God's blueprint for happiness.

HAPPINESS!

The Christian today has joy but very little happiness because happiness depends on external surroundings. It is difficult to be happy when so many are dying lost without God in continuous rebellion that brings forth so much sorrow and heartache. Even the Messiah, when looking upon such in His earthly sojourn, was *"a man of sorrows, and acquainted with grief"* (Isa. 53:3).

Down through the many, vast centuries, men have longed for David's prayer to be answered. On that glad morn when Jesus comes back (Rev., Chpt. 19), Satan will then be locked away along with all his minions of darkness. The government will then be on the Shoulder of Jesus Christ (Isa. 9:6), and, thankfully, of the *"increase of His Government and Peace there will be no end"* (Isa. 9:7). The and only then will the people be happy. As well, such happiness will spread over the entirety of the Earth because *"God is the Lord."*

At that time, there will be no more worship of Buddha, Mohammad, Joseph Smith, or any other fake luminary. As well, all false religions such as Hinduism, Spiritism, Humanism, and other such false lights will be locked away with their sponsor, Satan. Over the entirety of the Planet, *"God is the LORD."*

PSALM 145

The Author is David:
Great is the Lord, and Greatly to be Praised

(1) "I WILL EXTOL YOU, MY GOD, O KING; AND I WILL BLESS YOUR NAME FOR EVER AND EVER.

NOTES

(2) "EVERY DAY WILL I BLESS YOU; AND I WILL PRAISE YOUR NAME FOR EVER AND EVER."

David wrote this Psalm but exactly when he wrote it is not clear. It seems to be after he had gained the Throne, with all enemies being subdued.

EVERY ENEMY DEFEATED

Even though David is king, still, he will address God as the True King of Israel. He gives God all praise and glory for bringing him (David) to this desired place. For such he will *"praise Your name for ever and ever."*

The struggle for David to finally arrive at the Throne which God had intended from the very beginning was long, hard, bloody, and painful. Satan spared no expense in hindering that which God had ordained. Nevertheless, David maintained his faith in God, and the Lord brought him through, as the Lord will bring us through.

As the Holy Spirit gave this Psalm to David, still, even in greater fulfillment it speaks of the Messiah Who will grace the throne of Israel on that glad day when all enemies are finally under His Feet. This is a Song addressing that Millennial Morn.

In Psalms 22:25 the Messiah said, *"My praise shall be of You in the great congregation."* This vow He fulfills here upon ascending the Throne of Jehovah at Jerusalem (I Chron. 29:23). As Viceroy He acts for God the Great King, addressing Him as *"My God the King,"* even as it is given in the original Hebrew. Before Him stands *"the great congregation,"* composed of the princes and people of Israel and the representatives of all nations. At this time, the time of the coming Kingdom Age, this mighty anthem will be sung. The Messiah will lead the Song, and the great congregation will respond.

(3) "GREAT IS THE LORD, AND GREATLY TO BE PRAISED; AND HIS GREATNESS IS UNSEARCHABLE."

The world will then look out upon the landscape that for the first time in human history is bathed in peace. The praise for such will be given to *"the LORD."* Regrettably, down through the ages men, even if recognizing the existence of God, continuously limited Him. Now the entirety of the world will say, *"His greatness is unsearchable."*

(4) "ONE GENERATION SHALL PRAISE YOUR WORKS TO ANOTHER, AND SHALL DECLARE YOUR MIGHTY ACTS."

The greatest problem of the Church has been that even though God gives great Revival to one generation, still, most of the time the blessed generation fails to pass it on to the one following. In the great Kingdom Age to come, the greater topic of conversation will always be *"Your works,"* and *"Your mighty acts."* This, the conversation of the world will not be on sports, entertainment, the stock market, or any other such like thing, but only upon the One Who can truly provide the great blessings of the previous Psalm that David asked for in his prayer (Ps. 144:12-14).

(5) "I WILL SPEAK OF THE GLORIOUS HONOUR OF YOUR MAJESTY, AND OF YOUR WONDROUS WORKS."

In these Passages Christ extols the Father, while the people extol the Messiah. The great congregation worships the Messiah as God; the Messiah worships God. Thus, the Holy Spirit in this Psalm testifies to Christ's Deity and humanity.

The great congregation sings without misgiving of the character, perfection, and duration of the Government which the Messiah will administer and of which Daniel also speaks (Dan. 7:22-27).

(6) "AND MEN SHALL SPEAK OF THE MIGHT OF YOUR TERRIBLE ACTS: AND I WILL DECLARE YOUR GREATNESS.

(7) "THEY SHALL ABUNDANTLY UTTER THE MEMORY OF YOUR GREAT GOODNESS, AND SHALL SING OF YOUR RIGHTEOUSNESS."

In the coming Kingdom Age, the entirety of the Earth will speak of God's great Power. The Messiah will proclaim the truthfulness of the statements of men and say, *"I will declare Your greatness."*

Men today talk little of God's Goodness. Then, the topic of conversation all over the world will be *"Your great goodness."* As well, the song on a worldwide basis will be *"Of Your righteousness."*

(8) "THE LORD IS GRACIOUS, AND FULL OF COMPASSION; SLOW TO ANGER, AND OF GREAT MERCY.

NOTES

(9) "THE LORD IS GOOD TO ALL: AND HIS TENDER MERCIES ARE OVER ALL HIS WORKS."

Verses Eight and Nine are the Song. The Song concerns the Character of Jehovah. His Name is linked with *"Grace," "Compassion,"* and *"Mercy."* As well, everything that He does is covered by Mercy and tender Mercy at that.

(10) "ALL YOUR WORKS SHALL PRAISE YOU, O LORD; AND YOUR SAINTS SHALL BLESS YOU."

The great price that was paid at Calvary for the Redemption of man is here called, *"Your works."* For that we will ever praise Him. The Saints who will offer this praise will be a testimony to the worth and value of all that He did to redeem fallen humanity.

(11) "THEY SHALL SPEAK OF THE GLORY OF YOUR KINGDOM, AND TALK OF YOUR POWER."

Such will be the topic of all conversation, the headlines of every newspaper, the subject content of every magazine, and the substance of every newscast over television and radio, which will be one hundred percent different than that which we presently observe.

(12) "TO MAKE KNOWN TO THE SONS OF MEN HIS MIGHTY ACTS, AND THE GLORIOUS MAJESTY OF HIS KINGDOM."

During the Kingdom Age, the priority of Jehovah will be the Evangelization of the world. It is God's priority now, but, sadly, the far greater majority of the Church is little engaged in such. Then, the determination will be that every human being on the face of the Earth knows of *"His mighty acts"* and of *"His glorious majesty."*

(13) "YOUR KINGDOM IS AN EVERLASTING KINGDOM, AND YOUR DOMINION ENDURES THROUGHOUT ALL GENERATIONS."

There have been some good kingdoms in Earth's long history, but only a few. Sadly, they have been short-lived. By and large, the kingdoms of this world has been despotic, dictatorial, self-serving, unmerciful and, thereby, enslaved the majority of the people. This glorious Kingdom will be different.

First of all, its people will be happy (Ps. 144:15), and second, it will be a Kingdom that will never end, becoming greater as God ultimately transfers His Headquarters from

Heaven to Earth, which will take place at the conclusion of the Kingdom Age (Rev., Chpts. 21-22).

(14) "THE LORD UPHOLDS ALL WHO FALL, AND RAISES UP ALL THOSE THAT BE BOWED DOWN."

The sense of this Verse is that during the days of the Kingdom Age, the weak and the infirm who have suffered so much will in that day be supported by *"the Lord."*

Spiritually speaking, most of the world presently is *"bowed down"* with sorrow, burden, sickness, disease, and heartache. It has been such since the Fall of man. But at long last the Messiah *"raises up."*

THE ORIGINAL CREATION

Man has never seen this Earth as God originally created it and intended for it to be. Neither has He beheld man as God originally intended man to be. Because of the terrible curse of sin, man has been *"bowed down."* In that day, this will end, and the landscape will be such as has never been viewed by man in all of history.

(15) "THE EYES OF ALL WAIT UPON YOU; AND YOU GIVE THEM THEIR MEAT IN DUE SEASON."

In that coming glad day, the eyes of the whole world will be directed toward the Messiah. Because of this the Earth will then yield her increase, which will guarantee a world without hunger, want, or poverty. Abundance will be the order of the day.

(16) "YOU OPEN YOUR HAND, AND SATISFY THE DESIRE OF EVERY LIVING THING."

As Jesus touched the bread and fed the great multitudes and they were all satisfied, He will, likewise, satisfy the hunger of every heart. In effect, He is and always has been the only One Who could *"satisfy."* The hand that He opens will be an abundant hand.

The cry of the present world's system is the *"clenched fist."* In that day, it will be the *"open hand"* because the Hand belongs to Christ.

(17) "THE LORD IS RIGHTEOUS IN ALL HIS WAYS, AND HOLY IN ALL HIS WORKS."

After some six thousand years of recorded history and with man's repeated failure in government, society, religion, and in all else, men upon seeing the wonder of His Government along with the provision of His open Hand will say, *"The Lord is Righteous."* In this Passage the entirety of the world will admit that *"His Ways"* are right and *"His Works"* are Holy.

(18) "THE LORD IS NEAR UNTO ALL THEM WHO CALL UPON HIM, TO ALL WHO CALL UPON HIM IN TRUTH."

In this Passage we are told that all of the servants of God may personally foretaste in their hearts the sweetness and Power of Christ's future, Perfect, earthly government. Tragically, few do.

(19) "HE WILL FULFILL THE DESIRE OF THEM WHO FEAR HIM: HE ALSO WILL HEAR THEIR CRY, AND WILL SAVE THEM."

Not only will the Lord do this in the coming Kingdom Age, but also and as always, He will do it now.

Man has a burning desire in his heart which he with all of his efforts cannot fill. If he would only *"taste and see that the Lord is good,"* he would then have his desires fulfilled, and only then!

(20) "THE LORD PRESERVES ALL THEM WHO LOVE HIM: BUT ALL THE WICKED WILL HE DESTROY."

This is a statement, in fact, that says that despite all of the evil in this world, in the end Righteousness will prevail, and wickedness will be destroyed.

(21) "MY MOUTH SHALL SPEAK THE PRAISE OF THE LORD: AND LET ALL FLESH BLESS HIS HOLY NAME FOR EVER AND EVER."

This was David's commitment; it should be our commitment as well; however, its greater fulfillment will come during the Kingdom Age. The result of His Administration shall be that all flesh shall bless His Holy Name for ever and ever. As well, He will cast out of His Kingdom all who offend.

At present, the majority of that which comes from *"all flesh"* is profanity, blasphemy, and iniquity. The day is coming when there will be no more profanity, blasphemy, or iniquity on the face of the Earth. *"All flesh"* will bless *"His Holy Name."* They will not only do so at that time, but *"for ever and ever."*

PSALM 146

Author Unknown:
Praise to God, Mighty Creator

(1) "PRAISE YE THE LORD. PRAISE THE LORD, O MY SOUL.

(2) "WHILE I LIVE WILL I PRAISE THE LORD: I WILL SING PRAISES UNTO MY GOD WHILE I HAVE ANY BEING."

Who wrote this Psalm is not known.

As the five Books of the Psalms correspond to the five Books of the Pentateuch, so the five closing Hallelujah Psalms also correspond. This Psalm is, therefore, the Genesis Psalm. It recalls the formation of man and the creation of the worlds.

Each Psalm begins and ends with Hallelujah. All five are, as well, Millennium Psalms. They connect the Books of Genesis and Revelation. They will be sung by the happy subjects of Christ's future Kingdom.

(3) "PUT NOT YOUR TRUST IN PRINCES, NOR IN THE SON OF MAN, IN WHOM THERE IS NO HELP.

(4) "HIS BREATH GOES FORTH, HE RETURNS TO HIS EARTH; IN THAT VERY DAY HIS THOUGHTS PERISH."

The great struggle that goes on in the Christian always concerns itself in trusting man or God.

TRUST IN THE LORD

One putting total trust in God does not refer to the ordinary commerce that must be undertaken in business in the normal course of life. Paul said, *"For then must you needs go out of the world"* (I Cor. 5:10). Nor does it mean that it is wrong or showing a lack of trust in God for Christians to engage the services of medical doctors. Luke himself was a physician, although there is no Scriptural record that he maintained any type of practice while with Paul. As well, God heals people in hospitals constantly, and while taking medicine. If such were wrong, the Lord simply would not do these types of things.

Some might refer to King Asa of Judah who the Scripture said, *"Sought not the LORD, but to the physicians"* (II Chron. 16:12).

This is the first mention of such among the Hebrews. Although it is not known for sure, the ones here could have been Egyptian physicians, who were in high repute at foreign courts in ancient times and who pretended to expel diseases by charms, incantations, and mystic arts.

If such was the case, one can see why Jehovah would be angry in such cases (Jer. 17:5-10). Such would have been looked at by the Lord as witchcraft and, in fact, that's exactly what it would have been.

Also, as it concerns the coming Kingdom Age, the Scripture tells us that trees shall grow beside the river that issues out from under the Sanctuary, and it says, *"And the fruit thereof shall be for me, and the leaf thereof for medicine"* (Ezek. 47:12).

If it is wrong now to take medicine, well then the Lord would be doing something wrong in the coming Kingdom Age, which we know isn't the case. In fact, most medicines come from *"leaves,"* or other types of plants or even the bark of trees. The evidence is, such medicine will be used copiously in the coming Kingdom Age which will be from the leaves of the trees that grow beside that particular River. More than likely, these particular *"leaves"* will probably be more preventative than anything else.

Once again as it regards consulting man, while the Christian should certainly seek the prayers, counsel, and advice of fellow Christians concerning matters, still, the Word of God and the leading of the Holy Spirit must be the criteria. Of course, the Holy Spirit will never abrogate the Bible in any manner.

ACCOUNTABILITY

One of the greatest faults in the Ministry is Preachers who love to lord it over other Preachers, and Preachers who love to be lorded over. Many Preachers are comfortable in having other Preachers tell them what to do; somehow, they think this absolves them from responsibility.

In the last few years, *"accountability"* has become very big in Church circles. In fact, the very name *"accountability"* seems to be very positive, as everyone should desire to be accountable; however, the meaning is totally different.

The idea is, that Preachers should be

accountable to another Preacher, etc. As well, the laity falls into the same category.

The idea is, whatever the one in charge demands to be done, is to be done without question. That is what they refer to as *"accountability."*

The truth is, such has led millions to Hell. That's a blunt statement, but it is true.

While in a sense, all Believers, Preachers included, are accountable to all other Believers, still, it is only in the sense of *"love."* Concerning this, Paul said, *"Owe no man anything but to love one another: for he who loves another has fulfilled the Law"* (Rom. 13:8).

Correct accountability is always to the Lord which is done through the Word of God. In other words, the Word of God always is the final authority on all things. As we have stated, some Preachers rather enjoy lording it over others, and believe it or not, some Preachers love to be lorded over.

Jesus addressed this by saying to His Disciples, and to all others as well, *"You know that the princes of the Gentiles exercise dominion over them, and they who are great exercise authority upon them* (worldly greatness, which is the opposite of spiritual greatness).

"But it shall not be so among you (the Believer is not to aspire to worldly greatness); *but whosoever will be great among you, let him be your minister* (servant)" (Mat. 20:25-26).

All, both Preachers and laity alike, should seek the Lord earnestly and constantly for guidance and direction. God has promised to give such (Jn. 14:26). As well, everything that one receives from the Lord or thinks is from the Lord should be checked against the Word. We are commanded by the Holy Spirit to *"try the spirits"* (I Jn. 4:1).

HUMANISTIC PSYCHOLOGY

As well, the modern Church has opted almost entirely to trust man instead of God. I speak of the fields of Psychology and Psychotherapy which stem entirely from humanism and evolution. It is impossible to meld such with the Word of God. The Lord takes the same dim view of this as He did of Asa's heathenistic physicians.

In these Passages we are plainly told to look to God and not to man. The Holy Spirit plainly says concerning man and from this direction, *"there is no help."*

The Fourth Verse portrays man's pitiful frailty and his ability, which is very short-lived. The next Verse gives us direction.

(5) "HAPPY IS HE WHO HAS THE GOD OF JACOB FOR HIS HELP, WHOSE HOPE IS IN THE LORD HIS GOD."

This Psalm opens and closes with the voice of a great multitude as the voice of many waters and as the voice of mighty thunderings shouting *"Hallelujah!"* Between these Hallelujahs the singer contrasts man and the Messiah, showing the inability of the one and the sufficiency of the Other as the Saviour. Thus, Man: faithless, powerless, and mortal; Messiah: faithful, all-powerful, eternal.

The Old Testament title, *"God of Jacob,"* corresponds to the New Testament title, *"God of all Grace."* He met Jacob when he deserved nothing and promised him everything. The Millennial Reign of Christ will prove the faithfulness of the Promise.

(6) "WHICH MADE HEAVEN, AND EARTH, THE SEA, AND ALL THAT THEREIN IS: WHICH KEEPS TRUTH FOR EVER."

Verses 6 through 10 contrast what God can do versus what man can do (Vss. 3-4). God is portrayed here as the Maker of Heaven and Earth.

(7) "WHICH EXECUTES JUDGMENT FOR THE OPPRESSED: WHICH GIVES FOOD TO THE HUNGRY. THE LORD LOOSES THE PRISONERS."

We are shown here how God uses His mighty Power. He uses it to bless, help, and strengthen poor, fallen man. Man's ways are the opposite. If he has any power, he generally uses it to enrich himself.

(8) "THE LORD OPENS THE EYES OF THE BLIND: THE LORD RAISES THEM WHO ARE BOWED DOWN: THE LORD LOVES THE RIGHTEOUS."

Since this Passage is very similar to Verse Fourteen of the previous Psalm, and inasmuch as David wrote that Psalm, quite possibly he wrote this one as well.

THE BLESSINGS OF THE LORD

Down through the ages, God has blessed,

helped, and given Redemption to those who would come to Him. Regrettably, most do not, but rather trust in man; consequently, the sorrow and pain of this Planet have been acute. This, which was portrayed in this Psalm and the previous Psalm, will be brought to full flower during the Millennial Reign.

(9) "THE LORD PRESERVES THE STRANGERS; HE RELIEVES THE FATHERLESS AND WIDOW: BUT THE WAY OF THE WICKED HE TURNS UPSIDE DOWN."

All that is portrayed in these Passages could have been the way of Earth for all these Millennia, but, instead, man in his rebellion has made it mostly a Hell instead of a Heaven. The *"way of the wicked"* is just about over, and then *"the Way of the Lord"* will be the covering of the entire world.

(10) "THE LORD SHALL REIGN FOR EVER, EVEN YOUR GOD, O ZION, UNTO ALL GENERATIONS, PRAISE YE THE LORD."

This Kingdom that is soon to come will not be as the government of man which comes and goes but will, in effect, last forever.

In this Passage the Holy Spirit informs Israel that the God Who revealed Himself to Abraham and to so many others will keep every Promise that He has ever made. He seals it with the exclamation, *"O Zion."* As the Psalm began, it closes — with a Hallelujah. Every Saint of God must look forward to this coming day.

PSALM 147

Author Unknown:
Great is Our God

(1) "PRAISE YE THE LORD: FOR IT IS GOOD TO SING PRAISES UNTO OUR GOD; FOR IT IS PLEASANT; AND PRAISE IS COMELY."

Who wrote this Psalm is not known.

PRAISE

As Psalm 146 was a symbol of the Book of Genesis, likewise, this Psalm is symbolic of the Book of Exodus, portraying Israel's great Deliverance which will point to her even greater deliverance from the Antichrist in the not-too-distant future.

NOTES

In effect, this is a Millennial Song and, therefore, points to that coming glad day or else portrays the actual occupation of that glorious moment which will enrapture the entirety of the Earth; hence, praise is its doctrine, as are all the last five Psalms, as well as many others.

Praise, in that glad day, will not be forced or retiring because the spiritual level of the entirety of the Planet is at a high that it has never previously known. And with prosperity abounding on every hand, along with a solution to sickness and all diseases (Ezek. 47:12), there will be fomented a constant cacophony of praise from the entirety of Planet Earth. Then all of mankind will say concerning praise to God, *"It is 'good' and 'pleasant,' and 'comely.'"*

(2) "THE LORD DOES BUILD UP JERUSALEM: HE GATHERS TOGETHER THE OUTCASTS OF ISRAEL."

Two things will happen at the outset of this glad day of the Millennial Reign as it pertains to this Scripture:

JERUSALEM

First of all, Jerusalem will become the capital city of the Earth. No longer will Washington, Tokyo, London, or any other city have the preeminence. The entirety of the world will look toward Jerusalem because the Prince of Peace reigns there.

It will be a city unlike any other city on the face of the Earth because Christ will be its dominant Personality. The Millennial Temple itself, as described by Ezekiel with the Water of Life flowing out from under its threshold, symbolic of the Holy Spirit, and with Christ at its Head, thereby, containing the solution for every problem on the face of the Earth, will be a wonder to behold.

ISRAEL

Second, Israel for nearly two thousand years has lived as *"outcasts"* all over the world. Only since 1948 can they call the Promised Land their home. Even now, the West Bank, the Gaza Strip, and in certain parts of Jerusalem there are constant problems with the Arab world; nevertheless, in that glad hour the Messiah will gather the majority, if not all, of the Jews from all over the world. At that time they will except Him as their Messiah. Of course, this is at the beginning of the coming Kingdom Age. The Promises that God made to the Patriarchs of old will now be fulfilled (Gen. 12:1-3). Israel will become at that time, the premier people on the face of the Earth, and all because of the Messiah — the very one they rejected and Crucified (Isa. 66:18-21).

(3) "HE HEALS THE BROKEN IN HEART, AND BINDS UP THEIR WOUNDS."

For all of this to brought about, a great healing will have to take place. He (the Messiah) will be the One Who will carry out this miraculous Restoration.

When Jesus healed the man born blind (Jn., Chpt. 9), this was a type of Israel in her blindness and an Israel that will wash and finally be able to see — washed in the Blood of the Lamb. The portrayal of this great miracle in John, Chapter 9 is a portrayal of this Third Verse.

(4) "HE TELLS THE NUMBER OF THE STARS; HE CALLS THEM ALL BY THEIR NAMES."

The implication of this particular Verse is astounding to say the least, in fact, light years beyond our comprehension.

THE OMNISCIENCE OF GOD

In the 1950's Astronomers claimed that there are over forty sextillion stars which are suns to other planets. That's a forty with twenty-one zeros behind it. With modern telescopes such as the Hubbell, that number, no doubt, has swelled considerably. And yet, it is declared here in this verse that God knows the exact number which He has created, ever how many that is (Isa. 45:18).

As well, we are here told that He has named each and every one of these stars, which means that there are forty to eighty sextillion names of these stars that are given, which again, defies all description.

First of all, to think that God created all of these stars, and at the same time, names them, which within itself speaks of the number of such names as eclipsing, in fact billions of times over, all the words in every language on this Planet.

(5) "GREAT IS OUR LORD, AND OF GREAT POWER: HIS UNDERSTANDING IS INFINITE."

The proper understanding of Verses Four and Five proclaim to us a greatness of God that is beyond human comprehension. No wonder, the Holy Spirit says, *"Great is our LORD!"*

How the world has suffered to have traded such power, such wisdom, and such knowledge for man's pitiful excuses for fabricated deity, whether made by his hands or conjured up in his mind. The suffering that such error has brought about is incalculable.

(6) "THE LORD LIFTS UP THE MEEK: HE CASTS THE WICKED DOWN TO THE GROUND."

The strict interpretation of this Passage portrays Israel as *"the meek."* The Antichrist is portrayed as *"the wicked."*

RELIGIOUS PRIDE

In this Passage, and in the broader sense, we find the reason for man's rebellion and, therefore, the pain, sickness, suffering, and sorrow that has plagued the Planet. Man is lifted up in his own pride, placing himself above God. Humanistic psychology and evolution are but two of man's sick ways. Of this pride, religious pride is the worst of all. It is the cause of all spiritual blindness in the world.

The far greater majority of that which calls itself *"Christian"* is, instead, a victim of spiritual pride. Great stock is placed in their good works, denominationalism, and their religion. Jesus Christ is tacked on to that which religious man worships. God will have no part of it. Paul said if we do such, *"We are fallen from Grace"* (Gal. 5:4).

The only personal thing that Jesus ever said about Himself was, *"For I am meek and lowly in heart"* (Mat. 11:29). We have here His Promise that He will *"lift up the meek."* We also have His Promise that He will *"cast the wicked (the proud) down to the ground."*

The greatest characteristic of the Christlike life is *"meekness."* Without such there cannot be love or any other great attribute of Christ.

THE CROSS OF CHRIST AND MEEKNESS

In fact, it is impossible for the Christian to know true humility and meekness unless that Christian understands the Cross of Christ as it refers to *"spiritual growth"* and *"the bearing of proper fruit,"* i.e., *"Sanctification."*

The Righteousness of God is found only in Christ and the Cross. Such Righteousness is obtained solely by the Believer evidencing Faith in Christ and the Cross, and in nothing else. If faith is registered, in fact, in something else, self-righteousness will be the result, which is the bane of the modern Church. It is the opposite of *"humility and meekness."*

That is the reason that Paul said, *"But God forbid that I should glory* (boast), *save in the Cross of our Lord Jesus Christ* (what the opponents of Paul sought to escape at the price of insincerity is the Apostle's only basis of exultation), *by Whom the world is crucified unto me, and I unto the world* (the only way we can overcome the world, and I mean the only way, is by placing our Faith exclusively in the Cross of Christ and keeping it there, which then gives the Holy Spirit latitude to work mightily within our lives)" (Gal. 6:14).

(7) SING UNTO THE LORD WITH THANKSGIVING; SING PRAISE UPON THE HARP UNTO OUR GOD."

Some six times, we are given such commands in the Psalms as it regards worshipping the Lord, accompanied by musical instrumentation (Ps. 33:2; 57:8; 98:5; 147:7; 149:3; 150:3).

The Millennial Reign in which this Song will be sung, will be a time of music. Satan has been very successful in perverting music, even Christian music. At that glad day, Satan will be no more. Then, music will fill the hearts and lives of the billions of Planet Earth. All will be in thanksgiving and praise unto our God.

(8) "WHO COVERS THE HEAVEN WITH CLOUDS, WHO PREPARES RAIN FOR THE EARTH, WHO MAKES GRASS TO GROW UPON THE MOUNTAINS."

This world and its climate does not function as God originally created it to do so. Due to the Fall, which effected the entirety of God's Creation, much of the world does not receive suitable rain, then some parts receive too much.

As well, much of the world is desert, which is little good to anyone. Once again, all of this was brought about by the Fall.

In the coming Kingdom Age, when Jesus will rule and reign from Jerusalem, the climates of the Planet will function as God originally ordered them to do so. At that time, every part of Earth will receive its due allotment of rain. This will cause even the deserts to blossom as a rose, in which the world will be able to bring forth harvests which are unimaginable at the present. In other words, there will be no more hunger or want!

(9) "HE GIVES TO THE BEAST HIS FOOD, AND TO THE YOUNG RAVENS WHICH CRY."

The animal kingdom is portrayed here as not only created by God but, as well, superintended by God. The terrible problems that presently beset the human family, which also have dealt havoc with the ecology of the Planet, have been caused by man's rebellion against God. Tragically, this problem will not be solved despite the efforts of the *"earth-firsters"* until Christ returns. Everything hinges on the return of Christ!

(10) "HE DELIGHTS NOT IN THE STRENGTH OF THE HORSE: HE TAKES NOT PLEASURE IN THE LEGS OF A MAN."

The sense of this Passage is that those things in which man trusts, in that, God takes no delight.

TRUST IN THE LORD

In Bible days men thought that if they had enough horses they could win any battle. As well, without modern technology the strength of man (his legs) was greatly dependent on in times of warfare. In modern times nations depend on modern technology. The difference is the same.

The warning is given: Those who place their trust in such will ultimately lose their way. Those who place their trust in God will know His Protection, Blessing, and Prosperity.

(11) "THE LORD TAKES PLEASURE IN THEM WHO FEAR HIM, IN THOSE WHO HOPE IN HIS MERCY."

So, if we want to know what pleases God, we find it in this Passage.

THAT WHICH PLEASES THE LORD

First of all, we are to fear Him. When we consider that He is Omnipotent (All-Powerful), Omniscient (All-Knowing), and Omnipresent (Everywhere), then we certainly should fear Him.

Second, we should hope in His Mercy. Man must approach God realizing that God owes us nothing, and that if we received our just deserts, we should be destroyed; therefore, we plead for Mercy, and God delights in our doing so and, thereby, grants an abundance of such.

(12) "PRAISE THE LORD, O JERUSALEM; PRAISE YOUR GOD, O ZION."

Israel's redemption from Egypt, the healing of the wounds inflicted there, and her formation into a nation illustrate the greater deliverance that she now experiences.

(13) "FOR HE HAS STRENGTHENED THE BARS OF YOUR GATES; HE HAS BLESSED YOUR CHILDREN WITHIN YOU."

This will be the glad time of the coming Kingdom Age.

TRUE POWER AND PROTECTION

"The bars of Your gates" refers to Israel's and Jerusalem's true power and protection. The gates are now strengthened because *"He has blessed your children within you."*

He would have done such so a long time ago if Israel had only humbled themselves before Him. That they would not do and have, thereby, suffered untold agony and pain. Now they realize from Whom their blessings come and will come before Him with meekness and praise, thereby, receiving His Blessings.

This pattern, although outlined for Israel on that coming glad day, will, as well, function exactly for any Christian.

(14) "HE MAKES PEACE IN YOUR BORDERS, AND FILLS YOU WITH THE FINEST OF THE WHEAT."

God delights in giving good things to His children. He Alone can bring *"peace"* and *"prosperity."* Israel was a long time in learning this. Modern man is a long time in learning it as well!

(15) "HE SENDS FORTH HIS COMMANDMENT UPON EARTH: HIS WORD RUNS VERY SWIFTLY."

"His Commandment" is the Bible. Within its pages is the wisdom of the ages. It alone contains the only revealed Truth in the world today and, in fact, ever had been. Tragically, it is denied by the world and, basically, ignored by the Church; consequently, there is very little *"peace and prosperity."* When His Word *"runs very swiftly,"* *"peace and prosperity"* are not far behind.

(16) "HE GIVES SNOW LIKE WOOL: HE SCATTERS THE HOARFROST LIKE ASHES."

We are told that there is nothing in nature which resembles wool more than large snowflakes. The sense of this Passage is that God controls all. When we properly understand His Power, Wisdom, and Knowledge (Vs. 4), then it is possible to understand the glory of His Creation.

(17) "HE CASTS FORTH HIS ICE LIKE MORSELS: WHO CAN STAND BEFORE HIS COLD?"

In Verses 16 and 17 we have the snow, frost, hail, and cold of the winter season; in Verse Eighteen we have the springtime pictured. The cold is driven away, the snow and ice melt, and the frost leaves the ground. All of this is superintended by God and functions according to His Word.

(18) "HE SENDS OUT HIS WORD, AND MELTS THEM: HE CAUSES HIS WIND TO BLOW, AND THE WATERS FLOW."

We are told here that everything is held up by the glorious and beauteous Word of God. By that we mean *"the Bible."* Sadly, the majority of Christians have not even read the Bible through once, much less made it a part of their daily spiritual diet. The Bible never grows old because it is the Word of God.

(19) "HE SHOWS HIS WORD UNTO JACOB, HIS STATUTES AND HIS JUDGMENTS UNTO ISRAEL."

His election of Israel as the depository of His Word and as the channel of its communication to the world moved both Moses and Paul to wonder and worship (Deut. 4:8; Rom. 3:2; 11:33).

(20) "HE HAS NOT DEALT SO WITH ANY NATION: AND AS FOR HIS JUDGMENTS, THEY HAVE NOT KNOWN THEM. PRAISE YE THE LORD."

As we have said repeatedly in these Volumes, God chose Israel for three great purposes:

1. That He might through them give the world the Word of God. Every writer of the Books of the Bible was Jewish. (Some think that Luke may have been a Gentile; however, there is no proof that he was. Inasmuch as

it plainly tells us in these Passages that God *"showed His Word unto Jacob."* Then we might conclude that Luke was a Jew as well.)

2. To be the womb of the Messiah.

3. To evangelize the world.

In the first two Israel succeeded; in the last one they failed, but they will accomplish their mission of Evangelism in the coming Kingdom Age.

The Psalm closes with *"Hallelujah,"* which in the Hebrew means, *"Praise You Jah."*

PSALM 148

Author Unknown:
Let All Creation Praise God

(1) "PRAISE YE THE LORD. PRAISE YE THE LORD FROM THE HEAVENS: PRAISE HIM IN THE HEIGHTS."

This is the third of the five Hallelujah Psalms. It corresponds to the Leviticus Book of the Pentateuch and as such ordains Worship as the subject of that Book.

The place of this worship is vast. It reaches from the depths beneath the Earth (Vs. 7) to the heights above the heavens (Vs. 1).

(2) "PRAISE YE HIM, ALL HIS ANGELS: PRAISE YE HIM, ALL HIS HOSTS."

In the coming Kingdom Age and for the first time, the entirety of God's vast creation will praise Him and continue to praise Him.

At this time, His Angels are praising Him, as well as *"all His Hosts,"* however, man, at least for the most part, rarely praises God. In the coming Millennial Reign that will change. Man will then praise Him as both His animate and inanimate creation praise Him.

(3) "PRAISE YE HIM, SUN AND MOON: PRAISE HIM, ALL YE STARS OF LIGHT.

(4) "PRAISE HIM, YOU HEAVENS OF HEAVENS, AND YOU WATERS THAT BE ABOVE THE HEAVENS."

All of these things praise Him by functioning in the orderly manner in which they were created. All are upheld and function strictly according to His Word. Moses relayed it, *"And God said, Let there be light: and there was light"* (Gen. 1:3). Some nine times in Genesis 1 alone it says, *"And God said."* His Word brought into being that which He commanded, and it upholds it now and forever.

(5) "LET THEM PRAISE THE NAME OF THE LORD: FOR HE COMMANDED, AND THEY WERE CREATED.

(6) "HE HAS ALSO STABLISHED THEM FOREVER AND EVER: HE HAS MADE A DECREE WHICH SHALL NOT PASS."

Verse Five proclaims what we have stated about Genesis 1. Verse Six proclaims that all the creation is upheld (stablished) and continues functioning according to God's Word.

EVOLUTION?

Modern man little recognizes that which we are given here in the Scriptures. Instead, school children are taught the mindless drivel of evolution as the origin of all things. Men do not praise Him today because God is given little credit, if any at all.

In the coming Kingdom Age and on that happy day, the entirety of the world will know and understand Who God is, and what He has done, and His Greatness. There will be no evolution taught in the public school systems or anywhere else. All philosophy such as psychology, psychotherapy, science (falsely so-called), along with the whole of Satan's lies, will be no more. Then the whole Planet will praise God for Who He is, and for what He has done!

(7) "PRAISE THE LORD FROM THE EARTH, YOU DRAGONS, AND ALL DEEPS:

(8) "FIRE, AND HAIL; SNOW, AND VAPOURS; STORMY WIND FULFILLING HIS WORD:

(9) "MOUNTAINS, AND ALL HILLS; FRUITFUL TREES, AND ALL CEDARS:

(10) "BEASTS, AND ALL CATTLE; CREEPING THINGS, AND FLYING FOWL."

The laws which govern the countless worlds revolving in space and which confine them to their orbits are pointed to in Verse Six.

The *"dragons,"* which actually refer to *"sea monsters,"* also refer to all kinds of fish and fish-like creatures which live in the oceans.

Verses 2 through 6 proclaim the heavens and their inhabitants praising the Messiah. And then in Verses 7 through 13, the Earth and its inhabitants praise Him.

(11) "KINGS OF THE EARTH, AND ALL

PEOPLE; PRINCES, AND ALL JUDGES OF THE EARTH:

(12) "BOTH YOUNG MEN, AND MAIDENS; OLD MEN, AND CHILDREN."

Verse Eleven speaks of the most powerful of men praising Him.

Verse Twelve speaks of all the population, even the children, praising Him. Praise at that time will be constant, unending, vocal, unashamed, and involving itself in the whole of God's Creation of both man and beast, as well as the inanimate.

Presently it is strange to the unconverted to hear people praise the Lord. Then, and we speak of the coming Kingdom Age, not only will praise be common, but the lack of such will be as strange then, as the opposite now.

(13) "LET THEM PRAISE THE NAME OF THE LORD: FOR HIS NAME ALONE IS EXCELLENT; HIS GLORY IS ABOVE THE EARTH AND HEAVEN.

(14) "HE ALSO EXALTS THE HORN OF HIS PEOPLE, THE PRAISE OF ALL HIS SAINTS; EVEN OF THE CHILDREN OF ISRAEL, A PEOPLE NEAR UNTO HIM. PRAISE YE THE LORD."

Verse Fourteen speaks of Israel being restored and called *"a people near unto Him."*

THE ETERNAL CREATOR

Verse Fourteen reveals that this Mighty God, Who both the heavens and the Earth are eternally to adore, is the Messiah, the God if Israel. The heavens are to adore Him because He created them, and He maintains them. The Earth and all that is therein adores Him, for His Name Alone is excellent. This Song of Millennial worship opens and closes with a Hallelujah as the noise of many waters.

The phrase, *"The Earth and Heaven,"* is noteworthy. This order is only found here and in Genesis 2:4. It is connected with the Divine title, Jehovah Elohim (The Eternal Creator). This title, as it occurs in Genesis 2:4 and Verse Thirteen (the Lord), expresses God's relationship to man as a Redeeming Saviour. The Earth is, therefore, made to precede the heavens, because Earth is where the Lord Jesus Christ paid the price on Calvary's Cross in order for man to be redeemed, and everything to be brought back as it originally was before the Fall. It is ever the Cross!

NOTES

The Psalm ends with the Hebrew *"HALLELU–JAH,"* which means, *"Praise You JAH."*

This Song pictures the happiest state of man and all living creatures under the Messiah's Coming Reign.

PSALM 149

Author Unknown:
Let All the Saints Praise God

(1) "PRAISE YE THE LORD, SING UNTO THE LORD A NEW SONG, AND HIS PRAISE IN THE CONGREGATION OF THE SAINTS."

Who wrote this Psalm is not known. It is the fourth Hallelujah Psalm and corresponds to the Book of Numbers. At the close of that Book, Israel stood at the entrance of Canaan, her brows wreathed with victory over the Moabites and the Amorites. In this Psalm she stands at the entrance of the Millennial Kingdom, crowned with victory over the Antichrist and the False Prophet.

The *"new song"* cannot be entered into without a *"new creation."* The Child of God today can sing this *"new song"* because he has entered into the *"new creation"* (II Cor. 5:17).

(2) "LET ISRAEL REJOICE IN HIM WHO MADE HIM: LET THE CHILDREN OF ZION BE JOYFUL IN THEIR KING."

The whole of this Passage is a prophetical prayer for God's people and applies to their Restoration and reign with the Messiah.

First, we have four requests concerning the Saints (Israel) and their duties unto the Messiah (Vss. 2-4). Then we have four requests concerning heavenly Saints (the Church) and their duties unto the Messiah (Vss. 5-9). Regrettably, Israel has been at war with God almost from her inception (Gen. 12:1-3). Now and at long last, they will be in harmony with their Lord and Messiah.

(3) "LET THEM PRAISE HIS NAME IN THE DANCE: LET THEM SING PRAISES UNTO HIM WITH THE TIMBREL AND HARP."

Israel's worship was always demonstrative. This relates back to the time the Ark was brought into Jerusalem (II Sam., Chpt. 6).

As the Ark was then a symbol of Christ and instigated worship, now Israel will worship even more grandly upon the enthronement of her King. That King is Jesus.

(4) "FOR THE LORD TAKES PLEASURE IN HIS PEOPLE: HE WILL BEAUTIFY THE MEEK WITH SALVATION."

There has not been many times in Israel's history when it could be said that the Lord took pleasure in *"His people;"* however, in this future happy day and at long last, Israel will have come home. The pride and haughtiness are gone. Now they are *"meek;"* consequently, the Lord of Glory will beautify them with His great and glorious Salvation.

The last phrase of Verse Four could be translated, *"He will adorn the meek with victory."*

(5) "LET THE SAINTS BE JOYFUL IN GLORY: LET THEM SING ALOUD UPON THEIR BEDS."

The word *"beds"* or couches of glory here means *"thrones."*

Even though these Verses (5-9), no doubt, pertain to the glorified Saints of God and to the Church, still, its statements apply to Israel as well.

In one sense, this section (5-9) foretells the efficiency, the piety, and the equity of the government which Israel will exercise over the nations of the Earth.

(6) "LET THE HIGH PRAISES OF GOD BE IN THEIR MOUTH, AND A TWO-EDGED SWORD IN THEIR HAND."

This Government will be efficient because of the two-edged sword; it will be pious, for the high praises of God will be in their mouths; it will be just, for it will exact vengeance; it will be impartial, for it will bind kings; it will be legal, for it will execute the judgment written in the Statute Books of Heaven.

(7) "TO EXECUTE VENGEANCE UPON THE HEATHEN, AND PUNISHMENTS UPON THE PEOPLE;

(8) "TO BIND THEIR KINGS WITH CHAINS, AND THEIR NOBLES WITH FETTERS OF IRON;

(9) "TO EXECUTE UPON THEM THE JUDGMENT WRITTEN: THIS HONOR HAVE ALL HIS SAINTS. PRAISE YE THE LORD."

These features of honesty and integrity are not prominent in man's government. History records the feebleness of man's government; that the mouths of the magistrates are more usually filled with cursing than with praising; that their administration is unjust rather than just; that they show partiality to the rich and great; that they inscribe unrighteous laws upon their statute books.

THE GOVERNMENT OF THE LORD

The sword of this Verse is two-edged. It can reach and punish with equal effect if an escape is attempted on the right hand or on the left. It has an edge as well, for the evildoer and the unfaithful wielder. So, Israel proved this in Joshua's day, for one edge judged the debauched Canaanite and the other edge the disobedient Israelite.

The glorified Saints, who comprise all who are part of the First Resurrection, which will include every single Believer both Jew and Gentile who has ever lived, will not be troubled by the *"unfaithful wielder,"* for such cannot be. Even though the Church is not mentioned in these Passages except only in shadow, still, the glorified Saints of God will help the Messiah rule the Planet (Rev. 20:6).

Incidentally, the Saints of the First Resurrection will include every single person who has ever evidenced faith in Christ, i.e., *"born-again."* There is no such thing as some being there and some not being there. All will be there!

In the glorious day of the Millennial Reign, the Apostles will sit on twelve Thrones judging the twelve Tribes of Israel. As is evident, Israel will sit on thrones judging the nations of the Earth, along with the glorified Saints.

In the Millennium, the nations of the Earth will be allocated by God in correspondence with and in relation to the boundaries of the sons of Jacob (Deut. 32:8).

That the Church will reign with Christ is plainly taught in Scripture as well (II Tim. 2:12; Rev. 5:10).

PSALM 150

Author Unknown:
Final Doxology

(1) "PRAISE YE THE LORD. PRAISE

GOD IN HIS SANCTUARY: PRAISE HIM IN THE FIRMAMENT OF HIS POWER."

This is the Fifth and, therefore, the last Hallelujah Psalm. As well, it should be described as the Deuteronomy Psalm of the Deuteronomy Book.

THE ALMIGHTY

In this glad day of the coming Kingdom Age with Christ reigning supreme in Jerusalem, praise will be offered unto God continually all over the world. As we have stated previously, since the Fall of man, about all that has ascended up from this Planet has been blasphemy, profanity, and filth. God has had little praise; however, in this glad time, the former things of evil are gone, and praise ascends up from the gladdened hearts of Earth's population — praise for God.

The Divine titles used are *"El"* and *"Jah." "El"* is essentially the *"Almighty,"* and *"Jah"* signifies the *"Ever-existing One,"* for example, Jesus Christ, the same yesterday, today, and forever.

This place of worship will have two platforms — the Sanctuary and the Firmament. The Sanctuary is earthly; the Firmament is heavenly.

Moses and David were commanded to construct the earthly Sanctuary according to the heavenly pattern shown to them. Nothing was left to their taste, style, or imagination. Here, both (the earthly and the heavenly) are united and form one place of worship. Then Heaven and Earth will finally be reconciled, with the prophecy of Jacob's Ladder being fulfilled (Gen. 28:12; Jn. 1:51).

(2) "PRAISE HIM FOR HIS MIGHTY ACTS: PRAISE HIM ACCORDING TO HIS EXCELLENT GREATNESS."

The theme of Praise will be twofold: first, what He does — His mighty acts; second, what He is — His excellent greatness. These express His Glory as Creator, as Redeemer, as the Lamb of God, and as the Son of God. The scene of worship in the Book of Revelation is Heaven; in this Psalm it is the Earth in unison with Heaven.

(3) "PRAISE HIM WITH THE SOUND OF THE TRUMPET: PRAISE HIM WITH THE PSALTERY AND HARP.

(4) "PRAISE HIM WITH THE TIMBREL AND DANCE: PRAISE HIM WITH STRINGED INSTRUMENTS AND ORGANS.

(5) "PRAISE HIM UPON THE LOUD CYMBALS: PRAISE HIM UPON THE HIGH SOUNDING CYMBALS."

These praises portray to us the fact that the worship is not only spontaneous, but orchestrated.

PRAISE

That which the world has previously thought foolish now is routine, glorious, visible, and constant. By and large, the musicians of the world have formerly dedicated their talents to the evil one. Now these talents will be dedicated to God's Glory.

What will it sound like with every city, town, village, and community ringing with the dedicated music of *"Amazing Grace"* or *"The Old Rugged Cross"* or *"Blessed Assurance?"* Be it far from the thought that this worship will be forced. Never! It will be desirous, beauteous, enraptured, joyful, happy, devoted, and rhythmic. That the Holy Spirit would devote this much space in the final Psalm denotes to us the type of worship and the enraptured joy that will cultivate the Earth on that coming glad day.

(6) "LET EVERY THING THAT HAS BREATH PRAISE THE LORD. PRAISE YE THE LORD."

In this coming day when Christ appears, everything that has breath will praise Him.

THE GLORY OF THE SON OF GOD

The appearance of our Lord will vindicate Him. At that time, it will be recognized that His Government of the world and His Plan for the ages was and is the highest wisdom and the most Perfect Love. Men will have nothing but praise for Him. The Book of Psalms assures this. Its pages are wet with tears, and its music broken with sighs, but its last song is a burst of satisfied rapture. Its five Volumes fitly close with a loud *"Hallelujah!"*

The world's system objects to praises to God. Sadly, even the majority of the Church follows suit, for there is very little praise, if any, heard in most Churches. The objections are many, hypocrisy being claimed on the part of some; however, this last Passage, which is the last breath of the Holy Spirit concerning the most glorious prophetic literature ever devised by the Heart of God, brushes such objections aside by claiming that if it has breath, it should praise the Lord. In this present day, there are objections. In that glorious future time, there will be only praise.

THE BLESSED MAN AND THE BLESSED GOD

The very First Psalm calls the Messiah *"The Blessed Man."* In the last Psalm He is worshipped as *"The Blessed God."* All of the one hundred and forty-eight intervening Psalms sing of the countless perfections of His Nature and of His Actions, as both Son of Man and Son of God.

All the Psalms should be a reminder to the Church that the Holy Spirit is presently preparing the Body of Christ for the glorious time when there will be nothing but praise. If praise is now an embarrassment, it is a good sign that we are not acquainted with the One to Whom the praise is directed.

So let us close this wonderful Book called *"Psalms,"* this conglomerate of Songs written by the Holy Spirit, with a resounding *"Hallelujah!"*

BIBLIOGRAPHY

[1] Williams, George, *The Student's Commentary on the Holy Scriptures* (Kregel, 1971), pg. 298.
[2] Spence, H.D.M. and Joseph Exell, *The Pulpit Commentary: Vol. 8* (Eerdmans, 1977), Vol. 1, pg. 2.
[3] Ibid., pg. 18.
[4] Ibid., pg. 43.
[5] Ibid., pg. 57.
[6] Ibid., pg. 173.
[7] Ibid., pg. 237.
[8] Ibid., pg. 246.
[9] Ibid., pg. 256.
[10] Ibid.
[11] Ibid., pg. 275.
[12] Ibid., pg. 287.
[13] George Williams, *The Student's Commentary on the Holy Scriptures*, pg. 331.
[14] H.D.M. Spence, *The Pulpit Commentary: Vol. 8*, Vol. 1, pg. 385.
[15] George Williams, *The Student's Commentary on the Holy Scriptures*, pg. 357.
[16] Ibid.
[17] Ibid.
[18] Ibid., pg. 360.
[19] Ibid.
[20] Ibid.
[21] H.D.M. Spence, *The Pulpit Commentary: Vol. 8.*, Vol. 2, pg. 125.
[22] Ibid., pg. 126.
[23] Ibid., pg. 127.
[24] Ibid., pg. 128.
[25] George Williams, *The Student's Commentary on the Holy Scriptures*, pg. 361.
[26] Ibid., pg. 362.
[27] H.D.M. Spence, *The Pulpit Commentary: Vol. 8*, Vol. 2, pg. 157.
[28] George Williams, *The Student's Commentary on the Holy Scriptures*, pg. 363.
[29] Ibid., pgs. 363-364.
[30] Ibid., pg. 364.
[31] Ibid., pg. 365.
[32] Ibid., pg. 366.
[33] Ibid.
[34] Ibid., pgs. 368-369.
[35] H.D.M. Spence, *The Pulpit Commentary: Vol. 8*, Vol. 2, pg. 241.
[36] George Williams, *The Student's Commentary on the Holy Scriptures*, pg. 369.
[37] Ibid., 370.
[38] Ibid.
[39] Ibid.
[40] Ibid.
[41] Ibid., 371.
[42] Ibid.
[43] Ibid., 372.
[44] H.D.M. Spence, *The Pulpit Commentary: Vol. 8*, Vol. 2, pg. 300.
[45] George Williams, *The Student's Commentary on the Holy Scriptures*, pg. 374.
[46] Ibid., 376.
[47] Ibid.
[48] Ibid., 377.
[49] Ibid., 378.
[50] Ibid., 379.
[51] Ibid., 378-379.

[52] H.D.M. Spence, *The Pulpit Commentary: Vol. 8*, Vol. 2., pg. 414.
[53] George Williams, *The Student's Commentary on the Holy Scriptures*, pg. 380.
[54] Ibid., pg. 380.
[55] H.D.M. Spence, *The Pulpit Commentary: Vol. 8.*, Vol. 2., pg. 426.
[56] George Williams, *The Student's Commentary on the Holy Scriptures*, pg. 382.
[57] Ibid.
[58] Ibid., 383.
[59] Ibid., 386.
[60] Ibid.
[61] Ibid., pg. 387.
[62] Ibid.
[63] Ibid., pg. 391.
[64] Ibid., pg. 392.
[65] Ibid.
[66] Ibid.
[67] Ibid., pg. 396.
[68] Ibid., pg. 391.
[69] Ibid., pg. 402.
[70] Ibid., pg. 405.
[71] Ibid., pg. 408.
[72] H.D.M. Spence, *The Pulpit Commentary: Vol. 8*, Vol. 3., pg. 362.

REFERENCE BOOKS

Atlas Of The Bible
Expository Dictionary Of New Testament Words
Interlinear Greek-English New Testament
New Bible Dictionary
Strong's Exhaustive Concordance Of The Bible
The Complete Word Study Dictionary Of The New Testament
The International Standard Bible Encyclopedia
The Zondervan Pictorial Encyclopedia Of The Bible
Vine's Expository Dictionary Of New Testament Words
Webster's New Collegiate Dictionary
Young's Literal Translation Of The Holy Book

NOTES

INDEX

The index is listed according to subjects. The treatment may include a complete dissertation or no more than a paragraph. But hopefully it will provide some help.

As well, even though extended treatment of a subject may not be carried in this Commentary, one of the other Commentaries may well include the desired material.

ABANDONMENT OF CHRIST 636
ABIDES FOREVER 589
ABORTION 335, 627
ABORTION AND EVOLUTION 625
ABRAHAMIC COVENANT 317
ABSALOM SPIRIT 14
ACCEPTED BY GOD 552
ACCOUNTABILITY 649
ACTION OF OUR LORD 189
ADULTERERS 238
AFFLICTIONS 555, 563, 600
AGE-OLD CONFLICT 506
AHITHOPHEL AND JUDAS 200, 508
ALL BLESSINGS COME FROM CHRIST 504
ALL DELIVERANCE IS FOUND IN THE CROSS OF CHRIST 209
ALL PRAISE AND WORSHIP MUST HAVE AS THEIR FOUNDATION THE CROSS OF CHRIST 38
ALL THE KINDREDS OF THE NATIONS 106
ALL-SEEING EYE OF GOD 48
ALL-SUFFICIENT HIGH PRIEST 129
ALMIGHTY 658
ALMIGHTY GOD 135
ALTAR 127
ALTAR OF GOD 206
ALTARS 387
AMERICA AND ISRAEL 198
AMERICA'S GREATEST DANGER! 322
ANCIENT HEBREWS 82
ANGER AND WRATH OF GOD 417
ANGER OF GOD 33, 279, 347, 369
ANIMAL SACRIFICES 258
ANOINTED WITH FRESH OIL 430
ANOINTING 112

ANOTHER JESUS 39, 127
ANSWERED PRAYER 166, 337
ANTICHRIST 263, 432, 445, 477
ANTICHRIST AND ISRAEL 199
ANTICHRIST AND THE TEMPLE 385
ANTICHRIST AND THE WORD OF GOD 47
APOSTATE CHURCH 326
APOSTLE PAUL 534
APPEARANCES OF CHRIST AFTER THE RESURRECTION 637
ARABS 595
ARE THERE DIFFERENT STANDARDS FOR DIFFERENT PEOPLE? 252
ARK OF THE COVENANT 600
ARMAGEDDON 45, 316
AUTHORITY AND SUFFICIENCY OF THE BIBLE AS THE RULE OF LIFE 532
AUTHORSHIP OF THE PSALMS vii (Introduction)
AVENGER OF BLOOD 43
BAAL 491
BANNERS 91
BATTLE OF ARMAGEDDON 444
BEING IN THE WILL OF GOD 274
BELIEVER AND THE CROSS 609
BELIEVERS 129, 595
BIBLE 153, 562
BIBLE AND ITS AUTHOR 546
BIBLE, THE ONLY REVEALED TRUTH 538
BIBLE WORSHIP 565
BLANK CHECK 381
BLASPHEMING THE HOLY SPIRIT 328
BLASPHEMY OF THE ANTICHRIST 434
BLESS THE LORD 612
BLESSED FOREVER 94
BLESSED IS THE MAN 148

BLESSED NATION 153
BLESSED SONG 532
BLESSING 178
BLESSING FROM THE LORD 265
BLESSING OF CONFESSED SIN 147
BLESSING THE LORD 156
BLESSINGS 17, 25, 121, 340
BLESSINGS OF GOD 305
BLESSINGS OF GOODNESS 93
BLESSINGS OF THE LORD 650
BLOOD OF CHRIST, THE PRICE OF REDEMPTION 230
BOASTING 210
BOASTING IN THE LORD 157
BOASTING OF SATAN 259
BOUND IN AFFLICTION AND IRON 498
BRIDE 217
BROKEN HEART 53
BROKEN VESSEL 145
BUILDUP OF ZION 461
BURNT OFFERINGS 308
CAIN AND ABEL 275
CALL OF GOD IS WITHOUT REPENTANCE 336
CALLING UPON THE LORD 73
CALVARY 592, 623, 641
CALVARY ACCOMPLISHED 230
CALVARY, WHERE SATAN WAS DEFEATED 12
CAPTIVES OF SATAN 618
CAPTIVITY 617
CAPTIVITY MADE CAPTIVE 318
CAST YOUR BURDEN UPON THE LORD 273
CATHOLIC CHURCH 605
CATHOLIC PRIESTS 185
CENTRAL SONG OF DEGREES 591
CERTITUDE OF BLESSING 607
CHASTISEMENT 110, 211, 412
CHIEF SHEPHERD 114
CHILDREN AND THE WORD OF GOD 360
CHRIST AND HIM CRUCIFIED 236
CHRIST AND JERUSALEM 398
CHRIST AND JUDAS 508
CHRIST AND SIN 626
CHRIST AS THE MAN 558
CHRIST IS THE LIGHT IN THE DARKNESS 517
CHRIST, OUR EXAMPLE 558
CHRIST OUR SUBSTITUTE 597
CHRIST, THE LAMB OF GOD 162
CHRIST, THE TRESPASS OFFERING 321
CHRIST, THE TRUE MAN 36
CHRISTIAN PSYCHOLOGY? 545
CHRIST'S PERFECT OBEDIENCE TO THE WILL OF GOD AS THE SIN-BEARER 193
CHURCH 81, 439, 464, 628

CLASS STRUGGLE 450
CLEAN HEART 254
CLOSE OF THE CHURCH AGE 351
CLOUDS OF DARKNESS 443
COMING BATTLE OF ARMAGEDDON 214
COMING JUDGMENT 625
COMING KINGDOM AGE 305, 592, 621
COMMAND OF THE LORD 361
COMMANDMENTS OF THE LORD 568
COMPLAINING 345
COMPLETE VICTORY 80
COMPOSITION OF MUSIC 151
COMPROMISE 605
CONDITIONS FOR MERCY 496
CONFLICT 477
CONFLICT OVER THE LAND OF ISRAEL 476
CONSTANT PRAISE 156
CONTEMPORARY CHRISTIAN MUSIC 449
CONTEST BETWEEN GOD AND SATAN 471
CONTINUOUS PRAISE AND WORSHIP 607
CONVERTING THE SOUL 86
CORE OF THE DETERIORATION OF THE UNITED STATES 179
CORRECT ATTITUDE TOWARD THE LORD 298
CORRUPTION OF THE WORD OF GOD 426
COUNSELOR 542
COUNSELS OF GOD 381
COURTS OF THE HOUSE OF THE LORD 608
COVENANT 350, 413, 476
COVENANTS 405
CRAFTY 384
CREATION 113, 152, 471
CREATION AND THE CREATOR 523
CREATION OF MAN 36
CREATION OF PLANET EARTH 473
CROSS 52, 114, 535
CROSS AND DELIVERANCE 236
CROSS AND ELEMENT JUDGMENTS 446
CROSS AND SANCTIFICATION 22, 417
CROSS AND THE ALTAR OF INCENSE 580
CROSS AND UNBELIEF 364
CROSS OF CALVARY 235
CROSS OF CHRIST 2, 39, 65, 73, 90, 128, 175, 194, 249, 250, 265, 313, 322, 332, 355, 391, 399, 417, 425, 445, 466, 485, 488, 492, 522, 529, 538, 544, 583, 618, 626
CROSS OF CHRIST AND LIMITING GOD 367
CROSS OF CHRIST AND MEEKNESS 652
CROSS OF CHRIST AND PSYCHOLOGY 578
CROSS OF CHRIST IS DIVIDING LINE BETWEEN CHURCH AND APOSTATE CHURCH 237
CROSS OF CHRIST IS THE MEANS OF DELIVERANCE 467

CROSS OF CHRIST, THE DIVIDING LINE 170
CROSS OF CHRIST, THE DIVIDING LINE OF THE CHURCH 331
CROSS OF CHRIST, THE ONLY THING BETWEEN MAN AND ETERNAL HELL 401
CROSS PAID IT ALL 417
CROSS, THE SECRET OF ALL PROSPERITY 107
CROWN OF PURE GOLD 93
CRUCIFIXION 102, 511
CRY OF THE MESSIAH IS HEARD 74
CRY OF THE SOUL 205, 355
CRYING TO THE LORD 498
CUP 352
DARK SAYING 228
DARKNESS 481
DAVID 26, 27, 76, 165, 371
DAVID AND THE MESSIAH 300
DAVID AND THE SON OF DAVID 41
DAVID, MANKIND, THE ANTICHRIST 263
DAVID, THE AUTHOR OF THE 119TH PSALM? 533
DAVID, THE LORD JESUS CHRIST, AND ISRAEL 203
DAVID THE MESSIAH 74
DAVID'S DISCIPLINE 505
DAVID'S PROCLAMATION TO THE LORD 29
DAY OF TROUBLE 89
DEATH 488, 526
DEATH OF CHRIST ON THE CROSS 182
DEATH OF THE WICKED 344
DECEPTION 46, 167, 261, 269
DEDICATION TO PRAYER AND TO THE BIBLE 572
DEEP CALLS UNTO DEEP 204
DEFEAT OF ALL ENEMIES 341
DEFINITION OF REDEMPTION 229
DEGREES OF SUFFERING 98
DEITY OF THE MESSIAH 451
DELIGHT OF THE WORD OF GOD 560
DELIVERANCE 99, 161, 286, 334, 467, 501, 573, 577
DELIVERANCE FROM OPPRESSION 569
DELIVERANCE THROUGH THE WORD OF GOD 573
DEMON OPPRESSION 157
DEMON SPIRITS 494
DENIAL OF GOD 56
DENOMINATIONALISM 632
DEPENDENCE ON GOD 415
DEPENDENCE ON THE LORD 221, 296
DESCRIPTION OF THE WICKED 68
DID GOD FORSAKE CHRIST TOTALLY WHEN JESUS WAS ON THE CROSS? 96
DID JESUS DIE SPIRITUALLY? 143
DISPENSATION OF GRACE 30
DISPENSATIONAL ASPECT OF THE PSALMS vii (Introduction)
DISPENSATIONS 42

DISTRESS 580
DIVIDING LINE IS THE CROSS 126
DIVINE HEALING 465
DIVINE IMAGE OF GOD 83
DIVINE TITLES 375, 389
DIVISION 290
DIVISION OF THE LAND 60
DOCTRINE OF SUBSTITUTION AND IDENTIFICATION 11
DOGS 103
DOING THE WILL OF GOD 61
DOUBLE THOUGHTS 565
DUST OF DEATH 102
DWELLING PLACE OF GOD 386
EAGLE 467
EARTH'S FIRST SONGBOOK vi (Introduction)
EGYPT 480, 616
EIGHT TITLES FOR JEHOVAH IN THIS SONG 108
EMBRACING THE WORD 545
EMPHASIS PLACED ON THE BIBLE BY THE HOLY SPIRIT 570
ENEMIES 28, 117, 124, 209, 313, 592
ENEMIES OF GOD 200
ENEMIES OF OUR LORD 132, 513
ENEMIES OF THE CROSS OF CHRIST 239, 418
ENEMY 497
ENIGMA OF MAN 227
ENTRANCE OF THE WORD GIVES LIGHT 568
EQUITY 451
ESAU AND JACOB 619
ETERNAL CREATOR 656
ETERNAL DESTINY OF BABIES 248
ETERNAL LIFE 106, 107
ETERNAL SECURITY 254
ETERNITY OF THE GOVERNMENT OF GOD 429
EVENING SACRIFICE 606
EVERY ENEMY DEFEATED 646
EVERYTHING EITHER IS CAUSED OR ALLOWED BY THE LORD 212
EVIL ANGELS 369
EVIL FOR GOOD 164
EVIL HEARTS OF MEN 201, 327
EVIL OF RELIGION 628
EVIL OF SELF-RIGHTEOUSNESS 301
EVOLUTION 655
EXALTATION OF CHRIST 94
EXALTATION OF THE LORD 221
EXALTED CHRIST 37
EXAMINATION 125
EXAMPLE OF CHRIST 633
EXCELLENCY OF JACOB 223
EXECUTING OF GOD'S WRATH 620
EXPERIENCING THE WORD 576

EXPOSITOR'S STUDY BIBLE 209, 539
EYES OF THE LORD 160
FACE OF THE LORD SHINING UPON
    BELIEVERS 146
FACT OF CREATION 462
FACT OF THE RESURRECTION 636
FAILURE 128
FAILURE TO FORGIVE 270
FAITH 17, 114, 345
FAITH IN GOD 334
FAITHFULNESS 406
FAITHFULNESS OF THE MESSIAH 405
FALLEN ANGEL 47
FALLEN FROM GRACE 464
FALSE APOSTLES 456
FALSE BIBLES 52
FALSE DIRECTIONS 126
FALSE DOCTRINE 196, 440
FALSE DOCTRINE AND THE CROSS 565
FALSE TEACHING 565
FALSE WAYS 562
FASHIONING OF THE HEARTS OF MEN 154
FAT AND PROSPEROUS 106
FAVOR 551
FAVOR AND SALVATION 484
FEAR 16, 130, 219, 228
FEAR AND THE CROSS OF CHRIST 16
FEAR OF THE LORD 88, 121, 468
FEAR THE LORD 104
FEARFULNESS AND TREMBLING 267
FEAST OF TABERNACLES 441
FIDELITY TO THE WORD 563
FIGURATIVE LANGUAGE OF THE HOLY
    SPIRIT 620
FINAL AUTHORITY 632
FINISH THE COURSE AND KEEP THE FAITH 338
FIRSTBORN 410
FIRSTBORN OF MANY BRETHREN 63
FLESH 366
FOOL 55, 262
FOOLISHNESS OF SIN 182
FOOLS 500
FOOT OF PRIDE AND THE HAND OF THE
    WICKED 173
FORGETTING WHAT GOD HAS DONE 487
FORGIVENESS 251, 268, 463
FORGIVING GOD? 356
FORMULA GIVEN BY THE HOLY SPIRIT 175
FORSAKEN BY THE LORD? 131
FOUNDATIONS 50
FOUR COMPANIES 497
FRAILTY OF MAN 190
FREE MORAL AGENCY OF MAN 623

FREE WILL 56
FROM THIS DAY WILL I BLESS YOU 140
FRUIT 4
FULFILLMENT OF BIBLE PROPHECY 506
FULLNESS OF JOY 64
FURNISHING A TABLE IN THE WILDERNESS 363
FUTURE OF CREATION 84
FUTURE RESTORATION 316
GENTLENESS OF OUR LORD 79
GLORIOUS PETITION 91
GLORY OF GOD 440
GLORY OF THE SON OF GOD 658
GOD ALONE MUST BE WORSHIPPED 445
GOD AND ETERNITY 416
GOD AND MAN 279, 470
GOD IN CREATION 82
GOD IN ORDINATION 86
GOD IN REVELATION 86
GOD IN THE THOUGHTS OF MAN 46
GOD IS HOLY 98
GOD OF JACOB 377, 388
GOD OF OUR STRENGTH 377
GOD THE FATHER ALWAYS HEARS GOD THE
    SON 92
GOD, THE RIGHTEOUS JUDGE 33
GOD UPHOLDS HIS WORD 559
GOD'S ANSWER TO THE ARAB WORLD 240
GOD'S ATTITUDE TOWARD MAN 393
GOD'S CHILDREN 113
GOD'S JUDGMENT IS ALSO AN ACT OF
    MERCY 614
GOD'S PRESCRIBED ORDER OF VICTORY 219,
    333, 424, 534, 587
GOD'S SHIELD 32
GOD'S WAYS 468
GOD'S WAYS AND GOD'S ACTS 468
GOD'S WILL AND GOD'S ACTION 358
GOD'S WORD BUILDS FAITH 438
GOD-BREATHED SCRIPTURES 553
GOOD FIGHT OF FAITH 378
GOODLY HERITAGE 60
GOODNESS AND MERCY 112
GOVERNMENT OF THE LORD 657
GOVERNMENT OF THE WORLD 407
GOVERNOR 106
GRACE AND MERCY 529
GRACE OF GOD 389
GREAT COMMISSION 71
GREAT CONTEST BETWEEN GOD AND SATAN 307
GREAT EARTHQUAKE 74
GREAT FEAR 57
GREAT IS THE LORD 225
GREAT QUESTIONS 413

GREAT SHEPHERD 174
GREAT TRIBULATION 220, 434
GREAT VICTORY OF CHRIST IS OBVIOUS TO ALL 526
GREAT WHITE THRONE JUDGMENT 95
GREATER SON OF DAVID 292
GREATEST CRISIS 361
GREATEST OPPOSITION TO THE WORK OF GOD 459
GREATNESS AND GLORY OF GOD 314
GREATNESS OF OUR LORD 353
GREEN PASTURES 109
GUARANTEE 566
GUARANTEE OF THE WORD 559, 579
GUARANTEED INTERCESSION 134
HABITS OF THE MASTER 572
HALLELUJAH! 607
HAPPINESS! 646
HARDENED HEART 100
HATRED FOR CHRIST 581, 634
HEART OF MAN 32
HEAVENLY MONARCH 599
HELL 272, 395
HELP GIVEN BY THE LORD 134, 292
HELP OF THE LORD 181
HEZEKIAH 603
HIS ANOINTED 92, 134
HIS VICTORY IS OURS 539
HISTORY AND THE FALL 245
HISTORY OF ISRAEL 375
HOLINESS 135, 224, 446
HOLY OF HOLIES 424
HOLY SPIRIT 535, 610
HOLY SPIRIT CONVICTION 346
HOUSE OF THE LORD 113
HOW CAN GOD BRING GOOD OUT OF SUCH TRAGEDY? 19
HOW CAN THE POWER OF GOD COME TO THE BELIEVER? 296
HOW CAN WE HAVE THE POWER OF GOD MANIFESTED IN OUR LIVES? 208
HOW COULD DAVID COMMIT SUCH A SIN? 257
HOW COULD THE LORD UPHOLD THE LAW, AND, AT THE SAME TIME JUSTIFY DAVID? 250
HOW COULD THERE BE AN OFFENSE IN THE CROSS? 575
HOW DID GOD BRING CREATION INTO EXISTENCE? 82
HOW DOES ONE FULLY TRUST IN HIS HOLY NAME? 156
HOW DOES ONE WALK IN THE SPIRIT? 4
HOW DOES SATAN THINK HE CAN OVERTHROW GOD? 8

HOW DOES THE BELIEVER GO ABOUT ASKING FORGIVENESS? 252
HOW DOES THE HOLY SPIRIT BRING OUR STATE OF HOLINESS UP TO OUR STANDING IN HOLINESS? 136
HOW DOES THIS LAW OPERATE WITHIN OUR LIVES? 486
HOW IS JUSTIFICATION BY FAITH CARRIED OUT? 253
HOW MANY MODERN CHRISTIANS PRESENTLY ARE BOASTING IN THE CROSS? 211
HOW THE HOLY SPIRIT WORKS 409
HOW TO PRAY 394
HUMAN SACRIFICE 493
HUMANISTIC PSYCHOLOGY 42, 169, 650
HUMANISTIC PSYCHOLOGY AND JUDGMENT 44
IDOLATRY 60, 444, 521
IDOLATRY IN THE NEW TESTAMENT 440
IDOLS 440
IDOLS AND IMAGES 370
IDOLS AT THE PRESENT 611
IF JESUS ATONED FOR ALL SIN, HOW CAN SATAN CONTINUE TO HOLD MEN IN BONDAGE? 12
IF MEN DO NOT KNOW THE LORD, THEY DO NOT UNDERSTAND THE SPIRIT WORLD 233
IF SATAN IS DEFEATED, WHY IS HE STILL CAUSING SO MANY PROBLEMS? 424
IF SIN WAS MADE INEFFECTIVE BY THE SACRIFICE OF CHRIST, WHY ARE BELIEVERS STILL TROUBLED BY SIN? 183
IMMACULATE CONCEPTION 249
IN THE KINGDOM AGE, THE WORLD WILL BE ONE 453
INCARNATION 10, 622, 623, 625, 627
INCARNATION OF CHRIST 402
INCREASE 368
INDIGNATION 550
INIQUITY 243
INIQUITY IN THE HEART 309
INSPIRATION 276
INSPIRATION OF THE BIBLE 578
INSTRUCTION 150
INSTRUCTION IN THE WORLD 237
INSTRUMENTS OF DEATH 34
INTEGRITY 125, 202
INTERCESSION 54, 132, 596
INTERCESSION FOR SIN 133
INTERCESSION OF CHRIST 25, 392
INTERCESSORY MINISTRY OF CHRIST 348
INTERCESSORY PRAYER 65
INTERCESSORY WORK OF CHRIST 191, 242, 323
INVESTIGATING THE BIBLE 569

IS IT WRONG TO ASSOCIATE ONESELF WITH A CHURCH DENOMINATION? 465
ISLAM 312
ISRAEL 105, 340, 372, 379, 433, 480, 594, 651
ISRAEL AND EGYPT 480
ISRAEL AND HER MESSIAH 203
ISRAEL AND THE CHURCH 154
ISRAEL AND THE LORD JESUS CHRIST 215, 528
ISRAEL BELONGS TO GOD 506
ISRAEL DURING THE TIME OF DAVID 188
ISRAEL IN THE LAST DAYS 284
ISRAEL'S COMING VICTORY 594
ISRAEL'S GREAT FEAST DAYS 454
IT IS TIME FOR YOU, LORD, TO WORK 567
JACOB 115, 209, 520
JACOB AND ISRAEL 57, 608
JEHOVAH'S SERVANTS 398
JERUSALEM 225, 397, 460, 584, 651
JERUSALEM AND BABYLON 617
JERUSALEM AND PROSPERITY 585
JESUS AND THE LAW 184
JESUS AND THE RELIGIOUS LEADERS OF ISRAEL 294
JESUS AS A BOY 561
JESUS CHRIST AND HIM CRUCIFIED 578
JESUS CHRIST AND THE CROSS 101, 447
JESUS CHRIST, KING OF KINGS 107
JESUS CHRIST, THE ONLY GOOD MAN WHO EVER LIVED 197
JESUS CHRIST, VERY MAN 142
JESUS DIED SPIRITUALLY DOCTRINE 62, 639
JESUS, THE APPLE OF GOD'S EYE 67
JESUS WAS FORSAKEN BY ALL EXCEPT HIS FATHER 197
JEWISH ILLUSTRATION 110
JONAH, THE GREAT SIN 400
JOSEPH 482
JOYFUL NOISE 448
JUDAS 271, 510
JUDGE 64
JUDGMENT 24, 30
JUDGMENT AND JUSTICE 458
JUDGMENT OF GOD 80, 489
JUDGMENT OF ISRAEL 235
JUDGMENT OF THE LORD 44
JUDGMENTS OF THE LORD 172
JUSTIFICATION 638
JUSTIFICATION BY FAITH 31, 243, 253, 301, 488
KEEPING OF THE LAW 534
KEEPING THE PRECEPTS 554
KEY IS CHRIST 343
KING OF GLORY 116
KING OF THE HEAVENS 585
KINGDOM 106
KINGDOM AGE 303, 521
KINGDOM NOW? 645
KINGDOM NOW PHILOSOPHY 310
KNOWLEDGE OF THE LORD 56
LACK OF UNDERSTANDING 420
LAMB FOR SACRIFICE 125
LAMP AND THE LIGHT 563
LAND OF ISRAEL 290
LARGE PLACE 529
LARGE ROOM 144
LAST ADAM, THE SECOND MAN 58
LAST DAYS 606
LAST HEAD 384
LAW 359, 465
LAW AND THE MODERN BELIEVER 86
LAW IN ISRAEL 361
LAW OF GOD 536
LAW OF MOSES 379
LAW OF REGRESSION 493
LAW OF THE LORD 1
LEADING AND GUIDANCE 142
LEARNING OF THE COMMANDMENTS 554
LEAVING VENGEANCE TO GOD 644
LESSON EVERY BELIEVER SHOULD LEARN 191
LIBERTY 549
LIE OF FALSE DOCTRINE 51
LIFE OF A MAN 417
LIGHT 471
LIMITING GOD 367
LONGSUFFERING OF THE LORD 48
LORD AND ISRAEL 384
LORD ANSWERS PRAYER 91
LORD CAN CHANGE MEN AND SITUATIONS 451
LORD IS NO RESPECTER OF PERSONS 304
LORD JESUS AND HIS FIRST ADVENT 298
LORD JESUS CHRIST 570
LORD JESUS CHRIST AND THE LAW OF GOD 537
LORD JESUS CHRIST, OUR GREAT HIGH PRIEST 117
LORD JESUS CHRIST, THE CROSS, AND THE HOLY SPIRIT 644
LORD JESUS CHRIST, THE TRUE ISRAEL! 138
LORD OUR VICTOR 35
LORD REIGNS 430, 443, 451
LORD WILL MAKE A WAY 20
LORD WILL TEACH US THE WORD 567
LOVE 72
LOVE OF GOD 366
LOVINGKINDNESS 125
LOVINGKINDNESS OF GOD 173
LUST 487
LYING VANITIES 143

MAGISTRATES AND RULERS 382
MAGNIFYING GOD'S WORD ABOVE HIS NAME 620
MAGNIFYING THE LORD 158
MAN 469
MAN'S PLACE IN CREATION 83
MANNER IN WHICH CHRIST INTERCEDES FOR US 324
MANNER IN WHICH THE HOLY SPIRIT WORKS 110
MANNER OF DELIVERANCE 193
MANNER OF GOD'S CREATION 623
MANNER OF SPIRITUAL WARFARE 642
MEANING OF THE INCARNATION 10
MEANS OF THE CROSS 207
MEDITATE IN THE WORD DAY AND NIGHT 3
MEDITATION 21, 45, 299, 474, 541, 561
MEEK 105, 120
MERCIES 547
MERCIFUL 77
MERCY 26, 119, 586, 613
MERCY AND TRUTH 391
MERCY OF GOD 281
MERE PROFESSORS OF RELIGION 237
MESSAGE OF THE CROSS 50
MESSIAH 60, 89, 104, 262, 483, 505, 540, 595
MESSIAH AND REDEMPTION 637
MESSIAH IS UPRIGHT 517
MESSIANIC PSALMS vii (Introduction)
MIGHTY GOD OF JACOB 601
MIGHTY POWER 484
MIGHTY THINGS DONE BY GOD 368
MILLENNIAL REIGN 339
MIRACLE WORKING GOD 613
MIRACLES AND UNBELIEF 363
MISCHIEVOUS DEVICE 96
MODERN BELIEVER AND THE CROSS 409
MODERN CHURCH 488
MODERN DOMINION TEACHING 435
MODERN FADS 136
MODERN PSYCHOLOGY 122
MORAL LAW 87
MOSAIC LAW 250
MURDER 179
MUSIC 151, 449
MUSIC AND WORSHIP 338
MUSIC AS IT REGARDS WORSHIP AND PRAISE 475
MUSIC AS USED BY THE LORD IN PRAISE AND WORSHIP 428
MYSTERY RELIGIONS 441
NAME OF ISRAEL 384
NAMES BLOTTED OUT OF THE BOOK OF LIFE 329
NATIONS OF THE WORLD 442
NATURE 450
NEW COVENANT 358
NEW CREATION IN CHRIST 84
NEW JERUSALEM 602
NEW SONG 193, 439, 446
NIGHT SEASON 98
NO IMPUTATION OF INIQUITY 148
OBEDIENCE TO THE BIBLE 569
OBJECT OF FAITH 278
OBJECT OF ONE'S FAITH 255
OFFENSE OF THE CROSS 275, 575
OIL OF GLADNESS 216
OIL OF HEALING 634
OIL RICHES OF THE MIDDLE EAST 261
OLD TESTAMENT NAMES GIVEN TO THE LORD AND THEIR MEANING 408
OMNIPOTENT AND OMNISCIENCE OF GOD 154
OMNISCIENCE OF GOD 652
ONLY ANSWER FOR SIN IS THE CROSS OF CHRIST 169
ONLY BEGOTTEN SON 103
ONLY THING STANDING BETWEEN THE CHURCH AND APOSTASY IS THE CROSS OF CHRIST 251
OPPOSITION 629, 635
OPPRESSION 26
ORDER OF MELCHIZEDEK 514
ORDINANCES AND TESTIMONIES 452
ORIGINAL CREATION 648
ORIGINAL SIN 245, 248
OUR DEFENSE 294
OUR GREAT HIGH PRIEST 122, 181, 252
OUR GREAT INTERCESSOR 591
OUR HELP COMES FROM THE LORD 582
OUR TIMES ARE IN HIS HAND 146
PALESTINIANS? 199
PARABLE 360
PATHS OF RIGHTEOUSNESS 110
PATHS OF THE LORD 120
PATIENCE 192
PAUL 630
PEACE 221
PEACE OF GOD 180
PEOPLE OF HIS PASTURE 437
PERFECT WISDOM AND INFINITE LOVE 547
PERFECTION OF CHRIST 301
PERFECTION OF THE SCRIPTURES 577
PERFECTION OF THE SON OF GOD 65
PERSECUTION 558, 595
PERSONAL PERFECTION OF CHRIST 455
PESTILENCE AND DESTRUCTION 425
PETRA 291

PLACE FOR THE LORD 601
PLAN OF GOD 45, 482
PLANS OF THE EVIL ONE 7
PLEA OF THE MESSIAH 192
PLIGHT OF THE LOST 232
PORTION ASSIGNED BY THE HOLY SPIRIT 61
PORTIONS 551
PORTRAYAL OF OUR LORD 392
POSSESSION 290
POSSESSION OF THIS EARTH 11
POWER OF GOD 208, 520, 616
POWER OF THE LORD 177
PRAISE 138, 258, 303, 311, 335, 387, 651, 658
PRAISE AND WORSHIP 38
PRAISE OF UNDERSTANDING 224
PRAISE THE LORD 104, 517, 518, 527
PRAISING GOD 98
PRAISING THE LORD 105, 427
PRAYER 14, 17, 264, 294, 303, 394, 400
PRAYER OF OUR LORD 572
PRAYER OF THE SON OF GOD 189
PREACHER OF RIGHTEOUSNESS 196
PREDISTINATION 155
PREOCCUPATION WITH SELF 343
PREPARATION OF THE TABLE 111
PRESENCE OF GOD 388
PRESENCE OF THE LORD 20
PRICE THAT WAS PAID 401
PRIDE 68, 287, 509, 557
PROCLAMATION OF KNOWLEDGE 85
PROHECY v (Introduction)
PROMISE 593
PROMISES OF GOD 139, 158, 430
PROMISES OF GOD ARE MORE THAN ENOUGH 194
PROMOTION 352
PROPER TRUST 59
PROPHECY 39, 97
PROPHETIC 198
PROPHETIC ANALYSIS OF THIS PSALM 266
PROPHETIC PSALM 148
PROPHETICAL MEANING OF THE FEASTS 454
PROSPERITY 4, 140, 312, 382, 496
PROTECTION 643
PROTECTION IS IN THE WORD 542
PROTECTION OF JEHOVAH 583
PROTECTION OF THE LORD 155, 163
PROTECTION OF THE WORD 560
PROUD 194, 550, 558
PROUD WILL BE PUT TO SHAME 556
PROVISION 108
PSYCHOLOGY, A ROMAN CIRCUS 544
PUNISHMENT! 187

PURE AND PERVERSE 77
PURPOSE OF THE GREAT TRIBULATION 435
PURPOSE OF THE HOLY SPIRIT 499
RAPTURE OF THE CHURCH 310, 432
REASON FOR HATRED 201
REASON JESUS CAME 460
RECOURSE OF THE CHILD OF GOD 70
REDEEMING THE LIFE 466
REDEMPTION 229, 463, 496, 624
REFUGE 42, 218, 423
REJECTED SAVIOUR 458
REJECTION OF CHRIST 142
REJECTION OF THE CROSS OF CHRIST IS ALWAYS MORAL AND NEVER THEOLOGICAL 333
REJOICING 151, 290
REJOICING IN THE LORD 93, 222
REJOICING THE HEART 88
RELATIONSHIP 343
RELIGION 23, 459, 629
RELIGION AND THE CROSS OF CHRIST 630
RELIGIOUS LEADERS 101, 142, 457
RELIGIOUS LEADERS OF ISRAEL 300
RELIGIOUS PRIDE 652
REMEMBER 119
REMEMBERING WHAT GOD HAS DONE FOR US 203
REMNANT 605
REMOVAL OF OUR TRANSGRESSIONS 469
REPENTANCE 242, 365, 459
REPROACH 324
REPROACH OF CHRIST 144
REQUIREMENTS FOR RIGHTEOUS LIVING 421
RESHAPING OF THE EARTH 474
RESPONSE OF FRIENDS AND KINSMEN WHILE JESUS WAS ON THE CROSS 185
RESTORATION 109, 187, 255, 385, 613
RESTORATION OF ISRAEL 436, 461
RESULT OF SIN 123
RESURRECTION 72, 108, 524
RESURRECTION OF THE LORD JESUS CHRIST 403
REWARD OF THE WICKED 425
RICHES CANNOT REDEEM THE SOUL 228
RIGHT ATTITUDE OF THE HEART 32
RIGHTEOUS 25
RIGHTEOUS JUDGMENT 339
RIGHTEOUS JUDGMENT OF GOD 40
RIGHTEOUSNESS 31, 115, 152, 391, 448, 531, 547
RIGHTEOUSNESS AND PEACE 390
RIGHTEOUSNESS AND SELF-RIGHTEOUSNESS 266
RIGHTEOUSNESS IS ACQUIRED 171
RIGHTEOUSNESS OF GOD 171

RIVER OF GOD 219, 305
ROADMAP FOR LIFE IS THE BIBLE 541
ROARING LION 70
ROCK 483
ROD AND THE STAFF 111
ROMAN ARMY 637
ROMANS, CHAPTER SIX 378
SACRIFICE OF PRAISE 501
SACRIFICES 259
SACRIFICES OF THE DEAD 491
SACRIFICIAL SYSTEM OF OLD 195
SAINTS 234
SALVATION 92, 341, 448, 579
SANCTIFICATION 334
SANCTUARY 90, 297, 343, 358, 386
SATAN 485, 530
SATAN AND HIS OPPPOSITION 477
SATAN'S DEFEAT 426
SATAN'S TACTICS 357
SCEPTER OF POWER 216
SEARCHING OF GOD 622
SEARCHLIGHT OF THE HOLY SCRIPTURES 543
SECOND COMING 39, 351
SECOND COMING AND THE BATTLE OF ARMAGEDDON 443
SECOND COMING OF THE LORD 10
SECRET OF ALL VICTORY 539
SECRET PLACE OF THE MOST HIGH 422
SECRET SINS 419
SECURITY 583
SEED 330
SEEKING THE LORD 158, 297
SELAH 14
SELF-RELIANT 421
SELF-RIGHTEOUS 120
SELF-RIGHTEOUSNESS 114, 323, 459, 631, 639
SEPARATION 128, 380
SEVEN METAPHORS USED OF GOD 73
SEVEN TIMES A DAY 576
SEVENFOLD ANOINTING 134
SEVENFOLD VICTORY 486
SHADOW OF DEATH 111, 213
SHADOW OF HIS WINGS 67
SHED BLOOD OF THE LORD JESUS CHRIST 304
SHEPHERD 108
SHIELD 25
SHIELDS OF THE EARTH 224
SHINING FACE OF THE LORD 51
SHINING OF GOD'S FACE 310
SHORT HISTORY OF THE ARK OF GOD 602
SHOUTINGS AND DANCINGS 399
SIGNS 349
SIN 55, 243

SIN, A LOSS OF FREEDOM 244
SIN AND FREEDOM 243
SIN AND GRACE 246
SIN AND ITS EFFECT ON THE BELIEVER! 183
SIN AND PUNISHMENT 247
SIN AND THE CHARACTER OF GOD 121
SIN AND THE CROSS 597
SIN AND THE DIVINE SOVEREIGNTY 244
SIN DEBT PAID 624
SIN IS THE PROBLEM 168
SIN NATURE 99
SIN OF MURDER 257
SIN OF PRESUMPTION 426
SIN, THE CAUSE OF ALL PROBLEMS 503
SINGING 314
SINGING AND MUSICAL INSTRUMENTS IN PRAISE TO GOD 378
SINLESS PERFECTION! 629
SINLESS PERFECTION? 255, 628
SINLESS SON OF GOD 76
SINNERS 119
SINNING AGAINST GOD 244
SINS OF IGNORANCE 419
SIXTH CHAPTER OF ROMANS 99
SLANDER 145, 456
SMITING OF THE ROCK 492
SMITTEN OF GOD 328
SMITTEN OF GOD AND AFFLICTED 401
SNARE 564
SNARE OF THE FOWLER 423
SOCIAL CHARACTER OF SIN 247
SOLITARY 315
SOME OF THE GREATEST PROBLEMS OF THE CHRISTIAN 633
SON OF DAVID 20
SON OF GOD 623
SON OF GOD AND SON OF MAN v (Introduction)
SONG OF BLESSING 306
SONG OF PRAISE 223
SONG OF SAINTS 139
SONG OF TRUST 598
SONGS OF DEGREES 580
SONGS OF DELIVERANCE 149
SOUL AND THE SPIRIT 254
SOUL OF MAN 231
SOUL SLEEP? 27
SOVEREIGN LORD 35
SPIRIT AND THE FLESH 477
SPIRIT OF GOD 474
SPIRITUAL ADULTERY 58, 238
SPIRITUAL DETERIORATION 601
SPIRITUAL JOURNEY OF EVERY BELIEVER 584
SPIRITUAL WARFARE 78, 641

SPIRITUAL WICKEDNESS IN HIGH PLACES 564
SPIRITUALITY OF ISRAEL 601
STATEMENT OF FAITH 265
STATUTES OF GOD 554
STATUTES OF THE LORD 557
STILL WATERS 109
STONE 531
STORY OF THE BIBLE 228
STRANGE GODS 381
STRENGTH 388
SUBSTITUTION AND IDENTIFICATION 621
SUFFERING OF THE MESSIAH 29
SUFFERING OF THE WORK OF GOD 54
SUFFERINGS OF CHRIST 97, 404
SWEETNESS OF THE WORD OF GOD 562
SYMBOL OF THE HOLY SPIRIT 220
SYNAGOGUES 349
TABERNACLE 370
TABLE 327
TASTE AND SEE 159
TEACH US, O LORD 546
TEACHING 85
TEACHING AS GIVEN BY THE LORD 121
TEARS OF ISRAEL 374
TEMPLE 130, 371
TEMPLE OF GOD 297
TEMPTING GOD 364
TEN WORDS 533
TERROR BY NIGHT 424
TESTIMONIES OF THE LORD 568
TESTIMONY OF THE LORD 87
TESTING 556
TESTING OF FAITH 50, 479
THANKSGIVING 236, 437
THAT WHICH PLEASES THE LORD 653
THE BAPTISM WITH THE HOLY SPIRIT 323
THE BLESSED MAN 1
THE CROSS, THE ONLY CURE FOR DECEPTION 8
THE MOST HIGH 35
THE PRESENCE OF EMMANUEL 397
THE RIGHTEOUS 589
THE SECRET OF THE LORD 122
THIRST AFTER GOD 202
THOSE WHOM THE LORD CHOOSES 457
THOUGHTS OF JESUS WHILE HE WAS ON THE CROSS 181
THREE EFFORTS OF SATAN AGAINST THE CHILD OF GOD 186
THREE FUNDAMENTAL DOCTRINES OF THE GOSPEL 321
THREEFOLD MINISTRY OF CHRIST 192
THRESHINGFLOOR 5
THRONE OF GOD 40
THROUGH CHRIST BY THE MEANS OF THE CROSS 380
TIME OF JACOB'S TROUBLE 46, 431
TO BE BLESSED IS TO PROSPER 523
TONGUE 260, 309
TONGUE OF THE REDEEMED 214
TORMENTS OF SATAN REGARDING THE DEATH OF CHRIST 403
TOTAL AND COMPLETE VICTORY 486
TOTAL DEPENDENCE ON THE WORD 550
TOTAL DEPRAVITY 245
TOTAL DEPRAVITY OF MAN 56
TOTAL TRUST 293
TOUCH NOT MY ANOINTED AND DO MY PROPHETS NO HARM 24
TRANSLATIONS 555
TRAP OF THE ENEMY 68
TREASURES 592
TREE PLANTED BY THE RIVERS OF WATER 3
TRINITY 152, 513, 613
TRIUMPH AND SUNSHINE OF THE RESURRECTION AND MILLENNIAL MORNINGS 641
TROUBLE 218, 344
TRUE AND FALSE MESSIAH vi (Introduction)
TRUE AND RIGHTEOUS 88
TRUE CHURCH AND THE APOSTATE CHURCH 556
TRUE ISRAEL 115
TRUE POWER AND PROTECTION 654
TRUE PRIEST AND ADVOCATE 553
TRUE PROPHETS 478
TRUE REPENTANCE 213
TRUE VINE 375
TRUST 59, 99, 117, 277, 586
TRUST AND THE CROSS 587
TRUST IN GOD 65, 280, 331
TRUST IN THE LORD 92, 186, 588, 649, 653
TRUST IN THE WORD 549
TRUSTWORTHINESS OF THE PROMISES 621
TRUSTWORTHINESS OF THE SCRIPTURES 555
TRUSTWORTHINESS OF THE WORD OF GOD 620
TRUTH 71, 126, 516
TURN AGAIN OUR CAPTIVITY 591
TURNING ASIDE FORM THE WORD OF GOD 456
TURNING THE CAPTIVITY 590
TWELVE TRIBES 585
TWO DIVINE PRINCIPLES 452
TWO REASONS FOR THE GREAT DISTURBANCE OF THE ELEMENTS 447
TWO TYPES OF SIN 147
TWOFOLD SORROW OF CHRIST 460

TYPE OF CHRIST 264
UNBELIEF 170, 193, 364, 438, 490, 526, 615
UNBELIEF COMES IN MANY WAYS 438
UNCONFESSED SIN 149
UNDERSTANDING OF THE WORD 577
UNDERSTANDING THE INTERCESSORY MINISTRY OF CHRIST 348
UNDERSTANDING THE SONGS OF DEGREES 582
UNDERSTANDING THE WORD 553
UNGODLY DESIRE 365
UNITED STATES AND ISRAEL 435
UNITY 604
UNITY BETWEEN THE BIBLE AND ITS AUTHOR 548
UNMOVEABLE 588
UPRIGHT IN HEART 173
URIM AND THUMMIM 206
VAIN HELP OF MAN 292
VALIDITY OF THE WORD OF GOD 548
VALLEY OF BACA 387
VANITY OF MAN 190
VENGEANCE BELONGS TO THE LORD 264
VERY GOD AND VERY MAN 64
VICTORIOUS CHURCH 79
VICTORY 41, 79, 223, 354, 427, 447, 513
VICTORY IN JESUS 39
VICTORY OF THE CROSS 282
VICTORY OF THE MESSIAH OVER THE ANTICHRIST 514
VIOLENCE AND FALSEHOOD 51
VOWS 293, 303
WAITING ON THE LORD 132
WALKING AFTER THE FLESH AND WALKING AFTER THE SPIRIT 172, 313, 337
WAY OF PSYCHOLOGY IS THE WAY OF LYING 543
WAY OF SIN 168
WAY OF TRUTH 545
WAY OF VICTORY 130
WAYS OF GOD 55, 381, 438
WAYS OF THE EVIL ONE 205
WAYS OF THE LORD 33, 118, 427, 536, 551, 595
WAYS OF THE WORLD 493
WE MUST NEVER BLAME GOD! 204
WEALTH AND HEALTH 481
WHAT DID THE KING OF GLORY DO? 116
WHAT DO WE MEAN BY THE WAY OF THE CROSS? 207
WHAT DOES BIBLICAL TRUST ACTUALLY MEAN? 66
WHAT DOES IT MEAN FOR ONE TO PUT ONE'S TRUST TOTALLY IN THE LORD? 66
WHAT DOES IT MEAN TO FALL FROM GRACE? 238
WHAT DOES IT MEAN TO PREACH THE CROSS? 9
WHAT DOES IT MEAN TO PUT ONE'S TRUST IN THE LORD? 278
WHAT GOD HAS BLESSED CANNOT BE CURSED 596
WHAT IS GOD REALLY LIKE? 396
WHAT IS GOD'S WAY? 6
WHAT IS HOLINESS? 135
WHAT IS LAW? 268
WHAT IS MEANT BY THE EXPRESSION, *"JESUS DIED SPRITUALLY"*? 63
WHAT IS SIN? 184
WHAT IS SPIRITUAL WARFARE? 642
WHAT IS THE LAW OF THE SPIRIT OF LIFE IN CHRIST JESUS? 485
WHAT IS THE SIN NATURE? 2, 535
WHAT IS TRUE PROSPERITY? 4
WHAT THE ANTICHRIST WILL BE LIKE? 260
WHATEVER ONE NEEDS IS IN THE CROSS 212
WHEN WILL THE TIMES OF THE GENTILES BE FULFILLED? 216
WHERE IS HEAVEN? 232
WHO IS THIS KING OF GLORY? 116
WHY CHRISTIANS ARE IN BONDAGE? 467
WHY DID ISRAEL REBEL AGAINST DAVID? 18
WHY DO MEN HATE CHRIST? 322
WHY DO SOME ACCEPT THE LORD AND SOME REJECT THE LORD? 155
WHY DOES MAN NEED REDEMPTION? 229
WHY IS ISRAEL SO IMPORTANT? 317
WHY IS IT SO HARD FOR PREACHERS TO ACCEPT THE CROSS? 9
WHY IS THE CROSS OF CHRIST SO IMPORTANT? 238
WHY THE PSYCHOLOGICAL WAY? 544
WHY WERE DAVID AND OUR LORD HATED? 275
WICKED SIN OF ABORTION 625
WILDERNESS 380
WILL OF GOD 212, 365
WILL OF MAN 83, 277
WILLPOWER 100
WISDOM 178, 249
WISDOM OF GOD 613
WISE BEHAVIOUR 455
WISE WILL UNDERSTAND 504
WITHOUT A CAUSE 508, 575
WORD OF GOD 76, 89, 310, 444
WORD OF GOD, HIDDEN IN THE HEART AND OBEYED IN THE LIFE 533
WORD OF GOD IS DESIGNED TO CHANGE THE HEARTS AND LIVES OF MEN 571
WORD OF GOD IS TO BE LOVED ABOVE GOLD 568
WORD OF GOD, THE ONLY TRUE MAP 570

WORD OF GOD WILL POINT OUT WEAKNESSES WITHIN OUR LIFE 543
WORK OF MEN'S HANDS 611
WORK OF THE FINGERS OF GOD 35
WORK OF THE LORD, PRESENT AND FUTURE! 30
WORKERS OF INIQUITY 22
WORKS OF THE LORD 515, 516
WORKS SALVATION 638
WORLD AND THE CHURCH 379
WORLD EVANGELISM BIBLE COLLEGE 538
WORM 100
WORSHIP 451
WORSHIPPERS OF IDOLS BECOME LIKE THE IDOLS THEY WORSHIP 522
WRATH OF GOD 421
YOU ARE GOD ALONE 394
YOUR ANOINTED, THE LORD JESUS CHRIST 388

For all information concerning the *Jimmy Swaggart Bible Commentary*, please request a Gift Catalog.

You may inquire by using Books of the Bible.

- Genesis (639 pages) (11-201)
- Exodus (639 pages) (11-202)
- Leviticus (435 pages) (11-203)
- Numbers
  Deuteronomy (493 pages) (11-204)
- Joshua
  Judges
  Ruth (329 pages) (11-205)
- I Samuel
  II Samuel (528 pages) (11-206)
- I Kings
  II Kings (560 pages) (11-207)
- I Chronicles
  II Chronicles (528 pages) (11-226)
- Ezra
  Nehemiah
  Esther (288 pages) (11-208)
- Job (320 pages) (11-225)
- Psalms (688 pages) (11-216)
- Proverbs (320 pages) (11-227)
- Ecclesiastes
  Song Of Solomon (245 pages) (11-228)
- Isaiah (688 pages) (11-220)
- Jeremiah
  Lamentations (688 pages) (11-070)
- Ezekiel (508 pages) (11-223)
- Daniel (403 pages) (11-224)
- Hosea
  Joel
  Amos (496 pages) (11-229)
- Obadiah
  Jonah
  Micah
  Nahum
  Habakkuk
  Zephaniah *(will be ready Spring 2013)* (11-230)

- Matthew (625 pages) (11-073)
- Mark (606 pages) (11-074)
- Luke (626 pages) (11-075)
- John (532 pages) (11-076)
- Acts (697 pages) (11-077)
- Romans (536 pages) (11-078)
- I Corinthians (632 pages) (11-079)
- II Corinthians (589 pages) (11-080)
- Galatians (478 pages) (11-081)
- Ephesians (550 pages) (11-082)
- Philippians (476 pages) (11-083)
- Colossians (374 pages) (11-084)
- I Thessalonians
  II Thessalonians (498 pages) (11-085)
- I Timothy
  II Timothy
  Titus
  Philemon (687 pages) (11-086)
- Hebrews (831 pages) (11-087)
- James
  I Peter
  II Peter (730 pages) (11-088)
- I John
  II John
  III John
  Jude (377 pages) (11-089)
- Revelation (602 pages) (11-090)

For telephone orders you may call 1-800-288-8350 with bankcard information. All Baton Rouge residents please use (225) 768-7000. For mail orders send to:

Jimmy Swaggart Ministries
P.O. Box 262550 • Baton Rouge, LA 70826-2550
Visit our website: www.jsm.org

NOTES

NOTES

NOTES

NOTES

NOTES